GROLIER INTERNATIONAL
Encyclopedia

Grolier Incorporated
Danbury, Connecticut

PHOENICIAN

EARLY HEBREW

EARLY ARAMAIC

EARLY GREEK

CLASSICAL GREEK

MODERN LATIN

ETRUSCAN

EARLY LATIN

CLASSICAL LATIN

RUSSIAN-CYRILLIC

GERMAN-GOTHIC

K

K/k is the 11th letter of the English alphabet. Both the letter and its position in the alphabet are derived from the Latin, which in turn came from the Greek by way of the Etruscan. The Greeks call the letter *kappa* and took its name, form, and position from a Semitic writing system in which the name of the sign was *kaph*.

In both Semitic and Greek writing systems the letter represents the sound *k,* a voiceless velar stop. Early Latin writing, under the influence of Etruscan, used three letters for this sound: *c* before *e* and *i, k* before *a,* and *q* before *u*. The use of *K/k* was eventually dropped, however, in favor of *C/c,* except for a few well-known and often abbreviated words.

When the Latin alphabet was introduced into the British Isles, the letter *C/c* was used to write all *k* sounds (thus modern *kind* and *king* were *cynd* and *cyning* in Old English), but the use of *K/k* for this sound before *e, i,* or *y* was soon revived in English. As a consequence, almost all English words that have the spelling *K/k* before *a, o, u, l,* or *r* are of foreign origin (for example, *kangaroo, kosher, kumquat, blitzkrieg*). In modern English, initial *K/k* followed by *n* is silent, as in *knee* and *knot,* although earlier both sounds were pronounced, as they still are in German.   I. J. GELB AND R. M. WHITING

Kaaba

Kaaba (Arabic, "a square building"), ISLAM's most sacred sanctuary and pilgrimage shrine, is located in the courtyard of the Great Mosque of MECCA. According to the Koran, the cubic-shaped structure was built by Adam according to a divine plan and rebuilt by Abraham and Ishmael. A trough in which they reputedly mixed mortar stands near the door and is a popular place of prayer. The Kaaba houses the Black Stone, the most venerated object for Muslims. Probably of meteoric origin, the stone is reputed to have been given to Ishmael by the angel Gabriel. When MUHAMMAD began to preach to the Meccans, the Kaaba was a shrine for the pagan deities of the Arabs. After the Prophet established control of Mecca, the shrine was rededicated to Allah. All Muslims face toward the Kaaba during their daily prayers.

Kabalevsky, Dmitri   [kah-buh-lef'-skee, duh-mee'-tree]

The Soviet composer Dmitri Borisovich Kabalevsky, b. Dec. 30 (N.S.), 1904, d. February 1987, attended the Scriabin Music School and then the Moscow Conservatory, where he studied composition with Nikolai Myaskovsky Kabalevsky spent much of his life as a professor of composition at the Moscow Conservatory, winning high academic and official distinction. He was appointed to the Ministry of Culture in 1954 and was named People's Artist in 1963. He wrote much educational music and several operas, including *Colas Breugnon* (1938), *The Family of Taras* (1950), *Nikita Vershinin* (1955), and *The Sisters* (1969). In addition to much music for film and occasional theater music, his compositions include two string quartets, a number of songs, including fine settings of some Shakespeare sonnets in Marshak's Russian translation, four symphonies, and three concertos for piano, one for violin, and two for cello. His *Requiem* for two choruses, soloists, and orchestra won the Glinka Prize in 1966.   MARTIN COOPER

Bibliography: Krebs, Stanley D., *Soviet Composers and the Development of Soviet Music* (1970).

Kabbalah   [kab-uh-lah']

Kabbalah, the Hebrew word for tradition, originally designated the legal tradition of JUDAISM, but it was later applied to the Jewish mystical tradition, especially the system of esoteric mystical speculation and practice that developed during the 12th and 13th centuries. The speculative aspects of Kabbalah (*Kabbalah iyyunit*) were stressed in southern European schools; more practical, socioethical, and sometimes magical themes (*Kabbalah maasit*) were emphasized in northern European circles. Kabbalistic interest, at first confined to a select few, became the preoccupation of large numbers of Jews following their expulsion from Spain (1492) and Portugal (1495). The teachings of Kabbalah, as developed by the visionary Isaac ben Solomon LURIA, are credited with giving rise to the Sabbatean movement led by SABBATAI ZEVI.

Like every other Jewish religious expression, Kabbalah was based on the Old Testament revelation. The revealed text was interpreted with the aid of various hermeneutic techniques. Of the many methods available, the Kabbalists most frequently used three forms of letter and number symbolism: *gematria, notarikon,* and *temurah*.

The Kabbalists developed distinctive doctrines of creation and of redemption. Their doctrine of creation was built on a theory of emanations and asserted that the world derived from the transcendent and unknowable God (*En Soph*) through a series of increasingly material manifestations (*sephirot*). The manifestations were repeated, in some versions of Kabbalah, in four interlocking series or "worlds": emanation (*atzilut*), creation (*beriah*), formation (*yetzirah*), and action or making (*assiyah*). By the sin of Adam and the later sins of humankind, the immanent aspect of God, or the *Shekhinah* (divine presence), was exiled in the final *sephirah, malkhut* (kingdom). The sexual imagery of Kabbalah treats *Shekhinah* (the word is feminine in gender) as the female aspect of divinity; it symbolically expresses the idea of the restoration of harmony (*tikkun*) as the reunion of the male and female aspects of the divine, that is, as the reunion of divine transcendence and immanence.

The classic document of the Kabbalistic tradition, the *Zohar,* was compiled by Moses de León about 1290. A more systematic presentation of the basic doctrine is contained in Moses Cordovero's *Pardes rimmonim* (Garden of Pomegranates, 1548). Kabbalah was a major influence in the development of HASIDISM and still has adherents among Hasidic Jews.

JOSEPH L. BLAU

Bibliography: Dan, Joseph and Keiner, Ronald, eds., *The Early Kabbalah* (1986); Epstein, Perle, *Kabbalah* (1978); Scholem, Gershom, *Kabbalah* (1974); Meltzer, David, ed., *The Secret Garden* (1976); Weiner, Herbert, *Nine and One Half Mystics* (1969).

Kabuki [kah-boo'-kee]

Elaborate masklike makeup and intricately decorated costumes are integral parts of Kabuki, a form of Japanese drama that evolved during the late 17th century and that remains popular today. The Kabuki performance combines dance, mime, music, and melodrama.

Kabuki is a popular Japanese theater form in which stylized acting is combined with lyric singing, dancing, and spectacular staging. The characters with which the word *Kabuki* is written in fact mean song, dance, and acting.

The female entertainer Okuni first performed Kabuki dances and comic sketches in 1603. Since 1629, however, when women were banned from professional stages, both Kabuki and the puppet drama BUNRAKU have been performed only by men. In Tokyo, ICHIKAWA Danjuro I (1660–1704) created a bravura acting style for such history plays as *Saint Narukami* (1684), while in Kyoto the elegant actor Sakata Tojuro (1644–1709) created a gentle, comic style for romantic domestic plays such as *Love Letter from the Licensed Quarter* (1678). Bunraku plays were adapted for Kabuki actors in the 18th century, and dance plays such as *The Subscription List* (1840) were adapted from KYOGEN and NŌ DRAMA in the 19th. Gangster plays, with thieves and murderers as heroes, were the invention of playwrights Tsuruya Namboku IV (1755–1829) and Kawatake Mokuami (1816–93). The classic Kabuki plays are still performed at commercial theaters in Japan, and some modern authors have tried to create new Kabuki plays.

Following the custom of No drama, the all-day Kabuki program provides variety by alternating play types and acting styles. *Hanamichi*, or walkways, revolving stages, elevators, trap doors, curtains, and rapid costume changes are used for theatrical effect. The female impersonator (*onnagata*) stylizes feminine traits into a half-real, half-artificial art. Actors use the *mie*, a pose, as the visual climax of a scene. Background music appropriate to the scene is selected from among some 500 melodies and rhythms and is played by an offstage ensemble consisting of No drums and flute, the three-stringed *shamisen*, plus a score of other drums, gongs, bells, and flutes. During a dance play, this ensemble—or one playing *Joruri* music—is seated on stage. JAMES R. BRANDON

Bibliography: Brandon, J. R., et al., *Chushingura* (1982), *Kabuki: Five Classic Plays* (1975), and *Studies in Kabuki* (1978); Ernst, Earle, *The Kabuki Theatre*, rev. ed. (1974); Leiter, Samuel, *Kabuki Encyclopedia* (1980); Toshio, Kawatake, ed., *Kabuki* (1985).

Kabul [kuh-bool']

Kabul, the capital and the largest city of Afghanistan as well as the capital of Kabul province, is located on the Kabul River in the northeast of the country, about 80 km (50 mi) east of the border with Pakistan. The population is 1,179,341 (1984 est.). The city, in a valley about 1,800 m (5,900 ft) above sea level, faces the HINDU KUSH to the northwest.

Ancient and modern elements coexist in Kabul. Manufactures include building materials, machinery, textiles, and processed food, while local craftspeople use methods that have changed little over thousands of years. Architecture ranges from small frame huts to modern high-rise hotels. The city has a university (1932), several technical institutes, and a large museum and is a transportation center.

Kabul (called Kabura by Ptolemy) has existed for more than 3,000 years. In AD 664 it was conquered by Arabs, and in the 13th century it was sacked by Genghis Khan. In 1504 the city was conquered by BABUR, under whom it was capital of the Mogul Empire until 1526. In 1773, Kabul became the capital of Afghanistan. Kabul was captured by the British in both 1842 and 1879 during the Afghan Wars. During the 1980s the city was a major Soviet military base.

Kabyle [kuh-byl']

The Kabyle, the largest BERBER-speaking tribe in Africa, occupy the mountainous coastal area of Kabylia, in northern Algeria. They number approximately 2 million. Their historical origins, like those of other Berber peoples, are only vaguely known. Principally agriculturists who cultivate cereal grains and olives, the Kabyle also maintain their subsistence economy through goat herding. Patrilineal clans characterize the marriage-family structure, with the husband's mother occupying a dominant position in the household. Councils composed of male elders govern each village, drawing upon a well-developed legal code to deal with property disputes and other offenses. Kabyle social organization includes a lower caste of butchers and smiths and a class of serfs (formerly slaves). Islam is the dominant religion. JAMES W. HERRICK

Bibliography: Wysner, Glora, *The Kabyle People* (1945).

kachina [kuh-chin'-uh]

A kachina is an ancestral spirit in the religion of the PUEBLO Indians of present-day Arizona and New Mexico. In certain ceremonies kachinas, or kachinam, are impersonated by masked dancers wearing colorful costumes. The HOPI believe that when a person dies his or her ghost may be metamorphosed into a kachina and live on as such in the underworld. A particular kachina does not, however, represent an individual but is instead a generalized mythical conception. No one knows how many different kachinas there are, but more than 250 have been identified. The kachinas are believed to spend half of every year in the Hopi villages, returning each July to underground dwelling places. The carved-wood kachina dolls of the Hopi and Zuñi are considered representations of the kachina spirits. KENNETH M. STEWART

Bibliography: Colton, Harold S., *Hopi Kachina Dolls with a Key to Their Identification*, rev. ed. (1987); Jacobs, Martina, *Kachina Ceremonies and Kachina Dolls* (1980).

Kádár, János [kah'-dahr, yahn'-ohsh]

The Hungarian political leader János Kádár, b. May 26, 1912, d. July 6, 1989, became the Soviet-appointed premier of Hungary after the HUNGARIAN REVOLUTION of 1956 and remained in power until 1988. Kádár joined the Communist party in 1929. Following the Communist takeover in 1948 he became minister of internal affairs and deputy chief secretary of the party. Arrested and imprisoned (1951–54) as a pro-Titoist he returned to lead the Budapest party organization in 1956. Kádár joined Imre NAGY's reform government during the 1956 Hungarian uprising but soon sided with the Soviets and formed a countergovernment. When the rebellion was put down, Kádár became premier and first secretary. Although he remained loyal to Moscow, his regime gradually introduced comparatively liberal domestic policies.

Kael, Pauline [kayl]

Pauline Kael, b. Petaluma, Calif., June 19, 1919, is a film critic whose sharp, analytical, sometimes eccentric opinions have won her a large following. She is particularly known for her reviews in the *New Yorker* (1968–   ), which relate movies to wide-ranging aspects of culture as well as to the audience itself. Her collections of essays and reviews include *I Lost It at the Movies* (1965), *Going Steady* (1970), *Deeper into Movies* (1973; National Book Award), *Reeling* (1976), *5001 Nights at the Movies* (1982), and *Taking It All In* (1984).

Kaesong   [kay'-suhng]

Kaesong is a special city with provincial status in southwestern North Korea, near the 38th parallel (the demarcation line between North and South Korea). It has a population of 259,000 (1980 est.). An agricultural trade center, Kaesong is also noted for porcelain and for locally grown ginseng. The walled city, called Songdor, was the capital of the Koryo dynasty from 938 until 1392. It was taken by North Korean forces during the Korean War, and the first truce talks were held there in 1951. Its special administrative status was attained when a military installation was built along the truce line.

Kaffir cat

The Kaffir cat, F. libyca, *may be the ancestor of modern domestic cats. Its markings are similar to those of the tabby cat.*

The Kaffir cat, *Felis libyca*, also known as the African wildcat, closely resembles the domestic cat and is often regarded as its primary ancestor. The Kaffir cat is sometimes classified as a subspecies of the European wildcat, *F. sylvestris*. Its color ranges from yellowish gray to orangy brown, with narrow, dark stripes. It reaches about 65 cm (27 in) in length and weighs up to 4.5 kg (10 lb) or more.   EVERETT SENTMAN

Kafir   [kaf'-ur]

The Kafir (Nuri) people occupy parts of the Hindu Kush in northern Pakistan and Afghanistan and number nearly 70,000. A Caucasoid people, they speak Kafiri—an Indo-European language—and subsist through agriculture, hunting, and the raising of livestock. Although a large number of Kafirs were forcibly converted to Islam in the late 19th century, others still practice their traditional religion, which includes the propitiation of a number of gods, the practice of shamanism, and elaborate funeral practices. Although the term *Kafir* (Arabic for "infidel") was originally used to denote non-Muslims in a derogatory fashion, the Asian Kafirs now consider the name a badge of their distinctive identity.

The name *Kafir*, or *Kaffir*, was also applied to the XHOSA peoples of southern Africa by early white settlers. It was later used in a pejorative sense by white South Africans to refer to all black Africans.   HILARY STANDING AND R. L. STIRRAT

Bibliography: Jones, Schuyler, *Men of Influence in Nuristan* (1974); Robertson, G. S., *Kafirs of the Hindu-Kush* (1896, repr. 1971).

Kafka, Franz

Franz Kafka, b. Prague, Bohemia (then belonging to Austria), July 3, 1883, d. June 3, 1924, has come to be one of the most influential writers of this century. Virtually unknown during his lifetime, the works of Kafka have since been recognized as symbolizing modern man's anxiety-ridden and grotesque alienation in an unintelligible, hostile, or indifferent world.

Kafka came from a middle-class Jewish family and grew up in the shadow of his domineering shopkeeper father, who impressed Kafka as an awesome patriarch. The feeling of impotence, even in his rebellion, was a syndrome that became a pervasive theme in his fiction. Kafka did well in the prestigious German high school in Prague and went on to receive a law degree in 1906. This allowed him to secure a livelihood that gave him time for writing, which he regarded as the essence—both blessing and curse—of his life. He soon found a position in the semipublic Workers' Accident Insurance institution, where he remained a loyal and successful employee until—beginning in 1917—tuberculosis forced him to take repeated sick leaves and finally, in 1922, to retire. Kafka spent half his time after 1917 in sanatoriums and health resorts, his tuberculosis of the lungs finally spreading to the larynx.

Kafka lived his life in emotional dependence on his parents, whom he both loved and resented. None of his largely unhappy love affairs could wean him from this inner dependence; though he longed to marry, he never did. Sexually, he apparently oscillated between an ascetic aversion to intercourse, which he called "the punishment for being together," and an attraction to prostitutes. Sex in Kafka's writings is frequently connected with dirt or guilt and treated as an attractive abomination. Nevertheless, Kafka led a fairly active social life, including acquaintance with many prominent literary and intellectual figures of his era, such as the writers Franz Werfel and Max Brod. He loved to hike, swim, and row, and during vacations he took carefully planned trips. He wrote primarily at night, the days being preempted by his job.

None of Kafka's novels was printed during his lifetime, and it was only with reluctance that he published a fraction of his shorter fiction. This fiction included *Meditation* (1913; Eng. trans., 1949), a collection of short prose pieces; *The Judgment* (1913; Eng. trans., 1945), a long short story, written in 1912, which Kafka himself considered his decisive breakthrough (it tells of a rebellious son condemned to suicide by his father); and *The Metamorphosis* (1915; Eng. trans., 1961), dealing again with the outsider, a son who suffers the literal and symbolic transformation into a huge, repulsive, fatally wounded insect. *In the Penal Colony* (1919; Eng. trans., 1961) is a parable of a torture machine and its operators and victims—equally applicable to a person's inner sense of law, guilt, and retribution and to the age of World War I. *The Country Doctor* (1919; Eng. trans., 1946) was another collection of short prose.

Franz Kafka, a 20th-century Czech author, wrote such intense, symbolic tales as The Metamorphosis *(1915) and* The Trial *(1925), in which he portrays people as tormented by isolation and ineffectuality. Himself burdened by mental conflict and tuberculosis, Kafka remained virtually unknown during his lifetime. Most of his works were published posthumously.*

At the time of his death Kafka was also preparing *A Hunger Artist* (1924; Eng. trans., 1938), four stories centering on the artist's inability to either negate or come to terms with life in the human community.

Contrary to Kafka's halfhearted instruction that his unprinted manuscripts be destroyed after his death, his friend Max Brod set about publishing them and thus became the architect of his belated fame. The best known of the posthumous works are three fragmentary novels. The TRIAL (1925; Eng. trans., 1937) deals with a man persecuted and put to death by the inscrutable agencies of an unfathomable court of law. The CASTLE (1926; Eng. trans., 1930) describes the relentless but futile efforts of the protagonist to gain recognition from the mysterious authorities ruling (from their castle) the village where he wants to establish himself. *Amerika* (1927; Eng. trans., 1938) portrays the inconclusive struggle of a young immigrant to gain a foothold in an alien, incomprehensible country. In all of these works, the lucid, concise style forms a striking contrast to the labyrinthine complexities, the anxiety-laden absurdities, and the powerfully oppressive symbols of torment and anomie that are the substance of the writer's vision. Kafka's fiction, somewhat like inkblot tests, elicits and defeats attempts at conclusive explanation.   PETER HELLER

Bibliography: Brod, Max, *Franz Kafka*, trans. by G. H. Roberts and Richard Winston, 2d ed. (1960); Flores, Angel, ed., *The Kafka Debate* (1977); Hayman, Ronald, *Kafka* (1982); Heller, Erich, *Franz Kafka* (1975); Lawson, R. H., *Franz Kafka* (1987); Politzer, Heiny, *Franz Kafka: Parable and Paradox* (1962); Udoff, Alan, ed., *Kafka and the Contemporary Critical Performance* (1987).

kagu   [kah'-goo]

The kagu bird, *Rhynochetos jubatus*, lives in the forests of New Caledonia. Classified as the sole member of the family Rhynochetidae, order Gruiformes, the kagu is perhaps a relic of a formerly more successful ancient group. It is about 55 cm (22 in) long. The loose-webbed plumage is pale gray and brown, the tail is a darker gray, and the wings are marked with white, chestnut, and black. There is a long crest on the head. The legs are fairly long and red. The bright red bill is strong and slightly decurved.

The nocturnal kagu feeds on worms, insects, snails, and similar prey. Nearly incapable of flight, it escapes enemies by running rapidly. Both sexes build the nest of twigs and leaves, which is placed on the ground, and incubate the single rust-colored egg. Formerly abundant, the kagu faces extinction because of hunting by humans and dogs.   ROBERT J. RAIKOW

Kahn, Albert   [kahn]

The American architect Albert Kahn, b. Rhaunen, Germany, Mar. 2, 1869, d. Dec. 8, 1942, was best known for his strikingly novel approach to factory design, especially for the assembly-line plants that he designed for the Ford Motor Company in the Detroit area. Kahn's buildings were the practical outcome of the ideas of Henry Ford (see FORD family), who revolutionized manufacture by combining all production under one roof. Kahn's Highland Park Plant, Detroit (1908–10), was the first truly autonomous industrial plant in the world. His River Rouge Plant, Detroit (begun 1917), was planned as a single-story structure, allowing the assembly line to proceed in a continuous flow from raw material to finished product.

So great was Kahn's fame as an industrial architect that the Soviet government commissioned him to design hundreds of factories built during the 1930s.   RON WIEDENHOEFT

Bibliography: Detroit Institute of Arts, *Legacy of Albert Kahn* (1970).

Kahn, Louis

Louis Isadore Kahn, b. Estonia, Feb. 20 (N.S.), 1901, d. Mar. 17, 1974, was one of the major architects of the 20th century. Kahn emigrated with his parents to Philadelphia in 1905, and studied architecture at the University of Pennsylvania. Kahn's first building to achieve international recognition was the Yale University Art Gallery, New Haven, Conn. (1952–54), built while he was professor of architecture at Yale (1947–57). From 1957 until his death he taught at the University of Pennsylva-

nia, where he designed the Richards Medical Research Building, which was quickly recognized as a challenge to the INTERNATIONAL STYLE of modern architecture.

Kahn's buildings are thought to reveal his interest in mystical philosophy. They are characterized by bold, clearly defined shapes, which achieve a massive, monumental effect through the use of large blocks of concrete. The functional aspects of the building, such as stairways, are sometimes isolated from the remainder of the structure in towers. Some of his most important buildings are the Salk Institute for Biological Studies, La Jolla, Calif. (1959–65); the library at Phillips Exeter Academy, Exeter, N.H. (1967–72); the Kimbell Art Museum, Fort Worth, Tex. (1966–72); and the Yale Center for British Art, New Haven (1969–74).   JOHN LOBELL

Bibliography: Giurgola, R., and Mehta, J., *Louis I. Kahn* (1975); Lobell, J., *Between Silence and Light* (1979); Ronner, H., et al., *Louis I. Kahn: Complete Works, 1935–1974* (1977; repr. 1983); Scully, Vincent, *Louis I. Kahn* (1962); Wurman, Richard S., *What Will Be Has Always Been: The Words of Louis Kahn* (1986).

K'ai-feng   (Kaifeng)   [ky'-fuhng]

K'ai-feng is a city in east central China in Honan (Henan) province. It has a population of 450,000 (1982). Located on the Lunghai Railroad and on several canals south of the Hwang Ho (Yellow River), it is a shipping point for trade with the interior. K'ai-feng is also an industrial center, with automotive, metallurgical, chemical, and food-processing plants. It served as the country's capital during the period of China's Five Dynasties (907–60) and then of the Northern Sung Dynasty until 1127. From 1368 until 1954 it was the capital of Honan province. A colony of Chinese Jews lived in the city from at least the 12th century; few traces of it remained by the 19th.

Kaifu Toshiki   [ky'-foo' toh'-shih-kee]

Kaifu Toshiki, b. Jan. 2, 1931, became prime minister of Japan on Aug. 8, 1989. Elected to successive terms in parliament from 1960, he served two terms as education minister. Kaifu, Japan's third prime minister in three months, was untainted by an influence-peddling scandal that forced Prime Minister TAKESHITA NOBORU to resign in June 1989. His successor, Uno Sosuki, stepped down after July elections in which his Liberal Democratic party (LDP) lost its majority in the upper house of parliament for the first time in 35 years. Kaifu remained in office after LDP gains in the February 1990 elections.

Kaigetsudo   [ky-get'-soo-doh]

Kaigetsudo is the collective name taken by a school of early-18th-century Japanese painters and printmakers who specialized in large, boldly executed portraits of courtesans. Among those who signed their works ''Kaigetsudo,'' scholars have identified Ando as founder of the school and Anchi, Dohan, Doshin, and Doshu as his pupils. Nothing definite is known of their biographies, but their works reflect a development of the UKIYO-E style of populist genre prints and a certain debt to the Torii school (see KIYONOBU I). Kaigetsudo prints, with sweeping lines and boldly decorative emphasis, set an enduring standard in popular Japanese art.   HOWARD A. LINK

Bibliography: Lane, Richard, *Kaigetsudo* (1959).

Kaiser, Georg   [ky'-zur, gay'-ork]

Georg Kaiser was a German dramatist. He was born in Magdeburg on Nov. 25, 1878, and died in Ascona, Switzerland, on June 4, 1945, an exile from Nazi Germany. Kaiser was the leading dramatist among the German expressionists and a consistent experimenter and innovator of theater forms. Early in his career he dealt with themes of sexuality in *Die jüdische Witwe* (The Jewish Widow, 1911), school tyranny in *Rektor Kleist* (Headmaster Kleist, 1905), and impotence in *König Hahnrei* (King Cuckold, 1913). Then Kaiser turned to the expressionistic mode of excitement, energy, and emotion that characterized his greatest works: *Die Bürger von Calais* (The Citizens of Calais, 1914), *From Morn to Midnight* (1916; Eng. trans., 1920), and the extraordinary trilogy *The Coral* (1917;

Eng. trans., 1929), *Gas I* (1918), and *Gas II* (1920; Eng. trans., 1924). The *Gas* trilogy remains the best example of the frenzy of German expressionist theater. The characters are given abstract labels instead of names, the sets appear to come from the easel of a modern painter, and the enemy is an unreal, modern technology—the result of a civilization out of control. Kaiser left Germany, where his works had been banned, in 1938.　　　　　　　　　　　　　　　　SOL GITTLEMAN

Bibliography: Benson, R., *German Expressionist Drama: Ernst Toller and Georg Kaiser* (1984); Schürer, Ernst, *Georg Kaiser* (1972).

Kaiser, Henry John

Henry John Kaiser, b. Sprout Brook, N.Y., May 9, 1882, d. Aug. 24, 1967, was a California industrialist who pioneered in the mass production of prefabricated cargo vessels during World War II. He had previously been a builder of dams and bridges including the Hoover Dam, the San Francisco–Oakland Bay Bridge, and the Grand Coulee Dam. During the war his shipyards built 1,460 vessels. After the war Kaiser Industries grew to include steel, cement, and aluminum plants. Kaiser was also a founder of the Kaiser-Frazer Corporation, an unsuccessful automobile manufacturer. In 1945 he established the Kaiser-Permanente Medical Care Program, a nonprofit health maintenance organization.

Bibliography: Kaiser Industries Corporation, *The Kaiser Story* (1968).

kala-azar　　[kah'-lah-ah-zar']

A form of leishmaniasis, kala-azar is a tropical disease caused by infection with protozoan parasites of the genus *Leishmania*. It is transmitted by the bite of sandflies that have fed on infected persons or animals. The parasites, multiplying inside body cells called macrophages, cause fever and may damage the spleen, liver, bone marrow, and lymph nodes. Treatment consists of diamidine drugs, good nutrition, and bed rest. Kala-azar is fatal in 90 percent of untreated cases.
　　　　　　　　　　　　　　　　PETER L. PETRAKIS

Kalahari Desert　　[kah-lah-har'-ee]

The Kalahari Desert, 260,000 km² (100,000 mi²) in area, covers the western two-thirds of Botswana and adjoining areas of eastern Namibia and South Africa's Cape Province. It is mostly a flat tableland (altitude 915–1,220 m/3,000–4,000 ft) that was once covered by an inland sea. The most prominent surface features, all of them in Botswana, are isolated salt pans and dry river courses, the OKAVANGO SWAMP (a remnant of the inland sea), the Makgadikgadi Pans (an ancient drainage basin), and Lake Ngami. Much of the region is covered by sand, generally reddish brown in the south and grayish white in the north. Flora consists of grasses and acacias typical of a steppe environment. Rainfall is light and erratic, decreasing from about 660 mm (26 in) per year in the northeast to 153 mm (6 in) in the southwest. Summers are very hot, with highs of 47° C (117° F), and winters are cool, as low as −13° C (8° F). The natural fauna includes giraffe, lion, impala, gemsbok, and wildebeest. The Kalahari Gemsbok National Park (20,800 km²/ 8,030 mi²), in South Africa, is a huge game preserve. Sparsely populated, the region is inhabited by nomadic KHOIKHOI, SAN (Bushmen), and TSWANA. It is believed that the first white men to cross the Kalahari were David Livingstone and W. C. Oswell in 1849.　　　　　　　　　　ALAN C. G. BEST

Bibliography: Silberbauer, G. B., *Hunter and Habitat in the Central Kalahari* (1981).

Kalámai　　[kah-lah'-may]

Kalámai (Kalamáta) is the capital of the department of Messenia in southern Greece. It has a population of 42,075 (1981). The city is a major port on the Gulf of Messenia and a market center for the Peloponnesus. Trade is dominated by olives, figs, currants, mulberries, and oranges. The city's industries produce flour, tobacco, liquor, and silk.

Kalámai developed during the period (1210–78) when the Peloponnesus (Morea) was a fief of the French Villehardouin family. The city was controlled by Venice during the 15th century and then by the Turks until 1821.

Kalamazoo　　[kal-uh-muh-zoo']

Kalamazoo is a city in southwestern Michigan on the Kalamazoo River. It is the seat of Kalamazoo County and has a population of 79,722 (1980). In addition to its role as market center for the surrounding farms, Kalamazoo has industries engaged in the production of paper and the manufacture of drugs, clothing, musical instruments, and metal products. It is the seat of Western Michigan University (1903).

The site was a fur-trading post in the late 1700s; permanent settlement began in 1829. The city's name is Indian for "boiling water." The arrival of the Michigan Central Railroad in 1846 accelerated population growth in the area.

kalanchoe　　[kal-uhn-koh'-ee]

Kalanchoes, genus *Kalanchoe* of the orpine family, Crassulaceae, are shrubby, succulent plants often called life plants because new plants can be propagated from their fleshy leaves. They are native to tropical Africa and Asia but are now cultivated in other warm areas; several species are popular houseplants. The yellow, scarlet, or purple flowers are tubular in shape.

Kalb, Johann　　[kahlp, yoh'-hahn]

Johann Kalb, b. June 29, 1721, d. Aug. 19, 1780, was a German-born officer, known as Baron de Kalb, in the Continental Army during the American Revolution. While serving in the French army, Kalb was sent (1768) to America on a secret mission to make observations for the French government. After his return to Paris, Kalb, the marquis de LAFAYETTE, and other American sympathizers were offered (1776) commissions by Silas DEANE. When Kalb arrived in Philadelphia in 1777, the Continental Congress was reluctant to confirm the commission; however, he became a major general, served at VALLEY FORGE (1777–78), and distinguished himself under Horatio GATES in the Carolina campaign. He was mortally wounded at the Battle of Camden.

kale　　[kayl]

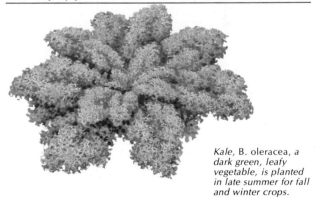

Kale, B. oleracea, a dark green, leafy vegetable, is planted in late summer for fall and winter crops.

Kale is a nonheading leaf vegetable, *Brassica oleracea,* of the Cruciferae family, which is eaten as a cooked green and is an excellent source of minerals and vitamins A and C. One of the oldest cultivated vegetables, kale closely resembles wild cabbage and may be the ancestor of all the common CABBAGE crops. It is hardy in cold weather—in fact, its flavor is improved after it has been touched by frost. Some types of kale are raised for cattle fodder and may grow more than 2.1 m (7 ft) in height. Garden kale usually grows about 0.6 m (2 ft) in height.　　　　　　　　　　　　　　O. A. LORENZ

Kalevala　　[kah'-le-vah-lah]

The *Kalevala,* Finland's national epic, is based on an oral tradition that dominated the epic, lyric, magic, and aphoristic poetry of the Balto-Finnish peoples (Finns, Karelians, Votes, Estonians) for some 2,500 years. Characteristic of this poetry are the use of trochaic tetrameter, highly developed alliteration, and many kinds of parallelism. The *Kalevala* owes its existence to Elias Lönnrot (1802–84), a country doctor who compiled it from oral poetry collected principally in Karelia. The first edition, published in 1835, consisted of 12,078 lines arranged in 32 cantos. A later edition (1849) had 22,795 lines in 50 cantos. The 1849 edition has had an enormous impact on all the arts in Finland, particularly on the music of Jean Sibelius; it also influenced Henry Wadsworth Longfellow's long narrative poem *Hiawatha* (1855).   MATTI KUUSI

Kalff, Willem   [kahlf, vil'-em]

Willem Kalff (or Kalf), b. 1619, d. July 31, 1693, was a leading Dutch still-life and genre painter. After early work in his native Rotterdam, Kalff painted (1642–46) in Paris and then settled (1653) in Amsterdam. In his mature work Kalff used a rich color tonality and impasto combined with clear linearity. These techniques accent the textures of the sumptuous decorative objects and fruit that he frequently used in his elegant compositions, for example, *The Nautilus Cup* (c.1660; Thyssen Collection, Lugano, Switzerland).   CHARLES I. MINOTT

Bibliography: Bergström, Ingvar, *Dutch Still-Life Painting in the Seventeenth Century,* trans. by Christina Hedström and Gerald Taylor (1956); Rosenberg, Jakob, et al., *Dutch Art and Architecture, 1600–1800* (1966).

Kalgoorlie   [kal-gur'-lee]

Kalgoorlie, a famous mining town in south central Australia on the Nullarbor Plain, merged with Boulder in 1947 and is now officially known as Kalgoorlie-Boulder. Kalgoorlie has a population of 9,145; the population of the metropolitan area is 19,818 (1981). Kalgoorlie is located over huge gold deposits, and gold mining has long been the economic mainstay, although nickel deposits discovered in 1966 are now also economically significant. Other industries include engineering, brewing, and metal fabricating. Kalgoorlie was settled (1894) after gold was discovered (1893); the town was originally called Hannan's Find.

Kali   [kah'-lee]

Among the many metamorphoses of the wife of the Hindu god SHIVA is that of Kali (the Black One). She represents one facet of SHAKTI, the divine creative power or mother goddess, but also the power of destruction. The rituals of her cult, which is particularly strong among the lower castes in India, focus both on sensual pleasure and on fertility. The THUGS, an Indian subcaste, were devoted to Kali. Her most famous legend concerns her struggle with Raktavija, head of an army of demons. Failing to wound him mortally with any of her weapons, Kali finally overcame him by drinking all his blood.

Kalidasa   [kah-li-dah'-suh]

India's foremost Sanskrit dramatist and poet Kalidasa flourished around AD 400, during the reign of Chandragupta II, the height of Indian classical civilization. The most famous of his three extant plays, *Shakuntala,* reveals his supreme command of poetic language. The play is a dramatization of part of the MAHABHARATA and deals with King Dusyanta's love for the hermit girl Shakuntala, their parting, and their eventual reunion. It evokes love in highly idealized terms as a spiritual force. The courtly comedy *Malavikagnimitra* (*Malavika and Agnimitra*) and the heroic *Vikramorvasiya* (*Vikrama and Urvashi*) show the author's keen sense of characterization and humor.

Kalidasa's "nature" poetry culminated in *Meghaduta* (*Cloud Messenger*), in which a *yaksa* (exiled spirit) sends messages to his wife by a passing cloud. Its intense lyricism greatly appealed to the early European romantics, particularly Schiller and Goethe. Kalidasa also wrote several court epics, all of them based on the legend of Rama. Kalidasa's originality in each genre remains unsurpassed.   GAUTAM DASGUPTA

Bibliography: Krishnamoorthy, *Kalidasa* (1972); Sabnis, S. A., *Kalidasa: His Style and His Times* (1966); Singh, A. D., ed., *Kalidasa: A Critical Study* (1977).

Kalimantan: see INDONESIA.

Kaline, Al   [kay'-lyn]

Baseball Hall of Fame member Albert William Kaline, b. Baltimore, Md., Dec. 19, 1934, was a star right fielder for the American League's Detroit Tigers, for whom he played exclusively (1953–74). In his career, Kaline accumulated 3,007 hits, 1,583 runs batted in, 399 home runs, and a .297 batting average (AL leader in 1955, at .340). An excellent defensive player, he won 10 Gold Glove awards.

Kalinin   [kuhl-yee'-neen]

Kalinin (1984 est. pop., 437,000) is the capital of Kalinin oblast in the Russian republic of the USSR. It is situated on the upper Volga River and is served by the Moscow-Leningrad highway and railroad. Kalinin evolved as a diversified industrial city during the Soviet period, producing textiles and a wide range of machinery. Originally named Tver, it was the center of a separate Russian principality until absorbed by Moscow in 1485. In 1931 it was named for Mikhail I. Kalinin, an early Soviet president.   THEODORE SHABAD

Kaliningrad   [kuhl-yee'-neen-graht]

Kaliningrad is the capital of Kaliningrad oblast in the Russian republic of the USSR. The city, situated on the Pregolya River near the Baltic Sea, has a population of 380,000 (1984 est.). Kaliningrad (formerly Königsberg) was the capital of the German province of East Prussia until 1945. At the end of World War II, East Prussia was partitioned with the northern half, including Königsberg, passing to the USSR and the southern half to Poland. The city was renamed for Soviet President Mikhail I. Kalinin in 1946. The inhabitants are now predominantly Russians; most Germans were removed after the war.

Kaliningrad has been almost entirely rebuilt after near total destruction in the war. From a historic German city with distinctive Gothic architecture, it has been transformed into a Soviet manufacturing and fishing center producing railroad equipment, ships, and paper. It is the base for the Soviet Baltic fleet. Its port is linked by a deep-water canal with the outer Baltic port of Baltisk, formerly Pillau. The city has the Kaliningrad State University (1967) and research institutes specializing in fisheries and oceanography. Among the few vestiges of its German past are the tomb of Immanuel Kant.

Königsberg grew around a castle built (1255) by the Teutonic Knights. It developed into a major trading center and joined the Hanseatic League in 1340. Both in the German period and under Soviet rule, it has been a strategic military base.   THEODORE SHABAD

Kalmyk   [kal'-mik]

The Kalmyk, formerly called the Oyrat, are a Central Asian people who dwell in the Kalmyk Autonomous Soviet Socialist Republic on the northwestern shore of the Caspian Sea. Smaller numbers of Kalmyk live in neighboring oblasts (provinces) of the Russian Soviet Federated Socialist Republic (RSFSR) and in central Siberia. Numbering 200,000, the Kalmyk bear classic Mongoloid features. They speak a Mongol derivative of the Altaic languages.

As Oyrat MONGOLS, the Kalmyk served as loyal warriors of Genghis Khan. They were strongest in the 14th century, when in Western Mongolia they became an independent political power. In the late 16th and early 17th centuries they were driven from Dzungaria by the Manchus. Kalmyk ethnic affiliation reputedly crystallized during the migrations to their present homeland. In World War II, the Kalmyk were accused of pro-German sentiments and many were deported to Siberia.

Still over 60 percent rural, the Kalmyk traditionally are nomadic herdsmen and Caspian fishermen, although today these activities are collectivized. Kinship is patrilineal, and family relations are patriarchal. Native Kalmyk architecture, art, and dress—Sino-Mongolian in style—and their traditional Lamaist religion recall their historic roots.   VICTOR L. MOTE

Bibliography: Rubel, P. G., *The Kalmyk Mongols* (1967); Symmons-Symonolewicz, Konstantin, ed., *The Non-Slavic Peoples of the Soviet Union* (1972); Wixman, R., *The Peoples of the U.S.S.R.* (1984).

Kamasutra   [kah-muh-soo'-truh]

The *Kamasutra* is a Hindu treatise on the art of love, composed sometime between the 1st and 4th centuries AD (Eng. trans., 1883). Written in Sanskrit, it is attributed to Vatsyayana, also known as Mallanaga. *Kama* is the Hindu word for love, pleasure, and sensual gratification; *sutra* are aphorisms. The work is partly a marriage manual, with specific sexual information. But the enormous influence of the *Kamasutra* stems from its wider discussion of women, courtship, and the place of erotic pleasure in the urbane life of a man or woman of leisure.   JANE COLVILLE BETTS

Kamba   [kahm'-buh]

The Kamba are a Bantu-speaking people living in Kenya, where they number about 2,000,000 (1985 est.). Primarily agriculturalists raising sorghum, maize, and millet as principal crops, they are also found as traders throughout East Africa today. Their history of long-distance trade dates back to precolonial times, when they traded in ivory and, to a lesser extent, in slaves and food. Formerly, they were the only tribe of Kenya to dominate every phase of trade between the interior and the coast, from collection of goods to final export.

Since World War II, the Kamba have also been known as itinerant woodcarvers who make carvings to order for customers as far off as Europe and America. They produce thousands of highly standardized objects either in original Kamba styles or in styles that imitate those of their neighbors, such as the Kikuyu and Masai. The Kamba are divided among about 25 totemic clans and may not marry within the clan. Descent is traced through the father's line.   RICHARD WERBNER

Bibliography: Lindblom, Gerhard, *The Akamba in British East Africa*, 2d ed. (1920); Middleton, John, *The Kikuyu and Kamba of Kenya* (1972); Munro, J. Forbes, *Colonial Rule and the Kamba* (1975); Muthiani, Joseph, *The Akamba from Within* (1973).

Kamchatka Peninsula   [kahm-chaht'-kuh]

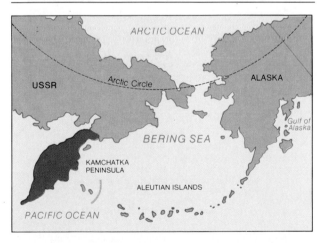

The Kamchatka Peninsula, part of the far eastern Russian republic of the USSR, extends about 1,200 km (750 mi) southward between the Sea of OKHOTSK and the BERING SEA, ending in Cape Lopatka, 11 km (7 mi) north of the KURIL ISLANDS. The peninsula has an area of 370,000 km² (140,000 mi²). Its two great volcanic ranges, Sredinnyi and Vostochnyi, run from north to south, separated by a central valley where the Kamchatka River flows. Twenty-eight of the volcanoes are active; the highest, Klyuchevskaya Sopka, rises to 4,750 m (15,600 ft). Winters are harsh, with severe winds and heavy snows; summers are cool and foggy.

Petropavlovsk-Kamchatsky, a fishing center, is the main settlement. The peninsula is sparsely populated. About 90% of the inhabitants are Russian, and most of the rest are Koryak and Kamchadal. Lumbering, fur trapping, and fishing are the major economic activities. The peninsula is noted for its giant crabs. Some grains and potatoes are grown in the central valley. Kamchatka has oil, coal, and copper deposits, but little exploitation has taken place. The peninsula was visited (1697) by a Russian expedition under Vladimir Atlasov (d. 1711) and annexed to Russia.

kame   [kaym]

A kame is a mound or irregular hill of stratified glacial debris originally deposited by glacial streams or in glacier ponds in a wide variety of positions on, in, or under a glacier. When the ice melts, the stream or pond bottom deposits are left as kames. Sand and gravel are the most common components; kames may also include silt, varved clay, or till that has flowed downslope from the original surrounding ice. The sediment is commonly collapsed and distorted from the melting of the ice walls.   JOSEPH R. HARTSHORN

Bibliography: Embleton, Clifford, and King, C. A. M., *Glacial Geomorphology,* 2d ed. (1975).

See also: ESKER; GLACIER AND GLACIATION.

Kamehameha   (dynasty)   [kah-may'-hah-may'-hah]

Kamehameha was the name of the first five monarchs of the Hawaiian Islands (see HAWAII, state). **Kamehameha I,** b. *c.*1758, d. May 8, 1819, known as Kamehameha the Great, conquered most of the Hawaiian islands and by 1810 became ruler of a united Hawaii. He brought law and order and prosperity to his realm. While encouraging the visits of traders and the introduction of modern technology, he insisted on preserving native customs and religious beliefs. He was succeeded (1819) by his son, **Kamehameha II,** also called Liholiho, 1797–1824. During Kamehameha II's reign the ancient Kapu system of laws and taboos was abolished, and in 1820 the first American missionaries were admitted to Hawaii.

Kamehameha II was succeeded (1825) by his brother, **Kamehameha III,** also called Kauikeouli, b. Mar. 7, 1814, d. Dec. 15, 1854. He permitted adoption (1840) of a charter making Hawaii a constitutional monarchy. Another landmark of his reign was the *Great Mahele* (1848), a policy that replaced the ancient feudal landholding system by giving land to the cultivator. In 1852 a new constitution granted suffrage to adult males and specified that the king must share power with a partially elected legislature.

Kamehameha III was succeeded by his nephew, Alexander Liholino, or **Kamehameha IV,** b. Feb. 9, 1834, d. Nov. 30, 1863. In 1855, Kamehameha IV signed a commercial treaty with the United States, but Congress declined to ratify it. The king's brother, b. Dec. 11, 1830, d. Dec. 11, 1872, ascended the throne in 1863 as **Kamehameha V.** He abrogated (1864) the constitution of 1852 and promulgated instead a charter that strengthened royal power, weakened the legislature, and restricted suffrage. U.S. missionary influence ebbed greatly during his reign. Kamehameha V died without an heir, and the legislature chose his successor, thus ending the dynasty.

Bibliography: Daws, Gavan, *Shoal of Time: A History of the Hawaiian Islands* (1968); Kuykendall, Ralph S., *The Hawaiian Kingdom, 1778–1854: Foundation and Transformation* (1938); Pole, James T., *Hawaii's First King* (1959); Tregaskis, Richard, *The Warrior King: Hawaii's Kamehameha the Great* (1973).

Kamenev, Lev Borisovich   [kah'-min-yif, lyef buh-ree'-suh-vich]

Lev Borisovich Kamenev, b. July 22 (N.S.), 1883, d. Aug. 24, 1936, was a Soviet political leader who briefly formed a ruling triumvirate with Joseph STALIN and Grigory ZINOVIEV in 1924. Originally named Rosenfeld, he joined the Russian Social Democratic Workers' party in 1901 and soon aligned himself with Vladimir Ilyich LENIN in the split between the BOLSHEVIKS and MENSHEVIKS. At the time of the RUSSIAN REVOLUTION of November 1917, Kamenev advocated a coalition of all the socialist parties. Although overruled, he became a member of the Politburo of the Communist party and held high office.

The triumvirate with Stalin and Zinoviev was formed on Lenin's death to exclude Leon TROTSKY from power. In 1925, however, Stalin began to ease out his colleagues. Kamenev was expelled from the party in 1927, readmitted, and expelled twice again. In 1936 he was tried for treason in the first show trial of the GREAT PURGE and executed. He was posthumously rehabilitated in 1988.   K. M. SMOGORZEWSKI

Bibliography: Ulam, Adam, *Stalin: The Man and His Era* (1987).

Kamerlingh Onnes, Heike   [kah'-mur-ling oh'-nes, hy'-kuh]

The Dutch physicist Heike Kamerlingh Onnes, b. Sept. 21, 1853, d. Feb. 21, 1926, received the 1913 Nobel Prize for physics for his pioneering work in CRYOGENICS and his discovery of SUPERCONDUCTIVITY. He studied under Gustav Kirchhoff and Robert Bunsen at Heidelberg, became professor of physics at Leiden in 1882, founded the famous Cryogenic Laboratory there in 1894, and succeeded in liquefying helium in 1908. Kamerlingh Onnes noticed in 1911 that the electrical resistivity of certain metals approached zero at a low temperature characteristic of each material, so that a current would continue to flow for hours or even days—a phenomenon known as superconductivity.   CARL A. ZAPFFE

Kaminaljuyú   [kahm-ee-nuhl-hoo-yoo']

Kaminaljuyú, an archaeological site on the outskirts of Guatemala City and now largely encompassed by it, dominated the MAYA highlands during the Late Preclassic (300 BC–AD 300) and flourished in the Early Classic (AD 250–550). Early relief sculpture there contributed to the patterns followed by the Classic Maya, including low-relief portraiture and accompanying hieroglyphic inscriptions, but the Kaminaljuyú texts, unlike later Maya ones, cannot yet be read.

Archaeological investigations carried out in the 1930s revealed that during the Early Classic, pots in tombs there were made in a hybrid Maya-TEOTIHUACÁN style, with gods and lords figured in Maya style on cylinder tripods of Teotihuacán type. Teotihuacán often had been identified as the home of the later TOLTEC (fl. 9th–12th centuries), but this discovery confirmed the contemporaneity of the Maya and Teotihuacán. Kaminaljuyú declined along with Teotihuacán after that city was sacked in the 7th century.   MARY ELLEN MILLER

Bibliography: Coe, Michael D., *The Maya*, 4th ed. (1987).

Kamloops   [kam'-loops]

Kamloops is a city in southern British Columbia, Canada, at the confluence of the North Thompson and South Thompson rivers; it has a population of 61,773 (1986). Accessible by rail, air, and highway, the city attracts many visitors who hunt and fish amid the rugged scenery of the surrounding Cariboo region. Kamloops also serves the area's extensive lumbering, mining, ranching, and farming interests. Local industries include the manufacture of food products and wood and pulp processing.

The trading post of Fort Kamloops, earlier called *cumeloups* (Indian for "meeting of the waters"), was established there about 1812. The gold seekers of the 1850s, the coming of the "overlanders" (1862), and the arrival of the railroad (1885) contributed to the town's growth.

Kampala

Kampala (1980 pop., 458,423), capital and largest city of Uganda, is the nation's commercial, financial, and industrial center. The city has rail and road connections to the rest of the country and to the Indian Ocean through Kenya. Port Bell on Lake Victoria and the ENTEBBE airport, 34 km (21 mi) to the south, serve the city. Kampala is a processing center for livestock and agricultural products; exports include cotton, coffee, and sugarcane. Makerere University (1922) is located there. In 1890, Frederick, Lord LUGARD, chose the site as headquarters for the British East Africa Company. Kampala became capital of Uganda in 1962.   G. N. UZOIGWE

Kampuchea   [kahm-poo-chah']

Kampuchea, also known as Cambodia, is located in mainland Southeast Asia between Vietnam, Laos, Thailand, and the Gulf of Thailand. From the 9th to the 15th century, the KHMER EMPIRE extended its sway far beyond the present boundaries of Kampuchea. This period produced the glorious temple complex and royal palace at ANGKOR. The Khmer kingdom gradually declined; it accepted French protection in 1863 and was later incorporated into French INDOCHINA. Cambodia became independent in 1953, but it was soon entangled in the VIETNAM WAR. In April 1975, Cambodian Communists known as the KHMER ROUGE took control of the country, which they renamed Democratic Kampuchea, and instituted policies that led to the deaths of at least 1,000,000 people. The Khmer Rouge were driven out in 1979 by the Vietnamese army and Kampuchean exiles. The Vietnamese-backed People's Republic of Kampuchea (renamed State of Cambodia in 1989) was opposed by the Chinese-backed coalition government of Kampuchea (in exile), which included the Khmer Rouge and two non-Communist factions. In August 1990 the UN Security Council approved a comprehensive peace plan calling for internationally supervised elections for a new government.

LAND AND RESOURCES
Kampuchea is heavily forested; only a small portion (16%) of the land is cultivated. Most of the country is low-lying. The Dangrek Mountains provide a watershed escarpment boundary with Thailand in the north. The Cardamom Range dominates the southwest, rising to 1,771 m (5,810 ft) at Phnom Aral, the highest point in the country. Adjacent to the coast is the Elephant Range, and highlands adjoin Laos and Vietnam east of the Mekong River in northern Kampuchea.

KAMPUCHEA

LAND. Area: 181,035 km² (69,898 mi²). Capital and largest city: Phnom Penh (1987 est. pop., 750,000).

PEOPLE. Population (1990 est.): 7,000,000; density: 38.7 persons per km² (100.1 per mi²). Distribution (1989): 11% urban, 89% rural. Annual growth (1989): 2.2%. Official language: Khmer. Major religion: Buddhism.

EDUCATION AND HEALTH. Literacy (1983): 48% of adult population. Universities (1990): 1. Hospital beds (1985): 17,856. Physicians (1985): 506. Life expectancy (1989): women—50; men—47. Infant mortality (1989): 134 per 1,000 live births.

ECONOMY. GDP (1984 est.): $570 million; $80 per capita. Labor distribution (1989): agriculture and fishing—80%; manufacturing—3%; commerce and services—17%. Foreign trade (1986): imports—$17 million; exports—$3 million; principal trade partners—Vietnam, USSR, Eastern Europe, Japan, India. Currency: 1 new riel = 100 sen.

GOVERNMENT. Type: republic (State of Cambodia); coalition government in exile (Democratic Kampuchea). Legislature: National Assembly. Political subdivisions: 19 provinces, 1 autonomous municipality.

COMMUNICATIONS. Railroads (1986): 612 km (380 mi). Roads (1986): 13,351 km (8,296 mi) total, 20% paved. Major ports: 2. Major airfields: 1.

Soils. Two types of soil predominate in Kampuchea: alluvium deposited by riverine flooding and soil resulting from rock decay. The former is fertile and supports rice production; the latter is mostly forested and has limited agricultural potential.

Climate. Monsoon rains prevail from mid-April to October, followed by drier and cooler air until March. Average annual rainfall in the central lowlands is 1,400 mm (55 in) and may be three or more times greater in the southwestern mountains. Temperatures range from 20° to 36° C (68° to 97° F).

Drainage. The MEKONG RIVER bisects and irrigates the eastern lowlands of Kampuchea. Close to the center of the country is the largest lake in Southeast Asia, the Tonle Sap ("great lake"), which acts as a natural reservoir for the Mekong. Only a few of Kampuchea's rivers, in the southwest, lie outside the drainage system of the Mekong and the Tonle Sap.

Vegetation and Animal Life. Dense tropical rain forests cover the uplands, while mangroves predominate along the coast. The natural vegetation of the central plains is prairie grass.

Larger species of wildlife, including buffalo, elephants, rhinoceroses, bears, tigers, and panthers, are found at higher elevations. Exotic birds and reptiles are common.

Resources. Hardwood forests have long been exploited for timber. Phosphate, salt, and gems (rubies, sapphires, and zircons) have been exported, and there are iron ore deposits. The Mekong has great hydroelectric and irrigation potential.

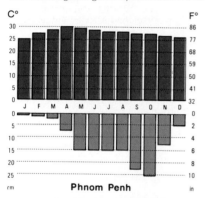

Bars indicate monthly ranges of temperature (red) and precipitation (blue) in Phnom Penh, the capital of Kampuchea. Phnom Penh, which is situated at the confluence of the Tonle Sap and Mekong rivers, has a tropical wet-dry climate.

PEOPLE

Kampuchea's population is unusually homogenous, with the KHMER constituting more than 85%. The Khmer are thought to have migrated from southern China prior to 200 BC. The chief minority groups are the Chinese and the Vietnamese. Although most Vietnamese were driven out or killed under Khmer Rouge rule, several hundred thousand Vietnamese have settled in Kampuchea since 1979. Vietnam's neighbors have raised charges that it is trying to colonize Kampuchea. It is unclear how various upland minorities, such as the Oham-Malays and Khmer Loeus, fared under the Khmer Rouge.

Theravada Buddhism has been the religion of almost all Khmer since the 13th century, when it replaced animism and ancestor worship among the peasants and Brahmanic beliefs at the royal court. The Khmer Rouge banned all religions, disrobed and punished thousands of monks, and desecrated hundreds of temples and monasteries. Since 1979 the practice of Buddhism has been permitted, and monasteries are being restored with government support.

Kampuchea is overwhelmingly agricultural and rural. The largest cities are PHNOM PENH, the capital, BATTAMBANG, and Kompong Cham. The Khmer Rouge evacuated the refugee-swollen cities and towns in 1975 with great loss of life. Massive population shifts again took place after 1979 as the new government allowed people to rejoin their families and return home. The population of Phnom Penh (1975 est., 3,000,000) increased from less than 200,000 in 1979 to 600,000 in 1984.

Formal education was abandoned during the Khmer Rouge period in favor of basic task training and political indoctrination in agricultural communes. Since 1979, with Vietnamese assistance, public schools have been reopened and adult literacy courses have been widely promoted.

Health care was very limited under French rule, and many physicians did not survive the Khmer Rouge revolution. Hospitals in the major towns have since been reopened.

The greatest monuments of Khmer culture are the ruins of Angkor Wat and Angkor Thom, which were inspired by a Hinduized worldview and indigenous sculptural idioms. The Vietnamese-backed government prides itself on having started to restore some of Kampuchea's lesser architectural monuments and temples. It has also organized classical- and folk-dance performances, song troupes, and shadow plays.

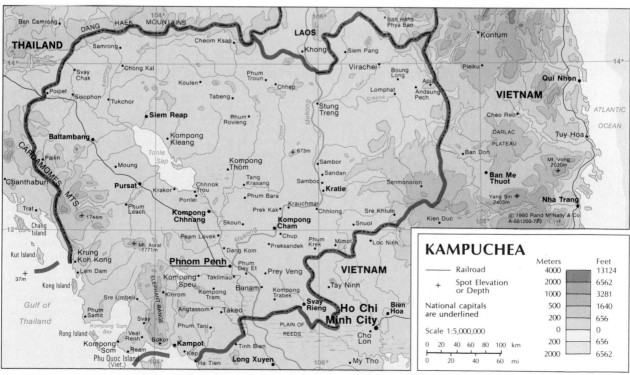

KAMPUCHEA

	Meters	Feet
Railroad	4000	13124
	2000	6562
Spot Elevation or Depth	1000	3281
	500	1640
National capitals are underlined	200	656
	0	0
Scale 1:5,000,000	200	656
	2000	6562

Scale 0 20 40 60 80 100 km
0 20 40 60 mi

(Above) *Phnom Penh, the capital and largest city of Kampuchea, is located in the south central portion of the country on the Mekong River. The city has become a major port as well as a processing and distributing center serving the surrounding provinces.*

(Left) *Buddhist monks in Phnom Penh light sticks of incense before offering prayers for peace. Theravada Buddhism, which was brought to Kampuchea by Indian merchants centuries ago, was sanctioned as the state religion prior to 1975, when the Khmer Rouge regime began to discourage religious practices, and again from 1989.*

ECONOMY

Kampuchea's myriad small plots, primitively cultivated once a year, traditionally produced an exportable surplus of rice. During the Vietnam War, dikes were destroyed and rubber plantations and processing plants were crippled by military damage; corn, groundnut, sugar, and livestock production also suffered. A large refugee population became dependent on imported rice. The Khmer Rouge, who emphasized economic self-sufficiency, abolished money and personal property and forcibly collectivized agriculture. By 1978, renewed civil war caused further economic disruption. After the Khmer Rouge were driven out in 1979, a massive international relief effort provided Kampuchea with food and other aid. The Vietnamese-backed government abandoned its efforts to collectivize agriculture in 1989, and much small enterprise is in private hands. Fish harvesting has increased dramatically, although the country is still not self-sufficient in rice.

Manufacturing facilities are also being rehabilitated. The surviving industries process agricultural and forest products and produce consumer goods. Transportation lines are slowly being restored. The road from Phnom Penh to Kompong Som is a vital link in the economy.

Under the Khmer Rouge, foreign trade was almost nonexistent. The Vietnamese-backed government depended almost exclusively on aid from Vietnam, the USSR, and its allies, but this aid declined after the breakup of Communism in Eastern Europe. Khmer Rouge attacks on economic targets further hampered recovery, driving up to 130,000 people from their homes by mid-1989.

GOVERNMENT

On Jan. 8, 1979, Vietnamese-backed opponents of the Khmer Rouge proclaimed the foundation of the People's Republic of Kampuchea (now State of Kampuchea), headed by a People's Revolutionary Council. In 1981 the newly elected National Assembly, whose members serve 5-year terms, ratified a constitution providing for a council of state and a council of ministers. The sole political party is the Kampuchean People's Revolutionary party, an offshoot of the Indochina Communist party dating from 1951. It rules through the Kampuchean United Front for National Construction and Defense.

The Coalition Government of Democratic Kampuchea (in exile) was formed in 1982, with Prince NORODOM SIHANOUK as president, Khieu Samphan (Khmer Rouge) as vice-president in charge of foreign affairs, and former premier Son Sann as prime minister. These leaders meet infrequently, and the armed forces of each faction operate independently.

HISTORY

Five significant periods can be discerned in the history of Kampuchea. From the 1st century AD, the kingdoms of Funan organized life in support of royal courts that adopted the Indian Brahmanic cult of the god-king; Indic culture spread into the legal code and an alphabet. During the 6th and 7th centuries, kingdoms of Khmer origin known as Chen-la kept the institutions of Funan while conquering neighboring kingdoms in present-day Laos, Vietnam, and Thailand. Chenla was succeeded by the classical (Angkor) period of Khmer history, which lasted from the 9th to the mid-15th century. During this period, Kampuchean artistic, architectural, and military achievements reached their zenith. A gradual decline in the coercive authority of the Khmer Empire was followed by losses of territory to the Vietnamese and the Thais.

The French protectorate began by treaty in 1863 and became a colonial relationship with Cambodia's incorporation into the Union of Indochina in 1887. Indochina fell to the Japanese during World War II, but France reclaimed it in 1945 as part of the newly conceived FRENCH UNION. King Norodom Sihanouk (installed by France in 1941) was pressed by new nationalist parties to gain full independence, which was granted in 1953.

After independence, opposition groups continued to demand further political and social reforms, although the Cambodian offshoot of Ho Chi Minh's Indochina Communist party withdrew its cadres to North Vietnam in 1954 following the Geneva cease-fire agreements for Indochina. Sihanouk gave up the throne to his father in 1955, but he remained a prince, premier, leader of the dominant political movement (the *Sangkum*), and, after 1960, elected head of state. He tried to minimize the risk of involvement in the Vietnam conflict by rejecting membership in the SOUTHEAST ASIA TREATY ORGANIZATION (SEATO), accepting military aid from China, breaking relations with South Vietnam and the United States, and allowing the North Vietnamese use of his seaport to support their forces in South Vietnam. A new Communist group under Soloth Sar (POL POT) sprouted secretly in 1960. This group, later named the Communist party of Kampuchea (Khmer Rouge), moved away from their North Vietnamese mentors, launching an armed struggle to topple the government in 1968.

The United States began secretly bombing North Vietnamese sanctuaries in Cambodia in 1969, and in April 1970, U.S. and South Vietnamese forces launched a limited incursion to wipe them out. By this time Sihanouk had been overthrown by one of his top generals, LON NOL. The new Khmer Republic's government became increasingly authoritarian and corrupt, and it fought a losing battle against the North Vietnamese on its territory and the Khmer Rouge guerrilla forces.

The Paris Peace Accords for Vietnam in January 1973 failed to halt the fighting in Kampuchea, and in April 1975 the Khmer Rouge took Phnom Penh. Without hesitation they drove the entire urban population out among the poor peasants of the countryside, in whose name a revolutionary leveling was to take place. For the next three and a half years the population was conscripted into agricultural communes by zonal and local Khmer Rouge commanders, referred to only as *Angkar* ("Organization"). A few light industries were maintained in the otherwise empty cities and towns. Hundreds of thousands of people died of exhaustion, malnutrition, revolutionary and disciplinary executions, and paranoid purges within the movement itself. Conservative estimates have put

Homes in this village along the Mekong River, like many throughout Kampuchea, are supported on stilts several feet above the water. These villages permit farmers to maximize cultivable land for rice, the nation's staple food crop, on fertile riverbank property.

the toll at about 1,000,000 persons; it may have been much higher. The Khmer Rouge almost totally isolated Kampuchea from the outside world. China was its chief ally.

In January 1979, following violent disputes with Vietnam over boundaries and revolutionary leadership, Phnom Penh was overrun by the Vietnamese army. Khmer Rouge defectors headed by HENG SAMRIN established a Vietnamese-style people's republic backed by the authority of up to 180,000 Vietnamese troops and myriad advisors. The Khmer Rouge forces staggered to the western boundary with Thailand, where the United Nations eventually organized camps for further waves of Kampucheans variously seeking food, haven, or resettlement. The Khmer Rouge launched guerrilla resistance with arms supplied by the Chinese. In 1982, Prince Sihanouk and Son Sann formed a coalition government with the Khmer Rouge. The Association of Southeast Asian Nations (ASEAN), opposed to the growing Soviet and Vietnamese influence in the region, helped to arm this more acceptable resistance group, which held Kampuchea's seat in the United Nations. In May 1989 constitutional revisions restored the right to private property and reinstated Buddhism as the official religion. The Vietnamese withdrew almost all of their forces from Kampuchea by September 1989 despite the collapse of multinational peace talks on the future of the country. In July 1990, as the Khmer Rouge intensified their guerrilla war, the United States withdrew diplomatic recognition from the government in exile, but it still aided the non-Communist rebel factions; China continued to aid the Khmer Rouge. Although many obstacles to peace remained, the four factions were pressed by their allies into forming an interim national council as part of a peace plan approved in August by the UN Security Council. The plan called for disarming the warring groups and holding UN-supervised elections, with international guarantees of Kampuchean neutrality.   MACALISTER BROWN

Bibliography: Becker, E., *When the War Was Over* (1986); Chanda, N., *Brother Enemy* (1986); Chandler, D. P., *A History of Cambodia* (1983); Etheson, C., *The Rise and Demise of Democratic Kampuchea* (1984); Kiernan, B., *How Pol Pot Came to Power* (1985); Kiernan, B., and Boua, C., eds., *Peasants and Politics in Kampuchea: 1942–1981* (1982); Shawcross, W., *Sideshow: Kissinger, Nixon, and the Destruction of Cambodia* (1980); Vickery, M., *Kampuchea* (1987).

Kanchenjunga   [kahn-chuhn-jung'-guh]

Kanchenjunga, the third highest mountain in the world (8,598 m/28,208 ft) after Mount Everest and K2 (Godwin Austen), is located in the HIMALAYAS on the border between Nepal and Sikkim, 75 km (47 mi) northeast of the city Darjeeling, in India. Its name, which means "Five Treasuries of the Great Snow" in Tibetan, refers to its five peaks, four of which are arranged symmetrically around the highest summit. Several attempts to climb the mountain have ended in fatal accidents,

but in 1955 a British team led by Charles Evans almost reached the top. The party stopped 1.5 m (5 ft) below the summit out of respect for local religious traditions.

Kandahar   [kan-duh-hahr']

Kandahar (Qandahar) is the seat of Kandahar province and the second largest city in Afghanistan, with a population of 225,500 (1988 est.). It lies in the south on a broad, irrigated plain high above sea level. The commercial center for a fruit-growing and sheep-raising region, Kandahar has fruit-processing plants and textile mills. Trade in hides, tobacco, textiles, and carpets is also important. The city has many mosques; its imposing mausoleums include that of Ahmad Shah Durrani, who founded the Kandahar Afghan kingdom in 1747.

Allegedly founded by Alexander the Great in the 4th century BC, Kandahar was subsequently conquered by Arabs, Turks, Moguls, and Persians and was the capital of Afghanistan from 1747 to 1773. The city was a rebel base and suffered much damage during the Soviet occupation of Afghanistan.

Kandinsky, Wassily   [kuhn-deen'-skee, vah-see'-lee]

The Russian-born painter Wassily Kandinsky, b. Dec. 4 (N.S.), 1866, d. Dec. 13, 1944, is often regarded as the originator of ABSTRACT ART. In 1896, Kandinsky abandoned a legal career to study painting in Munich. Trips to Paris familiarized him with neoimpressionism and the work of Paul Gauguin and the Fauves. In 1907 he exhibited with the German expressionist group Die BRÜCKE, and in 1909 he founded the New Association of Munich Artists. In 1910, Kandinsky executed his first abstract painting and wrote his famous theoretical study *Concerning the Spiritual in Art* (1912), developing his ideas about nonrepresentational painting, the psychological power of pure color, and the analogy between art and music. In 1911, Kandinsky, with August Macke, Franz Marc, and, later, Paul Klee, founded Der BLAUE REITER group. That same year Kandinsky and Marc published their theories of abstract art and in 1911 and 1912 held exhibitions of their work.

After spending some time in Switzerland, Kandinsky returned (1914) to Moscow, where he taught and organized numerous artistic activities. He moved (1921) to Germany once again and became a teacher at the Bauhaus in 1925. In 1926 he wrote *Point and Line to Plane*, an analysis of geometric forms in art. During this decade Kandinsky's painting evolved from the more expressionistic and highly colored improvisations of his early work toward more precisely drawn and geometrically arranged compositions.

When the Bauhaus was closed (1933) by the Nazis, Kandinsky moved to Paris, where he lived for the rest of his life. His later works are arrangements of organically shaped forms re-

The linear activity of Wassily Kandinsky's Improvisation 33 (Sketch for "Orient") (1913) demonstrates that his abstract art continued to be based on images. The painting represents a reclining couple. Influenced by cubism in the direction of greater abstraction, Kandinsky used swirling colors that show his continuing allegiance to Fauvism.

sembling microscopic creatures. Kandinsky's paintings and theoretical writings exercised a strong influence on the subsequent development of modern art, especially on the development of ABSTRACT EXPRESSIONISM.   BARBARA CAVALIERE

Bibliography: Grohmann, Will, *Wassily Kandinsky: Life and Work* (n.d.); Kandinsky, Wassily, *Concerning the Spiritual In Art* (1947; repr. 1976) and *Complete Writings on Art,* 2 vols. (1982); Overy, Paul, *Kandinsky: The Language of the Eye* (1969); Picon, Gaetan, Washton, Rose-Carol, and Kandinsky, Nina, *Kandinsky: Parisian Period 1934–1944* (1969); Weiss, P., *Kandinsky in Munich* (1982; repr. 1986).

Kandy   [kan'-dee]

Kandy, the capital of Central province, Sri Lanka, is located at an elevation of 490 m (1,600 ft) on the Kandy Plateau in the middle of the island, on the banks of the Mahaweli River. The city has a population of 114,000 (1983 est.). The surrounding area is mountainous and densely forested, cut by numerous rivers and streams. Rain is very heavy, averaging about 2,030 mm (80 in) per year; temperatures vary little, with an annual average of 24° C (75° F). The economy of the city and of the region is based primarily on tea and rice production. The inhabitants, mostly Sinhalese, are Buddhists. Kandy is the site of the University of Sri Lanka; the National Academy of Dance, where the Kandyan dance is taught; and the Dalada Maligawa, or Temple of the Tooth, where a relic, allegedly a tooth of the Buddha, is kept.

Kandy, which dates from the early centuries AD, was the capital of the kingdom of Kandy, a Sinhalese domain, from 1592. It remained the last anti-British holdout until 1815, when the British finally succeeded in taking the region.

Kane, Paul

Paul Kane, b. Sept. 3, 1810, d. Feb. 20, 1871, was a Canadian painter best known for his depictions of North American Indian life. Originally a furniture and sign painter in Toronto, he decided to become a serious artist after encountering, on a visit (1841–43) to Europe, George Catlin's paintings of American Indians. Kane returned to Canada inspired by Catlin's works, and he made (1845) a sketching trip among the Ojibwa tribe of the Lake Huron area, executing numerous portraits and genre works in the romantic tradition. Under the auspices of the Hudson's Bay Company, he journeyed (1846–48) to western Canada to paint the Indians and buffalo herds. Kane gained considerable fame through his 1848 exhibition in Toronto of 100 of these works. He wrote an account of these travels, *Wanderings of an Artist among the Indians of North America* (1859).   DAVID WISTOW

Bibliography: Harper, J. Russell, *Paul Kane's Frontier* (1971); National Gallery of Canada, *Paul Kane, 1810–1871* (1971–72).

Kanem-Bornu   [kah'-nem bohr'-noo]

Kanem-Bornu is the name applied to territories around Lake Chad (within modern Nigeria, Niger, Chad, and Cameroon) that were ruled from about 800 to 1846 by the Sefuwa line of kings. The original Sefuwa kings were probably nomad-warriors from the Sahara, but they ruled over large populations of farmers. An 11th-century *mai* (divine king) named Humai was converted to Islam. All his successors depended heavily on Muslim officials to regulate the state's important long-distance trade across the Sahara.

The state was originally centered on the farming lands of Kanem, the region northeast of Lake Chad, but invasions by Saharan nomads caused the Sefuwa to move their capital to Bornu, on the lake's southwestern shore, probably in the 14th century. The language and culture that developed in the new locale is called KANURI.

In the late 16th century Kanem-Bornu experienced a major revival of power and extended its dominion over the Hausa cities to the west. The Muslim FULANI revolutions of the early 19th century threatened the Sefuwa throne, but it was saved by a dynamic minister, al-Kanemi (d. 1835). The ancient Sefuwa dynasty died out in 1846, however, and the state fell in 1893 to the Sudanese conqueror Rabiyh Zubayr. In 1898, Kanem-Bornu was partitioned between the British, French, and German colonial spheres.   ROBERT R. GRIFFETH

Bibliography: Ajayi, J. F., and Crowder, Michael, *The History of West Africa,* vol. 1 (1972); Osae, T. A., and Odunsi, A. T., *A Short History of West Africa,* 2 vols. (1973).

Kanesh: see KÜLTEPE.

K'ang-hsi, Emperor of China   (Kangxi)
[kahng'-shee']

K'ang-hsi, b. May 4, 1654, d. Dec. 20, 1722, second CH'ING (Manchu) emperor of China, is famous both for his astute management of civil and military affairs and for his patronage of scholars. Succeeding to the throne in 1661, he assumed personal rule in 1669.

K'ang-hsi's armies pacified southern China (1673–81), conquered Taiwan (1683), and, led by the emperor himself, defeated the Dzungar Mongol chieftain Galdan in 1696. By 1720, Tibet was also under imperial control. In addition, the emperor established (1689) diplomatic relations with Russia and encouraged trade with the West. He tolerated Christian missionary activity in order to take advantage of the Jesuits' scientific knowledge. K'ang-hsi patronized Chinese as well as Manchu scholars, who compiled such literary monuments as the K'ang-hsi dictionary of the Manchu language, a geography of China, and an encyclopedia of 5,000 volumes.

Bibliography: Hummel, Arthur W., ed., *Eminent Chinese of the Ch'ing Period, 1644–1912,* 2 vols. (1943–44); Spence, Jonathan D., *Emperor of China: Self-Portrait of K'ang-hsi, 1654–1722* (1974).

K'ang Yu-wei   (Kang Youwei) [kahng yoo wee]

K'ang Yu-wei, b. Mar. 19, 1858, d. Mar. 31, 1927, was the dominant figure of the reform movement that briefly gained ascendancy in China following that country's humiliating defeat in the SINO-JAPANESE WAR of 1894–95. A Cantonese scholar, he published a series of books reinterpreting Confucian thought in such a way as to justify radical changes in the Chinese imperial system. Despite repression his ideas spread, and in 1898 the Kuang-hsü emperor adopted K'ang's program, issuing edicts covering such matters as the creation of a public school system, the modernization of the bureaucracy, the promotion of commerce and industry through the construction of railroads and factories, and military reorganization under a central administration. Dowager Empress TZ'U-HSI, however, was enraged by this threat to old court ways. Backed by conservative officials, she imprisoned the emperor and abruptly ended the so-called "Hundred Days of Reform." K'ang escaped abroad. He returned to China in 1914 and spent the rest of his life teaching his philosophy of progress.

Bibliography: Cameron, M. E., *The Reform Movement in China, 1898–1912* (1931; repr. 1963); Hsiao Kung-Chuan, *A Modern China and a New World: K'ang Yu-wei, Reformer and Utopian, 1858–1927* (1975); Jung-Pang Lo, ed., *K'ang Yu-wei: A Biography and a Symposium* (1967).

kangaroo   [kang-guh-roo']

A kangaroo is a marsupial mammal in the family Macropodidae. Typically, it has greatly enlarged hind legs, a strong, muscular tail, small forelegs, a relatively small head, and large ears. It usually moves in a hopping gait. The forepart of the kangaroo's stomach has been modified for the bacterial fermentation of plant cellulose, which makes that material digestible. Female kangaroos have an abdominal pouch for carrying their young, which are born in a rather undeveloped state. Although the period of gestation, or pregnancy, may be short, generally ranging from 27 to nearly 40 days, the young may spend a long period in the pouch; in the case of the red kangaroo, *Macropus rufus,* they remain nearly eight months. Kangaroos also demonstrate embryonic diapause, or the de-

In combat, a male red kangaroo, M. rufus, grabs its opponent with its forearms and kicks the abdomen with its hindlegs, while balancing on its heavy tail. Female red kangaroos are actually bluish gray in color.

layed birth of the young. Immediately after giving birth, a female kangaroo will mate, but the resulting new embryo stops its development at the blastocyst stage, where it consists of about 100 cells and measures about 0.25 mm (0.01 in). The embryo may continue its development after the previous young grows old enough to leave the pouch or if it dies prematurely.

The 50 or more species of kangaroos are distributed from Tasmania and Australia proper to New Guinea and adjacent islands, and some have been introduced into New Zealand. The Macropodidae family is divided into two subfamilies, Macropodinae, containing the large and small kangaroos (wallabies and wallaroos), and Potorinae, containing the small and primitive rat kangaroos.

The largest kangaroo, and the largest marsupial, is the gray kangaroo, *Macropus giganteus,* also called *M. major* or *M. cangaru,* which inhabits open forest or bushland in eastern Australia and Tasmania. It may stand more than 2 m (7 ft) tall, be 2.9 m (9.6 ft) long, including its tail, and weigh nearly 80 kg (200 lb). It can leap 1.5 m (5 ft) when moving at a slow pace and more than 9 m (30 ft) at high speeds. For short distances a gray kangaroo can travel at 48 km/h (30 mph). Gray kangaroos feed on grasses and other herbaceous material. The smallest kangaroo is the musky rat kangaroo, *Hypsiprymnodon moschatus,* of northeastern Australia, which grows to 33.5 cm (13 in) long, has a 17-cm (6.7-in) hairless tail, and weighs about 500 g (1 lb). Its limbs are nearly equal in size, and its foot structure is quite different from the other species.

Bibliography: Dawson, T. J., "Kangaroos," *Scientific American,* August 1977; Frith, H. J., and Calaby, J. H., *Kangaroos* (1969); Time-Life Books, *Kangaroos and Other Creatures from Down Under* (1978).

kangaroo rat

Kangaroo rats are about 22 species of North American rodents of the genus *Dipodomys,* family Heteromyidae. They are found in arid areas west of the Missouri River from Canada to central Mexico. Kangaroo rats are stocky animals with long

Kangaroo rats, such as D. merriami, *feed on most parts of available vegetation and some insects.*

hind legs, short front legs, and a long tail, which is tufted at the tip. The hind legs are used for hopping, in the manner of kangaroos. The small front feet are used to gather food, which is stuffed into two external, fur-lined cheek pouches, each with an opening in the skin near the side of the mouth. The largest kangaroo rats are 20 cm (8 in) long, plus a slightly longer tail, and weigh up to 140 g (5 oz). The coat is yellowish to dark brown, with white underparts and a white stripe on each side of the tail.

Kangaroo rats seldom or never drink, obtaining sufficient water from the breakdown of their food. Mating may occur at any time under favorable climatic conditions. Gestation is about 29 to 33 days, with usually 2 to 4 young to a litter and as many as 3 litters per year.

kangaroo thorn

Kangaroo thorn, *Acacia armata*, is classified in the mimosa subfamily of the pea family, Leguminosae. It is a spiny, bushy shrub, growing to 3 m (10 ft) tall, and is native to the dry regions of New South Wales, Australia. The spines, about 13 mm (0.5 in) long, are found at the bases of the leaves. The leaves are actually phyllodes, consisting only of expanded leaf stalks (petioles), with no true leaf blades. Small yellow flowers, grouped into solitary globular heads, appear in early spring. DIANNE FAHSELT

Kania, Stanisław   [kahn'-yuh, stahn'-ees-wahv]

Stanisław Kania, b. Mar. 8, 1927, succeeded Edward Gierek as first secretary of the Polish Communist party in September 1980. He joined the party in 1945 and became a member of the politburo in 1975, in charge of national security. As first secretary, Kania managed with considerable deftness to respond to the demands of the Polish workers while averting the threat of Soviet invasion. He was reelected by an unprecedented secret ballot at a party congress in July 1981 but ousted by the party's central committee in October.

Kano   [kay'-noh]

Kano, a city in northern Nigeria, lies about 860 km (535 mi) northeast of Lagos and has a population of 565,800 (1989 est.). For centuries it has been the largest and most important commercial center of the savanna zone. Kano serves as a distribution center for skins (especially tanned goatskins from which morocco leather is made), eggs, and livestock. Industries include textile milling, oil refining, printing, and brewing. The city has several high schools. The old town, inhabited mainly by Hausa people, is surrounded by a 20-km-long (12-mi) wall, probably dating from the 15th century. The modern district is called Nassarawa.

Tools found in Kano suggest that a Stone Age settlement existed there. A permanent city can be traced back about 1,000 years. From the 12th century, Kano was the center of one of the seven Hausa city-states. It was first visited by Europeans in the 1820s and was captured by the British in 1903.

RONALD D. GARST

Kano   (family of Japanese painters):   see EITOKU; MASANOBU; MOTONOBU; SANRAKU; TANYU.

Kanpur   [kahn'-pur]

Kanpur, an industrial city in the state of Uttar Pradesh, northern India, lies on the right bank of the Ganges River about 400 km (250 mi) southeast of New Delhi. With a population of 1,481,789 (1981), Kanpur is the largest city in the state. A booming industrial, rail, and trade center, Kanpur leads the nation in the production of wool textiles and leather goods; its cotton mills, in operation since 1869, are the most productive in northern India. The population is largely Hindu, but there are some Muslims and Sikhs. Kanpur University (1966) and the Indian Institute of Technology (1960) are located there.

Kanpur, originally a small village, was taken over by the British in 1801. Then known as Cawnpore, the village was the scene of a massacre during the INDIAN MUTINY (1857), when the entire British garrison and its dependents were killed by Indian rebels. ASHOK K. DUTT

Kansa   [kan'-saw]

The Kansa, or Kaw, are North American Indians who speak a Siouan dialect closely related to the languages of the OSAGE and QUAPAW. According to their own tradition they originated in the east; they crossed the Missouri and ascended the Kansas until forced back by the CHEYENNE. When first encountered by white traders, they lived in a village of 130 earth lodges near Council Grove (Kansas) and numbered about 2,500. Clan membership appears to have been determined according to female ancestry. Women owned the lodges, took charge of sacred burial customs, and had considerable influence in village affairs. Young men established links with a variety of mysterious powers, or *wakans,* through the sacred rite of the vision quest. Traditions were maintained until the late 19th century despite intensive Christian missionary efforts.

SAUK and IOWA tribesmen raided the Kansa from the east; Sioux and Cheyenne threatened them from the north and west. U.S. attempts to maintain peace were ineffective. After ceding land in a peace treaty of 1825 and settling on a reservation in Kansas, the Kansa were attacked by Pawnee and Cheyenne. In 1846 they ceded two million acres for only $200,000. After their last bison hunt in 1873, they left the Neosho Valley for Indian Territory (present-day Oklahoma). In 1905 only 204 Kansa remained, although by the late 1980s those living on the Kaw Reservation near Pawnee had increased to nearly 600. ERNEST L. SCHUSKY

Bibliography: Unrau, William E., *The Kansa Indians* (1971; repr. 1986).

Kansas

Occupying the central position in the conterminous United States, Kansas is one of the nation's leading agricultural states. It is 14th in size among the states but 32d in population rank. Kansas is bordered by Nebraska, Missouri, Oklahoma, and Colorado. The area was first explored by Europeans with the Coronado expedition of 1541, but significant Anglo settlement did not occur until 1855. After a 6-year struggle over the slavery issue, the "Sunflower State" entered the Union in 1861 on the free side. Today it is a prosperous, conservative, rural state with an economy well balanced between agriculture and industry. TOPEKA is the capital. The name *Kansas* is a Sioux word meaning "people of the south wind."
LAND AND RESOURCES
Kansas has a reputation for flat topography, but this stereotype is correct only for the western quarter of the state; most of the land is rolling and hilly. The highest point, Mount Sunflower, in Wallace County in the west, is 1,231 m (4,039 ft); the lowest elevation is 207 m (679 ft) in Montgomery County in the southeast. The rock strata are arranged in the manner of shingles. The oldest rocks, Mississippian (345–320 million-year-old) limestones, outcrop only in the southeastern corner of the state. To the west newer surface materials are found, first Pennsylvanian and Permian (320–225 million-year-old) limestones and shales, then recent Cretaceous (135–65 mil-

lion-year-old) and Quaternary (less than 2.5 million-year-old) deposits. The western two-thirds of Kansas is part of the GREAT PLAINS, the eastern third belongs to the Central Lowlands, and the tiny Mississippian outcrop is part of the Ozark Upland.

The flat topography of the Great Plains is commonly attributed to a lack of water for erosion, but the recentness of surface deposits is probably a more important factor. The plains surface is actually an outwash "apron" deposited after the Rocky Mountains were uplifted. Wind-deposited soil, called loess, was placed to a depth of about one meter on top of this apron at the time of the last ice age, and it provides an excellent, stone-free medium for agriculture. Streams have dissected the plains in central Kansas to form the Blue and Smoky hills in the northern part of the area and the Gypsum Hills in the south; the latter contain scenic buttes and mesas.

The Central Lowlands portion of Kansas is commonly divided into four subregions. South of the Kansas River are the Osage Cuestas, a plains area broken by limestone escarpments exceeding 60 m (200 ft) in height. To the west, in a belt from Washington County to Cowley County, these escarpments become bolder and more frequent. Kansans call this area the Flint Hills, a name referring to a mineral commonly found in the limestone layers. Sandstone replaces limestone in the Chautauqua Hills, a small area along the Chautauqua-Montgomery County line. North of the Kansas River is the Till Plain, where the rock escarpments are masked by a layer of glacial debris. The terrain there is gently rolling. Soils in eastern Kansas are not quite as good as those in the west, because they have generally been subjected to leaching and erosion for a longer period of time. Humus-rich chernozems predominate in the glaciated area of the northeast.

Climate. Kansas's "big sky," dramatic sunsets, and great variability in temperature and precipitation are all important aspects of the regional personality. Because the state is remote from the moderating influences of oceans, it has a wide annual temperature range. The average January temperature is −1° C (30° F); the July average is 26° C (79° F). Diurnal ranges are also broad. Precipitation is highly variable and has a marked regional pattern. Average rainfall increases from 380 mm (15 in) in the extreme west to 1,140 mm (45 in) in the southeast, a pattern related to distance from the Gulf of Mexico moisture source. About 75% of the annual precipitation falls between April and September, but summer is often a moisture-deficient season because of high evaporation rates. Because precipitation is dependent on the chance meeting of moist air from the Gulf of Mexico and low-pressure systems, yearly totals are highly variable, especially in western Kansas. Thus, the region of greatest variability coincides with that of lowest average rainfall totals, and the combination produces doubled risks for local farmers. Sharply contrasting air masses frequently clash over the Kansas plains, bringing violent weather and adding to the variability.

Drainage. The Kansas (Kaw) River in the north and the ARKANSAS RIVER in the south drain most of the state. The Kaw is a short stream (275 km/170 mi) formed by the junction of the Smoky Hill and the Solomon and the Republican rivers; it enters the Missouri River at Kansas City. Principal tributaries of the long Arkansas River (2,348 km/1,459 mi) in Kansas are the Cimarron, Neosho, and Verdigris. The Arkansas occupies an especially wide and fertile lowland from the Hutchinson area in the south central part of the state to the Oklahoma border. None of the Kansas waterways is used for navigation. The state has 20 major reservoirs and more than 70,000 farm ponds. Extensive groundwater reserves are being depleted by heavy irrigation.

Vegetation and Animal Life. Prairie vegetation was the dominant pattern encountered in Kansas by the first explorers. Blue grama and buffalo grass grew in the west, and taller bluestem species dominated elsewhere. Timber, especially cottonwoods, sycamores, and walnut trees, was common in the river valleys. Currently a debate exists concerning the origin of the Kansas prairie. Some say that grass is the natural vegetation under the state's highly variable climatic conditions, but others claim that trees would predominate over

KANSAS

LAND. Area: 213,096 km² (82,277 mi²); rank: 14th. Capital: Topeka (1988 est. pop., 122,000). Largest city: Wichita (1988 est. pop., 295,000). Counties: 105. Elevations: highest—1,231 m (4,039 ft), at Mount Sunflower; lowest—207 m (679 ft), at Verdigris River.

PEOPLE. Population (1990 prelim.): 2,467,000; rank: 32d; density: 11.6 persons per km² (30.2 per mi²). Distribution (1988 est.): 53.4% metropolitan, 46.6% nonmetropolitan. Average annual change (1980–90): +0.4%.

EDUCATION. Public enrollment (1988): elementary—306,751; secondary—119,845; higher—138,700. Nonpublic enrollment (1980): elementary—22,200; secondary—6,700; combined—3,100; higher (1988)—14,147. Institutions of higher education (1987): 54.

ECONOMY. State personal income (1988): $39.3 billion; rank: 31st. Median family income (1979): $19,707; rank: 26th. Nonagricultural labor distribution (1988): manufacturing—181,000 persons; wholesale and retail trade—259,000; government—206,000; services—212,000; transportation and public utilities—64,000; finance, insurance, and real estate—58,000; construction—42,000. Agriculture: income (1988)—$6.6 billion. Forestry: sawtimber volume (1987)—3 billion board feet. Mining: value (1987)—$1.9 billion. Manufacturing: value added (1987)—$12.9 billion. Services: value (1987)—$7.6 billion.

GOVERNMENT (1991). Governor: Joan Finney, Democrat. U.S. Congress: Senate—2 Republicans; House—2 Democrats, 3 Republicans. Electoral college votes: 7. State legislature: 40 senators, 125 representatives.

STATE SYMBOLS. Statehood: Jan. 29, 1861; the 34th state. Nickname: Sunflower State; bird: western meadowlark; flower: sunflower; tree: cottonwood; motto: *Ad Astra per Aspera* ("To the Stars through Difficulties"); song: "Home on the Range."

large portions of Kansas had it not been for widespread burning by the Indians, who set fire to the land to induce the early growth of pasturage for buffalo. The common occurrence of oak, hickory, elm, hackberry, juniper, and other tree species on rocky, droughty (but fire-protected) escarpments supports the latter view, as does the sprouting of trees on abandoned farmland in the eastern half of the state. Animal life is highly diverse in Kansas and includes both woodland and grassland species. Pheasants are a popular game bird in the west, and antelope have recently been reintroduced there. Squirrels, raccoon, and deer occur in the east.

Resources. Petroleum and natural-gas deposits are widespread in the southern half of Kansas. The fields are in decline but still produce over half of the state's mineral output. The exploitation of the Hugoton gas field in the 1950s

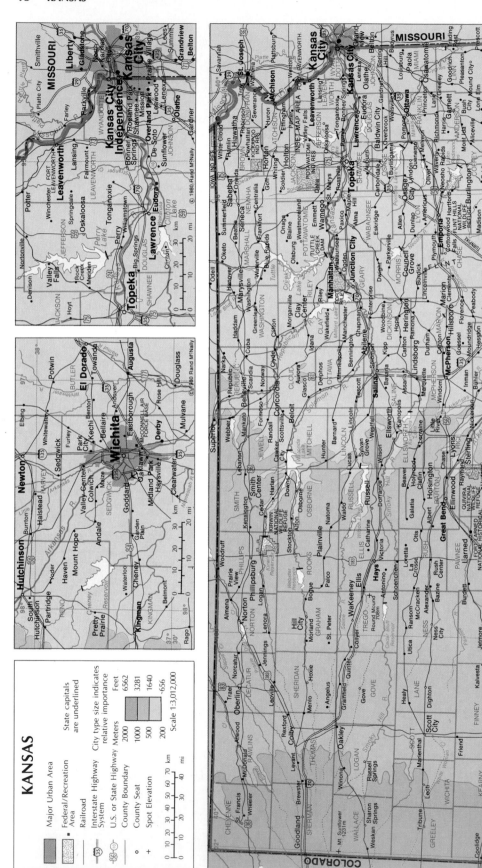

KANSAS

Major Urban Area

Federal/Recreation Area

Railroad

Interstate Highway System

U.S. or State Highway System

County Boundary

County Seat

+ Spot Elevation

State capitals are underlined

City type size indicates relative importance

Meters	Feet
2000	6562
1000	3281
500	1640
200	656
	-656

Scale 1:3,012,000

km 0 10 20 30 40 50 60 70
mi 0 10 20 30 40

© 1980 Rand McNally & Co.

The cultivation of wheat, which is grown in each of Kansas's 105 counties, annually injects millions of dollars into the state economy. Although Kansas has acquired a traditional image as the agrarian heartland of the United States, manufacturing has recently superseded agriculture as the state's most important economic activity.

and '60s made southwestern Kansas one of the wealthiest areas per capita in the state. Most of the oil and gas is shipped out of Kansas to power-manufacturing plants in states east of Kansas. Before World War II the state was, with Oklahoma and Missouri, a major producer of lead and zinc. No mines now operate in the district, and a moderate economic depression exists locally. Salt, from the Hutchinson area, and coal, in the southeast, are other resources.

PEOPLE
The population density of Kansas is less than half the national average. Natural increase along with a net inmigration produced a modest growth rate from 1970 to 1980 of 5.1%, also well below the national norm of 11.4% (1970–80). About two thirds of the population live in urban areas. These figures do not imply a lack of prosperity, however, for Kansas ranks above the national average in per-capita income.

Most of the major cities in the state are located on early transportation routes, principally the Kaw Valley–Union Pacific line due west from KANSAS CITY and the path of the Santa Fe Railroad from ATCHISON through TOPEKA, Emporia, HUTCHINSON, and Garden City. A major exception is WICHITA, a city whose initial prosperity can be attributed more to promotion than to transportation advantages. Today, thanks principally to the petroleum and aircraft industries, Wichita is the largest city in the state, followed by Kansas City and Topeka.

Most early Kansans were born in Illinois, Indiana, Ohio, and Pennsylvania, but there was also an influential minority from New England. Today 5% of the people are blacks, many of whom are descendants of the "exodusters," former slaves who came to Kansas just after the Civil War. A substantial majority of church members in Kansas are Protestant. Roman Catholicism and the United Methodist church are the largest single denominations. Kansas has a small Jewish population.

Education and Cultural Activity. Education has always enjoyed a high level of local support, a fact that some attribute to the role of pioneer settlers from New England. In the 1980s nearly 75% of adults had completed high school and 7% were college graduates. There are more than 50 institutions of higher learning in Kansas. Six are state universities. The University of Kansas in Lawrence, with about 26,000 students, is known for its liberal arts program and medical school. Kansas State University in Manhattan enrolls some 18,000 students and enjoys national stature for its agricultural and other applied-science programs. Other public universities are located in Empo-

ria, Hays, Pittsburg, and Wichita (see KANSAS, STATE UNIVERSITIES AND COLLEGES OF). Significant libraries outside the universities are housed at the state historical society in Topeka and at the Eisenhower Library in Abilene.

Because Kansas lacks cities of great size, most cultural activities are concentrated in the universities. Notable art museums are at the University of Kansas and in Wichita; the State Historical Society in Topeka has a historical museum; and the University of Kansas has an excellent museum of natural history. Historical sites include various forts and stations along the Santa Fe and Oregon trails and on the Pony Express route, and John Brown Memorial Park in Osawatomie, containing the log cabin where the abolitionist John BROWN lived. Outdoor recreational areas are less spectacular than in some states, but many people enjoy touring the lush, peaceful grazing areas of the Flint Hills. An annual rodeo at Strong City in June attracts a large crowd. Other recreational centers are the federal reservoirs and the state parks. Local sports interest is concentrated on the two major universities and the professional teams in Kansas City, Mo.

Perhaps because of a low population density, local communications have always been well developed. A number of daily newspapers are published, led in circulation by the *Wichita Eagle-Beacon*. The state has several commercial television stations, along with many radio stations.

ECONOMIC ACTIVITY
The Kansas economy has been based on agriculture since settlement. Meat packing, milling, and processing of other food products are the leading industries. Warehouses exploit the state's central location, and transportation equipment is an important product.

Agriculture. Kansas ranks among the top ten U.S. states in the value of its total farm marketings and traditionally leads the nation in wheat production. The production of wheat is ideal for the central plains climate. Farmers plant winter wheat in September to take advantage of autumn rains and cool temperatures, and after a winter dormancy, the crop resumes growth in the spring. Wheat harvest is in June, just as the summer dry weather begins. Other leading crops include grain sorghum (a drought-resistant feed grain), hay crops, corn, and soybeans in southeastern Kansas, and irrigated crops of various types in the western half of the state. Through irrigation more corn is now grown in western than in eastern Kansas, and the irrigation acreage has increased rapidly. The

development of giant sprinkler systems, each pivoting around a well and capable of watering 65 ha (160 acres), started this expansion about 1960.

In spite of Kansas's reputation as a wheat state, beef cattle are a more important part of the economy. Typically, cattle account for a greater share of the total agricultural receipts than does wheat. Cattle are found throughout the state, but the highest concentration occurs in the Flint Hills. This area traditionally was controlled by Texas cattle ranchers who used the bluestem grass to build up their herds after long drives north to the railheads. The region is still controlled by absentee owners, but cow and calf herds predominate instead of transient beef cattle. Kansas cattle used to be shipped east for fattening and slaughter, but today the trend is to keep these operations in the cattle-producing areas. Feedlots are now common throughout the state, and meat packers are abandoning their large and antiquated facilities in cities such as Chicago and Kansas City in favor of smaller plants in

Topeka, the capital of Kansas, is an important agricultural marketing and shipping center. Topeka's landmarks include the Menninger Clinic, Mulvane Art Museum, an Episcopal cathedral, Washburn University (1865), and many parks.

places such as Dodge City and Emporia.

Manufacturing and Transportation. One of the nation's first natural-gas booms occurred in southeastern Kansas in the 1890s. Glass and portland-cement factories, zinc smelters, brick and tile works, and other concerns were attracted to the area in large numbers. The glass and zinc industries eventually left the area, but southeastern Kansas remains an area of small manufacturing cities. The production of transportation equipment is the state's leading industry, and Wichita manufactures about two-thirds of all American general-aviation aircraft. Nonelectrical machinery and chemicals production, coal and gas products, printing and publishing, and food processing are also leading industries.

Excellent transportation has always characterized this crossroads of the nation. Main lines of the Union Pacific and Santa Fe railroads bisect the state, as do interstate highways 35 and

(Left) The huge grain elevators that dot the Kansas landscape are used to store the state's annual harvest of wheat. Ranking among the top ten states in revenue derived from farm products, Kansas is also a major producer of corn, sorghum grain, and hay.

(Below) Hereford cattle penned in a commercial feedlot are fed a diet of corn and sorghum to fatten them for market. Livestock have played a formative role in the history of Kansas, which was the northern terminus of the 19th-century cattle drives originating in Texas.

(Below) The grasslands of Kansas, which are among the finest natural grazing regions in the world, are dotted with oil pumps that provide wealth for the state. Kansas is a major producer of petroleum, natural gas, helium, and petroleum-related chemicals.

70. Many large manufacturers use this transportation system to market their products across large sections of the United States.

Tourism. Kansas attracts some tourism dollars each year, mostly from people in transit to and from Colorado and the West. In recent years there has been a statewide debate over the merits of establishing a Prairie National Park somewhere in the Flint Hills. Proponents talk of capturing more tourist dollars and preserving a major natural ecosystem; opponents say that development would destroy the serenity of the prairie and that Kansas ranchers are already doing a good job of preserving the grasslands.

Power. Most of the electrical power sold in Kansas annually is generated by coal- and gas-fired power plants. The state has one nuclear power plant, and many residents have explored the potentials of solar and wind power. These last two sources may be especially appropriate for Kansas, given the state's relatively high percentage of sunshine, its windy climate, and its dispersed population.

GOVERNMENT

Kansas is governed under its original constitution (1859), one of the oldest still in use. Legislators represent districts set up under the one-person–one-vote principle. The state senate has 40 members; the house of representatives has 125. Elected boards of commissioners head the 105 county governments.

Local politics has traditionally been Republican because that party was initially associated with the free-state cause and with the popular Homestead Act of 1862; since statehood only a small number of Democratic governors have been elected. Notable Republican figures with Kansas roots include Alf Landon, 1936 presidential nominee, and Dwight Eisenhower. Pockets of Democratic strength are Wyandotte County, an urbanized, blue-collar area; Ellis County, a German Catholic center; and the coal-mining area of southeastern Kansas.

HISTORY

When Francisco Vásquez de CORONADO explored the area in 1541, Kansas was occupied primarily by Osage, Pawnee, and Kansa peoples. A Pueblo group, fleeing Spanish rule in New Mexico, occupied a site in western Kansas from about 1664 until 1730. (The Pueblo site and a Pawnee village in northern Kansas have now been restored.)

Kansas was part of the area claimed by France as Louisiana at the end of the 17th century. It was ceded to Spain in 1762, restored to France in 1800, and sold to the United States in 1803 in the Louisiana Purchase. Many of the famous expeditions to the West in the early 19th century passed through Kansas, including those of Zebulon Montgomery PIKE in 1806 and Stephen H. LONG in 1819–20. Reports from the Long party led to the erroneous use of the term "Great American Desert" to describe the plains region.

Primarily because of this image, Kansas was considered an unlikely place for Anglo settlement, and the government decided to use the land for reservations for displaced Indians from the East. Westward-bound migrants were passing through Kansas, however, on both the OREGON TRAIL and the SANTA FE TRAIL. Soon tremendous pressure developed to open Kansas itself for settlement, and in the early 1850s the Indians were moved to what became Oklahoma. Three small reservations in northeast Kansas are relics from that earlier time: the Potawatomi, the Kickapoo, and the Iowa-Sac-Fox.

The U.S. government opened Kansas to settlement in 1854 under the terms of the KANSAS-NEBRASKA ACT, which allowed the territory to determine its own position on slavery. The peopling of Kansas thus immediately became a national issue. Organizations like the EMIGRANT AID COMPANY promoted immigration by antislavery Northerners, while proslavery groups mounted a similar drive. The two groups of settlers established rival governments, violence erupted, and the territory soon became known as "Bleeding Kansas." After much controversy within both the territory and the U.S. Congress, the proposed proslavery LECOMPTON CONSTITUTION was rejected by the electorate, and Kansas entered the Union in 1861 under the terms of the Wyandotte Constitution (1859). Guerrilla raids continued along the Missouri-Kansas border throughout the Civil War.

A major land boom occurred in the 1870s, as adequate rainfall, good soil, postwar mobility, and rapidly expanding railroads brought thousands to the state, including many immigrants from Germany, Sweden, Russia, and elsewhere. One

(Above) *An auctioneer* (right) *acknowledges a bid at the Rezac Livestock Auction in Saint Marys, Kans. Livestock and related products are the state's most valuable agricultural commodities, contributing significantly to the state's economy.*

(Right) *Wichita, located at the confluence of the Arkansas and Little Arkansas rivers, is the largest city in Kansas.*

group, the German-Russian Mennonites, introduced the hard winter wheat that transformed Kansas agriculture.

Settlers dealt with the dry Western environment much as they had with the humid East, plowing the land and establishing small farms. Ranching was viewed as an undesirable, seminomadic way of life, and so small farms were extended westward. Tree planting was thought to increase rainfall because leaves would transpire large amounts of water into the atmosphere; irrigation was believed to have almost limitless potential; and techniques of dry farming were proposed to enable even the western counties to be cultivated easily. These beliefs were the products of unfounded optimism and wet years. When especially dry conditions occurred in the 1930s, widespread winds blowing across thousands of acres of nearly unprotected soil produced the infamous DUST BOWL. Since the 1930s, improved tillage techniques, enlarged land holdings, increased use of irrigation, rural-to-urban migration, and other factors have improved the situation greatly.

Nineteenth-century Kansas was noted for its activism. Abolitionist concern was followed by major involvement in the Temperance movement and Populist party. Populism ended as a formal political movement about 1900, but it brought about many innovations including federal grain inspection and stockyard regulation. More recently, the case of BROWN V. BOARD OF EDUCATION OF TOPEKA, KANSAS led to the 1954 Supreme Court ruling that racial segregation in the public schools was unconstitutional. At least one observer has called modern Kansas the "eclipsed state," contrasting past activity with present complacency. The state is certainly conservative politically and has a net out-migration of the young and highly educated. Other Kansans, however, believe that the state possesses what many Americans value today: smaller urban centers; clean air; an emphasis on self-reliance; and a reputation for good government and progressive education.

JAMES R. SHORTRIDGE

Bibliography: Davis, Kenneth S., *Kansas: A Bicentennial History* (1976); Drury, James W., *The Government of Kansas*, rev. ed. (1970); Federal Writers' Project, *Kansas: A Guide to the Sunflower State* (1939; repr. 1973); Muilenburg, Grace, and Swineford, Ada, *Land of the Post Rock* (1975); Richmond, Robert W., *Kansas: A Land of Contrasts* (1974); Rydjord, John, *Kansas Place Names* (1972); Self, Huber, *Environment and Man in Kansas: A Geographical Analysis* (1978); Shortridge, James R., *Kaw Valley Landscapes: A Guide to Eastern Kansas* (1977); Socolofsky, Homer, and Self, Huber, *Historical Atlas of Kansas* (1977); Zornow, William F., *Kansas* (1957; repr. 1971).

Kansas, state universities and colleges of

All the state schools of higher learning in Kansas are coeducational and grant both undergraduate and graduate degrees. The **University of Kansas** (1865; enrollment: 23,450; library: 1,850,000 volumes) at Lawrence has a college of liberal arts and sciences and schools of architecture, journalism, education, pharmacy, business, and social welfare, and, at Kansas City, a school of medicine. **Kansas State University** (1863; enrollment: 19,045; library: 825,000 volumes), a land-grant school at Manhattan, offers programs in arts and sciences and is a major center for agricultural studies. Four state institutions offer liberal arts and teacher education curricula: **Emporia Kansas State College** (1863; enrollment: 6,390; library: 560,000 volumes), at Emporia; **Fort Hays Kansas State College** (1902; enrollment: 5,700; library: 275,000 volumes), at Hays; **Pittsburg State University** (1903; enrollment: 5,285; library: 400,000 volumes), at Pittsburg; and **Wichita State University** (1895; enrollment: 15,725; library: 550,000 volumes), at Wichita, which until 1963 was the University of Wichita.

Kansas City

Two separate political units, Kansas City, Kans., in the northeastern part of its state, and Kansas City, Mo., on the western side of its state—each located on opposite banks of the Kansas River where it meets the Missouri River—comprise the Kansas City metropolitan area. Although separate politically, the two cities form one economic unit. Kansas City, Mo., has always been two or three times the size of its companion city in Kansas. The population of the former is 448,159; the latter

Kansas City, Mo., at the confluence of the Kansas and Missouri rivers, was settled in 1821 by French traders. The city's commercial future was assured by the arrival (1865) of the railroad, and Union Station (foreground) is a stately reminder of the railroad's importance.

has 161,087 inhabitants (1980). The population of the 7-county greater metropolitan area is 1,327,020. Kansas City, Kans., is the seat of Wyandotte County.

After the completion (1869) of the first bridge across the Missouri River, Kansas City became a transportation hub. Today it is a junction of rail, highway, and water routes and an inland port. From the end of the Civil War to the beginning of World War II the local economy was based primarily upon the handling, processing, and marketing of grain and cattle. Kansas City, Kans., has the world's largest grain elevator. The leading industries today are flour milling, meat packing, automobile assembly, oil refining, printing, and the manufacturing of steel and aluminum products, airplane engines, furniture, apparel, agricultural equipment, and chemicals.

The city's educational institutions include the University of Kansas Medical Center (1899) and the University of Missouri at Kansas City (1963). The Nelson-Atkins Art Gallery, one of the nation's leading art museums, and an extensive municipal park system of more than 1,200 ha (3,000 acres) grace Kansas City, Mo.

The first permanent settlement at this river junction was a trading post established in 1821. A succession of small villages was founded in the decades that followed, but the prosperity they enjoyed as the beginning point for westward expeditions was continually interrupted by disease epidemics. Economic stability was ensured by the arrival of railroad lines in 1865. The name Kansas City became official in the Kansas settlement in 1886 and in the Missouri town in 1889. Recent industrial and commercial expansion has established both cities as the second largest in their respective states. In one of the worst hotel disasters in U.S. history, the collapse (July 17, 1981) of suspended walkways in the lobby of the new Hyatt Regency Hotel in Kansas City, Mo., killed more than 100 persons.

TOM MCKNIGHT

Kansas-Nebraska Act

On May 30, 1854, the U.S. Congress passed the Kansas-Nebraska Act, establishing the territories of Kansas and Nebraska. This controversial legislation repealed the MISSOURI COMPROMISE of 1820–21 and reopened the controversy over the extension of slavery in the western territories. The Missouri Compromise had prohibited slavery north of a line drawn at latitude 36° 30′ through the Louisiana Purchase. Four attempts to organize a single territory for the area west of Missouri and Iowa and north of the 36° 30' line had failed in Congress due to southern opposition to the Missouri Compromise and competition between northern and southern advocates of a TRANSCONTINENTAL RAILROAD.

In January 1854, Sen. Stephen A. DOUGLAS of Illinois introduced a bill dividing the land into two territories, Kansas and Nebraska, and leaving the question of slavery to be decided by the settlers. This latter provision, known as POPULAR SOVEREIGNTY, enraged antislavery people. But after months of bitter debate, the bill passed. This solution did not defuse the slavery issue. Kansas was soon rent by conflict, and the sectional split between North and South was aggravated to a point that made reconciliation virtually impossible. The Republican party was founded by opponents of the act, and the United States was pushed further toward CIVIL WAR.   DOUGLAS T. MILLER

Bibliography: Malin, James C., *The Nebraska Question, 1852–1854* (1953); Ray, P. Orman, *The Repeal of the Missouri Compromise: Its Origins and Authorship* (1909; repr. 1965).

Kansu   (Gansu)   [kan'-soo]

Kansu, a province in northwestern China, is bounded on the north by the Republic of Mongolia. Kansu has an area of 530,000 km² (204,600 mi²) and a population of 19,880,000 (1983 est.). Ninety percent of the people are Chinese, and the remainder consists of Tibetan, Mongol, Turkic, and Chinese Muslim minorities. The capital, LAN-CHOU (Lanzhou), is a trading, industrial, and refining center.

Kansu lies on a high plateau, which has an average elevation of about 1,830 m (6,000 ft). The eastern part of the province is the principal center of earthquakes in China. Kansu has very little arable land (less than 10%), and its most valuable resources are petroleum, coal, and iron. New road and railroad systems have been built in the last decades. The region became a part of the Chinese territory in the 3d century BC. An ancient route, the Kansu corridor, for centuries provided the link between China and Central Asia.

Kant, Immanuel   [kahnt, i-mahn'-oo-el]

A pivotal force in the history of philosophy, the German philosopher Immanuel Kant, b. Apr. 22, 1724, d. Feb. 12, 1804, radically altered the nature of philosophic inquiry. Kant was born in Königsberg, East Prussia, to lower-middle-class parents who were devout pietists (see PIETISM). At the age of 8 he entered the Collegium Fridiricianum, a pietistic Latin school; he remained there for 8½ years and then entered the University of Königsberg in 1740 to study theology and, subse-

Immanuel Kant, an 18th-century German philosopher, achieved what he called a "Copernican revolution in philosophy" through his probe of the limitations inherent in speculative philosophy and in the rationalism of his day. His works, which explore the rule of reason and experience and define the sphere of philosophical inquiry, have had profound impact on Western thought. (Staatliches Kantgymnasium, Berlin.)

quently, natural science and philosophy. While at the university he was greatly influenced by a follower of Christian Wolff, the German rationalist. He also read the works of Gottfried Wilhelm von Leibniz and Isaac Newton. Other important influences on Kant's later thought were the writings of David Hume and Jean Jacques Rousseau. The death of his father forced him to interrupt his studies, and he became a tutor for private families from 1746 to 1755. In 1755 he returned to the University of Königsberg, where he remained for the rest of his life. In 1756 he was granted a degree and made a lecturer, and in 1770 he was appointed a professor.

Pre-Critical Period (1755–81). By 1755, Kant had written *Principiorum Primorum Cognitiones Metaphysicae Nova Dilucidato* (The First Principles of Metaphysical Knowledge), which was somewhat critical of the Leibnizian philosophy, and *The General Natural History of the Heavens* (Eng. trans., 1900), in which he employed Newtonian laws to formulate the Kant-LaPlace hypothesis of the origin of the solar system. In this period his works were primarily scientific, but some contained discussions of methodology. For example, in 1756 he published *Physical Monadology* (Eng. trans., 1928), which contrasted Leibnizian with Newtonian ways of thinking and introduced the distinction between things-in-themselves and things-as-they-appear.

In his writings during the 1760s he was explicitly critical of the Leibnizian-Wolffian philosophy. In 1763, in *An Attempt to Introduce the Concept of Negative Magnitudes into Philosophy* (Eng. trans., 1911), he argued that some physical relations, such as causality, cannot be reduced to logical relations, and in *Enquiry into the Proofs for the Existence of God* (1763; Eng. trans., 1836), he rejected René Descartes's attempt to prove existence by logic. In *Inquiry into the Distinctness of the Principles of Natural Theology and Morals* (1764; Eng. trans., 1949), he directly attacked the Leibnizian methodology of modeling philosophy solely on the deductive method. Kant's inaugural dissertation, *The Forms and Principles of the Sensible and Intelligible Worlds* (1770; Eng. trans., 1928), marked a complete breach with the Leibnizian metaphysics.

Critical Period (1781–90). Between 1770 and 1781, Kant published very little. Between 1781 and 1790, however, he produced his most important works, representing the full development of his critical powers. In 1781 he published the CRITIQUE OF PURE REASON (Eng. trans., 1838), his most famous work. It is divided into two major parts: "The Transcendental Doctrine of the Elements," which deals with the sources of human knowledge, and the "Transcendental Doctrine of Method," which deals with the proper and improper uses of reason. Kant used the word *transcendental* to designate that method which examines the necessary but nonempirical conditions of knowledge. In 1785 he published *The Foundations of the Metaphysics of Morals* (Eng. trans., 1969) and, in 1787, *The Critique of Practical Reason* (Eng. trans., 1949), both of which examine moral philosophy. The third critique, *The Critique of Judgment* (1790; Eng. trans., 1895), deals with aesthetic and teleologic, or purposive, judgments. During this period Kant also published seven other major works.

Philosophy. From Kant's point of view, the philosophical traditions of both EMPIRICISM and RATIONALISM had reached a "dark, confused, and useless" dead end. What he proposed was a radical, new synthesis in which he would incorporate both experience and reason without falling into the skepticism of the empirical school or the vast, unverifiable metaphysical structure of the rationalist school. The problem of knowledge, as he saw it, was how to connect the "is" of sense experience with the "must" of necessary and universal truth. His starting point was the distinction between analytic and synthetic judgments. An analytic judgment is one in which the predicate is contained in the subject—for instance, "Triangles have three sides." The truth of such a judgment can be known by an analysis of the subject. A synthetic judgment is one in which the predicate adds to or expands the subject—for instance, "Triangles were the earliest figures to be discovered in geometry." The truth of such a statement cannot be known through an analysis of the subject.

Kant also distinguished two ways in which judgments can

be known: something is known *a priori* if it is neither derived from nor testable by sense experience; it is known *a posteriori* if it is derived from or testable by experience. Philosophers before Kant had held that analytic judgments were known *a priori* and that synthetic judgments were known *a posteriori*. Analytic *a priori* judgments were always and necessarily true—but true only about the meaning and relations of words, not about the world. Synthetic *a posteriori* judgments, on the other hand, were about the world—but they could only be contingent or probable truths. This meant that we could have no certain knowledge about experience, and Kant believed that we had such knowledge. Thus he formulated this problem: "How are synthetic *a priori* judgments possible?" His solution, in essence, was that experience provides the content (the synthetic element) and the mind provides the structure (the *a priori* element) that determines the way in which the content will be organized and understood.

Kant calls the contribution of the mind a "category." He distinguishes four groups of categories by which the contents of experience are ordered: quantity, quality, relation, and modality. Examples of specific categories within these groups are space, time, causality, and substance. These categories are contentless and only prescribe the structure for objects of possible experience. Space, for example, is not something external to us but a structure in the mind that relates objects to one another. The active contribution of the mind gives meaning to the external material of experience. Whether things really are the way they appear to us is something we can never know, for all our knowledge comes prestructured through the filter of the mind. This is the basis for Kant's famous distinction between the unknowable NOUMENON, or thing-in-itself, and the PHENOMENON, or thing-as-it-appears.

Kant held that synthetic *a priori* judgments were possible in mathematics and physics but not in metaphysics. Thus he thought it a mistake for metaphysicians to attempt to go beyond sense experience in order to define concepts like God, freedom, or the immortal soul. All theoretical knowledge consists in applying the categories to perceptual material located in space and time, and these concepts lie outside the spatio-temporal categories. Such ideas have, for Kant, an indispensable function. Whereas most concepts have a "constitutive" function (they classify experience), concepts like God, freedom, or soul have a "regulative" function: they guide us toward certain goals useful for science and ethics. They are held "as if" they were true.

In the moral sphere Kant says that he has denied knowledge to make room for faith. Because moral law cannot be justified by reason it can only be obeyed for its own sake. Kant's ethical theory thus rests on the concept of duty. A good person acts out of duty, not because he or she fears punishment or hopes for reward or happiness, but only because it is his or her duty. Like other concepts, moral laws are only mental structures, so the primary moral law will be a contentless form of judgment that can be applied universally; Kant calls this the CATEGORICAL IMPERATIVE. The categorical imperative states that a person should "act in such a way that it is possible for one to will that the maxim of one's action should become a universal law." Kant gives the example of someone who borrows money, promises to repay it, but has no intention of doing so. If this were a universal law—that is, if everyone behaved this way—promises would be meaningless, and no one would lend money to anyone.

In his aesthetic theory, Kant holds that judgments that ascribe beauty to something, although they rest on feeling, do have a claim to validity and are not merely statements of taste or opinion. When a person judges something to be beautiful, imagination, perception, and understanding are in harmony; there is a harmony of the experienced object with mental structure. The concepts involved in such judgments are purpose and purposiveness.

Influence. Kant called his radical redefinition of philosophic problems and procedures a "Copernican Revolution" in philosophy. As Copernicus had reversed the way subsequent scientists thought about the relationship of the Earth and the Sun, so Kant reversed the way subsequent philosophers

thought about the relationship of the world of experience and the mind. The mind is not shaped by the world of experience; rather the world of experience is shaped by the patterns set by the mind. Kant's influence and his stature as a philosopher can be measured by the fact that, since Kant, few have been able to philosophize without taking his work into account. His philosophy was the spring from which German IDEALISM flowed. The works of Johann Gottlieb Fichte, Friedrich Wilhelm von Schelling, Arthur Schopenhauer, G. W. F. Hegel, and Ernst Cassirer were greatly influenced by Kant's philosophy. Even those who have opposed Kant's views have tended to deal with philosophical questions as he framed them.

DONALD GOTTERBARN

Bibliography: Ameriks, Karl, *Kant's Theory of Mind* (1982); Arendt, Hannah, *Lectures on Kant's Political Philosophy* (1982); Beck, Lewis White, *Commentary on Kant's Critique of Practical Reason* (1960), *Essays on Kant and Hume* (1978), and *Studies in the Philosophy of Kant* (1965); Cassirer, H. W., *Kant's First Critique: An Appraisal of the Significance of Kant's Critique of Pure Reason* (1954; repr. 1978); Deleuze, Gilles, *Kant's Critical Philosophy*, trans. by Barbara Habberjam and Hugh Tomlinson (1985); Ewing, Alfred C., *Short Commentary on Kant's Critique of Pure Reason*, 2d ed. (1967); Findlay, Joan, *Kant and the Transcendental Object* (1981); Galston, William A., *Kant and the Problem of History* (1965); Goldman, Lucien, *Immanuel Kant* (1972); Heidegger, Martin, *Kant and the Problem of Metaphysics*, trans. by James S. Churchill (1962); Jaspers, Karl, *Kant* (1966); Korner, Stephan, *Kant* (1975); Schlipp, Paul A., *Kant's Pre-Critical Ethics*, 2d ed., ed. by Lewis W. Beck (1960; repr. 1977); Wilkerson, T. E., *Kant's Critique of Pure Reason* (1976).

Kantorovich, Leonid V.   [kuhn-tahr'-uh-vich, lay'-oh-need]

The Soviet economist Leonid Vitalyevich Kantorovich, b. Saint Petersburg, Jan. 19 (N.S.), 1912, d. Apr. 7, 1986, won the Nobel Prize for economics (with Tjalling Koopmans) in 1975 for his work in econometrics, specifically his contributions to the theory of optimum allocation of resources. He graduated from the University of Leningrad in 1930 and then taught there, first as an instructor (1932–34) and later as a professor (1934–60). From 1958 to 1971 he worked at the Siberian division of the Academy of Sciences of the USSR at Novosibirsk (Akademgorodok), and in 1971 he became head of the Institute for Economic Management in Moscow. He became a full member of the USSR Academy of Sciences in 1964 and won the Lenin Prize for Economics in 1965. Kantorovich gained fame in 1939–40 for a paper entitled "Mathematical Methods for the Organization and Planning of Production," which advocated a method of improving the Soviet system of central planning by applying the econometric tool of linear programming. His principal work is *Economic Calculation and the Use of Resources* (1959; Eng. trans., 1965). He was also coauthor (with G. P. Akilov) of *Functional Analysis* (2d ed., 1982).

Kanuri   [kuh-noo'-ree]

The Kanuri, speakers of a Saharan group of Sudanic languages, inhabit most of Bornu Province in northeastern Nigeria. In addition to the more than 3,000,000 Kanuri in Nigeria in the mid-1980s, an estimated 400,000 lived in Niger and Chad, chiefly in cities and towns. Since the 11th century, the Kanuri have adhered to Islam. Being strategically located along the trans-Saharan trade routes, they early developed a stratified, state-organized empire (see KANEM-BORNU) that reached its peak of influence during the 16th century. Traditional Kanuri society included a hereditary nobility and socially mobile commoner and slave classes. Their political unity helped them to resist successfully the jihad (holy war) waged by the FULANI in the early 19th century.

Kanuri villages consist of square, sun-dried brick dwellings with thatched roofs. Polygyny is practiced, with plural wives and their children occupying separate households. The Kanuri subsistence economy is based on agriculture, with peanuts grown as a cash crop. Longstanding trade networks with neighboring Fulani, Arab, and Berber peoples are well developed.

JAMES W. HERRICK

Bibliography: Cohen, Ronald, *The Kanuri of Bornu* (1967).

Kaohsiung   (Gaoxiong)   [gow'-shyoong']

Kaohsiung is a major seaport in southwestern Taiwan. The population is 1,250,000 (1982 est.). The city is a commercial and industrial center, manufacturing chemicals, paper and food products, aluminum, and ships. The main exports are rice, sugar, and fruit. Settled in the early 17th century, Kaohsiung was opened as a treaty port in 1863 and underwent major development as a port during the Japanese occupation (1895–1945) of Taiwan.

kaolinite: see CLAY MINERALS.

kaon   [kay'-ahn]

A kaon, or K-meson, is a FUNDAMENTAL PARTICLE classified as both a boson and a hadron; it has a mass between that of the electron and that of the proton. Four kaons exist: two electrically charged, K^+ and K^- (antiparticles of each other), and two neutral, K^0 and $\bar{K}^0$ (also a pair of antiparticles).

See also: MESON.

Kapital, Das

Das Kapital ("Capital," 3 vols., 1867, 1885, 1894; Eng. trans., 1886, 1907, 1909), a monumental politico-economic study written by Karl MARX and edited in part by Friedrich ENGELS, served as the theoretical basis of modern socialism and COMMUNISM. In it Marx attempted to show that the capitalist system contained within itself the seeds of its own destruction. He assumed that the value of a product is determined by the amount of labor needed to produce it (the labor theory of value), and that the capitalist's profit depends on his ability to keep the worker's wages lower than the value of the goods he or she produces. Marx called the difference between the two amounts "surplus value." He predicted that competition among capitalists would lead to an inevitable decline in surplus value, causing a crisis in the system. From this would come a revolution that would replace capitalism with socialism.

Kapitza, Peter   [kah'-peet-sah]

The Russian physicist Peter Leonidovich Kapitza, b. June 26, 1894, d. Apr. 8, 1984, received the 1978 Nobel Prize for physics for his work in the field of low-temperature physics, especially his discovery (1938) that helium II (a form of helium that is a stable liquid below 2.174° K, or −270.976° C) is a superfluid—it has almost no viscosity. Kapitza received (1923) his Ph.D. degree from Cambridge University, where he worked until 1934, when he was detained in the USSR by Stalin. In 1935 he was made director of the S. I. Vavilov Institute for Physical Problems in Moscow. Except for 1946–54, when he fell out of favor with Stalin, Kapitza remained there, later working on controlled thermonuclear fusion.   CRAIG B. WAFF

Bibliography: Parry, Albert, ed. and trans., *Peter Kapitsa on Life and Science* (1968).

Kaplan, Mordecai Menahem   [kap'-luhn, mor'-duh-ky]

The American-Jewish philosopher, educator, and rabbi Mordecai Menahem Kaplan, b. Lithuania, June 11, 1881, d. Nov. 8, 1983, founded the Society for the Advancement of Judaism (1922) and the Jewish Reconstructionist Foundation (1940). Kaplan also served as dean of the Teachers Institute of the Jewish Theological Seminary of America (1931). In some of his writings—*A New Approach to the Problem of Judaism* (1924), *Judaism as a Civilization* (1934; rev. ed., 1957), *Judaism in Transition* (1936), *The Future of the American Jew* (1948), and *A New Zionism* (1935; rev. ed., 1959)—Kaplan originated the concept of reconstructionism. He argued that Judaism is a dynamic civilization based on nationhood, not religion. Zionism and Israel, therefore, are central components of Judaism that serve to revitalize the pride of diaspora Jews.   SAUL S. FRIEDMAN

Bibliography: Libowitz, Richard, *Mordecai M. Kaplan and the Development of Reconstructionism* (1983).

kapok   [kay'-pahk]

The kapok tree, C. pentandra, *a deciduous tree of the tropics, has seedpods that produce a floss still used for stuffing and clothing insulation. The seeds also yield an oil used in manufacturing soap.*

The kapok is a large deciduous tree, *Ceiba pentandra,* family Bombacaceae, with spines on its branches and young trunks. The irregularly shaped tree has a wide-spreading crown and has prominent buttresses at its base. It is native to tropical Asia, although it is now grown throughout the tropics in both the New and Old Worlds. The flowers are white or rose and occur in dense clusters, usually blooming before the leaves appear. Each seed within the fruit is surrounded by a dense mat of cottony fibers. These fibers are almost pure cellulose although, unlike cotton fibers, they do not lend themselves to spinning. Buoyant, impervious to water, and with a low thermal conductivity, kapok fibers were extensively used for stuffing, padding, and insulation but have been somewhat replaced by synthetic fibers. A mature tree yields up to 42 kg (92 lbs) of fiber per harvest. Kapok seeds contain an oil used in the manufacture of soap.   DIANNE FAHSELT

Kaprow, Allan   [kap'-roh]

Allan Kaprow, b. Atlantic City, N.J., Aug. 23, 1927, is an American painter, assemblage artist, and art theorist who created the art form called HAPPENINGS. Kaprow's early paintings were abstract expressionist in style and were influenced by his studies with Hans Hofmann in New York City. In addition to paintings, Kaprow also experimented with collages and assemblages composed of nontraditional art materials such as straw, wadded newspapers, and flashing lights. Inspired by ABSTRACT EXPRESSIONISM's emphasis on the act of painting and by the avant-garde composer John Cage, who advocated chance and indeterminacy as valid means of artistic organization, Kaprow began (1957–58) to create environmental works that integrated space, materials, time, sound, color, and even spectators. Kaprow called these works happenings, and they were intended to inject spontaneity and improvisation into art. During the 1960s he devoted himself to creating and publicizing happenings and establishing them as a viable art form. He also taught.   DIANA KURZ

Bibliography: Kaprow, Allan, *Assemblages, Environments and Happenings* (1966) and, ed. by S. S. Shaman, *Standards* (1979).

Kapteyn, Jacobus Cornelius   [kahp-teen', yah-koh'-buhs kor-nay'-lee-uhs]

Jacobus Cornelius Kapteyn, b. Jan. 19, 1851, d. June 18, 1922, was a Dutch astronomer who made the first major contributions since William and John Herschel to an understanding of the distribution and motions of the stars in the Milky Way galaxy. In a 13-year collaboration (1885–98) with Sir David Gill, he measured the position and brightness of almost a half-million stars. In 1902, Kapteyn discovered that stars do not move randomly but stream in two opposite directions. Kapteyn coordinated a worldwide effort to gather data on parallaxes, proper motions, and radial velocities of stars and used statistical methods to determine stellar distances. This work yielded the first approximation of the size and structure of the Milky Way.

Kapustin Yar [ka-poos'-tin yahr]

Kapustin Yar, the Soviet Union's oldest space center (see BAIKONUR), lies several kilometers below Volgograd near the Volga River. The site of rocketry experiments in the 1930s and of ballistic missile and early space tests in the 1940s and 1950s, its location was known to other nations but not publicly acknowledged by the Soviet Union until 1983.

Kara Kum [kar-uh-kum']

Kara Kum, a major desert of the USSR, lies east of the Caspian Sea, covering 60% of the Turkmen Soviet Socialist Republic as well as the southwestern Kazakh Soviet Socialist Republic. With an area of about 300,000 km^2 (116,000 mi^2), it extends approximately 965 km (600 mi) from east to west and 400 km (250 mi) from north to south. Its name means "black sands."

The low-lying Kara Kum is dominated by sand dunes, except for clay-covered sections in the west. Sulfur is mined at Sernyy Zavod in central Turkmenistan. Rainfall averages less than 255 mm (10 in) a year. The Tedzhen and Murgab rivers flow into the southern Kara Kum, where they eventually sink into the sand. Their waters irrigate oases such as Tedzhen and Mary, as does water from the AMU DARYA, diverted along the 837-km (520-mi) Kara Kum Canal, which was constructed in the 1950s. Scrub cover grows along the borders and cereal grains are grown in the oases. Seminomadic herders of Turkmen (Turcoman) descent raise camels, sheep, and goats.

Karachi [kuh-rah'-chee]

The port city of Karachi, the former capital of Pakistan, retains its position as the major industrial and communications center. The two minarets in this view of the city belong to the Memon mosque.

Karachi, the largest city and the major seaport of Pakistan, is situated on the Arabian Sea just northwest of the Indus River delta. The population of the city proper is 5,103,000 (1981), and that of the Karachi Division is 5,353,000. Together with its suburbs, Karachi encompasses an area of 591 km^2 (228 mi^2). Karachi has grown rapidly because of its port and its industries. Manufactures include textiles (jute and cotton), footwear, food products, and handicraft items. A sophisticated road-, rail-, and air-route system makes the city an important transportation junction. Its port also serves landlocked Af-

ghanistan. Migration from other parts of Pakistan and India has been significant since the two countries gained independence. The University of Karachi (1951) and several colleges and technical schools are located there.

Karachi was founded in 1729 on the site of a fishing village. During the 18th century it became a port and expanded rapidly. The British captured the city in 1839 and annexed it to their Indian territories in 1842. By 1914 it was the largest grain-exporting port in the British Empire. It was the capital of independent Pakistan until 1959. RICHARD ULACK

Karaites [kair'-uh-yts]

Karaites are members of a Jewish sect founded by Anan ben David in Babylonia in the 8th century AD. Their name (from the Hebrew *qara,* "to read") refers to the sect's concentration on the written Law (TORAH), as distinct from the majority of Jews' emphasis on the TALMUD and the rabbinic traditions (the Rabbanites). The Karaites avoided dealings with Rabbanites, forbade intermarriage, replaced Jewish liturgy by selected biblical readings, and developed an extensive polemic literature. From Palestine and Babylonia, Karaism spread to Egypt, Syria, the Crimea, Constantinople, and Spain. Today the sect has dwindled to a few thousand adherents, most of them in Israel and the USSR. NAHUM N. GLATZER

Bibliography: Ankori, Zvi, *Karaites in Byzantium* (1959); Birnbaum, P., ed., *Karaite Studies* (1971); Mann, J., *Texts and Studies in Jewish History and Literature,* 2 vols., rev. ed. (1970); Nemoy, L., ed. and trans., *Karaite Anthology* (1952).

Karajan, Herbert von [kahr'-ah-yahn]

The Austrian Herbert von Karajan, b. Apr. 5, 1908, d. July 16, 1989, is acknowledged as one of the foremost conductors of his generation. He studied at the Salzburg Mozarteum and the Academy of Music in Vienna. His first appointment as conductor was at the opera house in Ulm, and he quickly became one of Germany's most prominent conductors. Although he had been a member of the Nazi party, after the war an Allied commission cleared him of charges of political collaboration. In 1955 he became conductor-for-life of the Berlin Philharmonic, a post he held for 35 years before resigning in 1989, primarily because of conflicts with the orchestra members. From 1957 to 1964 he was artistic director of the Vienna State Opera and he conducted at the Salzburg Festival from 1951. A prolific recording artist, von Karajan was celebrated for his renditions of Beethoven, Wagner, Bruckner, and Richard Strauss. STEPHANIE VON BUCHAU

Bibliography: Holmes, J. L., *Conductors on Record* (1982); Vaughan, Roger, *Herbert von Karajan: A Biographical Portrait* (1986).

Karakalpak [kah-ruh-kul-pahk']

The Karakalpak are a Kipchak Turkic-speaking people who are distantly related to the PECHENEGS, marauders of Kievan Russia. Basically Mongoloid, they exhibit mixed racial features, the result of numerous subjugations. They number several hundred thousand, most of whom live in the USSR, with the balance in Turkey, Iran, and Afghanistan. They are concentrated primarily along the lower Amu Darya and in the contiguous Kyzyl Kum desert. *Karakalpak* means "black hat," in reference to the group's typical headwear.

Before 1900 the Karakalpak were semisedentary, combining irrigated agriculture with nomadic herding. Today they are collective farmers and fishers. Their religion is Sunnite Islam.

Known from the 16th century, they had migrated to their present homeland by the 18th century. They are distinguished from the UZBEK and KAZAKH peoples principally through their dialect. Living in adobe-type houses instead of yurts, the Karakalpak remain rural and rarely intermarry with anyone except the Kazakh. VICTOR L. MOTE

Bibliography: Bacon, E. E., *Central Asians under Russian Rule* (1966; repr. 1980); Meakin, Annette, *In Russian Turkestan* (1903; repr. 1976); Weekes, R. V., ed., *Muslim Peoples* (1978); Wheeler, G., *The Modern History of Soviet Central Asia* (1975).

Karakoram Range [kah-ruh-kohr'-uhm]

The Karakoram Range, a high (mean elevation: 6,096 m/20,000 ft) mountain range in the HIMALAYAS of Central Asia, extends 483 km (300 mi) southeast from the Pamir Knot in northern Kashmir to southwestern Tibet. The tallest peak, GODWIN AUSTEN, or K2, is the second highest mountain in the world. Young geologically, the Karakoram mountains emerged in the Cenozoic Era. Because of their steep slopes and alpine glaciers, the summits are almost inaccessible. The dry, harsh climate supports little vegetation or wildlife, but pastoral Tibetans inhabit the lower elevations.

Karamanlis, Konstantinos G. [kah-rah-mahn-lis']

Konstantinos G. Karamanlis, b. Feb. 23, 1907, is a conservative politician who served as premier and president of Greece. Karamanlis was elected to parliament in 1935 and entered the cabinet in 1946 as minister of labor. Appointed prime minister in 1955, Karamanlis formed his own party, the National Radical Union, and won three elections. He resigned as prime minister in 1963 and went into exile in France. After the fall (1974) of the military regime that had come to power in 1967, he returned to Greece and founded another party, New Democracy, which he led as prime minister from 1974 until 1980. Karamanlis held the presidency from 1980 to 1985 and was reelected to that post in 1990.

Bibliography: Woodhouse, C. M., *Karamanlis* (1982).

Karamzin, Nikolai Mikhailovich [kuh-ruhm-zeen', nee-kuh-ly' mee-ky'-luh-vich]

Nikolai Mikhailovich Karamzin, b. Dec. 12 (N.S.), 1766, d. June 3 (N.S.), 1826, is considered the greatest prose writer of 18th-century Russia. His *Letters of a Russian Traveler* (1790, 1801; Eng. trans., 1951), written after a trip (1789–90) to western Europe, is a monument of Russian literary sentimentalism. Karamzin also wrote a number of fictional works, the most famous of which is *Bednaia Liza* (Poor Liza, 1791–92). Appointed Russian historiographer in 1803, he concentrated thereafter on his great *Istoriya Gosudarstva Rossiyskogo* (History of Russia, 12 vols., 1819–29). Karamzin refined Russian prose by bringing literary usage into greater conformity with the French-oriented speech of polite society. HAROLD B. SEGEL

Bibliography: Black, J. L., ed., *Essays on Karamzin* (1975); Cross, A. G., *N. M. Karamzin* (1972); Segel, Harold B., *The Literature of 18th-Century Russia: A History and Anthology,* 2 vols. (1967).

karate: see MARTIAL ARTS.

Karatepe [kah-rah'-te-pe]

Karatepe (Hittite: Azitawattia) is a Hittite archaeological site north of Osmaniye in south central Turkey. Excavated (1947–52) by the German archaeologist Helmuth Bossert, it yielded parallel 8th-century BC texts in Phoenician and Hittite, which helped in the difficult process of deciphering Neo-Hittite hieroglyphic script.

Karelia [kuh-ree'-lee-uh]

Karelia is a region adjoining Finland in northwestern USSR, politically constituted as the Karelian Autonomous SSR within the Russian SFSR. Its area is 172,400 km² (66,546 mi²). Its population is 792,000 (1989), of which about 11% are Karelians, a Finnish-speaking people. The capital is Petrozavodsk (1989 pop., 270,000). The area is heavily forested, and much of the land is covered with swamps. Karelia is a major supplier of wood and paper products, including prefabricated housing, furniture, skis, and paper.

In 1923, Karelia was constituted as an autonomous republic. After the USSR acquired borderlands from Finland as a result of the RUSSO-FINNISH WAR (1939–40), the new territory was combined with Karelia to form the Karelo-Finnish SSR. In 1956, however, it reverted to the status of an autonomous re-

public. The Karelian Isthmus, a neck of land linking the USSR and Finland, lies to the south of the Karelian ASSR, on the opposite side of Lake Ladoga. All but the southernmost section became part of Finland in 1917 but was ceded to the USSR in 1940. This region is now part of the Leningrad oblast of the Russian SFSR. THEODORE SHABAD

Karen

The Karen people of Burma, who numbered about 3,267,000 in the mid-1980s, are, with the Shans, one of the two largest non-Burmese ethnic groups in that country. A Karen state lies east of Rangoon along the Thai border, but only a minority of Karens live there; the rest are mainly dispersed in the densely populated deltas of the Irrawaddy, Sitang, and Salween rivers. Some speak a Karen dialect, and others have adopted Burmese. Although many leading Karens are Christians, the majority (about two-thirds) are Buddhist.

The influence of the Karens under British rule was out of proportion to their numbers. Many of them, especially those who were Christian, came to hold important positions in the colonial army, and they were disliked by the Burmese who led the nationalist movement that gained independence for Burma in 1948. Unwilling to submit to Burmese rule, the Karens rebelled unsuccessfully in 1949, and Karen insurgency has persisted since then. RICHARD BUTWELL

Karinska, Barbara [kuh-rinz'-kuh]

Barbara Karinska, b. Russia, Oct. 3 (N.S.), 1886, d. Oct. 19, 1983, worked in Paris during the 1930s realizing the costume designs of such painters as Salvador Dalí and André Derain. She moved to New York in 1938, executed costumes for Broadway shows and the Metropolitan Opera, won an Academy Award (1948) for her costumes for the film *Joan of Arc,* and in 1948 became resident costume maker and designer for the new New York City Ballet (NYCB). She was responsible for the costumes in every major ballet presented by the NYCB, including *The Nutcracker, Jewels,* and, her last production, the 1977 *Vienna Waltzes.* DAVID VAUGHAN

Bibliography: Kirstein, Lincoln, *The New York City Ballet* (1973).

Karl-Marx-Stadt [karl-marks'-shtaht]

From 1953 to 1990, Karl-Marx-Stadt was the name of Chemnitz, a city in the German state of Saxony. It lies southeast of Leipzig, on the Chemnitz River at the foot of the Erzgebirge (Ore Mountains). With a population of 313,095 (1988 est.), it was one of the largest cities in the former East Germany. Known since medieval times for its textiles, the city also manufactures automobiles, machine tools, electrical equipment, chemicals, and furniture. It is a transportation hub. Several technical schools and a college are located there.

Originally settled by the Slavic Wends on a trade route through the Erzgebirge, the city began to flourish as a textile center in the 12th century. Heavily damaged during the Thirty Years' War (1618–48), it recovered its prosperity with the advent of cotton manufacturing. During the 19th century, Chemnitz was a pioneer in machine construction, producing machine tools, railroad locomotives, and textile machinery. Although damage during World War II was severe, a few historic buildings remain or have been reconstructed. They include several Gothic churches and the 15th-century town hall. A 12th-century Benedictine monastery houses the city museum.

Karlfeldt, Erik Axel [kahrl'-felt, ay'-rik ahk'-sel]

The poet Erik Axel Karlfeldt, b. July 20, 1864, d. Apr. 8, 1931, was one of the principal figures of modern Swedish literature. Elected to the Swedish Academy in 1904, he was posthumously honored with the Nobel Prize for literature in 1931. A poet of his native Dalarna province, Karlfeldt was known for his sensitivity to nature and familiarity with local peasant traditions, qualities that characterize *Fridolins visor* (Fridolin's Songs, 1898) and *Fridolins lustgård* (Fridolin's Pleasure Garden, 1901). Selections from his poetry were translated in *Arcadia Borealis* (1938). VIRPI ZUCK

Karloff, Boris   [kahr'-lawf]

Although his name became synonymous with horror, Boris Karloff, b. Nov. 23, 1887, d. Feb. 2, 1969, was actually a tall, quiet, charming Englishman, originally named William Pratt, who after a wandering theatrical career became a Hollywood extra and was chosen to play the Frankenstein monster. His best films include *Frankenstein* (1931), *The Old Dark House* (1932), *The Mummy* (1932), *Bride of Frankenstein* (1935), *The Body Snatcher* (1945), and *The Raven* (1935, 1963).

LESLIE HALLIWELL

Bibliography: Jensen, Paul M., *Boris Karloff and His Films* (1975); Lindsay, Cynthia, *Dear Boris: The Life of William Henry Pratt, a.k.a. Boris Karloff* (1975).

Karlovy Vary   [kahr'-law-vee vah'-ree]

Karlovy Vary (Carlsbad) is a resort city in northwestern Czechoslovakia on the Teplá River. It has a population of 59,183 (1984 est.). Manufactures include porcelain and food products. Founded (1347) as a spa by Emperor Charles IV, the city still attracts visitors to its warm mineral springs. The Carlsbad Decrees (1819), discouraging liberal teachings in German universities, were drawn up there.

Karlsruhe   [kahrls'-roo-e]

Karlsruhe is an industrial city and inland port in Baden-Württemberg state, southwestern West Germany. It lies about 65 km (40 mi) northwest of Stuttgart and is connected with the Rhine River to the west by a 6.5-km (4-mi) canal. The population is 271,236 (1982 est.). The city's industries include oil refining, metalworking, machinery construction, printing, chemical production, brewing, and food processing. Since 1956, Karlsruhe has been a center for nuclear research. The city is the seat of the Federal Supreme Court and the Federal Constitutional Court. Fridericiana Technical College (1825) is located there.

Established in 1715, Karlsruhe was laid out in a fan shape, with streets lined by imposing neoclassical buildings radiating outward from the margrave's palace; notable among these buildings are the town hall and the Protestant church. The city was heavily bombed during World War II.

Karlstadt   [kahrl'-shtaht]

The German theologian Andreas Rudolf Bodenstein, b. *c.*1480, d. Dec. 24, 1541, was later called Karlstadt (or Carlstadt) for his birthplace. He became a professor at the University of Wittenberg, where he played an important role in the early years of the Reformation. Karlstadt and Martin Luther together debated the Catholic apologist Johann Eck at Leipzig in 1519, but Karlstadt later became increasingly radical, favoring the destruction of religious images and reinterpretation of the Eucharist. In 1525, Luther directly criticized Karlstadt in his treatise *Against the Heavenly Prophets, on Images and Sacrament.* Expelled from Saxony for political reasons, Karlstadt later became a professor of the Old Testament at Basel.

Bibliography: Edwards, Mark, *Luther and the False Brethren* (1974); Rupp, Gordon, *Patterns of Reformation* (1969); Sider, Ronald J., *Andreas Bodenstein von Karlstadt: The Development of His Thought, 1517–1525* (1974).

karma   [kahr'-muh]

Karma is a fundamental concept in all Indian religions. Its meaning has shifted through the centuries but has always revolved around the notion of action, especially religious or ritual action. In the early Brahmanical tradition (see HINDUISM), this meant primarily the act of sacrifice addressed to the gods, but later, particularly in BUDDHISM, the concept was mixed with moral notions and came to refer to acts, good or bad, that resulted in correspondingly positive or negative fruits either in this or in a future life. As such, karma also came to be viewed as a metaphysical principle, a law of karma, that bound beings to the cycle of rebirth (see TRANSMIGRATION OF SOULS).

JOSEPH M. KITAGAWA AND JOHN S. STRONG

Karmal, Babrak   [kahr-mahl', bahb-rahk']

Babrak Karmal, b. 1929, headed the Soviet-sponsored regime in Afghanistan from 1979 to 1986. Leader of the pro-Soviet wing of Afghanistan's ruling People's Democratic (Communist) party, he was installed as party chief and president when Soviet troops occupied the country in December 1979. After more than five years of Soviet military operations failed to end resistance to his rule, Karmal was replaced as party leader by Muhammad Najibullah in May 1986. He retained the ceremonial post of president.

Kármán, Theodore von   [kahr'-mahn]

The Hungarian-born physicist Theodore von Kármán, b. May 11, 1881, d. May 7, 1963, analyzed the phenomenon known today as the Kármán vortex street. This phenomenon is the periodic production of vortices, or regions of rotation, by a cylindrical object in a moving fluid. The vortices are generated by first one side of the object and then the other and can cause serious damage to structures not designed to withstand such oscillations.

Kármán received his Ph.D. from the University of Göttingen in 1908. From 1912 to 1929 he was director of the Aeronautical Institute at the University of Aachen. During this time he discovered a new law of turbulence, which allowed the prediction of drag on the surface of aircraft and rockets, as well as permitting description of fluid flow in pipes.

In 1930, Kármán became director of the Guggenheim Aeronautical Laboratory at the California Institute of Technology, where he remained until 1949. He became a citizen of the United States in 1936. Later he cofounded the institute's Jet Propulsion Laboratory, a government-funded center for rocket research and space exploration. Aerodynamic work by Kármán and his students became the basis for the design of supersonic aircraft. His autobiography, *The Wind and Beyond* (1967), was posthumously edited by Lee Edson.

JEAN SILVERMAN

Karnak   [kahr'-nak]

Karnak, a village on the Nile at the northern extremity of LUXOR, is the site of the greatest assembly of ancient temples in Egypt. They are spread over about 48 ha (120 acres) and range in date over about 2,000 years. By far the largest and most important is the temple of Amun (Amon). In origin, it probably dates back to the Old Kingdom (*c.*2686–2181 BC), but the earliest surviving building is a pavilion of Sesostris I (*c.*1971–1928 BC). Amun, called king of the gods, was the state god in the New Kingdom (*c.*1570–1085 BC). During this period kings with such famous names as Amenhotep, Thutmose, Seti, and Ramses conducted campaigns in Western Asia and Nubia, bringing back vast quantities of booty, some of which paid for building the Amun temple and made its priesthood the richest religious organization in the land. Architecturally, the temple's most impressive element is the colossal Hypostyle Hall of Seti I (*c.*1318–1304 BC). Its walls are decorated with scenes carved in relief and hieroglyphic inscriptions that primarily depict religious ceremonies or record historical events, such as conquests.

I. E. S. EDWARDS

Bibliography: Michalowski, Kazimierz, *Karnak,* trans. by Henryk Krzeczkowski (1969); Nims, C. F., *Thebes of the Pharaohs* (1965).

Karnataka   [kahr-nah-tah'-kah]

Karnataka (formerly Mysore) is a state located on the southwest coast of India. It has an area of 192,204 km^2 (74,210 mi^2) and a population of 37,135,714 (1981); its capital city is BANGALORE. Just inland from the coastal plain along the Arabian sea, the Western GHATS rise to an average altitude of 760 m (2,500 ft). The fertile plateaus and plains to the east of the hills are irrigated by the Cauvery, Tunga, and Badhra rivers. Coffee, tea, rice, sugarcane, cotton, and peanuts are the main crops. Gold, iron ore, manganese, bauxite, and copper are mined. The major industries include iron, steel, and machinery manufacturing, production of hydroelectric power, food processing, cotton and silk textile manufacturing, and sandal-wood oil processing.

The area was controlled by a succession of Hindu dynasties from the 3d century BC, and later, by both Hindu and Muslim rulers. In the mid-18th century, HYDER ALI, a Muslim, conquered the region. In 1767 the four Mysore Wars between Ali and the British began; they continued under Hyder Ali's son TIPPU SULTAN until 1799, when the victorious British assumed control. In 1947 the state of Mysore became part of independent India. In 1973 its name was changed to Karnataka.

Bibliography: Chandrasekhar, S., *Dimensions of Socio-Political Change in Mysore, 1918–40* (1985).

Karpov, Anatoly   [kahr'-pohf]

The Soviet Anatoly Yevgenievich Karpov, b. May 23, 1951, was world chess champion from 1975 to 1985. Karpov won the world junior championship in 1969 and a year later became the world's youngest international grand master. His game is noted for economy and precision. In 1975, Karpov was awarded the world championship by default, after Bobby Fischer refused to defend his title. In 1978 and again in 1981, Karpov retained the world title against Soviet expatriate Viktor Korchnoi. In 1985, however, he lost the title to his countryman Gary Kasparov; he was beaten again by Kasparov in 1986 and 1987.

Bibliography: Byrne, Robert, *Anatoly Karpov* (1976).

Karrer, Paul   [kar'-ur]

The Swiss chemist Paul Karrer, b. Apr. 21, 1889, d. June 18, 1971, was one of the two winners of the 1937 Nobel Prize for chemistry; his portion of the award was for his research on the chemical structure of the carotenoids and flavins (yellowish red and light yellow pigments, respectively) and on vitamins A and B_2. The carotenoid research led to his successful isolation (1931) of vitamin A from cod-liver oil. Karrer received (1911) his doctorate from the University of Zurich, to which he returned later, becoming professor (1918) of chemistry and director (1919) of the Chemical Institute.

Karsavina, Tamara Platonovna   [kur-sah'-veen-uh, tuh-mar'-uh pluh-toh-noh'-vuh]

Tamara Platonovna Karsavina, b. Saint Petersburg, Mar. 10 (N.S.), 1885, d. London, May 26, 1978, one of the greatest dancers of the BALLETS RUSSES DE SERGE DIAGHILEV, became a ballet legend in her own lifetime. Daughter of the dancer Platon Karsavin, she graduated from the Saint Petersburg Imperial School in 1902 and immediately entered the Maryinsky Ballet (now Kirov Ballet) as a soloist. From 1909, when she was given star roles, until 1912, Karsavina divided her time between the Maryinsky company and Diaghilev's touring group, where she was the frequent partner of Vaslav Nijinsky. Influenced by Mikhail Fokine's ideas of expressive dance, she excelled in his ballets, notably *Les Sylphides* (1909), *Carnaval* (1910), *Petrushka* (1911), *Le Spectre de la Rose* (1911), and *L'Oiseau de Feu* (The Firebird, 1910).

After the Russian Revolution, Karsavina emigrated to the West, where she worked with Diaghilev in Paris and was for many years associated with the Royal Academy of Dancing in London.   MICHAEL ROBERTSON

Karsh, Yousuf   [kahrsh, yoh'-zuf]

The Canadian photographer Yousuf Karsh, b. Mardin, Turkey, Dec. 23, 1908, specializes in revealing and dramatic portraits of prominent men and women. Using a battery of studio lights and a large view camera, he poses his subjects against a plain background and illuminates them in a way that emphasizes their psychological makeup. His portrait *Winston S. Churchill* (1941) not only made Karsh famous but became a symbol of British resistance to the Nazis. *Marian Anderson* (1948), *Jawaharlal Nehru* (1949), and *Ernest Hemingway* (1958) all embody his strong yet quiet style. Karsh's portraits have been collected in such books as *Faces of Destiny* (1946), *Portraits of Greatness* (1959), *Faces of Our Time* (1971), and *A Fifty-Year Retrospective* (1983).   MELINDA BOYD PARSONS

Yousuf Karsh is one of the leading photographers of the 20th century, renowned for portraits such as those of the American artist Georgia O'Keeffe (1956). Karsh uses strong lighting contrasts and simple settings in meticulously composed portraits that suggest his subjects' personalities and historical significance. (Karsh, Ottawa.)

Kasavubu, Joseph   [kas-uh-voo'-boo]

Joseph Kasavubu, b. 1910 or 1917, d. Mar. 24, 1969, was the first president of the Congo republic (now Zaire). A teacher and junior civil servant under the Belgian government in the Congo, he became active in various political and cultural associations during the 1940s. Initially, Kasavubu worked to reunify the Bakongo people. In 1955 he became president of Abako, a powerful Bakongo association, and a spokesman for Congolese independence.

When the Congo became independent in 1960, an uneasy coalition government was formed, with Kasavubu as president and Patrice LUMUMBA as premier. Later that year, Kasavubu had Lumumba removed from office. Kasavubu himself was toppled from power in 1965 by Gen. Joseph Mobutu (now MOBUTU SESE SEKO).   L. H. GANN

Bibliography: Young, Crawford, *Politics in the Congo: Decolonization and Independence* (1965).

Käsebier, Gertrude   [kay'-ze-beer]

Gertrude Käsebier, b. Des Moines, Iowa, May 18, 1852, d. Oct. 12, 1934, a founding member (1902) of the PHOTO-SECESSION, began taking photographs in 1893 and opened a highly successful portrait studio in New York City in 1897. Building her compositions in contrasting tones, she created evocative, soft-focused platinum prints that far surpassed contemporary camera portraiture. As her business became larger and more commercial, however, her portrait work suffered the loss of careful composition and ingenuity. This weakening of her style brought her into conflict with Alfred STIEGLITZ and precipitated a break (1912) with the Photo-Secession group. One of the founders of the Pictorial Photographers of America, she continued to photograph until 1929.   ELIZABETH POLLOCK

Bibliography: Naef, Weston, *The Collection of Alfred Stieglitz: Fifty Pioneers of Modern Photography* (1978).

Kashgar

Kashgar—in Chinese, k'a-shih (Kashi)—is a city in the western part of China's Sinkiang (Xinjiang) Autonomous Region, near the Soviet border. Its population of 150,000 (1982) is largely UIGHUR and Muslim. A fertile oasis in the Takla Makan desert, Kashgar historically was one of the main commercial centers on the SILK ROAD between China and the west. It marked the westernmost point of Chinese cultural and political influence. Today the city produces cotton, silk, and leather goods and is known for its fine carpets.

Kashmir   [kash-mir']

Kashmir is a mountainous region at the extreme north of the Indian subcontinent. The territory of about 223,000 km² (86,000 mi²) is divided into the Indian state of Jammu and

Kashmir, a former princely state, has become the focus of several international disputes since 1947 because of its politically strategic location in India and Pakistan, bordering Afghanistan and China. The area was accorded autonomy in 1848 under the terms of two treaties and served as a buffer zone separating tsarist Russia and Britain's empire in India.

Kashmir (139,000 km²/53,700 mi²) and the Pakistani Azad (Free) Kashmir (83,800 km²/32,400 mi²). Its population is 5,987,389 (1981). Famous for its natural beauty, Kashmir is sometimes called the "Switzerland of India." Almost half the population lives in the fertile Vale of Kashmir (India), between the Great Himalaya and the Pir Panjal ranges.

The capitals of the Indian section are SRINAGAR in summer and Jammu in winter; the capital of the Pakistani Kashmir is Muzaffarabad. More than 65% of the inhabitants are Muslims, who live in the Vale of Kashmir and in the central and western parts. Hindus reside mostly in the south, around the city of Jammu. In the east is the region of Ladakh, where many of the people are of Tibetan ethnic stock and Buddhists.

Historically, Kashmir was part of the Indian kingdoms. During the Asokan period (273–232 BC), Buddhism was introduced; between the 9th and 12th centuries, the area was a center of Hindu culture. Muslim rule began in AD 1341 and initiated mass conversion to Islam. In 1846 the territory became the princely state of Jammu and Kashmir, belonging to British India. Since 1947 the state has been the object of several armed conflicts between India and Pakistan—India claiming the territory on historical and legal grounds, and Pakistan maintaining that this Muslim-majority state rightfully belongs to Pakistan (see INDIA-PAKISTAN WARS). The 1962 Chinese invasion of India resulted in the Chinese takeover of a northern, uninhabited section of Ladakh known as Aksai Chin. A "line of control," agreed on in 1972, divides the Indian and Pakistani sections of Kashmir. Subsequent efforts to resolve the conflicting Indian, Pakistani, and Chinese territorial claims in Kashmir met with little success. Mounting violence by militant Muslim separatists in Jammu and Kashmir increased tensions between India and Pakistan in 1990.   ASHOK K. DUTT

Kasparov, Gary   [kahs'-pah-rawf]

The Soviet chess player Gary Kimovich Kasparov, b. Apr. 13, 1963, became the world champion in 1985 by defeating his countryman and then-champion Anatoly KARPOV. Kasparov became a grand master in 1980; his first challenge to Karpov came in 1984–85, when their match was halted inexplicably after 48 games, with Karpov retaining the title. In 1985, 1986, and 1987, however, Kasparov was victorious. His autobiography, *Fighting Chess*, was published in 1985.

Kassel   [kah'-sul]

Kassel (1986 est. pop., 184,200) is an industrial city in Hesse state, Germany. It is located on the Fulda River about 20 mi (32 km) west of the former border between West and East Germany. The city's manufactures include locomotives, automobiles, electrical machinery, synthetic textiles, and optical and precision instruments. Lignite is mined nearby. The city is also a transportation center and a river port.

Originally a Roman settlement, Kassel was chartered in 1180. The city flourished after the landgraves of Hesse established their residence there in 1277; in 1567 it became the capital of Hesse-Kassel. The city was heavily damaged during World War II, but most historic buildings were rebuilt. Notable among them are the Rathaus and the State Theater and the 17th- and 18th-century castles of Karlsaue, Wilhelmshöhe, and Wilhelmstal. The Federal Art Collection houses one of Germany's finest collections of paintings.

Kassites   [kas'-yts]

The Kassites (or Cassites) were a nonnative population of the ancient Near East who infiltrated southern Mesopotamia from the Zagros Mountains of Iran in the 18th century BC. They were political masters of Babylonia for 500 years (c.1600–1100 BC). Their origins were probably central Asiatic. The Kassites' language is insufficiently recorded and only poorly understood. Between 1450 and 1200 BC, Kassite Babylonia interacted diplomatically with New Kingdom Egypt, the Hittite empire, and the Middle Assyrian kingdom.   LOUIS L. ORLIN

Bibliography: Saggs, H. W. F., *The Greatness That Was Babylon* (1962).

Kastler, Alfred   [kahst-lair', ahl-frayd']

The French physicist Alfred Kastler, b. May 3, 1902, d. Jan. 7, 1984, won the 1966 Nobel Prize for physics for his discovery and development of methods for optically studying Hertzian resonances in atoms. This work led to the measurement of nuclear spins and magnetic moments and the development of the maser and laser. Kastler received his doctorate from the University of Bordeaux and taught there before becoming professor and co-director of the physics laboratory at the École Normale Supérieure, where he taught from 1941 to 1968. He served (1958–72) as director of the Atomic Clock Laboratory, Centre National de la Récherche Scientifique.

Katanga: see SHABA.

Katayev, Valentin Petrovich   [ka-ty'-yuhf, vuhl-yin-teen' pee-troh'-vich]

Russian novelist Valentin Petrovich Katayev, b. Jan. 28 (N.S.), 1897, d. Apr. 12, 1986, has been called "the licensed humorist of the Soviets." *The Embezzlers* (1926; Eng. trans., 1928) dealt with Soviet bank tellers who escape their drab jobs by taking along the cash; *Squaring the Circle* (1928; Eng. trans., 1934) was about two mismatched couples who exchange partners. Katayev, also a popular playwright, adapted both novels for the stage. *Time Forward!* (1932; Eng. trans., 1933), by contrast, was a serious novel about the building of a cement plant. His *Lonely White Sail* (1936; Eng. trans., 1937), a partly autobiographical novel, was the first in a series of four chronicling life in Odessa from 1910 through World War II. Personal reminiscences from early childhood to old age were the subject of three of his later books, *The Holy Well* (1965; Eng. trans., 1967), *The Grass of Oblivion* (1967; Eng. trans., 1970), and *A Mosaic of Life; or, The Magic Horn of Oberon* (1972; Eng. trans., 1976).   MAURICE FRIEDBERG

Katmai, Mount   [kat'-my]

Mount Katmai is a 2,047-m (6,715-ft) volcano located on the Alaska Peninsula in southern Alaska. Katmai erupted in 1912, blowing off the top of the mountain and scattering volcanic ash to a depth of 300 mm (1 ft) in some areas as far as 160 km (100 mi) away. The wasteland it created became known as the VALLEY OF TEN THOUSAND SMOKES because of the millions of steam vents that dot its surface. The area was declared a national monument in 1918. The crater measures 13 km (8 mi) in circumference and 1,130 m (3,700 ft) deep.

Katmandu   [kaht-mahn-doo']

Katmandu, the capital of Nepal, is located in the southern foothills of the Himalayas. Its population is 235,160 (1981). Katmandu is the commercial and transportation center of Nepal; its economy is based on jute, sugar, hides, and textiles. A 1934 earthquake severely damaged the city, forcing the construction of new buildings. Historical landmarks include many Hindu temples and a palace housing a 1549 temple that is a pilgrimage site for Tibetan Buddhists. Tribhuvan University was established in 1959.

Katmandu (also spelled Kathmandu) was founded in 723. In 1768 the city was captured by Gurkha kings and became their capital.

Kato Takaaki　[kah'-toh tah-kah-ah'-kee]

Kato Takaaki, b. 1860, d. Jan. 28, 1926, also called Kato Komei, was a leading Japanese statesman in the early 20th century. He began (1887) his political life as private secretary to the statesman OKUMA SHIGENOBU and, like Okuma, was associated throughout his career with the Mitsubishi business cartel.

Kato was twice ambassador to Great Britain (1894–99, 1908–13) and several times minister of foreign affairs (1900, 1906–08, 1913, 1914–15). In 1915 he sent the so-called Twenty-one Demands to China, calling for increased Japanese privileges in that country. As leader of the Kenseikei party after World War I, Kato became prime minister in 1924. His government introduced universal male suffrage and reduced the power of the army. At the same time, however, it included military training in the ordinary school curriculum and suppressed political radicalism. Kato died in office.

Katowice　[kah-toh-veet'-se]

The city of Katowice (1984 est. pop., 363,300) is located in the Silesian coal mining region of southwest Poland, about 120 km (75 mi) northwest of Kraków. Katowice is a major rail junction. Its industries include the manufacture of iron, steel, chemicals, textiles, and heavy machinery. Several colleges and technical schools are located in the city. Settled in the late 16th century, Katowice was annexed by Prussia in 1742. It grew rapidly after the discovery of coal in the late 19th century. It became a part of Poland in 1921.

Katsura Taro　[kaht'-soo-rah tah-roh']

Katsura Taro, b. 1847, d. Oct. 10, 1913, was a leading Japanese statesman in the period preceding World War I. A supporter of the MEIJI RESTORATION (1868), by which the shogunate was overthrown and the emperor restored to authority, Katsura rose to prominence as a protégé of the statesman YAMAGATA ARITOMO. He was minister of the army under Yamagato from 1898 to 1900.

As prime minister from 1901 to 1906, Katsura concluded an alliance (1902) with Britain and presided over Japan's victory in the RUSSO-JAPANESE WAR (1904–05). After a period in opposition to ITO HIROBUMI, he returned to office for a second term and carried out the annexation of Korea in 1910. A third term as premier lasted only seven weeks (December 1912 to February 1913) because of opposition to his armaments program and to the oligarchical basis of his power. Although he opposed the concept of party politics Katsura founded (1913) the Rikken Doshikai party to counter the power of Ito's Seiyukai party. He thus contributed to the development of two-party politics in Japan.

Katsushika Hokusai:　see HOKUSAI.

Kattegat　[kat'-ih-gat]

The Kattegat is a north-south strait separating the JUTLAND peninsula of Denmark from Sweden; it reaches the North Sea through the SKAGERRAK and the Baltic Sea through the Øresund and the Great and Little Belts. The shallow passage is 220 km (137 mi) long and has a maximum width of about 145 km (90 mi). With the Skagerrak, the Kattegat constitutes the shipping passage into and out of the Baltic Sea.

katydid　[kayt'-ee-did]

Katydids are stout-bodied grasshoppers of the family Tettigoniidae, order Orthoptera. They are usually green in color,

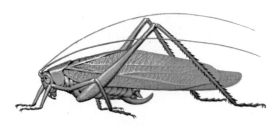

The bush katydid, Scudderia curvicauda, *is also called a long-horned grasshopper because its antennae are as long as its body (4 cm/1.6 in).*

with long, hairlike antennae, the front wings draped over the sides of the body, and a long, bladelike ovipositor (egg-laying tube) extending from the rear of the body in females. The raspy *katy-did* song is produced only by males and serves to attract females. The sound is made by rubbing together the roughened areas at the bases of the two front wings.

Katz, Sir Bernard

German-British biophysicist Sir Bernard Katz, b. Mar. 26, 1911, was awarded, with Julius AXELROD and Ulf Svante von Euler, the 1970 Nobel Prize for physiology or medicine for his contribution to the understanding of the chemistry of nerve impulse transmission. Katz investigated the chemical acetylcholine: its storage, release from nerve endings during impulse transmission, and inactivation. This work has greatly aided the development of neurophysiology and the search for drugs that act upon the nervous system.

Kauffmann, Angelica　[kawf'-muhn, ahng-gay'-lee-kah]

The Swiss artist Angelica Kauffmann, b. Oct. 30, 1741, d. Nov. 5, 1807, was one of the most important neoclassical painters. The daughter of the muralist and portraitist J. J. Kauffmann, she demonstrated her artistic ability at an early age. While in Rome in 1763 she first encountered neoclassicism and became friends with Benjamin West and J. J. Winckelmann. Although she became (1765) a member of the Accademia di San Luca, Kauffmann was not allowed to take part in the nude drawing classes because she was a woman. Nevertheless, she undertook a career as a history painter. In 1766, Kauffmann traveled to England, where she became one of the founding members of the Royal Academy of Art and a close friend of Sir Joshua Reynolds. In Britain Kauffmann made a sizable income from the production of allegorical portraits as well as from her designs for the interiors of numerous houses, especially those designed by Robert Adam. In 1781 she married the Venetian painter Antonio Zucchi (1762–95) and settled in Rome, where she became (1795) the unofficial head of the Roman school of painting. Kauffmann painted more than 500 paintings during her lifetime, including numerous self-portraits, for example, *Self-Portrait Hesitating between Painting and Music* (c.1794; Nostell Priory, Yorkshire), and history paintings such as *Cornelia, Mother of the Gracchi* (1785; Virginia Museum of Fine Arts, Richmond).　THOMAS WILLIAM SOKOLOWSKI

Bibliography: Harris, Ann Sutherland, and Nochlin, Linda, *Women Artists, 1500–1950* (1976); Manners, Lady Victoria, and Williamson, G. C., *Angelika Kauffmann, R. A.* (1924; repr. 1976); Mayer, Dorothy Moulton, *Angelika Kauffmann, R. A., 1741–1807* (1972).

Kaufman, George S.　[kawf'-muhn]

One of the most successful playwrights and directors in the history of Broadway, George Simon Kaufman, b. Pittsburgh, Pa., Nov. 16, 1889, d. June 2, 1961, is best remembered for his many imaginatively plotted and staged comedies. He left law school to become drama critic of the *New York Times* (1917–30) and retained that post even after achieving success as a playwright. His first successful play, *Dulcy* (1921), was written with Marc CONNELLY, who was also his coauthor on *To the Ladies* (1922), *Merton of the Movies* (1922), *Beggar on Horseback* (1924), and *The Butter and Egg Man* (1925). With

George S. Kaufman, an American playwright, comedy writer, and director, helped create some of the most popular plays and musicals of the 1930s. Working in collaboration with many distinguished partners, Kaufman was twice a cowinner of the Pulitzer Prize for drama.

Edna FERBER, Kaufman wrote *The Royal Family* (1927), *Dinner at Eight* (1932), *Stage Door* (1936), and *The Land Is Bright* (1941). His best plays, *Once in a Lifetime* (1930), *You Can't Take It with You* (1936), which won him a Pulitzer Prize, and *The Man Who Came to Dinner* (1939), were joint ventures with Moss HART. He also collaborated with Morrie Ryskind on the book for the Gershwins' *Of Thee I Sing* (1932), with Howard Dietz and Arthur Schwartz on *The Band Wagon* (1931), with Ring Lardner on *June Moon* (1929), and with Alexander Woollcott on *The Dark Tower* (1933).

Bibliography: Goldstein, Malcolm, *George S. Kaufman* (1979); Meredith, Scott, *George S. Kaufman and His Friends* (1974).

Kaunas   [kow'-nahs]

Kaunas (1987 est. pop., 417,000) is the second largest city of the Lithuanian Soviet Socialist Republic of the USSR. It is situated at the juncture of the Neman and Neris rivers. Kaunas is an industrial center, with textile mills and diversified manufacturing. Part of its electric power is derived from the Kaunas hydroelectric station, upstream on the Neman.

First mentioned in the 11th century, the city has the remains of a castle, basilica, and church dating from the 14th and 15th centuries. Annexed by Russia in the third partition of Poland (1795), it was called Kovno and served as the provincial capital. From 1918 until 1940, Kaunas was the capital of independent Lithuania.   THEODORE SHABAD

Kaunda, Kenneth D.   [kown'-duh]

Kenneth David Kaunda, b. Apr. 28, 1924, became the president of Zambia (formerly Northern Rhodesia) after it won independence from Great Britain in 1964. He was reelected in 1968, 1973, 1978, 1983, and 1988. Kaunda began his career as a teacher but in 1949 joined the anticolonial African National Congress and eventually became the leader of the independence movement. He supported liberation movements in southern Africa and tried to reduce tribal factionalism by making (1972) Zambia a one-party state. In the 1980s he focused chiefly on Zambia's huge foreign debt.

Bibliography: Hall, R. S., *Kaunda, Founder of Zambia* (1965); MacPherson, Fergus, *Kenneth Kaunda of Zambia* (1975).

kauri pine   [kow'-ree]

The beautiful, massive kauri pine is a New Zealand cone-bearing evergreen tree, *Agathis australis*, of the family Araucariaceae. Although its maximum height may not exceed 46 m (150 ft), the diameter of the trunk may exceed 6 m (20 ft). The trunk is free of branches for much of its length and yields high-quality wood. The kauri pine is also a source of kauri gum, or copal, used in varnishes, paints, and printing inks. The finest copal, however, is dug from the soil in fossil form. Because of their poor growth, kauri pines are seldom cultivated. Plants grown commercially are usually the Australian *A. robusta*, the Queensland kauri.

Kautsky, Karl Johann   [kowt'-skee]

Karl Kautsky, b. Oct. 16, 1854, d. Oct. 17, 1938, was an influential German socialist theorist. A staunch Marxist, he founded (1883) the journal *Die neue Zeit*, which he edited until 1917, and was the author of much of the Erfurt program (1891), by which the German Social Democratic party upheld revolutionary Marxism. Kautsky opposed the revisionist theories of Eduard BERNSTEIN but later condemned the Bolshevik Revolution (1917) in Russia as antidemocratic. He lost influence after World War I.

Bibliography: Goode, P., *Karl Kautsky: Selected Political Writings* (1983); Salvadori, M., *Karl Kautsky and the Socialist Revolution* (1979).

Kaw: see KANSA.

Kawabata Yasunari   [kah-wah'-bah-tah yah'-soo-nar-ee]

Kawabata Yasunari, b. June 11, 1899, d. Apr. 16, 1972, was one of the greatest modern Japanese novelists and the first Japanese to receive (1968) the Nobel Prize for literature. His evocative, haunting descriptions, his emphasis on setting as much as on character, and his open-ended plots made him the most "Japanese" of modern writers, because these qualities also distinguish many classical works.

Kawabata began his literary career as a standard-bearer for European expressionism in Japan, but his lyrical qualities soon came to the fore, beginning with "The Dancing Girl of Izu" (1926; Eng. trans., 1955) and continuing with *Snow Country* (1937–48; Eng. trans., 1956), *Thousand Cranes* (1952; Eng. trans., 1959), *The Sound of the Mountain* (1954; Eng. trans., 1970), and *The Old Capital* (1962; Eng. trans., 1987). Man in his starkest isolation, nature at its most poignantly beautiful, and the paradoxical relationship between the two are nowhere more powerfully depicted than in the pages of his novels. He died by his own hand.   EDWARD B. FOWLER

Bibliography: Miyoshi, Masao, *Accomplices of Silence* (1974; repr. 1975); Petersen, G. B., *The Moon in the Water* (1979); Ueda, Makoto, *Modern Japanese Writers* (1976).

Kawasaki   [kah-wah-sah'-kee]

Kawasaki is an industrial city in Japan, adjacent to Tokyo on the north and to Yokohama on the south. The city has a population of 1,121,000 (1987 est.). As one of Japan's leading centers of heavy industry, Kawasaki has many petrochemical, steel, oil-refining, and other industrial plants. Lying on Tokyo Bay, it is also a port city whose major imports are mineral fuels, foodstuffs, and raw materials.

Founded about 1150, Kawasaki was a residential town for noblemen during the Tokugawa period (1603–1868). In the 1930s it developed as an industrial center, and after the mid-1950s it also became a bedroom community for the sprawling Tokyo-Yokohama metropolis.   JAMES CHAN

Kawasaki disease

Kawasaki disease is an unusual childhood disease characterized by a rash, swollen lymph glands, and fever. First described in 1967 by Tokyo pediatrician Dr. Tomisaku Kawasaki, the disease strikes a few hundred children in the United States each year. Most cases pass without permanent ill effects, but in about 20 percent of the cases the walls of the coronary arteries are at least temporarily weakened. In about 1 percent of U.S. cases, this leads to heart attack and death. The cause of the disease is unknown. A bacterial origin has been suggested, but in the late 1980s some evidence was gathered suggesting a RETROVIRUS.

Kay, John

The English engineer John Kay, b. July 16, 1704, d. 1764, invented the flying shuttle, which paved the way for power-loom weaving. Kay invented several minor textile improvements before patenting a carding (combing) machine and the flying shuttle in 1733. The shuttle, equipped with a mechanical attachment that sent it flying through the weft at the jerk of a cord, increased the speed of weaving and made it possible for a double width of cloth to be woven by one person.

kayaking: see CANOEING AND KAYAKING.

Kaye, Danny

An American stage, film, and television comedian who developed scat singing into a fine art, Danny Kaye, b. Daniel David Kominsky, Brooklyn, N.Y., Jan. 18, 1913, d. Mar. 3, 1987, received his comedy training in the resort hotels of the Catskills. Here he met Sylvia Fine, who became his wife and the arranger of the special material that showcased his talent for dialects and patter songs. Their cooperation led to such strong Kaye vehicles as *The Court Jester* (1956) and *The Five Pennies* (1959). Kaye also starred in *The Secret Life of Walter Mitty* (1947) and *Hans Christian Andersen* (1952) and was known around the world for his work on behalf of UNICEF.

LEONARD MALTIN

Bibliography: Freeland, M., *The Secret Life of Danny Kaye* (1986).

Kazakh

The Kazakh are a Central Asian people whose ancestors had occupied grasslands in the contemporary Kazakh Soviet Socialist Republic (SSR) since Bronze Age times. Not until the 16th century, however, did the Kazakh people establish their own khanate and tribal associations. Before 1917, they comprised three tribes: the Great, Middle, and Little Kazakh. Today, nine-tenths of the over 7 million Kazakh live in the USSR. Others reside in northwest China, Mongolia, and Afghanistan. They speak a Kipchak Turkic language of the Altaic family and are sometimes mistakenly called ''Kirghiz'' or ''Kirghiz-Kazakh.''

The Kazakh are traditionally nomadic Sunnite Muslims. Racially Mongoloid, they give the impression of classic Mongol warriors when mounted on horseback and garbed in their traditional clothing. Their way of life, the least Islamized of any of the Central Asian Turks, is richly infused with shamanistic, Islamic, and Soviet heritage. Week-long festivals and the practice of bride-price payment, dowries, arranged marriages, and polygamy survive. Kinship is determined according to male ancestry, and families are patriarchal. Traditional culture is expressed in oral epics, legends, ritual songs, and from the 19th century in a written literature strongly influenced by Russian traditions. Today 70 percent of the Kazakh are rural dwellers, and only 500,000 Kazakh remain shepherds. Modern herding is restricted, but felt yurts (tents) for temporary quarters still exist.

VICTOR L. MOTE

Bibliography: Bacon, E. E., *Central Asians under Russian Rule* (1980); Katz, Zev, et al., eds., *Handbook of Major Soviet Nationalities* (1975); Weekes, R. V., ed., *Muslim Peoples: A World Ethnological Survey* (1978); Wixman, R., *The Peoples of the U.S.S.R.* (1984).

Kazakh Soviet Socialist Republic [kah-zahk']

The Kazakh Soviet Socialist Republic is one of the 15 constituent republics of the USSR. The second largest in area, it extends from Siberia in the north to Central Asia in the south, and from the Caspian Sea in the west to the Chinese border in the east. The area is 2,717,200 km² (1,049,100 mi²), and the population is 15,842,000 (1985 est.). The republic's capital is ALMA-ATA, with a population of 1,068,000 (1985 est.). The republic is commonly called Kazakhstan.

The topography of Kazakhstan is varied, with a predominance of lowland and upland plains and rolling hill country. High mountains occur only in the northeast, where the republic reaches into the ALTAI MOUNTAINS, and southeast, where it extends into the TIEN SHAN. The climate becomes progressively drier from north to south, as the natural vegetation changes from grassland steppe in the north to desert with irrigated oases in the south. Average January temperatures range from −2° C to −19° C (29° F to −2° F) and July temperatures from 20° C to 29° C (68° F to 84° F). Annual precipitation varies

from 200 mm to 500 mm (8 to 20 in). The lowlands are drained by the IRTYSH RIVER, the SYR DARYA, the URAL RIVER, the Tobol, and the Ishim River. In addition to bordering on the CASPIAN SEA, Kazakhstan also includes part of the ARAL SEA and all of Lake BALKHASH.

The Kazakh are in the minority, constituting 33% of the population. Traditionally a nomadic stock-herding group of Muslim religion and Turkic language, they still live principally in rural areas, with only one-quarter residing in cities. The ethnic Russians, 42% of the population, provide most of the urban and industrial labor force and are concentrated in cities. Other large minorities are Ukrainians and ethnic Germans. The principal cities, in addition to Alma-Ata, are the coal and steel center of Karaganda (608,000), Chimkent (360,000), Semipalatinsk (307,000), Ust-Kamenogorsk (302,000), and Pavlodar (309,000; all 1984 ests.).

Aside from Siberia, Kazakhstan is the USSR's richest depository of mineral resources and industrial raw materials, development of which has given rise to a highly diversified mineral industry. The republic has some of the USSR's largest coal basins, which provide fuel for an important electric-power industry. Kazakhstan is a major producer of iron ore, nonferrous metals (chromite, copper, lead, zinc), bauxite for the aluminum industry, and other metals. Petroleum is now being produced. Kazakhstan has over 16% of the USSR's agricultural land, producing much of its grain. Animal husbandry is also still important. The USSR's nuclear-testing grounds and the Baikonur space-launching center are in Kazakhstan.

Except for the southern margins, Kazakhstan was a sparsely populated region of nomadic herdsmen until the Russians gained control in the mid-19th century. After the Bolshevik Revolution the region was constituted in 1920 as the Kirghiz ASSR, the name Kirghiz having been mistakenly applied to the Kazakh in the past. It was renamed Kazak (the original spelling) in 1925, and in 1936 its status was raised to that of full Soviet republic.

THEODORE SHABAD

Bibliography: Allworth, Edward, ed., *Central Asia: A Century of Russian Rule* (1967) and *The Nationality Question in Soviet Central Asia* (1973); Demko, George J., *The Russian Colonization of Kazakhstan, 1896–1916* (1969).

Kazan [kuh-zahn']

Kazan, the capital of the Tatar ASSR in the Russian republic of the USSR, is situated on the left bank of the Volga River and is a major river port. Its population is 1,047,000 (1985 est.). Although Kazan is nominally the capital of the TATARS, ethnic Russians outnumber Tatars in its population.

Kazan is an important industrial center, with diversified manufacturing including aircraft and machine tools, petroleum refining, chemical plants, and the USSR's largest fur-dressing factory. The old town, on the high, left bank of the Kazanka River, a small Volga tributary, contains a kremlin, or fortress, built in the 16th century, where the Tatar ASSR's government now sits. Nearby is the 18th-century Cathedral of Saint Peter and Saint Paul. Kazan is one of Russia's oldest educational centers, with a noted university dating from 1804.

The city was established in the early 15th century as the capital of the Tatar khanate of Kazan, one of the successor states of the GOLDEN HORDE. After its conquest by IVAN IV of Russia in 1552, Kazan developed into a military, administrative, and economic center of the Volga. It became a provincial capital in 1708. Following the Russian Revolution, when a republic was established (1920) for the Tatar minority, Kazan became the capital.

THEODORE SHABAD

Kazan, Elia [kuh-zan', eel'-yuh]

An American stage and film director, Elia Kazan (originally Kazanjoglous), b. Istanbul, Turkey, Sept. 7, 1909, to Greek parents, became a director after a brief career as an actor with New York's Group Theater in the 1930s. His greatest success was directing plays by Arthur Miller and Tennessee Williams, including *A Streetcar Named Desire* (1947) and *Death of a Salesman* (1949). He also directed the Academy Award-winning films *Gentleman's Agreement* (1947) and *On The Water-*

front (1954). His two autobiographical novels, *America, America* (1962) and *The Arrangement* (1967), were turned into films in 1963 and 1968.

Bibliography: Koszarski, Richard, *Hollywood Directors, 1941–1976* (1977).

Kazantzakis, Nikos [kah-zahnd-zah'-kees, nee'-kohs]

The Greek writer Nikos Kazantzakis is placed by many critics in the vanguard of modern Greek literature. Works such as The Odyssey: A Modern Sequel *(1938) and* Zorba the Greek *(1946) present sophisticated philosophical thought in colloquial language and explore the conflict between passion and asceticism.*

The Greek novelist, poet, and thinker Nikos Kazantzakis, b. Crete, 1883, d. Oct. 26, 1957, spent half his life living in Germany, the USSR, and France. He also traveled widely throughout Europe, Japan, and Communist China. Influenced early by Nietzsche and Bergson, he owed a debt to Marxism and Buddhism as well as to Christianity and attempted to synthesize these apparently disparate world views. His career started out more philosophical and pedagogical than literary. He came to the fore as a poet only in 1938 with his vast philosophical epic *The Odyssey: A Modern Sequel* (Eng. trans., 1958), which takes up the hero's story where Homer leaves off.

Even more successful were his novels, which he did not begin writing until after his 60th year. His first, *Zorba the Greek* (1946; Eng. trans., 1952; film, 1965), is the most popular. In it Kazantzakis embodies Bergsonian ideas of the *élan vital* in the exuberant figure of Zorba.

His other novels are perhaps deeper, if less exuberant. *Freedom and Death* (1953; Eng. trans., 1956) deals with the concept of liberty, told through the story of a dour resistance fighter in the Cretan struggle for independence from the Turks. *The Greek Passion* (1954; Eng. trans., 1954) is a reenactment of Christ's passion, set in a Greek village. Kazantzakis also wrote the novels *The Last Temptation of Christ* (1955; Eng. trans., 1960) and *God's Pauper: Saint Francis of Assisi* (1956; Eng. trans., 1962); a large number of plays; and an autobiography, *Report to Greco* (1961; Eng. trans., 1965).

P. A. MACKRIDGE

Bibliography: Bien, Peter, *Nikos Kazantzakis* (1962) and *Nikos Kazantzakis and the Linguistic Revolution in Modern Greek Literature* (1972); Kazantzakis, Helen, *Nikos Kazantzakis*, trans. by Amy Mims (1968); Prevelakis, Pandelis, *Nikos Kazantzakis and His Odyssey*, trans. by Philip Sherrard (1961).

Kazin, Alfred [kay'-zin]

With the publication of *On Native Grounds: An Interpretation of Modern American Prose Literature* (1942), Alfred Kazin, b. Brooklyn, N.Y., June 5, 1915, established himself in the center of New York intellectual life. As literary critic, editor, and teacher, Kazin continued his examination of American writing with works such as *The Inmost Leaf* (1955), *Contemporaries* (1962), and *Bright Book of Life: American Novelists and Storytellers from Hemingway to Mailer* (1973).

His autobiographical trilogy—*Walker in the City* (1951), *Starting Out in the Thirties* (1965), and *New York Jew* (1978)—evokes New York life from the 1920s through the 1970s.

C. CANTALUPO

kea [kay'-uh]

The kea, *Nestor notabilis*, is a large, powerful parrot native to the South Island of New Zealand. Like other parrots, it belongs to the family Psittacidae. The kea is up to 55 cm (22 in) in length. Its body plumage is olive green marked with black bars, but its rump and wing undersides are bright red. It has a long, deeply hooked bill that crosses at the tip. During the warmer months of the year, the bird feeds on fruits, plant buds, and a variety of insects. During the winter, when plants and insects are scarce, it has been known to feed on the carcasses of dead sheep. The kea has even been known to attack live sheep, using its powerful bill to slash through the sheep's back to pluck out the kidney fat on which it feeds. Although stories of such sheep attacks are believed to be greatly exaggerated, sheep farmers have practically exterminated the birds.

Kean (family) [keen]

The Kean family was one of the most illustrious theatrical families in 19th-century England. Edmund Kean, b. London, Mar. 17, c.1787, d. May 15, 1833, became the greatest tragic actor of the period, excelling particularly in Shakespearean roles. His son, Charles John Kean, b. Waterford, Ireland, c.1811, d. Jan. 22, 1868, established himself as an actor during his father's lifetime and went on to become a notable manager and director. In 1842 he married another performer, the highly acclaimed actress Ellen Tree, b. Ireland, December 1805, d. Aug. 20, 1880.

An illegitimate child, **Edmund Kean** made his debut at the age of four as Cupid in a Covent Garden ballet. In 1808 he married the actress Mary Chambers and a few years later began touring the provinces with an acting troupe. In 1814 he played Shylock at Drury Lane and was immediately accepted as a major star. Kean was not good in roles requiring elegance or comedy, but he excelled in portraying nobility—usually with a touch of malignancy, marked by outbursts of emotional, almost murderous, frenzy. "To see him act," wrote Coleridge, "is like reading Shakespeare by flashes of lightning."

Audiences enjoyed Kean's passionate, romantic style; but his wild exploits off the stage and bouts of drunkenness diminished both his popularity and skill. He gave his last performance on Mar. 25, 1833, playing Othello to the Iago of his son Charles. Gravely ill, he collapsed in his son's arms during the fourth act, was carried from the theater, and died less than two months later.

Although lacking his father's explosive genius as an actor, **Charles Kean** contributed significantly to the English theater

Edmund Kean, an English tragedian who made his stage debut at the age of four, became a celebrity in 1814 with his memorable performance as Shylock at London's Drury Lane Theatre. Although subsequent roles established him as England's finest dramatic actor, Kean lost favor with his audiences over a scandal in 1825, when he was successfully sued for adultery.

as both a manager and director. He began acting in 1827 and achieved fame in 1838 as Hamlet. Kean directed his first production, *Romeo and Juliet,* in 1841. A year later he married Ellen Tree, who remained his costar for the rest of his career. In 1848 he was appointed master of revels by Queen Victoria, and he also managed (1850–59) London's Princess's Theatre, where he staged productions notable for their historical authenticity. The increasing patronage of Victoria revived theatergoing as a respectable pastime. More than anyone else in England, Kean established the director as the theater's primary artist.

Ellen Tree Kean became a successful comedienne with her first performance at Covent Garden in 1823. Regarded as one of the best actresses of her time, she retired from the stage when her husband died.   ANDREW KELLY

Bibliography: Cole, John W., *The Life and Theatrical Times of Charles Kean* (1859); Fitzsimons, Raymund, *Edmund Kean: Fire from Heaven* (1976); Fletcher, Ifan Kyrle, *The Life and Theatrical Career of Edmund Kean* (1938); Playfair, Giles, *Kean* (1939; repr. 1973).

Kearny, Philip   [kar'-nee]

Philip Kearny, b. June 1, 1814, d. Sept. 1, 1862, was a Union general in the U.S. Civil War who became renowned for his courage and for the rapport he enjoyed with his men. A nephew of Stephen Watts Kearny, he joined (1837) the army as a lieutenant, went to Europe to study the French cavalry service, and served with French forces in Algeria (1840). He lost an arm in the Mexican War. At the beginning of the Civil War, Kearny commanded a New Jersey brigade in the Army of the Potomac. Later he was cavalry commander in the Peninsular Campaign and at Second Bull Run. He was killed when he unwittingly crossed enemy lines at Chantilly.

Bibliography: Werstein, Irving, *Kearny, the Magnificent* (1962).

Kearny, Stephen Watts

Stephen Watts Kearny, b. Aug. 30, 1794, d. Oct. 31, 1848, led the U.S. forces that occupied New Mexico and pacified California in the MEXICAN WAR. Commissioned in the army in 1812, he won distinction during the War of 1812. A series of frontier assignments followed, including service in the Yellowstone expedition of 1825 and, after 1833, in the First Dragoons, for which he has been called the "father of the U.S. Cavalry."

Stationed at Fort Leavenworth at the beginning of the Mexican War, Kearny was given command of the Army of the West in May 1846. He entered New Mexico without resistance and organized a civil government there. He then proceeded to California, guided by Kit Carson. Although wounded in the Battle of San Pascual near San Diego on Dec. 6–7, 1846, he linked forces with Commodore Robert F. STOCKTON and defeated the Mexicans at San Gabriel on Jan. 8, 1847. After a bitter dispute with Stockton, who had appointed John C. Frémont as governor of California, Kearny was recognized as governor in March and served until June 1847. He subsequently went to Mexico, where he was military governor, first of Veracruz and then of Mexico City.   SEYMOUR V. CONNOR

Bibliography: Clarke, Dwight L., *Stephen Watts Kearny* (1961).

Keaton, Buster   [keet'-uhn]

Joseph Francis "Buster" Keaton, b. Piqua, Kans., Oct. 4, 1895, d. Feb. 1, 1966, actor and director, was one of the giants of silent film comedy. Raised in a vaudeville family, Keaton entered the film industry in 1917 as a protégé of Fatty Arbuckle and quickly mastered film technique on both sides of the camera. A superb acrobat from youth, Keaton developed both a keen appreciation for movie sight gags and the perfectionist's desire to execute them without flaw. In 1921, under the banner of his own company, he began his solo starring career and refined his unique deadpan character—a loner caught in the flurry of modern life who somehow manages to triumph over even the most mind-boggling disasters. Such classic shorts as *One Week* (1920), *The High Sign* (1921), *The Boat* (1921), *Cops* (1922), and *The Balloonatic* (1923) led to feature

This scene from The General *(1926), picturing Buster Keaton, the master of silent film comedy, in his typical role as an impassive loner and hero who triumphs over unbelievable odds, well illustrates Keaton's nickname, "the great stone face." Keaton produced, directed, wrote, and starred in this classic, a tightly structured series of hectic exploits based on an actual event during the U.S. Civil War.*

films in which he expanded his highly individual comic views: *Our Hospitality* (1923), *The Navigator* (1924), *Seven Chances* (1925), *The General* (1926), and his cinematic tour de force, *Sherlock Jr.* (1924). Bad business advice coupled with personal problems sabotaged his career in the early 1930s. He continued to work in films and television the rest of his life, but after his move to MGM in 1928, he never again exercised the creative control he had enjoyed in the silent era. His memoirs, *My Wonderful World of Slapstick,* appeared in 1960.   LEONARD MALTIN

Bibliography: Anobile, Richard J., ed., *The Best of Buster* (1976); Blesh, Rudi, *Keaton* (1966); Dardis, Tom, *Keaton: The Man Who Wouldn't Lie Down* (1979); Maltin, Leonard, *The Great Movie Comedians* (1978); Moews, Daniel, *Keaton: The Silent Features Close Up* (1977); Wead, George, and Lellis, George, eds., *The Film Career of Buster Keaton* (1977).

Keaton, Diane

The film actress Diane Keaton, b. Diane Hall in Los Angeles, Jan. 5, 1946, first came to notice in *The Godfather* (1972) and its sequel (1974). It was as a comedienne, however, that Keaton became famous, playing opposite Woody Allen in a series of his movies during the 1970s, winning an Academy Award for *Annie Hall* (1977). The funny, kooky, half-awkward urban types in these films gave way to more dramatic roles in *Looking for Mr. Goodbar* (1977), *Interiors* (1978), *Reds* (1981), *Shoot the Moon* (1983), and *The Little Drummer Girl* (1984).

Keats, John   [keets]

John Keats, one of England's greatest poets and literary theoreticians, together with Lord Byron and Percy B. Shelley, formed the second generation of British romantic poets (see ROMANTICISM). Noted for the rich, sensuous texture of his poetry as well as for his ability to identify with and render the thing contemplated, Keats was also a strenuous thinker, as revealed by his letters; in these he speculated on the nature of poetry and the poet and struggled with the problems of suffering and death.

Born in London, Oct. 31, 1795, the son of a livery stable keeper, Keats was orphaned while still a child, and in 1811 he was apprenticed to a surgeon. As soon as he was qualified,

John Keats, one of the outstanding English romantic poets, appears in this study by a close friend, Joseph Severn. Despite Keats's short career (he died at the age of 25), his is some of the most thematically and poetically complex writing in the English language.

however, Keats left surgery for poetry, influenced by his friend the poet Leigh Hunt, who encouraged him to write and also introduced him to many of the most famous poets of the day.

After producing several mediocre poems, Keats suddenly composed the remarkably assured sonnet "On First Looking into Chapman's Homer" (1816), soon to be followed by his long, ambitious allegorical poem ENDYMION (1818). Written in the lush style of Hunt—which Keats soon rejected—this work described the poet's search for ideal beauty. After its publication he was attacked as a member of Hunt's "Cockney School" of poetry in an article in *Blackwood's Magazine*. This and other severe attacks on Keats later gave rise to the myth, embodied most notably in Shelley's great elegy *Adonais* (1821), that Keats had been killed by criticism.

Actually he died of tuberculosis, a disease against which both he and his brother Tom long struggled; in 1818, Tom died, and shortly afterwards Keats became aware that he too had contracted consumption. His misery was exacerbated by his love for Fanny Brawne; because of his increasing ill health, marriage was impossible. Throughout this anguished time, however, Keats was producing his masterpieces. During 1819 alone, he composed *The Eve of St. Agnes, La Belle Dame sans Merci, Lamia,* the six great *Odes* (including "Ode on a Grecian Urn" and "Ode to a Nightingale"), and reworked his unfinished epic *Hyperion* into *The Fall of Hyperion,* in which he examined his own poetic career and rededicated himself to the strenuous art of poetry.

By early 1820, Keats understood clearly that he was dying and in the fall traveled with his friend the painter Joseph Severn to Rome in an attempt to delay the workings of the disease. From there he wrote agonized letters lamenting his loss of love and the failure of his hopes of poetic excellence. He died on Feb. 23, 1821, in the house on the Spanish Steps that now forms a memorial to him and Shelley.

Keats's short poetic life is unprecedented in English literature; between the ages of 18 and 24 he wrote poems of such power that they rank with the greatest in the language. Taking in all the senses, they lyrically render the totality of an experience and catch in their packed phrases the complexity of life in which pain and pleasure are inextricably joined. The theory that complements this poetry is expounded in Keats's appealing letters; in these he speculates on the truth of the imaginative world and proposes a theory of negative capability requiring that the poet open himself to all experience.

JANET M. TODD

Bibliography: Bate, W. J., *John Keats* (1963); Bush, Douglas, *John Keats* (1966); Gittings, Robert, *John Keats* (1968); Hewlett, Dorothy, *A Life of John Keats*, 3d ed. (1970); Ryan, Robert M., *Keats: The Religious Sense* (1976); Sperry, Stuart M., *Keats the Poet* (1973).

Keble, John   [kee'-bul]

The English theologian and poet John Keble, b. Apr. 25, 1792, d. Mar. 29, 1866, is considered the founder of the OXFORD MOVEMENT. A fellow of Oriel College, Oxford, he was ordained in the Church of England in 1815. In 1827 he published a volume of poems, *The Christian Year*, which went through 95 editions during his lifetime and led to a professorship of poetry at Oxford (1831–41). In his poetry Keble exhibited fervent faith in the authority of the church and its sacraments, and he was believed by John Henry NEWMAN to have begun the Oxford movement with a sermon on "National Apostasy" preached on July 14, 1833. Although absent from Oxford as vicar of Hursley, Hampshire, Keble was a steadying force through all the movement's troubles. After his death a college was created at Oxford and named for him.

JOHN EVERITT BOOTY

Bibliography: Battiscombe, Georgina, *John Keble: A Study in Limitations* (1963); Beek, W. J. A. M., *John Keble's Literary and Religious Contributions to the Oxford Movement* (1959); Martin, Brian W., *John Keble: Priest, Professor and Poet* (1976).

Keeling Islands: see COCOS ISLANDS.

keeshond   [kays'-hahnd]

The keeshond is a Dutch breed of dog of the spitz type characterized by a dense, rough coat, erect ears, and a tightly curled tail carried over its back. It is a squarely built dog, standing about 46 cm (18 in) high at the shoulders and weighing up to 18 kg (40 lb). Its coat color is a mixture of gray and black, with a very pale gray undercoat. The keeshond was originally developed as a barge dog, accompanying the small vessels on the rivers and canals of Holland.

JOHN MANDEVILLE

Bibliography: Peterson, Clementine, *The Complete Keeshond* (1971).

The keeshond, or Dutch barge dog, has long been considered the national dog of Holland, where it is widely used as a watchdog. The breed, similar to the German wolfspitz, has a dense coat and arches its tail over its back.

Kefauver, Estes   [kee'-faw-vur, es'-teez]

Carey Estes Kefauver, b. Madisonville, Tenn., July 26, 1903, d. Aug. 10, 1963, was a U.S. senator from Tennessee whose investigations into organized crime in 1950-51 were nationally televised and created great public interest. A lawyer, Kefauver sat in the U.S. House of Representatives from 1939 to 1949. In 1948 he won election to the Senate despite the opposition of the Tennessee Democratic boss Ed Crump, who had called him a "pet coon." After chairing the Special Committee to Investigate Organized Crime in Interstate Commerce, Kefauver sought the Democratic nomination for president in 1952 but lost to Adlai E. Stevenson. He lost to Stevenson again in 1956, but he was the vice-presidential nominee. Despite his support for civil rights for blacks, an anomalous position for a Southern politician in that era, Kefauver remained in the Senate until his death.

Bibliography: Gorman, Joseph B., *Kefauver: A Political Biography* (1971); Moore, William H., *The Kefauver Committee and the Politics of Crime, 1950-52* (1974).

Keino, Kipchoge   [kay'-noh, kip-choh'-gay]

Kipchoge Keino, b. Jan. 17, 1940, was the first great distance runner to come from Kenya, a country now known for its talented runners. He joined the Kenya police force in 1958 and competed for the police track team. In the 1964 Olympics he placed fifth in the 5,000-m (5,500-yd) run. The next year he ran the mile in 3 min 54.2 sec. He surpassed the American Jim Ryun at the 1968 Olympic Games in the 1,500-m (1,650-yd) event with a world-record time of 3 min 34.9 sec. Keino won the 3,000-m (3,300-yd) steeplechase, an event in which he had little experience, at the 1972 Olympics. In 1973, Keino became a professional runner but retired about 1975.

Keir, James   [kir]

The Scottish industrial chemist James Keir, b. Sept. 29, 1735, d. Oct. 11, 1820, discovered a method of extracting caustic soda from waste sulfates, predating the Leblanc process, and pioneered the scientific chemical industry. After serving as an army physician in the West Indies, Keir operated a glass factory at Stourbridge from 1771 to 1778, then became manager in 1778 of Boulton and Watt's engineering works. In 1780, Keir began the manufacture of alkali at his Tipton Chemical Works, founded in partnership with Alexander Blair.

Keitel, Wilhelm   [ky'-tuhl]

Wilhelm Keitel, b. Sept. 22, 1882, d. Oct. 16, 1946, was chief of the high command of the German Armed forces during World War II. Hitler's closest military advisor, he dictated the terms of the French surrender in 1940 and signed Germany's surrender to the Allies in May 1945. He was convicted of war crimes at the Nuremberg Trials and executed.

Kekkonen, Urho K.   [kek'-oh-nen, oor'-hoh]

Urho Kaleva Kekkonen was president of Finland for 25 years. He was first elected in 1956; in deference to the USSR, which favored his retention in office, he was reelected without serious opposition in 1962 and 1968; in 1974 Parliament extended his third term by 4 years to 1978. He was then reelected to another 6-year term, but declining health caused his resignation in October 1981.

As president of Finland from 1956 to 1981, Urho Kaleva Kekkonen, b. Sept. 3, 1900, d. Aug. 31, 1986, pursued a policy of neutrality in international affairs, trying to maintain good relations with the West without antagonizing the neighboring USSR. Kekkonen was educated at the University of Helsinki and worked as a lawyer until he was elected to Parliament in 1936. He served as minister of justice (1936–37) and minister of the interior (1937–39). After the Russo-Finnish War Kekkonen handled the resettlement of 420,000 refugees from Karelia, the territory ceded to the USSR. As leader of the Agrarian party (later renamed Center party), he was prime minister four times in the years 1950–56.   K. M. SMOGORZEWSKI

Kekulé von Stradonitz, Friedrich August
[kay'-koo-lay fuhn strah'-doh-nits]

Friedrich August Kekulé von Stradonitz, b. Sept. 7, 1829, d. July 13, 1896, was a German chemist best known for his work

Friedrich August Kekulé, a 19th-century German chemist, brought the science of organic chemistry into the modern era with his work on the molecular structure of compounds. His best-known discovery concerned the circular configuration of carbon atoms in benzene, an idea that first occurred to Kekulé in a dream.

on the structure of the BENZENE molecule. An energetic man with great personal charm, Kekulé became a leading and dominant figure among 19th-century chemists.

Kekulé was a student of architecture at the University of Giessen in 1847, when the influence of Justus LIEBIG attracted him to chemistry. He became a professor at Ghent in 1858 and while there developed his benzene theory and wrote his famous textbook, *Lehrbuch der organischen Chemie* (Handbook of Organic Chemistry).

Kekulé's first important work was carried out in London in 1854, when he found thioacetic acid, the first known organic acid containing sulfur. He also gave the first satisfactory structure for the diazo compounds (1866). In 1857 he deduced the key concept that carbon always forms four bonds and introduced the fundamentally important idea that carbon atoms can bond with one another, a concept independently proposed by Archibald Couper (1858).

The structure of benzene was given by Kekulé in 1865 as a simple hexagon, and in 1866 he postulated a pair of structures differing in the location of the alternate double bonds. Later he showed that the two possible arrangements are identical, the benzene ring behaving as if there were oscillation between the double and single bonds, by which he anticipated the concept of RESONANCE of the early 1930s.

VIRGINIA F. McCONNELL

Bibliography: Anschutz, Richard, *August Kekulé*, 2 vols. (1929); Farber, Eduard, ed., *Great Chemists* (1961); Toulmin, Stephen, and Goodfield, June, *The Architecture of Matter* (1962; repr. 1974); Partington, J. R., *A History of Chemistry*, vol. 4 (1964).

Keller, Gottfried   [kel'-ur, gawt'-freet]

The stories of the Swiss author Gottfried Keller, b. July 19, 1819, d. July 15, 1890, are among the best examples of the trend in German literature that came to be known as poetic realism. Keller set out initially to become a painter, then tried his hand at writing poetry, tragedy, and an autobiographical novel, *Green Henry* (1854–55; Eng. trans., 1960), which brought him a measure of success; both his poetry and novel have attracted increasing interest. The basis for Keller's literary renown, however, was his collection of village tales, *The People of Seldwyla* (1856; Eng. trans., 1931), which contained his best-known story, "Romeo und Julia auf dem Dorfe," an adaptation of the Shakespearean theme to a rural setting. Keller has long been considered a master of the novella form.

JAMES M. McGLATHERY

Bibliography: Lindsay, James M., *Gottfried Keller: Life and Works* (1968).

Keller, Helen

Helen Adams Keller, b. Tuscumbia, Ala., June 27, 1880, d. June 1, 1968, was an author, lecturer, and humanitarian

Helen Keller graduated cum laude from Radcliffe College in 1904, despite being stricken, at the age of 19 months, by an illness that left her blind, deaf, and mute. With the determined help of her young teacher Anne Mansfield Sullivan, Keller overcame these disabilities. She spent her exemplary life writing and speaking to benefit the handicapped.

whose unusual life and dedicated work had an international influence on the lives of the handicapped. She became blind and deaf at the age of 19 months through a damaging brain fever and could communicate only through hysterical laughter or violent tantrums. Nevertheless, with the help of her teacher Anne Mansfield Sullivan, Keller learned to read braille and to write by using a special typewriter. Their early relationship was the subject of *The Miracle Worker,* a 1960 Pulitzer Prize–winning play and 1962 film by William Gibson. In 1904, Keller graduated with honors from Radcliffe College and began a life of writing, lecturing, and fund raising on behalf of the handicapped.

Bibliography: Keller, Helen, *The Story of My Life* (1903; repr. 1954) and *Teacher* (1955); Waite, H. E., *Valiant Companions: Helen Keller and Anne Sullivan Macy* (1959); Weiner, M., *Helen Keller* (1970).

Kelley, Edgar Stillman

Edgar Stillman Kelley, b. Sparta, Wis., Apr. 14, 1857, d. Nov. 12, 1944, once heralded as a potential successor to Edward MacDowell as a composer, is today better known as an educator and writer on music. He studied in Chicago and in Stuttgart, Germany. He was the music critic (1893–95) for the *San Francisco Examiner* and taught in New York and at Yale University before returning to Germany, where he taught piano and theory in Berlin. In 1910 he became dean of the composition department at the Cincinnati Conservatory and remained there until his death. With his former student and wife, the pianist Jessie Stillman, Kelley organized the Kelley Stillman Publishing Co. His compositions, mostly written in an immediately accessible musical style, include a comic opera, *Puritania* (1892); incidental music to *Ben Hur* for chorus, soloists, and orchestra (1900); and many choral works, mostly on American subjects. KAREN MONSON

Kelley, Florence

Florence Kelley, b. Philadelphia, Sept. 12, 1859, d. Feb. 17, 1932, strove to improve industrial working conditions. A graduate (1882) of Cornell University, she later studied in Switzerland, where she became a socialist and translated Friedrich Engels's *The Condition of the Working Class in England* (1887), and at Northwestern University, from which she earned (1894) a law degree. A forceful advocate of protective wage and labor laws for women and an end to child labor, Kelley served as the first chief factory inspector in Illinois (1893–97) and, from 1899, as secretary of the National Consumers' League. BARBARA CUNNINGHAM

Bibliography: Blumberg, D. R., *Florence Kelley* (1966); Goldmark, Josephine, *Impatient Crusader* (1953).

Kelley, William Melvin

The novelist William Melvin Kelley, b. the Bronx, N.Y., Nov. 1, 1937, is well known for his understated, bitterly ironic, sharply intelligent stories of black American lives. *A Different Drummer* (1962), regarded as his best novel, imagines the effect on a southern state of a sudden exodus of all its black citizens. *A Drop of Patience* (1965) follows the life of a blind musician, and *dem* (1967) attacks the myths white Americans live by. Kelley's novel *Dunfords Travels Everywheres* (1970) uses linguistic play and fantasy to explore the resemblances between a black writer in Paris and a black hustler in Harlem.

Kellogg, Frank B.

Frank Billings Kellogg, b. Potsdam, N.Y., Dec. 22, 1856, d. Dec. 21, 1937, was an American politician and diplomat, best known as the sponsor of the KELLOGG-BRIAND PACT (1928). He began his career as a corporation lawyer in Saint Paul, Minn. In 1904 he became a special counsel to the federal government in the antitrust suits against the General Paper Company and Standard Oil.

A Republican, Kellogg served in the U.S. Senate from 1917 to 1923. He was an ambassador to Britain (1924–25) and then became Calvin Coolidge's secretary of state (1925–29). In the latter office Kellogg not only promoted the Kellogg-Briand Pact, by which 62 nations renounced war, but also improved relations with Mexico and settled the TACNA-ARICA DISPUTE between Chile and Peru. He was awarded the 1929 Nobel Peace Prize. From 1930 to 1935, Kellogg was a judge on the Permanent Court of International Justice.

Bibliography: Ellis, Lewis E., *Frank B. Kellogg and American Foreign Relations, 1925–1929* (1961; repr. 1974).

Kellogg, W. K.

Will Keith Kellogg, b. Battle Creek, Mich., Apr. 7, 1860, d. Oct. 6, 1951, was the creator of Kellogg's Corn Flakes. As a young man he worked with his brother, Dr. John H. Kellogg, at the latter's Battle Creek Sanitarium, where they developed toasted wheat flakes and other vegetarian health foods. In 1906 he organized the Battle Creek Toasted Corn Flake Company and merchandised his product with heavy advertising. He added other breakfast foods to the company's line, making it the world's largest manufacturer of prepared cereals. He established the philanthropic W. K. Kellogg Foundation in 1930 and gave it a total of $47 million.

Bibliography: Powell, Horace B., *The Original Has This Signature—W. K. Kellogg* (1956).

Kellogg-Briand Pact

The Kellogg-Briand Pact was an agreement to renounce war as an instrument of national policy. It was signed in Paris by 15 nations on Aug. 27, 1928. Almost every country in the world soon joined the pact, which was hailed as an important step toward peace. Aristide BRIAND, the French foreign minister, led the way to this pact by proposing that France and the United States renounce war with each other. The U.S. secretary of state, Frank B. KELLOGG, then suggested that other nations be invited to pledge to settle all disputes peacefully. Because the pact did not provide for enforcement, it was useless in stopping undeclared wars, such as the Japanese invasion of Manchuria in 1931. DONALD S. BIRN

Bibliography: Ferrell, Robert, *Peace in Their Time; The Origins of the Kellogg-Briand Pact* (1952; repr. 1968).

Kelly, Ellsworth

American abstract painter Ellsworth Kelly, b. Newburgh, N.Y., May 31, 1923, is a prominent figure in the so-called hard-edge movement (see HARD-EDGE PAINTING), which developed in New York in the late 1950s. He is best known for large paintings composed of brilliant monochrome areas of color juxtaposed with two or three precisely edged and intensely colored two-dimensional images. Underlying this formula is an effort to demonstrate that the image and the field are interchangeable elements that can be interpreted as either figure or ground—as positive or negative space. Kelly developed this personal style while living in Paris from 1948 to 1954.

Yellow-Blue, painted by the American artist Ellsworth Kelly in 1963, is an example of the hard-edge trend in abstract art. Although he was a native of New York State, Kelly was working in Paris when he evolved his style. Image-field ambiguities fill his paintings. (Private collection.)

In 1966 he did a series of monochrome paintings arranged in pairs and began experimenting with geometrically shaped canvases that play shape and color against color.

BARBARA CAVALIERE

Bibliography: Coplans, John, *Ellsworth Kelly* (1973); Goosen, E. C., *Ellsworth Kelly* (1973); Waldman, Diane, *Ellsworth Kelly; Drawings, Collages, Prints* (1971).

Kelly, Emmett

An American circus clown, Emmett Kelly, b. Sedan, Kans., Dec. 9, 1898, d. Mar. 28, 1979, became famous as Weary Willie, a sad-faced hobo in ragged clothing. Kelly first created Willie as a cartoon character in 1920 and later assumed the role with the Ringling Brothers circus, on television, and in films and Broadway shows. In contrast to the traditional white-faced clown, the laughter Willie provoked was directed more at life's pitfalls than at its pratfalls.

Kelly, Gene

A dancer, singer, and actor whose cheerful manner and innovative dance sequences enlivened some of Hollywood's most memorable musicals, Eugene Curran Kelly, b. Pittsburgh, Pa., Aug. 23, 1912, turned choreography into a virile, athletic American art. Synthesizing ballet with the tattoo of tap, the rhythms of jazz, and a sense of fun and grace, he was at his best in *The Pirate* (1948), *On the Town* (1949), *An American in Paris* (1951), *Singin' in the Rain* (1952), and *Brigadoon* (1954). Kelly has also directed films, including *Hello Dolly*

Gene Kelly displays his atletic dancing style in the classic street scene from Singin' in the Rain (1952). A leading Hollywood dancer and actor during the 1940s and '50s, Kelly has since turned to film directing, scoring popular successes wth Gigot (1963) and Hello Dolly (1969).

(1969), and was a principal in the MGM reprise *That's Entertainment* (1974).   ELEANOR M. GATES

Bibliography: Hirschhorn, Clive, *Gene Kelly: A Biography* (1975); Thomas, Tony, *Films of Gene Kelly* (1974).

Kelly, Grace

Grace, Princess of Monaco, b. Philadelphia, Nov. 12, 1929, as Grace Patricia Kelly, d. Sept. 14, 1982, first achieved fame as an American film star. She appeared in *High Noon* (1952) and *High Society* (1956) and won an Academy Award for her performance in *The Country Girl* (1954). Her cold beauty and aristocratic bearing were perhaps most successfully exploited in three Alfred Hitchcock thrillers—*Dial M for Murder* (1954), *Rear Window* (1954), and *To Catch a Thief* (1955). Grace Kelly's acting career ended when she married Prince Rainier III of Monaco in 1956, but she remained an international celebrity until her death following an automobile accident at the age of 52.

Bibliography: Lewis, Arthur H., *Those Philadelphia Kellys, with a Touch of Grace* (1977).

Kelly, Ned

Edward "Ned" Kelly, b. June 1855, d. Nov. 11, 1880, was Australia's most notorious BUSHRANGER and folk hero. After serving time in prison for stealing horses, he was later hunted for killing three policemen in Victoria. The Kelly gang—Ned, his brother Dan, and two friends—took to the bush, seizing a sheep station, robbing two banks, and capturing a hotel. Encased in roughly made armor, they eventually fought it out with the police. His companions were killed, and Ned was captured and hanged in Melbourne.   E. J. TAPP

Bibliography: Jennings, M. J., *Ned Kelly, the Legend and the Man* (1968).

Kelly, William

An iron manufacturer, William Kelly, b. Pittsburgh, Pa., Aug. 21, 1811, d. Feb. 11, 1888, invented (1851) a pneumatic process for making steel by blowing air through molten iron. His "air-boiling process" was identical with the one patented in England by Sir Henry BESSEMER in 1856. When he learned that Bessemer had applied for an American patent for the process, Kelly filed his own claim and in 1857 won a patent on the basis of priority.

Bankrupted by the panic of 1857, Kelly recovered and helped found a steel company, although his fame was obscured by that of Bessemer, whom Kelly allowed to make steel under the Kelly patents.   FRANCES GIES

Bibliography: Burlingame, Roger, *Inventors behind the Inventor* (1947); Gies, Joseph and Frances, *Ingenious Yankees* (1976).

See also: IRON AND STEEL INDUSTRY.

Kelmscott Press   [kem'-skuht]

The Kelmscott Press, founded in Hammersmith, London, in 1891, was the crowning achievement of the artist, poet, writer, and social reformer William MORRIS. Morris rebelled against the shoddy goods produced by an increasingly mechanized, industrial England. Books particularly had suffered in the decline of handicrafts. To reintroduce high-quality craftsmanship, Morris in 1861 formed a furniture and interior decorating company and in 1890 established his own printing press together with the Pre-Raphaelite artist Sir Edward BURNE-JONES, as designer and illustrator. Their textiles, furnishings, and stained glass were justly famous, but their most lasting impact was the interest they stimulated in improved book illustration and typography. Morris interested himself in the history of bookmaking from manuscript calligraphy to papermaking and typeface design. The first edition from the Kelmscott Press was his own *Story of the Glittering Plain* (1891), handprinted on handmade paper in the first of his new typefaces. *The Golden Legend,* in Golden typeface, followed in 1892. The glory of the Press, however, was the *Kelmscott Chaucer* (1896). Using the third (Chaucer) typeface and illustrated by Burne-Jones, it took 5 years to plan, 2 years to print, and crowned a lifelong love of literature, art, and craftsmanship. The Press was closed (1898) 2 years after Morris's death.   MARJORIE COLLINS

Bibliography: Needham, Paul, and Dunlap, Joseph, eds., *William Morris and the Art of the Book* (1976); Sparling, Henry H., *The Kelmscott Press and William Morris, Master-Craftsman* (1975).

See also: ARTS AND CRAFTS MOVEMENT; BOOK; PRE-RAPHAELITES.

kelp

Kelp are any of a number of genera of seaweeds belonging to the brown algae, division Phaeophyta, order Laminariales. Kelp tend to grow in large, offshore beds in the temperate oceans. They vary in size from 0.5 m (1.65 ft) up to 60 m (198 ft). Most kelps consist of at least three distinguishable parts: the holdfast, stipe, and blade. The holdfast is a basal growth that secures the kelp to its substrate. The blade is the large, laminar portion of the plant that is the principal location of photosynthesis. Trumpet cells, a special modification of kelp, translocate photosynthates about the plant. This translocation is performed in the blade and stipe. The stipe is the stemlike portion connecting the holdfast to the blade. Reproduction is accomplished via ALTERNATION OF GENERATIONS, with the sporophyte generation dominant.

Kelp are important sources of detritus in the marine food chain. They are a source of potash, iodine, and alginic acid. Alginic acid is used for treating latex in tire manufacturing, in paints, in ice cream, and as fillers for confections. Kelp are used extensively as a food in the Far East because of their high mineral and vitamin content.   STEPHEN FAUER

Bibliography: Abbott, Isabella, and Dawson, E. Yale, *How to Know the Seaweeds,* 2d ed. (1978); Chapman, V. J., *Seaweeds and Their Uses,* 2d ed. (1970); Duddington, C. L., *Flora of the Sea* (1966).

kelpie   [kel'-pee]

The Australian kelpie is a medium-sized dog used primarily for herding sheep in Australia. It is considered an excellent stock dog. The kelpie's ancestry most likely includes the border collie and possibly the dingo, a wild dog native to Australia.

The Australian kelpie is a breed of dog whose primary function today is that for which it was originally bred—herding sheep in Australia. The breed is descended from Scottish shepherd dogs, most probably border collies, sent to Australia around 1870, with the likely infusion of dingo blood during the early stages of its development. The kelpie grows to 50 cm (20 in) high at the shoulders and weighs about 18 kg (40 lb). Its short, straight, harsh coat is usually black or black and tan, although red, brown, and bluish gray also occur. The breed is placed in the Miscellaneous Class by the American Kennel Club.   JOHN MANDEVILLE

Bibliography: Braund, Kathryn, *The Uncommon Dog Breeds* (1975).

Kelsey, Henry   [kel'-see]

Henry Kelsey, b. *c.*1667, d. 1724, was an English explorer of the Canadian west. In 1684 he joined the Hudson's Bay Company and was stationed at York Factory on Hudson Bay. His many expeditions included one (1690–92) into what is now Saskatchewan, and Kelsey was probably the first white man to see the western prairies, bison, and grizzly bears. Appointed governor of all the company's Hudson Bay posts in 1718, he made two attempts (1719, 1721) to find the Northwest Passage before being recalled (1722) to England.

Kelvin, William Thomson, 1st Baron   [kel'-vin]

The Scottish physicist and mathematician Lord Kelvin calculated that molecular motion stops at −273° C. He called this temperature absolute zero, the lowest possible temperature that can be obtained. A prodigy in mathematics, Kelvin gained greatest renown in thermodynamics.

The thermodynamics studies of the Scottish physicist William Thomson, b. June 26, 1824, d. Dec. 17, 1907, led to his proposal (1848) of an absolute scale of TEMPERATURE. The Kelvin absolute temperature scale, developed later, derives its name from the title—Baron Kelvin of Largs—that he received from the British government in 1892. Thomson also observed (1852) what is now called the JOULE-THOMSON EFFECT—the decrease in temperature of a gas when it expands in a vacuum.

Thomson served as professor of natural philosophy (1846–99) at the University of Glasgow. One of his first projects was to calculate the age of the Earth, based on the rate of cooling of the planet—assuming it had once been a piece of the Sun. (His result—20 to 400 million years—was far short of the current estimate of 4.5 billion years.) Greatly interested in the improvement of physical instrumentation, he designed and implemented many new devices, including the mirror-galvanometer that was used in the first successful sustained telegraph transmissions in transatlantic submarine cable. Thomson's participation in the telegraph cable project formed the basis of a large personal fortune.   SHELDON J. KOPPERL

Bibliography: Burchfield, Joe D., *Lord Kelvin and the Age of the Earth* (1975); Gray, Andrew, *Lord Kelvin: An Account of His Scientific Life and Work* (1908; repr. 1973); Sharlin, Harold and Tiby, *Lord Kelvin: The Dynamic Victorian* (1978); Thompson, Silvanus P., *The Life of Lord Kelvin,* 2 vols., 2d ed. (1977).

Kelvin scale

The Kelvin, or absolute temperature, scale is defined so that 0 K is absolute zero, the coldest theoretical temperature (−273.15° C/−459.67° F), at which the energy of motion of molecules is zero. Each absolute degree is equivalent to a Celsius degree, so that the freezing point of water (0° C/32° F) is 273.15 K, and its boiling point (100° C/212° F) is 100° higher, or 373.15 K. The scale is named for the physicist William Thomson, 1st Baron Kelvin, who first proposed an absolute temperature scale.

Bibliography: Castle, John G., *Science by Degrees: Temperatures from Zero to Zero* (1965); Mendelssohn, Kurt, *The Quest for Absolute Zero: The Meaning of Low Temperature Physics,* 2d ed. (1977).

Kemble (family) [kem'-bul]

Son of an itinerant actor-manager, **John Philip Kemble**, b. Feb. 11, 1757, d. Feb. 26, 1823, first appeared on the London stage in 1783 and was considered England's leading actor of his time. With his sister Sarah SIDDONS he practiced the "classical style," although he lacked her emotional intensity. As manager (1803–17) of the Covent Garden, he turned it into the English-speaking world's leading theater. Faced with financial problems and Edmund KEAN's rivalry, he retired in 1817. His brother **Charles Kemble**, b. Nov. 25, 1775, d. Nov. 12, 1854, a noted Shakespearean actor, managed Covent Garden from 1817 to 1832, encouraging the use of historically accurate costumes and scenery.

Charles Kemble's eldest daughter, the beautiful **Fanny (Frances) Kemble**, b. Nov. 27, 1809, d. Jan. 15, 1893, was interested in a literary career but became an actress in 1829, when she appeared at Covent Garden to save her father from bankruptcy. Her three years there temporarily brought back the theater's prosperity, as she proved an accomplished comedic and tragic actress. She toured the United States with her father (1832–34), then married the owner of a plantation and retired. Her *Journal of a Residence on a Georgian Plantation in 1838–1839* (1863) later gained fame for its harrowing account of slave life. Divorced, she resumed a career as a writer of plays, journals, and poems. She also gave stage readings of Shakespeare in England and the United States, residing intermittently in both countries. ANDREW KELLY

Bibliography: Baker, Herschel C., *John Philip Kemble* (1942); Marshall, Dorothy, *Fanny Kemble* (1977); Williamson, Jane, *Charles Kemble* (1970); Wister, Fanny K., ed., *Fanny, the American Kemble* (1972).

Kemp, Jack

Jack French Kemp, b. Los Angeles, July 13, 1935, served in Congress (1971–89) as a Republican from upstate New York and then (1989–   ) as U.S. secretary of housing and urban development. He graduated (1957) from Occidental College and was a professional football quarterback for 13 years, becoming active also in Republican politics. Kemp gained national prominence by championing supply-side economics. He ran unsuccessfully for his party's presidential nomination in 1988.

Kendall, Amos [ken'-dul]

An influential American journalist, Amos Kendall, b. Dunstable, Mass., Aug. 16, 1789, d. Nov. 12, 1869, was a Democratic political figure for nearly 40 years. Kendall migrated to Kentucky, where he edited *Argus of Western America,* an influential newspaper published in Frankfort, Ky. Breaking his earlier allegiance to Henry Clay, Kendall campaigned for Andrew Jackson's election to the presidency in 1828. He became a leading member of Jackson's informal KITCHEN CABINET and reputedly wrote a number of Jackson's state papers.

After serving as auditor of the Treasury, Kendall was postmaster general (1835–40) and instituted the pony express service, originally between New York and Philadelphia, and the money-order system. He later became (1845) the business agent for Samuel F. B. Morse and grew wealthy through investments in the Morse telegraph. CHARLES T. DUNCAN

Bibliography: Kendall, Amos, *Autobiography of Amos Kendall* (1872; repr. 1949); Schlesinger, Arthur M., *The Age of Jackson* (1949).

Kendall, Edward

The biochemist Edward Calvin Kendall, b. South Norwalk, Conn., Mar. 8, 1886, d. May 4, 1972, isolated many hormones, including cortisone, from the adrenal cortex. He was awarded, with Philip Hench and Tadeus Reichstein, the 1950 Nobel Prize for physiology or medicine for their discoveries about these hormones and their uses (see GLUCOCORTICOID). Kendall also isolated the thyroid hormone THYROXINE.

Kendall, George Wilkins

The American journalist George Wilkins Kendall, b. Mt. Vernon, N.H., Aug. 22, 1809, d. Oct. 21, 1867, is remembered mainly for his eyewitness coverage (1846–48) of U.S. conflicts in Mexico. His reports were first published in the *New Orleans Picayune,* which Kendall founded in 1837. *The War between the United States and Mexico* (1851) is based on his experiences. Kendall County, Tex., is named for him.

kendo: see MARTIAL ARTS.

Kendrew, John Cowdery [ken'-droo]

The English biochemist John Cowdery Kendrew, b. Mar. 24, 1917, used X-ray diffraction methods to determine (1960) the structure of the complex protein myoglobin. This led his colleague, Max Perutz, to determine the structure of related hemoglobin, for which the two men shared the Nobel Prize for chemistry in 1962. HENRY M. LEICESTER

Kennan, George F. [ken'-uhn]

George Frost Kennan, b. Milwaukee, Wis., Feb. 16, 1904, was a U.S. diplomat and scholar known for advocating the policy of "containment" of Soviet expansionism. After graduating (1925) from Princeton University he entered the foreign service and became an expert on Russian affairs.

In an influential article in *Foreign Affairs* in 1947, Kennan called for the application of counterforce to contain the Soviet Union. Although this remained U.S. policy toward the USSR for decades, Kennan himself eventually turned away from U.S. COLD WAR policies; he opposed the Vietnam War. He had served briefly (1952) as U.S. ambassador to Moscow, then joined the Institute for Advanced Study in Princeton, N.J. He was also ambassador to Yugoslavia in 1961–63. Author of numerous works on history and foreign relations, including *American Diplomacy* (1951; rev. ed., 1985), Kennan published *Sketches from a Life* in 1989.

Kennedy (family)

The Kennedys, one of the most influential families in the American political arena, convened for a portrait photograph at their home in Hyannis Port, Mass., on Nov. 9, 1960, the day after John Fitzgerald Kennedy (standing, center) won election to the presidency.

The Kennedy family of Massachusetts has achieved a prominence in American political life comparable only to that of the Adams family in the late 18th and early 19th centuries. In 1960, John F. KENNEDY was elected president of the United States. His term in office was cut short by assassination in November 1963, and the same fate befell his brother Robert F. KENNEDY when he campaigned for the Democratic nomination for the presidency in 1968. A third brother, Edward M. KENNEDY, remains an influential figure in the Democratic party.

These brothers came from a family of nine, the children of **Joseph Patrick Kennedy,** b. Sept. 6, 1888, d. Nov. 18, 1969, and **Rose Fitzgerald Kennedy,** b. July 22, 1890. The son of a Boston saloonkeeper turned politician, Joe Kennedy graduated from Harvard in 1912 and married (1914) Rose Fitzgerald, daughter of a mayor of Boston. A bank president at the age of 25, he made a fortune by investment in stocks, importing, shipbuilding, and moviemaking. He became chairman (1934–35) of the newly created Securities and Exchange Commission, head (1937) of the U.S. Maritime Commission, and then U.S. ambassador to Britain (1937–40). As ambassador he became known as an isolationist and a pessimist about Britain's chances of resisting Nazi German conquest.

Although Joe Kennedy never ran for elective office, he and his wife had great ambitions for their children. Set against a record of extraordinary talent and accomplishment, however, is a haunting recurrence of tragedy. The oldest son, Joseph P. Jr. (1915–44), was killed in wartime service over England. Rosemary (b. 1918), the oldest daughter, was mentally retarded. The next daughter, Kathleen (1920–48), died in an airplane crash in Europe. The assassinations of John, who had fulfilled his family's political ambition, and then Robert, who inherited his mantle, continued the pattern of tragedy. The youngest of this generation is Edward Kennedy. The three other Kennedys of the same generation are Eunice (b. 1921), who married R. Sargent SHRIVER, director of the Peace Corps (1961–66) and ambassador to France (1968–70); Patricia (b. 1924), who was for a time married to the actor Peter Lawford; and Jean (b. 1928), who married businessman Stephen Smith.

The 28 cousins of the next generation—the children of John, Eunice, Patricia, Robert, Jean, and Edward—have shown promise but also shared grief: Edward Jr. lost a leg to bone cancer in 1973, and Robert's son David died in 1984 of multiple-drug ingestion. In 1986, Robert's son Joseph II was elected to Congress from Massachusetts.   JOHN F. STACKS

Bibliography: Collier, P., and Horowitz, D., *The Kennedys* (1984); Goodwin, Doris Kearns, *The Fitzgeralds and the Kennedys* (1987); Wills, G., *The Kennedy Imprisonment* (1982).

Kennedy, Anthony M.

Anthony McLeod Kennedy, b. Sacramento, Calif., July 23, 1936, was appointed to the U.S. Supreme Court by President Reagan on Nov. 11, 1987, and sworn in on Feb. 18, 1988. A graduate of Stanford University (1958) and Harvard Law School (1961), Kennedy had served 12 years as a U.S. Court of Appeals judge, acquiring a reputation as a legal conservative.

Kennedy, Cape: see CAPE CANAVERAL.

Kennedy, Edward M.

The younger brother of President John F. Kennedy and U.S. senator Robert F. Kennedy, Edward Moore Kennedy, b. Boston, Feb. 22, 1932, is a leader of the liberal Democrats in the U.S. Senate. He entered Harvard, as had his brothers, but was suspended for cheating on an examination. After serving 2

Edward "Ted" Kennedy has served as a U.S. senator from Massachusetts since 1962. Kennedy, noted as a sponsor of liberal legislation, was the Democratic whip, or assistant majority leader, from 1969 to 1971. In 1980 he was an unsuccessful contender for his party's presidential nomination.

years in the armed forces, he returned to Harvard and received his degree in 1956. With his brother John in the White House, "Teddy" was elected to John's Senate seat in 1962.

Ted Kennedy suffered a major political setback in the summer of 1969, when he drove his car off a bridge on Chappaquiddick Island, Mass. His companion in the car, 28-year-old Mary Jo Kopechne, was drowned. He was later found guilty of leaving the scene of an accident, and his explanations of the tragedy were unconvincing to many. Despite the accident, he was regularly reelected to the Senate. Although considered a strong potential contender for the Democratic presidential nomination, Kennedy declined to seek the nomination until 1980, when he challenged the incumbent, Jimmy Carter. Defeated by Carter in most of the primaries, Kennedy nonetheless remained in the race until the convention in August nominated Carter, whom Kennedy then endorsed. Kennedy made no subsequent bid for his party's nomination.

Kennedy, John F.

John Fitzgerald Kennedy, the 35th president of the United States (1961–63), was, at the age of 43, the youngest man and the first Roman Catholic ever elected to the presidency. Rich, handsome, elegant, and articulate, he aroused great admiration at home and abroad. His assassination in Dallas, Tex., in November 1963 provoked outrage and widespread mourning. His term of office as president was too short, however, to permit safe judgments about his place in history.

Early Life. Kennedy was born in Brookline, Mass., on May 29, 1917, a descendant of Irish Catholics who had immigrated to America in the 19th century. His father, Joseph P. Kennedy, was a combative businessman who became a multimillionaire, head of the Securities and Exchange Commission, and ambassador to Great Britain (see KENNEDY family).

Kennedy graduated from Choate School in Wallingford, Conn., briefly attended Princeton University, and then entered Harvard University in 1936. At Harvard he wrote an honors thesis on British foreign policies in the 1930s; it was published in 1940, the year he graduated, under the title *Why England Slept*. In 1941, shortly before the United States entered World War II, Kennedy joined the U.S. Navy. While on active duty in the Pacific in 1943, the boat he commanded—PT 109—was sunk by the Japanese. Kennedy performed heroically in rescuing his crew, but he aggravated an old back injury and contracted malaria. He was discharged in early 1945.

Congressman and Senator. In 1946, Kennedy ran successfully for a Boston-based seat in the U.S. House of Representatives; he was reelected in 1948 and 1950. As a congressman he backed social legislation that benefited his working-class constituents. Although generally supporting President Harry S. Truman's foreign policies, he criticized what he considered the administration's weak stand against the Communist Chinese. Kennedy continued to advocate a strong, anti-Communist foreign policy throughout his career. Restless in the House, Kennedy challenged incumbent Republican senator Henry Cabot Lodge, Jr., in 1952. Although the Republican presidential candidate, Dwight D. Eisenhower, won in Massachusetts as well as the country as a whole, Kennedy showed his remarkable vote-getting appeal by defeating Lodge.

A year later, on Sept. 12, 1953, Kennedy married Jacqueline Bouvier (see ONASSIS, JACQUELINE BOUVIER KENNEDY). The couple had three children: Caroline Bouvier (b. Nov. 27, 1957), John Fitzgerald, Jr. (b. Nov. 25, 1960), and a second son who died in infancy in August 1963.

Kennedy was a relatively ineffectual senator. During parts of 1954 and 1955 he was seriously ill with back ailments and was therefore unable to play an important role in government. Critics observed that he made no effort to oppose the anti–civil-libertarian excesses of Sen. Joseph R. McCarthy of Wisconsin. His friends later argued, not entirely persuasively, that he would have voted to censure McCarthy if he had not been hospitalized at the time. During his illness Kennedy worked on a book of biographical studies of American political heroes. Published in 1956 under the title *Profiles in Courage*, it won a Pulitzer Prize for biography in 1957. Like his earlier book on English foreign policy, it revealed his admiration for forceful political figures. This faith in activism was to become a hallmark of his presidency.

In 1956, Kennedy bid unsuccessfully for the Democratic vice-presidential nomination. Thereafter, he set his sights on the presidency, especially after his reelection to the Senate in 1958. He continued during these years to support a firmly anti-Communist foreign policy. A cautious liberal on domestic issues, he backed a compromise civil rights bill in 1957 and devoted special efforts to labor legislation.

By 1960, Kennedy was but one of many Democratic aspirants for the party's presidential nomination. He put together, however, a well-financed, highly organized campaign and won on the first ballot. As a northerner and a Roman Catholic, he recognized his lack of strength in the South and shrewdly chose Sen. Lyndon Baines JOHNSON of Texas as his running mate. Kennedy also performed well in a series of unprecedented television debates with his Republican opponent, Vice-President Richard M. NIXON. Kennedy promised tougher defense policies and progressive health, housing, and civil rights programs. His New Frontier, he pledged, would bring the nation out of its economic slump.

Presidency. Kennedy won the election, but by a narrow margin. He lacked reliable majorities in Congress. Primarily for these reasons, most of his domestic policies stalled on Capitol Hill. When advocates of racial justice picked up strength in 1962-63, he moved belatedly to promote civil rights legislation (see CIVIL RIGHTS ACTS). He also sought a tax cut to stimulate the economy. At the time of his assassination, however, these and other programs such as federal aid to education and MEDICARE remained tied up in Congress. It was left to his successor, President Johnson, to push this legislation through the more compliant congresses of 1964 and 1965.

Kennedy's eloquent inaugural address—in which he exhorted the nation: "Ask not what your country can do for you—ask what you can do for your country"—sounded cold war themes. Soon thereafter, the president acted on his anti-Communism by lending American military assistance to the BAY OF PIGS INVASION of Cuba in April 1961. The amphibious assault had been planned by the Central Intelligence Agency under the Eisenhower administration. The actual invasion was Kennedy's decision, however, and he properly took the blame for its total failure. Later in his administration he tried to diminish anti-Americanism in the Western Hemisphere by backing development projects under the ALLIANCE FOR PROGRESS, but the small sums involved had little impact. The Peace Corps program was developed with similar goals in mind (see ACTION).

Kennedy's chief adversary abroad was the Soviet leader Nikita Khrushchev. As early as June 1961 the two men talked in Vienna, but the meeting served only to harden Soviet-American hostility. Khrushchev then threatened to sign a treaty with East Germany that would have given the East Germans control over western access routes to Berlin. Kennedy held firm, and no such treaty was signed. The Soviets responded, however, by erecting a wall between East and West Berlin. Kennedy used the crisis to request from Congress, and to receive, greatly increased appropriations for defense.

By far the tensest overseas confrontation of the Kennedy years occurred with the CUBAN MISSILE CRISIS. In October 1962, U.S. intelligence discovered that the Russians were constructing offensive missile sites in Cuba. Kennedy recognized that such missiles would add little to Russian military potential, but he regarded the Soviet move as deliberately provocative. Resolving to show his mettle, he ordered a naval and air quarantine on shipments of offensive weapons to Cuba. At first armed conflict seemed likely. But the Soviets pulled back and promised not to set up the missiles; the United States then said it would not attack Cuba.

As if chastened by this crisis, the most frightening of the cold war, the Soviets and Americans in 1963 signed a treaty barring atmospheric testing of nuclear weapons. Kennedy nevertheless remained as ready as before to stop Communist advances. He continued to bolster American defenses and stepped up military aid to South Vietnam, where revolutionary forces were increasingly active. By November 1963, the

JOHN FITZGERALD KENNEDY
35th President of the United States (1961-63)

Nickname: "JFK"; "Jack"
Born: May 29, 1917, Brookline, Mass.
Education: Harvard College (graduated 1940)
Profession: Author, Public Official
Religious Affiliation: Roman Catholic
Marriage: Sept. 12, 1953, to Jacqueline Bouvier (1929-   )
Children: Caroline Bouvier Kennedy (1957-   ); John Fitzgerald Kennedy (1960-   ); Patrick Bouvier Kennedy (1963)
Political Affiliation: Democrat
Writings: *Why England Slept* (1940); *Profiles in Courage* (1956)
Died: Nov. 22, 1963, Dallas, Tex.
Buried: Arlington National Cemetery, Arlington, Va.

Vice-President and Cabinet Members
Vice-President: Lyndon Baines Johnson
Secretary of State: Dean Rusk
Secretary of the Treasury: C. Douglas Dillon
Secretary of Defense: Robert S. McNamara
Attorney General: Robert F. Kennedy
Postmaster General: J. Edward Day (1961-63); John A. Gronouski, Jr. (1963)
Secretary of the Interior: Stewart L. Udall
Secretary of Agriculture: Orville L. Freeman
Secretary of Commerce: Luther H. Hodges
Secretary of Labor: Arthur J. Goldberg (1961-62); W. Willard Wirtz (1962-63)
Secretary of Health, Education, and Welfare: Abraham A. Ribicoff (1961-62); Anthony J. Celebrezze (1962-63)

United States had sent some 16,000 military personnel to Vietnam. His administration also intervened in South Vietnamese politics by at least conniving at the overthrow of Ngo Dinh Diem in November 1963.

Assassination. By this time Kennedy was thinking ahead to the presidential campaign of 1964. In order to promote harmony between warring factions of the Democratic party in Texas, he traveled there in November 1963. While driving in a motorcade through Dallas on November 22, he was shot in the head and died within an hour.

President Johnson appointed the WARREN COMMISSION to investigate the assassination. It concluded that the killer, acting alone, was 24-year-old Lee Harvey OSWALD. No motive was established. Speculation about the assassination persisted, however. In 1978 a special Congressional committee concluded that "probably" Kennedy had been the victim of a conspiracy but that Oswald was the killer.   JAMES T. PATTERSON

Bibliography: Bradlee, Benjamin C., *Conversations with Kennedy* (1984); Brauer, Carl M., *John F. Kennedy and the Second Reconstruction* (1977); Kern, Montague, et al., *The Kennedy Crises* (1984); Schlesinger, Arthur M., Jr., *A Thousand Days: John F. Kennedy in the White House* (1965; repr. 1975); Sorensen, Theodore C., *Kennedy* (1965); Thompson, Kenneth W., ed., *The Kennedy Presidency* (1986).

Kennedy, Robert F.

Robert F. Kennedy served as attorney general of the United States during the presidency of his brother John F. Kennedy. Later he became (1965) a U.S. senator from New York, and in 1968 he campaigned for the Democratic nomination for president. He won five out of the six presidential primaries he entered. On the night of his victory in the California primary, however, he was assassinated while leaving Los Angeles's Ambassador Hotel.

Robert Francis ("Bobby") Kennedy, b. Brookline, Mass., Nov. 20, 1925, d. June 6, 1968, younger brother of U.S. President John F. Kennedy, was U.S. attorney general (1961–64) and a U.S. senator (1965–68). Like his brother, he was assassinated.

After graduating from the University of Virginia Law School in 1951, Bobby Kennedy was a Justice Department lawyer before resigning to manage his older brother's successful 1952 senatorial campaign. He became an assistant counsel to Sen. Joseph McCARTHY's Permanent Investigations Subcommittee in 1953. With one interruption to protest McCarthy's methods, he worked for the panel into 1956. Subsequently (1957–59) Kennedy was chief counsel for the Senate Rackets Committee and exposed the underworld connections of Teamsters Union officials James Hoffa and Dave Beck.

In 1960, Bobby managed the presidential campaign of John Kennedy, earning a reputation for considerable ruthlessness as well as skill. Appointed attorney general in his brother's administration, he stressed civil rights enforcement and a drive against organized crime. He was subsequently criticized for his extensive use of wiretaps, including one on Martin Luther King. Kennedy was also a close advisor to his brother.

After President Lyndon B. Johnson declined to choose Kennedy as his 1964 running mate, the attorney general resigned and won a U.S. Senate seat from New York. He focused increasingly on the needs of poor minorities and, beginning in 1966, became a sharp critic of the Vietnam War. In March 1968, Kennedy announced his candidacy for the Democratic

presidential nomination. Possessing a forceful, earnest, and charismatic personality, he forged a broad coalition of enthusiastic supporters that included young people, blacks, professionals, and blue-collar workers. On the night (June 4–5) of his victory in the California primary, however, Kennedy was fatally shot. His assassin, an immigrant from Jordan named Sirhan B. Sirhan, was arrested at the scene and later convicted of first degree murder.

Bibliography: Halberstam, David, *The Unfinished Odyssey of Robert Kennedy* (1968); Kennedy, Robert F., *Robert Kennedy: In His Own Words* (1988); Navasky, Victor, *Kennedy Justice* (1971; repr. 1977); Schlesinger, Arthur M., *Robert Kennedy and His Times* (1978; repr. 1985).

Kennedy, William

The American writer William Joseph Kennedy, b. Albany, N.Y., Jan. 16, 1928, has received critical acclaim for realistic fiction infused with an essentially comic spirit. In the novels *The Ink Truck* (1969), *Legs* (1975), *Billy Phelan's Greatest Game* (1978), *Ironweed* (1983; Pulitzer Prize; film, 1987), and *Quinn's Book* (1988), Kennedy evokes a powerful sense of time (1930s) and place (Albany) through fresh, vibrant language, acute feel for setting, and a marvelous ear for conversation. Kennedy also writes short stories and has published a volume of essays, *O Albany!* (1983).

Kennedy Center for the Performing Arts

The John F. Kennedy Center for the Performing Arts, in Washington, D.C., was created by an act of Congress as a memorial to the slain president. The center officially opened on Sept. 8, 1971, with the world premiere of Leonard Bernstein's *Mass*. The center was financed by the federal government as well as by private and corporate contributions, and was furnished in part by generous gifts from countries throughout the world. With a concert hall, opera house, several theaters, restaurants, and various spaces for exhibitions and conferences, the center has become a national cultural institution. It regularly presents programs by eminent U.S. music and dance organizations, as well as by famous groups from abroad, including the Bolshoi, Vienna, and La Scala opera companies. The Performing Arts Library of the Library of Congress and the American Film Institute also operate from the center.

In 1983 the AMERICAN NATIONAL THEATER AND ACADEMY (ANTA) founded the American National Theater Company, which offered its own productions, many of them experimental or new works. Despite the efforts of its artistic director Peter Sellars, however, the group failed to attract an audience; it was dissolved in 1986.

Bibliography: Coxe, Warren J., et al., eds., *A Guide to the Architecture of Washington, D.C.*, 2d ed. (1974).

Kennedy Space Center

Kennedy Space Center (KSC) is the chief civilian space launch facility in the United States. It is located adjacent to Cape Canaveral Air Force Station at Cape Canaveral, Fla. The center began operation in 1951 as the Experimental Missile Firing Branch of the Army Ordnance Guided Missile Center in Huntsville, Ala. In 1960 these became, respectively, the Launch Operations Directorate and the Marshall Space Flight Center. The directorate was made the independent launch operations center in July 1962 and was renamed in 1963 for President John F. Kennedy, who had committed the United States to landing astronauts on the Moon before 1970.

Because of this commitment, larger space launch facilities were built on nearby Merritt Island and were incorporated as part of the space center in July 1965. New facilities, called Launch Complex 39, included a vehicle assembly building for vertical assembly of the SATURN V rocket, two launch pads, and a launch control center. A complex for administrative and operational support was also built.

In addition to sending men to the Moon and orbiting the first U.S. space station, Kennedy Space Center is responsible for smaller civilian launches that must use air force launch pads at the cape. The center was designated (1973) as the eastern launch site for the reusable SPACE SHUTTLE. Launch Complex 39 was modified to accommodate the shuttle, and a new airstrip and special hangars were built for recovering and refurbishing it.   DAVID DOOLING

Kennelly-Heaviside layer: see IONOSPHERE.

Kenosha   [kin-oh'-shuh]

Kenosha, the seat of Kenosha County, is a city in southeastern Wisconsin on Lake Michigan at the Pike River estuary. It has a population of 77,685 (1980). A manufacturing city of automobiles, metal parts, and furniture, it is also an important port on the Saint Lawrence Seaway. Kenosha is the site of Carthage College (1847) and the University of Wisconsin Parkside campus (1965). The city was founded in 1835; its name means "pike" in Potawatomi dialect.

Kensett, John Frederick   [ken'-set]

The American painter John Frederick Kensett, b. Cheshire, Conn., Mar. 22, 1816, d. Dec. 14, 1872, belonged to the HUDSON RIVER SCHOOL and was an important exponent of LUMINISM. Trained as an engraver, he began painting under the guidance of John W. Casilear and in the 1840s undertook a 7-year trip to Europe, accompanied part of the time by the painter Asher Brown Durand. In his early paintings Kensett used thick brushstrokes to depict dense forest scenes. By the mid-1850s, however, he was concentrating on typical Hudson River school compositions in which broad expanses of shore, water, and sky are viewed from a height. The atmospheric haze enveloping these vistas produces the subdued and delicate color effects that are Kensett's trademark. The poetic rendering of fall colors in his *View Near Cozzens Hotel from West Point* (1863; New-York Historical Society, New York City) exemplifies his technical mastery, as does the limpid, almost magically still surface of the water in his *Lake George* (1869; Metropolitan Museum of Art, New York City).
                                    ABRAHAM A. DAVIDSON

Bibliography: Kettlewell, James, et al., *John Frederick Kensett* (1967); Howat, J. K., *John Frederick Kensett* (1968).

Kensington Rune Stone   [ken'-zing-tuhn roon]

The Kensington Rune Stone is a 91-kg (200-lb) slab of graywacke rock that a farmer found near Kensington, Minn., in 1898. It contains an inscription in runes (an angular script used by Germanic tribes beginning in the 3d century AD) that purportedly records an Indian attack on Norse explorers in the year 1362. Although its authenticity was disputed from the time of its discovery, the inscription was cited by some as evidence to support the claim that Norsemen explored the interior of North America in pre-Columbian times. The stone is now generally regarded as a forgery. It is housed in a museum in Alexandria, Minn.   JAMES W. HERRICK

Bibliography: Blegen, Theodore C., *The Kensington Rune Stone: New Light on an Old Riddle* (1968); Holand, Hjalmar R., *Norse Discoveries and Explorations in North America: Leif Ericson to the Kensington Stone* (1940; repr. 1969); Pohl, Frederick J., *The Viking Explorers* (1966).

Kent

Kent is a county in southeastern England on the English Channel. Its area is 3,711 km² (1,433 mi²), and its population is 1,463,055 (1981). Maidstone is the county town. The relief of Kent is dominated by the North Downs—long, low, chalk hills culminating in the white cliffs of Dover. The Weald, an elevated, formerly forested area, is southwest of the Downs. The rivers Thames, Medway, and Stour flow through Kent, and numerous marshes, including Romney Marsh, are along the coast.

Shipping is an important part of Kent's economy; ports are at DOVER and Folkstone. Fruits (apples and cherries), hops and other grains, and truck-farm crops for London are grown. Grazing land for sheep and cattle is extensive. Paper, heavy machinery, cement, and chemicals are manufactured, and petroleum is refined on the Isle of Grain. There is a small coal-

field near Dover. Many resorts, such as Margate, are located along the coast. Because of Kent's proximity to London, many of the towns are commuting suburbs. CANTERBURY is the seat of the primate of the Church of England.

Because of Kent's coastal location, it has been the site of many invasions into Britain, including those of the Romans (AD 43) and the Saxons and Jutes (5th century). The Jutes established the independent kingdom of Kent (5th–7th century). In 1170, Archbishop Thomas BECKET was murdered in Canterbury Cathedral, and it became a major pilgrimage center during the Middle Ages. (See CANTERBURY TALES, THE.)

Kent, James

James Kent, b. near Brewster, N.Y., July 31, 1763, d. Dec. 12, 1847, was a U.S. jurist whose *Commentaries on American Law* (4 vols., 1826–30) made him known as "the American Blackstone." After graduating from Yale University, he studied law and was admitted to the bar in 1785. He practiced law in Poughkeepsie, N.Y., and then taught law at Columbia College, New York City, from 1794 to 1798. In 1798 he was appointed to the New York Supreme Court, becoming chief judge in 1804. In 1814 he was made chancellor of the New York Court of Chancery, where his opinions contributed to development of the law of equity in the United States. His *Commentaries* were published in five editions during his lifetime.

Kent, Rockwell

Rockwell Kent, b. Tarrytown Heights, N.Y., June 21, 1882, d. Mar. 13, 1971, was an American painter, printmaker, and writer whose theme was the vastness and grandeur of nature, and often the heroic loneliness of humans before it, as seen in *The Road Roller* (1909; Phillips Collection, Washington, D.C.). He was a wanderer and adventurer who wrote several books recording and illustrating his travels. As a printmaker, Kent favored wood engravings; his style, influenced by William Blake, used marked contrasts of light and dark for dramatic effect, as in his *Northern Night* (1930; one version, Philadelphia Museum of Art). Kent is best known as the illustrator of numerous books, including a special edition (1930) of Herman Melville's *Moby-Dick*.   ABRAHAM A. DAVIDSON

Bibliography: Jones, Dan Burne, *The Prints of Rockwell Kent: A Catalogue Raisonné* (1975); Kent, Rockwell, *Rockwell Kent* (1945).

Kent, William

William Kent, b. c.1685, d. Apr. 12, 1748, was an English architect, decorator, and landscape gardener. As a landscapist he created the first English landscape garden at Stowe in Buckinghamshire; as a building architect he continued the neo-Palladian style (see Andrea PALLADIO) initiated by Inigo JONES. On a trip (1709–19) to Italy Kent met the architect Richard Boyle, 3d earl of BURLINGTON, who on returning to England employed Kent as a painter, furniture designer, and decorator. Their most notable collaboration was Chiswick House (begun 1725) in London, based on Palladio's Villa Rotonda (1566–67) near Vicenza, Italy. After editing and publishing (1727) a book of designs by Jones, Kent began practicing architecture about 1730 under the patronage and guidance of Lord Burlington. A neo-Palladian preoccupation with symmetrical design marks Kent's masterpiece, Holkham Hall, Norfolk (begun 1734), as well as his major architectural works in London, the Treasury (1734–36) and the Horse Guards building (1750–58). His best-presented works of landscape gardening are at Rousham, Oxfordshire, and at Stowe, Buckinghamshire.
                                    VALENTIN TATRANSKY

Bibliography: Colvin, H. M., *A Biographical Dictionary of English Architects, 1660–1840* (1954; repr. 1978); Harris, John, *The Palladians* (1982); Jourdain, M., *The Work of William Kent* (1948); Wittkower, Rudolf, *Palladio and Palladianism* (1974).

Kentucky

Kentucky presents a mixture of both the Midwest and the South. The northern, more urban portion of the state, particularly the Ohio Valley corridor, is characterized by manufacturing and is oriented to the Midwest. Southern Kentucky tends to be rural in nature, concentrating on agriculture and mining; it is generally associated with the South. The state's abundant natural resources, scenic beauty, historic treasures, and proud people contrast with Kentucky's problems of poverty, poor housing, and low levels of education.

Kentucky is centrally located within the eastern United States, bordered by the seven states of Illinois, Indiana, Ohio, West Virginia, Virginia, Tennessee, and Missouri. The state has an extreme width of 290 km (180 mi) and a length of 676 km (420 mi). Kentucky was once an Indian hunting ground. The name is believed to come from an Indian word meaning "prairie." White men had explored the area by 1750, but the first permanent settlement was not established until 1774 in Harrodsburg. In 1792, Kentucky separated from Virginia to become the 15th state.

LAND

Kentucky shows diversity in its terrain. Considerable areas of plains, many hills, and a limited mountainous area in southeastern Kentucky, the highest part of the state, can be found in the state. Elevations generally decrease to the west and north, varying from 610 to 914 m (2,000 to 3,000 ft) in the southeast to between 122 and 183 m (400 and 600 ft) in the northwest and 396 m (1,300 ft) in the north. The highest point is Black Mountain, 1,262 m (4,139 ft), located near the Virginia border; the lowest elevation, 78 m (257 ft), is the Mississippi River along the state's western tip.

The state may be divided into six regions that closely conform to geologic structure. The Pennyroyal region, named for a type of mint native to the area, is a flat-to-rolling limestone agricultural area at the heart of Kentucky. It extends nearly two-thirds of the distance across the state and accounts for about 30% of the total area.

To the east of the Pennyroyal, the Eastern Mountain and Coalfield claims more than 25% of the land. This part of the state, Kentucky's Appalachia, is characterized by vast coal resources, rugged terrain, and widespread poverty. North of the Pennyroyal is the Knobs, a narrow crescent-shaped belt of conical hills containing less than 10% of Kentucky's area. It surrounds the limestone-based Bluegrass region, centered on Lexington. The Bluegrass region covers about one-fifth of the state along the Ohio River. It is famous for its horse farms, tobacco, and cattle.

The Western Coalfield, more than 10% of the state, is a relatively rolling sandstone and shale area west of the Pennyroyal where agriculture and area stripping of coal takes place. To its west, the Jackson Purchase, 6% of Kentucky, is that region lying west of the Tennessee River which was bought from the Chickasaw Indians in 1818 by Andrew Jackson and former governor Isaac Shelby. It is characterized by large farms developed on unconsolidated floodplain deposits.

The state is geologically simple: rocks are sedimentary and consist primarily of limestones, sandstones, and shales. The strata are nearly horizontal except for deformation associated with thrust faulting in mountainous southeastern Kentucky. Rocks vary in age from the recent (less than 10,000 years) in the Jackson Purchase to more than 420 million years, found in the Ordovician limestones of the Bluegrass.

Soils are primarily woodland residual, but extensive areas possess alluvial and aeolian, or wind-borne, soils. The most fertile soils are associated with alluvial deposits along the Mississippi and Ohio rivers and their tributaries. The poorest soils are in the coalfield regions.

Climate. The climate is moderate but variable. Kentucky's weather is influenced by warm air from the Gulf of Mexico in summer and by cyclonic storms during winter. The state's location in the path of major storm tracks contributes to frequent weather changes.

The west is slightly warmer than the east in summer, and the south is marginally warmer than the north in winter. Summer temperatures range from highs of 33° C (92° F) to lows of 17° C (62° F). Winter highs average 10° C (50° F) and lows −3° C (26° F). The growing season extends from 206 days in the west to 165 days in the southeast.

Annual precipitation decreases from south to north, with

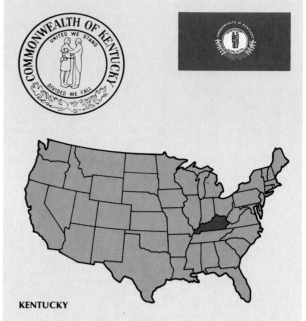

KENTUCKY

LAND. Area: 104,661 km² (40,410 mi²); rank: 37th. Capital: Frankfort (1980 pop., 25,973). Largest city: Louisville (1988 est. pop., 282,000). Counties: 120. Elevations: highest—1,262 m (4,139 ft), at Black Mountain; lowest—78 m (257 ft), at the Mississippi River.

PEOPLE. Population (1990 prelim.): 3,665,220; rank: 23d; density: 35.7 persons per km² (92.4 per mi²). Distribution (1988 est.): 46.1% metropolitan, 53.9% nonmetropolitan. Average annual change (1980–90): +0.01%.

EDUCATION. Public enrollment (1988): elementary—451,805; secondary—185,822; higher—129,225. Nonpublic enrollment (1980): elementary—42,100; secondary—14,700; combined—11,000; higher (1988)—30,643. Institutions of higher education (1987): 60.

ECONOMY. State personal income (1988): $47.8 billion; rank: 26th. Median family income (1979): $16,444; rank: 45th. Nonagricultural labor distribution (1988): manufacturing—274,000 persons; wholesale and retail trade—328,000; government—244,000; services—292,000; transportation and public utilities—73,000; finance, insurance, and real estate—59,000; construction—63,000. Agriculture: income (1988)—$2.5 billion. Forestry: sawtimber volume (1987)—34.1 billion board feet. Mining: value (1987)—$4.8 billion. Manufacturing: value added (1987)—$18.1 billion. Services: value (1987)—$9 billion.

GOVERNMENT (1991). Governor: Wallace Wilkinson, Democrat. U.S. Congress: Senate—1 Democrat, 1 Republican; House—4 Democrats, 3 Republicans. Electoral college votes: 9. State legislature: 38 senators, 100 representatives.

STATE SYMBOLS. Statehood: June 1, 1792; the 15th state. Nickname: Bluegrass State; bird: cardinal; flower: goldenrod; tree: Kentucky coffee tree; motto: United We Stand, Divided We Fall; song: "My Old Kentucky Home."

northern Kentucky receiving an average of 1,016 mm (40 in) and southern Kentucky more than 1,270 mm (50 in). Much of the state's rainfall occurs between March and June; the least amount occurs in October. Severe storms can occur any time of the year but are most common from March to September. Kentucky averages six tornadoes yearly.

Drainage. Three streams mark Kentucky's western, northern, and eastern boundaries: the MISSISSIPPI, OHIO, and Big Sandy rivers. Other important streams include the CUMBERLAND, TENNESSEE, Green, Kentucky, Licking, and Salt rivers. Virtually all of Kentucky's streams flow from the south or southeast to the north or northeast and into the Ohio River. The stream pattern is mainly dendritic.

Kentucky has a large number of lakes and countless smaller natural ponds or sinks. The best-known lakes include Cumberland (205 km²/79 mi²), Kentucky (194 km²/75 mi²), and

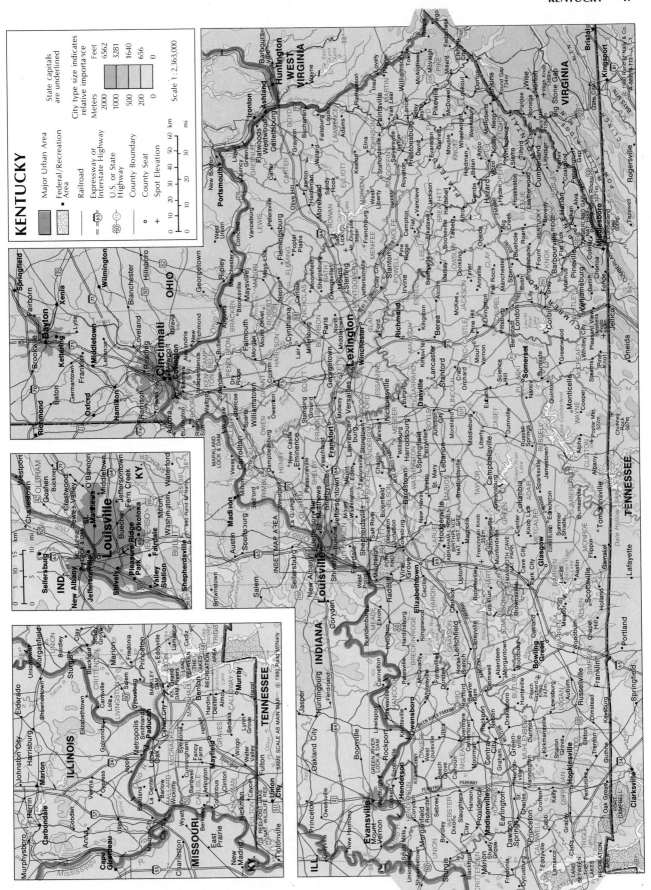

Barkley (184 km²/71 mi²). Lakes Cumberland and Barkley were formed by damming the Cumberland River, while Kentucky Lake was formed on the Tennessee and is part of the TENNESSEE VALLEY AUTHORITY. The state's best-known natural water body is Reelfoot Lake, formed as a result of an 1811 earthquake. The most productive groundwater areas are in the Jackson Purchase, in the Ohio River floodplain, and in the Pennyroyal. Relatively little groundwater is associated with the coalfield and Bluegrass regions.

Vegetation and Wildlife. The state lies at the center of the Eastern Deciduous Forest and is about 48% tree covered. Little of the original forest remains, however. Dominant trees include oak, tulip poplar, hickory, beech, buckeye, maple, pine, cedar, and hemlock. Animal life consists largely of deer, rabbit, squirrel, opossum, raccoon, skunk, woodchuck, snake, and quail. Fish include crappie, bass, perch, catfish, and darters.

Resources. Kentucky's most abundant natural resources include reserves of bituminous coal, limestone, sand and gravel, and water and forest resources. Also present are reserves of natural gas, petroleum, oil shale, clay, and fluorspar.

PEOPLE

Kentucky's population grew by more than the national average in the decade between 1970 and 1980, and to some extent that growth appeared to be related to the Sun Belt phenomenon, which has spurred rapid migration to the South and Southwest. In recent years, however, the growth rate has slowed. The state's population density is lower than that of the eastern United States in general. The farm population continues to decrease.

Kentucky has a relatively large rural and small-town population. Few cities are of significant size. The state has two large cities, LOUISVILLE and LEXINGTON, and one other city with a population in excess of 50,000—OWENSBORO. A number of other cities have more than 20,000 people, including Covington, Bowling Green, PADUCAH, Hopkinsville, Ashland, FRANKFURT, and Henderson.

The state's population is mostly white. Blacks form the largest nonwhite group, followed by persons of Spanish origin, who account for less than 1% of the state's population; Asian and Pacific Islanders; and American Indians. Of the state's foreign-born residents, most originated from Germany, the United Kingdom, Italy, and Canada.

Baptists constitute the largest religious group. Other large denominations are the Roman Catholics, Presbyterians, Methodists, and Disciples of Christ.

Education. Kentucky's first school opened in Harrodsburg in 1775, and the public school system was established in 1838 by the state legislature. The state department of education is in charge of the public school system; it is headed by a superintendent of public instruction.

Higher education can be traced to the 1780 chartering of Transylvania Seminary, now Transylvania University. The state's largest school, the University of Kentucky, dates to 1865 (see KENTUCKY, STATE UNIVERSITIES OF). The Kentucky community college system, administered by the University of Kentucky, has branches located in several cities. In addition to the state schools, a number of private institutions of higher education are located in Kentucky.

Many public libraries, along with college and specialized libraries, serve Kentucky. The largest library collections are found at the University of Kentucky, the University of Louisville, the Kentucky State Library, and the Louisville Public Libraries.

Culture. The state's museums contain natural history, science, and art collections. Historic houses, planetariums, and nature centers are also part of Kentucky's cultural life. The J. B. Speed Art Museum is in Louisville. Examples of unique museums in the state include the John James Audubon Museum in Henderson and the Kentucky Derby Museum in Louisville. The state's three principal symphony orchestras are located in Louisville, Lexington, and Owensboro; other cities support university or community orchestras. One opera company and one resident theater are located in Louisville, and ballet companies are headquartered in Lexington and Louisville.

Louisville is Kentucky's largest city and one of the South's leading manufacturing centers. It is noted for its bourbon, producing almost half of the world's supply. A restoration project along the Ohio River protects an important historic district.

Historical Sites. Federal, state, and local historic attractions total about 2,000 in number. Some of the more significant include reconstructed forts Harrod and Boonesboro; Cumberland Gap; the Abraham Lincoln and Jefferson Davis birthplaces; Ashland, home of Henry Clay; Federal Hill, known as Stephen Foster's "My Old Kentucky Home"; and the communities of Danville and Frankfort, the state capital.

Communications. Kentucky has a number of daily newspapers, including the influential Louisville Courier-Journal. There are also commercial television and radio stations and an educational television system in the state.

ECONOMY

Contrary to popular opinion, manufacturing contributes far more to Kentucky's economy than agriculture and mining combined. The greatest single source of income is derived from manufacturing. Agriculture is still important to the state, and Kentucky ranks among the leading U.S. states in the production of tobacco. Eastern Kentucky is highly dependent on coal mining and is the poorest region of the state. Beginning in the 1960s both the state and federal governments established poverty-combating programs in Kentucky's Appalachian region, but income has remained lower and unemployment higher in that area than elsewhere in the state.

Agriculture. Kentucky's agriculture is confined generally to the western two-thirds of the state. Crops and livestock activities each account for about half of farm income. By far the most valuable crop is tobacco—primarily burley; the crop is grown in almost every county in the state. Also significant are corn, soybeans, and hay. Livestock is dominated by cattle with associated dairy products, hogs, horses, and poultry.

Although Kentucky is a leader in hardwood production, forestry contributes relatively little to the state's economy except on a local level in eastern and southern Kentucky.

Mining. The only state with two distinct coalfields—the Appalachian in eastern Kentucky and the Eastern Interior in western Kentucky—Kentucky is the nation's leading bituminous coal-producing state. Coal is obtained both by underground and surface, or strip, methods. Contour stripping dominates hilly eastern Kentucky; area stripping is more common in the west. Other leading mineral activities, by value of production, include stone, petroleum, natural gas, sand and gravel, and clay.

Manufacturing. Manufacturing in Kentucky, employing more than 250,000 people, is dominant along the Ohio River corri-

Cumberland Gap is a natural passageway through the scenic Cumberland Mountains of the Appalachians. Daniel Boone, with a group of pioneers, built (1775) the Wilderness Road through the gap, creating a route for western-bound settlers. It is the principal feature of the Cumberland Gap National Historical Park.

(Left) *Kentucky tobacco is as famous as Kentucky horses, and Lexington's tobacco exchange is the nation's largest burley market. The state ranks second after North Carolina in tobacco production.*

(Below) *Coal is extracted from a Kentucky strip mine after the strata overlying a coal seam are removed to expose the coal. Strip mining is environmentally devastating, and today, once an area is mined, its original topography is regularly re-created and replanted.*

dor between the Ashland–Catlettsburg area in northeastern Kentucky and the PADUCAH–Calvert City area in the extreme western part of the state. An additional manufacturing area is centered on Lexington. Louisville is the state's principal center of manufacturing; other important industrial cities are Owensboro and the Newport-Covington area. The leading types of manufacturing include metals (steel and aluminum), machinery, transportation equipment, chemicals, food (including Bourbon whiskey and other alcoholic beverages), tobacco products, and lumber and wood products.

Tourism. Four federal parks lie wholly or partly within the state: Mammoth Cave National Park, Cumberland Gap National Historical Park, Abraham Lincoln Birthplace National

Historic Site, and Land Between the Lakes National Recreation Area. The Kentucky state park system supervises 17 areas, the newest of which is Kentucky Horse Park, near Lexington. Breaks Interstate Park is jointly operated by Kentucky and Virginia.

Six areas are significant to tourism: the Kentucky and Barkley lakes area, the Mammoth Cave area, scattered locations in and near Daniel Boone National Forest, the Lake Cumberland area, Lexington and the Bluegrass area, and Louisville. The state has three Thoroughbred and four standardbred, or harness, race tracks. The best known include the Thoroughbred tracks at Churchill Downs in Louisville, site of the KENTUCKY DERBY, and Keeneland Race Course in Lexington, one of the country's most beautiful racing facilities. Also popular is the historic Red Mile in Lexington, site of many record-setting harness races. Rupp Arena, the nation's largest college basketball facility, is in Lexington.

Transportation. Kentucky has 112,651 km (70,000 mi) of highways, of which 1,997 km (1,241 mi) are freeways providing easy access to other states. An extensive system of toll roads also crosses the state. Local roads, however, are considered poor when compared with those of adjacent states. The Mississippi and Ohio rivers and intrastate rivers provide 2,575 km (1,600 mi) of navigable waterway. In addition, 5,954 km (3,700 mi) of railroad track cross the state, and scheduled flights are provided to seven major airports. In all, 67 airports, including Greater Cincinnati International Airport in northern Kentucky and Standiford Field in Louisville, service the state.

Energy. Kentucky, with coal reserves presently estimated at 66 billion tons, will play a nationally important energy role in future years. At present coal provides more than 90% of the state's electric generating capacity. A total of 51 electric generating plants operate in the state; 33 are steam generating plants, 9 are hydroelectric, and 9 internal combustion. Kentucky has no nuclear generating plants.

GOVERNMENT AND POLITICS

Kentucky is organized as a commonwealth rather than a state and operates under its fourth constitution, adopted in 1891. Elected officials include the governor, lieutenant governor,

Mammoth Cave's subterranean depths extend circuitously beneath Kentucky's Green River for 245 km (150 mi). Its caverns feature limestone stalagmites and stalactites, and underground rivers, lakes, and waterfalls. Mammoth Cave National Park was established in 1936.

The annual "Run for the Roses," the Kentucky Derby, is held at Louisville's Churchill Downs on the first Saturday in May. Since its inception in 1875, the Derby has been a racing classic. It is the first leg of the Triple Crown, before the Preakness and the Belmont Stakes.

secretary of state, attorney general, treasurer, auditor of public accounts, commissioner of agriculture, and superintendent of public instruction—all of whom are elected for 4-year terms. The legislature consists of 38 senators, elected for 4 years, and 100 representatives, elected for 2 years. The judiciary is composed of one court of justice, which, in turn, is composed of four courts: supreme, appeals, circuit, and district.

Kentucky has 120 counties, a number exceeded only by Texas and Georgia, averaging 855 km² (330 mi²) in area. Counties are governed by a fiscal court, composed of an elected judge-executive, who serves as county administrator, and three or more magistrates. Cities in Kentucky are delegated powers according to one of six class assignments based on population. Recently a new legal entity was approved by the legislature that permitted the city of Lexington and Fayette County to merge, thus forming a metropolitan government. For planning purposes, the state is divided into 15 multicounty planning regions called Area Development Districts (ADDs).

Politically, the state is dominated by Democrats, who have a two-to-one registration margin over Republicans. Republican strength is greatest in a 15-county area in southeastern Kentucky.

Kentucky, "the Bourbon whiskey capital of the world," is conservative with the sale of alcoholic beverages. Of Kentucky's 120 counties, 84 totally prohibit alcoholic beverage sales. These dry counties are located primarily in the rural, southern part of the state.

HISTORY

Indians established civilizations in Kentucky more than 13,000 years ago. When the first white people entered the area, it was being used as a hunting ground by the SHAWNEE and CHEROKEE Indians.

One of the early explorers, Dr. Thomas Walker, entered Kentucky after discovering Cumberland Gap in 1750. The gap provided a relatively easy route through the Cumberland Mountains, and in subsequent years countless explorers and settlers were to move through it. One of the best-known explorers was the legendary Daniel BOONE, who first arrived in 1767. Others reached Kentucky via the Ohio River and established settlements at Maysville and Louisville.

The first settlement of Fort Harrod, now known as Harrodsburg, was established by James Harrod in 1774. Boonesboro was settled in 1775 by Daniel Boone and his companions. Increased settlement brought pressures for statehood. Following

Many of the finest Thoroughbreds, standardbreds, and saddle horses in the United States have been bred in Kentucky. Most of the horse farms are located near Lexington in the Bluegrass region, where fertile soils produce a silver blue grass that gives the state its nickname.

conventions in Danville, the first constitution was approved in April 1792; Kentucky became the 15th state on June 1, 1792. In what was essentially a compromise between Lexington and Louisville, Frankfort was selected the state capital. The new state legislature adopted a strong STATE RIGHTS position when it adopted (1798) resolutions opposing the Alien and Sedition Acts (see KENTUCKY AND VIRGINIA RESOLUTIONS).

Between statehood and the Civil War, Kentucky increased its population from about 75,000 to more than 1 million. Slavery became the dominant social and political issue as the state expanded its farm production. An agricultural market downstream on the Mississippi River was assured by the Louisiana Purchase in 1803. The steamboat provided transportation on the Ohio River by 1815, and a rail system was developed before 1860.

A border state, Kentucky attempted to remain neutral during the Civil War but was unsuccessful because of its strategic location and the divided loyalties of its citizens. Farmers who used the Ohio and Mississippi rivers for transporting their produce wanted access to both waterways and the international port of New Orleans. If the South separated itself from the North, this free access would be impeded. On the other hand, influential plantation owners and state rights advocates sided with the Confederacy. As a result, Kentuckians could be found in both Union and Confederate armies. Confederate forces invaded Kentucky in 1861. Most of the fighting within the state's boundaries, however, had ceased by 1863, after the Confederate army was driven out.

After the Civil War, the state changed economically and socially. Tobacco replaced hemp as the major agricultural crop. Coal mining was stimulated by the extension of rail lines into the coalfields of the eastern part of the state. Increased employment opportunities arose in manufacturing and services, and the major cities grew rapidly. After 1920 the state began a 50-year trend of marked decreases in rural population and growth in urban areas.

From World War II to the present day, Kentucky has changed with the nation. Certain internal events, however, have had a particular impact on Kentucky's historic development. A modern highway system of interstate routes and an extensive toll-road network connecting all parts of the state have been established. The creation of the Kentucky Program Development Office and the authorization for the 15 Area Development Districts, beginning in 1968, showed serious efforts to plan for the state's future. Aggressive state involve-

ment with industrial development and stimulation of tourism was begun, particularly with the promotion of the state park system. The state joined in the formation of the Appalachian Regional Commission in 1965 and obtained assistance from the Tennessee Valley Authority in the western part of the state. Higher education was upgraded through the creation of regional universities and community colleges, along with the Kentucky Educational Television Network. A coal severance tax was enacted, to be levied at the time of extraction on an industry whose technological changes have resulted in an increased use of machinery rather than human labor, a major shift from underground mining to surface mining, and an increase in pollution. The state's judicial system was revamped in 1976, and the long-established pattern of out-migration appears recently to have been reversed.

In order to realize its potential, Kentucky must solve a number of problems: regional economic inequality; poor transportation in certain areas; widespread pollution problems, particularly with regard to the mining industry; and an agricultural base overly dependent on tobacco.

Kentucky's future looks promising, however. Continued economic development is possible because of the state's advantages in energy, natural resources, transportation, water, scenery, and climate. With intelligent land-use planning, the state's abundant resources, coupled with a relatively low population density, should provide Kentuckians with an improved economy and a better overall quality of life.

DENNIS E. QUILLEN

Bibliography: Caudill, Harry M., *A Darkness at Dawn: Appalachian Kentucky and the Future* (1976) and *Night Comes to the Cumberlands* (1963); Clark, Thomas D., *Agrarian Kentucky* (1978), *A History of Kentucky*, 4th ed. (1961), and *Kentucky: Land of Contrast* (1968); Coleman, J. Winston, ed., *Kentucky: A Pictorial History*, 2d ed. (1971); Dykeman, Wilma, and Stokely, James, *The Border States* (1968); Federal Writers' Project, *Kentucky: A Guide to the Bluegrass State* (1939; repr. 1973); Harvey, Curtis E., *The Economics of Kentucky Coal* (1977); Jewell, Malcolm E., and Cunningham, Everett W., *Kentucky Politics* (1968); Karan, P. P., ed., *Kentucky: A Regional Geography* (1973); Karan, P. P., and Mather, Cotton, eds., *Atlas of Kentucky* (1977); Rice, Otis K., *Frontier Kentucky* (1975); Schwendeman, Joseph R., *The Geography of Kentucky*, 3d ed. (1970); Van Hook, Joseph O., *The Kentucky Story*, 3d ed. (1970); Weller, Jack E., *Yesterday's People: Life in Contemporary Appalachia* (1965).

Kentucky, state universities of

Kentucky's state universities are coeducational and grant undergraduate and graduate degrees. The **University of Kentucky** (1865; enrollment: 22,365; library: 1,640,500 volumes), at Lexington, a land-grant institution, has colleges of agriculture, arts and sciences, architecture, engineering, business, and nursing. A medical center, the National Tobacco Research Laboratory, and schools of law and engineering are at the university. The **University of Louisville** (1798; enrollment: 17,800; library: 931,000 volumes), at Louisville, has schools of law, engineering, business, dentistry, and medicine.

Other universities, with liberal arts and teacher education curricula, are: **Eastern Kentucky** (1906; enrollment: 13,510; library: 503,000 volumes), at Richmond; **Morehead State** (1922; enrollment: 7,050; library: 345,000 volumes); **Murray State** (1922; enrollment: 8,000; library: 504,000 volumes); **Northern Kentucky** (1908; enrollment: 7,000; library: 272,000 volumes), at Highland Heights; **Western Kentucky** (1906; enrollment: 13,490; library: 490,000 volumes), at Bowling Green; and **Kentucky State** (1886; enrollment: 2,300; library: 165,000 volumes), at Frankfort, a land-grant college founded for blacks and having a predominantly black enrollment.

Kentucky and Virginia Resolutions

In 1798 the legislatures of Kentucky and Virginia adopted resolutions opposing the ALIEN AND SEDITION ACTS, which Congress, dominated by the FEDERALIST PARTY, had passed earlier in the year. The Democratic-Republicans (see DEMOCRATIC PARTY) regarded these acts as a dangerous denial of individual liberty. Although his authorship was not known at the time, Thomas JEFFERSON, then U.S. vice-president, had drafted (Nov. 16, 1798) the resolutions adopted in Kentucky, and James

MADISON had authored Virginia's set (adopted Dec. 24, 1798).

The Kentucky Resolutions, the more radical of the two sets, declared specifically that the Alien and Sedition Acts were unconstitutional and that a state had the right to make that determination. An additional resolution passed by the Kentucky legislature in 1799 declared that formal NULLIFICATION was the proper remedy for a federal law that a state deemed unconstitutional. The Virginia Resolutions referred to the duty of a state to ''interpose'' its authority when the federal government assumed powers not granted by the Constitution. Both sets of resolutions also called upon other states to concur; no other states did so, however. The resolutions were later viewed as the first significant statement of STATE RIGHTS.

MORTON BORDEN

Bibliography: Koch, Adrienne, *Jefferson and Madison: The Great Collaboration* (1950); Miller, John C., *Crisis in Freedom: The Alien and Sedition Acts* (1951; repr. 1964).

Kentucky coffee tree

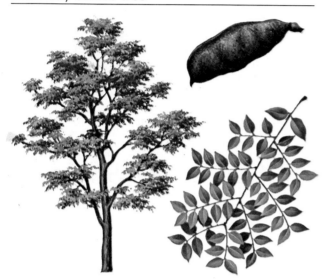

The Kentucky coffee tree, G. dioica, is cultivated as an ornamental tree valued for the handsome silhouette of its bare branches during winter. It grows in rich soil along stream banks.

The Kentucky coffee tree, *Gymnocladus dioica,* is native to forests of the eastern United States—mostly west of the Appalachian Mountains. This tree is about 30 m (100 ft) in height and bears twice-compound leaves. Early settlers roasted the tree's seeds—contained in pods—as a coffee substitute.

Kentucky Derby

The Kentucky Derby, first run on May 17, 1875, is the most important and prestigious Thoroughbred horse race in the United States. Called ''the run for the roses,'' it is held each year on the first Saturday in May at the 1-mi (1.6-km) Churchill Downs racetrack in Louisville, Ky.; it is the first and most acclaimed of the Triple Crown races (the others are the Belmont Stakes and Preakness Stakes). Each year more than 150,000 people attend this 1.25-mi (2-km) race for a field of up to about 20 three-year-old horses. Since the 1960s millions have watched the Derby on television. The winner's purse of some races in the mid- and late 1980s has exceeded $500,000; the winner also receives a gold trophy. Some of the greatest racehorses in history have won the Derby: Sir Barton (1919), Gallant Fox (1930), War Admiral (1937), Whirlaway (1941), Citation (1948), Swaps (1955), Needles (1956), Secretariat (1973), Seattle Slew (1977), and Affirmed (1978).

Bibliography: Bolus, Jim, *Run for the Roses: 100 Years at the Kentucky Derby* (1974); Bryant, B., and Williams, J., *Portraits in Roses* (1984); Chew, Peter, *The Kentucky Derby* (1974).

Kenya [ken'-yuh]

Kenya, a republic of East Africa, is bordered by the Indian Ocean on the southeast, Somalia on the east, Ethiopia on the north, Sudan on the northeast, Uganda on the west, and Tanzania on the south. It is named for Mount Kenya, the second highest mountain in Africa, located in the south central part of the country at the equator. Kenya was a colony of Great Britain before becoming independent on Dec. 12, 1963.

LAND AND RESOURCES

The only lowlands in Kenya are located along the Indian Ocean in a narrow belt that is 3 to 16 km (2 to 10 mi) wide in the south and widens to about 160 km (100 mi) north of the Tana River. Inland are three upland areas, which include a belt of low plateaus in the east, the Kenya Highlands and the GREAT RIFT VALLEY in the west central regions, and the broad uplands of the Lake Victoria Basin in the west. The low eastern plateaus begin abruptly at the edge of the coastal plain and rise gradually westward to 1,525 m (5,000 ft) in the Yatta Plateau. Located west of the Yatta Plateau, the Kenya Highlands are divided by the spectacular tectonic trough of the eastern arm of the Great Rift Valley, which cuts across the highlands from north to south. The Kenya Highlands rise to more than 3,950 m (13,000 ft) in the Aberdare Range, which forms the steep eastern edge of the rift valley, and to more than 3,000 m (10,000 ft) in the Mau Escarpment, which forms the western edge of the rift; they rise to a high point of 5,199 m (17,058 ft) in Mount KENYA. The Great Rift Valley varies in width from about 50 to 65 km (31 to 40 mi), and the floor of the trough, which is 600 to 900 m (2,000 to 3,000 ft)

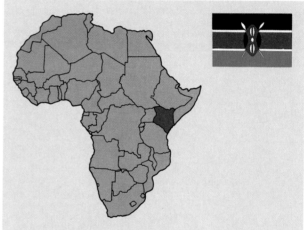

REPUBLIC OF KENYA

LAND. Area: 582,646 km² (224,961 mi²). Capital and largest city: Nairobi (1984 est. pop., 1,103,600).

PEOPLE. Population (1987 est.): 22,400,000; density (1987 est.): 38 persons per km² (100 per mi²). Distribution (1986): 16% urban, 84% rural. Annual growth (1986): 3.9%. Official language: Swahili. Major religions: traditional religions, Protestantism, Anglicanism, Roman Catholicism, Islam.

EDUCATION AND HEALTH. Literacy (1985): 59% of adult population. Universities (1987): 2. Hospital beds (1984): 29,294. Physicians (1984): 2,057. Life expectancy (1980–85): women—54.7; men—51.2. Infant mortality (1986): 76 per 1,000 live births.

ECONOMY. GNP (1985): $5.96 billion; $290 per capita. Labor distribution (1984): services—29%; agriculture—21%; manufacturing—14%; public administration—13%; trade—8%. Foreign trade (1984): imports—$1,549 million; exports—$1,034 million; principal trade partners—United Kingdom, West Germany, United Arab Emirates, Japan. Currency: 1 Kenya shilling = 100 cents.

GOVERNMENT. Type: one-party state. Legislature: National Assembly. Political subdivisions: 7 provinces, Nairobi area.

COMMUNICATIONS. Railroads (1986): 2,654 km (1,649 mi) total. Roads (1984): 54,500 km (33,900 mi) total. Major ports: 1. Major airfields: 2.

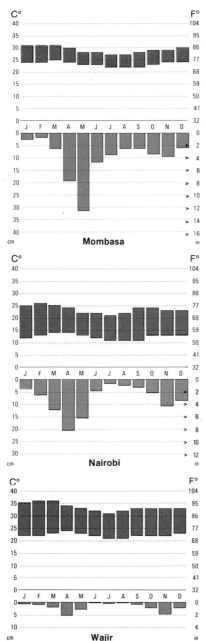

Mombasa

Nairobi

Wajir

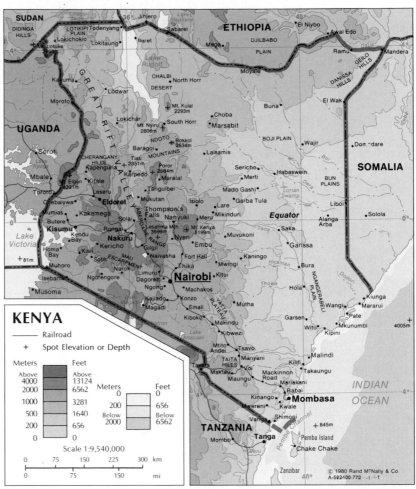

KENYA

— Railroad

+ Spot Elevation or Depth

Meters	Feet
Above 4000	Above 13124
2000	6562
1000	3281
500	1640
200	656
0	0

Meters	Feet
0	0
200	656
Below 2000	Below 6562

Scale 1:9,540,000

0   75   150   225   300 km

0   75   150 mi

© 1980 Rand M⁀Nally & Co.
A-582400-772 -1-1-1

Bars indicate monthly ranges of temperatures (red) and precipitation (blue) in three cities in Kenya. Mombasa, bordering the Indian Ocean, and Nairobi, in the highlands, have a tropical wet-dry climate. Wajir, on the northern plateau, has a steppe climate.

below the surrounding landscape, falls from an elevation of between 900 and 1,800 m (3,000 and 6,000 ft) in the south to 385 m (1,280 ft) in the north near Lake RUDOLF, where it is broader and less well defined.

West of the highlands, elevations drop to about 1,200 m (4,000 ft) in the Lake Victoria Basin, which is part of a broad uplifted area between the eastern and western arms of the Great Rift Valley. The Lake Victoria Basin is composed of the Kericho Highlands in the south; the Nandi and Elgeyo plateaus in the north; the Kano Plain, located at an elevation of 1,130 m (3,720 ft) on Lake VICTORIA's Kavirondo Gulf; and the Kisii and Luyla highlands, located to the south and north, respectively, of the Kavirondo Gulf.

Soils. Thin sandy soils cover about three-fourths of Kenya; because of dry climatic conditions, these soils are unsuitable or marginally suitable for agriculture. By contrast, the soils of the Lake Victoria Basin are generally fertile, well watered, and of high agricultural potential. The rich volcanic soils of the Kenya Highlands are also good for agriculture.

Climate. Kenya's low-lying coastal plain has a humid equatorial type of climate characterized by high humidity and little temperature variation from month to month. Inland the northern region has a semiarid climate with near-desert conditions in the drier areas. The higher inland regions receive more rainfall, and temperatures range from subtropical to temperate depending on elevation. The average annual temperature along the coast is 27° C (80° F), but in the Kenya Highlands it is only 14° C (57° F). The average annual temperature for the Lake Victoria Basin and the Great Rift Valley is 21° C (70° F), and for the low plateaus in the eastern parts of the nation it is 20° C (68° F).

About three-fourths of Kenya is semiarid and receives less than 500 mm (20 in) of rain a year; many northern and eastern sections along the borders with Ethiopia and Somalia receive less than 250 mm (10 in) of rain a year. Rainfall is greater in the narrow coastal belt near Mombasa, where 1,000 to 1,525 mm (40 to 60 in) of rain falls every year, and in the Kenya Highlands, where total precipitation varies from 900 to 1,525 mm (35 to 60 in), according to elevation and exposure to moisture-bearing winds. Most precipitation occurs during the "long rains," the rainy season from March to May.

Drainage. Kenya's principal river is the Tana, which rises in the Highlands and flows southeastward to the Indian Ocean. Western sections of Kenya are drained by the Nzoia and Kuja rivers. Lake Victoria, Lake Rudolf, and other smaller lakes in the Great Rift Valley drain much of the interior of Kenya.

Vegetation and Animal Life. Tropical savanna grasslands cover most of the low-altitude regions of Kenya; the savanna takes on a semidesert aspect in the dry northern areas. Trees increase in size and number in better-watered areas, and dense forests are found along some water courses. In the highlands, savanna predominates at lower altitudes, giving way to forest at altitudes between 1,500 m (5,000 ft) and 3,300 m (11,000 ft).

Herbivores, ranging in size from the small dik-dik to the eland, and carnivores, such as lions, leopards, and cheetahs, are abundant in Kenya, and large areas have been set aside as national parks and wildlife preserves. The principal national parks—where tourists may see a wide range of animals in a natural setting—are Tsavo, Mount Kenya, Amboseli, and Aberdare. Poaching of protected species, however, remains a major problem in Kenya, as in other African nations. Black rhinoceros, elephant, leopard, zebra, and giraffe populations became so reduced in number that a government ban on the sale of skins, tusks, and other hunting trophies went into effect in 1978. In 1985 the government began moving the still-endangered black rhinoceroses into heavily guarded sanctuaries to protect them from poachers.

PEOPLE

Kenya's population is divided by language and culture into more than 40 different ethnic groups. The largest and traditionally the most important group politically is the KIKUYU, which constitutes about 21% of the population and is one of the Bantu-speaking peoples. Other important Bantu peoples are the KAMBA (11%), the Luhya (14%), and the Kisii.

The LUO, a people of Nilotic origin who speak a non-Bantu language, constitute about 13% of the population. The second largest non-Bantu ethnic group comprises several tribes of Nilotic origin who have taken the name Kalenjin to indicate their common identity and cultural origins. The Kalenjin, about 10% of the total population, includes among its members the Kipsigis, Nandi, Elgey, Tugen, and Marakwet. The MASAI, a cattle-herding people of the Great Rift Valley, are also of Nilotic origin. Arabs and SWAHILI, a people of mixed Arab and black African origin, predominate in the coastal areas, and there are small numbers of nomadic Somali and Galla in northern sections of the nation. Several thousand Europeans, most of them of British origin, and Asians live in Nairobi and other cities.

Language and Religion. Swahili, which became the official language of Kenya in 1974, is grammatically a Bantu language, although it is heavily influenced by Arabic and is written with the Roman alphabet. English is also an official language and is still widely used. Bantu and Nilo-Hamitic languages, consisting of numerous dialects associated with individual ethnic groups, predominate in the highlands.

Kenya has no official religion. The majority of Kenyans follow traditional religious practices, but about one-third of the population is Christian. Islam is prevalent in areas of Arab and Asian influence along the coast and among the nomadic tribes of the north.

Demography. The overall population density figure for Kenya obscures the fact that four-fifths of the country is occupied by less than 15% of the population, and the remaining one-fifth is occupied by more than 85% of the total population. The most densely populated areas are the Kenya Highlands and the Lake Victoria Basin, where densities in some places reach 407 per km^2 (1,055 per mi^2). More than eight out of every ten Kenyans live in rural areas, mostly as farmers or pastoralists in dispersed settlements rather than in villages. Some 70% of the urban population is concentrated in the cities of NAIROBI, the capital, and MOMBASA.

Kenya has one of the highest rates of population growth in the world, and it is predicted that the population may reach 120 million by 2050. This rapid rate of increase is due primarily to the high birthrate and low death rate; more than half the population is under the age of 15.

Education and Health. Kenya's educational goal is the provision of 8 years of free primary education for all children, but only about 75% of school-age children in urban areas, and a much lower percentage in rural areas, attend classes. The University of Nairobi (1956) was the only university until 1985, when it was announced that one of its constituent colleges, Kenyatta College, would receive university status.

Rapid population growth has placed great strains on health facilities and other social services, particularly in rural areas of the country.

The Arts. Although black Africa has no ancient traditions of written literature, traditional oral histories of the tribal peoples have had a significant effect on literature in Kenya, as elsewhere in Africa. Among the country's best-known contemporary authors are James NGUGI WA THOINGO, Muga Gicaru, and Josiah Kariuki. The Kamba are known for their wood carvings and the Kisii for soapstone carvings. Drums and plucked instruments provide musical accompaniment to traditional dancing.

The principal cultural institutions are in Nairobi and include the National Museum, which is noted for its collections in paleontology and prehistory, the Kenya Cultural Center, and the National Theater.

Nairobi, the capital of Kenya since 1905, has expanded rapidly since its founding in 1899 and is today the nation's most populous city. Located in the highlands of southeastern Kenya, the city is a trade center for the agricultural produce of the fertile region.

This large plantation on Kenya's coastal strip produces sisal, one of the nation's cash crops. Major agricultural exports, such as coffee, tea, and sugar, once grown exclusively on large estates, are now also produced by smaller, independent farming cooperatives.

ECONOMIC ACTIVITY

The Kenyan economy is predominantly agricultural. Although only about 80% of the land can be cultivated, farming provides about 30% of the gross domestic product, employs more than 80% of the total labor force, and accounts for about 65% of all export earnings. The rapid economic growth of the first postindependence decade later slowed, due chiefly to pressures created by the rapidly growing population. Once able to feed itself and sell surplus to its neighbors, Kenya now imports large quantities of food, particularly wheat. Unemployment is high, especially in urban areas.

Agriculture. About 45% of the area under cultivation is occupied by large farms. These large farms and cooperatives involving about 20% of all smallholders grow cash crops for export markets, and their income from farming is thus subject to the wide price swings associated with world trade in agricultural commodities. Some 20% of the best agricultural land was reserved for whites until 1960; much of this land has since been redistributed to Africans. About 60% of all smallholders are subsistence farmers. Population growth and drought have led to soil erosion on marginal lands.

Kenya's altitudinal and climatic differences allow for cultivation of a wide variety of subtropical and temperate crops. The most valuable cash crop is coffee, which is grown mainly in the Kenya Highlands on both large and small farms. Tea is the other principal cash crop grown in the highlands, in areas where conditions are unsuitable for coffee; it is the nation's second most valuable crop. Tea and coffee together accounted for 41% of all foreign exchange earnings in 1984. Corn (the chief subsistence crop), pyrethrum, and wheat are also grown in the highlands. Kenya is the world's leading producer of pyrethrum extract, which is used in the manufacture of pesticides. The principal crops grown on the subtropical coastal lowlands are sisal, cashew nuts, sugar cane, cotton, and rice. Stock raising is the chief activity in the three-fourths of Kenya that is too dry for cultivation.

Forestry and Fishing. Forests cover only about 4% of the total land area and are located mostly on the slopes of Mount Kenya, the Aberdare Range, Mount ELGON, and other high areas. In 1984, Kenya produced 29,330,000 m³ (1,035,780,00 ft³) of roundwood, mostly softwoods used domestically for fuel. Fishing is locally important along the shores of Lake Victoria, Lake Rudolf, and the Indian Ocean.

Manufacturing and Energy. After independence Kenya pursued a policy of fast growth and industrialization aimed at meeting domestic demand for industrial products and providing an exportable surplus. Although the growth of the industrial sector has slowed, Kenya is the most highly industrialized nation in East Africa. Industries include agricultural processing plants, a petroleum refinery at Mombasa, a pulp and paper mill at Webuye, and several textile and automobile assembly plants. Among the chief manufactured products are processed foods, textiles and clothing, and cement.

Lake Nakuru, a shallow saline lake located in the Great Rift Valley of East Africa, is a noted refuge for such species of waterfowl as the flamingo, which nests there in huge flocks. Lake Nakuru National Park is one of Kenya's many preserves.

Kenya has no coal or petroleum. There are hydroelectric plants along the Tano River and an oil-fired plant on the coast. About 10% of the nation's power supply is imported from Owen Falls Dam in Uganda. A geothermal plant, the first in Africa, began operation near Lake Naivasha in 1981.

Tourism. With its many national parks and wildlife preserves and the added attractions of the Indian Ocean coast, Kenya draws more visitors than any other country in tropical Africa. Tourism is the second largest foreign-exchange earner.

Transportation and Trade. In 1967, Kenya, Tanzania, and Uganda formed the East African Community (EAC). By 1977, however, the organization's once-flourishing customs unit, common market, and joint postal, air, rail, and telecommunications systems had collapsed due to political and economic differences between the three countries. Kenya, which took control of its railways and harbors in 1976 and its airways in 1977, suffered from the loss of the regional trade and transportation network in which it had provided the larger share of manufactured goods and services. In 1983 agreement was reached on the disposition of EAC assets and liabilities, and the border between Kenya and Tanzania, closed in 1977, was reopened.

Kenya's principal exports are primarily agricultural products, as in the colonial period, but processed industrial goods are also economically important. In 1983 the principal exports were coffee, which accounted for 25% of all exports by value; tea, 20%; refined petroleum products, 19%; vegetables and fruit, 9%; and cement, 4%. The leading imports were petroleum, 31%; machinery and transportation equipment, 23%; and chemicals, 14%. Since the early 1970s Kenya has generally had an unfavorable balance of trade and has borrowed to finance food imports for the growing urban population. A shortage of foreign exchange has led to restrictions on the import of raw materials and equipment by industry.

GOVERNMENT

Independence was achieved on Dec. 12, 1963, and in 1964, Kenya became a republic within the British Commonwealth of Nations. The president leads the nation; Daniel Arap MOI was elected to this office in 1978. Kenya has a unicameral National Assembly consisting of 158 members who are elected by universal adult suffrage at least once every 5 years and 14 members appointed by the president. Kenya effectively became a one-party state of the Kenya African National Union (KANU) in 1964, when the Kenya African Democratic Union (KADU) joined KANU. Another party, the Kenya People's Union (KPU), was proscribed in 1969. In 1982 the constitution was changed to legalize Kenya's status as a one-party state.

HISTORY

Bantu tribes are believed to have migrated eastward and southward across the continent from West Africa and to have entered Kenya about 1,000 years ago. The Nilotic peoples began to enter from the north at about the end of the 15th century and were still migrating when the Europeans arrived. Arabs dominated the coastal areas from the 7th century until the Portuguese took possession of the coast following Vasco da GAMA's visit to Mombasa in 1498 and reestablished their control after the Portuguese were ousted in 1729. From then until 1963 the Arabs retained nominal control of the coastal regions, first as part of the sultanate of Muscat (Oman) and after 1861, when the Muscat empire was divided, as part of the sultanate of Zanzibar.

Modern European interest in Kenya began in the 1850s, when Europeans explored the interior in search of the source of the Nile and Christian missionaries began their efforts to convert the inhabitants and to end the Arabs' flourishing trade in slaves. By 1855 there were about 300 missionaries in East Africa, and the slave trade was ended by the sultan in 1873. In 1885, Karl Peters received a charter for his German East Africa Company and initiated a scramble among the European nations to establish colonies in East Africa. The Anglo-German agreements of 1886 recognized the sultan's authority over the coastal areas and placed the southern coastal strip (now Tanzania) in the German sphere of influence and the northern coastal strip (now Kenya) in the British sphere of influence. In 1887 the sultan leased the northern coastal strip to the Imperial British East Africa Company, and when that company was dissolved in 1895 the British government established the East Africa Protectorate. The railroad from Mombasa to Nairobi and Lake Victoria was built in the last decade of the 19th century, and as white settlers began to enter Kenya, large areas of the Kenya Highlands—later known as the White Highlands—were subsequently alienated from the Africans and reserved for white-only settlement. In 1920 the interior regions were organized as the British crown colony of Kenya while the coastal strip remained a British protectorate over lands nominally ruled by the sultan of Zanzibar.

The African population did not submit easily to British authority, and there were countless clashes between the two groups. The British appointed African chiefs and village headmen to carry out some administrative duties, but efforts to enlist black leaders into legislative bodies met with little success. An educated African elite began to emerge, however, from the schools established primarily by the Christian missionaries, and in 1944 black Kenyans, especially Kikuyu, concerned about their political future formed the Kenya African Union (KAU), which 3 years later came under the leadership of Jomo KENYATTA. In the early 1950s open revolt against the British took the form of a terrorist campaign against the settlers by the so-called MAU MAU movement. Jomo Kenyatta was imprisoned in 1953, but the terrorism continued and a state of emergency was in effect from 1952 to 1960.

In 1960 a constitutional change replaced the system of multiracial representation in the government with one of majority rule. Kenyatta was freed in 1961 and in May 1963 led the Kenya African National Union (KANU) in a decisive victory at the polls, thereby establishing black control of the government and paving the way for independence. Kenya became internally self-governing on June 1, 1963, and full independence was achieved on Dec. 12, 1963, with Jomo Kenyatta as the first prime minister. On Dec. 12, 1964, Kenya became a republic and Kenyatta the first president. Kenyatta remained head of the highly centralized government until his death in August 1978. He was succeeded by his vice-president, Daniel arap MOI, a member of the Kalenjin minority. Moi, who ran unopposed in the 1979 presidential elections, gradually reduced Kikuyu dominance of political life.

Since independence Kenya has followed a policy of nonalignment with a definite westward tilt. Kenya has been unusual among African nations in that the highly nationalistic and socialistic route to economic development has been shunned, and private ownership and investment in land and industry actively encouraged. By the early 1980s, however, Kenya's once-flourishing economy was no longer able to keep pace with rapid population growth. Rural poverty and poor nutrition were widespread, and food shortages and unemployment led to unrest in urban areas. In 1982 economic woes and opposition to the legalization of the one-party state sparked an attempted coup against Kenya's government—the first in 19 years. Moi cracked down on dissent and was reelected in 1983 and 1988. He stressed the role of foreign investment and the private sector in improving the economy, but he faced growing opposition from students and the underground Mwakenya movement.   RONALD D. GARST

Bibliography: American University, *Kenya: A Country Study* (1984); Arnold, G., *Modern Kenya* (1981); Fedders, A., and Salvadori, C., *Peoples and Cultures of Kenya* (1980); Gertzel, C., *The Politics of Independent Kenya* (1970); Hazelwood, A., *The Economy of Kenya* (1979); Huxley, E., and Perham, M., *Race and Politics in Kenya* (1956; repr. 1975); Kitching, G., *Class and Economic Change in Kenya* (1980); Knappert, J., *East Africa* (1987); Leys, N., *Kenya*, 4th ed. (1973); Miller, N., *Kenya* (1984); Spenser, J., *The Kenya African Union: 1944–1953* (1985).

Kenya, Mount

Mount Kenya, an extinct volcano in central Kenya, with an elevation of 5,199 m (17,058 ft), is Africa's second highest mountain. The crater is eroded and contains several small receding glaciers. Mount Kenya National Park includes the area above 3,290 m (10,800 ft) and most of the forested (cedar, bamboo) slopes below. The summit was first reached (1899) by the party of the British geographer Sir Halford Mackinder.

Kenyatta, Jomo   [ken-yah'-tuh, joh'-moh]

Jomo Kenyatta (Kamau wa Ngengi), b. *c.*1891, d. Aug. 22, 1978, was the leader of Kenya's struggle for national independence and president of the Republic of Kenya from 1964 until his death. A Kikuyu, he was born in the Kikuyu tribal area

Jomo Kenyatta, an African nationalist and Kenyan political leader, became the first prime minister (1963) and, later, first president (1964) of Kenya following its establishment as a state independent of Great Britain. Kenyatta, following a nominal "nonalignment" policy in international affairs, developed a strong central government and contributed greatly to Kenya's stability.

near Nairobi and educated at a Church of Scotland mission school. In 1928 he became general secretary of the Kikuyu Central Association (KCA) and pressed for the return of land taken by British settlers. In 1931 he went to London to represent the KCA at the Colonial Office and stayed there for 15 years. He shared an apartment with the actor Paul Robeson, appeared in the 1935 film *Sanders of the River*, and studied anthropology at the London School of Economics under Bronislaw Malinowski. In 1938 he published an anthropological study, *Facing Mount Kenya*. He also made two trips to Moscow, studying at the Lenin School.

Kenyatta returned to Kenya in 1946 to fight for *uhuru* (independence). After the bloody MAU MAU rebellion broke out, he was imprisoned in 1952 as the leader, a charge which he always denied. He was released in 1961 and became president of the opposition Kenya African Nationalist Union (KANU). With KANU's electoral victory in 1963 he became the first prime minister of self-governing Kenya and the president of the Republic of Kenya in 1964. As Kenya's unchallenged ruler (known to his people as *Mzee*, or the "old man"), he maintained political stability, a fairly free press, pro-Western policies, and a prosperous mixed economy. He encouraged foreign private investment and greatly advanced public education and health. Kenya, however, remained a one-party state with significant tribal divisions and rural poverty, and Kenyatta was unable to control corruption, especially in his own family. He was succeeded as president by Daniel Arap Moi.   K. M. SMOGORZEWSKI

Bibliography: Arnold, Guy, *Kenyatta and the Politics of Kenya* (1974); Delf, George, *Jomo Kenyatta* (1961; repr. 1975); Howarth, Anthony, *Kenyatta; A Photographic Biography* (1967); Kenyatta, Jomo, *Suffering Without Bitterness* (1968); Murray-Brown, Jeremy, *Kenyatta* (1973).

Kenyon, Dame Kathleen   [ken'-yuhn]

British archaeologist Kathleen Mary Kenyon, b. Jan. 5, 1906, d. Aug. 24, 1978, conducted extensive excavations at Jericho, Jerusalem, and other sites in the Near East. While excavating the biblical site of JERICHO, she also explored the early occupation levels of the site, which include remains of farming cultures dating from more than 9,000 years ago. Kenyon's writings include *Digging up Jericho* (1957) and *Archaeology in the Holy Land* (1960; 3d ed., 1970).   STEPHEN KOWALEWSKI

Kenzan

Ogata Kenzan, 1663–1743, a master ceramicist, firmly established pottery as one of Japan's major art forms. After a comfortable and cultivated youth as the son of a wealthy clothier in Kyoto, he opened (1699) his own kiln at Narutaki, where he produced pottery that until 1701 was decorated by his brother, the painter KORIN. From the location of the kiln in the northwest hills of Kyoto, he took the name Kenzan, or Northwest Mountain.

Along with works produced in Edo (modern Tokyo) in his later years, Kenzan's Narutaki ceramics were highly valued for their superbly executed decorative designs, which were inspired by the paintings of his brother. Kenzan also produced lacquer ware and small paintings that reflected his interests in literature, calligraphy, and Zen. His assimilation of decorative painting into the potter's craft set a trend in Japanese ceramics that still thrives today.   BARBARA BRENNAN FORD

Bibliography: Sato, Masahiko, *Kyoto Ceramics*, trans. by A. O. Towle and U. P. Coolige (1973).

Kepes, Gyorgy   [kep'-ish]

Gyorgy Kepes, b. Selyp, Hungary, Oct. 4, 1906, is an influential designer, painter, photographer, and art educator. Already in the 1920s he was experimenting with photograms, abstract images of objects recorded directly on photosensitive paper without a camera. A cofounder (1937) with László Moholy-Nagy of the New Bauhaus in Chicago, he later became professor of visual design and director of the Center for Advanced Visual Studies at Massachusetts Institute of Technol-

ogy. His light workshop emphasized the emotional impact of light and color, especially in abstract photography, as in his untitled cliché verre (*c.*1943) or *Light Texture* (1950). *The Language of Vision* (1944) and *Structure in Art and Science* (1965) are two of his numerous theoretical works.

                                    MELINDA BOYD PARSONS

Bibliography: Benthall, J., "Kepes's Center at M.I.T.," *Art International*, January 1975; Pollack, Peter, *The Picture History of Photography* (1969).

Kepler, Johannes   [kep'-lur]

Johannes Kepler, a German mathematician, formulated the three laws of planetary motion that bear his name by using the astronomical observations recorded by Tycho Brahe, for whom he worked briefly. Kepler was instrumental in the development of early telescopes. He invented the convex eyepiece, which allowed an expanded field of vision, and discovered a means of determining the magnifying power of lenses.

The German astronomer Johannes Kepler, b. Dec. 27, 1571, d. Nov. 15, 1630, was the first strong supporter of the heliocentric theory of COPERNICUS and the discoverer of the three laws of planetary motion. He attended seminaries at Adelberg and Maulbronn before studying theology, philosophy, and mathematics at the University of Tübingen. At Tübingen, Kepler's scientific ability attracted the notice of the astronomer Michael Maestlin. Through Maestlin, Kepler became a supporter of the Copernican theory, although his teacher continued to expound officially the old Ptolemaic system. Kepler had planned to enter religious life, but he accepted a chair in mathematics and astronomy at Graz.

At the age of 24, Kepler published *Mysterium cosmographicum* (Cosmographic Mystery, 1596), in which he defended the Copernican theory and described his ideas on the structure of the planetary system. Influenced by the Pythagoreans, Kepler viewed the universe as being governed by geometric relationships that conform to the inscribed and circumscribed circles of the five regular polygons.

Although he was not a Copernican himself, Tycho BRAHE, the mathematician at the court of Emperor Rudolph II at Prague, was so impressed with Kepler's work that in 1600 he invited Kepler to come to Prague as his assistant. Confronted with the Catholic persecution of the Protestant minority in Graz, Kepler gladly accepted. When Brahe died the following year, Kepler was appointed his successor and thus inherited Brahe's scientific legacy.

This legacy included many accurate positional determinations of the planets, especially those of Mars. Kepler now embarked on an intensive study of the true orbits of the planets. Abandoning the ancient belief that the planets must move in perfect circles, Kepler concentrated on Mars. He proved that the orbit of Mars is an ellipse, with the Sun occupying one of its two foci. This, the first of Kepler's laws of planetary motion, appeared in *Astronomia nova* (New Astronomy) in 1609, with the second "law of areas" governing planetary velocity.

Always guided by the concept of beauty in the structure of the universe, and specifically by a theory of harmony in geometric figures, numbers, and music, Kepler, in his *Harmonices mundi* (Harmonies of the World, 1619), announced his third law—a relationship between the orbital periods and the distances of the planets from the Sun. His belief that the Sun regulates the velocity of the planets was a milestone in scientific thought, laying the foundation for Newton's theory of universal gravitation.

Among Kepler's numerous scientific contributions are an influential treatise on the theory of optics (1604), a treatise on optics as applied to telescope lenses (1611), a work offering physical explanations of the appearance of a nova in 1604, and an enthusiastic acceptance of and elaboration on Galileo's observations with a telescope (1610). His *Epitome astronomiae Copernicanae* (Introduction to Copernican Astronomy, 1618–21) became one of the most widely read treatises on astronomy in Europe. Kepler's last great work, known as the *Rudolphine Tables* (1627), was a widely used compilation of accurate tables of planetary motion.

The posthumous *Somnium* (Dream, 1634), on which Kepler labored until shortly before his death, is indicative of his fertile mind. In this work, Kepler describes a journey to the Moon and discusses the existence of lunar inhabitants. A crucial link between the thought of Copernicus and that of Newton, Kepler was an important figure in the 17th-century scientific revolution.   STEVEN J. DICK

Bibliography: Beer, Arthur, ed., *Kepler* (1974); Caspar, Max, *Kepler*, trans. by C. D. Hellmann (1959; repr. 1962); Jardine, Nicholas, *The Birth of History and Philosophy of Science: Kepler's "A Defense of Tycho Against Ursus" with Essays on its Provenance and Significance* (1984); Koestler, Arthur, *The Watershed* (1960); Koyré, Alexander, *The Astronomical Revolution*, trans. by R. E. Madder (1961).

Kepler's laws   [kep'-lurz]

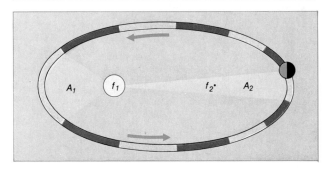

Johannes Kepler was the first to describe the planetary orbits as ellipses with the Sun at one of the two focal points (f_1 and f_2). Although a planet's speed varies, the line joining the Sun and a planet sweeps out equal areas (A_1 and A_2) in equal time periods, represented by the colored section of the orbit.

Formulated by the German astronomer Johannes Kepler, Kepler's laws of planetary motion describe the shape of the orbit, the velocities, and the distances of the planets with respect to the Sun. The laws were announced after Kepler's long and elaborate analysis of Tycho BRAHE's observations of the planets; they may be stated as follows: (1) the planets move in ellipses with the Sun at one focus; (2) the line joining the Sun and a planet sweeps out equal areas in equal intervals of time; (3) the square of the time of revolution of a planet divided by the cube of its mean distance from the Sun gives a number that is the same for all the planets. The second law, enunciated (1609) along with the first law, is known as the law of areas; the third law, announced in 1619, is sometimes referred to as the harmonic law.

Kepler's laws were generalized and corrected by Sir Isaac Newton so that they apply to any motion associated with the so-called two-body problem. In this problem two bodies are idealized as point masses, or small rigid spheres, and the motion of one about the other is subject to Newtonian mechanics (see LAWS OF MOTION) and to Newton's law of GRAVITATION; no force other than the mutual gravitational attraction is considered. The possible forms of motion in this problem are now called Keplerian motion.

Kepler's second law required no amendment by Newton; in the generalized form of the first law, however, orbits can be ellipses, parabolas, or hyperbolas. The amended third law applies only to elliptic orbits. Let *a* be the semimajor axis of the orbit of one body about the other, and *P* its period; let m_1 and m_2 be the masses of the two bodies and *G* the constant of gravitation. Then $P^2/a^3 = \pi G (m_1 + m_2)$.

The amended laws can be applied to a satellite revolving around a planet or to two stars that form a binary system (see BINARY STARS). The amended third law is important in determining the masses of binary stars.   J. M. A. DANBY

Bibliography: Abell, G. O., *Exploration of the Universe*, 4th ed. (1982); Pasachoff, J. M., and Kutner, M. L., *Contemporary Astronomy*, 3d ed. (1985); Roy, A. E., *Orbital Motion*, 2d ed. (1982).

kepone: see POLLUTANTS, CHEMICAL.

Keppel, Francis   [kep'-ul]

Francis Keppel, b. New York City, Apr. 16, 1916, d. Feb. 19, 1990, was an American educator. As dean of Harvard's Graduate School of Education (1948–62), he quadrupled the enrollment and raised the school to a position of national leadership. He redesigned the Master of Arts in Teaching (MAT) degree and expanded the program. He created the School and University Program for Research and Development (SUPRAD), which conducted pilot projects on topics such as team teaching and the use of teaching machines. Keppel was U.S. Commissioner of Education from 1962 to 1965, and he worked for greater federal support of education until leaving government in 1966 to direct private programs in educational development. He later headed (1966–74) the General Learning Corporation and the education program of the Aspen Institute for Humanistic Studies (1974–84), both in New York City.

Kerala   [ker'-uh-luh]

Kerala, a state on the Arabian Sea in southwestern India, is bordered on the north by Karnataka and on the east by Tamil Nadu. Kerala has a population of 25,453,680 (1981) and an area of 38,855 km^2 (15,005 mi^2); it thus has the highest population density in the country: 655 persons per km^2 (1,696 per mi^2). The capital is Trivandrum, and the leading ports are COCHIN and Quilon. Most of the population speaks Malayalam, the official language, and most are Hindus. Kerala has a large and ancient Christian community (21%; see MALABAR CHRISTIANS), as well as a substantial Muslim minority (20%).

The land rises from the 580-km-long (360-mi) Malabar Coast to an alluvial plain, where crops of rice, coconuts, cassava, and cashew nuts are grown. To the east, tea, rubber, coffee, and pepper plantations extend in the foothills of the Western GHATS. The mountains have forests of teak, ebony, and rosewood and a wide variety of wildlife.

Kerala became a powerful state in the 9th century. Its history from the 15th to the 20th century was marked by Arab, Portuguese, Dutch, and British intervention. In the state elections of 1957, the Communist party won a majority, giving Kerala the first Communist government in the country. The Communists have participated in several governments since.

keratin   [kair'-uh-tin]

A hard PROTEIN substance, keratin is a major structural material of the skin, hair, nails, claws, feathers, hooves, scales, and horns of animals. Hair and nails are almost totally keratin. Because of the presence of keratin, the outermost layer of mammals' skin is waterproof; this layer is designated the *stratum corneum*, or horny layer. The keratin molecule is a rigid, cylinder-shaped helix.

Kerensky, Aleksandr Fyodorovich   [kuh-ren'-skee, uhl-yik-sahn'-dur fyoh'-dor-uh-vich]

Aleksandr Kerensky, b. Apr. 22 (N.S.), 1881, d. June 11, 1970, headed the Russian provisional government from July to October 1917, during the interim between the overthrow of the tsar and the Bolshevik Revolution. A lawyer and a democratic moderate, Kerensky joined the Socialist Revolutionary party in 1905 and was elected to the fourth DUMA in 1912. As premier, Kerensky was personally identified with Russia's abortive military offensive in World War I, a fact that further weakened his already shaky coalition government. In a vain effort to maintain control, Kerensky ordered V. I. LENIN's arrest as well as that of the right-wing general Lavr KORNILOV. Beleaguered by radicals and reactionaries alike, he fled Russia in October. He lived in Paris until 1940, after which he settled in New York City. WILLIAM G. ROSENBERG

Bibliography: Kerensky, A. F., *Prelude to Bolshevism: The Kornilov Revolt* (1919), *The Catastrophe* (1927), *The Crucifixion of Liberty* (1934), and *Russia and History's Turning Point* (1965); Whitman, Alden, *The Obituary Book* (1971).

Kerguelen cabbage   [kur'-guh-lin]

Kerguelen cabbage is a herbaceous plant, *Pringlea antiscorbutica,* of the mustard family, Cruciferae. It is found on Kerguelen and Crozet islands in the southern Indian Ocean, near Antarctica. The plant has a cabbagelike head and produces a pungent essential oil. It may be eaten as a cooked vegetable. Apparently because these small, windy islands have no flying insects, the flowers of the Kerguelen cabbage have been modified for pollination by wind. Petals, which may obstruct the wind, are usually lacking and, when present, are behind the pollen-bearing anthers.

kermes   [kur'-meez]

Kermes is a genus of oak-infesting scale insects in the family Kermidae, order Homoptera. The bright red dye obtained from the dried bodies of these insects is also called kermes. Adult females are legless and wingless and are covered by a nearly spherical protective scale resembling a tiny gall. Males look like small gnats. JAMES R. BAKER

Kern, Jerome

Jerome David Kern, b. Jan. 27, 1885, d. Nov. 11, 1945, was one of the most innovative composers for the American musical theater. His *Show Boat* (1927), with book and lyrics by Oscar Hammerstein II, marked the beginnings of the musical play as distinguished from musical comedy. Among Kern's other successful musicals were *Sally* (1920), *Music in the Air* (1932), and *Roberta* (1933). He received Oscars for his film songs "The Way You Look Tonight" and "The Last Time I Saw Paris." His other songs include the classic "Ol' Man River," "Smoke Gets in Your Eyes," and "All the Things You Are." DAVID EWEN

Bibliography: Ewen, David, *The World of Jerome Kern* (1960); Freedland, Michael, *Jerome Kern* (1978).

kerosene   [kair'-uh-seen]

Kerosene, also known as paraffin oil or coal oil, is a liquid hydrocarbon fuel commonly obtained from the fractional distillation of PETROLEUM. Originally used as a fuel for lamps, kerosene is now used primarily as a heating fuel, especially in domestic heating systems, and as an aviation fuel. It is also used as a solvent and thinner.

The quality of kerosene is determined by its burning properties, which depend on the mixture of components present in the particular sample. The number of carbon atoms in the molecules of these components may vary from 9 to 16. The important properties of kerosene are represented by two parameters: the smoke point, which is determined by burning kerosene in a standard wick-fed lamp and measuring in millimeters the height of the flame at which it starts to smoke, and the char value, which is a measure of the tendency to form carbon deposits when burned. Both of these properties can be improved by removing aromatic hydrocarbons from the kerosene either by solvent extraction with liquid sulfur dioxide or by acid treatment.

Because kerosene has a high boiling point (150–300° C/

300–570° F), it shows no tendency to evaporate at room temperature and must therefore be encouraged to vaporize for most efficient combustion.

Stringent constraints are placed on the performance of kerosene when it is used as a fuel for aviation gas turbine engines. The most important constraints relate to thermal stability, so that the fuel can be heated to relatively high temperatures without leaving gummy deposits in the fuel system. J. T. McMULLAN

Kerouac, Jack   [kair'-oo-ak]

Jack Kerouac, a leading author and theorist of the beat generation, epitomized the questioning, rebellious spirit of American youth during the 1950s. On the Road (1957), a novel based on Kerouac's adventures while traveling through the United States, is considered a major document of beat-generation thinking and writing.

The American writer Jack Kerouac, b. Jean Louis Kerouac, Lowell, Mass., Mar. 12, 1922, d. Oct. 21, 1969, became the leading chronicler of the beat generation, a term that he coined to label a social and literary movement in the 1950s. After studying briefly at Columbia University, he achieved fame with his spontaneous and unconventional prose, particularly the novel *On the Road* (1957). After the success of this work Kerouac produced a series of thematically and structurally similar novels, including *The Dharma Bums* and *The Subterraneans* (both 1958), *Doctor Sax* (1959), *Lonesome Traveler* (1960), and *Big Sur* (1962). His loosely structured, autobiographical works reflect a peripatetic life, with warm but stormy relationships and a deep social disillusionment assuaged by drugs, alcohol, mysticism, and biting humor.

Bibliography: Charters, Ann, *Kerouac: A Biography* (1973); Gifford, Barry, and Lee, Lawrence, *Jack's Book: An Oral Biography of Jack Kerouac* (1978); Jarvis, Charles E., *Visions of Kerouac* (1975); Tytell, *Naked Angels: The Lives and Literature of the Beat Generation* (1976).

Kerr, Clark   [kur]

Clark Kerr, b. Stony Creek, Pa., May 17, 1911, has been a labor economist, an arbitrator, a university official, and an advisor on higher education. He began arbitrating labor disputes in 1942 and, over the next few decades, became one of the busiest arbitrators in the United States. In 1945 he joined the faculty of the University of California at Berkeley and also became director of the Institute of Industrial Relations.

In 1949, as head of the Berkeley Academic Senate committee on tenure, he vigorously protested the board of regents' policy requiring special loyalty oaths from university teachers. He was named the first chancellor of the Berkeley campus in 1952 and was the president of the University of California (1958–67). As president he helped arrange a compromise solution to disputes between the state colleges and the university. He was president when the Berkeley Free Speech Movement inaugurated a period of turbulent and controversial student-

Clark Kerr, an influential American educator, oversaw the expansion and specialization of the state university system during his nine years as president of the University of California. Formerly an extremely successful arbitrator, he has written numerous works on both labor relations and higher education.

administration relations in the mid-1960s. From 1967 to 1973 he was chairman of the Carnegie Foundation Commission on Higher Education, and since 1974 he has been chairman of the Carnegie Council Policy Studies in Higher Education.

Kerr, Sir John Robert   [kar]

Sir John Robert Kerr, b. Sept. 24, 1914, was governor general of Australia from 1974 to 1977. Previously he had been a lawyer and judge, serving (1972–74) as chief justice of the supreme court of New South Wales. As governor general, because of a parliamentary deadlock, he took the unprecedented and controversial step of dismissing Prime Minister Gough WHITLAM's Labor government and dissolving Parliament in 1975.   K. M. SMOGORZEWSKI

Kerry

Kerry, a county in southwestern Ireland in MUNSTER province, is bounded by the Atlantic Ocean on the west and south and the River SHANNON on the north. It has an area of 4,700 km² (1,815 mi²) and a population of 122,770 (1981). Tralee is the county seat. Three long, mountainous peninsulas give the coastline a rugged and picturesque appearance. Farming, stock breeding, and fishing are the major occupations. Tourism is also important because of Kerry's beautiful scenery, including·Macgillicuddy's Reeks, Ireland's highest mountains, and the lovely lakes of KILLARNEY. The area was ruled by the Fitzgeralds from the 13th century until the 16th century, when it became part of the Munster plantation.

Kerry blue terrier

The Kerry blue terrier, a native of Ireland, has apparently been known in County Kerry, southwestern Ireland, at least since

The Kerry blue terrier, declared the national dog of Ireland, originated in County Kerry, Ireland, where it was used for herding, hunting, retrieving, and killing vermin and as a watchdog and pet.

the mid–19th century. The breed was not officially recognized until the 20th century—in 1922 by the English Kennel Club and in 1924 by the American Kennel Club. The Kerry, as its name indicates, is a ''blue'' dog, ranging from deep slate to light gray; it is born black, but solid black is unacceptable in the show ring. A medium-sized and long-legged terrier, it reaches 50 cm (19.5 in) high at the shoulder, and about 18 kg (40 lb) in weight. Its coat is dense, abundant, wavy, soft, and silky.   JOHN MANDEVILLE

Bibliography: Izant, Edith, *Your Kerry Blue Terrier* (1978).

Kertész, André   [kair'-tesh]

André Kertész, b. Budapest, Hungary, July 2, 1894, d. Sept. 27, 1985, was one of the inventors of modern PHOTOJOURNALISM. He moved to Paris in 1925 and 3 years later purchased a Leica miniature camera that enabled him to work with both speed and discretion. Kertész contributed photographs to the first French picture magazines, including *Vu,* where he formulated and edited his own stories. His ability to expose the significant details and communicate the essence of a subject directed the future trend of journalistic photography.

In the United States from 1936, Kertész earned a living as a free-lance magazine photographer until 1962, when he became sufficiently prosperous to photograph, for his own interest, subjects related to his early work. His best-known images are of ordinary places; in these, irrational elements are exposed so as to obtain a suddenly witty and unfamiliar situation. His photographs can be seen in *Paris Vu Par André Kertész* (1934) and *André Kertész: Sixty Years of Photography, 1912–1972* (1972).   ELIZABETH POLLOCK

Bibliography: Kismark, Carole, *André Kertész* (1977).

The Hungarian photographer André Kertész, a pioneer in modern photojournalism, took this photograph called Broken Bench *in New York City in 1962. The depiction of a lone man confronting a broken bench conveys a moment of sudden, humorously disconcerting experience with fresh immediacy and wit typical of Kertész's work.*

Kerwin, Joseph

The American astronaut Joseph Peter Kerwin, b. Oak Park, Ill., Feb. 19, 1932, was the first U.S. physician to fly in space. He received his medical degree from Northwestern University Medical School in 1957. After his internship he trained as a Navy flight surgeon.

Kerwin was selected with the first group of scientist-astronauts in 1965. As science pilot of SKYLAB II (the first manned Skylab), he spent 28 days observing crew physiology during extended zero gravity in May and June 1973. He was later placed in charge of the mission specialist group of astronauts at Johnson Space Center in Houston, Tex.   DAVID DOOLING

Kerwin, Patrick

Patrick Kerwin, b. Sarnia, Ontario, Oct. 25, 1889, d. Feb. 2, 1963, was chief justice of the Supreme Court of Canada from

1954 to 1963. A well-known criminal lawyer, he was appointed to the Ontario Supreme Court in 1932 and became a justice of the Canadian Supreme Court in 1935.

Kesey, Ken   [kee'-zee]

Ken Kesey, an American writer and a spokesman for the counterculture of the 1960s, achieved fame with his book One Flew over the Cuckoo's Nest *(1962), which was made into a Broadway play and film. His more ambitious novel,* Sometimes a Great Notion *(1964), received critical acclaim, and his life with the Merry Pranksters was celebrated in Tom Wolfe's book* The Electric Kool-Aid Acid Test *(1968).*

The novelist and screenwriter Ken Kesey, b. La Junta, Colo., Sept. 17, 1935, is best known for his first novel, ONE FLEW OVER THE CUCKOO'S NEST (1962; film, 1975), which is based partly on his experience as a hospital ward attendant. After writing *Sometimes a Great Notion* (1964; film, 1971), a saga of the Northwest, Kesey achieved notoriety as an LSD advocate and member of the Merry Pranksters, a group that toured the country in a converted school bus. *Demon Box* (1986) is a mixture of essays and short stories.

Kesselring, Albert   [kes'-ul-ring, ahl'-bairt]

Albert Kesselring, b. Nov. 20, 1885, d. July 16, 1960, was one of the leading German generals in World War II. After commanding air force operations in the conquest of Poland (1939) and the invasion of the Low Countries and France (1940), he was promoted to field marshal (June 1940). He then commanded the Luftwaffe in the Battle of Britain (August–October 1940) and on the central sector of the Russian front (1941–42). Sent to Italy, he became commander in chief of the German forces there in 1943. In this capacity he was responsible for the massacre of 335 Italian hostages in the Ardeatine Caves near Rome in 1944. In March 1945, Kesselring became supreme German commander on the Western front. He was sentenced to death by a British military court in 1947, a sentence that was later commuted to life imprisonment. In 1952, Kesselring was released because of ill health.

Bibliography: Kesselring, Albert, *Kesselring: A Soldier's Record,* trans. by Lynton Hudson (1954).

kestrel: SEE FALCON.

ketone   [kee'-tohn]

Ketones are organic compounds that contain a carbonyl group (an oxygen atom doubly bonded to a carbon atom) bonded to two other organic groups. Closely related are ALDEHYDES, in which the carbonyl group is bonded to one organic group and one hydrogen atom. Ketones are commonly named by appending the suffix *-one* to a descriptive prefix, or by naming the groups attached to the carbonyl carbon atom. Thus the mixed ketone called methyl ethyl ketone ($CH_3COCH_2CH_3$) is also called butanone.

The first and simplest member of the ketone series, CH_3COCH_3, has the common name ACETONE. Acetone is manufactured industrially from isopropyl alcohol. It is also a by-product of the synthesis of phenol (carbolic acid) from cumene. Acetone is by far the most important industrial ketone. More than one million U.S. tons of acetone are produced each year in the United States. Half of this amount is used for the synthesis of other chemicals such as methyl isobutyl ketone and methyl methacrylate. Methyl isobutyl ketone is used as a solvent for paints and lacquers. Polymerization of methyl methacrylate using peroxide initiators gives a strong, highly transparent, thermoplastic solid polymer that is sold under such trade names as Lucite and Plexiglas.

In the laboratory, ketones are prepared by oxidizing secondary alcohols with chromic oxide (CrO_3) or sodium dichromate ($Na_2Cr_2O_7$) in dilute sulfuric acid (H_2SO_4).

$$CH_3—\underset{\underset{\text{2-butanol}}{OH}}{\overset{|}{CH}}—CH_2CH_3 \quad \xrightarrow[H_2SO_4]{Na_2Cr_2O_7} \quad CH_3—\underset{\underset{\text{butanone}}{O}}{\overset{\|}{C}}—CH_2CH_3$$

Methyl ketones can be made from acetylenes by the mercuric sulfate catalyzed addition of water. Mixed ketones can be prepared by the reaction of dialkyl cadmium reagents with carboxylic acid chlorides.

One of the characteristic reactions of ketones is the addition of various reagents to the atoms of the double bond. For example, acetone adds hydrogen cyanide (HCN) to form a cyanohydrin.

The blood ketone level in humans, normally low, increases in response to starvation, diabetes mellitus, or a high-fat, low-carbohydrate diet. This condition is known as ketosis. Dietary changes and, in diabetes, the administration of insulin, usually correct the condition.   HERMAN E. ZIEGLER

Bibliography: Morrison, Robert T., and Boyd, Robert N., *Organic Chemistry,* 5th ed. (1983).

Kettering, Charles Franklin   [ket'-ur-ing]

Charles Franklin Kettering, b. near Loudonville, Ohio, Aug. 29, 1876, d. Nov. 25, 1958, was an American engineer and inventor. He is also known as a cofounder of the Sloan-Kettering Institute for Cancer Research. While working at the National Cash Register Co., he designed (1905) the first electric cash register. In 1908 he developed an improved IGNITION SYSTEM. In 1912 the Cadillac Division of General Motors turned to Kettering's newly formed Dayton Engineering Laboratories Company (Delco) for components that combined ignition, lighting, and the first practical electric self-starter. His starter system used a small, yet powerful, electric motor, similar to that developed for the cash register. Kettering became (1919) the director of research at General Motors and guided many important research projects, including high-octane, knock-free gasoline (which reduces knocking in high-compression engines) and the lightweight two-cycle diesel engine (which made the diesel locomotive practical).   DENNIS SIMANAITIS

Bibliography: Boyd, Thomas A., *Professional Amateur: The Biography of Charles Franklin Kettering* (1957; repr. 1972); Donovan, Frank, *Wheels for a Nation* (1965); Lavine, Sigmund A., *Kettering: Master Inventor* (1960); Leslie, Stuart W., *Boss Kettering* (1986); Young, Rosamond M., *Boss Ket: A Life of Charles F. Kettering* (1961).

kettledrum

Kettledrums (*timpani*), which produce sounds of definite pitch, are the most important percussion instruments of the orchestra. They consist of a calf-skin or plastic sheet mounted on a hoop that is fitted over a hemispherical shell of brass or copper with a hole in the bottom to relieve the stress of concussion. The skin is tightened by screws, formed with T-shaped handles for efficiency. The player uses two sticks with heads ranging from hard (wooden) to soft (felt) that, along with the positioning of the stroke, can produce a gentle roll, a harsh, explosive effect, or any shade between. Kettledrums come in two basic sizes: one with a 28-in-diameter (71-cm) head and the other with a 25-in-diameter (63.5-cm) head.

Kettledrums originated in the Near East before AD 600. Crusaders brought small drums to Europe in the mid-13th century; the large size did not arrive before the mid-15th century. At first used only with trumpets, and carried on horses during displays of military pomp, kettledrums began to appear in opera and church orchestras during the 17th century.

Changing the pitch on a hand-tuned kettledrum (top right) involves turning the T-shaped screws that control the tension of the drum head. The pitch of the pedal kettledrum is controlled by moving the pedal (6), which controls six tuning rods (3). The tuning rods tighten or loosen their grip on the head (1), changing the tuning almost instantaneously. Other parts of the pedal drum include the flesh hoop and metal counterhoop (2), the shell (4), crown (5), and castor (7).

Two kettledrums were standard in the 18th-century orchestra, three by the mid-19th century. Only rarely did their number exceed five. Hector Berlioz, however, used ten pairs in his *Requiem* (1837). Following early failures in quick tuning devices, a satisfactory pedal was finally developed in the 20th century, making possible chromatic passages and even glissandi (rapid "sliding" up and down the scale).

ROBERT A. WARNER

Bibliography: Blades, J., *Percussion Instruments and Their History,* rev. ed. (1984); Sadie, S., *New Grove Dictionary of Musical Instruments,* 3 vols. (1984).

Kew Gardens

Kew Gardens, or the Royal Botanic Gardens, in Kew, near London, England, is one of the major botanical gardens in the world. It contains more than 40,000 different kinds of plants, with particularly noteworthy collections of Australian plants, succulents, tropical orchids, and ferns. The Gardens also has three museums, a taxonomy laboratory, an extensive library, and a large herbarium of dried species. Formerly a royal estate, Kew Gardens became a government institution in 1841.

key

The term *key* in music has two meanings. (1) A key is that movable part of a keyboard or woodwind instrument which, when activated, produces the desired pitch. On keyboards (such as that of a piano or organ) each key corresponds to a string or pipe of different pitch; to sound a note the key is depressed. On woodwinds the keys open or close holes in the instruments, an action that shortens or lengthens the column of air vibrating in a tube, thus altering the pitch. (2) The key of a musical composition denotes the pitch (keynote) of its tonal center (TONALITY). A composition in the key of C, for example, has the note C as its tonal center.

Music has always had a tonal center, at least since medieval times, but the concept of tonality—of music being in a key—emerged only in the early 18th century with the dominance of the major-minor system and its accompanying key "signatures" (arrangements of sharps or flats at the beginning of a composition to indicate the key). Even though a piece may modulate or change its key (perhaps even its key signature) during its course, it normally returns to its original key and is considered to be in that key. Some 20th-century music is written in more than one key simultaneously (polytonality) or completely without key (ATONALITY).

WILLIAM HAYS

Key, Francis Scott

Francis Scott Key, a lawyer and poet from Maryland, composed the lyrics to "The Star-Spangled Banner" in 1814, shortly after witnessing the British shelling of Baltimore's Fort McHenry. Key's patriotic verses, set to the melody of an old drinking song, became the national anthem of the United States in 1931.

A Maryland lawyer and poet, Francis Scott Key, b. Carroll City, Md., Aug. 1, 1779, d. Jan. 11, 1843, wrote the words of THE STAR-SPANGLED BANNER (1814), which became the U.S. national anthem by an act of Congress in 1931. Key also wrote other songs and verse as well as a study entitled *The Power of Literature and Its Connection with Religion* (1834).

Key West

Key West, Fla. (1980 pop., 24,382), is the southernmost city of the continental United States and the seat of Monroe County. The city is located approximately 95 km (60 mi) southwest of the Florida mainland, in the Florida Keys. Its economy is dependent on fishing, tourism, and U.S. naval installations. Key West was settled during the 1820s.

keyboard, computer

The keyboard is the main device by which an operator enters information into a COMPUTER. Keyboards consist of an array of keys that can be manually depressed, activating the entry of specific data. Based roughly on the classic design of the typewriter key arrangement, computer versions include not only keys for letters, numbers, and punctuation, but also a variety of keys and functions necessary for computer operation. Keys are switching mechanisms that generate electrical signals upon contact. Capacitance switches and ferrite core switches use electrical properties that ensure that a depressed key will generate a single signal. Mechanical switches are simpler in concept and incorporate safeguards against creating multiple signals.

keyboard instruments

Musical instruments in which the vibrator (sound generator) is activated indirectly by a mechanical or electrical linkage (the action) controlled by a keyboard are known as keyboard instruments. The keyboard itself is a system of levers, buttons, or knobs arranged for convenient manipulation usually by the fingers but occasionally by the hands or the feet. Typically, the manipulation of a key causes the vibrator(s) for one perceptible pitch, or note, to sound. The action of the finger, hand, or foot may supply the mechanical force necessary to activate the vibrator (for example, the hammer action of the PIANO), or it may only direct some secondary force that will actually excite the vibrator (for example, the wind supply of the ORGAN). A keyboard-action mechanism can be fitted to

The piano (A) and the clavichord (B) both produce sound when their strings are struck—by a felt-covered wooden "hammer" in the case of the piano, by the clavichord's thin metal "tangent." The harpsichord (C) has leather "quills" to pluck the strings. Using two keyboards, or manuals, each of which controls two or more sets of strings, the harpsichordist can produce rapid changes in sound volume.

instruments from any of the four major classes of acoustical MUSICAL INSTRUMENTS; keyboards are also frequently used in electronic instruments.

Keyboards offer several advantages over direct physical control of the vibrator. The playing technique required simply to produce a sound reliably is minimized. The sounding of vibrators too large or unwieldy or too numerous to be played directly is made possible with a keyboard action. The sounding of several pitches simultaneously, otherwise difficult or even impossible on some types of instruments, is greatly facil-

itated by a keyboard, as is the playing of rapid and complicated patterns of pitches and rhythms. Against these advantages is the serious disadvantage of the loss of direct and intimate physical control over the process of sound generation caused by the introduction of a mechanical medium between the body of the player and the vibrator. The subtle flexibility of intonation, tonal coloration, and attack and release of notes available, for example, to the violinist or the flutist in the sounding of a single tone is to a great extent denied to the keyboard player. The compromise implied by these advantages and disadvantages seems to have been acceptable to musicians of the West. The exclusive development of keyboard instruments in Europe may be explained in part by the relatively fixed, stable scale system and the preoccupation with polyphony present in European music since the Middle Ages.

All evidence indicates that the first keyboard instrument developed was the organ, specifically the *hydraulos*, attributed to Ktesibios of Alexandria (3d century BC). The keyboards of these ancient organs were direct extensions of the sliders that admitted air into the pipes. In some cases the key had to be pushed or pulled to sound a note and then returned manually to terminate the note; other keyboards were furnished with springs to return the key to rest position and stop the flow of air through the pipe.

During the Middle Ages the balanced keyboard was developed, in which a series of small balanced levers was linked to the action mechanism. This invention was crucial to the advancement of keyboard instruments, because it allowed a more efficient manipulation of the keys by the fingers, thus facilitating rapid execution and polyphonic playing. Initially taking the form of a row of flat ("white") keys, each representing a degree of the diatonic scale, the chromatic notes were soon introduced as raised, slightly recessed, alternative ("black") keys placed between the natural keys. With minor variations as to size and ornamentation this arrangement of the keyboard pertains to the present.

During the late Middle Ages the keyboard was fitted to stringed musical instruments of the board ZITHER family. The three keyboard-activated mechanisms for exciting strings into vibration resulted in the distinctive actions of the CLAVICHORD, HARPSICHORD, and PIANO. The late Middle Ages also saw the development of pedalboards, which are keyboards played by the feet. Most frequently employed in the organ, pedalboards have been fitted occasionally to the stringed keyboard instruments as well.

The keyboard instruments quickly gained a dominant position in European musical history. Their major shortcomings (lack of dynamic inflection in the case of the organ and harpsichord and the inability of the stringed keyboard instruments to truly sustain a tone) were more than offset by their ability to realize with relative facility a complete polyphonic texture. They have accordingly been favored as solo and accompanimental instruments, as well as the ideal pedagogical instruments and studio instruments of composers. In the 20th century the keyboard has been adapted to various systems of electronic and synthetic sound production, from those of the various electronic organs to the more recent synthesizers (see ELECTRONIC MUSIC).

NICHOLAS RENOUF

Bibliography: Grover, David S., *The Piano: Its Story from Zither to Grand* (1976); Marcuse, Sybil, *A Survey of Musical Instruments* (1975); Russell, Raymond, *The Harpsichord and Clavichord* (1973); Sumner, William Leslie, *The Organ* (1962; repr. 1973).

Keynes, John Maynard [kaynz, may'-nurd]

John Maynard Keynes, b. June 5, 1883, d. Apr. 21, 1946, was one of the most influential economists in the 20th century. Keynes's range of activities was exceptional. In addition to his work as an economist, he was—often simultaneously—a high government official, an editor of an academic journal, a businessman (who managed his investments in bed each morning at breakfast), a teacher at Cambridge University, a college bursar, a collector of rare books, a patron of the arts, and a member of the literary set called the BLOOMSBURY GROUP.

John Maynard Keynes, perhaps the most influential economist of the 20th century, achieved world fame in 1919 with the publication of his Economic Consequences of the Peace, *an indictment of reparations exacted by the Treaty of Versailles. Keynes's reputation was established by his later, widely adopted theories advocating government spending to relieve protracted unemployment.*

Keynes was educated at Eton and Cambridge. After service in the India Office and the Treasury, he became the principal British financial representative to the Paris Peace Conference that followed World War I. Resigning in protest at the reparations imposed on Germany, he published *The Economic Consequences of the Peace* (1919), which gave him an international reputation. Keynes predicted that Europe would be economically ruined as a result of harsh economic conditions imposed on Germany. His subsequent writings covered a wide canvas, including *A Treatise on Probability* (1921; a dissertation in mathematical logic), his graceful *Essays in Biography* (1933), and his classic work in economic theory, *The General Theory of Employment, Interest and Money* (1936).

The last book was Keynes's answer to the riddle of the Great Depression of the 1930s—that millions of people, willing to work, could not find employment—and the analysis offered in it is the basis of his enduring reputation. A central proposition of the *General Theory* is that times exist in a market economy when the total demand of consumers and investors may be insufficient to purchase all the goods the society has produced. (Traditional economics had held that supply creates its own demand.) Business managers, finding that they cannot sell all they have on hand, will cut back on production and employment, and a depression will result. Keynes held that part of the solution during periods of high unemployment was for the government to increase the money supply, thus lowering interest rates and stimulating business investment. But Keynes also advocated an active government FISCAL POLICY of deficit spending on public works and other projects and the maintenance during depressions of an unbalanced budget to increase the aggregate demand for goods and services.

Keynes's opinions were a sharp departure from conventional economics, and his theory remains controversial. In the years after World War II, however, his views in one form or another became widely accepted among economists in England and the United States, while his critics were in the minority.

An intensely active man, Keynes returned to government service during World War II. In 1942 he was raised to the peerage as Baron Keynes of Tilton. He played an important role at the Bretton Woods Conference of 1944, which established the basis of the postwar international monetary system, and he negotiated the multibillion-dollar U.S. loan to Britain in 1945. Keynes is one of a handful of social scientists who, through their writings, have substantially affected the course of history.   RICHARD T. GILL

Bibliography: Gilbert, J. C., *Keynes's Impact on Monetary Economics* (1982); Harrod, R. F., *The Life of John Maynard Keynes*, 2d ed. (1952; repr. 1982); Johnson, Elizabeth S. and Harry G., *The Shadow of Keynes* (1979); Keynes, Milo, ed., *Essays on John Maynard Keynes* (1975); Lekachman, Robert, *John Maynard Keynes* (1986) and, as ed., *Keynes'

General Theory: Reports of Three Decades,* rev. ed. (1968); Patinkin, Don, *Anticipations of the General Theory and Other Essays on Keynes* (1982); Skidelsky, Robert S., ed., *The End of the Keynesian Era* (1977); Vicarelli, F., *Keynes' Relevance Today* (1985).

See also: ECONOMY, NATIONAL.

keypunch: see PUNCHED CARD.

Keyser, Hendrik de   [ky'-sur]

Hendrik de Keyser, b. May 15, 1565, d. May 15, 1621, one of the most prominent Amsterdam architects and sculptors of his time, is credited with introducing various Italian Renaissance elements into that city. The head of a family of artists—his son Thomas was a noted portrait painter—de Keyser was appointed city mason and sculptor in 1594. After absorbing the lessons of English Jacobean architecture during a visit (1607) to London, he incorporated numerous Italianate motifs into his Amsterdam Exchange (1608–11; destroyed). From 1614 until his death, he worked on the tomb of Prince William I (Nieuwe Kerk, Delft), a complex marble-and-bronze project that recalls Francesco Primaticcio's tomb for Henry II. De Keyser's designs for the Westerkerk in Amsterdam (1620–38) mark a break from picturesque Dutch architecture and the beginning of Dutch classicism. He also simplified domestic architecture by downgrading gables and introducing classical orders.   ROBERT F. CHIRICO

Keystone Kops

Virtually synonymous with silent-film comedy, Mack SENNETT's Keystone Kops were inspired bunglers whose slapstick antics concentrated on wild chases featuring an out-of-control paddy wagon and death-defying acrobatic stunts. Sennett explored the idea for the zany policemen at his Keystone studio in December 1912, and the original seven uniformed Keystone Kops made their formal debut in a two-reeler in 1914. Their most famous madcap leader was Ford Sterling.   FRANK MANCHEL

Bibliography: Lahue, Kalton C., and Brewer, Terry, *Kops and Custards: The Legend of Keystone Films* (1968).

KGB

The KGB (*Komitet Gosudarstvennoy Bezopasnosti*, Committee for State Security) controls both the political and federal police and the intelligence and counterintelligence activities of the USSR. Founded in 1954, the KGB succeeded the NKVD (1934) and the MGB (1946) of the repressive Stalin era, and the earlier secret-police organizations the Cheka (1917) and the OGPU (1922). The KGB concentrates on INTELLIGENCE OPERATIONS—even making heroes of its master spies—and places less emphasis on its predecessors' policy of systematic terrorism. It also polices Soviet borders, operates prison camps and mental hospitals, and directs a large network of internal informers. It is estimated that in the 1980s the KGB had a budget of $6–12 billion and employed 500,000 people. Unlike the earlier secret police organizations, which attained a degree of autonomy, the KGB is firmly controlled by the Communist party. Well-known leaders of the various Soviet security organizations include Feliks DZERZHINSKY, Genrikh Yagoda, Nikolai Yezhov, and Lavrenti BERIA. Yuri V. ANDROPOV, who was general secretary of the Soviet Communist party from 1982 to 1984, headed the KGB from 1967 to 1982.

Bibliography: Barron, John, *KGB: The Secret Work of the Soviet Secret Agents* (1974) and *KGB Today* (1983); Freemantle, Brian, *KGB* (1982); Myagkov, Aleksei, *Inside the KGB* (1977).

Khafre, King of Egypt   [kah'-fruh]

Khafre, also called Chephren, fl. 1st half of the 26th century BC, was the fourth king of the 4th dynasty (c.2613–c.2498 BC) of ancient Egypt. The son of Khufu, he built at Giza the second of the three Great Pyramids and the Great SPHINX, whose colossal facial image may be a representation of Khafre's features.

Khajuraho   [kaj-rah'-hoh]

Khajuraho, in north Madhya Pradesh, India, about 600 km (360 mi) southeast of New Delhi, is the site of a magnificent series of Hindu temples built by the Chandella Rajputs from about AD 950 to 1050. The complex originally contained 85 buff-colored sandstone and granite temples, of which about 25 remain today.

Each temple, set upon a lofty terrace, comprises a sequence of halls, foyers, and porches fused into a single architectural fabric and coordinated along a common axis. The interior spaces progress from open to closed in a modulated sequence, from the full light of the entrance to the profound darkness of the sanctum. On the exterior, the pyramidal superstructures echo a natural mountain range, rising from the low, broad shapes of the porch in regular stages, peaking in the high, phallic form that covers the sanctum. The stone surfaces are animated with myriad representations of the gods and of erotic scenes, intended as concrete demonstrations of the potency of the icon originally enshrined within.

DIRAN KAVORK DOHANIAN

Bibliography: Lal, Kanwar, *Immortal Khajuraho* (1967); Zannas, Eliky, and Auboyer, Jeannine, *Khajuraho* (1960).

khaki   [kak'-ee]

Khaki is a durable cotton or wool fabric distinguished by its color, a yellowish or greenish brown. The fabric is in common use for military uniforms. Khaki was first used as a military color by the British army in India, in 1848 (the name is derived from the Hindi for *dusty*). An excellent camouflage color, the dust-hued khaki also concealed the effects of India's dirt roads. It became the official color of British army uniforms and, eventually, of the military dress of many other countries. During World War I, an olive tint was added to the khaki shade to help camouflage soldiers fighting on European battlegrounds.

ISABEL B. WINGATE

Khalid, King of Saudi Arabia   [kah'-leed]

Khalid ibn Abd al-Aziz, b. Riyadh, 1913, d. June 13, 1982, became king of Saudi Arabia after the assassination (Mar. 25, 1975) of his half brother King FAISAL. Khalid was one of several dozen sons of Ibn Saud, who founded the Saudi kingdom in 1926. Preceded on the throne by his brothers Saud (1953–64) and Faisal (1964–75), he was said to be a self-effacing man who had played a conciliatory role among the royal princes. He was succeeded by his crown prince, FAHD ibn Abd al-Aziz.

K. M. SMOGORZEWSKI

Khalkhas   [kal'-kuhz]

The Khalkha people are the principal inhabitants of Outer MONGOLIA (the Mongolian People's Republic). Their language, spoken by one million people, represents several closely related dialects. Like all Mongol tongues, Khalkha is subsidiary to Altaic. Descendants of GENGHIS KHAN's hordes, the Khalkha are true Mongoloids, with light yellow skin, high cheekbones, and a pronounced epicanthic fold of skin over the eye.

Khalkha society was traditionally based on nomadic patriarchal clans, which were determined according to male ancestry. Married sons lived near their fathers and other male relatives. A landowning nobility existed as a result of land grants received in exchange for military service. Tribes lived in herding camps that were moved from pasture to pasture several times a year. Dwellings were circular felt tents, called *gers* or YURTS. Meat and dairy products, including kumiss, characterized their diets. Dried dung was the fuel used on the treeless Khalkha steppes. Traditionally shamanists or pagans, the Khalkha became Lamaist Buddhists in the 17th century.

Loose-knit Khalkha-Tatar tribal confederations, originating in 300 BC, became united under Genghis Khan in the 13th century. On horseback, the MONGOLS conquered Central Asia, southern Russia, and eastern Europe. Their empire collapsed in the 1500s. Since 1920 the Khalkha people have been influenced by the USSR. Resisting collectivization, more than

half of the Khalkha are still herders. Yurts are common, even in cities.

VICTOR L. MOTE

Bibliography: Bitsch, J., *Mongolia, Unknown Land,* trans. by R. Spink (1963); Lattimore, O., *Nomads and Commissars* (1962); Phillips, E., *The Mongols* (1969); Street, J., *Khalkha Structure* (1963).

Khamseh   [kham'-seh]

The Khamseh (Arabic for "five together") is a federation of five tribes of pastoral nomads in the province of Fars in southern Iran. The five tribes, numbering about 75,000, are the Persian-speaking Arab and Basseri (in recent times the dominant tribe of the group) and the Turkish-speaking Ainalu, Baharlu, and Nafar. All are Shiite Muslims and are physically indistinguishable from other Iranian populations.

With their sheep and other livestock, the Khamseh nomads migrate semiannually across the Zagros Mountains between the low-lying valleys and plains close to the coast of the Persian Gulf and the high, summer pastures on the Iranian Plateau. The federation was formed under the leadership of a wealthy merchant family in the mid-19th century to check the power of the neighboring QASHQAI tribes and to provide protection for the trade routes from the plateau to the Gulf ports. The organization of the federation was not institutionalized and depended on personal relations with tribal leaders. Allegiance was never secure, and force was often needed to keep individual tribes in submission. The Khamseh no longer has any political function. Their numbers may be decreasing as a result of a growing preference for city life, but their pastoral production remains important to the national economy.

BRIAN SPOONER

Bibliography: Barth, Fredrik, *Nomads of South Persia* (1961; repr. 1968).

Khants   [kahnts]

Khants, a Mongoloid people linguistically related to Hungarians, are native to the Ob River Valley and adjacent swamps in the Russian Soviet Federated Socialist Republic of the USSR. They are also sometimes called Ostyaks. With yellowish white skin, straight or concave noses, high cheekbones, and short stature, they scarcely resemble the MAGYARS of Europe. Both peoples, however, speak a Ugrian dialect of Uralic. The Khants number about 21,000. Without a written language until after 1917, only two-thirds of them still speak their native tongue. Southern Khants converse in Russian or Tatar.

Traditionally, Khants were sedentary fishermen and hunters. Their early dwellings were riverbank pit-houses in winter and birchbark tents and stilt houses in summer. Distinctively harnessed dog sleds were used for transportation on snow. Dugout canoes were employed in summer. Clothing was primitive, but Khant women were expert weavers of nettle thread. Social structure was patriarchal; kinship was patrilineal. Khant religion was shamanistic.

The ethnic origins of the Khant people can be traced to the Ob Valley during the 1st millennium BC. Gradually, they expanded downstream. Still rural fishermen, today they also engage in collective farming, reindeer herding, and dairying. Khants are skilled woodcarvers. Now the leading Soviet petroleum producer, their homeland is among the fastest-growing regional economies in the USSR.

VICTOR L. MOTE

Bibliography: Levin, M. G., *Ethnic Origins of the Peoples of Northeastern Asia* (1972); Symmons-Symonolewicz, Konstantin, ed., *The Non-Slavic Peoples of the Soviet Union* (1972).

Kharkov   [kar'-kuhf]

Kharkov is the second largest city of the Ukrainian Soviet Socialist Republic, in the USSR, and the administrative center of Kharkov oblast. Located in the northeast Ukraine, the city has a population of 1,464,000 (1980). Kharkov is one of the largest economic centers of the USSR and, after Moscow and Leningrad, the most important transport hub. It is situated at the confluence of the Kharkov, Lopan, and Udy rivers and the junction of eight rail lines; highways run north to Moscow, west to Kiev, and southeast to the Caucasus.

The city's population is about two-thirds Ukrainian and one-third ethnic Russian. A modern industrial city that only developed during the second half of the 19th century, Kharkov has few sites or monuments of historical significance. Its importance for the Soviet economy lies entirely in the manufacturing of diversified machinery products. Kharkov produces tractors, heavy electrical equipment, power-generating turbines, engines, and mining equipment. The city's large electric power demand has been met both by coal-fired power stations and, since the discovery of the Shebelinka gas field nearby in the mid-1950s, by gas-burning power plants. Kharkov is a major educational and industrial research center, with the Kharkov A. M. Gorky State University (1805) and technical schools training engineers for the city's industries. It has an opera and ballet theater, Ukrainian and Russian drama theaters, and historical and fine arts museums.

Kharkov arose originally in 1656 as a military stronghold along the Russians' southern defense line against the Crimean Tatars. After the end of the 18th century, when Russia conquered the Crimea, Kharkov lost its military significance and gradually turned into a town of artisan industry and commerce. Its modern industrial development, beginning in the 1860s, was due both to the rise of the coal and steel industry in the nearby DONETS BASIN and to the construction of railroads. After the Bolshevik Revolution, Kharkov served as the capital of the Ukraine from 1917 to 1934. The city was heavily damaged in World War II and has since been rebuilt.

THEODORE SHABAD

Khartoum [kar-toom']

Khartoum is the capital of Sudan and of Khartoum province. Situated at the confluence of the White and Blue NILE rivers, it is connected by bridges to the neighboring suburbs of OMDURMAN and Khartoum North. The population is 476,218 (1983), the majority of which is Arabic, although a large portion is black African. The climate is very hot and dry.

Khartoum is the commercial and transportation hub of the country. It has rail links to the north and west, and the two Nile rivers carry a large volume of traffic. Khartoum's industries include oilseed, gum Arabic, and food processing, printing, and textile and glass manufacturing. The city is laid out with wide avenues, and the presidential palace and the parliament building are the principal landmarks. The University of Khartoum (1956) and a branch of Cairo University (1955) are there.

Khartoum was founded in 1821 by Muhammad Ali of Egypt, and it grew rapidly as a trade and military center. It was destroyed (1895) when the Mahdists massacred the Anglo-Egyptian garrison under Charles George GORDON. The city was recaptured (1898) by Lord KITCHENER, who rebuilt it to serve as the administrative center of Anglo-Egyptian Sudan. When Sudan became independent in 1956, Khartoum became the capital. Devastating floods in 1988 left 1.5 million people in the Khartoum area homeless.

Khasi [kah'-see]

The Khasi are one of the major tribal groups inhabiting the Khasi and Jaintia Hills district of Meghalaya state, bounded by Assam state, in eastern India. They number more than 400,000 and speak a language of the Mon-Khmer family. Their cultural tradition sets them off from the plains Assamese, their neighbors to the south, and suggests different ethnic affinities. At the time of British takeover (1825–35), the Khasi were divided into some 25 chiefly states, each presided over by a Siem, or ruler, of the aristocratic lineage. The Khasi rule of succession is traced through the female line, with kingly succession through the eldest son of the eldest sister and property inheritance through the youngest daughter. Many religious rites were in the hands of women.

Khasi society has changed radically with the introduction of Christianity and the intrusion of the modern state. Christianity has affected traditional inheritance rules and such distinctive Khasi customs as the erection of standing stones to honor the dead. The introduction of the potato in the early 19th century changed the base of the Khasi economy. The potato crop is now a major source of trade for the flourishing town of Shillong, the administrative headquarters, and contributed to improved communications over much of the Khasi Hills.

R. L. STIRRAT AND HILLARY STANDING

Bibliography: Bareh, Hamlet, *The History and Culture of the Khasi People* (1967) and *Khasi Democracy* (1964).

Khatchaturian, Aram [kah-chah-toor-yahn', uh-rahm']

Aram Khatchaturian, b. June 6 (N.S.), 1903, d. May 1, 1978, was a Soviet composer of Armenian birth best known outside the USSR for the "Sabre Dance" from his ballet *Gayane* (1942) and for two concertos—one for piano (1936), the other for violin (1940). The latter was popularized in Western Europe and the United States by the Russian violinist David Oistrakh. Khatchaturian made extensive use of Oriental melodic and rhythmic forms borrowed chiefly from Armenia, but also from neighboring Caucasian (Georgian and Azerbaijani) folk music. Brilliant orchestral coloring plays an important part in all his music, which includes popular choral songs, balalaika pieces, military marches, film and incidental music for plays, as well as compositions in classical forms. MARTIN COOPER

Bibliography: Krebs, Stanley D., *Soviet Composers and the Development of Soviet Music* (1970); Shneerson, Grigory, *Aram Khachaturian*, trans. by Xenia Danko (1959).

Khazars [kah'-zars]

The Khazars, a Turkic people, created a commercial and political empire that dominated substantial parts of South Russia during much of the 7th through 10th centuries. During the 8th century the Khazar aristocracy and the *kagan* (king) were converted to Judaism. The Khazars established their capital at Itil (or Atil), in the Volga delta, and for four centuries thereafter this Jewish empire held the balance of power between the Christian BYZANTINE EMPIRE and the Muslim CALIPHATE. The fortified Khazar city of Sarkil on the lower Don River was built with Byzantine help and served as a crossroads to central Asia. The Khazars controlled many of the trade routes to the Orient; some of the Radhanites (Jewish merchants from Gaul), for example, were accustomed to crossing the Khazar empire while traveling to and from China and India. During the late 10th and early 11th centuries an alliance of Byzantines and Russians broke the power of the Khazars in the Crimea. In 965, SVYATOSLAV I, duke of Kiev, decisively defeated the Khazar army. Further to the east new waves of Turkic invaders overran the remains of the Khazar state.

BERNARD S. BACHRACH

Bibliography: Dunlop, D. M., *The History of the Jewish Khazars* (1954; repr. 1967); Koestler, Arthur, *The Thirteenth Tribe: The Khazar Empire and Its Heritage* (1976).

Khiva

Khiva is a town in Khorezm oblast of the Uzbek SSR of the Soviet Union. Its population is 26,000 (1974 est.). Although it is of little importance today, its history goes back to the 6th century AD and it was a major city of Muslim Central Asia in medieval times. From the 16th to the 19th century it was the capital of the Khanate of Khiva, an Uzbek principality. Annexed by Russia in 1873, it was the capital of the Khorezm People's Soviet Republic from 1920 to 1924. Khiva's Ichan-Kala (Inner City) contains the 14th-century tomb of Seyid Ala-ud-Din, the Kunya-Ark fortress (17th century), the former palace of the khans (19th century), and many historic mosques and *madrasahs* (Islamic schools).

Bibliography: Burnaby, Fred, *Ride to Khiva* (1877; repr. 1988).

Khmer [kmair]

The Khmer people make up about 93 percent of the population of 6,540,000 (1987 est.) of Kampuchea (formerly the Khmer Republic, or Cambodia). Many Khmer also live in southeast Thailand and southern Vietnam. Their language is affiliated with the Mon-Khmer linguistic family. The ancestors of the Khmer migrated to their present homeland in early times from the north or west. Later, Indian civilization brought Hinduism and Buddhism to the region. For centuries the country experienced the rise and fall of various empires that built such famous monuments as the temples at ANGKOR.

The Khmer traditionally practiced rice farming in the lowland of their nation through which flow the Mekong and Tonle Sap rivers. They resided in villages of raised houses of bamboo and thatch. Genealogical descent is traced through both parents. Traditional religious belief was Theravada Buddhist, although pre-Buddhist beliefs and practices concerning numerous spirits and demons were also maintained. The arts of music, dance, and silk weaving were highly developed. The Khmer culture and way of life were badly disrupted during the period of Khmer Rouge rule.   DONN V. HARTT

Bibliography: Chandler, David P., *The Land and People of Cambodia* (1972); Edmonds, I. G., *The Khmers of Cambodia* (1970).

Khmer Empire

The Khmer Empire, which occupied contemporary Kampuchea (Cambodia) and parts of present-day Thailand, Laos, and Vietnam, existed between the 6th and 15th centuries.

The Khmers, whose descendants are today's Cambodians, are first known to have lived along the lower and middle Mekong River in northern Kampuchea and southern Laos. Their capital was initially near Kompong Thom, but under King Yasovarman I (r. 889–900), it was moved to ANGKOR, which became a magnificent city. The architectural splendor of the famed Angkor Wat temple and the lesser-known Bayon and Banteay Srei monuments was not subsequently equaled by other mainland Southeast Asian cultures. Khmer art, architecture, and culture were strongly Indian-influenced but included distinct local contributions.

The Khmers warred constantly with the adjacent Mon, Cham, Annamese, and Thai peoples. Their dominant role in continental Southeast Asia was ended by the Thais, coming out of southwest China, in the 14th and 15th centuries. After repeated raids by the Thais, Angkor was abandoned c.1434 and the capital moved to Phnom Penh. The period of Khmer greatness was ended.   RICHARD BUTWELL

Bibliography: Audric, John, *Angkor and the Khmer Empire* (1972); Coedes, G., *Angkor*, trans. by E. F. Gardner (1986).

Khmer Rouge   [kmair roozh']

The Khmer Rouge, or Cambodian Communist army, emerged as a significant rebel group during the late 1960s. With the aid of the North Vietnamese and the Viet Cong, and using the mountains of southern Cambodia as their retreat, the Khmer Rouge carried on a systematic war against the government of Prince NORODOM SIHANOUK and his successor, LON NOL. By 1970, when the Sihanouk government fell, the Khmer Rouge controlled about two-thirds of Cambodia.

Despite massive economic and military aid from the United States—including bombing of Khmer Rouge positions—the Lon Nol government continued to lose territory. Phnom Penh, the capital, fell to the Khmer Rouge on Apr. 16, 1975.

A Communist government under President Khieu Samphan and Prime Minister POL POT was then established, and the name of the country was changed to Kampuchea. The new regime immediately implemented a program of radical social change in which entire city populations were evacuated to rural areas. It was charged with responsibility for the deaths of at least one million Cambodians before border clashes with Vietnam culminated early in 1979 with a full-scale Vietnamese invasion and the installation of a Vietnamese-backed government in Phnom Penh. The Khmer Rouge, aided by China, retreated to remote villages along the Thai border and joined Sihanouk and former prime minister Son Sann in an uneasy coalition government in exile. It had the largest rebel army when Vietnamese troops withdrew in 1989.   JOHN CADY

Bibliography: Chandler, D. P., and Kiernan, B., eds., *Revolution and Its Aftermath in Kampuchea* (1983).

Khoikhoi   [koy'-koy]

The Khoikhoi are a southern African people who have often been called *Hottentot*. The latter name, used principally by white South Africans, now connotes a derogatory stereotype. A seminomadic pastoral people who were also hunters and gatherers, the Khoikhoi once inhabited the southern part of Namibia and the northwestern, southern, and southeastern parts of South Africa. They speak a Khoisan language noted for the four clicks—dental, alveolar, cerebral, and lateral—occurring in many words (see CLICK LANGUAGES).

In 1650, when contacted by Dutch settlers, the total Khoikhoi population was an estimated 35,000–50,000. The largest political unit was the tribe, varying in size from 500 to 2,500 people. Traditionally, each tribe consisted of a federation of clans united by the institution of chieftainship. Descent and residence were determined according to male ancestry. Each nuclear family occupied separate beehive-shaped huts. The Khoikhoi were monotheists and worshiped a celestial god. Their material culture was simple and adapted to their seminomadic life.

As a result of European colonization the traditional Khoikhoi social system collapsed, and many Khoikhoi intermarried with the settlers, thus forming part of the Cape COLOURED population. The Republic of South Africa now has fewer than 500 Khoikhoi-speakers. In Namibia more than 50,000 Khoikhoi were reported in the mid-1980s.   PETER CARSTENS

Bibliography: Elphick, Richard, *Kraal and Castle* (1977); Schapera, Isaac, *The Khoisan Peoples of South Africa* (1930; repr. 1960).

Khoisan language: see AFRICAN LANGUAGES.

Khomeini, Ayatollah Ruhollah   [koh-may-nee', roo-hoh'-lah]

The Ayatollah Khomeini ruled Iran with an iron hand from 1979 until his death in 1989. He was succeeded as spiritual leader of Iran by Ali Khamenei, but temporal power passed to the new president, Hashemi Rafsanjani. One of Khomeini's legacies was the death sentence that he pronounced (1989) upon the Indian-born British author Salman Rushdie for his novel Satanic Verses, which was deemed offensive to Muslims.

The Ayatollah (Arabic, "Reflection of Allah") Ruhollah Khomeini (Ruhollah Hendi), b. Khomein, Iran, May 27, 1900?, d. July 3, 1989, became leader of Iran in 1979 by forcing the overthrow of the shah (see MUHAMMAD REZA SHAH PAHLAVI) and Prime Minister Shahpur Bakhtiar. The son of an ayatollah of the SHIITE sect, he studied theology and by 1962 was one of the six grand ayatollahs of Iran's Shiite Muslims. Exiled in 1963 for his part in religious demonstrations against the shah, he was expelled from Iraq in 1978 and moved to France, where he emerged as the leader of the antishah movement. In January 1979, after the shah left Iran, he returned to lead the country, becoming *faqih* (supreme religious guide) of Iran's Islamic republic for life in December.

In his efforts to transform Iran into an Islamic state, Khomeini was hostile to the West. In November 1979 he supported militant students who invaded the U.S. embassy and precipitated the IRANIAN HOSTAGE CRISIS. Khomeini and other fundamentalist clerics faced opposition from Western-educated moderates, from minorities within the country, and from various leftist guerrilla groups but gradually consolidated control, imposing rigid censorship, executing members of the opposition, and banning Western customs. Khomeini used the GULF WAR initiated by Iraq in 1980 to help unify the country, although he was less than successful in exporting his revolution and reluctantly accepted a cease-fire in the costly conflict in 1988. After his death, which prompted an outpouring of religious fervor, Iran remained a theocracy, although the constitution was revised to grant more power to the president.

Khond   [kahnd]

The Khond (or Kandh) people are dispersed throughout the hill areas of Orissa state in northeastern India. Their population is estimated at more than 700,000, and they are classified as a "scheduled tribe" by the government of India. They speak Kui, an unwritten Dravidian language, although today many Khond are bilingual, having been educated in the state language, Oriya. The largest of the Orissan hill tribes, the Khond attained a particular notoriety because of their traditional practices of warfare and human sacrifice. The latter practice was suppressed by the British. Influenced by Hindu Oriyas who settled in the region, may Khond have abandoned shifting slash-and-burn cultivation in favor of wet rice agriculture. Their traditional life-style, based on land-owning clans and a religious cult of the earth, has largely disappeared in many areas.   R. L. STIRRAT AND HILLARY STANDING

Bibliography: Banerjee, Sukumar, *Ethnographic Study of the Kuvi-Khanda* (1969).

Khorana, Har Gobind   [kuh-rahn'-uh, goh'-bind]

The Indian-American geneticist Har Gobind Khorana, b. Jan. 9, 1922, shared with M. W. Nirenberg and Robert Holley the 1968 Nobel Prize for physiology or medicine for his contribution to knowledge of how genes determine cell function. In 1976, Khorana synthesized an artificial gene and laid the foundation for recombinant-DNA technology. Khorana discovered that the GENETIC CODE consists of nonoverlapping triplets, read in sequence with no gaps between them.

Khorezm   [kuh-rez'-uhm]

Khorezm (Khwarizm) is a historic region of the USSR located along the Amu Darya (Oxus River) south of the Aral Sea. From ancient times its rulers were known as the Khwarizm-shahs. In the late 12th and early 13th centuries, under the fourth Khwarizm-shah dynasty, Khorezm was the center of an empire that included most of Iran and Central Asia. From the 16th to the 19th century it was ruled by the Khanate of KHIVA. Annexed by Russia in 1873, it existed briefly as the Khorezm People's Soviet Republic from 1920 to 1924; today it is an oblast of the Uzbek Soviet Socialist Republic.

Khorsabad   [kohr'-suh-bahd]

The village of Khorsabad, 20 km (12 mi) northeast of Mosul in Iraq, is the site of the ancient neo-Assyrian capital Dur Sharrukin (Fortress of Sargon). Founded (717 BC) by Sargon II of ASSYRIA (721–705 BC), it was virtually abandoned, unfinished, after his death.

The well-planned ancient city, almost 4 km^2 (1.5 mi^2) in area, was surrounded by a wall about 24 m (80 ft) thick, fortified with towers. The seven entrances were guarded by huge, winged human-headed bulls of carved stone. Little remains of the inner city except for ruins of the imperial arsenal beside the southwest wall and the fortified citadel at the northwest wall. On the upper terrace of the citadel, together with temples and a ziggurat, stood Sargon's palace. Below were official residences and a temple to the god Nabu.

Discovered (1843) by Paul Émile BOTTA, the site was excavated by the French (1851–55) and by a University of Chicago expedition (1929–35). Superb examples of Assyrian imperial art and architecture have been found at Khorsabad. Palace

sculptures are in the collections of the British, Baghdad, Louvre, and University of Chicago museums.   KATE FIELDEN

Bibliography: Frankfort, Henri, *The Art and Architecture of the Ancient Orient*, rev. ed. (1969); Loud, Gordon, *Khorsabad I* (1936); Loud, Gordon, and Altman, C. B., *Khorsabad II* (1938).

Khosru I, King of Persia   [kahs-roo']

Khosru I, d. 579, called Chosroes in the West, succeeded his father, Kavad, as ruler of Persia in 531. A SASSANIAN, he is known in Eastern sources as Anushirvan (of immortal soul) because of his fame. For the Arabs his name, rendered as Kisra, became the generic name for all the Sassanian kings.

Khosru reformed the taxation of the Sassanian empire, as well as its military and social structure. He successfully fought the Byzantine Empire, briefly occupying Antioch in 540, and in the east he crushed the nomadic Hephthalites and established Sassanian hegemony over present-day Afghanistan. His troops conquered areas as far away as Yemen and in the Caucasus. A patron of learning, Khosru invited Greek philosophers to his court after their academy was closed in Athens in 529. During his long reign many works were translated from Greek and Sanskrit into Persian. Khosru also built many structures.   RICHARD N. FRYE

Khotan   [koh-tahn']

Khotan (Chinese: Ho-t'ien or Hotan) is a city in the western part of China's Sinkiang Autonomous Region, near the Indian border. Its population is 73,540 (1982). Historically, it was important as the center from which Buddhism spread from India into China. Today it has a mostly UIGHUR and Muslim population, and produces textiles, metalwork, and jewelry.

Khrushchev, Nikita Sergeyevich   [kroos'-chef or krus-chawf', nyi-kee'-tuh syir-gay'-uh-vich]

Nikita Khrushchev achieved political supremacy in the USSR by 1956, three years after Joseph Stalin's death. His policies of "destalinization" at home and "peaceful coexistence" abroad eased relations with the West but antagonized China. Foreign-policy failures, notably the Cuban Missile Crisis (1962), and agrarian problems led to his ouster in 1964.

Nikita Sergeyevich Khrushchev was first secretary of the Soviet Communist party from 1953 to 1964 and effective leader of the USSR from 1956 (premier from 1958) to 1964. He was born on Apr. 17 (N.S.), 1894, in a mud hut in the village of Kalinovka, Kursk province. As a young boy, Khrushchev worked long hours in the coal mines. According to his memoirs, he had a strict religious upbringing, becoming a revolutionary under the influence of one of his teachers. In 1918 he joined the Bolshevik party and fought in the Civil War. Afterward, he was sent by the party to a technical institute.

Khrushchev rose steadily up the party ladder, always combining his talents as an administrator with his technical training. After assignments in the Ukraine, he became head of the Moscow regional party committee, and in 1934 he became a member of the Central Committee of the Soviet Communist party. In these positions he directed the construction of the Moscow subway.

Although increasingly influential, Khrushchev was never an intimate associate of Joseph STALIN; he concentrated on technical rather than political accomplishment. Perhaps for that reason he escaped the Great Purge of the 1930s. In 1938 he returned to the Ukraine as first secretary of the Ukrainian Communist party and focused his attention primarily on agriculture, in which he gained a reputation as an expert. After World War II he was brought again to Moscow, where he served in the Secretariat and the Politburo and was again head of the Moscow regional committee. It was those positions, and his reputation as an agricultural expert, that soon propelled him to power.

Khrushchev in the Post-Stalin Era. Stalin died on Mar. 5, 1953, and the resulting power vacuum was filled by a "collective leadership," consisting primarily of Khrushchev, Lavrenti BERIA, Nikoli BULGANIN, Georg MALENKOV, Vyacheslav MOLOTOV, and Lazar Kaganovich. Malenkov was named premier and Khrushchev first secretary of the Communist party. The collective leadership was not long in existence. Beria was forced out of the party in July 1953 (and later executed). In 1955, Malenkov was replaced as premier by Bulganin, who was nominated to the post by Khrushchev. By 1956, Khrushchev was paramount in the party. At the 20th party congress that year, he gave his famous six-hour "secret speech" denouncing the "crimes of the Stalin era." Many old-time party leaders felt that Khrushchev had gone too far; but, despite two attempts on his life later that year, he continued to consolidate his power. In 1957, Malenkov, Molotov, and Kaganovich were purged from the party after an abortive attempt to oust Khrushchev from leadership. In 1958, Bulganin resigned, and Khrushchev became premier as well as party secretary.

Khrushchev's Domestic Policies. Khrushchev set bold new economic goals for "overtaking the West" and the United States in particular. In 1954, under his supervision, vast new virgin lands were opened to cultivation, and the result was a dramatic increase in food production. Two outstanding harvests (1956, 1958) enabled him to push ahead with rapid industrial development, especially in the production of consumer goods. He also introduced a series of important administrative reforms. In 1957 he set up a new system of regional economic councils (Sovnarkhozy) and invited debate and discussion on various economic, educational, and legal reforms. He also relaxed censorship somewhat, allowing some dissident intellectuals, like Aleksandr Solzhenitsyn, to publish previously suppressed works. In 1962 he attempted to reorganize the entire party apparatus on the basis of the "production principle," dividing local committees into separate agricultural and industrial sections. Problems soon developed, however. The good harvest years were followed by bad ones, his administrative changes led to much confusion, and his policy of more open discussion provoked new opposition. Dissidence grew along with popular frustration, as expectations outstripped accomplishments.

Foreign Affairs. Energy, ebullience, and lofty goals also characterized Khrushchev's foreign policy. After a dramatic reconciliation with President TITO of Yugoslavia in 1955, he met with Western leaders at a Geneva summit conference in 1955. He also traveled to the United States (in 1959 and 1960), the first Soviet leader to do so. These activities did much to thaw the COLD WAR and to build commercial and cultural ties between East and West.

Despite Khrushchev's relaxed relations with the West, he maintained strong Soviet control over the Communist nations of Eastern Europe. This fact was emphasized by his brutal suppression in 1956 of the HUNGARIAN REVOLUTION. The WARSAW TREATY ORGANIZATION, which binds the Eastern bloc militarily to Moscow, was a creation of the Khrushchev era. Meanwhile, his insistence on "peaceful coexistence" with the capitalist West and his generally unorthodox interpretation of classic Marxist doctrine contributed to a rupture with the Communist government of China. Cuba represented both a triumph and a failure of Khrushchev's foreign policy. The triumph lay in Cuba's alignment, under Fidel CASTRO, with the USSR, giving the latter its first ally in the Western Hemisphere. The failure resulted from the CUBAN MISSILE CRISIS (1962), when Khrushchev, with a great loss of face, was forced to remove Soviet missiles from the island.

Khrushchev's Decline. Khrushchev's unorthodox policies and his colorful behavior had created opposition from the beginning, especially among the old guard party members. His early successes tended to neutralize that faction, but as his failures began to mount, both domestically and internationally, his opponents in the Politburo gained strength. Finally, in October 1964, he was forced out of office. His remaining years were spent in quiet retirement in the outskirts of Moscow. The vast changes he had unleashed in the USSR could not be undone, however, and his years in power have had a lasting effect on the Soviet Union. He died on Sept. 11, 1971.

WILLIAM G. ROSENBERG

Bibliography: Ebon, Martin, *Nikita Khrushchev* (1986); Frankland, Mark, *Khrushchev* (1966); Khrushchev, Nikita S., *Khrushchev Remembers*, ed. and trans. by Strobe Talbott, 2 vols. (1970–74); Linden, Carl, *Khrushchev and the Soviet Leadership, 1957–1964* (1966); McCauley, Martin, ed., *Khrushchev and Khrushchevism* (1987); Medvedev, Roy and Zhores, *Khrushchev: The Years in Power* (1976).

Khufu, King of Egypt [koo'-foo]

Khufu, or Cheops, fl. *c.*2680 BC, was the king of ancient Egypt who directed the construction of the Great Pyramid at Giza (see PYRAMIDS), the largest tomb-pyramid ever built. He was the son and successor of King Snefru, who founded the 4th dynasty (*c.*2613–2498). In 1954 remains of the 43-m (142-ft) funerary ship of Khufu were discovered near the Great Pyramid; a second boat was found in 1987. An ivory statuette found in the temple at Abydos and thought to depict Khufu is in the Egyptian Museum in Cairo.

Khwarizm-shahs: see KHOREZM.

Khyber Pass [ky'-bur]

The Khyber Pass, a strategically important pass, is on the border between Pakistan and Afghanistan. Cutting through the Safed Koh Range, it is 53 km (33 mi) long, 5 m to 5 km (15 ft to 3 mi) wide, and reaches 1,067 m (3,500 ft) in elevation. The pass, controlled by Pakistan, links the cities of Peshawar, Pakistan, and Kabul, Afghanistan, by railroad, paved highway, and caravan route. For centuries the pass has been used by invaders into India. On the northwest frontier of British India, it was the scene of frequent fighting between British forces and local PATHAN tribes.

kiang [kih-ang']

The kiang is the largest and most numerous of the wild asses found in Asia. Native to high plateaus in the mountains of Tibet, kiangs are hardy animals that travel in fast-moving herds.

The kiang, a wild ass and a member of the horse family, Equidae, lives on the Tibetan Plateau in Asia at altitudes of 4,100 to 4,800 m (13,500 to 16,000 ft). It is classified either as a separate species, *Equus kiang,* or as a subspecies of the Asiatic wild asses, *E. hemionus kiang.*

The largest of the wild asses, the kiang stands 14 hands high (142 cm/56 in) at the withers and weighs up to 400 kg (900 lb). It lives in herds of about five to several hundred. It has a black stripe down its back, and its coat varies from red in summer to brownish in winter.   EVERETT SENTMAN

Kiangsi   (Jiangxi)   [jyang'-see']

Kiangsi is a landlocked province in south central China. It has an area of 164,700 km² (63,600 mi²) and a population of 33,840,000 (1983 est.). The capital is Nanchang. The Kan River provides a natural north-south corridor through many mountain ranges before emptying into P'o-yang Hu, the second largest lake in China.

A fertile province, Kiangsi produces two crops of rice every year. Other crops include tea, sugarcane, cotton, fruit, and ramie fiber. Its mines yield tungsten, coal, tin, and manganese. The most notable provincial product, however, is Kiangsi porcelain, made since the 11th century from high-quality kaolin from the banks of P'o-yang Hu. From the early Chou dynasty (770–453 BC) to the Long March of the Communists in the 1930s, the Kan River valley has provided an important route for migration, commerce, and military conquest.

Kiangsu   (Jiangsu)   [jyang'-soo']

Kiangsu is a province on the Yellow Sea coast in eastern China. Most of the region's 102,300-km² (39,500-mi²) area lies on a low fertile alluvial plain crossed by the YANGTZE RIVER, the Huai Ho, the GRAND CANAL, and an intricate network of lakes, canals, and streams. The capital is NANKING. The population, consisting entirely of Han Chinese, is 61,350,000 (1983 est.). Modern SHANGHAI, the largest urban center in China, lies within the province but is administered by the central government in Peking.

Major crops include rice, wheat, barley, corn, cotton, and sweet potatoes. The growing of silkworms and raising of fish are also important. Kiangsu was part of Nanking province under the Ming dynasty (1368–1644); during the 18th century under the Ch'ing, it became a separate province. Kiangsu was the center of the Taiping Rebellion (1850–64). During the Japanese occupation in 1937–45, the province was greatly damaged, but it has since recovered.

kibbutz   [kih-buts']

A kibbutz is one type of collective settlement in Israel whose members own or lease land together and practice farming. Agricultural work, cooking, and decision making are carried out in common. Children are raised by the community in many kibbutzim, seeing their own parents a few hours a day.

The first kibbutz (Degania) was founded in 1910 as an experiment by seven agricultural workers, and it generated considerable international interest. Other kibbutzim soon followed; they played an important role in the Jewish settlement of Palestine as part of the international Zionist movement, which stressed the need to create agricultural roots in the Jewish homeland. Most immigrants to Palestine were familiar with middle-class occupations but not agriculture, and a period of life in a kibbutz, run on principles that emphasized equality and the dignity of manual work, served both to accustom settlers to a raw country where group work was essential to survival and to settle territory in Palestine.

From the mid-1930s to 1945 growth of the kibbutzim was particularly rapid as European Jews fled persecution and the Nazi Holocaust. Kibbutz members were frequently in the vanguard of Jewish socialist thinking, and they continue to play an important political role in the government of modern Israel, although the character of most kibbutzim has become less intimate with growth. In the mid-1980s Israel had nearly 300 kibbutzim, most of which owned their own factories or processing plants. Recently, financial setbacks have occurred due to poor investment practices. About 3% of the Israeli population live in kibbutzim.

Bibliography: Bettelheim, Bruno, *Children of the Dream* (1969); Leon, Dan, *The Kibbutz: A New Way of Life* (rev. ed., 1969); Rosner, Menachem, *Democracy, Equality, and Change,* ed. by Joseph R. Blasi (1982); Spiro, Melford E. and Audrey G., *Children of the Kibbutz: A Study in Child Training and Personality* (1975); Vitaler, Harry, *A History of the Co-Operative Movement in Israel,* 7 vols. (1966–70).

Kickapoo   [kik'-uh-poo]

Noted as ''great pedestrians'' by the first French traders to meet this Algonquian-speaking Indian tribe of North America, the Kickapoo endured numerous relocations in their drive to remain free of white domination. Originally from central Michigan, by 1670 they had migrated to the portage of the Fox and Wisconsin rivers (southwestern Wisconsin), where they became closely allied with the SAUK and FOX. They were decimated by OJIBWA, OTTAWA, and POTAWATOMI attacks during the Fox wars in the early 18th century, but changing their affiliations they aided in the final conquest of the ILLINOIS tribes, whereupon they settled south of present-day Peoria, Ill., and in adjacent parts of Indiana.

The Kickapoo adopted horses earlier than other neighboring tribes and adapted themselves to the great belt of prairie lands stretching from central Illinois to northern Mexico. They supported the Shawnee chief TECUMSEH against the Americans in the War of 1812 and the Americans against the SEMINOLE in Florida a decade later. They fought bitterly with their prairie rivals, the OSAGE, in the early 1820s. In 1852 a large number of Kickapoo migrated to Texas and later to Mexico; an estimated 500 Kickapoo were living in East Coahuita, Mexico, in the early 1970s. Other reservation groups are located in central Oklahoma, northeast Kansas, and Texas, where the Kickapoo number about 2,000 (1987 est.).   JAMES CLIFTON

Bibliography: Gibson, A. M., *The Kickapoos: Lords of the Middle Border* (1963); Ritzenthaler, Robert, and Peterson, F. A., *The Mexican Kickapoo* (1956; repr. 1970).

Kid, Thomas: see KYD, THOMAS.

Kidd, Captain

William Kidd, known as Captain Kidd, b. Scotland, c.1645, d. May 23, 1701, was a British pirate whose life has been much romanticized by literature. Kidd became a privateer and by 1690 was an affluent shipowner in New York. While engaged in a privateering mission off East Africa in 1696–97, he turned to piracy, capturing several ships. He returned (1699) to Oyster Bay, Long Island, thinking that his privateering commission would shield him from arrest. He was induced to sail to Boston, however, where he was detained and sent to London. Kidd was tried for piracy and murder and executed.

The disappearance of most of his booty gave rise to legends about Kidd and his buried treasure. The only treasure actually recovered was found on Gardiners Island, off Long Island, in 1699. Literary treatments of the Kidd legend include Edgar Allan Poe's *The Gold Bug* (1843).

Bibliography: Winston, Alexander P., *No Man Knows My Grave* (1969); Ritchie, Robert C., *Captain Kidd and the War against the Pirates* (1986).

Kidder, Alfred Vincent

Alfred Vincent Kidder, b. Marquette, Mich., Oct. 29, 1885, d. June 11, 1963, was one of the most eminent American archaeologists of the early 20th century. Working in the southwestern United States and later in Mesoamerica, he developed the first truly systematic approach to American prehistory.

Kidder was educated at Harvard University (A.B., 1908; A.M., 1912; Ph.D., 1914), where he became a specialist in southwestern archaeology. In 1915, as newly appointed director of excavations for Phillips Academy, in Andover, Mass., he began long-term investigations at the large Pecos pueblo in New Mexico. After his appointment to the Carnegie Institution of Washington in 1926, Kidder's interests shifted to

Mesoamerica. He was active in Carnegie projects in the MAYA region, especially the KAMINALJUYÚ excavations near Guatemala City. Kidder retired from the Institution in 1950.

Kidder's work at Pecos led him to develop a classification system that served as a vital framework for later investigations of PUEBLO culture. His *Introduction to the Study of Southwestern Archaeology* (1924), a model of archaeological reasoning, had an enormous impact on the field. As director of the Carnegie investigations in Mesoamerica, Kidder produced a body of multidisciplinary research that is a major contribution to knowledge of the Maya.   JOHN S. HENDERSON

Bibliography: Woodbury, Richard B., *Alfred V. Kidder* (1973).

kidnapping

Kidnapping (from *kid* plus *napper,* thief) is carrying away a person against that person's will and often holding him or her for ransom. The ransom demanded is usually monetary, but kidnapping has also been used for political extortion—to draw attention to a cause or to demand the release of political prisoners. In the 1970s and '80s political kidnapping internationally was increasingly linked to various practitioners of TERRORISM. Victims ranged from U.S. publishing heiress Patricia Hearst (in California in 1974) to former Italian prime minister Aldo MORO (in Italy in 1978) to numerous foreigners abducted and held hostage in turbulent Lebanon during the 1980s.

After the kidnapping of Charles A. LINDBERGH's 20-month-old son in 1932, federal kidnapping laws with severe penalties were enacted in the United States. In most states the penalty for kidnapping for ransom is life imprisonment. A recent trend in the United States has been an increased number of kidnappings of their own children by parents involved in child-custody disputes.

Bibliography: Abrahams, Sally, *Children in the Crossfire* (1983); Cassidy, E. B., *Political Kidnapping* (1986); Clutterbuck, Richard, *Kidnap and Ransom: The Response* (1978).

kidney, artificial

Artificial kidneys remove toxic wastes and fluids that build up in the blood of patients with impaired KIDNEY function. The procedure in blood filtering—termed *hemodialysis*—is employed in acute situations resulting from drug overdose, burns that can cause kidney shutdown, and circulatory shock following surgery. Chronic dialysis treatment was begun in 1960 at the University of Washington by Dr. Belding Scribner. It is used by patients with end-stage renal failure, which results from disorders such as glomerulonephritis (an immunological reaction to a strep infection resulting in kidney inflammation). Chronic patients are treated for 4 to 6 hours, 3 times a week, on the average, usually for the rest of their lives or until a kidney transplant can be performed (see TRANSPLANTATION, ORGAN). In the United States about 100,000 patients regularly receive hemodialysis.

The artificial kidney was first used on humans in 1943 by Dr. Willem Kolff in the Netherlands. He used a drum apparatus with a cellophane membrane that rotated through a saline solution. Blood from the patient was allowed to flow, via tubing, through the closed membrane. Because the saline solution was on the external side, the processes of osmosis and diffusion removed waste products and fluids, respectively. The more than 30-year delay from the time dialysis was first performed on animals in 1913 was due to the lack of a blood anticoagulant, heparin, a commercially made membrane, and a delivery machine for the solution.

Since the 1940s the saline solution bath has been replaced by sophisticated machines that deliver a solution, dialysate, to the artificial organ and have a number of safety monitors. The artificial kidney was made presterilized, disposable, and commercially available in 1955, an innovation that led the way to chronic treatment programs. Such programs grew significantly after 1973, when the U.S. government passed legislation guaranteeing 80 percent reimbursement through Medicare to all patients. In the 1980s, emphasis shifted to home dialysis. Continuous ambulatory peritoneal dialysis (CAPD), which uses a small, portable dialysis unit and allows patients greater movement, is less traumatic to the body, requires less time, and costs about 50% less than traditional dialysis.

In the late 1980s a natural kidney hormone, erythropoietin, became available in quantity through genetic engineering. Clinical trials have indicated that the protein can reverse the anemic condition observed in most dialysis patients, a condition that requires about one-fourth of them to receive periodic blood transfusions.   HOWARD GALER

Bibliography: Cogan, M. G., and Garovoy, M. E., eds., *Introduction to Dialysis* (1985); Gabriel, Roger, *A Patient's Guide to Dialysis and Transplantation,* 3d ed. (1987).

kidney disease

The kidneys are subject to numerous disorders. Some, present at birth, are called developmental and hereditary abnormalities; some arise as a result of uncontrolled cell growth and are called tumors. The majority of disorders, however, occur secondary to physiologic, anatomic, metabolic, or immunologic alterations within the body, or to toxic or infectious agents acquired from the environment. For instance, preliminary studies have shown a link between the overuse of two common painkillers, ibuprofen and acetaminophen, and kidney failure in some patients. Kidney disorders can be categorized according to the anatomic site they involve: those interfering with the blood flow of the kidneys, those directly damaging the nephrons (the functional units of the kidneys), and those obstructing the outflow of urine from the kidneys.

Developmental and Hereditary Abnormalities. Congenital abnormalities of size, shape, and number of the kidneys are quite common. These abnormalities cause problems only if they interfere with the passage of urine. A rather devastating hereditary condition is adult polycystic kidney disease. The kidneys become filled with large cysts, and the disease usually becomes apparent in the fourth or fifth decade of life. Scientists are very close to isolating the gene responsible.

A more unusual condition is hereditary nephritis, the most common variety being Alport's syndrome. Red blood cells and protein are present in the urine, deafness frequently develops, and progressive loss of renal function occurs. There are several hereditary renal tubular functional defects (the Fanconi syndrome) involving excretion of amino acids, monosaccharides, phosphate, and hydrogen ions; the Fanconi syndrome does not usually lead to renal failure.

Tumors. The two important malignant tumors of the kidney are: Wilm's tumor, which occurs primarily in the early years of life, and hypernephroma (renal cell cancer), which is more common in later years. Wilm's tumor occurs as a painful abdominal mass. Patients with hypernephroma have weight loss, weakness, and anemia. Surgical excision of these tumors is curative if it is done before they spread outside of the kidney.

Disorders of Renal Blood Flow. A decrease in renal blood flow may be secondary to primary (prerenal) events, including a reduced cardiac output (such as in heart failure), a decreased blood volume (hemorrhage or dehydration), decreased blood pressure, or hypotension (as in shock from severe infection). Correction of the primary event allows renal function to return to normal. Disease of the renal arteries also reduces renal blood flow, thereby decreasing renal function. Arteriosclerosis of the renal arterioles, due to severe hypertension, may rapidly reduce renal blood flow and impair renal function. Toxemia of pregnancy and renal vein thrombosis also may cause renal failure.

Disorders Directly Damaging the Nephrons. Each nephron in the kidney is composed of a glomerulus and its tubule. Some diseases, such as glomerulonephritis, primarily attack the glomerulus; others attack the tubulointerstitial portions of the kidneys. Acute glomerulonephritis occurs one to three weeks after a streptococcal skin infection or an upper-respiratory-tract infection and is manifested by scanty urine, red blood cells in the urine, edema, hypertension, and impaired renal function. The majority recover completely. Systemic diseases such as diabetes mellitus, multiple myeloma, and amyloidosis also may cause damage that can progress to renal failure.

The causes of tubulointerstitial disease of the kidneys are even more numerous. Acute tubular necrosis (cell death) is caused by toxic substances, circulating blood or muscle pigments, or shocklike states. It is an acute reversible form of renal tubular cell damage that is quite common. Interstitial nephritis may be due to toxic agents (analgesics, antibiotics, heavy metals), metabolic abnormalities (high levels of calcium or uric acid in the blood), infectious diseases (bacterial pyelonephritis, infectious mononucleosis), hypersensitivity reactions to drugs (sulfonamides, penicillins), vascular lesions (arteriosclerosis, sickle-cell anemia), obstruction of urine flow (stones), tumors (leukemia, lymphoma), and hereditary disorders (familial nephritis). Hemolytic uremia syndrome, a rare disease that is the most common cause of kidney failure in infants, was found in 1986 to be caused by a particular form of the bacterium *Escherichia coli.*

Disorders Obstructing the Urine Outflow. Obstruction of the urinary tract that causes blockage of the outflow of urine leads to renal damage. Numerous types of lesions can cause obstruction, such as congenital malformations and hereditary disorders (for example, cysts), infectious processes causing strictures (tuberculosis in the kidneys, gonorrhea in the urethra), stones, and tumors. Bladder dysfunction due to a neurologic lesion and bladder outlet obstruction due to prostatic hypertrophy also are common obstructive events. Some lesions lead to acute and others to chronic renal failure.

When end-stage renal failure, that is, complete loss of excretory function, ensues, patients may be kept alive by hemodialysis (see KIDNEY, ARTIFICIAL) or by receiving a renal transplant. When kidney failure occurs, toxic wastes build up in the body and cause UREMIA. If untreated, patients may die from such complications as infection, hemorrhage, resistant congestive heart failure, and hypertension.   JOHN M. WELLER

Bibliography: Cameron, Stewart, *Kidney Disease: The Facts,* 2d ed. (1986); Garrell, Dale C., and Snyder, Solomon H., eds., *Kidney Disorders* (1989); Kinsey, E., and Smith, M., *Renal Disease* (1987); Rose, B. D., ed., *Pathophysiology of Renal Disease,* 2d ed. (1987); Schrier, R. W., and Gottschalk, C. W., *Diseases of the Kidney,* 3 vols., 4th ed. (1988).

kidney stone

Stones, or calculi, commonly form in kidney tissue or the draining structures of the urinary tract as a result of diseases, infections, or incompletely defined problems of mineral excretion. The most common types of stones contain various combinations of calcium, magnesium, phosphorus, or oxalate. Kidney stones frequently form once without recurrence, but in extreme cases they may enlarge to fill the entire draining structure of the kidney. Uric-acid stones complicate gout, and they occasionally develop in the absence of other manifestations of that disease. Less common types are due to inherited disorders characterized by excretion of abnormal amounts of cystine or xanthine (see CYSTINURIA). In 1983 a drug, sodium cellulose phosphate, was introduced to reduce recurrence of stones formed from excessive calcium. Recurrence of most stones can be prevented by therapy based on analysis of the stones, the urine, and the blood.

When a stone causes erosion of tissue, blood appears in the urine; when one lodges in the draining tubes, there may be severe pain in the flank extending to the lower abdomen and groin. Other complications include obstruction to urine flow, persistent infection of the kidneys, and progressive tissue damage with loss of kidney function.

Most solitary stones are passed in the urine, but others require medical treatment. In the 1980s new procedures were developed that proved more effective than traditional surgical removal. Percutaneous removal employs a fiberoptic nephroscope, through which forceps, a basket, or a loop is inserted to extract the stone through the skin. A noninvasive technique uses narrowly focused acoustic shock waves to break up the stones (see LITHOTRIPSY). To break up stones in the lower ureter, the narrow canal between the kidney and the bladder, a laser light guided by optical fibers is used.

RICHARD B. FREEMAN

Bibliography: Pak, C. Y., ed., *Renal Stone Disease* (1987).

kidneys

The two kidneys are the major organs of excretion in vertebrates. Excess water, toxic waste products of metabolism such as UREA and URIC ACID, and inorganic salts are disposed by the kidneys in the form of URINE. The kidneys are also largely responsible for maintaining the water balance of the body and the acidity (pH) of the blood (see EXCRETORY SYSTEM). The kidneys and associated organs that produce and eliminate urine are collectively called the urinary system. The kidneys also play important roles in other body activities, such as in releasing the protein erythropoietin—which stimulates the bone marrow to increase the formation of red blood cells—and in helping to control blood pressure. Some drugs or their breakdown products are eliminated through the kidneys.

ANATOMY

Human kidneys are paired, reddish brown, bean-shaped structures about 11 cm (4.4 in) long. They are located in back of the body cavity, one on each side of the spine just above the waist. The kidneys are loosely held in place by a mass of fat (perirenal fat) and by two layers of fibrous tissue (renal fascia) between which the kidneys are placed. The outer margin is convex and the inner border concave. Located on the inner surface is a slit called the hilus, through which passes the arteries, veins, nerves, and the renal pelvis, a funnellike structure. Urine from each kidney is collected in the renal pelvis and passes into a hollow tube, the ureter, which is 40–45 cm (16–18 in) long and extends downward, emptying into the urinary bladder. A shorter, single tube, the urethra, eliminates urine from the bladder.

The cut surface of the kidney reveals two distinct areas: the cortex—a dark band along the outer border, about 1 cm (0.4 in) in thickness—and the inner medulla. The medulla is divided into 8 to 18 conical tissues termed renal pyramids. The apex of each pyramid, the papilla, extends into the renal pelvis, through which urine is discharged. The cortex arches over the bases of the pyramids (cortical arches) and extends down between each pyramid as the renal columns.

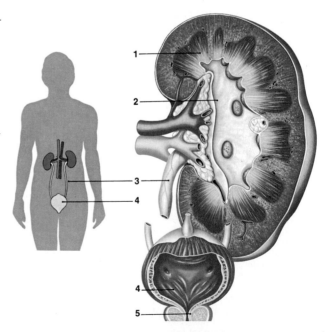

The kidneys, which are the most important organs of the excretory system, are located in the upper abdomen. Each kidney contains about one million nephrons (1), which purify the blood of the waste products that form urine. Urine travels from the nephrons to the renal pelvis (2) and into a ureter (3). The ureter of each kidney moves urine toward the bladder (4) by means of peristalsis, wavelike muscular contractions. The bladder, an elastic, baglike tissue, contracts when it is full, pushing the urine through the urethra (5) and out of the body.

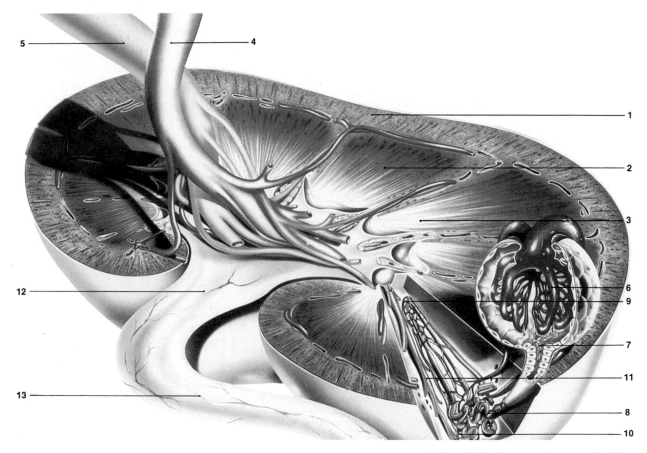

The kidneys filter out waste products from blood and maintain the salt and water balance of the body. A kidney has an outer cortex (1) and an inner medulla (2), which is divided into 8 to 18 segments known as pyramids (3). A renal artery (4) carries blood to the kidneys, and a renal vein (5) carries purified blood back into the general system. The nephron, which is the basic unit of the kidney, includes a glomerulus (6) that filters waste products from the blood. The waste products form a concentrated fluid (7) that passes through a descending tubule (8) to the loop of Henle (9) and into an ascending tubule (10). These tubules are surrounded by blood vessels that absorb and recycle water and salts from the fluid. A collecting tubule (11) carries the product, urine, from the nephron to the renal pelvis (12), which connects to a ureter (13).

Nephrons. Each kidney contains at least 1 million microscopic structures called nephrons, or renal tubules. These are the basic functional, or urine-forming, units of the kidney. Each nephron, about 4 cm (1.6 in) long, has thin walls of epithelial cells and is divided into a Bowman's capsule and a tubule. Each nephron begins with a renal corpuscle, which is a granular body found in the cortex. Each corpuscle is composed of a double-walled, cuplike structure called Bowman's capsule, and this surrounds a tuft or knot of blood vessels called a glomerulus (pl. glomeruli). A winding, convoluted section of the nephron tubule extends from Bowman's capsule toward the medulla region of the kidney and is called the proximal convoluted tubule. This region of the tubule is followed by Henle's loop. This loop, a relatively straight portion of the tubule, extends into the medulla and loops back in a sharp turn to the cortex. The final section, the distal convoluted tubule, is also convoluted and winding and is located close to the proximal convoluted portion. It continues on to connect other tubules in a branching structure called the collecting tubules. The collecting tubules descend into the medulla and terminate at the papillae, thus conducting the formed urine to the renal pelvis.

Blood Circulation. Arterial blood enters the kidneys, at the hilus, by renal arteries, which subdivide into smaller and yet smaller arteries, and finally to afferent arterioles. They lead into the 30 to 40 capillary loops of the glomerulus. Blood is recollected from each glomerulus by the efferent arterioles, which are much smaller in diameter than the afferent arterioles and therefore create a relatively higher backup blood pressure in the capillaries of the glomerulus than in other capillaries of the body. This is significant in the efficient filtering function of the nephron. The efferent vessels divide into capillaries surrounding the tubules, thus supplying blood to the medulla. Eventually they rejoin into veins and exit through the renal hilus.

URINE PRODUCTION

The initial site of urine production is the glomerulus. Arterial blood pressure, originally generated from the heart, drives a filtrate of plasma across the porous capillary walls of the glomeruli into the open space around the capillary tuft, called Bowman's space, and is collected in Bowman's capsule. The filtered plasma, now called glomerular filtrate, is mainly water but also contains salts, glucose, amino acids, nitrogenous wastes such as urea, and a small amount of ammonia. Proteins, fats, and cellular elements (red blood cells, white blood cells, and platelets) are filtered out so that they remain in the general blood circulation. In normal kidneys 100 to 140 milliliters (0.21 to 0.29 pt) of filtrate is formed each minute, for a total of about 170 liters (180 qt) per day.

As the glomerular filtrate passes along the proximal convoluted tubule, the majority of its water content and some of its dissolved materials are reabsorbed through the walls of the tubule into the blood of the surrounding capillaries. This reabsorption process is highly selective. Water, sodium and chloride ions, most of the bicarbonate, and all of the glucose are reabsorbed into the bloodstream, while other products, such as urea and ammonia, remain in the tubule.

During the later stage, through Henle's loop and the distal convoluted tubule, most of the remaining filtrate is further selectively reabsorbed, so only about 1 percent of the volume of the original filtrate is finally excreted as urine. The urine is considerably different in composition from the original filtrate.

The kidneys excrete 400 to 2,000 milliliters (0.84 to 4.2 pt) of urine or more per day; excretion varies in volume and composition depending on the needs of the host. Kidneys maintain the internal fluid environment within narrow limits and are capable of adapting to a wide range of environmental situations. The cells lining the tubules are under the influence of regulating factors such as the hormones aldosterone (from the adrenal gland), antidiuretic hormone, parathyroid hormone, and atrial natriuretic factor (from the heart).

The distal tubule regulates the overall acidity of the urine, and ultimately of the blood, by excretion of hydrogen ions. Ammonia combines with hydrogen to form ammonia ions that are secreted into the urine. The removal of hydrogen ions decreases the acidity.

All the blood glucose will be removed unless the blood glucose exceeds normal concentrations by a considerable amount. Other mechanisms remove most, if not all, of the other solutes, such as sodium. Much of the sodium ion in kidney filtrate is transported back to the blood, but 3 to 5 g (0.1 to 0.17 oz) pass into the urine each day. As a result, most animals have strict salt requirements and must consume several grams of sodium chloride daily in order to live. The retention of sodium is enhanced by the presence of aldosterone. This hormone is secreted into the bloodstream when the body's supply of sodium falls below normal. When there is an excess of sodium, aldosterone secretion is reduced and more sodium is excreted.

When excessive amounts of fluid are lost from the body, or the blood pressure falls below normal, the kidneys release the enzyme renin into the blood, where it promotes the formation of angiotensin. Within minutes, angiotensin causes vasoconstriction, which increases blood pressure and stimulates the secretion of aldosterone.

EVOLUTION OF THE KIDNEY

The structure of the nephron is basically the same in the kidneys of all vertebrates and has even been identified in the fossils of the oldest known vertebrates. The kidney has gone through a series of changes, however, in the course of evolution from invertebrates. In invertebrates, the excretory organ is a simple absorbing tubule called a nephridium. Among lower vertebrates, such as the fishes, there exists a primitive kind of kidney, called the holonephros, that consists of three to five kidney tubules near the heart. Most adult fishes and amphibians have a posterior kidney, or opisthonephros, containing a more-complicated type of tubule. Adult reptiles, birds, and mammals have the most advanced form of kidney, called a metanephros.

During human embryonic development, a holonephros appears in the third week of gestation and begins degenerating by the fourth week without ever having functioned as a kidney. A true kidney, an opisthonephros, forms during the fourth week, and a metanephros takes its place during the fifth or sixth week and remains as the functional kidney for life.

It is generally believed that the kidney first evolved in the original vertebrates, which were freshwater life forms requiring some means for pumping excess water from the body. In keeping with the laws of OSMOSIS, there is a continual flow of water into the bodies of freshwater fish. This excess water must be disposed of once it has entered. At the same time that the nephron first evolved and developed, it became capable of reabsorbing glucose, salts, and other materials that otherwise would have been lost in pumping out surplus water.

In the case of freshwater fishes that returned to the sea and in the evolution of land animal forms (reptiles and birds), the situation became reversed: water conservation, rather than disposal, became the problem, and the nephron became a liability instead of an asset. This difficulty appears to have been solved during evolution in a number of ways. Nearly all marine teleosts (bony fishes) show more or less reduction in the number and size of glomeruli, culminating in some forms

having no glomeruli in the nephrons. These fishes also eliminate large amounts of salt through the gills, thus retaining fresh water. Retaining their large glomeruli, the marine elasmobranchs (sharks and rays) are similar to the fresh-water teleosts in that they take in water and excrete copious amounts of urine.

The reptilian-avian line patterns itself after the marine teleosts by reducing the glomerular system, although no aglomerular kidney occurs. Mammals adapted to dry land are able to conserve water by producing extremely concentrated urine. The kangaroo rat, an extremely efficient water conserver, can produce urine six times as concentrated as sea water.

RICHARD B. FREEMAN

Bibliography: Crowley, L. V., *Introductory Concepts in Anatomy and Physiology* (1976); DeWardner, H. E., *The Kidney*, 5th ed. (1985); Hladky, S. B., and Rink, T. J., *Body Fluids and Kidney Physiology* (1986); Lote, Christopher, *Principles of Renal Physiology* (1982); Marsh, D. J., *Renal Physiology* (1983); O'Connor, W. J., *Normal Renal Function* (1982); Riegel, J. A., *Comparative Physiology of Renal Excretion* (1972); Smith, Homer W., *The Kidney: Structure and Functions in Health and Disease* (1951); Vander, Arthur J., *Renal Physiology* (1975).

See also: KIDNEY DISEASE.

Kiel   [keel]

Kiel is the capital of Schleswig-Holstein state in northern West Germany. It is located about 90 km (55 mi) north of Hamburg, on the Kiel Fjord, where the Kiel Canal enters the Baltic Sea. Its population is 246,900 (1983 est.). The climate is temperate, with a July average temperature of 17° C (63° F) and a January average of 6° C (33° F). Annual rainfall averages 710 mm (28 in). The city's industries include shipping, shipbuilding, electrical engineering, food processing (especially fish), printing, and the manufacture of textiles and precision instruments. Christian Albrecht University (1665) has noted schools of economics, international law, and oceanography. The naval base at Kiel was of major importance to Germany during both world wars.

First mentioned in the 10th century, Kiel was chartered in 1242 and became a member of the HANSEATIC LEAGUE in 1284. It was the seat of the powerful dukes of Holstein until 1773, when it came under Danish control. In 1866 it passed, with all of Holstein, to Prussia. Construction of the canal, linking the North and Baltic seas, began in 1887 and the canal began operating in 1895. The city was heavily bombed during World War II, but the damaged sections have been rebuilt.

Kielland, Alexander Lange   [kel'-lahn, ahl-ek-sahn'-dur lahng'-eh]

A Norwegian novelist, short-story writer, and dramatist, Alexander Lange Kielland, b. Feb. 18, 1849, d. Apr. 6, 1906, came from an upper-class background but devoted his literary life to pointing out social inequality and social ills. Despite his intent to voice social indignation, Kielland's writing is infused with a general air of optimism, an elegant style, wit, and irony. His major works include two collections of short stories, published in 1879 and 1880, which are characterized by their dramatic structure and well-turned point; three works in which he attacked conditions in various social institutions; and three novels portraying Norwegian social and cultural life: *Garman and Worse* (1880; Eng. trans., 1885); *Else* (1881; Eng. trans., 1894), and *Skipper Worse* (1882; Eng. trans., 1885).

KJETIL A. FLATIN

Bibliography: Beyer, Harald, *A History of Norwegian Literature* (1956).

Kienholz, Edward   [keen'-hohlts]

Edward Kienholz, b. Fairfield, Wash., 1927, is an American artist best known for his complex, often bizarre assemblages, or tableaux, of found objects. Originally a creator of wall and panel collage assemblages, Kienholz in the mid-1950s belonged to a Los Angeles–based group of artists who sought to create a nonelitist art for the public. He also helped organize (1957) the innovative Ferus Gallery, which exhibited works of West Coast abstract expressionist (see ABSTRACT EXPRESSIONISM) artists. By 1962, Kienholz's own relief assemblages had grown so complex that they could no longer be placed on walls, and he began making his environmental tableaux.

BARBARA CAVALIERE

Bibliography: Calas, Nicolas and Elena, *Icons and Images of the Sixties* (1971); Tuchman, Maurice, *Edward Kienholz* (1966).

Kierkegaard, Søren   [kyair'-kuh-gawr, sur'-en]

Søren Kierkegaard, a 19th-century Danish philosopher and religious writer, sought to differentiate among the truly religious, the aesthetic, and the ethical modes of life. His emphasis on subjective commitment to truth made him the forerunner of existentialism.

Søren Aabye Kierkegaard, b. May 5, 1813, d. Nov. 11, 1855, was a Danish philosopher and religious thinker whose reaction against the depersonalization of society and against the established church of Denmark took the form of brilliant literary and philosophical essays. He is regarded by philosophers today as a precursor of EXISTENTIALISM, although not all existentialists are directly influenced by him.

Kierkegaard studied philosophy and theology at the University of Copenhagen and received a master's degree in 1840. The next year he shocked Copenhagen's society by breaking his engagement to Regine Olsen, the daughter of a treasury official. Although he broke the engagement for fear that he and his fiancee might lack common philosophic interests, he gave the impression of acting out of a brutal and indifferent selfishness in order to make the breach definitive. Thereafter he lived a life of seclusion, devoted to writing. The impact on his career of the broken engagement, as well as his austere Lutheran upbringing and his melancholia, is evident in virtually everything he wrote thereafter.

Many of Kierkegaard's books, such as *Either/Or* (1843; Eng. trans., 1944) and *Philosophical Fragments* (1844; Eng. trans., 1936), were written under pseudonyms. He adopted this practice in order to avoid giving the impression that the views expressed in the books constituted any definitive religious position, or even that they necessarily represented his own position.

Kierkegaard's unifying theme was that there are three spheres of existence—the aesthetic, the ethical, and the religious—in constant tension. He found the first of these, personal aesthetic enjoyment, in the fickle search for pleasure that is essentially egoistic. The second, the ethical sphere, is not egoistic; rather it is an impersonal ideal, a law based on reason rather than personal preference and convenience. In this stage, life is not a series of separate moments of pleasure but a long-range project to be organized according to rational principles. These principles include not only the rules of ultimate self-interest but also the abstract principles of morality that describe what an individual ought to do. In the third stage, that of true religious choice, no automatic, rational decision procedure can be employed, but rather a "leap of faith" provides the grounds for decision. Thus in *Fear and Trembling* (1843; Eng. trans., 1941) Kierkegaard retold the sto-

ry of Abraham's dilemma in such a way as to present the two alternatives of an abstract ethical universal (the abstract rule that one should not kill one's child) and a concrete religious commitment (the unjustifiable but undeniable command of God to Abraham that he should slay Isaac).

For Kierkegaard, the highest level of human life consists of recognizing the need for RELIGION as a subjective commitment to truth, as opposed to the Hegelian philosophy of pure thought. Kierkegaard attacked what he considered to be the sterile METAPHYSICS of G. W. F. HEGEL, who attempted to systematize the whole of existence and create an objective theory of knowledge. Kierkegaard's often repeated statement, "truth is subjectivity," should not be understood in the sense of a shallow individualism. Rather, it links truth with the subject instead of with its object, making the full communication of truth to other subjects impossible. Kierkegaard drew the only logical conclusion from his principle—that it is impossible to establish an objective system of doctrinal truths.

Although few 19th-century thinkers have surpassed Kierkegaard's influence on 20th-century thought, there is no "Kierkegaardian school" of philosophy, theology, or literary criticism. This is due largely to the fact that he did not develop an all-embracing system, but instead deliberately developed his ideas from several often incompatible points of view at the same time. But lack of an explicit following is itself a confirmation of Kierkegaard's philosophy, for he insisted that the individual was the repository of truth.

THOMAS E. WREN

Bibliography: Collins, James, *The Mind of Kierkegaard* (1953; repr. 1965); Elrod, John W., *Kierkegaard and Christendom* (1981); Hannay, Alastair, *Kierkegaard* (1982); Lowrie, Walter, *A Short Life of Kierkegaard* (1942); Stendahl, Brita K., *Søren Kierkegaard* (1976).

Kiesler, Frederick John   [kees'-lur]

The Austrian architect Frederick John Kiesler, b. Vienna, Sept. 2, 1896, d. Dec. 27, 1965, was a visionary "nonbuilding" architect noted for his development of freely flowing spaces in sculptured forms. His unorthodox approach to architecture was first expressed in a 1923 design for a City in Space, which he based on the principles of bridge building. In the late 1920s and early '30s he carried these ideas forward in designs for an Endless Theater and a House in Space, culminating eventually in his plan for an Endless House, which was exhibited (1959–60) at the Museum of Modern Art in New York City. According to Kiesler the rounded shapes of these revolutionary architectural forms could be created by applying a plastic substance, such as concrete, to a sculptured mesh of steel. Kiesler's avant-garde aesthetics were put to most direct use in his work as director of scenic design (1934–37) at the Juilliard School of Music, New York City.

RON WIEDENHOEFT

Bibliography: Guggenheim Museum, *Frederick Kiesler* (1964).

Kiev   [kee'-yuhf]

Kiev, the third-largest city of the USSR, is the capital of the Ukrainian Soviet Socialist Republic and the administrative center of Kiev oblast. Located in the north central Ukraine, it is on the DNEPR RIVER just below the mouth of the Desna. Kiev's population is 2,355,000 (1983 est.), and its area is 707 km² (300 mi²). One of the largest industrial, cultural, and educational centers of the USSR, the city is also a major transport hub at the junction of railroads, highways, and the navigable Dnepr. The city's main airport is situated at Borispol, to the east. Kiev was originally built and is still largely located on the higher, west bank of the Dnepr. More recently it has spread over the lower, east-bank section known as Darnitsa.

Contemporary City. The city's population is predominantly Ukrainian (65% of the total); ethnic Russians constitute 23% and Jews 9%. The historical heart of Kiev, on the west bank of the Dnepr, falls into three distinctive districts. They are the Upper Town, the city center with the main business street, the Kreshchatik; Pechersk, to the south, with a noted 11th-century cave monastery and the government buildings; and Podol, to the north, the old commercial and Jewish district.

Kiev's important industries are situated mainly in Darnitsa, on the eastern side of the Dnepr, downwind from the city proper, thus reducing air pollution in the city. The principal manufacturing establishments produce river and seagoing vessels, airplanes, motorcycles, cameras, synthetic fibers, building materials, and a wide range of machinery and metal products. Electricity needs are met both by heat and power plants within the city and by the Kiev hydroelectric station, just upstream on the Dnepr River.

As the national center of the Ukraine, Kiev has a wide network of educational and cultural institutions. It is the seat of the Ukrainian Academy of Sciences and many of its affiliated research institutes. The Kiev State University (1834) has a student enrollment of about 20,000. Its Polytechnical Institute (1898) heads a long list of engineering schools. Cultural facilities include the Shevchenko Theater of Opera and Ballet and both Ukrainian and Russian drama theaters, as well as the Kiev State Historical Museum and museums of both Ukrainian and Russian fine arts. Historical sites are St. Sophia Cathedral, dating from 1037; the 11th-century Golden Gate, one of the original city gates; and the ruins of the 11th-century Kiev-Pechersk cave monastery, long an important pilgrimage site and now a museum. The Babi Yar monument (1976) marks a site where thousands of Jews and Soviet prisoners of war were massacred by the Germans during World War II.

History.   One of the oldest cities in Europe, Kiev was probably founded by the 7th century and was first mentioned in 9th-century chronicles. It flourished from the 9th to the 12th century as a trade center and the capital of an early Russian state known as Kievan Russia (see RUSSIA/UNION OF SOVIET SOCIALIST REPUBLICS, HISTORY OF). Kiev was virtually destroyed by Mongol invaders in 1240. It fell under the rule of Lithuania (c.1362) and then Poland (1569) before passing to Russia in 1654. With the development of steam navigation on the Dnepr and the building of railroads, Kiev became an important financial and commercial city in the mid-19th century. Industrial development dates mainly from the Soviet period, especially after the capital of the Ukraine was moved there in 1934. German forces occupied the city from September 1941 to November 1943, during World War II, and it suffered extensive damage.   THEODORE SHABAD

Kigali   [kee-gah'-lee]

Kigali is the capital and commercial center of Rwanda, in central Africa (1980 est. pop., 139,900). An international airport and the École Technique Officielle Don Bosco (1956) are located there. Tin and tungsten are mined nearby.

Kikuyu   [ki-koo'-yoo]

The Kikuyu (Gikuyu) are an East African people of the Kenya highlands. They speak a Bantu language of the Benue-Congo subfamily of the Niger-Congo stock; in the mid-1980s they numbered more than 4,000,000. A farming people, they traditionally live in hilltop villages of dispersed homesteads. Political authority rests in a council of elders. Males are organized in age grades, progressing from initiation in adolescence to political office in mature adulthood. Descent is patrilineal, residence patrilocal. Polygyny is the general rule, with each wife having her own dwelling. Bride price is paid by the husband to the wife's people in the form of livestock.

The Kikuyu have long been subject to competition for land, first with neighboring Masai raiders and later with English settlers. By the mid-1900s many Kikuyu were working as laborers on European farms or in Nairobi. From 1952 to 1956 under the leadership of Jomo KENYATTA, the MAU MAU movement aimed at recovering land taken by Europeans, obtaining self-government for Africans, restoring traditional customs, and driving out all foreigners. Kenya's largest tribal group, the Kikuyu have continued to play a strong role in national affairs since Kenyan independence (1963).   PHOEBE MILLER

Bibliography: Gatheru, R. M., *Child of Two Worlds: A Kikuyu's Story* (1972); Kenyatta, Jomo, *Facing Mount Kenya: The Life of the Gikuyu* (1938; repr. 1962); Lambert, H. E., *Kikuyu Social and Political Institutions* (1956; repr. 1965); Leakey, Louis S. B., *Mau Mau and the Kikuyu* (1952); Muriuki, Godfrey, *A History of the Kikuyu, 1500–1900* (1974); Turnbull, Colin, *Man in Africa* (1976).

Kilauea   [kee-lah-way'-uh]

Kilauea is the world's largest active volcano crater. Part of MAUNA LOA, it is located on south central Hawaii island in Volcanoes National Park. The summit of Kilauea reaches 1,247 m (4,090 ft), and the crater is 13 km (8 mi) in circumference. Kilauea's eruptions are generally in the form of molten lava lakes, with little escaping gas and few explosions.

Kildare   [kil-dair']

Kildare is a county in eastern Ireland, located in Leinster province. It covers 1,694 km^2 (654 mi^2) and has a population of 104,122 (1981). Kildare is the county seat, but the county council meets at Naas. Most of the area is flat farmland. The principal crops are wheat, barley, oats, and root vegetables. Kildare is famous for racehorse breeding, and cattle raising is also important. Manufactures include textiles, paper products, and cutlery. Naas was the home of the kings of Leinster from the 2d to the 12th century. The town of Kildare grew up around a religious house founded in the 5th century.

Kilimanjaro   [kil-ih-muhn-jah'-roh]

Kilimanjaro, the highest mountain in Africa, is a snow-covered inactive volcano on the plains of northeastern Tanzania close to the border with Kenya. It has two peaks: the taller, Kibo, is 5,895 m (19,340 ft) high, and the lower, Mawenzi, is 5,149 m (17,564 ft). Kibo and Mawenzi are connected by a ridge. The crater of Kibo, 2 km (1.2 mi) wide and up to 300 m (984 ft) deep, is covered by a thick, slowly decreasing ice cap. Members of the Masai tribe inhabit the lower parts of the mountain, where there are also coffee plantations.

The first Europeans to discover Kilimanjaro, the legendary burial place of King Solomon, were two German missionaries, Johannes Rebmann and Ludwig Krapf, in 1848. Their tales of a snow-covered peak near the equator, however, were not initially believed. Later two other Germans were the first to reach (1889) the Kibo summit.

Kilkenny   (city)   [kil-ken'-ee]

Kilkenny (Gaelic: Cill Choinnigh) is the seat of County Kilkenny in southeastern Ireland, located in the valley of the River Nore. Its population is 9,473 (1981). The commercial center of a rich agricultural region, it is also an industrial city with beer brewing and other diversified light manufactures. During the 6th century Saint Canice established a monastery there. Later, Kilkenny was the capital of the kingdom of Ossory. From the Norman period until 1843, Kilkenny was divided into Englishtown and Irishtown, with much strife between the two. Anglo-Norman parliaments were held there from 1293 to 1408, and from 1642 to 1648 (during the English Civil War) Kilkenny was the capital of the Roman Catholic confederacy. It surrendered to Oliver Cromwell in 1650.

Kilkenny   (county)

Kilkenny is a county in Leinster province, located in southeastern Ireland. Its 2,061-km^2 (796-mi^2) area consists of low hills and plains watered by the Barrow, Nore, and Suir rivers. The population is 70,806 (1981). Kilkenny is the county town. Grains, vegetables, and livestock are raised, anthracite coal is mined, and brewing is a well-established industry. The county has numerous ancient sites including Iron Age fortifications, inscribed stones and crosses, castles, and abbeys. It became a part of Leinster province in 1210.

Killarney   [kil-lar'-nee]

Killarney (1981 pop., 7,678) is the market town of County Kerry, southwestern Ireland. Many tourists are attracted by Killarney's mild climate and scenic location. The town is surrounded by lakes and mountains, with Macgillycuddy's Reeks—the highest mountains in Ireland—nearby and the Lakes of Killarney only 2.5 km (1.5 mi) away. Lace, shoes, woolens, and other light manufactures are produced. The cathedral (built 1846) was designed by Augustus Pugin.

killifish [kil'-ih-fish]

Killifish are about 300 species of small, minnowlike fishes in the family Cyprinodontidae. Also called topminnows or toothcarps, killifish are found in warmer fresh, brackish, or salt water throughout most of the world. Killifish are stout or slender fishes typically with flattened heads and upturned lower jaws, the mouth opening upward. One group of killifishes, found in Africa and South America, are known as annual fishes because they pass through a complete life cycle—birth, reproduction, and death—in less than one year. This brief lifespan is an adaption of the species for surviving in ponds and other waters that dry up every year. When water levels fall, these fishes, such as *Cynolebias*, spawn and produce eggs that are extremely resistant to drying. The eggs and developing young remain in the pond bottom until the following rainy season and hatch when the waters rise.   ALAN R. EMERY

Killy, Jean Claude [kee-leé, zhawn klohd]

Jean Claude Killy, b. Aug. 30, 1943, was a French downhill skier who, during the 1968 Winter Olympic Games in Grenoble, France, became only the second skier ever to win all three gold medals for men's Alpine skiing. Killy also won the World Championship combined titles in 1965 and 1966 and the World Cup in 1967 and 1968. He was world professional champion in 1972 and retired soon thereafter. Killy served as copresident of the Olympic organizing committee for the 1992 Winter Games, in Albertville, France.

Kilmer, Joyce [kil'-mur]

The poet and journalist Alfred Joyce Kilmer, b. New Brunswick, N.J., Dec. 6, 1886, d. July 30, 1918, is famous for his poem "Trees" (1914), a work full of sentiment and confused simile. Kilmer wrote war poems that were far better, such as "Rouge Bouquet" (1918). His collections include *Trees and Other Poems* (1914) and *Main Street and Other Poems* (1917). Kilmer died in battle during World War I.   JAMES HART

kiln

The unfired pottery shown here is moving through a continuous kiln, where the temperature gradually increases until a maximum is reached at the kiln's center. Temperature levels are varied according to the nature of the composition of the materials being fired.

A kiln is an oven or furnace specially designed to bake, dry, harden, or burn various materials. Kilns that operate at relatively low temperatures are used to dry hops, cure tobacco, and season wood; high-temperature kilns may operate at temperatures up to 1,200° C (2,192° F) and are used to fire BRICK and POTTERY. A basic distinction between kilns is their method of firing. An intermittent kiln is loaded with the material to be fired, and the temperature is raised to the required level for the necessary time; the kiln is then allowed to cool before the fired material is unloaded. In continuous kilns, the firing temperature is maintained continuously. The material to be fired is drawn slowly into the firing zone, where the temperature is highest, and then into gradually cooler areas until it is cool enough to be removed. Rotary kilns, such as those used to make cement, are heated cylinders inclined at a slight angle,

that revolve slowly as the raw materials are fed into the top. The materials gradually descend through the firing zone and cool by the time they reach the bottom.

Kilpatrick, William Heard

William Heard Kilpatrick, b. White Plains, Ga., Nov. 20, 1871, d. Feb. 13, 1965, was an American philosopher widely regarded as the father of progressive education. After studying at Mercer and Johns Hopkins universities, Kilpatrick taught in the Georgia public schools and at Mercer. He taught at Teachers College, Columbia University, from 1909 until he retired in 1938. A colleague of the philosopher John Dewey, whose ideas he popularized, Kilpatrick developed the project method of teaching, emphasizing a child-centered rather than subject-oriented approach. By the time he retired, he had taught 34,000 graduate students. His books include *The Educational Frontier* (1933; repr. 1969) and *Philosophy of Education* (1951).

Kim Il Sung [keem eel sung]

Kim Il Sung, originally Kim Sung Chu, b. Apr. 15, 1912, became premier of the People's Republic of Korea (North Korea) on its establishment in 1948. Kim, who joined the Communist party in 1931, fought the Japanese occupation forces in the 1930s and commanded a Korean unit in the Soviet army in World War II. As premier, Kim directed the invasion of South Korea that led to the KOREAN WAR (1950–53). He became president in 1972 under a revised constitution. Promoting self-reliance, he has isolated his country from the outside world. Kim, known in North Korea as "Great Leader," has designated his eldest son, Kim Jong Il, as his successor.

Bibliography: Suh, Dae-Sook, *Kim Il Sung* (1988); Tai Sung An, *North Korea in Transition: From Dictatorship to Dynasty* (1983).

Kimberley [kim'-bur-lee]

Kimberley, a city of 74,061 (1985) in Cape province, central South Africa, is the nation's leading diamond center. Several diamond mines are located there, and all diamonds mined in South Africa are sold in Kimberley. Iron, manganese, and gypsum are also mined, and textiles and construction materials are manufactured. The city is an important rail junction. Kimberley was founded in 1871, after diamonds were discovered there. The mines were held by De Beers Consolidated Mines, headed by Cecil Rhodes. The famous Open Mine produced about 14,508,000 carats of diamonds between 1871 and 1914, when it closed.   ALAN C. G. BEST

kimberlite [kim-bur-lite]

Kimberlites are fragmented igneous rocks that occur as narrow, pipelike fissures extending through plates of continental crust. Relatively low in silica, they differ from surrounding rocks and apparently were explosively emplaced by forces deep within the Earth's mantle. In minerological terms, kimberlites are PERIDOTITES of serpentinized mica content (see SERPENTINE). They contain a variety of high-pressure minerals, including DIAMOND. The most notable are found in South Africa, Tanzania, Angola, and Siberia.

Most kimberlite pipes were emplaced in the range about 100 million years ago, although the Premier in South Africa dates from 1,150 million years. The pipe at the famous Kimberley diamond mine in South Africa is the archetype, typifying their narrow surface area (approximately 40,000 m²/450,000 ft²) and great depth (from more than 1,000 m/3,500 ft below the present land surface to the limit of mining). At the time of the eruption, the Kimberley pipe extended an estimated additional 1,400 m (4,600 ft) through now-eroded layers of overlying sediments and formed a deep, narrow funnel of debris and kimberlite magma.   JAMES A. WHITNEY

Bibliography: Cox, Keith G., "Kimberlite Pipes," *Scientific American*, April 1978.

Kimbundu: see MBUNDU.

Kincardine   [kin-kar'-din]

Kincardine, also known as The Mearns, is a former county on the North Sea coast of Scotland. To the west the rugged Grampians rise to more than 610 m (2,000 ft). Along the coast and in the river valleys potatoes and oats are grown; livestock raising is also important. Stonehaven (1981 pop., 7,885), the area's largest town, was once an important fishing village; now tourism and the wool industry are significant. The Picts were the first known inhabitants of the area, which also has some Roman remains. In 1296 a document was drawn up at Kincardine, turning over the Scottish crown to King Edward I, king of England. Kincardine became a part of the new administrative region of GRAMPIAN in 1975.

kindergarten: see PRESCHOOL EDUCATION.

Kindi, al-   [kin-dee, ahl]

Known as al-Arab because of his southern Arabian origins, al-Kindi, d. *c.*873, served as a translator and editor of Greek philosophical works at the court of the Abbasid caliphs al-Mamun and Mutasim. He was well versed in ancient learning and devoted his life to its dissemination in all areas of Muslim culture. Al-Kindi's name was closely associated in the Middle Ages with astrology and alchemy, but in fact he was more interested in astronomy than astrology, and always maintained a skeptical attitude toward alchemy.

In his philosophical and scientific writings, al-Kindi was eclectic, although he regarded Neopythagorean mathematics as the foundation of all science; and like al-FARABI, he attempted to reconcile the views of Plato and Aristotle. According to al-Kindi, revealed and natural theology (philosophy) reached the same conclusions, but he maintained that philosophy was inferior to revelation. He believed in the immortality of the individual human soul, but could not give philosophical proofs for the resurrection of the body, which, he declared, was a matter of faith, not reason.   TAMARA M. GREEN

Bibliography: Boer, Tjitze de, *The History of Philosophy in Islam,* trans. by Edward R. Jones (1903; repr. 1967); Sarton, George, *Introduction to the History of Science,* vol. 1 (1927; repr. 1975); Weinberg, Julius, *A Short History of Medieval Philosophy* (1964).

kinematics   [kin-eh-mat'-iks]

Kinematics is the branch of physics concerned with the description of motion. (The analysis of the causes of motion is a separate subject called DYNAMICS.) The standard way to describe motion is to give the position of an object as a function of time. In one dimension, the displacement *x* from the origin is given in terms of the time *t* after zero time. The velocity *v* is the time rate of change of position. Similarly, acceleration is the time rate of change of velocity. When objects move in three dimensions, the speeds and accelerations in each perpendicular direction can be treated separately, since both velocity and acceleration are vectors.   CLIFFORD E. SWATZ

See also: LAWS OF MOTION; MOTION, PLANAR.

kinetic art   [kin-et'-ik]

The term *kinetic art* is applied to sculpture in which physical motion plays an important role. The parts of a kinetic sculpture may be moved mechanically or by natural means. Kinetic art is a 20th-century phenomenon and was created by artists who saw it as valuable metaphor for the rhythms of a mechanical age. The Italian futurists (see FUTURISM) were the first to emphasize physical motion as the dominant element of an aesthetic theory. Similar ideas were put forward by Marcel DUCHAMP, whose *Mobile: Bicycle Wheel* (1913; Philadelphia Museum of Art) is thought to have been the first sculpture to use physical movement. After World War I, Soviet constructivist sculptors (see CONSTRUCTIVISM) incorporated the idea of

motion into their dynamic works. Vladimir Yevgrafovich TATLIN conceived a completely kinetic *Monument to the Third International,* which was never executed. Ideas of kinetic art were developed further by László MOHOLY-NAGY, who, while working during the 1920s at the Bauhaus in Weimar, Germany, experimented with light and color. In 1932, Alexander CALDER created the first true MOBILE, whose parts move in air currents. Calder's mobiles inspired a resurgence of kinetic art, whose possibilities were explored in the 1950s and 1960s by such artists as Jean TINGUELY.   BARBARA CAVALIERE

Bibliography: Apollonio, Umbro, ed., *Futurist Manifestos* (1973); Kepes, Gyorgy, *The Nature and Art of Motion* (1965); Malina, Frank J., ed., *Kinetic Art: Theory and Practice* (1974); Moholy-Nagy, László, *Vision in Motion* (1947); Popper, Frank, *The Origins and Development of Kinetic Art* (1969); Selz, Peter, *Directions in Kinetic Sculpture* (1966).

kinetic energy

Kinetic energy is the energy of motion. Both solid objects in motion and flowing fluids possess kinetic energy simply because of their motion. This kinetic energy arises from, and is equivalent to, the work expended to bring about the motion. For example, work is done in the act of throwing a baseball; not counting air friction, the kinetic energy of the baseball in flight is equivalent to the work required to throw it. Mathematically, the kinetic energy of a moving object is expressed as half the product of the object's mass and the square of its speed, or $\frac{1}{2}mv^2$. Thus, massive objects traveling at high speeds possess large amounts of kinetic energy.

Kinetic energy is only one of several types of energy that are important in the study of physics, and engineers seek efficient ways to convert one to the other. The kinetic energy of waterfalls and spinning turbines is converted to electrical energy; to stop a speeding automobile, its kinetic energy is dissipated by frictional heating in the brakes.   GARY S. SETTLES

See also: CONSERVATION, LAWS OF; ENERGY; POTENTIAL ENERGY.

kinetic theory of matter

The kinetic theory of matter is an attempt to explain and predict all measurable properties of gases, liquids, and solids, based on a knowledge of their atomic and molecular compositions. This largely has been achieved for simple, low-density gases, and considerable progress is being made toward a similar understanding of more complex gases, liquids, and solids.

The kinetic theory of matter is based upon three fundamental assumptions. First, all matter is composed of atoms and molecules, even though other successful methods treat matter as uniform, continuous substances. Second, these atoms and molecules are not at rest but are in constant thermal motion, of which heat is a manifestation. Third, any macroscopic sample contains a large enough number of atoms or molecules so that statistical concepts can be used to determine their properties, eliminating the necessity of calculating the motion of each individual molecule. These postulates, in a more precise and mathematical form, are the basis of the kinetic theory of matter.

Development. The kinetic theory of gases was developed in the 19th century to explain a number of diverse experiments on gases carried out during the 17th and 18th centuries. (See GAS LAWS.) Among the first of these was the observation by Robert Boyle that, at constant temperature, a gas's pressure is proportional to its density. Jacques Charles and Joseph L. Gay-Lussac showed that if a gas is heated at constant volume, its pressure is proportional to the temperature measured from absolute zero, and the rate of increase of the pressure is independent of the gas studied. These two observations can be expressed in one form of the ideal gas law $PV = Nk_BT$, where P is the pressure, V the volume, N the number of atoms or molecules, T the absolute temperature, and k_B the BOLTZMANN CONSTANT.

Daniel Bernoulli explained (1738) Boyle's law on the basis of the molecular hypothesis; he assumed that pressure arises from collisions by gas molecules with the container walls. When the density is increased at constant temperature, the number of collisions increases and with it the pressure. Julius

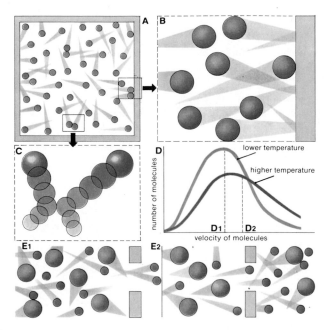

According to the kinetic theory of matter, a gas consists of molecules in constant motion (A). The molecules collide with the container walls (B) and with one another (C) to account for temperature and pressure. At any given temperature, the molecules in a gas (D) have a definite distribution of speeds about an average value D_1. If the temperature rises, the average speed of the molecules increases to D_2. In mixed gases (E_1), low-mass molecules move faster than those of high mass. Thus, the mixture can be separated by diffusion (E_2) because lighter molecules can escape through small holes faster than heavier ones.

L. Mayer suggested (1842) that heat is simply a result of molecular motion; this equivalence of heat energy and molecular kinetic energy was verified experimentally (1843) by James P. Joule. Observations, during the 19th century, of BROWNIAN MOTION confirmed that the atoms and molecules in matter are in constant thermal motion.

Rudolf Clausius calculated (1857) that, if the molecules are all moving with the same speed, v, but in random directions, the rate of collisions with the wall can be calculated statistically, and the amount of momentum transferred during each collision is obtained from the laws of classical mechanics. The pressure is then found to be $PV = \frac{1}{3}Nmv^2$, where m is the mass of the molecules. Combining this with the ideal gas law gives the important relationship $\frac{1}{2}mv^2 = \frac{3}{2}k_BT$, showing that a gas's temperature is directly related to the velocities of the molecules that compose it.

James C. Maxwell showed that a gas's molecules have different velocities; he used probability theory to calculate their distribution. The relationship between temperature and velocity is still valid, but v^2 must be replaced by the average of the square of the velocity of the molecules. Ludwig Boltzmann used classical mechanics to put Maxwell's results on a more rigorous dynamical basis; he also derived the equation that describes the return of a dilute gas toward its equilibrium state. The Boltzmann equation is the basis of the kinetic theory of gases.

Josiah Willard Gibbs generalized Boltzmann's work and in so doing established the foundations of statistical mechanics; instead of restricting his attention to the dynamical evolution of dilute gases, he developed a formalism that is applicable as well to liquids and solids. His statistical description of matter not only satisfied the laws of thermodynamics, but also gave a prescription for calculating the thermodynamic properties of matter. The hypotheses that underlie his work have in recent years been given a more rigorous mathematical foundation and have been tested and verified by a wide variety of experiments.

Transport of Matter and Energy. Kinetic theory also treats the description of transport on a molecular scale. Experiments show that if a density or concentration gradient is created in a gas or liquid (that is, the density or concentration is slightly higher in one part of the container than in another), matter will flow to restore the system to equilibrium. If the gradient is small, the rate of net flow will be proportional to this gradient, and the proportionality constant is called the diffusion coefficient.

If the molecules in one part of the fluid move relative to those in another, shear force will be exerted, tending to restore the system to equilibrium; the shear viscosity is the proportionality constant that determines the restoration. A third example of transport is the heat flow that occurs in the presence of a temperature gradient; if two surfaces of a sample are maintained at different temperatures, heat flow will occur from the hotter to the cooler side. Thermal conductivity is the transport coefficient that relates the heat flow to the temperature difference. Kinetic theory allows the calculation of these transport coefficients for dilute gases.

Mean Free Path. Although very accurate and general methods are available, the simple "mean free path" approach allows an estimate of the magnitude of the transport coefficients of a dilute gas. The mean free path is the average distance a molecule travels between collisions.

The thermal conductivity, for example, may be estimated from the mean free path. If a temperature gradient exists, an imaginary surface can be considered in which molecules within a mean free path on one side of the surface are slightly hotter (they are moving faster and have higher energies) and those within a mean free path on the other side are cooler and have lower energies. If equal numbers of molecules cross the surface in a given time, a net flow of energy (and therefore of heat) will take place from the hotter to the cooler side.

In this way the thermal conductivity can be determined from the mean free path; similar calculations are possible for the diffusion constant and viscosity. Results of this simple approach lie within a factor of two or three of more accurate theoretical or experimental values when reasonable choices of the molecular diameter are made.

Gases. The kinetic theory of gases has been extensively tested and verified experimentally. If the forces between atoms or molecules are known independently, such properties as the dependence of viscosity on temperature can be calculated using kinetic theory and compared with experiment, resulting in a high rate of agreement.

The reverse procedure is often used: forces between molecules can be determined from transport measurements on gases. The way in which light is scattered by a gas is also predicted correctly by kinetic theory.

Liquids and Solids. The kinetic theory of liquids and solids is at a much less developed state than that of gases. At low temperatures molecules form regular crystalline lattices, and their motion can be described in terms of oscillations about equilibrium positions. As the temperature increases, these oscillations become larger in amplitude, defects form in the ordered lattice, and diffusion can occur. At the melting point the lattice structure disappears and the material forms a liquid, in which molecules can diffuse throughout the sample.

The kinetic theory of liquids is an area of active research that is particularly difficult, because a molecule in a liquid interacts simultaneously with many other molecules, rather than simply undergoing binary collisions as in a gas. Major advances in the understanding of the dynamics of simple liquids have been made since 1960 through the development of the method of molecular dynamics. High-speed computers are used to solve the equations of motion of a small number of molecules (typically 500–1,000). Many questions about liquid-state dynamics can be asked and answered through these computer simulations.

DAVID W. OXTOBY

Bibliography: Frenkel, J., *Kinetic Theory of Liquids* (1946); Hirschfelder, J. O., et al., *Molecular Theory of Gases and Liquids* (1965); Present, R. D., *Kinetic Theory of Gases* (1958); Reif, F., *Fundamentals of Statistical and Thermal Physics* (1965).

kinetics: see CHEMICAL KINETICS AND EQUILIBRIUM.

king

A king is a male ruler who reigns usually for life. Originally kings were often elected, although hereditary kingship generally became the rule. In some civilizations, such as in ancient Egypt, the king was believed to be a god. Christian kings during the Middle Ages considered themselves as representatives of God's will. Absolute monarchs, such as those of the 16th to the 18th century in Europe, claimed to rule by DIVINE RIGHT. Today the power of most kings is limited by constitutions, and they function mainly as symbols of national unity.

Bibliography: Hocart, A. M., *Kingship* (1927); Kern, Fritz, *Kingship and Law in the Middle Ages* (1950); Strayer, J. R., *On the Medieval Origins of the Modern State* (1970).

See also: MONARCHY; QUEEN.

King, B. B.

The blues singer and guitarist Riley "B. B." King, b. Itta Benna, Miss., Sept. 16, 1925, is acknowledged as a major influence on the development of ROCK MUSIC. At 16, King began to work as a Memphis, Tenn., disk jockey and a singer in local clubs using his stage name, Blues Boy. He cut his first record in 1949 and by the mid-1960s had achieved wide recognition. His subsequent career has produced a long list of hits and a series of triumphal tours.

King, Billie Jean

Billie Jean Moffitt King, b. Long Beach, Calif., Nov. 22, 1943, is an American professional tennis star who became one of the most recognizable personalities in the sport. In 1979, King surpassed the record of Elizabeth Ryan (an outstanding doubles player of the 1920s) by accumulating 20 Wimbledon titles, 6 in singles (the latter total surpassed only by Helen Wills Moody and Martina Navratilova). King won the Wimbledon women's doubles title 10 times with 5 different partners in the period 1961–79. She was the U.S. Open singles champion 4 times, first as an amateur in 1967, then as a professional in 1971, 1972, and 1974. She won the French Open in 1972 and the Australian Open in 1968. King turned professional in 1968, and in 1971 she became the first woman athlete to earn $100,000 in a year. In 1973 she won a famous "mixed singles" victory over 1939 Wimbledon champion Bobby Riggs in the Houston Astrodome before a crowd of 30,472, the largest ever to watch a tennis match.   STEVE FLINK

Bibliography: King, Billie Jean, and Chapin, Kim, *Billie Jean* (1974).

Billie Jean King, shown about to return a shot at Wimbledon in 1982, was one of the most highly regarded players in tennis during the 1960s and '70s. As a player, she was powerful and aggressive on the court. Off the court, largely through her outspokenness and leadership qualities, King was probably the individual most responsible for women's tennis gaining monetary parity with men's in the 1970s.

King, Carole

Songwriter and recording artist Carole King, b. Carole Klein in Brooklyn, N.Y., Feb. 9, 1942, began her career with her first husband, lyricist Gerry Goffin, by writing songs in the Brill Building on Broadway, rock-and-roll's version of Tin Pan Alley. From their cubbyhole workspace, the team turned out over 100 songs and their first hit, the rhythm-and-blues ballad "Will You Love Me Tomorrow?" (1960). King composed in almost every pop style, and her songs were recorded by eminent artists in such pop genres as jazz-rock, folk-rock, gospel, and rhythm and blues. Divorced in 1968, and now writing her own lyrics and performing her own songs, King recorded *Tapestry* (1971), which sold some 13 million copies and won four Grammy awards. Later albums include *Pearls* (1980), featuring some of her most famous collaborations with Goffin.

King, Ernest Joseph

Ernest Joseph King, b. Lorain, Ohio, Nov. 23, 1878, d. June 25, 1956, was a U.S. naval officer who began his career as a midshipman during the Spanish-American War (1898). In World War I he was assistant chief of staff to Adm. Henry T. Mayo, commander of the Atlantic Fleet. King was promoted to admiral in 1941. In World War II he became the first officer to serve as commander in chief of the U.S. Navy and chief of naval operations at the same time. In 1944 he was made a fleet (five-star) admiral and retired the next year. *Fleet Admiral King: A Naval Record* (1952) is his autobiography.

King, Martin Luther, Jr.

Martin Luther King, Jr., was a man of impressive moral presence who devoted his life to the fight for full citizenship rights of the poor, disadvantaged, and racially oppressed in the United States. Born on Jan. 15, 1929, in Atlanta, Ga., he was the second of three children of the Rev. Michael (later Martin) and Mrs. Alberta Williams King. He received a bachelor's degree in sociology (1948) from Morehouse College, a B.D. (1951) from Crozer Theological Seminary, and a doctorate in philosophy (1955) from Boston University.

In 1954, King accepted his first pastorate—the Dexter Avenue Baptist Church in Montgomery, Ala. He and his wife, Coretta Scott King, whom he had met and married (June 1953) while at Boston University, had been resident in Montgomery less than a year when Mrs. Rosa Parks defied the ordinance concerning segregated seating on city buses (Dec. 1, 1955). King's successful organization of the year-long Montgomery bus boycott, with the assistance of the Rev. Ralph ABERNATHY and Edward Nixon, catapulted him into national prominence as a leader of the CIVIL RIGHTS movement.

King studied the life and teachings of Mahatma Gandhi and further developed the Indian leader's doctrine of *satyagraha* ("holding to the truth"), or nonviolent civil disobedience. In the aftermath of Montgomery he traveled, delivered speeches, and wrote his first book, *Stride toward Freedom* (1958). In 1960 he accepted copastorship with his father of the Ebenezer Baptist Church in Atlanta and became president of the Southern Christian Leadership Conference (SCLC). Although he continued to travel and speak widely and firmly committed the SCLC to voter-registration campaigns throughout the South, King's major campaigns were those in Albany, Ga. (December 1961–August 1962), Birmingham, Ala. (April–May 1963), and Danville, Va. (July 1963). He organized the massive March on Washington (Aug. 28, 1963) where, in his brilliant "I Have a Dream" speech, he "subpoenaed the conscience of the nation before the judgment seat of morality." In January 1964, *Time* magazine chose King Man of the Year, the first black American so honored. Later that year he became the youngest recipient of the Nobel Peace Prize.

After supporting desegregation efforts in Saint Augustine, Fla., in 1964, King concentrated his efforts on the voter-registration drive in Selma, Ala., leading a harrowing march from Selma to Montgomery in March 1965. Soon after, a tour of the northern cities led him to assail the conditions of economic as well as social discrimination. This marked a shift in SCLC

Martin Luther King, Jr., the Baptist minister recognized as the leading figure of the civil rights movement in the United States, employed the nonviolent tactics espoused by Mahatma Gandhi in his struggle to end segregation and discrimination against American blacks. King, who in 1964 became the youngest recipient of the Nobel Peace Prize, was assassinated in 1968 while visiting Memphis to support a strike by city sanitation workers.

strategy, one intended to "bring the Negro into the mainstream of American life as quickly as possible." Having begun to recognize the deeper relationships of economics and poverty to racism, King now called for a "reconstruction of the entire society, a revolution of values." Along with demands for stronger civil and voting rights legislation and for a meaningful poverty budget, he spoke out against the Vietnam War. On Apr. 4, 1967, he told an audience that "The Great Society [President Lyndon Johnson's antipoverty program] has been shot down on the battlefields of Vietnam."

Early in 1968, King began to plan a multiracial poor people's march on Washington to demand an end to all forms of discrimination and the funding of a $12-billion "Economic Bill of Rights." In the midst of organizing this campaign, he flew to Memphis, Tenn., to assist striking sanitation workers. There, on Apr. 4, 1968, King was felled by an assassin's bullet. The violent death of this man of peace brought an immediate reaction of rioting in black ghettos around the country. Although one man, James Earl Ray, was convicted of King's murder, the question of whether he was the paid agent of conspirators has not been conclusively resolved. It is clear only that the United States was deprived of a towering symbol of moral and social progress. In 1983, King's birthday was designated a national holiday.   DAVID LEVERING LEWIS

Bibliography: Ansbro, J. J., *Martin Luther King, Jr.* (1984); Fairclough, A., *To Redeem the Soul of America* (1987); Garrow, D., *Bearing the Cross* (1986); Lewis, D. L., *King: A Biography*, 2d ed. (1978); King, M. L., Jr., *A Testament of Hope*, ed. by J. M. Washington (1986); Oates, S. B., *Let the Trumpet Sound* (1982).

King, Rufus

Rufus King, b. Scarborough, Mass. (now in Maine), Mar. 24, 1755, d. Apr. 29, 1827, was an American statesman who took an active part in framing the federal Constitution. After graduating from Harvard in 1777, he practiced law in Newburyport, Mass., and was elected to the legislature in 1783. He was a leading delegate (1784–87) to the Continental Congress, and he introduced the prohibition on slavery in the Northwest Ordinance of 1787 (see NORTHWEST TERRITORY). An advocate of strong central government, he was an active member of the Constitutional Convention of 1787 and urged ratification of the Constitution by Massachusetts.

After his marriage to Mary Alsop, the daughter of a wealthy merchant, King settled in New York City and worked closely with Alexander Hamilton in the formation of the FEDERALIST PARTY. As U.S. Senator (1789–96), he vigorously supported the Washington administration. In 1796 he was appointed minister to Great Britain, where he was so successful in easing ten-

sions that President Thomas Jefferson kept him in that post until 1803. When King returned to the United States, he was an unsuccessful vice-presidential candidate on the Federalist ticket in 1804 and 1808. Reelected to the U.S. Senate in 1813, he at first opposed all measures in support of the War of 1812; after the British invasion of Washington, however, he shifted his position. In 1816, as the Federalist presidential candidate, he lost by a wide margin to James Monroe.

Although he was a Federalist in an era of Democratic-Republican domination, King's moderation and fairness earned him wide respect. Because of his strong antislavery views, he took the lead in the Senate in 1820 in opposing the admission of Missouri as a slave state (see MISSOURI COMPROMISE).

                                                HARRY AMMON

Bibliography: Ernst, Robert, *Rufus King, American Federalist* (1968); King, Charles, ed., *The Life and Correspondence of Rufus King*, 6 vols. (1894–1900; repr. 1971).

King, Stephen

Stephen Edwin King, b. Portland, Maine, Sept. 21, 1949, a writer of supernatural horror novels, has won both critical acclaim and enormous popular success. Several of his many novels have been filmed, most notably *Carrie* (1974; film by Brian De Palma, 1976) and *The Shining* (1977; film by Stanley Kubrick, 1980). Among his other novels are *Firestarter* (1980), *Pet Sematary* (1983), and *Misery* (1987). His *Danse Macabre* (1981) is an overview of the horror genre from 1950 to 1980.

King, W. L. Mackenzie

William Lyon Mackenzie King was three times prime minister of Canada (1921–26, 1926–30, 1935–48). Born in Berlin (now Kitchener), Ontario, on Dec. 17, 1874, he was named for his mother's father, William Lyon MACKENZIE. He was educated at the universities of Toronto, Chicago, and Harvard, specializing in political economy. In 1900 he was invited by William Mulock, postmaster general in Sir Wilfred Laurier's Liberal government, to establish the Department of Labor. Having won a seat in the House of Commons in 1909, he became minister of labor the same year.

King believed in the rational conciliation of labor disputes. One of the first Canadian politicians to recognize the importance of improving labor conditions, he attempted to persuade management to recognize labor unions. He expressed many of his ideas in *Industry and Humanity* (1918).

King lost his parliamentary seat when the Laurier government fell in 1911. During World War I he spent most of his time investigating industrial relations for the Rockefeller

Mackenzie King, prime minister of Canada for a total of 21 years (1921–26, 1926–30, 1935–48) and leader of Canada's Liberal party for nearly 30 years (1919–48), did much to solidify Canadian independence and to strengthen relations with the United States. During World War II he participated with Roosevelt and Churchill in several Allied conferences.

Foundation in the United States. In 1919, after the death of Laurier, he was chosen leader of the Liberal party and found a parliamentary constituency in Prince Edward Island. In the federal election of December 1921, King and his party won a plurality of seats and, with the support of some Progressives, were able to form a minority government. In 1925 the Liberals were narrowly defeated at the polls, but continued support from the Progressives enabled King's administration to survive until a scandal in the Customs Department brought it down in June 1926.

A general election in October 1926 returned King to power with a Liberal majority. He was defeated in 1930 and led the opposition to Richard Bedford Bennett's Conservative government until 1935. Gaining political advantage by being out of office during the worst years of the Depression, the Liberals won a clear victory in 1935, and King remained prime minister until he retired undefeated in 1948.

King was isolationist in thought and sympathy, and he underestimated the danger from the European Fascist powers. For much of his career he could also be described as anti-British. In the 1920s his governments pushed for total Canadian autonomy within the British Empire, the dominion status finally recognized by the Statute of Westminster in 1931. When World War II broke out, therefore, Canada entered the conflict on its own authority. Throughout the war, King sought to cooperate with Britain and the United States without allowing Canada to be taken for granted. He formed an able war cabinet and succeeded in maintaining national unity by delaying the introduction of conscription, which was bitterly opposed by French Canadians, until late in 1944.

King was a prime minister who operated by consensus politics. He disliked hard, clear policies, and his thoughts often seemed to be expressed in woolly terms. Not for him the eloquent phrases that characterized the other Allied leaders, Winston Churchill and Franklin Roosevelt. His personal life was unusual. A bachelor, he lived in Laurier's old house with his dog, his butler, and his benign ghosts, whom he consulted from time to time, especially his mother and Laurier. He thought of himself as a rebel, like his grandfather Mackenzie, but to others he seemed a rather conventional liberal. Mild in manner, he could be, and was, politically ruthless. King died on July 22, 1950. P. B. WAITE

Bibliography: Dawson, R. M., *William Lyon Mackenzie King, 1874–1923* (1958); Esberey, Joy E., *Knight of the Holy Spirit: A Study of William Lyon Mackenzie King* (1980); Granatstein, J. L., *Mackenzie King: His Life and World* (1977); Neatby, H. Blair, *William Lyon Mackenzie King, 1924–1932* (1963) and *William Lyon Mackenzie King, 1932–1939* (1976); Pickersgill, J. W., *The Mackenzie King Record*, 4 vols. (1960–70).

King, William Rufus de Vane

William Rufus de Vane King, b. Sampson County, N.C., Apr. 7, 1786, d. Apr. 18, 1853, was briefly vice-president of the United States under President Franklin Pierce. After serving (1811–16) as a Democratic congressman from North Carolina, he moved to Alabama and became (1819) one of that state's first senators. He resigned to serve as ambassador to France (1844–46), but returned to the Senate in 1848. Elected vice-president in 1852, King was sworn into office while in Cuba for his health. He died just after his return to the United States.

King George's War: see FRENCH AND INDIAN WARS.

King Lear [leer]

William SHAKESPEARE's *Tragedy of King Lear* has affinities with classical Greek tragedy, as it is described in Aristotle's *Poetics*. *King Lear* has a lofty theme that pits man against the powers of nature and the gods and develops, in both the king and the duke of Gloucester, a tragic recognition of human frailty and folly. The main action, concerning Lear and his daughters, is paralleled by a second series of events involving Gloucester and his sons. The story is deeply rooted in folklore. Shakespeare used Raphael Holinshed's *Chronicles* (1577) as the basis for his historical setting in pre-Roman Britain, and

he also relied on the old play *The True Chronicle History of King Leir* (publ. 1605). Shakespeare's play, which was probably written about 1605, was first performed in 1606 and published in 1608. The madness of King Lear leads him to tragic awareness. He is schooled in the ways of adversity by his acerbic, witty Fool. MAURICE CHARNEY

King Philip's War

King Philip's War (1675–76) was the most destructive Indian war in New England's history. It was named for Philip (Metacom), the son of MASSASOIT and sachem (chief) of the WAMPANOAG tribe of Plymouth Colony from 1662. Philip deeply resented white intrusion and domination. After maintaining peace with the colonists for many years, he finally became a leader in open resistance. Fighting first broke out at the frontier settlement of Swansea in June 1675, after which the conflict between Indians and whites spread rapidly across southern New England, involving the colonies of Plymouth, Massachusetts, Connecticut, and, to a limited extent, Rhode Island. Some tribes, including the NARRAGANSETTS and Nipmucks, became active on Philip's side; others gave valuable assistance to the whites. Indian raiding parties burned many New England towns and killed or captured hundreds of colonists. Eventually, colonial forces imposed even greater destruction upon the Indians, until finally all resistance was crushed. Philip himself was trapped and killed in August 1676.

DOUGLAS EDWARD LEACH

Bibliography: Leach, Douglas, *Flintlock and Tomahawk: New England in King Philip's War* (1958; repr. 1966); Rich, Louise, *King Philip's War, 1675–76* (1972).

king snake

The prairie king snake, L. calligaster, *lives in open woodlands and prairies. Some older snakes have a melanistic (dark) phase.*

King snakes, *Lampropeltis,* in the family Colubridae, are moderately sized, powerful constrictors and have smooth scales and single anal plates (the scale in front of the vent). Their diet consists of a variety of vertebrates, including other snakes. Six species occur in the United States. The prairie king snake, or mole snake, *L. calligaster,* is distributed from Maryland westward to Nebraska and Texas and southward to Florida. It is brown or tan with darker blotches. Most subspecies of the common king snake, *L. getulus,* are dark brown or black with white or yellow bands, stripes, or spots. This species occurs from coast to coast. Two species, the Sonora mountain king snake, *L. pyromelana,* and the California mountain king snake, *L. zonata,* are restricted to mountainous regions in the western United States and Mexico. They are tricolored with red, black, and white. The Mexican king snake, *L. mexicana,* is marked with gray, black, and sometimes orange and is found in southwestern Texas and northern portions of the Mexican Plateau. Two species in the genus *Lampropeltis, L. triangulum* and *L. doliata,* are often known as MILK SNAKES. JONATHAN CAMPBELL

Bibliography: Mattison, Christopher, *Snakes of the World* (1986).

King William's War: see FRENCH AND INDIAN WARS.

kingbird

The western kingbird (left), T. verticalis, *and the eastern kingbird* (right), T. tyrannis, *are named for their domineering behavior.*

The kingbird comprises the genus *Tyrannus* of the New World family, Tyrannidae, known as tyrant flycatchers. Despite their relatively small size, kingbirds are boldly aggressive against intruders, especially birds of prey. They measure 20-24 cm (8-9.5 in) in length and are brown- or gray-backed birds with white or yellowish undersides and gray heads. Some have a small crown spot of bright red, which is usually concealed. The eastern kingbird, *T. tyrannus,* has a dark gray back, a white underside, and a white band on its tail's tip. During the summer it ranges throughout the northern United States east of the Rocky Mountains to central Canada. It winters in tropical South America. In the Midwest its range overlaps that of the western kingbird (*T. verticalis*), which has a lighter gray back and yellow underside and has white on the sides of its tail. This bird winters in Central America, primarily Mexico.   WILLIAM D. SANDFORD

kingfisher

The belted kingfisher, M. alcyon, *is a common North American bird that lives near streams and rivers. The female* (bottom) *differs from the male* (top) *by having a band of dark-colored feathers on its belly.*

Kingfisher is the common name for members of the cosmopolitan avian family Alcedinidae, order Coraciiformes, which also includes the Australian kookaburra, *Dacelo gigas.* The greatest number of species are found in the tropics and subtropics. These birds measure 10 to 46 cm (4 to 18 in) in length and have a large, usually crested head and a compact body. The bill is usually straight, long, and powerful, and the front toes are characteristically fused at the base. Kingfisher plumages are green, blue, purple, reddish brown, or white; several species have iridescent feathers. The majority of species do not eat fish, but rather insects and other invertebrates. Many kingfishers hover in search of prey before they swoop to the ground or dive into the water. Most species are solitary. Their unlined nests are in tree cavities or in embankments.

Kingfishers are usually classified into three subfamilies. The belted kingfisher, *Megaceryle alcyon,* and the giant kingfisher, *M. maxima,* of tropical Africa are included in the subfamily Cerylinae, most members of which eat mainly fish. The belted kingfisher is named for the band of color across the bird's breast. The common kingfisher, *Alcedo atthis,* of Europe, Asia, and Africa is in the subfamily Alcedininae, which includes many insect-eating species. The most familiar of the tree kingfishers, subfamily Daceloninae, is the kookaburra, known for its variety of loud calls, some of which are reminiscent of human laughter.   GARY D. SCHNELL

Bibliography: Steinbacher, J., "The Coraciiformes," in H. B. Grzimek, ed., *Grzimek's Animal Life Encyclopedia,* vol. 9 (1972).

kinglet

The golden-crowned kinglet (male, at bottom), R. satrapa, *a delicate, active bird, lives in North American coniferous forests.*

The kinglet is a common name for birds of the genus *Regulus* of the Old World warbler family, Sylviidae, including two very small, active North American birds. Both measure about 10 cm (4 in) in length and have olive gray backs, light wing bars, and paler undersides. The golden-crowned kinglet, *R. satrapa,* has white stripes over its eyes and a bright cap, orange in the male, yellow in the female, that is bordered with black. The male ruby-crowned kinglet, *R. calendula,* has a small, bright red head spot. Kinglets feed almost exclusively on insects. Found from coast to coast, they nest in northern coniferous forests and winter south to Guatemala.
                                            WILLIAM D. SANDFORD

Kings, Books of

The two books of Kings, labeled 1-2 Kings in the Hebrew and English versions of the BIBLE, but 3-4 Kings in the Greek and Latin, are so designated because of their contents. They follow and are a continuation of the books of SAMUEL (1–2 Kings in Greek and Latin) and narrate the history of Israel and Judah from SOLOMON's accession to the destruction of Jerusalem and the exile of Judah in 587 BC. The Books of Kings give a detailed account of Solomon's wisdom and wealth and the building of the Temple at Jerusalem. They also narrate the decline that began during his reign and culminated in the exile. These books conclude the Deuteronomistic History, the name given to the books from DEUTERONOMY to Kings, all of which appear to have been compiled on the same principle. The hand of the Deuteronomistic editor or editors is evident in the stereotyped evaluation of each king by the often anachronistic standards of the Deuteronomic law; the editor(s) also composed the greater part of Solomon's Temple dedication prayer, as well as the long explanation for the fall of Israel. The compiler(s) did use earlier sources, however. These include lost works called the Acts of Solomon, the Chronicles of the Kings of Judah, and the Chronicles of the Kings of Israel; some official lists; an account of the temple construction; and a summary of the official annals of both Israel and Judah. The compiler(s) also incorporated a number of early prophetic legends, including the Elijah-Elisha cycles. The original work dates from c.615 BC, but it was updated and reedited c.550 BC.

J. J. M. ROBERTS

Bibliography: Cross, F. M., *Canaanite Myth and Hebrew Epic* (1973); Gray, John, *I–II Kings: A Commentary*, 2d ed. (1970).

Kingsley, Charles

The Victorian writer and social reformer Charles Kingsley, b. June 12, 1819, d. Jan. 23, 1875, was an Anglican country clergyman, a canon of Westminster Abbey, and from 1860 to 1869 professor of modern history at Cambridge. An early supporter of Charles Darwin's theory of evolution, Kingsley was one of the few clergy of the period to enlist in the ranks of the Darwinians. His remedy for the ills of society, which he propounded in lectures, sermons, pamphlets, and novels, was "Christian Socialism," a call for cooperative enterprise and morality in social action. In the novel *Yeast* (1851), Kingsley described the distress of agricultural labor; in *Alton Locke* (1850), another novel, he attacked the exploitation of urban workers. *The Water Babies* (1863), a popular children's fantasy, was both a moralizing fable and a speculation on evolution. Of Kingsley's historical fiction, *Westward Ho!* (1855) and *Hereward the Wake* (1866) are the best known.

Bibliography: Colloms, Brenda, *Charles Kingsley: The Lion of Eversley* (1975); Martin, Robert B., *The Dust of Combat: A Life of Charles Kingsley* (1960); Pope-Hennessy, Una, *Canon Charles Kingsley: A Biography* (1949; repr. 1973); Uffelman, L. K., *Charles Kingsley* (1979).

Kingston   (Jamaica)

Kingston (1982 pop., 494,227), the capital and largest city in Jamaica, lies on the southeastern coast of the island. One of the leading ports of the West Indies, it exports sugar, rum, molasses, and bananas. Other industries include tourism, oil refining, shoe and clothing manufacturing, and food processing. The average annual temperature is 25° C (77° F), and yearly rainfall is 813 mm (32 in). The University of the West Indies (1962) is there.

Founded in 1692 after nearby Port Royal was destroyed by an earthquake, Kingston became the capital of Jamaica in 1872. Points of interest include Rockfort, a 17th-century fortress; the Church of Saint Thomas; and Headquarters House (18th century), once the seat of government.

Kingston   (New York)

Kingston, the seat of Ulster County, New York, is located 145 km (90 mi) north of New York City in the fertile Hudson River valley. It has a population of 24,481 (1980). A distribution center for fruits and dairy products produced on the surrounding farms, Kingston has also become a gateway to the summer and winter resorts of the upper CATSKILL MOUNTAINS. It also has light manufacturing, including computers and apparel.

Henry Hudson's party landed near the site of Kingston in 1609, and it was first settled by the Dutch about 1652 as Esopus. In 1664 it came under British control and was renamed Kingston (1669). In 1777 it was chosen as the first state capital, and the legislature met there once before the British burned the city during the American Revolution.

Kingston   (Ontario)

Kingston, a Canadian city located in southeastern Ontario, has a population of 55,050 (1986). It is located on the north shore of Lake Ontario, where the St. Lawrence Seaway and Rideau Canal join the lake. It is a busy port and industrial city, where locomotives, ships, aluminum, synthetic fibers, and ceramics are manufactured. Queen's University (1841) and the Royal Military College (1876) are there. Fort Henry, built during the War of 1812, is now a military museum.

The city was founded (1673) as Fort Frontenac by Louis de Buade, comte de Frontenac. It was destroyed (1758) by the British and resettled (1784) by United Empire Loyalists, who renamed the city for King George III. From 1841 until 1844 the city served as the seat of government of the united provinces of Upper and Lower Canada.

Kingston upon Hull: see HULL.

kinkajou   [kink'-uh-joo]

The kinkajou, P. flavus, is the only member of the raccoon family possessing a prehensile tail. Called the "night monkey" in Mexico, it has tawny or brown fur, which is soft and woolly.

The kinkajou, *Potos flavus,* sometimes called a honey bear, is a member of the raccoon family, Procyonidae. Its slender, short-legged body may reach 58 cm (23 in) in length (plus a 56-cm/22-in prehensile tail) and 2.7 kg (6 lb) in weight. The kinkajou is one of only two carnivores (the other is the binturong) that have prehensile tails. Kinkajous are arboreal and inhabit forests from southern Mexico to Brazil. They are nocturnal and feed on fruit, insects, and small mammals.

EVERETT SENTMAN

Kinnock, Neil

Neil Gordon Kinnock, b. Mar. 28, 1942, is the leader of Britain's Labour party. The son of a Welsh miner, he was educated at University College, Cardiff, and elected to Parliament in 1970. Kinnock was a close associate of former Labour leader Michael Foot, whom he succeeded in 1983. Taking charge of a party weakened by division, he moved to strengthen its position with moderate voters by disassociating himself from Labour's left wing. Labour was defeated in the 1987 general election, however.

Kino, Eusebio Francisco   [kee'-noh, ay-oo-say'-byoh frahn-sees'-koh]

Eusebio Francisco Kino, b. Tyrol, c.1644, d. Mar. 15, 1711, was a Jesuit missionary and explorer who directed the establishment of Spanish missions among the PIMA Indians in Pimería Alta (in what is now northern Sonora, Mexico, and southern Arizona). He was admitted to the Society of Jesus in 1669 and distinguished himself in studies in mathematics, cartography, and astronomy. He chose the calling of a missionary and was sent to New Spain in 1681. After an abortive mission to Baja California in 1683, he began his longtime mission to the Pima Indians in Pimería Alta. From headquarters established at Nuestra Señora de los Dolores in Sonora in 1687, he founded a number of missions, including San Xavier del Bac (1700), near Tucson, Guevavi, and Tumacacori (now a U.S. National Monument). Explorations of the area around the mouth of the Colorado River in 1701 persuaded him that Baja California was a peninsula, not an island. His 1705 map was the standard reference for the area for more than a century. Kino aided the Pimas in diversifying their agriculture and in their constant wars with the Apaches.

Bibliography: Bolton, H. E., *Kino's Historical Memoir of Pimería Alta* (1919), *The Padre on Horseback* (1932), and *Rim of Christendom* (1936); Burros, E. J., *Kino and the Cartography of Northwestern New Spain* (1965); Smith, F. J., et al., *Father Kino in Arizona* (1966).

Kinross   [kin-raws']

Kinross is a former county in central Scotland. The level terrain, surrounded by hills, supports stock farms and produces barley, oats, wheat, and potatoes. The principal cities, Kinross and Milnathort, have important textile mills and food-processing plants. Some coal is mined in the Benarty and Cleish hills, which border Loch Leven, noted for its trout fishing. Mary, Queen of Scots was imprisoned on the island in the loch in 1567, but escaped the following year. In 1975, during the reorganization of local government in Scotland, Kinross became part of the TAYSIDE administrative region.

Kinsey reports   [kin'-zee]

The Kinsey reports, *Sexual Behavior in the Human Male* (1948) by Alfred C. Kinsey, Wardell B. Pomeroy, and Clyde E. Martin, and *Sexual Behavior in the Human Female* (1953) by the same authors and Paul H. Gebhard, were the first large-scale empirical studies of sexual behavior. The Kinsey investigators questioned 5,300 white males and 5,490 white females from many different backgrounds about sexual behavior such as the frequency of masturbation, petting, marital and extramarital intercourse, oral sex, and female orgasm. Today, the Kinsey reports are not only respected for breaking new ground in sex research, but are considered authoritative in most of their findings. Kinsey was a professor of zoology at the University of Indiana when the reports were prepared, and sex research is still conducted at the university's Institute for Sex Research, Inc., in Bloomington. Kinsey died in 1956.

Bibliography: Christenson, Cornelia V., *Kinsey: A Biography* (1971); Robinson, Paul, *The Modernization of Sex: Havelock Ellis, Alfred Kinsey, William Masters and Virginia Johnson* (1976).

Kinshasa   [keen-shah'-suh]

Kinshasa (formerly Leopoldville) is the capital and largest city of Zaire, with a population of 2,338,246 (1981 est.). It is located on the CONGO RIVER, where it widens to become Malebo Pool (formerly Stanley Pool) and at the point where upstream navigation of the Congo River becomes possible. A rail line, completed in 1898, links the city to the ocean port of Matadi. The leading industries are food processing and paper, textile, and chemical manufacturing. Kinshasa was founded as a supply depot by Henry Morton Stanley in 1881 at a Humbo village site. In 1923 it replaced Boma as the capital of the Belgian Congo. When the Congo gained its independence in 1960, Kinshasa became the new capital of Zaire.

EDOUARD BUSTIN

kinship

Kinship is the network of human relationships created by genealogical connections as they are conceived of in particular societies and by social ties—for example, those based on

adoption—modeled after natural genealogical relations. Because kinship is universal, it plays an important role in regulating behavior and in the formation of social groups. The most important of these is the FAMILY, which provides children with emotional roots, socialization and training, and their initial position in and orientation to the social world. Kinship is especially important in small-scale and middle-range societies, where it regulates much behavior of community members, even beyond the immediate family; often it is the basis for the formation of important social, political, and territorial groups, and it may be the basis for office holding of many kinds. The study of kinship is a major field of anthropological and sociological investigation.

Kin Terms. Kinship comprises two categories of relatives. The first are consanguines, often referred to as blood relatives, whose links to each other are rooted ultimately in the link between parents and children. Consanguines include descendants—an individual's children or other persons of succeeding generations linked to that person through his or her children, such as a grandchild or great-great grandchild. An ascendant is a person of a preceding generation to whom an individual is linked by parent-child ties, such as to a grandmother. Ascendants and descendants together are called lineal relatives. Collaterals, another type of consanguine, are the siblings of lineal relatives or their descendants, such as an uncle, an aunt, or a cousin by blood. The second major type of relative is an affine, a person related by marriage, such as a brother-in-law or an aunt by marriage.

Kinship does not depend on factual knowledge of conception and genetics; such knowledge, especially about the role of paternity, was unknown in most societies throughout most of history. Consequently, cultures have developed varying beliefs about genealogical relationships that often differ from strict biological fact. A kinship system consists of a society's cultural beliefs about how the genealogical relationships of consanguinity and affinity are to be categorized and labeled and about what rights, duties, and expectations are linked with each kinship category. These labels make up a system of kinship terminology consisting of terms of reference—the terms the culture applies to various genealogical categories—and terms of address—the terms used to address kinspersons in particular categories. An example of how cultural categories differ from genealogical ones is our use of the term *aunt* for both the consanguineal genealogical category, mother's sister, and the affinal category, mother's brother's wife.

Descent. One of the most common ways in which the constructed kinship systems of various cultures differ from biological reality is in conceptions of descent. Very common is the notion of unilineal descent, in which a person is counted as being descended from only one parent. If descent is traced through the male line (through the father), it is called patrilineal; if it is traced through the mother it is called matrilineal. Double unilineal descent is traced through the mother's mother and the father's father. Bilateral descent, used by U.S. society, is traced through both the mother and father.

Because the principle of unilineal descent assigns an individual unequivocally to a kinship group, it can be used to form corporate groups, such as a LINEAGE or a CLAN. Corporate groups often assume such functions as holding land or providing representatives for office on a village or tribal council. Societies in which kinship is used as a broad organizing principle for many aspects of life are sometimes called kin-dominated societies. They exist throughout the world, notably among preliterate, middle-range social groups, such as the pastoral nomads of Asia and the Middle East, traditional African agriculturalists, and the Australian Aborigines.

Unilineality is also used as a principle for the inheritance of property or position. In a patrilineal society, positions—such as head of the household and major property (land, in many societies)—are inherited by a man's patrilineal heir, usually his son or a younger brother. In matrilineal societies the heir will also be a male, but one with whom the link is traced matrilineally, usually a man's sister's son. Unilineal inheritance has the advantage of keeping the inherited position or property within the unilineal descent group. In American society property is inherited bilineally, but last names are normally inherited patrilineally.

Kinship has its origins in MARRIAGE, the socially recognized union of a man and a woman, and reflects the particular form of marriage practiced, whether POLYGAMY, MONOGAMY, or other kinds of unions (see CONCUBINAGE). Some forms of marriage, such as the sororate, the levirate, and ghost marriage, are based on the cultural belief that marriage extends beyond the lifetime of one of the partners, another example of how cultural conceptions about kinship differ from biological fact.

Artificial or fictive kinship refers to customs in which a person is given kin status by attribution rather than by birth. The prime example is ADOPTION. In another type of pseudo-kinship, called figurative usage, kinship terms are extended to non-kin in order to stress an aspect of the person's role that is similar to that of a kinsperson. Children are taught, for example, to call a close female friend of their parents "aunt" because she plays an avuncular role. Ritual kinship, a third type of pseudo-kinship, entails a formalized relationship that is similar to but distinct from actual kinship, such as bloodbrotherhood and ritual coparenthood, or compadrazgo, a kind of mutual cogodparenthood.

JAMES LOWELL GIBBS, JR.

Bibliography: Fox, Robin, *Kinship and Marriage: An Anthropological Perspective* (1967); Goody, Jack, *Comparative Studies in Kinship* (1969); Keesing, Roger M., *Kin Groups and Social Structure* (1975); Pasternak, Burton, *Introduction to Kinship and Social Organization* (1976); Van den Berghe, P. L., *Human Family Systems* (1979).

Kintpuash   [kint'-poo-ahsh]

Kintpuash, c.1837–73, also called Captain Jack, was a MODOC headman and leader in the Modoc War (1872–73), a series of battles between the Modoc and the U.S. Army. A native of northeastern California, Kintpuash was settled (1864) with other Modoc on the Klamath reservation in Oregon. He and others later returned to their California homeland, requesting a reservation there. In late 1872 a detachment of U.S. troops attempted to arrest Kintpuash and his small band and force them to return to the Klamath reservation. The Indians resisted; several soldiers and Indians were killed. Kintpuash fled with his band to the nearby Lava-beds, where they met other Modoc runaways.

White authorities arranged a peace conference. Kintpuash, formerly an advocate of peace, was asked by other leaders to prove his commitment to resistance by killing white negotiators if they did not meet Indian demands. When the whites refused to compromise, Kintpuash shot Gen. Edward Canby and another commissioner and fled. A large military force besieged the Indians in the Lava-beds. Kintpuash skillfully directed the Indian defense; his 50-odd warriors and their families stood off nearly 1,000 U.S. troops for more than 9 months. Kintpuash was finally captured, however, and he and three other headmen were summarily tried and hanged. The surviving warriors and their families were shipped to Indian Territory (now Oklahoma).

PHILIP DRUCKER

Kiowa   [ky'-uh-wuh]

The Kiowa are a North American tribe of Plains Indians who speak a Kiowa-Tanoan language. Kiowa tradition speaks of a migration in the company of the Kiowa APACHE into the Plains from the headwaters of the Missouri River during the 18th century. At that time they were organized in 10 independent bands and numbered an estimated 3,000. The ARAPAHO, CHEYENNE, and Dakota (SIOUX) pushed them out of the Black Hills region southwestward into their historic range along the headwaters of the Arkansas, Cimarron, Canadian, and Red rivers. There they met and at first fought the COMANCHE, but, from c.1790, Kiowa and Comanche shared territories and together raided settlements in Texas and New Mexico. Their raids furnished horses and mules for trade with northern Plains tribes. Although the Kiowa accepted a restricted range between the Washita and Red rivers at the Medicine Lodge Treaty of 1867, tribal resistance continued. Since 1875, however, the Kiowa have adapted to reservation life in Oklahoma.

The Kiowa played an important role in the spread of the peyote religion (see NATIVE AMERICAN CHURCH). Also, they have produced outstanding contemporary writers on Indian life; in 1969, N. Scott MOMADAY won a Pulitzer Prize for his novel, *House Made of Dawn* (1968). In 1981 their population was about 4,000 on or near the reservation.

FRED W. VOGET

Bibliography: Corwin, Hugh D., *The Kiowa Indians* (1958); Horr, David A., ed., *The Kiowa-Comanche Indians,* 2 vols. (1974); Mayhall, Mildred P., *The Kiowa,* 2d ed. (1971); Nye, Wilbur S., *Bad Medicine and Good: Tales of the Kiowas* (1980).

Kipling, Rudyard   [kip'-ling, ruhd'-yard]

Rudyard Kipling, who in 1907 became the first English writer to win the Nobel Prize for literature, strikes a pensive pose in this portrait by Sir Philip Burne-Jones. Kipling achieved enormous popularity for his poems and short stories, many of which defend the righteousness of British colonialism. (National Portrait Gallery, London).

The English novelist, short-story writer, and poet Joseph Rudyard Kipling, b. Dec. 30, 1865, d. Jan. 18, 1936, was a literary giant in his own time, although the value of his works is now a source of considerable critical debate. He is most widely known for his works for children, especially the two "Jungle Books" (*The Jungle Book*, 1894, and *The Second Jungle Book*, 1895), and his celebration of British imperialism. He was, however, no crude jingoist and wrote on many subjects in a highly imaginative fashion.

Born in Bombay, India, Kipling was educated in England, where he spent several unhappy childhood years later described in the short story "Baa, Baa, Blacksheep" (1888) and in the autobiographical *Something of Myself* (1937). From 1882 to 1889 he worked for Indian newspapers but then returned to England, where he gained rapid acceptance by London literary society, initially with the semiautobiographical novel *The Light that Failed* (1890).

Many of Kipling's works were derived from his experience of India—among them the "Jungle Books," *Kim* (1901), and the *Just So Stories* (1902). He was perhaps most characteristic when, mainly through the medium of the short story, he used a variety of settings—India, London, the sea, the jungle—to convey his ideals of duty and self-abnegation; the importance of law and of action was shown in such works as *Actions and Reactions* (1909), *Debits and Credits* (1926), and *Limits and Renewals* (1932). These themes also occur in *Captains Courageous* (1897), which was stimulated by a visit to America, and in the school story *Stalky & Co.* (1899).

Kipling gained a reputation as a humorist with "The Village That Voted the Earth Was Flat" (1913). In *Puck of Pook's Hill* (1906) and *Rewards and Fairies* (1910), he expressed his love of England's past. His collections of verse, including *Barrack-*

Room Ballads (1892), *The Seven Seas* (1896), and *The Five Nations* (1903), display a great range of technical achievement and a variety of subject matter.   RICHARD M. FORD

Bibliography: Amis, Kingsley, *Rudyard Kipling and His World* (1975); Birkenhead, Lord, *Rudyard Kipling* (1978); Carrington, Charles E., *Rudyard Kipling: His Life and Work* (1955); Cornell, Louis L., *Kipling in India* (1966); Dobrée, Bonamy, *Rudyard Kipling: Realist and Fabulist* (1967); Gilbert, Elliot L., *The Good Kipling* (1971) and, as ed., *Kipling and the Critics* (1965); Green, Roger L., *Kipling: The Critical Heritage* (1971); Mason, Philip, *Kipling: The Glass, the Shadow and the Fire* (1975); Orwell, George, "Kipling" in *Critical Essays* (1946); Rutherford, Andrew, ed., *Kipling's Mind and Art* (1964); Trilling, Lionel, "Kipling" in *The Liberal Imagination* (1950); Wilson, Angus, *The Strange Ride of Rudyard Kipling* (1977).

Kirchhoff, Gustav Robert   [kirk'-hawf]

The German physicist Gustav Robert Kirchoff, b. Mar. 12, 1824, d. Oct. 17, 1887, discovered (1859) a fundamental law of electromagnetic radiation: the emissive power of the radiation of a BLACKBODY is represented by a universal function of wavelength and temperature. The search for a theoretical explanation of this function later led to Planck's quantum hypothesis in 1900. Along with the experimental results obtained in collaboration with Robert Bunsen, Kirchhoff's discovery put spectroscopy on a firm scientific basis. In the 1860s, using spectral analysis, Kirchhoff and Bunsen detected new elements on the Earth and identified terrestrial elements in the solar atmosphere. The latter accomplishment signaled the birth of astrophysics.   RICHARD HIRSH

Kirchhoff's laws

Kirchhoff's two laws are the basis of analysis of electrical circuits. (See CIRCUIT, ELECTRIC.) The laws were first formulated by the German physicist Gustav Kirchhoff (1824–87) working in collaboration with the German chemist and physicist Robert Bunsen (1811–99). Because the laws are a generalization of OHM'S LAW and the law of conservation of charge (see CONSERVATION, LAWS OF), they do not state any new principles; but they do give two rules that can be systematically applied to the current, voltage, and resistance of any complex electrical circuit, or network, to determine the electrical values of any portion of the network.

A simple electrical circuit is composed of a single loop without branch points (junctions of wires). It may contain a source of electromotive force (emf), such as a battery, and one or more resistances. Adding more components in parallel creates additional loops and branch points. When only a single source of emf exists, the apportionment of current can generally be determined easily by applying Ohm's law. Kirchhoff's laws, however, which can be applied to such simple circuits, are needed for more complex networks.

To analyze electrical networks using Kirchhoff's laws, scientists assign an algebraic symbol for the current in each loop and for an arbitrary direction. Kirchhoff's laws are then applied: (1) The net sum of the currents at each branch point is zero. This is the branch point (or node) rule. (2) The net sum of the emfs in each loop equals the net sum of the voltage drops, which is the product of resistance and current, in each loop. This is the loop rule. Applying these two rules results in a series of equations that can be solved algebraically.

Kirchhoff's laws apply to both direct current and alternating current circuits. In alternating current circuits, IMPEDANCE is used in place of resistance.

A. G. ENGELHARDT AND M. KRISTIANSEN

Bibliography: Gibson, W. M., *Basic Electricity*, 2d ed. (1976); Mandl, Matthew, *Basics of Electricity and Electronics* (1975).

Kirchner, Ernst Ludwig   [kirsch'-nur]

Ernst Ludwig Kirchner, b. May 6, 1880, was a leading German expressionist painter and a master of graphics, especially the woodcut. He first studied architecture but turned to painting in Munich (1903–04) and then, in Dresden (1905), became a founding member of Die BRÜCKE (The Bridge) with Erich HECKEL and Karl SCHMIDT-ROTTLUFF. This group was strongly in-

In Self-portrait with Model (1907), an early work by the German expressionist Ernst Ludwig Kirchner, the formal simplification stems from the artist's study of Egyptian and primitive art. In expressionist painting naturalism is always subordinated to expressive purposes. (Kunsthalle, Hamburg.)

fluenced by Vincent van Gogh's intense color and heavy IMPASTO (thickness of paint) as well as the color experiments of the French Fauves (see FAUVISM). Kirchner also learned from the works of Albrecht Dürer, woodcuts of the late Gothic period, and primitive sculpture.

Kirchner painted female nudes, mountainous landscapes, and city streets. His *Self-Portrait with Model* (1907; Kunsthalle, Hamburg) shows the artist wearing a brightly striped robe—like his model's—shadowed with green, and his expression violent and masklike. In *Five Women on the Street* (1913; Wallraf-Richartz Museum, Cologne) the expression of pain is even more aggressive. Kirchner transforms the long dresses and feather boas of the time into sinister, barbaric costumes. During this period he replaced his bright palette with a darkly shadowed range of colors. Kirchner's bitter view of his world is expressed all the more sharply in his starkly savage and highly acclaimed woodcuts, lithographs, and etchings of which he produced about 2,000.

Drafted into the German army during World War I, Kirchner suffered a nervous breakdown. On his release from the army he settled in Switzerland and returned to intense color for a time. By the late 1920s, however, his palette had become subdued. The forms of his landscapes and portraits became less angular and more serene and the emotional urgency of his earlier works disappeared, although an undercurrent of melancholy remained. By the mid-1930s his works were being attacked (and many were later confiscated) by the Nazis, who were unsympathetic to the avant-garde. On June 15, 1938, in despair and poor health, he committed suicide.

CARTER RATCLIFF

Bibliography: Gordon, Donald E., *Ernst Ludwig Kirchner: A Retrospective Exhibition* (1968); Grohmann, Will, *Ernst Ludwig Kirchner* (1961); Haftmann, Werner, *Painting in the Twentieth Century*, 2 vols. (1965); Selz, Peter, *German Expressionist Painting* (1957).

Kirghiz   [kir-geez']

The Kirghiz are mountain tribespeople who originated in the upper Yenisey River valley of Central Asia. They number about 2 million, of which about three-quarters live in the Kirghiz Republic in the USSR. The rest reside in other Soviet republics, in northwest China, and in Afghanistan. A Mongoloid people of short stature and stocky build, the Kirghiz speak a Kipchak Turkic language of the Altaic family.

The Kirghiz are transhumant nomadic herdsmen. Their society remains patrilineal, patriarchal, and patrilocal. These patterns are reinforced by Sunni Muslim beliefs. About half of the Kirghiz population still adheres to Islam. Certain pre-Islamic religious elements also persist. An estimated 300 itinerant mullahs exist in Kirghizia. They preserve Muslim shrines, schools, and festivals, and also help to maintain pre-Islamic folk beliefs. In addition, shamans traditionally serve as intermediaries between the living and the dead. Female Kirghiz almost never marry Russian men. Child marriage and the payment of bride-price and dowries prevail. Polygamy is sometimes practiced.

Historically, the Yenisey Kirghiz have been linked to the BURYAT people. In AD 840, Kirghiz warriors defeated the UIGHUR in Mongolia. In the 10th century the Kirghiz themselves were routed by the Chinese. Some of them returned to the Yenisey, and others migrated to their present homeland. Soviet and Chinese Kirghiz are collectivized. VICTOR L. MOTE

Bibliography: Bacon, Elizabeth E., *Central Asians under Russian Rule* (1988); Katz, Zev, et al., eds., *Handbook of Major Soviet Nationalities* (1975); Kozlof, Viktor, *The Peoples of the Soviet Union* (1988); Weekes, Richard V., ed., *Muslim Peoples: A World Ethnographic Survey* (1978).

Kirghiz Soviet Socialist Republic

The Kirghiz Soviet Socialist Republic, or Kirghizia, is one of the 15 constituent republics of the USSR. It is located in Central Asia and borders China on the east. Its area is 198,500 km² (76,600 mi²), and its population is 4,291,000 (1989). The capital is FRUNZE, with a population of 616,000 (1989).

Kirghizia is situated largely in the high mountain country of the TIEN SHAN. The mountains, which rise to 7,437 m (24,400 ft) in Pobeda (Victory) Peak on the Chinese border, contain some of the USSR's largest mountain glaciers. The Naryn River, a headstream of the Syr Darya, drains the region. A distinctive feature is a large mountain lake, Issyk-Kul, with an area of about 6,200 km² (2,400 mi²).

The republic's population and economic activities are concentrated in the Chu River valley in the north and in the west around the margins of the Fergana Valley, most of which lies in the neighboring Uzbek SSR. The Kirghiz people speak a Turkic language and are Muslim. With only 41% of the total population, they are a minority in their own republic. A majority of the Kirghiz are nonurban dwellers, who continue their traditional nomadic stock-herding activities. Russians, 22% of the population, live mainly in cities, and Uzbeks, 10%, are cotton farmers. Kirghizia is important mainly for its mineral production, including petroleum and natural gas, uranium, mercury, antimony, and coal. Light industry (food processing and textile manufacturing) takes place in the cities. Electric power needs are met in part by the large Toktogul hydro station on the Naryn.

The Kirghiz people began migrating to the region during the 16th century. It came under Russian control in the second half of the 19th century. After the Bolshevik Revolution it was constituted in 1924 as an autonomous oblast, initially called Kara-Kirghiz (the past name given to the Kirghiz people). It was renamed Kirghiz in 1925 and raised to the status of autonomous republic the following year. In 1936 it became a full soviet socialist republic. In 1990 tension between the Kirghiz and the Uzbek minority erupted into rioting in which more than 100 people were killed. THEODORE SHABAD

Kiribati [kir'-uh-bahs]

The Republic of Kiribati, formerly the Gilbert Islands, straddles both the equator and the international date line in the Pacific Ocean. The national territory extends over 5 million km² (2 million mi²), but the land area is less than that of New York City. Kiribati's 33 islands are grouped into the Gilbert Islands (including Tarawa, the capital, and Banaba, or Ocean Island), the Line Islands, and the PHOENIX ISLANDS. Kiribati was a part of the Gilbert and Ellice Islands colony until 1975, when the Ellice Islands gained independence as TUVALU.

LAND AND PEOPLE

All of the islands except volcanic Banaba are low coralline structures with few elevations above 4 m (12 ft). The soil is poor, composed of coral sand and rocks. Vegetation is limited to coconut palms and pandanus trees. Temperatures in Kiribati vary more during a 24-hour period than during the year,

REPUBLIC OF KIRIBATI

LAND. Area: 712 km² (275 mi²). Capital and largest city: Tarawa (1988 est. pop., 22,833).
PEOPLE. Population (1989 est.): 68,828; density: 97 persons per km² (250 per mi²). Distribution (1985): 67% rural, 33% urban. Annual growth (1989): 1.5%. Official language: English. Major religions: Roman Catholicism, Protestantism. •
EDUCATION AND HEALTH. Literacy (1985): 90% of adult population. Universities (1990): none. Hospital beds (1986): 283. Physicians (1986): 16. Life expectancy (1989): women—57; men—53. Infant mortality (1989): 58 per 1,000 live births.
ECONOMY. GDP (1988): $40 million; $650 per capita. Labor distribution (1985): services and public administration—47%; construction—6%; trade—13%; transportation and communication—15%; agriculture—5%. Foreign trade (1987): imports—$17.5 million; exports—$2.3 million; principal trade partners—Australia, Japan, New Zealand, United Kingdom. Currency: 1 Australian dollar = 100 cents.
GOVERNMENT. Type: republic. Legislature: House of Assembly. Political subdivisions: 6 districts.
COMMUNICATIONS. Railroads (1990): none. Roads (1988): 640 km (398 mi) total. Major ports: 3. Major airfields: 1.

with minima of 26° C (79° F) and maxima of 32° C (89° F). The mean annual rainfall near the equator is about 1,020 mm (40 in), whereas the extreme northern and southern islands average about 3,050 mm (120 in).

The i-Kiribati are overwhelmingly Micronesian, with some Polynesians and Europeans. Many inhabitants migrate to other Pacific island nations in search of employment.

ECONOMY
Phosphate, mined on Banaba, was once the leading source of income; the economy suffered severely when phosphate mining ceased in 1979, and efforts to revive the industry are being pursued. Copra is now the leading export. Fishing, handicrafts, and small-scale businesses are being developed, and a causeway linking Tarawa's two main islands was completed in 1987. Kiribati's fishing rights are among its most valuable resources. Remittances from locally trained seamen working on overseas vessels provide additional income.

HISTORY AND GOVERNMENT
Kiribati's earliest inhabitants are thought to have been Samoans, who sailed there in the 13th century. The United Kingdom established the High Commission for the Western Pacific in 1877 to oversee the islands and their European inhabitants. Gradually all the present islands were brought under the commission's jurisdiction. Kiribati was granted independence in 1979. Later that year the United States renounced its claims to the Line and Phoenix islands. Ieremia Tabai, Kiribati's first president, was reelected to successive terms. MARJORIE JOYCE

Bibliography: Carter, John, ed., *Pacific Islands Yearbook*, 15th ed. (1984); Mason, Leonard, ed., *Kiribati: A Changing Atoll Culture* (1986) and *Kiribati: Aspects of History* (1979).

Kirin: see MANCHURIA.

Kirk, Norman Eric

Norman Eric Kirk, b. Jan. 6, 1923, d. Aug. 31, 1974, was prime minister of New Zealand from 1972 to 1974. Elected to Parliament in 1957, he became president of the Labour party in 1964. In 1972, when Labour won the general election for the first time in 12 years, Kirk became prime minister. During his short term in office, he pulled New Zealand troops out of the Vietnam War, recognized the People's Republic of China, and attempted to block French nuclear tests in the Pacific.

Bibliography: Eagles, Jim, and James, Colin, *The Making of a New Zealand Prime Minister* (1973).

Kirkcaldy [kur'-kaw'-dee]

Kirkcaldy is a town in County Fife, eastern Scotland. Located on the Firth of Forth about 16 km (10 mi) north of Edinburgh, it has a population of 46,314 (1981). Coal mining is the area's most important economic activity. Linoleum, malt, textiles, rope and twine, farm machinery, and furniture are manufactured. It is the birthplace of the architect Robert Adam and the economist Adam Smith. Kirkcaldy dates from its grant in 1334 to nearby Dunfermline Abbey; it became a royal burgh in 1450 and grew rapidly as a commercial port.

Kirkcudbright [kur-koo'-bree]

Kirkcudbright is a former county in southwestern Scotland. Castle Douglas and Kirkcudbright are the largest towns. The low coastal plain on the Irish Sea is fertile land for dairy farms and mixed agriculture. Inland, to the northwest, the terrain rises to a maximum elevation of 843 m (2,765 ft) at Merrick. Sheep and cattle graze in these highlands, and reforestation projects are increasing timber yields. Hydroelectric plants have been built on the River Dee where it flows out of the highlands. Tourism is growing in importance in the area. As part of the reorganization of Scotland's local government in 1975, Kirkcudbright was incorporated into the administrative region of DUMFRIES AND GALLOWAY.

Kirke, Sir David

Sir David Kirke, b. c.1597, d. January or February 1654, was an English merchant and adventurer in Canada. In 1627 and 1629, Kirke and his four brothers led expeditions against the French at Quebec, forcing Samuel de CHAMPLAIN to surrender the colony in 1629. It was restored to France in 1632. Kirke was knighted (1633) and from 1639 to 1651 served as the first English governor of Newfoundland. F. J. THORPE

Bibliography: Biggar, H. P., *The Early Trading Companies of New France*, rev. ed. (1934; repr. 1972).

Kirkland, Gelsey [gel'-see]

Gelsey Kirkland, b. Bethlehem, Pa., Dec. 29, 1953, is a ballerina renowned for the technical purity of her dancing. Kirkland entered the New York City Ballet (NYCB) at the age of 15, was given her first principal role in *The Firebird* in 1970, and by 1972 was a principal dancer. She danced with American Ballet Theatre (1974–81, 1982–84), where she triumphed in *Giselle* and *The Sleeping Beauty*. Her autobiography, *Dancing on My Grave*, was published in 1986. MICHAEL ROBERTSON

Kirkland, Lane

Joseph Lane Kirkland, b. Camden, S.C., Mar. 12, 1922, was elected president of the American Federation of Labor and Congress of Industrial Organizations (AFL-CIO) on Nov. 19, 1979. Kirkland joined the AFL staff in 1948 and for many years was chief assistant to AFL-CIO president George MEANY. As Meany's successor, he vigorously criticized the Reagan administration's economic policies. In 1984 and 1988 he led union support for the losing Democratic presidential candidates. In 1987 he welcomed the TEAMSTERS back to the AFL-CIO.

Kirkpatrick, Jeane

Jeane Jordan Kirkpatrick, b. Duncan, Okla., Nov. 19, 1926, served (1981–85) as U.S. ambassador to the United Nations under President Ronald Reagan. Educated at Columbia University and the University of Paris, Kirkpatrick has taught political science at Georgetown University. A forceful advocate of conservative positions, she caused controversy by her distinction between "authoritarian" (friendly right-wing) governments and "totalitarian" (hostile left-wing) regimes.

Kirlian photography [kur'-lee-uhn]

Kirlian photography, sometimes called electrophotography or corona discharge photography, uses high-voltage electricity to produce an image. The technique was known in the late 1800s but was perfected in the 1940s by Soviet electrician Semyon Kirlian. In a typical procedure the object being photographed is placed directly on an unexposed sheet of photographic film. The film rests on an electrode coated with a thin layer of a nonconductive material such as glass or plastic. When voltage is applied to the electrode, a corona discharge occurs between the electrode and the object. A corona discharge is an ionization phenomenon (see ION AND IONIZATION) that occurs at electric field strengths lower than the threshold at which a spark can form. The discharge is invisible to the eye, but is recorded on film.

In Kirlian photographs, objects appear to be surrounded by a glow or "aura." In photographs of living objects this glow is quite pronounced, leading some parapsychologists to claim that Kirlian photographs are evidence of the existence of "psychic" energy. The intensity of the glow, however, can be explained by the presence of moisture, which heightens the corona discharge effect. Researchers have attempted to develop Kirlian photography as an analytic tool, but the technique has proven to have little scientific usefulness.

Bibliography: Edelson, E., "Aura Phenomenon Puzzles Experts," *Smithsonian*, April 1977; Krippner, S., and Rubin, D., eds., *The Energies of Consciousness* (1975); Pehek, J., Kyler, H., and Faust, D., "Image Modulation in Corona Discharge Photography," *Science*, Oct. 15, 1976.

Kirov [kee'-rawf]

Kirov is the capital of Kirov oblast in the Russian Soviet Federated Socialist Republic of the USSR. Located on the west bank of the Vyatka River in northern European Russia, the city has a population of 421,000 (1987 est.).

Kirov is an important manufacturing center served by several railroads and by shipping on the Vyatka. Its principal industries are machine-building and metal-fabricating plants producing construction equipment, agricultural equipment, and heavy machinery. The city's location in the forested zone has given rise to a wood-products industry, including a large match factory. Kirov also has a tire plant. Artificial leather is also produced. A number of buildings dating from the 17th and 18th centuries have been preserved, including the Uspensky Cathedral.

Originally known as Khlynov, the city was renamed Vyatka for its river in 1780. In 1934 its name was changed to Kirov in honor of Sergei M. Kirov, a high Soviet official, whose assassination that year formed the pretext for the Great Purge. THEODORE SHABAD

Kirov Ballet

The Kirov Ballet, of Leningrad (formerly Saint Petersburg), was the most important ballet company in Russia until 1944, when the Kirov's chief choreographer, Leonid Lavrovsky (1905–67), and its prima ballerina, Galina ULANOVA, were transferred to Moscow's Bolshoi Ballet. The company's weakened artistic standing gave eventual preeminence to Moscow.

Founded during the reign (1730–40) of Empress Anna as a ballet school for the children of court servants, the Imperial Ballet Company was originally housed in the Bolshoi Theater of Saint Petersburg. It moved in 1889 to the Maryinsky Theater, which was renamed Kirov Theater in 1935.

The company's first ballet masters and choreographers came from abroad. Among them were the Austrian Franz Hilverding (1710–68), the Italian Gaspero Angiolini (1731–1803), and the Frenchman Charles Louis Didelot (1767–1837). At the same time, most of the company's dance stars, such as Marie Taglioni (see TAGLIONI family), Fanny ELSSLER, and Lucile GRAHN, were from western Europe.

Although Russian artists gradually made their mark, it was a Frenchman—Marius PETIPA—who dominated ballet in Saint Petersburg from 1862 until his retirement in 1903, and it was a series of Italian virtuoso dancers—for example, Virginia Zucchi (1849–1930), Enrico Cecchetti (1850–1928), Carlotta Brianza (1867–1930), and Pierina Legnani (1863–1923)—who captured the public's admiration. Only toward the end of the 19th century, with such ballerinas as Matilde Kshessinska (1872–1971) and Olga Preobrazhenska (1870–1962), did Russian dancers gain ascendancy. The first native choreographer acclaimed at the Maryinsky (Kirov) was Mikhail FOKINE.

After the 1917 Revolution the Kirov encouraged experimental ideas for a time but soon reverted to conservatism. In the 1960s and '70s the company lost some of its finest dancers, among them Mikhail BARYSHNIKOV, Natalia MAKAROVA, and Rudolf NUREYEV, who chose to live and work in the West. Despite such problems the Kirov has remained one of the world's finest classical ballet companies. DALE HARRIS

Bibliography: Doeser, Linda, *Ballet and Dance: The World's Major Companies* (1978); Gregory, J., and Ukladnikov, A., *Leningrad's Ballet* (1982); Roslavleva, Natalia, *The Era of the Russian Ballet* (1966).

Kirstein, Lincoln [kur'-steen]

Lincoln Edward Kirstein, b. Rochester, N.Y., May 4, 1907, is a renowned American dance writer and ballet administrator. Educated at Harvard University, Kirstein has acute intellectual gifts and aesthetic discernment. He was responsible in 1933 for bringing choreographer George BALANCHINE to the United States. With Balanchine he established (1934) the School of American Ballet, the U.S. equivalent of the professional dance academies of Russia and Europe. This school was to become the base for a series of performing companies—including the American Ballet and Ballet Society—culminating in the NEW YORK CITY BALLET (founded 1948). The latter, with Balanchine as chief choreographer (until his death in 1983) and Kirstein as patron, policy maker, and policy defender (he was general director until his retirement in 1989) was probably the single most significant force in shaping the style of contemporary ballet. Kirstein earlier was a founder-director (1936–39) of Ballet Caravan and founder and editor (1942–48, except for World War II military service) of the periodical *Dance Index*. His writings include *Dance* (1935), *Three Pamphlets Collected* (1967), *Movement and Metaphor* (1970), *The New York City Ballet* (1973), *Nijinsky Dancing* (1975), *Quarry* (1986), and with Muriel Stuart, *The Classic Ballet: Basic Technique and Terminology* (1952). TOBI TOBIAS

Kisangani [kee-san-gah'-nee]

Kisangani (previously Stanleyville) is a city in northeastern Zaire located on the Congo River. The population of the city is 282,650 (1984 est.). Kisangani owes its importance to its location at the base of Stanley Falls, making it the river's head of navigation. It is a busy port, and major industries are brewing, the manufacture of furniture and clothing, and food processing. The University of Zaire (1963) is there.

A settlement was established there in 1880 by Henry Morton Stanley. Patrice Lumumba, before becoming Zaire's first prime minister, made Kisangani his seat of power; it was also the seat of a Lumumbist government in exile (1960–61) and was briefly held by Lumumbist sympathizers in 1964. Army mutinies occurred there in 1966 and 1967, during the civil war in the Congo. EDOUARD BUSTIN

Kish

Kish (modern Uhaimir), situated 14 km (9 mi) east of Babylon in Iraq, was the most important Sumerian city-state during the formative years of Mesopotamian civilization (c.2800–2370 BC). An ancient list of Sumerian kings records Kish as the first postdiluvian kingdom (c.2750–2370 BC). Although some of the kings mentioned are mythical, others, including Enmebaragesi and Mesilim, are known from contemporary inscriptions. Kish was occupied almost continuously from late prehistoric times (c.3500 BC) until the Sassanian period (AD c.600), but it was no longer paramount after the removal (c.2371 BC) of political power to the city of Agade.

The site, about 8 by 3 km (5 by 2 mi), contains the mounds of twin cities: Kish and to the east, Hursagkalama (modern Ingharra), where a deep sounding produced shards and flint tools from the earliest levels of occupation. Remains of the flourishing 3d-millennium-BC city include three ziggurats, a temple, a residential palace, and chariot burials. Religious and secular buildings of the Old Babylonian (early 2d millennium) and neo-Assyrian (8th century BC) periods contained important collections of cuneiform tablets. Later remains include the foundations of two 6th-century-BC neo-Babylonian temples at Ingharra. Excavations at Kish were conducted by the French (1852, 1912) and by a joint Oxford University–Chicago Field Museum expedition (1923–33). KATE FIELDEN

Bibliography: Gibson, McGuire, *The City and Area of Kish* (1972); Moorey, P. R. S., *Kish Excavations, 1923–1933* (1978).

Kishinev [kish-in-yef']

Kishinev (1987 est. pop., 663,000) is the capital of the Moldavian Soviet Socialist Republic of the USSR. It is situated on the Byk River, a Dnestr tributary. Under Soviet rule, Kishinev developed into a diversified manufacturing center specializing in the processing of produce, particularly wines, canned goods, and tobacco, from the agriculturally rich hinterland.

First mentioned in 1466, Kishinev received the status of city during the 17th century. It developed into the economic and political center of the disputed historical province of Bessarabia, which was seized by Russia from the Ottoman Empire in 1812. Between the two world wars the city was part of Romania and was known as Chísinau. THEODORE SHABAD

Kissinger, Henry A. [kis'-in-jur]

Henry Kissinger, a professor of government at Harvard, entered the Nixon administration in 1969 and was secretary of state from 1973 to 1977. During his tenure the United States entered a period of détente with the USSR, reestablished ties with China, and withdrew its forces from Vietnam. In 1983 he headed a commission to study U.S. policy in Central America.

Henry Alfred Kissinger, b. Fürth, Germany, May 27, 1923, was chief foreign policy advisor and secretary of state to Presidents Richard NIXON and Gerald FORD. In these positions he attained unusual power and prestige. Among his achievements were the restoration of U.S. relations with the People's Republic of China and the arrangement—by "shuttle diplomacy" between the parties—of a cease-fire between the Israelis and Arabs in the Arab-Israeli War of 1973. He also negotiated a cease-fire in Vietnam, sharing the Nobel Peace Prize for 1973 with the North Vietnamese negotiator Le Duc Tho.

Kissinger came to the United States in 1938 and became (1943) a U.S. citizen. He served in the U.S. Army in World War II and in the U.S. military government of Germany in 1945–46. He studied political science at Harvard University and taught there from 1954 until 1969. His doctoral dissertation was later published as *A World Restored* (1973). His *Nuclear Weapons and Foreign Policy* (1957) brought him recognition as an expert on nuclear strategy; he advocated the development of conventional forces as an alternative to sole reliance on nuclear weapons. Kissinger served as a consultant on foreign policy for Presidents Kennedy and Johnson.

As assistant to President Nixon for national security affairs (1969–73), Kissinger gathered most of the reins of foreign policy into his own hands. He controlled the National Security

Council, greatly expanding its staff; he outweighed the secretary of state (William P. Rogers) in discussions of policy; and he played an active role in diplomacy, negotiating with heads of state and prime ministers. He succeeded Rogers as secretary of state in September 1973, continuing to hold the post of director of the National Security Council until 1975. He remained as secretary of state after Gerald Ford succeeded Richard Nixon in August 1974.

Kissinger's diplomacy was a politics of maneuver, characterized by a distrust of bureaucracy and a preference for dealing personally with statesmen abroad and leaders of Congress at home. He was most successful in the period 1971–73, when new relationships were established with China and the USSR, the first strategic arms limitation agreement (SALT I) was signed, and U.S. troops were withdrawn from Vietnam. In his subsequent period (1974–77) as secretary of state he encountered domestic and foreign opposition to his policies.

After retiring as secretary of state, Kissinger remained active as a commentator on foreign affairs, a teacher, and a consultant. His memoirs, *White House Years* and *Years of Upheaval,* appeared in 1979 and 1982, respectively.

Bibliography: Caldwell, D., ed., *Henry Kissinger: His Personality and Policies* (1983); Hersh, S., *The Price of Power: Kissinger in the Nixon White House* (1983); Nutter, G. W., *Kissinger's Grand Design* (1975); Starr, H., *Henry Kissinger: Perceptions of International Politics* (1984).

Kitagawa Utamaro: see UTAMARO.

Kitakyushu   [kee-tah'-kyoo-shoo]

Kitakyushu (1984 est. pop., 1,065,078) is a city located at the northernmost tip of Kyushu island, Japan, across a narrow strait from Honshu island. Kitakyushu was created in 1963 from the formerly independent cities of Moji, Kokura, Yawata, Tobata, and Wakamatsu.

Kitakyushu is one of Japan's major centers of heavy industry. It is near the western end of the Tokaido megalopolis, the urban-industrial region stretching westward along the southern coast of Honshu from Tokyo. Iron and steel, chemical fertilizers, paper and pulp products, machinery, and metal products predominate; ceramics, textiles, and foodstuffs are among the lesser products. Shipbuilding is another of the city's industries. Yawata is near the country's largest coal mine and is the site of Japan's first steel plant. The rapid rate of industrial development in the Kitakyushu region since the mid-1950s has created serious problems of air pollution, particularly the accumulation of falling soot.   JAMES CHAN

Kitchen Cabinet

In U.S. history, Kitchen Cabinet was the name given by critics of President Andrew JACKSON to an informal group of advisors who influenced him on matters of policy. Before the cabinet reorganization of 1831, Jackson never held official cabinet

meetings. Members of the Kitchen Cabinet included Martin VAN BUREN, John H. EATON, and Amos KENDALL.

kitchen gods

In China, the kitchen gods, or *ma-chungs,* are paper images of the god of the kitchen stove or hearth, Tsao Chün. The annual New Year's eve feast is spread before an ornate *ma-chung* of red cardboard placed above the stove. That image is then burned to send the god to heaven; it is replaced the next morning with a cheaper paper *ma-chung* for daily use.

Kitchener

Kitchener, a city in Canada with a population of 150,604 (1986), is located in southern Ontario in the Grand River Valley. It is the seat of Waterloo County. The economy is based on the meatpacking, brewing and distilling, and textile industries. It has close ties with its nearby twin city of Waterloo. Kitchener was settled about 1806 by German Amish and Mennonite farmers from Pennsylvania; it was known as Berlin until the name was changed (1916) during World War I. Kitchener retains much of its original Pennsylvania-Dutch flavor.

Kitchener, Herbert Kitchener, 1st Earl

Horatio Herbert Kitchener, 1st Earl Kitchener, b. June 24, 1850, d. June 5, 1916, was Britain's foremost general at the beginning of the 20th century. Commissioned in the Royal Engineers in 1871, he was attached to the Egyptian army in 1883 and became its commander in chief in 1892. In that capacity he established his reputation by reconquering the Sudan from the Mahdists, winning the famous Battle of Omdurman in 1898. That same year his tactful treatment of the French in the FASHODA INCIDENT may have avoided a war with France.

After serving as governor of the Sudan, Kitchener became (1899) chief of staff to Frederick Sleigh ROBERTS in the SOUTH AFRICAN WAR and succeeded as commander in chief in 1900. He was much criticized for interning Afrikaner civilians in concentration camps. As commander in chief in India (1902–09), Kitchener quarreled with the viceroy, Lord CURZON, over military policy, but the London government supported him and made him a field marshal. From 1911 to 1914 he was the virtual ruler of Egypt as British consul general.

At the start (1914) of World War I, Kitchener became secretary of state for war, the first serving officer to hold this post. He expanded the army from 20 divisions to 70, but he was blamed for the munitions shortage on the western front. Kitchener was drowned when his ship was torpedoed while on a mission to Russia.   DON M. CREGIER

Bibliography: Arthur, George, *Life of Lord Kitchener,* 3 vols. (1920); Warner, Phillip, *Kitchener: The Man behind the Legend* (1986).

kite   (bird)

Both the Mississippi kite, Ictinia mississipiensis *(left), and the swallow-tailed kite,* Elanoides forficatus *(right and in flight), are graceful birds of prey found near wetlands from the southeastern United States to South America. These birds seldom perch during daylight hours and are most commonly seen in flight.*

Kite is the common name for about 30 species of typically lightly built birds of the hawk family, Accipitridae, widely distributed over warmer regions of the world. They are distinguished by their graceful, gliding flight and occur most commonly near water or wetlands. Kites are classified in three subfamilies: Elaninae, or the white-tailed kites; Perninae, or the fork-tailed kites (and honey buzzards); and Milvinae, or the true kites. The swallow-tailed kite, *Elanoides forficatus,* found from the southeastern United States and the West Indies to northern Argentina, is slim, black above, and white below and has a white head and a long, deeply forked tail. It spends most of the time on the wing, feeding on the larger flying insects and skimming the water to bathe and drink. The Everglade kite, *Rostrhamus sociabilis,* found from southern Florida into Argentina, is heavier-bodied, dark, with a broad white band across the tail. It feeds exclusively on snails. Some Old World species are scavengers.   WILLIAM F. SANDFORD

kite   (object)

A kite consists of a lightweight frame that is covered with paper, plastic, or cloth; it is designed to be flown in the wind at the end of a long cord wound on a stick or drum. In Eastern countries, kites have been flown since before recorded history and have deep-rooted cultural and historical associations. Although kites are used primarily for recreation, they have also been employed in war and in scientific research. In 1752, Benjamin Franklin, the U.S. statesman and inventor, flew a kite during a thunderstorm to demonstrate the electrical nature of lightning. Kites have been used for military observation and for meteorological experiments, but today airplanes and balloons have replaced the kite for such work.

Common kite shapes are the diamond, hexagon, box, and tetrahedron. Kites with a single flat surface, such as the diamond, must have a tail hanging from the bottom to control the kite. The box kite, which was invented in the 1890s in Australia by Lawrence Hargrave, has a rectangular frame that is twice as long as it is wide. The ends of a box kite are uncovered, and it needs no tail. The best wind for kite flying ranges between 13 and 32 km/h (8 and 20 mph) and is steady close to the ground.

Bibliography: Hart, Clive, *Kites* (1967); Newman, Lee S. and Jay H., *Kite Craft* (1974); Thomas, Bill, *The Complete World of Kites* (1977); Yolen, Will, *The Complete Book of Kites and Kite Flying* (1976).

(Left) *This o-dako, or giant fighting kite, is typical of those flown during the kite-dueling festivals,* tako-kichi matsuri, *held throughout Japan. The movements of these giant kites are controlled by 42 or 49 bridles, or ropes, operated by eight to twelve people.*

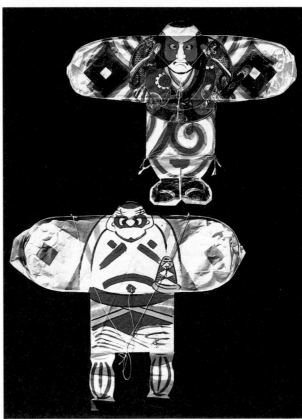

(Above) *Two of the foremost traditional kitemakers in Japan today created these* yakko *kites, vivid evocations of the footmen of the samurai. This* shosuke yakko *kite (top), by Matsutaro Yanese, bows at the waist. Teizo Hasimoto designed this* yakko *kite (bottom).*

(Left) *The designs of many Edo kites are derived from ukiyo-e woodblock prints. This Edo kite, portraying a breaking wave, was created by Teizo Hashimoto. During the 1700s, Tokyo formerly called Edo, was one of the major centers of kitemaking.*

A contestant in Baltimore's annual kite festival prepares a Rogallo kite for flight. This kite, developed by Francis Rogallo, is today one of the most popular styles of kite. The principles governing the Rogallo kite have been successfully applied to aircraft designs.

kithara   [kith'-uh-ruh]

The kithara was used by the ancient Greeks to accompany singing and for professional solo performances. A large, heavy lyre, the kithara had as many as 12 strings, which were plucked with a plectrum. It was held against the musician's body and was supported by a leather band.

The largest of the ancient Greek LYRES, the kithara was a wooden instrument with from three to usually seven strings. Its base was a sound box from which two upthrust arms, straight or curved, were connected at the top with a crossbar. The strings, which ran from top to bottom, crossed a bridge that provided tension, and they were plucked with a plectrum. Associated with the cult of Apollo, the instrument was used by professionals as a solo instrument and as an accompaniment for solo singers. It was usually heavy enough to require support by a strap or band. Its smaller counterpart, the lyre, was the instrument of amateurs. Plucked instruments of this variety are known to have existed in Egypt as early as 1500 BC.   ELWYN A. WIENANDT

Bibliography: Baines, Anthony, ed., *Musical Instruments through the Ages*, rev. ed. (1975); Sachs, Curt, *The History of Musical Instruments* (1940).

Kitt Peak National Observatory

Kitt Peak National Observatory, located 84 km (52 mi) southwest of Tucson, Ariz., on top of the 2,100-m (7,000-ft) Kitt Peak, is one of the world's major astronomical research centers. It was founded in 1958 by the Association of Universities for Research in Astronomy (AURA), a nonprofit consortium of 17 universities that operates the observatory under contract with the U.S. National Science Foundation.

The observatory does research in solar, planetary, stellar, galactic, and extragalactic astronomy. It has 15 telescopes, among them reflectors with apertures of 158 in (4 m), 84 in (2.1 m), and 51 in (1.3 m), the 60-in (1.5-m) Robert McMath solar telescope (the world's largest), and a 24-in (61-cm) solar vacuum telescope. The National Radio Astronomy Observatory also operates a 36-ft-diameter (11-m) radio telescope at Kitt Peak. Using INTERFEROMETERS and image-enhancement techniques (see IMAGE PROCESSING), astronomers at Kitt Peak photographed for the first time the surface of a star (Betelgeuse) other than the Sun.

kittiwake   [kit'-ee-wayk]

One of the more unusual gulls, the kittiwake, *Rissa tridactyla*, is classified in the family Laridae, order Charadriiformes. It has a white head, tail, and underparts; the top of the wings and the back are gray; and the wingtips and feet are black. Kittiwakes live along the coasts of northern Europe, Asia, and North America. Unlike most gulls, kittiwakes travel far out to sea, feeding on fish and crustaceans and often following ships. They nest on cliff ledges. Unlike other gulls, the young remain in the nest until able to fly; possibly this is an adaptation to prevent fatal falls.   ROBERT J. RAIKOW

Kitwe   [kee'-tway]

Kitwe, Zambia's leading commercial and industrial center, is located near the Kaufe River about 48 km (30 mi) south of the Zaire border. Its population is 314,794 (1980 est.). Kitwe was founded in 1936 and grew on the basis of the copper mining industry that dominates the region. Foodstuffs, plastics, and clothing are also produced.

kiva   [kee'-vuh]

Kivas (Hopi for "old house") are sacred ceremonial chambers of the present-day PUEBLO Indians of Arizona and New Mexico; they are also found in the ruins of the prehistoric ANASAZI culture. The kivas traditionally belong to the religious fraternities in Pueblo society, whose members perform secret rites from which the uninitiated are excluded. Most kivas are semisubterranean, built along clefts on the edge of the mesa with the roof of the kiva level with the ground surface. These rectangular or circular stone rooms have no doors and can be entered only by hatchways, descending by ladders through the roof. In addition to being used for the performance of esoteric rituals, the kivas also traditionally serve as council chambers and workshops, where the men do the weaving.

KENNETH STEWART

Bibliography: Vivian, Gordon, and Reiter, Paul, *Great Kivas of Chaco Canyon and Their Relationships* (1972).

Kivu, Lake   [kee'-voo]

Lake Kivu is located in Africa's Great Rift Valley, 1,460 m (4,790 ft) above sea level, on the border between Zaire and Rwanda. It has an area of 2,700 km² (1,042 mi²), with an uneven coast and many islands. The average depth is 220 m (722 ft). In 1958 a hydroelectric plant was built at the lake's outlet into the Ruzizi River. A German explorer, Count Adolf von Götzen, was the first European to visit the lake in 1894.

kiwi   (bird)   [kee'-wee]

The common, or brown, kiwi, Apteryx australis, *a strange-looking bird, lays an egg approximately 10 percent of its weight, the largest of any bird. The kiwi is the national emblem of New Zealand and is pictured on that country's coins, bills, and stamps.*

The kiwi is a flightless, solitary, nocturnal bird found only in New Zealand. Three living species, all in the genus *Apteryx,* comprise the family Apterygidae. They are usually classified in their own order, Apterygiformes. Named for their cry, kiwis are brownish or grayish in color and may be streaked or barred. They have small heads, hairlike plumage, minute wings, and no external tail. The bill is long and slender, with nostrils near the tip. Kiwis range from 1.25 to 4 kg (2.75 to 9.0 lb) in weight and from 45 to 84 cm (18 to 33 in) in length and stand up to 30 cm (1 ft) high. They inhabit humid forests or swamps, where they feed on insects, snails, berries, and especially earthworms. Recent experiments confirm that kiwis locate food by smell, which is unusual for birds. The one or two very large eggs, about 13 cm (5 in) in length and 400 g (14 oz) in weight, are laid in a burrow, and the smaller male incubates them for about eleven weeks. The little spotted kiwi, *A. oweni,* seems to be disappearing.   FRED E. LOHRER

Bibliography: Calder, William A., "The Kiwi," *Scientific American,* July 1978.

kiwi   (fruit)

The kiwi fruit is the fruit of a grapelike, deciduous vine, *Actinidia chinensis,* native to south central China, where it grows on trees to heights of 10 m (30 ft) or more. About 1906 it was introduced into New Zealand, which is now the principal producer of the fruit, although plantings have also been made in California. The small, round fruit has a fuzzy, greenish brown skin roughly resembling the plumage of the kiwi bird;

its flesh is a translucent emerald green, with a refreshing lime-like flavor. Kiwi fruit is eaten fresh or cooked, and, like the papaya, its juice may be used as a meat tenderizer.

W. B. STOREY

Kiyomasu   [kee-yoh-mah'-soo]

Kiyomasu, or Torii Kiyomasu, 1696–1716, was a Japanese painter and printmaker who worked during the formative period of UKIYO-E, a printmaking style featuring decorative representations of genre subjects, especially those reflecting the world of popular entertainment in Edo (present-day Tokyo). His style is distinguished by rugged, vividly handcolored portraits of actors, one of the hallmarks of the Torii school of Ukiyo-e prints. Although Kiyomasu's numerous prints of actors sometimes follow the curvilinear manner associated with Torii school founder KIYONOBU I, they often display a finer and more accomplished calligraphic line.   HOWARD A. LINK

Bibliography: Link, H. A., *The Theatrical Prints of the Torii Masters* (1977).

Kiyonaga   [kee-yoh-nah'-gah]

Kiyonaga, or Torii Kiyonaga, 1752–1815, was a Japanese UKIYO-E (a print style featuring populist genre subjects) artist and the fourth titular head of the Torii school founded in the early 18th century by Kyonobu I. Generally regarded as the greatest Ukiyo-e master of the 1780s, Kiyonaga executed a wide range of paintings, prints, and illustrated books. Tutored by Kiyomitsu, his predecessor as head of the Torii School, Kiyonaga developed an elongated, linear style that he used to depict statuesque courtesans and stylish Edo (modern Tokyo) men and women during the middle phase (1781–85) of his career. The idealized feminine beauty celebrated in these prints had a profound influence on contemporary Japanese artists. Following Kiyomitsu's death and the official acceptance (1787) of Kiyonaga's titular status as Torii IV, Kiyonaga concentrated on prints of Kabuki actors that exhibit a new, realistic portrait style.   HOWARD A. LINK

Bibliography: Hirano, Chie, *Kiyonaga, A Study of His Life and Works* (1939); Narazaki, M., *Kiyonaga,* trans. by John Bester (1969).

Kiyonobu I   [kee-yoo-noh'-boo]

Kiyonobu I, or Torii Kiyonobu I, 1664–1729, was a major Japanese painter and printmaker in the UKIYO-E style who specialized in illustrations of Kabuki actors for the three theaters of Edo (modern Tokyo). The son of an Osaka Kabuki actor, Kiyonobu I moved (1687) to Edo and came under the influence of MORONOBU, whose lively woodblock prints of populist genre subjects typified the Ukiyo-e style. Building on Moronobu's legacy, Kiyonobu I founded the Torii school of Ukiyo-e prints, which greatly advanced Japanese printmaking. His greatest works were two books (1700) dazzlingly illustrated in black and white, one portraying actors and the other depicting courtesans. The fluidly contoured and highly decorative style of these illustrations influenced Ukiyo-e masters for decades to come. One of his numerous pupils was his son, Kiyonobu II, who helped carry on his father's tradition.

HOWARD A. LINK

Bibliography: Link, H. A., *The Theatrical Prints of the Torii Masters* (1977).

Klamath   [klam'-uhth]

The Klamath are North American Indians who in the 19th century lived on the shores of Upper Klamath Lake, Klamath Marsh, and the lower Sprague and Williamson rivers in south central Oregon. Their language, like closely related Modoc, belongs to the Sahaptin stock of the Penutian linguistic family. More closely related to the Plateau than to the Great Basin or Californian culture areas, their economy was highly adapted to their lake and marsh environment. Lakes and rivers provided abundant fish. Water lily seeds, camas roots, and berries were vegetal staples. The Klamath built substantial semisubterranean earth lodges at their main village sites, mat lodges at temporary camps. They used dugout canoes for lake and river transport. The guardian spirit quest and associated dances were the principal religious activities, along with shamanistic curing. Traditionally aggressive, Klamath raided nearby California Indian villages for captives to be traded.

By the treaty of 1864 with the United States, a reservation was created comprising much of the original Klamath home area; later, however, the Modoc and some Paiute and Pit River Indians were forced onto the same reservation. Members of these groups eventually merged with the Klamath to form a cohesive Klamath Tribe; this body retained control of extensive timberlands until termination of the reservation in 1954. In 1986 the Klamath tribe was reorganized. Its population is about 2,500.   PHILIP DRUCKER

Bibliography: Gatschet, Albert S., *The Klamath Indians of Southwestern Oregon* (1890; repr. 1966); Howe, Carrol B., *Ancient Tribes of the Klamath Country* (1968); Spier, Leslie, *Klamath Ethnography* (1930); Stern, Theodore, *The Klamath Tribe* (1965).

Klaproth, Martin Heinrich   [klahp'-roht]

Martin Heinrich Klaproth, b. Dec. 1, 1743, d. Jan. 1, 1817, was a German chemist who discovered the elements uranium, zirconium, and cerium in their oxide forms. He began his career as an apothecary and studied chemistry independently. Klaproth was assessor of pharmacy to the Collegium Medicum (Prussia's highest medical board) from 1782, professor of chemistry to the Royal Field Artillery School from 1787, and professor to the Royal Artillery Academy from 1791. He was appointed (1810) professor of chemistry at the newly established University of Berlin. Klaproth at first favored the standard PHLOGISTON THEORY, but on repeating Antoine Lavoisier's experiments before the Berlin Academy of Science in 1792 he became one of the first converts outside France to Lavoisier's antiphlogistic theory. A prolific and careful analytical chemist, he examined many minerals, confirmed the existence of strontium, established the identity of tellurium, and determined the properties of the minerals yttria and beryllia.
                                                    RALPH GABLE

Klebsiella   [kleb-see-el'-uh]

Klebsiella is a genus of bacteria, family Enterobacteriaceae, containing at least 200 strains of gram-negative rods. The species *K. pneumoniae* is the most important medically. It frequently causes pneumonia and is associated with infectious diseases of the lungs, genitourinary tract, and liver.

Klee, Paul   [klay]

A Swiss-born painter and graphic artist whose personal, often gently humorous works are replete with allusions to dreams, music, and poetry, Paul Klee, b. Dec. 18, 1879, d. June 29, 1940, is difficult to classify. Primitive art, surrealism, cubism, and children's art all seem blended into his small-scale, delicate paintings, watercolors, and drawings.

Klee grew up in a musical family and was himself a violinist. After much hesitation he chose to study art, not music, and he attended the Munich Academy in 1900. There his teacher was the popular symbolist and society painter Franz von STUCK. Klee later toured Italy (1901–02), responding enthusiastically to Early Christian and Byzantine art.

Klee's early works are mostly etchings and pen-and-ink drawings. These combine satirical, grotesque, and surreal elements and reveal the influence of Francisco de Goya and James Ensor, both of whom Klee admired. Two of his best-known etchings, dating from 1903, are *Virgin in a Tree* and *Two Men Meet, Each Believing the Other to Be of Higher Rank*. Such peculiar, evocative titles are characteristic of Klee and give his works an added dimension of meaning.

After his marriage in 1906 to the pianist Lili Stumpf, Klee settled in Munich, then an important center for avant–garde art. That same year he exhibited his etchings for the first time. His friendship with the painters Wassily Kandinsky and August Macke prompted him to join Der BLAUE REITER (The Blue Rider), an expressionist group that contributed much to the development of abstract art.

Paul Klee's *Fish Magic* (1925) exemplifies the imagination, humor, and thematic use of small motifs characteristic of much of his work. Klee, one of the most inventive artists of the 20th century, was a major figure in the evolution of modern art. (Philadelphia Museum of Art.)

A turning point in Klee's career was his visit to Tunisia with Macke and Louis Molliet in 1914. He was so overwhelmed by the intense light there that he wrote: "Color has taken possession of me; no longer do I have to chase after it, I know that it has hold of me forever. That is the significance of this blessed moment. Color and I are one. I am a painter." He now built up compositions of colored squares that have the radiance of the mosaics he saw on his Italian sojourn. The watercolor *Red and White Domes* (1914; Collection of Clifford Odets, New York City) is distinctive of this period.

Klee often incorporated letters and numerals into his paintings, as in *Once Emerged from the Gray of Night* (1917–18; Klee Foundation, Berlin). These, part of Klee's complex language of symbols and signs, are drawn from the unconscious and used to obtain a poetic amalgam of abstraction and reality.

Klee taught at the BAUHAUS school after World War I and in 1925, in his *Pedagogical Sketchbook,* he tried to define and analyze the primary visual elements and the ways in which they could be applied. In 1931 he began teaching at Dusseldorf Academy but was dismissed by the Nazis, who termed his work "degenerate." Klee left Germany for Switzerland in 1933. The mood of his later work is increasingly melancholic and characterized by heavy black lines that in the painting *Revolution of the Viaduct* (1937; Kunsthall, Hamburg) become independent, ponderous forms.   MANUELA HOELTERHOFF

Bibliography: Geelhaar, Christian, *Paul Klee and the Bauhaus* (1973); Grohmann, Will, *Paul Klee,* trans. by N. Gutermann (1967); Jordan, Jim M., *Paul Klee and Cubism* (1984); Kagan, Andrew A., *Paul Klee—Art and Music* (1983); Klee, Paul, *The Diaries of Paul Klee,* ed. by Felix Klee (1964); Lanchner, Carolyn, ed., *Paul Klee* (1987); Plant, Margaret, *Paul Klee: Figures and Faces* (1978).

Klein, Calvin: see FASHION DESIGN.

Klein, Felix

Felix Christian Klein, b. Apr. 25, 1849, d. June 22, 1925, was both a sound mathematician and a great promoter of mathematical activity in his native Germany and internationally as well. He is best known for his work in NON-EUCLIDEAN GEOMETRY, for his studies on the connections between geometry and group theory, and for results in function theory. Klein received his doctorate in 1868 from the University of Bonn, where he had studied mathematics and physics. After teaching at a number of universities, he went (1886) to the University of Göttingen, were he remained until his retirement in 1913.   J. W. DAUBEN

Klein, Melanie

Melanie Klein, b. Vienna, Mar. 30, 1882, d. London, Sept. 24, 1960, pioneered in the psychoanalysis of children and invented play therapy. Klein's analyses of infantile and child development have been of key importance to psychoanalytic theory on personality development. In particular, she studied the earliest beginnings of the Oedipus complex and superego and analyzed personality origins in terms of paranoid-schizoid and depressive patterns.

Bibliography: Segal, Hanna, *Introduction to the Work of Melanie Klein*, 2d ed. (1974).

Klein, Yves

Yves Klein, b. Apr. 28, 1928, d. June 6, 1962, was one of the most unusual artists of postwar France. Although Klein had no formal artistic training, he developed elaborate metaphysical theories about art. He was fascinated by the process of making art, and his public demonstrations—for example, nude girls covering themselves with blue paint and rolling across canvases, or flamethrowers directed at various materials—caused a sensation. His 1958 Void show, in which he presented an empty gallery that had been "cleansed" of the signs of previous artists' shows, nearly caused a riot.

PHIL PATTON

Klein bottle

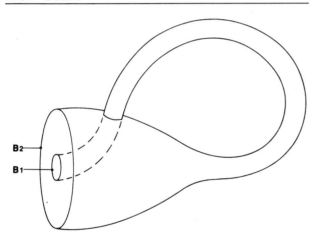

A Klein bottle, first described by Felix KLEIN, is a certain closed surface that is of interest in TOPOLOGY as well as for amusement. It represents a one-sided surface that is closed and has no boundary. It cannot be constructed in ordinary Euclidean three-dimensional space, but it is possible to describe how such a surface could be constructed. Let C be a flexible cylinder with boundary curves labeled B_1 and B_2. If the cylinder is bent around and B_1 is attached to B_2, a torus (surface of a doughnut) is obtained. If, however, B_1 is attached to B_2 with "other orientation"—in other words, with the other points of C not being attached together—the surface obtained is a Klein bottle. This would be a strange surface to live on. A person making a round-trip journey would find at the end of the trip that his directions of North and South would agree with the local residents, but East and West would have been reversed.

MORTON L. CURTIS

Bibliography: Lietzmann, Walther, *Visual Topology* (1968).

Kleist, Heinrich von

Bernd Heinrich Wilhelm von Kleist, b. Oct. 18, 1777, d. Nov. 21, 1811, driven to suicide largely because he failed to achieve fame as an author in his lifetime, ironically is today considered one of the greatest poets ever produced by Germany. Kleist did not go unnoticed even during his lifetime; his genius was recognized, with qualifications, by most of the lead-

ing German authors of the day, but Kleist's plays and stories were puzzling and disturbing to audiences that were more accustomed to moralistic and sentimental literature and that therefore found the turbulent, self-expressive writing of the troubled young aristocrat often in shockingly bad taste. His principal dramatic works included the one-act comedy *The Broken Pitcher* (1806; pub. 1811; Eng. trans., 1961), the Amazon tragedy *Penthesilea* (1808; Eng. trans., 1959), and his masterpiece, *The Prince of Homburg* (1810; pub. 1821; Eng. trans., 1956). His best-known novellas were *Michael Kohlhaas* (1810; Eng. trans., 1913–15) and *The Marquise of O.* (1810; Eng. trans., 1960).

The meaning, if no longer the quality, of Kleist's works is still much debated, with existentialists seeing in him a forerunner of Kierkegaard and other philosophers of *Angst,* and Marxists claiming him as an early critic of feudalism in his native Prussia. The intense erotic feeling that characterizes many of his portrayals has interested psychoanalytic critics, and there has recently been a renewed appreciation of the comic and ironically humorous elements in his works.

Kleist was determined to support himself by his writing, and, partly because he was unable to achieve that aim, he never married. By 1811 the Prussian government had suppressed his journal, the *Berliner Abendblätter,* and his hopes of a German uprising against Napoleon became increasingly forlorn. His suicide involved the fulfillment of a promise to a friend's wife, who believed she was incurably ill, that he would kill her and join her in death whenever she wished.

JAMES M. McGLATHERY

Bibliography: Dyer, Denys, *The Stories of Kleist: A Critical Study* (1977); Gearey, John, *Heinrich von Kleist: A Study in Tragedy and Anxiety* (1968); Helbling, Robert E., *Heinrich von Kleist: The Major Works* (1975); Silz, Walter, *Heinrich von Kleist* (1977); Stahl, Ernst L., *Heinrich von Kleist's Drama* (1961).

Klemperer, Otto   [klem'-pur-ur]

The German conductor Otto Klemperer, b. May 14, 1885, d. July 6, 1973, was only 22 when, on the recommendation of Gustav Mahler, he was named to conduct the German National Theater in Prague. After conducting opera in Hamburg, Bremen, Strasbourg, Cologne, and Wiesbaden, he joined (1927) the Kroll Opera in Berlin and in 1931 the State Opera. He left Germany in 1933 and became conductor (1933–39) of the Los Angeles Philharmonic; he also directed the reorganization of the Pittsburgh Symphony. In 1959 he was appointed principal conductor "for life" of the London Philharmonia (later New Philharmonia) Orchestra, with which he made many memorable recordings, particularly of the German repertoire. Klemperer was also the composer of six symphonies, nine string quartets, and a mass.

KAREN MONSON

Bibliography: Ewen, David, *Famous Modern Conductors* (1967); Heyworth, Peter, ed., *Conversations with Klemperer* (1973); Klemperer, Otto, *Minor Recollections*, trans. by J. M. Brownjohn (1964).

Discography: Beethoven, L. v., *Fidelio, Missa Solemnis, Symphonies nos. 1–9;* Brahms, J., *Symphonies nos. 1–4;* Bruckner, A., *Symphonies nos. 4 and 6;* Haydn, F. J., *Symphonies nos. 88, 100, 102, and 104;* Mozart, W. A., *Don Giovanni, The Magic Flute, Symphonies nos. 24, 29, 31, 33–41;* Wagner, R., *Overtures and Preludes, Wagner Concert.*

Klenze, Leo von   [klent'-se]

The German architect Franz Karl Leo von Klenze, b. Feb. 29, 1784, d. Jan 27, 1864, was an influential exponent of NEOCLASSICISM and of Renaissance Revival styles. Klenze began his career as a court architect in the new kingdom of Westphalia under Jérôme Bonaparte, Napoleon I's brother. He was called to the Bavarian court of Maximilian I in 1815 and was ennobled in 1833 after serving as royal building director for King Louis I of Bavaria.

As a proponent of neoclassicism Klenze was similar to Karl Friedrich SCHINKEL, his contemporary in Berlin, in his eclectic borrowings from and transformations of architectural forms from classical antiquity and the High Renaissance. Although he had a particular affinity for the Greek heritage, Klenze also adapted styles from the Middle Ages for his church designs.

Klenze's many important designs for Munich contributed significantly to establishing its noble architectural character. These include his plans for streets and squares; the Glyptothek (sculpture museum; 1816-30); the Alte Pinakothek (old painting collection, 1826-36); the Allerheiligen-Hofkirche (court church, 1836-37); and portions of the Residenz palace (Königsbau, Festsaalbau, 1826-42). Other important structures outside Munich were the Walhalla, a Doric memorial temple above the Danube near Regensburg (1830-42), completion of the Hall of Freedom near Kelheim (after 1847), and the New Hermitage in Saint Petersburg (Leningrad), Russia (1839-51).

RON WIEDENHOEFT

Bibliography: Hederer, Oswald, *Leo von Klenze* (1964); Hitchcock, Henry-Russell, *Architecture: 19th and 20th Centuries*, 3d ed. (1968).

kleptomania

Kleptomania is the obsessive impulse to steal, in the absence of any need or desire for the articles stolen. According to psychoanalytic theory, the stolen objects have sexually symbolic value; other theories view kleptomania as revenge for emotional deprivation in infancy or an attempt to extend the limits of power.

See also: NEUROSIS.

Klimt, Gustav   [kleemt]

The Austrian Secessionist painter Gustav Klimt painted the watercolor-gouache study Fulfillment (The Kiss) *for a mosaic mural in a Brussels residence. Klimt was known for sensual forms and elegant linear patterns that reflect both Art Nouveau decorative taste and symbolist erotic undertones. (Musée d'Art Moderne, Strasbourg.)*

The work of the painter and illustrator Gustav Klimt, b. July 14, 1862, d. Feb. 6, 1918, embodies the high-keyed erotic, psychological, and aesthetic preoccupations of turn-of-the-century Vienna's dazzling intellectual world. He has been called the preeminent exponent of ART NOUVEAU. Klimt began (1883) as an artist-decorator in association with his brother and Franz Matsoh. In 1886-92, Klimt executed mural decorations for staircases at the Burgtheater and the Kunsthistorisches Museum in Vienna; these confirmed Klimt's eclecticism and broadened his range of historical references. Klimt was a cofounder and the first president of the Vienna Secession, a group of modernist architects and artists who organized their own exhibition society and gave rise to the SECESSION MOVEMENT, or the Viennese version of Art Nouveau. He was also a frequent contributor to *Ver Sacrum,* the group's journal.

The primal forces of sexuality, regeneration, love, and death form the dominant themes of Klimt's work. His paintings of *femmes fatales,* such as *Judith I* (1901; Österreichische Galerie, Vienna), personify the dark side of sexual attraction. *The Kiss* (1907-08; Österreichische Galerie) celebrates the attraction of the sexes; and *Hope I* (1903; National Gallery, Ottawa) juxtaposes the promise of new life with the destroying force of death.

The sensualism and originality of Klimt's art led to a hostile reaction to his three ceiling murals—*Philosophy* (1900), *Medicine* (1901), and *Jurisprudence* (1902)—for the University of Vienna.

Other important decorative projects undertaken by Klimt were his celebrated *Beethoven frieze* (1902; Österreichische Galerie), a cycle of mosaic decorations for Josef Hofmann's Palais Stoclet in Brussels (1905-09), and numerous book illustrations.

Klimt's style drew upon an enormous range of sources: classical Greek, Byzantine, Egyptian, and Minoan art; late-medieval painting and the woodcuts of Albrecht Dürer; photography and the symbolist art of Max Klinger; and the work of both Franz von Stuck and Fernand Khnopff. In synthesizing these diverse sources, Klimt's art achieved both individuality and extreme elegance.

JEFFERY HOWE

Bibliography: Comini, Alessandra, *Gustav Klimt* (1975); Hofmann, Werner, *Gustav Klimt* (1972); Novotny, Fritz, and Dobai, Johannes, *Gustav Klimt* (1968; repr. 1976).

Klimuk, P. I.   [kli'-muk]

The Soviet cosmonaut Pyotr Ilyich Klimuk, b. July 10, 1942, became a leading member of a new generation of Soviet space pilots. Klimuk was one of several young jet pilots enrolled in the cosmonaut program at an early age in late 1965 and then sent to special engineering schools. He was the command pilot of the 8-day SOYUZ 13 mission in December 1973, the youngest man ever to be in command of a spaceship.

Later, he was the backup commander of SOYUZ 18 when the spaceship crashed on blast-off on Apr. 5, 1975. Consequently, he and flight engineer Vitaly SEVASTIANOV were launched on the make-up mission six weeks later and spent two months in space on board Salyut 4. In mid-1978 he visited Salyut 6, along with a Polish copilot, on Soyuz 30.

JAMES OBERG

Kline, Franz

Franz Kline, b. Wilkes-Barre, Pa., May 23, 1910, d. May 13, 1962, was an important member of the New York school of ABSTRACT EXPRESSIONISM. After studies (1930s) in Boston and London and a period of representational still lifes and cityscapes, he worked in New York City. Through most of the 1950s, Kline limited his vast nonobjective canvases to hurtling black streaks or bars surrounded by areas of white, for example, *Mahoning* (1956; Whitney Museum of American Art, New York City).

The critic Dore Ashton described Kline's black figures as energies or forces spanning an immeasurable wilderness, and he argued that their effectiveness lay in their refusal to take

The American artist Franz Kline's Copper and Red *(1959)* shows the vehemence and bold movement characteristic of his work. Kline, one of the leading exponents of abstract expressionism, is best known for his forceful and massively structured compositions. *(Private collection.)*

on a coherent compositional format. About 1959, Kline abandoned his starkly simple scheme to add middle tones and color.

ABRAHAM A. DAVIDSON

Bibliography: Ashton, Dore, *The Unknown Shore* (1962); Gordon, Jack, *Franz Kline: 1910-1962* (1968).

Klinefelter's syndrome

A congenital disease of males, Klinefelter's syndrome is characterized by small size and firmness of the testes, lack of sperm cells, breast development, and increased excretion of sex hormones; mental retardation often occurs. A relatively common syndrome, it occurs in about 1 out of 500 live male births. The plasma concentration of the male hormone testosterone is often low. The diagnosis is rarely made before puberty, and many affected males may still appear mentally and physically normal.

The fundamental abnormality is an excess of X-type (female) sex chromosomes in the body cells. A body cell in a normal male has an X chromosome and a Y chromosome, the latter determining maleness. Body cells in patients with Klinefelter's syndrome have more than one X chromosome along with the Y.

The excess female chromosomes interfere with full development of male characteristics. Generally, as the number of X chromosomes increases the severity of mental retardation and malformations also increases.   PETER L. PETRAKIS

Klondike   [klahn'-dyk]

The Klondike is a sparsely populated area in west central Yukon Territory in Canada, near the Alaskan border. It was the site of a great gold rush in the 1890s. The Klondike, which encompasses an area of about 2,070 km² (800 mi²), takes its name from the Klondike River. Gold mining has continued on a small scale, along with lead, silver, and zinc extraction. The Alaska Highway passes through the southern part of the Klondike, offering a reliable overland connection with Alaska and other parts of Canada.

Gold was discovered at Rabbit Creek (later Bonanza Creek) ih 1896, and a great gold rush began in 1897. More than 30,000 people streamed into the area. Dawson, still the major town of the Klondike, served the needs of the prospectors. By 1910, when the great strike was over, more than $100,000,000 worth of gold had been taken from the Klondike.

Bibliography: Berton, Pierre, *Klondike Fever: The Life and Death of the Last Great Stampede* (1958); Bronson, William, *The Last Grand Adventure* (1977); Hunt, William R., *North of 53 Degrees* (1975); Wharton, David D., *The Alaska Gold Rush* (1972).

Klopstock, Friedrich Gottlieb   [klawp'-shtawk]

A German epic, lyric, and dramatic poet, Friedrich Gottlieb Klopstock, b. July 2, 1724, d. Mar. 14, 1803, produced a literary landmark with his most substantial work, *The Messiah* (Eng. trans., 1788)—an epic on the Passion in 20 cantos, which appeared between 1748 and 1773 and strongly reflected the religious enthusiasm of the day.

The inspiration was Miltonic, although Klopstock's canvas was narrower. His plays include three on biblical themes and a trilogy (1769-87) concerning the German national hero Hermann. The influence of his *Odes* (1747-80; Eng. trans., 1848) was perhaps more lasting. Some are pietistic-ethical reflections; others extol the pleasures of rural life or explore Ossianic themes. In these poems hexameters give way to free verse, in which the line, as a unit of sense, is also a rhythmical unit, with sporadic echoes of classical cadences. Klopstock's use of language was individual; he boldly coined new words on a Homeric model and strikingly exploited the resources of German word order. A major contributor to developments among the next generation of German poets, seen especially in Hölderlin's use of language and in the melancholy devotion of Novalis, Klopstock can be considered a link between German classicism and romanticism.

PAUL SALMON

Bibliography: Adler, Frederick Henry, *Herder and Klopstock* (1914); Closs, August, *The Genius of the German Lyric,* rev. ed. (1962); Kuehnemund, Richard, *Arminius, or the Rise of a National Symbol in Literature, from Hutten to Grabbe* (1953).

Kluckhohn, Clyde   [kluk'-hohn]

Anthropologist Clyde Kay Maber Kluckhohn, b. Le Mars, Iowa, Jan. 11, 1905, d. July 29, 1960, was a leading figure in the study of cultural values and personality. He taught at the University of New Mexico (1932-34) and at Harvard University (Ph.D., 1936) from 1935 until his death.

A noted authority on the Navajo Indians, Kluckhohn published numerous works on them and on other anthropological topics. *Navaho Witchcraft* (1944) is regarded as a classic in anthropological research. His other writings include *Mirror for Man* (1949) and *Culture: A Critical Review of Concepts and Definitions* (1952), which he coauthored with Alfred L. Kroeber.   STEPHEN KOWALEWSKI

Bibliography: Kluckhohn, Richard, ed., *Culture and Behavior: Collected Essays of Clyde Kluckhohn* (1962); Taylor, Walter W., et al., eds., *Culture and Life: Essays in Memory of Clyde Kluckhohn* (1973).

klystron   [klis'-trahn]

A klystron is a specialized vacuum tube (ELECTRON TUBE) capable of amplifying MICROWAVE signals. The tube is generally cylindrical in shape. An electron gun at one end serves as the CATHODE; it generates an intense ELECTRON BEAM that is directed toward a collector; as it travels along the axis of the tube the beam is focused by an electromagnet that surrounds the tube.

The beam passes through an open chamber called the input buncher cavity; the input signal (the microwave signal that is to be amplified) is coupled to this cavity in such a way that it modulates the velocity of individual electrons in the beam, converting the initially steady current in the beam into a fluctuating current. One or more intermediate cascade cavities along the beam's path encourage the formation of bunches of electrons by allowing faster electrons to catch up with slower ones. The fully modulated beam, whose current is an amplified version of the incoming microwave signal, then enters an output cavity in which part of its energy passes to an output WAVEGUIDE. This is the desired amplified output signal. The electron beam continues out the end of the tube into a collector chamber. This chamber may require water cooling, because considerable heat is produced by the dissipating beam. Klystrons can also be used as microwave oscillators if a portion of the output signal is fed back into the input cavity. They find practical application in high-power radar systems, radio transmitters, and particle accelerators.

FORREST M. MIMS, III

Bibliography: Baden-Fuller, A. J., *Microwaves*, 2d ed. (1979).

knee: see JOINT (in anatomy).

Kneller, Sir Godfrey   [nel'-ur]

Sir Godfrey Kneller, b. Lübeck, Germany, Aug. 8, 1646, d. Oct. 26, 1723, was a prolific court painter to five monarchs of England. Originally named Gottfried Kniller, he studied with Ferdinand Bol (a pupil of Rembrandt) in Amsterdam and traveled (1672–74) in Italy and Germany, executing portraits in Rome and Venice. In 1674 he arrived in England, where he met and painted a portrait of James Vernon (1677; National Portrait Gallery, London), secretary to the duke of Monmouth.

Through Monmouth he obtained the opportunity to paint King Charles II, thus launching a highly successful career as a painter to the courts of Charles II, James II, William III, Queen Anne, and George I; he became court painter (1688) and principal painter (1692) and was knighted (1692) by William III. Kneller served (1711–18) as governor of the Academy of Painting and Drawing in London and received a baronetcy from George I in 1715. During his lifetime he painted many important people, including not only the monarchs of England but those of several European countries—for example, Louis XIV of France and Peter I of Russia.   ALVIN R. MARTIN

Bibliography: Killanin, Lord, *Sir Godfrey Kneller and His Times 1646–1723* (1948); Stewart, J. Douglas, *Sir Godfrey Kneller* (1971); Waterhouse, E. K., *Painting in Britain,* rev. ed. (1978).

Knickerbocker group   [nik'-ur-bahk-ur]

Named after Diedrich Knickerbocker, a pseudonym assumed by Washington Irving in his *History of New York* (1809), the Knickerbocker group was a loose-knit school of writers that flourished in New York City during the first half of the 19th century. Its members shared similar literary tastes, writing more to entertain than to instruct, and a similar goal—to make New York City an important literary center in the United States and to nurture a national literature. The principal figures in the group, in addition to Irving, were James Fenimore Cooper and William Cullen Bryant. Among the others were George P. Morris (author of "Woodman, Spare That Tree!"), John Howard Payne (author of "Home, Sweet Home"), Samuel Woodworth (author of "The Old Oaken Bucket"), James K. Paulding, and the editor and writer Nathaniel Parker Willis.

WAYNE R. KIME

Bibliography: Callow, James T., *Kindred Spirits: Knickerbocker Writers and American Artists, 1807–1855* (1967); Taft, Kendall, ed., *Minor Knickerbockers: Representative Selections* (1947).

Knidos: see CNIDUS.

Knievel, Evel   [kuh-neev'-ul, ee'-vul]

Robert Craig "Evel" Knievel, b. Butte, Mont., Oct. 17, 1938, began doing tricks on a motorcycle as a teenager and later became a professional motorcycle stuntman. A natural athlete, Knievel was a ski-jump champion and also played briefly with the Charlotte (N.C.) Clippers of the professional Eastern Hockey League. Knievel gained fame, however, under his assumed name, for zooming on his motorcycle up a ramp and over parked cars for distances of more than 45 m (150 ft). The daredevil sustained serious injuries in a crash landing after jumping over fountains at a Las Vegas hotel. He was unsuccessful in attempting (1974) to jump the Snake River Canyon, Idaho, in a rocket-powered motorcycle.

Bibliography: Spiegel, Marshall, *Evel Knievel* (1978).

knife: see SWORD.

knife fish

The knife fish Notopterus notopterus, *found in weed-infested rivers and backwaters of Southeast Asia, achieves great mobility by undulating its anal fin to propel itself either forward or backward.*

Knife fish is the common name for members of the African and Asian fish family Notopteridae, also called featherbacks. The family consists of three genera (the Asian *Notopterus* and the African *Papyrocranus* and *Xenomystus*), with six species, all of which are characterized by a deep, thin, bladelike body, a long anal fin extending nearly the full length of the underside of the body, and a distinctly narrow or pointed tail. All but *Xenomystus* also have a small, slender dorsal fin in the center of the back (the "feather"). They range in size from 15 cm (6 in) to about 1 m (3 ft) and are typically freshwater fishes, but a few enter brackish water.

Knife fish is also the common name for an unrelated group of New World fishes collectively known as GYMNOTID eels, although they are not true eels.

knight

In medieval Europe the term *knight* referred to a mounted warrior of secondary noble rank. The name is sometimes also applied to the *equites* of ancient Rome, a similar class of mounted soldiers who ranked below senators. The Roman class was formed to provide a means of advancement for men who were not born into a noble family (or *gens*). The medieval rank, however, probably originated with the barbarian tribes of northern Europe, and the English term was derived from the Old English *cniht,* meaning "youth" or "military follower." Often the younger son of a hereditary peer, the knight began his training as a young boy by entering the service of an overlord. At age 15 or 16 he was raised to the rank of squire and began his period of trial. When his overlord considered him worthy, the prospective knight received his accolade, traditionally a tap on the shoulder with a sword, which proclaimed him a knight. Once knighted he was entitled to the honorific title "Sir" and continued in the military service of his overlord.

As FEUDALISM developed, the rank of knight (in French, *chevalier*; in German, *Ritter*) became a landholding rank. The knight held his land by what was known as military tenure. That is, in return for a land grant the knight was expected to render military service to his overlord. Knighthood also took on a religious significance, and a vigil before the altar became part of the initiation into knighthood.

At the time of the CRUSADES the great military and religious orders of knighthood were established. They included the Knights of St. Lazarus (formed as early as the 4th century but militarized during the 12th century); the Knights HOSPITALERS (formed in the 12th century); the Knights TEMPLARS (1118); the

TEUTONIC KNIGHTS (1190); and the Knights of the Sword (Livonian Order; 1204). The Spanish orders of Alcántara, Calatrava, and Santiago were founded in the 12th century, and the Portuguese Order of Saint Benedict of Avis evolved during the following century.

Later secular knightly orders were established in Europe. They included the Order of the Garter (c.1349) in England, the Order of Saint Michael (1469) in France, and the Burgundian Order of the Golden Fleece (c.1430; later split into Austrian and Spanish branches). As modern weapons and battle techniques diminished the military effectiveness of the armored knight, his title became primarily honorary. Increasingly, the military service required of a landholding knight was converted to money payments to the overlord—known as scutage in England.

In modern times many monarchies established purely honorific orders of knighthood. In Great Britain they included the

An artist's rendering of a knight in armor is based on the effigy of Sir Edmund de Thorpe, who fought under the English king Henry V and was killed in Normandy in 1418. A tunic worn over the knight's breastplate, or cuirass, bears his quarterly arms (A). For such ceremonial functions as jousting or for actual warfare, the knight might have worn a great helm (B), in which the basinet (pointed helmet) and visor were decorated with a panache of peacock feathers and a tassled mantle. The well-armed knight was equipped with several specialized weapons. The pointed face of the war hammer (C) was used to pierce an opponent's armor. The mace (D) was capable of shattering armor and incapacitating an enemy. The knight's war sword (E) was kept close at hand, worn in a sheath, or scabbard (F).

Order of the Bath (1725) and the Order of the Thistle (for Scots; reformed in 1687). The French Legion of Honor was established by Napoleon I in 1802 and the Japanese Supreme Order of the Chrysanthemum in 1888.

Honorary knighthood still exists. Practices vary from country to country, however. In Britain the title of knight is not hereditary but is conferred by the monarch (with the advice of the government). The British feminine equivalent of knight is dame commander.   ROBERT GAYRE OF GAYRE AND NIGG

Bibliography: Barber, Richard, *The Knight and Chivalry,* 2d ed. (1975; repr. 1982); Beeler, John, *Warfare in Feudal Europe, 730–1200* (1971); Broughton, B. B., *Dictionary of Medieval Knighthood and Chivalry* (1986); Herlihy, David, ed., *The History of Feudalism* (1970).

See also: CHIVALRY; HERALDRY.

Knight, Bobby

Robert Montgomery Knight, b. Orrville, Ohio, Oct. 25, 1940, became during the 1988–89 season the youngest collegiate basketball coach to attain 500 career victories. After being a successful defense-oriented head coach at Army (1966–71), Knight went on to Indiana University (1972–   ), where he has won a National Invitation Tournament title (1979), three National Collegiate Athletic Association titles (1976, 1981, 1987), and three College Coach of the Year awards (1975–76, 1989). When he led the U.S. team to a gold medal in the 1984 Olympics, Knight became only the second coach in history to win NIT, NCAA, and Olympic championships.

Knight, Etheridge

The poet and teacher Etheridge Knight, b. Corinth, Miss., Apr. 19, 1931, was an inmate at Indiana State Prison when he began to write about the brutality of prison life. A Korean War veteran, Knight shows an impressive sensitivity to the psychological effects of a racially divided society. Among the best known of his books are *Poems from Prison* (1968) and *Black Voices from Prison,* which he edited in Italian in 1968 and published in English in 1970. Other verse is found in *Belly Song and Other Poems* (1973) and *The Essential Etheridge Knight* (1986).

Knights Hospitalers: see HOSPITALERS.

Knights of Columbus

The Knights of Columbus (K. of C.), a U.S. fraternal order of Roman Catholic men, was founded in 1882 by Michael J. McGivney, a Connecticut priest. The K. of C. provides social activities, insurance, and other benefits for its members, sponsors athletic events, contributes to various charitable and educational projects, and works to promote Catholic interests. With headquarters in New Haven, Conn., it has a total membership (1989) of about 1.45 million organized in nearly 8,000 local councils, most of them in the United States, but also in Canada, the Philippines, Mexico, and other countries. The K. of C. magazine, *Columbia,* is published monthly.

Knights of Labor

The Knights of Labor was the major national workers' organization in the United States from about 1880 to 1890 and the first to try to bring all workers into one centralized LABOR UNION. It was founded in Philadelphia in 1869 by Uriah S. Stephens and other garment workers as a secret fraternal lodge to protect its members against abuse from employers. When Terence V. Powderly replaced Stephens as master workman in 1879, membership was below 10,000. Soon the Knights dropped its secret and ritual aspects and attempted to draw together the entire labor movement. Successful strikes against the Union Pacific Railroad in 1884 and Jay Gould's railroads the next year increased membership to 700,000 in 1886.

Unsuccessful strikes in 1886 and antilabor sentiment generated by the HAYMARKET RIOT brought setbacks. A more fundamental cause of the organization's decline was confusion over goals. On the one hand, the Knights favored a weekly pay law, an 8-hour workday, and industrial safety measures. On the other, the Knights of Labor was unreconciled to large-scale industrial enterprise and unwilling to make a clear distinction between capital and labor; the Knights established producers' cooperatives and even admitted the owners of small businesses as members. The national leadership opposed strikes, which were from time to time forced upon it by rank-and-file action. By 1890 the organization had been overshadowed by the craft-union-oriented American Federation of Labor, and in 1893 membership was only 75,000. The Knights persisted ineffectively until the organization was formally dissolved in 1917.

Bibliography: Browne, H. J., *The Catholic Church and the Knights of Labor* (1949; repr. 1976); Meltzer, Milton, *Bread and Roses: The Struggle of American Labor, 1865–1915* (1967; repr. 1977); Ware, N., *The Labor Movement in the United States, 1860–1895* (1929; repr. 1964).

knitting

Knitting is the making of fabric by using special needles to interlace yarn in a series of loops, or stitches. Knit patterns are produced with two basic stitches: a knit stitch is a loop pulled to the front of the work; a purl stitch is pulled to the back. By varying knit and purl stitches, by slipping, casting off, or adding stitches, and by using different yarn colors and textures, a large variety of patterns can be made.

The origins of knitting are unknown, but knitted fabric and pointed knitting needles have been found among ancient Egyptian and Roman remains. Hand knitting, using two single-pointed needles for flat work and a flexible circular needle with points at each end or several double-pointed needles for circular work, remains a popular hobby. Unusual and attractive hand-knit items can command high prices. Most knit fabrics and garments today, however, are produced by machine.

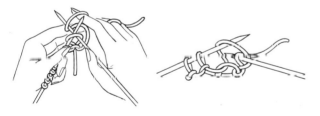

To form a knit stitch, the tip of the right-hand needle is inserted from left to right through the front of the first stitch on the left-hand needle and the yarn is looped under, then over, the tip of the right-hand needle (above left). This loop is then drawn through the stitch on the left-hand needle (above right), and the original stitch is slipped off the left-hand needle behind the new stitch on the right-hand needle. The stitches should be loose enough to slide easily along the needle and the tension consistent to maintain even size.

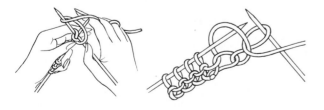

The purl stitch is the reverse of the knit stitch. To form a purl stitch, the right-hand needle is inserted from right to left through the front of the stitch on the left-hand needle; the yarn is then looped over and under the tip of the right-hand needle (above left). This loop is drawn through the stitch on the left-hand needle (above right), and the original stitch is slipped off the left-hand needle in front of the new stitch formed on the right-hand needle. Alternate rows of knit and purl stitches create the smooth surface known as stockinette. Alternating knit and purl stitches in the same row creates a ribbed effect.

William Lee, an English clergyman, invented the first knitting machine in 1589. His "stocking frame," based on an early form of hand knitting that used hooked needles mounted side by side on a frame, allowed an operator to form an entire row of loops with a single stroke of a foot pedal. It remained essentially unaltered until the mid-18th century, when mechanisms were added for making ribbed knitting and even types of lace. The stocking frame produced a weft fabric, where the stitches were built up horizontally. The first warp-knitting machine, invented in 1775, knit yarn together vertically and could produce fabric far more quickly than the older machines.

Modern knitting machines belong to either the weft or warp category. Weft machines are often circular—the needles are mounted on a rotating cylinder, and a tubular fabric is produced as the cylinder turns. Warp machines are usually flat-bed, with the needles mounted in a straight line. These machines knit a flat fabric that is less elastic than fabrics knitted on weft machines and are used for knitting full-fashioned garments. Some of the huge computer-controlled knitting machines used by the textile industry today can knit several million stitches per minute.　　　　　RICHARD HILLS

Bibliography: Abbey, Barbara, *The Complete Book of Knitting* (1972); Gartshore, Linda, *The Craft of Machine Knitting* (1978); Phillips, Mary W., *Creative Knitting* (1980).

Knopf, Alfred A.　[kuh-nahpf']

A noted American publisher, Alfred Abraham Knopf, b. New York City, Sept. 12, 1892, d. Aug. 11, 1984, began his career with Doubleday, Page & Company in 1912 and started his own firm three years later. Blanche Wolf, whom he married in 1916, was his copublisher until her death in 1966. The Knopf firm, noteworthy for quality printing and binding, introduced to U.S. readers many foreign authors, among them André Gide, Thomas Mann, and Sigrid Undset. Among the American writers who were published by Knopf are Willa Cather, John Hersey, George Jean Nathan, and H. L. Mencken. By its 35th anniversary the firm had published the works of nine Nobel Prize winners. After it was sold to Random House in 1960, the Knopf firm retained its own imprint.

Knossos　[nahs'-uhs]

Knossos, home of the legendary King MINOS and the MINOTAUR, was from earliest times the leading settlement of Crete and center of Minoan culture during the Aegean Bronze Age. Concealed by low hills from the sea 5 km (3 mi) to the north, it dominated the fertile central region of the island, of which its successor, Herakleion (Iráklion), remains the commercial

The Great Palace, built on the debris of a Neolitihic settlement, dominates the ancient site of Knossos, near modern Iráklion on Crete. Knossos, home of the legendary King Minos, was the largest Cretan city of the Bronze Age. Its excavation by Sir Arthur Evans in 1900–05 provided the first archaeological evidence of the brilliant Minoan phase (2500–1450 BC) of Aegean civilization.

capital. A hill west of the Kairatos stream was settled by a group of the first people to land in Crete at the end of the 7th millennium BC. The settlement gradually expanded, especially after the transition to the Bronze Age (*c.*3000 BC). From the end of the 3d millennium BC the original hill was occupied by a great palace, named the Palace of Minos by Sir Arthur EVANS, who excavated it in 1900–05. With its elaborate plan and winding corridors, this sprawling complex may have been the reality behind the myth of the labyrinth built by DAEDALUS for Minos. The palace at Knossos, the finest surviving example of Minoan architecture, has been extensively restored.

The Bronze Age city surrounding the palace, at its greatest extent in the 16th century BC, is thought to have covered an area of 600,000 m² (718,000 yd²), with a population of about 20,000. By that time Knossos apparently exercised authority over the whole of Crete; it remained the chief center after the island was conquered by the Mycenaeans from the Greek mainland (*c.*1450 BC). The palace was destroyed in the 14th or early 13th century BC and never rebuilt, but the city continued to be inhabited until the end of the Bronze Age (*c.*1100 BC), and Knossos rivaled Gortyna for predominance among the Dorian Greek states of Crete from *c.*1000 BC until the Roman conquest in 67 BC. After the Battle of Actium in 31 BC, Augustus settled some of his veterans at Knossos, making it a Roman colony. Ruins of an aqueduct and Roman public buildings are still visible. By the time of the Arab conquest (AD *c.*827), Knossos had been replaced by Herakleion on the coast. In the Middle Ages even the ancient name was forgotten.　　　　　　　　　　　　　　　　　SINCLAIR HOOD

Bibliography: Evans, Arthur J., *The Palace of Minos*, 4 vols. (1921–35); Palmer, L. R., *A New Guide to the Palace of Knossos* (1969).

See also: AEGEAN CIVILIZATION; MINOAN ART.

knotweed: see SMARTWEED.

Know-Nothing party

A wagon filled with Know-Nothing party members runs down a political foe on the streets of Baltimore as witnesses stand idly by. The party gained strength in many states during the 1850s as a xenophobic response to the expanding political role of immigrants and Catholics.

The Know-Nothing party was an antiforeign, anti-Roman Catholic political organization that flourished in the United States between 1852 and 1856. Nativism had been growing since the mid-1840s in response to massive immigration, especially from Ireland and Germany. Many of these immigrants had become part of urban Democratic political machines, much to the resentment of non-Democratic old-stock Americans. In the early 1850s, various secret, antiimmigrant organizations joined to form a new political party. Officially called the American party, it was popularly known as the

Know-Nothing party because members answered "I know nothing" when asked about the exclusive, native-Protestant organization.

Advocating exclusion of Catholics and foreigners from public office and seeking to increase the naturalization period from 5 to 21 years, the Know-Nothings won national prominence chiefly because the two major parties—Whigs and Democrats—were at that time breaking apart over the slavery issue. The party reached its zenith in 1854–55, but then soon became factionalized over the slavery issue. In 1856 Millard FILLMORE, the American party presidential candidate, received 21 percent of the popular vote, but the party rapidly disintegrated thereafter. Most of its Northern members joined the ranks of the newly formed Republican party.

　　　　　　　　　　　　　　　　　DOUGLAS T. MILLER

Bibliography: Beals, Carleton, *Brass-Knuckle Crusade* (1960); Billington, Ray A., *The Protestant Crusade, 1800–1860* (1938; repr. 1964); Overdyke, W. D., *The Know-Nothing Party in the South* (1950; repr. 1968).

Knowth

Knowth, a hamlet in County Meath, Ireland, is the site of a major Neolithic passage grave in the Boyne River valley. The principal burial mound measures 90 by 78 m (300 by 250 ft), stands 11 m (36 ft) high, and covers an area of nearly 6,500 m² (70,000 ft²). This extensively excavated BARROW was found to contain two stone passages, 33 and 34 m (108 and 111 ft) long and larger than any others known in Europe. One of the passages terminated in a characteristically cruciform-shaped chamber with side recesses, in one of which was a large ornamental stone basin of presumed ritual purpose. Around the central tomb were grouped 16 satellite tombs of simpler construction. The whole group belongs to the later Neolithic Period of the 3d millennium BC.　　　　　　D. W. HARDING

Bibliography: O'Ríordáin, S. P., and Daniel, Glyn, *New Grange and the Bend of the Boyne* (1964).

Knox, Fort: see FORT KNOX.

Knox, Henry

Henry Knox, b. Boston, July 25, 1750, d. Oct. 25, 1806, a bookseller before the outbreak of war, served with distinction as an artillery officer in the American Revolution and later became secretary of war. In 1775, Knox helped save Boston from capture by the British when he brought 55 pieces of badly needed artillery from Fort Ticonderoga. Using oxen and horses, he transported the guns 480 km (300 mi) overland to the besieged city under difficult winter conditions. He later commanded artillery forces in several operations, including the battles of Trenton, Monmouth, and Yorktown, and organized (1779) a temporary artillery school at Pluckemin, N.J. Commander of West Point (1782–84), Knox also founded (1783) the Society of the Cincinnati (see CINCINNATI, SOCIETY OF THE), an organization for officers who were veterans of the Revolution. He served (1785–94) as secretary of war under the Articles of Confederation and also, in George Washington's administration, under the U.S. Constitution.

Bibliography: Callahan, North, *Henry Knox: General Washington's General* (1958).

Knox, John

John Knox, b. *c.*1514, d. Nov. 24, 1572, was the key figure of the REFORMATION in Scotland as the founder of Scottish PRESBYTERIANISM. After serving briefly as a Roman Catholic priest, he became a Protestant through the efforts of the Scottish reformer George Wishart. After Wishart was burned at the stake at St. Andrews in 1546, and after Protestant conspirators assassinated Wishart's judge, Cardinal David Beaton, that same year, Knox joined other rebellious Protestants barricaded in St. Andrews castle. There he was urged to preach. His zeal and obvious ability made him an immediate leader of the Protestant cause.

When the castle of St. Andrews fell to Scottish and French Roman Catholics in July 1547, Knox was sentenced to serve

John Knox, leader of the Scottish Reformation, was largely responsible for the establishment of Presbyterianism in Scotland. Author of The First Blast of the Trumpet against the Monstrous Regiment of Women (1558), a denunciation of women rulers, Knox debated with the Catholic Mary, Queen of Scots, and, by his preaching, helped sustain the opposition that finally forced her abdication.

on French galleys. After 19 months his release was secured by English Protestant influence. Knox then lived for four years in England, serving as a parish preacher in Berwick and Newcastle and becoming (1551) a chaplain to King Edward VI. His objections to the Second Book of Common Prayer in 1552 paved the way for the later Puritan movement in England.

Knox fled to the Continent in 1553 when the Catholic Mary I succeeded to the throne in England. He served as minister to English refugees in Frankfurt, met John CALVIN in Geneva, and returned for a 9-month preaching tour in Scotland before settling (1556) as the minister of the English refugee church in Geneva. Knox's theology, which stressed God's sovereignty, continued to develop along Calvinistic lines. He went well beyond Calvin in his political theory, however. In 1554, Knox had begun to justify resistance to faithless rulers who attack their dutiful subjects. While in Geneva, Knox published a notorious work, The First Blast of the Trumpet against the Monstrous Regiment of Women (1558), in which he denounced rule by women. It was directed at the queen regent of Scotland, Mary of Guise, MARY, QUEEN OF SCOTS (then also queen of France), and England's Mary I—all Catholic monarchs. The work's major effects, were to embarrass Calvin, to offend the Protestant Elizabeth I, who succeeded Mary I to the English throne in 1558, and to make Knox persona non grata in England.

Knox returned to Scotland in May 1559 at the height of conflict between Catholics and Protestants. His inspirational preaching and timely aid from England allowed Protestant forces to triumph. The return of the widowed Mary, Queen of Scots, in 1561 led to a famous series of face-to-face confrontations between the young queen and Scotland's foremost preacher. When Mary was forced to abdicate in 1567, Protestantism was secured in Scotland. Knox played the leading role in formulating the constitution of the reformed Church of Scotland (see SCOTLAND, CHURCH OF), and he remained an outspoken preacher until his death.

While Knox was not as consistent a Presbyterian or as devout a nationalist as later Protestants in Scotland, his work set the Church of Scotland on its Calvinistic and Presbyterian path. His principal work was his History of the Reformation in Scotland, published posthumously (1st complete ed., 5 vols., 1644). His only complete theological work was the Treatise on Predestination (1560).   MARK A. NOLL

Bibliography: McEwen, J. S., The Faith of John Knox (1961); Muir, Edward, John Knox: Portrait of a Calvinist (1930; repr. 1978); Percy, Eustace, John Knox (1964); Reid, W. S., Trumpeter of God: A Biography of John Knox (1974); Ridley, Jasper, John Knox (1968).

Knox, Philander Chase

Philander Chase Knox, b. Brownsville, Pa., May 6, 1853, d. Oct. 12, 1921, U.S. secretary of state (1909–13) under President William Howard Taft, is remembered for advancing "dollar diplomacy," whereby the protection of U.S. financial interests abroad became a major goal of the nation's foreign policy. A Pennsylvania lawyer, Knox served (1901–04) as U.S. attorney general and instituted several important antitrust actions under President Theodore Roosevelt. From 1904 to 1909, Knox, a Republican, sat in the U.S. Senate. After serving as secretary of state he returned to the Senate (1917–21), where he opposed U.S. membership in the League of Nations.

Bibliography: Bemis, S. F., ed., The American Secretaries of State, vol. 9 (1928; repr. 1963); Graebner, N. A., An Uncertain Tradition: American Secretaries of State in the Twentieth Century (1961; repr. 1980); Mowry, G. E., The Era of Theodore Roosevelt, 1900–1912 (1958).

Knoxville

Knoxville is the seat of Knox County in eastern Tennessee. Located along the Tennessee River about 280 km (175 mi) east of Nashville, the city has a population of 175,030 (1980). Knoxville is a center for industry and agricultural trade and the headquarters of the Tennessee Valley Authority (TVA). Its manufacturing is concentrated in textiles and chemicals. Marble quarrying, zinc mining, and food processing are also important. A significant number of tourists come to Knoxville en route to the Great Smoky Mountains National Park, Cumberland Mountains, and several TVA lakes. The OAK RIDGE NATIONAL LABORATORY is nearby. Knoxville is the site of the University of Tennessee (1794) and of Knoxville College (1875). A world's fair was held there in 1982.

Knoxville was settled permanently in 1785. It was named for Maj. Gen. Henry Knox, secretary of war, in 1791. Knoxville twice served as the state capital (1796–1812 and 1817–19).

Knyphausen, Wilhelm, Baron von
[knip'-how-zen]

Baron von Knyphausen, b. Nov. 4, 1716, d. Dec. 7, 1800, was a German general who commanded the Hessians in British service during the American Revolution. He fought at the battles of White Plains, Brandywine, and Monmouth and was temporarily (1779–80) British commander in New York. He returned to Germany in 1782.

koala   [koh-ah'-luh]

The koala, Phascolarctos cinereus, is a marsupial mammal in the phalanger family, Phalangeridae. It is sometimes placed in a separate family, Phascolarctidae. It has a large head, hairy ears fringed with white, and a large nose. It has dense, woolly, grayish white fur and a vestigial tail. It grows up to 84 cm (33 in) long, and weighs up to 14 kg (30 lb). Selective eaters of eucalyptus leaves and young bark, koalas are solitary or live in small harems led by a single male. The young are born after a gestation period of 25 to 30 days and weigh about 5.5 g (0.2 oz) at birth. They spend about 6 months in the mother's pouch and are weaned on predigested eucalyptus leaves, devoid of fecal material, that have passed through the mother's digestive tract. Nearly exterminated by epidem-

The koala, P. cinereus, is often found in eucalyptus trees, the leaves of which are its basic diet. The animals avoid young leaves, which are poisonous. Koalas are permeated with the pungent odor of eucalyptus.

ics around the turn of the century, by massive slaughter for their fur into the 1920s, and by human-caused fires, koalas are now found only in the eucalyptus forests of eastern Australia. They are now fully protected by law.

Bibliography: Lee, Anthony, and Martin, Roger, *The Koala: A Natural History* (1988); Williamson, H. D., *The Year of the Koala* (1975).

koan   [koh'-ahn]

In Zen Buddhism, a koan (literally, a public case) is a theme for meditation used by masters to help their disciples break through the barriers of the intellect to achieve enlightenment. There are about 1,700 popular koans, which usually consist of a saying from a great Zen master or his answer to a question. For example, a monk asked Tung-shan ''Who is Buddha?'' and received the reply ''Three *chin* of flax.'' By meditating on such a koan, which is nonrational, Zen students open their minds to spiritual intuition. Koan practice was developed in China and transmitted to Japan in the 13th century.

Bibliography: Miura, Isshu, and Sasaki, Ruth, *The Zen Koan* (1966); Suzuki, D. T., *The Essentials of Zen Buddhism*, ed. by Bernard Phillips (1962; repr. 1973); Watts, Alan, *The Way of Zen* (1988).

kob   [kahb]

The male Uganda kob, Adenota kob thomasi, *an antelope, is easily distinguished from the female by his long, graceful horns.*

Kobs are ANTELOPES in the genus *Kobus,* of the ox and antelope family, Bovidae. The kob is a graceful, long-nosed animal 1 m (3 ft) high at the shoulders and weighing about 112.5 kg (250 lb). The coat is smooth and yellowish brown to almost black, with whitish underparts. The long horns of the male curve backward with an upward tip. The kob lives in Africa south of the Sahara and in the upper Nile valley. It favors high, dry plains, where it is found in small herds or singly.

EVERETT SENTMAN

Kobe   [koh'-bay]

Kobe, a city in south central Honshu, Japan, lies on a coastal lowland facing the Inland Sea, about 32 km (20 mi) west of Osaka. The population is 1,426,838 (1988). Kobe is one of the largest and busiest ports in Japan, handling much of Japan's foreign trade. Kobe exports mostly manufactured or semimanufactured goods and imports raw materials and foodstuffs. It is also an industrial city with shipbuilding and steel, rubber, and textile manufacturing. Tourist attractions include the Municipal Museum of Arts, Suma Temple, Suma Aquarium, Minatozawa Shrine, and Sorakuen Park. Several universities and colleges are located there. A port since the 13th century, Kobe was opened to foreign trade and residence in 1868.

JAMES CHAN

Koblenz   [koh'-blents]

Koblenz, a city in the West German state of Rhineland-Palatinate, lies between Bonn and Mainz at the confluence of the Mosel (Moselle) and Rhine rivers. Its population is 110,843 (1986 est.). Long a commercial and industrial center, Koblenz produces aluminum, machinery, chemicals, furniture, textiles, and clothing. It is also a popular tourist and conference site. The church of Saint Castor dates from AD 836. The Ehrenbreitstein Castle houses a Rhine museum.

The Romans fortified the site about 9 BC. It became the headquarters of the Franks in the 6th century and in the 11th century was presented to the archbishops of Trier by Holy Roman Emperor Henry II. France took control of the city in 1794 and held it until 1815, when it became part of Prussia. From 1824 to 1945, Koblenz was the capital of the Rhine province. It was heavily bombed during World War II, but most of its historic buildings have been restored.

Kobo Abe: see ABE KOBO.

Koch, Edward I.   [kahch]

Edward Irving Koch, b. New York City, Dec. 12, 1924, was a three-term mayor (1978–90) of New York City. The son of Polish immigrants, he became a lawyer and entered New York City Democratic politics in 1962. Prior to his election as mayor, Koch served on the city council (1967–68) and as a member of Congress (1969–77). Known for his brash, colorful manner, Koch maintained his popularity despite New York's problems of unemployment, steadily declining services, and cutbacks necessitated by successful efforts to balance the city's budget. He was reelected in 1981, running as a Republican-Democratic fusion candidate, and again in 1985, overwhelming his Republican opponent. His support had slipped among many minority voters, however, by 1989, when he was defeated in the Democratic primary election by David Dinkins. Koch wrote (with William Rauch) the autobiographical *Mayor* (1984) and *Politics* (1985) and, with John Cardinal O'Connor, *His Eminence and Hizzoner* (1989).

Koch, Marita   [kohk]

The career of East German sprinter Marita Koch, b. Feb. 18, 1957, was one of sustained excellence and versatility. From her first world record (200 m), in 1978, to her last (400 m), in 1985, Koch set 10 individual world marks at 200 m and 400 m, and took part in 5 others in all 3 sprint relays. Her best time for 200 m was 21.71 sec, and for 400 m, 47.60 sec, a record that still stands. Koch won the 1980 Olympic gold medal at 400 m. She retired in 1986.

Koch, Robert

The German bacteriologist Robert Koch, b. Dec. 11, 1843, d. May 27, 1910, made many contributions to bacteriology, including his important discovery (1882) of the bacillus responsible for tuberculosis. He was awarded the 1905 Nobel Prize for physiology or medicine for his work. In 1876, Koch discovered the ANTHRAX bacillus and later found a way of preventing the disease through preventive inoculation. In the early 1900s, Koch worked in Africa, studying the transmission of several diseases, including African sleeping sickness. His many achievements also include his development of improved microscopic techniques and bacterial staining and culturing methods. Koch set forth four principles known as Koch's Postulates, for locating disease-causing microorganisms; these are now considered fundamental in bacteriology.

Bibliography: De Kruif, Paul, *The Microbe Hunters* (1926; repr. 1976); Knight, David C., *Robert Koch: Father of Bacteriology* (1961); Reid, Robert, *Microbes and Men* (1975).

Kocher, Emil   [koh'-kur]

The Swiss surgeon Emil Theodor Kocher, b. Aug. 25, 1841, d. July 27, 1917, pioneered in the treatment of goiter by removal of the thyroid gland and developed improved techniques for many other surgical procedures. As professor of surgery and director of the surgical clinic at the University of Bern for most of his career, Kocher taught goiter surgery, methods for treating hernia and shoulder dislocation, and techniques for improved surgery of the stomach, spinal cord, and gallbladder. He also pioneered in stressing the importance of asepsis in surgical care. Kocher was awarded the 1909 Nobel Prize for physiology or medicine.

Bibliography: Sourhes, Theodore L., *Nobel Prize Winners in Medicine and Physiology* (1966).

Kodály, Zoltán   [koh'-dy, zohl'-tahn]

Zoltán Kodály, b. Dec. 16, 1882, d. Mar. 6, 1967, was, after Béla Bartók, the foremost Hungarian composer and ethnomusicologist of the 20th century. As a scholar of Magyar music, Kodály collected, arranged, and published folk songs and wrote extensively about Hungarian folk music. As a teacher at the Academy of Music in Budapest, he inspired dozens of students, some of whom became well-known musicians. Kodály later specialized in teaching children, and his methods have been organized into the widely used Kodály Method. He collaborated with Bartók in studies of folk music; his compositions were influenced by Bartók's style, although Kodály used folk elements, harmony, and rhythm more conservatively than Bartók. One of Kodály's most popular works is the orchestral suite *Háry János* (1926). His other compositions include a symphony, a concerto for orchestra, music for the stage, chamber music, solos for piano and other instruments, folksong arrangements, choral music, songs, church music, and educational music. He is also the author of books on pedagogic and historical subjects. In the summer of 1965, Kodály was composer-in-residence at Dartmouth College.

FARLEY K. HUTCHINS

Bibliography: Chosky, Louis, *Kodály Context* (1981); Eösze, László, *Zoltán Kodály: His Life and Work*, trans. by Istrán Farkas and Gyula Gulyás (1962); Young, P. M., *Zoltán Kodály: A Hungarian Musician* (1964; repr. 1976).

Kodiak Island   [koh'-dee-ak]

Kodiak is an island located in the Gulf of Alaska, off the southern coast of Alaska. The island has an area of 13,895 km² (5,365 mi²) and a population of 9,939 (1980). The city of Kodiak is the island's main commercial center. The eastern part of the island is mountainous and heavily forested; the western lowlands are covered by grasses. The island is volcanic in origin. Three-quarters of the area is a national wildlife refuge (established 1941) inhabited by the Kodiak brown bear. Due to the proximity of the Japan Current, the climate is warm and humid. Fishing, mining, grazing, and fur trapping are economic mainstays.

Discovered in 1763, Kodiak was settled in 1784 by Grigory Ivanovich SHELEKHOV, who founded a Russian colony at Three Saints Bay. It remained under Russian jurisdiction until 1867, when the United States purchased Alaska.

Koestler, Arthur   [kest'-lur]

Arthur Koestler, b. Budapest, Hungary, Sept. 5, 1905, d. Mar. 3, 1983, established his reputation with novels in English such

Arthur Koestler rose to literary prominence through his expressions of disillusionment with the totalitarian features of communism. After a prolific career as a writer on a wide variety of subjects, he committed suicide, with his wife, in 1983.

as *Darkness at Noon* (1940), which examine the totalitarian and revolutionary politics of the 20th century. Koestler became disillusioned with communism after his membership in the German Communist party (1931–38); he became a British subject in 1945. Much of Koestler's work dealt with psychology and the creative process and includes *The Sleepwalkers* (1959) and *The Act of Creation* (1964). Other recent books are *The Thirteenth Tribe* (1976), *Janus: A Summing Up* (1978), *Bricks to Babel* (1980), and *Kaleidoscope* (1981).

Bibliography: Hamilton, Iain, *Koestler: A Biography* (1982); Sperber, Murray, ed., *Arthur Koestler: A Collection of Critical Essays* (1977).

Koetsu   [koh'-ayt-soo]

The Japanese artist Honnami Koetsu, 1558–1637, was one of the principal founders of *Rimpa*, a school of Japanese decorative art that emerged in the early Edo period (1615–1868). A distinguished calligrapher and tea master, he was also one of Japan's finest potters and designers of lacquer ware. Koetsu designed a series of printed books of No dramas and classic literary works during the period from 1606 until 1615. That year he was granted an estate at Takagamine, outside Kyoto, by the Tokugawa shogun Ieyasu. There various artisans worked together under Koetsu's direction. As a tea master, he favored the simple *raku* ware that he made himself.

Koetsu collaborated with the painter SOTATSU in revitalizing the ancient tradition of the decorated poem scroll. The products of this dual effort, in which Koetsu inscribed classic poetry in his bold hand over Sotatsu's gold and silver designs of birds, flowers, or deer, introduced a new decorative style into Japanese art. A notable example of calligraphy by Koetsu appears in the *Deer Scroll* (early 17th century; Seattle Art Museum, Wash.).

BARBARA BRENNAN FORD

Bibliography: Yoshikawa, Itsuji, *Major Themes in Japanese Art*, trans. by Armius Niskouskis (1976).

Koffka, Kurt   [kohf'-kah]

Kurt Koffka, b. Berlin, Mar. 18, 1886, d. Nov. 22, 1941, was one of the three major figures identified with the origin and spread of GESTALT PSYCHOLOGY. Educated at the universities of Berlin, Edinburgh, Freiburg, and Würzburg, he was at the Psychological Institute in Frankfurt in 1910 when Max Wertheimer began his experiments in apparent motion that launched the Gestalt school. Together with Wertheimer and Wolfgang Köhler, Koffka elaborated the new approach. From 1911 to 1924, Koffka taught at the University of Giessen, publishing many experimental studies within the Gestalt paradigm. He wrote a major Gestalt treatise on developmental psychology in 1921 (Eng. trans., 1924) and the first substantial paper on Gestalt theory in a U.S. journal (*Psychological Bulletin*, 1922). After teaching at Cornell University and the University of Wisconsin, Koffka became a professor of psychology in 1927 at Smith College, where he remained until his death. His *Principles of Gestalt Psychology*, the fullest and most systematic statement of the Gestalt approach to psychology, was published in 1935.

Koffka was an effective proselytizer who helped Gestalt psychology become widely known. He applied the theory in many areas, particularly perception and developmental psychology.   MICHAEL WERTHEIMER

Kohl, Helmut

Helmut Kohl, b. April 3, 1930, is the Christian Democratic chancellor who presided over the reunification of Germany in 1990. Kohl succeeded Helmut Schmidt as West German chancellor in 1982, and won endorsement from the electorate in 1983 and 1987. When the Communist East German regime began to disintegrate early in 1990, he gained a following among East German voters as a champion of rapid and total German reunification within NATO. Overcoming strong opposition both at home and abroad, he achieved the incorporation of East Germany into the Federal Republic in a few months, thus greatly increasing the size and prestige of his country and ending more than four decades of German disunity.

Kohler, Kaufmann   [koh'-lur, kowf'-mahn]

Kaufmann Kohler, b. Bavaria, May 10, 1843, d. Jan. 28, 1926, was a rabbi and a leading theologian of Reform Judaism. He studied at universities in Munich, Berlin, Leipzig, and Erlangen. The radicalism of his doctoral thesis, "The Blessing of Jacob," created such controversy that he was barred from the pulpit. After emigrating (1869) to the United States he served congregations in Detroit and Chicago. In 1879 he succeeded his father-in-law, David Einhorn, as rabbi of Temple Beth-El in New York City. Kohler helped formulate (1885) the so-called Pittsburgh Platform, the original code of Reform Judaism. It emphasized moral teachings and social justice and rejected many traditional ideas, including sacrificial cults, resurrection, and the concept of a national restoration of Israel to Palestine. Between 1903 and 1921, Kohler served as president of Hebrew Union College, Cincinnati, Ohio, and as editor of the *Hebrew Union Annual*. Among his many writings *Jewish Theology Systematically and Historically Considered* (1910) was his major work.   SAUL S. FRIEDMAN

Bibliography: Marx, R. J., *Kaufmann Kohler as Reformer* (1951).

Köhler, Wolfgang   [ker'-lur]

The psychologist Wolfgang Köhler, b. Tallinn, Estonia, Jan. 21, 1887, d. June 11, 1967, was—with Kurt Koffka and Max Wertheimer—one of the originators of GESTALT PSYCHOLOGY. Köhler was educated at the universities of Tübingen, Bonn, and Berlin. In 1910 he was at the Psychological Institute in Frankfurt when Wertheimer began his apparent-motion experiments that started the Gestalt school of psychology. From 1913 to 1920, on Tenerife in the Canary Islands, Köhler undertook pioneering studies of intelligent problem solving ("insight learning") by chimpanzees, published as *The Mentality of Apes* (1917; Eng. trans., 1925). He directed the Psychological Institute at the University of Berlin from 1921 to 1935. Thereafter he taught at Swarthmore College until 1955 and at Dartmouth College from 1958 until his death. His many works include *Gestalt Psychology* (1929), *The Place of Value in a World of Facts* (1938), and *Dynamics in Psychology* (1940).

Köhler was the natural scientist of the early Gestalt trio. He applied the Gestalt approach in physics, animal and human learning and problem solving, memory, perception, brain processes, and other areas.   MICHAEL WERTHEIMER

Bibliography: Henle, Mary, ed., *The Selected Papers of Wolfgang Köhler* (1971).

Koko Nor   [koh'-koh nohr]

The Koko Nor (Chinese: Ching Hai), a large glacial lake in Central Asia, is located in the Nan Shan mountain system of west central China at an altitude of 3,205 m (10,515 ft). It is approximately 105 km (65 mi) long and 64 km (40 mi) wide and has a maximum depth of 37 m (123 ft). The name is derived from the Mongolian for "blue sea."

Formed during the Pleistocene Epoch, the lake was originally filled with glacial meltwater; today it receives water from

23 rivers and streams. It has no outlet. The azure water is brackish and is frozen from November through March.

Kokoschka, Oskar   [koh-kohsh'-kuh, ohs'-kur]

Vienna, State Opera *(1956) is an example of Kokoschka's later, more decorative style. (Österreichische Galerie, Vienna.)*

Oskar Kokoschka, b. Mar. 1, 1886, d. Feb. 22, 1980, was a leading Austrian painter, printmaker, and writer. While a student (1904–09) at the Vienna School of Arts and Crafts, he was influenced by the Vienna Secession movement, especially the work of Gustav Klimt. Kokoschka soon evolved his own highly personal style in which was reflected the anxious, decadent atmosphere of prewar Vienna. A nervous linearity and psychological intensity characterize *The Portrait of August Forel* (1909; Städtische Kunsthalle, Mannheim, Germany); such early expressionist portraits are among his most memorable paintings. A public performance (1909) of his sadistic play *Mörder, Hoffnung der Frauen* (Murder, the Hope of Women; 1907), about the battle of the sexes, provoked scandal, and in 1910, seeking a less hostile milieu, Kokoschka moved to Berlin. There he joined the artist group associated with the influential magazine *Der Sturm*.

Returning (1911) to Vienna, Kokoschka began a relationship with Alma Mahler that inspired *Bride of the Winds* (1914; Kunstmuseum, Basel, Switzerland). In part to escape this affair, he joined the Austrian army, only to be severely wounded in 1916. After a painful convalescence, he taught (1919–24) at the Dresden Academy. The work of this period is typified by *The Power of Music* (1919; Staatliche Gemäldegalerie, Dresden), with its bold colors and broad, crude forms. After 1924, Kokoschka traveled through Europe, North Africa, and the Near East, painting spatially distorted, somewhat impressionistic cityscapes. In 1934 he moved to Prague but, perceiving the Nazi menace, fled to London in 1938. When the Nazis included some of his works in the Exhibition of Degenerate Art (1937), Kokoschka responded with his *Self-Portrait of a Degenerate Artist* (1937; Emil Korner Collection, Port William, Scotland). He became a British citizen but lived in Switzerland after 1953.   IDA K. RIGBY

Bibliography: Gombrich, E. H., *Homage to Kokoschka* (1984); Hodin, J. P., *Oskar Kokoschka: The Artist and His Time* (1966); Leshko, Jarslaw, *Orbus Pictus: The Prints of Oskar Kokoschka* (1987); Schvey, Henry, *Oskar Kokoschka: The Painter as Playwright* (1982).

kola nut   [koh'-luh]

Kola "nuts" are the edible, fleshy seeds of tropical trees of the *Cola* genus. The most important species, *Cola acuminata*, is native to rain forests of tropical West Africa. Wild trees, often preserved during forest clearance, have been a source of kola nuts up to modern times. Cultivation began in the late 19th century, principally in West Africa, although the trees were introduced into the New World during the 17th and 18th centuries and are now also cultivated in Brazil and Jamaica. Nigeria produces most of the world crop.

The nuts contain the stimulant CAFFEINE, and in Africa and South America they are chewed to dispel hunger and to alleviate fatigue. They are commercially valuable as a source of flavor and caffeine in cola drinks and medicines. Cultivated trees bear fruit for up to 50 years, sometimes twice annually. Vegetative propagation of the higher-yielding trees results in considerably less variation than in those grown from seed.

PHILIP M. SMITH

Kolbe, Georg   [kohl'-be]

The German sculptor Georg Kolbe, b. Apr. 15, 1877, d. Nov. 20, 1947, is best known for his graceful nude figure studies in bronze, dating from the 1920s. His work was strongly influenced by the impressionistic style of Auguste Rodin and by the classical idealization of such German sculptors as Adolf von Hildebrand. Although some of Kolbe's sculptures were removed from display during the Nazi era, he was permitted to continue to work and exhibit. His later work has been criticized for its dullness and empty monumentality as opposed to the lyricism of his earlier sculptures, such as *Standing Nude* (1926; Walker Art Center, Minneapolis, Minn.).

ELIZABETH PUTZ

Bibliography: Andrew Dickson White Museum of Art, Cornell University, *Georg Kolbe: Sculpture from the Collection of B. Gerold Kantor; Drawings from the Georg Kolbe Museum, Berlin* (1972).

Kollantai, Aleksandra   [kuh-luhn-ty']

The Russian Marxist feminist Aleksandra Kollantai, b. Apr. 1 (N.S.), 1872, d. Mar. 9, 1952, became the first woman accredited as a foreign ambassador. An advocate of free love and full equality for women, she served (1917–18) as Soviet commissar of social welfare but resigned in protest against the authoritarianism of the Bolshevik regime and joined the "Workers' Opposition." Later reconciled with the regime, she headed (1923–45) the Soviet diplomatic missions to Norway, Mexico, and Sweden; in 1944 she negotiated the Soviet-Finnish armistice.

Bibliography: Clements, Barbara Evans, *Bolshevik Feminist* (1979).

Kollwitz, Käthe   [kawl'-vits, kay'-te]

The distinguished German graphic artist Käthe Kollwitz, b. July 8, 1867, d. Apr. 22, 1945, took as her theme the suffering caused by poverty, rebellion, war, and death. Kollwitz's urgent social and political concern is evident in her major print cycles: *The Weavers' Uprising* (1895–98), a series of three lithographs and three etchings based on a play by Gerhardt

Käthe Kollwitz's lithograph Woman with a Blue Shawl *(1903) exemplifies the realism and compassion characteristic of her moving portrayals of the poor and oppressed. Kollwitz's work is noted for its strong social and political content. (Wallraf-Richartz Museum, Cologne.)*

Hauptmann; *Peasants' War* (1902–08), etchings; *War* (1922–23) and *Proletariat* (1925), both comprising woodcuts in an expressionist style reminiscent of Ernst Barlach; and *Death* (1934–35), lithographs that combine the theme of mortality with self-portraiture. Kollwitz is also known for her sculpture, notably her war monument (unveiled 1933) in Belgium's Roggevelt Military Cemetery.

BARBARA CAVALIERE

Bibliography: Klein, Mina D., and Arthur, H., *Käthe Kollwitz: Life in Art* (1972); Kollwitz, Hans, ed., *Diaries and Letters of Käthe Kollwitz*, trans. by Richard and Clara Winston (1955); Nagel, Otto, *Käthe Kollwitz* (1971); Zigrosser, Carl, ed., *Prints and Drawings of Käthe Kollwitz* (1969).

Komarov, Vladimir   [kuh-mahr'-awf]

The Soviet cosmonaut Vladimir Mikhalovich Komarov, b. Mar. 16, 1927, d. Apr. 24, 1967, was the first person to die during a spaceflight. A Soviet air force jet pilot with an academic background in engineering, Komarov was chosen (1960) as a member of the first group of Soviet cosmonauts. He commanded *Voskhod 1* (see VOSKHOD), the world's first multimanned spaceship, which was launched on Oct. 12, 1964, and remained in orbit for 24 hours. Komarov was launched into space aboard *Soyuz 1* (see SOYUZ) on Apr. 22, 1967, but the launch of a second spacecraft, with which he was to dock, was cancelled, and Komarov was killed the following day while attempting to return to Earth. According to published reports, the parachute of his command module snarled, and the module struck the ground at a velocity of several hundred kilometers per hour.

JAMES OBERG

Bibliography: Oberg, James, "Soyuz 1 Ten Years After: New Conclusions," *Spaceflight,* May 1977.

Komodo dragon   [kuh-moh'-doh]

The komodo dragon, V. komodoensis, *is a relative of the extinct 7-m (23-ft) reptile* V. priscus, *whose remains have been found in Quaternary deposits in Australia.*

The largest living lizard, the Komodo dragon, *Varanus komodoensis,* attains a total length of up to 3 m (10 ft) and an average weight of 136 kg (300 lb). These giant lizards live only in the vicinity of Indonesia, for example, on Komodo island, for which they are named. They are representative of the MONITOR lizard family, Varanidae. Like other monitors, Komodo dragons are carnivorous, feeding on animals as large as small deer and bush pigs. They will eat smaller members, and sometimes other adults, of their own species and also feed on eggs and carrion. Their long, sharp claws enable them to disembowel large animals, and their jagged teeth aid them in tearing pieces from their prey. Komodo dragons, like other large monitors, can be formidable adversaries, even for humans, if these lizards are actually cornered. Young Komodo dragons climb trees, but adults—far too large to be arboreal—dig burrows or spend hot daylight hours under bushes, coming out in the morning and evening. Like several other monitors, Komodo dragons swim well, sometimes swimming to small islets a half kilometer from shore to prey on domestic goats. These reptiles are endangered and are under strict protection by the Indonesian government.

STEVEN C. ANDERSON

Bibliography: Burden, William, *Dragon Lizards of Komodo: An Expedition to the Lost World of the Dutch East Indies* (1927).

komondor   [kahm'-uhn-dohr]

The komondor is a large working dog used in Hungary to guard livestock. It may be a descendant of Asian dogs brought to Europe by the Magyars during the 9th century. The komondor has also been used in Europe for police and military work.

Komondors are large, shaggy, working dogs native to Hungary and used as sheep dogs, as well as police and guard dogs. As a herdsman's dog, the komondor usually protects the flocks and herds, while smaller dogs do much of the routine work. They are rarely seen in the United States. Komondors stand about 70 cm (28 in) tall at the shoulder and weigh about 40 kg (90 lb). Their thick, woolly coats are pure white. Their ears hang down from the face, and their long tails are carried in a low curve.

Kon-Tiki   [kahn-tik'-ee]

The *Kon-Tiki* is the raft on which a six-member crew, led by the Norwegian explorer Thor HEYERDAHL, sailed across 6,900 km (4,300 mi) of the Pacific Ocean from Peru to Polynesia in 1947. The purpose of the expedition, which lasted 101 days, was to support Heyerdahl's theory that ancient South American mariners could have successfully negotiated the vast expanse of open ocean in their large sailing rafts, thus populating the islands of the South Pacific.

In constructing the *Kon-Tiki*, named for a legendary Inca sun-god, Heyerdahl tried to duplicate as closely as possible the sailing rafts used by the ancient Incas. Nine thick logs of Peruvian balsa were lashed together with hemp rope. The raft measured 13.7 m (45 ft) long in the center but tapered to 9.1 m (30 ft) at the sides, producing a bluntly pointed bow. Two masts supported a large rectangular sail, and a bamboo cabin was built near the raft's center. A large steering oar at the stern and five centerboards completed the design of the *Kon-Tiki*, in which no metal was used.

After being towed out of Callao harbor on Apr. 28, 1947, the raft was set adrift 80 km (50 mi) off the Peruvian coast. On July 30, 1947, 93 days after the start of the voyage, the *Kon-Tiki* sailed past the island of Puka Puka in the Tuamoto group east of Tahiti. Eight days later, on Aug. 7, 1947, after the *Kon-Tiki* crashed into a reef in the Tuamoto Archipelago, the crew waded ashore to an uninhabited island, from which they were rescued a week later. The *Kon-Tiki* is now preserved in a museum in Oslo. A complete account of the voyage appears in Heyerdahl's book *Kon-Tiki* (1948; Eng. trans., 1950).

Konarak   [kohn-ah'-ruhk]

The enormous black-granite temple of Konarak, dedicated to the sun-god Surya, was built along a remote stretch of beach on the eastern coast of India, about 380 km (240 mi) south of Calcutta, during the reign of Narasimhadeva (AD 1238–64). It was originally designed as a series of halls and pavilions ranged along a common axis and leading to a tower rising above the sanctum. The complex was never completed, and little survives except the massive assembly hall that stood in front of the sanctuary tower and the base of an open pavilion.

A striking feature of the temple's design is that the hall and tower complex was intended as an architectural replica of Surya's solar chariot; around its high platform are placed 12 great wheels intricately carved in stone and, flanking the main approach to the platform, 7 colossal freestanding figures of horses, placed as though pulling the temple through space. Life-size sculptures of lions and elephants stand in the courtyard, and along the walls are carved scenes of battle and the hunt, music making and the dance, and erotic couples portrayed in various, often unusual, sexual poses. Set into each lateral face of the exterior of the assembly hall are finely carved images of the sun-god standing in a horse-drawn car and attended by the maidens of dawn.

Bibliography: Ebersole, Robert, *The Black Pagoda* (1957); Elisofon, Eliot, and Watts, Alan, *Erotic Spirituality* (1971).

Kongo, Kingdom of

The Kingdom of Kongo emerged as a centralized state during the late 14th and early 15th centuries in a large area around the lower course of the Congo River in what is modern Zaire and Angola. It was one of the first major African kingdoms contacted by the Portuguese (in 1482) in the course of their maritime expansion. During the first decades of relations between Portugal and the mani-kongos, as the monarchs of Kongo were known, efforts were made by both sides to stimulate peaceful relations based on trade and missionary activity. The mani-kongos themselves converted to Christianity and adopted Portuguese reign names beginning with Alfonso I (r. 1505–43), whose African name was Nzinga Mbemba. However, the Portuguese promise to supply artisans and teachers to continue the process of peaceful Christianization of the kingdom was never properly fulfilled. Instead, commerce became increasingly centered on the slave trade, which was highly profitable both to Portuguese soldier-merchants and to officials of the mani-kongo.

The increasing rapaciousness of the slave trade led to deterioration of relations between the Kongo and Portugal. All efforts at collaboration ended by the middle of the 17th century when the Portuguese, from their base in nearby Angola, invaded the kingdom and killed the reigning monarch, Antonio I (r. 1661–65). Although claimants continued to assert their rights to the title of mani-kongo through the 19th century, the kingdom actually disintegrated into a number of small vassal states that eventually formed parts of the colonies of Portuguese West Africa and the Belgian Congo.

ROBERT R. GRIFFETH

Bibliography: Davidson, Basil, *The African Slave Trade* (1961); Scholefield, Alan, *The Dark Kingdoms: The Impact of White Monarchies on Three Great African Monarchies* (1975); Vansina, Jan, *The Kingdoms of the Savannah* (1966).

Königsberg bridge problem   [kur'-nigs-burg]

In the Pregel River in Königsberg (present-day Kaliningrad) an island was formed by digging a connecting channel between its two branches. In the 18th century a total of seven bridges spanned the river. According to folklore, a person could not take a round-trip walk in which each bridge was crossed exactly once. This problem is one of the earliest examples of a problem that was recognized as being "topological"—it did not involve distances in any significant way, but rather it was concerned with how things fit together, which is an aspect of TOPOLOGY. The problem was analyzed and solved mathemati-

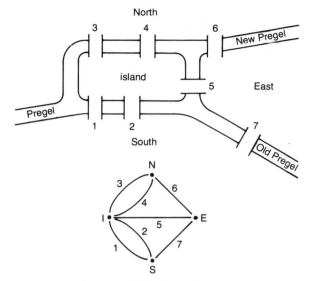

the equivalent topological graph

The Königsberg bridge problem—ascribed to the mathematician Leonhard Euler—involves an island in Königsberg, which can be reached by seven bridges. Euler asked if it would be possible to start from any land point, N, S, E, or I, cross each of seven bridges only once, and return to the initial point. The answer is no.

cally by Leonhard EULER, who proved that folklore was correct. Euler showed that making such a walk was equivalent to traversing a simple figure called a topological graph with no retracings. He reduced the land masses to points (vertices) and represented the bridges as line segments. The study of such topological graphs is called graph theory.

MORTON L. CURTIS

Bibliography: Barr, Stephen, *Experiments in Topology* (1972); Lietzmann, Walther, *Visual Topology* (1968).

Konoe Fumimaro   [kohn'-oh-ay foo'-mee-mah-roh]

Konoe Fumimaro, b. Oct. 12, 1891, d. Dec. 16, 1945, twice prime minister of Japan (1937–39, 1940–41), outlined Japan's expansionist aims for a "new order in East Asia" but sought to avoid war with the United States. A member of a noble family, he entered politics as a protégé of the statesman SAIONJI KIMMOCHI. As a prince he sat in the house of peers, of which he became president in 1933. In his early career he was known as a liberal.

Konoe became prime minister in 1937, a month before the outbreak (July 7) of the Second SINO-JAPANESE WAR. Thereafter he cooperated with the army in extending government controls in Japan, securing passage (1938) of the National General Mobilization Law, which gave the premier broad emergency powers. In 1938 he also issued a statement expounding Japan's aims for a "new order." When he returned to power in 1940, Konoe announced the formation of a New National Structure to create an "advanced national defense state"; political parties were dissolved and replaced by one mass organization, the Imperial Rule Assistance Organization.

In September 1940, Konoe concluded a military alliance with Germany and Italy and in April 1941 a nonaggression pact with the USSR. Fearing American intervention, he then pursued negotiations with the United States. When these failed, he resigned in October 1941, to be replaced by Gen. TOJO HIDEKI. After Japan's defeat in 1945, Konoe became a member of the first postwar cabinet. However, he was issued an arrest warrant as a possible war criminal and committed suicide.

Bibliography: Butow, Robert J. C., *Tojo and the Coming of War* (1961); Toland, John, *The Rising Sun* (1970).

Konya   [kohn'-yah]

Konya (ancient Iconium) is the capital city of Konya province, central Turkey. Located on a plateau about 1,027 m (3,370 ft) above sea level, the city has a population of 329,129 (1980). Known for its handwoven carpets since the 13th century, Konya also produces sugar, flour, textiles, leather goods, and aluminum. Tourism is important.

One of the oldest cities in the world (excavations reveal settlement in the 3d millennium BC), Konya was settled by the Phrygians in the 3d century BC and was visited three times by Saint Paul. It became the capital of Lycaonia in the 4th century AD. In the late 11th century, the SELJUKS gained control of the area, and the city became the seat of the sultanate of Iconium or Rum. The city reached the peak of its prosperity in the 13th century; it retains a number of buildings (now used as museums) from this period, including the monastery of the mystical sect known in the West as Whirling Dervishes. Konya was captured by the Il-Khan Mongols in the late 13th century and was part of the Turkoman principality of Karaman before it was annexed (1472) by the Ottoman Empire. After a period of decline, it grew as a result of the construction (1896) of the Istanbul–Baghdad railroad, which passes through Konya.

Kook, Abraham Isaac   [kohk]

Abraham Isaac Kook, b. Latvia, 1865, d. Sept. 1, 1935, a Jewish philosopher, mystic, and Zionist, was the first chief rabbi in British-mandated Palestine. He emigrated to Palestine in 1904. He was at a conference in Germany when World War I began; he made his way to England, where he spent the war years and stirred popular support for the BALFOUR DECLARATION. He returned to Palestine in 1919 and was elected chief rabbi in 1921, a post he held until his death.

Kook's form of Zionism was based on his mystical doctrine of inclusion; as he understood it, even secularist Jews working to build up the Jewish homeland were doing God's work. He held that the fire of Israel blazes in every Jew and that a Jew's imagination could only be "lucid and clear, clean and pure" in the Holy Land. Once Jews returned to their native land, he claimed, the "Universal Light, in all its power" could radiate from "the unique source of our being." Some Orthodox Jews denounced his policy of treating all branches of Judaism and even anti-Zionists as a part of Jewish culture. Many of his essays were published posthumously under the title *Orot hakodesh* (Lights of Holiness, 1963–64).   SAUL S. FRIEDMAN

Bibliography: Agus, Jacob B., *The High Priest of Rebirth: The Life, Times and Thought of Abraham Isaac Kuk,* 2d ed. (1972).

kookaburra   [kook'-uh-bur-uh]

The kookaburra, D. gigas, is also called the "bushman's clock" in Australia.

The kookaburra, or laughing jackass, *Dacelo gigas*, is a large and noisy bird of the Australian forests. Although a member of the kingfisher family, Alcedinidae, order Coraciiformes, the kookaburra does not eat fish but feeds mainly on large insects and small reptiles and amphibians. At a maximum of 47 cm (18.5 in) in length, and with a 10-cm (4-in) bill, the kookaburra is larger than most kingfishers, but its brown and tan plumage is drab by the standards of the family. Kookaburras nest during the spring and lay 2 to 4 white eggs in tree holes or termite nests. Their loud cries, which resemble human laughter and are typically chorused at dawn and dusk, are one of the characteristic sounds of the Australian forests.

ROBERT J. RAIKOW

Koopmans, Tjalling C.

The Dutch-American economist Tjalling Charles Koopmans, b. 's Graveland, the Netherlands, Aug. 28, 1910, d. Feb. 26, 1985, shared (1975) the Nobel Prize for economics with Leonid V. Kantorovich for his work in econometrics—the application of statistics, probability, and other quantitative techniques to economics. He focused on devising mathematical solutions to the problems of minimizing the cost of producing goods and of maximizing production with limited resources. This field, called linear programming, has wide applicability. Koopmans received a doctorate from the University of Leiden in 1936, taught in Rotterdam (1936–38), and worked for the League of Nations (1938–40). He moved to the United States in 1940. In 1944 he began his association with the Cowles Commission for Research, first at the University of Chicago and then, from 1955, at Yale University. He retired from Yale as a professor emeritus in 1981.

Kootenai: see KUTENAI.

Köppen, Wladimir Peter   [kur'-pen, vlahd'-ee-mir pay'-tur]

Wladimir Peter Köppen, b. St. Petersburg (now Leningrad), Russia, Sept. 25, 1846, d. June 22, 1940, was a German climatologist and meteorologist widely known for his classification and mapping of world climatic regions. As a young student in the Crimea, Köppen became interested in the influence of climate on vegetation. From 1875 to 1919 he served as director of meteorological services at the German Naval Observatory in Hamburg, where he organized weather warnings and upper-air observations. He published a world map of heat zones in 1884 and introduced in 1900 his first version of a climatic classification based on vegetation. Recognizing that plants require more moisture under higher temperatures, he established numerical limits for five major climatic types and their subdivisions in terms of monthly values of temperature and precipitation. From 1926 until his death, Köppen was a coeditor with Rudolf Geiger of the five-volume *Handbuch der Klimatologie* (Handbook of Climatology).

Bibliography: Oliver, John E., *Climate and Man's Environment* (1973).

Köprülü   (family)   [kurp-roo-loo']

The Köprülü family formed a dynasty of Turkish grand viziers (chief executive officers) who sought to revive the OTTOMAN EMPIRE by restoring traditional institutions and practices during the late 17th century. **Mehmed Köprülü Pasha,** 1583–1661, who became grand vizier in 1656, used forceful methods, executing and banishing dishonest or incapable officials and confiscating their properties. His son and successor, **Fazil Ahmed Pasha,** 1635–76, modified Mehmed's methods while stabilizing finances, curbing inflation, and restoring direct control over the provinces. He also brought the empire to its territorial peak by conquering Crete (1669) and the southern Ukraine (1676).

Ahmed was succeeded by his brother-in-law, **Kara Mustafa Pasha,** d. 1683. Deceived by an apparent revival of Ottoman military power, he overextended the army by trying to conquer Vienna in 1683. Defeated by a European coalition, Mustafa was ordered to commit suicide by the sultan. Ahmed's brother **Mustafa Köprülü,** 1637–91, and cousin **Hüseyin Köprülü,** d. 1702, tried in vain to halt the ensuing Austrian drive into Ottoman territory. The latter finally concluded the Treaty of Karlowitz (1699), by which the empire lost Hungary and was left exposed to further weakness and losses during the 18th century.

STANFORD J. SHAW

Bibliography: Shaw, Stanford J., *Empire of the Gazis: The Rise and Decline of the Ottoman Empire, 1280–1808,* vol. 1 in *History of the Ottoman Empire and Modern Turkey* (1976).

Koran

The Koran, or Qur'an (Arabic for "recital"), is the Sacred Scripture of ISLAM. Muslims acknowledge it as the actual words of God revealed to the Prophet MUHAMMAD between *c.*610 and his death (632). The text contains 114 chapters (*suras*), arranged—except for the opening sura—approximately according to length, beginning with the longer chapters.

The Koran, termed glorious and wonderful (50:1; 72:1), describes itself as a healing and mercy, as light and guidance from God (17:82; 27:77; 41:44; 42:52), as the absolute Truth (69:51), and as a perspicuous Book sent down from heaven in Arabic (12:1–2), part by part (17:106; 25:32), upon Muhammad. Presented as a blessed reminder and an admonition to people everywhere (21:50; 38:87; 80:11–15), it calls for grateful recognition of the many signs, around us and in us (51:20–21), of the goodness of him from whom all good comes (4:79) and urges a total commitment to him who alone is God (112:1–4). Announcing Judgment Day as the final fulfillment of God's threat and his promise (21:97–104), it warns evildoers and those who are ungrateful (17:89; 25:50) but brings good tidings to those who accept the guidance to the straightest path (17:9) and who live in accord with its message and its commandments (regarding marriage and divorce, children and inheritance, lawful foods, spoils of war, and so on). The text asserts that its message is neither a human invention (as its inimitability proves, 17:88) nor an innovation, since it confirms and clarifies the Scripture that Jews and Christians had received earlier (3:3; 5:15, 48; 35:31).

It is generally believed that the standard text of the Koran, adopted during the reign (644–56) of the caliph Uthman, is based on the compilation of one of Muhammad's secretaries, Zayd Ibn Thalbit. By calligraphic copying of its verses, and in many other ways as well, Muslims express their devotion to this Scripture over which, they trust, God himself watches (15:9).

WILLEM A. BIJLEFELD

Bibliography: Ali, Abdullah Yusuf, *The Holy Qur'ān,* 2 vols. (1937–38; repr. 1973); Arberry, A. J., *The Koran Interpreted,* 2 vols. (1955; repr. 1969); Bell, Richard, *Introduction to the Qur'ān,* ed. by W. Montgomery Watt, 2d ed. (1970); Jeffery, Arthur, *The Qur'ān as Scripture* (1952); Pickthall, Marmaduke, trans., *The Meaning of the Glorious Koran* (1930; repr. 1970).

korat

The korat, a breed of cat from Thailand, has a close-lying coat of shimmering blue, each hair tipped with silver.

The korat, a breed of cat from Thailand, has a close-lying, light coat of silvery blue. There is virtually no undercoat. The head is heart shaped, the ears large and round tipped, and the eyes large and changing from blue in the kitten, through amber, to green gold in the adult. The breed was recognized in the United States in the late 1960s.

EVERETT SENTMAN

Korbut, Olga   [kohr'-buht, ohl'-guh]

The Soviet gymnast Olga Korbut demonstrates remarkable flexibility in a routine on the balance beam during the 1976 Olympic games in Montreal. Korbut's performance at the previous Olympics in Munich earned her three gold medals and stimulated interest in gymnastics.

Olga Korbut, b. May 16, 1955, was a 17-year-old Soviet whose gymnastic mastery and vivacity impressed and charmed both judges and spectators at the 1972 Olympics in Munich. That year she won 3 gold medals, 1 each for the team competition and the floor and balance-beam events. She also won a silver medal on the uneven parallel bars. She was selected Associated Press Female Athlete of the Year for 1972. At the 1976 Olympics in Montreal, Korbut garnered two additional medals—a silver for the balance beam and a gold as a member of the winning Soviet female team. Korbut retired in 1977.

Korda, Sir Alexander   [kohr'-duh]

Alexander Korda, the professional name of Sándor Kellner, b. Sept. 16, 1893, d. Jan. 23, 1956, was a major figure in British cinema for almost 25 years. He began his producing and directing career in Hungary but left his native land in 1919 to embark on an international career in Europe and Hollywood. After establishing London Film Productions in Britain in 1932, Korda achieved world recognition with *The Private Life of Henry VIII* (1933). Specializing in historical films and using international directors, he turned out such successes as *Rembrandt* (1936), *The Four Feathers* (1939), *The Third Man* (1949), and *Richard III* (1956). He was knighted in 1942.

ROY ARMES

Bibliography: Korda, Michael, *Charmed Lives: A Family Romance* (1979); Kulik, Karol, *Alexander Korda: The Man Who Could Work Miracles* (1975).

Kordofanian language: see AFRICAN LANGUAGES.

Korea   [kuh-ree'-uh]

Korea is a small, strategically important, and politically divided country occupying a narrow peninsula of the East Asian mainland. It shares land borders with China on the north and with the USSR on the northeast, and it reaches to within 195 km (120 mi) of the largest Japanese island, Honshu. Formerly a united kingdom, Korea was divided (1948) at about the 38th parallel of latitude into the Communist-controlled Democratic People's Republic of Korea, otherwise known as North Korea, and the U.S.-supported Republic of Korea, or South Korea. Both republics seek eventual reunification of the peninsula through the political overthrow of the other. Seoul is the capital of South Korea, and Pyongyang is the capital of North Korea.

Korea has a long history as a cultural bridge across which Chinese culture was transmitted to Japan and Japanese influences reached the mainland. Korean culture was greatly enriched by this contact, but Korea was dominated politically by both China and Japan for part of its history. Nevertheless, the Koreans have maintained their identity as a separate and distinct people. The name is derived from Koryo, the dynasty that ruled the peninsula from 913 to 1392. Following the devastation of the KOREAN WAR (1950–53), both nations had to rebuild their economies. South Korea looked outward, developing a successful export-oriented economy. North Korea, one of the world's most highly regimented and isolated societies, focused on economic self-sufficiency.

LAND AND RESOURCES
Korea occupies a predominantly mountainous peninsula, about 320 km (200 mi) wide, that extends southward from the Asian mainland for about 965 km (600 mi). The peninsula is bordered by the Yellow Sea on the west and the Sea of Japan on the east. More than 3,000 islands, most of them small and uninhabited, border the irregular, 8,700-km-long (5,400-mi) coastline; the largest of these is Cheju (Quelpart) Island, located about 120 km (75 mi) off the southwest coast. Only about 20% of the Korean peninsula is occupied by lowlands suitable for settlement and cultivation, and most of the population is concentrated in small, discontinuous coastal plains and inland valleys that open onto the western coast. The remaining 80% is too rugged for cultivation.

The mountains drop steeply along the east coast, forming a narrow plain with few good harbors except in the northeast. To the west, the descent is more gentle and the land opens to the largest and richest agricultural lands. The highest mountains are the Paektu-san (Ch'ang pai Mountains), which are located northeast of the western lowlands; these mountains extend from northeast to southwest along the Chinese border, where they reach 2,744 m (9,003 ft) at Mount Paektu, Korea's highest point.

To the east of the lowlands are the T'aebaek Mountains, the backbone of the peninsula, which extend southward from Wonsan to form the main watershed. These mountains rise steeply from a narrow coastal plain along the Sea of Japan and reach 1,709 m (5,604 ft) at Diamond Mountain. To the south, separating the western lowlands from the south coast and Pusan's Naktong Valley, is the Sobaek Range, which extends from northeast to southwest across the southern end of the peninsula.

Soils. Korea's best agricultural soils are alluvial and are found in river valleys and coastal plains. Even these, however, tend to be somewhat infertile and sandy and require heavy fertilizing. Soils in the mountains are generally thin and suitable only for cultivation by the slash-and-burn technique.

Climate. The climate of Korea is both continental and monsoonal. During the winter, the peninsula is usually swept by cold, dry north and northwest winds blowing from the interior of the Asian continent. As a result, North Korea has long, cold, and snowy winters, with an average January temperature of about −8° C (17° F) at Pyongyang; milder, shorter winters occur farther south, with an average January temperature of −5° C (23° F) at Seoul. During the summer, southerly monsoon winds, blowing onshore from the surrounding seas, predominate. Temperatures in July average 27° C (80° F) throughout the peninsula except in mountainous regions. The frost-free period, or growing season, ranges from 220 days in the south, making double cropping possible there, to less than 175 days, suitable for only one crop a year, in the north.

DEMOCRATIC PEOPLE'S REPUBLIC OF KOREA (NORTH)

LAND. Area: 120,538 km² (46,540 mi²). Capital and largest city: Pyongyang (1986 est. pop., 1,275,000).

PEOPLE. Population (1988 est.): 21,900,000; density (1988 est.): 181.7 persons per km² (470.7 per mi²). Distribution (1988): 64% urban, 36% rural. Annual growth (1979–86): 2.5%. Official language: Korean. Major religions: Buddhism, Confucianism, shamanism, Chundo Kyo.

EDUCATION AND HEALTH. Literacy (1984): 95% of adult population. Universities (1986): 1. Hospital beds (1982): 244,000. Physicians (1982): 45,000. Life expectancy (1984): women—72; men—65. Infant mortality (1987): 33 per 1,000 live births.

ECONOMY. GNP (1986): $20.1 billion; $1,123 per capita. Labor distribution (1987): manufacturing—39%; agriculture and fishing—43%; government and public authorities—18%. Foreign trade (1985): imports—$1.72 billion; exports—$1.38 billion; principal trade partners—USSR, China, Japan. Currency: 1 won = 100 chon.

GOVERNMENT. Type: Communist state. Legislature: Supreme People's Assembly. Political subdivisions: 9 provinces, 3 cities, 1 special district.

COMMUNICATIONS. Railroads (1985): 4,473 km (2,779 mi) total. Roads (1985): 22,000 km (13,670 mi) total. Major ports: 6. Major airfields: 1.

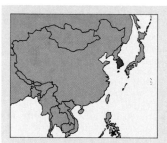

REPUBLIC OF KOREA (SOUTH)

LAND. Area: 98,484 km² (38,025 mi²). Capital and largest city: Seoul (1985 est. pop., 9,645,932).

PEOPLE. Population (1988 est.): 42,600,000; density (1988 est.): 432.6 persons per km² (1,120.3 per mi²). Distribution (1987): 65% urban, 35% rural. Annual growth (1979–86): 1.4%. Official language: Korean. Major religions: Buddhism, Christianity, Confucianism, shamanism, Chundo Kyo.

EDUCATION AND HEALTH. Literacy (1984): 94% of adult population. Universities (1986): 31. Hospital beds (1985): 74,265. Physicians (1985): 29,596. Life expectancy (1986): women—71.5; men—65.2. Infant mortality (1987): 30 per 1,000 live births.

ECONOMY. GNP (1986): $95.0 billion; $2,296 per capita. Labor distribution (1987): commerce and services—22%; manufacturing—25%; agriculture and fishing—24%; construction—5%; government and public authorities—24%. Foreign trade (1987): imports—$35.3 billion; exports—$46 billion; principal trade partners—United States, Japan. Currency: 1 won = 100 chon.

GOVERNMENT. Type: republic. Legislature: National Assembly. Political subdivisions: 9 provinces, 4 cities.

COMMUNICATIONS. Railroads (1986): 6,299 km (3,914 mi) total. Roads (1986): 52,264 km (32,475 mi) total. Major ports: 11. Major airfields: 4.

Annual precipitation is heaviest in the south, which receives more than 1,525 mm (60 in), and decreases to about 510 mm (20 in) in the north. Most precipitation occurs during the summer months.

Drainage, Vegetation, and Animal Life. The rivers of Korea are short and swift. They are widely used for irrigation and for generation of hydroelectricity but are of limited value for navigation. The most important rivers are the YALU and T'umen in the north; the Taedong, Han, and Kum in central Korea; and the Naktong in the southeast.

Coniferous forests, including pine, fir, larch, and spruce trees, grow extensively in the north and at higher elevations farther south. Deciduous trees and pine forests predominate in warmer areas. Overcutting, fire from slash-and-burn agriculture, and insects have depleted much of the original forest cover, however, and have resulted in serious soil erosion in many areas. Such wild animals as wolves, bears, leopards, and tigers are still found in some sparsely settled northern and peninsular upland areas.

Resources. Korea is well endowed with mineral resources, including large deposits of coal, iron ore, copper, gold, silver, and tungsten. Because of the political division at the 38th parallel most coal and metals, as well as most of the commercial forests and hydroelectric power resources, are located in North Korea; South Korea, on the other hand, possesses the best agricultural land and a larger labor force.

PEOPLE

Koreans are an ethnically homogenous Mongoloid people who have shared a common history, language, and culture since at least the 7th century AD, when the peninsula was first unified. The official language of both North and South is Korean (see KOREAN LANGUAGE), which is believed to have developed from a Tungusic base thousands of years ago, although many words have been borrowed from the Chinese and Japanese languages. The Korean alphabet, called *hangul,* was developed during the 15th century and is believed to have been the first phonetic alphabet in East Asia.

North Korea officially adheres to Marxism as the national ideology, and organized religion is reportedly suppressed. The majority of South Koreans profess (as did most North Koreans, until the Communists came to power) Buddhism and Confucianism, the latter of which was Korea's official religion from the 14th to the early 20th century. About 22% of South Koreans are Christians. Also important are shamanism, a widely practiced belief in natural spirit, and the strongly nationalistic religion known as Chundo Kyo (Tonghak before 1905), which was founded in the 19th century and combines elements of Confucianism, Taoism, and Buddhism.

Demography of North Korea. About 34% of all Koreans now live in North Korea. The population density is greatest in the plains along the western coast, where it can exceed 385 per km² (1,000 per mi²). The population is growing rapidly due to a high birthrate of 30 per 1,000 accompanied by a low death rate of 6 per 1,000 (1984). Despite this natural increase, however, North Korea experiences a severe labor shortage, partly because of heavy casualties during the Korean War and also because of the migration of more than 3,000,000 persons from North to South Korea since 1948. The population is more urban than rural, and urban migration continues. The largest cities are PYONGYANG (the capital), KAESONG, Chongjin, and Hungnam.

Demography of South Korea. About 66% of all Koreans now live in South Korea, which ranks among the world's most densely populated nations. As in North Korea, the lowlands along the western coast are the most densely populated areas. Although the overall rate of population growth (3% a year at the end of the Korean War) has slowed, South Korea is experiencing an urban growth rate of 5% a year. The largest cities are SEOUL (the capital, with about 23% of South Korea's total population), PUSAN, TAEGU, INCHON (Seoul's port), Kwangju, and TAEJON.

Education and Health in North Korea. Nearly 100% of those reaching school age since 1948 are literate. Education is free and compulsory for all students between the ages of 5 and 16, and about 20% pursue some form of higher education. The

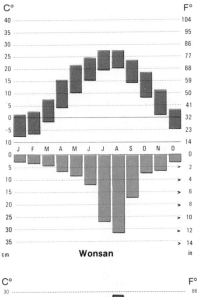

Wonsan

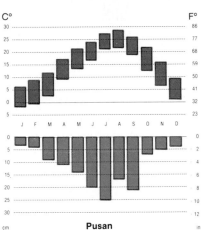

Pusan

Annual climate charts for two cities in Korea illustrate the climate zones of the peninsular nation. Bars indicate monthly ranges of temperature (red) and precipitation (blue). Wonsan, a major North Korean port on the Sea of Japan, has the continental humid climate that characterizes much of Korea, with extreme temperature variation and generally high precipitation. Pusan, South Korea's largest port, has the moderate temperatures and high precipitation of the region's subtropical humid climate.

Seoul, the capital and largest city of South Korea, lies in a basin flanked on the north and south by low mountainous ridges. Founded in 1392 and extensively rebuilt following the Korean War, the city is South Korea's major industrial, commercial, and cultural center.

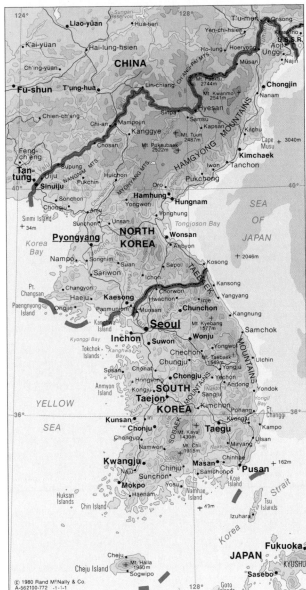

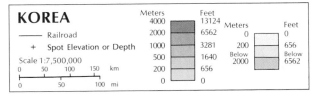

KOREA

—— Railroad

+ Spot Elevation or Depth

Scale 1:7,500,000

Meters	Feet
4000	13124
2000	6562
1000	3281
500	1640
200	656
0	0

Meters	Feet
0	0
200	656
Below 2000	Below 6562

© 1980 Rand McNally & Co.
A-562100-772 -1-1-1

largest institution of higher learning is Kim Il Sung University (1946), in Pyongyang (see KOREAN UNIVERSITIES). Free medical treatment is available, and paramedics supplement the care provided by physicians.

Education and Health in South Korea. Elementary education is free and compulsory for all students between the ages of 6 and 11, and 100% of this age group is enrolled in school. More than 75% of all children also attend secondary school. Opportunities for higher education have been greatly expanded since 1948, and South Korea now has more than 200 institutions of higher learning. Health care has improved dramatically since 1948, with a consequent increase in life expectancy at birth. Traditional medical treatment, using herbs and acupuncture, now complements Western medicine.

The Arts. Korea's rich artistic and cultural heritage has been strongly influenced by centuries of close contact with China. Buddhism, which dominated Korean life from the 7th to the 12th century, has influenced the arts. Buddhist temples, monasteries, shrines, palaces, fine metalwork, and other art treasures still bear witness to the achievements of this golden age and are valuable to South Korea's growing tourist industry. Under the Koryo dynasty (918–1392), delicate celadon ceramics of outstanding beauty and craftsmanship were produced. Folk tales, music, poetry, and drama all draw heavily on the Buddhist and Confucian traditions. (See also KOREAN ART.)

ECONOMIC ACTIVITY

North Korea. After the North-South division, North Korea possessed most of the industrial plant, iron, and other ores, coal reserves, and electrical installations developed during the Japanese occupation (1910–45). Damage inflicted during the Korean War was rapidly repaired with financial and technical assistance from the USSR and other Communist nations, and in the 1960s economic growth in the north took place at a rapid pace. By the end of the 1970s, however, economic growth had slowed, and the gross national product by the mid-1980s was less than one-fourth that of South Korea. Under Communist control, all industry has been nationalized and agriculture collectivized.

Manufacturing and Power. In the early years of Communist control, expansion of the iron and steel, chemical, metallurgical, and machine industries was stressed in an effort to build an industrially self-sufficient and militarily strong economy. Since the 1970s, the emphasis has shifted from heavy industries to the development of previously neglected consumer products. Major products currently include heavy machinery, trucks, tractors, bulldozers, farm implements, and electrical generators. The major industrial centers are Pyongyang, Chongjin, Kimchaek, and Kangson and Kangso (both near Pyongyang), which are all diversified metallurgical centers; Hungnam, the center of the petrochemical industry; and Sinuijul, a pulp and paper manufacturing center.

Electricity is produced at large hydroelectric power installations on the Yalu River and its tributaries in the north. Thermal electric plants fueled by coal and imported oil supplement hydroelectric power during the dry season and are extensively used in heavily industrialized areas. In 1985, North Korea had a kW capacity of 5.9 million, and 40 billion kW h were produced.

Agriculture, Fishing, and Forestry. It is estimated that less than half of the total labor force works in agriculture, reduced from 75% in 1948. The chief crop is rice. Agriculture is heavily mechanized, partly in response to the labor shortage, and irrigation is widely used. Land along tidal flats on the west coast is being reclaimed to increase the amount of cultivable land area. Commercial fishing is a major industry along the east coast, where the main fishing ports are Wonsan and Simpo. Much of the catch is exported. Commercial forestry is well developed, especially in the northern mountain regions.

Transportation. An extensive rail network links North Korea with China and also connects the country's major ports and cities; most freight and passengers are carried by rail. Road transportation is less well developed, although highways link Pyongyang with Kaesong and the ports of Wonsan and Nampo.

Trade. The principal imports are petroleum, coking coal, wheat, cotton, and machinery. The principal exports are rice, metals, cement, machinery, and chemicals. Efforts to develop trade with Sweden, Finland, and other Western nations in the 1970s resulted in major balance-of-trade problems, and North Korea was forced to default or defer payments on many of its Western purchases. In the mid-1980s, after several years of renewed emphasis on economic self-reliance, the government again sought to develop trade and technical links with capitalist countries.

South Korea. Since the Korean War the South Korean economy has been revitalized and greatly expanded with the aid of capital investment from the United States and, since the mid-1970s, from Japan. During the 1960s and 1970s the economy grew at a rate between 7% and 10% a year. The real growth rate fluctuated during the 1980s, although overall growth con-

Pyongyang, the capital of North Korea, is located on the Taedong River. The city was almost completely destroyed during the Korean War but has since been rebuilt. Among its modern buildings is the Korean Revolutionary Museum, shown in the background of this photo.

tinued. Overseas construction contracts, particularly in the Middle East, provide a significant source of income.

Manufacturing and Power. Manufacturing now employs more than 20% of the labor force and provides most of the nation's exports. Early postwar industrial development focused on Korea's low labor costs and included such labor-intensive industries as electronics, footwear, and textile manufacturing. Today Korean-made televisions, stereos, tape recorders, and textiles successfully compete with those made in Japan. In addition, emphasis is now placed on industries producing high value-added items, such as petrochemicals, steel, ships, cement, and automobiles and trucks. Seoul is the principal industrial center, followed by Pusan and the oil-refining and shipbuilding center of Ulsan.

In 1948, North Korea stopped electricity transmission to the South, and South Korea began a massive construction effort to develop electrical generating facilities. In 1985, 56.5 billion kW h of electricity were produced (ten times the 1966 output). Only 7% of the nation's energy is derived from hydroelectric power, and 7% from nuclear power; the remainder is produced primarily at thermal plants fueled with imported petroleum. To reduce the country's dependence on imported oil, the government launched an expansion of nuclear power facilities, which are expected to provide more than 40% of South Korea's electricity by the 1990s.

Agriculture, Fishing, and Forestry. About 22% of the land is farmed; agriculture provides less than 25% of the national income and employs about one-third the labor force. Rice is the principal summer, or wet-season, crop; wheat, barley, corn, potatoes, and sweet potatoes are the major dry-season crops. South Korea's rice yields, among the highest in the world, are obtained through heavy use of fertilizers, hybrid seeds, irrigation, and mechanization, plus a strong system of cooperatives. Animals, including cattle, pigs, and poultry, provide an increasing share of farm income. Fish, a traditional part of the Korean diet, are abundant offshore and in the Sea of Japan. Since the 1950s fish production has increased tremendously, and South Korea now ranks third (following Japan and China) among Asian fish producers. Forests cover about 66% of the total land area, but demand greatly exceeds the yearly wood output. Extensive reforestation efforts have been launched.

Transportation. The principal rail line connects Seoul, Taejon, Taegu, and Pusan. A second rail line runs from Seoul to the south and west, and a third serves the east coast. The

Korean villages frequently are situated near foothills, which protect them from severe monsoon winds. Although Korea's terrain is quite mountainous and only about 20% of the land is suitable for agriculture, nearly half of all Koreans live in small villages.

construction of an extensive network of superhighways has led to a decline in the use of rail transportation. Roads, subways, and other facilities were built in preparation for the 1988 Olympic Games, which were held in Seoul.

Trade. The keystone of South Korea's growing prosperity is foreign trade. Exports have increased dramatically since the 1960s and include a wide range of manufactured goods from electronic goods to textiles. Because the country must import all of its petroleum and most of its industrial raw materials, imports generally exceed exports in value. In the 1980s, South Korean exports faced increasing competition from other industrializing nations and were threatened by protectionist legislation in the United States and elsewhere.

GOVERNMENT

North Korea. North Korea is a Communist state in which political power rests with the leadership of the Korean Workers' party. According to the constitution of 1972, top policy-making power rests with the Central People's Committee. Legislative power nominally belongs to the Supreme People's Assembly, whose members are directly elected; this body, however, only ratifies decisions of the Central People's Committee. Executive power rests with the president and the State Administrative Council, headed by a premier named by the president. KIM IL SUNG has served as president since 1948.

South Korea. According to the 1987 constitution, the sixth since 1948, legislative power is vested in the mostly popularly elected National Assembly and executive power in the president. The latter is elected to a single 5-year term. The president appoints the cabinet, headed by a prime minister. ROH TAE WOO was elected president in 1987 under the new constitution, which curtailed presidential powers, strengthened the legislature, and pledged military neutrality in politics.

HISTORY SINCE 1945

Korea, one of the oldest nations in the world, was first unified in the 7th century AD (see KOREA, HISTORY OF). The country was occupied by Japan in 1905 and formally annexed by that state in 1910. During World War II, Korea was promised independence following the defeat of Japan. At the end of the war, however, it was divided at the 38th parallel of latitude; Soviet troops occupied Korea north of this line, and American forces were south of the parallel. Subsequent reunification efforts failed. In 1947 the United Nations agreed to supervise country-wide elections for a new government but were denied ac-

A Korean musician plays the a chaing, a bowed, 7-stringed zither thought to have originated in China but that survives today only in Korea. The traditional ensemble, which includes drums, oboes, flutes, fiddles, and zithers, performs the distinctive traditional Korean music.

cess to North Korea. Elections proceeded in the south, and on Aug. 15, 1948, the U.S. military government ended, and the Republic of Korea, with Syngman RHEE as president, was proclaimed. On Sept. 9, 1948, a Communist-controlled government in North Korea proclaimed the independence of the Democratic People's Republic of Korea under President Kim Il Sung. Both governments claimed jurisdiction over the entire peninsula. In 1950, North Korea invaded the South in the first phase of the Korean War, and the United States quickly came to the aid of the South. In 1953 the war ended inconclusively, and the cease-fire line was placed at about the 38th parallel, with a 2,000-m-wide (6,560-ft) demilitarized zone (DMZ) on either side. The truce has been an uneasy one, marked by frequent border skirmishes. Reunification talks have been held and proposed periodically since 1972 without result.

North Korea since 1953. Chinese troops aided North Korea during the Korean War, but North Korea tried to disassociate itself from the dispute between China and the USSR during the 1960s; in 1966, North Korea declared its political independence. In 1968 tensions increased when the crew of the U.S. ship *Pueblo* were held and charged with spying, but neither

Moscow nor Peking intervened (see PUEBLO INCIDENT). President Kim Il Sung, raised to demigod status, chose his eldest son, Kim Jung Il, as his eventual successor. Tensions between North and South increased in the late 1980s due to North Korea's construction of a giant dam on the North Han River and its boycott of the 1988 Olympics when it was unable to cohost the event. The two held talks on trade links and cross-border visits, however, and in September 1990 their prime ministers met for the first time since the Korean War.

South Korea since 1953. In 1960, student-led riots forced the resignation of President Syngman Rhee. The new president, Chang Myun, was overthrown in 1961 in a military coup that brought Gen. PARK CHUNG HEE to power. Park, elected president in 1963, did much to restore economic prosperity. Rising protests against his increasing powers, however, led to the imposition of military rule in 1972. In 1975 all political opposition was banned. The Park regime ended with his assassination by the head of the Korean Central Intelligence Agency in 1979. Premier Choi Kyu Hah was then elected president.

In May 1980 protests against the reimposition of martial law led to an uprising in Kwangju that was harshly suppressed by the army. Soon after, a military committee led by CHUN DOO HWAN assumed power. A new constitution was approved in October, and Chun became president in 1981. His army-backed Democratic Justice party (DJP) lost seats in the 1985 legislative elections, and in June 1987 the worst political protests since 1980 erupted. Roh Tae Woo, Chun's successor as head of the DJP, reached an agreement with opposition leaders Kim Dae Jung and Kim Young Sam in September on a new constitution providing for direct presidential elections. Roh won the elections on Dec. 20, 1987, but with only 37% of the vote over a divided opposition. He assumed office on Feb. 25, 1988. In the April 1988 legislative elections, 3 opposition parties won 164 of the 299 seats. In November former president Chun apologized to the nation for abuses of power by his regime. President Roh established diplomatic relations with the Soviet Union and announced compensation for victims of the 1980 Kwangju incident. A January 1990 merger of the DJP and the two leading opposition parties collapsed in July, when opposition members resigned from parliament.

ROBERT B. HALL, JR.

Bibliography:
KOREA (NORTH AND SOUTH): Hoare, J., and Pares, S., *Korea* (1988); Kim, J., *Divided Korea* (1975); Koh, B. C., *The Foreign Policy Systems of North and South Korea* (1984); McCune, S., *Korea's Heritage* (1956; repr. 1964); Macdonald, D. S., *The Koreans* (1988); Osgood, C. B., *The Koreans and Their Culture* (1951; repr. 1983); Young, W. K., *Politics and Policies in Divided Korea* (1983).
NORTH KOREA: American University, *North Korea: A Country Study* (1981); An, T. S., *North Korea: A Political Handbook* (1983); Brun, E., and Hersh, J., *Socialist Korea* (1976); Merrill, J., *North Korea: Politics, Economics, and Society* (1986); Scalapino, R. A., and Lee, H., eds., *North Korea in a Regional and Global Context* (1986).
SOUTH KOREA: American University, *South Korea: A Country Study* (1982); Bartz, P., *South Korea: A Descriptive Geography* (1972); Curtis, G. L., and Sung Joo Han, eds., *The U.S.-South Korean Alliance* (1983); Hinton, H. C., *Korea under New Leadership* (1983); Kang, T. P., *Is Korea the Next Japan?* (1989); Kwan, J. K., ed., *Korean Economic Development* (1990); Shapiro, M., *The Shadow in the Sun*; Steinberg, D. I., *South Korea Profile* (1986); Stephens, M., *Lost in Seoul* (1990).

Korea, history of

Korean history is thought to have begun with the settlement of the peninsula by Tungusic tribes, who spoke a Ural-Altaic language, followed shamanic religion, and had a paleolithic culture, about 3000 BC. Tangun, a legendary figure, is said to have established the first Korean "kingdom" of Choson in 2333 BC. The introduction of bronze tools from China and the establishment of Chinese military colonies in Korea in 108 BC led to the sinicization of Korea and the rapid development of agriculture.

Three Kingdoms. Meanwhile, three loosely organized Korean tribal federations, which emerged in the 3d century BC, were transformed into kingdoms. The establishment of the kingdoms of Silla in 57 BC, of Koguryo in 37 BC, and of Paekche in 18 BC (traditional dates) marked the beginning of the Three

Kingdoms period in Korean history. Koguryo, initially based in southern Manchuria, expanded southward and in AD 313 overthrew Lo-lang, the last Chinese stronghold in Korea.

During this period, the influence of CONFUCIANISM, TAOISM, and other forms of Chinese culture increased in Korea; BUDDHISM also grew, particularly in Paekche and Silla. Silla expelled (562) the Japanese—who had established a foothold on the coast in the 4th century—and between 660 and 668 destroyed both Paekche and Koguryo with Chinese help. Having unified Korea, Silla became a highly centralized state in which Buddhism and the arts flourished.

In the 9th century, however, serious provincial rebellions broke out, and in 936 the kingdom was finally overthrown by rebels who had established the Koryo dynasty, with its capital at Kaesong, in 918.

Koryo. Under the Koryo dynasty power was initially wielded by civilian administrators, and the political, social, economic, and educational systems of Korea became increasingly sinicized. In 1170 the military seized control and suppressed Buddhism. By the end of the 12th century a military family, the Ch'oe, ruled the country, but opposition to it mounted, especially after the MONGOLS began their invasions in 1231. In 1258 the Ch'oe were deposed, and their civilian successor submitted to the Mongols.

A relatively peaceful period of Koryo rule under Mongol suzerainty followed. The invention (1234) of a new printing system with movable type allowed the ready dissemination of Buddhist and Confucian writings, and Korean potters manufactured high-quality green Koryo ware (see KOREAN ART). A revolt against Mongol rule in 1356 brought another period of disorder. Finally, in 1392, the Koryo king was overthrown by the Yi dynasty, aided by the new Ming dynasty in China, to whom the Yi swore allegiance.

Yi. The Yi dynasty, which established a new capital at Hanyang (now Seoul), rejected Buddhism and established Chu Hsi Confucianism as a national orthodoxy. It also improved relations with its Chinese overlords and brought about economic and social reforms. A well-functioning Confucian bureaucracy, an orderly social structure, rapid development of the educational system accompanied by the publication of many books, and the growth of science and technology seemed to promise a bright future. The adoption of the Korean writing system, called *hangul,* by King Sejong (r. 1418–50) in 1443 marked the high point in cultural development.

From the early 16th century, however, growing factionalism among scholars, mismanagement of state affairs by officials, court intrigues and power struggles, usurpation of power and privileges by the landed gentry, decline of foreign trade, and increasing tax burdens brought about political instability as well as economic decline and social upheavals. A reform school known as Silhak arose among scholars and officials, but Confucian conservatism prevented change.

The devastating but unsuccessful invasions (1592–98) by the Japanese under HIDEYOSHI and the wars of conquest (1627–37) by the Manchu worsened the internal situation. Vassalage to the Manchu, who went on to overthrow the Ming and establish the Ch'ing dynasty in China, fostered the antiforeign sentiments of the Koreans. The state of the nation continued to deteriorate as rebellions and peasant uprisings erupted.

Contact with the West and Japan. Roman Catholicism was brought to Korea from China in the 17th century, and what was called Western Learning developed. A new native religion called Tonghak (Eastern Learning) arose in 1860 and won the support of the underprivileged and mistreated peasantry. Persecution of the Christians and the destruction of a U.S. merchant ship in 1866 helped provoke Western assaults by the French in 1866 and the United States in 1871.

The Koreans resisted these attacks, but in 1876 the Japanese took advantage of the governmental disruption within Korea to force a commercial treaty on the Yi. Six years later Korea, the "hermit kingdom," also opened its doors to the Western nations, beginning with a treaty with the United States.

After the opening of Korea, rivalries developed—particularly among China, Japan, and Russia—for predominance of influence over the weak Korean state. In 1894 followers of

Tonghak revolted against the government, and China sent troops to suppress the rebellion. Japan also sent troops to Korea. The First SINO-JAPANESE WAR ensued (1894–95), and victorious Japan established hegemony over the nominally independent Korea. After defeating the Russians in the RUSSO-JAPANESE WAR (1904–05), Japan was strong enough to force Korea to become a protectorate. After some Korean resistance Japan formally annexed the country in 1910.

Modern History. During the Japanese colonial period (1905–45) the Koreans endured political suppression, economic exploitation, and social and educational discrimination, in addition to attempts to Japanize their culture. The so-called March movement of 1919 mounted massive demonstrations against colonial rule and was brutally suppressed. Subsequent independence movements were similarly treated. In the meantime Korea became an important economic and military base for Japan's continental expansion.

The Japanese surrender to the Allies in 1945 liberated Korea from Japan, but the country was divided along the 38th parallel of latitude between the U.S. and Soviet occupation forces. In November 1947 the United Nations adopted a resolution to set up a unified independent Korean government, but the UN commission responsible was able to hold elections only in the southern (U.S.) zone. On Aug. 15, 1948, the Republic of Korea was inaugurated, ending U.S. military rule in the South. In North Korea the Communists established their own regime and inaugurated the Democratic People's Republic of Korea in September 1948. Thus the temporary military demarcation line became the boundary between two Korean states. Since the devastating KOREAN WAR (1950–53), which resulted from a North Korean invasion of the South, there has been only an uneasy truce along the line.

For the history of North and South Korea since 1948, see KOREA.   ANDREW C. NAHM

Bibliography: Choy, Bong-Youn, *Korea: A History* (1971); Gregor, J. A., and Hsia Chang, M., *The Iron Triangle* (1984); Han, Woo-Keun, *The History of Korea*, trans. by Grafton Mintz and Kyung-Shik Lee (1971); Henthorn, William E., *A History of Korea* (1971); Hulbert, Homer B., *History of Korea*, ed. by Clarence Weems, 2 vols., rev. ed. (1962); Kim, C. I. Eugene and Han-kyo, *Korea and the Politics of Imperialism, 1876–1910* (1967); Kim, Jeong-Hak, *The Prehistory of Korea*, trans. by Richard and Kazue Pearson (1978); Lee, Chong-sik, *The Politics of Korean Nationalism* (1963); Lee, Kai-baik, *A New History of Korea*, trans. by E. W. Wagner and E. J. Schultz (1984).

Korean art

The arts of Korea, although a distinct entity, were profoundly influenced by Chinese art and architecture. Korean traditions in turn formed an important early link between Chinese and Japanese culture; it was through Korea that Buddhist art forms first reached Japan during the 6th century.

The earliest Korean art, dating from about 3000 BC, appeared in the form of Neolithic pottery impressed with simple geometric decoration. Metalworking developed in Korea after the 10th century BC. From the 3d century BC on cast-bronze mirrors and other utilitarian objects were made that attest to the marked influence of Chinese styles.

With the Chinese conquest of northwestern Korea in 108 BC, Lo-lang, near modern Pyongyang, North Korea, became a provincial outpost of the Han dynasty (206 BC–AD 220). Richly furnished burial chambers discovered at Lo-lang have revealed many of the finest surviving examples of Han decorative arts.

During the Three Kingdoms period (late 1st century BC–AD 668), the local powers of Koguryo in the north, Paekche in the southwest, and Silla in the southeast vied for control over the Korean peninsula. Koguryo art survives principally in the form of fresco-type mural paintings decorating 5th- and 6th-century tomb chambers along the middle Yalu River. The vigorous polychrome paintings depict lively everyday scenes, real and fantastic animals, and other stylized motifs, some of which display Central Asian influences. The Paekche kingdom maintained close ties with Japan in the 6th and 7th centuries; its art is primarily known from gracefully sculpted Buddhist images preserved in Japan. The finest example from this period

Chinese influence on Korean culture became prominent during the 2d century BC with the founding of colonies of the Han dynasty. This painted lacquer basket from Lo-lang is representative of Han dynasty art. (National Museum of Korea, Seoul.)

is the painted wood figure of *Kudara Kannon* (Horyuji, Nara), which either was brought from Korea or was carved by one of the many Paekche artisans then working in Japan. Silla art of the Three Kingdoms period is noted for the refinement of its metalwork. Monumental tomb mounds surrounding Kyongju, the Silla capital, have yielded a striking array of uniquely Korean ornaments, including a group of gold crowns richly embellished with masses of comma-shaped jade pendants and gold discs.

Silla unified the Korean kingdoms into a single realm in 668, marking the start of the Great Silla period (668–918). Impressive granite monuments were erected, including the mid-8th-century pagoda of the Pulgaksa monastery and the cave-temple of Sukkalam (both near Kyongju), the latter containing an immense stone Buddha figure and fine relief carvings exhibiting T'ang Chinese influence. Silla-period metalworkers excelled in the creation of large bronze temple bells, which were often as much as 4 m (13 ft) high; also noteworthy are the elegant gilt-bronze figurines of Buddhist deities, such as that of *Maitreya* (7th century; National Museum of Korea, Seoul).

Royal patronage of Buddhism during the Koryo dynasty (918–1392) encouraged the renewed construction of temples and monasteries, the most important extant example being the Hall of Eternal Life at the 13th-century Pusoksa, believed to be the oldest wooden building in Korea. Although sculpture and stonework declined during the Koryo period, the aristocratic arts—precious metalwork, lacquer inlaid with mother-of-pearl, and above all, ceramics—reached new levels of quality and refinement. Porcelain making, introduced (late 11th century) from Chekiang, China, was rapidly transformed by native artisans into a distinctly Korean variant—the "kingfisher-colored" Koryo CELADONS. These subtle blue green wares are regarded as among the most serenely beautiful Asian porcelains ever produced. In the 12th century the Koreans invented the technique of inlaying black or white clays into the celadon wares to produce delicate bird, flower, and cloud patterns.

With the founding of the Yi dynasty (1392–1910), Buddhism

This 5th–6th-century AD pottery vessel in the form of a warrior and horse exemplifies the type of unglazed Silla stoneware that was crafted during the Three Kingdoms period. Although influences from Chinese mortuary sculpture are apparent, the execution remains distinctively Korean. (Academy of Arts, Honolulu.)

The Koryo period (918–1392) of Korean art is renowned for its exquisite porcelain wares. This 12th-century water bowl with a peony design is typical of the uniquely Korean technique of inlaying black and white clay on celadon ware. (Museum of Fine Arts, Seoul.)

was replaced by a Chinese-inspired Neo-Confucianism. Under the conservative formalism of Confucian concepts, the arts suffered a steady decline in the early centuries of Yi rule. The autocratic monarchy strove to maintain close ties with the court of Ming China, and grandiose buildings, such as the 15th-century Kyongbok Palace, were erected in the new capital of Seoul in emulation of even grander Peking prototypes. In painting, both the professional court artists and the scholar-gentry painters relied heavily on Chinese themes and conventions. Not until the 18th century did distinctively Korean tendencies emerge in the work of a number of Yi artists. The most prominent of these was CHONG SON, who eschewed the traditional Chinese-styled landscape for the depiction of rugged Korean scenery, as in *The Diamond Mountains* (private collection, Seoul). Genre painting represents another mode in which Yi artists broke from the slavish imitation of academic Chinese painting. A characteristic example, displaying typically Korean deftness and wit, is *Boating Scene* (Kangsong Museum of Fine Arts, Korea), part of an album by Sin Yunbok (b. *c.*1758).

In Yi decorative arts, the delicate celadons of the preceding period were replaced by *pun-ch'ong,* a coarsely made pottery often enhanced by freely applied patterns in white or blue slip. Highly prized by collectors in Japan, the rustic Yi wares exhibit qualities of vitality and freshness that characterize much of Korean folk art, from inlaid lacquer objects to charming painted illustrations of Korean folk tales.

K. A. PETERSON

Bibliography: Eckardt, Andreas, *A History of Korean Art* (1929); Kim, Chewon, *Treasures of Korean Art* (1966); Kim, Chewon, and Lee, Kim L., *Arts of Korea* (1974); McCune, Evelyn, *The Arts of Korea: An Illustrated History* (1961); Moes, Robert J., *Korean Art* (1987); Sun-u, Ch'oe, et al., *Traditional Korean Painting* (1983); Won-Yong, Kim, et al., *Traditional Korean Art* (1983).

Korean language

Korean is the language spoken by approximately 65 million people living on the Korean peninsula: 43 million of them in the Republic of Korea (South Korea) and 22 million in the Democratic People's Republic (North Korea). The current political partition of the country, along with the resulting different economic and social systems, has tended to strengthen long-standing linguistic divergences between north and south.

A member of the URAL-ALTAIC family of languages, Korean was brought down into the peninsula by early invaders who first entered the region during the diffusion of the Altaic peoples in Neolithic times. Each of the three kingdoms (18 BC–AD 935) of Silla, Koguryo, and Paekche appears to have

(Above) Tombs of the Korean Koguryo dynasty were decorated with polychrome wall paintings. This hunting scene from the Tomb of the Dancing Figures (c.400) exemplifies the bold lines and heavy brushstrokes of this period of Korean painting.

(Left) This ink-monochrome landscape painting by Chong Son (1676–1759) reflects the innovations in painting introduced during the later Yi period. Chong Son was one of the first Korean artists to depict distinctly Korean scenes. (University Museum, Seoul.)

had a different variety of Old Korean, but the sources for these earliest stages of the language are too fragmentary to make clear whether Old Korean was one language with three dialects or three different, but probably related, languages.

Middle Korean was apparently the final stage in the historical development of the variety of Old Korean used in the Silla kingdom, especially as that language had survived into the period of Unified Silla, from the 7th to the 10th century. Not until late Middle Korean are there extensive records, written in an indigenous phonetic script of great precision and efficiency, called *hangul,* the development of which about 1443–44 remains one of the major achievements of Korean civilization. Today the north employs *hangul* exclusively. In the south, the use of borrowed Chinese characters to supplement *hangul* is discouraged but continues to be tolerated.

ROY ANDREW MILLER

Bibliography: Martin, S. E., et al., *Beginning Korean* (1969); Miller, Roy A., *Japanese and Other Altaic Languages* (1971); Woong, Hub, et al., *The Korean Language* (1983).

Korean universities

The State Institute of Higher Learning was established in Korea in 1922. Until the late 19th century, China provided Korea's intellectual inspiration and educational leadership. At that time Korea began to modernize its educational system, and American Protestant missionaries founded colleges there.

Because Korea was part of the Japanese empire from 1910 to 1945, Korean education on all levels was designed for the Japanese there; the language of instruction was Japanese.

From 1945 to 1948, when the Republic of Korea (South Korea) was set up, the U.S. military government in Korea and the United Nations oversaw the establishment of a new, democratic educational system that came to be based on that of the United States. In accordance with the country's economic and social goals, the goals of the educational system emphasized teacher education and scientific and technological education. The number of universities and their enrollments increased rapidly and continued to do so even during the Korean War (1950–53). From 1945 to 1960 the number of colleges grew from 19 to 85. There were 459 universities, colleges, and junior colleges in 1986–87, a vast majority of which were co-educational. In 1986–87 more than 1.3 million students attended these schools. South Korean state universities and colleges are under the minister of higher education; public institutions are administered by local governments; and there are many private universities and colleges.

SELECTED KOREAN UNIVERSITIES

University and Location	Date Founded	Enrollment
Republic of Korea		
Chosun University, Kwangju	1946	22,873
Chung-ang University, Seoul	1918	19,501
Chungnam University	1952	20,107
Dongguk University, Seoul	1906	15,979
Ewha Women's University, Seoul	1886	12,730
Hanyang University, Seoul	1939	27,000
Korea University, Seoul	1905	23,417
Kyung Hee University, Seoul	1949	25,000
Kyungpook National University, Taegu	1946	21,343
Pusan National University	1946	29,000
Seoul National University	1946	24,536
Sookmyung Women's University, Seoul	1938	7,465
Yeungnam University, Gyongsan	1967	22,506
Yonsei University, Seoul	1885	26,681
Democratic People's Republic of Korea		
Kim Il Sung University, Pyongyang	1946	16,000

The area of the present Democratic People's Republic of Korea (North Korea) had no colleges before 1945. The earliest ones were modeled on those in the USSR, but ideological differences between the countries have enabled North Korea to be freer in establishing its own educational system. There are nearly a million students in about 175 colleges and institutes and Kim Il Sung University. Higher education, which is under the jurisdiction of the minister of higher education, is divided between work-study and all-study programs.

Bibliography: Adams, Don, *Higher Educational Reforms in the Republic of Korea* (1965); McGinn, Noel F., et al., *Education and Development in Korea* (1979).

Korean War

In the Korean War (1950–53) a U.S.-dominated United Nations coalition came to the aid of South Korea in responding to an invasion by North Korea, which was aided by the USSR and allied with Communist China; the war ended in a military stalemate and the restoration of the political status quo. Concurrently, the United States was assuming increasing leadership of the Western nations against what were perceived as the expansionist intentions of its former ally, the USSR. As this COLD WAR heated up, it brought the United States into a military confrontation with Communist forces in Korea.

BACKGROUND

The Korean peninsula was a Japanese possession from 1910 to 1945.

When World War II ended in the Pacific in 1945, the USSR administered the surrender of Japanese forces north of the 38th parallel in Korea, and the United States supervised the surrender in the South. The two allies established a joint commission to form a provisional Korean government. The Soviets and the Americans soon disagreed, however, on the

legitimacy of the competing political groups that sought to govern Korea, and mutual suspicions mounted.

In 1947 the United States asked the United Nations to attempt to unify the northern and southern halves of the country. The 38th parallel hardened ominously, however, into an international boundary in 1948 with the establishment of Syngman RHEE's Republic of Korea in the South and the Democratic People's Republic of Korea under KIM IL SUNG in the North. The arbitrarily set border split the peninsula both politically and economically into a Communist industrial North and a primarily agricultural South, which was dependent on U.S. aid. By 1949 both the USSR and the United States had withdrawn most of their troops, leaving behind small advisory groups; the North Korean troops were much better trained and equipped than those in the South, however. Increasing hostility led to sporadic border clashes between North and South Koreans throughout 1949 and into 1950. In September 1949 a UN commission, after trying unsuccessfully to unify the country, warned of the possibility of civil war.

THE INVASION OF SOUTH KOREA

The withdrawal of U.S. forces and a speech (Jan. 12, 1950) by Secretary of State Dean ACHESON excluding South Korea from the U.S. defensive perimeter in the Pacific encouraged North Korea to take a bold military action. At approximately 4 AM on June 25, 1950, artillery of the North Korean Army opened fire on South Korean units standing watch south of the 38th parallel. About 30 minutes later the first of about 80,000 North Korean troops crossed the border. At 5:30 AM the main attack, consisting of North Korean infantry and tanks, advanced along the shortest route between the 38th parallel and Seoul, the capital of South Korea. North Korean divisions also struck in the mountains of central Korea and along the east coast.

Reacting to initial reports of the fighting, the United States requested (June 25) an emergency meeting of the UN Security Council to discuss the situation. After confirming the details of the invasion and deciding that the attack was a breach of the peace, the Security Council called on the North Korean government to cease hostilities. Because it seemed clear by June 27 that the North Koreans intended to disregard the UN request, the Security Council met again to consider a new resolution—one recommending that "the members of the United Nations furnish such assistance to the Republic of Korea as may be necessary to repel the armed attack and to restore international peace and security in the area." After some

United Nations troops follow tanks through the rubble-strewn streets of Seoul. The city, which had fallen to the North Koreans on June 28, 1950, was recaptured in the UN counteroffensive of September 1950, spearheaded by an amphibious landing at Seoul's port of Inchon.

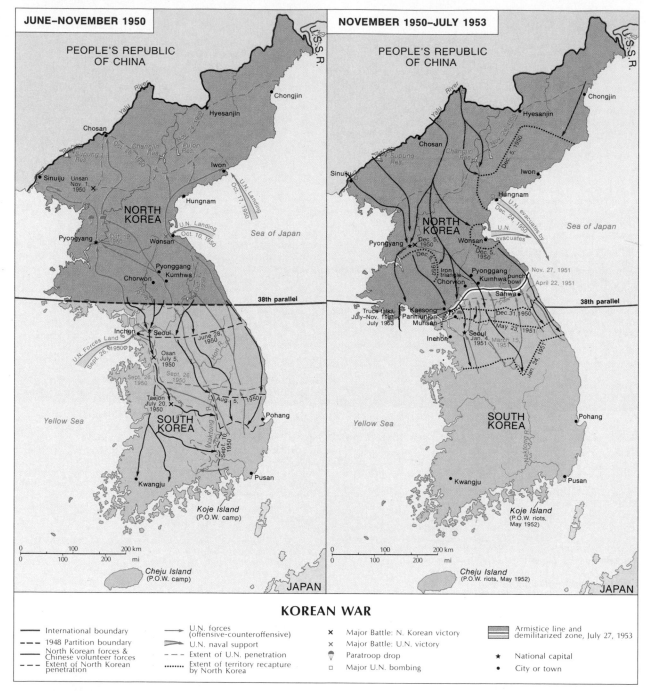

KOREAN WAR

—— International boundary	→ U.N. forces (offensive-counteroffensive)	✕ Major Battle: N. Korean victory
– – – 1948 Partition boundary	▷ U.N. naval support	✕ Major Battle: U.N. victory
—— North Korean forces & Chinese volunteer forces	– – – Extent of U.N. penetration	⍨ Paratroop drop
– – – Extent of North Korean penetration	···· Extent of territory recapture by North Korea	□ Major U.N. bombing

Armistice line and demilitarized zone, July 27, 1953

★ National capital

● City or town

debate the resolution passed. The USSR was not represented in the Security Council because it was boycotting that body in protest over the exclusion of Communist China from the United Nations.

In the meantime, U.S. President Harry S. TRUMAN conferred with Acheson and concluded that the USSR had directed the invasion. On June 27, Truman, without a congressional declaration of war, committed U.S. military supplies to South Korea and moved the U.S. Seventh Fleet into the Formosa Strait, a show of force meant to intimidate China. The Chinese, however, preoccupied since World War II with internal affairs and concerned with regaining Taiwan, had so far remained aloof from the Korean problem, as they had during the 1904–05 war. Proceeding unilaterally, the U.S. Joint Chiefs of Staff (JCS) directed (June 30) General of the Army Douglas

MACARTHUR, the American commander in East Asia, to commit his ground, air, and naval forces against the North Koreans. On July 7 the UN Security Council passed a resolution requesting that all member states wishing to aid South Korea make military forces and assistance available to the United States, which would designate the commander of the unified forces. By this resolution, President Truman became the executive agent for the UN on all matters affecting the war in Korea, and MacArthur became the commander in chief, UN Command. Although the United States ultimately contributed most of the air and sea power and about half of the ground forces (with South Korea supplying the bulk of the remainder), MacArthur controlled the allied war effort of a total of 17 combatant nations (the largest contributors, after the United States and South Korea, being Australia, Canada, Great

Britain, and Turkey). Five additional nations provided medical units.

DELAY AND DEFENSE

MacArthur's sole hope of saving the South Koreans from the superior Soviet- and Chinese-trained North Korean forces was to hold the port of PUSAN at the southern tip of the Korean peninsula until help arrived. He rushed reinforcements north to bolster the hard-pressed South Korean Army; on July 5, American units made contact with North Korean tanks and infantry just north of Osan. The Eighth Army, commanded by Lt. Gen. Walton H. Walker (1889–1950), delayed the North Koreans north and west of the Naktong River, the last natural barrier protecting Pusan. As the North Koreans pushed south toward the Naktong, however, Walker moved the Eighth Army into what came to be known as the Pusan Perimeter, a two-sided front (240 km/150 mi long), which survived only because of the timely arrival of reinforcements and American air superiority over the battlefield.

Beginning on August 5 the North Koreans launched a series of violent attacks against the perimeter in an effort to capture Pusan. By September 12, however, reinforcements had greatly increased the combat power of the allies, and the North Korean offensive had spent itself.

THE INCHON LANDING

With virtually all enemy units concentrated against Pusan, the time for a counteroffensive had arrived. MacArthur had long planned a counterstroke against the port of Inchon, on the west coast of Korea behind the North Korean line. For several weeks he had diverted forces to Japan in preparation for this counterattack, committing to Korea just enough men and material to impede the North Korean attack on Pusan. His sense of how much to send and how much to withhold helped transform his greatest gamble into his most striking professional accomplishment.

Inchon, with its appalling array of tides and currents, was the worst sort of amphibious objective. The harbor was dominated by Wolmi-do, a small island which, if defended, could impede the landing and prevent tactical surprise. Disregarding strong objections to his plan, MacArthur remained convinced that the advantages of seizing the Inchon-Seoul area were worth the risks of landing in Inchon Harbor. He made a daring amphibious landing at Inchon on September 15, successfully cutting the North Korean supply lines. In the days that followed, the marines seized Kimpo Airport and the city of Seoul while the infantry turned south to meet the Eighth Army, which was pursuing a fleeing enemy north from the Pusan Perimeter. By Oct. 1, 1950, the North Koreans had been pushed out of South Korea, and the UN forces were poised south of the 38th parallel.

CROSSING THE 38TH PARALLEL

In the meantime, President Truman's National Security Council advised against crossing the 38th, arguing that the ejection of the North Koreans from South Korea was a sufficient victory. The Joint Chiefs of Staff objected; contemporary military doctrine demanded the destruction of the North Korean Army to prevent a renewal of the aggression. MacArthur, they argued, would have to pursue it into North Korea. On September 11—four days before the Inchon landing—the president adopted the arguments of his military advisors while retaining restraints recommended by the National Security Council to avoid provoking the Chinese and the Soviets: no UN troops should enter Manchuria or the USSR; only South Koreans should operate along international borders; and if the Soviets or Chinese intervened before the scheduled crossing, it should be canceled.

On October 7 the UN General Assembly passed a resolution calling for the unification of the peninsula and authorized MacArthur to send his forces into North Korea. In a conference with Truman at Wake Island on October 15, MacArthur was optimistic about an early victory. The North Korean capital of PYONGYANG fell on October 19, and the allied UN troops streamed north virtually unopposed. They pushed the North Korean forces to the YALU RIVER, which formed the North Korean border with the Manchurian region of China.

By the end of the month, the fall of North Korea seemed imminent.

CHINESE INTERVENTION

In retrospect, the decision to cross the 38th parallel seems to have been the turning point in the Korean War. Beginning in late September, Communist China had warned of possible Chinese intervention if UN forces crossed the border, and between October 14 and November 1 about 180,000 Communist "volunteers" had secretly crossed the Yalu. Not knowing the full extent of the Chinese commitment, MacArthur believed that a furious counterattack on October 25 was a limited gesture rather than a serious intervention. By November 2, however, intelligence officers had accumulated undeniable evidence that Chinese Communist forces had intervened. The UN Security Council was soon notified of their presence.

After his troops replenished their depleted supplies, MacArthur launched a "home-by-Christmas" offensive on November 24. Although some UN forces reached the Yalu, the Chinese army struck quickly and with full force. Stunned, American and South Korean units began a long retreat that ended in early January 1951, only after the UN forces had recrossed the 38th parallel and the city of Seoul had once again fallen.

CHANGING WAR AIMS

Lt. Gen. Matthew B. RIDGWAY, who took over the Eighth Army after General Walker died (Dec. 23, 1950) in a jeep accident near the front line, brought the UN withdrawal to a halt south of Seoul. Beginning on Jan. 7, 1951, allied units began to probe north, opening an offensive that frontline troops came to call the "meatgrinder." Throughout January, February, and March, Ridgway's men pushed on relentlessly until they once again crossed the 38th parallel. In early April the UN advance slowed temporarily as units consolidated strong defensive ground and braced themselves for an expected enemy counteroffensive.

In the meantime the defeat in North Korea had forced the UN to reexamine its war aims in light of Chinese involvement. MacArthur quickly charged that he was facing "an entirely new war" and that the strategy for war against North Korea did not apply in a war against China. MacArthur wanted more forces and a broader charter to retaliate against the Chinese, especially to conduct air operations against the "privileged sanctuary" of Manchuria. In this strategy, he was completely at odds with President Truman and other UN leaders who wanted a lesser commitment and a cease-fire. The UN General Assembly branded Communist China an aggressor in February 1951 and voted to subject it to economic sanctions. Its new war aim was to contain the Communist forces along the 38th parallel while negotiating an end to the conflict. Even in the darkest days before the Inchon landing, American leaders believed that restraint was necessary to avoid widening the war. Now that China was involved, the administration feared that it might invoke the Sino-Soviet treaty and cause the Soviets to unleash their nuclear capability against the United States or mount a conventional strike in Europe. MacArthur's proposals to expand his force and to retaliate against the Chinese were, therefore, not favorably considered by the administration. MacArthur disagreed, too, with Acheson and Truman's policy of giving priority to Europe at the expense of the shooting war in Korea; he openly appealed to the public and Congress in an attempt to reverse the new war policy. During this period of cold-war tensions many Americans—most notably Joseph R. MCCARTHY, U.S. senator from Wisconsin—agreed with MacArthur's stand.

THE DISMISSAL OF MACARTHUR

MacArthur had been a difficult subordinate. He had clashed with Truman over U.S. policy toward Taiwan early in the war and complained about the restrictions placed on his forces and his freedom to wage the war. He publicly suggested that the policies of the Truman administration had been responsible for military setbacks. On Mar. 25, 1951, just as President Truman put the finishing touches on a new initiative seeking a cease-fire, MacArthur broadcast a bellicose ultimatum to the enemy commander that undermined the president's plan. Truman was furious; MacArthur had pre-empted presidential prerogative, confused friends and enemies alike about who was directing the war, and directly challenged the president's authority as commander in chief. On April 5, while Truman considered ways to handle the problem, Joseph W. Martin, minority (Republican) leader of the House of Representatives, released the contents of a letter from MacArthur in which the general repeated his criticism of the administration. The next day Truman began the process that was to end with MacArthur's relief from command on April 11. On his return to the United States, MacArthur received a hero's welcome.

STABILIZING THE FRONT

After MacArthur's dismissal Ridgway moved to Tokyo to replace him, and Lt. Gen. James A. VAN FLEET took command of the Eighth Army. On April 22, while Van Fleet's army edged north, the more than 450,000 Chinese opened a general offensive. Followed closely by this formidable force, Van Fleet withdrew below the 38th parallel, finally halting only 8 km (5 mi) north of Seoul.

On May 10, the Chinese launched a second offensive, concentrating their main effort on the eastern sector of the UN line. Van Fleet attacked in the west, north of Seoul. The surprised Communist units pulled back, suffering their heaviest casualties of the war, and by the end of May they were retreating into North Korea. By late June, a military stalemate had developed as the battle lines stabilized in the vicinity of the 38th parallel. Both sides dug into the hills and for the next 2 years waged a strange and frequently violent war over outposts between their lines.

NEGOTIATIONS

In late June 1951 the Soviets proposed a conference among the belligerents. Although both sides wanted a cease-fire, negotiating held different meanings for each side. The UN wanted above all to bring an end to the fighting and to defer political questions to a postwar international conference. The Communists wanted to deal with political questions while negotiating a cease-fire. The Communists had their way, and the truce talks dragged on for two years before an armistice was finally concluded.

Negotiations were initially hampered by haggling over matters of protocol and the selection of a truly neutral site. On July 10, 1951, the full armistice delegations met at Kaesong, with Vice Adm. C. Turner Joy representing the UN command and Gen. Nam Il of North Korea representing the Communists.

On July 26 the two sides finally reached agreement on an agenda containing four major points: fixing a demarcation line and demilitarized zone, supervision of the truce, arrangements for prisoners of war, and recommendations to the governments involved in the war. Numerous problems arose, however, causing frequent suspensions of the talks, which in October resumed at a new site, Panmunjon.

One by one the issues were resolved until the only remaining obstacle was the handling of prisoners of war (POWs). The UN wanted prisoners to decide themselves whether or not they would return home; the Communists insisted on forced repatriation. A lengthy stalemate developed, reflecting the battlefield stalemate along the 38th parallel. A series of Communist POW riots that erupted in May 1952 on Koje and Cheju islands only complicated the issue. In order to force the Communists to negotiate in good faith, Gen. Mark CLARK, who succeeded Ridgway, increased air attacks over North Korea. On June 23, 1952, UN air attacks destroyed major hydroelectric installations on the Yalu.

By April 1953 the POW deadlock was finally broken, and the first prisoners were exchanged at Panmunjon under a compromise that permitted prisoners to choose sides under supervision of a neutral commission. Not satisfied with a truce that did not result in the unification of Korea and totally voluntary repatriation, Syngman Rhee disrupted the proceedings on June 18 by releasing about 25,000 North Korean prisoners who wanted to live in the South. To gain Rhee's cooperation, the U.S. government promised him a mutual security pact, long-term economic aid, expansion of the South Korean Army, and coordination of goals and actions in the international conference to follow (see GENEVA CONFERENCES).

On July 27, 1953, an armistice was signed, without the participation of South Korea, and the shooting phase of the Korean War came to an end. Although the precise number of Chinese and North Korean casualties is unknown, estimates of total losses range between 1.5 and 2 million, plus perhaps a million civilians in the north. The UN command suffered a total of 88,000 killed, of whom 23,300 were American. Total casualties for the UN (killed, wounded, or missing) were 459,360, including 300,000 South Koreans. Another million civilian casualties were incurred in South Korea. In addition over 40 percent of the industry and a third of the homes in that country were ruined.

Politically and militarily the war was inconclusive. For years the two armies continued watching each other over the demilitarized zone, a 4-km-wide (2.5-mi) band stretching 250 km (155 mi) across the Korean peninsula, waiting for the day when the fighting might begin again. Korea was no closer to unification; the war only served to intensify bitterness between North and South. The Korean War had other important results in the arena of international diplomacy. It contributed to the strained relations between Washington and Peking. In addition it added a new military dimension to the U.S. foreign policy of containment, which had heretofore been implemented by political and economic measures, including military aid. Originally formulated by George F. KENNAN, developed by Dean Acheson, and advanced by John Foster DULLES, the containment policy helped lead to U.S. military involvement in Vietnam during the 1960s.   ROY K. FLINT

Bibliography: Appleman, Roy E., *The United States Army in the Korean War* (1961); Cumings, Bruce, *The Origins of the Korean War* (1981); Field, James A., *A History of United States Naval Operations: Korea* (1962); Forty, George, *At War in Korea* (1982); Futrell, Robert F., *The United States Air Force in Korea, 1950–1953* (1961); Gardner, Lloyd C., *The Korean War* (1972); Hoyt, Edwin P., *The Pusan Perimeter: Korea* (1984); Marshall, S. L. A., *The River and the Gauntlet* (1953); Middleton, H. J., *The Compact History of the Korean War* (1965); Rees, David, *Korea: The Limited War* (1964; repr. 1970); Ridgway, Matthew B., *The Korean War* (1967); Spanier, John W., *The Truman-MacArthur Controversy and the Korean War*, 2d ed. (1965).

Korematsu v. United States   [kohr-e-maht'-soo]

The case of *Korematsu* v. *United States* (1944) involved the treatment by the government of persons (both citizens and aliens) of Japanese descent during the early years of World War II. Amid fears that an invasion of the West Coast was imminent, President Franklin D. Roosevelt had issued Executive Order 9066, which permitted various restrictions on the Japanese residing along the coast. Within this framework Lt. Gen. John L. DeWitt, who was in charge of the Western Command, had barred all persons of Japanese descent from the military area of San Leandro, Calif. For his failure to comply with the order, Fred Toyosaburo Korematsu, an American citizen, had been arrested and convicted.

In upholding Korematsu's conviction the Supreme Court, speaking through Justice Hugo Black, concluded that Congress and the president, under constitutional war powers, might exclude persons of Japanese ancestry from areas of the West Coast during a wartime emergency. Korematsu, said Black, was not excluded because of hostility to him or to his race but because military judgment feared invasion of the West Coast or espionage and sabotage by Japan. The Court was not unmindful of the hardships imposed, but, said Justice Black, "hardships are a part of war, and war is an aggregation of hardships." Justices Owen Roberts, Frank Murphy, and Robert Jackson registered strong dissents.

In 1983 a federal district court judge overturned Korematsu's conviction on the grounds that the government had knowingly withheld critical information. The 1944 decision nonetheless remains on the books.   ROBERT J. STEAMER

See also: NISEI.

Korin   [koh'-reen]

Japanese artist Ogata Korin, 1658–1716, crystallized the sophisticated taste of Kyoto's prosperous urban culture in his paintings, textile designs, fans, and lacquer ware. Heir to the artistic ideas of KOETSU and SOTATSU, he worked in the classical mode of those masters, eliminating superfluous decorative elements in favor of concise designs rendered in clear outline and brilliant color.

A wealthy merchant's son, Korin quickly exhausted his inherited fortune after his father's death (1687). He then turned to painting for a livelihood, beginning (1699) by painting the ceramics produced by his brother KENZAN. By 1701, Korin's painting skill had been recognized officially by the award of the honorary title of *Hokkyo*, with which he signed all his paintings. During sojourns (1704–05 and 1707–09) in Edo (modern Tokyo) he developed an ink-painting style based on his study of SESSHU, SESSON, and Kaiho Yusho, earlier painters favored by the military class.

For his large-scale compositions Korin drew on the classical Japanese traditions as revitalized by Sotatsu. His *Iris Screens* (Nezu Museum, Tokyo), which alludes to a poignant theme from the 10th-century *Tales of Ise*, exhibits Korin's unique synthesis of Sotatsu's bold forms and gorgeous color with an elegant simplicity. Korin's radically concise designs and his use of brilliant color patches set against gold leaf profoundly influenced Rimpa, the tradition of Japanese art that emerged in the early Edo period (1615–1868); it also had some influence on 19th-century European artists, who took Korin's style to be representative of all Japanese painting.

BARBARA BRENNAN FORD

Bibliography: Hiroshiji, Mizuo, *Edo Painting: Sotatsu and Korin*, trans. by J. M. Shields (1972); Randall, Doanda, *Korin* (1960).

Kornberg, Arthur   [kohrn'-burg]

The biochemist Arthur Kornberg, b. Brooklyn, N.Y., Mar. 3, 1918, shared the 1959 Nobel Prize for physiology or medicine with Severo Ochoa for his work in contributing to an understanding of the enzymatic synthesis of deoxyribonucleic acid (DNA). In 1956 he successfully formed copies of DNA molecules *in vitro*, but they were biologically inactive. Heading a research team at Stanford University, Kornberg succeeded in producing (1967) the first *in vitro* replication of infective viral DNA with full biological activity.

Bibliography: Moore, Ruth E., *The Coil of Life: The Story of the Great Discoveries in the Life Sciences* (1961).

Kornilov, Lavr Georgiyevich   [kur-nee'-luhf, lah'-vur gee-ohr'-gee-vich]

Lavr Georgiyevich Kornilov, b. July 30 (N.S.), 1870, d. Apr. 13, 1918, was a Russian general who led White Russian resistance to the Bolsheviks in the Russian Civil War (1918–20). He served in the Russo-Japanese War (1904–05) and commanded a division in World War I. After the RUSSIAN REVOLUTION of March 1917, Kornilov was made commander in chief by the provisional government. In September, however, he attempted a military coup to establish a more conservative regime and was arrested. After the Bolshevik Revolution in November, he escaped to assume command of a volunteer White Russian army on the Don River. He was killed while attacking Ekaterinodar (now Krasnodar).

K. M. SMOGORZEWSKI

Korolev, Sergei   [kuh-rahl-yawf', sair-gay']

Sergei Pavlovich Korolev, b. Dec. 30, 1906, d. Jan. 14, 1966, was the chief designer of the Soviet space program during the period 1954 to 1966. A rocket engineer in the 1930s, Korolev was arrested during the Stalin purges and sent to a Gulag prison in Siberia. During World War II he was kept in a special prison, where scientific and engineering prisoners could work on projects of military significance. During this period he helped design the Katyusha bombardment rockets and a rocket unit to assist aircraft in taking off.

After the war, Korolev was released from prison to oversee the exploitation of captured German V-2 rockets and to direct the recruitment of German engineers and technicians from that missile program. Korolev personally dealt with Nikita Khrushchev in applying for funding for missile and space

projects and, with the approval of Khrushchev, began work on the "semyorka" intercontinental ballistic missile in 1954. After its successful flight in June 1957, Korolev received permission to proceed with additional plans to use the rocket to launch artificial earth satellites called SPUTNIKS.

Impressed with the international political impact of the first Sputnik, Khrushchev compelled Korolev to conduct a series of space shots almost solely devoted to publicity, such as the twin VOSTOK flights (1962), the first woman-in-space flight (1963), and the three-man VOSKHOD flight (1964). Korolev's plans for sending probes to the moon were frustrated by engineering failures, and the first successful automated landing did not come until two weeks after his death. Korolev received posthumous honors and publicity, although while he was alive his identity had never been revealed by Moscow.

JAMES OBERG

Bibliography: Golovanov, Iaroslav Kirillovich, *Sergei Korolev: the Apprenticeship of a Space Pioneer*, trans. by M. M. Samokhvalov and H. C. Craighton (1975); Oberg, James E., "Korolev and Khrushchev and Sputnik," in *Spaceflight*, April 1978.

Koryak: see CHUKCHI.

Kosciusko, Mount   [kah-zee-uhs'-koh]

Mount Kosciusko, located in the Snowy Mountains (also called the Muniong Range) of the Australian Alps, in southeastern New South Wales, is Australia's highest peak (2,228 m/7,309 ft). From May to September it is a center for winter sports. The first European to discover the mountain was P. E. Strzelecki in 1840, who named the peak for his fellow Pole, Tadeusz Kościuszko.

Kościuszko, Tadeusz   [kah-see-uhs'-koh, tuh-dush']

Tadeusz Andrzej Bonawentura Kościuszko, b. Feb. 4, 1746, d. Oct. 15, 1817, was a Polish military and national leader who also served in the Continental Army during the American Revolution. After education as a military engineer in Poland and France, a disappointment in love and sympathy for the American cause led him to seek a commission in the Continental Army. His fortification of Bemis Heights helped win the victory at Saratoga (see SARATOGA, BATTLES OF); he also fortified West Point.

Kościuszko is best known in Polish history for his brilliant leadership of the 1794 revolt against Russia following the Second Partition (1793) of Poland. He raised peasant armies by granting the peasants land for service and defeated a Russian army at Raclawice (Apr. 4, 1794). Defeated by Russian and Prussian forces six months later, he was imprisoned (1794–96) in St. Petersburg. After a visit to America in 1797–98 he lived in France and later in Switzerland. Kościuszko made Thomas Jefferson executor of his will, bequeathing his property to buy freedom and education for slaves. The will, however, was later contested by his relatives. His *Manual on the Maneuvers of Horse Artillery* (1808) was for many years used by the U.S. Army.

ANNA M. CIENCIALA

Bibliography: Gardner, Monica, *Kościuszko*, rev. ed. (1942); Haiman, Miecislaus, *Kościuszko in the American Revolution*, ed. by George Billias (1943; repr. 1975), and *Kościuszko: Leader and Exile* (1946; repr. 1977).

See also: POLAND, PARTITIONS OF.

kosher   [koh'-shur]

A rabbinic term, usually applied to food permitted to be eaten by traditionally observant Jews, *kosher* (or *kasher*) is a Hebrew word that means "fit, proper." The Jewish dietary laws, based on the Bible (Leviticus 11; Deuteronomy 14) as interpreted in the Talmud, concern animal products only. Kosher foods include barnyard fowl, the meat of cattle, sheep, and goats (and their milk), and such fish as have fins and scales—excluding shellfish, eels, and so on. Poultry and quadrupeds must be killed by specially trained and licensed slaughterers in accordance with detailed rules; the carcasses are drained of blood and inspected to ensure that the animals were not diseased. Unless it is to be broiled, meat must be thoroughly salted and later rinsed before cooking, to remove any remaining blood. The hindquarter of animals may be eaten only if certain nerves and sinews are first removed. Meat and milk products may not be cooked and eaten together or immediately after one another, and the use of the same utensils in their preparation and consumption is forbidden. The dietary laws were not hygienic in original intent, but they have probably been so in effect; the Bible describes them as a means of sanctification.   BERNARD J. BAMBERGER

Bibliography: Kemelman, Y. A., *A Guide to the Jewish Dietary Laws*, 3d ed. (1971); Rubinstein, S. L., *The Book of Kashrut* (1967).

Košice   [kaw'-shih-tsee]

Košice, an industrial city in Czechoslovakia, is a regional capital of the Eastern Slovak republic. It lies on the Hornád River, about 310 km (195 mi) east-northeast of Bratislava, and has a population of 214,270 (1984 est.). The climate is moderate continental. Košice is an important metallurgical center and a major railroad junction. Its principal industries are petroleum refining and the manufacture of iron, steel, heavy machinery, magnesite, clothing, and wood products. The old section of the city has several 14th- and 16th-century churches.

Settled in the 9th century, Košice was chartered in 1241 by Hungarians and was later occupied at various times by Austrians, Hungarians, Russians, and Turks. It was ceded to Czechoslovakia by Hungary in 1920. In the spring of 1945, Košice was a seat of the provisional Czechoslovak government, and it gave its name to a postwar reconstruction program.

Kosinski, Jerzy   [kuh-zin'-skee, yur'-zee]

Jerzy Kosinski's stark, surrealistic novels assume the role of treatises on the process of dehumanization and the need for self-definition. The Painted Bird (1965), one of his most powerful works, is a tale of savage beauty written in a lucid style that increases the impact of the story. Steps (1968) received the 1969 National Book Award.

A Polish-born novelist who has written all his books in English, Jerzy Nikodem Kosinski, b. Łódź, June 14, 1933, emigrated to the United States in 1957 and published his first two works, the nonfictional *The Future Is Ours, Comrade* (1960) and *No Third Path* (1962), under the pseudonym of Joseph Novak. *The Painted Bird* (1965), his powerful and bitter first novel, is a nightmarish depiction of childhood during World War II, which reflects the years he spent hiding from the Nazis in the Polish countryside. Its sequel, *Steps* (1968), for which he won a 1969 National Book Award, is in a similar vein. Kosinski's sardonic humor and grim pessimism are also evident in such later novels as *Being There* (1971), *The Devil Tree* (1973), *Cockpit* (1975), *Blind Date* (1977), *Passion Play* (1979), and *Pinball* (1982).

Bibliography: Kosinski, Jerzy, *The Art of the Self: Essays à propos "Steps"* (1968) and *Notes of the Author on "The Painted Bird"* (1965).

Kosmos: see COSMOS.

Kossel, Albrecht   [kohs'-ul, ahl'-brekt]

Albrecht Kossel, b. Sept. 16, 1853, d. July 5, 1927, was a German biochemist whose early studies on NUCLEIC ACIDS, the constituents of DNA and genes, led to the isolation and identification of many of the simple nitrogenous bases of which these are composed. He also studied the proteins that are part of the genes themselves. For this work he received the Nobel Prize for physiology or medicine in 1910.

HENRY M. LEICESTER

Kossuth, Lajos   [koh'-shoot, lah'-yohsh]

Lajos Kossuth, a 19th-century Hungarian national hero, is revered as the leader of Hungary's 1848 revolution against Austrian rule. In 1849 he declared Hungary's independence. Although his forces blunted Austrian invasion, Russia forced Hungary to surrender and Kossuth to flee into exile.

Lajos Kossuth, b. Sept. 19, 1802, d. Mar. 20, 1894, was a Hungarian liberal statesman and the foremost leader of the REVOLUTION OF 1848 in Hungary. Brought up in the anti-Habsburg Protestant traditions of northeastern Hungary and sent to the national Diet at Pozsony (now Bratislava) in 1832, Kossuth soon emerged as one of the leaders of the liberal opposition against oppressive Austrian rule. His main goal was the establishment of a liberal, ultimately independent Hungarian national state. A brilliant orator and publicist, he soon became the idol of the Magyars, but his refusal to grant recognition to the aspirations of the other nationalities of Hungary brought him into conflict with the non-Magyars.

After serving as the minister of finance in Hungary's first constitutional government (Apr. 7–Sept. 28, 1848), Kossuth assumed full control of the revolution. While the revolution inflicted defeats on the Austrians, Kossuth's declaration of Hungary's independence on Apr. 14, 1849, triggered Russian intervention, which brought about Hungary's defeat.

After his flight from Hungary on Aug. 11, 1849, and two years in Turkey, Kossuth toured Britain and the United States in a well-publicized but unsuccessful effort to gain Western support for Hungary's independence movement. Later he proposed a Danubian confederation but found no takers. After Ferenc DEÁK and the moderate Hungarian leaders concluded the Compromise of 1867, establishing the Dual Monarchy of Austria-Hungary, Kossuth's hopes faded altogether. Although he retained much influence over the Magyar masses, his political role ceased. He died in exile in Turin, Italy.

S. B. VARDY

Bibliography: Deak, Istvan, *The Lawful Revolution: Louis Kossuth and the Hungarians, 1848–1849* (1979); Komlos, John H., *Kossuth in America, 1851–1852* (1973); Lengyel, Emil, *Lajos Kossuth: Hungary's Great Patriot* (1969); Sebestyén, Endre, *Kossuth: A Magyar Apostle of World Democracy* (1950); Zarek, Otto, *Kossuth*, trans. by Lynton Hudson (1937; repr. 1970).

Kostenki   [kahs-tenk'-ee]

Kostenki is a village along the Don River, about 40 km (25 mi) south of Voronezh, in the USSR, near which Soviet archaeologists have intermittently excavated since 1922. In its vicinity are numerous Upper Pleistocene open-air campsites belonging to the Eastern GRAVETTIAN phase of the Upper Paleolithic period and dating from 25,000 to 11,000 years ago. These sites were repeatedly occupied by groups of *Homo sapiens* (the modern human species) hunting mammoths, horses, red deer, and rhinoceroses. Circular living areas (5–7 m/16–23 ft in diameter) suggesting huts with a central hearth were made of branches, mammoth bones and tusks, and skins. Larger oval areas (up to 16 by 35 m/52 by 116 ft) with rows of hearths and many pits may have functioned as shared domestic working areas. A remarkable bone and ivory tool industry including awls, points, and polishers, as well as mattocks, shovels, and numerous other incised artifacts were found at Kostenki and its environs. Burials were discovered as were female figurines and many other small sculptures and ornaments of stone, bone, and ivory.   JACQUES BORDAZ

Bibliography: Klein, Richard, *Man and Culture in the Late Pleistocene: A Case Study* (1969).

Kosygin, Aleksei N.   [kuh-see′-gin]

Aleksei Nikolayevich Kosygin, b. Saint Petersburg (now Leningrad), Feb. 20 (N.S.), 1904, d. Dec. 18, 1980, was premier of the USSR from October 1964 until his resignation on grounds of ill health in October 1980. He joined the party in 1927 and became a member of the ruling politburo in 1948. Stalin demoted him to candidate member in 1952, but Kosygin returned to the politburo in 1960, when he became first deputy premier under Nikita Khrushchev. After Khrushchev's downfall, in 1964, Kosygin took over as premier, while Leonid BREZHNEV succeeded Khrushchev as first party secretary. Together they dismantled many of the reforms of their predecessor and introduced a more steady and sophisticated foreign policy. Kosygin's diplomatic talents were used on numerous assignments, such as negotiating the India-Pakistan cease-fire in 1966 and meeting U.S. president Lyndon B. Johnson in Glassboro, N.J., in 1967.   K. M. SMOGORZEWSKI

Bibliography: Tatu, Michel, *Power in the Kremlin: From Khrushchev to Kosygin* (1969).

koto   [koh′-toh]

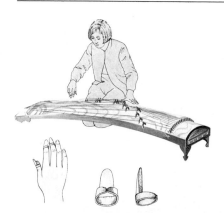

The Japanese koto is a long zither with 13 strings that are usually made of silk. It is tuned by movable bridges, one for each string. The player plucks the strings with three ivory plectra worn on the right hand and with the left hand alters the pressure on the strings to produce different tones.

The koto is a Japanese zither derived from the Chinese *ch'in* (or *chyn*). Its common use in Japan dates back to the 17th century, although its use at court began much earlier. When played, the 2-m-long (6-ft) instrument rests on the floor with the upper end raised a few centimeters above the lower. Its 13 strings are supported by individual movable bridges and plucked by three ivory plectra on the player's right hand. The koto is used for purely instrumental music or to accompany singing or dancing. The performer can raise the pitch of each string by a half step or whole step by applying pressure beyond the bridge. In this way the 12 half steps of the Pythagorean scale can be used over its two-octave range even though the instrument is tuned to a pentatonic (five-tone) scale.
                                        ELWYN A. WIENANDT

Bibliography: Adriaansz, Willem, *The Kumiuta and Danmono Traditions of Japanese Koto Music* (1973); Malm, William P., *Japanese Music and Musical Instruments* (1959).

Kotzebue, Otto von   [koht′-suh-byoo]

Otto von Kotzebue, b. Dec. 30 (N.S.), 1787, d. Feb. 15 (N.S.), 1846, was a navigator in Russian service who explored extensively in the Pacific and Arctic. Son of the German dramatist August von Kotzebue, he took part in A. J. KRUSENSTERN's circumnavigation in 1803–06. He subsequently commanded two circumnavigations (1815–18, 1823–26) himself, discovering Kotzebue Sound off northwest Alaska and collecting much scientific information.   ROBIN BUSS

Bibliography: Buck, Peter H., *Explorers of the Pacific* (1953); Kotzebue, Otto von, *A Voyage of Discovery, into the South Sea and Bering's Straits,* 3 vols. (1821; repr. 1967), and *A New Voyage Round the World in the Years 1823–1826,* 2 vols. (1830; repr. 1967).

Koufax, Sandy   [koh′-faks]

Sandy Koufax delivers a pitch to a Minnesota Twins batter during the final game of the 1965 World Series. Relying on his blazing fastball and baffling curve, Koufax led the Los Angeles Dodgers to victory in the series. Koufax was forced to retire after the following season because of a painful and chronic arthritic condition afflicting his pitching arm.

Sanford Koufax, b. Brooklyn, N.Y., Dec. 30, 1935, an American professional baseball player, was the most dominating pitcher of the mid-1960s. Many baseball authorities believe that he might have established himself as the greatest pitcher ever had not chronic arthritis in his left elbow forced his early retirement in 1966. From 1955 to 1960, Koufax, who played for 12 years with the Dodgers baseball organization, was an unimpressive pitcher. He changed his style, however, and in 1961 won 18 games and led the National League in strikeouts with 269. For the next 5 years he had the lowest earned-run average in the league (1.97), won 111 games, lost 34, pitched 4 no-hit games (including one perfect game), and led the Los Angeles Dodgers to 3 pennants and 2 World Series titles. He also won 3 Cy Young Awards as baseball's best pitcher. In 1972, at age 36, he entered the Baseball Hall of Fame, the youngest inductee ever.

Bibliography: Koufax, Sanford, and Linn, Ed, *Koufax* (1966); Mitchell, Jerry, *Sandy Koufax* (1966).

Koussevitzky, Serge   [koo-suh-vits′-kee, serzh]

The Russian-born conductor Serge Koussevitzky, b. July 26, 1874, d. June 4, 1951, achieved his greatest fame as the director (1924–49) of the Boston Symphony Orchestra. His talent and determination were apparent from his youth. For example, the abundance of performers who played the more common orchestral instruments prompted him to take up (1888) the double bass at the Moscow Conservatory, and he became a virtuoso on that neglected instrument. For his performances he composed several valuable solo works for double bass, including a concerto, which have become standard study pieces. His marriage in 1905 to Natalie Ushkov, the daughter of a wealthy tea merchant, gave him the opportunity to achieve his next objective, to become a conductor. Koussevitzky conducted the Berlin Philharmonic in 1908; thereafter, he soon established himself as a brilliant conductor in Russia and Europe (1909–20). In 1921 he moved to Paris, where he introduced a unique series of orchestral programs, the Concerts Koussevitzky, in which he introduced many important new works by French composers. He was named permanent conductor of the Boston Symphony in 1924, a post he held for 25 years. In 1940 he established a music school at the Berkshire Music Center, and in 1942 he founded the Koussevitzky Music Foundation, which continues to commission works and support contemporary music.   DELMER D. ROGERS

Bibliography: Leichtentritt, Hugo, *Serge Koussevitzky, the Boston Symphony Orchestra and the New American Music* (1946; repr. 1976); Lourié, Arthur, *Sergei Koussevitzky and His Epoch,* trans. by S. W. Pring (1931; repr. 1971); Schonberg, Harold, *The Great Conductors* (1967); Smith, Moses, *Koussevitzky* (1947).

Kovacs, Ernie

Television comic Ernie Kovacs, b. Trenton, N.J., Jan. 23, 1919, d. Jan. 13, 1962, was the first comedian to put television's potential for sight effects to creative use. An actor and gag writer, Kovacs first appeared on Philadelphia TV as the chef in an unscripted cooking show. His mad goulash chatter aroused the notice of NBC-TV, and in 1951 he starred in the first of several short-lived comic series. Equipped with cigar and horn-rimmed glasses, Kovacs shrank and expanded, disappeared and zoomed back into focus, pantomimed to extraordinary effect, and, in fact, opened TV's visual possibilities for succeeding comic shows such as *Laugh-In.*

Kovalenok, Vladimir: see IVANCHENKOV, ALEKSANDR.

Kovno: see KAUNAS.

Kowal, Charles T.

The American astronomer Charles Thomas Kowal, b. Buffalo, N.Y., Nov. 8, 1940, is known for his discovery on Nov. 1, 1977, of CHIRON, an asteroid with an unusual orbit between Saturn and Uranus. The discovery was made using a BLINK MICROSCOPE on photographic plates from Palomar Observatory. Associated with the California Institute of Technology since 1963, Kowal has also discovered a 13th satellite of Jupiter, named Leda, and numerous supernovas.   STEVEN J. DICK

Kowloon

Kowloon (Chiou-lung) is a town on the west shore of Kowloon Peninsula, southeastern China, in the British crown colony of HONG KONG. Its population of 799,123 (1981) consists primarily of Chinese. Kowloon is located 1.6 km (1 mi) from Hong Kong Island and is a free-trade area, manufacturing center, and tourist town.

Kozintsev, Grigory   [koh-zint'-sef]

Grigory Kozintsev, b. Mar. 22 (N.S.), 1905, was a noted Russian filmmaker whose career began soon after the revolution and ended only with his death on May 11, 1973. In 1921 he helped organize a theater workshop in Petrograd, called Factory of the Eccentric Actor (FEKS); according to the manifesto of the workshop it was influenced by circus, vaudeville, carnival, and cinema. A group from the workshop soon entered film production, collaborating to make their first "politico-eccentric" film, *Adventures of Oktyabrina* (1924). Kozintsev's best-known collaborative efforts include *Shinel* (The Cloak, 1926, from Gogol's story); *S.V.D.* (1927, on the Decembrist revolt of 1825); and *The New Babylon* (1929, on the Paris Commune). The most notable films he made on his own were *Don Quixote* (1957), *Hamlet* (1964), and *King Lear* (1972).
                                        JAY LEYDA

Kracauer, Siegfried   [krah'-kow-ur, zeek'-freet]

Siegfried Kracauer, b. Feb. 8, 1889, d. Nov. 26, 1966, was an influential German-Jewish film historian and theoretician best known for his championship of realism as the truest function of cinema. Cultural affairs editor (1920–33) of the *Frankfurter*

Zeitung, Kracauer left Germany after the rise of Adolf Hitler, and during World War II he conducted research into Nazi propaganda films for New York's Museum of Modern Art. His *From Caligari to Hitler* (1947) was an exploration of the roots of nazism in the German cinema of the 1920s. Kracauer's most important work, *Theory of Film: The Redemption of Physical Reality* (1960), argues—with more intensity than consistency—for a cinema devoted to the presentation of real-life people in real-life situations in a style from which all theatrical or aesthetically formal elements would be excluded.
                                        ROGER MANVELL

Kraepelin, Emil   [krep-uh-leen', ay'-mil]

Emil Kraepelin, b. Feb. 15, 1856, d. Oct. 7, 1926, was a German psychiatrist who developed an influential classification of psychoses into two types: dementia praecox, now called SCHIZOPHRENIA, and manic-depressive psychosis. Kraepelin was the first to use objective tests and measurements to study drug effects and mental disorders.

Kraft, Adam

Adam Kraft, c.1455–1509, an outstanding German sculptor of the late Gothic period, produced a number of realistic, expressive, yet stylistically restrained stone carvings, of which all known examples are in Nuremberg, where he lived. His earliest works are reliefs (1490–92) in the church of Saint Sebald; they are unusual in that they duplicate paintings above the tombs of the Schreyer and Landauer families in the same church. Kraft's most spectacular creation is the tabernacle (1493–96) in Saint Lorenz, a tower about 19 m (62 ft) high. Its Gothic architectural forms include numerous reliefs and statues, among which are portraits of the artist and two apprentices. These figures are seen kneeling at the foot of the structure, supporting its base. Other major works are the monuments of the Pergenstörffer (1498–99) and Rebeck (1500) families in the Frauenkirche; the Landauer tomb (1503) in the Egidienkirche; and the sandstone reliefs representing the Stations of the Cross (1505–08; Germanisches National Museum, Nuremberg).   MARK J. ZUCKER

Bibliography: Müller, Theodor, *Sculpture in the Netherlands, Germany, France, and Spain, 1400–1500,* trans. by Elaine and William Robson Scott (1966).

krait   [krite]

The banded krait, B. fasciatus, *is a nocturnal ground dweller. The snake has potent venom; because it is sluggish during the day and is not aggressive, however, it does not often bite humans.*

Kraits are venomous South Asian snakes of the genus *Bungarus,* family Elapidae. There are about a dozen species, most of which reach 1.2 m (4 ft) in length, except for two species that reach 2.1 m (7 ft). Kraits are usually colorful, with alternating light and dark bands. They feed mainly on other snakes and have highly toxic venoms, for which antivenins are available.

Krak des Chevaliers   [krahk day shev-ahl-yay']

The well-preserved Krak des Chevaliers (French for "Krak of the Knights") is a Crusader fortress in Syria near the northern border of Lebanon. It is one of the world's finest surviving monuments of medieval military architecture. Originally a Saracen castle, the Krak (from the Levantine Arabic *Karak*, meaning "fortress") was garrisoned by Kurds in 1031. In 1110, Crusaders took over the site, making it part of a chain of fortresses protecting approaches to their County of Tripoli. The HOSPITALERS manned the Krak from 1142 until its capture by the Mameluke sultan Baybars I in 1271.

Krak stands on a mountain spur with ravines on three sides. Its defenses consist of a walled lower suburb and two lines of walls with open wards between them. Gigantic taluses make it an artificial mountain, with walls faced with bossed masonry blocks. Rounded towers provided flanking fire from loopholes. The main entrance is protected by a huge moat, drawbridge, and sloping covered passageway with portcullis. Inside are large vaults and the castle keep, in which is located the chamber of the Grand Master of the Order and a chapel with Gothic arched windows.   JEAN MACINTOSH TURFA

Bibliography: Boase, T. S. R., *Castles and Churches of the Crusading Kingdom* (1967); Fedden, Robin, and Thomson, John, *Crusader Castles*, 2d ed. (1957); Lawrence, T. E., *Crusader Castles*, 2 vols. (1936).

Krakatoa [krak-uh-toh'-uh]

Krakatoa is an active island volcano located in the Sunda Strait, south of Sumatra and west of Java, Indonesia. About 813 m (2,667 ft) above sea level at present, the cone is believed to have once reached 1,800 m (6,000 ft). The island is 3.2 km (2 mi) long and 6.5 km (4 mi) wide.

The earliest recorded eruptions on Krakatoa were in 1680–81. Activity next began on May 20, 1883, culminating in four gigantic explosions on August 27. The third of these was the most violent explosion on Earth in modern times. Heard as far away as Rodrigues Island, about 4,800 km (3,000 mi) away in the Indian Ocean, the eruption blew away the northern two-thirds of the island, produced tidal waves as high as 37 m (120 ft) that resulted in 36,000 deaths, and sent a dust cloud 80 km (50 mi) into the atmosphere. The cloud had encircled the Earth by September 9 and caused atmospheric effects for over a year. The amount of ejected material is estimated to have been 21 km³ (5 mi³); the total energy released was equivalent to 200 megatons of TNT. The size of the explosion was due to the collapse of the volcano walls and the steam produced when sea water rushed into the cone.

Bibliography: Furneaux, Rupert, *Krakatoa* (1964).

Kraków [krah'-koof]

Kraków (English: Cracow), the capital of the Polish province of the same name, lies on the Vistula River about 260 km (160 mi) south of Warsaw. With a population of 740,300 (1984 est.), it is Poland's third largest city.

The center of the old town is the large marketplace, with the impressive 13th-century Cloth Hall. The royal Wawel castle and a 14th-century Gothic cathedral are located on a rocky promontory close to the old town. Until 1764 the cathedral served as the coronation and burial place of the Polish kings.

Kraków is today an important industrial (chemicals and metallurgy) and trading center as well as a major railroad junction, but it is known primarily because of its prominent role in Polish history and cultural life. Between 1320 and 1609 the city was Poland's capital. In 1364 the prestigious Jagiellonian University, the second oldest university in central Europe, was established there. In 1794 the famous Polish revolutionary hero Tadeusz KOŚCIUSZKO led an uprising against the Russians who had occupied the city; this unsuccessful revolt led to the third partition of Poland (1795), in which Kraków was given to Austria. In 1815, Kraków and the surrounding territory became a free republic. As the only independent part of Poland, Kraków became the focus of Polish national aspirations, and its inhabitants took part in several Polish uprisings. In 1846, in order to put an end to this defiance, Austria, Prussia, and Russia decided that the Kraków free state should be incorporated into Austria. Following World War I, Kraków became part of the reconstituted Polish state.

EDWARD TABORSKY

Kramer, Jack

The American John Albert Kramer, b. Las Vegas, Nev., Aug. 1, 1921, was a tennis champion who, more than anyone else, through his play and promotion elevated the status of the professional game when it was unfashionable to do so. After winning at Wimbledon (1947) and Forest Hills (1946–47), Kramer successfully turned professional, witnessing the establishment (1968) of open play 10 years after retirement.

Krasner, Lee

The American painter Lee Krasner, b. Brooklyn, N.Y., Oct. 27, 1908, d. June 19, 1984, was a leading figure in ABSTRACT EXPRESSIONISM. Her chief contribution to post–World War II American painting was her distinctive use of surging, overlapping forms that charge the surfaces of her works with intimations of organic energy. Krasner was married (1945–56) to the abstract expressionist painter Jackson POLLOCK.   CARTER RATCLIFF

Bibliography: Baro, Gene, *Lee Krasner: Collages and Works on Paper 1933–1974* (1975); Friedman, B. H., *Lee Krasner: Paintings, Drawings and Collages* (1965); McKinney, D., *Lee Krasner: Recent Paintings* (1973); Rose, Barbara, *Lee Krasner: A Retrospective* (1983).

Krasnodar [kruhs'-nuh-dah]

Krasnodar, a town in the southwest of the Russian republic of the USSR, is situated on the north bank of the Kuban River, in the Northern Caucasus region. Its population is 595,000 (1983 est.). An important manufacturing center, the city has food-processing industries, textile, machinery, furniture, and garment factories, and an oil refinery. Kuban State University (1970) is there. Founded in the 1790s by Cossacks, the city was known until 1920 as Yekaterinodar, named for Empress Catherine II.   THEODORE SHABAD

Krasnoyarsk [kruhs-nuh-yarsk']

Krasnoyarsk is a city in Siberia, in the Russian republic of the USSR. The city's population is 872,000 (1985 est.). It is situated at the junction of the Trans-Siberian Railroad and the Yenisei River. One of Siberia's largest cities, Krasnoyarsk produces heavy mining equipment and truck trailers, synthetic rubber, chemicals, and tires, as well as aluminum. The Krasnoyarsk hydroelectric station, on the Yenisei, is one of the largest in the world. The city is the seat of Krasnoyarsk State University (1970).

Founded in 1628 as a fortified outpost during the Russian advance through Siberia, Krasnoyarsk became an administrative center in 1822. Its growth accelerated after 1895, when the railroad arrived, and again after World War II.

THEODORE SHABAD

Kraus, Karl

One of the most gifted and feared critics in Austria, Karl Kraus, b. Apr. 28, 1874, d. June 12, 1936, severely denounced the spoilers of language, whom he viewed as representative of the moral turpitude of his time. His famous satirical literary journal *Die Fackel* (The Torch), founded in 1899, included works by the finest German-speaking writers at the turn of the century; Kraus then wrote it entirely during 1911–36.

Sprüche und Widersprüche (*Sayings and Contradictions*, 1909) and *Nachts* (*In the Night*, 1919), collections of aphorisms, denounced the fashionable trends of his society. His magnum opus was a drama entitled *Die Letzten Tage der Menschheit* (*The Last Days of Mankind*, 1922), which portrayed the corruption in Europe through newspaper reports, expressionist images, and quotations and also prophesied another world war. The plays *Traumtheater* (Dreamtheater, 1932) and *Die Unüberwindlichen* (The Unconquerable Ones, 1928) criticized the craze for psychoanalysis in Vienna. His poetry, *Worte in Versen* (Words in Verses, 1916–30), adhered to his dicta of purity and ethics, as did his essays.   JACK ZIPES

Bibliography: Grimstad, Kari, *Masks of the Prophet: The Theatrical World of Karl Kraus* (1982); Iggers, Wilma, *Karl Kraus*, rev. ed. (1967); Timms, Edward, *Karl Kraus: Apocalyptic Satirist* (1986); Zohn, Harry, *Karl Kraus* (1971; repr. 1982).

Krebs, Sir Hans Adolf   [krebz]

Sir Hans Adolf Krebs, b. Aug. 25, 1900, d. Nov. 22, 1981, a German-British biochemist, discovered the citric acid cycle in sugar metabolism, sharing a part of the 1953 Nobel Prize for physiology or medicine for his work. In 1932, Krebs discovered how urea is formed in the liver; four years later he elucidated the steps involved in converting foodstuffs, chiefly carbohydrates, into usable energy. These steps, known as the citric acid cycle, or Krebs cycle, are essential to metabolism. Krebs became professor of biochemistry at Oxford University in 1954 and was knighted in 1958.

Krebs cycle

The Krebs cycle (also known as the citric acid cycle) is a series of chemical reactions in cells for the oxidation of carbohydrate, fat, and protein. It is named for the biochemist Sir Hans Adolf Krebs. The net effect of the Krebs cycle is to remove energy bit by bit from cellular fuels by a series of chemical reactions. Energy is withdrawn at several steps and stored in chemical form in adenosine triphosphate (ATP), the chief storehouse of energy in all organisms.

As a result of oxidation reactions in the cycle, carbon-carbon bonds in fuel molecules are broken, and the energy that held the carbon atoms together is released. Fuel molecules—the carbohydrates, fats, and proteins in foodstuffs—are not fed directly into the Krebs cycle, however. They are first broken down to acetyl coenzyme A, which enters at the start of the cycle and, after reaction with oxaloacetic acid, is progressively transformed into CITRIC ACID (containing 6 carbons), ketoglutaric acid (5 carbons), succinic acid (4), and oxaloacetic acid (4). The starting product, acetyl coenzyme A, reenters the cycle and reacts with oxaloacetic acid, and the cycle "turns" again.

See also: ATP; BIOCHEMISTRY; METABOLISM.

Krefeld   [kray'-felt]

Krefeld is a city in northwestern Germany in the state of North Rhine–Westphalia; the city has a population of 216,598 (1987 est.). When Uerdingen and several other nearby towns were annexed to Krefeld during the early 20th century, the city gained access to the Rhine River, about 8 km (5 mi) to the east. Until 1940 it was known as Krefeld-Uerdingen am Rhein. Noted for the production of silks and velvets, it maintains a textile school and textile museum. Other manufactures include steel, boilers, chemicals, rugs, clothing, and dyes. Chartered in 1373, Krefeld passed to Prussia in 1702. The city was heavily damaged during World War II.

Kreisky, Bruno   [kry'-skee, broo'-noh]

Bruno Kreisky, b. Jan. 22, 1911, d. July 29, 1990, was chancellor of Austria from 1970 to 1983, remaining in office longer than any of his predecessors in the postwar period. A socialist and a Jew, Kreisky fled to Sweden when Austria was annexed by Nazi Germany in 1938. Returning after the war, he helped negotiate (1955) Austrian independence and neutrality, was elected to the Nationalrat (parliament) in 1956, and served as foreign minister from 1959 to 1966. As chancellor he took a prominent part in international affairs, particularly as an advocate of compromise in the Arab-Israeli conflict.

Kreisler, Fritz   [kry'-slur]

Fritz Kreisler, b. Feb. 2, 1875, d. Jan. 29, 1962, was a celebrated Austrian violinist whose compositions for his instrument became popular showpieces for violin virtuosos. He entered the conservatory in Vienna at age 7 and won the gold medal at age 10. He subsequently studied in Paris with Lambert Joseph Massart (violin) and Léo Delibes (composition), made his American debut in New York in 1888, and enjoyed a successful career. For a decade (1889–99) he retired from music to study medicine and art. He also served for a time in the Austrian army. When he resumed his musical career he met with greater acclaim than ever, toured extensively, and settled (1940) in the United States, where he became a citizen in 1943. His best-known compositions include "Caprice Viennois," "Liebesfreud," and "Schön Rosmarin" for violin and two operettas. He published his reminiscences of World War I, *Four Weeks in the Trenches: The War Story of a Violinist* (1915).   KAREN MONSON

Bibliography: Lochner, Louis P., *Fritz Kreisler* (1951; repr. 1988).

Kremlin   [krem'-lin]

The Kremlin of Moscow, a triangular walled enclave situated on the Moskva River, contains the offices of the government of the Soviet Union. The complex of ornate cathedrals and palaces, which was originally constructed as a citadel, housed the royal court of Russian tsars until the capital was removed to Saint Petersburg in 1712.

In many old Russian cities, such as Novgorod, the fortified area, or kremlin (from the Russian *kreml,* meaning "fortress"), still stands; that of Moscow, occupying a hillside that abuts Red Square, is the largest and most famous. First mentioned in monastic chronicles in 1331, the Moscow Kremlin has served as a defense post, residence of monarchs and patriarchs, and seat of government. Its triangular area of 36.4 ha (90 acres) is enclosed by a 2.25-km-long (1.4-mi) brick wall built (1485–95) during the reign of Grand Duke IVAN III (r. 1462–1505); with the help of Italian architects, Ivan converted the Kremlin into the symbol of his power.

Within the walls the oldest ensemble is set around the Cathedral Square. The Assumption (Uspenski) Cathedral (1475–79), where rulers were crowned, was modeled on the Assumption Cathedral (1158–61) in the city of Vladimir. The private church of the tsars, the Annunciation (Blagoveshchenski) Cathedral (1484–89), was created by master builders from the city of Pskov. The architecture of the Archangel Cathedral (1505–08), however—burial place of the royal family until Tsar Peter I—first incorporated Italian decorative devices. Some original frescoes survive in the Assumption Cathedral, and the iconostases (altar screens) of all three display fine 15th-century icons. The Hall of the Facets (Granovitaya Palata, 1487–91), with a magnificent vaulted throne room, is the sole remnant of the Grand Ducal Palace. The 81-m (266-ft) Bell Tower of Ivan III completes the ensemble.

In the 17th century, when the Kremlin ceased being a fortress, its defense towers were capped with tentlike cupolas. Three residential buildings from this period survive, all fine examples of the heavily ornamental Moscow baroque style: the Terem Palace (1635–36), where the tsar held audiences; the Poteshnyi Palace (1651–52), site of Russia's first theater; and the large Patriarch Palace (1642–56). Although Peter I (r. 1689–1725) moved the seat of government to the new city of Saint Petersburg (now Leningrad) in 1712, construction continued in the Moscow Kremlin. Added were such buildings as the stark Arsenal (1702–36); the neoclassical Senate (1776–87), which now houses the Council of Ministers; the Great Kremlin Palace (1839–49), with large reception halls and private chambers for the imperial family; and the new Armory (1844–51).

After the Bolshevik Revolution the capital was moved back (1918) to Moscow, and the Soviet government was centered in the Kremlin. Lenin's apartment and office are preserved in the Senate building. Many smaller structures were razed; architectural and artistic treasures were restored to their original design and splendor. Only two new buildings were added in the 20th century: the Presidium of the Supreme Soviet (1932–34) and the Palace of the Congresses (1959–61). After Stalin's death (1953) the grounds of the Kremlin were opened to the public. The major churches are now museums of medieval art, and the new Armory displays rich collections of weapons, costumes, silver, and state regalia dating from the 12th century. ELIZABETH KRIDL VALKENIER

Bibliography: Burian, Jiri, and Shvidkovsky, Oleg A., *The Kremlin of Moscow*, trans. by Greta Mǎsková (1975); Duncan, David Douglas, *Great Treasures of the Kremlin* (1968); Meares, Bernard, trans., *Around the Kremlin* (1967); Voyce, Arthur, *The Moscow Kremlin, Its History, Architecture and Art Treasures* (1954).

Krenek, Ernst   [kren'-ek]

Twentieth-century European music is reflected in microcosm in the works of the Austrian composer Ernst Krenek, b. Aug. 23, 1900. He studied (1916–23) with Franz Schreker. The success of Krenek's jazz-influenced opera, *Jonny spielt auf* (Johnny Strikes Up; 1925–26), brought him international recognition: it was translated into at least 18 languages and performed in more than 100 cities. Krenek emigrated to the United States in 1937, and after teaching at Vassar College (1939–42) in Poughkeepsie, N.Y., and Hamline University (1942–47) in Saint Paul, Minn., he settled in California, having become a U.S. citizen in 1945.

Krenek's compositional style has varied greatly. He wrote dissonant, atonal music from 1921 to 1923. During the next few years he absorbed neoclassic influences, and from 1926 to 1931 he incorporated jazz and an almost Schubertian romanticism into his work. Since 1931 he has been composing in the twelve-tone and other serial techniques that he learned from Arnold Schoenberg and his school. He has also experimented with tape and electronic music. Krenek's orchestral compositions include five symphonies and four piano concertos; outstanding among his many choral works is the impressive *Lamentations of Jeremiah* (1941–42); *Karl V* (first performed in 1938) ranks high among his operas; his chamber music includes eight string quartets.

Bibliography: Krenek, Ernst, *Horizons Circled (1974)* and *Music Here and Now*, trans. by Barthold Fles (1939; repr. 1967); Stuckenschmidt, H. H., *Twentieth Century Composers: Germany and Central Europe* (1970).

krennerite   [kren'-ur-ite]

The gold TELLURIDE MINERAL krennerite ($AuTe_2$) has the same chemical composition, occurrences, and associations as the more abundant tellurides CALAVERITE and SYLVANITE; it has, however, orthorhombic rather than monoclinic symmetry. Krennerite is brittle and silver white to pale yellow. Hardness is 2–3, luster is metallic, and specific gravity is 8.6. Silver is a frequent impurity.

Kresge Foundation   [krez'-gee]

The Kresge Foundation, in Troy, Mich., was established in 1924 by Sebastian S. Kresge as a general-purpose charitable foundation. Its chief activities have been providing grants for major capital equipment, construction, and renovation to educational, medical, and artistic institutions. In 1978 it had assets of $586,902,197 and made 219 grants totaling $28,667,585.

Kress, Samuel H.

Samuel Henry Kress, b. Cherryville, Pa., July 23, 1863, d. Sept. 22, 1955, founded one of the most successful retail chains in the United States. Having observed the success of F. W. Woolworth (see WOOLWORTH family), Kress decided in 1896 to start a similar chain of stores in the South. He opened the "S. H. Kress and Co. 5, 10, & 25 cent store" in Memphis,

Tenn., and by 1900 the company had 12 such stores. When Kress died in 1955, the number had risen to 264. An avid collector, Kress amassed art masterpieces of the Middle Ages and Italian Renaissance, most of which he donated to museums, particularly the National Gallery of Art in Washington, D.C., whose president he became in 1945.

Kreutzer, Rodolphe   [krut-sair', roh-dohlf']

Rodolphe Kreutzer, b. Nov. 16, 1766, d. Jan. 6, 1831, was a French violinist and composer of German parentage. After his debut at the age of 13, he played in various Paris opera houses. He was appointed solo violinist (1801) and principal conductor (1817) of the Paris Opéra. He composed more than 40 operas, most of them performed in Paris, but none entered the permanent repertoire. His most enduring contribution was the *Forty Études* for unaccompanied violin, a mainstay of violin instruction. Kreutzer is the dedicatee of Beethoven's sonata, opus 47, for violin and piano, the so-called Kreutzer Sonata. HOMER ULRICH

Bibliography: Chapin, Victor, *The Violin and Its Masters* (1969).

Krieghoff, Cornelius   [kreeg'-hahf, kor-neel'-ee-uhs]

The Dutch-born Canadian painter Cornelius Krieghoff, b. Amsterdam, June 19, 1815, d. Mar. 8, 1872, specialized in small genre works reminiscent of the 17th-century Dutch tradition that depicted the life of the Quebec habitant, for example, *The Habitant Farm* (1856; National Gallery of Canada, Ottawa). After 1840, Krieghoff worked in Toronto; in Longueuil, Quebec; and in Quebec City. His precisely rendered canvases were popular as souvenirs. During his travels Krieghoff also executed dramatic, richly colored autumn and winter landscapes. DAVID WISTOW

Bibliography: Harper, Russell, *The Habitant* (1977); Jouvancourt, Hugues de, *Cornelius Krieghoff*, trans. by Nancy Côté (1971).

krill

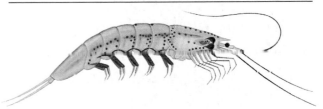

The krill, Euphausia similis, *a small, shrimplike marine crustacean, lives in the sub-Antarctic oceans. It comprises the diet of baleen whales.*

Shrimplike marine crustaceans of the order Euphausiacea, krill comprise about 90 species; more particularly, the term *krill* refers to species of the genera *Euphausia, Thysanoessa,* and *Meganyctiphanes,* which constitute major elements in the diets of certain whales. Krill range from 8 to 80 mm (0.3 to 3 in) in length and are pelagic, inhabiting open seas from the surface to depths of about 2,000 m (6,500 ft). The krill's body is divided into a head, thorax, and abdomen, and, characteristically, the head and thorax are covered by a shallow, shieldlike carapace that does not enclose the featherlike gills protruding beneath it. None of the thoracic legs are modified into maxillipeds (chewing mouthparts), as in lobsters; instead, these legs commonly bear long, hairlike setae, which are used to strain the krill's food of microplankton from the water. *E. superba,* the common krill of the southern polar seas, feeds largely on tiny diatoms (algae).

Some species of krill live in huge swarms. Heavy concentrations may contain as many as 63,000 individuals per cubic m (48,000 per cubic yd), weighing a total of about 20 kg (34 lb). It is upon these heavy concentrations that whales feed, sometimes consuming 1,800 to 2,400 kg (4,000 to 6,000 lb) at one feeding.

Krill are generally luminescent, having photophores that produce a brilliant blue green light. Luminescence is thought to be used as a form of communication in swarming and re-production. During reproduction, eggs are typically freely re-leased into the sea. A female may lay as many as 11,000 eggs. Most krill reach maturity in one year, some in two years. In 1982 the Antarctic Treaty signers ratified the Maritime Living Resource Convention, which provides an ecological approach to the managment of krill fishing.   STEPHEN C. REINGOLD

Bibliography: Barnes, Robert D., *Invertebrate Zoology*, 4th ed. (1980); Hamner, William M., "Krill," *National Geographic*, May 1982.

Kripke, Saul

Saul Aaron Kripke, b. Bay Shore, N.Y., Nov. 13, 1940, a pro-fessor of philosophy at Princeton University, is a leading con-temporary analytic philosopher. He is particularly noted for his invention of "possible world semantics," a form of modal logic by which the "possible" or "necessary" truth of state-ments can be mathematically proved. He has also advanced a new theory of truth that attempts to avoid the problem of par-adox in truth statements. Kripke has made major contributions to set theory; he wrote *Naming and Necessity* (1980).

Krishna   [krish'-nuh]

Krishna, the eighth avatar (incarnation) of the Hindu god Vishnu, displays two distinct characters—one sensual, one wise and awe-inspiring. This Indian bronze statuette depicts the young Krishna as a cowherd playing the flute to amuse the cowmaidens. Krishna's youthful deeds are celebrated in India each spring during the Holi festival.

Perhaps the most popular god of Hinduism, Krishna is cele-brated in literature, art, music, and dance throughout India. He may be depicted as the blue, flute-playing beloved of the cowmaidens (gopis) of Brindaban, as a prince consorting with his lover Radha, or as a small child caught stealing butter. The basic source for this Krishna is the Puranas, especially the Bhagavata Purana. In Krishna the most sensitive sentiments of erotic love, yearning for salvation, elements of folk legends, and the tradition of Sanskrit literature are blended.

Connected in popular belief but of a quite different temper-ament is the Krishna of the BHAGAVAD GITA, an AVATAR (incar-nation) of VISHNU, who discourses to the hero Arjuna on the battlefield of Kurukshetra. Although this Krishna is the focus of a number of devotional cults (see BHAKTI), the spirit is one of the awesome might and all-encompassing nature of God, displayed to Arjuna in a dazzling vision by Krishna, and de-votion is taught as only one of three disciplines (the others are knowledge and nonattached action) leading to release.
KARL H. POTTER

Bibliography: Archer, William G., *The Loves of Krishna* (1957).

Krishna Menon, Vengalil Krishnan   [krish'-nuh men'-in, ven-gah'-leel krish'-nuhn]

Vengalil Krishnan Krishna Menon, b. May 3, 1897, d. Oct. 6, 1974, was the defense minister of India (1957–62) and a lead-ing exponent of his country's neutralist foreign policy. A British-educated friend of Prime Minister Jawaharlal NEHRU, he was India's high commissioner in London (1947–52) and then the chief Indian delegate at the United Nations (1952–62), where he was a vigorous spokesman for neutrality and a sharp critic of the United States. He became a minister of de-fense in 1957. Blame for India's crushing military setbacks during the 1962 border dispute with China was placed on Krishna Menon. Forced to resign from the cabinet in Novem-ber 1962, he was never again a major political figure.
MARCUS FRANDA AND VONETTA J. FRANDA

Bibliography: Brecher, Michael, *India and World Politics: Krishna Me-non's View of the World* (1968); George, T. J. S., *Krishna Menon* (1964).

Krishnamurti, Jiddu   [krish-nu-mur'-tee, yid'-oo]

Jiddu Krishnamurti, b. May 22, 1895, d. Feb. 17, 1986, was an Indian Hindu religious philosopher linked with the Theosoph-ical Society. Annie BESANT, a leader of the society, met Krish-namurti in 1909 and proclaimed him an incarnation of Mai-treya, the messianic Buddha. In 1911 he founded the World Order of the Star, based on the claim that he was Buddha re-incarnated. Although he dissolved this movement in 1929, fol-lowing a tour of the United States and England with Besant during which he repudiated her claim, Krishnamurti contin-ued to write and lecture on THEOSOPHY. He later settled (1969) in Ojai, Calif., where he directed the Krishnamurti Founda-tion. His writings include *The Urgency of Change* (1970) and *The Awakening of Intelligence* (1973).

Bibliography: Dhopeshwarkar, Atmaram D., *J. Krishnamurti and Awareness in Action* (1967); Lutyens, Mary, *Krishnamurti: The Years of Awakening* (1975) and *Krishnamurti: The Years of Fulfillment* (1983); Vas, L. S. R., *The Mind of Jiddu Krishnamurti* (1971).

Kristiansand   [kris-tyahn-sahn']

Kristiansand is a city in southern Norway, about 242 km (150 mi) southwest of Oslo. The population is 61,834 (1983). Situat-ed on the Skagerrak, an arm of the North Sea, at the mouth of the Otra River, it is a commercial and transportation center, with a busy port and rail and air connections. Industries in-clude shipbuilding, textile manufacturing, and wood and food processing. Kristiansand has many notable landmarks, includ-ing the Church of the Holy Trinity (1618–28) and the Lutheran cathedral (1685–87; rebuilt 1882–85).

Founded by King Christian IV of Denmark and Norway in 1641, Kristiansand was fortified in 1660 with the construction of a huge fortress (Christiansholm). In 1682 it was made a Lu-theran episcopal see. The city's growth was stimulated by the arrival of the railroad in the late 19th century.

Krivoi Rog   [kree-voy' rawk]

Krivoi Rog, which means "crooked ravine," is a city of Dne-propetrovsk oblast in the Ukrainian Soviet Socialist Republic of the USSR. It is situated on the Ingulets River, a tributary of the Dnepr. The city has a population of 680,000 (1984 est.). Krivoi Rog is the center of the USSR's largest iron-ore mining region, accounting for more than half of the nation's ore pro-duction. Iron ore is mined both underground and, since the 1950s, increasingly in huge open pits. A small steel plant dat-ing from the 1930s was greatly expanded in the 1960s and has become one of the nation's largest. Much of the ore is shipped to the DONETS BASIN. The city was founded by Zapo-rozhye Cossacks in the 17th century.   THEODORE SHABAD

Kroeber, Alfred L.   [kroh'-bur]

Alfred Louis Kroeber, b. Hoboken, N.J., June 11, 1876, d. Oct. 5, 1960, is generally considered the most influential American anthropologist after Franz BOAS, one of his teachers. During his tenure (1901–46) at the University of California at Berke-ley, he advanced the study of California Indians and devel-oped important theories about the nature of culture. A major figure in the emergence of anthropology as an academic discipline, he held that human culture could not be entirely explained by psychology, biology, or related sciences. Kroeber was immensely prolific, publishing continuously until the time of his death, in Paris at the age of 85. His major works include *Anthropology* (1923; rev. ed. 1948); *Handbook of the Indians of California* (1925); *Configurations of Culture Growth* (1944); *Culture; a Critical Review of Concepts and Definitions* (1952), coauthored with Clyde Kluckhohn; and *Style and Civilizations* (1957). STEPHEN KOWALEWSKI

Bibliography: Driver, Harold, *The Contribution of A. L. Kroeber to Culture Area Theory and Practice* (1962); Kroeber, Theodora, *Alfred Kroeber: A Personal Configuration* (1970); Steward, J. H., *Alfred Kroeber* (1973).

Kromdraai: see STERKFONTEIN.

Kronos: see CRONUS.

Kropotkin, Pyotr Alekseyevich [kruh-poht'-kin, pyoh'-tur uhl-yik-syay'-eh-vich]

Pyotr Kropotkin, a leading anarchist speaker and theorist, was born to a noble Russian family and served for a year as page to Tsar Alexander II. Arrested in 1874 for his libertarian beliefs, Kropotkin escaped and lived in England for 30 years. His writings had considerable impact on anarchist movements in England and Russia.

Prince Pyotr Alekseyevich Kropotkin, b. Moscow, Dec. 21 (N.S.), 1842, d. Feb. 8, 1921, was a Russian political philosopher and anarchist whose work inspired European anarchist groups in the late 19th century (see ANARCHISM). Kropotkin's early writing was on scientific subjects. From his study of zoology he developed a theory of mutual cooperation that was set forth in *Mutual Aid* (1902). According to Kropotkin, cooperation, not competition, leads to evolution in the higher species. On the basis of this belief Kropotkin attacked Social Darwinism and developed a theory of nonviolent anarchistic social organization. Exiled from Russia in 1876 because of his political views, he lived in France, where he was imprisoned (1883–86), and then in England (1886–1917). Kropotkin returned to Russia at the beginning of the Russian Revolution (1917) but he was soon disillusioned with the authoritarian Bolshevik regime.

Bibliography: Avrich, Paul, *The Russian Anarchists* (1967), and *The Anarchists in the Russian Revolution* (1973); Kropotkin, Pyotr, *Memoirs of a Revolutionary* (1899; repr. 1968); Miller, Martin A., *Kropotkin* (1976).

Kru

The Kru are a West African ethnic population occupying the southeast coastal area of Liberia. They are composed of about 20 subtribes and speak a Kwa-Kru language of the Niger-Congo family. Because of the continual migrations of tribal members to urban centers, population figures are difficult to determine but are estimated at about 50,000.

The Kru migrated to their present homeland from an area to the northwest during the 15th to the 17th century. A great seafaring people, they presently constitute the largest segment of the Port of Monrovia work force. Fishing dominates their subsistence activities, but the production of rice and cassava is also important. Their compact villages or towns are politically autonomous. The principal unit of social organization is the patrilineal clan built upon the small polygynous family. Nonhereditary chiefs are aided by a council of clan heads and titled officials. Since the 1920s, however, their traditional political organization has been increasingly supplanted by the national governmental administration. Although the Kru did not traditionally keep slaves, they are believed to have exported slaves from neighboring tribes during the slave trade era.

Belief in a supreme deity and in nature deities as well as ancestor worship characterize their religious system. They possess a rich oral literature that has produced thousands of folktales, proverbs, morality tales, and humorous stories. JAMES W. HERRICK

Bibliography: Schwab, George, *Tribes of the Liberian Hinterland* (1947; repr. 1968).

Kruger, Paul

The South African statesman Paul Kruger headed the Boer republic of the Transvaal in the confrontation with Great Britain that led to the SOUTH AFRICAN WAR. Born on Oct. 10, 1825, in Cape Colony, Stephanus Johannes Paulus Kruger moved north with his family on the GREAT TREK (1835, 1840) and settled in the Transvaal. A stern Calvinist, he entered public life, becoming commandant-general of the Transvaal in 1863. In 1877, when the country was temporarily annexed by Britain, Kruger accepted office under the new government, but he was dismissed in 1878. The Transvaal regained its independence after a brief war in 1880–81, and, in 1883, Kruger became president of the republic.

During Kruger's term of office the Transvaal underwent far-reaching changes as a result of the discovery of gold at the Witwatersrand (1886). Kruger welcomed European, especially British, immigrants to develop the mines, but he refused to grant political rights to these so-called *uitlanders* (foreigners). His anti-British sentiments were intensified by the unofficial British raid launched against the Transvaal by Leander Starr JAMESON in 1895.

Faced with far-reaching British demands on behalf of the *uitlanders,* Kruger became convinced that war with Britain was inevitable. In 1899 he struck the first blow in the South African War by invading the Cape Colony and Natal. When the fortunes of war turned against him, Kruger went to Europe in 1900 in an unsuccessful effort to secure foreign aid. He died in Switzerland on July 14, 1904. L. H. GANN

Bibliography: Juta, Marjorie, *The Pace of the Ox: A Life of Paul Kruger,* rev. ed. (1975); Kruger, Paul, *The Memoirs of Paul Kruger* (1902; repr. 1969); Meintjes, Johannes Stephanus, *The Fall of Kruger's Republic* (1961) and *President Paul Kruger* (1974); Nathan, Manfred, *Paul Kruger: His Life and Times,* 5th ed. (1946).

krummhorn [krum'-horn]

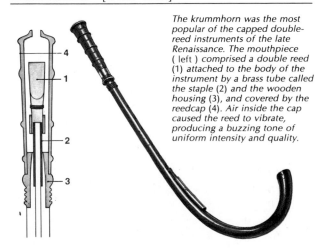

The krummhorn was the most popular of the capped double-reed instruments of the late Renaissance. The mouthpiece (left) comprised a double reed (1) attached to the body of the instrument by a brass tube called the staple (2) and the wooden housing (3), and covered by the reedcap (4). Air inside the cap caused the reed to vibrate, producing a buzzing tone of uniform intensity and quality.

The krummhorns (English, crumhorn; also known by various regional names) were a family of woodwinds bent at the lower end like a fishhook that were popular in the 16th and 17th centuries. A double reed was enclosed by a wooden cap with a hole into which the player blew as on a recorder, the player's lips never touching the reed; the fingering also is similar to that of the recorder. Krummhorns accompanied shawms, trombones, and viols in secular and religious music.

ELWYN A. WIENANDT

Bibliography: Baines, Anthony, *Woodwind Instruments and Their History*, rev. ed. (1963).

Krupa, Gene

The most famous drummer of the SWING era, Gene Krupa, b. Chicago, Jan. 15, 1909, d. Oct. 16, 1973, achieved international celebrity as a drum virtuoso with Benny GOODMAN's band during the 1930s. Krupa was the first who dared to use the base drum on recordings in the 1920s. He formed his own band in 1938 but continued to perform occasionally with other jazz groups, including those of Goodman and Tommy Dorsey.

Krupp (family) [krup]

The Krupp family were German steel and armament manufacturers based in Essen. **Friedrich Krupp**, b. July 17, 1787, d. Oct. 8, 1826, is considered to have founded the family business, although his ancestors had been in the armaments and iron business since the 16th century. In 1810, Friedrich set up a forge in Essen and began experimenting in the production of cast steel. He subsequently turned out fine quality steel in a plant he built in 1818. The business expanded considerably under Friedrich's son **Alfred Krupp**, known as the "Cannon King," b. Apr. 26, 1812, d. July 14, 1887. An inventor and metallurgist, Alfred discovered how to cast steel in large masses. He sent a steel casting weighing over 2 tons to the Great Exhibition of 1851 in London. Although he manufactured a great variety of articles, he became famous mainly for his enormous siege guns, which were used in the Franco-Prussian War (1870–71). His son, **Friedrich Alfred Krupp**, b. Feb. 17, 1854, d. Nov. 22, 1902, focused on the financial side of the business and vastly increased the Krupp holdings. He acquired other steel works, coal and iron mines, shipyards, engine shops, and a fleet of steamships. After his death, management of the Krupp works was taken over by **Gustav Krupp von Bohlen und Halbach**, b. Aug. 7, 1870, d. Jan. 16, 1950, a Prussian diplomat who married Friedrich's daughter Bertha (for whom the large World War I artillery pieces called "Big Berthas" were named) and assumed the family name.

After Hitler's assumption of power in 1933, the Krupp works provided the foundation for German rearmament. During World War II the company employed a large number of slave laborers, including Jews and prisoners of war. Conditions in the camps where the workers were housed were terrible and the death rate high. The company also maintained a large fuse factory at the Auschwitz concentration camp in Poland, where, after being worked to exhaustion, prisoners were gassed. At the Nuremberg war crimes trials, Gustav was indicted as a major war criminal, but because of his failing health he was not tried. His son, **Alfried Krupp von Bohlen und Halbach**, b. Aug. 13, 1907, d. July 30, 1967, who had taken over the firm in 1943, was tried along with 11 leading members of the company. On July 31, 1948, he was sentenced to 12 years in prison and confiscation of all his property. He was released, following a general amnesty, on Feb. 3, 1951. His corporate property was returned to him, and he again took command of the Krupp works. By 1959 the company was acquiring new industries. In 1967, however, Alfried's son **Arndt von Bohlen und Halbach** (d. 1986) renounced his rights to the succession, and in 1968 the company became a corporation owned by the stockholding public.

Bibliography: Batty, Peter, *The House of Krupp* (1966); Manchester, William, *The Arms of Krupp, 1587–1968* (1968); Mühlen, Norbert, *The Incredible Krupps* (1959); Young, Gordon, *The Fall and Rise of Alfried Krupp* (1960).

Krupskaya, Nadezhda Konstantinovna [krup'-skuh-yuh, nuh-dezh'-duh kuhn-stahn-tee-noh'-vuh]

Nadezhda Konstantinovna Krupskaya, b. Feb. 26 (N.S.), 1869, d. Feb. 27, 1939, was a Russian revolutionary and the wife of Vladimir Ilich LENIN, whom she married in 1898. She helped organize the Bolshevik party and, after the party seized power (October 1917), held various posts in the education commissariat. When Lenin died (1924), Krupskaya presented to the Politburo his so-called Testament, in which he recommended the removal of Joseph STALIN from the party leadership. No action was taken, and Krupskaya lost all influence, although she continued to serve in the government.

Bibliography: McNeal, Robert H., *Bride of the Revolution* (1972).

Krusenstern, Adam Johann [krooz'-en-shtairn, ah'-dahm yoh'-hahn]

Adam Johann Krusenstern, b. Nov. 19 (N.S.), 1770, d. Aug. 24 (N.S.), 1846, commanded the first Russian expedition that sailed around the world. The voyage, which lasted from 1803 to 1806, took a westward course by way of Cape Horn, Japan, and the Cape of Good Hope. Krusenstern described the trip in *Voyage Round the World* (1809–13; Eng. trans., 1813).

Krutch, Joseph Wood [kruch]

A critic and teacher, Joseph Wood Krutch, b. Knoxville, Tenn., Nov. 25, 1893, d. May 22, 1970, was a prolific author of books on literature, society, science, and nature. From 1924 to 1952 he was an editor and drama critic for *The Nation* and also a professor at Columbia University. Among his best-known works are *Edgar Allan Poe: A Study in Genius* (1926), *The Modern Temper* (1929), and *The Measure of Man* (1954), which won the National Book Award in 1955. *More Lives than One* (1962) is his autobiography.

Krylov, Ivan Andreyevich [krih-lawf', ee-vahn' uhn-dray'-uh-vich]

Ivan Andreyevich Krylov, b. Feb. 13 (N.S.), 1769, d. Nov. 21 (N.S.), 1844, was Russia's greatest writer of fables. He began publishing them, together with translations of La Fontaine's fables, in 1809, and in 1843 nine volumes of the collected fables were in print. Touching almost every aspect of Russian life, as well as the universal human condition, they have remained popular in the USSR down to the present. Apart from fables, Krylov was also interested in the theater and wrote comic operas, comedies, and tragedies. The only play of his to achieve theatrical success, however, was *Modnaya lavka* (The Fashion Shop, 1806). Krylov's other outstanding literary enterprise was a satirical journal known as *Pochta dukhov* (The Spirit's Mail, 1789), which spared no institution of contemporary Russian society. Conceived in the same spirit was *Kaib* (1792), subtitled "An Eastern Tale," an allegory alluding to the autocracy of Catherine II.

HAROLD B. SEGEL

Bibliography: Stepanov, Nikolay, *Ivan Krylov* (1973).

krypton [krip'-tahn]

The chemical element krypton is the fourth member of the noble gases, group O of the periodic table. The word *krypton* is derived from the Greek *kryptos*, meaning "hidden." Krypton's symbol is Kr, its atomic number 36, and atomic weight 83.80. Krypton is a monatomic gas. Along with neon and xenon, it was discovered in 1898 by Sir William Ramsay and Morris W. Travers in the residue from the fractional distillation of liquid air. It is present in the Earth's atmosphere at concentrations of about 1 part per million by volume. Naturally occurring krypton is composed of six stable isotopes.

Krypton has a melting point of $-156.6°$ C, a boiling point of $-152.30°$ C, and a gas density of 3.733 g/l at $0°$ C. The electronic formula of krypton is argon-$3d^{10}4s^24p^6$. The element was originally believed to be truly inert, but a few compounds such as krypton difluoride, a hydrate, and clathrates have since been synthesized. The commercial separation of krypton from liquid air is the most difficult of the noble gas separations, and consequently the high cost of the gas has limited its uses. Its principal use is in filling various fluorescent and incandescent lighting devices.

Krypton is characterized spectroscopically by brilliant green and orange lines. In 1960 it was internationally agreed that the fundamental unit of length, the meter, should be redefined so that 1 meter equals 1,650,763.73 wavelengths of the orange-red line of ^{86}Kr. This definition replaced the former standard, the platinum-iridium alloy bar kept in Paris.

J. ALISTAIR KERR

Bibliography: Cotton, F. A., and Wilkinson, Geoffrey, *Basic Inorganic Chemistry* (1976); Holloway, J. H., *Noble Gas Chemistry* (1968); Porterfield, William W., *Inorganic Chemistry* (1984); Purcell, K. F., and Kotz, J. C., *An Introduction to Inorganic Chemistry* (1980).

Ku K'ai-chih   (Gu Kaizhi)   [goo' ky'-jre]

Ku K'ai-chih, AD 344–406, was the earliest recorded figure painter in China. His style of depicting figures, for which he is renowned, became a major source of the classical tradition of Chinese figure painting. Ku, who lived during a time of political turmoil, held various posts at court in Nanking. His contemporaries admired him for his talent as a painter and for his wit as a political figure. Ku was considered to be the first portrait artist to capture the spirit of his subject. His elegant, refined figures were drawn in fine, even lines, a style that profoundly influenced later Chinese painters. None of Ku's works survive, but the famous hand scroll *Admonitions of the Instructress to the Court Ladies* (British Museum, London) is a faithful copy of the original.   LOUISA SHEN TING

Bibliography: Acker, William, *Some T'ang and Pre-T'ang Texts on Chinese Painting,* vol. 2 (1974); Sirén, Osvald, *Chinese Painting: Leading Masters and Principles,* vol. 1 (1956).

Ku Klux Klan   [koo kluhks klan]

Members of the Ku Klux Klan, clad in their traditional white robes, parade through the streets of Washington, D.C., in 1925. The Klan, a secret terrorist society devoted to maintaining white supremacy, has undergone periodic declines and revivals since its inception in 1866.

The Ku Klux Klan is the name of two distinct groups of white racists in U.S. history. During the RECONSTRUCTION era, when the votes of newly enfranchised black Southerners put Republicans in power in the Southern states, white Southerners resorted to force to preserve white supremacy. From 1866 to 1872 they organized into secret societies that terrorized local white and black Republican leaders and blacks whose behavior violated old ideas of black subordination. Especially strong in Tennessee and North and South Carolina, many of these organizations coalesced under the largest, the Ku Klux Klan, which was for a time led by former Confederate general Nathan B. FORREST. Sworn to secrecy, its members wore white robes and masks and adopted the burning cross as their symbol. They were most active during election campaigns, when their nighttime rides to murder, rape, beat, and warn were designed to overcome Republican majorities in their states.

In most states Republican authorities were unable to suppress the violence, fearing that they would provoke outright race war if they sent their mostly black state militias against the Klan. In many areas Democratic law-enforcement officials were themselves Klan members or sympathizers. Even where local officers took action, Klan members sat on juries and acquitted accused night riders.

By 1871 the violence was so serious that Republicans in Congress gave President Ulysses S. Grant authority to use national troops to restore order in affected districts. Faced with trained soldiers empowered to arrest suspects and hold them without trial, the Klan collapsed with surprising swiftness. Although Southern whites resorted to violence to regain control of their states from 1874 to 1877, the Klan as an organization disappeared by the end of 1872.

In the 1870s most Americans repudiated the methods of the Ku Klux Klan, even Southerners agreeing that the organization had become out of control. However, at the turn of the century the story of the Klan was popularized in Thomas B. Dixon's *The Clansman* (1905) and D. W. GRIFFITH's powerful movie *The Birth of a Nation* (1915). This led to the establishment of a new Ku Klux Klan, which spread throughout the nation and preached anti-Catholic, anti-Jewish, antiblack, antisocialist, and anti-labor-union "Americanism." Often taking the law into their own hands, mobs of white-robed, white-hooded men punished "immorality" and terrorized "un-American" elements. At its height in the early 1920s, the Klan had over 2 million adherents and exercised great political power in many Southern, Western, and Midwestern states.

In many ways a response to the great changes taking place in American society in the post-World War I years, the Klan began to wane as people adjusted to the new environment in which they lived. By the 1930s it had lost nearly all of its power. Some remnants of the Klan continue to exist; there was a membership spurt in the South in response to the civil rights movement of the 1960s. The various independent Klan groups competing for publicity probably numbered fewer than 10,000 members by the late 1980s.   MICHAEL LES BENEDICT

Bibliography: Chalmers, David M., *Hooded Americanism: The First Century of the Ku Klux Klan, 1865–1965* (1965); Katz, William L., *The Invisible Empire: Impact of the Ku Klux Klan on History* (1986); Lowe, David, *KKK: The Invisible Empire* (1967); Rice, Arnold S., *The Ku Klux Klan in American Politics* (1962; repr. 1972); Sims, Patsy, *The Klan* (1978; repr. 1982).

Kuala Lumpur   [kwah'-luh lum-poor']

Kuala Lumpur, the capital city of Malaysia, is 40 km (25 mi) from the coast of the Malay peninsula. Its population of 1,103,200 (1985 est.) is about two-thirds Chinese; a large number of Indians also reside in the city.

Kuala Lumpur is located at the confluence of the Kelang and Gombak rivers. Its port city, Port Swettenham, is at the coast along the Strait of Malacca. The city is also served by rail and air. Due to its central location, Kuala Lumpur is the commercial and transportation center for the surrounding tin-mining and rubber-plantation region. Industries include iron, tin, rubber and food processing, and railroad equipment and cement manufacturing. Two universities are in the city. Notable landmarks include the National Mosque, Chinese temples, and many buildings built in a distinctive style combining British Victorian and Islamic elements.

Kuala Lumpur was settled in 1857 by Chinese tin miners and grew rapidly because of its location. It became the capital of Selangor state (1880), the capital of the British colony of the Federated Malay States (1896), the capital of the independent Malaya (1957), and the capital of Malaysia (1963). Kuala Lumpur was designated a separate federal territory in 1974; a new capital for Selangor was established (1977) at Shah Alam.

Kuan Han-ch'ing   (Guan Hanqing)   [gwahn' hahn ching]

One of China's earliest and most popular dramatists, Kuan Han-ch'ing, c.1220–c.1300, lived in north China when it was under Mongol rule. Though a member of the scholar-official class, he had close dealings with the professional stage and wrote many *tsa-chü*, or "variety plays," based on lyrics sung in a developed theatrical tradition.   GLEN DUDBRIDGE

Bibliography: Yang, Hsien-yi and Gladys, trans., *Selected Plays of Kuan Han-ch'ing* (1958).

Kubasov, Valery N.   [koob'-ah-sawf']

The Soviet cosmonaut Valery Nikolayevich Kubasov, b. Jan. 7, 1935, was a civilian engineer in the Soviet spacecraft design bureau when he was chosen (1966) to become a cosmonaut. He was the flight engineer of the SOYUZ 6 mission (Oct. 11–16, 1969), during which maneuvers were held with *Soyuz 7* and *Soyuz 8* (Oct. 12–17 and 13–18). He evidently trained for Salyut missions in 1971–73 but was switched to the APOLLO-SOYUZ TEST PROJECT; he made his second space flight on *Soyuz 19* (July 15–21, 1975), which linked up with an Apollo spacecraft. Kubasov's third flight was made aboard *Soyuz 36*, with Hungarian air force pilot Bavtalan Farkas. Launched on May 26, 1980, the craft linked up with SALYUT 6 and returned eight days later.   JAMES OBERG

Kubin, Alfred

The Austrian graphic artist, writer, and philosopher Alfred Kubin, b. Apr. 10, 1877, d. Aug. 20, 1959, was a member of the BLAUE REITER group. He began his career as a photographer's apprentice (1892–96) in Klagenfurt and then studied art (1898–1901) in Munich. After traveling for a time he joined Der Blaue Reiter in 1911. The visionary pessimism of his fertile imagination, charged with a strong sense of the macabre and burlesque, is recorded in numerous drawings, prints, and book illustrations, for which he won considerable acclaim, including a prize at the 1952 Venice Biennale and the International Prize for Drawing at the 1955 São Paolo Biennale.   STEPHANIE WINKELBAUER

Bibliography: Kubin, Alfred, "Alfred Kubin," *Art and Artists*, December 1970; Schmeid, Wieland, *Alfred Kubin*, trans. by Jean Steinberg (1969).

Kubitschek, Juscelino   [koo'-buh-chek, zhoo-suh-lee'-no]

Juscelino Kubitschek de Oliveira, b. Sept. 12, 1902, d. Aug. 22, 1976, was president of Brazil from 1956 to 1961 and the person chiefly responsible for the construction of BRASÍLIA, the country's new modern capital. One of his aims in pushing for the development of Brasília was to open up the interior of the country to development.

Trained as a doctor, Kubitschek entered politics in the 1930s and in the ensuing years held various elective offices. During his term as president he attempted to develop the country's industrial base and to increase food production. He also initiated public works projects to improve transportation.

Bibliography: Bourne, Richard, *Political Leaders of Latin America* (1970); Medaglia, Francisco, *Juscelino Kubitschek, President of Brazil: The Life of a Self-Made Man* (1959).

Kublai Khan, Mongol Emperor   [koob'-ly khan]

Kublai Khan, b. 1215, d. February 1294, grandson of the first great Mongol conqueror GENGHIS KHAN, established China's YÜAN dynasty and extended the empire of the MONGOLS to its widest dimensions. The fourth son of Genghis Khan's son Tolui, he was proclaimed great khan in 1260, but another six years passed before he consolidated his control over the eastern Mongol territories.

In 1279, Kublai Khan conquered the SUNG dynasty in southern China, and he subsequently directed military expeditions against Indochina, Burma, the island of Java, and Malacca (Melaka) on the western coast of the Malay Peninsula. Attempted invasions of Japan in 1274 and 1281 failed partly because of bad weather. Kublai made no efforts to extend his rule to the west into territory ruled by other descendants of Genghis Khan.

Kublai Khan moved his capital from Karakorum to Peking, where his lavish court was visited by Marco POLO and other

Kublai Khan, founder of the Mongol dynasty in China, receives the Venetian travelers Nicolò, Marco, and Maffeo Polo at his court in Peking. This illustration is taken from a 15th-century French edition of The Travels of Marco Polo. *(Bibliothèque Nationale, Paris.)*

Europeans. Although educated by Confucian scholars, he adopted Buddhism; he came to practice—and bequeathed to his successors—a type of Buddhism blended with traditional shamanism that was later known as Mongolian Lamaism.   RICHARD BUTWELL

Bibliography: Martin, Bernard, and Shui, Chien-tung, *Makers of China* (1972); Saunders, J. J., *History of the Mongol Conquests* (1971).

Kubrick, Stanley   [koob'-rik]

Stanley Kubrick, b. New York City, July 26, 1928, is an American film writer, director, and producer with a virtually legendary status as an idiosyncratic master. While working as a photojournalist for *Look* magazine, Kubrick made an inconspicuous entrance into filmmaking with a documentary short, *The Day of the Fight*. Other early films include *Fear and Desire* (1953) and *Killer's Kiss* (1955). With *The Killing* (1956), critics began to take notice of his taut, brilliant style and bleakly cynical outlook. *Paths of Glory* (1957) solidified his reputation as a filmmaker interested in depicting the individual at the mercy of a hostile world. In *Spartacus* (1960), Kub-

The American film director Stanley Kubrick directs the camera on the set of A Clockwork Orange *(1971). A still photographer for* Look *magazine before directing his first film—a 15-minute documentary entitled* The Day of the Fight—*at the age of 22, Kubrick has won critical acclaim for such films as* Paths of Glory *(1957),* Lolita *(1962),* Dr. Strangelove *(1963), and* 2001 *(1968).*

rick met the challenge of bringing a costume spectacle to the screen. *Lolita* (1962), based on the novel by Vladimir Nabokov, received mixed reviews. But *Dr. Strangelove, or How I Learned to Stop Worrying and Love the Bomb* (1964) was enthusiastically hailed for its black-comedy vision of atomic-age apocalypse. His *2001: A Space Odyssey* (1968) and *A Clockwork Orange* (1971), both made in England where Kubrick has worked since 1961, engendered critical controversy, but the former has now become accepted as a landmark in modern cinema. His later films are *Barry Lyndon* (1975), a visually arresting adaptation of a minor Thackeray novel; *The Shining* (1980), a domestic horror tale based on a Stephen King novel; and *Full Metal Jacket* (1987), about the Vietnam War.

WILLIAM S. PECHTER

Bibliography: Nelson, Thomas A., *Kubrick: Inside a Film Artist's Maze* (1982); Phillips, Gene, *Stanley Kubrick: A Film Odyssey* (1975); Walker, Alexander, *Stanley Kubrick Directs*, rev. ed. (1972).

kudzu

Kudzu, *Pueraria lobata* (formerly *P. thunbergiana*), of the pea family, Leguminosae, is a trailing or climbing, semiwoody vine with hairy stems and with leaves divided into three large, broadly oval leaflets, each up to 15 cm (6 in) long. Its fragrant flowers, which smell of grapes, are reddish purple with a yellow patch at the base of the uppermost petal and are borne in spikelike clusters (racemes) up to 30 cm (12 in) long. The fruit is a hairy pod, up to 10 cm (4 in) long, containing many seeds.

Kudzu is native to China and Japan, where it is cultivated for its edible roots and for its stem fibers, known as ko-hemp. It was introduced as an ornamental under its Japanese name into the southern United States during the 1870s; the related *P. tuberosa* and *P. phaseoloides* were introduced about 1911. Kudzu is now found as far north as Pennsylvania, but it rarely flowers north of Virginia. It is a rampant plant, growing as much as 30 cm (12 in) per day under ideal conditions, and may climb 18 m (60 ft) high, with a total length of 30 m (100 ft) and roots 3.5 m (12 ft) deep.

Kudzu is useful as forage and hay for livestock, for control of soil erosion, and for enriching the soil by adding nitrogen and leaf litter. It is, however, often considered a pest because it may completely cover trees and other objects with its rapid growth, and it is difficult to eradicate. EDWIN E. ROSENBLUM

Kuhn, Richard [koon, rik'-art]

The German chemist Richard Kuhn, b. Dec. 3, 1900, d. Aug. 1, 1967, was awarded the Nobel Prize for chemistry in 1938 for his investigation of the structure of vitamins and the cartenoids. He determined the structure of vitamin B (riboflavin) and vitamin B_6 (pyridoxine) and synthesized them. He also showed that ordinary carotene (isolated from carrots) consisted of three isomers and demonstrated a relationship between the cartenoids and vitamin A. In Kuhn's early studies, he synthesized diphenylpolyenes; his later work involved synthesizing pantothenic acid and ascorbic acid (vitamin C).

O. B. RAMSAY

Kuibyshev [koo'-ib-ih-shef]

Kuibyshev (also Kuybyshev) is the capital of Kuibyshev oblast in the western Russian republic of the USSR. It is situated along the left bank of the Volga River at the mouth of the Samara River. Kuibyshev has a population of 1,280,000 (1987 est.). A major river port, Kuibyshev is the largest city of the Volga River valley and an industrial and transportation center. Its diversified manufacturing industries produce equipment for the oil industry and for construction and ball-bearings. The southwest satellite city of Novokuibyshevsk (1983 est. pop., 109,000) is a major oil-refining and petrochemical center. The automotive and chemical center of Togliatti (1986 est. pop., 610,000) is to the northwest, near Zhigulevsk hydroelectric station, one of the largest in the USSR.

Kuibyshev, originally named Samara, was founded in 1586 as a Russian fortress guarding the eastern margins of the Rus-

sian state and the trade route along the Volga. In the mid-17th century it became a major flour-milling center. Modern industrial development and urban growth began during World War II. Kuibyshev was the temporary capital of the USSR from 1941 until 1943. It was renamed in 1935 for Valerian Kuibyshev, an expert on economic affairs. THEODORE SHABAD

Kuiper, Gerard [keh-oo'-pur, kay'-rard]

The Dutch-born American astronomer Gerard P. Kuiper, b. Dec. 7, 1905, d. Dec. 23, 1973, is best known for his study of the surface of the Moon. A graduate of the University of Leiden (1927, 1933), Kuiper went to the United States in 1933. He joined the faculty of the University of Chicago in 1936 and from 1947 to 1949 and again from 1957 to 1960 headed the university's YERKES OBSERVATORY and McDONALD OBSERVATORY. Kuiper also founded (1960) and directed the Lunar and Planetary Laboratory of the University of Arizona. He discovered a satellite of Uranus in 1948 and one of Neptune in 1949, found an atmosphere on Titan, and advanced theories of planetary formation.

STEVEN J. DICK

Bibliography: Abbott, David, ed., *The Biographical Dictionary of Scientists, Astronomers* (1984).

Kukenaam Falls [kur'-ken-ahm]

Kukenaam (Spanish: Cuquenán) Falls, on the Venezuela-Guyana border, are the second highest falls in South America. They spill 610 m (2,000 ft) down the sandstone face of Mount Kukenaam, a flat-topped 2,627-m (8,620-ft) mountain in the Guyana Highlands. The falls continue as the Kukenaam River, a tributary of the Caroni River in the Orinoco Basin.

Kula Ring [koo'-luh]

The Kula Ring is a route of ceremonial exchange established in southeastern Papua between the Trobriand Islanders and the Dobu-speaking people of the D'Entrecasteaux Islands. Two kinds of valuables symbolic of wealth and prestige—red-shell necklaces and white-shell armbands—were the customary Kula gifts passed in reciprocal exchange. The exchanges took place annually, with the objects circulating along a fixed trade route. The necklaces were passed clockwise from island to island, the armbands counterclockwise.

Much magic, ritual, and mythology were associated with the Kula, and great excitement attended the arrival and departure of the special canoe fleets bearing the Kula gifts. An interisland Kula expedition was both a collective ritual and a competitive undertaking, involving much organization and having political implications. All interisland trade was conducted under the auspices of the Kula exchange. Lifelong trade relationships were established between a man and his Kula partners. First studied by the anthropologist Bronislaw MALINOWSKI in the 1920s, the Kula exchange has declined somewhat in recent years with the introduction of a cash economy and other European influences.

RONALD M. BERNDT

Bibliography: Firth, Raymond W., ed., *Man and Culture* (1957); Harding, Thomas G., *Voyagers of the Vitiaz Strait* (1967); Malinowski, Bronislaw, *Argonauts of the Western Pacific* (1922; repr. 1984); Uberoi, J. P. Singh, *Politics of the Kula Ring* (1962); Weiner, Annette, *The Trobrianders of Papua New Guinea* (1987).

kulaks [koo-laks']

In Russian history the term *kulaks* was used to connote relatively prosperous peasants. After the 1917 Bolshevik Revolution the Soviet government regarded the kulaks as being more attached to private property and other attributes of capitalism than the peasantry as a whole. Under the NEW ECONOMIC POLICY (NEP) introduced in 1921, Soviet policy favored the kulaks for a time. Toward the end of the 1920s, however, the government placed increasing economic restrictions on them. In 1929, Soviet dictator Joseph STALIN launched a drive to "liquidate the kulaks as a class"—dekulakization—in order to collectivize agriculture. A kulak came to be defined as any peasant who opposed the system of socialism as defined by

Stalin. Many kulaks forcibly resisted collectivization; countless numbers burned crops and slaughtered livestock. It is estimated that by the mid-1930s more than 5 million peasant households had been eliminated. Many were sent to forced labor camps in Siberia, and famine caused many deaths.

Kulmbach, Hans von   [kulm'-bahk, hahns fuhn]

Hans von Kulmbach, 1480–1522, whose real name was Hans Süss, was a painter and graphic artist whose works reflect the influence of his mentor, Albrecht Dürer. After studying with Jacopo de' Barbari, Kulmbach became (c.1500) assistant to Dürer in Nuremberg. His masterpiece, the *Tucher Altarpiece* (1513; Saint Sebald Church, Nuremberg), contains many of Dürer's stylistic forms and ideas but lacks some of the power and scope of the great master's works. Some Kulmbach works were probably executed from Dürer designs, though revealing a more delicate style. Kulmbach was an outstanding colorist and a gifted and sensitive portraitist, as seen in *Margrave Casimir of Hohenzollern* (1511; Alte Pinakothek, Munich).

Bibliography: Cuttler, C. D., *Northern Painting from Pucelle to Breugel* (1968); von der Osten, G., and Vey, H., *Painting and Sculpture in Germany and the Netherlands, 1500–1600,* trans. by M. Hottinger (1969).

Kültepe   [kul-tuh-pay']

Kültepe, a tell (mound site) 20 km (12 mi) northeast of Kayseri in central Turkey, is identified as ancient Kanesh by texts from an adjacent Assyrian merchants' quarter (*karum*) of the early 2d millennium BC. Distinguishable solely by their cuneiform tablets and use of cylinder seals, these foreign merchants of Kanesh traded primarily in metals and textiles. The records from karum Kanesh, the principal colony within a larger network, provide invaluable data about the Old Assyrians and their Anatolian contemporaries; however, reasons for the karum's abandonment remain obscure. Systematic excavations conducted at Kültepe since 1948 have revealed mud-brick houses, graves, and shops in the karum, and deep deposits on the mound, the seat of the local ruler, with monumental buildings extending back into the 3d millennium BC. Artifacts from the site are displayed in the Archaeological Museum in Ankara, Turkey.   LOUISE ALPERS BORDAZ

Bibliography: Orlin, Louis L., *Assyrian Colonies in Cappadocia* (1970); Özgüç, Tahsin, "An Assyrian Trading Outpost," *Scientific American,* February 1963.

Kulturkampf   [kul-toor'-kahmpf]

The *Kulturkampf* ("cultural struggle") is the name given to the attempt by Otto von BISMARCK to subordinate the Roman Catholic church in Germany to the state. Fearing Catholic political influence, Bismarck imposed (1871–78) a series of restrictive laws on the church. They proved ineffective and after 1878, were rescinded or allowed to lapse.

Kumin, Maxine

American writer and teacher Maxine Winokur Kumin, b. Philadelphia, June 6, 1925, is best known for her poetry but writes novels, essays, and short stories as well. She has also authored twenty books for children, three of them with the poet Anne Sexton. *Up Country: Poems of New England* (1972) received the 1973 Pulitzer Prize for poetry. *Our Ground Time Here Will Be Brief* (1982) is a collection of new poems and others gathered from her six earlier books of verse. Kumin became poetry consultant to the Library of Congress in 1981.

kumquat   [kuhm'-kwaht]

The kumquat, genus *Fortunella* of the rue family, Rutaceae, is an evergreen shrub or tree belonging to the citrus group and native to eastern Asia and Malaysia. Its sweet-scented white flowers produce small, orange fruits, whose mildly acid-flavored pulp and rind are edible. Of the several kumquat varieties grown, the oval Nagami, *F. margarita,* is the most common. The Marumi, *F. japonica,* has acidic juice and a sweet rind. The egg-shaped Meiwa, *F. crassifolia,* is a sweet variety

The kumquat, genus Fortunella, *is a small Chinese evergreen of the citrus group. Both the rind and the pulp of its fruit can be eaten.*

that is cultivated in China.

The kumquat is the hardiest of the CITRUS FRUITS and is grown for its fruit and as an ornamental shrub in areas that may be too cold for oranges. The fruit is eaten fresh and is used as an ingredient in marmalades. Preserved in sugar syrup, it is a staple dessert in Chinese cookery.

Kun, Béla   [koon, bay'-lah]

Béla Kun, b. Feb. 20, 1886, d. Nov. 30, 1939, was one of the founders of the Hungarian Communist party and the de facto head of the short-lived Communist regime established in Hungary in 1919. Having been converted to Bolshevism as a prisoner of war in Russia (1916–18) during World War I, Kun returned to Hungary as an agitator. On the fall of the government of Count Mihály Károlyi, he became commissar for war and foreign affairs in the Communist administration established on Mar. 22, 1919. His radical reforms and repression of dissent created both internal and external antagonism. The regime fell on Aug. 1, 1919, when Romanian troops occupied Budapest. Kun went eventually to Moscow, where he was a leader of the Comintern. Arrested (1936) during the Stalinist purges, he died in prison.   S. B. VARDY

Bibliography: Tõakés, R. L., *Béla Kun and the Hungarian Soviet Republic* (1967); Völgyes, I., ed., *Hungary in Revolution 1918–19* (1971).

K'un-ming   (Kunming)   [kwen ming]

A city in southwestern China on the northern shore of Tien Ch'ih, K'un-ming is the capital of Yünnan province; it has a population of 1,990,603 (1982). An important transportation and industrial center, it has iron and steel mills and industries producing textiles, chemicals, and machinery. K'un-ming is the site of China's major copper-smelting operations. Educational institutions include Yünnan University (1923).

Although K'un-ming is an ancient city, its modern development began with the completion of the railroad to Indochina (1910). Refugees from Japanese-occupied China moved their industries there during World War II. It was the eastern terminus of the Burma Road.

Kundera, Milan   (kun'-duh-ruh)

The Czech writer Milan Kundera, b. Apr. 1, 1929, has lived in France since 1975, persuaded to self-exile by the censoring or suppression of his work by the government of his native country. Kundera has long denied any political motivation in his writings, however. His work is always humorous, skeptical, and fundamentally pessimistic in describing the universal human condition, whether under Communism or elsewhere. *The Book of Laughter and Forgetting* (1979; Eng. trans., 1980) is Kundera's most celebrated novel. Other highly regarded works include *The Joke* (1967; Eng. trans., 1982); *Laughable Loves,* a collection of short stories originally published in the 1960s (Eng. trans., 1974); *Life Is Elsewhere* (1969; Eng. trans., 1974); and *The Unbearable Lightness of Being* (1984; Eng. trans., 1984).

Küng, Hans [koong, hahns]

Hans Küng, b. Mar. 19, 1928, is a Swiss Roman Catholic theologian who has been censured by The Vatican. Director of the Institute of Ecumenical Research at the University of Tübingen, he first gained international attention with the publication of his doctoral dissertation, showing the convergence in thought between Protestant theologian Karl BARTH and the Council of Trent (see TRENT, COUNCIL OF) on the central Reformation issue of justification by faith. Küng made his greatest impact upon the Roman Catholic church through the publication of his *The Council, Reform and Reunion* (1960; trans. 1961) on the eve of the Second Vatican Council. His later works include *The Church* (1967), *Infallible? An Inquiry* (1971), *On Being a Christian* (1976), and *Does God Exist?* (1980). At the insistence of Pope John Paul II, who objected to his questioning of basic Catholic doctrines, Küng was dismissed from Tübingen's faculty of Catholic theology in 1979.

RICHARD P. MCBRIEN

kung fu: see MARTIAL ARTS.

Kunitz, Stanley J. [kyoo'-nits]

The American poet, scholar, and critic Stanley Jasspon Kunitz, b. Worcester, Mass., July 29, 1905, published his first book of poems, *Intellectual Things,* in 1930. He has compiled biographical dictionaries of English and American writers, served as editor of the Yale Series of Younger Poets, and collaborated with Max Hayward on translations of the works of the Russian poets Anna Akhmatova and Andrei Voznesensky. Kunitz's *Selected Poems 1928–58* won the Pulitzer Prize for poetry in 1959.

Kuniyoshi [kun-ee-yoh'-shee]

The Japanese painter and printmaker Utagawa Kuniyoshi, 1798–1861, has been hailed as the last great master of the Japanese color print to work in the tradition of the UKIYO-E printmaking style. After studying in Edo (modern Tokyo) under Katsukawa Shun'ei, he became a pupil of Utagawa Toyokuni and a member of the Utagawa school. Reappraised in recent years as an artist of great originality, he depicted a wide range of subjects, including atmospheric landscapes, actors, and animals, as well as heroic episodes from Japanese history. His taste tended toward the dramatic and bizarre, and his later works are extraordinarily complex. HOWARD A. LINK

Bibliography: Robinson, B. W., *Kuniyoshi* (1961).

Kuniyoshi, Yasuo [yah-soo-oh']

The Japanese-born painter Yasuo Kuniyoshi, b. Sept. 1, 1893 or 1889, d. May 14, 1953, settled in the United States in 1906 and became a major figure in his field during the 1930s and '40s. He studied at the Art Students League and later taught there for 20 years. His early paintings (1920s) were generally flattened, symbolic landscape fantasies containing animals and figures. During the 1930s he painted thickly impastoed still lifes and figures directly from life. His melancholy, reflective women, however, were meant to be universal symbols, not portraits.

Kuniyoshi was deeply affected by World War II; as a result, his paintings of the 1940s became ominous, surrealistic fantasies, peopled by grotesque, harshly modeled, and garishly colored carnival figures. He was the first living American artist to be given a retrospective exhibition (1948) at New York City's Whitney Museum. LISA M. MESSINGER

Bibliography: Goodrich, Lloyd, *Yasuo Kuniyoshi* (1969).

Kunlun Mountains [kwen lwen]

The Kunlun Mountains (K'un-lun Shan), the longest mountain chain in Asia, extend over 2,400 km (1,500 mi) between the HIMALAYAS to the south and the TIEN SHAN to the north. Their western edge is the PAMIRS, in the USSR; as they stretch eastward through Tibet to Tsinghai province, China (where they end), they become broader and higher. The highest peak, Ulugh Muztagh, which reaches 7,724 m (25,340 ft), is in Tibet.

Although the main system was formed about 230 million years ago, seismic activity is common. The extremely arid climate results in hot desert at low altitudes and cold desert in the higher altitudes. Melting snow and glaciers during the summer months feed several major rivers, among them the HWANG HO (Yellow River), the MEKONG, and the YANGTZE. The steep slopes, harsh environment, and high passes make access difficult, and the sparse population is concentrated in the river valleys.

Kunstler, William

The radical American lawyer William Moses Kunstler, b. New York City, July 7, 1919, is best known for his 1969–70 work in defending the "Chicago Seven," who were charged with conspiracy to incite a riot at the 1968 Democratic National Convention. Among other notable cases, Kunstler defended American Indian militants in the 1974 WOUNDED KNEE case and acted for the prisoner-defendants in the ATTICA PRISON RIOT trial (1975).

Kuo Hsi (Guo Xi) [gwoh see]

Kuo Hsi, c.1020–c.1100, was an influential landscape artist of the Northern Sung period (960–1127) in China. His style of painting was later classified as being one of the three founding schools of Chinese landscape painting. A pupil of Li Ch'eng, Kuo developed his own style in which he depicted the austere terrain of northern China. He was also an art theorist, stressing in his essays on landscape painting the need for the artist to study every aspect of nature. Kuo's large-scale hanging scroll, *Early Spring* (1072; National Palace Museum, Taipei) is regarded as a masterpiece of monumental landscape art. LOUISA SHEN TING

Bibliography: Sakanishi, Shio, *An Essay on Landscape Painting* (1935); Sirén, Osvald, *Chinese Painting: Leading Masters and Principles,* vol. 1 (1956).

Kuo Mo-jo (Guo Moruo) [kwoh moh-joh']

The Marxist intellectual Kuo Mo-jo, originally Kuo K'ai-chen, b. November 1892, d. June 12, 1978, was a major figure in Chinese culture. Founder (1921) of the Creation Society, a literary group that greatly influenced modern Chinese literature, Kuo himself wrote prolifically on a wide range of topics, establishing himself as China's most versatile intellectual. Portions of his 1921 poetry collection *Nü-shen* (The Goddesses) have been translated into English. In 1949 he became director of the Chinese Academy of Sciences, and in 1951 he was awarded the Stalin Peace Prize.

Bibliography: Průšek, Jaroslav, ed., *Studies in Modern Chinese Literature* (1964); Roy, David Tod, *Kuo Mo-jo: The Early Years* (1971).

Kuomintang (Guomindang) [kwoh'-min-tahng']

China's Kuomintang (Nationalist party) played an active political role on the Chinese mainland for more than three decades; since 1949 it has been the ruling party in Taiwan. Also known as the KMT, it was organized in 1912 by Sung Chiao-jen as the successor to the secret revolutionary league T'ung Meng Hui (Together-Sworn Society). The latter had been founded in 1905 by SUN YAT-SEN to overthrow the CH'ING (or Manchu) dynasty. Although Sun had been elected (1911) provisional president of the new Chinese republic, he reluctantly yielded the presidency to the north China military leader YÜAN SHIH-K'AI. Sun Yat-sen became director of the Kuomintang, which was organized as a political party advocating a system of parliamentary government. After the first KMT election victory, however, Yüan had Sung, who had engineered the victory, killed and all Kuomintang members, including Sun, expelled from the assembly. Many fled the country, and Yüan became virtual dictator by 1914.

Not until Yüan's death, in 1916, did the exiles dare to resume political leadership. Sun's Kuomintang government, which assumed control at Canton in 1917, accepted aid from Soviet advisors to help enlist mass support for the party. In 1923, Sun sent CHIANG KAI-SHEK to Moscow to study political organization and military training. In 1924 the Kuomintang party congress, which included Communists, accepted Sun's "Three Principles of the People": nationalism, democracy (realized in stages), and livelihood (guaranteed through collectivization of land and industry).

Such was the Kuomintang legacy when Sun died in 1925, leaving Chiang in control. At the completion of Chiang's NORTHERN EXPEDITION (1926) against the Peking warlords, he dismissed (1927) both the Russian advisors and the Chinese leftists, thus beginning a long civil war between the two Chinese factions. In 1928 the Kuomintang captured Peking and won diplomatic recognition for its government at Nanking. Chiang took on Shanghai business groups as allies and advocated the active pursuit of democracy and the revision of unequal treaties.

For a time, Chiang tolerated Japanese intervention to the north—until Kuomintang forces clashed with the Japanese, who had invaded China proper, at the Marco Polo Bridge in July 1937 (see SINO-JAPANESE WARS). The Kuomintang governed China throughout World War II, although it was greatly weakened militarily by campaigns against the Chinese Communists, who were able to establish strongholds in the north. After the war, Chiang's exhausted and demoralized Kuomintang was unable to maintain control. The Communists, now led by MAO TSE-TUNG, took over the mainland in 1949, and the exiled Kuomintang retreated to the island of Formosa (now Taiwan).   JOHN F. CADY

Bibliography: Hsieh Jan-chih, ed., *The Kuomintang* (1970); Yu, G. T., *Party Politics in Republican China: The Kuomintang, 1912–1924* (1966).

Sun Yat-sen, a Chinese scholar educated in Hawaii and England, returned to China in 1911 to become the leading figure of the republican revolution that deposed the Ch'ing dynasty in 1911–12. His political organization, the Kuomintang, which was dominated by Chiang Kai-shek after Sun Yat-sen's death in 1925, functioned as the legitimate government of China from 1926 to 1949.

Kupka, František   [kup'-kah]

The Czech painter František Kupka, b. Sept. 23, 1871, d. June 24, 1957, explored the psychological effects of abstract color and is credited with painting the first totally abstract work, *Fugue in Red and Blue* (1912; National Gallery, Prague). The painting is composed of concentric, rhythmical masses of color or that seem to emerge from one another and radiate isolated lines. After 1895, Kupka lived primarily in Paris, where he was greatly influenced by the ORPHISM of Robert Delaunay. He also drew cartoons for the current periodicals and illustrated several books. Kupka exhibited his *Diagrams and Whirling*

The Czech artist František Kupka, influenced by his experience of cubism in Paris and inspired by his interest in astronomy and the colors of the prism, produced one of the earliest abstract paintings, Fugue in Red and Blue, in 1912. (National Gallery, Prague.)

Arabesques paintings in 1924 and in 1936. This pioneer abstractionist was not widely recognized, however, before a 1946 retrospective exhibition in Czechoslovakia.
BARBARA CAVALIERE

Bibliography: Barr, Alfred, *Cubism and Abstract Art* (1966); Messer, Thomas M., et al., *František Kupka: 1871–1957* (1975); Seuphor, Michel, *Abstract Painting from Kandinsky to the Present* (1962).

Kuprin, Aleksandr Ivanovich   [koop'-rin, uhl-yik-sahn'-dur ee-vahn'-uh-vich]

Aleksandr Ivanovich Kuprin, b. Sept. 7 (N.S.), 1870, d. Aug. 25, 1938, was a Russian writer, sometimes referred to as the Russian Kipling. He was educated in military schools and served in the army for several years before committing himself to literature. He is best known for his novel *The Duel* (1905; Eng. trans., 1916), portraying the senselessness of army life in starkly realistic detail. His other novel, *Yama: The Pit* (1924; Eng. trans., 1927), is an exposé of prostitution that suggests its affinities with bourgeois life-styles. Kuprin emigrated after the Bolshevik Revolution and lived in Paris until 1937, when he returned to the Soviet Union.

Bibliography: Luker, N. J. L., *Alexander Kuprin* (1978).

Kurdistan   [kur'-dis-tahn]

Kurdistan, which means "land of the Kurds," is a large, mountainous plateau region encompassing parts of eastern Turkey, northern Iraq, northwestern Iran, and areas of Syria and Soviet Azerbaijan. The area measures about 720 km (450 mi) from north to south and 600 km (375 mi) from east to west at the broadest part. The region is bounded by the ZAGROS

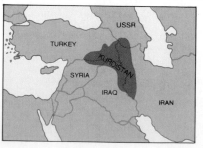

Kurdistan occupies portions of Turkey, Syria, Iraq, Iran, and the USSR. The Kurds, who are ethnically closest to the Iranians, traditionally are nomadic herders. Saladin, the great opponent of the Crusaders, was of Kurdish descent.

MOUNTAINS in Iran and Iraq and by the TAURUS MOUNTAINS in eastern Turkey. The TIGRIS and EUPHRATES rivers rise in eastern Kurdistan, as do many other smaller rivers and streams. The average elevation is about 2,500 m (8,300 ft), but some peaks reach over 4,000 m (13,100 ft). The climate is extreme, with bitterly cold, harsh winters and hot, dry summers.

Kurds have lived in Kurdistan since about 2400 BC. Traditionally, the Kurds were nomads. In recent times, however, most of them have settled down because the separate governments have introduced sedentary agriculture and have forced Kurds to move their goat herds within national boundaries. Barley, wheat, cotton, corn, and fruits are grown in the lowlands.

Kurdistan (Kordestan) is also the name of a province in western Iran, with an area of 24,998 km^2 (9,652 mi^2), which lies mainly in the Zagros Mountains. The capital is Sanandaj. Most of the inhabitants of the province are Kurds.

Kurds   [kurdz]

Kurd is the ethnic name of a number of tribal groups inhabiting the mountainous border regions of southeast Turkey, northwest Iran, north Iraq, northeast Syria, and Soviet Azerbaijan. These tribes speak various dialects of Kurdish, an Indo-Iranian language. They call their rugged homeland Kurdistan. Most Kurds are Sunni Muslims of the Shafi rite; various heretical and mystical sects also exist locally. Physically, they resemble neighboring southwest Asian populations except that the Kurds tend to show a somewhat higher incidence of fair coloring. Although reliable statistics are lacking, their total population is estimated at 10 to 20 million, of which the greatest number are in Turkey, Iraq, and Iran.

Most Kurds are agricultural-village dwellers, cultivating wheat, barley, cotton, and fruit. Some live in nomadic communities that emphasize pastoralism, but such groups have dwindled since the closing of national frontiers and the Kurdish political struggles of the last several decades. The traditional Kurdish tribal system generally resembles that of the Arabic BEDOUIN in its emphasis on patrilineal genealogy and endogamous marriage, but it is marked by greater status differentiation of leaders.

Although the Kurds have never been united politically, Kurdish autonomy has had a long history. Kurd as a collective name was first applied to the tribal groups in the 7th century AD when the Arabs converted them to Islam. Three short-lived Kurdish dynasties with more than local power existed in the 10th to 12th centuries; the 12th-century Kurdish warrior SALADIN, a prominent foe of the Christian Crusaders, founded another dynasty that lasted into the 13th century. During succeeding centuries numerous Kurdish principalities vied for local power, showing little interest in achieving unity. Only in the late 19th and early 20th centuries did a nationalist movement emerge. With the breakup of the Ottoman Empire after World War I, Turkey agreed to the establishment of an independent Kurdistan under the Treaty of Sèvres (1920). This part of the treaty was never ratified, however, and the autonomy clause was completely eliminated from the Treaty of Lausanne (1923) through Turkish efforts under Kemal Ataturk.

Sporadic uprisings by Kurds occurred in Iraq (1922–24) and Turkey (1924). Since 1946 most nationalist activity has been in Iraq, where Kurds waged continuous guerrilla warfare (1961–70) and open rebellion (1974–75) against the Iraqi government. This movement collapsed when unofficial Iranian support was withdrawn after a 1975 Iran-Iraq border accord. In Iran, Kurds began pushing for cultural and political autonomy after the 1979 Islamic revolution. Iraqi Kurdish separatists later backed Iran in the GULF WAR. In 1988 the Iraqi government was accused of using chemical weapons against the Kurds, on whom it launched a major assault following the ceasefire in the Gulf war. More than 70,000 Iraqi Kurds fled to Turkey.

BRIAN SPOONER

Bibliography: Bois, Thomas, *The Kurds*, trans. by M. W. M. Willard (1966); Hassan, Arfa, *The Kurds* (1966); Kinnane, Derek, *The Kurds and Kurdistan* (1964); O'Ballance, Edgar, *The Kurdish Revolt: 1961–70* (1973); Pelletiere, S. C., *The Kurds* (1984).

Kuril Islands   [koo'-reel]

The Kuril (or Kurile) Islands, a chain of 30 major plus many smaller islands with a total land area of 15,600 km^2 (6,025 mi^2), extend 1,200 km (745 mi) from the KAMCHATKA PENINSULA, USSR, to Hokkaido, Japan. They are part of the Russian republic of the USSR. The chain separates the Pacific Ocean from the Sea of OKHOTSK. Most of the islands are of volcanic origin; 38 volcanoes are still active. Vegetation ranges from sparse tundra on the northern islands to forests and farmlands on the southern islands. The climate is cold and wet, averaging 4° C (40° F), with 900 mm (35 in) of precipitation. Fishing, sulfur mining, whaling, and hunting are the chief occupations. The principal town is Kurilsk, on Iturup, the largest island. Dutch sailors discovered the Kurils in 1634. Japan and Russia penetrated the islands in the 18th century, and both claimed them in the 19th century. Japan acquired them in 1875 in exchange for Sakhalin. After World War II they were occupied (1945) by the USSR in accordance with the Yalta agreement, but Soviet possession is disputed by Japan.

Kurosawa, Akira   [koo-roh'-sah-wah, ah-kee'-rah]

The most famous Japanese film director in the West, Akira Kurosawa, b. Mar. 23, 1910, first achieved international recognition with *Rashomon* (1950), a brilliant study of a crime of violence told from four different points of view. His reputation soared with a series of sword-fight epics set in feudal times: such movies as *The Seven Samurai* (1954) inspired a host of Western imitations. Kurosawa has been equally influenced by Western themes and has made screen adaptations of Dostoyevsky's *The Idiot* (1951), Gorky's *The Lower Depths* (1957), and two of Shakespeare's blackest dramas—Macbeth (*Throne of Blood,* 1957), and King Lear (*Ran,* 1986). These are cinematic spectaculars (Kurosawa built a $1.6-million castle for *Ran* and used 1,400 extras and 250 horses); yet, despite their overwhelming physical beauty and the monumental cruelty they display, they demonstrate compassion and an awareness of human nobility as well as its weakness. Two modest but moving Kurosawa films are his *Ikiru* (1952), about a lonely, dying old man; and *Derzu Uzala* (1975), a story set in Russian Siberia.

Bibliography: Kurosawa, A., *Something Like An Autobiography* (1982); Richie, D., *The Films of Akira Kurosawa,* rev. ed. (1984).

Kusch, Polykarp   [koosh, pahl'-ee-karp]

The German-born American physicist Polykarp Kusch, b. Jan. 26, 1911, shared the 1955 Nobel Prize for physics with Willis LAMB for work at Columbia University on precise determinations of the magnetic moment of the electron, using atomic beams of radio frequency. Kusch chaired the Department of Physics at Columbia (1949–52, 1960–63) and since 1972 has been at the University of Texas.

CARL ZAPFFE

Kutenai   [koot'-en-ay]

The Kutenai (or Kootenay, a Blackfoot term) are North American Indians who inhabited northwest Montana and British Columbia in the 18th century. Their own name is Sanka. Upper Kutenai occupied territory around the Columbia River headwaters and adopted Plains traits when ranging eastward to hunt bison; Lower Kutenai maintained a distinct Plateau culture centered on fishing the Lower Kootenay River. Both Upper and Lower Kutenai used digging sticks to gather bitter root and camas bulbs; nuts and berries, deer, elks, and fish supplemented their food supply. After obtaining horses both groups exploited seasonal bison herds. Because of resistance from other Plains bison hunters, the Kutenai formalized war honors and gloried in acts of bravery. Slavery was practiced following the introduction of war captives, but the traditional social organization remained simple. Northwest Coast and Plains cultures influenced the religion of the Kutenai, who adopted a modified form of the SUN DANCE ritual.

When first contacted by white traders in the early 1800s, the Kutenai were scattered widely across their territory. The white threat united them briefly, but a series of misunderstandings led to their dispersion. One band joined the FLATHEAD; others took a reservation in Idaho. The majority scattered into communities along the Kootenay River in British Columbia. Kutenai descendants in Canada are employed as ranchers, guides, and laborers. The enrolled population of the Kootenai Reservation in Idaho was 118 in 1987.

ERNEST L. SCHUSKY

Bibliography: Johnson, O. W., *Flathead and Kootenay* (1969); Turney-High, H. H., *Ethnography of the Kutenai* (1941; repr. 1974).

Kutuzov, Mikhail Illarionovich   [ku-too'-zuhf, mee-kuh-yeel' ee-luh-ryohn'-uh-vich]

Mikhail Illarionovich Kutuzov, b. Sept. 16 (N.S.), 1745, d. Apr. 16 (N.S.), 1813, was the Russian military commander who repulsed NAPOLEON I's invasion of Russia in 1812. After service in the Russo-Turkish Wars, he rose to prominence as the Russian commander against the French at the Battle of AUSTERLITZ in 1805; he advised a retreat but was overruled by Russian emperor ALEXANDER I and was badly defeated. Thereafter, Alexander I disliked Kutuzov. When Napoleon began his invasion in 1812, however, Alexander recalled Kutuzov and appointed him field marshal. After the Russian defeat at Borodino on Sept. 7 (N.S.), 1812, forced on him by the emperor's determination to fight, Kutuzov adopted his own tactics of retreat, evacuated Moscow, and saved his army. When Napoleon began his own retreat for lack of supplies, Kutuzov harried the French army out of Russia.

L. JAY OLIVA

Bibliography: Parkinson, Roger, *Fox of the North* (1976); Tarlé, Eugene, *Napoleon's Invasion of Russia* (1942).

See also: NAPOLEONIC WARS.

kuvasz   [kuv'-ahs]

The kuvasz, the most popular native breed in Hungary, is a shepherd, guard, and hunting dog. King Matthias I (r. 1458–90) raised dogs of this type and is said to have kept one near at all times as his bodyguard.

The kuvasz is a Hungarian working breed of dog that generally resembles the Great Pyrenees. Both breeds are large, white, and heavily coated and were originally used as guard dogs, especially of flocks of sheep. The kuvasz stands 76 cm (30 in) high at the shoulders and weighs up to 52 kg (115 lb), with females slightly smaller. It has a compact body, with a rather long head, close-hanging ears, and a long, thickly haired tail. Its coat is slightly wavy and reaches 13 cm (5 in) long. Although the kuvasz is Hungarian, its name is a corruption of Turkish and Arabic words for guardian, possibly reflecting an Asiatic origin for the breed.

JOHN MANDEVILLE

Bibliography: American Kennel Club, *The Complete Dog Book*, 17th ed. (1985).

Kuwait   (country)

Kuwait, an oil-rich Arab sheikhdom in the northeastern corner of the Arabian Peninsula at the head of the Persian Gulf, was independent from 1961 to Aug. 2, 1990, when it was occupied by Iraq. The world community condemned the Iraqi invasion and continued to recognize the exiled emir as Kuwait's legal ruler. The United States and other nations sent troops to neighboring Saudi Arabia, and an international embargo was imposed upon Iraq in an effort to force it to withdraw.

Kuwait is bordered on the north and west by Iraq, on the east by the Persian Gulf, and on the south by Saudi Arabia. It ranks fourth in proven oil reserves (after Saudi Arabia, the USSR, and Iraq) and was a founding member of the ORGANIZATION OF PETROLEUM EXPORTING COUNTRIES (OPEC). Its name is derived from *kut*, the Arabic word for fort. The capital, Kuwait, is located on an inlet of the Persian Gulf.

LAND AND PEOPLE

Kuwait is a virtually flat desert; the highest point in the country is a hill in the south rising to 299 m (981 ft). Of its few oases Al-Jahrah is the largest. Nine offshore islands are included in the national territory, but only one, Failaka, is inhabited. Most of the nation lies below an elevation of 200 m (656 ft). The red desert soils do not favor agriculture. The average daily temperature is 33° C (91° F), with maxima of 52° C (126° F). Rainfall ranges from 25 to 175 mm (1 to 7 in) annually, falling mostly in the winter months when cyclones occur. Fierce dust storms, called *kaus*, may last several days in winter. Most vegetation consists of low bushes and scrub; the marshy coastal areas support halophytic, or salt-loving, plants. Less than 9% of the land is arable, and most water is obtained through massive desalination efforts.

Kuwaiti society is composed of five strata: the ruling family, old Kuwaiti merchant families, former Bedouins who have become city dwellers, Arabs from other countries who have ob-

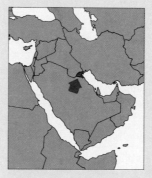

STATE OF KUWAIT

LAND. Area: 17,818 km² (6,880 mi²). Capital: Kuwait (1985 pop., 44,224). Largest city: al-Salimiya (1985 pop., 153,220).
PEOPLE. Population (1990 est.): 2,123,711; density: 119.2 persons per km² (308.7 per mi²). Distribution (1989): 94% urban, 6% rural. Annual growth (1990): 3.8%. Official language: Arabic. Major religion: Islam.
EDUCATION AND HEALTH. Literacy (1990 est.): 71% of adult population. Universities (1990): 1. Hospital beds (1987): 5,503. Physicians (1987): 2,799. Life expectancy (1990): women—76; men—72. Infant mortality (1990): 15 per 1,000 live births.
ECONOMY. GNP (1988): $26.25 billion; $13,680 per capita. Labor distribution (1986): services—45%; construction—20%; trade—12%; manufacturing—9%; finance and real estate—3%. Foreign trade (1988): imports—$5.2 billion; exports—$7.1 billion; principal trade partners—Japan, United States, Italy, Germany. Currency: 1 Kuwaiti dinar = 1,000 fils.
GOVERNMENT. Type: constitutional emirate (occupied by Iraq Aug. 2, 1990, and declared part of Iraq Aug. 28, 1990; emir heads government in exile recognized by the world community). Legislature: National Assembly (suspended). Political subdivisions: 4 districts.
COMMUNICATIONS. Railroads (1990): none. Roads (1988): 3,871 km (2,405 mi) total. Major ports: 3. Major airfields: 1.

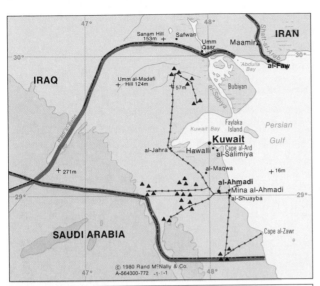

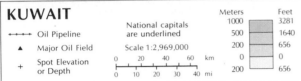

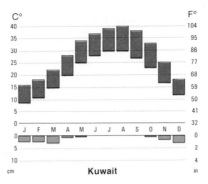

Bars indicate monthly ranges of temperature (red) and precipitation (blue) for the city of Kuwait. Located on Kuwait Bay, the city has the high temperatures and minimal precipitation that characterize the climate of the desert nation.

KUWAIT

⊶⊶⊷	Oil Pipeline
▲	Major Oil Field
+	Spot Elevation or Depth

National capitals are underlined

Scale 1:2,969,000

© 1980 Rand McNally & Co.
A-564300-772 -1-1-1

Meters	Feet
1000	3281
500	1640
200	656
0	0
200	656

or vote. After the invasion, nearly half of all Kuwaitis were in exile, mostly in Saudi Arabia and other Gulf states. Hundreds of thousands of foreign workers, many of whom lost everything they owned, also fled. Many Westerners were taken to Iraq as hostages (later released), while thousands of Iraqis were ordered to occupy dwellings vacated by fleeing Kuwaitis.

ECONOMIC ACTIVITY
The economy of modern Kuwait was based almost totally on petroleum. Agricultural activity was minimal, but some consumer goods and fertilizer were manufactured. By law, 10% of all petroleum revenues were deposited in a special reserve fund to provide for the time when oil reserves were exhausted. Exports from Iraqi-occupied Kuwait were halted by an international embargo. Kuwait's substantial overseas assets remained under control of the government in exile, which contributed to the cost of U.S. forces in the Gulf and aided poorer Arab nations backing the effort to liberate Kuwait.

HISTORY AND GOVERNMENT
The Sabah dynasty was established in 1756 after Arab tribes settled the area. Kuwait was nominally a province in the Ottoman Empire, but the sheikh received British protection in 1899 when the Turks threatened actual control. Kuwait achieved independence in 1961, but when Iraq claimed the area, it again received a British pledge of protection. Under the 1963 constitution, executive power is vested in the emir and exercised by a council of ministers. Sheikh Jabier al-Ahmad al-Sabah became emir in 1977. The legislature was suspended from 1976 to 1981 and again in 1986; an interim council without legislative powers was elected in June 1990. In the 1980s Kuwait was subject to terrorist attacks by Shiite Muslim extremists, includ-

tained citizenship, and foreigners. Arabic is the official language, although many people speak English. Muslims comprise 99% of the population and Christians less than 1%.

Prior to the Iraqi invasion, Kuwait had one of the highest per capita incomes in the world, financed by petroleum revenues. Kuwaiti citizens made up less than 40% of the population and about 19% of the labor force. The population was growing at almost three times the world rate, a result of both natural increase and immigration. The non-Kuwaitis—mostly Palestinians, Egyptians, and South Asians—enjoyed most of the welfare benefits of Kuwaiti citizens (including free education and low-cost medical care) but could not own property

The city of Kuwait experienced rapid growth after the discovery of vast petroleum reserves. Once a small fishing and trading village, the city became a major port on the Persian Gulf. Many of its inhabitants fled following the August 1990 Iraqi invasion of Kuwait, and much of its wealth was shipped to Iraq. The international embargo imposed after the invasion left the city short of food and other necessities.

ing a 1985 attempt to assassinate the emir; it supported Iraq against Iran in the GULF WAR (1980–88). On Aug. 2, 1990, after a dispute over oil, money, and boundaries, Iraq invaded Kuwait. On August 28 it incorporated the oil-producing northern third of Kuwait into the Iraqi province of Basra and created a new province from the rest. As the United States and other nations sent troops to the region to end the Iraqi aggression, war threatened to engulf the entire Middle East.　　IRA M. SHESKIN

Bibliography: Abu-Hakima, A. M., *The Modern History of Kuwait* (1983); Al-Moosa, A., and McLachlan, K., *Immigrant Labor in Kuwait* (1985); Assiri, A. -R., *Kuwait's Foreign Policy* (1990); Crystal, J., *Oil and Politics in the Gulf* (1990); Ismael, J. S., *Kuwait* (1982).

Kuybyshev:　see KUIBYSHEV.

Kuznets, Simon S.

Simon Smith Kuznets, b. Kharkov, Russia, Apr. 30 (N.S.), 1901, d. Aug. 8, 1985, was awarded (1971) the Nobel Prize in economics for his work in economic statistics, notably the study of national income and economic growth. Kuznets is credited with developing the concept of gross national product. He taught at the University of Pennsylvania, Johns Hopkins, and Harvard and served (1927–63) on the National Bureau of Economic Research.

Kuznetsk Basin

The Kuznetsk Basin (abbreviated Kuzbas) is one of the USSR's major coal fields. Extending along the Tom River in southwestern Siberia, between the Kuznetsk Ala-Tau and the Salair ranges, it has an area of approximately 26,000 km² (10,000 mi²). The basin's immense coal reserves are among the highest-quality deposits in the world. The proximity of iron-ore deposits has made the Kuzbas one of the USSR's leading industrial areas, producing iron and steel, chemicals, and heavy machinery. The Kuzbas is densely populated, with many cities, including Kemerovo and Novokuznetsk. Large-scale mining began in the mid-19th century. Industrial development began in the 1930s and continued during World War II to replace industrial areas held by the Germans. The population has declined somewhat as other energy sources have replaced coal.

Kwakiutl　[kwah'-kee-oo'-tul]

The Kwakiutl are a group of closely related North American Indians who traditionally have occupied both Vancouver Island and the adjacent mainland shores and islands of southern British Columbia, Canada. The mainland north to Douglas Channel was the traditional homeland of the Bella Bella and Haihais, speakers of linguistically related Heiltsuk. Far up Douglas and Gardner channels at Kitimat and Kitlope, lived the Xaisla, speakers of a variant Heiltsuk dialect. The Kwakiutl language family (Kwakiutl and Heiltsuk/Xaisla), with NOOTKA, forms the Wakashan linguistic stock (see INDIAN LANGUAGES, AMERICAN). Before European contact the Kwakiutl numbered an estimated 7,000, the Heiltsuk/Xaisla-speakers about 10,000. With the introduction of European diseases in the 19th century, their combined population was reduced to less than 1,900 in 1929. After that time, their population gradually increased. By the 1980s they numbered about 3,400.

With the aid of anthropologist Franz BOAS in the late 1800s, thousands of pages of information on Kwakiutl life were recorded in the Kwakiutl language and in English translation by George Hunt and his Kwakiutl-raised Tlingit wife. Thus Kwakiutl culture is among the most documented of all American Indian cultures. Skilled canoeists, fishers, and sea hunters, the Kwakiutl also excelled as carvers of TOTEM poles and other ritual objects. With their Heiltsuk kin they originated the most spectacular ceremonials of the Northwest Coast culture area. Although these ceremonies and the POTLATCH exchange were prohibited by Canada's much amended Indian Act (1876), the Kwakiutl still staged them to preserve the formal ranked statuses valued by their society. Since repeal of the law in 1951, both institutions have been performed in modified form as affirmations of Kwakiutl identity.　　PHILIP DRUCKER

Bibliography: Boas, Franz, *Kwakiutl Ethnography*, ed. by Helen F. Codere (1967); Goldman, I., *The Mouth of Heaven: An Introduction to Kwakiutl Religious Thought* (1975; repr. 1981); Kirk, Ruth, *Tradition and Change on the Northwest Coast* (1986; repr. 1988); Walens, S., *Feasting with the Cannibals: An Essay on Kwakiutl Cosmology* (1981); Wolcott, H., *A Kwakiutl Village and School* (1984).

Kwangsi　(Guangxi)　[gwang'-see']

Kwangsi is an autonomous region in southern China, bounded on the south and southwest by Vietnam and the Gulf of Tonkin. It has an area of about 220,400 km² (85,100 mi²) and a population of 40,164,000 (1988 est.). The capital, Nan-ning, lies on the Siang Chiang (West River), which runs through the region. Irrigation has increased the rice production so much that the surplus crop is shipped to other parts of the country. New highway and railroad facilities have contributed to industrial development. Fishing and timber are also important. Han Chinese constitute over half of the population, and the Chuang, a Thai people, are the largest minority group.

Kwangtung　(Guangdong)　[gwang'-tung']

Kwangtung is a province of southern China, on the South China Sea, west of the Taiwan Strait. The province has an area of 197,100 km² (76,100 mi²), excluding the island of HAINAN, which became a separate province in 1988. The population is 58,321,000 (1988 est.), of which 3,420,000 (1988 est.) live in CANTON (Guangzhou), the chief city and capital. British Hong Kong and Portuguese Macao are enclaves surrounded by Kwangtung.

The province is generally hilly and mountainous, although the Pearl River Delta, the Luichow Peninsula, and several delta plains and inland basins are lowland areas. The climate is subtropical; yearly rainfall averages 1,600 mm (65 in). Two crops of rice can be harvested each year. Sweet potatoes are the leading crop for drier soils; sugarcane is also extensively grown. About 300 species of fruit are grown. Mineral resources, including tungsten, iron, and manganese, are considerable. Industries, primarily in Canton, include steel, textiles, shipbuilding, canning, and sugar refining.

The population, about 98% ethnic Chinese, is divided into several language groups, constituting the largest group of non-Mandarin (official standard Chinese) speakers in the country. The Cantonese dialect is spoken by almost two-thirds of the population.

Kwangtung had earlier contact with the West than did most other parts of China, and crowded conditions in the farming villages near Canton led to the emigration of many Cantonese, especially to Southeast Asia and the United States. In 1979, Kwangtung was one of the first provinces to be designated a Special Economic Zone. It has prospered due partly to its proximity to Hong Kong as it has carried out new pragmatic economic policies aimed at attracting foreign capital and stimulating exports.　　JOHN E. MACDONALD

Kwanzaa　[kwahn'-zuh]

Kwanzaa is a seven-day festival observed by some black Americans in late December and early January. Inspired by a traditional African harvest festival, it was originated in 1966 by M. Ron Karenga, a Los Angeles–based black activist, to increase awareness of the African heritage and encourage qualities such as unity, self-determination, and cooperation in the black community. The observance includes exchanging gifts and an African-style meal known as *karamu*.

kwashiorkor　[kwash-ee-or'-kor]

Kwashiorkor is a form of malnutrition common in developing countries among those living on a diet inadequate in calories and grossly deficient in PROTEIN. The signs of this nutritional disease are anemia, edema (swelling), liver damage, muscle wasting, loss of appetite, and general apathy. The disease occurs mainly in children, especially those already suffering from parasitic disease or infectious diarrhea. The principal cause, however, is a mainly carbohydrate diet that provides inadequate protein. (The name *kwashiorkor* is derived from the Ga language of West Africa and means "the disease of the displaced child.") The disease is particularly prevalent in Africa, Latin America, and Asia. It is associated with poverty and diets of plantains or starchy roots, such as cassava. Treatment consists of a well-balanced, protein-rich diet; the disorder is often fatal, however; those who survive may have physical stunting and mental retardation.

A related disease, nutritional MARASMUS, results from an extremely low intake of all nutrients, including protein, and calories. The symptoms are similar to those of kwashiorkor, but edema is not present. The child with marasmus is underweight, wasted, and often emaciated, whereas the so-called sugar baby case of kwashiorkor shows little weight loss because energy stores are preserved.   MICHAEL C. LATHAM

Kweichow   (Guizhou)   [gwey'-jrow]

Kweichow is a province in southwestern China, encompassing an area of 174,048 km² (67,200 mi²). The population is 29,010,000 (1983 est.), and the capital is Kuei-yang (Guiyang). About 70% of the inhabitants are Han Chinese, but there are numerous tribal minorities. Traditionally an isolated region, Kweichow has become more accessible because of new roads and railways. Rice and corn cultivation are the main occupations. Manufactures include iron and steel, heavy machinery, chemicals, textiles, liquor, and processed foods. Kweichow became a province under the Ming dynasty (1368–1644). Before the Communist takeover in the 1940s, it was the scene of many revolts against the central government.

kyanite   [ky'-uh-nyt]

Kyanite, a blue, white, or sometimes green aluminum silicate mineral, is found as distinctive, long-bladed crystals in gneisses and mica schists. It has the unusual characteristic of showing a marked variation in hardness in different directions.

The aluminum SILICATE MINERAL kyanite (derived from the Greek *kyanos,* meaning "blue") is used in the manufacture of spark plugs, porcelain, and other refractories; it has the same chemical composition ($AlAlOSiO_4$) as ANDALUSITE and SILLIMANITE. Its long-bladed, usually blue crystals (triclinic system) are distinctive. Hardness is 4–5 along the length of the crystal and 6–7 across it, luster is vitreous to pearly, specific gravity is 3.5–3.7, and cleavage is perfect in one direction. Kyanite occurs in GNEISSES, SCHISTS, and granite PEGMATITES; it is an indicator of deep-seated, regional metamorphism of clay-rich sediments.

Kyd, Thomas

The Elizabethan playwright Thomas Kyd (1558–94) was the author of *The Spanish Tragedy* (c.1586), the first revenge tragedy in English literature and easily the most popular play of the day. *The Spanish Tragedy* owes much to the Roman writer Seneca. Kyd was imprisoned in 1593 on a false charge of atheism and died soon after his release.

Bibliography: Freeman, Arthur, *Thomas Kyd: Facts and Problems* (1967); Murray, Peter B., *Thomas Kyd* (1969).

Kyogen   [kee-oh'-gen]

Kyogen are short comic plays that developed in Japan alongside the serious NO DRAMA. Originally they were improvised

by the actors, but a repertoire gradually accumulated so that today about 160 Kyogen plays are performed. They dramatize warmly humorous incidents taken from 14th- and 15th-century life—for example, two servants tricking their master (*Poisoned Sugar*), a henpecked lord fooling his wife (*The Zen Substitute*), and a trainer doing tricks with his monkey to save its life (*The Monkey Quiver*).   JAMES R. BRANDON

Bibliography: Sakanishi, Shio, trans., *Japanese Folk Plays* (1960); McKinnon, Richard, ed. and trans., *Selected Plays of Kyogen* (1968).

Kyoto   [kyoh'-toh]

Kyoto is one of Japan's largest cities. Located on south central Honshu, it has a population of 1,480,000 (1985 est.) and an area of 611 km² (236 mi²). The climate is temperate, with warm, humid summers and cool, dry winters.

Kyoto served as Japan's imperial capital for more than a thousand years (794–1868) and is still Japan's leading cultural center. It is also the manufacturing center for traditional handicrafts, such as silk, dyed fabric, damascene, porcelain, dolls, lacquerware, and for sake-brewing. Heavy manufacturing includes copper smelting, chemicals, and machinery. The city is located at the center of the vast urban and industrial region covering southern Honshu and has well-developed transportation links to Osaka, Tokyo, and Nagoya. Because of the numerous Buddhist temples, Shinto shrines, gardens, and traditional houses that preserve Kyoto's rich history, it is a leading tourism center visited by an estimated 20 million persons annually. The Kyoto National Museum, Imperial Palace, Yasaka Shrine, and Kinkakuji (Temple of the Golden Pavilion) are noted landmarks. There are over 20 universities and colleges in Kyoto, including the prestigious Kyoto University (1897).

Adopted as the site of the imperial capital by the Emperor Kammu, Kyoto (or Heian) was built in 794. Like nearby Nara, the previous capital, the city was modeled after Ch'ang-an, capital of the T'ang dynasty in China. Before the rise of Edo (present-day Tokyo) as the capital of the Tokugawa shogunate (1603–1868), Kyoto enjoyed more than eight centuries of unrivaled glory among all Japanese cities. Finally, in 1868, Tokyo became the imperial capital. Kyoto is so rich in historic relics that it was spared Allied bombing during World War II.   JAMES CHAN

Kyushu   [kyoo'-shoo]

Kyushu, the southernmost and most densely populated of the four main islands of Japan, encompasses 42,023 km² (16,225 mi²). It has a population of 13,230,000 (1984 est.). The island's volcanic mountains, part of the Ryukyu range, reach a height of 1,788 m (5,866 ft) at Kuju-san. Abundant rainfall of over 2,000 mm (80 in) annually and a mean average temperature of 15° C (60° F) enable cultivation of tropical fruits and vegetables as well as grains, soybeans, tea, and tobacco. Fishing, mining, and the production of raw silk and porcelain are also important industries. The chief cities include FUKUOKA, KITAKYUSHU, NAGASAKI, and Omuta. Inhabited at least since the Stone Age, Kyushu became the seat of the Yayoi civilization in the 1st century BC.

Kyzyl Kum   [kuh-zul' koom]

The Kyzyl Kum is a desert of the USSR, lying southeast of the Aral Sea and covering about half of the Uzbek republic and a southern strip of the Kazakh republic. Stretching 800 km (500 mi) east to west and 725 km (450 mi) north to south, it has an area of 300,000 km² (115,000 mi²). Its name means "red sands."

Generally low, the Kyzyl Kum has scattered peaks over 915 m (3,000 ft). Rainfall averages only 100 mm (4 in) a year, so there is little vegetation to hold the shifting sand dunes. More than 410 km² (158 mi²) of trees have been planted to prevent the sands from spreading. Shepherds tend Karakul sheep, and at oases along rivers—particularly the SYR DARYA and the AMU DARYA at the desert's borders—cotton, rice, and wheat are grown. Sulfur, gold, and natural gas are extracted.

PHOENICIAN				ETRUSCAN	
EARLY HEBREW		**Ll**		EARLY LATIN	
EARLY ARAMAIC				CLASSICAL LATIN	
EARLY GREEK		MODERN LATIN		RUSSIAN-CYRILLIC	
CLASSICAL GREEK				GERMAN-GOTHIC	

L

L/l is the 12th letter of the English alphabet. Both the letter and its position in the alphabet were derived from the Latin alphabet, which in turn are derived from the Greek by way of the Etruscan. The Greeks call the letter *lambda* and took its name, form, and position from a Semitic writing system, in which the name of the sign was *lamedh*.

L/l is a liquid consonant; that is, it is frictionless and can be prolonged like a vowel. In English, *L/l* is regularly voiced, as in *like*, *lip*, and *fall*. When the letter is preceded by a voiceless consonant, the beginning of voicing is normally delayed until after the *l* sound has already begun, as in *please* or *slip*. In some words, *L/l* is not pronounced, although it affects the pronunciation of the preceding vowel, as in *walk* and *should* (compare *shoulder*). I. J. GELB AND R. M. WHITING

L'Amour, Louis

One of the best-selling American authors ever, Louis Dearborn L'Amour, b. Jamestown, N.Dak., 1908, d. June 10, 1988, wrote 86 novels—almost all westerns—that sold over 160 million copies in his lifetime, as well as more than 400 short stories. Establishing his western format early—*Hondo* (1953; film, 1954) is an example—L'Amour produced heroic action tales that reflect scrupulous historical research. *The Walking Drum* (1984), however, is set in medieval Europe, and *Last of the Breed* (1986) in contemporary Siberia.

L'Anse aux Meadows   [lawnse oh med-doh']

L'Anse aux Meadows, on the northernmost tip of Newfoundland, is the site of a Viking settlement dating from about AD 1000; it may have been the VINLAND settlement described in the early Norse sagas about the explorer LEIF ERIKSSON. Excavation of the site, begun in 1961, revealed the remains of eight turf-walled houses, one of which was a longhouse 22 m by 15 m (72 ft by 50 ft) containing five rooms including a "great hall," and a smithy, where bog iron was smelted. Several of the houses had stone ember pits identical with those found in Norse houses in Greenland. Among the artifacts unearthed was a soapstone spindle whorl similar to those discovered in Norse ruins in Greenland, Iceland, and Scandinavia; this find suggests that women as well as men were present at the site. Other artifacts point to a brief, much earlier occupation of the site by Maritime Archaic Indians and a later occupation by Dorset Eskimo. MARGARET P. ROESKE

Bibliography: Ingstad, Anne S., *Discovery of a Norse Settlement in America* (1977); Ingstad, Helge M., *Westward to Vinland*, trans. by Erik J. Friis (1969).

La Brea Tar Pit   [bray'-uh]

La Brea Tar Pit is a natural accumulation of tar that formed over the site of an ancient oil seep in what is now Los Angeles's Hancock Park. For about 40,000 years, petroleum from rock strata deep beneath the ground has oozed upward to form pools on the surface. With the passing of time, the oil lost its volatile elements and gradually formed a thick deposit of asphalt. First reported by Spanish explorers in 1769, the asphalt was mined commercially for many years. Today, the asphalt of Rancho La Brea ("Ranch of the Tar") is better known for the array of fossil vertebrates it has yielded.

During Early Pleistocene time (about 2.5 million years ago), animals coming to the seeps for water or attempting to cross the tarry surface became mired in this natural death trap. Permeated with asphalt, these PREHISTORIC ANIMALS are in a remarkable state of preservation. Larger herbivorous animals trapped in the tar pits include horses, mastodons, bison, camels, and the giant ground sloth. Carnivores attracted by these

An artist's conception of the La Brea Tar Pit about 20,000 years ago depicts a probable scene of the period. Since 1906 archaeologists have found thousands of well-preserved, tar-impregnated bones and teeth of various extinct creatures that became mired and entombed. Some of the specimens are of large animals, but others are of tiny insects and even rats and rabbits like those of today.

herbivores include mountain lions, SABER-TOOTH CATS, the giant California jaguar, and dire wolves. Birds, including a vulture with a 3.6-m (12-ft) wingspan and the California stork, and many smaller species of animals have also been found.

WILLIAM H. MATTHEWS III

Bibliography: Heric, T. M., "Rancho La Brea," *Journal of the West*, April 1969; Stock, C., *Rancho La Brea*, 6th ed. (1956; repr. 1972).

La Bruyère, Jean de   [lah bru-yair']

The French moralist Jean de La Bruyère, b. Paris and baptized Aug. 17, 1645, d. May 10, 1696, became famous as the result of one work, *The Characters, or the Manners of the Age, with the Characters of Theophrastus* (Eng. trans., 1699), in which he sarcastically depicted 17th-century Paris and the life of the French court. Although less profound than his contemporaries Blaise Pascal or La Rochefoucauld, La Bruyère nevertheless displayed considerable wit and stylistic originality in his portraits. The tutor of the duc de Bourbon (grandson of the Great Condé), La Bruyère served (1686–96) as head of the Condé library at Chantilly.

MADELEINE ALCOVER

Bibliography: Gosse, Edmund William, *Three French Moralists and the Gallantry of France* (1918); Knox, Edward C., *Jean de la Bruyère* (1973); Yarrow, P. J., "La Bruyère," in *The Seventeenth Century*, vol. 2 of *A Literary History of France*, ed. by P. E. Charvet (1967).

La Coruña   [lah kor-oon'-yah]

La Coruña is located on an inlet of the Atlantic Ocean in northwest Spain. A major commercial port for trade with North and South America, the city is also the capital of La Coruña province. Its population is 232,356 (1981). La Coruña's port primarily exports agricultural products, and it has Spain's second largest fishing industry. There is also some light manufacturing of fish, tobacco products, and paper. Historical landmarks include a lighthouse probably built by the Romans in the 1st century AD and the churches of Santiago (12th century) and Santa María del Campo (13th century). Called Brigantium by the Romans, La Coruña was ruled by the Moors (8th–10th century) and the Portuguese (14th century) until annexed to Spain in the 15th century. During the 16th century the port was the site of several battles between English and Spanish fleets. The death of the British general Sir John Moore (1761–1809) at La Coruña is the subject of a poem by Charles Wolfe, "The Burial of Sir John Moore" (1817).

La Crosse   [luh kraws]

La Crosse (1980 pop., 48,347), a city in western Wisconsin on the Mississippi River at the influx of the Black and La Crosse rivers, is the seat of La Crosse County. Rubber footwear and air-conditioning equipment are manufactured, and lumber is milled there. The University of Wisconsin has a branch at La Crosse. Settled as a trading post in 1841, La Crosse became an important lumbering center after the arrival of the railroad in 1858.

La Farge, John   [luh farzh]

John La Farge, b. New York City, Mar. 31, 1835, d. Nov. 14, 1910, was an American muralist, stained-glass designer, landscape painter, and writer. He studied briefly in Paris under the French academic painter Thomas COUTURE and in Newport, R.I., under the American landscapist William Morris HUNT. An offer to complete (1876) the mural decorations of Trinity Church in Boston led to a succession of important commissions for murals, such as his *Ascension* (1888; Church of the Ascension, New York City), and *Athens* (1898; Bowdoin College, Brunswick, Maine). He also experimented with stained glass, and, by eliminating much of the leading, he achieved a shimmering, incandescent effect with stained glass that is best represented in his *Old Philosopher* window (1880; Crane Memorial Library, Quincy, Mass.). Another facet of his talents is revealed in the watercolor and oil paintings he made after trips to Japan (1886) and the South Seas (1890–91). Most of these paintings are topographically accurate, but some, such

as his watercolor *The Strange Thing Little Kiosai Saw in the River* (1897; Metropolitan Museum of Art, New York City), take a visionary turn.

ABRAHAM A. DAVIDSON

Bibliography: Cortissoz, Royal, *John La Farge: A Memoir and a Study* (1911; repr. 1971); Kennedy Galleries, *John La Farge* (1968); Weinberg, Helene Barbara, *The Decorative Work of John La Farge* (1972; repr. 1977).

La Farge, Oliver Hazard Perry

Oliver Hazard Perry La Farge, b. New York City, Dec. 19, 1901, d. Aug. 2, 1963, an anthropologist, writer, and fervent spokesman for the American Indian, is best known for his novel *Laughing Boy* (1929), winner of a Pulitzer Prize. Among several other works dealing with American Indian culture are *All the Young Men* (1935) and *The Enemy Gods* (1937).

F. M. PAULSEN

Bibliography: McNickle, D'Arcy, *Indian Man: A Life of Oliver La Farge* (1971); Pearce, T. M., *Oliver La Farge* (1972).

La Fayette, Comtesse de   [lah fah-yet', kohn-tes' duh]

Marie Madeleine Pioche de La Vergne, comtesse de La Fayette, baptized Mar. 18, 1634, d. May 25, 1693, wrote the first analytical novel in French literature. The simplicity of style and lack of sentimentality characteristic of her work, particularly as compared with that of her predecessors of the 1640s and '50s, made her a true French classicist. Because of an aristocratic prejudice she never signed her works of fiction; they were published either anonymously or under the name of her friend and fellow writer Jean Segrais. Both LA ROCHEFOUCAULD, with whom she had a long liaison, and Segrais were unquestionably involved in the creation of her novels. In all of them—*La Princesse de Montpensier* (1662), *Zaÿde* (1670), her masterpiece *La Princesse de Clèves* (1678), and the posthumous *La Comtesse de Tende* (1724)—she dealt with the same theme: the dangers of passionate love. She also produced two historical works, the *Histoire de Madame Henriette d'Angleterre* (The Story of Henrietta of England, 1720) and *Mémoires de la Cour de France* (Reminiscences of the French Court, 1731).

MADELEINE ALCOVER

Bibliography: Haig, Stirling, *Madame de Lafayette* (1970); Raitt, Janet, *Madame de Lafayette and La Princesse de Clèves* (1971); Scott, J. W., *Madame de Lafayette. La Princesse de Clèves* (1983).

La Follette, Robert M.   [luh fahl'-et]

Robert "Fighting Bob" La Follette became a leader of reform-minded progressive Republicans during his three terms as governor of Wisconsin and later as a U.S. senator from that state. La Follette opposed U.S. participation in World War I and voted against ratification of the Treaty of Versailles, thus rejecting the League of Nations.

As governor of Wisconsin, U.S. senator, and presidential candidate, Robert Marion La Follette, Sr., was one of the leading progressive politicians in the United States. He was born in Primrose, Wis., on June 14, 1855, the son of a prosperous, politically active Republican farmer. He graduated from the University of Wisconsin in 1879 and from its newly founded law school in 1880, and he won election (1880) as district attorney of Dane County. In 1881 he married Belle Case.

In 1884, La Follette was elected to Congress. His speeches against the "pork barrel" rivers and harbors bill and in favor of a protective tariff brought him to the attention of the Republican congressional leadership. Placed on the prestigious Ways and Means Committee, he helped William McKinley draft the Tariff Act of 1890. Its unpopularity caused both of them to lose their seats in the 1890 election.

In 1891, La Follette refused a bribe offered by the dominant Wisconsin Republican, Senator Philetus Sawyer. The incident was leaked to the press, and La Follette's response to Sawyer's public account made him a political pariah. In the following years he campaigned against the corrupt party machine in Wisconsin. Twice rejected (1896, 1898) for the Republican gubernatorial nomination, he took his campaign to the people, focusing on the novel idea of a direct primary for party nominations. In 1900 he was elected governor.

As governor La Follette had to fight a recalcitrant legislature to redeem his campaign pledges. Finally gaining control over the legislature, he enacted a program that included direct primaries, more equitable taxation, a more effective railroad commission, civil service reform, conservation, control of lobbyists, a legislative reference library, and bank reform.

In 1905 the Wisconsin legislature elected La Follette to the U.S. Senate. He was a controversial senator almost from the beginning. In a long freshman speech he sought to strengthen the Hepburn bill (1906) regulating railroad rates. In 1908 he conducted a record, but unsuccessful, filibuster against the Aldrich-Vreeland bill, charging that creation of the National Monetary Commission was meant to enrich bankers. After William Howard Taft became president, La Follette forged the progressive Republican opposition to the Payne-Aldrich Tariff and became a persistent critic of the administration. In 1911 he was chosen as the progressive Republican candidate to displace Taft, but he was superseded by Theodore Roosevelt in 1912.

La Follette supported most of the policies of Democratic President Woodrow Wilson until the question of U.S. entry into World War I arose. Vigorously opposed to entry, he was the victim of an unsuccessful attempt to expel him from the Senate for an antiwar speech. After the war he voted against ratification of the Treaty of Versailles because it failed to allow colonial self-determination and equity for weak nations. By this vote he also rejected U.S. participation in the League of Nations. In the postwar period La Follette resisted the anti-Communist scare and fought for the interests of workers and farmers against the business-oriented Republican administrations. He initiated the investigation into the TEAPOT DOME scandal in 1922. The following year he made an independent race for the presidency on the PROGRESSIVE PARTY ticket and received almost 5 million votes. He died on June 18, 1925, still a fervent believer in democracy. Direct popular government would, he was convinced, prevent control by the powerful few, permit greater economic equity, and enable society's underdogs to organize for their own improvement.

FRED GREENBAUM

Bibliography: Greenbaum, Fred, *Robert Marion La Follette* (1975); La Follette, Belle Case and Fola, *Robert M. La Follette*, 2 vols. (1953); Manéy, Patrick J., *Young Bob La Follette* (1978); Maxwell, R., *La Follette and the Rise of the Progressives in Wisconsin* (1956); Thelen, David, *Robert M. La Follette and the Insurgent Spirit* (1976; repr. 1986).

La Fontaine, Jean de   [lah-fohn-ten', zhawn duh]

One of the world's greatest fabulists, the Frenchman Jean de La Fontaine, baptized July 8, 1621, d. Apr. 13, 1695, modeled himself after two classic predecessors, Aesop and Phaedrus, to create incomparable, deceptively simple poetic masterpieces of humor and penetrating psychological observation. In contemporary France he ranks, along with Molière, as one of the two most popular 17th-century writers.

A native of Champagne, La Fontaine in 1652 bought a com-

The 17th-century French poet and fabulist Jean de La Fontaine is renowned for his 12 books of collected fables (1668–94), derived from ancient and modern sources. La Fontaine used diverse narrative techniques and rhyme schemes to convey the satirical and allegorical tone of the fables.

mission as inspector of forests and waterways and subsequently divided his time between Paris and the provinces. Thanks to his witty and pleasing personality, he received financial support from wealthy patrons, such as Nicolas Fouquet, Louis XIV's minister of the treasury, and later, Madame de la Sablière. In the latter's salon he met philosophers, scientists, and writers. Because of his nonconformist views he made friends with others in marginal religious, philosophical, and ethical groups, such as Jansenists, disciples of Gassendi, and libertine society.

La Fontaine's first literary piece was a comedy, *L' Eunuque* (The Eunuch, 1654), an imitation of a play by Terence. It was followed by his well-known *Tales and Novels in Verse* (Eng. trans., 1898), short licentious tales adapted from Boccaccio and Ariosto, which, starting in 1664, La Fontaine continued to publish until his death. He then turned to his masterwork, *Fables* (pub. in 3 parts, 1668–94; Eng. trans., 1806), in which he depicted human vanity, stupidity, and aggressiveness in animal guise. Like his countryman Montaigne, La Fontaine was a nonacerbic moralist who, in contrast to his ancient predecessors, avoided didacticism by suggesting his intention without underlining it. In this he was typical of the best French classical writers. La Fontaine also produced some miscellaneous verse works, further comedies, and a narrative piece in prose and verse, *The Loves of Cupid and Psyche* (1669; Eng. trans., 1744).

MADELEINE ALCOVER

Bibliography: Guiton, M. O., *La Fontaine* (1961); King, Ethel, *Jean de La Fontaine* (1970); Lapp, J. C., *The Esthetics of Negligence* (1971); Mackay, Agnes E., *La Fontaine and His Friends* (1973); Sutherland, Monica, *La Fontaine* (1953; repr. 1974).

La Fresnaye, Roger de   [lah fren-ay', roh-zhay' duh]

Roger de La Fresnaye, b. July 11, 1885, d. Nov. 27, 1925, was a French cubist painter. He attended the École des Beaux-Arts (1904–08) and then studied with members of the Nabi group. Shortly afterward he was exposed for the first time to the art of Paul Cézanne and Paul Gauguin, both of whom were to have lasting influence on his work.

When La Fresnaye began (1910) to experiment with cubist ideas he retained much of the linear and coloristic stylization that he had learned from Gauguin—so much so that even his most cubist works appear to compromise the strict principles of CUBISM and the looser dictates of naturalistic painting. Although La Fresnaye did adopt the fragmented planes of the cubist idiom, he preferred to retain a traditional perspective and expressive contours. La Fresnaye's artistic career was interrupted by World War I, which destroyed his health and led to his early death, at age 40. In his postwar works he adopted a stylized linear realism.

IRMA B. JAFFE

Bibliography: Seligman, Germain, *Roger de La Fresnaye* (1969).

La Guaira   [lah gwy'-rah]

La Guaira (1981 pop., 21,815), the leading port city of Venezuela, is situated on the Caribbean Sea coast about 15 km (10 mi) north of Caracas by highway. Its harbor, formed by an artificial breakwater, is used to export coffee, cacao, bananas, tobacco, and hides. The city has facilities for shipbuilding and repair, along with textile manufacturing. La Guaira was founded in 1589.

La Guardia, Fiorello [luh gwar'-dee-uh, fee-oh-rel'-oh]

Fiorello La Guardia, an American public official, distinguished himself during seven terms in Congress (1916-18; 1923-33) and three consecutive terms as mayor of New York (1934-45) by liberal legislation and wide-reaching reform. In Congress he cosponsored the prolabor Norris–La Guardia Act (1932); as mayor he introduced many civic and administrative improvements.

The public career of Fiorello Henry La Guardia, b. New York City, Dec. 11, 1882, d. Sept. 20, 1947, an American political reformer, congressman, and mayor of New York City, spanned three decades. Although he never received a high school diploma, La Guardia studied law at New York University and was admitted to the bar in 1910. He was first elected to Congress as a Republican in 1916, and after service in the U.S. air force during World War I and a term as president of the New York City Board of Aldermen, he served again in the House of Representatives from 1923 to 1933. In Congress, La Guardia defended the interests of his predominantly immigrant, working-class constituency. He condemned legislation establishing national-origins quotas for the admission of immigrants, and he cosponsored the Norris–La Guardia Act (1932), which barred the use of injunctions to prevent strikes.

Elected mayor of New York City in 1933 on a Fusion ticket and reelected twice, he held that office until 1945. As mayor, La Guardia (known as "The Little Flower," from his name Fiorello) led a drive against political corruption, modernized the city's administrative structure, and introduced major improvements in the fields of health, housing, recreation, and the arts. He was equally well known for bravely attempting to conduct the New York Philharmonic Orchestra, reading comic strips over the radio to entertain children during a newspaper strike, and banning organ-grinders from the city's streets in order to remove a source of prejudicial stereotypes concerning Italians. La Guardia served briefly as director of the Office of Civilian Defense (1941–42) and as head of the United Nations Relief and Rehabilitation Administration (1946). He published an autobiography of his early years, *The Making of an Insurgent* (1948; repr. 1986). RICHARD POLENBERG

Bibliography: Garrett, Charles, *The La Guardia Years* (1961); Heckscher, August, and Robinson, Phyllis, *When La Guardia Was Mayor: New York's Legendary Years* (1978); Mann, Arthur, *La Guardia: A Fighter against His Times*, 2 vols. (1959–65; repr. 1969) and *La Guardia Comes to Power: 1933* (1965); Manners, William, *Patience and Fortitude: Fiorello La Guardia* (1976).

La Guma, Alex [luh goo'-muh]

The South African novelist Justin Alexander La Guma, b. Feb. 20, 1925, d. Oct. 11, 1985, was a critic of the political, economic, and social realities that exist for nonwhites in South

Africa. His literary reputation was established with the novelette *A Walk in the Night* (1962), which focuses on ghetto life in a South African city. La Guma resided in London and later in Cuba, having first been imprisoned in South Africa for his political activities and then exiled from the country, where all of his writings are banned. His novels include *And a Threefold Cord* (1964), *The Stone Country* (1967), *In the Fog of the Season's End* (1972), and *Time of the Butcherbird* (1979). La Guma also wrote short stories and edited *Apartheid: A Collection of Writings on South African Racism by South Africans* (1972). RICHARD K. PRIEBE

La Hire, Laurent de [lah eer', loh-rahn duh]

Laurent de La Hire (or La Hyre, Lahire), b. Feb. 27, 1606, d. Dec. 28, 1656, was a painter and etcher in the French classical tradition. Francesco Primaticcio's work at Fontainebleau greatly influenced his style, as did the classical decorations of Simon Vouet and Nicolas Poussin. A knowledge of classical art and literature, as well as great skill in perspective, marks La Hire's best works, such as his *Mercury Entrusting the Infant Bacchus to the Nymphs* (1638; The Hermitage, Leningrad). Most of his career was spent in the service of the French royal government, for which he executed numerous decorative designs, portraits, and historical paintings. SUZANNE J. WILSON

Bibliography: Blunt, Anthony, *Art and Architecture in France, 1500 to 1700* (1973).

La Meri [lah mair'-ee]

La Meri, b. Russell Meriwether Hughes, Louisville, Ky., May 18, 1898, d. Jan. 7, 1988, was an ethnic dancer, teacher, choreographer, lecturer, and writer who began her career in 1923 as a dancer in silent-movie houses in Texas and the New York City area. In 1928, La Meri embarked on world tours, performing solo ethnic dances and studying native dances to add to her repertory. She founded the School of Natya with Ruth ST. DENIS in New York in 1940, and in 1941 she organized her own company. When St. Denis departed for California in 1942, La Meri renamed the school the Ethnologic Dance Center and expanded the curriculum. In addition to teaching in the school until 1956, La Meri choreographed, lectured, and performed; she also toured with her company and served as a resident teacher at Jacob's Pillow (Mass.). As one of the world's experts on the ethnologic or art dance, she wrote many books and articles for periodicals and encyclopedias. BARBARA BARKER

Bibliography: Hughes, Russell Meriwether (La Meri), *Dance as an Art Form* (1933), *Dance Composition: The Basic Elements* (1965), *Dance Out the Answer: An Autobiography* (1977), *The Gesture Language of the Hindu Dance* (1941), *Principles of the Dance Art* (1933), and *Total Education in Ethnic Dance* (1977).

La Paz (Bolivia) [lah pahs']

La Paz is the administrative capital and leading commercial center of Bolivia and the capital of La Paz department. It has a population of 953,634 (1984 est.). Located 3,658 m (12,001 ft) above sea level in a canyon carved out of the Altiplano (Bolivia's high plateau) by the La Paz River, it is the world's highest capital city. It has a cool, dry climate.

In addition to its governmental function, La Paz serves as the Altiplano's major trade and market center. Its industries are food processing and light manufacturing (textiles, glass, furniture, and electrical equipment). Since space is extremely limited in the canyon, many of the older buildings have been torn down to make way for modern office buildings. The center of city life is the Plaza Murillo, on the north side of the river. Facing its formal gardens are the huge cathedral, the presidential palace, the national congress building, and the national museum of art. La Paz is the site of the University of San Andrés (1830).

La Paz was founded by the Spaniards in 1548—on the site of an Inca village—as a way station along the caravan route from the silver mines at Potosí to Lima. The town's location, in the

La Paz, the administrative capital of Bolivia and the country's most populous city, lies in a narrow valley at the foot of the Cordillera Real, with Mount Illimani towering in the distance. At an altitude of 3,658 m (12,001 ft), the city is the world's highest capital.

valley, was selected as a means of escaping the harsh climate of the Altiplano, and the town was named Nuestra Señora de La Paz to commemorate the peaceful conditions existing in Bolivia at that time. During the 18th and 19th centuries La Paz developed into a leading commercial center and supply point for the numerous mining activities carried out on the Altiplano. The importance of the city was further enhanced by the construction of railroads from La Paz to Chile and to Argentina and by the building of roads linking La Paz to other regions of Bolivia. RAY HENKEL

La Paz (Mexico)

La Paz (1982 est. pop., 130,427), the capital and largest city of the state of Baja California Sur in northwestern Mexico, lies on La Paz Bay, an inlet of the Gulf of California, about 150 km (95 mi) from the tip of the Baja California peninsula. The city is a major pearl fishing and agricultural processing center in the area and a popular winter resort. It was permanently settled in 1811.

La Pérouse, Jean François de Galaup, Comte de [lah pay-rooz', zhawn frahn-swah' duh guh-loh, kohnt duh]

The French navigator Jean François de Galaup, comte de La Pérouse, b. Aug. 22, 1741, d. c.1788, discovered the strait north of Japan named for him. In 1785 he was given command of two ships, *La Boussole* and *L'Astrolabe,* to find the NORTHWEST PASSAGE from the Pacific side. Sailing from France, he rounded Cape Horn and went on to Hawaii and other Pacific islands, Alaska, Macao, and the Philippines. After discovering (1787) La Pérouse Strait, he landed on Kamchatka and sent an overland party back to France with his journals. Some of his party were murdered in the Samoan Islands, but La Pérouse sailed on to Australia. After leaving Botany Bay in March 1788 he disappeared. In 1826–27 a few remains from his ships were found on the Melanesian island of Vanikoro. ROBIN BUSS

Bibliography: Allen, E. W., *The Vanishing Frenchman* (1959).

La Plata [lah plah'-tah]

La Plata, the capital of the province of Buenos Aires, Argentina, is located 56 km (35 mi) south of Buenos Aires near the south shore of the RÍO DE LA PLATA estuary. Its population is 564,750 (1980). La Plata is closer to the Atlantic Ocean than Buenos Aires and has a deeper, artificial, nontidal port at Ensenada that accommodates larger ships, thus making it the main outlet for the produce of the Pampas. The city is also served by rail, road, and air routes. Textile, chemical, meatpacking, refining, and packaging industries supplement the export-import trade.

A model of planned urban development, La Plata was laid out as the new capital of the province in 1882 after Buenos Aires was named the national capital (1880). Cultural life is dominated by the National University (1897), theater, natural science displays, and government operations.

RICHARD W. WILKIE

La Rochefoucauld, François, Duc de [lah rohsh-foo-koh']

François VI, duc de La Rochefoucauld, b. Sept. 15, 1613, d. Mar. 17, 1680, was a French classical moralist whose literary fame rests on one sparkling book, *The Maxims.* His early years, both in the army and at the French court, and involving many fights and amorous escapades, participation in the Fronde (1648), and an attempt (1651) to assassinate Cardinal Retz, were recorded soberly in his *Memoirs* (1662; Eng. trans., 1684).

In 1652, following his recovery from a severe head wound that kept him in retirement for three years, La Rochefoucauld returned to Paris and the literary salons. In the meantime, influenced by JANSENISM, he had begun to think seriously about the meaning of a Christian life. Encouraged to write out his thoughts, he did so in maxims, a peculiarly French literary form of epigram that expresses in a clear, impersonal image an often paradoxical truth that surprises or shocks. The first edition of La Rochefoucauld's *Maxims* was published in 1665, after which he began a 15-year liaison with the novelist Madame de LA FAYETTE, who was much influenced by the association. He completed four later editions of the *Maxims*—revisions and expansions of his original work—in 1666, 1671, 1675, and 1678.

Believing self-interest to be the root of all human action, La Rochefoucauld, expressing the Christian view of man's unregenerate nature, attributed the imperfections found in individuals and in society to self-deception, which he considered the natural outcome of self-love. Among his most famous maxims are "Self-love is the greatest of flatterers" and "Hypocrisy is the homage vice pays to virtue." Acclaimed for the perfection of their form, the *Maxims* were subsequently widely translated.

Bibliography: Bishop, Morris, *The Life and Adventures of La Rochefoucauld* (1951); La Rochefoucauld, François, *The Maxims of La Rochefoucauld,* trans. by Louis Kronenberger (1959); Lewis, Philip, *La Rochefoucauld* (1977); Moore, Will G., *La Rochefoucauld* (1969).

La Rochelle [lah roh-shel']

La Rochelle (1982 pop., 75,840) is the capital city of Charente-Maritime department in western France. Located on the Bay of Biscay, it is an important Atlantic coast fishing port and a popular summer resort. Major industries include petroleum refining and chemical, aircraft, and automobile manufacturing.

La Rochelle was made a commune in 1199 when it was already a busy port. During the 16th century it was a center of HUGUENOT resistance to the crown. Conceded by treaty to the Huguenots in 1573, the city was besieged by Cardinal RICHELIEU in 1627–28. During the 18th century La Rochelle's port handled most of France's trade with Canada, but with the loss of Canada port activity declined. The old section of the city contains the 16th-century town hall and 14th-century towers guarding the harbor entrance. Occupied by the Germans during World War II, La Rochelle withstood an Allied siege from September 1944 to May 1945.

La Salle, Robert Cavelier, Sieur de [lah sahl, roh-bair' kah-vul-yay', syur duh]

Robert Cavelier, sieur de La Salle, was the first European to navigate the length of the Mississippi River to its mouth. La Salle then claimed the entire basin for France, naming the area Louisiana, for the French monarch Louis XIV.

The French fur trader and explorer René Robert Cavelier, sieur de La Salle, was the European discoverer of the lower Mississippi. Born at Rouen, France, on Nov. 21, 1643, he spent 9 years as a Jesuit novice, studying logic, physics, and mathematics. In 1667, however, he left the order and emigrated to Canada. There he became consumed with ambition to discover the elusive route to the Orient through the interior of North America. Many people with whom La Salle came in contact in succeeding years looked upon him as a visionary—some even doubted his sanity—so obsessed was he with becoming famous as a discoverer.

La Salle's travels did not develop seriously until about 1673 when he became an instrument of the comte de FRONTENAC's policy of western commercial and military expansion for New France. He was appointed commandant of Fort Frontenac on Lake Ontario and charged with the development of the fur trade in that area. Under Frontenac's sponsorship he traveled in 1679 to Lake Michigan, in 1680 to the Illinois country, and in 1682 from the Illinois River down the Mississippi to its mouth. Four new forts—Niagara (1679), Saint Joseph and Crèvecoeur (1680), and Saint Louis (1682)—were established in the northwest, and the first sailing vessel, the *Griffon,* built (1679) by La Salle's associate Henri de TONTY, was launched on the Great Lakes above Niagara.

Profits from the fur trade were intended to finance these explorations, but political setbacks, bad luck, and bad organization turned such expectations into debts. After Frontenac's recall (1682), La Salle lost an important source of patronage and had to spend a year lobbying at the French court to regain official support. When it came, in 1684, it was generous. La Salle was to lay claim, on behalf of France, to the territory that he had named Louisiana, stretching from the Illinois country to the Gulf of Mexico, and beyond into the interior of New Spain (Mexico). To this end he was supplied with ships and men to sail into the Gulf of Mexico, penetrate Spanish territory, and exploit the mines he was expected to find. The expedition, which set sail in 1684, was a failure. La Salle did not succeed in rediscovering the Mississippi delta from the Gulf, and he was finally murdered by mutineers in Texas on Mar. 19, 1687.   F. J. THORPE

Bibliography: Cox, I. J., ed., *The Journeys of René Robert Cavelier, Sieur de La Salle,* 2 vols. (1922; repr. 1973); Delanglez, Jean, *Some La Salle Journeys* (1938); Eccles, W. J., *Canada under Louis XIV* (1964); Osler, E. B., *La Salle* (1967); Parkman, Francis, *La Salle and the Discovery of the Great West* (1889; rep. 1968); Weddle, Robert S., *Wilderness Manhunt: The Spanish Search for La Salle* (1973).

La Scala [lah skah'-lah]

La Scala, or the Teatro alla Scala, in Milan, Italy, has been one of the world's most prestigious opera houses since the 18th century, when on Aug. 3, 1778, a new theater was built by order of the Empress Maria Theresa to replace one that had burned down. The theater was so named because it was built on the former site of Santa Maria alla Scala, a 14th-century church. An air raid in 1943 during World War II was responsible for the virtual destruction of the theater, but it was rebuilt after the war in 1946; it now seats an audience of 3,600.

Every great Italian composer since the 18th century has composed for La Scala. The house was host to the first productions of Rossini's *La Gazza Ladra,* Donizetti's *Lucrezia Borgia,* Bellini's *Norma,* Verdi's *Otello* and *Falstaff,* Puccini's *Madama Butterfly* and *Turandot,* and Giordano's *Andrea Chenier.* Arturo Toscanini served La Scala (periodically from 1898) as principal conductor (with director-general Giulio Gatti Casazza), and after a break (1929) with Mussolini and the fascists he returned to conduct at the opening of the rebuilt theater in May 1946. Other conductors who built their careers in this opera house include Tullio Serafin, Victor De Sabata, Guido Cantelli, and Carlo Maria Giulini; the list of singers La Scala has called its own is as impressive as it is long.   KAREN MONSON

Bibliography: Jacob, Naomi E., and Robertson, James C., *Opera in Italy* (1948; repr. 1970).

La Spezia [lah spayt'-syah]

La Spezia (formerly Spezia), the capital of La Spezia province in Liguria, northwest Italy, lies southeast of Genoa on the Ligurian Sea at the eastern end of the Riviera. Its population is 112,606 (1983 est.). The area is a summer and winter resort. Along the Gulf of La Spezia near the city are the picturesque villages of Lerici and Portovenere.

Although the city has been inhabited since Roman times, it remained a small fishing village until it was fortified in the

LA SALLE'S ROUTE
1679-80, 1682

Middle Ages. La Spezia was badly damaged by Allied bombing in World War II, but the medieval Castel San Giorgio survived, and a 15th-century cathedral was rebuilt.

DANIEL R. LESNICK

La Stampa: see STAMPA, LA.

La Tène [lah ten]

La Tène is an important early Iron Age site on the east side of Lake Neuchâtel, Switzerland. Excavations at the site between 1907 and 1917 revealed that the CELTS had driven piles into the edge of the lake and constructed two timber causeways there. Numerous objects were also found in the shallow waters of the lake, including iron swords and other weapons and everyday ironwork and wood objects. Some of the finds were decorated with abstract, curvilinear patterns that appear in widely distributed examples of later CELTIC ART.

The site of La Tène has given its name to the second phase of the Celtic Iron Age in Europe, which followed the HALLSTATT period and lasted from the mid-5th century BC until the Roman conquest. Its earliest remains, found in the Marne and Middle Rhine region of west central Europe, consist of chariot burials accompanied by imported Etruscan and Greek drinking vessels, which reached Celtic lands over the Alpine passes. During the La Tène phase, prehistoric Celtic culture was at its zenith. La Tène culture existed in France, Germany, Austria, Switzerland, Bohemia, Britain, Ireland, parts of Iberia, the Low Countries, and Italy north of the Po River. Its influence was also felt in northern and eastern Europe. From the 5th century BC the La Tène Celts are mentioned by classical writers. In 387 BC the Romans were defeated by the Celts at the Battle of the Allia, and Rome was sacked. Thereafter the Celts were a serious threat to Roman Italy until their defeat in 295 BC. During the La Tène period Celts also raided the Carpathians, Bulgaria, and Macedonia, which they laid waste in 279 BC. They sacked Hellenistic Delphi and carried off booty to their shrine at Massilia (present-day Marseille) in France. Some Celts were employed as mercenary soldiers in Hellenistic armies, and a Celtic shield has been found in Egypt. Some also settled in Turkey, where they founded the kingdom of GALATIA.

From the 3d century BC on the far-flung world of the La Tène Celts shrank considerably. During the early 1st century BC the Romans began pressing on Celtic lands in GAUL. A series of political upheavals gave Julius Caesar an opportunity to begin conquering Gaul in 58 BC; he finally met a united force of Celts under VERCINGETORIX at Alesia in 52 BC where his victory meant the collapse of Celtic dominance of Gaul. Independent Celtic kingdoms were maintained in southern Britain until their conquest by Claudius in AD 43, and in Ireland and parts of Scotland until the Middle Ages.

LLOYD R. LAING

Bibliography: Chadwick, N. K., *The Celts* (1970); Filip, Jan, *Celtic Civilization and its Heritage*, trans. by Roberta F. Samsour (1962); Navarro, J. M. de, *The Finds from the Site of La Tène* (1972).

La Tour, Georges de [lah toor', zhorzh duh]

The paintings of the Lorraine artist Georges de La Tour, baptized in Vic-sur-Seille, Mar. 14, 1593, d. Jan. 30, 1652, are a unique and personal expression of the far-reaching influence of the Italian painter Caravaggio.

Nothing is known of La Tour's early life or artistic training. Except for some parallels with Nancy artists such as Jacques Callot and Jean Le Clerc, his early style closely resembles that of the Dutch Caravaggists, especially Hendrick Terbrugghen. Historians believe that he traveled north rather than to Italy in his youth. *The Fortune Teller* (c.1621; Metropolitan Museum, New York City) displays an interest in naturalistic detail and plastic form, which is like that of Terbrugghen. La Tour, however, demonstrates a greater concern for formal, large-scale composition, with dramatic effects of light and color.

In 1639, La Tour is described as an official painter to the

In The New Born *(1646–49) by the French painter Georges de La Tour, sharp, simplified forms are illuminated dramatically by controlled artificial light, turning his everyday genre subjects into spiritual images of stoic dignity. (Musée des Beaux-Arts, Rennes.)*

French king Louis XIII, suggesting that he had been to Paris, if only briefly, before this date. Whereas no trace of Parisian influence is evident in his paintings, in the late 1630s a change occurred in his style. The early daylight compositions gave way to nocturnal scenes illuminated by candles or torches, a device popularized by the Utrecht Caravaggist, Gerrit van Honthorst. *The Flea Hunt* (c.1635; Museum of Lorraine, Nancy) is a typical example. The mundane subject is enhanced by a quiet intimacy achieved through disciplined reduction of detail and controlled color and lighting. This figure is reduced to a series of nearly geometric planes echoing the pattern of horizontals and verticals that dominates the painting. This abstracting tendency creates a serenity that is characteristically French and is developed further in La Tour's mature style.

By 1620, La Tour had established a prosperous career in the town of Lunéville, summer residence of his patron the duke of Lorraine, and but for an absence between 1639 and 1641 he appears to have spent most of his life there. The artist closest to him spiritually is the Provençal painter Trophime Bigot the younger, who was active in Rome during the 1630s, but it is uncertain whether the two ever met. La Tour's late style is remarkable for its subtlety, and his masterpiece, *Saint Irene Mourning Saint Sebastian* (c.1649; Staatliche Museen, Berlin), is an exquisitely balanced study of stylized figures arrested in a moment of intense, spiritual repose.

NANETTE SALOMON

Bibliography: Blunt, Anthony, *Art and Architecture in France, 1500–1700,* 2d ed. (1970); Furness, S. M. M., *Georges de la Tour of Lorraine, 1593–1652* (1949); Nicholson, Benedict, and Wright, Christopher, *Georges de la Tour* (1974).

La Tour, Maurice Quentin de

Maurice Quentin de La Tour, b. Sept. 5, 1704, d. Feb. 17, 1788, was the most popular French portrait painter of his day. The majority of his portraits were done in pastels, a technique engendered by the pastels of the Venetian Rosalba Carriera during her triumphant Parisian visit in 1721, and one that enjoyed a great vogue in France throughout the 18th century. A virtuoso technician with a flair for capturing the inner qualities of his sitters, La Tour quickly rose to prominence. His gifts are revealed fully in his *Self-Portrait* (1751; Amiens Museum). La Tour's lucid and well-composed works reflect his ties to the Enlightenment thinkers, many of whom sat for him. Although *Voltaire* (1736; National Museum, Stockholm) is only a preliminary study of the famous man's features, it succeeds in representing the tremendous energy and vitality of the sitter. A similar vivacity animates most of La Tour's other portraits, among which his *Madame de Pompadour* (1755) and *Philibert Orry* (1745)—both in the Louvre, Paris—stand out.

Bibliography: Bury, Adrian, *Maurice Quentin de La Tour: The Greatest Pastel Portraitist* (1971); Thuiller, Jacques, and Chatelet, Albert, *French Painting from Le Nain to Fragonard*, trans. by James Emmons (1964).

La Venta   [lah vayn'-tah]

La Venta, on an island in the Tonalá River near the Gulf coast in western Tabasco, Mexico, was one of the two great OLMEC capitals. Between 900 and 400 BC it was the most powerful center in Mesoamerica.

La Venta was a modest civic-ceremonial center between 1200 and 900 BC. With the collapse of SAN LORENZO, the first Olmec capital, La Venta flourished, dominating the Olmec world until 400 BC. Its political and economic influence spread far beyond the Gulf coast Olmec heartland, reaching almost every part of Mesoamerica. La Venta's architecture features clay platforms for temples and perhaps palaces. The main pyramid, which may be an effigy volcano, is more than 30 m (100 ft) tall. La Venta is best known for its monumental stone sculpture, especially colossal human heads, and for its many caches of jade figurines and ornaments. The Smithsonian Institution and the National Geographic Society sponsored the major investigations at La Venta in 1955.

JOHN S. HENDERSON

Bibliography: Coe, Michael D., *America's First Civilization* (1968).

La Vérendrye, Pierre Gaultier de Varennes, Sieur de   [lah vay-rahn-dree', pyair goh-tyay' duh vah-ren', syur duh]

The soldier, fur trader, and explorer Pierre Gaultier de Varennes, sieur de La Vérendrye, b. Trois Rivières (now in Quebec), Nov. 17, 1685, extended the frontiers of New France well into the present Canadian province of Manitoba, visited part of the area that is now the northern U.S. Plains states, and approached the foothills of the Rockies. The son of René Gaultier, sieur de Varennes, the longtime governor of Trois Rivières, he pursued a military career in New France and France until 1712. He subsequently tried to be a farmer and worked part-time as a fur trader (on the Saint-Maurice River) until 1726 and then became the partner of his brother Jacques René in the fur trade north of Lake Superior. There he met Indians whose reports convinced him that the water route to the fabled Western Sea led through the lakes and rivers to the northwest.

Between 1731 and 1738, with the backing of the governor and intendant of New France and accompanied by three of his sons and a nephew, he established posts at Rainy Lake, the Lake of the Woods, Lake Winnipeg, the Red River, and the Assiniboine River. Unable to discover a river flowing toward the western ocean, La Vérendrye reaped an impressive fur-trade harvest, convincing the French minister of the marine, Jean Frédéric, comte de Maurepas, that his real interest was commercial gain rather than the advancement of knowledge. In late 1738 he visited the Mandan Indian villages on the Missouri River in present North Dakota, entering the main village with an escort of 600 Assiniboins and 30 Mandans and with drums beating and colors flying.

In the 1740s his sons claimed (1743) for France the area around modern Pierre, S.Dak., and added to the number of trading posts in the area that is now Manitoba. In spite of this expansion, La Vérendrye's operations were a financial failure; he resigned in 1744, leaving his sons and his nephew to carry on at the western posts. He died at Montreal on Dec. 5, 1749; that year the new French minister of the marine, Antoine Louis Rouillé, had him decorated with the cross of the order of Saint Louis. La Vérendrye had failed to persevere westward into the mountains and had lacked adequate support for his posts from the Canadian suppliers of trade goods, but he had won new Indian tribes to the French allegiance, luring

their trade away from the British HUDSON'S BAY COMPANY and toward Montreal. The journals and letters of La Vérendrye and his sons were edited and published in 1927.

F. J. THORPE

Bibliography: Crouse, N. M., *La Vérendrye, Fur Trader and Explorer* (1956; repr. 1972); Kavenagh, Martin, *La Vérendrye, His Life and Times* (1967); Rich, E. E., *The Hudson's Bay Company, 1670–1870*, 3 vols. (1960).

Laban, Rudolf von   [lah'-bahn, roo'-dohlf fuhn]

Rudolf von Laban, b. Dec. 15, 1879, d. July 1, 1958, was a Hungarian dancer, teacher, and theorist who codified the laws of physical expression and in 1928 invented a system of dance notation, *Kinetographie Laban*, now known as Labanotation. Born in Bratislava, Laban studied painting in Munich and ballet in Paris. In 1930 he was appointed director of movement in the Berlin State Opera and choreographed large productions. Reacting against what he saw as the artificiality of ballet, Laban sought freer methods of bodily expression in plastic rhythms and movement for its own sake. Working with his students Kurt Jooss and Mary Wigman, he evolved eukinetics, a system of controlling the dynamics and expressiveness of human movement. Laban sought to spread his philosophy to a lay audience and set up teaching centers all over Europe. Hitler's rise to power forced him to go (1938) to England, where, during World War II, Laban adapted his work to teach factory workers corrective exercises. BARBARA BARKER

Bibliography: Laban, Rudolf von, *A Life for the Dance*, 2d ed. (1975), *The Mastery of Movement*, 3d ed. (1971), and *Laban's Principles of Dance and Movement Notation*, 2d ed. (1975); Ullman, Lisa, *Modern Educational Dance*, 2d ed. (1973).

labeled compound: see NUCLEAR MEDICINE.

Labiche, Eugène Marin   [lah-beesh', u-zhen' mah-reen]

A writer of comedy and farce, Eugène Labiche, b. May 5, 1815, d. Jan 23, 1888, was one of the most prolific and popular 19th-century French dramatists. He produced many light, charming plays, which ranged from short sketches to full-length comedies such as *The Italian Straw Hat* (1851; Eng. trans., 1956) and *Monsieur Perrichon's Journey* (1860; Eng. trans., 1957). STUART E. BAKER

Bibliography: Labiche, Eugène, *Monsieur Perrichon's Journey*, in *Let's Get A Divorce! and Other Plays*, ed. by Eric Russell Bentley (1958).

See also: BOULEVARD THEATER.

Labille-Guiard, Adélaide   [lah-bee'-gee-ar', ah-day-lah-eed']

The French painter Adélaide Labille-Guiard, b. Apr. 11, 1749, d. Apr. 24, 1803, was a major portraitist whose forte was depicting her sitters in unselfconscious attitudes. Her first teacher was the miniaturist François Elie Vincent; subsequently (1769–74), she learned the techniques of pastels from famed portraitist Maurice Quentin de La Tour. In pre-Revolutionary years she received commissions from many members of the royal family, and her talents remained in great demand throughout the Revolutionary and Directory period.

Her detailed and vividly colored compositions were often quite ambitious in format. Rather than emulate the grand, flattering style of many 18th-century portraits, she sought to inject a sense of spontaneity and life into her subjects' poses. Representative of her lively style are her *Portrait of Mme Adélaide* (1787; Versailles) and *Self-Portrait* (1785; Metropolitan Museum of Art, New York City). ELEANOR TUFTS

Bibliography: Harris, Ann S., and Nochlin, Linda, *Women Artists: 1550–1950* (1976).

Labor, U.S. Department of

The U.S. Department of Labor was established in 1913 to "foster, promote, and develop the welfare of the wage earners of the United States, to improve their working conditions, and to advance their opportunities for profitable employment." Today the department administers more than 130 federal laws involving wages, hours, working conditions, unemployment insurance, workers' compensation, and freedom from discrimination in employment. It also publishes statistical information and engages in other activities concerned with jobs and labor unions. In 1983 it had more than 19,000 employees and a budget of about $39 billion.

The department's Employment and Training Administration assists the states in maintaining public employment services intended to help workers find jobs. It operates manpower training programs and emergency job programs for the unemployed and sets standards for apprenticeship and other forms of industrial training.

The Labor-Management Services Administration administers laws that require regular reports from labor unions and private pension plans. It helps veterans exercise their reemployment rights and supervises labor-management relations in the federal government.

The Employment Standards Administration administers the minimum-wage and hour laws and various other laws concerning the compensation of workers. In 1970 the OCCUPATIONAL SAFETY AND HEALTH ADMINISTRATION was established by Congress to enforce safety and health standards in industry.

The Bureau of Labor Statistics compiles the Consumer Price Index and indexes of wholesale prices and publishes information on employment and earnings. Its *Monthly Labor Review* is found in most reference libraries.

Labor Day

Labor Day is a holiday set aside to celebrate and honor working people. Inaugurated in 1882 by the Knights of Labor, it is now a legal holiday observed on the first Monday in September in the United States, Puerto Rico, and Canada. In Europe the day on which the history and accomplishments of labor are celebrated is May 1, MAY DAY.

labor force

The term *labor force* in its broadest sense refers to all adults within a population who work or seek work. As used by a government agency—to indicate, for example, the percentages of EMPLOYMENT AND UNEMPLOYMENT—the term is more rigorously defined. For the Bureau of Labor Statistics (BLS) of the U.S. Department of Labor, the total labor force includes both military personnel and all civilians over the age of 16 who work for pay or within a family enterprise, as well as unemployed persons actively seeking work. "Discouraged" job seekers, those who no longer look for work, are not counted as part of the labor force. According to BLS statistics, the total United States labor force in mid-1982 was 112.4 million persons; the civilian labor force totaled 110.2 million, of which 43.4% were women; 99.8 million were employed. (The total labor force, including military personnel, has been used since 1983 to determine the percentage of unemployment in the figures released monthly by the BLS.)

During the 20th century a dramatic rise in the number of women in the labor market has increased the size of the labor force. In the United States 21% of all women worked in 1900; 53% worked in 1980. Longer periods of education and earlier retirement have reduced the average number of working years for all workers and have shrunk the age span among workers. In less-developed countries the labor force includes larger proportions of persons aged less than 20 or more than 65 years, as well as more unskilled workers.

Bibliography: Berg, Ivar, *Sociological Perspectives on Labor Markets* (1981); International Labor Organization, *Labor Force Participation and Development* (1982); Rima, Ingrid, *Labor Markets, Wages, and Employment* (1980).

Labor-Management Relations Act

The Labor-Management Relations Act of 1947, better known as the Taft-Hartley Act, was intended to limit some of the activities of labor unions in the United States. It amended the NATIONAL LABOR RELATIONS ACT of 1935 (the Wagner Act), which had defined unions' rights to organize and to bargain with employers. The Taft-Hartley Act was amended by the Labor-Management Reporting and Disclosure Act of 1959.

The Taft-Hartley Act forbade unions to force employees to become members. It also banned closed shops (requiring prior union membership as a condition of being hired) and secondary boycotts. The act placed other limitations on union activities. It authorized the president of the United States to impose an 80-day delay on any strike found to imperil the national health or safety; it required unions to provide information on their finances and to give a 60-day notice before striking; it allowed employers to replace striking workers; and it imposed a ban on union contributions to political campaigns. The ban on union contributions was virtually nullified later by court rulings that it infringed the constitutional right of citizens to free expression. The act retained the provisions of the Wagner Act for voting by employees on whether they wish to be represented by a union but restricted representation elections for craftsworkers, professionals, supervisors, and custodial employees.   JACK BARBASH

Bibliography: Lee, R. Alton, *Truman and Taft-Hartley* (1966).

Labor-Management Reporting and Disclosure Act

The Labor-Management Reporting and Disclosure Act of 1959, also known as the Landrum-Griffin Act, undertakes to "eliminate or prevent improper practices on the part of labor organizations, employers, labor relations consultants and their officers or representatives." It was enacted after extensive congressional investigation into union racketeering, especially in the TEAMSTERS Union, and amends the Labor-Management Relations (Taft-Hartley) Act. The act has five principal titles.

Title I is a "bill of rights" for union members—specifically, protection against discrimination, the right to freedom of speech and assembly, and the right to sue. Procedures are established for setting dues and initiation fees, for disciplinary action, and for access to the collective-bargaining agreement.

Title II deals with disclosures of information: disclosure by the union of finances, disclosure by union officials of conflict-of-interest involvements, disclosure by employers and their consultants of payments to union officials and employees.

Title III protects trusteeships from abuse. In a trusteeship the national union typically sets aside the self-government of a subordinate body and installs a trustee to take over the organization. Title IV establishes standards for democratic union elections. Title V aims to protect union finances from mishandling, including bonding of financial officers. It prohibits bribes and payoffs in employer-union dealings. Former Communist party members and ex-convicts are prohibited from holding union office until 5 years have elapsed.   JACK BARBASH

labor union

A labor union is an organization of employees whose purpose is to bargain with an employer or a group of employers over pay and working conditions. In the United States about 23 percent of all employees belong to unions and employee associations. In other countries, especially in Western Europe, union membership is higher. It is not uncommon, as in the Scandinavian countries, for a large majority of all employees to belong to unions. West European unions reinforce their power by affiliating with labor, socialist, and, in a few countries, communist political parties. In some countries labor unions are divided into Christian and socialist groups. Frequently, labor-supported parties control the governments in their respective countries. Although U.S. unions are politically active, they have no such direct affiliations with political parties.

The four functions of unions in the United States are to recruit new members, negotiate with employers, occasionally conduct strikes to achieve their purposes, and engage in politics by supporting political candidates who are favorable to them and by working to influence legislation. Unions maintain professional staffs to manage these various operations.

In 1980 about 22.8 million workers belonged to unions and employee associations in the United States. They constituted 23 percent of the total labor force, or 25.2 percent of the employees in nonagricultural work. Union membership has been generally increasing since the early 1960s, largely because of the growth of public employee unions. At the same time, the proportion of all workers and employees enrolled in unions has been declining. This decline is probably due to the shift of the labor force away from manufacturing and manual work—areas in which unions have always been strongest—and into service occupations.

The importance of labor unions in American life cannot be measured by the number of workers who are represented by them. Many nonunion employers are influenced by the standards set in collective-bargaining agreements between unions and other employers. Unions also have great political influence both in Washington, D.C., and in the state capitals. They are the major organized force behind government policies on employment and social welfare. By means of lobbying, testimony before congressional committees, and general public relations they also influence government decisions on other economic matters and foreign affairs.

UNION STRUCTURE

Unions are classified either as craft unions, industrial unions, or public employee unions. Membership in a craft union is limited to those who practice an established craft or trade, for example, bricklayers, carpenters, and plasterers. The major craft unions are composed of workers in the building, printing, metal, and maritime trades and of railroad employees. The primary employers of craft union members are nonfactory businesses and small-scale, highly competitive, local enterprises.

The membership of an industrial union is composed of skilled, semiskilled, or unskilled workers in a particular workplace, industry, or group of industries. Industrial unions are primarily found in the more technologically advanced industries and in large-scale national and international corporations.

The craft union is likely to be more powerful than the industrial union in relation to employers, and craft union locals are likely to be more powerful than the national organization. However, the industrial union's national organization is likely to be more powerful than the local unions.

Public employee unions are organizations of municipal employees such as firefighters, teachers, and police. The major difference between unions in the private sector and those in the public sector is that the latter generally do not have the right to strike. They often strike anyway, or circumvent the ban on strikes by proclaiming that their members have been taken ill. (President Ronald Reagan's controversial reaction to the 1981 strike of the Professional Air Traffic Controllers Organization was unprecedented. He fired 11,500 controllers and decertified the union.) One of the most important issues in union-management relations today is that of what to do about strikes in the public sector. A closely related problem is how to settle disagreements without a strike and on terms that are fair both to the employees and to the public.

The typical union operates on five organizational levels. In the plant, a shop committee discusses day-to-day, on-the-job problems with management. One or more shop units make up a local union, which in urban industrial areas may have many members. The local union is the basic unit and has authority to levy dues or fees, discipline its members, and enter into written agreements with management. Sometimes local unions in a geographical or industrial area form an association (known as a district council, joint council, and so on) to coordinate their efforts on matters of common interest. The national union is composed of locals and intermediate bodies and is the kingpin in the trade union structure. The national (frequently called the international if it has Canadian locals) typically exerts the decisive influence in collective bargaining with local employers.

The federation of national unions is the top organizational body. The principal U.S. federation at present is the AMERICAN FEDERATION OF LABOR AND CONGRESS OF INDUSTRIAL ORGANIZATIONS (AFL-CIO), which is mainly an association of autonomous national unions and is financed ultimately by the dues of union members. Funds are disbursed in specified proportions to affiliated groups, with the national and local unions usually getting the largest shares. (Some major U.S. unions remain independent of the AFL–CIO, for example, the TEAMSTERS and the UNITED MINE WORKERS. The UNITED AUTO WORKERS, which had withdrawn from the AFL-CIO in 1969, rejoined in 1981.) In Canada the Canadian Congress of Labour (CCL) is the counterpart of the AFL-CIO. In 1982 a split within the CCL resulted in a new federation of building trade unions, the Canadian Federation of Labor (CFL). Canada also has a federation of Catholic labor organizations called the Confédération des Travailleurs Catholiques du Canada (CTCC).

Unions are self-governing organizations. Major decisions at all levels are made by the elected leadership. In the administration of their internal affairs, however, and in their relations with employers, many unions have developed a high degree of professionalism. Leaders often devote full time to their union positions. In addition, unions occasionally employ lawyers, doctors, economists, educators, and publicists.

COLLECTIVE BARGAINING

The major function of U.S. unions is collective bargaining, a process by which unions and employers negotiate terms of employment. The terms are set forth in a written agreement that the union and the employer promise to enforce. The collective agreement is a fairly large document that is divided into five main sections: (1) wages and wage supplements; (2) workers' rights on the job; (3) union rights in relation to the employer; (4) management rights in relation to the union; and (5) machinery for enforcing these rights, that is, the GRIEVANCE PROCEDURE.

About 200,000 labor-management agreements exist in the United States at the present time, and each is unique. Its specific provisions depend on the employer's ability to pay, the condition of the economy and the industry, the needs of the employees, and the abilities of the union and the employer negotiators.

Wages and Wage Supplements. The wage provisions of the agreement specify how much the employees are to be paid in relation to particular job classifications and types of work. The provisions cover paid holidays, paid vacations, overtime rates, and hours of work. Most agreements specify minimum daily or weekly pay guarantees.

Among the most important provisions of collective bargaining agreements are those covering so-called fringe benefits, such as health insurance, sick leave, and pensions. These benefits are no longer "fringe" but are of central importance and in the United States are evolving into a private social security system. The pay rate negotiated by unions and management is, therefore, not a matter of simply deciding on the hourly rate but a complex structure of wages, job classifications, and wage supplements.

Job Rights. Unions are also interested in workers' rights on the job, which give employees a voice in determining work conditions and protect them from arbitrary acts of their superiors. Workers have the right to complain to management without fear of reprisal if they have reason to believe that some provision of the collective agreement has been violated. Another important job right concerns discharge and discipline. In such cases, the employee must be given "just cause," or a good reason; if the employer fails to show just cause, the worker has the right of redress through the grievance machinery. Workers are also entitled to seniority rights; length of service must be considered in determining layoffs, transfers, promotions, and vacation time.

Union Rights. A collective bargaining agreement also contains union security provisions that establish the union's right to recognition as long as it represents a majority of the employees in a bargaining unit. Most agreements provide for a union shop, where workers are hired on the condition that they join the union and pay dues. (In a CLOSED SHOP, all persons hired must already be union members. OPEN SHOPS,

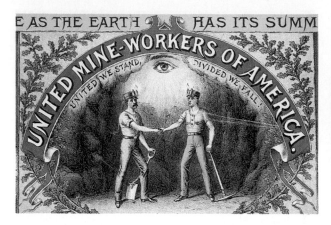

This detail of an early United Mine Workers membership certificate testifies to the idealism that animated the American labor movement during the late 19th century. Such idealism also led many 19th-century unions to incorporate social and political causes into their platforms.

"Breaker" boys employed (c.1900) in U.S. coal mines often worked 10-hour shifts, sorting coal under deplorable conditions. Labor unions were among the chief supporters of the earliest state and federal attempts to regulate child labor through legislation.

which are mandatory in states that have RIGHT-TO-WORK LAWS, do not require union membership as a condition of employment.) A check-off clause requires management to withhold union dues from employees' pay and forward them to the union. Under federal law a union has exclusive representation in any collective bargaining unit where it has been selected by a majority of the employees. The employer may not bargain with any other union or employee group claiming to represent workers in that unit, which may be an occupation, craft, department, plant or plants, company, or companies, depending on the scope of the agreement.

Management Rights. An agreement will also contain provisions designed to protect "management's right to manage" from union penetration. Unions in the United States say that they seek only to review management decisions, and then only those decisions that affect the terms of employment. Nonetheless, employers feel strongly that they need protection from union invasion of their prerogatives. A typical management rights provision will read, "The management of the plant and the direction of the working force, including the right to establish reasonable rules and regulations and production schedules, to hire, to promote outside the bargaining unit, and to discharge for just cause, shall be vested exclusively in the company, subject to the agreement."

Enforcement. Many unionists believe that enforcing the agreement is the most important part of the collective bargaining process and that without enforcement the written agreement is ineffective. Enforcement is administered through a functioning grievance procedure that culminates in ARBITRATION.

POLITICAL ACTION
Most unions have found that political and legislative activity are necessary complements to collective bargaining. They work to elect candidates for federal, state, and local offices who favor union positions, and they usually support candidates on the basis of their records rather than their party. However, Democrats seem more likely to favor labor programs than do Republicans. In the 1930s, Franklin D. Roosevelt turned to organized labor for political support, and in most presidential elections since then the unions have favored the Democratic nominee. For many candidates, union support is often crucial. In comparison with other interest groups that help fund election campaigns, labor union POLITICAL ACTION COMMITTEES (PACS) have donated the largest aggregate amounts.

The legislative side of union activity consists of lobbying for union policies in the state legislatures and in Congress and of monitoring the enforcement of these policies. Full employment, improved Social Security benefits, fuller health insurance coverage, protection from foreign imports, equal opportunity, taxation, occupational health and safety, minimum

wages, and the reform of labor laws are some of the major legislative interests of unions. Legislation and politics are the primary concern of the staff of the AFL–CIO.

DEVELOPMENT OF UNIONS
In the Middle Ages the GUILDS—economic organizations of craftsmen—set price and quality standards and fended off competition. The 16th-century journeyman's societies carried out extensive lobbying and some strikes. The labor union in England developed in response to the changed conditions of the Industrial Revolution, but attempts to organize unions were largely unsuccessful until the formation (1868) of the TRADES UNION CONGRESS and the passage of the Trade Union Act. In the late 19th century British unions allied with socialists in the Independent Labour party (later the LABOUR PARTY). German unions began to organize after 1848 but attained no lasting significance until after World War II; in France labor union groups formed in the early 19th century. In Russia labor unions developed for a brief time in 1905 and again under state supervision after 1917. Developing countries in the second half of the 20th century have spawned politically important mass union movements.

Unions have existed in the United States since the late 18th century, when the growing distance between masters and workers encouraged the formation of unions. The early unions were local units organized by skilled craftsmen to protect themselves against the competition of half-trained workers ("green hands").

After about 1830 the unions became reform-minded and sought to change the economic and social system rather than simply to bargain with employers. The skilled craftsmen in the unions had not fully reconciled themselves to the status of wage earners; they clung to the ideal of self-employed artisan, which they saw being threatened by the growth of large industry. The spokesmen of this movement were middle-class intellectual reformers who, even before the time of Karl Marx, sought to direct the workers along anticapitalist and antiindustrialist lines. Producers' cooperatives, currency reform, temperance, and independent labor parties were popular causes. The KNIGHTS OF LABOR, which flourished between 1869 and 1886, marked the full flowering and then the rapid decline of this kind of reformism in the American labor movement. As the Industrial Revolution got fully under way in the

(Above) *Samuel Gompers, who helped to found the American Federation of Labor in 1886, served as that organization's president for 37 years. His emphasis on "bread and butter" unionism, with its rejection of political activism, did much to shape the goals of organized labor in the United States.* (Below) *The 1937 strike of Chrysler auto workers in Detroit, following a successful strike against General Motors earlier that year, gained industry recognition of the newly formed United Auto Workers.*

George Meany, then president of the AFL, and Walter Reuther of the CIO join hands victoriously at the 1955 convention that proclaimed the merger of the two labor federations. The AFL-CIO is today a major force in American economic and political life.

post–Civil War period, the Knights of Labor gave way to the emerging craft unions. The American Federation of Labor, formed in 1886 under Samuel Gompers, became the symbol of the new unionism. The AFL unionists believed that industrial capitalism was here to stay and grow, that there was no retreat from the wage system, and that the primary purpose of the unions had to be improving the workers' lot through collective bargaining. This was called "pure and simple" or "bread and butter" unionism, in contrast with socialist or rev-olutionary unionism, the primary objective of which was transforming society. Although craft unions dominated this period, radical voices, both within and outside the AFL, argued that no permanent solution to the problems of the worker was possible in a capitalist society. The most dramatic challenges came from such socialist leaders as Eugene V. Debs and Daniel De Leon. Another radical was William D. (Big Bill) Haywood, the leader of the militant Industrial Workers of the World (IWW).

Neither pure-and-simple unionism nor radical unionism gained a foothold in the mass production sectors of the economy. However, the craft unions flourished in the construction, printing, and railroad industries, where employers' bargaining power was weak and the ties of the craftsmen were strong. The craft unions also managed their organizations in a more businesslike way and attracted and held members through a system of unemployment, sickness, and death benefits that the workers themselves financed.

New Deal Era. Trade unions reached their lowest point during the Great Depression that began in 1929 and continued into the early 1930s; however, Franklin D. Roosevelt's New Deal (1933) changed their fortunes. The New Deal permitted government intervention in the economy, and much of it was designed to strengthen the unions and the workers. For the unions the most significant part of the New Deal was the National Labor Relations Act of 1935, better known as the Wagner Act, which strengthened the unions' rights to organize and bargain with employers. Leaders such as John L. Lewis, Walter P. Reuther, David Dubinsky, and Sidney Hillman brought great personal abilities to the creation of new unions

THE 30 LARGEST U.S. LABOR ORGANIZATIONS, 1988

Name of Organization	Members
Teamsters, Chauffeurs, Warehousemen, and Helpers of America, International Brotherhood of	2,000,000
National Education Association	1,600,800
Food and Commercial Workers, United	1,300,000
State, County, and Municipal Employees, American Federation of	1,200,000
United Automobile, Aerospace, and Agricultural Implement Workers of America, International Union	1,197,000
Electrical Workers, International Brotherhood of	1,000,000
Service Employees' International Union	850,000
Machinists and Aerospace Workers, International Assoc. of	800,000
Steelworkers of America, United	750,000
Carpenters and Joiners of America, United Brotherhood of	700,000
Teachers, American Federation of	660,000
Communications Workers of America	650,000
Engineers, International Union of Operating	420,000
Hotel Employees and Restaurant Employees International Union	370,000
Postal Workers Union, American	320,000
Plumbing and Pipefitting Industry of the U.S. and Canada, United Association of Journeymen and Apprentices of the	320,000
Printing Trades Association, International Allied	300,000
Clothing and Textile Workers Union, Amalgamated	280,560
Civil Service Employees Association	240,000
Letter Carriers of the United States of America, National Association of	277,500
Government Employees, American Federation of	250,000
Mine Workers of America, United	240,000
Paperworkers International Union, United	240,000
Retail, Wholesale, and Department Store Union	225,000
Electronic, Electrical, Salaried, Machine, and Furniture Workers, International Union of	200,000
Graphic Communications International Union	200,000
Musicians of the U.S. and Canada, American Federation of	200,000
School Employees, American Association of Classified	200,000
Transportation Communications International Union	200,000
Government Employees, National Association of	195,000

SOURCE: *Encyclopedia of Associations 1989.*

UNION MEMBERSHIP IN THE UNITED STATES, 1955-86

Year	Union Membership	Union Membership as % of Labor Force
1955	17,749,000	24.4
1960	18,177,000	23.6
1965	18,519,000	22.4
1970	20,752,000	22.6
1974	21,643,000	21.7
1978	21,784,000	19.7
1980	19,843,000	18.2
1983	17,717,000	20.1
1986	16,975,000	17.5

SOURCE: U.S. Bureau of Labor Statistics.

in the mass-production industries. These unions affiliated in the Congress of Industrial Organizations, which in 1955 merged with the American Federation of Labor under the leadership of George MEANY.

The membership of national unions grew from less than 3 million in 1933 to more than 8 million in 1938. During World War II it continued to increase and reached more than 14 million in 1945. Growth subsequently leveled off, and some observers asked whether unionism had reached a point of stagnation and decline. Beginning in the 1960s the growth of public employee unionism did stimulate union development, but through the 1980s overall union membership declined.

Internationally, two large organizations—the WORLD FEDERATION OF TRADE UNIONS (1945) and the INTERNATIONAL CONFEDERATION OF FREE TRADE UNIONS (1949)—have come to dominate the scene. The INTERNATIONAL LABOR ORGANIZATION (1919), an agency of the United Nations, promotes better working conditions and collective bargaining, among other things.

Labor Legislation. The Wagner Act and other laws, mostly federal laws reinforced by court interpretations, have protected and regulated labor unions. The Norris-La Guardia Act (1932) prohibited the granting of injunctions in labor disputes in federal courts. The LABOR-MANAGEMENT RELATIONS ACT (1947), more often called the Taft-Hartley Act, prohibited certain unfair practices by unions against employers. The LABOR-MANAGEMENT REPORTING AND DISCLOSURE ACT of 1959, called the Landrum-Griffin Act, protected the rights of union members as against union officers and sought to eliminate union racketeering. The CIVIL RIGHTS ACT of 1964 prohibited discrimination by unions and employers on the basis of race, sex, or age. Federal executive orders have given federal employees the right to form unions as well as to bargain with their employer. State laws have done the same for state employees. RIGHT-TO-WORK LAWS in many states prohibit union-shop agreements.

Recent federal laws and regulations determine not only how bargaining is to be accomplished but what the parties should bargain about. Since World War II, the federal government has occasionally stepped in to restrict the wage increases that unions could ask for, in an effort to curb inflation. The federal government is increasingly setting standards for specified areas previously covered only by the collective agreement, for example, in occupational health and safety and in PENSION plans.   JACK BARBASH

Bibliography: Barbash, Jack, *American Unions: Structure, Government, and Politics* (1966); Brierley, W., *Trade Unions and the Economic Crisis of the 1980's* (1986); Estey, Marten, *The Unions: Structure, Development, and Management,* 3d ed. (1981); Fink, Gary M., *Labor Unions* (1977); Freeman, Richard B., and Medoff, James L., *What Do Unions Do?* (1984); Goldfield, Michael, *The Decline of Organized Labor in the United States* (1987); Lipset, Seymour M., ed., *Unions in Transition: Entering the Second Century* (1986).

Labour party

The Labour party, one of Great Britain's two major political parties, came into being in 1900 as the offspring of the British trade union and socialist movements of the late 19th century. The Reform Acts of 1867 and 1884, which enfranchised the workers, the founding (1868) of the TRADES UNION CONGRESS (TUC) to coordinate the burgeoning labor movement, and the forming of the socialist FABIAN SOCIETY (1883) and of the Independent Labour party (ILP, 1893) laid the groundwork for a viable Labour party. In 1900 the TUC and the ILP—at the urging of the Fabian Society and of Keir HARDIE, who had founded the Scottish Labour party in 1888—merged to form the Labour Representation Committee. In 1906 this organization was renamed the Labour party. Its early development was hampered by poor organization and by widely divergent political views. In World War I the pacifist stand of the Labour party's leader Ramsay MACDONALD led to his replacement in 1914 by Arthur HENDERSON. The party joined in the coalition governments during the war, but it withdrew in 1918. By 1922, growing postwar economic and social problems, a split in the Liberal party, and the resolution of many of the differences between the trade union and the socialist factions resulted in Labour becoming the second strongest party in Great Britain.

The MacDonald Governments. In 1924, with Liberal support, the first Labour government was formed, led by Ramsay MacDonald. MacDonald encountered political difficulties over the question of relations with the USSR, and the government fell before the year was out. Labour returned to power in 1929–31 with another minority government. Faced with the world economic crisis, MacDonald turned to conservative policies that were rejected by his own cabinet; he formed (1931) a new coalition with Liberals and Conservatives. Although the Labour party expelled him from its ranks, he continued as prime minister with support from other parties until 1935. Labour did not return to power until 1940, when it joined Winston Churchill's wartime coalition government.

The Attlee Era. By the 1940s the party had developed a broad program of social reform involving nationalization of key industries. In July 1945 it won a decisive victory at the polls, and Clement ATTLEE became prime minister in Labour's first majority government. Attlee's able cabinet included Ernest BEVIN as foreign secretary, Sir Stafford CRIPPS as chancellor of the exchequer, and Aneurin BEVAN as minister of health. The government passed a comprehensive national health bill and nationalized the Bank of England and major industries. By 1951 nationalization extended to one-fifth of the economy. Labour also oversaw the granting of independence to India in 1947 and supported the formation of NATO.

The 1950 elections severely reduced Labour's parliamentary majority, and in 1951 the Conservatives returned to power for 13 years. Ensuing years were marked by ideological conflict within Labour's ranks. Left-wingers, led by Aneurin Bevan, advocated further nationalization of industry and a reduced dependence on the United States. They lost to those led by Hugh GAITSKELL, who wanted a less doctrinaire program. A change also took place in party membership, with suburban and middle-class people joining in greater numbers.

The 1960s and After. The Labour party was in power again from 1964 to 1970 under Harold WILSON and returned once more in 1974. The country's economic difficulties were a continuing burden. Great Britain's participation in the European Economic Community troubled many members, and inflationary wage demands by unions that form the core of the party caused considerable friction. An energy crisis, low productivity, and the huge costs of the welfare state compounded its difficulties. James CALLAGHAN, who succeeded Harold Wilson in 1976, had some success in fighting inflation, but a series of strikes and renewed economic problems in the winter of 1978–79 led to Labour's losing a vote of confidence in the House of Commons (March 1979) and then to the party's crushing defeat by the Conservatives in May 1979. The split between the left- and right-wing factions of the party widened decisively in 1980 over issues of party organization. In November Callaghan was succeeded by Michael FOOT, a left-wing moderate. In 1981, amid great controversy, the party voted to adopt a system of choosing a leader in which representatives of the unions and local organizations participated as well as members of Parliament (who had previously been the sole electors). This left wing victory caused four former cabinet members, including Roy JENKINS, David Owen, and Shirley Williams, to leave the party and form the new Social Democratic party. (The Social Democrats subsequently allied with the Liberal party.) Weakened by this defection, Labour was again defeated at the polls in the general elections of 1983 and 1987. In 1983, Neil KINNOCK replaced Foot as party leader. JOHN H. FENTON

Bibliography: Cole, G. D. H., *History of the Labour Party from 1914* (1948); Drucker, H. M., *Doctrine and Ethos in the Labour Party* (1979); Foote, Geoffrey, *The Labour Party's Political Thought,* 2d ed. (1986); Pelling, Henry, *A Short History of the Labour Party,* 3d ed. (1968), and *Origins of the Labour Party,* 2d ed. (1965).

Labrador   [lab'-ruh-dohr]

Labrador is the northeastern sector of mainland Canada encompassing parts of the provinces of Quebec and Newfoundland. It covers about 1,620,000 km² (625,000 mi²). Labrador is bounded by Hudson Strait (north), Hudson Bay (west), the Gulf of St. Lawrence and Eastmain River (south), and the Atlantic Ocean (east). The name Labrador is often applied only to the Newfoundland coast, while the Quebec portion is called UNGAVA. The principal towns are Schefferville in Quebec and Labrador City and Wabush in Newfoundland.

Mining of iron ore along the Ungava-Newfoundland border is the main economic activity. Lumbering and its products are important, and some income is derived from fishing and fur trapping. Hydroelectric resources are being developed, with plants at Menihek and Churchill Falls.

By about the 10th century AD, Vikings who had sailed across the Atlantic established a settlement (L'ANSE AUX MEADOWS) on the Labrador coast. The settlement was subsequently deserted. In 1498, John Cabot visited Labrador. Political control of the region was not settled until 1927, when the border between Newfoundland and Quebec was established.

Labrador retriever

A strongly built, medium-sized, all-purpose dog, the Labrador retriever has become one of the world's most popular breeds. Males stand 57.2–62.2 cm (22.5–24.5 in) at the shoulder and weigh 27–34 kg (60–75 lb); females are 54.6–59.7 cm (21.5–23.5 in) and weigh 25–31.7 kg (55–70 lb). The Labrador's tail is medium in length, thick at the base, and tapering toward the tip. The short, dense coat has no feathering and is black, yellow, or chocolate. The Labrador originated in Newfoundland, where it aided fishermen. The dogs' express job was to swim to shore with the drag ends of fishing nets in their mouths. The men then took over the nets and the dogs swam back to the boats. JOHN MANDEVILLE

The Labrador retriever is an accomplished swimmer. Originating in Newfoundland, it is used to retrieve waterfowl and to flush out and retrieve pheasant, grouse, and other upland game birds.

Bibliography: Howe, Lorna, and Waring, Geoffrey, *The Labrador Retriever,* rev. ed. (1975).

labradorite: see FELDSPAR.

Labrouste, Henri   [lah-broost', ahn-ree']

Henri Labrouste, b. May 11, 1801, d. June 24, 1875, was a rationalist architect whose chief legacy consists of work at two major libraries in Paris. Labrouste studied at the École des Beaux-Arts, won the Prix de Rome in 1824, and returned (1830) to Paris, where he worked and taught until his death. His Bibliothèque Sainte Geneviève (1843–50) was one of the first large-scale public buildings to feature visible iron construction in the interior; its arcade of slender columns supports a delicately ornamented vault. The masonry exterior is one of the finest examples of Renaissance revival. Labrouste's discipline and taste also characterize his Reading Room and stacks (1858–68) within the complex of the Bibliothèque Nationale: the succession of fragile domes carried on metal columns is ethereal in effect. ROBERT NEUMAN

Bibliography: Giedion, S., *Space, Time and Architecture,* 5th ed. (1967).

labyrinth and maze   [lab'-uh-rinth, mayz]

The labyrinth was, in ancient times, a structure composed of an intricate series of passageways and chambers, probably at first designed to baffle enemies. A labyrinth either had branched paths with misleading goals or one long circuitous path that led to a central goal. A maze is a form of labyrinth.

Labyrinth. The largest and most complex of the ancient labyrinths was that of the temple of the dead, adjoined to the tomb of the Egyptian pharaoh Amenemhet III at Hawara (19th century BC). The most famous of legendary labyrinths was in KNOSSOS on Crete. According to Greek mythology, MINOS, king of Crete, yearly chose 14 Athenian youths as food for the MINOTAUR, the monster confined in the labyrinth built by DAEDALUS. So artfully was his maze of passageways designed that no one entering it could find a way out, until THESEUS succeeded in escaping after killing the Minotaur. Homer describes the Cretan labyrinth as a setting for a ritual dance that was probably associated with the coming of spring.

Both angular and rounded labyrinth designs appear as rock carvings in Europe and the New World, on ancient pottery, in mosaics on pavements and in homes throughout the Roman Empire, and in art in Africa, Australia, and India.

Maze. A maze, which is labyrinthine in design, generally refers to a feature of formal gardens in England and in Europe. Turf mazes, commonly found in England, are often called Troy-towns, either for the name of the city or from the Celtic word *tro*, ''to burn.'' Mazes are depicted in such medieval churches as the parish church at Saint Quentin and Chartres Cathedral in France, and at San Vitale, Ravenna, and Lucca cathedrals in Italy; they are thought to have been incorporated into churches as copies of stone or turf mazes to show the difficult way to heaven.

Formal gardens of the 16th and 17th centuries often contained topiary mazes of box or yew trees. Such mazes were found in many countries, including Italy, at the Villa d'Este in Tivoli; Belgium; and at the emperor's summer palace, Yüan Ming Yüan, in China. André LE NÔTRE created at Versailles a maze (since destroyed) whose intersections contained 39 fountains in the form of animals from Aesop's fables. The maze at HAMPTON COURT, near London, was constructed in 1690 and is the oldest surviving one in England. The original 17th-century holly maze at the Governor's Palace in Williamsburg, Va., was re-created in the 20th century.

Bibliography: Bord, Janet, *Mazes and Labyrinths of the World* (1976); Matthews, Wilham H., *Mazes and Labyrinths* (1922; repr. 1969).

Lacaille, Nicolas Louis de   [lah-ky']

Nicolas Louis de Lacaille, b. Mar. 15, 1713, d. Mar. 21, 1762, was a French astronomer and mapmaker whose measurements helped to confirm the disputed Newtonian belief that the Earth bulges at the equator. Lacaille's career was climaxed by an expedition to the Cape of Good Hope where, from 1751 to 1753, he charted the stars of the southern skies.

Lacan, Jacques

The French psychiatrist Jacques Marie Émile Lacan, b. Apr. 13, 1901, d. Sept. 9, 1981, was as highly controversial as he was influential in his field. Considering himself a strict Freudian but taking ideas also from structuralist linguistics, he revived interest among French intellectuals in Freudian ideas. He held that a child's acquisition of language begins the repression of thoughts and emotions that later could result in mental illness. In 1953 he and his followers were expelled from the International Psychoanalytic Association for unorthodoxies that included using analytic sessions as short as five minutes. He founded the Freudian School of Paris in 1964 and disbanded it in 1980, after it had fallen into ''deviations and compromises.'' Lacan's writings include *The Four Fundamental Concepts of Psycho-Analysis* (Eng. trans., 1981) and *Speech and Language in Psychoanalysis* (Eng. trans., 1981).

Lacandón   [lah-kahn-dohn']

The Lacandón are Maya Indians living in the mountainous, heavily forested area of eastern Chiapas, Mexico, near the Guatemalan border. Their history is relatively unknown, but there are indications that the Lacandón had a complex sociopolitical organization in pre-Columbian times. Today they number only about 200 and live in tiny, widely scattered villages composed of several related families. Slash-and-burn agriculturalists, the Lacandón are forced to move every few years, when the cultivable land becomes exhausted. Their principal crop is maize; fishing is also important.

The Lacandón are noted for their fierce resistance to the introduction of Roman Catholicism. Each village contains a crudely built temple in which copal (incense) is burned to propitiate the traditional gods.   LOUIS C. FARON

Bibliography: Baer, Philip, and Merrifield, William, *Two Studies on the Lacandónes of Mexico* (1971).

Laccadive Islands   [lak'-uh-dive]

The Laccadive Islands, renamed Lakshadweep in 1973, are located in the Arabian Sea about 320 km (200 mi) from the south Indian coast; they are a union territory of India. The 27 coral islands and numerous reefs have a total area of about 29 km² (11 mi²) and a population of 40,237 (1981). The main islands are Kavarrati, Minicoy, and Amindivi. The people, mostly Muslims, fish and produce copra and coconut fiber. The Portuguese discovered the islands in 1498.

laccolith   [lak'-uh-lith]

A laccolith is a large, mainly concordant, mushroom-shaped, intrusive body of IGNEOUS ROCK with a flat bottom and a dome-shaped top. It is made up of coarse-grained plutonic rocks, often in the range from granite to gabbro. Most laccoliths are thought to form by deep igneous activity in which magma rises through a feeder pipe or dike into sedimentary rocks domed up by the intrusion.   WILLIAM D. ROMEY

lace

True laces are decorative openwork fabrics made of very fine threads of linen, cotton, silk, or similar material. If the thread is worked with spools, or bobbins, the lace is called bobbin or pillow lace; lace made with a needle is called needle lace, point lace, or needlepoint lace. Composite laces are made using a combination of the two techniques. Laces that are produced using the techniques of macrame, crochet, or knitting are not considered true laces, although Irish crocheted lace is highly esteemed. Almost all modern lace is made by machine and closely imitates the techniques and motifs of handmade types.

In making needle lace, one or more threads are laid down on a piece of parchment according to a pattern drawn on it. Some of the areas between the tacked-down threads are filled in with a regular meshwork of stitching to form the lace's background, called the net ground or reseau. The remaining open areas are filled in with more ornamental needlework to produce the primary design elements (toile).

To make bobbin lace, individual threads, each wound on a bobbin, are twisted and plaited together around an intricate network of pins placed in a paper pattern attached to a pillow. The pattern shows where the pins are to be placed and how the bobbins are to be manipulated. For some bobbin laces both the net ground and toile are worked at the same time; for others, individually worked pieces of lace, called sprigs, are appliquéd to an existing net ground. Composite laces usually entail appliquéing needleworked sprigs to bobbin-worked or machine-made grounds.

Bobbin lace and needle lace both probably originated in Italy during the early part of the 16th century. Bobbin lace developed from macrame and other types of fancy knotting that flourished in Genoa, Venice, and the other Italian textile centers. Needle lace evolved from drawn-thread work, cutwork, and other openwork embroidery techniques. Knowledge of the new techniques quickly spread to Belgium, and the artisans there were soon making bobbin laces as fine as those made in Italy. By the middle of the 16th century, exceptional needle laces were being produced in Spain and Switzerland. Lace making spread to England and France in the 17th century and also was important in Germany and Austria.

The important bobbin laces include Belgian Mechlin, Bruges, Point de Lille, Valenciennes, Antwerp, and Binche; Italian Milanese; French Chantilly and Point de Paris; and English Honiton, Buckinghamshire, and Bedfordshire. The needle laces include the Italian Point de Venice, the Spanish Point d'Espagne, the Flemish Point de Venise and Point

(Above) *The naturalistic motifs characteristic of bobbin lace are exemplified in this linen cravat end (1720–30) from Brussels. By the early 1700s the lace makers of the Low Countries, aided by the development of a regular ground mesh, or reseau, excelled in the creation of bobbin lace. (Cooper Hewitt Museum, New York City.)*
(Left) *The floral patterns of this early-18th-century cravat are typical of needle lace of the baroque period. Symmetry distinguishes the needle lace of the 17th and early 18th centuries from that of the Renaissance. (Cooper Hewitt Museum, New York City.)*

Chantilly lace, a silk bobbin lace, is characterized by elaborate pictorial designs executed against a hexagonal double-mesh background. The use of black silk thread in the design of Chantilly lace, exemplified in this French fan (c.1850–70), is more common than that of white silk thread. (Victoria and Albert Museum, London.)

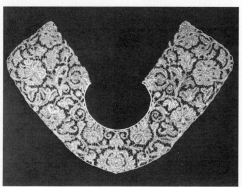

The heavy ornamentation characteristic of the baroque period is seen in this collar (c.1650; Victoria and Albert Museum, London; left) of gros point de Venise, a scrolled needle lace worked in relief, and in the Italian bobbin-lace collar (c.1650; Cooper Hewitt Museum, New York City; center), in which metallic threads accentuate the floral designs. The Belgian handkerchief (late 19th century; Metropolitan Museum of Art, New York City) shown on the right is of linen and Valenciennes bobbin lace, a delicate lace distinguished by its flat texture.

d'Angleterre, and the French Point d'Argentan and Point d'Alençon.
MARK DITTRICK

Bibliography: Bath, Virginia C., *Lace* (1974); Jackson, Emily N., *History of Handmade Lace* (1900; repr. 1971); Meulen-Nulle, L. W. van der, *Lace* (1964); Nottingham, Pamela, *Complete Book of English Bobbin Lace* (1977); Pethebridge, Jeanette, *A Manual of Lace* (1947); Pfannschmidt, Ernest-Eric, *Twentieth-Century Lace* (1977); Powys, Marian, *Lace and Lace-making* (1953); Wardle, Patricia, *Victorian Lace* (1969).

lacertid   [luh-surt'-id]

Lacertids are about 20 genera and 160 species of lizards of the family Lacertidae. They occur in Europe, Asia, and, most abundantly, in Africa. Characteristic of this family is a complete bar at the rear of the skull; bony plates (osteoderms) cover the opening above the bar and obscure its presence. Osteoderms fused to the skull also underlay the large scales (shields) on top of the head.

For the most part, lacertids are small, agile lizards. The largest species, the jeweled lizard, *Lacerta lepida*, reaches only about 75 cm (29.5 in) in total length. The viviparous lizard, *L. vivipara*, is live-bearing through most of its extensive range, but there is some evidence that it is egg-laying in the Pyrenees mountains of western Europe. The European fence lizard, *L. agilis*, is representative of many Eurasian species, breeding in the spring (May or June) and laying eggs in early summer (June or July). Incubation takes two to three months, depending upon temperature. Lacertids feed mainly on insects and other small invertebrates.
JONATHAN CAMPBELL

lacewing   [lays'-wing]

The giant lacewings, such as Osmylus fulvicephalus, *are the largest types of lacewing, with wingspans up to 75 mm (nearly 3 in).*

Lacewings (family Chrysopidae) are common insects that are important predators of aphids. They are usually greenish, often with copper-colored eyes, and mostly 10–20 mm (0.4–0.8 in) in length. The common name refers to the lacy character of the wings, which at rest are held rooflike over the body. The eggs are laid on foliage, each at the end of a tiny stalk. Adult lacewings give off a disagreeable odor when handled.
DONALD J. BORROR

Lachaise, Gaston   [lah-shez', gahs-tohn']

The French-American sculptor Gaston Lachaise, b. Paris, Mar. 1, 1882, d. Oct. 18, 1935, contributed a contemporary Venus—imperious, erotic, yet full of grace—to modern art. After his training in the classical mode of sculpture at the École des Beaux-Arts, Paris, Lachaise went (1906) to the United States and worked in New York City and Boston. He emigrated in order to follow Isabel Dutaud Nagle, after whom his powerful vision of womanhood was modeled. They were married in 1913. The innovative *Standing Woman: Elevation* (1912-27; Albright-Knox Art Gallery, Buffalo, N.Y.) announces his mature style. His ornamental sculptures include work on the RCA Building and the International Building at Rockefeller Center in New York City. The voluptuous and iconic *Heroic Woman* (1932; Museum of Modern Art, New York City) marks the culmination of Lachaise's treatment of the monumental female nude.
DAVID TATHAM

Bibliography: Kramer, Hilton, *The Sculpture of Gaston Lachaise* (1967); Norland, Gerald, *Gaston Lachaise, the Man and His Work* (1974) and *Gaston Lachaise, 1882-1935: Sculpture and Drawings* (1964).

Lachish   [lay'-kish]

Lachish, identified at the mound of Tell ed-Duweir, in present-day Israel, southwest of Jerusalem, was a major city of ancient Palestine during the Bronze Age (2d millennium BC). Caves beneath the mound proper were occupied as early as the 4th millennium BC; they were subsequently used for burials. During the Middle Bronze Age (c.1900–1500 BC) the city was fortified with a glacis and provided with a moat. In the Late Bronze Age (c.1550–1200 BC) this moat was the location for three successive temples. Known as the "Fosse Temples," they contained ivory carvings, scarabs, ritual vessels, and a wealth of imported Cypriot and Mycenaean pottery.

At the end of the 13th century BC, Lachish was destroyed, perhaps by the Israelites. The city was rebuilt (928-911 BC) by Rehoboam, and a palace was founded above the earlier buildings of the Late Bronze Age. The city was fortified with a double wall with buttresses and towers, and a rock-cut water system was started but was never completed. After the city's violent destruction by Sennacherib in 701 BC, the events of which are recorded on a relief from Nineveh, this palace was abandoned. The gateway of the succeeding 7th-century BC city contained rooms in which were found the famous Lachish Letters. Written (c.589 BC) in ink on potsherds, they vividly describe the conditions of the city immediately prior to its destruction by Nebuchadnezzar II in 587 BC.

Late remains of a large public building date from the Persian period (mid-5th century BC). The site was excavated from 1932 to 1938 by the British archaeologist J. L. Starkey. Renewed excavations by the University of Tel Aviv were begun in 1967.
JONATHAN N. TUBB

Bibliography: Thomas, D. Winton, ed., *Archaeology and Old Testament Study* (1967).

Lackawanna River   [lak-uh-wahn'-uh]

The Lackawanna River flows through northeastern Pennsylvania. Its east and west branches meet just south of Uniondale and flow 56 km (35 mi) southwest, crossing a major anthracite coal-mining region, to join the SUSQUEHANNA RIVER near Pittston. SCRANTON is the largest city on the Lackawanna's banks.

lacquer   [lak'-ur]

Lacquer is a fast-drying, high-gloss varnish used as a protective and decorative coating on objects made, usually, of wood and known as lacquer ware. It is also used in industrial applications on metal, fabric, leather, and paper. Lacquers originated in China, perhaps as early as the Chou dynasty (1027–256 BC), although the Ming period (AD 1368-1644) pro-

This early-15th-century red lacquer box was created during the Ming dynasty (1368-1644), when carved red lacquer ware attained full expression. The design is characteristic of lacquer ware of the period. (Smithsonian Institution, Freer Gallery of Art, Washington, D.C.)

duced the most diverse and beautiful lacquered objects, including the famous red, carved lacquer ware. Japanese lacquerers probably learned the art from the Chinese, and surpassed them in the development of a new technique for the incorporation of gold and silver inlays (see CHINESE ART AND ARCHITECTURE; JAPANESE ART AND ARCHITECTURE).

Although the word *lacquer* is derived from *lac*, a resin secreted by an insect (*Laccifer lacca*) found largely in Southeast Asia (see SHELLAC), the first true lacquers were exudates collected from the sap of a sumac tree, *Rhus vernicifera*, native to China, Japan, and the Himalayas. After being boiled down and mixed with coloring pigments, the sap would dry to a high, hard gloss when painted on a surface. A soft, smooth wood was usually used as the base of the lacquered object. The wood was coated with pastes made of starch, clay, and resin and then covered with a thin cloth, over which successive layers of lacquer were painted, allowed to dry, and then rubbed to a glossy, smooth polish. Layers of clear lacquer separated the layers of colored lacquer. A finished piece might have as many as 250 layers of lacquer which, if carved, revealed the colors of the lower layers. Incredibly intricate designs could thus be obtained.

Modern lacquers are almost entirely synthetic. Many industrial lacquers are made from cellulose compounds, especially nitrocellulose, with resins added for durability and adhesion and plasticizers such as linseed or castor oil to improve flexibility. Cellulose-based lacquers are used in the manufacture of inks and furniture coatings. For many other applications vinyls, acrylics, or other synthetic polymers are used to produce lacquers of great clarity and durability.   JOHN J. OBERLE

Bibliography: Huth, Hans, *Lacquer of the West* (1971); Kuwayama, George, *Far Eastern Lacquer* (1982); Rague, Beatrix von, *A History of Japanese Lacquerwork* (1976); Yonemura, Ann, *Japanese Lacquer* (1979); Yu-Kuan, Lee, *Oriental Lacquer Art* (1972).

See also: PAINT.

lacrosse   [luh-kraws']

Lacross is a team sport in which players use a netted stick, the crosse, to throw or bat a ball into a goal; players may also kick the ball into the goal. The game originated in contests among various North American Indians. The Indian game, haggataway, received its modern name from French Canadians who saw in the crosse's shaft a resemblance to a bishop's crosier (*la croix*). Intertribal Indian games used as many as 200 men to a side, and the goal area was designated by the place where the senior medicine man from each tribe stood. A modern lacrosse game with a set of rules was first played in an enclosed field by two Indian teams in 1834. Soon many whites played the game, and in 1867, Dr. George W. Beers, a native of Montreal, codified the first lacrosse rules. The game spread to other English-speaking countries, and in North America it remains a popular club and school sport.

The modern lacrosse field is 110 yd (100.58 m) long and from 60 to 70 yd (54.86 to 64 m) wide. The goals have 6-ft (1.82-m) square openings with net backings and are 80 yd (73.15 m) apart. Each goal is centered in a circle 18 ft (5.48 m) in diameter called the goal crease. A lacrosse ball is made of India rubber, is slightly smaller than a baseball, and weighs about 5 oz (141.74 g). A crosse is from 3 to 6 ft (.91 to 1.82 m) long, and its net is walled on either one or both sides to form a pocket in which a player carries the ball. The crosse face is 7 to 12 in (17.78 to 30.48 cm) wide, depending on the player's position.

A lacrosse team consists of 10 players—3 attackers, 3 midfielders, 3 defenders, and 1 goalie. Players try to move the ball in the direction of the opponents' goal by carrying the ball with the crosse, passing it to a teammate by using a wrist-flipping motion, or kicking it. Only the goalie may use his hands to stop shots at the goal. Games are divided into four 15-minute periods, and in the event of a tie at the end of regulation play, two 5-minute overtime periods are played.

Women's lacrosse, which was first played in England, differs from the men's version in its restrictions on impeding a player's progress by body blocking.

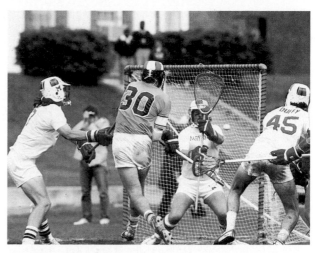

A goalkeeper tries to block a shot during a lacrosse match. Although the sport has been sponsored by the National Collegiate Athletic Association since 1971, its popularity in the United States has remained largely regional.

Bibliography: Boyd, Margaret, *Lacrosse* (1959); Evans, G. Heberton, and Anderson, Robert E., *Lacrosse Fundamentals* (1966); Morrill, W. Kelso, *Lacrosse*, rev. ed. (1966); Scott, Bob, *Lacrosse: Technique and Tradition* (1976).

Lactantius, Lucius Caecilius Firmianus   [lak-tan-shuhs, loo'-shuhs ky-see'-lee-uhs furm-ee-ay' nuhs]

Lucius Caecilius Firmianus Lactantius, *c.*240–*c.*320, a North African Christian apologist distinguished for his Latin prose style, was called the "Christian Cicero" by Renaissance scholars. Appointed (*c.*290) teacher of rhetoric at Nicomedia by the Roman emperor Diocletian, he resigned (*c.*305) his post when the emperor began persecuting Christians. Later, he was tutor to Crispus, the son of Constantine I. His principal work was *Divinae institutiones* (Divine Institutions, *c.*304–*c.*313), the first systematic Latin summary of Christian teaching. His work was meant for the well educated; hence the elegant and careful style of his writing.

Bibliography: Lactantius, *Excerpts from the Works of Lactantius*, trans. by W. Fletcher (1972).

lactic acid   [lak'-tik]

Lactic acid, or 2-hydroxypropionic acid ($CH_3CHOHCOOH$), is an odorless, colorless liquid produced in metabolism by almost all living cells as an end product of fermentation, or anaerobic respiration. It is reconverted to glycogen in the liver, or it can be used directly for energy. Lactic acid is produced industrially for use in manufacturing drugs, plastics, and other products.

Lactobacillus   [lak-toh-buh-sil'-uhs]

Lactobacillus is a genus of rod-shaped BACTERIA belonging to the family Lactobacillaceae and found in fermenting animal and plant products and in the mouth, vagina, and intestinal tract of some warm-blooded animals. Commonly called lactic acid bacteria, they produce the acid from carbohydrates. *Lactobacillus* is important industrially in the production of dairy products such as buttermilk.

lactone   [lak'-tohn]

Lactones are a class of organic compounds that can be described as intramolecular, cyclic ESTERS. The size of the ring is important in determining its ease of synthesis; five- and six-atom rings often form spontaneously when a hydroxycarboxylic acid is heated, whereas both smaller and larger lactones usually require special techniques.

The chemistry of lactones is similar to that of other esters. Lactones are widely distributed in nature. Some, such as penicillic acid lactone, ascorbic acid (vitamin C), and mycin antibiotics, have physiological activity. The musk odor of large-ring lactones is important in perfumes.   K. THOMAS FINLEY

lactose: see MILK; SUGAR.

Ladewig, Marion   [lad'-wig]

Marion Ladewig, b. Grand Rapids, Mich., Oct. 30, 1914, is generally regarded as the greatest woman bowler of all time. Nicknamed "the Lady of the Lanes," Ladewig won eight National All-Star Tournaments from 1949 to 1963, and from 1950 to 1963 she was named Woman Bowler of the Year a record nine times. She was elected to the National Bowling Hall of Fame in 1964, three years before retiring from national competition.

ladies' tresses

Ladies' tresses, *Spiranthes,* are about 200 widely distributed species of the orchid family, Orchidaceae, commonly found in damp woods and meadows. They are characterized by small whitish flowers, typically grouped in a twisted spike, and by usually clustered, tuberous roots. The leaves either closely surround the stem or are restricted to its base.

Ladislas I, King of Hungary   [lad'-is-luhs]

Saint Ladislas I, b. *c.*1040, d. July 29, 1095, was one of the early Árpád kings of Hungary. He reigned from 1077 to 1095 and is held in high esteem by the Hungarian people. The second son of Béla I (r. 1060–63), and the successor to his brother Géza I (r. 1074–77), Ladislas is looked upon as the embodiment of Christian knighthood, able statesmanship, and effective military leadership. Internally, he resumed the work of STEPHEN I by consolidating royal power and further strengthening Hungary's nascent Christianity. In his foreign policy he supported the popes against the Holy Roman emperors. Yet, when his conquest of Croatia (1089–91) was opposed by Pope URBAN II, he did not hesitate to change sides. To advance Hungarian interests in the Balkans, Ladislas also sought Byzantine connections, and his daughter Piroska (Irene) married the future Byzantine emperor JOHN II Comnenus. Ladislas was canonized in 1192.   S. B. VARDY

Bibliography: Kosáry, D. G., and Vardy, S. B., *History of the Hungarian Nation* (1969); Sinor, Denis, *History of Hungary,* 5th ed. (1977).

Ladoga, Lake   [lah'-doh-guh]

Lake Ladoga, the largest lake in Europe, is located in the northwest European region of the USSR about 40 km (25 mi) east of Leningrad. Approximately 220 km (135 mi) long, it has a maximum width of 124 km (77 mi) and a maximum depth of 230 m (754 ft). Its area is 17,679 km^2 (6,826 mi^2).

Formed by glacial action, the lake's basin and northern shores are rocky and indented; its southern shores are low and marshy. The lake contains more than 650 islands. It is fed by many rivers, principally the Volkhov, the Svir, and the Vuoksa, and drains into the Gulf of Finland via the Neva River. Fishing and water transport (it is part of the VOLGA-BALTIC WATERWAY) are the main economic activities. The lake freezes along the shore from December to May.

Ladrone Islands: see MARIANA ISLANDS.

Lady Chatterley's Lover

Lady Chatterley's Lover, a novel by D. H. LAWRENCE first published (1928) in a privately printed edition in Italy, has been one of the most controversial books of the 20th century. Lady Chatterley is the wife of a British industrialist who, paralyzed below the waist by war wounds, serves as a metaphor for upper-class impotence. Constance Chatterley finds fulfillment in a sexual union with Mellors, her husband's gamekeeper, thus portraying the author's belief in the health of physical life freed from social constraint. Lawrence's explicit but lyrical descriptions of the sexual act led to expurgations and prosecution for obscenity in the United States, England, and Canada between 1959 and 1962.   JANE COLVILLE BETTS

Bibliography: Lawrence, D. H., *A Propos of "Lady Chatterley"* (1930; repr. 1973); Rolph, C. H., *The Trial of "Lady Chatterley"* (1961); Spilka, Mark, ed., *D. H. Lawrence: A Collection of Critical Essays* (1963).

ladybug

The seven-spot ladybug, Coccinella 7-punctata, *is one species of brightly colored beetle that fascinates children. The ladybug serves to rid gardens of aphids and other pests.*

Ladybugs, or ladybird beetles, are insects of the family Coccinellidae, order Coleoptera. They are small, usually 10 mm (0.4 in) or less in length; oval to nearly circular in longitudinal cross section; and highly curved above and flat below. Although some ladybugs are unmarked, most are brightly marked and colored. Both adults and larvae are voracious eaters of aphids, scale insects, and other plant pests. With the exception of two plant-eating species, which are large and downy, ladybugs are extremely beneficial.

Bibliography: Borror, D. J., et al., *Introduction to the Study of Insects,* 4th ed. (1976).

lady's slipper

Lady's slipper C. calceolus *is a wild orchid commonly found in woodlands, especially under groves of pines.*

Lady's slippers are a genus, *Cypripedium,* of flowers belonging to the orchid family, Orchidaceae. The approximately 50 species are found throughout the Northern Hemisphere. Flowers are often large and showy and are characterized by the formation of the lower petal into an elongated pouchlike lip said to resemble a slipper or a moccasin. The leaves are broad and pleated and surround the stem at their bases. The stem of the showy lady's slipper, *C. reginae,* is covered with hairs containing a fatty acid that causes blistering similar to that caused by poison ivy.

Laënnec, René Théophile Hyacinthe   [lah-ay-nek', ruh-nay' tay-oh-feel' ee-yah-sant']

The French physician René Théophile Marie Hyacinthe Laënnec, b. Feb. 17, 1781, d. Aug. 13, 1826, invented the STETHO-

SCOPE and developed the anatomical-clinical method of diagnosing diseases of the chest. Laënnec studied medicine at Nantes and Paris and received his doctorate in 1804. He joined the staff of the Necker Hospital in 1816, and while there he invented (c.1817) the stethoscope.

During the next three years he listened to the chest sounds of patients and learned to correlate different sounds to various diseases. He published his findings in one of the important books of medical literature, *Traité de l'auscultation médiate* (1819).

Laer, Pieter van   [lar, pee'-tur vahn]

The Dutch painter Pieter van Laer, b. 1592 or 1593, d. June 30, 1642, was popularly known as Bamboccio ("the simpleton"). He left his native city of Haarlem in 1623 for Italy; between about 1625 and 1638 he lived and worked in Rome, where his nickname was bestowed on him by his Dutch and Italian colleagues. He became the leader of their group—called the BAMBOCCIANTI—who adopted and popularized his genre subjects and realistic style. He painted street scenes and landscapes peopled with lively peasants, soldiers, and brigands. From this period comes *The Morra Players* (n.d.; Galleria Nazionale, Rome). Van Laer also was influenced by Nicolas Poussin and Claude Lorraine in Rome. On his return to Haarlem in 1638 his naturalistic genre paintings had a considerable impact on his contemporaries.   CHARLES I. MINOTT

Bibliography: Rosenberg, Jakob, et al., *Dutch Art and Architecture, 1600–1800* (1966; rev. ed. 1972).

Laetolil   [lay'-toh-lil]

Laetolil is an archeological site located 40 km (25 mi) south of Olduvai Gorge in Tanzania. First excavated by Mary Leakey (see LEAKEY family) in 1975, the site consists of numerous layers of volcanic ash in which fossil animal bones and hominid remains were found. The technique of potassium argon dating was used to assign an age of about 3.75 million years to the fragmentary jaws and crania found at the site. These remains are nearly a million years older than the hominid fossils found by Richard Leakey in the East Turkana area of Kenya. Mary Leakey believes that these finds are of the genus *Homo* and not of the genus AUSTRALOPITHECUS. Because of this, she suggests, the australopithecines are not the direct ancestors of humans. Instead, she believes that the australopithecines were an offshoot of the hominid evolutionary line and that they gradually became extinct. More important discoveries are likely to emerge from Laetolil as excavations continue.   BRIAN M. FAGAN

laetrile

Laetrile has been purported by some authorities to be an effective cure or remedy in cancer treatment. The name has been used incorrectly and interchangeably with amygdalin, the chief component of laetrile, which is found in the seeds of many fruits, notably apricots and bitter almonds. Laetrile as originally prepared and patented (1949) by the California physician Ernest T. Krebs, Sr., and his son, Ernest T. Krebs, Jr., was an extract of apricot pits. A less toxic, purified form was subsequently developed.

According to the Krebses, the chief proponents of laetrile as an anticancer drug, amygdalin is broken down in the body by enzymes known as beta glucosidases to yield dextrose and mandelonitrile, a compound containing hydrogen cyanide. Cyanide-containing compounds are the components allegedly active against cancer. Proponents claim that tumor cells are selectively killed by laetrile because they contain more of the beta glucosidase enzymes than do healthy tissues. They also claim that tumors contain less of the enzymes that convert toxic hydrogen cyanide to nontoxic compounds than do healthy tissues. Laetrile has also been claimed to be a vitamin—so-called Vitamin B_{17}.

The use of laetrile for the treatment of cancer is a controversial and emotional issue. Reports of anticancer activity are said to consist of individual case reports without adequate controls, objective measurements, or sufficient follow-up. Published studies of trials with animal tumors, with one exception that has since been refuted, have shown no evidence of anticancer activity. From the medical and scientific viewpoint, no objective, acceptable evidence is said to exist today to indicate that laetrile has any activity as an anticancer agent or as a vitamin.

The U.S. Food and Drug Administration prohibited importation and interstate sale of laetrile in 1963, and use of the substance has been banned in Canada and Mexico since the mid-1970s. Despite these rulings and the negative scientific reports, numerous U.S. states have approved the manufacture and sale of laetrile, which is widely used.

DANIEL P. GRISWOLD

Bibliography: Richardson, John A., and Griffin, Patricia, *Laetrile Case Histories: The Richardson Cancer Clinic Experience* (1977); United States Congress Senate Committee on Human Resources, *Banning of the Drug Laetrile from Interstate Commerce by the Food and Drug Administration* (1977).

Lafayette   (Indiana)   [lah-fee-et']

Lafayette (1980 pop., 43,011), a city on the Wabash River in west central Indiana, is the seat of Tippecanoe County. Surrounded by a livestock- and grain-producing region, Lafayette is a meat-packing and shipping center; metal products, pharmaceuticals, beer, and sponge-rubber products are manufactured there. Railroad shops serve three major lines. Purdue University (1865) is across the river in West Lafayette. Lafayette was laid out in 1825.

Lafayette   (Louisiana)

Lafayette, a city on the Vermilion River in south central Louisiana, is the seat of Lafayette Parish. Settled about 1770 by exiled Acadians from Nova Scotia, the city of 81,961 (1980) retains a Cajun character. It is a commercial and shipping center for an area that produces cane, cotton, corn, livestock, and petroleum. Heymann Oil Center, headquarters for many oil companies, is here, as is the University of Southwestern Louisiana (1898).

Lafayette, Marie Joseph Paul Yves Roch Gilbert du Motier, Marquis de   [lah-fuh-yet', mah-ree' zhoh-zef pohl eev rohk zheel bair' dih moh-tyay', mar-kee' duh]

The French general the marquis de Lafayette, called the hero of two worlds, was prominent in both the American Revolution and the French Revolution. Born on Sept. 6, 1757, to a noble family in the Auvergne, he defied the French authorities in 1777 by crossing the Atlantic to offer his services to

The marquis de Lafayette, hero of the American Revolution and a key figure in the early phase of the French Revolution, is here portrayed by J. B. Le Paon. In America, Lafayette participated in the final defeat of the British at Yorktown (1781). Appointed (1789) commander of the National Guard at the beginning of the French Revolution, Lafayette sought to play a moderating role. He lost popularity, however, and was impeached (1792) after military failure against the Austrians. He fled France.

the Continental Congress at Philadelphia. He was a friend of George Washington, who became his model, and served under him at the Battle of the Brandywine and at Valley Forge. In 1779 he went to France to expedite the dispatch of a French army, but he returned to distinguish himself again at Yorktown (1781). Brave in battle and staunch in adversity, Lafayette won enduring popularity in America, and his fame did much to make liberal ideals acceptable in Europe.

As discontent in France mounted, Lafayette advocated the convocation of the States-General in 1789. He became a deputy, proposed a model Declaration of Rights, and was elected (July 15, 1789) commander of the National Guard. However, although he had enormous potential as a mediator, Lafayette had neither a realistic policy of his own nor the flexibility to support the more practical comte de MIRABEAU. Despised by the court as a renegade aristocrat whose bourgeois army was unable to protect the royal family, he was also hated by the populace for trying to suppress disorder.

In 1792, as an army commander, Lafayette made a futile attempt to save the monarchy and then deserted to the Austrians, who promptly imprisoned him as a dangerous revolutionary. Released in 1797 at Napoléon Bonaparte's insistence, Lafayette was allowed to return to France in 1799. In 1815 he was one of those who demanded NAPOLEON I's abdication.

In 1824, Lafayette made a triumphant U.S. tour. By then his home, La Grange, was a place of pilgrimage for liberals throughout the world. When the July Revolution of 1830 occurred, he was again called on, as a symbol, to command the National Guard. He died in Paris on May 20, 1834.

Bibliography: Bernier, Olivier, *Lafayette: Hero of Two Worlds* (1983); Gerson, Noel B., *Statue in Search of a Pedestal: A Biography of the Marquis de Lafayette* (1976); Gottschalk, Louis R., *Lafayette Comes to America* (1935; repr. 1974), *Lafayette Joins the American Army* (1937; repr. 1974), *Lafayette and the Close of the American Revolution* (1942; repr. 1974), *Lafayette between the American and French Revolution* (1950; repr. 1974), *Lafayette in the French Revolution, through the October Days* (1969), and *Lafayette in the French Revolution: From the October Days through the Federation* (1973); Idzerda, Stanley J., et al., eds., *Lafayette in the Age of the American Revolution: Selected Letters and Papers, 1776–1790*, 4 vols. (1977–81).

Lafitte, Jean   [lah-feet', zhawn]

Jean Lafitte, or Laffite, c.1780–c.1826, was a Louisiana privateer and smuggler. About 1810 he and his men settled in the area of Barataria Bay, near New Orleans, and preyed on Spanish ships in the Gulf of Mexico. In 1814, during the WAR OF 1812, the British attempted to buy Lafitte's aid in attacking New Orleans. Instead he passed their plans on to the Americans and helped Andrew Jackson defend the city in January 1815. Lafitte later returned to privateering.

Bibliography: De Grummond, Jane Lucas, *The Baratarians and the Battle of New Orleans* (1961).

Lafleur, Guy   [lah-flur', gee]

The professional ice hockey player Guy Damien Lafleur, b. Thurso, Quebec, Sept. 20, 1951, is one of the most prolific scorers in National Hockey League history. Playing for the Montreal Canadiens (1971–84), Lafleur led the NHL in scoring 3 times (1976–78), was league MVP twice (1977–78), and was a 1st-team All-Star 6 times. The Canadiens won 6 Stanley Cups—NHL titles—and he had amassed 1,246 career points (518 goals, 728 assists) when he retired in 1984. He returned in 1988, playing for the New York Rangers.

Lafontaine, Sir Louis Hippolyte   [lah-fohn-ten']

Sir Louis Hippolyte Lafontaine, b. Oct. 4, 1807, d. Feb. 26, 1864, was a Canadian political leader who helped to establish responsible, or cabinet, government, the constitutional principle that allowed British colonies to evolve into self-governing nations. A lawyer, Lafontaine was elected to the Legislative Assembly of Lower Canada (Quebec) in 1830. He supported the reformer Louis Joseph PAPINEAU but opposed his call for an armed uprising in 1837. His association with Papineau led him to flee to Europe after the failure of the REBELLIONS OF 1837,

Sir Louis Lafontaine, a leader of the French-Canadian Reform party, was joint prime minister of Canada with Robert Baldwin (1842–43; 1848–51). The second Baldwin-Lafontaine ministry, called the "great ministry," was noted for its reforms, including the Municipal Corporations Act, which reformed local government in Ontario, and an act to revise the judicial system.

but he returned in 1838 and, after a brief imprisonment, resumed his political career. Because Papineau was in exile, Lafontaine was now the leading French-speaking reformer, and he cooperated with Robert BALDWIN, who occupied a similar position in Upper Canada (Ontario), to secure control of the executive by the elected house of the legislature.

In 1841, Upper and Lower Canada were united into one province, and the following year Lafontaine joined with Baldwin in the first reform ministry. It collapsed in 1843 in a dispute with the governor, Charles (later 1st Baron) METCALFE, over the authority to make appointments. In 1848, however, a second Baldwin-Lafontaine ministry was formed, and this time it succeeded in establishing the principle that an appointed governor must accept the advice of a ministry holding the confidence of the legislature. The issue was tested decisively in the Rebellion Losses Bill, introduced by Lafontaine in 1849 and accepted by the governor, the 8th earl of ELGIN. The bill was designed to compensate people for property losses sustained during the Rebellion of 1837.

A period of constructive legislation in the areas of municipal government, railroads, and education followed until 1851, when Lafontaine and Baldwin retired. Lafontaine was appointed chief justice of Canada East (the former Lower Canada) in 1853 and was made a baronet in 1854.   D. M. L. FARR

Bibliography: Leacock, Stephen B., *Mackenzie, Baldwin, Lafontaine, Hincks*, rev. ed. (1926); Ryerson, Stanley B., *Unequal Union: Confederation and the Roots of Conflict in the Canadas, 1815–1873* (1968).

Laforgue, Jules   [lah-forg', zhool]

The French symbolist poet Jules Laforgue, b. Uruguay, Aug. 16, 1860, d. Aug. 20, 1887, was, with Rimbaud, among the inventors of *vers libre* (free verse)—poetry that is composed to the rhythm of speech and sound patterns, rather than to the traditional regular metrical phrases. Despite his short life, Laforgue had a significant influence on 20th-century poets such as Ezra Pound and T. S. Eliot. His *Complaints* (1885) and *The Imitation of Our Lady the Moon* (1886), with their plain speech and music-hall lyrics, did much to change the course of poetry in the years that followed.

Bibliography: Arkell, D., *Looking for Laforgue* (1980); Collie, M., *Jules Laforgue* (1977); Ramsey, Warren, ed., *Jules Laforgue* (1969).

Lafosse, Charles de   [lah-faws', sharl duh]

The paintings of Charles de Lafosse, b. June 15, 1636, d. Dec. 13, 1716, represent an important link between Italian and French baroque art. Lafosse's teacher, Charles Le Brun, played a decisive role in his career, getting him commissions as early as 1655. Lafosse traveled (1658–63) in Italy, visiting Rome, Venice, Parma, and Modena. The northern Italian influence, especially that of Correggio and Paolo Veronese, was crucial for Lafosse's mature style, as in *The Rape of Proserpine* (1673; École des Beaux-Arts, Paris). Lafosse entered the

Academy of Painting and Sculpture in 1673 and became chancellor by 1715. He worked with Le Brun at the Tuileries and Versailles in the 1670s. About 1680, Lafosse became an outspoken advocate of color in the theoretical dispute among baroque painters between the Poussinists and the Rubenists, involving line versus color. The combination of Flemish and north Italian influences in his late works, such as The Presentation of the Virgin (1682; Museum des Augustins, Toulouse), foreshadowed the airy, light rococo style.

NANETTE SALOMON

Bibliography: Blunt, Anthony, Art and Architecture in France: 1500 to 1700, 2d ed. (1970).

Lagash   [lay'-gash]

The ancient Sumerian city of Lagash (modern al-Hiba) lies about 200 km (120 mi) northwest of Basra, Iraq, and 10 km (6 mi) southeast of ancient Girsu (modern Tello), which was earlier believed to have been Lagash. The Lagash mounds are among the largest in areal extent in all of Mesopotamia; the earliest known levels are prehistoric (c.4000 BC). During the Early Dynastic period (c.2800–2400 BC) the city became the largest in SUMER; its kings are known from contemporary inscriptions including that of Girsu's famous Stela of the Vultures (now in the Louvre), which records Eannatum's victory over the neighboring state of Umma. Subject to the Agade Empire (c.2371–2230 BC), Lagash revived under the governorship of Gudea (c.2130 BC), whose monuments and inscriptions reveal a flowering of economic and artistic wealth. The city had declined by the Old Babylonian period (c.1900–1600 BC) and may not have been occupied after the mid-2d millennium BC. Excavations were conducted at Girsu primarily by the French (1877–1933); ongoing American investigations at Lagash were begun in 1968.

KATE FIELDEN

Bibliography: Kramer, S. N., The Sumerians (1963).

Lagerkvist, Pär   [lah'-gur-kvist, pair]

Pär Fabian Lagerkvist, b. May 23, 1891, d. July 11, 1974, was a Swedish novelist, poet, and dramatist. When he visited Paris in 1913, he was attracted to intellectual movements in art that were alien to his religious and traditional upbringing. In Ord-Konst och Bildkonst (Literary and Pictorial Art, 1913), he argued for the development in literature of a primitive vitality and an intellectual discipline characteristic of modern painting. He recommended as models the literary style of Homer, the Old Testament, and the Icelandic sagas. His pessimism about human nature and the individual's place in a meaningless world deepened during World War I; a view found in Ångest (Anguish, 1916), considered the first collection of expressionist poems in Swedish literature, and in Sista Människan (The Last Man, 1917) and The Secret of Heaven (1919; Eng. trans., 1966), plays that show the influence of Strindberg. Lagerkvist's bleak pessimism gradually gave way in the 1920s to a more hopeful view of life. Denilyckliges väg (The Happy Man's Way, 1921), a collection of poems and Guest of Reality (1925; Eng. trans., 1936), an idyllic description of his childhood, express his changing attitude.

A critic of totalitarianism in the 1930s, Lagerkvist protested against the brutality in the world in the novel The Hangman (1933; Eng. trans., 1936). The Dwarf (1944; Eng. trans., 1945) and Barabbas (1950; Eng. trans., 1951) were studies of the struggle between good and evil inherent in the human condition. The Sibyl (1956; Eng. trans., 1958) and The Death of Ahasuerus (1960; Eng. trans., 1962) speak of reconciliation with God. Lagerkvist was awarded the Nobel Prize for literature in 1951.

Bibliography: Sjoberg, Leif, Pär Lagerkvist (1976); Spector, Robert D., Pär Lagerkvist (1973).

Lagerlöf, Selma   [lah'-gur-lurv, sel'-mah]

Selma Ottiliana Lovisa Lagerlöf, b. Nov. 20, 1858, d. Mar. 16, 1940, a Swedish novelist and short-story writer, was the first woman to be awarded the Nobel Prize for literature (1909). Her first literary success was The Story of Gösta Berling (1891;

Eng. trans., 1898), a saga written in a romantic style that characterized all her later works. The Miracles of Antichrist (1897; Eng. trans., 1899) was a novel about socialism in Sicily. After a tour of Palestine, Lagerlöf published Jerusalem (1901–02; Eng. trans., 1915), a two-volume novel describing a settlement of Swedish farmers in Jerusalem. When Swedish school authorities commissioned her to write a Swedish geography, the result was a work later translated into English in two volumes: The Wonderful Adventures of Nils (1907) and Further Adventures of Nils (1911). Describing a boy's journey through Sweden, it captured the imagination of children the world over.

Bibliography: Berendsohn, Walter, Selma Lagerlöf (1931; repr. 1968); Larsen, Hanna, Selma Lagerlöf (1936; repr. 1975).

lagomorph   [lag'-uh-morf]

Lagomorphs, once considered rodents, are members of the order Lagomorpha, which includes RABBITS, HARES, and PIKAS. They are small, gnawing animals readily distinguished from rodents by the presence of two pairs of upper incisors (front teeth), one behind the other. Serological (blood) tests suggest that lagomorphs are distantly related to hoofed animals.

lagoon   [luh-goon']

Lagoons are marginal marine water bodies protected and partially isolated from the open sea by sand island barriers, coral reefs, or partially drowned preexisting topography.

Types. Along sandy coastal plains (such as the central Atlantic coast of the United States), lagoons are linear water bodies paralleling the coast, protected from the ocean by sand island barriers but usually connected with the ocean by one or more tidal inlets. The depth of these lagoons averages 2 m (7 ft), about half that of ESTUARIES. Coastal plain lagoons are valuable recreational and shellfish resources, but they are not suitable as shipping ports unless deepened by extensive dredging.

In tropical regions CORAL REEF growth may form effective seaward barriers to linear, curved, or circular lagoons. Such tropical lagoons, which may be over 30 m (100 ft) in depth

Lagoons are shallow bodies of seawater separated from the ocean by (A) coral barrier reefs; (B) curved, fingerlike extensions of deltas formed by sediment deposited from seaward-flowing rivers and ocean currents parallel to the shore; (C) shoreward-curving spits formed by extension of a headland by sediment deposition from longshore currents; (D) offshore bars built up above sea level by sediment-carrying waves that break well offshore; and (E) broad areas of seafloor brought up out of the water by an uplift of land or fall of sea level.

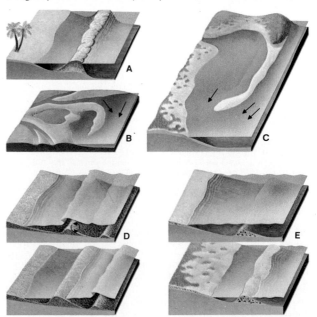

and dotted with pinnacle reefs, exchange a limited amount of water with the ocean by reef overwash. Reef barriers must generally be cut to make an artificial channel before the deeper lagoon behind can be reached by even small ships.

Characteristics. Lagoons in tropical and temperate climates differ in two important aspects. First, sediments accumulating in most tropical lagoons are calcium-carbonate skeletal remains of organisms that lived in or near the lagoon. Temperate and some tropical lagoons, in contrast, receive largely terrigeneous, or land-derived, sediment carried into the lagoon through tidal inlets, and they have only minor amounts of locally produced skeletal remains (see SEDIMENT, MARINE). Second, tropical carbonate lagoons tend to be underlain and bounded by rigid topography—whether modern reef, preexisting limestone rock, or volcanic terrain. Temperate-climate lagoons, on the other hand, are mostly bounded and underlain by unconsolidated muds, sands, and gravels that can be remolded by waves and currents. Major storms in temperate lagoons can create new inlets into the lagoon or produce sand washovers or tidal deltas that dramatically shift the lagoon's margins. In fact, with deficient sand supply, the entire sand island barrier will gradually shift landward.

Tidal currents actively scour lagoon bottoms only in the vicinity of inlets. Tides may dominate water circulation in lagoons that are subjected to a broad tidal range or that have multiple inlets. Tidal circulation is of limited influence in most other lagoons. Wind-generated waves dominate bottom agitation and circulation in most shallow lagoons. Lagoons may be gradually filled in both by general shallowing and by encroachment of marginal tidal flats, marshes, and swamps. The overall rate of lagoon infilling varies from about 10 to over 50 cm (about 4 to over 20 in) per hundred years and depends on the rate of sediment supply or production and the effectiveness with which a lagoon traps that material. Both linear and equidimensional shallow lagoons are commonly subdivided into smaller subcircular bays by sandspit or mudspit growth from the margins. Such lagoon partitioning appears to be caused by water-circulation gyres set up by winds.

HAROLD R. WANLESS

Bibliography: Bird, Eric, *Coasts,* 3d ed. (1984); Coates, D. R., ed., *Coastal Geomorphology* (1973); Komar, P. D., *Handbook of Coastal Processes and Erosion* (1983); Schwartz, M. L., ed., *The Encyclopedia of Beaches and Coastal Environments* (1982).

Lagos   [lah'-gohs]

Lagos, the capital and industrial and commercial center of Nigeria, lies in the southwestern part of the country. Located on the Bight of Benin, an inlet of the Gulf of Guinea, it occupies four islands (Lagos, Ikoyi, Victoria, and Ido) and parts of the mainland. The population is 1,097,000 (1983 est.), 80% of which is Yoruba. The city produces foodstuffs, automobiles, radios, metals, textiles, paints, soaps, and pharmaceuticals.

Population growth in Lagos has been overwhelming; transportation, utilities, housing, and port facilities are all seriously strained. Power failures, water-supply interruptions, and traffic jams are common. Water pollution is a serious problem because the surrounding lagoons have long been used as garbage dumps, and atmospheric pollution has worsened with increased numbers of factories and cars.

Many national institutions are located in Lagos, among them the National Museum, the National Library, the University of Nigeria (1960), and the University of Lagos (1962).

The Portuguese, who first visited the site of Lagos in 1472, later established a slave-trading center there. The area was under the domination of the Kingdom of Benin from the late-16th to the mid-19th century, and in 1861 it was taken over by the British. The city became the capital of the Colony and Protectorate of Nigeria in 1914 and the capital of independent Nigeria in 1960. In 1976 the government announced that within about 20 years the national capital will be moved to a newly created federal territory near Abuja in the central part of the country.

RONALD D. GARST

Bibliography: Baker, Pauline H., *Urbanization and Political Change: The Politics of Lagos, 1917–1967* (1975).

Lagrange, Joseph Louis de   [lah-grahnzh', zhoh-zef' lwee duh]

Joseph Louis, comte de Lagrange, was the preeminent mathematician of his age. The range of his groundbreaking research included studies in celestial mechanics, analytical mechanics, number theory, and calculus of variations. A lifelong teacher, he began lecturing at the age of 18 and helped to found two academies of science.

The French physicist Joseph Louis, comte de Lagrange, b. Jan. 25, 1736, d. Apr. 10, 1813, was one of the most important mathematical and physical scientists of the late 18th century. He invented and brought to maturity the calculus of variations and later applied the new discipline to CELESTIAL MECHANICS, especially to finding improved solutions to the THREE-BODY PROBLEM. He also contributed significantly to the numerical and algebraic solution of equations and to number theory. In his classic *Mécanique analytique* (Analytical Mechanics, 1788), he transformed mechanics into a branch of mathematical analysis. The treatise summarized the chief results in mechanics known in the 18th century and is notable for its use of the theory of differential equations. Another central concern of Lagrange was the foundations of calculus. In a 1797 book he stressed the importance of Taylor series and the concept of function. His search for rigorous foundations and generalization set the stage for Augustin Cauchy, Niels Henrik Abel, and Karl Weierstrass in the next century.

Lagrange served as professor of geometry at the Royal Artillery School in Turin (1755–66) and helped to found the Royal Academy of Science there in 1757. Because of overwork and poor pay, his health suffered, leaving him with a weakened constitution for life. When Leonhard Euler quit the Berlin Academy of Science, Lagrange succeeded him as director of the mathematical section in 1766. In 1787 he left Berlin to become a member of the Paris Academy of Science, where he remained (through its new form as the National Institute from 1795) for the rest of his career.

A diplomatic and amenable man, Lagrange survived the French Revolution. During the 1790s he worked on the metric system and advocated a decimal base. He also taught at the École Polytechnique, which he helped to found. Napoleon named him to the Legion of Honor and Count of the Empire in 1808.

RONALD CALINGER

Bibliography: Abbott, David, ed., *The Biographical Dictionary of Scientists: Mathematicians* (1985); Boyer, Carl B., *A History of Mathematics* (1968); Burzio, F., *Lagrange* (1942).

lahar: see MUDFLOW.

Lahontan, Lake: see LAKE, GLACIAL.

Lahore   [luh-hor']

Lahore, the second-largest city of Pakistan and the capital of Punjab province, is located in the northeastern part of the country on the Ravi River, about 25 km (15 mi) from the Indian border. Its population is 2,922,000 (1982), and it covers 332 km² (128 mi²).

Nearly 20% of Pakistan's industrial establishments are located in Lahore, producing iron and steel, textiles, rubber, processed foods, and gold and silver handicrafts. Large railroad yards are there, and Lahore is the center of Pakistan's motion-picture industry. In the fertile upper Indus plain, Lahore is the commercial and transportation center of the surrounding fertile agricultural region that produces rice and wheat.

The traditional center of the Punjab, Lahore is a cultural and educational city with important museums and libraries. The University of the Punjab (1882) is Pakistan's oldest university. Lahore has many important 17th-century landmarks, including the Wazir Khan, Pearl, and Golden mosques, the palace and mausoleum of the Mogul emperor Jahangir, and the famous Shalimar gardens.

Little is known of Lahore's early history, but in 1036 its ruling Brahmin dynasty was overthrown by the Muslim GHAZNAVIDS from Afghanistan, who made Lahore the capital of their empire in 1106. The city entered its most influential era following 1524, when it was taken by the Moguls and made one of their capitals. Most of Lahore's famous landmarks date from this period. In 1767 it passed to the SIKHS, who made it the capital of their kingdom until 1849, when the British annexed the whole Punjab. Lahore was the scene of fighting during the 1965 India-Pakistan War.　　　　　　　　　RICHARD ULACK

Lahr, Bert

Bert Lahr, b. Irving Lahrheim in New York City, Aug. 13, 1895, d. Dec. 4, 1967, was a popular comic on vaudeville and Broadway stages, as well as in motion pictures. Perhaps his most memorable role was that of the Cowardly Lion in the 1939 film *The Wizard of Oz.*

Laika　[ly'-kuh]

The female dog Laika was the first living creature to be sent into outer space. She was launched by the USSR on Nov. 3, 1957, in the 508-kg (1,120-lb) *Sputnik 2* satellite. Laika traveled in a sealed, cylindrical cabin that contained equipment for recording her pulse, respiration, blood pressure, and heartbeat. The craft was not designed to return her to Earth.

Laika is also the name of a group of northern Eurasian dogs of the spitz type raised as pets and for hunting.

Laing, R. D.

Psychiatrist Ronald David Laing, b. Glasgow, Scotland, Oct. 7, 1927, d. Aug. 23, 1989, applied existential philosophy to challenge prevailing conceptions of mental illness. Laing, through experiences in the British Army (1951–53) and Glasgow hospitals (1953–56), came to view SCHIZOPHRENIA, the most common PSYCHOSIS, as "a special strategy that a person invents in order to live in an unlivable situation." The medical model of mental illness, Laing claimed, strips a patient of power and dignity, subjects him or her to treatment devoid of compassion, and in labeling him or her "mad" may well be missing the point that the patient might be sane and the environment mad.

In 1957, Laing moved to the Tavistock Clinic in London, where he applied his theories and finished *The Divided Self: A Study of Sanity and Madness* (1960), a work that brought him fame as an existential and "radical" psychiatrist. In subsequent studies of schizophrenia, such as *The Self and Others* (1961) and (together with J. A. Esterson) *Sanity, Madness and the Family* (1964), Laing placed more stress on disturbed family environments as a cause, a view now widely discarded by the psychiatric community. In 1965 he helped found Kingsley Hall, a therapeutic community in London where patients and therapists live on an equal footing. Laing later withdrew many of his claims about the causes of and proper treatment for mental disorders, and he admitted that many of his own methods of treatment for schizophrenia had failed. Laing, however, particularly in his early insistence that schizophrenics be treated as human beings rather than as instances of a disease, presented a powerful challenge to mainstream psychiatry, and his work advanced the cause of humane treatment for all mental patients.　　　　　　　　　JERRY RALYA

Bibliography: Boyers, Robert, ed., *R. D. Laing and Anti-Psychiatry* (1974); Evans, Richard I., *Dialogue with R. D. Laing* (1981); Laing, R. D., *The Making of a Psychiatrist* (1985).

laissez-faire　[les-ay-fair']

Laissez-faire (French, "leave alone"), in economics, is the doctrine that the best economic policy is to let businesses make their own decisions without government interference. This doctrine of noninterference was first enunciated by the French PHYSIOCRATS of the 18th century as a reaction against the restrictionist policies of MERCANTILISM. Linked with the concept of FREE TRADE, it became the basis of Adam SMITH's classical economics. Later, Jeremy BENTHAM and John Stuart MILL applied the economic notions of laissez-faire CAPITALISM to utilitarian, individualistic political theory, and the Manchester school economists John BRIGHT and Richard COBDEN used them for practical political purposes.

Laissez-faire principles were strongest in the mid-19th century, but the increasing practice of monopoly and the social costs of the Industrial Revolution brought about greater government regulation. Modern proponents of laissez-faire stress the importance to economic growth of the profit incentive and the undeterred entrepreneur. The phrase, however, has been largely supplanted by such terms as *market economy* or *free enterprise.*

Bibliography: Hirst, Francis W., ed., *Free Trade and Other Fundamental Doctrines of the Manchester School* (1903; repr. 1968); Kanth, R. K., *Political Economy and Laissez-Faire Economics and Ideology in the Ricardian Age* (1986); Thirwall, A. P., ed., *Keynes and Laissez-Faire* (1978).

Lajos:　for Hungarian kings of this name, see LOUIS.

lake　(body of water)

Lakes are inland bodies of standing water. They are important for the storing of water, regulation of streamflow, navigation, and recreation (see WATER RESOURCES). Depending on the purpose, lakes have been classified according to the origin of their basins, their age, their permanency, the frequency of their water circulation, and their salt content.

ORIGIN

Lake basins may be formed in a variety of ways. Tectonically formed basins result from deformation of the Earth's crust—such as gentle crustal movements (for example, the CASPIAN SEA, a relict sea), folding (the Fählensee in Switzerland), or faulting (Lake BAIKAL). Basins of volcanic origin include those formed in extinct craters (such as CRATER LAKE in Oregon), and those located in basins either produced by the collapse of large lava flows (Yellowstone Lake) or dammed by lava or mud flows (Snag Lake in Lassen National Park). The two main types of glacial-lake basins (see LAKE, GLACIAL) are those formed by the scouring out of new or the deepening of existing basins in the native rock (for example, the English LAKE DISTRICT and the GREAT LAKES of North America), and those formed behind MORAINES, which are glacial deposits of soil and rock (such as the FINGER LAKES of New York State).

Basins may be formed by solutions of rock, such as the lakes in the Karst regions of Yugoslavia. River-action lakes include basins formed by release of materials held in suspension when the water velocity is decreased (as in Lake Pepin on the Mississippi); by abandoned river channels in mature floodplains, called OXBOW LAKES (common in the floodplains of the lower Mississippi); and by erosion of a pool at the foot of a waterfall, called plunge pools (for example, part of the former course of the Columbia River that now forms the Grand Coulee). Basins can also form by the obstruction of a river by a landslide, by the shifting of sediments by near-shore currents, by wind action in arid regions (either dammed between sand dunes or formed in a deflation basin), by the dense growth of plants, by the impact of a meteorite (see METEORITE CRATERS), and by the complex behavior of higher organisms such as beavers and humans.

LIFE CYCLE AND WATER CIRCULATION

Lakes are temporary features of the landscape. Many lakes in

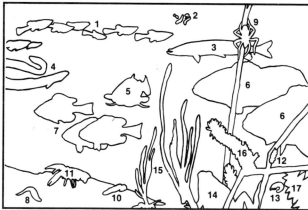

A North American lake harbors a closely interacting community of aquatic animals and plants. Mosquitofish (1), Gambusia affinis, eat mosquito larvae (2), genus Culex. The northern pike (3), Esox lucius, is a voracious predator. The American freshwater eel (4), Anguilla rostrata, is a true fish with a snakelike body. The brown bullhead catfish (5), Ictalurus nebulosus, ranges throughout all the United States and southern Canada. The largemouth black bass (6), Micropterus salmoides, is considered a challenge among sports enthusiasts because it is a good fighter when hooked. The pumpkinseed sunfish (7), Lepomis gibbosus, enjoys sunny waters. A dog leech (8), Erpobdella octoculata, attaches by its jaws to fishes or frogs. A fisher spider (9), Dolomedes triton, catches aquatic insects and small fish. Insects and crustaceans that are important food for fishes include the caddisfly (10), order Trichoptera, and such crustaceans as the American crayfish (11), Cambarus officinis, a freshwater isopod (12), Asellus aquaticus, and an amphipod, the scud (13), Gammarus fasciatus. The common bullfrog (14), Rana catesbeiana, is the largest of North American frogs. Plant life includes water celery (15), Vallisneria americana; waterweed (16), Elodea densa; and water lobelia (17), Lobelia dortmanna.

arid regions are intermittent, existing only for a short period after heavy rains. But even the "permanent" lakes will eventually disappear because of infilling by sediments, erosion of the barrier forming the lake basin (see EROSION AND SEDIMENTATION), or changes in the drainage pattern. In addition, a change to a drier climate will lower the lake level and may cause it to disappear (see PLAYA); a change to a wetter climate will do the opposite.

In addition to movement from inflow to outlet, there are two other principal causes of water circulation in lakes. Wind stress causes surface waves and, more importantly, SEICHES, which occur when a persistent wind leads to a piling up of water at the downwind end of the lake. When the wind ceases, the water flows back and forth in a periodic rocking motion.

Horizontal and vertical DENSITY CURRENTS occur because most lake water has its greatest density at a temperature close to 4° C (39° F). Lakes stratify into layers, with less dense water on top (the epilimnion) and denser water below (the hypolimnion). Seasonal warming and cooling of the upper layer increases its density and causes an overturning of the

waters. Some lakes turn over once a year (monomictic) and some twice (dimictic). Most lakes circulate at least once a year (holomictic), but in lakes with a strong salinity gradient (with heavy salty water at the bottom) the heating and cooling of the upper layer is not strong enough to produce overturning (meromictic).

COMPOSITION

Ions, gases, and organic compounds occur in the water in a dissolved state. The salinity—the total concentration of ions present—is determined by the nature of the inflowing water, which in turn reflects the composition of the drainage basin. Generally, the salinity of open lakes (from which water is drained by outflow) will not markedly change over time, while the salinity of closed lakes (which have no outlet and lose water only through evaporation) will increase over time. Salt lakes are found only in arid regions, but they differ greatly in their degree of salinity. The GREAT SALT LAKE has about four times the dissolved solids content of seawater and the DEAD SEA about seven times.

All lake waters contain at least some suspended matter, which settles slowly to the bottom and accumulates as sedi-

MAJOR LAKES OF THE WORLD

Lake	Surface Area		Volume		Mean Depth	
	km²	mi²	km³	mi³	m	ft
Caspian	371,000	148,000	79,340	19,035	182	597
Superior	82,100	31,700	12,088	2,900	149	489
Victoria	68,780	26,560	2,660	637	40	131
Huron	59,570	23,000	3,543	850	59	195
Michigan	57,750	22,300	4,918	1,180	85	279
Aral*	41,000	15,830	374	90	9	30
Tanganyika	33,990	13,120	19,420	4,659	572	1,876
Baikal	31,490	12,160	23,260	5,581	740	2,427
Nyasa (also Malawi)	30,790	11,890	8,370	2,009	273	895
Great Bear	30,400	11,740	2,200	529	72	238
Erie	25,670	9,910	480	116	19	62
Great Slave	25,390	9,800	1,550	373	62	204
Winnipeg	24,520	9,470	320	76	13	43
Ontario	19,554	7,550	1,640	393	86	283

*The fourth largest lake in area in 1960, the Aral Sea has shrunk 40% since then.

ments (see SEDIMENTS, MARINE). These consist of inorganic matter (erosion products from the rocks in the watershed), organic compounds, and chemical precipitates (when water becomes saturated). Deposits in saline lakes differ from those in freshwater lakes in the predominance of chemical precipitates and the relatively small fraction of organic matter. Lakes commonly have varved sediments (see VARVED DEPOSIT). During the summer the larger sediments form a coarse-grained layer, while in winter, when freezing stops the inflow and agitation within the lake, a fine-grained layer is formed. Sediment cores containing either varves or alterations of strata are studied to deduce the history of the lake basins and changes in climate.

ENVIRONMENTAL PROBLEMS

Lakes face two basic kinds of environmental problems: threats to water quality and the deterioration of shoreland. Pollution (see POLLUTION, ENVIRONMENTAL) by municipalities, industries, shipping, and poor agricultural practice has led to poisoning of the water, changes in its temperature, and acceleration of the natural process of EUTROPHICATION. The last is due to the enrichment of lakes with various nutrients, which support biological productivity to such an extent that an excessive demand is placed on the oxygen content of the water. Some of the world's major lakes currently suffer from such problems, including the Great Lakes of North America. Shorelines act as a buffer between the land and the water. Their development results in increased erosion, impairment of the WATER QUALITY, and scenic deterioration. Irrigation practices can likewise cause damage, as in the ARAL SEA, where substantial recession has occurred due to the diversion of water.

Some researchers have also recommended the monitoring of volcanic lakes similar to Cameroon's Lake Nyos, the site of a 1986 disaster where the escape of carbon dioxide gas killed 1,700 people.   WALTRAUD A. R. BRINKMANN

Bibliography: Brock, T. D., *A Eutrophic Lake* (1985); Burgis, M. J., and Morris, P., *The Natural History of Lakes* (1987); Cooke, G. D., et al., *Lake and Reservoir Restoration* (1986); Hutter, K., ed., *Hydrodynamics of Lakes* (1984); Payne, A. I., *The Ecology of Tropical Lakes and Rivers* (1986); Stumm, W., ed., *Chemical Processes in Lakes* (1985); Taub, F. B., ed., *Lakes and Reservoirs* (1984); Wetzel, R. G., *Limnology*, 2d ed. (1983).

See also: LIMNOLOGY.

lake   (dye)

Lake is the name given to a class of dyestuffs that are made by combining a soluble dye with a mordant, a metallic salt that renders the DYE insoluble in water. Many organic substances—such as the carmine derived from COCHINEAL insects or the violet color made from brazilwood—cannot be used as dyestuffs because, being soluble, they will wash out of the dyed material. Combined with a chromium, iron, or other metallic salt, however, these colors become the insoluble carmine lake and Vienna lake. Lakes are also made from synthetic, coal-tar–derived colors. Synthetic ALIZARIN combined with an aluminum salt produces the color Turkey red.

lake, glacial   [glay'-shul]

Glacial lakes include glaciogenic lakes, created by the action of glaciers (see GLACIER AND GLACIATION), and pluvial lakes (found today in desert and semidesert areas), whose water depths have fluctuated greatly in response to worldwide climatic changes during glacial-interglacial cycles (see ICE AGES).

GLACIOGENIC LAKES

Lakes that have originated directly from glacial action are of four chief generic types: glacier margin, glacial erosional, glacial depositional, and isostatic.

Glacier-Margin Lakes. A glacier may act as a dam to create a temporary lake along its margin. Some lakes of this type exist at present, but remnants of ancient ones are much more numerous. One type, the proglacial lake, forms where the land in front of a glacier slopes down toward the margin of the ice. Proglacial lakes along continental ice sheets tend to be broad and aligned along the ice front.

Long, narrow glacier-margin lakes are created when a valley glacier forms dams across tributary valleys, or when a glacier flowing out of a tributary valley blocks the main valley. The lakes in tributary valleys are generally small but commonly numerous.

Glacier-margin lakes tend to be short lived; they fluctuate in level with the waxing and waning of the glacier that dams the lake, and the water level can fall rapidly if lake-outlet streams melt and erode the glacier. Buildup of hydrostatic pressure in a lake may float a glacier off its bed, creating an outlet that suddenly drains the lake through release of a catastrophic flood. Such a flood is commonly designated by its Icelandic name, *jökulhlaup*. Proglacial lakes along the continental ice sheets commonly overflowed land barriers to the south. Fed by large volumes of glacial meltwater, these flows created spectacular spillway channels.

Glacial-Erosion Lakes. Glaciers are better able than streams to "overdeepen" their beds by selectively removing weak rock, mostly by ice scour and plucking; abrasion by powerful subglacial streams, however, can be significant locally. Both continental ice sheets and mountain glaciers produce such depressions, which, until filled with sediment, are sites of ponds and lakes from less than one to as many as thousands of square kilometers in area. CIRQUE lakes—also known as tarns in England, corries in Scotland, and cwms in Wales—in mountainous areas, and paternoster (or stairstep) lakes, created by selective erosion in valleys, constitute the most common category. The ability of glaciers to erode their beds increases with the rate of flow of the glacier and the thickness of the ice; ice-scoured lake basins are therefore most numerous in the deeper glaciated valleys and far from the margins of the continental ice sheets.

Glacial-Deposition Lakes. The sediments left after a glacier melts can produce lake basins of several types. Moraine-dammed lakes are caused by end MORAINES—ridges of till deposited during stillstands of the retreating glacier—that dam either a mountain valley or a sloping continental surface.

Classic examples (Lakes GARDA and COMO in Italy, Lake Zurich in Switzerland, Chiemsee in Bavaria, and Jackson and Jenny Lakes in Grand Teton National Park in Wyoming) are generally found in the piedmonts and lower ends of glaciated valleys.

Outwash-dammed lakes, such as Lakes McDonald and Kintla and the Lower Two Medicine Lakes in Glacier National Park, were created by plugs of glacial outwash—gravel and sand deposited by meltwater streams—in valleys. Finally, blocks of ice that have melted from within either a ground moraine—till deposited in irregular heaps by a stagnant, dying glacier—or an outwash plain beyond the ice margin may create small lakes, ponds, and swamps called KETTLE lakes.

Isostatic Glacial Lakes. Isostatic glacial lakes occupy the lowest parts of large areas that have been depressed isostatically by the weight of a large ice sheet (see ISOSTASY). During the last glaciation the Laurentide Ice Sheet depressed the land surface north of a line connecting Milwaukee, Cleveland, and New York by as much as 100 m (330 ft). Rebound from this depression has been in progress ever since the start of deglaciation about 17,000 years ago. The depression has tended to block drainage southward away from the ice sheets. This factor has usually not operated alone, but rather in combination with other factors, such as glacier or moraine damming, to accentuate the formation of lakes. It was an important factor in the development of proglacial lakes along the southern margin of the Laurentide Ice Sheet, and it is still significant in impeding the drainage of ice-scoured lake basins in the Canadian Shield.

Lakes Associated with Continental Ice Sheets. The greatest concentrations of glacial lakes by far were created by the Laurentide and Scandinavian Ice Sheets of North America and Europe. Interior parts of these ice sheets scoured deeply into bedrock, mostly granitic and gneissic rock, producing myriad large and small lakes, especially in southeastern Canada and Finland. Most of the lake basins originated by ice erosion, although many also are moraine-dammed.

In North America, just beyond the southern margin of the Laurentide Ice Sheet, a series of proglacial lakes developed during the waning of the last glaciation, between 14,000 and 10,000 years ago. These lakes fluctuated greatly in depth and extent but were often huge—much larger than the present GREAT LAKES. Most notable were Lake Agassiz (the largest), Lake Souris, and the ancestral Great Lakes, which at times extended most of the distance—more than 2,000 km (1,200 mi)—from Saskatchewan to the upper St. Lawrence River. Farther south, while the ice sheet was receding, short-lived and relatively small lakes existed in many places where moraines or plugs of outwash impeded drainage of the large volumes of meltwater.

PLUVIAL LAKES

A pluvial lake, always found in a semiarid or arid area, shows evidence of large fluctuation in water level, mainly in response to climatic changes corresponding to glacial-interglacial cycles; hence pluvial lakes are classed with glacial lakes. All known pluvial lakes are less than 2 million years old, that is, of Quaternary age.

Today, pluvial lakes are either PLAYAS, which are lake beds that are usually dry, or saline lakes, such as the Great Salt Lake, which are shrunken remnants of the expanded ancient lakes. STRANDLINES and shore deposits surrounding the present reduced lakes attest to former large increases in lake depth—commonly more than 10 m (33 ft) for the smaller lakes and 50 to more than 300 m (160 to more than 1,000 ft) for the larger ones—and expansions in lake volume of more than one order of magnitude. Stratigraphic studies of the shore and lake-bottom deposits show that the lake expansions alternated with times of major lake recession or complete desiccation.

The closed basins that are sites of pluvial lakes were formed by four kinds of geologic processes. Tectonic processes include high-angle faulting, which created many large basins, such as those in the basin and range region of western North America, and gentle folding, or warping, which formed large basins in South Africa and Australia. Some basins, including numerous examples in the Southern High Plains of the United States, originated by collapse of strata that overlie water-soluble deposits (salt, gypsum, and limestone) that were dissolved by groundwater. Many smaller basins, such as those found throughout the High Plains, have been created by wind erosion (deflation). Finally, basins may form when drainage channels are blocked by landslides, alluvial fans, or lava flows.

Distribution. Pluvial lakes occur in desert and semidesert regions, where the net runoff within their drainage basins is generally less than the annual precipitation. In North America they are numerous in the basin and range region, especially the Great Basin, the site of Lake Bonneville and Lake Lahontan (the largest and second-largest pluvial lakes in the Western Hemisphere). The largest pluvial lake in the world is the ARAL SEA–CASPIAN SEA–BLACK SEA system in the USSR and central Asia.

Evidence of Climatic History. The shore and bottom sediments of the larger pluvial lakes contain remarkably fine stratigraphic records of the climatic changes that caused the lake fluctuations. The sequences of Lakes Bonneville and Lahontan are especially complete and sensitive, surpassing all other types of land sequences—glacial, alluvial, and eolian. These records extend back more than a million years, vastly longer than that from any glaciogenic lake. They have yielded detailed information on the chronology, amplitude, and general climatic conditions of the lake cycles.

In addition, geologists and hydrologists have appraised the water budgets of various pluvial lakes in the Great Basin. Most investigators conclude that the highest Late Pleistocene lake levels could only have been attained by both higher precipitation and lower evapotranspiration (lower temperature) than now—an increase of 180 to 230 mm (7 to 9 in) in precipitation and a decrease of 2.7 to 5 C degrees (4.9 to 9 F degrees) in temperature.

Some parts of the lake-sediment sequences can be time-correlated—by means of radiometric age-dating, volcanic-ash chronology, and paleomagnetic correlation—with the glacial successions in various parts of North America and Europe. The time relationships of glacial and lacustrine cycles, however, remain controversial. Concrete evidence that their maxima were synchronous is available from only one place in the world, an area 20 km (12.5 mi) south of Salt Lake City, where end moraines of three successive advances of two mountain glaciers intertongue with high-shore deposits of Lake Bonneville. It is unlikely, however, that all pluvial lakes and all glaciers fluctuated exactly in unison. Undoubtedly, the times of inception and disappearance of lakes and of glaciers differed considerably with latitude, altitude, and other factors.

ROGER B. MORRISON

Bibliography: Embleton, Clifford, and King, C. A. M., *Glacial Geomorphology* (1975); Flint, Richard F., *Glacial and Quaternary Geology* (1971); Hough, Jack L., *Geology of the Great Lakes* (1958).

Lake Charles

Lake Charles (1980 pop., 75,226), a city on the Calcasieu River in southwestern Louisiana, is the seat of Calcasieu Parish. A deepwater port of entry, it is connected to the Gulf of Mexico by a 48-km-long (30-mi) channel. McNeese State University (1939) is located there. Settled in 1852 as a lumbering town, Lake Charles became the center of a rice-growing area after the arrival of the railroads brought Midwestern settlers. With the discovery of petroleum and natural gas nearby, it became an important petrochemical producer.

Lake District

The Lake District is a region of mountains, lakes, and waterfalls long famous for its beauty, in Cumbria, northwestern England. England's highest mountains, including the highest, Scafell Pike (978 m/3,210 ft), and largest lakes are there. The latter include Windermere, the largest, covering 16 km² (6 mi²), Ullswater, Bassenthwaite Lake, Derwent Water, and Coniston Water. The Lake District National Park, established in 1951, covers 2,243 km² (866 mi²). Tourism is the principal source of income, but sheep, dairy cattle, and poultry are raised, and some slate and building stone are quarried. The poet William Wordsworth lived here, as did Samuel Taylor Coleridge and Robert Southey, who together are called the Lake Poets.

Bibliography: Marshall, J. D., and Davies-Shiel, Michael, *The Lake District at Work* (1971); Millward, Roy, and Robinson, Adrian, *The Lake District* (1970); Pearsall, W. H., *The Lake District* (1973).

lake dwelling

Lake dwellings were villages or single houses built near the waters of a lake or a marsh, on platforms or artificial mounds. They have existed during several periods of human history. The most famous prehistoric lake dwellings are those of the late Neolithic and early Bronze Ages in Switzerland, France, and northern Italy.

The discovery of these lake villages occurred during the dry summer of 1853–54, when a drop in the level of the Lake of Zurich revealed the stumps of piles that had supported the platforms on which houses were built during the Neolithic Period. Because of the waterlogged conditions, materials not normally preserved at prehistoric sites, including wooden vessels and implements, were found intact. Subsequent research showed that these villages were built on marshy ground at the edge of lakes, not in open water. The earliest villages are datable to the 4th millennium BC. All produced similar, round-based, sparsely decorated or undecorated pottery, evidence that the lake dwellers belonged to a group of cultures usually designated the Western Neolithic. In France the lake villages belong to what is called the Chassey culture; in Switzerland they are characteristic of the Cortaillod culture, named after a site on Lake Neuchâtel. The north Italian variant is known as the Lagozza, although not all Lagozza sites are lake villages. Some lake villages of the Bronze and Iron Ages are also known in Europe. Two famous ones are the Iron Age villages of Gastonbury and Meare in Somerset, England, occupied from the 3d to the 1st century BC. When first excavated in the early 20th century, these Celtic villages were believed to have been built directly over the lakes and to have been occupied for a relatively short period. More recent excavation has shown that the remains belong to several phases and that the villages were built on marshy land rather than in open water. In its final stage Glastonbury contained some 90 huts, of which about 30 were occupied at one time. Circular in shape, the huts were constructed of close-set vertical timbers.

Lake dwellings in the form of single homesteads built on artificial islands are found in certain parts of Ireland and Scotland. Called *crannogs* (from the Irish *crann* or "tree"), they range in date from the late Bronze Age to the 17th century AD. The best known is Lagore, County Meath, Ireland, which was a royal residence from the 7th to the 10th century.

LLOYD R. LAING

Bibliography: Bulleid, Arthur, *The Lake Villages of Somerset,* 2d ed. (1926); Childe, V. Gordon, *The Dawn of European Civilization,* rev. ed. (1957; repr. 1967); Keller, Ferdinand, *The Lake Dwellings of Switzerland and Other Parts of Europe,* trans. by John E. Lee (1866).

Lake of the Woods

Lake of the Woods, located on the borders of Minnesota, Manitoba, and Ontario, covers 3,846 km² (1,485 mi²). The lake, shallow and irregularly shaped, has a heavily indented shoreline and over 14,000 islands. Located in an area forested with pines, the lake and four provincial parks along its shores are used for recreation.

Lakeland terrier

The Lakeland terrier, one of the oldest English working terriers, has been known in the English lake districts for centuries. The breed was developed to hunt fox and otter. It had to be small enough to go to ground (burrowing) yet big enough to run down its quarry.

A small working dog was the Lakeland terrier, developed in the Lake District of England to hunt foxes that were feeding on livestock. Packs composed of hounds and a few of these terriers would pursue a fox to its hiding place, where a Lakeland would enter and kill the predator.

The Lakeland is a small, square dog, sturdily built, with small V-shaped ears, wiry coat, and docked tail. The ideal height for a mature male is 36.25 cm (about 14.5 in) with a weight of 7.65 kg (17 lb); females are slightly smaller. The undercoat is soft, the outer or guard coat hard and wiry. Lakelands may be white, blue, black, liver, black and tan, blue and tan, red, red grizzle, grizzle and tan, or wheaten.

JOHN MANDEVILLE

Bibliography: Weiss, Seymour, *How to Raise and Train a Lakeland Terrier* (1966).

Lakshmi   [luhk'-shmee]

Wife of the Hindu god VISHNU, and one of the incarnations of the Mother-Goddess, or *Devi,* Lakshmi is the goddess of fortune and prosperity as well as the epitome of feminine beauty. According to Hindu legend, she was born radiant and fully grown from the churning of the sea. Lakshmi is portrayed as sitting on a lotus, her traditional symbol.

See also: SHAKTI.

Lalande, Joseph Jérôme Le Français de   [lah-lahnd', zhoh-zef' zhay-rohm' luh-frahn-say' duh]

Joseph Jérôme Le Français de Lalande, b. July 11, 1732, d. Apr. 4, 1807, was a French astronomer widely known for his improvement of astronomical tables and for his popular books on astronomy, navigation, and travel. He became involved in many astronomical controversies and took an active part in scientific and literary organizations.

Lalibela

Lalibela, named after its 13th-century royal founder, is the site of a spectacular complex of 11 rock-hewn Christian churches in the mountainous Eritrean region of northern Ethiopia. The churches are of two types—shrinelike grottoes, of which there are four, carved into natural cavities in the mountain slope, and seven monolithic freestanding structures, the foundations of which descend deep into the rock plateau. The freestanding churches are built on a cruciform plan. Three equilateral crosses, carved one inside the other, decorate the roofs, which are level with the plateau. The church interiors were originally covered with mural paintings of scenes from the life of Christ, few of which survive. Accompanying geometric and floral motifs bear the influence of COPTIC ART AND ARCHITECTURE.

Bibliography: Jager, Otto Arnold, and Pearce, Ivy, *Antiquities of North Ethiopia: A Guide,* 2d ed. (1974); Tamrat, Taddesse, *Church and State in Ethiopia, 1270-1527* (1972).

Lalique, René   [lah-leek', ruh-nay']

René Lalique, b. Apr. 6, 1860, d. May 5, 1945, was a French jewelry designer and glassmaker who is best known for his use of unusual materials and innovative styles in jewelry and glassware. An interest in glass resulted (1908) in his designs for mass-produced perfume bottles in molded forms. The success of these early designs allowed him to establish (1920) his own glass factory, where he developed a style that was initially called art modern and is now known as ART DECO. The sleek, stylized formulations of Lalique's Art Deco designs exerted a profound influence on his contemporaries, who saw in this style a bold statement of the drive and power of the industrial age expressed with singular elegance.

Lalique's innovative lighting fixtures were particularly influential in modern interior decoration. In his wall and ceiling lighting, angular pieces of etched and frosted glass concealed the light sources, and chandeliers were decorated with plant and animal forms or were designed to suggest fountains and jets of water. His most famous single commission (1931–35) was the palatial first-class dining salon of the S.S. *Normandie*, then the flagship of the French line.   MARION B. WILSON

Bibliography: Arwas, Victor, *Glass: Art Nouveau to Art Deco* (1977); McClinton, Katharine M., *Lalique for Collectors* (1975); Percy, Christopher V., *The Glass of Lalique* (1977).

Lalo, Édouard   [lah-loh']

The French composer Édouard Victor Antoine Lalo, b. Jan. 27, 1823, d. Apr. 22, 1892, is best known for his rhythmic and colorful *Symphonie espagnole* (1875) for violin and orchestra. He studied at the Lille and Paris conservatories, becoming a skilled violinist and violist, and in 1855 he became violist of the Armingaud-Jacquard string quartet. He achieved his first major success with the *Symphonie espagnole*, when Pablo de Sarasate performed the work in 1875. Lalo's Cello Concerto (1876) is one of the better known concerti for that instrument. The melodious suites from his ballet *Namouna* (1882) as well as excerpts from his opera *Le Roi d'Ys* (The King of Ys; 1888) are occasionally performed. His other works include the Symphony in G minor, concerti for violin and piano, chamber music, and songs. Lalo was a skillful orchestrator whose music, written in the late-romantic idiom, foreshadows the impressionist style.

Lamaism: see TIBETAN BUDDHISM.

Lamaist art and architecture

Lamaist art and architecture arose in areas that came under the influence of TIBETAN BUDDHISM (Lamaism) in addition to Tibet itself, Ladakh, Nepal, Sikkim, Bhutan, parts of Central Asia, Mongolia, parts of western China, and a small area in northern China near Peking. It was almost entirely devoted to the service of religion, mainly Buddhist but also, in Tibet, to Bön-po, the indigenous shamanistic religion that was centered on nature spirits and magic.

The Lamaist artistic tradition is derived from several sources, the most important being India, China, and Central Asia. Probably the earliest influence came from India and was

This 18th-century gilt-bronze statue of Avalokitesvara, the bodhisattva of infinite compassion and mercy, is representative of Lamaist art as it was interpreted in North China. The statue, which is sculpted in a seated meditative pose, was probably used for purposes of worship in a Lamaist monastery. (Philip Goldman Collection, London.)

This 18th-century mandala is an example of Tibetan bardo painting and is attributed to the Nying-ma-pa sect of Tibet. As explained in the Tibetan Book of the Dead, the bardo is the intermediate state between death and rebirth. (Gulbenkian Museum, Durham, England.)

received in Tibet, together with Buddhism, about the 7th century AD. Close links based on this religious association continued between India and Tibet until the 12th century, when the Muslims invaded India. Nepal and China became important influences on Tibetan culture after the Mongol domination of both China and Tibet in the 13th century. Eventually, Tibet's position changed from that of an importer of religious ideas from India to that of a custodian of Buddhism north of India, with a consequent increase in the prestige of its art among other northern Buddhist countries. Conservative, regional art styles continued until about the 17th century, when Tibet developed its own national style, which is sometimes difficult to distinguish from that of other traditions developed in the Himalayan area.

Architecture. Some Lamaist religious buildings are based on secular Tibetan architecture, being rectangular and having a courtyard. The most characteristic structures are in the form of deity groups (MANDALAS) or relic mounds (STUPAS). The first type was intended merely to house images and to provide space for ritual; in the second, known in Tibet as a *chorten*, images and paintings were more formally arranged (often in a circle or rectangle) to create a miniature cosmos around the central deity. Each architectural element of the stupa carried a particular religious symbolism, the whole representing the essential elements of Buddhahood. Building materials are generally of wood, stamped earth, stone, or sun-dried bricks; smooth surfaces (particularly on stupas) were often brightly painted.

Inward-tapering walls, flat roofs, and small windows are characteristic features of Tibetan architecture, a notable example being the magnificent Potala, former residence of the Dalai Lama, in Lhasa. Local variations are found outside Tibet, notably the Nepalese tiered roof that is closely related to the Chinese PAGODA.

Sculpture and Painting. The images placed in Lamaist buildings as objects of worship are generally made of metal or stucco; some wood sculpture is also found, principally in Nepal, and a small amount of stone carving. Metal images are usually of cast copper, bronze, or brass, but some of the larger figures are also of embossed copper. Gilding is common, especially on Buddha statues, which are typically rendered as slender figures with delicate, youthful features; jewelry may be simulated with semiprecious stones, of which turquoise and coral are the most popular, and imitation gems. Figures in all materials are often painted and adorned with jewelry, crowns, scarves or complete sets of outer clothes.

Paintings, the other principal category of Lamaist image-making, are often in the form of elaborate wall paintings, designed to augment the ritual significance of the three-dimensional images. Based on texts such as the *Mahavairochanasutra*, they function as the visual realization of these sacred doctrines. They not only have served to teach the illiterate but also to heighten religious awareness within the temple.

In addition to wall paintings, several forms of portable paintings are significant, of which temple banners, called tankas, are the most important. These scroll paintings are executed on prepared cotton cloth; they are mounted with blue silk borders and a round wooden rod at the top and bottom to make them hang flat. The tankas are also based on texts, such as those that describe the life of the Buddha. They often appear in sets of 3 to about 30 paintings and are embellished with stylized natural elements such as clouds and flame patterns or lush landscape settings, sometimes reflecting Chinese influence. Other frequent subjects include assemblies of deities, influential monks and their spiritual lineages, the wheel of life, assembly trees (*tshogs-shing*), and deity groups arranged to represent a diagram of the cosmos. Several stylistic traditions are recognized, including those of western Tibet (Guge), and the Nor monastery; Tibetan texts also mention Mendri (*sman-bris*), Gyadri (*rgya-bris*), Karmagardri (*skar-ma sgar-bris*), and other styles, which are, however, difficult to differentiate. The aim of the Lamaist artist was not to be creative in the Western sense, but to follow the conventional Lamaist iconographic traditions as closely as possible in order to produce an object that was effective in its religious purpose.

Images of tantric deities abound in Lamaist art, both in painted and sculpted form. They are usually portrayed in their ferocious aspect and are often accompanied by their female counterparts. A characteristic example is the fantastic demonic mask, produced in brightly painted papier-mâché, wood, or leather. A host of uniquely Lamaist ritual objects such as prayer wheels and altar lamps were made, often of exquisite workmanship, as well as items for secular use including brass and copper teapots and bowls, often gilded or inlaid with silver, and distinctive rugs and saddlery.

JOHN LOWRY

Bibliography: Gordon, Antoinette K., *Tibetan Religious Art*, 2d ed. (1952; repr. 1963); Lauf, Detlef Ingo, *Tibetan Sacred Art* (1976); Olschak, B. C., *Mystic Art of Ancient Tibet* (1973); Olson, Eleanor, *Catalogue of the Tibetan Collections and Other Lamaist Articles in the Newark Museum*, 5 vols. (1950-71); Pal, Pradapaditya, *The Art of Tibet* (1969) and *Nepal, Where the Gods are Young* (1975); Snellgrove, David, and Richardson, Hugh, *A Cultural History of Tibet* (1968); Tucci, G., *Tibetan Painted Scrolls*, 3 vols. (1949).

Lamar, Lucius [luh-mar', loo'-shuhs]

Lucius Quintus Cincinnatus Lamar, b. Putnam County, Ga., Sept. 17, 1825, d. Jan. 23, 1893, was a Mississippi political leader and U.S. official whose career spanned the Civil War. He served as a U.S. representative from Mississippi (1857-60), drafted Mississippi's ordinance of secession from the Union (1860), and returned to Washington as representative (1873-77), senator (1877-85), secretary of the interior (1885-88), and associate justice of the Supreme Court (1888-93). After the Civil War he promoted North-South reconciliation.

Bibliography: Cate, Wirt A., *Lucius Q. C. Lamar: Secession and Reunion* (1935; repr. 1969); Murphy, James B., *L. Q. C. Lamar* (1973).

Lamar, Mirabeau Buonaparte [luh-mar', mir'-uh-boh bwohn'-uh-parte]

Mirabeau Buonaparte Lamar, b. Aug. 16, 1798, d. Dec. 19, 1859, was the second president (1838-41) of the Republic of Texas. He moved to Texas from Georgia in 1836. During the TEXAS REVOLUTION he distinguished himself in the Battle of San Jacinto, and in 1836 he was elected vice-president of the republic. Two years later he was chosen to succeed Sam Houston as president. Serving until 1841, Lamar instituted some far-reaching policies in Texas, including the building of Austin, establishment of a system of public education, enactment of a law protecting homesteads from foreclosure, support for a Texas navy, and the much-criticized expulsion of the Cherokee Indians from East Texas. He later fought in the Mexican War, collected the materials for a history of Texas, and revived his early interest in poetry. He served as U.S. minister to Nicaragua (1857-59). SEYMOUR V. CONNOR

Bibliography: Gambrell, Herbert P., *Mirabeau Buonaparte Lamar: Troubadour and Crusader* (1934).

Lamarck, Jean Baptiste [lah-mark', zhawn bahp'-teest]

The French naturalist Jean Baptiste Lamarck is best known for his erroneous theory that organisms acquire new characteristics in response to environmental factors and pass along these traits to succeeding generations. Lamarck also contributed to comparative anatomy and the study of invertebrates and originated the term biology.

Jean Baptiste Pierre Antoine de Monet, Chevalier de Lamarck, b. Aug. 1, 1744, d. Dec. 18, 1829, was a French naturalist who became widely known for his theory of EVOLUTION. The theory, known as Lamarckism, was based on the idea, not unreasonable at the time, that plants and animals evolve by adjusting to changes in their environment. According to Lamarck, once a change occurred in a plant or animal, it could be passed on to the next generation. This theory, included in Lamarck's 2-volume *Zoological Philosophy* (1809; Eng. trans., 1914), was accepted by many contemporary scientists, but it was later proved to be incorrect. Today the generally accepted theory is that of Charles DARWIN, who proposed that changes in traits occur randomly, not directly in response to changes in the environment. Trofim D. LYSENKO, a Russian agronomist of the 20th century, however, adopted a Lamarckian viewpoint and, with Stalin's backing, established it as Soviet doctrine in genetics research and teaching. The result was a setback in genetics in the USSR during the Stalinist era.

Originally interested in botany, Lamarck wrote a 3-volume text, *Flore française* (French Flora, 1778). He was appointed the royal botanist in 1781 and became a professor of invertebrate zoology in 1793 at the Museum of Natural History in Paris.

The first scientist to distinguish between animals with backbones (vertebrates) and without backbones (invertebrates), he classified many invertebrates into the categories of arachnids, crustaceans, and echinoderms. He also wrote a text on invertebrate systems, *Système des animaux sans vertèbres* (1801), and a 7-volume treatise on the natural history of invertebrates (1815–22).   Reviewed by LOUIS LEVINE

Bibliography: Burkhardt, Richard W., *The Spirit of System: Lamarck and Evolutionary Biology* (1977); Cannon, Herbert Graham, *Lamarck and Modern Genetics* (1959; repr. 1975); Glass, Hiram B., et al., eds., *Forerunners of Darwin, 1745–1859* (1959).

See also: HEREDITY.

Lamarckism: see HEREDITY; LAMARCK, JEAN BAPTISTE.

Lamartine, Alphonse de

Alphonse de Lamartine, b. Oct. 21, 1790, d. Feb. 28, 1869, was a major French-romantic poet and a distinguished orator who commanded a large popular following during the Revolution of 1848. Lamartine, who came of an aristocratic family, had a genteel and untroubled upbringing. He served briefly in the military guard of Louis XVIII and in 1820 obtained a diplomatic post in the French embassy at Naples, where he married a wealthy Englishwoman, Maria Ann Birch. In the same year he published his first volume of verse, *Méditations poétiques* (1820). These lyrical, deeply personal effusions won him immediate acclaim. *Nouvelles Méditations poétiques* (1823) and *Mort de Socrate* (1823)—based on Plato's *Phaedo*—were less well received, but *Le Dernier Chant du pèlerinage d'Harold* (1825), a tribute to Lord Byron, was eagerly read by the English poet's French admirers. Lamartine was elected to the Académie Française in 1829 and in the following year published *Harmonies poétiques et religieuses,* plaintive and melancholy sentiments expressed in melodious verse.

Abandoning his diplomatic career ·in 1830, Lamartine tried unsuccessfully to win election as a deputy in the government. He was finally elected in 1833 after he had made an extensive tour of eastern Mediterranean countries and begun composing the long narrative poems *Jocelyn* (1836) and *La Chute d'un ange* (1838). During the next decade he became increasingly involved in politics, taking on the role of champion of the people and espousing the cause of republican liberty. His last volume of verse, *Les Recueillements poétiques* (1839), reflects compassion for the mass of humanity and regret for his own former egotism and isolation. During this period he made many of his finest speeches, which include discourses on political liberty and apologies for Napoleon—by then a symbol of all that was heroically French. When Louis Philippe was deposed in 1848, Lamartine was an idol of the people, but he failed to win election in 1849 and retired from public affairs. Lamartine's last years were devoted to writing, and he produced numerous volumes of autobiography, history, novels, and short tales.

Bibliography: George, Albert J., *Lamartine and Romantic Unanism* (1940); Lombard, Charles M., *Lamartine* (1973); Whitehouse, Henry R., *The Life of Lamartine* (1918; repr. 1973).

Lamb, Charles

Charles Lamb, b. London, Feb. 10, 1775, d. Dec. 27, 1834, a versatile writer, is best known as the author of the ingratiating *Essays of Elia* (1823, 1833). A small, stuttering man who devoted himself to a mentally unstable sister, Mary, and whose official career was clerking (1792–1825) for the East India Company, Lamb was a central figure in the first generation of British romantics and a particular friend of Samuel Taylor Coleridge.

In the mid-1790s, about the time Mary, during one of her seizures, killed their mother, he began writing poetry, chiefly album verse; the most reprinted is the tender "Old Familiar Faces" (1798). After a muted sentimental novelette, *A Tale of Rosamund Gray* (1798), he turned to drama. Of his five plays only one, *Mr. H: or Beware a Bad Name* (1806), was produced, and that failed; Lamb himself hissed the effort at the Drury Lane. With Mary he wrote some children's books, the best known being *Tales From Shakespear* (1807). He was proud of his *Specimens of English Dramatic Poets* (1808), which led to other dramatic criticism, notably "On the Trag-

Charles Lamb, a 19th-century English writer, appears in a portrait by his fellow essayist William Hazlitt. Although Lamb was unsuccessful as a poet and playwright, he achieved literary prominence through his critical dissertations on the works of Elizabethan dramatists and through satirical essays.

edies of Shakespeare," published (1811) in Leigh Hunt's *Reflector,* and "On the Artificial Comedy of the Last Century," which appeared (1822) in *The London Magazine.*

When Lamb was 45 years old he began publishing in *The London Magazine* a series of personal essays signed "Elia"—observing that the name was an anagram for "a lie." These essays, which include the familiar "Dream Children," "A Dissertation upon Roast Pig," "The South-Sea House," and "Christ's Hospital," are protectedly autobiographical, sometimes deriving from his franker, more vigorous letters, which are among the best to have survived from the 19th century. Although his style is charming, whimsical, slightly archaic, and often tender, Lamb resisted and does not deserve the name sometimes given him of "Gentle Charles."

JOHN E. JORDAN

Bibliography: Ainger, Alfred, *Charles Lamb* (1901; repr. 1970); Barnett, George L., *Charles Lamb* (1976) and *Charles Lamb: The Evolution of Elia* (1964; repr. 1972); Blunden, Edmund, *Charles Lamb and His Contemporaries* (1933; repr. 1973); Lamb, Charles, *The Life, Letters, and Writings of Charles Lamb,* ed. by Percy Fitzgerald, 6 vols. (1895; repr. 1971), and *The Letters of Charles and Mary Anne Lamb,* 3 vols., ed. by Edwin W. Marrs (1975, 1976, 1978); Lucas, Edward V., *The Life of Charles Lamb,* 5th ed. (1921; repr. 1968); McKenna, Wayne, *Charles Lamb and the Theatre* (1978).

Lamb, Willis Eugene, Jr.

The American physicist Willis Eugene Lamb, Jr., b. Los Angeles, Calif., July 12, 1913, shared the 1955 Nobel Prize for physics with Polykarp KUSCH for work on microwave spectroscopy and the fine structure of hydrogen and helium atoms. His work included the discovery in 1947 of the "Lamb shift," a minute characteristic observed in the absorption and emission behavior of photons relative to the quantized energy levels available to the electron in the hydrogen atom. Lamb also worked with lasers and masers, magnetron oscillators, and statistical mechanics.   CARL A. ZAPFFE

Lambert's law: see ABSORPTION, LIGHT.

lamb's-quarters: see GOOSEFOOT.

lame duck

In U.S. politics a lame duck is an officeholder who has not been reelected or who is prevented by law from running for office again. During the period between the election and the end of his or her term, the lame duck's political influence may be greatly reduced because the successor is not bound to follow the lame duck's policies and because the latter has few political levers, such as patronage, left to exercise. The 20TH AMENDMENT to the U.S. Constitution was adopted (1933) to shorten the presidential lame duck period between election and inauguration.

Lamennais, Félicité Robert de   [lahm-uh-nay', fay-lee-see-tay' roh-bair' duh]

Hugues Félicité Robert de Lamennais, b. June 19, 1782, d. Feb. 27, 1854, was a French religious and political writer who attempted to combine liberalism with Roman Catholic thought. Son of a shipowner in Brittany, he became a priest only after renouncing an earlier attraction to the Enlightenment. His initial writings, especially the widely read *Essay on Indifference in Matters of Religion* (1817–23; trans. 1895), were conservative and ultramontane (that is, pro-papal), reacting to the French Revolution with a plea for the return of power to the clergy. In the 1820s, however, he evolved toward a belief in liberalism and the separation of church and state as the only means of achieving a religious revival. He and his friends elaborated their liberal ideas in the newspaper *L'Avenir,* founded in 1830. After being censored by the pope, Lamennais gradually left the church altogether, became an ardent proponent of republicanism, and died unreconciled with the church. His liberal ideas have been much admired by many 20th-century Roman Catholics.   T. TACKETT

Bibliography: Stearns, Peter N., *Priest and Revolutionary: Lamennais and the Dilemma of French Catholicism* (1967); Vidler, Alexander R., *Prophecy and Papacy: A Study of Lamennais, the Church and the Revolution* (1954).

Lamentations, Book of   [lam'-en-tay'-shuhnz]

The Book of Lamentations in the Old Testament of the BIBLE is actually five poems that lament the destruction of Jerusalem in 586 BC. Often called "The Lamentations of Jeremiah," it is usually placed after the Book of JEREMIAH, despite its uncertain authorship. The poet vividly describes the devastation endured by Jerusalem. Although this recitation of laments faced the harsh realities of the present, the prayer-poems also stirred up continuing hope in Yahweh's promises for the future.

Lamia   [laym'-ee-uh]

In Greek mythology, Lamia was a beautiful woman whose children were taken away in jealousy by HERA because ZEUS had loved her. In revenge, Lamia began to steal and kill the children of others. She became a hideous creature. Because Hera had condemned her to sleeplessness, Zeus gave Lamia the ability to remove her own eyes at will in order to sleep. In later legend the lamia was a vampire that seduced young men; this version of the story inspired the poem *Lamia* (1820) by John Keats.

Lamont-Doherty Geological Observatory

The bequest (1948) of a large plot of land in Palisades, N.Y., to Columbia University by the widow of the financier Thomas W. Lamont, coupled with the need by a geology research group for a place to test sensitive seismic instruments, led to the establishment (1949) by the university of what later became known as the Lamont-Doherty Geological Observatory. Under the leadership of Maurice EWING, the first director (1949–72), and his successor Manik Talwani, the observatory—with a current staff of about 600—has placed a major emphasis on the study of the ocean floor and what lies beneath it. Through the use of their two research ships and their development and improvement of instruments, observatory staff members played a leading role in establishing the continuity of the mid-oceanic ridge system, the association of earthquake epicenters with its crest, and the existence of fracture zones. Staff members have also developed theories of seafloor spreading and plate tectonics.

The observatory's collection of deep-sea piston cores—the largest in the world—has been used to detect variations in past climates of the Earth.   CRAIG B. WAFF

lamp

A device for producing light by burning oils, fats, or combustible fluids, the lamp has been a part of all civilizations. The

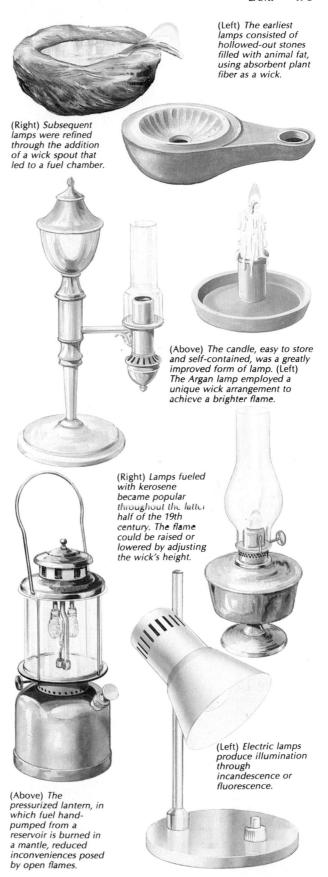

(Left) The earliest lamps consisted of hollowed-out stones filled with animal fat, using absorbent plant fiber as a wick.

(Right) Subsequent lamps were refined through the addition of a wick spout that led to a fuel chamber.

(Above) The candle, easy to store and self-contained, was a greatly improved form of lamp. (Left) The Argan lamp employed a unique wick arrangement to achieve a brighter flame.

(Right) Lamps fueled with kerosene became popular throughout the latter half of the 19th century. The flame could be raised or lowered by adjusting the wick's height.

(Left) Electric lamps produce illumination through incandescence or fluorescence.

(Above) The pressurized lantern, in which fuel hand-pumped from a reservoir is burned in a mantle, reduced inconveniences posed by open flames.

earliest lamps were shells or saucer-shaped pieces of stone that held oil or animal fat with crude wicks of vegetable fiber. (Both the lamp and the candle seem to have had a common origin in the torch and the rushlight—a rush dipped in tallow. The oil lamp, however, was used long before the candle.) Later, stone lamps were more purposefully shaped, with oil reservoirs and grooved lips to hold the wicks. Little improvement in lamps as sources of light, however, was made over many thousands of years, although many changes were made in the location of the wick. One such change was a wick spout, which led from the oil chamber. Lamps with two or more spouts became common.

Not until the 18th century was the wick finally moved from the edge of the oil reservoir to its center. In the 1760s the first central burner, a flat woven wick encased in a metal sheath, was developed. Benjamin Franklin devised a two-burner lamp of this type. Flat wicks burned far more efficiently than the round, solid wicks that had commonly been used. The first real improvement in lamp design, however, was the invention of a Swiss scientist, Aimé Argand (1753–1814). His oil lamp (1782) used a circular tubular wick that enabled air to reach the inner wick surface and a glass chimney that both sheltered the flame and improved its combustion.

Whale oil was an important source of lamp fuel during the early and middle 1800s; other fuels commonly used included various kinds of vegetable and fish oils and lard. After 1850, however, kerosene became the principal fuel. Kerosene lamps used a simple rack-and-pinion mechanism for raising and lowering the wick. The Welsbach mantle, which had been invented for the gas light (see LIGHTING DEVICES), was adapted for kerosene; suspended above the wick, the mantle burned the inflammable vapors produced by the wick flame.

Pressurized kerosene lamps were first used in the late 1860s and, in such forms as the Coleman lamp, are still popular. In these lamps hand-pumped air forces the oil through a coil that is heated by the flame; the heated oil is partially vaporized and burns with a bright light.

Bibliography: Allphin, Willard, *Primer of Lamps and Lighting,* 3d ed. (1973); O'Dea, William T., *The Social History of Lighting* (1958); Paton, James, *Lamps: A Collector's Guide* (1979); Robins, Frederick William, *The Story of the Lamp* (1939; repr. 1970); Withers, John C., *Principles of Illumination* (1966).

lampblack

Lampblack is a black pigment produced by the incomplete burning of liquid hydrocarbons such as creosote or kerosene. A related pigment, carbon black, is produced from natural gas. Both pigments are used in inks and paints and on carbon papers. Carbon black is widely used as a strengthening agent in the manufacture of vulcanized rubber for tires.

Lampedusa, Giuseppe di   [lahm-pay-doo'-zah, joo-zep'-pay dee]

Giuseppe Tomasi di Lampedusa, b. Dec. 23, 1896, d. July 23, 1957, was an Italian nobleman whose only novel, *The Leopard* (1958; Eng. trans., 1960; film, 1963), won worldwide acclaim. Drawn in part from his own family history, *The Leopard* is a vast panorama of aristocratic Sicilian society and the changes it underwent during the period 1860–1910. *Two Stories and a Memory* (1961; Eng. trans., 1962) was also published posthumously. Lampedusa's work is viewed by most critics as a continuation of the 19th-century literary tradition of Tolstoy and Proust.   LOUIS KIBLER

lamprey   [lamp'-ree]

Lampreys, family Petromyzontidae, and hagfishes are the two surviving groups of jawless vertebrates (class Agnatha). The earliest known lampreys, *Mayomyzon,* are from the Pennsylvanian Period, about 300 million years ago, and are thought to be closely related to an extinct group of jawless fishes, the ostracoderms, which flourished earlier. Lampreys are eellike in shape and lack scales and paired fins (pectorals and pelvics), but they do have a tail fin and one or two dorsal (top)

Lampreys are fish without jaws. The mouth is a circular, toothed, sucking disk, and the body skeleton consists almost entirely of cartilage. Shown are a sea lamprey (top), P. marinus; a river lamprey (center), Lampetra fluviatilis; and a brook lamprey (bottom), L. planeri.

fins. In place of jaws, lampreys have an oral sucking disk bearing teeth and a rasplike tongue. The internal body support consists of a notochord ("backbone") and a cartilaginous skeleton. Lampreys have seven separate gill openings on each side and a single nostril on the upper part of the head.

Some lampreys live only in fresh water. Other species are anadromous, living in marine waters but breeding in fresh water. Lampreys are found in cold to cool coastal and inland waters of both the Northern and Southern hemispheres, with the exception of all of Africa but the northwestern tip.

Although individuals in a single lamprey species may be either parasitic or nonparasitic, it is more usual for a species to be exclusively one or the other. When lampreys hatch they develop into small, blind, toothless, almost wormlike larvae called ammocetes, which burrow in the stream bottom. Ammocetes are filter feeders, straining tiny organisms from the water for food. After several years, varying with the species, and upon reaching usually between 10 and 20 cm (4 to 8 in) long, the ammocetes metamorphose, or change, into the adult form. If the species or individual is nonparasitic, the digestive system degenerates and the adult neither feeds nor grows, merely surviving long enough to reproduce. If parasitic, the adult will adhere to the bodies of other fish with its sucking disk and then rasp their flesh to feed on their blood and tissues.

The sea lamprey, *Petromyzon marinus,* spread to the Great Lakes in the 20th century and caused an immense amount of damage to the fisheries there by killing off lake trout and other species. It is now controlled by the use of a poison that kills the ammocete larvae in the streams.   EDWARD O. WILEY

Bibliography: Hardisty, M. W., and Potter, I. C., eds., *The Biology of the Lampreys,* 3 vols. (1971–1982).

lamprophyre   [lam'-proh-fire]

Lamprophyre is a dark-colored igneous rock composed of large crystals (phenocrysts) of iron and magnesium-rich minerals, such as hornblende (see AMPHIBOLE), biotite (see MICA), or PYROXENE, set in a fine-grained, dark-colored groundmass. Lamprophyres commonly occur as dikes or sills. Most of them contain less than 46% silica by weight and are high in sodium and potassium. Lamprophyric magma is commonly rich in volatile compounds such as water and carbon dioxide.
                                                    JAMES A. WHITNEY

lamp shell: see BRACHIOPOD.

Lamy, Jean Baptiste   [lah-mee', zhawn bap-teest']

The French missionary Jean Baptiste Lamy, b. Oct. 11, 1814, d. Feb. 13, 1888, was the first Roman Catholic bishop of Santa

Fe, N.Mex. After several years of parish work in France, he volunteered for missionary work in the United States. He labored among scattered Catholics, principally in southern Ohio, until he was sent (1850) to the Southwest as vicar apostolic. He became bishop (1853) and later archbishop (1878) of Santa Fe, a desert diocese with Indian, Spanish, Mexican, and American traditions. Willa CATHER's novel *Death Comes for the Archbishop* (1927) is based upon Lamy's career.

Bibliography: Horgan, Paul, *Lamy of Santa Fe* (1975).

Lan-chou (Lanzhou) [lahn-jrow]

Lan-chou is the capital of Kansu (Gansu) province in north central China. It is located on the upper Hwang Ho (Yellow River). With a population of 2,260,000 (1980 est.), it is the largest city, as well as the economic and cultural center, of the province, and it is connected by rail with all major parts of China. Since the Communist takeover in 1949, Lan-chou has been transformed from a small town into a thriving industrial city. Machine manufacturing, oil refining, metallurgy, textile weaving, and cement and chemical production are the major industries. New hydroelectric stations have supplied the city with enough energy for further industrial development.

Lan-chou flourished as a caravan center during the Han dynasty (202 BC–AD 220). Strategically located between China proper and Central Asia and between northern and southwestern China, the city was used by successive dynasties as a stronghold for controlling Central Asia. It became the capital of Kansu in 1666.   JAMES CHAN

Lanark [lan'-urk]

Lanark is a former county located in south central Scotland. The terrain rises from the Clyde River valley in the north to the hilly southern uplands. The major cities include GLASGOW; the former county town, also named Lanark; and Airdrie. Lanark is Scotland's most industrialized region; shipbuilding and textile, machinery, heavy-metals, and brick manufacturing take place there. Agriculture is important in the northern valley; wheat, oats, potatoes, and vegetables are grown. During the Middle Ages, Lanark became prominent because of its prosperous market towns. Lanark's growth was assured after the Industrial Revolution because it possessed large reserves of coal and iron and its rivers provided sources of power for the earliest factories. In 1975, during the reorganization of local government in Scotland, Lanark became part of the STRATHCLYDE administrative region.

Lancashire [lank'-uh-shur]

Lancashire is a county in northwestern England along the Irish Sea coast. Its population is 1,372,118 (1981), and the county covers 3,043 km² (1,175 mi²). Lancaster is the county seat. Until 1974, Lancashire included the industrial cities of MANCHESTER and LIVERPOOL and adjoining coal deposits, which made it the most industrialized and populous county in England. In the local government reorganization of 1974, however, these cities and their surrounds were constituted as separate metropolitan counties. Today Lancashire's principal industrial and commercial centers are Lancaster and Preston. Oats and vegetables are grown and dairy cattle raised in the county. Tourism is important at coastal resorts such as BLACKPOOL.

The Romans established military camps in Lancashire, which subsequently became part of the Anglo-Saxon kingdom of NORTHUMBRIA. Textile manufacturing became important in the Middle Ages. The Industrial Revolution made Lancashire the world's leading producer of cotton textiles, a position it held until the end of the 19th century. Since then, the county has suffered an economic decline due to decreased demand for its products, insufficient industrial diversification, and the decrease in size and resources after 1974.

Lancaster (dynasty) [lank'-uh-stur]

Lancaster was the family name of the 15th-century English kings HENRY IV, HENRY V, and HENRY VI, who were descended from JOHN OF GAUNT, duke of Lancaster.

The title earl of Lancaster was first bestowed (1267) on **Edmund Crouchback**, 1245–96, the younger son of HENRY III and brother of King EDWARD I. Edmund's son **Thomas, earl of Lancaster**, c.1277–1322, who possessed vast estates, led the baronial opposition to EDWARD II and dominated the government from 1314 to 1318 . Thomas was executed after defeat in the Battle of Boroughbridge (1322), and the title passed to his brother, **Henry**, c.1281–1345. Henry's son, **Henry of Grosmont**, c.1299–1361, was the first duke of Lancaster and an important commander in the Hundred Years' War. John of Gaunt, the fourth son of EDWARD III, acquired the title and the Lancastrian estates by his marriage to Duke Henry's heiress, Blanche.

The house of Lancaster acquired the throne when John's son Henry Bolingbroke overthrew RICHARD II in 1399. Crowned king as Henry IV, he sought legitimacy by claiming that Edmund Crouchback had actually been the elder son of Henry III—a clear fiction. Henry's eldest son, Henry V (r. 1413–22), was outlived by two brothers—John, duke of Bedford (1389–1435) and Humphrey, duke of GLOUCESTER—who played prominent roles during the long minority of Henry V's only son, Henry VI. The latter's rule was finally challenged by the rival royal house of YORK. Henry was overthrown (1461) by the Yorkist EDWARD IV during the Wars of the Roses, and the Lancastrian line ended with the deaths of Henry VI and his son, Edward, in 1471.   GEORGE HOLMES

Bibliography: Green, V. H. H., *The Later Plantagenets*, rev. ed. (1966); Jacob, E. F., *The Fifteenth Century, 1399–1485* (1961); Keen, M. H., *England in the Later Middle Ages* (1973); Maddicott, John R., *Thomas of Lancaster, 1307–1322: A Study of the Reign of Edward II* (1970); Storey, R. L., *The End of The House of Lancaster* (1967).

Lancaster (Pennsylvania)

Lancaster, the seat of Lancaster County, is 95 km (60 mi) west of Philadelphia in southeastern Pennsylvania. It has a population of 54,725 (1980). Lancaster is the market center for the surrounding fertile Piedmont plateau where tobacco, grain, and dairy products are produced. Lancaster also has many small industries including the manufacture of machinery, watches, building materials, and other electrical and metal products. It is the heart of the Pennsylvania Dutch region, and many residents belong to the Amish, Mennonite, and Dunkard sects. Tourists come to colorful farmers' markets and "Wheatland" (1828), the home of President James Buchanan, a national shrine. Franklin and Marshall Colleges merged there in 1853. Lancaster was settled in 1709 and laid out as a town in 1730. It was a munitions center during the American Revolution. From 1799 to 1812 it served as the state capital.

Lancaster, Burt

Burton Stephen Lancaster, b. New York City, Nov. 2, 1913, became in the 1950s a top Hollywood action star in such films as *Gunfight at the OK Corral* (1957). More demanding roles made him a critical success in *From Here to Eternity* (1955), *Elmer Gantry* (1960; Academy Award), and *1900* (1976), among others. In *Atlantic City* (1981) and *Local Hero* (1983) the mature Lancaster seemed at the height of his powers.

Lancaster, Joseph

The British educator Joseph Lancaster, b. Nov. 25, 1778, d. Oct. 24, 1838, was one of the developers of the monitorial system of education. While still in his teens, he began teaching poor children in London. No system of public education existed at the time, and as a result children flocked to his schools. To handle the large number of students, Lancaster had the more advanced pupils teach the others. He raised funds to support his work, and eventually 30,000 were enrolled in 95 Lancasterian schools. Lancaster went bankrupt and in 1818 emigrated to the United States. He founded schools in several cities before again overspending. Lancasterian schools were an important factor in the growth of mass education.

Bibliography: Kaestle, Carl F., *Joseph Lancaster and the Monitorial School Movement: A Documentary History* (1973).

lancelet: see AMPHIOXUS.

Lancelot, Sir   [lans'-uh-laht]

In the medieval stories about King Arthur (see ARTHUR AND ARTHURIAN LEGEND), Sir Lancelot of the Lake (du Lac) was King Arthur's bravest knight. As a baby he was rescued from a lake by MORGAN LE FAY, who prepared him to receive his surname—Lancelot. He was descended from kings named Galahad and was the father of Sir GALAHAD. When grown, Lancelot superseded Sir GAWAIN, as Arthur's champion. In later versions of the legend, Lancelot committed adultery with Queen GUINEVERE. Always a champion of women, he frequently saved her from danger. He eventually left Arthur's court altogether. The legend of Lancelot seems to have originated in ancient Ireland, where he was the Gaelic sun-god of summer, known at Tara as Lugh (Lug) Lamfada.

NORMA L. GOODRICH

Bibliography: App, A. J., *Lancelot in English Literature* (1929; repr. 1969); Weston, Jessie L., *Legend of Sir Lancelot du Lac* (1901; repr. 1972).

Lancet   [lan'-set]

A distinguished British medical magazine, the *Lancet* (founded 1823) is published weekly from London and New York. It carries technical articles on medical science and important news of the profession. The *Lancet*'s combined British and North American readership is about 55,500.

ROLAND E. WOLSELEY

lancet fish

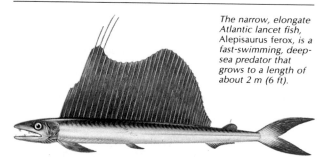

The narrow, elongate Atlantic lancet fish, Alepisaurus ferox, *is a fast-swimming, deep-sea predator that grows to a length of about 2 m (6 ft).*

Lancet fishes, family Alepisauridae, are large, slender-bodied, deep-sea fishes with long, high dorsal fins and large, dagger-like teeth. Two or three species are recognized. The Atlantic lancet fish, *Alepisaurus ferox,* is blackish in color and grows to 2 m (6 ft) long.

Lancret, Nicolas   [lahn-kray', nee-koh-lah']

Nicolas Lancret, b. Jan. 22, 1690, d. Sept. 14, 1743, was a French rococo painter who specialized in genre scenes. He studied in Claude GILLOT's workshop, where one of his fellow pupils was Antoine WATTEAU. Although he shared with Watteau a taste for festive scenes executed in the spirited and airy style of the rococo, Lancret lacked his famous contemporary's ability to invest a scene with visual poetry and haunting poignancy.

His works portray well the decorative and sentimental aspects of a scene, without attempting to explore what lies beneath the surface. Theatrical subjects fascinated him, and he had a keen eye for genre scenes, such as *Winter* (1738; Louvre, Paris) and *Fastening the Skate* (1741; Stockholm Museum). He also enjoyed a high reputation as a portrait painter, particularly of theatrical figures, such as *The Actor François-Charles Racot de Grandval* (1742; Indianapolis Museum of Art). Although not a great master, he displayed a charming and lighthearted touch in portraying the elegant society of 18th-century France.

SUZANNE J. WILSON

Bibliography: Kalnein, Wend Graf, and Levey, M., *Art and Architecture of the Eighteenth Century in France* (1972).

land: see PROPERTY.

Land, Edwin

Edwin Herbert Land, b. May 7, 1909, is an American scientist and industrialist known for inventing the single-step (one-step) method of developing and printing photographs. As a student at Harvard University he became interested in POLARIZED LIGHT. By the mid-1930s he was able to apply polarization to antiglare automobile headlights, camera filters, reduced-glare sunglasses, and three-dimensional motion pictures. He founded the Polaroid Corporation in 1937.

After World War II, Land developed a camera that took and developed photographs in a single-step process (see FILM PROCESSING). Known as the Polaroid Land Camera, it was demonstrated in 1947 and first marketed in 1948, with improved versions following. A camera that was able to take color photographs was marketed in 1963. A motion-picture system (Polavision), in which a movie could be viewed almost immediately after being taken, was demonstrated in 1977 and marketed in 1978. As a by-product of his work, Land developed a theory of COLOR PERCEPTION that holds that at least three independent image-forming mechanisms work together to indicate the color seen by the eye.

Bibliography: Heyn, Ernest V., *Fire of Genius* (1976).

land-grant colleges

Land-grant colleges are institutions of higher education founded or expanded with the assistance of federal lands granted to the states. The Land-Grant Act of 1862, often called the MORRILL ACT, was introduced by Justin S. Morrill, a Republican congressman and later a senator from Vermont. It offered tracts of federal lands to states as an incentive for establishing college programs in scientific, agricultural, industrial, and military studies. Some states applied the grants to a single institution, others to several institutions. Most of the colleges developed higher-education programs in addition to those required by the act. Awards generally went to public institutions, but in a few cases private colleges such as the Massachusetts Institute of Technology won them. Occasionally a state changed its mind: In Connecticut, farmer organizations protested the designation of Yale University as the grant recipient; the award was transferred to a state college that later became the University of Connecticut. The second Morrill Act, approved in 1890, continued to support land-grant colleges and required that states practicing racial segregation create black colleges as a precondition to receiving funds. In the 50 states, the District of Columbia, Guam, Puerto Rico, and the Virgin Islands, 72 land-grant colleges and universities have been established.

DONALD R. WARREN

Bibliography: Allen, Herman R., *Open Door to Learning: The Land-Grant System Enters Its Second Century* (1963); Guthrie, Edwin Ray, *The State University: Its Function and Its Future* (1957); Nevins, Allan, *State Universities and Democracy* (1962).

land reclamation

Land reclamation makes otherwise inaccessible areas available for human use. Swamps, deserts, and submerged coastal lands are naturally inaccessible; surface mines, waste-disposal sites, and municipal landfills are waste areas created by human activity. The land reclaimed from such areas has been used for agricultural and forest crops, recreation, wildlife, and industrial or residential development.

RECLAMATION OF NATURALLY INACCESSIBLE AREAS

Naturally inaccessible areas are frequently the result of moisture extremes. Wet areas must be either drained or land-filled. Drainage (see DRAINAGE SYSTEMS) is accomplished in several ways: by building a system of channels, by laying drainage pipes, and by pumping. In many cases embankments must be constructed to keep water out of the reclaimed areas. LANDFILL operations require large quantities of suitable fill material such as sand, which is often obtained by dredging adjacent areas. Water is supplied to arid areas either by pumping it from underground sources or by transporting it through an IRRIGATION system.

Irrigation of arid lands has a long history, having been practiced for thousands of years in the Middle East. It has been most intensively developed in Israel, where conduits carry water from the Jordan River and other freshwater sources in northern Israel to the Negev Desert, more than 200 km (125 mi) away. Although almost all of Israel's conventional water resources have been under exploitation for many years, the area under irrigation continues to increase because of the development of improved irrigation methods, such as drip irrigation. Attempts are also being made to use saline water as well as fresh water for irrigation.

Reclamation of wetlands has significantly enhanced the well-being of several nations. The Netherlands is an outstanding example. Over a period of centuries the amount of arable land has been significantly increased by the construction of dikes, enclosing portions of the shallow coastal waters, which are then drained off. The Zuider Zee project, the first phase of which was a 29-km (18-mi) dike completed in 1932, has creat-

Nearly 17% of the present surface area of the Netherlands has been recovered from the sea by land-reclamation projects, many of which have been ongoing since the beginning of the 12th century. About one-third of this land has been reclaimed during the 20th century.

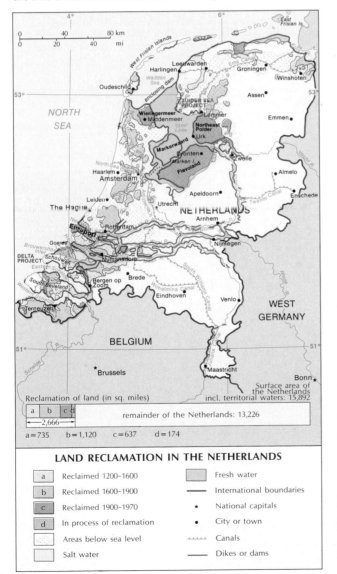

LAND RECLAMATION IN THE NETHERLANDS

a	Reclaimed 1200–1600	Fresh water
b	Reclaimed 1600–1900	International boundaries
c	Reclaimed 1900–1970	★ National capitals
d	In process of reclamation	● City or town
	Areas below sea level	Canals
	Salt water	Dikes or dams

ed nearly 200,000 ha (500,000 acres) of POLDERS (land reclaimed from the sea) thus far. Because much of this land is below sea level, continuous pumping is required to maintain the desired water-table level.

Considerable areas in salt marshes have also been reclaimed in eastern England by constructing embankments that separate the marshes from the sea, and draining the marshes both with ditches inside the embankments and through tidal sluices. Because the marshes are above sea level, pumping is not needed. Land reclaimed from the sea has such a high salt level that only salt-tolerant vegetation can be planted during the first few years. However, after several years, rain leaches out most of the sodium ions and soil conditions improve.

An example of large-scale reclamation of freshwater marshes is the drainage in the 1930s of the PONTINE MARSHES of Italy, a 75,000-ha (195,000-acre) region of dunes and marshes about 70 km (45 mi) southwest of Rome. The project not only opened new land for settlement and agriculture but also helped control malaria, a product of the marshes.

Reclamation of wetlands has been less actively pursued in the United States, because such areas are highly productive habitats for fish, shellfish, birds, and wildlife. Reclamation of arid lands, however, has been a major goal of the U.S. Bureau of Reclamation. The Lower Colorado River Project has transformed desert areas, such as the Imperial Valley of California, into some of the most productive cropland in the world.

RECLAMATION OF ARTIFICIALLY CREATED WASTE AREAS

The major problems associated with waste areas that are the result of human activity—industry, mining, and waste disposal—are slope instability, chemical leachates, and soil nutrient deficiencies. Such waste areas occupy only a small fraction of the land area, but they are frequently concentrated in highly populated regions and, in addition to their ugliness, often cause air and water pollution over widespread areas. In such cases the need for reclamation is particularly pressing; but when it is accomplished, it results in healthier environments as well as useful land.

Slope instability can be reduced by reshaping the waste areas into landforms with gentler slopes that will conform with the surrounding landscape features. Erosion is prevented through water-control measures and the establishment of a vegetative cover.

The Aberfan disaster in Wales in 1966—in which 170 people, mostly schoolchildren, were killed when a coal-refuse bank collapsed—resulted in one of the largest reclamation projects of derelict land. The piles of black wastes formerly so

Battery Park City, on 37.2 ha (92 acres) of landfill along the Hudson River in New York City, is considered a fine example of urban design.

common in many of the urban areas of England and Wales have been transformed into landscaped parks and preserves. Because of their proximity to heavily populated areas, costs have been high, but large numbers of people have benefited from the vastly improved environment.

Many disused mine-waste piles dot the landscapes of the older coal-mining regions of the United States, particularly in the East. Although most cause serious environmental problems, few have been reclaimed.

Reclamation of Surface-Mined Land. Of much greater magnitude in terms of the amount of land involved are the scars left by surface-mining operations, especially where coal has been mined. Federal and state laws now require the reclamation of land disturbed by strip-mining operations, and a concerted effort is underway to reclaim land disturbed in past operations. Most commonly mine operators are required to restore the land to a use at least as good as that which existed prior to mining. This restoration may involve stockpiling the upper soil layers, segregating and burying potentially toxic material, reshaping the piles to approximately the original contour, respreading the soil, and establishing a vegetative cover. Such reclamation is most efficiently done as part of the mining operation. Reclamation of old abandoned surface mines is more difficult and more costly.

Reclamation of surface-mined areas in the western United States and Canada is even more difficult because of the arid climate and, in some cases, high elevations. Nevertheless, surface mining will probably expand rapidly there in the next few decades, not only for coal but also for oil shale and oil sands.

Reclamation of Chemically Polluted Land. Methods used in alleviating problems of chemical pollution vary, depending upon the nature of the chemicals involved. High concentrations of soluble salts can be reduced by leaching the salts from the surface layers of the soil with water. Acidity can be lessened by applying calcium-containing material, such as

pulverized limestone, to the soil. The improvement may be only temporary, however. Mine wastes often contain large quantities of pyrite (FeS_2), which reacts with oxygen and water to form sulfuric acid and other toxic products. Acid is thus continuously produced, and a continuing need exists for periodic treatment following the initial reclamation.

The chemical and physical properties of the waste are sometimes so adverse to plant growth that the only satisfactory reclamation measure is to cover the waste with a thick layer of soil material. In other cases it may be possible to improve conditions by applying another waste material, such as the fuel ash produced by coal-burning electric-generating stations or sewage sludge from municipal treatment plants.

Landfill Reclamation. The most common reclamation problem throughout the world involves the disposal of urban wastes. Although most such wastes are inert or biodegradable and seldom contain hazardous toxic materials, they can constitute public-health problems. Many attempts have been made to reclaim valuable materials from the waste and to produce energy or new products from it; nevertheless, most of it is still disposed of on land. Ideally, such disposal sites are isolated from surface and subsurface waters, the wastes are compacted and covered with soil, and a vegetative cover is established. Unfortunately, there is a shortage of suitable sites, especially near large cities (see WASTE DISPOSAL SYSTEMS).

In addition to urban wastes, reclamation problems are created by highway and reservoir embankments, pulverized fuel ash, and wastes resulting from the removal and processing of such materials as sand and gravel, building stone, limestone, bauxite, china clay, iron ore, gold, and a variety of heavy metals.

Reclamation usually involves the establishment of vegetation. Selection of species and strains that are tolerant of adverse conditions can reduce site-modification costs and improve the chances for success. Where possible, time-tested methods of site preparation and plant establishment are used.

In the 1980s, artist Michael Heizer designed a huge earth sculpture for a land reclamation project in Illinois. Built on an abandoned strip mine that once looked like the photo on the left, his work includes the water strider, frog, and catfish shown on the right.

For example, success is more likely if lime and fertilizer are incorporated into the upper layers, a seedbed is prepared, seed is drilled into the soil, and a mulch is applied.

RUSSELL J. HUTNICK

Bibliography: Bradshaw, A. D., and Chadwick, M. J., *The Restoration of the Land* (1980); Chase, S., *Rich Land, Poor Land* (1936; repr. 1969); Flawn, P. T., *Environmental Geology* (1970); Golze, A. R., *Reclamation in the United States* (1952); Hutnick, R. J., and Davis, G., eds., *Ecology and Reclamation of Devastated Land*, 2 vols. (1973); Law, D. L., *Mined-Land Rehabilitation* (1984); Maltby, E., *Waterlogged Earth: Why Waste the World's Wet Places?* (1986); Reith, C. C., and Potter, L. D., eds., *Principles and Methods of Reclamation Science* (1986); Wagret, P., *Polderlands* (1968); Weiner, D. P., et al., *Reclaiming the West: The Coal Industry and Surface-Mined Lands* (1980).

land use: see CONSERVATION; ZONING.

Landau, Lev [luhn-dow', lef]

The Soviet scientist Lev Davidovich Landau made significant contributions to almost every area of modern theoretical physics. Landau's work ranged from nuclear physics and astrophysics to low-temperature physics—including his work with helium, which won him a Nobel Prize in 1962. Landau also worked on the first Soviet atomic bomb and contributed to the Soviet space program.

One of the most important Soviet scientists of the 20th century, Lev Davidovich Landau, b. Jan. 22 (N.S.), 1908, d. Apr. 1, 1968, made contributions to almost every field of theoretical physics. Landau studied physics and chemistry at Leningrad State University. After graduating at the age of 19, he worked at the Physico-Technical Institute in Leningrad. His first important contribution to theoretical physics, involving the theory of diamagnetism of metals, was made during his stay at Niels Bohr's Institute for Theoretical Physics in Copenhagen.

In 1931, Landau was appointed head of the Ukrainian Physico-Technical Institute of Kharkov, which under his leadership became the center for theoretical physics in the Soviet Union. At Kharkov he also began, in collaboration with his former student E. M. Lifshits, his multivolume treatise on theoretical physics, which even today remains an important work in the field. Landau received many honors in his own country, including the Stalin Prize, the Lenin Prize (1962), and the title Hero of Socialist Labor, but his critical statements outside the field of physics also made him many enemies. He was imprisoned in 1938, and only the personal intervention of the Soviet physicist Peter Kapitza saved him from deportation to a concentration camp. He subsequently received the Nobel Prize in 1962 for his pioneering work on the theory of liquids, especially liquid helium.

Landau's work in low-temperature physics includes a theory of superfluidity of liquid helium and a theoretical description of superconductivity. To solid-state physics Landau contributed the theory of diamagnetism and the theory of phase transitions. In plasma physics, which deals with the study of ionized matter, he gave a description of the motion of a system of charged particles. In astrophysics he predicted in the 1930s the existence of NEUTRON STARS, since confirmed by the discovery of pulsars. He also showed that when the mass of a star depleted of its nuclear fuel is greater than 1.5 solar masses, its material is subjected to pressures that the atomic forces can no longer overcome (see BLACK HOLE).

In nuclear physics Landau did important work on the scattering of mesons by nuclear forces and the scattering of light by mesons. He was also the first to describe how cosmic radiation in the Earth's atmosphere gives rise to electron "avalanches." Landau applied Heisenberg's uncertainty principle to relativistic quantum mechanics, contributed to the description of electron-positron annihilation, and studied quantum effects on the motion of electrons and mesons.

In 1962, Landau was severely injured in a car accident and was declared clinically dead several times. He lived until April 1968 but performed no further scientific work.

Bibliography: Cutler, Ann, *Four Minutes to Live* (1970); Dorozynski, Alexander, *The Man They Wouldn't Let Die* (1965); Livanova, Anna, *Landau: A Great Physicist and Teacher*, trans. by J. B. Sykes (1980).

Landau, Mark Aleksandrovich: see ALDANOV, M. A.

landfill

The sanitary landfill provides a way of safely disposing of solid wastes in a controlled manner. The landfill site is lined with an impermeable material such as clay, and soil is used to surround and contain the waste materials. Municipal solid wastes—the garbage collected from households—and, at times, certain industrial and agricultural wastes are spread in layers and compacted by heavy bulldozers to reduce their volume. At least once every 24 hours, a layer of soil of a minimum of 15 cm (6 in) in thickness is spread on top of the compacted waste and is itself compacted before more waste is added. When the waste-soil mound reaches a certain height, it is covered with a layer of soil at least 60 cm (2 ft) thick, which is then revegetated. The water table under the site must be at least 2 m (6 ft) deep and the site not subject to flooding. Soils vary greatly in their ability to contain and renovate the ordinary decomposition products of solid waste, so only a small proportion of potential sites are suitable for use as sanitary landfills.

The decomposition of organic wastes generates biogas, a mixture of methane and carbon dioxide and an inexpensive source of energy. A number of U.S. landfill sites are currently equipped to collect the gas, which is used to generate electricity.

The heterogeneousness of the material in landfills causes uneven settlement of the mound, and ordinarily a closed landfill cannot be used as a building site. It may be reclaimed, however, for recreational use.

It is estimated that at least one-third of the nation's landfills will have reached their capacity and be forced to close by the early 1990s. Today, large incinerators have replaced landfills in many municipalities. But incinerators produce pollution problems of their own, principally hazardous exhaust gases and a highly toxic ash, the final product of waste burning. The ash can safely be disposed of only by burying it in a landfill.

In future, it may be possible to reduce the total amount of solid waste. Plastic throwaway items, disposable diapers, plastic bottles, and packaging materials contribute most to the waste flow. Much of the plastic may eventually be made to self-destruct. Metal, glass, and paper may be recycled, if profitable markets can be found for the new materials. Landfills may then be used only for the burial of biodegradable wastes.

GUY W. MCKEE

Bibliography: Henstock, M., *Disposal and Recovery of Municipal Solid Waste* (1983) and *Garbage Management in Japan* (1987); Neal, H. A., and Schubel, J. R., *Solid Waste Management and the Environment* (1987); Smith, W. H., and Frank, J. R., eds., *Methane from Biomass* (1988).

See also: POLLUTION, ENVIRONMENTAL; WASTE DISPOSAL SYSTEMS.

landform evolution

The expression *landform evolution* applies to the time-dependent changes that occur in landforms in various settings. Schemes of landform evolution have been worked out for areas experiencing humid, arid, or glacial conditions, or the alternation of two or more types of climate. In addition, the role of crustal movements and mountain building have been worked into such schemes or considered in independent sequences of events. The evolution of coastal landforms has also been studied.

Effects of Humid Climates. William M. DAVIS, in his theories of landform evolution, cited (1899) presumably time-dependent stages of development keyed largely to stream erosion that occurred during periods of crustal stability (see PENE-PLAIN). Following subsequent discoveries indicating that crustal uplift accompanies erosion, John T. Hack (1913–   ) suggested (1960) that humid landforms in the Appalachian

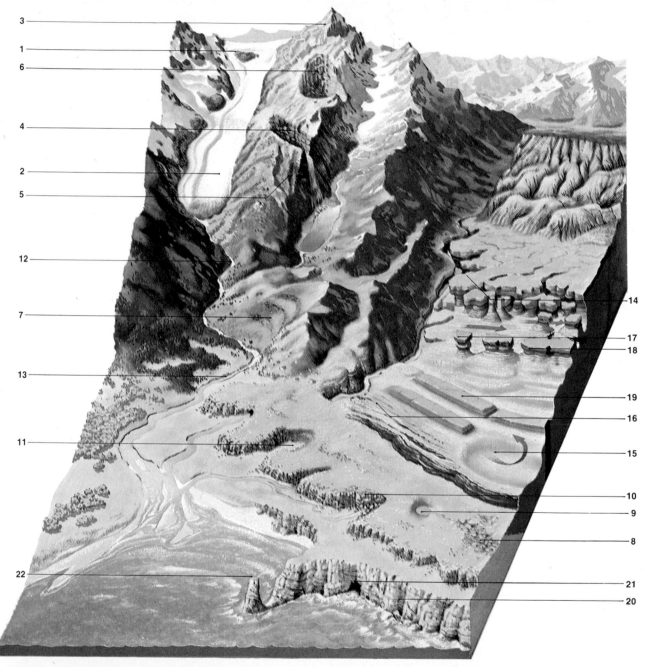

Processes of erosion, or the wearing away of land surfaces by ice, water, and wind, and of deposition have sculptured the land into various shapes called landforms. In mountainous areas, mass movements of ice caps (1) and glaciers (2) have abraded and carved out pyramidal peaks (3), hanging valleys (4), truncated spurs (5), and cirques (6), or bowl-shaped depressions. The impact of rain on surfaces with no protective vegetative cover causes slopewash (7), whereas the chemical action of rain and dissolved carbon dioxide on limestone results in grikes (8), or grooved surfaces, swallow holes (9), chasms (10), and dry valleys (11). A rapidly flowing river erodes its bed vertically and laterally (12) first to form steep and then wide river valleys (13) and canyons (14). Winds blowing across dry land create basinlike depressions, or deflation hollows (15). The sandblasting action of windblown soil particles may smooth pebbles and rocks and then fit them together closely to form a continuous layer, or desert pavement (16), or may abrade the base of a small rock mass to form a pedestal, or mushroom rock (17). It may also abrade larger rock masses to form zuegens (18), or may excavate long passageways between deeply undercut overhanging ridges, or yardangs (19). Along coastlines, wave action may result in cliffs (20), caves (21), and stacks (22).

Mountains develop toward a steady-state condition (see ERO-SION CYCLE; EROSION AND SEDIMENTATION).

In this scheme, topographic relief caused by incising streams (see RIVER AND STREAM) increases in areas of prolonged humidity, as long as uplift continues. A ridge-ravine (selva) topography results, which resembles Davis's "mature" developmental stage. Individual hillslopes, beneath vegetal cover, tend to be shaped by gravity erosion and solutional effects of percolating groundwater, and thus incline toward watercourses. Landform evolution substantially slows down when a steady state is reached.

Effects of Arid Climates. In DESERT regions the areas with steady-state landforms tend to be erosional plains (pediplains) and surfaces of alluviation generated by running water, which may be modified locally by wind erosion and deposition (see WIND ACTION). Such areas are found in parts of the Sahara and Australian deserts. Desert running water eventually evaporates and deposits sediment rather than eroding and extending drainage systems. Individual hillslopes in deserts tend to be worn back and down by a combination of gravity erosion and, where barren, by sheetwash erosion.

Effects on Climate Change. Geologically recent widespread climate changes restrict areas of possible steady-state landform evolution to little more than 10 percent of the Earth's land surface. In fact, landform evolution over most of the Earth has proceeded under a variety of alternating climates, and therefore tendencies toward steady-state morphologies are periodically interrupted, producing an array of polygenetic landforms. Valley cutting under humid conditions may give way to valley alluviation and pedimentation (see ALLUVIAL FANS; PEDIMENT, geology) under aridity, only to have the alluvial deposits incised upon a return to humid conditions by renewed streamflow. Resulting landscapes often exhibit stairstepped terrain that reflects alternating planation and valley deepening. The region of the southern Ozarks in the United States is an example.

The long-term evolution of terrain developed under changing climate may be determined by the degree to which the various climate types are expressed in intensity and duration. Thus, in a setting such as the North American High Plains, planation, or flattening, may eventually dominate and generate a plain, even with sporadic episodes of gully cutting. Alternatively, valley cutting may predominate despite sporadic intervals of alluviation, as recently occurred in west-central Tennessee. Intermediate examples also exist.

Effects of Glaciation. Glacial conditions (see GLACIER AND GLACIATION), as in Antarctica and Greenland, may dominate landform evolution. More commonly, in the lower latitudes, they may alternate with humid or arid conditions. Thus, valley cutting under humid conditions occasionally gives way to ice scour and drift deposition (see DRIFT, GLACIAL). Drainage systems are periodically disrupted in this fashion, and isolated glacial depressions often contain lakes that may gradually fill with sediment and evolve into swamps (see SWAMP, MARSH, AND BOG) and then prairies (see LAKE, GLACIAL). Northern portions of North America and Eurasia show many landforms that are products of alternating glaciation and aridity or humidity.

Effects of Crustal Movements and Volcanism. Effects of various types of crustal movement and volcanism (see DIASTROPHISM; VOLCANO) can be imposed on those of climate to determine landform evolution. MOUNTAIN landforms commonly evolve in response to a combination of climatic effects and those of rock deformation (see OROGENY). In newly formed mountains, the effect of climate may be slight. At lower latitudes, developing mountains initially experience arid or humid climates, but uplift to great elevations may induce sculpture by alpine glaciers. In oceanic settings near warm seas, mountain erosion may occur under predominantly humid conditions, whereas in midcontinental regions, such as those of central Asia, mountain sculpture at lower elevations may occur mainly under desert conditions. Often such mountains have glaciated peaks. Because mountains often influence wind directions and moisture distribution, the opposite sides of a given mountain range may simultaneously experience

distinct forms of evolution under different climates (see MOUNTAIN CLIMATES).

Ultimately, not only climate but also the way rocks are deformed governs landform evolution in mountains. In mountains formed by what is believed to be collisions between two continents, a mountain root is formed, which maintains the mountainous elevations in a buoyant crustal relationship, much as a cork sticks partly above the water in which it floats. The mountain root causes renewed uplift as erosion removes rock weight, but only as long as the root exists. Eventually, such mountains evolve by becoming lower and lower. In approximately 500 million years, they may be reduced to a low elevation and possibly take on some aspects of a plain.

When mountains are developed in continued association with an OCEANIC TRENCH, as in the case of the Andes, the evolution is altered by this association. Crustal movements near trenches apparently add new rock material through volcanism to the mountain root and crestal peaks. Such rock additions may counter the lowering effects of erosion. Depending on the amount of erosion versus added rock, trench-associated mountains may maintain their elevations through time in a sort of mountainous steady state; some may actually continue to increase in height despite continuing erosion.

Coastal Landform Evolution. Coastal landforms (see BEACH AND COAST) evolve in response to the exposure of shoreline rocks to erosion by waves and currents and to sediment accumulation. Deltas form and enlarge at river mouths as a result of the high influx of sediment that accompanies the onset of humid conditions on land. On the other hand, they are destroyed by marine erosion as sediment influx wanes. Sand beaches grow and dwindle largely in response to the same cycle. Shaping of coastal outlines and bedrock exposures varies with changes in sea level, which interrupt the normal cycles of evolution.   H. F. GARNER

Bibliography: Adams, George F., and Wyckoff, Jerome, *Landforms* (1971); Garner, H. F., *The Origin of Landscapes: A Synthesis of Geomorphology* (1974); Shimer, John A., *Field Guide to Landforms in the United States* (1972); Thornbury, William D., *Principles of Geomorphology*, 2d ed. (1969) and *Regional Geomorphology of the United States* (1965); Tuttle, Sherwood D., *Landforms and Landscapes*, 2d ed. (1975); Watts, May T., *Reading the Landscape of Europe* (1971).

See also: GEOMORPHOLOGY.

Landini, Francesco   [lahn-dee'-nee, frahn-ches'-koh]

Francesco Landini, b. c.1325, d. Sept. 2, 1397, was the most celebrated Italian poet-musician of the 14th century. Blinded at an early age by smallpox, he turned to music as a youth. He became the leading organist in Florence and was noted for his skill at the portative organ. Often compared in versatility and genius to his French contemporary Guillaume de MACHAUT, Landini wrote many of the texts he later set to music. Of his 154 preserved compositions, 140 are *ballate* and the rest are madrigals and *cacce*. Many of his works are preserved in an elaborate manuscript of the early 15th century that belonged to the Florentine organist Antonio Squarcialupi (1416–80) and that is therefore called the *Squarcialupi Codex*. Landini's music is characterized by free-flowing melody, consonant harmony, and technical refinement and sophistication.
                                                    ROBERT M. CAMMAROTA

Bibliography: Grout, Donald J., *A History of Western Music*, rev. ed. (1973); Hopping, Richard H., *Medieval Music* (1978); Reese, Gustave, *Music in the Middle Ages* (1940); Seay, Albert, *Music in the Medieval World*, 2d ed. (1975); Sternfeld, F. W., ed., *Music from the Middle Ages to the Renaissance* (1973).

Landis, Kenesaw Mountain

Kenesaw Mountain Landis, b. Millville, Ohio, Nov. 20, 1866, d. Nov. 25, 1944, was an American judge (1905–22) and commissioner of professional baseball from 1921 until his death. As U.S. district judge for northern Illinois he fined (1907) Standard Oil of Indiana $29,240,000 for illegal rebates. Although the fine was overturned on appeal, Landis's harsh treatment of the corrupt company was very popular. Appointed baseball commissioner after the bribery scandals of 1919, in which the Chicago White Sox allegedly lost the World Series intentionally, he restored baseball's integrity. Upon his death a special committee elected him to the Baseball Hall of Fame.

Bibliography: Spink, John G. T., *Judge Landis and 25 Years of Baseball* (1974).

landlord: see LEASE; TENANT.

Landon, Alf

Alfred Mossman Landon, b. West Middlesex, Pa., Sept. 9, 1887, d. Oct. 12, 1987, was a key figure in the U.S. Republican party in the 1930s and ran unsuccessfully for president in 1936. "Alf" Landon first entered the national political arena in 1912, campaigning for Theodore Roosevelt, who was the Progressive party candidate for president. Landon continued to be associated with progressive politics within the Republican party. In 1932 he was elected governor of Kansas, and two years later he was the only incumbent Republican governor to be reelected in an otherwise Democratic landslide. This success made Landon a strong candidate to oppose President Franklin D. Roosevelt in 1936. Although he won 17,000,000 votes, Landon carried only Maine and Vermont. Following his defeat Landon retired from national politics. His daughter Nancy Landon Kassebaum was elected U.S. senator from Kansas in 1978 and reelected in 1984.

Bibliography: McCoy, Donald R., *Landon of Kansas* (1966).

Landor, Walter Savage

The English poet and essayist Walter Savage Landor, b. Warwick, Jan. 30, 1775, d. Sept. 17, 1864, won renown for his lengthy prose work, *Imaginary Conversations* (1824–53)—a series of 152 dialogues between celebrated writers, statesmen, and philosophers of ancient and modern times. His early poetry includes the epic *Gebir* (1798) and the verse drama *Count Julian* (1812). During a writing career that spanned 68 years, Landor produced many fine short poems and epigrams that are terse, polished expressions of intense feeling. His violent republican beliefs made him an outcast from English society, and he lived in Spain and Italy for much of his life.

Bibliography: Dilworth, Ernest, *Walter Savage Landor* (1971); Elwin, Malcolm, *Savage Landor* (1941; repr. 1983).

Landowska, Wanda

The harpsichordist and pianist Wanda Landowska, b. Warsaw, July 5, 1877, d. Aug. 16, 1959, was the leading figure in the 20th-century revival of the harpsichord and was particu-

larly admired for her interpretations of Bach. She started her career as a pianist in 1891, but her interest in music of the baroque period drew her to the harpsichord. She made her debut as harpsichordist in 1903 in Paris and first performed in the United States in 1923. In Saint-Len-la-Forêt, near Paris, she established (1925) a world-famous school for the study of early music. World War II brought her to the United States, where she continued teaching, writing, and performing. Due in large part to her efforts, the performance of early music on instruments of the period is today an accepted practice.

Bibliography: Ewen, David, ed., *Musicians since 1900* (1978); Restout, Denise, ed., *Landowska on Music* (1965).

Landrum-Griffin Act: see LABOR-MANAGEMENT REPORTING AND DISCLOSURE ACT.

Land's End

Land's End, a peninsula in Cornwall, is the westernmost point of England. Spectacular granite cliffs looming more than 20 m (60 ft) above the water make Land's End a popular tourist attraction. A lighthouse completed in 1797 warns ships of the many rocky reefs located offshore.

Landsat

Landsat, formerly Earth Resources Technology Satellite (ERTS), is a series of U.S. satellites designed to observe the Earth's surface in different regions of the electromagnetic spectrum. Their applications include forecasting crop production around the world, assisting in soil and forestry management, locating energy and mineral resources, and assessing urban population densities.

Landsat 1 (launched July 23, 1972; turned off January 1978), *Landsat 2* (Jan. 22, 1975; turned off February 1982), and *Landsat 3* (Mar. 5, 1978; turned off March 1983) provided a total of more than 1 million pictures. On July 16, 1982, *Landsat 4* was launched into an orbit that brought it over the same point on Earth every 16 days, and on Mar. 5, 1984, *Landsat 5* was sent into a circular polar orbit.

Landsat evolved from the Tiros and Nimbus meteorological satellites and used some of their components. Each of the first three Landsats weighed about 900 kg (about 2,000 lb) and consisted of a cylindrical instrument section upon which was mounted an open-truss structure supporting a smaller housing and two solar panels. The next two Landsats each had a multimission design consisting of a communications module, attitude control module, and power module clustered around a central truss containing the propulsion module. Each weighed 1,996 kg (4,400 lb).

The first color photomosaic of the continental United States was compiled from 569 individual cloud-free photographs taken from an altitude of 917 km (570 mi) by an orbiting Landsat satellite. The Landsats, a series of spacecraft that transmit data to Earth-based stations, were launched by NASA but are now controlled by a private company. Setbacks in the space program and lack of government support have resulted in increased costs and have delayed further development of the Landsat project. Competing remote-sensing programs in France, Germany, and Japan have benefited from this delay.

Two images, developed from a single photograph taken by an orbiting Landsat satellite, of farmland in the San Joaquin Valley of California, one of the most important U.S. agricultural regions, demonstrate some of the spacecraft's capabilities. The left-hand photograph indicates the cultivated sections as base, or preliminary, data. The right-hand photograph displays a special color-enhancement process that enables scientists to identify specific crops. Fields of cotton are coded as red; safflower as yellow; wheat stubble as green; and fallow ground as blue.

Each of the first three Landsats carried a Multi-Spectral Scanner (MSS) and a Return Beam Vidicom (RBV) camera system. The MSS "sees" the Earth in the green, red, and infrared spectral regions. It relays signals to Earth or to Tracking and Data Relay Satellites (TDRS; see TRACKING STATION), or stores them for later sending. The MSS has a resolution of 70 m (230 ft). The RBV is a backup sensor that distinguishes objects as small as 100 m (330 ft). The next two Landsats also carried a Thematic Mapper (TM), a device that scans in seven narrower spectral bands and provides nearly three times the resolution of the MSS.

Landsats are the property of the federal government. In 1984 their management was transferred to a private firm, the Earth Observational Satellite Company (EOSAT), a joint venture of RCA Corporation and Hughes Aircraft Company. In 1979 federal responsibility for and financial support of the satellites was transferred from the National Aeronautics and Space Administration (NASA) to the National Oceanographic and Atmospheric Administration (NOAA). NOAA felt that land surveys did not belong within its purview and tried to end Landsat funding in 1989, an attempt that was blocked by the Bush administration.　　　　　　　　　　　　MITCHELL R. SHARPE

Bibliography: Jones, Pat, "Remote Sensing," *Space World,* November 1985; Knox, Charlie, "Remotely Incensed," *Ad Astra,* April 1989; Lindsay, E. J., ed., *Remote Sensing of Earth Resources* (1981).

landscape architecture

The art of landscape architecture is almost as old as that of architecture itself. In ancient Egypt, Mesopotamia, and Persia, immense efforts were devoted to creating verdant enclosures for temples and palaces, of which the most famous were the "Hanging Gardens" of Babylon, a complex of irrigated terraces erected *c.*605 BC by Nebuchadnezzar II (see MESOPOTAMIA; EGYPT, ANCIENT; PERSIAN ART AND ARCHITECTURE).

Ornamental horticulture first flourished in imperial Roman times in suburban villas around Rome. At HADRIAN'S VILLA open arcades and peristyles were used to weave together dwellings, gardens, and pools. Pliny the Younger's estates at Laurentium and Tusci (AD *c.*60) incorporated extensive pleasure gardens in which formal and informal gardens were mingled. Pliny's own descriptions inspired many reconstructions during the Renaissance and later. Excavations at Pompeii have also revealed formal courtyard gardens. The Romans seem to have regarded their gardens as unroofed living spaces and treated them as integral parts of domestic architecture.

The ancient tradition of the pleasure garden persisted in medieval Arab civilization (see MOORISH ART AND ARCHITECTURE), and exotic gardens of water, fruit trees, and flowers were also recorded in Persian miniature paintings from the 14th century. Some of the greatest Moorish gardens of Spain have partially survived at the ALHAMBRA and Generalife palaces, dating from the 13th century, where plantings, fountains, pools, and canals occupy the richly decorated courtyards. In northern Europe tiny, formally planted, walled gardens containing bathing pools and marble tables provided settings for courtly life;

flowers for such gardens were chosen for their symbolic values. Attention was also given, both in monasteries and in castle precincts, to practical gardens of herbs, useful flowers, and fruit trees.

Italy. The humanism of the Italian Renaissance brought about a dramatic change in the character of landscape architecture. As in Roman times, the garden was an integral part of a suburban dwelling, and the interior spaces of a house were often subordinated to the garden, allowing the occupants to regard themselves as a part of an ordered nature. Eminent architects took up the design of gardens under the patronage of the nobility and the popes. For Giovanni de'Medici (see MEDICI family), MICHELOZZO built one of the first great hillside villas with terraced gardens, at Fiesole, overlooking Florence, in 1458. The Medicis were also responsible for the most extensive gardens of Florence, the Boboli, which they developed over the course of 150 years behind the PITTI PALACE after their purchase of it in 1549. The Boboli Gardens cover a large hillside with formal plantings, sculptures, and basins, including a small formal island designed by Giorgio VASARI.

By the latter half of the 16th century, Rome and its environs contained the finest achievements of Renaissance landscape architecture. Those of the Villa Medici, built about 1580, progress from the rear façade of the house through an open entertainment area, to a low garden of formal beds flanked by sculpture galleries, and on to a formally planted woodland. In the hills north of Rome, water was used to cool and ornament the garden of the Villa d'Este at Tivoli, designed by Pirro Ligorio. Begun *c.*1550, this garden combines cascades, jets, and curtains of water with placid pools and channels on hillside terraces through which the visitor walks on ramps and stairways. At the Villa Lante at Bagnaia, designed about 1565, probably by Giacomo Barozzi da VIGNOLA, water is directed through basins and channels, appearing and disappearing along a densely planted hillside and finally emerging in reflecting pools in a formal garden. The villa itself, divided symmetrically into two buildings, is an integrated part of the composition. In contrast to such elegant gardens is the bizarre arrangement of sculptures in a landscape conceived in 1572 by Pierfrancesco Orsini at his villa at Bomarzo. There natural limestone outcroppings are cut into monsters, beasts, and river gods. During the baroque period in Italy, complex patterns of planting and varied combinations of plant types became popular. On the Isola Bella in Lake Maggiore, Carlo FONTANA created (1632–70) a terraced island garden combining clipped hedges in patterns, low trees, lawns, and grottos.

France. In 16th-century France the large terraces of Renaissance gardens were dominated by parterres, interlaced designs of low, clipped evergreens and flowers or colored earths; and by topiary, bushes trimmed in animal shapes. Unlike Italian gardens, those in France tend to stand apart from the châteaus they adorn. Fine examples survive at CHENONCEAUX and Villandry. Under the influence of Henry IV's garden designer Claude Mollet, who worked at the châteaus of Saint-Germain-en-Laye, Anet, FONTAINEBLEAU, and the TUILERIES, *parterres de broderie,* or "embroidery plantings"—ex-

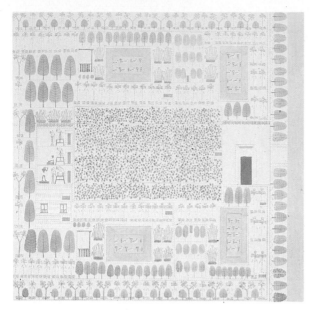

(Left) *The plan (c.1400 BC) of an Egyptian estate at Thebes, one of the earliest known landscape diagrams, depicts a symmetrical arrangement of fruit trees, artificial pools, and pavilions grouped around the axis of the main structure and the entrance gate. Such a plan was probably the product of a long tradition of Egyptian landscape design. (New York Public Library.)*

(Right) *The Court of the Pool in the Generalife, a Moorish palace in Granada, Spain, is bisected by a shallow, fountain-lined canal that extends to exterior gardens.*

tremely complex, curvilinear patterns in dwarf evergreens and low-growing flowers—became popular and were identified with French gardens. Under Louis XIV, French gardeners began to work on a grander scale and in closer relationship with architecture. The foremost landscape architect of this time was André LE NÔTRE. At the Château of VAUX-LE-VICOMTE, Le Nôtre used a gently sloping site to create broad walks, terraces of *parterres de broderie*, and a great basin extending toward vistas perfectly coordinated with the overall design of the château and its grounds. At the Palace of VERSAILLES, he laid out a vast expanse of basins, fountains, parterres, and woodland alleys along a broad central axis whose terminus was the horizon. The whole was bound together by sculpture and symbolic floral planting on the theme of Apollo, god of the Sun, and emblem of the "Sun King," Louis XIV. Le Nôtre also designed the garden of the Château of Chantilly, where vast basins and open lawns patterned with gravel paths contrast with a dense forest laced with walks and dotted with pavilions.

French 18th-century garden design responded to English naturalism with romantic woodland landscapes dotted with grottos and pseudo-antique ruins. Ermenonville, begun by the Marquis de Girardin in 1766, was also inspired by the naturalistic ideas of Jean Jacques ROUSSEAU. The Parc Monceau, built in the northern suburbs of Paris in the 1770s, incorporated

entertainments such as merry-go-rounds and a windmill among replicas of ruined classical temples. Perhaps the most famous garden complex of the period was the *Hameau* built at Versailles in 1782 for Marie Antoinette by Richard Mique (1728–1794) and the painter Hubert ROBERT; a curving pool and woodland surround an informal replica of a rustic farm.

England. English Renaissance gardens were characterized by intricate "knots" (a form of parterre), elaborate topiary, mazes, and areas of clipped lawn. Gardens such as those of HAMPTON COURT retained some of the intimacy of medieval gardens while incorporating Italian and French elements of design. In the late 17th century Charles Bridgeman (d. 1738) and Benjamin Wise (1653–1738) produced closer adaptations of the French formal garden on the grounds of Chatsworth House, Derbyshire, and BLENHEIM PALACE. Within a generation, however, a reaction to formal gardens had occurred. Joseph ADDISON wrote (1710–1712) of the "pleasures of the imagination" derived from broad expanses of natural scenery. In 1719 the poet Alexander POPE built a three-acre "natural" garden behind his house at Twickenham, Surrey, with curving paths and an elevation from which to admire the view. It was reached by a tunnel, the walls of which were embedded with shells and fossils.

In the 1740s the painter and architect William KENT produced a compromise between the formal, restricted garden

The 16th century garden at the Chateau de Villandry, France, partially enclosed in the manner of medieval gardens, embodies the early Renaissance fashion for precisely ordered geometric designs.

Gardens of the Villa Lante (c.1565) at Bagnaia, Italy, designed by Giacomo da Vignola, ascend in a linear sequence of structured terraces to the villa itself.

(Above) *The sunken gardens adjoining London's Kensington Palace, a symmetrical arrangement of flower beds and lawns, contrast with the less formal gardens surrounding the palace grounds.*

(Left) *The "natural" landscape of Blenheim Palace, designed during the late 18th century by Capability Brown, replaced the formal gardens created earlier by Benjamin Wise with carefully planned lakes, meadows, and groves. This informal style had great influence throughout England and the Continent.*

and natural scenery, coordinating vistas of buildings, replicas of classical temples, and trees in the grounds of Stowe (1736), Rousham (1738–41), and Kensington Gardens (c.1744). Many landowners then took up the style. In 1743, Henry Hoare, on his land at Stourhead, Wiltshire, set buildings in wooded surroundings beside a lake, using art to improve nature, but not to replace it. Hoare's landscape garden, like that of Stowe, is a carefully constructed framework of philosophical and literary allusion that the initiated observer may interpret like a symbolic text. In the same year the poet William SHENSTONE took possession of The Leasowes, Shropshire, which he left as a farm, setting out in its grounds a walk that connected pleasing natural vistas, each point of observation being supplied with a rustic seat and an appropriate poetic inscription.

The idea of the natural garden reached complete expression in the work of a professional gardener, Lancelot Brown, called "Capability" BROWN in recognition of his talent for seeing capabilities in even the least attractive situations. Brown's characteristic landscape design, applied throughout a long career that began in 1749, consisted of an irregular belt of trees surrounding the property; a curving walk providing views of the landscape; small clumps of trees irregularly placed about the lawn; and an expanse of water created by the damming of a stream. Brown avoided geometric patterning. Everything, he insisted, should curve in imitation of the beauty of nature.

Brown was immensely successful and prolific, but by the time of his death in 1783, his achievements were questioned. Sir Uvedale PRICE, in his *An Essay on the Picturesque* (1794), asserted that Brown's theory of beauty was inappropriate to landscape gardening and advocated another quality, the "picturesque," which was rough, irregular, and strong in contrasts. Price felt that the gardener, instead of imposing a pattern on nature, should examine each site individually and work with its peculiarities, articulating and extending existing features while leaving the ground covered with rocks and weeds. This theory was partially applied by Humphry REPTON, who set up as a landscape gardener in 1788 and in 1796 went into partnership with the architect John NASH; the two men produced a celebrated series of castles and Italianate villas in picturesque settings, such as Cronkhill, Shropshire (1801).

Price and Repton remained the masters of the natural landscape garden well into the 19th century. Their theories were refined in the publications of John Claudius Loudon (1783–1843) from the 1820s to the 1840s. In the 1880s, William Robinson (1838–1935) created the naturalistic flower garden of undulating perennial borders and woodland plantings of bulbs. His ideas were developed by Gertrude Jekyll (1843–1942) around the turn of the century, often with extraordinary effects of texture and color in very small gardens.

(Left) *Exquisite parterres of clipped shrubbery and flowers in the gardens at Versailles, designed by André Le Nôtre, contribute to the splendor of Louis XIV's palace.* (Below) *The gardens of the Château de Chenonceaux, influenced by the court style, form a brocade of elegant parterres. The central lawns aligned with the structure constituted the original Renaissance garden.*

The United States. In the United States during the mid-19th century, the tradition of formal gardening gave way to natural landscaping in the manner of Repton. This development was primarily due to the influence of Andrew Jackson DOWNING, whose gardens, intended to provide settings for picturesque country houses, consisted of irregularly grouped trees of varying heights, massed flowers, undulating contours, and curving walks and lakes.

The English tradition, as interpreted by Downing, was the inspiration for the great public parks and suburban housing developments laid out by Frederick Law OLMSTED in the second half of the 19th century. Olmsted's greatest work, New York's Central Park, begun in 1857, is a varied yet harmonious landscape of woods, meadows, lakes, and formal precincts dotted with pavilions and monuments: an ideal rural landscape in the center of the city.

The most notable landscape architecture of the 20th century is to be found in California, where the temperate climate allows for the close interrelationship of open, lightly constructed houses and simple, informal gardens arranged around lawns and patios. Many of the most characteristic of these were designed in the 1940s and '50s by Thomas Church.

More recently, Lawrence HALPRIN has devised a dramatic landscaping technique, barely differentiated from nature itself, at the California coastal development Sea Ranch, begun in 1962, and has revived the tradition of the water garden in his complex walk-through fountains in Portland and San Francisco.   ANN VAN ZANTEN

Bibliography: Brown, Jane, *Gardens of a Golden Afternoon* (1982); Chadwick, George F., *The Park and the Town* (1966); Church, Thomas, et al., *Gardens Are for People*, 2d ed. (1983); Coffin, David, ed., *The Italian Garden* (1972); Cowell, F. R., *The Garden as Fine Art* (1978); Eckbo, Garrett, *Urban Landscape Design* (1964); Hunt, John D., and Willis, Peter, ed., *The Genius of Place: The English Landscape Garden, 1620–1820* (1975); Hyams, Edward, *A History of Gardens and Gardening* (1971); Jellicoe, Geoffrey A., *Studies in Landscape Design*, 3 vols. (1960–1970); MacDougall, Elizabeth B., and Hazelhurst, F. H., eds., *The French Formal Garden* (1974); Mack, Maynard, *The Garden and the City* (1969); Newton, Norman T., *Design on Land: The Development of Landscape Architecture* (1971); Pevsner, Nikolaus, ed., *The Picturesque Garden and Its Influence Outside the British Isles* (1974); Tandy, Clifford R., ed., *Landscape and Human Life: The Impact of Landscape Architecture Upon Human Activities* (1966); Tobey, G. B., *A History of Landscape Architecture* (1973).

See also: FOUNTAIN; GARDEN.

landscape painting

Landscape elements played almost no part in Western painting until panoramas of nature began to appear in Roman wall painting of the late 1st century BC. One of two surviving examples from this period, the *Odyssey Landscapes* (Museo Profano, The Vatican), gives a panoramic account of the adven-

Sacral Landscape (AD c.50), a mural in Pompeian Style II, is an early attempt at aerial perspective, with its detailed foreground figures contrasted with sketchy, distant mountains. (Museo Nazionale, Naples.)

tures of Odysseus in eight compartments subdivided by pilasters. In the murals called *View of a Garden* (Villa Livia, Primaporta, Italy), the artist dispensed with the architectural framework to portray a lovely garden. Despite these early efforts, landscape painting did not achieve a prominent place in Western art until the mid-14th century—a circumstance that may reflect the lack of any deep-seated regard for nature in Christian thought.

In the great Eastern civilizations, on the other hand, a religious and mystical devotion to nature accorded landscape a leading role in painting. The era of the T'ang and Sung dynasties in China (c.618–1279) produced superb landscape views, particularly those by the great landscapist FAN K'UAN in the late 10th and early 11th centuries. Landscape was also a primary element in ISLAMIC ART—for example, in *Landscape Mosaic* (715; The Great Mosque, Damascus, Syria), in manuscript illuminations such as *Two Warriors Fighting in a Landscape* (1396; British Museum, London), and in *Summer Landscape*, from the famous *Album of the Conqueror* (15th century; Topkapi Palace Museum, Istanbul).

Traveling amid Mountains and Streams, a landscape scroll by the Chinese artist Fan K'uan, who flourished during the late 10th and early 11th centuries under the Sung dynasty (960–1279), reflects the yin-yang principle of complementary opposites. This religious and philosophic principle is embodied in the landscape paintings of the Far East, where landscape painting, called shan-shui, has held a prominent position in the arts since antiquity. (National Palace Museum, Taipei.)

The influence of Islamic landscapes may have spread to European painting, in which landscape began to assume a more independent aspect from the first half of the 14th century. Ambrogio Lorenzetti's (see LORENZETTI family) *Good and Bad Government* frescoes (1338–40; Palazzo Pubblico, Siena, Italy) and Simone MARTINI's frescoed *Guidoriccio da Fogliano* (1328; Palazzo Pubblico, Siena) contain the first landscape vistas seen in Western art since the Roman era. The LIMBOURG BROTHERS' series of views of life in nature in *Les Très Riches Heures du Duc de Berry* (c.1416; Musée Condé, Chantilly, France) unite landscape with architectural interiors and exteriors and display the first snow landscape in European painting (see BOOK OF HOURS). During the Renaissance, the study of PERSPECTIVE gave rise to further experimentation with landscape as a backdrop for human endeavors—the atmospheric settings of LEONARDO DA VINCI being a prime example. In some of the works by Venetian Renaissance painters, such as Gio-

(Left) *Ambrogio Lorenzetti's* Good and Bad Government *frescoes (1338–40) comprise one of the earliest modern landscapes in Western art.* "Good government in the city," *a detail from this work, is an allegorical evocation of medieval urban Siena. (Palazzo Pubblico, Siena.)*

The Tempest *(c.1503), one of the few paintings unquestionably by the Venetian painter Giorgione, is also his most enigmatic masterpiece. The subject is unknown; X-ray studies have revealed, however, that Giorgione painted out the figure of a woman bathing in the stream at left, substituting the man shown standing there. (Accademia, Venice.)*

The power and beauty of the wilderness, a theme prevalent in German landscapes, was first expressed by Albrecht Altdorfer. Danube Landscape near Regensburg *(c.1520–25) epitomizes the dramatic chiaroscuro and detail characteristic of Altdorfer's work. This romantic approach to nature was continued by German landscapists until c.1900. (Alte Pinakothek, Munich.)*

vanni Bellini's (see BELLINI family) *Saint Francis in Ecstasy* (c.1485; Frick Collection, New York City) and GIORGIONE's *The Tempest* (c.1505; Galleria dell'Accademia, Venice), the masterful pastoral vistas seem to overshadow the human characters.

Nowhere was the impact of Venetian landscapes more pronounced than in northern Europe, where 15th-century Flemish artists had already established a tradition of meticulously detailed landscapes. After he visited (1494–95) Venice, Albrecht DÜRER produced landscape watercolors such as his *Alpine Landscape* (1495; Ashmolean Museum, Oxford, England). Dürer's landscapes, in turn, influenced the Danube valley painter Albrecht ALTDORFER, whose *Danube Landscape near Regensburg* (c.1520–25; Alte Pinakothek, Munich) is often called the first pure landscape painting in Western art. Farther north, Flemish painter Gillis van Coninxloo (1544–1606) was instrumental in transmitting Venetian-type landscape painting to the Low Countries in the late 16th century. During the same period, Coninxloo's compatriot Pieter Bruegel the Elder (see BRUEGEL family) was incorporating detailed views of fields and forests into diagonally organized compositions whose landscape planes unfold into the distance.

The merging of the Venetian and local traditions produced the unrivaled pictorial realism of 17th-century Dutch landscape painting, in which landscape for the first time emerged as one of the most influential forces in art. Jan van GOYEN's naturalistically painted scenes of canals, harbors, riverbanks, and winter recreation, which represent a revolutionary move away from pure detail and toward atmospheric effects and

Hunters in the Snow (1565), by the Flemish artist Peter Bruegel the Elder, represents January in his series of landscapes devoted to the months of the year. The effect of deep space is enhanced by the pronounced diagonal that starts with the dogs and men in the lower left corner, extends down the steep hill with the row of trees, continues across the frozen ponds and through the village, and ends with the towering alpine crags at the upper right. Opposing diagonals define the foreground and carry the eye to the far horizon line. (Kunsthistorisches Museum, Vienna.)

The Jewish Graveyard (c.1660) is one of two versions of the subject by the Dutch landscapist Jacob van Ruisdael. Although this memento mori—a reminder of mortality—is an imaginary landscape, the tombs are exact renderings of those in a Portuguese Sephardic cemetery near Amsterdam; the rainbow symbolizes hope. (Detroit Institute of Arts.)

The subtle radiance and classical theme of Claude Lorrain's The Embarkation of Odysseus (1646) is typical of the idealized landscapes of the 17th century. Lorraine is considered one of the greatest masters of the evocation of atmosphere and light, which concerned him more than a faithful depiction of a mythological subject. (Louvre, Paris.)

spatial breadth, had a great impact on other Dutch landscapists. The influence of Goyen is manifest in the dynamic, imaginative compositions of Jacob van RUISDAEL, whose Jewish Graveyard (one version c.1660; State Picture Gallery, Dresden) is one of the masterpieces of landscape art, and in the works of Meindert HOBBEMA, whose work in England profoundly influenced 18th- and 19th-century English landscape painting.

The evolution in France of an idealized style of landscape painting that contrasted greatly with the naturalistic vein of Dutch art occurred during the 17th century. Supreme masters of the idealized landscape were Claude LORRAIN, who executed serene pastoral scenes such as A Pastoral (c.1650; Yale University Art Gallery, New Haven, Conn.), and Nicolas POUS-

SIN, who set heroic scenes from antiquity in carefully structured landscapes.

Idealized pastoral scenes remained in vogue in the 18th century—in the paintings of Antoine WATTEAU and Thomas GAINSBOROUGH, for example—but toward the end of that century a new school of landscapists emerged in Britain. Inaugurated by Gainsborough and Thomas GIRTIN, who was among the first to do naturalistic landscapes in watercolor, British landscape painting reached its peak in the early-19th-century works of John CONSTABLE and J. M. W. TURNER, who introduced a romantic and dramatic note to views of mountains and seas.

With the possible exception of German artist Caspar David FRIEDRICH, whose mystical and pantheistic landscapes repre-

(Left) Watermill with a Red Roof (c.1670) is by Meindert Hobbema, a pupil of Jacob van Ruisdael and the last of the great Dutch landscapists. The tranquility of this rustic scene, with tiny figures wandering among stately trees and tile-roofed farm buildings, is typical of his considerable oeuvre. (Art Institute of Chicago.)

(Below) The vivid and dynamic landscapes of J. M. W. Turner, exemplified by View of the Dogana and the Church of San Giorgio, Venice (1842), anticipated the brilliant color and diffuse light of the impressionist landscapes of the late 19th century. (Tate Gallery, London.)

(Above) Caspar David Friedrich's Oak Tree in the Snow (c.1810–12) is the epitome of romantic German landscape painting, with its strong evocation of spiritual values. (Wallraf-Richartz Museum, Cologne.)

(Right) Albert Bierstadt, in The Rocky Mountains (1863), by contrast sought primarily to convey the awesome beauty and grandeur of the American West. (Metropolitan Museum of Art, New York City.)

sent an isolated and unique achievement, every important landscapist of the 19th century owed some debt to the British romantics. The American HUDSON RIVER SCHOOL (c.1825–75) was influenced by the British masters. Equally indebted to Turner and Constable were the French landscapists of the BARBIZON SCHOOL (c.1830–70), who advocated a direct study of nature in reaction against the conventions of neoclassical landscape painting as exemplified by Poussin. The French trend toward painting directly from nature, which was greatly advanced by the painterly landscapes of Camille COROT, eventually gave rise to IMPRESSIONISM. Painting *en plein air* (outdoors), impressionist artists such as Claude MONET and Camille PISSARRO sought to capture the ephemeral effects of light on surfaces rather than the solid structures of objects, and thus altered radically the entire course of Western art. In addition to Western influences, the stylized landscapes of JAPANESE ART also contributed to the birth of impressionism.

Landscape was also a principal focus in the POSTIMPRESSIONIST works of Paul CÉZANNE, whose increasingly abstract landscapes influenced much of 20th-century painting. Early in this century, innovative movements such as FAUVISM and CUBISM explored abstracted depictions of landscape, most of which reflect Cézanne's impact. Later, surrealists such as Salvador DALÍ created fantasy landscapes populated with nightmarish figures. At the opposite end of the artistic spectrum, Andrew

The Bridge at Narni *(1826), an early study by Camille Corot painted directly from nature, anticipates such impressionist techniques as a limited palette and a vivid use of light effects. (Louvre, Paris.)*

Paul Cézanne's Landscape with Viaduct: Mont Sainte-Victoire *(c.1885–87) exemplifies the monumental and increasingly abstract forms found in his topographical paintings of the late 19th century. (Metropolitan Museum of Art, New York City.)*

WYETH and other American painters sought to render nature in photographic detail.   BARBARA CAVALIERE

Bibliography: Bouret, Jean, *The Barbizon School* (1973); Clark, Kenneth, *Landscape into Art* (1949; repr. 1961); Hind, Charles L., *Landscape Painting from Giotto to the Present Day*, 2 vols. (1923–1924); Lee, Sherman, *Chinese Landscape Painting* (1962); Novak, Barbara, *American Painting of the Nineteenth Century* (1974); Stechow, Wolfgang, *Dutch Landscape Painting of the Seventeenth Century* (1966); Turner, A. Richard, *The Vision of Landscape in Renaissance Italy* (1966; repr. 1974); Valsecchi, Marco, *Landscape Painting in the Nineteenth Century*, trans. by Arthur Coppotelli (1971).

Landseer, Sir Edwin   [lan'-seer]

The English painter Sir Edwin Henry Landseer, b. Mar. 7, 1802, d. Oct. 1, 1873, was a renowned Victorian artist particularly admired for his animal subjects. The son of John Landseer, a prominent engraver, he drew prodigiously, starting when he was four years old. He won the Society of Arts Silver Isis Medal for drawing in 1814; in 1815, while studying with the artist Benjamin Haydon, Landseer exhibited for the first time at the Royal Academy. In 1816 he entered the Royal Academy School, studying with Henry Fuseli and James Ward. Landseer's *Fighting Dogs Getting Wind* (1818; private collection) was praised by Fuseli and Théodore Géricault. From 1818 until 1840 his success was uninterrupted.

Landseer became an associate of the Royal Academy in 1826 and a fellow in 1831. He was knighted in 1850 and became the favorite artist of Queen Victoria. His popular *Monarch of the Glen* (1851; Dewar House, London) was a triumph at the Great Exhibition of 1851 in London, and in 1855 he received a gold medal at the Paris Exposition Universelle. In 1858, however, he suffered a mental breakdown from which he never fully recovered. His four monumental bronze lions in Trafalgar Square, London, the result of one of his last bursts of creative energy, were put in place in January 1867. Although Landseer's anthropomorphic animal paintings may seem overly sentimental, the faultless technique is clearly evident; his small oil studies and his drawings, among the finest of the 19th century, reveal his superlative draftsmanship.
                                                            ALVIN R. MARTIN

Bibliography: Hill, Ian B., *Landseer* (1973); Lennie, Campbell, *Landseer: The Victorian Paragon* (1976); Mass, Jeremy, *Victorian Painters* (1969).

landslide and avalanche   [av'-uh-lanch]

Landslides and avalanches are massive downward and outward movements of slope-forming materials; these masses may range from the size of cars to entire mountainsides. The term *landslide* is restricted to movement of rock and soil and includes a broad range of velocities, even slow movements that, although rarely a direct hazard to life, can destroy buildings or break buried utility lines. The term *avalanche* includes movement of snow and ice as well as rock and soil materials and applies only to movements rapid enough to threaten life.
Landslides. A landslide occurs when a portion of hillslope becomes too weak to support its own weight. The weakness is generally initiated when rainfall or some other source of water increases the water content of the slope, reducing the shear strength of the materials. Other causes of landslides include earthquakes and loud sounds. Landslides are abundant where erosion (see EROSION AND SEDIMENTATION) is most actively wearing away the terrain, as along some streams and seacoasts, but they also occur well away from areas of active downcutting. Many types of landslides move seasonally or sporadically and may lie dormant for years. Slow-moving landslides are distinguished from creep by having distinct boundaries with adjacent stable ground.

Ground that is stable in its natural state may slide after human alteration. Grading for roads or buildings on hillsides facilitates landsliding, both by cutting into the slope—removing support from materials higher up the slope—and by overloading the slope below with the excavated materials. Many damaging landslides occur where development alters natural slopes or groundwater conditions, especially within dormant landslide masses that are barely stable in their natural state.

Landslides are generally classified into slides, falls, and flows. Slides move as largely coherent bodies by slippage along one or more failure surfaces. Slumps are those slides which move largely by rotation along cylindrical slip surfaces. The resulting backward rotation of the slide mass commonly produces hillside flats in otherwise sloping terrain. Block glides, in contrast, slide along inclined planar slip surfaces. Slumps and block glides move up to 2 m/day (7 ft/day), though commonly much slower, and may involve the movement of enormous volumes of material. Debris slides and rockslides move slowly to rapidly down steep slopes. Falls of rock or soil originate on cliffs or steep slopes. Large rockfalls can be catastrophic events. An earthquake off the coast of Peru in 1970 started a rockfall from the northwest peak of HUASCARÁN. The descending mass, which incorporated material as it accelerated to more than 280 km/h (170 mph), buried more than 18,000 people.

Flows are landslides that behave like fluids. Many varieties are recognized. MUDFLOWS involve wet mud and debris. Earthflows involve wet clayey material. Slow earthflows are tongues of material up to hundreds of meters long that com-

monly move less than several meters a year. They are abundant on clayey hillslopes such as those in the California Coast Ranges. Rapid earthflows, in contrast, occur on very gentle slopes in sensitive silts and clays, as along Rivière Blanche, Quebec. Solifluction is the slow downslope flow of soil that occurs on arctic and alpine hillsides when thawed ice or snow saturates the soil cover. Dry flows occur where great kinetic energy, as from earthquake or fall from steep slopes, permits dry materials to flow unexpectedly long distances very rapidly. A large, rapid flow of dry loess (wind-deposited silt) accompanying an earthquake (1920) in Kansu Province, China, killed 100,000 people. A rockfall avalanche is a form of dry flow in which enormous rockfalls flow rapidly for kilometers across gentle slopes. Rockfall avalanche deposits are also recognized on the Moon.

Avalanches. Snow avalanches are caused by the added weight of fresh snow or by gradual weakening of older snow. They are often triggered by the weight of a skier or the impact of small masses of snow or ice falling from above. Snow avalanches are a major danger in high mountain areas. In the Dolomites of Italy during World War I, 6,000 troops were killed in a single day by snow avalanches.

Two principal types of snow avalanche are distinguished. A loose snow avalanche gathers more and more snow as it descends a mountainside. A slab avalanche consists of more compact, cohesive snow and ice that breaks away from the slope in a discrete mass, much like a block-glide landslide; this type is responsible for the great majority of accidents.

Prevention and Damage Limitation. A number of methods are employed to prevent landslides, such as the capture and drainage of water before it reaches the potential slide area; the pumping of water from wells in the slide area; and the filling in of cracks that could be pervaded by precipitation or surface water. Damage to buildings and other structures is limited through geologic exploration of construction sites and through the design and construction of earthworks.

The avalanche danger of unstable slope accumulations is reduced or prevented through detonation, from either the tossing of grenadelike explosives or the shooting of bazookalike shells into the slope. Structural damage is limited by the construction of various types of fencing and of splitting wedges, V-shaped masonry walls that split an avalanche around a structure located behind the walls.   STEPHEN ELLEN

Bibliography: Fraser, Colin, *The Avalanche Enigma* (1966) and *Avalanches and Snow Safety* (1978); Gilluly, James, et al., *Principles of Geology*, 4th ed. (1975); Sharpe, Charles, *Landslides and Related Phenomena* (1938; repr. 1960); Záruba, Quido, and Mencl, Vojtěch, *Landslides and Their Control* (1969).

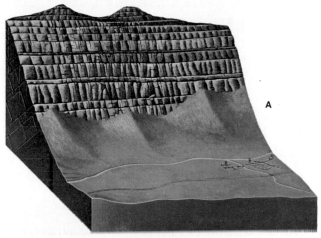

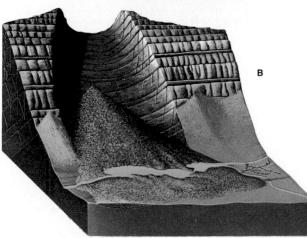

One of the best-known landslides in history occurred in Alberta, Canada, on Apr. 19, 1903. An estimated 31 million m³ (40 million yd³) of limestone rock suddenly slid down between two peaks of Turtle Mountain (A, B). The sliding mass buried part of the town of Frank below, killing 70 persons; it also dammed the river, forming a new lake. Coal excavation shafts had undermined the underlying rock foundation. Joints, or cracks, along the steep 50° sloping face had opened and fragmented the rock. An earthquake that had occurred two years before the fall had further loosened the rock fragments. Within the joints water from melting snows was frozen by a sudden cold spell, forcing the rock apart and starting the slide.

Landsteiner, Karl   [lahnt'-shty-nur]

The Austrian-American physician Karl Landsteiner, b. June 14, 1868, d. June 26, 1943, was a pioneer in the field of blood chemistry. His work led to the discovery of all four major blood groups (A, B, AB, and O), paving the way for the safe use of blood transfusions. He was awarded the 1930 Nobel Prize for physiology or medicine. In 1940 he helped discover the Rh factor in blood.

Lane, Fitz Hugh

The works of the American seascape painter Fitz Hugh Lane, b. Gloucester, Mass., Dec. 18, 1804, d. Aug. 13, 1865, are outstanding in the American movement now called LUMINISM. In his paintings of shore sites near his native Gloucester and on the coast of Maine, Lane sought to convey the purity of the air and the brilliance of the light while also retaining the distinctness and clarity of objects. Lane was crippled from infancy onward and confined to a wheelchair. Therefore, the vistas of his beautifully composed scenes are limited, enhancing the sense of almost magical concentration. An example is *Owl's Head, Penobscot Bay, Maine* (1862; Museum of Fine Arts, Boston).   ABRAHAM DAVIDSON

Bibliography: Wilmerding, John, *Fitz Hugh Lane* (1971) and *Fitz Hugh Lane: American Marine Painter* (1964).

Lane, James Henry

James Henry Lane, b. June 22, 1814, d. July 11, 1866, became known in U.S. history as the "liberator" of Kansas. As a U.S. congressman from Indiana (1853–55), he voted for the KAN-SAS-NEBRASKA ACT. Moving to Kansas, he presided over the Topeka convention (1855) that framed a free-state constitution and commanded the free-state militia in the ensuing guerrilla war against proslavery forces.

When Kansas was finally granted statehood under the free-state Wyandotte constitution, Lane became (1861) one of its U.S. senators. During the Civil War, he led the "Kansas brigade" in western Missouri and raised one of the first black regiments in the Union Army.

Bibliography: Bailes, K. E., *Rider on the Wind: Jimhare and Kansas* (1962); Rawley, James A., *Race and Politics: Bleeding Kansas and the Coming of the Civil War* (1969).

Lanfranc   [lan'-frank]

Appointed archbishop of Canterbury in 1070, Lanfranc of Bec, b. Pavia, c.1005, d. May 24, 1089, was a theologian and church reformer. A student and practitioner of civil law in Pavia, he later went to Tours to study theology under BERENGAR OF TOURS and by 1039 was teaching theology at his own school in Avranches. In 1042 he became a monk at Bec, in Normandy, where he founded a monastic school and became its prior. Lanfranc defended the eucharistic doctrine of the church against Berengar at the councils of Rome and Vercelli in 1050 and at Tours in 1055; he also wrote a treatise on the subject, *Liber de Corpore et Sanguine Domini* (Book on the Body and Blood of the Lord), which became a medieval classic. In 1063, William, duke of Normandy, appointed Lanfranc abbot of St. Stephen in Caen.

After William's conquest of England and assumption of the English crown as WILLIAM I, Lanfranc became archbishop of Canterbury. As archbishop he was particularly noted for his moral reform of the English clergy, for his strengthening of the monasteries, for the establishment of ecclesiastical courts, and for the transfer of sees from the towns to important cities.

DAVID HARRY MILLER

Bibliography: Daly, L. J., *Benedictine Monasticism* (1965); Gibson, Margaret T., *Lanfranc of Bec* (1978); Macdonald, Allan J., *Lanfranc: A Study of His Life, Work and Writing,* 2d ed. (1944).

Lanfranco, Giovanni   [lahn-frahng'-koh, joh-vah'-nee]

Giovanni Lanfranco, b. Jan. 26, 1582, d. Nov. 30, 1647, was one of the first and among the greatest artists to develop the high baroque style of painting. He was trained by Agostino Carracci in Parma. At the age of 20 he joined Annibale Carracci's shop in Rome, but he soon rejected Annibale's classical manner of painting in favor of intense animation, dramatic lighting, and strong colors in his canvases and frescoes. In Rome he developed illusionistic ceiling painting based on CORREGGIO's work in Parma; this may be seen in Lanfranco's earliest dome painting in the Buongiovanni Chapel, San Agostino (c.1616). His masterpiece is the dome of San Andrea della Valle (1625–28). Lanfranco's canvases, such as the *Ecstasy of Saint Margaret of Cortona* (1620; Pitti Palace, Florence), which foreshadow later sculptures by Giovanni Lorenzo BERNINI, are the epitome of high baroque colorism and heightened religious emotion. He executed many frescoes in Naples in his later years but returned to Rome shortly before his death where he painted the *Saint Charles Borromeo Received into Glory* (1646–47) in the apse of San Carlo ai Catinari.

EDWARD J. SULLIVAN

Bibliography: Posner, Donald, "Domenichino and Lanfranco: The Early Development of Baroque Painting in Rome," in *Essays in Honor of Walter Friedlaender* (1965); Salerno, Luigi, "The Early Work of Giovanni Lanfranco," *Burlington Magazine,* July 1952; Vitzthum, Walter, "A Project by Lanfranco for the Quirinal," *Burlington Magazine,* May 1964; Wittkower, Rudolf, *Art and Architecture in Italy, 1600 to 1750,* 3d rev. ed. (1973).

Lang, Andrew

Andrew Lang, b. Mar. 31, 1844, d. July 20, 1912, was a British journalist, translator, and poet, but he was best known as a folklorist and a writer of fairy tales. Born in Selkirk, Scotland, he grew up surrounded by folk legends and ballads. He studied classics and history at the University of Saint Andrews, where he began a scholarly study of folklore. In 1889 he published *The Blue Fairy Book,* an anthology of fairy tales for children. Lang responded to the immediate popularity of his book by producing a new collection of children's stories annually through 1913; among these are *The Yellow Fairy Book, The Red Fairy Book,* and *The Green Fairy Book.* Although he took liberties in "purifying" his sources, his fairy tales have long been regarded as classics of children's literature. Lang was also known for his literary criticism and his *History of English Literature* (1912). He collaborated with other scholars in the translations of Homer's *Odyssey* (1879) and *Iliad* (1883).

R. L. ABRAHAMSON

Bibliography: Green, Roger Lancelyn, *Andrew Lang* (1946; repr. 1973); Langstaff, Eleanor De Selms, *Andrew Lang* (1978).

Lang, Fritz

The German-American director Fritz Lang is considered one of the masters of film artistry and imaginative technique. His silent film classic Metropolis *(1927) envisions the class warfare that breaks out in a highly mechanized and dehumanized society of the year 2000.*

A long and distinguished career in Germany made Fritz Lang, b. Vienna, Dec. 5, 1890, d. Aug. 2, 1976, probably the most famous of the many European film directors who fled Hitler for Hollywood during the 1930s. Lang's early studies of painting and architecture clearly influenced the expressionist style and grand scale of such films as *Destiny* (1921), the two-part *Nibelung Saga* (1924), and his celebrated depiction of a futuristic slave society, *Metropolis* (1927). During the same period Lang was also making smaller-scaled studies of criminal society in *Dr. Mabuse the Gambler* (1922) and *The Spy* (1928), which, with *The Last Will of Dr. Mabuse* (1932), strongly suggested his anti-Nazi sentiments. Lang's interest in the criminal mind produced his masterpiece—the chilling portrait of a child killer, *M* (1931), Lang's first sound film, starring Peter Lorre. Lang left Germany for France in 1933.

Lang made a highly successful American debut with *Fury* (1936), an indictment of mob violence, followed by a plea for social justice in *You Only Live Once* (1937). These films gave way to a succession of melodramas, most notably *The Ministry of Fear* (1944), *The Woman in the Window* (1944), and *Scarlet Street* (1945), that painted a picture of society less in terms of social issues than of a nameless, oppressive sense of dread. These expressionist nightmares, along with *M,* constitute the height of Lang's achievement. Thereafter, although he directed an offbeat Western in *Rancho Notorious* (1952), a first-rate police thriller in *The Big Heat* (1953), and a stylish costume drama in *Moonfleet* (1955), his films were of diminishing interest. A distinctive stylist, Lang was much admired by the French New Wave directors.   WILLIAM S. PECHTER

Bibliography: Eisner, Lotte, *Fritz Lang* (1977; repr. 1986); Humphries, R., *Fritz Lang* (1988); Jenkins, Stephen, *Fritz Lang* (1981); Jensen, Paul M., *The Cinema of Fritz Lang* (1969).

Langdell, Christopher Columbus   [lang'-dul]

Christopher Columbus Langdell, b. New Boston, N.H., May 22, 1826, d. July 6, 1906, was an American legal educator who originated the case-study method for teaching law. As dean of the Harvard Law School from 1870 to 1895, he transformed legal education by introducing required courses and examinations. His students became familiar with legal principles by studying important judicial decisions. His method eventually became standard law-school procedure.

Langdon, John   [lang'-duhn]

John Langdon, b. Portsmouth, N.H., June 5, 1741, d. Sept. 18, 1819, was a political leader in New Hampshire during and after the American Revolution. He represented his state at the Second Continental Congress and helped organize and finance the expeditions of John STARK and the New Hampshire militia against Gen. John BURGOYNE in 1777. A delegate to the Constitutional Convention (1787), Langdon campaigned vigorously in New Hampshire for ratification of the U.S. Constitution. He served in the U.S. Senate (1789–1801) and later as governor of New Hampshire (1805–09, 1810–12).

Bibliography: Upton, R. F., *Revolutionary New Hampshire* (1936; repr. 1970).

Lange, David   [lahng'-ee]

David Lange, b. Aug. 4, 1942, became prime minister of New Zealand in 1984. A criminal lawyer, Lange entered parliament in 1977; in 1983 he became head of the Labour party. In July 1984 his party defeated the National party of Sir Robert MULDOON, and Lange became prime minister. After he forbade port visits from ships that might be nuclear armed, New Zealand was suspended from ANZUS. Lange remained prime minister after the 1987 elections but resigned in 1989.

Lange, Dorothea   [lang]

Dorothea Lange's bleak, realistic portraits of migrant workers, such as Migrant Mother, Nipomo, California *(1936), helped win public support for federal relief programs during the Depression. She collaborated with her husband, Paul Taylor, to produce a study of California's migrant workers in* An American Exodus: A Record of Human Erosion *(1939).*

Dorothea Lange, b. Hoboken, N.J., May 26, 1895, d. Oct. 11, 1965, was a documentary photographer noted for her ability to make the strangers in her photographs seem like familiar acquaintances. Her photographs for the Farm Security Administration, including *Migrant Mother, Nipomo, California* (1936), document the erosion of the land and people of rural America during the Great Depression and are her best-known images. Other significant projects included photo essays for *Life* magazine and a series of studies of justice in California. She often collaborated with her husband, the economist Paul Taylor.   ELIZABETH POLLOCK

Bibliography: Cox, Christopher, *Dorothea Lange* (1987); Meltzer, Milton, *Dorothea Lange: A Photographer's Life* (1978; repr. 1985); Ohrn, K. B., *Dorothea Lange and the Documentary Tradition* (1980).

Langer, Susanne K.   [lang'-ur]

Suzanne Knauth Langer, b. New York City, Dec. 20, 1895, d. July 17, 1985, was an American philosopher primarily known as an aesthetician. She was educated at Radcliffe, where she remained as a tutor from 1927 to 1942. She also taught at Columbia University (1945–50) and Connecticut College (1954–62). A major influence on her thought was the philosophy of Ernst CASSIRER, which she developed into a logic of signs and symbols, initially applied to music and later extended to the whole range of the fine arts. Langer defined art as the creation of apparent forms expressive of human feelings and held that each art creates its own particular kind of appearance. In her study of the mind, she maintained that all mental phenomena are modes of feeling. Among her major works are *Philosophy in a New Key* (1942), *Feeling and Form* (1953), *Problems of Art* (1957), and *Mind: An Essay on Human Feeling* (3 vols., 1967–82).   E. DARNELL RUCKER

Bibliography: Hardison, O. B., Jr., ed., *The Quest for Imagination* (1971); Kaelin, Eugene F., *Art and Existence* (1970).

Langer, William

William Leonard Langer, b. Boston, Mar. 16, 1896, d. Dec. 26, 1977, was an American historian recognized as an authority on diplomatic history. Coolidge professor of history at Harvard (1936–64), he wrote many books on the diplomatic background of the two world wars. His best-known volumes, *The Challenge to Isolation, 1937–1940* (1952) and *The Undeclared War, 1940–1941* (1953), both coauthored with S. Everett Gleason, were critical of American isolationism. Langer worked in the Office of Strategic Services (OSS; 1942–45) and the Central Intelligence Agency (CIA; 1945–46, 1950–52).

Bibliography: Langer, William L., *In and Out of the Ivory Tower: Autobiography* (1977).

Langevin, André   [lahn-zhuh-van']

With a series of novels that deal naturalistically with predestined losers, the French Canadian André Langevin, b. July 11, 1927, has gained a reputation as one of Canada's leading contemporary writers. For his first two novels, *Évadé de la nuit* (Fugitive of the Night, 1951) and *Dust over the City* (1953; Eng. trans., 1955), he won the Prix du Cercle du Livre de France. Later novels include *Le Temps des Hommes* (The Time of Men, 1956), *L'Élan d'Amérique* (The American Moose, 1972), and *Orphan Street* (1974; Eng. trans., 1976).

Langgaard, Rued

Rued Immanuel Langgaard, b. July 28, 1893, d. July 10, 1952, a Danish composer and keyboard performer, made his debut as an organist in 1905 and as a composer in 1908. Rooted in late romanticism, his works advanced remarkably over the next two decades into the fields of polytonality and atonality but held to the late romantic ideal of intense self-expression in art. These traits and his own character brought Langgaard into conflict with the forces then dominant in Danish music. As a result he retreated to a less tonally venturesome style, but his music still exhibited a sometimes bizarrely idiosyncratic composing technique. His works include 16 symphonies, an opera, and many chamber and vocal compositions, often designed for liturgical use.

Langhans, Carl Gotthard   [lahng'-hahns, gawt'-hart]

Carl Gotthard Langhans, b. Dec. 15, 1732, d. Oct. 1, 1808, was a major force in the transition from the baroque style to neoclassicism in German architecture. His early Schloss Trachenberg (1762–65) maintained baroque articulation, but the Hatzfeld Palace (begun 1765), with its references to 17th-century Roman palazzi, was a harbinger of neoclassicism. Although

Langhans's designs evoke ancient times, they are tempered by contemporary styles; an example is the influential BRANDEN-BURG GATE (1789–94).   ROBERT F. CHIRICO

Bibliography: Hempel, Eberhard, *Baroque Art and Architecture in Central Europe,* trans. by Elisabeth Hempel and Marguerite Kay (1965).

Langlade, Charles Michel de   [lahng-lahd', sharl mee-shel' duh]

Charles Michel de Langlade, b. May 1729, d. *c*.1801, a pioneer of mixed French and Indian descent in what is now Wisconsin, led an Indian detachment that took part in the defeat of British General Edward BRADDOCK near Fort Duquesne in 1755 during the FRENCH AND INDIAN WARS. He continued to lead Indian auxiliaries in aid of the French until 1761, when he surrendered the fort at Mackinac to the British and became a British subject. In 1763 he warned the British of PONTIAC'S REBELLION. During the American Revolution he fought George Rogers CLARK in the West.

Langland, William   [lang'-luhnd]

The 14th-century alliterative poet William Langland, b. *c*.1330, d. *c*.1400, author of the masterpiece PIERS PLOWMAN, is numbered with Geoffrey Chaucer and the anonymous author of *Sir Gawain and the Green Knight* as one of the three Middle English writers of sustained genius. Langland probably came from the West Midlands, perhaps Ledbury in Shropshire. Two shorter poems, *Piers the Plowman's Creed* (*c*.1394) and *Richard Redeless* (*c*.1399), once attributed to Langland, are now thought to be the work of others.   DAVID YERKES

Bibliography: Ryan, William M., *William Langland* (1968); Schmidt, A. V., *The Clerkly Maker* (1987).

Langley, Samuel Pierpont   [lang'-lee, peer'-pahnt]

The American astronomer Samuel Pierpont Langley, b. Boston, Aug. 22, 1834, d. Feb. 27, 1906, is most noted for his work on AERODYNAMICS and solar radiation. With only a high school education, he became professor of astronomy at the Western University of Pennsylvania (1867) and director of Allegheny Observatory in Pittsburgh. He served as secretary of the SMITHSONIAN INSTITUTION from 1887 and founded the SMITHSONIAN ASTROPHYSICAL OBSERVATORY in 1890. Langley's many attempts to build a full-size workable aircraft were all unsuccessful. He did, however, invent the heat-measuring BOLOMETER, and he used it to advance knowledge of infrared solar radiation.
                                                          STEVEN J. DICK

Bibliography: Vaeth, J. Gordon, *Langley* (1966).

Langmuir, Irving   [lang'-myoor]

Irving Langmuir, an American physical chemist, was awarded the Nobel Prize for chemistry in 1932 for his work on molecular films on solid and liquid surfaces. His studies in high-temperature chemistry led to the improvement of the tungsten-filament light bulb and the development of an atomic hydrogen blowtorch.

The American chemist Irving Langmuir, b. Brooklyn, Jan. 31, 1881, d. Aug. 16, 1957, excelled in both theoretical contributions and their practical applications in many fields of science. He conducted (1909–50) his research at the General Electric Company in Schenectady, N.Y. Langmuir's studies of chemical reactions at high temperature and low pressure led to the gas-filled tungsten lamp. Other research by Langmuir shed light on the properties of atomic hydrogen and resulted in the manufacture of the atomic hydrogen torch used for welding. In atomic structure he contributed to the modern theory of electronic bonding. His work on thermionic emission resulted in the construction of many electron tubes. For his pioneer work in the fields of catalysis and adsorption Langmuir was awarded the 1932 Nobel Prize for chemistry.

Bibliography: Jaffe, Bernard, *Irving Langmuir* (1948); Rosenfeld, Albert, *The Quintessence of Irving Langmuir* (1966); Wasson, Tyler, ed., *Nobel Prize Winners* (1987).

Langton, Stephen   [lang'-tuhn]

A major statesman of the English church, Stephen Langton, b. *c*.1155, d. July 9, 1228, was instrumental in securing King JOHN's concession of the MAGNA CARTA in 1215. He was created (1206) a cardinal by Pope INNOCENT III and appointed (1207) archbishop of Canterbury. King John, however, did not recognize the appointment, and England was placed under interdict until 1213, when the king was reconciled with the papacy. Stephen took his seat at Canterbury and from then on was active in English politics. His support of the barons against the king in securing the Magna Carta led to his suspension as archbishop, but he was restored to office in 1218. He was a prolific writer and the probable composer of the hymn *Veni sancte spiritus*.   DAVID HARRY MILLER

Bibliography: Lawrence, Clifford, ed., *The English Church and the Papacy in the Middle Ages* (1965; repr. 1984); Painter, Sidney, *The Reign of King John* (1949; repr. 1979); Powicke, F. M., *Stephen Langton* (1928; repr. 1965); Roberts, Phyllis B., *Studies in the Sermons of Stephen Langton* (1968).

Langtry, Lillie   [lang'-tree]

Emilie Charlotte Le Breton Langtry, b. Oct. 13, 1853, d. Feb. 12, 1929, better known as Lillie—or the Jersey Lily, a name bestowed by the painter John Millais because of her Channel Island origins—was the first of several women flaunted by the Prince of Wales, later Edward VII, as his mistress. She made her acting debut in 1881 and gained popular success through her beauty, style, and aura of scandal. Oscar Wilde wrote *Lady Windermere's Fan* (1892) for Langtry; her memoirs, *The Days I Knew*, appeared in 1925.

Bibliography: Aronson, Theo, *The King in Love* (1988); Brough, James, *The Prince and the Lily* (1975).

language and literature

Because all literature is created with words, the medium of literature is language. Not all combinations of words, however, result in literature. Literary combinations are differentiated from the enormous mass of casual discourse by some filtering device or set of rules. These words then pass into the permanent stock of preserved sounds or texts, forming the literary tradition of the group that produced them. One must therefore question what makes one group of words literature and another group not literature, and what the precise connection between language and literature is. This article addresses these questions. Further information may be found in AESTHETICS; CRITICISM, LITERARY; FIGURES OF SPEECH; LINGUISTICS; PHONETICS; PHONOLOGY AND MORPHOLOGY; PSYCHOLINGUISTICS; SEMANTICS; SEMIOTICS; STRUCTURALISM; SYNTAX; and VERSIFICATION.

Some linguists regard literary artifacts simply as preserved utterances, distinguished by the very fact of their preservation. The great mass of casual speech vanishes into air and out of memory just a few seconds after being uttered. Psycholinguists have demonstrated, for example, that, whereas most people can relate the gist of statements made a few minutes earlier, few can repeat the exact words they heard. By contrast, noncasual speech must be repeated word for word in order to achieve the total effect. The medium—the words chosen and their particular order—is part of the message. As the French poet Paul VALÉRY has indicated, ordinary discourse vanishes or dissolves as soon as it has done its work—as soon as it has communicated an idea and brought understanding—but literature is preserved and interpreted again and again, as if its usefulness can never be exhausted.

Even strictly defined, however, *literature* includes an astonishing variety of material. Besides poetry, plays, and novels, literature includes folk tales and songs, religious rituals, sermons, diaries, journals, political documents, essays, philosophical treatises, chronicles, and speeches in courts and legislatures. What all these kinds of discourse have in common is a formal setting: anything written or uttered in a situation recognized as artistic thereby acquires the status of art and loses its status as a casual, or transitory, expression. A printed passage entitled "Sonnet XI" cannot, by the rules of Western culture, be taken as a casual utterance. Artistic displacement—a fire hydrant removed to a museum, for example—assigns special status to the object displaced. The very fact of displacement suggests to the onlooker that someone became convinced enough of the value of the object in question to take it out of its casual setting. Hence any utterance, even a telephone book, if read or presented as literature on a literary occasion and surrounded by literary trappings, loses its utilitarian aspect and is interpreted for itself alone.

Another approach to defining *literature* starts with the assumption that preserved utterances have a special type of language or language organization that is not present, or at least not so prominent, in casual utterances. The elevated diction used in English and French poetry of the 17th and 18th centuries is an obvious example of literary language. Less elaborate means exist, however, to differentiate special linguistic devices from those found in ordinary discourse.

Roman JAKOBSON has distinguished three processes at work in the creation of language of any sort: selection, equivalence, and combination. Most expressions are produced semiautomatically, by unconscious mechanisms. This proposition can be illustrated by the following example: a person sees a 4-ft-high object made of wood slats hooped with steel, from the interior of which issues a sound like "Rowf! Rowf!"; further, the person looks inside the object and sees a small, four-legged creature with a tail, from which the sound seems to be coming. If the person decides to comment on the situation, then first, either semiconsciously or unconsciously, he or she selects certain words equivalent to the situation—*barrel, barking, dog*—and also a few functional or relational words—*in, a, the, and*. Second, almost always unconsciously, the person combines the words into a complete linguistic account of the experience. The words selected are strongly determined by the situation, but the ways of combining them are not. Here the speaker can choose, again unconsciously, among several possibilities, with the final choice based perhaps on personal style. For example, the speaker might choose from such expressions as *There's a dog in the barrel and he's barking; A barking dog is in the barrel over there; I think that a dog is barking in that barrel;* and *There's a barrel with a dog in it over there.*

Sometimes, however, the speaker selects the combination of words with as much care as he or she gave to selecting the words themselves. He might follow a rule such as "No odd syllable is to bear a strong stress." Then the only allowable sequence to describe the situation would be something like *a DOG is in the BARrel and he's BARKing*, with stress on the second, sixth, and tenth syllables. A more elaborate rule or set of rules would provide this alliterating sentence: *a Bloodhound's in the Barrel, and he's Barking and he's Baying.* A speaker looking for onomatopoeia—in this instance, the replication of the actual sound of the barking in the sounds of the utterance—might choose words with fricatives (consonants pronounced by forcing the breath through the teeth) and declare *a SCHnauZer'S in the HoGSHead; He SHoutS, He raGeS.*

In each of the foregoing examples the sound pattern of the utterance is distinctive and stands out as something worth preserving. The sentences cannot vanish or dissolve as soon as their meaning has been communicated—to repeat only the gist would be to miss the point. In their own humble ways, the sentences are literature.　EDMUND L. EPSTEIN

Bibliography: Bailey, Richard, and Burton, Dolores, *English Stylistics: A Bibliography* (1968); Chatman, Seymour, and Levin, Samuel, eds., *Essays on the Language of Literature* (1967); Culler, Jonathan, *Structuralist Poetics: Structuralism, Linguistics, and the Study of Literature* (1975); Cunningham, J. V., ed., *The Problem of Style* (1966); Epstein, Edmund, *Language and Style* (1978); Fowler, Roger, ed., *Style and Structure in Literature: Essays in the New Stylistics* (1975); Freeman, Donald, ed., *Linguistics and Literary Style* (1970); Hough, Graham, *Style and Stylistics* (1969); Milic, Louis, ed., *Stylistics: A Preliminary Bibliography* (1965); Sebeok, Thomas, ed., *Style in Language* (1960).

languages, artificial

Artificial languages are languages that have been deliberately invented, unlike typical world languages that have developed naturally and, for the most part, without conscious planning. The planning that has gone into many natural languages, especially into standard forms taught in schools, has merely involved controlling or modifying natural languages already in use. Artificial languages, on the other hand, introduce novel systems of symbols. They are used in such diverse fields as mathematics, formal logic, and computer science. These artificial languages are not to be compared with natural languages; they are designed to handle specific and special categories of subject matter and cannot serve to describe the whole range of human experience.

Less limited artificial languages have been proposed to create a more logical vehicle of thought than can be found in any natural language and to overcome the barriers to communication resulting from the multiplicity of languages spoken in the world today. The second goal has probably received more widespread attention.

The idea of artificially creating a more logical language goes back to such thinkers as the 17th-century philosopher René DESCARTES. Since his time hundreds of forms have been suggested. An interesting example was the language *Solresol*, developed by Jean François Sudre in 1817. All its words were formed of combinations of the syllables designating the notes of the musical scale. Two recent attempts are *Loglan*, invented by James Cooke Brown for use in exploring the relationship between language and thought, and Hans Freudenthal's *Lincos*, or *Lingua Cosmica*, intended as a program for establishing communication with extraterrestrial intelligent beings should they be located.

Although some natural languages have been widely used around the world at various times as a common means of communication among speakers of various languages, it is uncertain that any one language will ever be adopted universally. English and French, the most widespread international languages today, are difficult to learn and are too closely identified with particular national groups. C. K. Ogden's *Basic English*, which he proposed in 1932, is an attempt to remedy the first impediment by reducing the vocabulary to a core of 850 words. For example, *enter* is replaced by *go into*, and *precede* by *go in front of*. It remains distinctly English, however, and so cannot meet the second objection.

The first major movement for an international artificial language, called *Volapük*, was initiated by Johann Martin Schleyer in 1880. The vocabulary of Volapük is based on English, but the words are so distorted in form that it neither looks nor sounds like English. This was deliberately done in order to give it more neutral appearance. Volapük rapidly lost favor in competition with ESPERANTO, which was first presented by Ludwik Lazar Zamenhof in 1887. Esperanto has a highly regular system of word information, with roots drawn from French, English, German, and other Indo-European languages. It is the most widely used artificial language today.

Of the various rival systems that have been proposed for international adoption in the 20th century, the most successful has been Alexander Gode's *Interlingua*, the culmination of a collaborative effort inspired in part by the Latin-based "interlingua" originally proposed in 1903 by the Italian mathematician Giuseppe Peano. Interlingua is based largely on the international vocabulary of science and technology and can be read with little difficulty by those familiar with English or a Romance language. It has been widely employed at medical conferences and in scientific journals.

FRANKLIN E. HOROWITZ

Bibliography: Brown, James Cooke, *Loglan 1: A Logical Language,* 3d ed. (1975); Connor, George Alan, et al., *Esperanto: The World Interlanguage,* 2d rev. ed. (1966); Freudenthal, Hans, *Lincos: Design of a Language for Cosmic Intercourse* (1960); Gode, Alexander, and Blair, Hugh, *Interlingua: A Grammar of the International Language,* 2d ed. (1971); Ogden, Charles Kay, *Basic English: International Second Language* (1968), rev. version of *The System of Basic English*; Pei, Mario, *One Language for the World* (1958).

languages, extinct

Extinct languages are not limited to ancient times. Dalmatian, a Romance language, died out in 1898 when Anthony Udina, the last known native speaker, was killed in a mine explosion; Cornish became extinct when Dolly Pentreath died in Mousehole, England, in 1777. An extinct language, however, is not necessarily a forgotten one. Many Dalmatian and Cornish texts survive, for example, and several languages of the ancient world are preserved on clay tablets or papyrus.

Sumerian. The oldest written language of Mesopotamia, Sumerian, has no known relatives. Its CUNEIFORM writing system evolved from a pictographic stage that began about 3100 BC. Sumerian was largely replaced by Akkadian after 2000 BC, but it survived for another two millennia as a religious language among the Babylonians and Assyrians—in much the way that Latin survived in medieval Europe.

Elamite. First written in pictographs (2500 BC) and later in cuneiform (1600–400 BC), Elamite was spoken in the eastern part of Mesopotamia and in southwest Iran. Some evidence suggests that the language descended ultimately from Akkadian.

Hattic. A language of central Anatolia, Hattic, often called Hattian, Khattish, or proto-Hittite, is preserved largely in Hittite records, where both Hattic words and whole Hattic sentences are found. It became extinct about 1400 BC and has no affinities with any known language.

Hurrian. A language of southeast Anatolia that was still alive at the beginning of the 1st millennium BC, Hurrian is preserved both in its own inscriptions and in Hittite texts. Hurrian is related to Urartian.

Urartian. Urartian, sometimes called Vannic or Chaldean, was spoken in eastern Anatolia around Lake Van, and in what is now Soviet Armenia, in the environs of Yerevan. Additional inscriptions have been found in Persian Azerbaijan, and Urartian is also known from an important Urartian/Assyrian bilingual text. Written records date from 900–600 BC, after which time the Urartians suddenly disappeared, to be replaced almost immediately, in the same area of eastern Anatolia, by the Armenians. Urartian is closely related to Hurrian, though not derived from it.

Phrygian. Phrygian, a language of west central Anatolia, had two literary periods, Old Phrygian (730–430 BC) and New Phrygian (AD 100–350). The later stage used a Greek-like script; the earlier had an eclectic alphabet based on Northwest Semitic models. Though of INDO-EUROPEAN origin, Phrygian is poorly understood, especially in the writing of the earlier period. It seems to be more closely related to Greek than to any other Indo-European language, but it also shows certain affinities with Armenian. An older theory, no longer tenable, related Phrygian to Thracian, and posited a Thraco-Phrygian language family.

Thracian. Thracian was spoken along the west coast of the Black Sea, south of the Danube, in what is now Bulgaria, and in parts of Greece and Turkey. Although no significant inscriptions exist, numerous words are known from Greek and Roman texts. In addition, a large number of personal and place names have been recorded. Thracian is of Indo-European origin, but its affinities to any language other than Dacian and perhaps Phrygian are vague.

Dacian. Also referred to as Getic, Dacian was spoken in what is now Romania—on the west coast of the Black Sea, north of the Danube. Like Thracian, it is known both from words mentioned in Greek and Latin texts, and also from proper names.

It has recently been shown that Dacian became distinct from Thracian, but the differentiation took place probably only after 1500 BC. Some scholars believe that a Dacian layer underlies Albanian, and that perhaps Dacian, rather than Illyrian, was the original form of that language.

Illyrian. Illyrian was spoken north and west of Greece during the Greco-Roman period. Scholars are unsure whether the term refers to just one language or to many. Most of the evidence for Illyrian comes from proper names; the core of the material is now called Messapic. Traditionally, Illyrian has been considered an ancient form of Albanian, but this view is losing favor.

Etruscan. The Etruscans controlled large sections of the Italian peninsula, particularly in the northwest, from the 8th through the 4th century BC, before the rise and eventual domination of the Romans. Nearly 10,000 brief and often repetitious inscriptions, as well as a few longer examples, survive from their language. Etruscan was written in a Greek-like script, but the language itself does not have any relatives. Thus the etymological method, so helpful in translating Indo-European languages, is of no use in deciphering Etruscan. A few terms like *puia*, "wife," and *clan*, "son," are known, however, as are the numbers from one to six—*thu, zal, ci, śa, mach, huth*. The recovery of more Etruscan represents a great challenge to modern linguists.

THE HITTITE-LUWIAN GROUP

The six Anatolian languages that make up the Hittite-Luwian group show archaic Indo-European features. The languages are known from texts as early as 1800 BC, and as recent as 200 BC. Hittite, Palaic, and Lydian form one subgroup; Cuneiform Luwian, Hieroglyphic Luwian, and Lycian form a second. Three other languages of southern Anatolia—Carian, Pisidian, and Sidetic—have been proposed as additions to the Hittite-Luwian group, but the evidence remains scanty.

Hittite. The most important language of the Hittite-Luwian group is Hittite. It was translated early in this century by the Czech scholar Bedřich Hrozný, who showed, to the surprise of most linguists, that the language was Indo-European, although it maintained certain features that had been lost in all the other Indo-European languages. Hittite used a form of Akkadian cuneiform writing, the knowledge of which was most helpful to Hrozný in translating. The written language contains numerous loan words from Luwian, Hattic, and Hurrian and also seems to use, in a random fashion, vocabulary from both Sumerian and Akkadian.

Palaic. Related to Hittite, but very poorly substantiated, Palaic has survived in fewer than 200 words, all known through a cuneiform writing system.

Lydian. Lydian was spoken on the west coast of Anatolia and was written in the Greek script from 500 to 300 BC. An Aramaic/Lydian bilingual text has proved of great value in establishing an understanding of language. In addition to inscriptions in Lydian, about 50 other words are found in the writings of various Greek authors.

Cuneiform Luwian. The most thoroughly understood language of the Luwian subgroup, Cuneiform Luwian is known from 1400 BC in south central Anatolia. It is called "cuneiform" after the type of writing system in which it is preserved, and to distinguish it from its very close relative, Hieroglyphic Luwian. It differs from Hittite both in vocabulary and in its phonological system.

Hieroglyphic Luwian. Often called Hieroglyphic Hittite, Hieroglyphic Luwian is not yet well understood, and its pictographic script has not been wholly deciphered. The language is clearly related to Cuneiform Luwian, but it probably represents a later stage of development. A major breakthrough in decipherment came with the discovery of the Karatepe bilingual inscriptions, which provide a parallel Phoenician translation of a Hieroglyphic Luwian text. The language is recorded from 1200 to 700 BC in what is now northern Syria and south central Turkey. Scholars have suggested that some of the vocabulary of Hieroglyphic Luwian is preserved as loan words in classical Armenian.

Lycian. Spoken in the southwest corner of Anatolia, Lycian is recorded from 500 to 200 BC in about 150 short inscriptions written with a West Greek alphabet.   JOHN A. C. GREPPIN

Bibliography: Friedrich, Johannes, *Extinct Languages*, trans. by Frank Gaynor (1957); Katičić, Radoslav, *Ancient Languages of the Balkans* (1976); Lehmann, Winifred P., *Historical Linguistics: An Introduction*, 2d ed. (1973); Pedersen, Holger, *Linguistic Science in the Nineteenth Century* (1931); Pope, Maurice, *The Story of Decipherment* (1975).

Languedoc   [lahng-dohk']

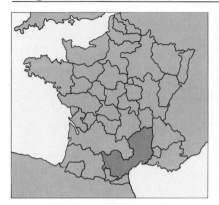

Languedoc, a historic region bordering the Gulf of Lions in southern France, was occupied during ancient times by a succession of invading peoples because of its strategic location separating Italy from the Iberian Peninsula. Languedoc was administered as a province until 1791, when it was subdivided into departments.

Languedoc is a historic province in southern France, bordering the Mediterranean Sea on the south and the Rhône River in the east. MONTPELLIER and TOULOUSE have long been the leading cities. The southern portion of the region, Bas (Lower) Languedoc, is composed of a low limestone plain, where almost half of all French wine is produced. In the north, in the Cévennes Mountains, sheep raising is the principal activity.

In 121 BC the area was incorporated into the Roman province of Gallia Narbonensis. By 924 it came under the control of the powerful counts of Toulouse. Under them, Languedoc developed a rich culture based on its distinctive language. The region's name is derived from this dialect of French, the language (*langue*) in which "yes" is rendered by *oc;* the language of northern France, where *oui* (formerly *oil*) is used for "yes," is called *langue d'oil*. The troubadour poetry of Langue d'oc flowered from the 10th to 12th century (see PROVENÇAL LITERATURE). During the same period, the ALBIGENSES, a religious sect, enjoyed a wide following in the area. In 1209, however, Pope INNOCENT III declared a crusade against the sect, and Languedoc was subsequently invaded by northern French troops. By the mid-13th century, Languedoc had been annexed by the French crown. During the French Revolution, Languedoc was divided into the departments of Ardèche, Gard, Hérault, Aude, and parts of Haute-Garonne, Lozère, Tarn-et-Garonne, Ariège, and Haute Loire.

TIMOTHY J. RICKARD

Bibliography: Le Roy Ladurie, Emmanuel, *The Peasants of Languedoc*, trans. by John Day (1977).

langur   [luhng-goor']

The langurs, *Presbytis*, also called leaf-eating or leaf monkeys, are a group of 14 species of long-tailed, tree-dwelling monkeys of southern Asia. Their habitats range from sea-level, dry-zone forests, through tropical rain forests, to snow-covered trees at altitudes of 4,000 m (13,000 ft). Langurs are 43 to 79 cm (17 to 31 in) long, have a tail 49.5 to 109 cm (19.5 to 43 in) long, and weigh from 3 to 21 kg (6.5 to 46 lb). The fur is rather long and often forms a crest or cap on the head and a prominent ridge above the eyes. Coloration is generally brownish, grayish, or blackish, with lighter underparts. Langurs subsist largely on a diet of leaves. They live in troops of 3 to 120 individuals. Four other species in the same family,

The hanuman langur, P. entellus, is considered in India a symbol of self-sacrifice. Folktales tell how this langur got its black face and hands by being scorched in a fire while helping a friend.

Cercopithecidae, are also called langurs: the douc langur, *Pygathrix nemaeus*, of Indochina; the snub-nosed langurs, *Rhinopitecus roxellanae* of western China and *R. avunculus* of North Vietnam; and the Mentawi Islands langur, *Simias concolor*, from islands off the west coast of Sumatra.

Lanier, Sidney   [luh-neer']

The American poet, novelist, critic, and musician Sidney Lanier, b. Feb. 3, 1842, d. Sept. 7, 1881, fought in the Confederate army and was captured (1864) and imprisoned. Sick and poor when released a year later, he published the novel *Tiger-Lilies* (1867) about his war experiences. In 1873 he became first flutist in the Peabody Orchestra in Baltimore. He augmented his income by delivering lectures—published posthumously in 1902 as *Shakspere and His Forerunners*—and these led (1879) to a teaching position at Johns Hopkins University. In 1880 he published *The Science of English Verse.* Many of his better poems, such as "Song of the Chattahoochee" (1877) and "The Marshes of Glynn" (1878), are set in his beloved South. A ten-volume centennial edition of Lanier's works appeared in 1945.   JAMES HART

Bibliography: DeBellis, Jack, *Sidney Lanier* (1972); Mims, Edwin, *Sidney Lanier* (1905; repr. 1968); Parks, Edd Winfield, *Sidney Lanier* (1968).

lanolin   [lan'-oh-lin]

A soft pale yellow wax, lanolin is a purified form of wool "grease," a by-product of the preparation of raw wool for spinning. Chemically, it is a mixture of cholesterol esters. Its resistance to rancidity, together with its emulsifying properties, slightly antiseptic effect, and capability of forming a stable emulsion with water, permit it to be widely used as a base for ointments, emollients, salves, cosmetics, soaps, and shampoos. Lanolin is extracted by washing raw wool in water or a soap solution and then separating wax from water in a centrifuge. The crude wool wax is purified, bleached, and mixed with water to form an emulsion. Lanolin can be mixed with almost twice its weight in water.

Lansdowne, Henry Charles Keith Petty-Fitzmaurice, 5th Marquess of   [lanz'-down, mar'-kwes]

Lord Lansdowne, b. Jan. 14, 1845, d. June 3, 1927, was a British statesman whose long career included service as governor general of Canada (1883-88), viceroy of India (1888-93), secretary of state for war (1895-1900), and foreign secretary (1900-05). While he was in Canada, the rebellion of Louis RIEL was suppressed (1885), the Canadian Pacific Railway was completed (1886), and negotiations were begun to settle the Newfoundland fisheries dispute with the United States.

Originally a Liberal, Lansdowne broke (1886) with that party over Irish Home Rule and aligned himself with the Conservatives. As foreign secretary in the Conservative government, he concluded an Anglo-Japanese alliance (1902) and the Entente Cordiale with France (1904; see TRIPLE ENTENTE). During World War I he served (1915–16) in the coalition government and in 1917 raised a storm of protest by publishing a letter calling for a negotiated peace.

Bibliography: Monger, George, *The End of Isolation: British Foreign Policy 1900–1907* (1963); Newton, Lord, *Lord Lansdowne: A Biography* (1929).

Lansing

Lansing, the capital of Michigan, is located at the junction of the Grand, Red Cedar, and Sycamore rivers in the southern part of the state. Lansing has a population of 130,414 (1980). In addition to being the seat of state government, the city is a major automobile production center and the commercial focus of a large agricultural area. Michigan State University (1857), the first agricultural college in the United States, is in East Lansing, which adjoins the city. The late-Renaissance-style capitol building, completed in 1878, stands in the center of the city.

Originally named Michigan, the city was settled in 1837 by settlers from New York State; it was renamed for Lansing, N.Y., when it was chosen state capital in 1847. Industrial growth was spurred by the arrival of the railroads in 1871. Ransom E. Olds began the automobile industry there in 1899; by 1904, Lansing was a leader in automobile production.

Lansing, Robert

Robert Lansing, b. Watertown, N.Y., Oct. 17, 1864, d. Oct. 30, 1928, was U.S. secretary of state (1915–20) under President Woodrow WILSON. Admitted to the bar in 1889, he married the daughter of John W. Foster, secretary of state in 1892–93. In 1892 he was asked to assist in the arbitration of the BERING SEA CONTROVERSY over fur seals, and thereafter he represented the United States in more international arbitrations than any other American lawyer of his time. In 1906 he helped found the American Society of International Law.

Appointed counselor of the Department of State in 1914, Lansing became secretary after the resignation of William Jennings Bryan during the crisis over the German sinking of the LUSITANIA. Lansing thereafter proved more anti-German than President Woodrow Wilson and welcomed the U.S. entry into World War I in 1917. He negotiated the Lansing-Ishii agreement (Nov. 2, 1917) with Japan, whereby the United States recognized Japan's special interests in China.

At the PARIS PEACE CONFERENCE, Lansing found himself largely ignored by Wilson. He protested strongly when the presi-

The American lawyer and statesman Robert Lansing gained international recognition as secretary of state (1915–20) under President Woodrow Wilson. Conflicts arising from Lansing's misgivings about many of the provisions of the Paris Peace Conference, including the establishment of the League of Nations, led to his resignation from office.

dent gave in to Japan's demands for extended rights in China. After the conference a disgruntled member of the U.S. delegation, William C. Bullitt, revealed to the Senate Foreign Relations Committee that Lansing considered the Treaty of Versailles too harsh on Germany, and that the secretary was not enthusiastic about the League of Nations. Several months later Wilson forced Lansing's resignation.   ROBERT H. FERRELL

Bibliography: Beers, B., *Vain Endeavor: Robert Lansing's Attempts to End American-Japanese Rivalry* (1962); Bemis, Samuel Flagg, *The American Secretaries of State and Their Diplomacy*, vol. 10 (1929); Smith, D. M., *Robert Lansing and American Neutrality, 1914–1917* (1958).

lantana   [lan-tan'-ah]

Lantana is a genus of mostly tropical, often aromatic, evergreen shrubs and herbs of the vervain family, Verbenaceae. The best known species—*L. camara*—is a hairy shrub, seldom more than 1.8 m (6 ft) high, with a prickly stem and dense, flat-topped clusters of flowers that open pink or yellow and change to red or orange. Cultivated varieties are sometimes used for hedges and bedding in warmer areas, but in Hawaii lantana has become a serious pest weed.

lantern fish

The lantern fish Myctophum punctatum, *found in the Mediterranean Sea and Atlantic Ocean, has light organs* (yellow) *on the lower body.*

Lantern fishes, family Myctophidae, are about 200 species of small, abundant oceanic fishes with strings of pearllike photophores, or light organs, along their sides (see BIOLUMINESCENCE). They average less than 15 cm (6 in) long and inhabit the mid-depths of the ocean, down to almost 1 km (0.6 mi), making upward feeding migrations each night.   C. P. IDYLL

lanthanide series   [lan'-thuh-nide]

The lanthanide series is the group of chemical elements that follow lanthanum in group IIIB in the periodic table. Their distinguishing feature is that they fill the 4f electronic subshell. Although only the elements cerium (atomic number 58) through lutetium (71) are lanthanide elements in principle, most chemists include yttrium (39) and lanthanum (57) in this group because they have similar physical and chemical properties. They are also called the rare earths, because they were originally discovered together in rare minerals and isolated as oxides, or "earths." In comparison with many other elements, however, they are not really rare, except for promethium (61), which has only radioactive isotopes with short half-lives. Lanthanide elements are found in many minerals, principally MONAZITE; in igneous rocks on the Earth's surface, cerium is the most abundant lanthanide.

In their elemental form, the lanthanides are silvery metals with high melting points. They tarnish slowly in air, except for samarium, europium, and ytterbium, which are much more reactive toward oxygen or moisture. The metals are prepared from fluorides or oxides by treatment with strongly reducing metals like calcium, or from molten chloride or fluoride salts by electrolysis at high temperatures. The lanthanides are typically isolated as a group by precipitating their insoluble hydroxides, oxalates, or phosphates. Until 1945, tedious, repetitive procedures such as fractional crystallization were required to separate these elements from one another. A much more effective separation technique, ion-exchange CHROMATOGRAPHY, has been used since 1945.

THE LANTHANIDE SERIES

Atomic Number	Atomic Weight	Element	Symbol	Melting Point, °C	Boiling Point, °C	Abundance in Earth's Crust
21	44.9559	scandium	Sc	1,539	2,830	5 ppm
39	88.9059	yttrium	Y	1,526	3,340	28
57	138.9055	lanthanum	La	920	3,460	18
58	140.12	cerium	Ce	798	3,430	46
59	140.9077	praseodymium	Pr	931	3,510	6
60	144.24	neodymium	Nd	1,016	3,070	24
61	(145)	promethium	Pm	1,168	2,460	4.5×10^{-20}
62	150.4	samarium	Sm	1,072	1,790	6
63	151.96	europium	Eu	817	1,600	1
64	157.25	gadolinium	Gd	1,312	3,270	6
65	158.9254	terbium	Tb	1,357	3,220	0.9
66	162.50	dysprosium	Dy	1,410	2,560	4
67	164.9304	holmium	Ho	1,470	2,695	1
68	167.26	erbium	Er	1,522	2,860	2
69	168.9342	thulium	Th	1,545	1,950	0.2
70	173.04	ytterbium	Yb	824	1,194	3
71	174.97	lutetium	Lu	1,663	3,395	0.8

Until recently the only commercial use of the rare earths was as misch metal, an alloy consisting principally of cerium, lanthanum, and neodymium, which is pyrophoric (catching fire in air) when finely divided and is used to make cigarette-lighter flints. Commercial production of the rare earths is now growing by approximately 20% each year. They are used as alloying materials in metallurgy (to remove sulfur and oxygen) and to make strong permanent magnets such as from $SmCo_5$. Other modern uses are as magnetic oxides such as yttrium iron garnet, $Y_6Fe_{10}O_{24}$; as phosphors in television screens (Eu^{3+} yields a red phosphor when "doped" into some oxides); as catalysts that decompose auto air pollutants, such as $La_{0.7}Sr_{0.3}MnO_3$; and as compounds that store hydrogen effectively, such as $LaNi_5H_6$.   LESTER R. MORSS

Bibliography: Cotton, F. Albert, and Dickinson, Geoffrey, *Advanced Inorganic Chemistry*, 4th ed. (1980); Fields, Paul R., and Moeller, Therald, eds., *Lanthanide-Actinide Chemistry* (1967); McCarthy, Gregory J., et al., eds., *The Rare Earths in Modern Science and Technology*, 3 vols. (1978–82); Subbarao, E. C., and Wallace, W. E., eds., *Science and Technology of Rare Earth Materials* (1980).

lanthanum   [lan'-thuh-nuhm]

Lanthanum is a chemical element, a white, malleable metal, and the first of the rare earths. Its symbol is La, its atomic number 57, and its atomic weight 138.9 (average weight of the two natural isotopes, ^{138}La and ^{139}La). ^{138}La is radioactive, with a half-life of 1.12×10^{11} years. Lanthanum is found with other lanthanides in monazite, bastnaesite, and other minerals. It was discovered in 1839 by Swedish chemist Carl G. Mosander. Scientists have created many radioactive isotopes of lanthanum. Because lanthanum increases the refractive index of glass, it is used in manufacturing high-quality lenses. Lanthanum is also used as a reagent, as a phosphor in fluorescent lamps, and as a catalyst for cracking crude petroleum (its largest use).

Lantian man

The remains of Lantian (or Lan-t'ien) man, a hominid belonging to the species *Homo erectus*, were uncovered in 1963 and 1964 by scientists from the Institute of Vertebrate Paleontology and Paleoanthropology in Peking. The first discovery, located near the Chinese town of Lan-t'ien, in Shensi province, was an almost complete lower jaw of a female. The following year an isolated molar tooth and a badly crushed skull cap, also female, were discovered 25 km (15 mi) away in deposits of roughly the same geological age, dating from the Middle Pleistocene Epoch, about 700,000 years ago. Lantian man is considered an early, less-evolved form of PEKING MAN. The jaw presents the earliest known incidence of third molar (wisdom tooth) absence and periodontal disease. Stone tools have been found in deposits close to, but not in direct association with, *Homo erectus lantianensis*, the official nomenclature of Lantian man.   ALAN MANN AND NANCY MINUGH

Lanvin, Jeanne   [lahn-van', zhawn]

Jeanne Lanvin, b. 1867, d. July 6, 1946, was a leading French couturière of the first half of the 20th century. She began designing for women in 1909, and she startled the fashion world in 1912 with a chemise dress to be worn without a corset. Her *robe de style* evening dress of the 1920s with its tight waist and long skirt evoked tradition and luxury through the use of expensive fabrics such as brocades and gold and silver lamé.   E. M. PLUNKETT

Bibliography: Calasibetta, Charlotte, *Fairchild's Dictionary of Fashion*, ed. by Lorraine Davis and Ermina Gable (1975); Garland, Madge, *The Changing Form of Fashion* (1970); Lambert, Eleanor, *The World of Fashion* (1976); Lynam, Ruth, *Couture* (1972).

lanxide

Lanxides are ceramic materials that are being developed for potential use in automobile and jet aircraft engines, as armor plating, and for other applications where strength, lightness, and high resistance to heat are of great importance. They differ from other ceramic composites in their novel mode of manufacture: oxidation of a molten metal and subsequent mixing of the oxide and metal under controlled conditions to produce a structure consisting of an oxide network suffused with pure metal. Named for a Maryland corporation that developed this process, lanxides are relatively inexpensive to make compared to the ceramics produced thus far for similar applications.

Lao   [low]

The Lao are the largest of the many ethnic groups in Laos, in Southeast Asia, constituting 48% of the 3,805,000 people in the country (1985 est.). There are even more Lao in neighboring Thailand than in Laos. Lao, or Laotian Tai, is the standard language of the nation, although upper-class Lao speak and write French. Most Lao live in villages. They grow rice, corn, coffee, tobacco, fruit, and vegetables and take fish from the Mekong River. Houses are raised above the swampy ground, and many have verandas. The Lao live in what is known as the "Golden Triangle," where a major cash crop is opium. The Lao trace their descent through the male line, and the family is the major social and economic unit. Although the Lao are Buddhists, they have retained many ancient beliefs in spirits that play a major role in their lives.

The Lao trace their history back to the ancient kingdom of Lan Xang. For some periods of Laotian history the country was dominated by the Burmese and Thai. In 1899 the French combined small kingdoms in the region and renamed the area Laos. Laotians obtained their independence from France in 1953.   DONN V. HART

Bibliography: Halpern, Joel M., *Government, Politics, and Social Structure in Laos: A Study of Tradition and Innovation* (1964); Le Bar, Frank, and Suddard, Adrienne, eds., *Laos* (1960; repr. 1967); McGilvary, Daniel, *A Half Century among the Siamese and the Lao* (1912; repr. 1977).

Lao-tzu   (Laozi)   [low'-dzu]

Lao-tzu, or Master Lao, is the name of the putative author of the Taoist classic *Tao-te Ching*. According to Taoist legend, Lao-tzu, the founder of TAOISM, was named Li Erh and had the courtesy name Lao Tan. An older contemporary of Confucius (551–479 BC), he was keeper of the archives at the imperial court. In his 80th year he set out for the western border of China, toward what is now Tibet, saddened and disillusioned that men were unwilling to follow his path to natural goodness. At the border (Hank Pass), however, the guard Yin Hsi requested that Lao-tzu record his teachings before he left, whereupon he composed in 5,000 characters the famous *Tao-te Ching* (The Way and Its Power). The essential teaching of Lao-tzu is the *Tao,* or Way, to ultimate reality—the way of the universe exemplified in Nature. The harmony of opposites (*T'ai Ch'ai*) is achieved through a blend of the *Yin* (feminine force) and the *Yang* (masculine force); this harmony can be cultivated through creative quietude (*wu wei*), an effortless action whose power (*te*) maintains equanimity and balance.

Bibliography: Chan, W. T., trans., *The Way of Lao Tsu (Tao te Ching)* (1963); Holmes, Welch, *The Parting of the Way* (1957); Kaltenmark, Max, *Lao-Tzu and Taoism,* trans. by Roger Greaves (1969).

Laocoön   [lay-ah'-koh-ahn]

The intense emotionalism of Hellenistic sculpture is epitomized in the Laocoön statue. Attributed to three Rhodian sculptors and generally considered to date from the 2d or 1st century BC, the sculpture portrays in dynamic movement the death struggle of the Trojan priest Laocoön and his sons. (Cortile del Belvedere, Vatican, Rome.)

The *Laocoön* is an ancient marble statue (n.d.; Cortile del Belvedere, Vatican) depicting Laocoön, the Trojan priest of Apollo, and his two sons being attacked by serpents. The Trojans saw the death of Laocoön not only as a portent for their city but also as Athena's punishment for the priest, who had hurled a spear at the wooden horse left behind by the Greeks on their feigned departure from Troy. The statue, which stands 2.42 m (8 ft) tall, was rediscovered in Rome in 1506 and was much admired and copied. In the late 16th century it was exalted as an example of unrestrained emotion; Titian, El Greco, and Peter Paul Rubens used it as a model; Johann Wolfgang von GOETHE wrote about it; and Gotthold Ephraim LESSING named his treatise (1766) on aesthetics for it. Pliny the Elder, in his *Historia Naturalis* (1st century AD), attributed the statue to the Rhodian sculptors Agesander, Athenodorus, and Polydorus. Its date is uncertain: if it is Hellenistic, it dates from the 2d or 1st century BC; if Roman (based on a Hellenistic prototype), from the first century of the Christian era.

ANASTASIA DINSMOOR

Bibliography: Bieber, Margarete, *Laocoön, the Influence of the Group since its Discovery,* 2d ed. (1967), and *The Sculpture of the Hellenistic Age,* 2d ed. (1961); Robertson, C. M., *A History of Greek Art* (1975).

Laoighis   [lay'-ish]

Laoighis (also Leix) is a county in Leinster province in central Ireland, covering an area of 1,720 km² (664 mi²); its population is 73,094 (1986). Major rivers are the Barrow and the Nore; the county town is Port Laoighis (Maryborough). The Slieve Bloom Mountains, with elevations to more than 520 m (1,700 ft), are in the northwest. Agriculture is the mainstay of the economy; wheat, barley, and sugar beets are the main crops, and dairy cattle are also important. A branch of the Grand Canal and the Cork-Dublin rail line pass through the county. Part of the kingdom of Ossory from the 1st to 11th century, Laoighis came under the English crown in the 16th century and was developed as a major agricultural region.

Laomedon   [lay-ahm'-ih-dahn]

In Greek mythology, Laomedon was a king of Troy and the father of PRIAM. When he refused to pay APOLLO and POSEIDON for building the walls of Troy, they sent a plague and a sea monster, respectively, to ravage the city. An oracle advised Laomedon to sacrifice his daughter Hesione to the monster. She was rescued by HERCULES, to whom Laomedon gave mortal horses rather than the immortal steeds that he had promised. In revenge, Hercules returned with six ships to destroy Troy, killed Laomedon, and carried Hesione away.

Laos   [lah'-ohs]

Laos is a small, landlocked country located in the interior of Southeast Asia's strategic Indochinese Peninsula. The People's Republic of China lies to the north, Vietnam to the east, Kampuchea (Cambodia) to the south, and Burma and Thailand to the west. Laos was a part of French INDOCHINA after 1893 and was granted full independence in 1953. After the French departed, a protracted civil war ensued. In 1975 the Communist forces gained control, the king was forced to abdicate, and Laos became a people's democratic republic.

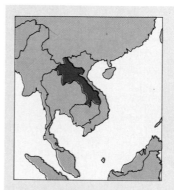

LAO PEOPLE'S DEMOCRATIC REPUBLIC

LAND. Area: 236,800 km² (91,429 mi²). Capital and largest city: Vientiane (1984 est. pop., 200,000).

PEOPLE. Population (1987 est.): 3,800,000; density (1987 est.): 16 persons per km² (42 per mi²). Distribution (1986): 16% urban, 84% rural. Annual growth (1978–85): 2.3%. Official language: Lao. Major religions: Buddhism, traditional religions.

EDUCATION AND HEALTH. Literacy (1980): 45% of adult population. Universities (1986): 1. Hospital beds (1985): 11,650. Physicians (1985): 430. Life expectancy (1985): women—52.4; men—49.4. Infant mortality (1986): 122 per 1,000 live births.

ECONOMY. GDP (1985): $600 million; $159 per capita. Labor distribution (1984): agriculture—71%; other—29%. Foreign trade (1985): imports—$163.3 million; exports—$47.6 million; principal trade partners—Thailand, Japan. Currency: 1 new kip = 100 at.

GOVERNMENT. Type: Communist one-party state. Legislature: National Congress of People's Representatives. Political subdivisions: 16 provinces, 1 municipality.

COMMUNICATIONS. Railroads (1987): none. Roads (1985): 12,983 km (8,067 mi) total. Major ports: none. Major airfields: 1.

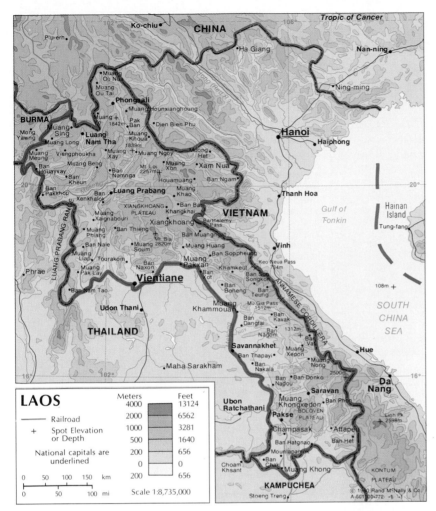

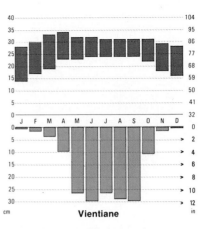

Bars indicate monthly ranges of temperature (red) and precipitation (blue) of Vientiane, the capital of Laos. Vientiane's climate, like that of the rest of this landlocked country, is tropical, with heavy monsoonal influences.

LAND

Laos is a predominantly mountainous land, with less than 10% of the total land area suitable for permanent agricultural settlement. It has a maximum north-south extent of 1,127 km (700 mi) and a maximum width of only 443 km (275 mi). Topographically, Laos has three areas. The northern half of the country is occupied by rugged mountains, which include Mount Bia (2,820 m/9,252 ft), the highest point in the country. The southern half of the country—sometimes referred to as the panhandle because of its long, narrow shape—is dominated by the mountains of the Annamese Cordillera, which extend from north to south along the eastern border. The Annamese mountains reach elevations of less than 2,438 m (8,000 ft) but are extremely rugged and are a major obstacle to travel and communication between Laos and Vietnam. The western half of the panhandle is occupied by most of the nation's principal lowlands, located on the alluvial floodplains along the MEKONG RIVER—Laos's major river—and its tributaries.

Laos has a monsoonal climate. Winters (November to April) are relatively cool and dry, and summers (May to October) are hot and wet. During the summer rainy season the average daily temperature is about 27° C (80° F), and rainfall is between 1,270 mm (50 in) and 2,286 mm (90 in). Temperatures during the dry season average between 16° C (61° F) and 21° C (70° F).

Forests cover almost two-thirds of Laos, but much of the valuable wood in the primary forest areas has been destroyed by slash-and-burn farming methods and replaced by economically unimportant trees and dense rainforest. Tin is commercially exploited, and deposits of coal, iron ore, copper, gold, lead, salt, and zinc await development. Laos's enormous hydroelectric potential is also undeveloped.

PEOPLE

The population of Laos is ethnically complex, with each ethnic group more closely tied to related groups outside the country's borders than to the Laotian nation. The dominant group are the LAO, who account for nearly 50% of the total population and are concentrated in the alluvial floodplains along the Mekong River valley and its tributaries. They practice a high-yielding wet-rice (paddy) form of agriculture. The Lao Teung, occupying middle elevations in the highlands, practice a low-yielding slash-and-burn form of agriculture. They are regarded as the original inhabitants and constitute about 25% of the total population. At higher elevations, above 1,067 m (3,500 ft), are the MEO and Man (YAO) hill tribes, which account for about 13% of the total population. Also separate are the tribal Tai, who practice a religion different from that of the lowland Lao. The official language is Lao, which is the language of the Lao ethnic group and is similar to Siamese. The Lao Teung all speak languages of the Mon-Khmer family, and the Meo and Man languages are regarded as belonging to the Miao-Yao language family. The official religion is Theravada Buddhism, which remains an important part of Lao life under the Communists. The Lao Teung, tribal Tai, and other hill tribes practice various forms of animism and ancestor worship.

By Southeast Asian standards, Laos is sparsely populated, even in the alluvial lowlands where most people are concentrated. The population is predominantly rural. The largest urban area is VIENTIANE, which is the capital and about four times as large as second-ranking Savannakhet. Other popula-

Women belonging to the Lao-Tai tribal group are differentiated as Red Tai and Black Tai by the color of their dress. Four major ethnic groups dominate the population of Laos. Cultural and tribal isolation is perpetuated by the mountainous terrain and poor transportation.

tion centers are Pakse and LUANG PRABANG. The birthrate is high and unlikely to fall to the level of advanced nations because of a government ban on birth-control practices. The death rate is also high, so the net population increase is moderate. Also, since 1975 an estimated 400,000 refugees, including most of the educated, wealthy elite and many tribespeople from the hills, have left the country.

Six years of schooling is compulsory. Primary school education begins at age six and lasts for five years. Secondary and senior high school last for three years each. Since 1975, Lao, has replaced French as the language of school instruction. Higher education is available at Sisavangvong University (1958) or may be sought abroad, primarily in the USSR.

Life expectancy is low and health-care facilities are inadequate, although new physicians are being trained. Malaria and malnutrition are widespread, and infant mortality is high.

ECONOMIC ACTIVITIES

Laos is economically underdeveloped, with one of the lowest per capita incomes in the world. Most of the people are dependent on subsistence farming. In 1979, in an attempt to revive the crippled economy, the ban on private trade was lifted and farmers were given incentives to increase production; further reforms were instituted in the late 1980s. By 1984 the government claimed to have achieved self-sufficiency in food, although shortages still exist in some areas. Rice is the chief food crop. Corn, wheat, vegetables, fruit, cotton, and tobacco are also raised, mainly for household consumption. The opium poppy is a major cash crop of the Meo and Man hill tribes. Fish from the Mekong and its tributaries and from local fish ponds provide an important source of protein.

Manufacturing is virtually nonexistent, limited to small-scale production of a few consumer items by primitive means, and economic development has been hampered by inadequate transportation. There are no railroads, and roads are often impassable during the rainy season. The main travel artery is the Mekong River, which is navigable between Savannakhet, Vientiane, and Luang Prabang. Most international traffic moves through the Vietnamese port of DA NANG and the airport at Vientiane. The 1986–90 development plan calls for investment in transportation, management training, and small- and medium-scale industrial projects.

Electricity from the Nam Ngum dam, exported to Thailand, is the leading source of foreign exchange. Tin, mined near Muang Khammouan (Thakhek), and small amounts of forest products are also exported. Laos has a chronic trade deficit and is heavily dependent on foreign aid.

GOVERNMENT

In 1975, King Savang Vatthana abdicated, and the coalition government led by Prince SOUVANNA PHOUMA was replaced by a Communist-controlled government led by Prime Minister Kaysone Phomvihan and President SOUPHANOUVONG, who retired in 1986. The Lao People's Revolutionary party is the only political party. In 1989, nationwide elections for an assembly to ratify a new constitution were held.

HISTORY

Laos was part of the KHMER EMPIRE before 1353 when the Laotian prince Fa Ngum assumed the throne of Muong Swa (Luang Prabang) and founded the kingdom of Lan Xang. Theravada Buddhism, adopted from the Khmers, became the state religion. The Lao kingdom reached its zenith under King Souligna Vongsa (r. 1637–94). After 1707 dynastic feuds divided the kingdom, and three competing kingdoms emerged—Vientiane, Luang Prabang, and Champasak. In the 19th century, annexation by Thailand was averted by an appeal for French protection. In 1893, Laos became part of French Indochina.

During World War II, Laos came under Japanese occupation. In April 1945, King Sisavang Vong of Luang Prabang proclaimed Laotian independence under Japanese protection. With the defeat of Japan, he accepted the French reassertion of control, despite the opposition of the Free Lao (Lao Issara) anti-French revolutionary movement, which formed a government in exile in Thailand. In 1949, Laos became a semiautonomous state within the FRENCH UNION, and in 1953 it was granted full independence. By this time, however, the Free Lao movement, regrouped as the Communist-backed PATHET LAO, had established control of northern Laos. Prolonged civil war ensued between the Pathet Lao and the royal government. The struggle was actually three-way because control of the royal government in Vientiane passed back and forth between the pro-Western rightists led by Gen. Phoumi Nosavan and the neutralists led by Prince Souvanna Phouma.

In 1961 a 14-power nation conference in Geneva sought to defuse the conflict by establishing a neutralist coalition government under Souvanna Phouma. Fighting soon broke out again, however, and Laos increasingly became a side theater in the VIETNAM WAR. The final coalition government, led by Souvanna Phouma and including his half-brother, the Pathet Lao leader Souphanouvong, was established in April 1974. After the fall of South Vietnam and Cambodia (now Kampuchea) to the Communists in 1975, the Pathet Lao assumed full control in Laos. In December, Souvanna Phouma's government was terminated, and the monarchy abolished. About 30,000 former police and government officials, including the former king, were sent to political reeducation centers.

Laos signed a treaty of peace and friendship (1977) and a border delineation treaty (1986) with Vietnam. Its alliance with Vietnam and the Soviet bloc has been strengthened since Vietnam's invasion (1979) of Kampuchea. By 1989, less than 2,000 Vietnamese soldiers remained in Laos. Their presence contributed to strained relations between Laos and Thailand and Laos and the United States.

ASHOK K. DUTT

Bibliography: Brown, MacAlister, and Zasloff, Joseph J., *Apprentice Revolutionaries: The Communist Movement in Laos, 1930–85* (1986); Dommen, A. J., *Laos* (1985); Jumsai, M. L., *The History of Laos*, 2d ed. (1971); Stuart-Fox, Martin, *Laos: Politics, Economics, and Society* (1987) and, as ed., *Contemporary Laos* (1982); Whittaker, D. P., et al., eds., *Laos: A Country Study* (1971; repr. 1985).

lapidary: see GEM CUTTING.

lapis lazuli [lap'-is laz'-u-lee]

Lapis lazuli has long been valued both as a deep blue ornamental GEM and as a source of ULTRAMARINE pigment. The col-

Lapis lazuli, an opaque, deep-blue stone, has been valued for ornamental purposes for more than 6,000 years. Of variable composition, it consists essentially of lazurite mixed with small amounts of other closely related aluminum silicate minerals.

or is due to lazurite, a blue variety of the SODALITE group of feldspathoid minerals; other minerals usually present include calcite, pyrite, amphibole, apatite, diopside, feldspar, sphene, and zircon. Lapis lazuli, a contact METAMORPHIC ROCK with variable composition and varying physical properties, usually occurs in altered limestones. Lapis lazuli is distinguished from artificially colored jasper by the presence of gold-colored flecks of pyrite and the lack of the tiny, colorless quartz crystals present in jasper. Major sources are at Badakhshan in Afghanistan, Lake Baikal in the USSR, and Ovalle in Chile.

Bibliography: Evans, Joan, *Magical Jewels of the Middle Ages and the Renaissance* (1922; repr. 1976); Kunz, George F., *The Curious Lore of Precious Stones* (1913; repr. 1971).

Laplace, Pierre Simon de   [lah-plahs', pyair see-mohn' duh]

The French mathematician and astronomer Pierre de Laplace made invaluable contributions to the development of probability theory and celestial mechanics. Laplace was elected to the Académie Française in 1816 and was renowned for his observations of planetary motions and their relation to Newton's gravitational theory. He contributed to the scientific acceptance of the hypothesis of gravitation.

The French astronomer and mathematician Pierre Simon de Laplace, b. Mar. 28, 1749, d. Mar. 5, 1827, is best known for his nebular hypothesis of the origin of the solar system. He also confirmed the long-term stability of the solar system by mathematically demonstrating the long-term periodicity of three apparently secular, or cumulative, sets of irregularities in the motions of solar-system bodies: the acceleration of the mean motions of the mutually perturbing planets Jupiter and Saturn; the acceleration of the mean motions of the mutually perturbing inner three Galilean satellites of Jupiter; and the acceleration of the mean motion of the Moon.

Laplace's monumental 5-volume work, *Traité de mécanique céleste* (Treatise on Celestial Mechanics, 1799–1825; Eng. trans., 1829–39), was the culmination of over a century of work devoted to the mathematical explanation, on the basis of gravitational theory, of the motions of the solar-system bodies. Earlier, in his popular-level *Exposition du système du monde* (Exposition of the System of the World, 1796), he presented his famous nebular hypothesis, which viewed the solar system as originating from the contracting and cooling of a large, flattened, and slowly rotating cloud of incandescent gas. Among his other findings in astronomy was the existence of an invariable plane in our solar system about which the whole system oscillates.

In mathematical analysis Laplace introduced the potential function and Laplace coefficients. He also brought the theory of mathematical probability to a mature stage. He conducted experiments on capillary action and specific heat with Antoine Lavoisier. In optics he opposed Thomas Young's theory of light. He also contributed to the foundations of the mathematical science of electricity and magnetism.

Laplace had a prosperous career. When he was 19, d'Alembert obtained an appointment for him as professor of mathematics at the École Militaire in Paris. He became an associate (1773) and then a pensioner (1785) of the Paris Academy of Sciences. During the French Revolution he helped to establish the metric system, taught the calculus at the École Normale, and was a member of the French Institute (1795). Under Napoleon he was a member, then chancellor, of the Senate, received the Legion of Honor (1805), and became Count of the Empire (1806). With his political suppleness, he was named a marquis (1817) after the Bourbon restoration. In his later years he lived in Arcueil, where he helped to found the Société d'Arcueil and encouraged the research of young scientists.

RONALD CALINGER

Bibliography: Bell, Eric T., *Men of Mathematics* (1937); Crosland, Maurice, *The Society of Arcueil* (1967); Hahn, Roger, *Laplace as a Newtonian Scientist* (1967); Numbers, Ronald, *Creation By Natural Law: Laplace's Nebular Hypothesis in American Thought* (1977); Todhunter, Isaac, *A History of the Mathematical Theories of Attraction and the Figure of the Earth From the Time of Newton to That of Laplace,* 2 vols. (1873; repr. 1962).

Lapland

Lapland (Finnish: *Lappi;* Swedish: *Lappland*), a vast area stretching across the northern part of Norway, Sweden, Finland, and the Kola Peninsula of the USSR, is the home of the Lapps. Lapland covers approximately 388,500 km² (150,000 mi²). The region lies mainly within the Arctic Circle and is bordered on the east by the White Sea, on the north by the Barents Sea, and on the west by the Norwegian Sea. The eastern portion is close to sea level and is dotted with lakes. The northeast is largely tundra, but other sections are mountainous and forested, and good pasturelands are to be found in some areas. The highest point is Kebnekaise Peak, in Sweden, with an altitude of 2,123 m (6,965 ft).

The climate is arctic, with an extremely short growing season. Part of the region is under ice and snow the year round. Minerals abound, and the iron ore deposits are among the world's richest. The Lapps, who now number about 42,800, came to Lapland from east central Europe in the middle of the first millennium BC. Today most are settled, but some are still nomadic, depending on reindeer for food, clothing, and shelter. Small numbers of Finns and Swedes came to the area in the 9th and 14th centuries AD, and mining was begun in the 17th century.

Bibliography: Marsden, Walter, *Lapland* (1976); Stalder, Valerie, *Lapland* (1971).

Lapps

The Lapps are a European people without a formal homeland of their own. Numbering about 42,800, they inhabit the arctic and subarctic regions of four countries: Norway, with around 20,000 Lapps; Sweden, with an estimated 17,000; Finland, with around 3,800; and the Soviet Union, with about 2,000. The name Lapp, from Finnish *lappalainen*, is a foreign term as far as these people are concerned. They prefer to be called Samit, their own name for themselves. The Lappish language belongs to the Finno-Ugric subfamily of the Ural-Altaic languages. It is thus unrelated to neighboring Scandinavian and Slavic languages with the exception of Finnish, Estonian, Latvian, and certain lesser-known tongues. Finnish is the closest of these to Lappish, but the two are not mutually intelligible. Lappish itself divides into three large language groups—east,

The Lapps, shown in traditional costume, inhabit an area of northern Europe known as Lapland, which borders on and lies within the Arctic Circle, including parts of Norway, Sweden, Finland, and the USSR. The Lapps are primarily a seminomadic herding or fishing people.

central, and south Lappish. Racially, the Samit are much intermixed with their neighbors but tend to be shorter and more round-headed, with a higher incidence of dark hair and brown eyes. They have been Christians since the 1600s.

The origins of the Samit are still uncertain, but they may be the oldest postglacial inhabitants in the Far North. Originally living as hunters, gatherers, and fishing people, some became pastoralists by the Middle Ages at the latest. Reindeer herding remains their most distinctive occupation. Reindeer herders today may frequently be seen in the traditional costume of colorful, decorated tunic and tasseled hat. Most Samit today, however, dress like other Europeans and live mostly in permanent houses and communities rather than in the tents and camps of their seasonal herding migrations. Many Samit live in fishing communities along arctic coasts and inland waters. Others have lived for generations as settled farmers. Some work at mining or forestry. ROBERT T. ANDERSON

Bibliography: Asbjorn, Nesheim, *Introducing the Lapps*, 2d ed. (1966); Bosi, Roberto, *The Lapps*, trans. by James Cadell (1960; repr. 1976); Spencer, Arthur, *The Lapps* (1978).

lapse rate

A lapse rate indicates how some variable—usually temperature—of the ATMOSPHERE or ocean changes with height or depth; it is positive when the variable decreases. Temperature lapse rate determines whether air will mix freely from low to high levels and carry pollutants away, or will be forced to cling to the surface. An unstable lapse rate, conducive to overturning, predominates in daytime. At night, when air near the ground often becomes colder than air higher up, a temperature INVERSION, or departure from the usual lapse rate, occurs, and strongly constrains air to remain very close to the ground. An average lapse rate is 6.5° C/km (11° F/mi).
HERBERT RIEHL

lapwing

Lapwing is a name given to several common species of birds of the PLOVER family, Charadriidae. It is most often associated with a large plover, *Vanellus vanellus*, a migratory species that breeds throughout Europe, Asia, and North Africa. This bird measures about 30 cm (12 in) in height and has a wispy crest and broad, rounded wings. Also known as the peewit or the green plover, it nests in plowed fields and usually produces four brownish, spotted eggs. Lapwings feed primarily on soil insects. STEPHEN C. REINGOLD

Laramie [lair'-uh-mee]

Laramie, a city in southeastern Wyoming on the Laramie River, is the seat of Albany County. Its population is 24,410 (1980). It serves as the commercial, industrial, and transportation center for the surrounding sheep- and cattle-raising region. The University of Wyoming (1886) is there. Laramie is the headquarters of Medicine Bow National Forest. It was settled in 1868 as a tent and shanty town for workers building the Union Pacific Railroad. The railroad and ranching brought prosperity to the area.

larceny [lar'-sen-ee]

Larceny is the taking and carrying away of another's personal property without legal claim to that property, without the owner's consent, and with the intent permanently to deprive the rightful owner of its use. Carrying away has been held to mean any movement of the property, however slight. Personal property includes tangible goods, fixtures attached to the land, crops, and legal documents. Persons who take property that they believe is their own are not guilty of larceny. Larceny has occurred if consent has not been freely given by the rightful owner or if it has been induced by trick or fraud (a process sometimes called larceny by false pretenses). A person who borrows property without the rightful owner's consent but with the intent to return it has not committed larceny. Larceny is commonly distinguished from robbery, in which force or violence is used or threatened.

Most states of the United States have statutes specifying what activities constitute larceny. Included among these are picking pockets, the receiving of stolen goods, the passing of checks drawn against insufficient funds or nonexistent bank accounts, the use of slugs in coin-operated machines, and, in some states, embezzlement. Laws generally distinguish among several kinds or degrees of larceny and punish them accordingly. Simple larceny, a MISDEMEANOR, is the taking of property; compound larceny, a FELONY, is the taking of property from a person or a person's business or dwelling house. The value of the stolen property distinguishes grand larceny from petit, or petty, larceny; the former is generally a felony, the latter a misdemeanor.

Bibliography: MacDonald, J. M., *Burglary and Theft* (1980).

larch

Larch is the common name for trees of the genus *Larix* of the pine family. Ten species occur naturally in cool, moist regions of the Northern Hemisphere. Two North American species—the eastern larch, or tamarack, *L. laricina,* and the western larch, *L. occidentalis*—have commercial value. The main dis-

The Japanese larch, L. kaempferi, *like other larches, loses its leaves in winter. Larches are among the few deciduous conifers.*

tinguishing characteristic of larches is that although they are pines they are deciduous, losing their foliage in the winter. The bark is thick and scaly, and the needles are pale or bright green, turning yellow in autumn. The European larch, *L. decidua*, is an important continental tree used for reforestation in the eastern United States. The Japanese larch, *L. kaempferi*, is used as a landscaping tree in the United States. Large forests of larch are sometimes destroyed by the larch sawfly.

Lardner, Ring

An American humorist who used the vernacular in his cynical short stories of ordinary people, Ringgold Wilmer Lardner, b. Niles, Mich., Mar. 6, 1885, d. Sept. 25, 1933, started his writing career as a columnist for the *Chicago Tribune*. A series of pieces for the *Saturday Evening Post* about a bush-league baseball pitcher turned pro became his first collection of short stories, *You Know Me, Al* (1916). Further collections, featuring prizefighters and other figures from the world of sports, secretaries, salesmen, Tin Pan Alley songsmiths, and Broadway chorus girls who revealed themselves in the idiom of their kind, included *Gullible's Travels* (1917), *Treat 'Em Rough* (1918), *How to Write Short Stories* (1924), and *The Love Nest* (1926). With George S. Kaufman, Lardner also wrote the comic play *June Moon* (1929). An unorthodox autobiography, *The Story of a Wonder Man*, appeared in 1927.

Bibliography: Evans, E., *Ring Lardner* (1980); Lardner, Ring, Jr., *The Lardners: My Family Remembered* (1976); Patrick, W. R., *Ring Lardner* (1963); Yardley, Jonathan, *Ring: A Biography of Ring Lardner* (1977).

Laredo   [luh-ray'-doh]

Laredo, Tex., stands on the Rio Grande opposite Nuevo Laredo, Mexico. It is the seat of Webb County and has a population of 91,449 (1980). A port of entry handling considerable trade, it is also the retail center for an extensive region of cattle ranches, irrigated farms, and petroleum and natural gas fields. Ceramics, electronics equipment, medical supplies, clothing, and leather goods are manufactured, and petroleum oil is refined. Tourism is also important.

Laredo was established in 1755 by Spanish settlers. After the Texas Revolution (1835-36), ownership of the city was disputed until the Treaty of Guadalupe Hidalgo (1848) established the Rio Grande as the border between Mexico and Texas.

lares   [lair'-eez]

The lares were Roman household gods who represented the spirits of the founding ancestors of a family. Each household had its own lar, to whom a portion of each meal was offered. Family lares were often represented by statues of a youth with a drinking horn and cup. Public lares were patrons of the state who presided over the major crossroads of the city.

large numbers, law of

The law of large numbers is a theorem in PROBABILITY theory that states that the average of the outcomes of independent repetitions of a chance phenomenon must approach the EXPECTED VALUE of the outcome as the number of repetitions increases without limit, or approaches infinity. It is also called Chebyshev's Theorem or Bernoulli's Theorem. For example, the actual average winnings per play in a game of chance in the long run must approach the expected winnings per play. Gambling houses, insurance companies, and other industries base their business practices on this assurance that the average result of many independent chance trials is quite predictable—even if the result of one individual trial is not.

The law of large numbers, popularly known as "the law of averages," is often thought to require that future outcomes balance past outcomes, but this assumption is not correct. A roulette wheel that has produced ten straight "reds" has no memory and so is no more likely to produce "black" than at any other time. It is a gambler's fallacy to think that the ten reds in a row will be balanced by extra blacks. The odds remain the same for each repetition, regardless of the past outcomes.   DAVID S. MOORE

Bibliography: Book, Stephen A., *Statistics* (1977).

Largillière, Nicolas de   [lar-zheel-yair', nee-kah-lah' duh]

Nicolas de Largillière was a leading French baroque portraitist, baptized Oct. 10, 1656, d. Mar. 20, 1746, who helped bring the coloristic influence of Rembrandt and Peter Paul Rubens to French court art. Having grown up and studied in Antwerp, Largillière felt at home with both the Dutch and Flemish masters. In his youth he worked in London (1674-80) with Sir Peter Lely, adding still life, drapery, and landscape to Lely's portraits. In Paris in the 1680s the influential artist Charles Le Brun helped him to obtain commissions among the lesser nobility and the newly rich bourgeoisie. Largillière's portrait of Le Brun (1686; Louvre, Paris) earned him a place in the Royal Academy, of which he later became director (1728-42) and chancellor (1743). Like his friend and contemporary Hyacinthe Rigaud, Largillière indulged his sitters' love of display by showing their opulent dress and accoutrements to the best effect. He also painted official group portraits such as those for the Paris Échevins (city fathers). His rare still lifes were precursors of Jean Baptist Chardin's work.

NANETTE SALOMON

Bibliography: Blunt, Anthony, *Art and Architecture in France, 1500 to 1700* (1953; repr. 1977); Muehsam, Gerd, ed., *French Painters and Paintings from the 14th Century to Post-Impressionism* (1978); Kalnein, Wend Graf, and Levey, Michel, *Art and Architecture of the Eighteenth Century in France* (1972).

Larionov, Mikhail Fyodorovich   [luh-rih-yaw' nawf, mee-kuh-yeel' fyoh-dor'-uh-vich]

Mikhail Fyodorovich Larionov, b. Teraspol, Ukraine, May 22 (N.S.), 1881, d. Paris, May 10, 1964, was an early leader of the Russian avant-garde movement in painting. He was instrumental in introducing and interpreting French and Italian art and ideas to Russia and by 1910 was the accepted leader of advanced Russian painting. In 1912 he issued the manifesto of rayonism, a style of abstract expressionist painting based on the disintegration of form into radiating beams of light. Although rayonism was short-lived, it provided the intellectual basis for the foundation of SUPREMATISM by Kasimir MALEVICH in the same year. In 1915, Serge Diaghilev asked Larionov and his wife, the artist Natalia Sergeyevna Goncharova, to join his ballet company in Paris to design stage settings. Not only did Larionov design ballets, but he also became Diaghilev's advisor on all aspects of production, including choreography.

ROWLAND ELZEA

lark

The common skylark, Alauda arvensis, of Eurasia, one of the most populous birds of Europe, has long been celebrated for its song. It is approximately 18 cm (7 in) long.

Lark is the common name for about 70 species of terrestrial, robin-sized songbirds belonging to the family Alaudidae. These birds are distributed worldwide, although most species are found in Africa. Larks are noted for the elaborate song of the males, which is performed during flight. Larks measure 13 to 23 cm (5 to 9 in) in height. They have long legs; the hind toe has a large, straight claw, making perching difficult.

The horned lark, *Eremophila alpestris,* which ranges throughout most of the Northern Hemisphere, is the only species native to North America. It has brown plumage on its back, is paler below, and has a pair of small, dark head tufts, or "horns." In the New World, it nests from the Arctic to South America. The common skylark, *Alauda arvensis,* of Eurasia, has also been introduced into the New World.

Larkin, Philip

Philip Arthur Larkin, b. Aug. 9, 1922, d. Dec. 2, 1985, was a highly regarded modern British poet. *The North Ship* (1945), a volume of his early verse, was followed by two novels, *Jill* (1946) and *A Girl in Winter* (1947). Larkin's fame as a poet was firmly established by *The Less Deceived* (1955). Larkin's portrayal of modern England concentrates on dejected and nondescript aspects of the industrial landscape, whose inhabitants he describes without sentiment but with unaffected compassion. Larkin's stoical, witty, and unpretentious style is seen to its greatest advantage in *The Whitsun Weddings* (1964) and *High Windows* (1974). His jazz criticism is collected in *All What Jazz* (1970), and he was the editor of *The Oxford Book of Twentieth-Century English Verse* (1973). Various essays are collected in *Required Writing: Miscellaneous Pieces, 1955–82* (1984).

Bibliography: Kuby, L., *An Uncommon Poet for the Common Man* (1974); Motion, A., *Philip Larkin* (1982); Thwaite, A., *Larkin at Sixty* (1982).

Larkin, Thomas Oliver

Thomas Oliver Larkin, b. Charlestown, Mass., Sept. 16, 1802, d. Oct. 27, 1858, was a U.S. merchant and diplomatic agent who helped prepare the way for the American acquisition of California. He settled in Monterey in 1832, opened a store, and conducted successful trade with Mexico and the Sandwich (Hawaiian) Islands. From 1844 to 1849, Larkin acted as U.S. consul, confidential agent, navy agent, and navy storekeeper. In these capacities, he helped protect Americans in the area and launched a propaganda campaign in favor of U.S. annexation. After the American seizure of California he was a member of the state constitutional convention in 1849.

Bibliography: Hammond, George P., ed., *The Larkin Papers,* 10 vols. (1951–64); Hawgood, J. A., ed., *First and Last Consul* (1962).

larkspur

Larkspur is the common name for about 40 species of annual herbs constituting the genus *Consolida* in the buttercup family, Ranunculaceae. Native to temperate regions of the Northern Hemisphere, larkspurs bear feathery leaves and loose racemes (clusters) of flowers, which range from purple to pink and white in color. The names larkspur and delphinium are sometimes used interchangeably, but botanists now place the DELPHINIUM—sometimes perennial—in a separate genus.

Larousse, Pierre [lah-roos', pyair]

Son of a village blacksmith, Pierre Athanase Larousse, b. Oct. 23, 1817, d. Jan. 3, 1875, became one of the most influential scholars and educators of 19th-century France. He published a series of reference works that, in their revised and updated forms, continue to be among the most popular in the world. His first book, a basic vocabulary list (1849), was followed by grammars and other school texts. In 1852, Larousse founded his own publishing house in Paris with Augustin Boyer. Four years later the firm published a compact dictionary. Larousse's masterwork, the comprehensive 15-volume encyclopedia the *Grand Dictionnaire,* came out in installments over a 10-year period from 1866 to 1876.

Lars Porsena, King of Clusium [lahrz-por-sen'-uh, klooz'-ee-uhm]

Lars Porsena was a quasi-historical Etruscan ruler of the 6th century BC. According to Roman tradition, this chieftain of Clusium (modern Chiusi) sought to restore the exiled TARQUINIUS SUPERBUS to the Roman throne but was deterred by the bravery of HORATIUS. Historians give more credence to the Etruscan legend of Mastarna (identified with Porsena), who conquered and ruled Rome until vanquished by the federated forces of the Latin League (see LATINS).

Lartet, Édouard Armand [lahr-tay']

Édouard Armand Isidore Hippolyte Lartet, b. Apr. 15, 1801, d. Jan. 28, 1871, although a magistrate by training, was one of the pioneers of modern paleontology. After his initial discovery (1834) of fossil remains in southwestern France, he began the first systematic investigation of French cave sites. During excavations at Aurignac he found evidence of human and extinct mammals existing in the same period. Beginning in 1863, Lartet and the English ethnologist Henry Christy worked together in the Dordogne area, where they excavated such famous prehistoric sites as Les Eyzies and La Madeleine. Lartet became (1869) professor of paleontology at the Musée d'Histoire Naturelle in Paris. *Reliquiae Aquitanicae* (1865–75), coauthored by Lartet and Christy, details their archaeological and paleontological work in southern France.

Lartigue, Jacques Henri [lahr-teeg']

Jacques Henri Lartigue, b. June 13, 1894, d. Sept. 12, 1986, is best known in his native France as a painter, his work having been exhibited in Paris, Marseilles, and Menton. But his photographs, which aim to capture the feeling of movement and to record the emotions of an era, are also highly acclaimed. Many of them appear in *Boyhood Photographs of J.-H. Lartigue: The Family Album of the Gilded Age* (1966); *Diary of a Century* (1970), edited by Richard Avedon; *Les Femmes* (1974); and *The Autochromes of J. H. Lartigue* (1981).

larva [lahr'-vuh]

A larva is an immature animal that occurs in the life cycle stage between the time certain animals hatch from eggs and the time they undergo development, or METAMORPHOSIS, into a markably different form, the adult. Larval stages occur in many kinds of invertebrates and in fish and amphibians. One kind of amphibian, the AXOLOTL, never passes from the larval stage to the adult stage. Although it becomes sexually mature and reproduces, its outward form is still larval and it even retains gills. This condition is called NEOTENY. Some insects first pass through a PUPA stage (seemingly inactive) before reaching the adult stage.

In contrast to adults, whose principal purpose is to reproduce, the principal purpose of larvae is to eat. For many insects the adult diet, if any, is completely different from the larval diet. This is thought to be biologically advantageous because larvae and adults do not compete for the same food. For many marine species the larval stage is also a time of dispersal.

Bibliography: Berrill, N. J., *Growth Development and Pattern* (1961).

laryngitis [lar-in-jy'-tis]

Laryngitis is an inflammation of the LARYNX, or voice box, usually associated with a common cold or overuse of the voice. It is commonly characterized by swelling, hoarseness, pain, dryness in the throat, coughing, and inability to speak above a whisper, if at all. Spasmodic laryngitis, most often seen in children with RICKETS, is characterized by crowing or whistling sounds while breathing in.

Complete recovery from common laryngitis can be expected within a few days if the patient refrains from speaking aloud. Chronic forms of laryngitis without respiratory infection or voice strain may be due to tuberculosis, syphilis, or tumors pressing on or in the larynx.   PETER L. PETRAKIS

larynx   [lair'-inks]

The larynx, or voice box, is a muscular tube in the throat of all mammals and some reptiles and amphibians. It contains the vocal cords, which produce sound that is converted into speech and other utterances by the lips, teeth, and tongue. Birds do not have a larynx, but most have a modified portion of the windpipe called the syrinx with which they vocalize.

The larynx has several segments of firm, elastic cartilage held together by muscle and ligaments. The cartilaginous wall is covered along its bore by a mucosa (moist membrane). The largest segment is the thyroid cartilage, which consists of two plates that form a ridge, called the "Adam's apple." The larynx extends from the pharynx (throat) above to the trachea (windpipe) below.

In mammals, including humans, the larynx has a flaplike structure, the epiglottis, at its inlet. The epiglottis causes swallowed food to pass from the throat into the esophagus rather than into the trachea.

The vocal cords, located in the upper region of the larynx, are two muscularized folds of mucous membrane that extend from the larynx wall. The gap between the folds is the glottis. Each fold encloses an elastic vocal ligament and muscle, which controls the tension and rate of vibration of the cords as air passes through them. In normal breathing the vocal muscles are held slack, allowing air to pass in and out of a wide slit. The tighter the vocal muscles contract the vocal cords, the higher the tone of the sound produced.

Cancers or other growths sometimes necessitate removal of the larynx, an operation known as a laryngectomy. After such an operation a patient usually breathes through a surgically formed opening in the neck, or tracheostoma. The patient may then be taught to speak again, using a so-called esophageal voice, by gulping down air into the esophagus and slowly releasing it through the mouth; gullet tissues can be made to produce a sound that is then modified by the mouth structures to yield recognizable speech. Alternatively, an artificial valve may be implanted between the esophagus and trachea, permitting air to be deflected through the esophagus for speech production.   ROY HARTENSTEIN

Bibliography: Fink, B. R., *The Human Larynx* (1975); Keith, R. I., *Handbook for the Laryngectomee*, 2d ed. (1983); Shedd, D. P., and Weinberg, Bernd, *Surgical and Prosthetic Approaches to Speech Rehabilitation* (1980); Singh, R. P., *Anatomy of Hearing and Speech* (1980).

Las Campanas Observatory   [lahs kahm-pah'-nahs]

Las Campanas Observatory, situated on a 2,500-m (8,250-ft) ridge in northern Chile, is operated by the Carnegie Institution of Washington. From 1970 to 1980 it was part of the Hale Observatories. The 2.5-m (100-in) Irenée du Pont telescope, opened in 1977, uses a complex optical system to reduce distortion and achieve an unusually wide field of view. It uses a deeply curved (f/3) primary mirror and a 74-cm (29-in) Gascoigne corrector to eliminate astigmatism. Also on the mountain are a 1-m (40-in) Swope reflector and the 61-cm (24-in) University of Toronto reflector, which was opened in 1971.
                                    NORMAN SPERLING

Las Casas, Bartolomé de   [lahs kah'-sahs]

The early-16th-century Spanish missionary Bartolomé de Las Casas was known as the Apostle of the Indies. He engaged in a lifelong struggle to make the Spanish court and church aware of the immorality of Indian oppression by the New World colonizers.

Known as the Apostle of the Indies, Bartolomé de Las Casas, b. 1474, d. July 1566, was one of the first Spanish missionaries in Latin America. His *Historia de las Indias* (History of the Indies) is a major source for the early period of colonization.

Las Casas first went to Hispaniola in 1502, and about 1512 he became a priest, probably the first to be ordained in the New World. (He later joined the Dominican order.) In 1514, Las Casas began a lifelong effort to improve conditions for the harshly treated Indians. He was generally supported by the Spanish crown and in 1542 secured enactment of the New Laws, by which the system of forced labor called the ENCOMIENDA was to be phased out. As bishop of Chiapas (1544–47), he met with bitter opposition trying to enforce the laws.

Bibliography: Hanke, Lewis, *Bartolomé de Las Casas* (1951); Helps, Arthur, *The Life of Las Casas* (1976); Wagner, Henry Roup, *The Life and Writings of Bartolomé de las Casas* (1967); Wright, Louis B., *Gold, Glory, and the Gospel: The Adventurous Lives and Times of the Renaissance Explorers* (1970).

Las Cruces   [lahs kroo'-sis]

Las Cruces, the seat of Dona Ana County, in southern New Mexico, is located on the Rio Grande, 60 km (37 mi) north of the Mexican border. Its population is 45,086 (1980). Las Cruces is the commercial center for an irrigated agricultural area growing vegetables, cotton, alfalfa, and pecans. New Mexico State University (1888) is there, and the White Sands Missile Range is to the northeast. Of interest are the nearby Organ Mountains, extinct volcanoes located in the West Potrillo Mountains, and the small Indian community called Tortugas.

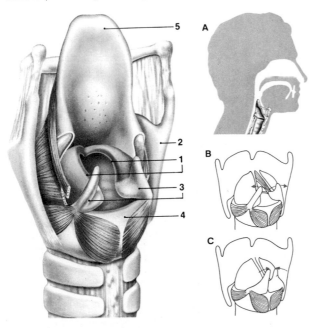

The larynx regulates voice production and prevents material from entering the windpipe during swallowing. Located at the entrance to the trachea (A), it is a framework of cartilages with different shapes and functions. The vocal cords (1) are stretched between the large thyroid cartilage (2) and two smaller moving cartilages (3). A large cartilaginous ring (4) at the top of the trachea supports the larynx. During swallowing, the vocal cords move together to close the windpipe, and the epiglottis (5) drops over the larynx. The vocal cords move apart during breathing (B). During speech (C) they are drawn together, and air forced through the larynx makes them vibrate.

Founded in 1848, the town was named for the wooden crosses (*Las Cruces*, in Spanish, "the crosses") marking the graves of an earlier band of settlers from Chihuahua, Mexico.

Las Palmas   [lahs pahl'-mahs]

Las Palmas, the largest city in Spain's Canary Islands, with a population of 366,454 (1981), is the capital of Las Palmas province on Grand Canary Island. It lies 7 km (4 mi) inland from the major port, Puerto de la Luz. The economy is based on tourism, shipbuilding, fisheries, food processing, and export of agricultural products. Of interest is the Cathedral of Santa Ana (begun in 1497). Las Palmas was founded in 1478.

Las Vegas

Las Vegas, a city in southeastern Nevada, is the seat of Clark County and, with a population of 164,674 (1980), is the largest city in the state. Because of its gambling casinos, it is a world-famous resort. Las Vegas is also the commercial center for a large mining and ranching area. The city lies at an altitude of 620 m (2,033 ft) on a desert plain surrounded by mountains. Income from luxury hotels, gambling casinos, and other entertainment used by approximately 15 million tourists a year forms the base of the city's economy. Livestock raising, mining (gold, silver, lime, borax, and gypsum), railroading, and the manufacture of beverages are also important industries. HOOVER DAM and the Nevada Test Site of Nellis Air Force Base are both nearby. A branch of the University of Nevada is in Las Vegas.

Artesian springs first attracted California-bound travelers to the site. Mormons from Utah settled there briefly (1855–57), and in 1864 the U.S. Army built Fort Baker. First part of Arizona Territory, Las Vegas was included in the state of Nevada in 1867. Arrival of the San Pedro, Los Angeles, and Salt Lake Railroad in 1905 encouraged the town's growth. Gambling was legalized in Nevada in 1931, and the population burgeoned after 1940 and again between 1960 and 1970, when the population almost doubled. In 1980 a fire at the MGM Grand Hotel in Las Vegas took 84 lives.

Lascaux   [lahs-koh']

Lascaux, a cave site near Montignac in Dordogne, France, ranks with ALTAMIRA as one of the most spectacular and famous examples of PREHISTORIC ART yet discovered. Superb paintings and drawings in black, brown, red, and yellow pigments, as well as rock engravings, appear on the walls and ceilings of the central cavern and in several side chambers and galleries within the cave. The main cavern, known as the Great Hall of Bulls, is in itself a complete work of art, containing what appears to be a deliberately planned frieze over the entire extent of its walls. The frieze consists of huge polychrome bulls and horses—the largest 5.5 m (18 ft) in length—and smaller bison, stags, a bear, and a curious, possibly

This cave painting of a cow and horses from Lascaux in southwestern France dates from the Upper Paleolithic Period (15,000–10,000 BC). The sensitively rendered representation is typical of the naturalistic cave art produced by the Cro-Magnons in ice-age Europe.

mythical, spotted and two-horned animal. In the left gallery are the most famous paintings of polychrome animals, including the so-called Frieze of Little Horses and, on the vaulted roof, a beautiful composition with horses and cows. Inside a small side chamber are several engraved cave lions. In the so-called Shaft of the Dead Man is a scene unique in cave art, depicting a two-horned rhinoceros, a schematically drawn dead man, a wounded bison, and a bird on a hooked instrument, possibly a spear-thrower. The significance of the scene and of the many engraved and painted latticelike signs that alternate with the painted animals is obscure.

The art of Lascaux is dated to the early MAGDALENIAN phases of the Upper Paleolithic Period (about 17,000 years ago). The cave was first discovered (1940) by four youths searching for their lost dog. Although initially the paintings were in perfect condition, subsequent atmospheric changes in the cave caused some of the paintings to deteriorate. Lascaux was closed to the public in 1963; an exact replica of the famous cave, Lascaux II, opened nearby in 1983.   LYA DAMS

Bibliography: Laming, Annette, *Lascaux* (1959).

laser   [lay'-zur]

The laser is a device that generates "well-organized" LIGHT, or COHERENT LIGHT (see also OPTICS). The mechanism relies on a process known as stimulated emission, and the word *laser* is derived from *Light Amplification by Stimulated Emission of Radiation*. The MASER uses the same principle to generate or amplify electromagnetic radiation in the longer-wavelength microwave region.

PRINCIPLES OF OPERATION

The essential components of a typical laser are (1) the active medium, such as a ruby rod or carbon dioxide gas; (2) a method of introducing energy into the active medium, such as a flash lamp; and (3) a pair of mirrors placed on each side of the active medium, one of which transmits part of the radiation that strikes it.

The principles of operation of the laser are the same whether its active medium consists of atoms of a gas, molecules in a liquid, ions in a crystal, or any of several other possibilities. To be specific, however, these principles are here described in terms of a gas made up of atoms. Each atom is characterized by a set of energy states, or energy levels, in which it may exist. These states may be pictured as unevenly spaced rungs of a ladder, with higher rungs representing states of higher energy. Left undisturbed for a long enough time, an atom will fall to its lowest energy state, or ground state. To simplify matters further, consider a fictitious atom having only two energy states, differing in energy by an amount ΔE, and consider how this atom interacts with light. According to quantum mechanics, the atom interacts with light of only one frequency ν (frequency is related to wavelength and color); this is determined by the equation $\nu = \Delta E/h$, where h is Planck's constant, equal to 6.62×10^{-34} joule-seconds.

Three kinds of interaction are possible: absorption, stimulated emission, and spontaneous emission. An atom in the lower state can absorb light and be excited to the upper state; an atom in the upper state can fall spontaneously to the lower state, emitting light in the process; or the atom can be stimulated by the presence of light to jump down to the lower state and emit additional light while doing so. Spontaneous emission is unaffected by the presence of light and occurs on a time scale characteristic of the states involved. This time is called the spontaneous lifetime. In stimulated emission the additional light that is emitted will have the same frequency and directional characteristics as the light that stimulates it. This is the crucial feature on which the properties of the laser are based, and, for the laser to work effectively, stimulated emission must predominate over both absorption and spontaneous emission.

The probabilities of occurrence of stimulated emission and absorption are both proportional to the light intensity; stimulated emission, however, can happen only to upper-state atoms, whereas absorption can happen only to lower-state atoms. For stimulated emission to dominate absorption,

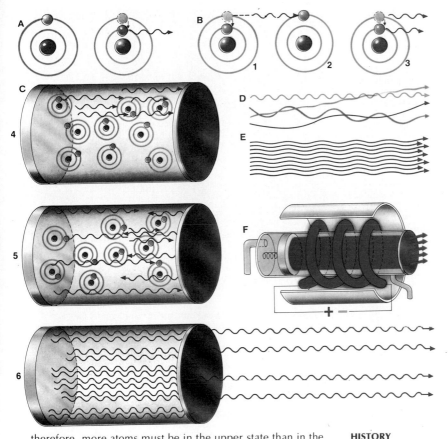

A B 1 2 3

C D E F

A laser is a device that produces an intense, highly concentrated beam of single-wavelength light. Most light is emitted by an excited atom (A) containing an electron in a higher-than-normal energy level. The electron soon returns spontaneously to its normal, or ground, state, releasing the excess energy in the form of light waves, or photons. In stimulated emission (B), a photon emitted from an atom (1) induces an electron in another excited atom (2) to fall immediately to a lower level and emit a photon identical to itself (3). Stimulated emission can thus be used to increase the number of emitted photons. Energy is first pumped into a laser material (C), raising most of the electrons to a level just above the ground state. Initially (4), only a few atoms will spontaneously radiate photons. Two silvered end mirrors, one partially transparent, reflect the radiation back and forth repeatedly (5), inducing a chain reaction of photon emission. All the electrons return to the ground state almost simultaneously, and a powerful pulse of laser light (6) emerges from the partially transparent end. Whereas light waves from conventional sources have a wide range of wavelengths and move in various directions (D), laser light waves have a single wavelength and are unidirectional and exactly in step with one another (F). A ruby laser (F) comprises a ruby rod with silver-coated ends spring-mounted in a liquid-cooled chamber. Energy for raising the atoms to the high-energy state is supplied by a coiled gas-discharge tube surrounded by a focusing reflector.

therefore, more atoms must be in the upper state than in the lower state. This unusual situation is called population inversion and can be achieved by supplying energy ("pumping" the laser) and carefully selecting the active medium. Typical pumping schemes include the use of light from flash lamps or other lasers, collisions of the lasing atoms with electrically accelerated electrons in a gas discharge tube, excitation with energetic particles from nuclear reactions, chemical reactions, and direct electrical input to a semiconductor. Continuous lasing is harder to achieve than pulsed lasing.

For stimulated emission to dominate spontaneous emission, it is necessary to ensure that the stimulating light is sufficiently strong. Stimulated emission then occurs in a time interval that is short compared to the spontaneous lifetime of the excited state. This situation is achieved by keeping a fraction of the laser light trapped between two mirrors enclosing the active medium. Domination of stimulated emission over spontaneous emission becomes more difficult to achieve as the spontaneous lifetime becomes shorter. Because shorter spontaneous lifetimes are associated with states that emit radiation of higher frequencies, it is difficult to make an ultraviolet-emitting laser, and an X-ray laser was not successfully demonstrated until 1984. Despite their complexity of construction, however, ultraviolet lasers, or excimers, have gained widespread use in industry. Emitting ultraviolet light when a halogen and rare gas atom combine temporarily, they are used in applications ranging from glass etching and photolithography to the sterilization of wines.

The sequence of events in generating a laser pulse is shown in the diagram. Atoms are raised to a higher energy state by a flash lamp or other pumping source. Light traveling perpendicular to the mirrors stays within the active medium long enough to stimulate emission from other atoms, whereas light traveling in other directions is soon lost. After further such stimulation by amplified light, some light reaching the output mirror is transmitted to form the laser beam, while some is reflected back through the medium to continue the stimulated-emission process.

HISTORY

The fundamental principles underlying the operation of the maser and laser were established long before these devices were successfully demonstrated: stimulated emission was proposed by Albert EINSTEIN in 1916, and population inversion was discussed by V. A. Fabrikant in 1940. These fundamental ideas, followed by two decades of intensive development of microwave technology, set the stage for the first maser, an ammonia maser, constructed in 1954 by J. P. Gordon, H. J. Zeiger, and Charles H. TOWNES. Over the next 6 years many workers, including Nikolai G. BASOV, Aleksandr M. Prokhorov, Arthur L. Schawlow, and Townes, made important contributions that helped to extend these ideas from the microwave to the optical wavelength region. These efforts culminated in July 1960 when Theodore H. MAIMAN announced the generation of a pulse of coherent red light by means of a ruby crystal—the first laser. In 1964, Townes, Basov, and Prokhorov were jointly awarded the Nobel Prize for physics. Schawlow received a later Nobel Prize, in 1981, for his development of laser spectroscopy, but Maiman, who had produced the first actual laser, received no prize.

Another aspect of laser history was finally resolved in 1987, when American physicist Gordon GOULD won his 30-year battle to obtain a patent for a gas-discharge laser he had conceived in 1957. He had written his ideas in a notebook at the time, and had them officially recorded, but failed to apply for a patent until 1959 because of poor legal advice. (In the notebook he had, in fact, coined the word "laser," as well.) Gould eventually did receive partial patents in 1977 and 1979, but the 1987 patent covers many types of laser, including the helium-neon laser.

LASER TYPES

A selection of laser types and characteristics is shown in the table on page 213. Many other types exist; for example, the free-electron laser uses a special magnet to produce a laser beam (ranging from infrared to visible wavelengths) from high-energy electrons emitted by a particle accelerator. Other types, listed without further discussion, include carbon-mon-oxide, color-center, gas-dynamic, helium-cadmium, hydrogen-fluoride, deuterium-fluoride, iodine, Raman spin-flip, and rare-gas halide lasers.

Many of these lasers may be operated so as to produce widely different pulse-duration, power, and wavelength characteristics; the numbers shown in the table are intended only to suggest the capabilities of each type rather than to indicate the complete range or maximum performance. Listed pulse-duration times range from 40 picoseconds (1 psec = 10^{-12} sec) to continuous-wave (cw), which is essentially infinite. A 1-nanosecond (10^{-9} sec) pulse is only about a third of a meter (1 ft) long as it travels through space. Pulse durations as short as 8×10^{-15} sec have been achieved, opening up possibilities for probing phenomena of very brief duration.

The tabulated power levels cover a range of a million to a billion in magnitude. The lowest tabulated power—3 milliwatts (mW)—refers to a cw laser, whose highly directional beam is so bright it can damage the eye. For power comparisons, electrical input to a typical light bulb is 100 watts (W), and electrical power generated by a power station is 1 billion watts, or 1 gigawatt. Power and energy must be distinguished. Power is the rate at which energy is transferred, so that one pulse from a 40-psec, 1-trillion-watt, or 1-terawatt laser provides the same amount of light energy as does a 40-W laser in 1 sec. By focusing high-power beams, enormous intensities can be reached for research purposes. For example, scientists are focusing 10-terawatt beams to provide intensities greater than 10^{17} watts/cm^2—power sufficient to compete for electrons with the electric attraction of an atomic nucleus.

The common helium-neon laser is also cheap, costing less than $200. The diode laser is the smallest, being packaged in a transistorlike enclosure. Dye lasers have a broad, continuously variable wavelength capability. The carbon-dioxide laser is the most efficient, with an up to 30% ratio of output light energy to input electrical energy.

CHARACTERISTICS OF LASER LIGHT

Light is a wave and as such can be characterized by its frequency (number of wavecrests passing a given point per second) or wavelength (distance between wavecrests). Coherence is also an important property. To understand the importance of a laser in various applications it will be useful to first list some characteristics of light in general, and laser-generated light in particular.

1. Nothing travels faster than light in empty space.
2. Light in empty space travels in a straight line at a known velocity. This is also approximately true for light traveling in the atmosphere.
3. Information can be carried by electromagnetic radiation; for example, Morse code can be sent using a blinking light. Light has a higher frequency than radio waves or microwaves, which gives it a greater information-carrying capacity.

An excimer laser threaded into a human heart through a catheter is used to break apart built-up deposits of plaque with brief, intense bursts of energy. Such medical uses of lasers are growing rapidly.

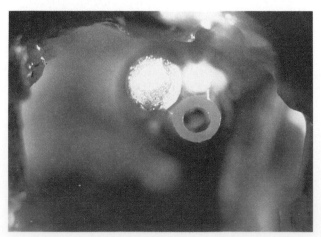

Above is one of the two power amplifiers of the huge carbon dioxide laser used in fusion research at Los Alamos National Laboratory. They deliver 20 trillion watts in pulses lasting a billionth of a second in experimental efforts to fuse the hydrogen isotopes deuterium or tritium.

4. All beams of radiation spread out as they travel (unless they are confined within a pipe or an optical fiber); however, this spreading can be minimized for coherent radiation. By using a large-diameter beam with a small wavelength, spreading can be reduced. Light has a shorter wavelength than radio waves or microwaves and therefore spreads less and can be usefully transmitted over larger distances. A related property is that coherent light can be focused into a smaller point than can radiation of longer wavelength.
5. Light beams can be readily manipulated by delicate, fast-moving mirrors and can be switched on and off quickly.
6. A laser can produce light of essentially a single frequency.
7. Pulsed lasers offer the possibility of power multiplication; that is, energy can be stored relatively slowly in the inverted population, and then some fraction can be retrieved in a very brief laser pulse—thus, the power (the rate at which energy is provided) can be much higher than that of the original energy source.
8. Swift application of modest amounts of energy to a small area can produce dramatic localized effects. For example, a small area of the surface of a metal block can be melted without causing permanent change to nearby regions.

APPLICATIONS

As laser technology advances, lasers continue to find new applications. For example, laser "atomic traps" were being developed in the late 1980s to slow down and study atoms; such traps are also used to examine living microorganisms. The following paragraphs discuss the types of lasers typically used for a number of applications, and the properties of laser light that are important to each application (referring by number to the preceding list).

Laser-Induced Controlled Thermonuclear Fusion (neodymium-glass and pulsed carbon-dioxide lasers; properties 4 and 7). The ability to control thermonuclear fusion on a scale much smaller than that typified by hydrogen bombs or the Sun would solve energy problems for the foreseeable future. One approach to this goal involves heating and compressing a microscopic pellet of hydrogen-isotope (deuterium or tritium) fuel by placing it at the focus of a high-power, short-pulse laser beam. Significant efforts are being devoted to fusion research in several countries.

Communications (diode and neodymium-yag lasers; properties 3, 4, and 5). Communications links using coded light pulses from lasers traveling in glass fibers are already in use in the Chicago Bell Telephone system (see FIBER OPTICS). A 144-fiber cable can carry 40,000 simultaneous telephone conversations. A soliton, or solitary wave, of laser light has recently been created and could lead to even better optical communications. Light also offers an attractive alternative to microwaves for satellite communications.

Materials Working (carbon dioxide, neodymium, and argon-ion lasers; properties 4, 5, and 8). A laser beam can be used to heat-treat or coat a surface layer of a metal component or to melt and weld a pair of components without introducing sufficient heat to distort them. Narrow cuts can be made, and holes can be drilled. Among the advantages over conventional techniques are that there is no cutting-tool edge to become dull with use, and computer control of cutting and drilling operations is straightforward. Delicate adjustments can be made to the size of microelectronic components while monitoring the desired electrical characteristics of the system.

In the late 1980s a novel process called selective laser sintering was being developed. Working from computer graphics, this "desktop manufacturing" device can produce prototype design models by a rapid buildup of fused layers of plastic or metal through use of a laser beam.

Medical Applications (carbon dioxide and argon-ion lasers; properties 4 and 8). A laser beam can be used to seal capillaries in a shallow surface layer without damaging deeper tissues. This can be done while painlessly vaporizing a surface tumor or cutting an organ. Noninvasive surgery of the retina (laser light enters through the eye lens) and cauterization of stomach ulcers (light enters via an endoscopic fiber) are important applications. Lasers have been used to clear cholesterol blockages in arteries (see ANGIOPLASTY).

Surveying and Ranging (helium-neon and ruby lasers; properties 2 and 4). A laser beam can be used as a straight line in surveying. Distances can be measured by timing a light pulse traveling from the laser to a mirror and back to a detector near the laser. This can be done for both terrestrial measurements and lunar ranging.

Holography (helium-neon and argon-ion lasers; property 6). Laser sources allow reproduction of three-dimensional images. This technique is known as HOLOGRAPHY. Holographic views of microscopic objects are now being made by using advanced X-ray lasers.

Isotope Separation and Spectrography (various; property 6). The detection, separation, and investigation of atoms and molecules based on the light frequencies that they absorb all benefit from the sophistication and tunability of laser light sources.

Military Applications (neodymium and carbon-dioxide lasers; properties 1, 2, 4, and 8). Lasers are used for range-finding and target designation, and are being developed as both antisatellite and ballistic missile defense weapons (see STRATEGIC DEFENSE INITIATIVE).

Information Applications (diode; properties 3, 5, and 8). Small laser beams are used in printing devices to trace reproducible images. Laser-etched discs are used for large-capacity audio, video, and data recording and playback (see COMPACT DISC; VIDEODISC).   JOHN F. WARD AND DANIEL S. ELLIOTT

Bibliography: Bertolotti, M., *Masers and Lasers: An Historical Approach* (1983); Griffiths, J., *Lasers and Holograms* (1983); Laurence, C. L., *The Laser Book* (1986); Luxon, James, *Lasers in Manufacturing* (1987); Measures, R. M., *Laser Remote Sensing* (1983); Metzbower, E. A., ed., *Lasers in Materials Processing* (1983); Whimmery, J. R., ed., *Lasers: Invention to Application* (1987); Young, M., *Optics and Lasers*, 3d rev. ed. (1986).

By using an impressive array of mirrors, tubes, and lenses, three laser beams are carefully aligned to intersect on an area within a flame. The resulting beam is then analyzed by spectrographic means to provide precise information about the combustion processes taking place. This advanced technique is called CARS, for coherent anti-Stokes Raman spectroscopy.

Lashley, Karl S.   [lash'-lee]

Karl Spencer Lashley, b. Davis, W.Va., June 7, 1890, d. Aug. 7, 1958, was a pioneer neuropsychologist in the United States especially known for his opposition to theories localizing complex psychological functions in the brain.

Lashley's formative academic years were spent, first as a zoologist at the University of Pittsburgh, then (1912–16) in animal behavior under John B. Watson, the founder of behaviorism, at The Johns Hopkins University in Baltimore. In 1917, Lashley became associated with S. I. Franz at Saint Elizabeth's Hospital in Washington, D.C., where he began his famous studies on brain function. This work culminated in a monograph published in 1929, *Brain Mechanisms and Intelligence,* in which Lashley proposed his theories of mass action (that learning involves the entire cortex) and equipotentiality (that parts of the cortex can take over the functions of other, damaged parts). This matter of equipotentiality of cortex function is still a subject of ongoing research.

Equally influential were his later papers, "The Problem of Serial Order in Behavior" (1951) and "In Search of the Engram" (1950). Less well known was Lashley's staunch support of sex research; he funded Kinsey's work and publications. It is for his brain research, however, that Lashley is best remembered—his opposition to the then-current reflexology (the explanation of behavior in terms of reflexes).

KARL H. PRIBRAM

Bibliography: Beach, F. A., et al., *The Neuropsychology of Lashley* (1960).

SOME LASERS AND THEIR CHARACTERISTICS

Active Medium	Type	Pulse Duration	Power	Wavelength	Year First Demonstrated	Pumping
Ruby	Crystal	20 nsec	10 MW	694 nm	1960	Lamp
Helium-neon	Gas	cw	3 mW	633 nm	1960	Discharge
Neodymium-glass	Glass	40 psec	1 TW	1.06 μm	1961	Lamp
Neodymium-yag	Crystal	15 nsec	10 MW	1.06 μm	1964	Lamp
Diode	Semiconductor	cw	100 mW	900 nm	1962	Electric
Nitrogen	Gas	6 nsec	500 kW	337 nm	1963	Discharge
Hydrogen cyanide	Gas	1 μsec	10 W	337 μm	1964	Discharge
Argon ion	Gas	cw	10 W	515 nm	1964	Discharge
Carbon dioxide	Gas	cw	1 kW	10.6 μm	1964	Discharge
Dye	Liquid	5 nsec	50 kW	450–900 nm	1966	Pulsed laser
Dye	Liquid	1 μsec	1 MW	450–900 nm	1967	Lamp
Dye	Liquid	cw	100 mW	450–900 nm	1969	cw laser
Molecular hydrogen	Gas	2 nsec	1.5 kW	160 nm	1970	Discharge
Methyl fluoride	Gas	cw	10 W	469 μm	1970	Laser

Laski, Harold   [las'-kee]

Harold Joseph Laski, b. June 30, 1893, d. Mar. 24, 1950, was a British political scientist, teacher, author of many books, and leader of the Labour party. He taught at McGill University (1914–16), Harvard University (1916–20), and the London School of Economics (1926–50). A lifelong socialist, he moved from an early belief in antistatist pluralism to an acceptance of Marxism, which he sought to adapt to British conditions. In 1945–46 he was chairman of the Labour party, which never accepted his Marxist philosophy. Laski was a close friend of Oliver Wendell Holmes, Jr., and selections from their correspondence were published as *Holmes-Laski Letters,* 2 vols. (1953). His numerous works include *Reflections on the Constitution* (1951) and *The Rise of European Liberalism* (1936).

Bibliography: Deane, Herbert A., *The Political Ideas of Harold J. Laski* (1954; repr. 1972); Martin, Kingsley, *Harold Laski* (1953); Zylstra, Bernard, *From Pluralism to Collectivism* (1968).

Laskin, Bora

Known for his brilliant legal scholarship, Bora Laskin, b. Fort William, Ontario, Oct. 5, 1912, d. Mar. 26, 1984, served (1973–84) as the 14th chief justice of Canada. Educated at the University of Toronto and at Harvard, he was appointed to the Supreme Court of Ontario, Court of Appeal, in 1965. In 1970 he joined the Supreme Court of Canada, its first Jew.

Lassalle, Ferdinand   [lah-sahl', fair'-dee-nahn]

Ferdinand Lassalle, b. Apr. 11, 1825, d. Aug. 31, 1864, was one of the founders of the German Social Democratic party. In his early twenties he undertook (1846–54) 35 lawsuits to obtain a divorce for Countess Sophie von Hatzfeldt, who made him financially independent. A Hegelian, Lassalle became a friend of Karl Marx, but differed from Marx in believing that the Prussian state would aid workers in establishing producer cooperatives. He helped establish the Universal German Workers' Association (1863), which became the Social Democratic party (1875). In conversations with Prussian minister president Otto von Bismarck, Lassalle tried to persuade him to introduce universal suffrage, which Lassalle believed would lead to state socialism. He died in a duel.   Frederic B. M. Hollyday

Bibliography: Brandes, Georg M. C., *Ferdinand Lassalle* (1911; repr. 1977); Footman, David, *Ferdinand Lassalle, Romantic Revolutionary* (1947; repr. 1977).

Lassell, William   [las-el']

The British astronomer William Lassell, b. June 18, 1799, d. Oct. 5, 1880, discovered Neptune's larger satellite, Triton, in 1846; discovered (simultaneously with William C. Bond) Saturn's eighth satellite, Hyperion, in 1848; and verified the existence of two satellites of Uranus—Ariel and Umbriel—in 1851. A successful brewer before turning to astronomy, Lassell ground many lenses for use in telescopes.   Steven J. Dick

Lassen Peak   [las'-en]

Lassen Peak, an active volcano in the Cascade Range in northeastern California, is 3,187 m (10,457 ft) high. It last erupted in 1921. The volcano's period of greatest recorded activity was in 1914–15, when massive mudflows and gaseous explosions destroyed large areas of forest. The Lassen Volcanic National Park, covering 430 km^2 (166 mi^2) and established in 1916, includes Lassen Peak, other volcanic cones, hot springs, mud pots, and fumaroles. Lassen Peak was discovered in 1821.

Lassus, Roland de   [lah-sues']

Roland de Lassus, b. 1532, d. June 14, 1594, was a great Flemish composer and one of the most prolific and cosmopolitan musical figures of the Renaissance. He was taken to Italy at an early age and, at the age of 21, was appointed choirmaster at the basilica of Saint John Lateran in Rome. He relinquished the post a year and a half later to Giovanni Pierluigi da Palestrina, who was destined to become his most celebrated contemporary and with whose music his own is often linked as embodying the ideals of Counter-Reformation polyphony. Lassus entered the service of Duke Albert V of Bavaria in 1556 and within a few years became chapelmaster at the court in Munich. He remained there, except for journeys to important musical centers including Venice, Paris, and Rome, until his death. He was held in such esteem throughout Europe that he was knighted by both emperor and pope.

Lassus' surviving works, many of which were published during his lifetime, include approximately 175 madrigals and lighter works with Italian texts, 150 French chansons, 90 German lieder, about 50 masses, and more than 500 motets. The principal source of the motets is the *Magnum opus musicum,* a collection of 516 pieces for 2 to 12 voices that was assembled from earlier prints and manuscripts by his sons and printed in 1604. His secular music, in which chordal and contrapuntal textures are often subtly blended within a rich harmonic background, is as formally varied as are the many different kinds of poems he set. It is by turns humorous, witty, noble, or sentimental, mirroring perfectly the mood of his chosen text. It is his sacred music, however, particularly his motets, for which Lassus is justly celebrated. Even in his earliest works his tendency to seek out and express the inner meaning of the words through the use of ingenious and ever-changing musical means was evident, and this quality became even more intensified and refined as his style matured. A famous example of this expressive style is his setting of the *Seven Penitential Psalms,* completed in 1570.   Frank D'Accone

Bibliography: Brown, Howard Mayer, *Music in the Renaissance* (1976); Craft, R., "Light on Lasso," *New York Review of Books,* May 4, 1978; Reese, Gustave, *Music in the Renaissance,* rev. ed. (1959).

Lasswell, Harold D.   [las'-wel]

Harold Dwight Lasswell, b. Donnellson, Ill., Feb. 13, 1902, d. Dec. 18, 1978, was an American political scientist renowned for his investigation of political power and of the relation between politics and personality. He received his Ph.D. from the University of Chicago in 1926 and taught at the University of Chicago (1924–38), the Washington School of Psychiatry (1938–39), Yale University (1946–71), the John Jay College of Criminal Justice (1970–73), and Temple University (1973–75). He was director of war communications research at the Library of Congress from 1939 to 1945. His works include *Propaganda Techniques in the World War* (1971), *Psychopathology and Politics* (1931; repr. 1977), *Politics: Who Gets What, When, How* (1936), *Power and Personality* (1948; repr. 1976), and, with Arnold Rogow, *Power, Corruption and Rectitude* (1963; repr. 1977).

Bibliography: Rogow, Arnold A., ed., *Politics, Personality, and Social Science in the Twentieth Century* (1969).

Last Supper

The meal shared by Jesus Christ and his disciples on the night before he was crucified is called the Last Supper (Matt. 26:20–29; Mark 14:17–25; Luke 22:14–38; John 13:1–17:26). It was the occasion of his institution of the Eucharist, when he identified the broken bread with his body and the cup of wine with his blood of the new Covenant. The ritual was that of a Jewish religious meal, which was given new meaning for Jesus' followers when they performed it in remembrance of him. Christians differ as to the meaning of the words of Jesus, the exact relationship of the bread and wine to his body and blood, and the frequency with which the rite is to be repeated. The Last Supper was also the occasion on which Jesus washed his disciples' feet and commanded them to wash one another's feet. It has been the subject of art from earliest times.   L. L. Mitchell

Bibliography: Cullman, Oscar, *Early Christian Worship* (1953); Dix, G., *The Shape of the Liturgy* (1945); Jeremias, J., *The Eucharistic Words of Jesus* (1955); Mitchell, L. L., *The Meaning of Ritual* (1977).

Latakia   [lat-uh-kee'-uh]

Latakia (1981 pop., 196,791) is the largest port of Syria and the capital of Latakia governorate. Situated on the Mediterranean in the northwest part of the country, Latakia has an artificial breakwater that protects it from the sea. It is a market center for cotton, tobacco, grain, fruits, olives, and vegetables, and produces ceramics, asphalt, and cotton and tobacco products. Sponge fishing is important. Because of earthquakes, the city lacks old landmarks.

Of ancient origin, the city was called Ramitha by the Phoenicians. In the late 4th century BC it was named Laodicea by the Macedonian conqueror Seleucus I; this name was altered in time to the present name. Latakia was later held by the Romans, Arabs, Crusaders, Egyptian Ayyubids, and Ottoman Turks in succession. After World War I it was capital of the French territory of the Alawites until it was incorporated into the French mandate of Syria in 1926. Latakia became part of the independent republic of Syria in 1942.

Lateran councils   [lat'-ur-uhn]

The Lateran councils were five ecumenical councils (see COUNCIL, ECUMENICAL) of the Roman Catholic church held during the 12th, 13th, and 16th centuries at the Lateran Palace in Rome. The First Lateran Council (1123) was called by Pope CALLISTUS II to ratify the Concordat of Worms (1122), which formally ended the lengthy INVESTITURE CONTROVERSY. The Second Lateran Council (1139) was convoked by Pope Innocent II to reaffirm the unity of the church after the schism (1130–38) of the antipope Anacletus II (d. 1138). It also condemned the teachings of ARNOLD OF BRESCIA. The Third Lateran Council (1179), convoked by Pope ALEXANDER III, ended the schism (1159–77) of the antipope Callistus III and his predecessors. It also limited papal electors to members of the College of Cardinals.

Although each of the first three Lateran councils decreed a number of reform measures, the Fourth Lateran Council (1215), convoked by Pope INNOCENT III, was the most important of the Lateran councils. Attended by well over 1,000 churchmen from throughout Christendom, the council sanctioned a definition of the EUCHARIST in which the word *transubstantiation* was used officially for the first time. The council also attempted to organize a new crusade to the Holy Land and to encourage crusading efforts against the ALBIGENSES and WALDENSES. Many precepts still binding on Roman Catholics (such as the Easter duty, or obligation, of annual confession and Holy Communion) were adopted at this council. In many respects the council marked a pinnacle in the power and prestige of the medieval papacy. The Fifth Lateran Council (1512–17), convened by Pope JULIUS II and continued by Pope LEO X, was convoked for the purpose of reform, but the main causes of the Reformation were left untouched. Its most significant decree was a condemnation of CONCILIARISM.   T. TACKETT

Lateran Treaty

The Lateran Treaty, signed on Feb. 11, 1929, by Benito MUSSOLINI for the Italian government and Cardinal Pietro GASPARRI for the papacy, settled the vexatious question of the relationship between the Holy See and Italy. The papacy accepted the loss of the PAPAL STATES, while Italy recognized the VATICAN CITY as an independent state.   ROBIN BUSS

laterite   [lat'-ur-ite]

The red, residual soil laterite is a weathering product comprised of a mixture of hydrated iron and aluminum oxides. Laterites are especially characteristic of the tropics and form under conditions of good drainage, high temperature, and extensive rainfall. The silica, alkalies, and alkaline earths of the parent rock are removed either by solution or colloidal processes. Iron tends to be oxidized and remains with the alumina. High-alumina laterites or high-iron laterites are sometimes used as ores. The name is derived from the Latin word (*later*) for brick, which can be made from hardened laterite.
                                                           HAYDN H. MURRAY

Bibliography: McFarlane, M. J., *Laterite and Landscape* (1977); Persons, Benjamin S., *Laterite: Genesis, Location, Use* (1970).

latex   [lay'-teks]

A latex is a colloidal suspension of very small polymer particles (see POLYMERIZATION) in water. Many polymers can be produced as latex, but RUBBER latexes especially are of great commercial importance. Natural rubber comes from the tree as a latex; several synthetic rubbers are produced as latexes because the polymerization process takes place in water. In both cases the water is a soapy solution that helps the particles to remain separate. Products such as gloves or contraceptives are made directly from rubber latex. Latex paints are essentially a solution of colored pigment and rubber latex.
                                                           P. W. ALLEN

lathe

A lathe, or turning machine, is a machine tool that removes unwanted material from a cylindrical workpiece by rotating it against a cutting tool. Common operations include shaping, boring, and threading. The lathe is the oldest, the most common, and the most important of all machine tools. Early wood-turning lathes, powered by a foot treadle, were used during the Middle Ages. The first screw-cutting lathe was developed by Jacques Besson in 1569, and the first practical all-metal screw-cutting lathe was built by Henry MAUDSLAY about 1800. Maudslay's machine developed into the modern engine lathe, so named because it was first driven by James Watt's steam engine. Early lathes were crude devices, but by 1830 such attachments as lead screws and change gears for reproducing screw threads, as well as power feed for moving the cutting tool, were in general use.

The engine lathe is one of the most useful machine tools. Its cutting tool can be power-driven along the edge and across the face of the workpiece for uniform cutting and to reproduce parts. Turret lathes provide a number of quickly indexed tools that can be used in sequence. Screw lathes synchronize the motion of the cutting tool with the rotation of

The invention of the turret lathe in 1850 was a major advance in mass production of metal components. Prior to that time a metal part (1) was machined by rotating it (red arrows) and slowly moving (blue arrows) a suitable cutting tool (2) against the work by means of a lever; a tool change required stopping the machine and replacing one tool with another, and then resetting the new tool before work could continue. The rotating turret (3) that was devised could hold up to eight different cutting tools. When the various tools were correctly adjusted in the turret by a skilled machinist, the lathe could be operated by an unskilled worker, who merely had to move the tool-feeding lever and turn the turret from one tool position to another according to a set procedure.

the workpiece. Some turning machines have a vertical spindle (that is, the part that revolves with the workpiece) instead of a horizontal spindle and have a large rotating table, sometimes measuring a few meters across. Such a lathe is called a vertical boring mill and is capable of holding and turning huge castings or weldments weighing many tons. Related types called vertical turret lathes are equipped with several interchangeable tools mounted on a turret. Speed lathes use a hand-manipulated cutting tool. These machines include metal-spinning lathes, used for forming and polishing. On these lathes, a thin disc or metal may be spun or formed into useful shapes (tubs, covers, and artistic forms).   JOHN E. NEELY

Bibliography: Bradley, Ian, *A History of Machine Tools* (1972); Westbury, Edgar T., *Metal Turning Lathes* (1967).

Lathrop, Rose Hawthorne   [lay'-thruhp]

After enjoying all the pleasures of genteel surroundings, Rose Hawthorne Lathrop, b. Lenox, Mass., May 20, 1851, d. July 9, 1926, became a nun and achieved her highest distinction by devoting herself to aiding the incurably ill. The youngest child of Nathaniel Hawthorne, she married George P. Lathrop in 1871 and spent the next two decades occupied mostly with literary activities. Her works include *Along the Shore* (1888), *A Story of Courage* (written with her husband, 1894), and *Memories of Hawthorne* (1897; 2d ed., 1923).

In 1891 both husband and wife became Roman Catholics. They became estranged, however, and, from 1896, Rose dedicated herself to caring for poverty-stricken cancer victims. She became a nun and in 1900 founded the Congregation of Saint Rose of Lima, a community of Dominican sisters. Taking the name Mary Alphonsa, she became superior of the nursing organization now known as the Servants of Relief for Incurable Cancer. In 1899, Rose had opened a small house on New York's Lower East Side; this institution was later enlarged and formally constituted (1912) as Saint Rose's Free Home for Incurable Cancer. Mother Mary Alphonsa also established (1901) the Rosary Hill Home in Hawthorne, N.Y.

HENRY WARNER BOWDEN

Bibliography: Burton, Katherine, *Sorrow Built a Bridge* (1937); Sheehan, Arthur T., and Sheehan, Elizabeth, *Rose Hawthorne: The Pilgrimage of Nathaniel's Daughter* (1959); Maynard, Theodore, *A Fire Was Lighted: The Life of Rose Hawthorne Lathrop* (1948).

Latimer, Hugh   [lat'-ih-mur, hyoo]

The English church reformer Hugh Latimer, b. c.1485, d. Oct. 16, 1555, was martyred with Nicholas RIDLEY under Queen MARY I. Ordained in 1522, he at first opposed Reformation ideas, but under the influence of the Cambridge reformer Thomas Bileny (c.1495-1531) he altered his opinions. Latimer's reforming zeal made him suspect to the ecclesiastical authorities, and he was twice imprisoned under HENRY VIII. His position improved with his defense of Henry's divorce and the king's subsequent break with Rome, following which Latimer was appointed (1535) bishop of Worcester. Latimer's career paralleled ecclesiastical developments in England. When the Roman Catholic Mary succeeded to the throne in 1553, he was confined to the Tower of London and, following a theological disputation, he was burned at the stake.

Bibliography: Chester, Allan G., *Hugh Latimer, Apostle to the English* (1954; repr. 1978); Darby, Harold S., *Hugh Latimer* (1953).

Latin America, history of

Latin America comprises the Spanish- and Portuguese-speaking areas of the Western Hemisphere—Mexico, most of Central and South America, and part of the West Indies. It is generally believed that humans first came to the Americas from Asia when a land connection existed between Siberia and Alaska; when they came is less certain, but archaeological findings indicate that humans may have been present as far back as 30,000 years ago. For thousands of years the Americas were sparsely inhabited by nomadic hunters and seed gatherers. The gradual development of cultivated plants, however, had made fairly high population densities possible in some

regions by the end of the 15th century, when European colonization began.

INDIAN CIVILIZATIONS

Three highly developed Indian cultures have attracted modern attention. These cultures are the AZTEC of central Mexico; the MAYA, who have lived since their origins until today in YUCATÁN, southern MEXICO, and GUATEMALA; and the INCAS of the Andean Highlands and coastal PERU.

Mesoamerican Civilization. The cultures of the Maya and the Aztecs are known as Middle American, or Mesoamerican, civilizations. Plants were being cultivated in MESOAMERICA at least as early as 7000 BC, although foraging and hunting were still the most important sources of food. By 3500 BC the population lived much of the year in a permanent location, and in the period 1500-900 BC a village agricultural economy was fully developed. The OLMEC culture of the southern Veracruz gulf coast is thought to have been the center from which the main Mesoamerican cultural patterns diffused.

The Maya culture, which dates from around 1200 BC, seems to have been of Olmec origin. Most of the Mayan monumental architecture, which includes pyramids and magnificently carved stelae and slabs, dates from the period AD 300-900. The Maya were responsible for great intellectual achievements, including a system of writing and a precise calendar based on a high level of mathematics.

The impressive Mayan sites were all ceremonial centers; scholars have deduced that the priesthood stood at the top of each local hierarchy. The largest center, TIKAL, reached its peak around 600-800. The Mayan centers showed no continuous settlement and were not true cities. Mayan political structure, methods of food production, and tools were typical of less advanced societies.

The exact extent of lands held by the Maya at their height is not known, but the Maya had constant contact, either cultural or commercial, with the central and coastal Mexican civilizations. Mayan civilization began to decline suddenly about 900; by 1000 much of the Yucatán was dominated by the TOLTEC. Today, however, the Mayan population is still readily identifiable, unlike the peoples who made up the Aztec state or the Inca empire at the time of Spanish conquest—probably because the Mayan lands were of less interest to the Spaniards.

In addition to the Olmec culture, the city of TEOTIHUACÁN, which flourished AD 350-650 in central Mexico, also influenced Mesoamerican civilization. The city, which became the center of a large empire, may have had a peak population of more than 150,000. Teotihuacán itself collapsed around 650. Its culture remained important, however, until its disintegration three centuries later, after a series of invasions by nomadic peoples from the north.

One northern nomadic group was the Mexica, or Meshica, later known as the Aztec. In 1325 they settled on a small island in Lake Texcoco that became the second great urban center of Mesoamerica, TENOCHTITLÁN. A series of alliances gave the Aztecs essential control of the central valley of Mexico by the 1420s. In the following years, Tenochtitlán grew from a small city-state into the center of a great empire, extending as far as present-day EL SALVADOR and Guatemala.

MONTEZUMA II, elected in 1502, was the Aztec emperor-god who was in power when the Spanish, under Hernán CORTÉS, arrived in 1519. The Spanish found in the Aztec domains an advanced civilization with an active commerce and a vast accumulation of wealth.

The military aristocrats, the priests, and the merchants held the most power, exerting authority over the freemen, who in turn ruled the landless bondsmen and slaves. For three centuries after the Spanish conquest of Tenochtitlán, the area of Aztec domination remained the focus for the Spanish occupation of America.

Andean Civilizations. When the Spanish arrived in the New World, the irrigated valleys of coastal Peru had supported agriculture for about 6,000 years. Their inhabitants had been producing finely woven cotton textiles since about 2500 BC. The most extensive of the pre-Inca coastal states, the CHIMU kingdom, had developed in these valleys; it was probably

This map of Villa de Valladolid, a Spanish settlement on the Yucatán peninsula of southeastern Mexico, dates from 1579. The Yucatán, which was the center of Mayan culture, remained unconquered for many years after the Spanish arrival in Mexico. The conquest of the Maya was finally realized in 1546, led by the conquistador Francesco de Montejo and his father. Small settlements such as this one came under the jurisdiction of the Council of the Indies, chartered in 1524 to administer Spanish colonial rule in the New World.

(Above) A 16th-century Mexican codex page shows a Spanish soldier meeting an emissary of the Aztec ruler Montezuma II.

(Below) Indians confront the Portuguese crew of Amerigo Vespucci during his 16th-century exploration of the South American continent.

consolidated in the first half of the 14th century AD.

The Incas, who were established in the valley of CUZCO after about 1250, began more extensive conquests in the early 15th century. They conquered the Chimu in the 1460s. Their northward expansion was still in progress when the Spanish, under the leadership of Francisco PIZARRO, appeared in northern Peru and, in 1532, captured the Inca king ATAHUALPA, along with a fortune in gold. The Inca empire then extended along the spine of the ANDES from the River Maule in south central CHILE to the northern border of present-day ECUADOR. At the top of the governmental hierarchy was an Inca ethnic elite in Cuzco, with a god-king at the pinnacle. By elaborate

terracing and irrigation, the Inca cultivated the mountainsides; they also erected amazing mountain citadels, including MACHU PICCHU.

COLONIAL ERA

The occupation of present-day Latin America and much of the western United States by the Spanish and Portuguese began in 1492 with the landing of Christopher COLUMBUS on SAN SALVADOR ISLAND in the Bahamas. He left a small group of settlers on the island of HISPANIOLA, and the following year he returned with a larger colonizing expedition. Columbus's first voyage was part of an effort by the Spanish kingdom of Castile to establish a sea route to the Indies in competition with the Portuguese. The Portuguese expedition of Pedro CABRAL landed at the easternmost bulge of BRAZIL in 1500, and trading posts were soon established.

The entire hemisphere became known as America once the European cosmographers became aware that a "new world" indeed existed. They used the name on their maps in honor of the Italian navigator Amerigo VESPUCCI, who mapped out the area in 1499–1501. The Treaty of TORDESILLAS (1494) had divided the world into Spanish and Portuguese halves for purposes of colonization. Vespucci, in the service of the Portuguese, determined that any lands south of the Brazilian bulge would lie in the Spanish half. Therefore, further exploration to the south was carried out by navigators working for Spain, one of whom, Ferdinand MAGELLAN, passed (1520) through the straits now bearing his name to reach the Pacific Ocean.

Portuguese Colonization. The Portuguese did not set up permanent colonies until 1532. Two permanent settlements, São Vicente (near present-day SÃO PAULO) and RECIFE, were established, and in 1549 the Portuguese crown sent a governor general to establish a capital at São Salvador, now SALVADOR, or Bahia. The Portuguese confined their settlements to the coastal area. Expeditions, known as bandeiras, however, helped establish Portugal's claim to lands lying far to the west of the line defined by the Treaty of Tordesillas. The bandeiras of the first half of the 17th century were generally forays in search of Indian slaves. Increasingly, however, these expedi-

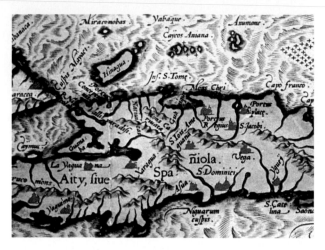

Hispaniola, the second largest island of the Caribbean, is the subject of this 15th-century map. The island was settled by Columbus on his second voyage in 1493, and it soon became the principal center for Spanish-American activity in the Caribbean. (Museo Amerigo, Madrid.)

The Spanish conquest of Cuba was initiated in 1511 by Diego de Velazquez, who subsequently founded settlements throughout the island, including Havana in 1515. This Havana street scene depicts the Spanish-dominated atmosphere of Cuba.

tions went in search of precious metals. At the end of the 17th century, after the discovery of gold fields in the present state of Minas Gerais, the first massive migration of Portuguese to America began. The capital of Brazil was moved (1763) from Bahia south to RIO DE JANEIRO, reflecting the southward shift of population and economic activity.

The first steps toward centralization of the Portuguese government along the coast were taken to expel French Huguenots who had established (1555) a colony at the site of present-day Rio de Janeiro. A more serious threat to Portugal's control over Brazil was mounted by the Dutch during the years 1580–1640, when Portugal was ruled by Spanish monarchs. The Dutch, in an effort to control the production of sugar as well as its processing and marketing in Europe, occupied the productive Portuguese sugar lands around Recife from 1630 to 1654. To the north of Brazil, the French, Dutch, and British all succeeded in establishing small colonies—FRENCH GUIANA, Dutch Guiana (now SURINAME), and British Guiana (now GUYANA). Thus, in its formative years the Portuguese colonization in America faced external threats. Spain, on the other hand, was able to establish control without serious interruptions from other European powers.

The Spanish in the Caribbean. The first focus of the Spanish occupation of America was the second largest island of the Caribbean, HISPANIOLA, which was fairly densely populated by ARAWAK tribes. The labor demands placed on them by the Spanish search for gold and their total lack of resistance to European diseases all but wiped out the Arawaks on Hispaniola. This rapid decline in the native labor source sent the Spaniards to CUBA, JAMAICA, the BAHAMA ISLANDS, and PUERTO RICO, where the native labor forces were also quickly depleted. In addition, the Spanish soon exhausted the meager gold deposits of Cuba, the largest of the Caribbean islands.

The role of Hispaniola and its capital city of SANTO DOMINGO in the conquest and colonization of continental Latin America was twofold. First, expeditions were organized and financed there. From Hispaniola and Cuba came most of the officers and men who made up the exploring expeditions to northern South America, PANAMA, Central America, Mexico, and much of what is today the United States. Second, the broad outline of the Spanish-American administrative structure was first established on Hispaniola.

An early settler's revolt against Columbus in Santo Domingo made it clear that Spaniards in America had no intention of being salaried employees or tenant farmers. They wanted wealth and control. The principal administrative instrument established to satisfy their demands was an adaptation of the old Spanish institution of the ENCOMIENDA—in essence, the allotment of a number of Indians to each settler.

As *encomendero,* the Spaniard was entitled to both personal services and tribute from Indians; in return he assumed responsibility for Christianizing them. The *encomienda* system assumed great importance on the mainland, where the high civilizations from Mexico to Peru were long accustomed to forced labor and the payment of tribute to local chiefs, who in turn made payments to the imperial hierarchy.

Once the Spaniards had exhausted the native Arawak labor supply on the islands, they began to import African slaves. The large-scale importation of African slaves for field labor did not become economically feasible, however, until plantation agriculture developed sufficiently to produce a substantial export crop of sugar during the late 17th century. This happened first in the smaller islands of the Lesser ANTILLES, settled by the British and French, and in Jamaica, invaded by the British in 1655. In the western third of Hispaniola (later HAITI), the French gradually built the most productive plantation export economy in colonial America, based on black slave labor.

In addition to the *encomienda,* a second important institution for the Spanish occupation of America was the *villa,* or city. The city was administered by a *cabildo,* or council, consisting first of elected and later of both elected and appointed members. The *cabildo* was the early Spanish settlers' chief instrument of contact with the royal government in Spain. The *cabildo* evolved into an important mechanism of local government. Although it declined in importance when Spain centralized control of its colonies, the *cabildo,* as a focus of local self-government, became a rallying point for the 19th-century nationalist movement. In the Caribbean, the city of Santo Domingo also served as the major regional administrative center. Its significance faded only when the human and mineral wealth of central Mexico and the Inca empire became evident.

Spanish Expansion. Conquests on the mainland brought the Spanish into close contact for the first time with America's high civilizations and their extraordinary mineral wealth. The conquest of Mexico began in 1519 with Cortés's capture of the Aztec king Montezuma II at Tenochtitlán. Pizarro's capture of the Inca emperor Atahualpa in 1532 led to the Inca ruler's execution and the Spanish occupation of Cuzco. In the next decades the Spaniards pushed into the areas of Chile, PARAGUAY, and COLOMBIA. Expeditions also went north into what is now the United States.

Relatively small bodies of Spanish CONQUISTADORS were able to conquer the Incas, Aztecs, and other Indian peoples quickly, for a variety of reasons. Three factors, however, seem fundamental. First, the Europeans arrived with advanced technology and domesticated animals—both of which the indigenous population found awesome. The Indians were particularly terrified to see warriors mounted on horseback. Secondly, the Spaniards brought new diseases against which the native peoples had no immunity. Third, the Aztec and Inca political structures were highly stratified, with a small and virtually impermeable group at the top of each. It was relatively easy for the conquistadors to substitute themselves at the pinnacle.

The Spanish crown spent the next 150 years establishing its own authority through an administrative structure with overlapping powers. This structure consisted of personal representatives such as viceroys and captains-general and a series of juntas ranging from the town *cabildo* through the AUDIENCIAS (royal courts of justice). The original viceroyalties were those of NEW SPAIN (1535) and Peru (1544), the former comprising all the territory north of Panama, the latter, all the territory from Panama south. Peru was later reduced by the creation of separate viceroyalties of NEW GRANADA (1717) and La Plata (1776).

In addition to the civil administration, Franciscan, Augus-

tinian, and Dominican missionaries were responsible for the Christianizing process. Some missionaries attempted to pacify the Indians by congregating them in *reducciones,* or reservations, the most notable of which were maintained by the Jesuits in Paraguay. The Jesuits also established themselves as the educators of the sons of the provincial landed aristocrats and urban merchants. The Jesuits, however, were seen as a threat to the centralized Spanish state, which, particularly after 1750, preferred to work through the hierarchy of the secular clergy (those ordained for parish service).

The crown sent its top administrators directly from Spain, and they frequently came into conflict with the criollos (CREOLES, or Spaniards born in America). An economic depression in America, the lack of technology for effective deep-vein · mining, the degeneration of the Habsburg line of Spanish rulers, and the increasing incursion of other European powers into the Caribbean trade lanes gave the regional Creole groups increasing opportunities to intrude themselves into high administrative positions.

Bourbon Reforms. When the Spanish Habsburg dynasty died out in 1700, it was replaced by that of the Bourbons, who hoped to set up a more efficient administrative structure. The impact on Spanish America was not fully felt until the 1760s, when CHARLES III sent José de Gálvez (1720–87) to New Spain as *visitador* (visitor general). The aims of the Gálvez reorganization were to replace all Creoles with new administrators, to increase revenues to Spain by reforming the tax structure and opening up intercolonial commerce, to protect frontiers in California and along the Gulf of Mexico from foreign incursions, and to expel the Jesuits on the grounds that they had effectively become a state within a state.

A number of such changes, known as the Bourbon Reforms, were put into effect throughout Spanish America in the 1770s. They produced greater revenue in bullion for Spain by revitalizing the colonial administrative system, centralizing tax collection, increasing production in the silver mines, and granting royal monopolies, particularly of tobacco. In addition, expeditions against the Indians to the north opened up new areas for future expansion, and more effective defenses provided security against other European powers.

The Bourbon Reforms, however, helped create many problems in Spanish America. For example, they drained many rural areas of the coins essential to local trade. Monopolies wiped out tobacco cultivation in all but a few designated centers. Local production of textiles and other manufactured goods was also hurt by increased imports from Spain. The exaction of surpluses and the loss of the better administrative positions hurt the prestige, and often the income, of many upper-class Creoles. This loss of long-held privileges was one factor leading such groups to urge a revolt against Spain when the occupation (1807–08) of the Iberian Peninsula by Napoleon I gave them their political opportunity. They could take encouragement from the example of Haiti, which had thrown off French rule to become (1804) the second independent nation (after the United States) in the Western Hemisphere.

WARS FOR INDEPENDENCE

The leaders of the independence movements in the areas of present-day ARGENTINA, VENEZUELA, Colombia, and Chile were people of means—usually merchants or landowners. In Mexico, however, where a populist mass uprising took place, the two most important leaders were the parish priests Miguel HIDALGO Y COSTILLA and José María MORELOS Y PAVÓN, both of whom felt they had been unjustly treated by the Spanish.

Mexico. Hidalgo led an Indian uprising in 1810 that sacked the city of Guanajuato before heading toward Mexico City under the banner of the Virgin of Guadalupe. At the same time, Morelos conducted a brilliant guerrilla campaign in the south, calling for a new government and the redistribution of wealth. Both of these priests were eventually captured and executed, Hidalgo in 1811 and Morelos in 1815, but large property owners remained in mortal fear of the Mexican masses thereafter.

The final declaration of independence in Mexico was made in 1821 by the Creole army officer Agustín de ITURBIDE, who

COLONIAL LATIN AMERICA c.1790

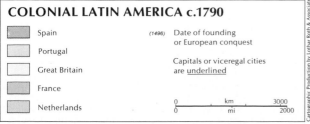

	Spain	*(1496)*	Date of founding or European conquest
	Portugal		
	Great Britain		Capitals or viceregal cities are <u>underlined</u>
	France		
	Netherlands		

0   km   3000
0   mi   2000

Cartographic Production by Lothar Roth & Associates

Separatist movements began in Mexico and other Latin American countries in reaction to Napoleon's invasion of Spain in 1808. The Mexican priest and social reformer Miguel Hidalgo y Costilla was the first revolutionary leader of the Mexican Wars for Independence. His army of Indians and peasant warriors was finally defeated by the royalist forces near Guadalajara in 1811. Hidalgo was defrocked and executed.

ruled briefly as Emperor Agustín I. He had fought against the popular insurgents, and his regime represented the interests of the traditional colonial Creole class, now unfettered by royal laws. It offered nothing to the mass of the population.

South America. The first armed efforts to defeat the Spanish in South America were organized in BUENOS AIRES, seat of the viceroyalty of La Plata, and in CARACAS, seat of a captaincy general. Both were centers of a newly emerging export economy largely in the hands of Spaniards in Venezuela and Creoles in Buenos Aires. Both armies suffered initial defeat at the hands of the Spanish, but their leaders were not captured.

In the south, the revolutionary forces reorganized under the Argentinian José de SAN MARTÍN, who, with the Chilean general Bernardo O'HIGGINS, led an attack from Mendoza across the Andes to the central valley of Chile. After the final defeat of the Spanish forces there in 1818, San Martín moved on to Peru by sea; the Spanish forces continued to hold the interior valleys.

In the north, Simón BOLÍVAR had massed an army in the Venezuelan interior and crossed the Andes to defeat the surprised Spanish forces in the Colombian highlands of Boyacá in 1819. Bolívar returned to Venezuela, where he was chosen president of the new Republic of Gran Colombia (present-day Colombia, Venezuela, Ecuador, and Panama) in 1821. With a large army, Bolívar proceeded south to Peru. After defeating the Spanish on a mountainside near Quito in 1822, Bolívar met with San Martín in Guayaquil. San Martín, who had formally declared Peru independent, then retired from public life, leaving the campaign to Bolívar and his principal lieutenant, Antonio José de SUCRE.

The merchants and landowners of Lima considered Bolívar more a troublemaking foreigner than a liberator. They wanted their pre-1750 authority reestablished and resented the separate treatment of Upper Peru (BOLIVIA). In 1826, Bolívar returned to his capital, BOGOTÁ, but, with his ideal of a single

LATIN AMERICAN INDEPENDENCE, 1810-38

✕ Battle site

1804 Date of independence

| 0 | km | 3000 |
| 0 | mi | 2000 |

continental state shattered by the strong regionalism that had emerged from a 15-year war, he was unable to keep the nation of Gran Colombia intact.

NATIONAL PERIOD

The independent nations of continental Latin America came into being within the large administrative units organized during Spanish and Portuguese rule.

Spanish-American Regionalism. During a relatively short period in the early 19th century, many areas threw off Spanish rule. In the viceroyalty of Peru, Chile became independent in 1818 and Peru in 1821. In the latter year, New Spain was transformed into Mexico and New Granada into Gran Colombia. Of the La Plata regions, Paraguay became independent in 1813, Argentina in 1816, Bolivia in 1825, and URUGUAY, after prolonged conflict with first Argentina and later Brazil, in 1828.

The overwhelming problem for most of the former Spanish territories was to establish authority over the various regions within their boundaries. Mexico quickly lost control of Guatemala, El Salvador, COSTA RICA, HONDURAS, and NICARAGUA, which banded together in the CENTRAL AMERICAN FEDERATION (1825–38) and then became separate states. The TEXAS REVOLUTION and the MEXICAN WAR (1846–48) resulted in Mexico ceding Texas, California, Arizona, and New Mexico to the United States. Like greater Mexico, Gran Colombia also disintegrated.

The early 19th century began the period of the Wars for Independence in Latin America. This relief portrays the meeting (1822) in Ecuador between the South American revolutionary leaders Símon Bolívar and José de San Martín. It was after this meeting that San Martín retired from public life, leaving the campaign for independence to Bolívar.

The Panama Canal, crossing the Isthmus of Panama and connecting the Atlantic and Pacific oceans, was constructed (1904–14) by the United States. Treaties signed in June 1978 ensured the canal's neutrality and gave Panama control of the canal on Dec. 31, 1999.

The 1960s witnessed revolutionary actions in the Dominican Republic. With the outbreak of civil war in 1965, the United States sent troops to ensure the safety of foreign nationals. The 1966 presidential election, organized by the OAS, resulted in troop withdrawal.

The secession (1830) of Venezuela and Ecuador spelled the end of Bolívar's dream. Panama also became independent (1903) of Colombia during the controversy over construction of the PANAMA CANAL.

The frontier areas of the new nations were sparsely populated, and national boundaries remained so vague that international problems ensued. Between 1879 and 1884, Chile fought against both Peru and Bolivia in the so-called War of the Pacific (see PACIFIC, WAR OF THE). The aftermath of this war was the TACNA-ARICA DISPUTE, which dragged on until 1929. Paraguay lost most of its male population in the devastating War of the Triple Alliance (1865–70; see TRIPLE ALLIANCE, WAR OF THE) against Argentina, Brazil, and Uruguay. It recovered, however, to defeat Bolivia in the CHACO WAR of 1932–35. In some instances boundary disputes between Latin American countries still remain unresolved. The early-19th-century dream of huge independent nations was largely unfulfilled in Spanish America; regional disputes displaced it.

Brazil. Portuguese America, on the other hand, was able to maintain its territorial unity despite regional variations. In 1822, Brazil became an independent empire under PEDRO I. When the empire was overthrown in 1889, and a republican government established, the states organized regional political parties. Although each party expressed local economic interests, these interests did not diverge greatly from region to region. Brazil's economy had been developed on the basis of slave labor and was confined to a relatively narrow coastal strip. The economy of the entire coast depended upon agricultural exports. Thus, each region supported the free-trade policies of the dominant world power, Britain. No national political organization emerged until the 1930s.

The Caribbean. Spain maintained Cuba and Puerto Rico as colonies until a Cuban revolt culminated in the independence of the island after the SPANISH-AMERICAN WAR of 1898. Puerto Rico then came under control of the United States. Haiti, the first nation of Latin America to establish firm independence, was also the first independent black nation in the modern world. Internal political control, however, passed back and forth between mulatto and black factions. The DOMINICAN REPUBLIC emerged from Haitian domination in 1844 but was occupied by the Spanish again during the U.S. Civil War and later was almost annexed by the United States.

The rest of the Caribbean remained in European political control and continued to be dominated by a plantation sugar economy. The older island colonies remained overwhelmingly black after the slave trade and slavery were abolished early in the 19th century. In the newer sugar colonies, such as Trinidad (see TRINIDAD AND TOBAGO), the large-scale introduction of East Indian indentured labor in the late 19th century resulted in racially divided populations.

Political and Socioeconomic Development. During the first half century of independence, the Latin American nations suffered from the debilitating effects of the long independence struggle, a lack of recognized political legitimacy at the national level, and localized economic development. These factors, along with local control of militia units, resulted in a diffusion of political power. Traditional Creole governments found it difficult to maintain control without the support of a national military leader, or CAUDILLO, often of MESTIZO (mixed European and American Indian) origin. In Mexico, Antonio López de SANTA ANNA emerged five times to provide the needed central authority; Venezuela's government called on José Antonio PÁEZ to maintain control.

Conservative political ideology was increasingly challenged by liberals, generally urban Creoles, who enjoyed an upsurge of influence in the mid-19th century. Liberal attacks helped to remove the Roman Catholic church from its traditional status in most Latin American nations by the end of the century. Countering liberal trends in the latter half of the century, some caudillos postponed elections until economic development could be consolidated. Mexico's Porfirio DÍAZ is a major example. Some former liberals, most notably Antonio GUZMÁN BLANCO in Venezuela, adopted a similar expediency.

In the last quarter of the 19th century the center of population in South America moved from the Pacific to the Atlantic coast. The economic boom generated by agricultural and processed exports to Europe increased the demand for labor in Argentina, Uruguay, and Brazil. A massive European migration from Italy, Spain, Portugal, and Germany resulted. The new immigrants settled in major cities, and by the time of World War I, a strong majority of the population of Buenos Aires was foreign born.

At about the same time, many nations began to build up their professional military forces to help elected civilian governments maintain control of the state. The professionalized army offered an attractive career to the children of immigrants. The strengthened armies, with their monopoly of modern weaponry, and the improvement in national transportation systems helped make the rise of a new type of caudillo possible.

The new officer class needed only a major crisis to assert its power and replace a political system that it considered inefficient. That crisis was offered by the worldwide Depression of the 1930s. In Brazil, Getúlio VARGAS instituted a form of state corporatism, *Estado Nova*, which relied on military support. In Argentina a series of army coups brought the rise of Juan PERÓN, whose first regime (1946–55), despite its considerable popular support, was a thinly disguised military dictatorship. Such dictators sought the support of urban labor rather than the support of the Indian and mestizo peasantry. Before the

The Marxist president of Chile, Salvador Allende (left), was deposed in a coup that ended his attempt to establish Chile as a socialist state. Apparent CIA connivance at Allende's 1973 overthrow renewed controversy concerning U.S. interference in Latin America.

1950s, only in Mexico had the peasants played a crucial political role and won substantial redistribution of the land.

With the victory of the Western democracies and the USSR over the fascist regimes in Europe during World War II, many Latin American governments came under attack for persistent inequalities. The success of Fidel CASTRO's revolution (1959) in Cuba, which soon joined the Communist bloc of nations, increased the pressure for social and economic reform. At the same time, however, it intensified the fear of left-wing revolution, a fear shared by the powerful United States, which sent troops into the Dominican Republic in 1965, apparently connived in the overthrow of the popularly elected Salvador ALLENDE in Chile in 1973, and in the 1980s supported anti-Marxist Nicaraguan rebels. (A peace plan to end that conflict was presented in 1987.) Also in the 1980s, the U.S. dispatch of military aid to the government of El Salvador signaled an end to the earlier U.S. policy of making its support of Latin American governments dependent on the latter's promotion of social reform and respect for human rights.

Contemporary Concerns. The nations of Latin America have a strong sense of nationalism. Territorial challenges continue in the boundary dispute between Peru and Ecuador (another between Argentina and Chile was settled in 1985) and the claim to BELIZE by Guatemala (under discussion in 1988 by a joint commission representing the two nations and Britain). The principle of national sovereignty also lay behind Latin America's support of Panama in its negotiations with the United States that resulted in the Panama Canal Treaty of 1977–78, granting Panama full control of the canal by 2000.

Economic development has dominated both domestic politics and international relations in Latin America since the 1940s; all governments have attempted to spur industrialization. Governments of both the right and left have been convinced that their sovereignty has been infringed on by international corporations whose investments in Latin America have not given priority to national development problems. In some countries, foreign-controlled extractive industries, such as copper, petroleum, and iron, have been nationalized.

Populous nations, such as Brazil and Mexico, with their large internal markets, had fared better than most other countries until their massive foreign debts, the largest in Latin America, hampered progress. Latin American nations have attempted to expand the market for their manufactured products by establishing regional customs unions, such as the Central American Common Market, the Andean Group, and CARICOM in the Caribbean. In international politics, economic problems have caused Latin America to identify its interest more with the Third World nations than with the centers of industrial production—particularly since the severe foreign-debt crisis of the 1980s.

Latin America's rapid population growth makes it difficult to mount a competitive capital-intensive technology and to provide adequate social services. Redistributing the land into smaller units is difficult when the expanding urban population makes large holdings necessary to produce food efficiently.

Proposals for combining economic development with social change have been put forward by certain Latin American governments, which since 1980 have shifted markedly from military to democratic, attempting a variety of social and economic programs. Despite such efforts, an ongoing, many-faceted problem in certain Latin countries is massive illegal drug trafficking. Especially active in the growth, processing, and exporting of drugs are Colombia, Bolivia, Mexico, and Panama, where in 1988 strongman Gen. Manuel Antonio Noriega was under a U.S. indictment for conspiring with drug dealers.

Economic independence appears at least as difficult to obtain as was political independence during the 1800s. The struggle is likely to continue, with the Latin American countries operating as a cultural-economic unit whenever it seems advantageous, but proceeding on individual routes, such as moves toward bilateral trade agreements, when they seem to serve particular national interests.   JOHN P. HARRISON

Bibliography: Bethell, Leslie, ed., *The Cambridge History of Latin America*, 5 vols. (1985–86); Bushnell, D., and Macaulay, N., *The Emergence of Latin America in the Nineteenth Century* (1987); Crow, J. A., *The Epic of Latin America* (1980); Falcoff, Mark, et al., *The Crisis in Latin America* (1984); Lowenthal, A. F., *Partners in Conflict: The United States and Latin America* (1987); McAlister, Lyle N., *Spain and Portugal in the World, 1492–1700* (1984); Rouquié, Alain, *The Military and the State in Latin America*, trans. by P. E. Sigmund (1987); Skidmore, Thomas E., and Smith, Peter H., *Modern Latin America* (1984).

Latin American art and architecture

Latin American art and architecture refers to the artistic traditions developed by the European colonizers of Mexico, Central America, and South America, and their descendants. Since the European discovery of the New World, the art and architecture of this vast area has evolved in two phases. The first was the colonial phase, beginning late in the 15th century and ending early in the 19th century, after the wars for independence were concluded. In Mexico the Revolution of the early 20th century marked the beginning of the second phase—the emergence of modern developments in architecture, painting, and sculpture. The rest of Latin America entered this phase at various times, although generally soon after it had begun in Mexico.

Highly developed civilizations existed in the New World thousands of years before the arrival of Europeans. Pre-Columbian American centers of great importance flourished in the Andes, central Mexico, and the MAYA area (Yucatán and Central America) up until the time of the Spanish conquest of the AZTECS (1519–21) and of the INCA (1531). On the desert coast of Peru the ruins of sun-dried mud brick buildings carved with polychromed relief sculptures can still be seen at CHAN CHAN (AD 1200–1450) and other sites; remains of expertly cut stone constructions exist at Cuzco, MACHU PICCHU (AD 1450–1532), and elsewhere in the Andean highlands. In Mexico pyramids of earthen rubble faced with stone and finished with brilliantly painted plaster dominated the architecture of the pre-Columbian period. TEOTIHUACÁN, a great urban center of the central valley of Mexico (200 BC–AD 750), was larger in area than Imperial Rome. A place of pilgrimage for many ancient peoples of Mesoamerica, it was a magnificent city of streets and palaces punctuated by pyramids and plazas laid out around a great central axis.

Generally characteristic of PRE-COLUMBIAN ART AND ARCHITECTURE was its skillful integration of architecture, sculpture, and painting into a style that presents a unique synthesis of all three aesthetic forms. This synthesizing tendency is also seen in the baroque style that appeared during the colonial period; it is likewise characteristic of much modern Latin American architecture even today.

Few of the native-American arts lasted long after the conquest. One of the best documented examples of a native art surviving past the 16th century is the art of manuscript paint-

(Right) *The ancient Inca site of Machu Picchu (AD 1450–1532), located near Cuzco, Peru, contains superb examples of Inca masonry construction and agricultural terracing.*

(Below) *This 16th-century painted wooden figure of San Guillermo from Quito, Ecuador, is representative of the statuary from the colonial period in Latin America.*

(Below) *The Codex Borbonicus is one of four surviving pre-Columbian Aztec painted manuscripts. (Bibliothèque du Palais Bourbon, Paris.)*

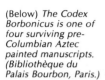

ing practiced among the Indians of Mexico. The earlier pre-Columbian styles with their abstract rendering of human figures gradually gave way to a more European approach to forms, the handling of the brush and pen, and even the use of European paper instead of tree bark and other native materials. Another survival of the pre-Columbian period in Mexico was the making of feather mosaics. Here the artists changed from making garments for the Aztec rulers and nobility to making decorations for bishops' miters and for other Christian ecclesiastical objects. In Peru the *keru*, a flared wooden drinking vessel decorated with carved and painted designs in the Inca tradition, continued into the colonial period with few changes except in subject matter.

Folk art traditions that began in the 16th century became widespread throughout Latin America. They represent an art based on the copying of styles over long periods of time in isolation from the innovating impulses emanating from vital artistic centers. The Santos, polychrome paintings and sculptures of saints, executed in a notably reverential yet primitive style, are typical examples of folk art, as is the carved facade of the Cathedral of Zacatecas (1752) in Mexico. Many church exteriors in the Andes region exhibit relief patterns resembling those found in local textiles. This distinctive folk style is sometimes called *mestizo* ("mixed") art because it combines traditional Indian features with Christian elements. Its main centers were the Peruvian towns of Ayacucho and Arequipa.

COLONIAL PERIOD

During the colonial period cities of great architectural splendor as well as local schools of painting and sculpture arose, especially in those parts of Latin America where the pre-Hispanic civilizations had thrived at the time of the conquest. In Peru the main Inca center of Cuzco became in the colonial period a splendid city with great churches, monastic buildings, and palaces. The School of Cuzco, a major colonial painting tradition noted for its profuse use of gold leaf, also developed there. TENOCHTITLÁN, the Aztec capital, became Mexico City, the seat of the richest New World viceroyalty (that of New Spain) and an archbishopric; it is still sometimes called the City of Palaces, and its school of painting became the most important in the colonial world. Cities that became in effect cultural satellites of these two early capitals include Bogotá and Quito for Cuzco and Puebla and Oaxaca for Mexico City. Colonial Buenos Aires in Argentina, Santiago in Chile, Monterrey in Mexico, and Antigua in Guatemala were

more or less frontier towns by comparison, depending primarily on mining, trade, or administration rather than cultural ascendancy for their importance in colonial times.

Unlike the other major New World colonies, the former Portuguese colony of Brazil was built upon no preexisting high Indian culture. Nevertheless, the architecture, painting, and sculpture of its principal colonial centers—Bahia, Recife, Belém—as well as of its mining towns in the province of Minas Gerais—all bear the imprint of having been created in a metropolitan environment rather than in provincial outposts. Perhaps the strict ties maintained between Lisbon and the overseas world helped keep Brazil abreast of European trends in the plastic arts; by contrast, in Mexico and Peru, where somewhat greater autonomy was given the local government, the arts remained in general more remote and more provincial in style.

Sixteenth Century. The 16th century marked the construction of a wide range of public building (of which few are still standing); many monastic establishments, mainly by the Augustinian, Dominican, and Franciscan men's orders; and the beginnings of the great cathedrals. The early military conquerors and religious orders in the New World brought with them works of art—paintings and sculptures—as well as knowledge of the main architectural styles then current in Spain. These styles included Late Gothic vaulted churches with pointed arches, buttresses, and traceried windows.

The Late Gothic style, dominant in the early monastic establishments, was often conjoined with external facades and interior altarpieces designed in the Plateresque, or early Renaissance, style of Spain. This combination of styles appears in the cathedral of Santo Domingo on Hispaniola, the oldest cathedral in the New World, begun in 1512. By the end of the 16th century more advanced construction techniques appeared and a number of triple nave cathedrals on a basilica plan were built, including those at Mexico City, Guadalajara, and Puebla, the latter designed by Claudio de Arciniega (*c.*1528–93).

Another style the Spanish brought to their new colonies was called Mudéjar, meaning the style of Moorish artisans working for Christians. The most prevalent form of Mudéjar art to reach the New World, seen especially in South America and in the Carribean Islands, are the elaborate carved and painted coffered ceilings with exposed wooden beams. These ceilings are decorated with abstract Moorish motifs that fea-

The architecture of Lima, Peru, the capital of Spain's New World empire until the 19th century, possesses a more profound Spanish influence than other Peruvian cities where Indian culture maintained its identity. The Palace of the Archbishop of Lima reflects Moorish architectural styles, duplicating contemporaneous building motifs in Spain.

right angles with a main plaza in the heart of the town. On this plaza were built the parish church or, depending on the importance of the town, cathedral, and other public buildings such as the city hall and jail, residences for important royal officials, and in the case of a cathedral town, the palace of the bishop or archbishop.

In painting, frescoes decorating some of the earliest colonial paintings were executed in grisaille (shades of grey that create the illusion of sculpture). Sixteenth-century painters who migrated from Europe included Italian-born Bernardo Bitti (1548–1610) in South America, and in Mexico, Flemish-born Simón Pereyns (active second half of the 16th century). Both painted in the Mannerist style characterized by attenuated body proportions, small heads, and a kind of withdrawn facial expression, as in Pereyns's *St. Christopher* (1588; Mexico Cathedral). In the colonies as in Spain, the subject matter of painting was mainly of a religious nature—saints of the church and scenes illustrating the life of Christ and the Virgin. Secular subjects were limited to portraits, and landscapes were unknown.

Seventeenth and Eighteenth Centuries. From the beginning of the 17th century to the end of the colonial period, the baroque styles dominated the artistic life of the Spanish and Portuguese colonies. Several phases of the baroque style are clearly evident in the monumental architecture and in the carved wooden retables (altarpieces) of the colonial church. The baroque retable is a painted and gilded screenlike construction placed behind the altar and often reaching from floor to ceiling. In the early 17th century appeared the so-called salamonic column, derived from the European Plateresque tradition. This spiral-shaped column, profusely carved with flower and fruit motifs, became a primary element in the 17th-century baroque altarpiece. The arrangement of the columns in relation to the wall behind them became markedly dynamic, with surface texture and color playing an important decorative role. Walls no longer appeared as flat surfaces but as convex and concave curves as the columns were projected further in space and piled one before or on top of another.

Colonial architectural projects were greatly expanded in the 18th century. Universities and other educational buildings were raised, as were numerous parish churches in the rich mining towns such as Taxco and Guanajuato in Mexico. Typically they were built on a cruciform plan with a dome over the crossing of nave and transepts. Golden altars were richly adorned with paintings and lifelike polychromed sculptures often garbed in silk, satin, or velvet garments.

ture interpenetrating linear designs meeting in elaborate star patterns. Modeled stucco decoration also using Moorish designs often appears on the outer walls of buildings. In Lima palaces having shuttered wooden balconies are reminiscent of the Moslem world of Spain or North Africa.

Throughout the colonial period, beginning with the first foundation of cities, military architecture played an important role. The castles and fortified city walls and forts of Havana, Cuba; Acapulco, Mexico; Lima, Peru; Veracruz, Mexico; Panama City; and San Juan, Puerto Rico, are among the major works of military architecture designed to protect the colonies from marauding pirates or foreign navies in time of war.

City planning was also of great importance because so many new towns and villages had to be founded from early in the colonial period. In Mexico, for instance, the Spaniards frequently relocated Indian villages from the low-lying hills to open and accessible locations so that they could be better controlled. When the new village or, as in the case of Puebla, Mexico, new town was laid out it followed the regular European Renaissance plan—a gridiron of streets intersecting at

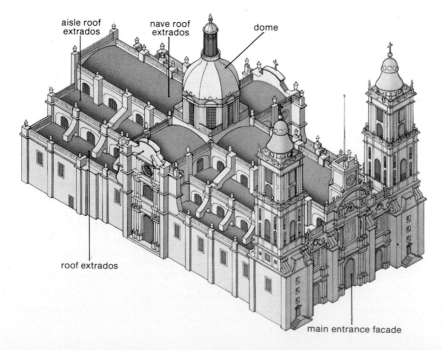

The Cathedral of Mexico City (1563–1667), which was built on the site of an ancient Aztec temple, is the largest church in Mexico. As master of architecture to King Philip II of Spain, Alonso Pérez de Castañeda based his design for the cathedral on the style of the 16th-century Jaén Cathedral in Spain. The cathedral plan is basilicalike and involves a fusion of architectural styles from Gothic to baroque. In the late 18th and early 19th centuries, the Spanish architect Manuel Tolsa designed the dome and lantern, along with adding exterior ornamentation and the clock on the cathedral's main facade.

(Left) *Churrigueresque style developed during the Spanish rococo period when architectural style was characterized by a baroque manner. The 18th-century facade of San Cayetano in Guanajuato, Mexico, exemplifies the influence that the style had on Spanish colonial architecture. The facade emphasizes rhythm and movement rather than a strict linear execution.*

(Right) *This 17th-century gilt-stucco relief of the Tree of Jesse is from the vault of Santo Domingo in Oaxaca, Mexico. Mexican art of this period was based on baroque styles, and interior design was characterized by ornamental facings in carved wood or stucco.*

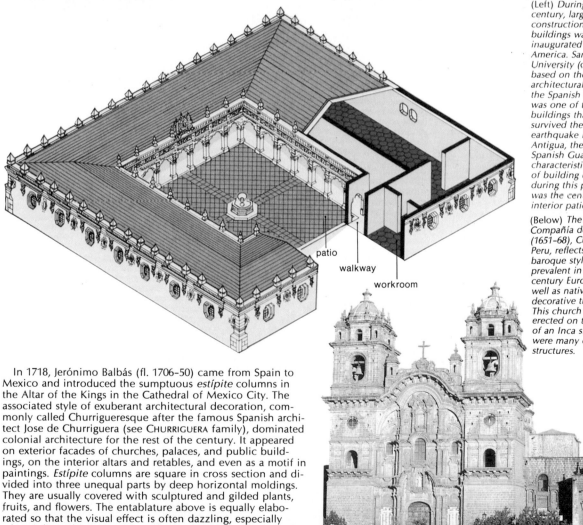

patio
walkway
workroom

(Left) *During the 18th century, large-scale construction of public buildings was inaugurated in Latin America. San Carlos University (c.1763), based on the architectural style of the Spanish baroque, was one of the few buildings that survived the 1773 earthquake in Antigua, the capital of Spanish Guatemala. A characteristic element of building design during this period was the central interior patio.*

(Below) *The Compañía de Jesús (1651–68), Cuzco, Peru, reflects the baroque style prevalent in 17th-century Europe as well as native decorative traditions. This church was erected on the ruins of an Inca site, as were many colonial structures.*

In 1718, Jerónimo Balbás (fl. 1706–50) came from Spain to Mexico and introduced the sumptuous *estípite* columns in the Altar of the Kings in the Cathedral of Mexico City. The associated style of exuberant architectural decoration, commonly called Churrigueresque after the famous Spanish architect Jose de Churriguera (see CHURRIGUERA family), dominated colonial architecture for the rest of the century. It appeared on exterior facades of churches, palaces, and public buildings, on the interior altars and retables, and even as a motif in paintings. *Estípite* columns are square in cross section and divided into three unequal parts by deep horizontal moldings. They are usually covered with sculptured and gilded plants, fruits, and flowers. The entablature above is equally elaborated so that the visual effect is often dazzling, especially when it lines the entire side wall of a church or the main altar in the apse.

The erection of countless palaces in the cities and grand haciendas in the country marked the agricultural wealth of the colonists in the 18th century. As seen in the elegant house of the Marqués de Jaral de Berrio (c.1760; Mexico City), the city palace typically had a large formal patio in the front part of the building with an entrance from the street large enough to admit horses and carriages. The formal staircase of the first patio led to the formal rooms on the first floor—dining room, salon, sitting rooms, bedrooms, and in the most affluent houses, even a private chapel. Other patios followed in the plan, often one for the stables and carriage house, one for the kitchen, and another for the laundry and other services. The sculptural decoration on the palace walls followed generally that used in churches—salamonic columns in the 17th and *estípite* columns in the 18th century. In addition to architectural sculpture on the exterior facade the family coat of arms invariably appeared and often, in a niche, the patron saint of the builder.

Portrait painting became immensely popular in the late 17th and 18th centuries. Wealthy members of the colonial nobility posed in all of their most rich and formal finery—silks from China, pearls from the Pacific, and the insignias of knighthood and nobility from Spain or Portugal. The foreground of such full-length or half-length portraits often includes a large painted shield or cartouche with the sitter's names and titles. An important Mexican painter was Baltasar de Echave Ibia (c.1585–c.1645), son of the Spanish-born painter Baltasar de Echave Orio (c.1548–1620) and father of the painter Baltasar de Echave Rioja (1632–82). Other prominent painters of the school of Mexico City were Cristobal de Villalpando (c.1652–1714) and Miguel Cabrera (1695–1768).

The main contribution of Brazil to the art of the baroque period was its magnificent churches and the sculptural creations of Antonio Francisco Lisboa, known as ALEIJADINHO. Brazilian architects endowed their churches with a forceful spatial expressiveness through the use of interconnecting oval interior spaces and contrasting concave and convex exterior walls. The octagonal nave, as seen in São Pedro dos Clérigos (1728) at Recife, was basic to much Brazilian church architecture. After 1755 the province of Minas Gerais became the center of architectural activity. Several churches were built at Ouro Prêto, including the São Francisco di Assis (1766–94), brilliantly decorated with carvings in wood and soapstone by Aleijadinho. His most renowned works are the dramatic statues of the Twelve Prophets at Congohas do Campo (1800–05), which highlight the monumental staircase leading to the church of Bom Jesus de Matozinhos.

POSTCOLONIAL PERIOD

At the end of the 18th century the Spanish colonies received a royal order to cease building altarpieces in the opulent

The Prophet Daniel (1800–05) is one of the Twelve Prophets at Congohas do Campo created by the Brazilian architect and sculptor Antonio Francisco Lisboa, called o Aleijadinho ("The Little Cripple"). The most influential and widely acclaimed sculptor of colonial Brazil, Aleijadinho produced works of great sensitivity reflecting the vivid emotionality and dramatic movement characteristic of baroque sculpture.

estípite style and also to destroy the ones in use and replace them with more chaste altars. Polychromed sculpture, lavish use of paintings, and the overwhelming profusion of gilding were all to be discontinued; the architectural elements were thenceforth to be made of white marble, alabaster, or of wood painted white to imitate marble. Columns were to be made in the simple forms associated with classical antiquity; the baroque predilection for carving plant decorations on the shaft was to be eliminated. This largely French-derived neoclassical style, reflected in such buildings as the College of Mines palace (1797–1813; Mexico City), emerged in both the Hispanic and Brazilian colonies in the late 18th and early 19th centuries, forming a bridge between the colonial period and the period of Latin American independence, which began in 1821.

Nineteenth Century. Architectural activity remained rather limited until the latter part of the 19th century, when the disturbances of the immediate postindependence period had abated and a new prosperity gained ground in Latin America. During the renewed period of building, new technologies

(Far left) Mexico's distinctive folk art has flourished since ancient times and has retained many preconquest characteristics. This scene of rural life, executed in bright colors on treated tree bark, epitomizes the vitality and originality of the Mexican folk art tradition.

(Left) The tradition of making handpainted wood and porcelain dolls has been part of Peruvian folk culture since the Spanish conquest. This elaborately costumed angel, depicted in a realistic style, was made by the 20th-century folk artist Hilario Mendivil.

David Alfaro Siqueiros is one of the original innovators in mural art, which dominates the postrevolutionary era of Mexican art. Siqueiros's abstract vision of natural unity is depicted in his mural The March of Humanity in Latin America. *(1971; Parque de Lama, Mexico City.)*

Diego Rivera's mural March to Tenochtitlan *(1929–35, 1944–50) is one of the scenes of Mexican history portrayed by the artist for the Palacio Nacional in Mexico City. Rivera's social emphasis and his bold narrative style made him one of Mexico's greatest mural painters.*

such as plumbing, electrical equipment, and elevators were imported from Europe or the United States. Another import was the eclectic style associated with the École des Beaux Arts of Paris. Decorative detailing is rich and varied in this Beaux Arts style, as exemplified in the Venetian Gothic–styled post office in Mexico City and, on a corner diagonally across from it, the baroque national theater (now the Palacio de Bellas Artes), both by the architect Adamo Boari. Bronze or wrought-iron balustrades, carved marble facades, finely finished interior wood paneling, as well as matching rugs, furniture, and draperies were all part of the architectural program in the many Beaux Arts–inspired urban buildings of the late 19th century. The Art Nouveau style stemming from France was also widespread at the turn of the century, although this phase of Latin American architecture has been little studied.

Latin American painting in the 19th century can be divided into three major categories: academic painting sponsored by the government or by members of the ruling elite; folk art, continuing the strong currents of popular art that originated in the earliest days of the colonies; and a new element, the painting of everyday life in Latin America by European or North American artists traveling through the New World.

Academic painting in Mexico reflected the styles of academic painting that arose in Europe. Early in the 19th century neoclassicism was introduced, the foremost representative being the Mexican painter Rafael Jimeno y Planes (1759–1825), who decorated (1810) the dome of the cathedral of Mexico City. A revival of the baroque in the mid- and late-19th century was characterized by the use of light and shade and by large, complex compositions depicting historical subjects. Whereas in Europe classical Greek or Roman subjects were generally portrayed, in Latin America subjects from its own past were favored, including scenes of Christopher Columbus, the Catholic kings, and other subjects from Spanish history. Uniquely New World subjects such as the invention of pulque (a Mexican fermented beverage) or the torture of Cuauhtemoc (an Aztec ruler) were also depicted, especially in Mexico.

Landscape painters also found much of their inspiration in European art styles . The landscapes of the great Mexican master José María VELASCO stand out as among the most impressive paintings of their genre in the European tradition on either side of the Atlantic. In such works as *The Valley of*

Mexico Seen from the Hill of Guadaloupe (1905; Museo Nacional de Arte Moderno, Mexico City), foreground details studied with the care of a geologist or a botanist appear alongside a sweeping distant view of almost epic dimensions.

Nineteenth-century folk art is represented not only by the continuation of rather stiff portraits but also by increasing numbers of *Ex-Votos,* a type of religious painting still being produced today. The *Ex-Voto* is rendered to offer thanks for a miraculous intervention by a particular saint or image of the Christ. Usually the account of what happened and the nature of the intercession is written out in detail, including the date and place in which the event occurred.

Among foreign artists who painted Latin American subjects were the German Johann Rugendas (1802–58) and the Englishmen Daniel Egerton (d. 1842) and Frederick CATHERWOOD, who excelled in making extraordinarily accurate views of Mayan ruins. The painters of the customs of the people, sometimes linked with native painters of similar subject matter who were called *costumbristas,* delighted in the picturesque character of country life. In Argentina they painted gauchos on the pampas, colonial buildings, and festive local costumes.

Twentieth Century. Following the Mexican Revolution of 1910 an entirely new trend emerged in Latin American art and architecture—first in Mexico and at various times thereafter in other Latin American countries. The academic salon painting of Hispanic or pre-Hispanic historical subjects disappeared from the scene. In its place mural painting portraying the revolution emerged as the representative type. While the Parisian school was experimenting with cubism and collages and the Bauhaus group in Germany was creating abstract geometric exercises in retreat from human meaning and significance, the Mexicans were returning to representational traditions of Late Gothic and Renaissance Italy—paintings with didactic, humanistic meaning, now charged with clear political overtones. Like the great quatrocento masters of the Italian Renaissance, the major Mexican muralists—Diego RIVERA, José Clemente OROZCO, and David Alfaro SIQUEIROS—painted large-scale figures using the fresco method; integrated painting into the framework of architecture; and recounted for the people large historical epics, the one religious, the other of contemporary history.

Diego Rivera, the most politically oriented of the three, painted dramatic scenes from the Mexican Revolution (such as the 1923–28 cycle in Mexico City's Ministry of Public Education building) and made comments on the life of his times in a style similar to that of the Renaissance. His clear figures were painted in a linear fashion and arranged in a series of planes, sometimes with landscape backgrounds derived from the majestic visions of the valley of Mexico conceived by Velasco. Orozco painted in a more baroque or expressionist style with great swirls of color defining the figures in painterly rather than linear fashion, as in his murals for the National Preparatory School (1923–26; Mexico City). Whereas Rivera suggests the careful and conscientious reporter, Orozco seems more like the epic poet, and Siqueiros, who also painted in an expressionistic, highly dynamic style, seems more like the intense pamphleteer. The artistic energy represented by the work of these three men surfaced in an entire school of painters, all focusing on the human form as their main artistic motif, some in terms of history, some in terms of sociological significance, some as painters of scenes from Mexican life and lore, some even as surrealists.

Cándido PORTINARI is the most widely recognized of Brazil's recent painters. A true modernist, he did fresco murals as well as panel paintings of the Brazilian people, especially cowboys and city workers. Although he was trained in Paris he abandoned his academic French training once he returned to Rio, where he developed his peculiarly Brazilian style. Emilio Pettoruti (1892–   ), on the other hand, studied for 12 years in Europe and on his return to Argentina continued as one of the foremost continental avant-garde painters. His cubist-styled painting *The Quintet* (1927; San Francisco Museum of Art) is startlingly similar to the work of Picasso. Other well-known avant-garde painters include the Chilean Roberto MATTA ECHAURREN and the Cuban Raúl Martinez (1927–   ).

Modern architecture in Latin America began as early as the 1920s with the functionalist principles of such Mexican architects as Juan O'GORMAN and José Villagrán Garcia (1901–   ). In Brazil the construction of the new Ministry of Education and Health building (1934–43; Rio de Janeiro) clearly signaled the inception of the modern international style. Among the participating architects were Lúcio COSTA, Oscar NIEMEYER, and Alfonso Eduardo Reidy (1909–64); Le Corbusier came from France to act as consultant.

Contemporary architecture in Latin America for the last several decades has been as vital as the architecture of the United States and Europe and, in some respects, even more imaginative. An almost baroque use of curving walls and dynamic definitions of internal and external space are found in much Latin American architecture, notably that of the Mexican architect Félix CANDELA. Furthermore, throughout much of Latin America the climate is so mild and even tropical that an openness to the environment unknown and impossible in Europe or the United States dominates design. The combination of painted murals or mosaic-work with sculpture often forms an integral part of the architecture, as in O'Gorman's mosaic-filled Library Building at the monumentally planned University of Mexico (1953), designed principally by Mario Pani (1911–   ) and Enrique de Moral (1907–   ). The University City in Caracas, Venezuela, built (1950–57) by Carlos Raúl VILLANUEVA, is another example of the focused campus in place of the older tradition of the university occupying scattered buildings in the heart of a metropolis.

Perhaps the greatest urban design of this century in Latin America and one of the major examples of urban planning in the world is that of Brasília, the new inland capital of Brazil by Lúcio Costa (1957). Here an entire city, with all of its administrative, legislative, and executive functions clearly planned, was designed to bring the life of Brazil inland from the old coastal cities of the colonial period. Most of the individual buildings have been executed since 1960, by Oscar Niemeyer.

DONALD AND MARTHA ROBERTSON

Bibliography: Bullrich, Francisco, *New Directions in Latin American Architecture* (1969); Castedo, Leopoldo, *A History of Latin American Art and Architecture from Pre-Columbian Times to the Present,* ed. and trans. by Phyllis Freeman (1969); Catlin, Stanton L., and Grieder, Terence, *The Art of Latin America since Independence,* rev. ed. (1966); Chase, Gilbert, *Contemporary Art in Latin America: Painting, Graphic Art, Sculpture and Architecture* (1970); Edwards, Emily, *Painted Walls of Mexico from Prehistoric Times until Today* (1966); Hitchcock, Henry-Russell, *Latin American Architecture since 1945,* 2d ed. (1972); Kelmen, Pal, *Art of the Americas, Ancient and Hispanic,* with a Comparative Chapter on the Philippines (1969) and *Baroque and Rococo in Latin America,* 2 vols., 2d ed. (1967); Kubler, George A., *Mexican Architecture of the Sixteenth Century,* 2 vols. (1948; repr. 1972), and, with Martin Soria, *Art and Architecture in Spain and Portugal and Their American Dominions, 1500 to 1800* (1959); Mann, Graciela, *The 12 Prophets of Aleijadinho* (1967); Museum of Modern Art in collaboration with the Mexican government, *Twenty Centuries of Mexican Art* (1940); Robertson, Donald, *Mexican Manuscript Painting of the Early Colonial Period: The Metropolitan Schools* (1959); Wethey, Harold E., *Colonial Architecture and Sculpture in Peru* (1949; repr. 1971).

Latin American Integration Association

On Aug. 12, 1980, the members of the Latin American Free Trade Association (LAFTA)—Argentina, Bolivia, Brazil, Chile, Colombia, Ecuador, Mexico, Paraguay, Peru, Uruguay, and Venezuela—signed a treaty that transformed LAFTA into the Latin American Integration Association. The intention of LAFTA, established in 1960, had been to eliminate tariff barriers between all members—originally by 1972, later by 1980. Failure to make substantial progress toward this goal was attributed in part to the differing levels of development among its members. The Latin American Integration Association, therefore, provides for tariff concessions to be made individually, taking into account each country's economic level. Continuing in existence within the association is the Andean Group, constituted in 1969 to promote regional integration. Its members are Bolivia, Colombia, Ecuador, Peru, and Venezuela; Chile withdrew in 1976.

Latin American literature

As the result of a boom in novel writing during the 1960s, Latin American literature finally captured world attention in the second half of the 20th century. Latin American novels, quickly translated into the major Western languages, caught the attention of critics and public alike both for the originality of their topics—all part of the present reality of Latin America—and for their rich, innovative styles. Despite earlier acknowledgement that Latin America had a substantial literary output, it took the "novels of the boom" to demonstrate that Latin American works were more than simply regional products and that many, in fact, altered the course of world literature.

Native and Early Colonial Writings. Except for the romances of chivalry they knew so well, and, to a lesser extent, the Bible, the Europeans who first came to Latin America in the 15th and 16th centuries had no literary models on which to

Alvorada Palace, the Brazilian presidential residence, is located in the inland capital city of Brasília. The palace is one of the many buildings designed for the city since 1960 by the architect Oscar Niemeyer. Brasília's master plan was laid out (1957) by Lúcio Costa.

base descriptions of what they found. Christopher Columbus and Amerigo Vespucci therefore described Latin America in terms of the literature they were familiar with. The chronicles of the first conquerors and colonizers likewise contain accounts of feats of courage and bouts of despair that are half-real, half-imagined in the light of the books they had read at home. The land and its inhabitants were often described in idealized terms that suggested the influence of the popular European notion of the noble savage. In practice, however, the natives were enslaved through excessive labor, and their cultures desecrated.

The degree of civilization represented by the indigenous tribes living in the New World varied widely. Some examples of the great Maya, Inca, and Aztec civilizations were preserved thanks to the efforts of sympathetic friars. The Maya sacred book *Popol Vuh* (Eng. trans., 1950), containing their philosophy, cosmology, and history, is an example of this extraordinary culture. The Franciscan Fray Bernardino de Sahagún (*c.*1500–90) wrote a history of New Spain, as Mexico was then called, basing his observations on material in Nahuatl, the language of the Aztecs; and a mestizo from the viceroyalty of Peru, Garcilaso Inca de la Vega, wrote his *Royal Commentaries* (1609–17; Eng. trans., 1869–71) to record life in pre-Columbian Peru as well as the conquest and civil wars that followed.

Most Latin American literature in the 16th and 17th centuries attempted to describe the newly conquered lands for the European reader. Writers wavered between awestruck amazement and hyperbolic language when describing the exotic birds, the vibrant hues of tropical plants, the strange inhabitants, and their rites and temples; at the same time, they recorded and sometimes enhanced their own major feat, the conquest. Perhaps the most engrossing account of this event is given by Bernal Díaz del Castillo (*c.*1492–1584) in his *The True Story of the Conquest of Mexico* (1632; Eng. trans., 1956). This amazing chronicle vividly recalls the adventures of the author as a young soldier in the army of Cortés. The writer's memory is prodigious, his writing lively and unencumbered by erudite pretentions.

Although the largest number of works dealt with the conquest as a feat of courage and faith, critics of the enterprise were not lacking. Fray Bartolomé de LAS CASAS, the most distinguished and successful critic, in his *Brevísima relación de la destrucción de las Indias* (1552; trans. 1953 as *The Tears of the Indians*) indicted the Spanish crown and its representatives for their maltreatment and eventual decimation of the native population. His advocacy prompted the king in Madrid to issue ordinances to temper the abuses perpetrated against the Indians.

Once colonization ended, picaresque accounts of travel and adventure, such as that written in 1690 by the Mexican Carlos de SIGÜENZA Y GÓNGORA, began to flourish. At the most sumptuous viceregal courts, in Mexico and Lima, baroque verse came into fashion, in imitation of the style then in vogue at the Spanish court.

A Mexican nun, Sor JUANA INÉS DE LA CRUZ, became well known as the "tenth muse" at the Mexican court for her dramatic pieces, poetry, and sophisticated scientific and philosophical writings. She is considered the most important literary figure of the Spanish colonial era.

The Literature of Independence. The 18th century and the beginning of the 19th saw the stirrings of a new pride among Latin Americans as independence approached. Most men of letters were by now members of the creole group, that is, descendants of Europeans born in the New World, with an allegiance to and sense of pride in their native land rather than Spain. In 1810 independence was declared in Venezuela, Mexico, and Buenos Aires. Not until the 1820s, however, did most of the continent free itself from Spanish rule. With autonomy a variety of national literatures emerged, and attention was focused on both the land and the Indian, mulatto, or mestizo as its native inhabitant. Poets, realizing at this point that they had to establish their cultural identity, set out to do so by addressing themselves to the battles and heroes of independence, *La Victoria de Junín: a Bolívar* (The Victory

of Junín: Hymn to Bolívar, 1825) of José Joaquín Olmedo (1790–1847) being the best-known example.

The Indian was the exalted topic of the poem *La Cautiva* (The Captive, 1837) by Esteban ECHEVERRÍA and of the collection of poems called *En el Teocalli de Cholula* (On the Pyramid of Cholula, 1820) by José María Heredia (1803–39). Andrés BELLO and, from a different point of view, Domingo Faustino SARMIENTO both grappled with the problem of creating a grammar for the Spanish used in the New World; both also wrote works of description of the land, whereas Sarmiento alone, in his study of the native leader Juan Facundo Quiroga, attacked *caudillismo* (military dictatorship). It is at this point that barbarism and civilization come to be identified as coexisting and contending forces in Latin American life. To secure the victory of the latter was the task most writers set themselves; at the same time, they evoked with a certain nostalgia the life of the gaucho and of the country dweller that was soon to disappear. The greatest work in this tradition, the epic *Martín Fierro* (1872) by José Hernández, became the national poem of Argentina.

Modernism. The last decade of the 19th century saw the emergence of a specifically Latin American literary movement, modernism. More directly affecting poetry, but involving prose fiction as well, this literary school was responsible for remarkable poetic innovation in both form and concept. Its main exponent was the Nicaraguan Rubén DARÍO. Steeped in the French poetic tradition, and in traditional Spanish verse as well, Darío managed to bring to Spanish verse a flexibility that was based on new combinations of sounds, kinesthesia, and evocation of moods, rather than on a direct expression of feelings. He also popularized the idea of Latin America as constituting one homeland, having himself lived in several sister nations as well as in Paris and Spain. Darío thus embodied both a universalization of formal innovations and a passion for the realities of Latin America's past and future. His predecessor, the Cuban José MARTÍ, had introduced these two concerns while actively participating in the struggle to liberate his native land.

Literature of the Land and of the Mexican Revolution. At the start of the 20th century the so-called novel of the land emerged; this undertook to describe without any romantic idealization the land and its peoples and the ways of life that were specific to the geographic conditions in which they lived. The gaucho in the pampas, the peon on the rubber plantation or in the sugarcane fields, the rancher of the Venezuelan plains, the Indian in his Andean hut—each was the subject of novels that appeared in the first decades of the 20th century: *Raza de bronce* (A Race of Bronze, 1919) by Alcides ARGUEDAS of Bolivia; *Don Segundo Sombra* (1926; trans. as *Shadows on the Pampas*, 1935) by Ricardo GÜIRALDES of Argentina; *Doña Bárbara* (1929; Eng. trans., 1931) by Rómulo GALLEGOS of Venezuela; *The Vortex* (1924; Eng. trans., 1935) by José Eustasio Rivera of Colombia; *Huasipungo* (1934; Eng. trans., 1962) by Jorge ICAZA of Ecuador; and stories of the jungle by Horacio Quiroga of Argentina.

At the same time, the Mexican Revolution received its own treatment both in poetry and in a series of novels that appeared during and after the conflict. The most famous novel was *The Underdogs* (1915; Eng. trans., 1929) by Mariano AZUELA. The author had fought in support of Madero, and his fictional work records the rise and fall of a peasant fighter for whom the Mexican Revolution (1910–20) brings only suffering and devastation. Unlike the romantic writers, the novelists of the land no longer stood in awe of the Latin American landscape. They began to perceive that injustice was the prevailing order, that it had not disappeared with the coming of political independence. Their not-so-new social institutions, combined with what had been accepted unquestioningly in the previous century as the beneficent influence of European thought, began to seem inadequate to the American reality—so different, varied, untamed, and underdeveloped. These novelists, while at times despairing of ever improving the lot of the downtrodden—even by violent, revolutionary means—ultimately stressed the innate purity of the people of the land, as revealed, for instance, by the peasant fighter in *The*

Pablo Neruda (1904–73)

Carlos Fuentes (1928–   )

Photo Jill Krementz © 1980

Gabriel García Márquez (1928–   )

Underdogs and by the Indian characters in Icaza's works. Even *Shadows on the Pampas*, produced by a writer refined in the Parisian manner, suggests that spiritual renewal is to be found in the land rather than in the salons.

The Brazilian Modernists. At the start of the 20th century the Brazilian modernist movement, centered on São Paulo, also began to achieve a similar cultural independence through different means. Brazil had gone through the same stages of development as the rest of Latin America, but its political and cultural independence came more gradually. The first emperor of Brazil, Pedro I, was a legitimate member of the royal Portuguese dynasty. Although he declared Brazil's independence from Portugal in 1822, the country remained under imperial rule and the dominance of the court in Rio de Janeiro until 1889.

With Brazil thus tied to Portuguese culture, Brazilian writers only little by little assumed responsibility for giving expression to their own landscape and ethnic mix of peoples. The presence of large numbers of former slaves added a distinctive African character to the culture; and subsequent infusions of immigrants of non-Portuguese origin helped the new nation to find its own voice and to use it.

Early in the century the novels of Joaquim Maria MACHADO DE ASSIS, such as *Dom Casmurro* (1899; Eng. trans., 1953), of Graça Aranna (1868–1931), and of Euclydes da Cunha (1866–1909) took stock of both urban and rural Brazilian life. About 1922 the modernist group (unrelated to the Spanish-language modernists of the 1890s) broke totally with this past, declaring themselves representatives of a new vanguard, and in numerous magazines and small publications experimented with verse and prose. A great deal of editorial and dramatic activity spread to areas remote from the coast, thus helping to upgrade the cultural validity of regions other than the largest urban centers. In the past the states of both Bahia and Minas Gerais had fostered active but relatively short-lived literary movements. Mário de ANDRADE was the foremost exponent of the modernist group.

Recent Latin American Literature. Brazil has given birth to a number of avant-garde schools since modernism, the best known of which is CONCRETE POETRY, and both poetry and prose fiction have continued to develop under local and European influence. Some of the best-known Brazilian authors of recent decades include Jorge AMADO, Érico VERÍSSIMO, Oswald de Andrade (1890–1954), Clarice Lispector (1925–77), João Guimães Rosa (1908–67), and Raquel de Queiros in prose; and Carlos Drummond de Andrade, João Cabral de Melo Neto, Vinicius de Moraes (1913–80), and Jorge de Lima (1893–1953) in poetry.

Puerto Rican literature, particularly in response to nationalist and racial concerns, has come into its own only within recent decades. A vibrant indigenous theater movement has been distinguished by the work of Emilio Belaval, Manuel Mendez Ballester, Francísco Arriví, and René Marqués (1919–79)—the last known especially for his play *The Oxcart* (1951; Eng. trans., 1960). Enrique Laguerre and Pedro Juan Soto have dominated the field of fiction. In poetry, Luis Palés Matos (1898–1959) pioneered with the theme of "primitivism" versus the cultural imperialism of "civilization."

In the rest of Latin America it is safe to say that contemporary prose ranks ahead of poetry in its general quality, particularly in view of the success many authors have had in experimenting with techniques introduced by French novelists and literary critics, such as the "new novel," and with the innovations of such U.S. writers as Faulkner—while retaining a very personal style and a distinctly Latin American voice. Novelists or short-story writers in this vein include Carlos FUENTES and Juan Rulfo of Mexico; Alejo CARPENTIER of Cuba; Jorge Luis BORGES, Julio CORTÁZAR, and Manuel Puig of Argentina; Juan Carlos Onetti of Uruguay; Gabriel GARCÍA MÁRQUEZ of Colombia; Mario VARGAS LLOSA and José Maria Arguedas (1911–69) of Peru; and José DONOSO of Chile. These writers, who are responsible for the boom of the 1960s, have finally managed to fuse the persistent need for self-definition with the need for modernity and universality. Although they have relinquished none of their Latin American specificity, they have expressed themselves in terms that were equally accessible to the much wider audience that is drawn from contemporary Europe and North America.

Many of their novels incorporate painful reassessments of the nation's immediate past as well as suggestions for new courses of action. These range from the creation of a new Latin-American-wide consciousness, which would thus obviate the need for European models, to a return to an almost apocryphal native past. At every turn of history, with every successful choice or error, Latin Americans have evolved their own particular sense of history, and writers have assumed an especially active role in forming this consciousness. The famous *Canto General* (1950) of Pablo NERUDA, for instance, is a summa of all Latin America: its land, its history, and its peoples. César VALLEJO in his poetry grieves for all the Christs of the continent; Nicanor Parra mocks the banality of ordinary experience; and Ernesto Cardenal exhorts Latin Americans to union and activism in the original Christian sense of setting all people free. Nicolás GUILLÉN is the poet who most successfully celebrates the infusion of African blood into the Hispanic cultural mainstream. Octavio PAZ, who has written lyric, surrealist, and even concrete poetry, remains the best-known exemplar of the cosmopolitan tradition.

Persecution and Exile. If Latin American writers have never been far from the historical events that shaped their lives and have borne witness to these in print, they have also had to bear the brunt of political persecution. From colonial times—when many Brazilian poets were banished to Angola—through independence—when many writers had to flee their countries—the price for writing about Latin American reality, as they saw it, has often been exile. Again today many younger Latin American writers are far from the source of their language and of their concerns, yet busily writing about both.

MARTA MORELLO-FROSCH

Bibliography: Arceniegas, G., *Latin America: A Cultural History* (1966); Bacarisse, S., *Contemporary Latin American Fiction* (1980); Bhalla, A., ed., *Latin American Literature: A Critical Biography of Major Writers* (1987); Englekirk, J. E., et al., *An Outline History of Spanish American Literature*, 4th ed. (1981); Foster, D. W., *Handbook of Latin American Literature* (1987); Franco, J., *An Introduction to Spanish American Literature* (1969) and *Spanish American Literature since Independence* (1973); Fuentes, C., et al., *Latin American Fiction Today: A Symposium* (1980); Kadir, Djelal, *Questing Fictions: Latin America's Family Romance* (1986); Lewis, M. A., *Afro-Hispanic Poetry, 1940–1980* (1984); Lindstrom, N., *Woman's Voice in Latin American Literature* (1987); Luby, B. J., and Finke, W. H., eds., *Anthology of Contemporary Latin American Literature, 1960–84* (1986); Manguel, A., ed., *Other Fires: Short Stories by Latin American Women* (1986); Monegal, Emir R., ed., *The Borzoi Anthology of Latin American Literature*, 2 vols. (1977); Torres-Rioseco, Arturo, *The Epic of Latin American Literature* (1942; repr. 1959) and *New World Literature: Tradition and Revolt in Latin America* (1949; repr. 1983).

See also: BRAZILIAN LITERATURE.

Latin American music and dance

The term *Latin American* as used here encompasses the Americas south of the United States, as well as the entire Caribbean. The musics of this vast area are perhaps most efficiently discussed not geographically but rather in terms of ethnic components—European (especially Iberian), Amerindian, African, and mestizo ("mixed" or acculturated).

During the colonial period in Latin America (16th–19th century) many Amerindian populations were considerably reduced, and much traditional Amerindian musical culture was destroyed or syncretized with Iberian. Little concrete evidence remains as to the real nature of pre-Conquest music in the Aztec, Inca, and Maya civilizations apart from the testimony of 16th-century Spanish chroniclers and what can be seen of instruments depicted in hieroglyphs and pottery decorations. Drums, rattles, scrapers, slit drums (hollowed logs), whistles, vertical flutes, and panpipes were found, with almost total absence of stringed instruments. In performing the *yaraví* song, the *huayno* song and dance form, and other genres, modern Andean Amerindians still make extensive use of vertical flutes and panpipes, along with European instruments such as bass drums, harps, and guitars of different sizes. In Mesoamerica Indians now play harps, fiddles, and guitars based upon archaic Spanish models, or MARIMBAS of African origin, all of which have largely replaced indigenous instruments. Only in certain tropical areas (as the Amazon basin) are virtually unacculturated Amerindian musics found.

The Iberian origins of many song and dance forms are evident in a widespread predilection for alternating 3/4 and 6/8 meters (hemiola), the use of harps, fiddles, guitars, and many song types derived from Spanish verse structures such as the romanze or villancico. Such song types include the corrido of Mexico, *desafio* of Brazil, *copla* of the Andean countries, and

The manman is a cylindrically shaped, single-headed drum whose membrane is secured by wooden pegs. Played by a bare hand and a stick known as a baquette guinée, the manman is one of the percussion instruments used in the voodoo rituals of Haiti.

The marimba is an upright percussion instrument featuring strips of hard wood mounted above resonating boxes. The Latin American marimba is distinguished from its African antecedent by the substitution of wooden sound boxes for gourds.

décima of South America, the Caribbean, and Mexico. Relatively few Iberian genres have been retained in their original forms; rather, acculturated song and dance genres are distinctly regional in text, structure, choreography, and spirit. They include the *zamba* of Argentina, cueca of Chile and Bolivia, bambuco of Colombia, joropo of Venezuela, jarabe and huapango of Mexico, and son and *punto* of Cuba. They are usually danced in couples and often incorporate such features as shoe tapping and scarf waving.

The largest black populations are found in tropical coastal lowlands, as in the Caribbean, Eastern Central America, Venezuela, Brazil, and the Colombian-Ecuadorian coasts. African musical features commonly retained include call and response singing, polyrhythms, extensive use of ostinatos (persistently repeated musical figures), and improvisation based on recurring short phrases. African instruments found in both unaltered and adapted forms, with many regional names and variations, include long drums, often in "family" sets of three (congas), iron gongs, gourd scrapers (guiro), concussion sticks (claves), internal or external rattles (maracas, shekere), sanza (*marimbula*), and marimbas. The "steel drum" (tuned metal barrel) of Trinidad has no direct African equivalent but evolved from drum ensembles. The most African forms are usually associated with African-derived religions, such as the Yoruba-oriented candomblé of Brazil, lucumí of Cuba, and voodoo of Haiti. More acculturated Afro-American musics such as the urban *samba de morro* (carnival samba) of Brazil, merengue of the Dominican Republic and Haiti, *bomba* and *plena* of Puerto Rico, and rumba, conga, guaracha, son, and *són montuno* of Cuba have become national folk musics. SALSA has evolved from the rumba as a popular music of New York's pan-Hispanic Caribbean population.

Still more cosmopolitan forms have become popular on the "pan-Latin" and international level through their diffusion by mass media. These include the BOLERO and danzón of Cuba, the TANGO of Argentina, the cabaret samba and *bossa nova* of Brazil, the CALYPSO of Trinidad, and the *cumbia* of Colombia. The REGGAE of Jamaica is closer in style and spirit to "soul" music than to Latin musics of the Caribbean.

From the 16th through the 19th century, most Latin American "art" music reflected contemporary European models. Indian and Creole (those of European ancestry born in the

Since precolonial times, dance has been an important aspect of the arts in Latin America. The Ballet Folklórica of Mexico uses the rich Mexican cultural heritage in exciting performances based on traditional themes and folk history.

colonies) composers and musicians composed and performed music much like that of their parent colonial cultures. In the 20th century, however, a number of composers discovered their "national voices," based partly upon traditional folk and tribal music (or their conception or reconstruction of it). These include Heitor VILLA-LOBOS in Brazil and Manuel Ponce, Carlos CHÁVEZ, Silvestre Revueltas, and Blas Galindo in Mexico. Other composers have tended to represent more universal, rather than nationalist, techniques: these include Alberto GINASTERA and Mauricio Kagel in Argentina, Camargo Guarnieri in Brazil, Domingo Santa Cruz Wilson and Juan Orrego-Salas in Chile, and Julián Carrillo in Mexico.

THEODORE SOLIS

Bibliography: Appleby, D. P., *The Music of Brazil* (1983); Béhague, Gérard, *Music in Latin America: An Introduction* (1979); Chase, Gilbert, *A Guide to the Music of Latin America*, 2d ed. (1962; repr. 1971); Hague, Eleanor, *Latin-American Music: Past and Present* (1934; repr. 1982); Orrego-Salas, Juan, *Music in Latin America* (1977) and *The Young Generation of Latin American Composers* (1963); Roberts, John S., *Black Music of Two Worlds* (1972); Slonimsky, Nicolas, *Music of Latin America* (1949; repr. 1972); Stevenson, Robert, *Music in Aztec and Inca Territory* (1968), *Music in Mexico: A Historical Survey* (1952), and *The Music of Peru: Aboriginal and Viceroyal Epochs* (1959).

Latin American universities

Latin American universities have historically reflected the social forces shaping the areas of the New World colonized by Spain and Portugal. The first Latin American university was founded in 1538 in Santo Domingo by Dominican friars. In 1551 the first royal and pontifical universities were established in Mexico City and Lima. Institutions of higher education in the New World were modeled after those of Salamanca in Spain and Coimbra in Portugal. With faculties of theology, law, arts, and medicine, their primary functions were the preparation of clergy to propagate the Catholic faith and the training of civil servants to administer a colonial empire.

Following the wars of independence (1810–25), Latin American countries adopted the Napoleonic model of secular, state-controlled universities, which had faculties to prepare individuals for service in law, medicine, and, later, engineering. During the 19th century, sciences were introduced into the curriculum and greater emphasis was placed on research. University development in the second half of the 19th

century, however, was greatly arrested by political instability and economic stagnation.

In the 20th century, nationalism, extension of the franchise, urbanization, and industrialization have contributed to the expansion and transformation of Latin American higher education. The population explosion and the expansion of primary and secondary education have led to increasing numbers of students demanding higher education and viewing it as a gateway to better employment and higher social status. The governments of Latin America look to institutions of higher education to prepare the professionals, scientists, and technicians they need to develop their economies.

The expansion of higher education has been most dramatic in the post–World War II period. There were 36 universities in Latin America at the end of the 19th century. By 1950, there were 105. Over the subsequent 25-year period, the number increased to nearly 300 universities among more than 1,000 institutions of higher learning. This increase has been achieved as a result of greater public expenditure and through the expansion and proliferation of private universities, where, unfortunately, the quality of education has varied.

While a greater number of students from low-income backgrounds have gained access to higher education, these students have for the most part enrolled in the less prestigious institutions. In recent years women have represented a significant percentage of postsecondary students as well.

Latin American postsecondary institutions offer degrees in virtually every field. Traditionally, fields of study such as law, medicine, and engineering have attracted large numbers of students. One consequence of these enrollment patterns is that the many graduates in fields like law have had greater difficulty in finding employment. Graduates in highly specialized scientific fields may also be unemployed because the national economies are not fully geared to employing professionals in newer fields. In an attempt to relate higher education to specific employment opportunities, many countries have introduced polytechnic institutes or established universities specializing in one subject area as alternatives to universities, but the problems persist.

Latin America has perhaps the oldest and most continuous tradition of student political activism; such activism has sometimes led to temporary closings of universities. Since 1918 in Córdoba, Argentina, students have championed university reforms and social changes that include student participation in the government of universities and in the selection and evaluation of faculty, academic freedom, university autonomy, tuition-free higher education, elimination of entrance examinations and attendance requirements, and greater opportunities for working-class people to attend college. Students have consistently opposed dictatorships and have fought for national independence, economic development, and social justice.

Since the 1950s a host of academic reforms, many financed by international technical assistance agencies, have begun to transform Latin American universities by creating full-time student bodies and full-time faculty, university cities with a central campus and main library, general studies courses, integration of teaching and research activities, more flexible curricula, regional university campuses, and extension programs that reach isolated areas by means of radio and correspondence materials. Militant Latin American students and faculty have resisted some of these reforms, which they claim represent the imposition of foreign models and have been designed to curb student political activity.

A truly indigenous Latin American university model has yet to emerge. Cuba comes closest to establishing a university system that serves national development purposes and the interests of the poorest members of society.

Latin American universities continue to be characterized by both change and turmoil, mirroring the continuing struggles of Latin American peoples to achieve self-determination and prosperity.

ROBERT F. ARNOVE

Bibliography: Benjamin, Harold R. W., *Higher Education in the American Republics* (1965); Levy, Daniel C., *Higher Education and the State*

LATIN AMERICAN UNIVERSITIES

University and Location	Date Founded	Enrollment	University and Location	Date Founded	Enrollment
Argentina			**El Savador**		
University of Buenos Aires	1821	190,000	University of El Salvador, San Salvador	1841	30,000
National Technological University,			José Simeon Canas Central American		
Buenos Aires	1959	47,430	University, San Salvador	1965	6,074
National University of Córdoba	1613	36,000			
National University of Cuyo, Mendoza	1939	11,289	**Guatemala**		
National University of La Plata	1905	30,000	University of San Carlos of Guatemala,		
National University of the Litoral, Santa Fe	1919	8,500	Guatemala City	1676	50,000
National University of Tucumán, San			Rafael Landivar University, Guatemala City	1961	7,313
Miguel de Tucumán	1914	36,673			
			Honduras		
Bolivia			National University of Honduras,		
University of San Andrés, La Paz	1830	37,000	Tegucigalpa	1847	26,889
University of San Simon, Cochabamba	1832	10,000			
Royal and Pontifical University of San			**Mexico**		
Francisco Xavier of Chuquisaca, Sucre	1624	9,600	Monterrey Institute of Technology and		
			Higher Education	1943	10,000
Brazil			National Autonomous University of		
Federal University of Bahia, Salvador	1946	18,431	Mexico, Mexico City	1551	327,000
Federal University of Fluminense, Niterói	1960	20,713	University of Guadalajara	1792	211,539
Federal University of Minas Gerais, Belo			University of Baja California, Mexicali	1957	22,772
Horizonte	1927	20,044	University of Veracruz, Jalapa	1944	64,689
Federal University of Pernambuco, Recife	1946	18,500			
Federal University of Rio de Janeiro	1920	30,000	**Nicaragua**		
Federal University of Rio Grande do Sul,			National University of Nicaragua,		
Pôrto Alegre	1934	17,626	Managua	1812	22,000
University of Brasília	1961	10,000	Central American University, Managua	1961	3,588
University of São Paulo	1934	44,159			
			Panama		
Chile			University of Panama, Panama City	1935	40,640
University of Chile, Santiago	1738	64,000	Santa Maria la Antigua University, Panama		
University of Concepción	1919	10,435	City	1965	3,905
Catholic University of Chile, Santiago	1888	16,115			
Catholic University of Valparaíso	1928	7,047	**Paraguay**		
			National University of Asunción	1890	19,443
Colombia			Our Lady of Asunción Catholic University,		
University of Antioquia, Medellín	1822	19,000	Asunción	1960	9,445
University of the Andes, Bogotá	1948	4,700			
National University of Colombia, Bogotá	1867	28,000	**Peru**		
University of Valle, Cali	1945	9,000	National University of San Marcos, Lima	1551	34,223
Xavier Pontifical University, Bogotá	1622	12,470	Pontifical Catholic University of Peru, Lima	1917	9,571
			National University of Liberty, Trujillo	1824	11,004
Costa Rica			National University of San Augustin		
University of Costa Rica, San José	1843	28,230	Arequipa	1828	15,200
National University, Heredia	1973	12,000			
			Puerto Rico		
Cuba			University of Puerto Rico, San Juan	1966	53,889
University of Havana	1728	15,980	Catholic University of Puerto Rico, Ponce	1948	13,308
University of Oriente	1947	6,000	Inter-American University of Puerto Rico,		
Central University of Las Villas, Santa Clara	1952	8,200	San Juan	1912	37,981
Dominican Republic			**Uruguay**		
University of Santo Domingo	1538	50,800	University of the Republic, Montevideo	1849	35,000
Catholic University Madre y Maestra,					
Santiago de los Caballeros	1962	7,100	**Venezuela**		
			University of Los Andes, Mérida	1785	35,256
Ecuador			University of Carabobo, Valencia	1852	41,360
Central University of Ecuador, Quito	1769	60,000	Central University of Venezuela, Caracas	1725	52,070
Pontifical Catholic University of Ecuador,			University of Zulia, Maracaibo	1891	64,000
Quito	1946	11,636	University of Oriente, Cumaná	1958	21,016
State University of Cuenca	1868	21,575	Andres Bello Catholic University, Caracas	1953	9,800

in Latin America: Private Challenges to Public Dominance (1986); Liebman, Arthur, et al., *Latin American University Students: A Six Nation Study* (1972); Mabry, Donald J., *The Mexican University and the State: Student Conflicts, 1910–1971* (1982); Maier, J., and Weatherhead, R., eds., *The Latin American University* (1979); Spencer, David E., ed., *Student Politics in Latin America* (1965); Suchlicki, Jaime, *University Students and Revolution in Cuba, 1920–1968* (1969); UNESCO, *New Trends and New Responsibilities for Universities in Latin America* (1980); Walter, R. J., *Student Politics in Argentina* (1968).

Latin language

Latin, originally the language spoken only in Rome and the surrounding region of LATIUM, gradually spread throughout the entire western Mediterranean region as more and more people came under Roman sway. Classical Latin was basically a learned language abstracted from the spoken vernacular by the educated upper classes in Rome. Regional varieties also existed, as did more popular forms, called Vulgar Latin, which can be seen on inscriptions and in the works of Plautus (2d century BC) and Petronius (1st century AD) and to some extent in the letters of Cicero (1st century BC).

Latin is a member of the INDO-EUROPEAN family of languages and retains many inherited features. Phonologically, initial syllables have shown the least change in Latin, no doubt because they are usually stressed.

Various weakenings of articulation occurred, however, in interior syllables, in which the short vowels tended to be raised or lost, and the fricatives *f* and *s* became voiced as *b* or *d* and *r*. Long vowels, however, retained their pronunciation. In fact, their number was increased by the monophthongization of diphthongs, when *ei* became *ī*, and *ou* became *ū*. The incidence of geminate consonants was increased by the simplification of consonant groups; *supmos*, for example, was simplified to *summos*.

Latin nouns were organized out of many earlier types into five basic declensions, and the number of cases, both singular and plural, also became fixed at five. Each noun incorporates a gender—masculine, feminine, or neuter—that governs the agreement of adjectives. Pronouns and adjectives are also declined, but adverbs, prepositions, and conjunctions are not. Because of these grammatical signals the word order in a Latin sentence can vary widely, conveying emphasis rather than grammatical meaning.

The Latin verbal system was organized into four conjugations. The four principal parts—present, infinitive, perfect, past participle—provide all the necessary information for deriving every form of the verb.

Each finite verb expresses three persons in two numbers, actively and passively, in the indicative (real), subjunctive (ideal), or imperative (command) mood, and in the two aspects, imperfective and perfective. Infinitives, participles, and verbal nouns complete the system. Distinctions of tense are possible only in the indicative and display considerable symmetry, as seen in the various indicative forms of the second person singular of *habeō*, "have":

	Imperfective	Perfective
Present	habē-s	habu-is-ti
Future	habē-b-is	habu-er-is
Past	habē-b-ās	habu-er-ās

Such clarity is not seen in the subjunctive, in which several original systems, including optative and subjunctive, seem to have coalesced:

Present or future	habe-ās	habu-er-is
Past	habē-r-ēs	habu-is-s-ēs

The major linguistic problem faced by the Romans was the creation of a vocabulary and syntax adequate to the requirements of world power and intellectual discourse. In this they were remarkably successful, and they created, partly on Greek models, a set of abstract nouns that continues to form the basis of learned discourse even today. Behind this vocabulary lies an earlier agricultural and military terminology that reflects the history of Roman institutions. For example, *grex*, "flock," became the root of both *congregatiō*, "association," and *ēgregius*, "outstanding."

Syntactically, the Romans were able to subordinate ideas by giving each complex sentence only one indicative verb. All subordinate notions were conveyed by participles or subjunctives.

Although Latin is no longer a living language in its own right, it survives in various modified forms in the ROMANCE LANGUAGES. Latin also remains the official language of the Roman Catholic church, and scientists habitually turn to Latin roots when looking for names for their latest discoveries.

WILLIAM F. WYATT, JR.

Bibliography: Hammond, Mason, *Latin: A Historical and Linguistic Handbook* (1976); Palmer, Leonard R., *The Latin Language* (1954); Pei, Mario, *The Story of Latin and the Romance Languages* (1976); Pulgram, Ernst, *The Tongues of Italy* (1958).

Latin literature

Classical Latin literature may be divided—more conveniently than accurately—into three major periods: from the beginnings to the appearance of Cicero (81 BC); from Cicero to the death of Emperor Augustus in AD 14; and from the close of the Augustan Age to the death of Juvenal, AD c.130. Latin continued to be written by both pagans and then Christians for another 1,500 years, but most of the better-known post-classical authors are categorized as early Christian, medieval, or Renaissance.

Although inscriptions and an assortment of laws and chants survive from as early as the 5th century BC, the formal beginnings of Latin literature are usually assigned to 240 BC, when LIVIUS ANDRONICUS presented at Rome his translations of two Greek plays, a tragedy and a comedy. He was followed by the epic poets Gnaeus NAEVIUS and Quintus ENNIUS and the inventor of satire, LUCILIUS. The works of all four writers survive only in fragments. CATO the Elder, called the father of Latin prose, and the comic playwrights PLAUTUS and TERENCE fall within the same period.

The hundred years following Marcus Tullius CICERO's first speech in 81 BC marked an extraordinary period of creativity. The philosophical poet LUCRETIUS and the lyricist CATULLUS both wrote during Cicero's lifetime. The next two generations—the Golden Age of Latin—saw the emergence of VERGIL, author of Rome's greatest epic, the AENEID; of HORACE, the master of satire and lyric poetry; of the elegists Sextus PROPERTIUS and TIBULLUS; of OVID, the cosmopolitan poet of the METAMORPHOSES; and of the historians of republican Rome, SALLUST and LIVY. Most of the works of these authors appeared during the relatively benign reign (31 BC–AD 14) of Augustus.

The following period, often termed the Silver Age, was marked by a falling-off in quality. Freedom of expression was circumscribed, and writing tended to become increasingly rhetorical. To this period belong the epic poets LUCAN, STATIUS, and Valerius Flaccus, the novelist PETRONIUS ARBITER, the satirists MARTIAL and JUVENAL, the tragedian Lucius Annaeus SENECA, the letter writer PLINY THE YOUNGER, the biographer of the emperors, SUETONIUS, and the towering historian of early imperial Rome, Cornelius TACITUS.

From the start, Latin literature was permeated by the influence of ancient GREEK LITERATURE. With the exception of satire, the Romans produced no genre that was untouched by the Greeks; and even when not imitating them, the Romans tended to define themselves in terms of Greek writers. The greatest Latin authors—Cicero, Vergil, Horace—however, accepted imitation as a challenge. They deliberately recalled their Greek predecessors, but often only to mark their departures from them. Of these writers it is fair to say that when they are most imitative, they are also most original.

STEELE COMMAGER

Bibliography: Copley, Frank O., *Latin Literature* (1969); Duff, John W., *A Literary History of Rome From the Origins to the Close of the Golden Age*, 3d ed. (1960), and *A Literary History of Rome in the Silver Age*, 3d ed. (1964); Hadas, Moses, *A History of Latin Literature* (1952); Rose, H. J., *A Handbook of Latin Literature* (1949).

Latins

The Latins, *Latini,* were the inhabitants of the ancient plain of Latium in western Italy. They may have absorbed the region's earlier inhabitants. Beginning from small communities, they banded together in religious and later political confederations, over which Rome became dominant by the 4th century BC.

The Latins maintained political and social autonomy even after being colonized by Rome. They were made Roman citizens in 90 BC during the Social War.

latite [lay'-tite]

Latite is a medium-colored IGNEOUS ROCK composed of large crystals of plagioclase and potassium feldspar set in a fine-grained groundmass. Latites commonly occur as dikes or sills. Chemically, latite is a fine-grained equivalent of MONZONITE.

JAMES A. WHITNEY

latitude [lat'-ih-tood]

The latitude of a point on the Earth's surface is its distance north or south of the equator. Lines of latitude, or parallels, extend east and west at precise intervals from the equator, which is the 0° parallel. Because the latitude lines are drawn around the Earth sphere, they can be divided as a circle into degrees, minutes, and seconds. The latitude of Times Square in New York City, for example, is calculated to be 40°45′12″ north. The length of a degree of latitude becomes larger as distance from the equator increases. When used in combination with lines of LONGITUDE, latitude lines give a unique designation to every point on the Earth.   ROBERT S. WEINER

Latium   [lay'-shuhm]

Latium (Italian: Lazio) is a region in west central Italy, stretching from the Tyrrhenian Sea to the Apennine Mountains and including Roma, Frosinone, Latina, Rieti, and Viterbo provinces. The population is 5,156,053 (1989 est.). ROME, the national capital, also serves as the capital of the region, and the main port is Civitavecchia. Agriculture is the region's economic mainstay; products include cereals, grapes, olives, and vegetables. Industry is concentrated around Rome, and fishing is carried on along the coast. Tourism also centers on Rome and at mountain and seaside resorts.

In the 3d century BC, Rome conquered Latium. After the fall of Rome, the region was occupied, successively, by the Visigoths, the Vandals, and the Lombards. It came under the control of the popes in the 8th century and remained a part of the PAPAL STATES until 1870, when Italy was unified. During World War II, Latium was the site of intense fighting during the Allied push toward Rome (1944), especially at the battles at ANZIO and CASSINO.

Latrobe, Benjamin Henry   [luh-trohb']

Baltimore's old Roman Catholic cathedral (now called the Basilica of the Assumption), designed by Benjamin Latrobe, is an outstanding example of early 19th-century American neoclassical architecture. The domes on the two steeples are later additions.

The leading figure in United States architecture during the early 19th century, Benjamin Henry Latrobe, b. England, May 1, 1764, d. Sept. 3, 1820, adapted the styles of ancient Greece to his own time and place. Educated from age 12 in Germany, he returned to England to study engineering and then took up architecture. During the 1790s he established an architectural practice in London before emigrating to Virginia in 1796.

After completing residential designs in Norfolk and the State Penitentiary in Richmond (1797–98), Latrobe moved to Philadelphia, where he won the design competition for the Bank of Pennsylvania. His plan (1798) for this building initiated the GREEK REVIVAL movement in American architecture. At the same time (1798–99) he inaugurated the GOTHIC REVIVAL with

his design for Sedgeley near Philadelphia, the first American mansion built in that style. In addition, he engineered Philadelphia's picturesque Waterworks, the first in America to employ steam pumps.

Latrobe's two most important commissions were the elegant, centrally domed Baltimore Cathedral (1804–18), the first Roman Catholic cathedral in the country, and the U.S. Capitol in Washington, D.C., to which he made major contributions. For the cathedral, Latrobe submitted alternative designs—one classical and the other Gothic. Although the latter was not executed, it became a model for neo-Gothic church designs in America. In 1803, President Thomas Jefferson appointed Latrobe surveyor of buildings and thus new architect of the CAPITOL OF THE UNITED STATES, which had been started in the 1790s. He completed the South Wing with magnificent interiors and was called back to rebuild the structure (1815–17) after it was largely razed by the British.

In 1818, Latrobe went to New Orleans to oversee his plan for the city's water supply. He died there of yellow fever.
          RON WIEDENHOEFT

Bibliography: Formwalt, Lee, and Van Horne, John, eds., *The Correspondence and Miscellaneous Papers of Benjamin Henry Latrobe*, 3 vols. (1985–88); Hamlin, T., *Benjamin Henry Latrobe* (1955); Norton, Paul, *Latrobe, Jefferson and the National Capitol* (1977).

Latter-Day Saints, Church of Jesus Christ of: see MORMONISM.

Latvia   [lat'-vee-uh]

Located on the eastern shore of the Baltic Sea, Latvia borders on Estonia in the north, the Russian and Belorussian republics in the east, and Lithuania in the south. Latvia has an area of 63,700 km² (24,600 mi²), and the population is 2,681,000 (1989). The capital city is RIGA, with a population of 915,000 (1989). From 1940 to 1990, Latvia was a soviet socialist republic, one of the 15 constituent republics of the USSR. Its current political status is ambiguous and transitional. On May 4, 1990, Latvia declared Soviet rule illegal and set a course for the gradual achievement of independence. It also changed its name to the Republic of Latvia.

Land and People. Latvia's landscape is of glacial origin, and has many lakes and rivers. The major river is the Daugava, or Western Dvina (se DVINA RIVER, WESTERN), which flows for 360 km (224 mi) in Latvia. The rivers empty into the Gulf of Riga or the Baltic Sea. Their estuaries provide ice-free commercial

and fishing harbors. Latvia has a moderate climate, with cool summers and mild winters. The highest elevation is under 300 m (984 ft).

The ethnic Latvians, or Letts, form 51.8% of the population (1989), down from 75% in 1923. Russians make up 34%, Belorussians 4.5%, Ukrainians 3.4%, and Poles 2.3%. The ethnic Latvians are mostly Lutheran in religion, and speak a Baltic language related to Lithuanian. Seventy-one percent of Latvia's population live in cities, of which Riga is the largest. Others are the industrial centers of Daugavpils (1989 pop., 127,000), Liepaja (114,000), and Jelgava (72,000), and the oil and chemicals port of Ventspils (52,000). Jurmala (65,000), near Riga, is the best-known beach resort.

Economy. More than two-thirds of Latvia's gross national product comes from industry. It is the USSR's main producer of telephone equipment, railroad and street cars, generators, mopeds, and washing machines. Light industry includes food processing. The rivers provide hydroelectric power, but most of Latvia's energy needs are supplied by Estonia and other republics. The agricultural sector concentrates on meat and dairy production; grains and flax are grown.

History. The Latvian people, along with the Lithuanians, have lived in the eastern Baltic region since ancient times. In the 13th century the Latvians were conquered and Christianized by the Germanic Knights of the Sword; their successors, the TEUTONIC KNIGHTS, founded the German-ruled state of LIVONIA, which dominated the area until the mid-16th century. In 1561–62, Latvia was divided between Poland and the duchy of Courland; the Swedes occupied part of the country in the 17th century, and between 1710 and 1721 the whole region was conquered by Russia under Peter the Great in the Great NORTHERN WAR.

The native German nobility continued to control Latvia under Russian rule, but a Latvian nationalist movement emerged in the 19th century, and independence was achieved (1918) after the collapse of the Russian Empire. Russian dominance was reestablished, however, when Latvia was annexed by the USSR in 1940. Soviet rule was harsh. More than 150,000 Latvians were either deported or perished in Soviet labor camps. The economy was industrialized, and Russian immigration reduced the Latvians almost to a minority in their own land.

The development of the PERESTROIKA reform movement of Soviet president Mikhail Gorbachev in the late 1980s presented Latvia with an opportunity to reassert itself, which it did beginning in 1988. The non-Communist Latvian People's Front, with wider popular support, was able to pressure the government into restoring Latvian as the official language and legalizing the use of the national symbols. Freedoms of speech, press, and religion were established, and private ownership of farms was legalized. In 1990, following the example of its Baltic neighbors, Lithuania and Estonia, Latvia began to move in the direction of independence. This met with opposition from the Soviet government and from the republic's own Russian minority. In June 1990 the Kremlin began negotiations with all three Baltic republics in search of a compromise solution.

V. STANLEY VARDYS

Bibliography: Bilmanis, Alfred, *A History of Latvia* (1951; repr. 1970); Misiunas, Romuald, and Taagepera, Rein, *The Baltic States: Years of Dependence, 1940–1980* (1983).

Latvian language: see BALTIC LANGUAGES.

Latynina, Larisa   [la-tee'-nee-nah]

Larisa Semyonovna Latynina, b. Dec. 27, 1935, was the dominant Soviet gymnast of her time and, as a world-class competitor from 1954 to 1966, won more Olympic medals than any athlete in any sport. In three Olympic Game, world, and European championship appearances she captured 9 gold, 15 silver, and 5 bronze medals. Her superb technique, beauty, and charm all contributed to her near invincibility in the 10 years after her debut at the world championships in 1954. She lost the combined exercises title at the 1964 Olympics to the Czech gymnast Vera Caslavska. Following her retirement, Latynina became the coach of the Soviet women's team.

Laud, William   [lawd]

William Laud, b. Oct. 7, 1573, d. Jan. 10, 1645, was archbishop of Canterbury and a close advisor of King CHARLES I. Educated at Oxford and ordained in 1601, he became bishop of Saint David's in 1621, bishop of London in 1628, and archbishop of Canterbury in 1633. As chancellor of Oxford (from 1629), he tried to restore some pre-Reformation forms of worship.

Laud maintained a strong position against Puritan pressures for further reform, insisted on the apostolic succession of bishops, and imposed his will by force and punishments. Increasingly, his administration became involved in political matters as he tried to carry his conservative program to Scotland and became identified with the Stuart royal cause. The notorious "etcetera oath" which he introduced at the Convocation of 1640, designed to prescribe the doctrine of the divine right of kings and the hierarchical government of the church, brought a reaction against his forceful policies. He was impeached (1641) by the LONG PARLIAMENT, imprisoned in the Tower of London, tried (1644–45) under questionable judicial circumstances, and executed.

FREDERICK A. NORWOOD

Bibliography: Carlton, Charles, *Archbishop William Laud* (1987); Trevor-Roper, Hugh, *Archbishop Laud, 1573–1645,* 2d ed. (1963).

Lauda, Niki   [low'-duh]

The Austrian Nikolaus-Andreas Lauda, b. Feb. 22, 1949, is one of only six men to win the Grand Prix car racing championship at least three times. Dedicated and fearless in pursuit of his sport, Lauda won his first title in 1975 and his second in 1977 (after a serious accident in 1976 left him close to death). He retired in 1979, returned to the circuit in 1982, and became three-time champion in 1984.

Laudonnière, René Goulaine de   [loh-dawn-yair', ruh-nay' goo-len' duh]

René Goulaine de Laudonnière, c.1529–c.1582, was a French Huguenot colonizer in Florida. After taking part in Jean RIBAUT's expedition to Florida in 1562, he led a second expedition that established the French Protestant colony of Fort Caroline on the Saint John's River in 1564. In 1565, as the feuding colonists were about to abandon the settlement, it was destroyed by the Spanish under Pedro MENÉNDEZ DE AVILÉS. The wounded Laudonnière escaped to France. His narrative of the expeditions was translated by Richard Hakluyt as *A Notable Historie Containing Foure Voyages Made by Certayne French Captaynes into Florida* (1587).

Bibliography: Bennett, C. E., *Laudonnière and Fort Caroline* (1964).

Laue, Max von   [low'-eh, mahks fuhn]

The German physicist Max Theodor Felix von Laue, b. Oct. 9, 1879, d. Apr. 24, 1960, received the 1914 Nobel Prize for physics for his discovery (1912) of the diffraction of X rays by crystals (see X-RAY DIFFRACTION). He showed that X rays are very short electromagnetic waves that can be used to study the structure of materials. He thus helped establish the field of X-ray structural analysis, an important branch of physics and chemistry. Professor of theoretical physics at Berlin from 1919 until his retirement in 1943, Laue was instrumental in rebuilding German science after World War II.

ROBERT PAUL

laughing gas: see ANESTHETICS.

Laughton, Charles   [lawt'-uhn]

Charles Laughton, b. July 1, 1899, d. Dec. 15, 1962, was a distinguished British-born character actor of stage and screen, best remembered for his work in the 1930s. On stage he performed with the Sadler's Wells Company (1933–34), the Old Vic (1935), and the Comédie Française (1937). His many British and American films include *The Private Life of Henry VIII* (1933), for which he won an Academy Award in the title role;

The British-born actor Charles Laughton is best known for his vigorous and convincing character portrayals on the stage and in such films as Mutiny on the Bounty *(1935),* Witness for the Prosecution *(1957), and* The Private Life of Henry VIII *(1933), for which he received an Academy Award.*

Mutiny on the Bounty (1935), in which he played Captain Bligh; *Rembrandt* (1936); *Jamaica Inn* (1938); *Witness for the Prosecution* (1957); and *Advise and Consent* (1961). From 1929 he was married to actress Elsa Lanchester.

Bibliography: Brown, William, *Charles Laughton: A Pictorial Treasury of his Films* (1970); Higham, Charles, *Charles Laughton: An Intimate Biography* (1976).

Laurana, Francesco [law-rah'-nah, frahn-ches'-koh]

The Italian Renaissance sculptor Francesco Laurana, c.1430–1503, grew up in a Venetian colony on the Dalmation coast of present-day Yugoslavia but executed most of his works in Italy, where his brother Luciano Laurana was also active as an architect. Employed initially by Ferdinand I of Naples, Francesco collaborated on the sculpture of the great Triumphal Arch of the Castelnuovo (1457–58), the only surviving 15th-century Italian triumphal arch. During the next two decades he moved from court to court in Italy and France, designing medals (1461–66) for René of Anjou, working (1467) on the complex sculptural program of the Mastrantonio Chapel at the church of San Francesco in Palermo, Sicily, and executing sculptures for the court of Federigo da Montelfeltro (1444–82), duke of Urbino. While in Urbino, Francesco mod-

eled at least some of the nine surviving portrait busts of women that represent perhaps his finest work. His bust of Battista Storza, duchess of Urbino (c.1475; Bargello, Florence), typifies his highly individual style, which owes more to the stylized elegance of Byzantine art than to the work of contemporary Florentine masters such as Donatello. Francesco was a master portraitist with a remarkable ability to simplify forms into almost abstract geometrical patterns that anticipate the more rigorous stylizations of much of 20th-century sculpture.   MARK J. ZUCKER

Bibliography: Kennedy, Clarence and Ruth W., *Four Portrait Busts by Francesco Laurana* (1962); Pope-Hennessy, John, *Italian Renaissance Sculpture* (1958; 2d ed., 1971); Seymour, Charles, Jr., *Sculpture in Italy: 1400 to 1500* (1966).

Laurasia: see PLATE TECTONICS.

laurel [lohr'-uhl]

Laurels are about 47 genera of mostly evergreen trees and shrubs in the laurel family, Lauraceae. They grow best in warm climates and are characterized by the aroma of their bark and their leathery, simple leaves. The true laurel, or sweet bay, *Laurus nobilis,* is native to Anatolia and has become naturalized in southern Europe. The dark green leaves of sweet bay are the BAY LEAF used in cookery. The flowers appear in yellow clusters, followed by black or dark purple berries. The other species of the genus, *L. canariensis,* is native to the Canary Islands. Members of other genera of the laurel family include the CALIFORNIA LAUREL, the CINNAMON tree, the AVOCADO, and the SASSAFRAS.

Certain other plants with similar leaves and bark are commonly referred to as laurels, but they do not belong to the laurel family. English laurel, *Prunus laurocerasus,* a large evergreen related to plum and cherry species of trees, is native from southeastern Europe to Iran. MOUNTAIN LAUREL, *Kalmia latifolia,* related to rhododendrons, grows naturally in the eastern United States. The Texas mountain laurel, or coralbean tree, *Sophora secundiflora,* grows in the southwestern United States. New Zealand laurel, *Corynocarpus laevigata,* has extremely poisonous orange fruit. A BEAUTY LEAF tree, *Calophyllum inophyllum,* native to Malaysia, is also called Alexandrian laurel.

Bibliography: Jaynes, Richard A., *The Laurel Book* (1975).

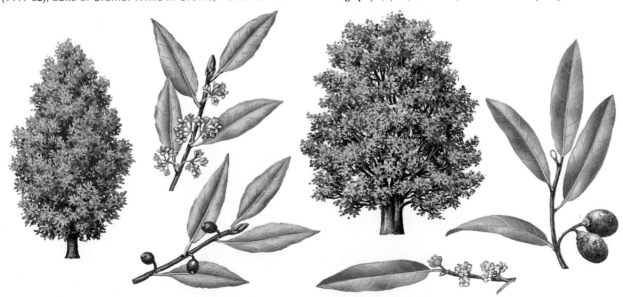

The sweet bay laurel, L. nobilis *(left), was grown in ancient Roman temple gardens, and its leaves were fashioned into crowns symbolizing accomplishment. Its leaves are now used to flavor food. The California laurel* Umbellularia californica *(right), is an evergreen whose timber is used to make high-quality furniture. Both trees bear tiny flowers and olive-shaped fruit.*

In this scene from the 1939 film The Flying Deuces, the slapstick comedy team of Oliver Hardy (left) and Stan Laurel (right) face a hilarious dilemma typical of their zany misadventures. Hardy was the irritable instigator, and Laurel was the amiable tragicomic "victim."

Laurel and Hardy   [lor'-ul, har'-dee]

Masters of slapstick buffoonery, Stan Laurel, b. Arthur Stanley Jefferson in Lancashire, England, June 16, 1890, d. Feb. 23, 1965, and Oliver Hardy, b. Harlem, Ga., Jan. 18, 1892, d. Aug. 7, 1957, were one of Hollywood's greatest comedy teams, with the skinny, sad-eyed Laurel playing the sensitive underdog to the obese, peevish Hardy. Laurel, the more creative of the two, began his career as a music hall comedian before settling in America in 1911 and teaming in 1927 with Hardy, a former singer and film heavy. On screen the pair portrayed clumsy, genteel misfits who turned minor problems into major disasters. Their mayhem can be seen in such short films as *Putting Pants on Philip* (1927), *From Soup to Nuts* (1928), *Two Tars* (1928), and *Big Business* (1929), as well as in the features *Pack Up Your Troubles* (1932), *Sons of the Desert* (1934), *Babes in Toyland* (1934), and *Way Out West* (1937). Although they made a successful transition from silent to sound films, their popularity waned after their departure (1940) from the Hal Roach studio.   FRANK MANCHEL

Bibliography: Everson, William, *The Films of Laurel and Hardy* (1983); Guiles, Fred L., *Stan: The Life of Stan Laurel* (1980); McCabe, John, *Mr. Laurel and Mr. Hardy*, rev. ed. (1985); Scagnetti, Jack, *The Laurel and Hardy Scrapbook* (1982).

Laurence, Margaret   [lor'-ens]

Margaret Laurence, b. Neepawa, Manitoba, July 18, 1926, d. Jan. 5, 1987, was considered by many critics the best novelist ever to write in Canada. A knowledgeable observer of African life and the author of books of short stories, travel, and translations, she has been most widely acclaimed for four linked novels of the Canadian west: *The Stone Angel* (1964), *A Jest of God* (1966; filmed as *Rachel, Rachel,* 1968), *The Fire-Dwellers* (1969), and *The Diviners* (1974). Her female protagonists are natives of a fictional prairie town called Manawaka; each is characterized sympathetically and compellingly, and each bespeaks courage in the face of adversity. Laurence has also published a volume of essays, *Heart of a Stranger* (1976).
        ROBERT COCKBURN

Bibliography: New, William, ed., *Margaret Laurence* (1977); Thomas, Clara, *The Manawaka World of Margaret Laurence* (1975).

Laurens, Henri   [loh-rahns', ahn-ree']

The French sculptor Henri Laurens, b. Feb. 18, 1885, d. May 5, 1954, pursued in sculpture the experiments that the cubist painters, his colleagues, were executing on canvas. His aim was to explore the possibilities of pure form without representational elements. Under the influence of Georges Braque, Juan Gris, and Pablo Picasso, Laurens became one of the most important cubist sculptors in Paris. Laurens produced his first cubist constructions of painted wood and metal in 1915. Laurens also made paper collages and sculptures in stone. He used color to define the volumes and planes of his sculpture and to offset the effects of reflected light. In his later career Laurens adopted more organic forms; after 1925 he produced many simplified representational works depicting female nudes and mythological personages—for example, his bronze *The Siren* (1945; Musée National d'Art Moderne, Paris).
        BARBARA CAVALIERE

Bibliography: Cooper, Douglas, *The Cubist Epoch* (1970); Goldschneider, Cecile, *Laurens* (1956); Kahnweiler, Daniel-Henry, *The Sculpture of Henri Laurens*, intro. by Werner Hofmann (1977).

Laurens, Henry   [lor'-ens]

Henry Laurens, a leading patriot during the American Revolution, appears in a portrait by John Singleton Copley. Laurens was captured by the British in 1780 but was freed (1782) in exchange for Charles Cornwallis. Laurens was one of the American peace commissioners.

Henry Laurens, b. Charleston, S.C., Mar. 6, 1724, d. Dec. 8, 1792, was a leading patriot during the American Revolution. A South Carolina merchant and planter, he was president of the Second Continental Congress from November 1777 until December 1778. In 1780 he was captured by the British while on his way to negotiate an agreement between the United States and Holland. The revelation of his mission led to war between Britain and the Dutch. After being imprisoned in the Tower of London, Laurens was exchanged in 1782 for General CORNWALLIS. That year he was one of the commissioners sent to Paris to negotiate peace with the British.

Bibliography: Wallace, David D., *The Life of Henry Laurens* (1915, repr. 1967).

Laurent, Auguste   [loh-rahn', oh-goost']

The French chemist Auguste Laurent, b. Nov. 14, 1807, d. Apr. 15, 1853, discovered phthalic acid, isatin, indene, and their substitution products. He also experimented with substitution and addition reactions in the aromatic series. Based on this work, and in opposition to the standard "dualistic" theory of J. J. Berzelius, Laurent developed a theory whereby organic compounds are built around atomic groupings known as radicals, rather than depending on electric charge. Leopold Gmelin and Alexander Williamson were interested in Laurent's ideas. In his famous *Methode de Chemie* (Method of Chemistry, 1854), published posthumously, Laurent used the hexagon to represent the chemical structure of different substances, including Friedrich Kekule's later views.

VIRGINIA F. McCONNELL

Laurentian Library   [luh-ren'-shuhn]

The Laurentian Library, or Biblioteca Medicea Laurenziana, derives from the personal library of the MEDICI rulers of Florence, Italy. It began with the manuscripts collected by Cosimo de Medici (1389–1464) and was later enriched by his sons Giovanni and Piero and by his grandson Lorenzo (1449–92). The library is housed in the Michelangelo-designed building in the cloisters of San Lorenzo. It was opened to the public in 1571 and now contains about 100,000 volumes, including 13,000 manuscripts and about 5,000 incunabula. Among the treasures are a collection of papyri from 300 BC to AD 600, the Ashburnham collection of codices and manuscripts, and one of the oldest extant Vergil manuscripts, from AD 494.

COLIN STEELE

Laurentian Mountains

The Laurentian Mountains, or Laurentides, located north of Montreal and the St. Lawrence River in southern Quebec, Canada, are part of the CANADIAN SHIELD. They are composed mainly of Precambrian igneous and metamorphic rocks and have deposits of valuable minerals. Worn down by Ice Age glaciers and time, the low, conifer-covered mountains are separated by streams and lakes. A popular ski and resort area, the Laurentides and Mount Tremblant provincial parks are there. Mount Tremblant, 960 m (3,150 ft), is the highest peak.

ALLEN R. SMITH

Laurentian Shield: see CANADIAN SHIELD.

Laurier, Sir Wilfrid   [law'-ree-ay]

Sir Wilfrid Laurier, the first French-Canadian prime minister of Canada (1896–1911), worked to achieve "unity and harmony and amity" between French- and English-speaking Canadians. Canada prospered during his tenure: the West was opened, railroads were built, and trade agreements were made with the United States and Great Britain. Laurier was knighted in 1897.

Wilfrid Laurier, b. Saint-Lin, Quebec, Nov. 20, 1841, d. Feb. 17, 1919, was the first French-Canadian prime minister of Canada. He served first in the Legislative Assembly of Quebec (1871–74) and then in the Canadian House of Commons until his death.

A Liberal, he was appointed (1877) minister of inland revenue in Alexander MACKENZIE's administration. With his colleagues, he went into the opposition in 1878. In 1887, Laurier was chosen leader of the Liberal party, and when his party won the election of 1896, he became prime minister. Heading a government described as "a ministry of all the talents," Laurier was returned to office in the elections of 1900, 1904, and 1908. He was finally defeated in 1911.

The "age of Laurier" was a period of great economic development. A flood of 2 million immigrants arrived in Canada, the West was opened, farming based on wheat and grains boomed in the prairies, the provinces of Alberta and Saskatchewan were created, and two transcontinental railways were built. The spectacular development of the West was accompanied by a tremendous increase in mining, lumbering, and manufacturing in the other parts of the country.

In the relations between English and French Canadians, Laurier tried to have diversity accepted as a characteristic of Canadian culture. He emphasized the need for cooperation and compromise, as exemplified by the settlement of the MANITOBA SCHOOLS QUESTION at the beginning of his administration. Laurier favored close ties with the British government, but after the French-Canadian outcry against the dispatch (1899) of Canadian troops to serve with the British forces in the South African War, he sought to balance imperial cooperation with the assertion of Canadianism. He therefore resisted the establishment of imperial defense forces but created in 1909 a separate Canadian Navy. In 1911 he concluded a tariff reciprocity agreement with the United States, a further assertion of detachment from the British Empire.

These key issues formed the central focus of the important election of 1911, which brought Laurier's downfall. On tariff reciprocity, Laurier lost Ontario, where manufacturing industries needed national protection. On Canada's involvement in the British Empire, a realignment of the parties in Quebec occurred: the Conservatives, who opposed Laurier's Canadianism, coalesced with the French-Canadian nationalists, who opposed Laurier's imperial cooperation as antinational.

As leader of the opposition, Laurier supported Canada's entry (1914) into World War I. However, he condemned conscription, which the French-Canadian constituency vehemently opposed. To prevent a complete ethnic split, he refused to join Sir Robert BORDEN's Union government, formed in 1917 of Conservatives and an important group of English-speaking Liberals. The shattered Liberal party had begun to coalesce again before his death.

ANDRÉE DÉSILETS

Bibliography: Bowsfield, Hartwell, *Laurier* (1969); Neatby, H. Blair, *Laurier and a Liberal Quebec* (1973); Robertson, Barbara, *Wilfred Laurier: The Great Conciliator* (1971); Schull, J. J., *Laurier, the First Canadian* (1965; repr. 1967).

Lausanne   [loh-zahn']

Lausanne is the capital of Vaud canton, western Switzerland, on Lake Geneva about 52 km (32 mi) northeast of Geneva. The population is 126,211 (1985 est.). An important tourist resort, rail center, port, and agricultural center, Lausanne also manufactures clothing, metalwork, leather goods, chocolate, and other products. The University of Lausanne (1891) was originally a theological school (1537) noted as a center for Calvinism. First settled by the Celts, Lausanne became the site of a Roman camp. A bishopric was established there in 590, and the city was ruled by prince-bishops until it came under Bernese rule in 1536 and the Reformation was introduced. Lausanne became the capital of Vaud in 1803.

Lausanne, Treaty of

The Treaty of Lausanne (1923) settled the boundaries of modern Turkey and resolved the territorial disputes raised in Anatolia by World War I. At the end of the war the Allies imposed the Treaty of Sèvres (1920) on the defeated OTTOMAN EMPIRE; it effectively dismembered the empire, leaving only Anatolia (minus a Greek enclave at Smyrna, or IZMIR) under Turkish rule. This settlement was rejected by the Turkish nationalists led by Mustafa Kemal (later Kemal ÁTATÜRK). Although they accepted the loss of Iraq, Syria, Arabia, and other non-Turkish areas, they objected to the loss of Smyrna to Greece. After driving the Greek troops out of Smyrna and ousting the sultan, Kemal's government was able to force the negotiation of a new treaty, which was finally concluded at Lausanne, Switzerland, on July 24, 1923.

According to the Treaty of Lausanne, Turkey regained not only Smyrna but also eastern Thrace and some of the Aegean islands. It also resumed control of the Dardanelles (internationalized under the previous treaty) on the condition that they were kept demilitarized and open to all nations in peacetime. A separate agreement between Turkey and Greece provided for the exchange of minority populations.

DONALD S. BIRN

Bibliography: Sontel, S. R., *Turkish Diplomacy, 1918–1923* (1975).

See also: CHANAK CRISIS.

Lautaro   [low-tah'-roh]

Lautaro, c.1536–57, called the Hannibal of Chile, led warriors of the Mapuche group of ARAUCANIANS against invading Spanish troops in 1553. As a youthful captive of the Spaniards, he became Pedro de VALDIVIA's head groom. Lautaro escaped and joined the Mapuche south of the Bío-Bío River, informing them that Spaniards were human and not, as they believed, part of their horses. He was named *toki* (supreme military leader) in 1553. After defeating the Spaniards that year and killing Valdivia, he razed Concepción in 1554. In 1557 he was leading 800 Mapuche toward Santiago when he was killed. Lautaro became a hero immortalized in the epic poem *La Araucana* by Ercilla y Zúñiga (1533–94).   LOUIS C. FARON

Bibliography: Edwards, Agustín, *Peoples of Old* (1929; repr. 1976).

lava   [lah'-vuh]

Streams of red-hot, molten lava flow down the sides of this volcano, which initially erupted underwater on Nov. 14, 1963, and within two days rose to form the new island of Surtsey off the coast of Iceland. The island is now flourishing with plant and animal life.

Lava is a general term for molten rock at the Earth's surface. It generally erupts from the vents and fissures of a VOLCANO at temperatures ranging from 850° to 1,250° C (1,500° to 2,300° F). Lava usually includes at least some crystals floating in the melt, even before it is erupted. Rapidly cooling lava generally forms OBSIDIAN, a volcanic glass. If lava cools slowly, as in the Hawaiian lava lakes, crystals may have time to grow to medium or coarse-grain textures. Occasionally, large crystals may grow in the magma before eruption, while fast cooling at the surface of a lava flow crystallizes the rest to a fine-grained matrix; this combination is called a porphyritic texture.

The composition of lavas ranges widely, from silica-rich RHYOLITES to the iron- and magnesium-rich (silica-poor) alkali BASALTS and basanites. Volatile content ranges from very low, as in Hawaiian basalts, to very high, as in SCORIAS and PUMICE.

The most fluid lavas are usually basaltic in composition and erupt at high temperatures. These basalts often form thin flows, called pahoehoe, of great lateral extent with relatively smooth surfaces. On the other hand, some basalt flows are jagged and blocky with very rough surfaces. These so-called

aa flows form from more viscous, lower-temperature lavas. In Hawaii some lava flows have been observed to start out as pahoehoe flows and then change to aa flows as they cool and become more viscous. (Both pahoehoe and aa are Hawaiian terms now in general use.) The more viscous a lava is—because of either lower temperatures or higher silica content or both—the more blocky and fragmented the flow becomes. The most viscous lava flows, such as rhyolite domes, may move only imperceptibly and are often little more than steep-sided piles of volcanic rubble.

JAMES A. WHITNEY

Bibliography: Cas, R. A. F., and Wright, J. V., *Volcanic Successions* (1987); Hyndman, D. W., *Petrology of Igneous and Metamorphic Rocks,* 2d ed. (1985); McBirney, A. R., *Igneous Petrology* (1985).

See also: IGNEOUS ROCK; MAGMA.

Laval   [lah-vahl']

Laval (1986 pop., 284,164) is an industrial and suburban city of Canada in Quebec province. It occupies the entire 230-km² (90-mi²) Île Jésus, just north of the Île de Montréal in the St. Lawrence River. The island, settled in 1681, was named for the Society of Jesus. In 1965, Laval was created by merging the 14 towns on the island.

Laval, François de

François de Laval, b. Apr. 30, 1623, d. May 6, 1708, was the first Roman Catholic bishop in Canada. He was born in France of a wealthy family and was educated by the Jesuits. Ordained a priest in 1647, he became a bishop in 1658 and was appointed vicar apostolic of New France. He arrived in Quebec in 1659.

A man of vision and character, Laval laid the foundations for the Catholic church in Canada. Afraid of having an inadequate number of diocesan priests, he founded (1663) a seminary in Quebec. Later the seminary became (1852) Laval University. He also organized an educational system that included a trade school and primary schools. His interest in Indian affairs and vigorous opposition to the sale of alcohol to Indians brought him into frequent conflict with the colonial authorities. In 1674, Laval succeeded in having Quebec declared a diocese and was named its first bishop. He resigned as bishop in 1688 but remained in Quebec until his death. The case for his canonization was begun in 1878; he was beatified in 1960. Laval is one of the main characters in *Shadows on the Rock* (1931), a novel by Willa Cather.

Bibliography: Scott, H. A., *Bishop Laval* (1926); Walsh, H. H., *The Church in the French Era: From Colonization to the British Conquest* (1966).

Laval, Pierre

Pierre Laval, b. June 28, 1883, d. Oct. 15, 1945, was a French statesman who figured significantly in the foreign and domestic affairs of the Third Republic and was vice-premier in the fascistic VICHY GOVERNMENT during World War II. At first a leftist socialist who defended trade unionists in his law practice, Laval entered in the Chamber of Deputies in 1914. In the 1920s he held a variety of governmental positions, but he was moving to the right and in 1926 was elected to the Senate as an independent.

Laval was premier in 1931–32 and both foreign minister and premier in 1935–36. In 1935 he formulated a plan with British foreign secretary Sir Samuel Hoare to halt the Italian invasion of Ethiopia by partitioning that country, giving much of it to Italy. Public indignation forced withdrawal of the plan, and Laval's government fell.

In 1940, Laval joined Marshal PÉTAIN's Vichy Government and helped persuade the Chamber of Deputies to give Pétain virtually unrestricted power. Appointed vice-premier, he pressed for closer ties with Nazi Germany. In 1941, Pétain replaced the independent-minded Laval with Adm. Jean DAR-LAN. Returning to power in 1942, Laval maneuvered to avoid deeper commitment to Germany, but with minimal success. In 1944 he was arrested by the retreating Germans, but he escaped to Spain in 1945. He was returned to France and tried for treason in a hostile court. After an abortive suicide attempt, he was executed. P. M. EWY

Bibliography: Laval, Pierre, *Diary of Pierre Laval* (1948; repr. 1976); Thompson, David, *Two Frenchmen* (1951; repr. 1975); Warner, Geoffrey, *Pierre Laval and the Eclipse of France* (1968).

Laval University

Established in 1663 as a seminary and made a university in 1852, Laval University (enrollment: 24,850; library: 1,540,600 volumes) is a private, coeducational francophone institution in Quebec City, Canada. It has a wide range of scholarly and professional faculties, as well as research institutes in northern studies, land planning, water, nutrition, atoms and molecules, and bilingualism.

Lavalleja, Juan Antonio [lah-vah-yay'-hah, hwahn ahn-tohn'-yoh]

Juan Antonio Lavalleja, b. June 24, 1784, d. Oct. 22, 1853, was a Uruguayan military officer and leader of the revolutionary group known as the Thirty-three Immortals who secured Uruguayan independence in 1828. They were successful in capitalizing on the longtime rivalry between Brazil and Argentina over control of Uruguay. The group precipitated a war (1825–28) between the two countries that resulted in a British-imposed peace guaranteeing the independence of Uruguay as a buffer state.

Lavalleja was never able to translate his revolutionary successes into political power in the new republic. A fellow Immortal, Fructoso RIVERA, became the first president and was succeeded by Manuel ORIBE. After two revolts (1832, 1834), Lavalleja sided with Oribe in the civil war that ensued (1843–51) between Rivera's faction, known as the Colorados (reds), and Oribe's faction, the Blancos (whites).

lavender [lav'-en-dur]

French lavender, L. dentata, is a shrub known for its fernlike leaves and purple flowers. Unlike some related species, it is not used to make perfume.

Lavender is the name given to 28 species of the genus *Lavandula,* a member of the MINT family. Grown for its fragrant flowers, it is used in perfumes, toilet preparations, and medicines. Lavender is native to the Mediterranean region and is cultivated commercially primarily in southern France and Italy. Important cultivated species include English or true lavender, *L. angustifolia,* with gray green foliage and small blue or white flowers; spike lavender, *L. latifolia,* a harsher smelling, broader-leaved type; and lavandin, a hybrid of true and spike lavenders. ARTHUR O. TUCKER

Laver, Rod [lay'-vur]

Rodney George Laver, b. Aug. 9, 1938, was an Australian tennis star who is considered by many experts to have been the greatest player in the game's history. Although he lacked an imposing physique, he was a spectacular shotmaker with an extremely effective topspin backhand. He is the only player in tennis history to win the Grand Slam of tennis (the Australian, British, French, and U.S. singles championships) twice, first as an amateur in 1962, then as a professional in 1969. He won 4 Wimbledon singles titles, 2 U.S. Open singles championships, and 3 Australian and 2 French singles titles between 1959 and 1969. He had a superb Davis Cup record, winning 10 of 12 Challenge Round matches. Laver had virtually retired from tournament play after 1976. STEVE FLINK

Bibliography: Laver, Rodney, *The Education of a Tennis Player* (1973).

Laveran, Charles [lah-vuh-rahn', sharl]

The French physician Charles Louis Alphonse Laveran, b. June 18, 1845, d. May 18, 1922, received the 1907 Nobel Prize for physiology or medicine for proving that certain diseases are caused by parasitic protozoa. He began his career as a French army doctor in 1867. In 1880, while stationed in Algeria, he discovered the causative organisms in the blood of malaria victims. Laveran also helped discover that KALA-AZAR, African sleeping sickness (TRYPANOSOMIASIS), and other tropical diseases are caused by protozoa. In 1907 he founded the Laboratory of Tropical Diseases at the Pasteur Institute in Paris.

Bibliography: Scott, H. H., *History of Tropical Medicine* (1939; repr. 1976).

Lavoisier, Antoine Laurent [lah-vwahz-yay', ahn-twahn' loh-rahn']

The French chemist Antoine Laurent Lavoisier, b. Aug. 26, 1743, d. May 8, 1794, was the founder of modern chemistry. Although he discovered no new substances and devised few new preparations, he described his experiments and synthesized chemical knowledge in his revolutionary textbook *Elements of Chemistry* (1789; Eng. trans., 1790). In this textbook he presented a new system of chemistry that was based on an essentially modern concept of chemical elements and that made extensive use of the conservation of mass in chemical reactions. Formerly, chemical theory had been based on either three or four elements, and negative mass was considered a possibility by some chemists.

Lavoisier demonstrated experimentally that oxygen gas in the air is involved in combustion, calcination (rusting), and respiration, thus disproving George STAHL's PHLOGISTON THEORY. The basic principles of the new nomenclature, devised in collaboration with Claude Louis BERTHOLLET, Antoine de FOURCROY, and Guyton de Morveau, are still used. Among Lavoisier's major mistakes were the exaggerated importance ascribed to the role of oxygen in acids and the inclusion of a weightless "heat substance" in his list of chemical elements.

Lavoisier's interest in science was developed during his education (1754–61) at the Collège Mazarin, where he studied mathematics, astronomy, chemistry, and botany, and during a

The French chemist Antoine Lavoisier was the founder of modern chemistry. He determined oxygen's role in combustion and respiration and was the first to distinguish between elements and compounds. Lavoisier also helped to establish the use of the metric system in France. He is shown here with his wife in a painting (1788) by J. L. David. (Rockefeller University, New York City.)

period (1761–64) of legal studies (a family tradition), when he listened to lectures on geology by Jean-Etienne Guettard (1715–86) and on chemistry by Guillaume-François Rouelle (1703–70), both members of the Académie Royale des Sciences. Lavoisier then worked for Guettard for 3 years, collecting details for a geologic map of France and participating in a geological survey (1767) of Alsace and Lorraine. His first paper (1764) on chemistry dealt with the properties of gypsum and the settling of plaster of paris. Another early essay, on the problem of lighting the streets of cities and large towns, was awarded a gold medal by the king of France.

Lavoisier was elected to the Academy of Sciences in 1768, the same year that he entered the Ferme Générale, a private firm that collected certain taxes for the government. He served (1775–91) on the Royal Gunpowder Administration and became a director of the Discount Bank and an administrator of the national treasury. During the period of the French Revolution Lavoisier served as an alternate deputy for the nobility—he had inherited a purchased title from his father in 1775—at the meeting of the Estates General; published reports on the state of French finances and on French agricultural resources; drafted with others a scheme for reforming the French educational system; and participated with other Academy members in establishing the metric system of weights and measures. Nevertheless, Lavoisier, a moderate constitutionalist, was subjected to attacks by radicals, such as Jean-Paul Marat, and his involvement with the unpopular Ferme Générale led to his execution by guillotine during the Reign of Terror.   RALPH GABLE

Bibliography: Guerlac, Henry, *Antoine Laurent Lavoisier: Chemist and Revolutionary* (1975) and *Lavoisier: The Crucial Year* (1961); McKie, Douglas, *Antoine Lavoisier* (1952).

law

Law can be defined broadly as a system of standards and rules of civil society: standards of human conduct that impose obligations and grant corresponding rights, and institutional rules regarding the ascertainment, creation, modification, and enforcement of these standards. The question "What is law?" has elicited a myriad of answers throughout human history, ranging from the Old Testament's assertion of law as the will of God to the thesis of Karl MARX and Friedrich ENGELS that law is an expression of class ideology.

CONCEPTIONS OF LAW

Notwithstanding the marked historical diversity in conceptions of law, many if not most of the conceptions of law can be placed in one of six broad categories: natural law, legal positivism, historical jurisprudence, sociological jurisprudence, Marxism, and legal realism.

Like Western philosophy in general, philosophy of law in particular first emerged in ancient Greece. In the 5th century BC the SOPHISTS and SOCRATES, along with his followers, took up the question of the nature of law. Both recognized a distinction between things that exist by nature (*physis*) and those which exist by human-made convention (*nomos*). The Sophists, however, tended to place law in the latter category, whereas Socrates put it in the former, as did PLATO and ARISTOTLE. Thus began the debate that continues even today over whether the essence of law is nature and reason on the one hand or convention and will on the other hand. Thinkers who believe the former belong to what can be loosely called the tradition of NATURAL LAW, and those who assert the latter belong to the tradition of legal positivism.

Natural Law and Legal Positivism. All of the early political philosophers were deeply concerned with the nature of justice and good government. The idea of natural law can be found in Plato's concept of the just state—governed by the good and the wise—which in his view reflects the naturally hierarchical structure of human society. Governed by wisdom, the ideal state has no need of conventional law because wisdom itself is the recognition of the primacy of natural order. Aristotle made a distinction, however, between paramount natural law that establishes general precepts and human-made law that merely imposes sanctions for violations of those precepts. Marcus Tullius CICERO, a Roman statesman and politician who was also a Stoic (see STOICISM) legal philosopher, put forward the first full-blown theory of natural law, in his *Commonwealth* (51 BC): "True law is right reason in accord with nature; it is of universal application, unchanging and everlasting. . . ."

Later, Saint AUGUSTINE combined Stoic legal thinking with Christian philosophy by identifying eternal, divine law with God's reason and will and by considering human law as being derived from and limited by divine law. The natural-law tradition culminated in the theory of Saint Thomas AQUINAS, which synthesized Aristotelian, Stoic, ROMAN LAW, and Christian elements. Aquinas formulated a fourfold classification of types of law: (1) eternal law—God's plan for the universe; (2) natural law—that part of the eternal law in which humans participate by their reason; (3) divine law—God's direct revelation to humankind through the scriptures; and (4) human law—particular determinations of certain matters arrived at through the use of reason from the general precepts of the natural law. Aquinas also argued—as Cicero had done—that an unjust law was not a genuine law but rather an act of violence. Later thinkers who may be placed in the natural-law tradition include Hugo GROTIUS, Thomas HOOKER, Gottfried LEIBNIZ, Baruch SPINOZA, Jean Jacques ROUSSEAU, and Jacques MARITAIN.

In marked contrast to natural-law jurists, legal positivists such as Thomas HOBBES argued that the essence of law is the command or will of the sovereign and that an "unjust law" is a contradiction in terms because the existing law is itself the standard of justice. Jean BODIN had anticipated Hobbes in the former respect when he claimed that "law is nothing else than the command of the sovereign in his exercise of sovereign power." Bodin had added, however, that the prince "has no power to exceed the law of nature," and he expected natural law to be found in constitutional restraints. Thus Bodin had not broken unequivocally from the natural-law tradition. John LOCKE's criticism of Hobbesian theory set the stage for modern theories of CIVIL DISOBEDIENCE and for independent government in the American colonies.

Many legal positivists after Hobbes have backed down from his extreme claims. For example, Jeremy BENTHAM and John AUSTIN agreed that law was the command of the sovereign but rejected the idea that law was necessarily the standard of justice or morality. Bentham was more interested in the law's utility in providing the greatest happiness for the greatest number. Hans Kelsen (1881–1973) and the English legal philosopher H. L. A. Hart repudiated the command theory of law, arguing respectively that laws are essentially derived from norms for the creation of law and rules that arise from society. Nonetheless the central point of contention between natural-law jurists and legal positivists remains the same: the former insist on a necessary connection between legal validity and moral value, whereas the latter hold that no such connection is necessary. As Hart put it in *The Concept of Law* (1961), natural law jurists hold that "there are certain principles of human conduct, awaiting discovery by human reason, with which man-made law must conform if it is to be valid," whereas legal positivists contend that "it is in no sense a necessary truth that laws reproduce or satisfy certain demands of morality though in fact they have often done so."

Historical Jurisprudence. In contrast with both natural-law jurists and legal positivists, members of the historical school of jurisprudence, most notably Friedrich Karl von SAVIGNY, maintained that "an organic connection [exists] between law and the nature and character of a people." In his view legislation is relatively unimportant except insofar as it declares customary law, which is the truly living law. Thus the spirit of the people and not the commands of the sovereign or right reason in accord with nature constitutes the essence of law. Other important juridical historians include Otto Friedrich von GIERKE, Sir Henry MAINE, and Frederick William MAITLAND. MONTESQUIEU may also be placed in this school, although he preceded it in time.

Sociological Jurisprudence. Akin to historical jurisprudence is sociological jurisprudence, which can be traced to the writings of Rudolf von Jhering (1818–92). He rejected Savigny's theory on the ground that the latter, in viewing law as a spontaneous expression of subconscious forces, overlooked the importance of conscious human purposes and the pursuit of interests embodied in the law. Jhering also emphasized that law must be understood in the context of social life. He thus foreshadowed the jurisprudence-of-interests school of thought and sociological jurisprudence. Both strains of Jhering's thought influenced the jurisprudential theory of Roscoe POUND and other American sociological jurists, who focused on the notion of "social engineering" law as a means of social control and the relationship between law and society.

Marxism. In contrast to historical and sociological jurists, Marxist jurists stress the relationship between law and the economic aspects of society rather than society generally and emphasize the pursuit of class interests instead of interests generally. Responding to critics, Marx and Engels wrote in *The Communist Manifesto* (1848): "Your law is but the will of your class exalted into statutes, a will which acquires its content from the material conditions of [the] existence of your class." Important Marxists who have refined the theory of law put forward by Marx and Engels include Andrei VYSHINSKY, E. Pashukanis (1891–1938), and Karl Renner (1870–1950).

Legal Realism. Legal realism, which has flourished in America, has been more of a movement than a school of thought. Its fundamental tenets were anticipated by Justice Oliver Wendell HOLMES, Jr., who remarked: "The life of the law has not been logic; it has been experience" and "Prophecies of what courts will do in fact, and nothing more pretentious, are what I mean by law." Like sociological jurists, legal realists revolted against analytic jurisprudence and formalism, or mechanical jurisprudence, but the realists were somewhat more extreme than the sociological jurists in their claims. They even went so far as to claim that legal rules are myths and that laws are really nothing more than particular judicial decisions. Realists combined behaviorism with this nominalism and thus aspired to the scientific study of law. The most influential of American legal realists include Karl Llewellyn (1893–1962), Jerome Frank (1889–1957), and Thurman Arnold (1891–1969). The most outspoken of its critics include Lon Fuller (1902–78), H. L. A. HART, and Ronald Dworkin (b. 1931).

TYPES OF LAW

Traditionally, law has been divided into public law and private law. Public and private laws that set forth the substance of rights and obligations are sometimes called substantive law in order to distinguish them from LEGAL PROCEDURE; the latter specifies the methods to be followed in adjudicating substantive law cases in order to ensure they are conducted in a manner protective of the rights of the participants. If procedural law relates to how the rights and duties of substantive law are to be vindicated and enforced, substantive law pertains to what the law is on a given matter.

Public Law. Public law concerns the structures, powers, and operations of a government, the rights and duties of citizens in relation to the government, and the relationships among nations. It can be divided further into constitutional law, ADMINISTRATIVE LAW, criminal law, and INTERNATIONAL LAW.

Constitutional law, the fundamental or paramount law of a nation, is derived from the nation's CONSTITUTION, which comprehends the body of rules in accordance with which the powers of government are exercised. Constitutions may be either written or unwritten—the United States's is an example of the former, Great Britain's of the latter. In some nations, courts have the power of JUDICIAL REVIEW, whereby they declare unconstitutional and therefore void laws that contravene the provisions or arrangements of the constitution.

Administrative law includes laws governing the organization and operation of agencies of the executive branch of government, the substantive and procedural rules that these agencies formulate and apply pursuant to their regulatory and other administrative functions, and COURT decisions involving public agencies and private citizens.

Criminal law consists of laws that impose obligations to do or forbear from doing certain things, the infraction of which is considered to be an offense not merely against the immediate victim but also against society. Most such laws are backed up by sanctions or punishments, which are applied in the event of conviction. Major breaches of the criminal law, usually defined as those punishable by imprisonment for more than 1 year, are termed FELONIES. Less serious crimes, called MISDEMEANORS, are punishable by imprisonment for a shorter period or by fines or both.

Finally, international law concerns the relationships among nations, including the use of the high seas, INTERNATIONAL TRADE, boundary disputes, warfare methods, and the like. Some legal theorists question whether international law is genuine law because it lacks an international legislature, centrally organized sanctions, and courts with involuntary jurisdiction, all of which characterize national legal systems.

Private Law. Unlike public law, private law does not involve government directly but rather indirectly as an adjudicator between disputing parties. Private law provides rules to be applied when one person claims that another has injured his or her person, property, or reputation or has failed to carry out a valid legal obligation. Private law also includes laws that confer powers or capabilities to create structures of obligations and rights on individuals who wish to achieve given legal objectives.

On the basis of the types of legal rights and obligations involved, private law is conventionally subdivided into six main categories: (1) TORT law; (2) PROPERTY law; (3) CONTRACT and BUSINESS LAW; (4) CORPORATION law; (5) INHERITANCE law; and (6) family law.

Sources of Law. Laws can also be subdivided on the basis of the sources of law from which they derive. The various legal systems of the world recognize as valid and therefore binding on their subjects some or all of the following major sources: constitutions and administrative rules, such as those described above; legislative statutes; judicial precedents; and customary practice. Although when a person thinks of law, the concept of statutes comes most readily to mind, statutes are now outnumbered by the innumerable administrative rules and regulations that have accompanied the growth of administrative government in modern times. Judicial precedents (also known as case law), which are recognized as valid law that later courts must follow in COMMON LAW but not in CIVIL LAW systems, are prior cases decided by courts. Finally, customary practice is a minor source of law in the legal systems of advanced industrial nations, but it is the primary if not the only source in primitive legal systems and is inextricably linked with kinship, taboo, religion, and traditional authority systems.

LAWYERS

The requirements for becoming a lawyer in the United States are set by each state (or the District of Columbia or Puerto Rico). In general, an individual must earn a bachelor's degree and then attend a recognized law school for either 3 years as a full-time day student or 4 years as a part-time evening student. Law schools grant the juris doctor (J.D.) degree, and many also offer a master of laws (LL.M.) program. Some also offer a doctoral program leading to the degree of doctor of the science of jurisprudence (J.S.D.). The basic J.D. degree is sufficient for either law practice, law teaching, or the judiciary. In order to become an ATTORNEY the individual must also pass the state's bar examination. A person who wishes to work in the law but does not wish to pursue the program leading to a law degree may train to be a paralegal assistant to lawyers (see PARALEGAL SERVICES). Various schools have been set up in recent years to train such persons.

Most lawyers are in private practice. In larger centers of population they tend to form partnerships that may range from two to hundreds of members. Because the law touches on all aspects of life, the work of lawyers is of infinite variety. Most lawyers specialize in a field such as tax law, estate planning, corporate law, workers compensation law, and so forth. Some lawyers specialize in trial work. Many work for federal, state, or local government or for administrative agencies. Some lawyers are employed by business firms; the legal department of a large corporation or bank may include dozens of lawyers.

In England legal representation is divided between solicitors, or attorneys, and barristers. A client goes to a solicitor, who drafts legal documents, advises, and handles matters that can be settled out of court or in lower courts. If a case must go to a higher court the solicitor employs a barrister, who is permitted to plead in superior courts. In these cases the solicitor and barrister form a legal team.

Reviewed by NICHOLAS D. CONSTAN, JR.

Bibliography: Abraham, Henry J., *The Judicial Process*, 3d rev. ed. (1975); Berman, Harold J., *Justice in the USSR*, rev. ed. (1963); Black, Donald, *The Behavior of Law* (1976); Bodenheimer, Edgar, *Jurisprudence* (1974); Cataldo, Bernard F., et al., *Introduction to Law and the Legal Process*, 2d ed. (1973); Corley, Robert N., *The Legal Environment of Business*, 4th ed. (1977); Frank, Jerome, *Law and the Modern Mind* (1930; repr. 1949); Freund, Paul A., *On Law and Justice* (1968); Friedrich, Carl, *The Philosophy of Law in Historical Perspective*, 2d ed. (1963); Hart, Herbert L. A., *The Concept of Law* (1961); Hoebel, Edward A., *Law of Primitive Man* (1954; repr. 1968); Llewellyn, Karl, *Jurisprudence: Realism in Theory and Practice* (1962); Merryman, John H., *The Civil Law Tradition* (1969); Pound, Roscoe, *An Introduction to the Philosophy of Law* (1921; repr. 1954).

See also: DIVORCE; EQUITY (law); EVIDENCE; GERMANIC LAW; HAMMURABI, CODE OF; JURY; JUSTINIAN CODE; JUVENILE DELINQUENCY; MAGNA CARTA; NAPOLEONIC CODE; SEAS, FREEDOM OF THE; SOCIALIST LAW; SPACE LAW.

law, history of

Law is a system of rules of conduct and rights formally recognized by society or prescribed by the authority in a state. It distinguishes between what is permitted and what is prohibited. The appearance of an organized court system in Egypt around 4000 BC marked the beginning of legal history. Under this system, the word of the king was law. The palaces were centers of law with judges administering justice. Records of wills, contracts, titles, and boundaries to land were maintained, and all legal actions were filed in the palaces. The Egyptian legal system endured until Egypt was conquered by Rome in the 1st century BC.

The oldest written code of law, the Code of Hammurabi (see HAMMURABI, CODE OF), came from the Mesopotamian legal system. Composed in approximately 2100 BC, the 285 provisions of the Code of Hammurabi controlled commerce, family, criminal, and civil law. Under the code, written pleadings began legal actions and testimony was given under oath.

Roman Law. The greatest contribution of the Roman Empire was the introduction of a legal system to the nations it conquered. The unified, written law of the Roman Empire—which at its height extended from England to Egypt—replaced unwritten native customs and rules.

The Egyptian goddess of truth and justice, Maat, was the personification of the concept of physical and spiritual order, ma'at, the basis of Egyptian life. It was the function of the pharaoh, the highest judicial and religious authority, to maintain ma'at. The administration of justice was usually delegated to a vizier, the representative of the pharaoh.

ROMAN LAW had its recorded beginnings in the law of the Twelve Tables, formulated in 451–450 BC. These laws, primarily procedural, were cast in bronze and attached to the "Rostra," or orator's platform, in the Roman Forum so that all Roman citizens—especially the plebeians—might read and understand the law and be protected from arbitrary patrician justice.

Roman legal development ended with the codification known as the *Corpus Juris Civilis* (Body of Civil Law), which consolidated all existing law into a single written code. It was promulgated (AD 533–34) by the Byzantine emperor Justinian I and was known as the JUSTINIAN CODE. The code was a collection of past laws and opinions of Roman jurists and also included new laws enacted by Justinian. The Code of Justinian became the foundation of the present CIVIL LAW system. Civil law and COMMON LAW, formed in England, are the two major legal systems in the world today outside the Communist or socialist countries (see SOCIALIST LAW).

Other legal systems developed prior to the Middle Ages—the Chinese and Greek legal systems, for example. The Hebrew (see TALMUD), Islamic, Hindu (see MANU), and Roman Catholic canon (see CANON LAW) legal systems were rooted in religion, but their influence extended to the secular world. The Roman law system had, however, the greatest influence on Western legal development.

This 6th-century mosaic shows the Byzantine emperor Justinian I with members of his court. Justinian sponsored the compilation of Roman law into the Corpus Juris Civilis, which formed the basis of western civil law. (San Vitale, Ravenna, Italy.)

Law in the Middle Ages. The decline of the Roman Empire in Western Europe in the 5th century and the rise of the Germanic tribes suppressed legal development throughout much of Europe. The conquering Germanic tribes brought little to replace Roman law. GERMANIC LAW began as the unwritten custom of the tribe, not the enactment of any supreme authority in the state. The *Lex Salica*, composed about AD 500, was the most important of the written Germanic tribal codes; compared with the Code of Justinian, however, the *Lex Salica* was crude and rudimentary. Each Germanic tribe was governed by its own customs and rules. The uniformity and systematic jurisprudence of the Roman legal system contrasted sharply with the differing rules among the tribes.

The early Middle Ages saw little progress in the development of law. Few schools of law existed. Learning was left to monks and clergy. The feudal system of land ownership, from the 8th century through the 14th century, was comprised of petty domains (see FEUDALISM). Systematic justice was destroyed. Each region administered, developed, and recorded its own local laws. The Roman Catholic church and its canon law system became increasingly influential during the Middle Ages in the vacuum of legal advancement. Canon law borrowed from Roman law and thereby preserved the Roman system until its revival in the late 11th century.

In Bologna, Italy, around the year 1100, an awakening of learning in the field of law occurred. Under the guidance of

This miniature from a 15th-century illuminated manuscript shows proceedings at the court of the King's Bench. The King's Bench, a court of law originally administered by clerics assigned by the sovereign, contributed to the development of common law in England.

Irnerius and his students, Justinian's works were resurrected and studied. Within another one hundred years, thousands of law students were studying in Bologna. These students spread through Europe. Commentators wrote opinions and treatises on legal cases and the law. They applied the principles of Roman law to Germanic and feudal customs, transforming Roman law into Italian law. During the 13th, 14th, and 15th centuries, faculties of law were founded in Spain, France, Germany, and the Netherlands. The studies conducted there were to form the basis of the modern civil law systems of these countries. Various interpretations of legal thought inevitably began to spring up. In the 16th century, for example, a school of law called legal humanism emphasized the importance and flexibility of classical Roman law. In the 17th and 18th centuries, legal scholars such as Hugo GROTIUS and Samuel von PUFENDORF put forward theories of NATURAL LAW, and advocated the use of reason in combination with tenets of Roman law.

The Dutch scholar Hugo Grotius, one of the most eminent jurists and humanists of the 17th century, is considered a founder of modern international law. In On the Law of War and Peace (1625), the earliest comprehensive text on international law, Grotius presented a humanitarian legal philosophy, based on natural law, applicable to both individuals and nations.

Modern Civil Law. Despite the renewed respect for law, the weakness of royal governments and the strength of the feudal system in the Middle Ages militated against any unified national law. Royal absolutism and growing nationalism in the 16th, 17th, and 18th centuries, however, began to unite nations and thus provided the foundation for unified legal sys-

tems. The French Revolution in 1789 and the rise to power of Napoleon I gave birth to the French civil code, or NAPOLEONIC CODE, in 1804. Spread throughout Europe by Napoleon's conquests, it became the most influential of the civil law national codes and was the basis of other national codes that followed: the Austrian Civil Code in 1811, the Italian Civil Code in 1865, the Spanish Civil Code in 1888, and the German Civil Code of 1900. Other comprehensive codes were compiled in Belgium, Romania, Bulgaria, Japan, Egypt, and many nations in Latin America. Even the law in the state of Louisiana, originally settled by the French in 1682, is heavily based on the French Civil Code.

The modern civil law systems that arose from ancient Roman law are distinguished by codification—the systematic and comprehensive statutory treatment of the law. The civil law COURTS base their decisions on enactments rather than on judicial precedent; the latter is the basis of common law. If the civil court ruling is attacked, the attack is on the ground that the statute has been misinterpreted or misapplied.

Modern continental European law resulted from the fusion of Germanic customary law and Roman law. To these were added contributions from feudal law, canon law, and the law of the merchant. It was a gradual process molded by nationalism, war, and revolution and revised and amended to meet the challenges of modern society.

The Napoleonic Code Crowned by Time (1833) celebrates the first modern codification of civil law, enacted (1804) by the French emperor as the Code Napoléon. This code became the basis for civil law throughout Europe and parts of the Americas.

Common Law. In England, however, a second system of legal justice, known as common law, evolved. Unlike the civil law system, common law is not a written code but is based on written judicial decisions that constitute precedent. This doctrine of following precedents is called stare decisis (Latin, "to stand by decided matters"). Statutes modify the law rather than embody it as in the civil law systems.

English law was initially based on the Germanic tribal customs. When the Normans invaded England in 1066, they found a legal system more advanced than their own. The Normans under William I (r. 1066–87) and his successors Henry II (r. 1154–89) and Edward I (r. 1272–1307) consolidated the conflicting local customs into the common law. Their objective was to curb the power of the feudal land owners and ensure the supremacy of the king. Trial by JURY was instituted, and the MAGNA CARTA (1215) placed the king under the rule of law. Magistrates, or justices, traveled from town to town to hear cases. The office of judge became a full-time career. Admission to the bar was contingent upon legal knowledge. Pleas to the king's chancellor for fair solutions to wrongs not righted by common law courts created a separate body of law called EQUITY, which was not merged with common law in England until 1873, and which survives in the United States in a few states.

As the revival of Roman law and its resulting codification spread through continental Europe during the later part of the Middle Ages, it stopped at the English Channel. Strong nationalism and a unified legal profession preserved the common law system in England. A guild of lawyers and their apprentices appeared in the 14th century. The INNS OF COURT provided education for law students. Court decisions were published (1300–1535) in Year Books, and these decisions were referred to in arguing and deciding cases. The Year Books provided a common and continuous legal record, ensuring the development of a uniquely English system.

Common law advanced through the teaching and writing of English legal scholars. Henry de Bracton (d. 1268) and Sir Edward COKE (1552–1634) advocated the common law system in their legal treatises. Sir William BLACKSTONE's *Commentaries on the Laws of England* (1765–69) analyzed English law and became the basis of legal education in the New World.

John Marshall, the fourth chief justice (1801–35) of the U.S. Supreme Court, established the judicial branch of the U.S. government as a powerful expositor of constitutional law. With landmark decisions such as that in Marbury v. Madison *(1803),* Marshall articulated the doctrine of judicial review, whereby the Supreme Court may rule on the constitutionality of legislative acts.

Sir William Blackstone, the most eminent British jurist of the 18th century, is best known for the historical analysis and systematization of English law contained in his Commentaries on the Laws of England *(1765–69). This work greatly influenced both legal procedure and legal education in Great Britain and the United States. (National Portrait Gallery, London.)*

The common law system spread through English colonization and conquest. The United States was one of the first to adopt and defend this system. Common law also exists in the British Commonwealth nations and in former colonies such as India. Flexible and adaptable to change, common law proved a viable legal system.

Law in the North American Colonies. Because the majority of the colonists who first settled America came from England, the common law system was introduced in many colonies. More important was the reliance on Blackstone's *Commentaries.* The influence of this work, along with the lack of any law schools in America until 1784, a fact that necessitated the training of lawyers in England, established English common law in America.

Lawyers led the fight for independence and were instrumental in composing the CONSTITUTION OF THE UNITED STATES (1787) and the BILL OF RIGHTS (1791). Of the 56 signers of the DECLARATION OF INDEPENDENCE (1776), 25 were attorneys; so were 31 of the 55 members of the CONSTITUTIONAL CONVENTION (1787). After the Revolutionary War, common law survived despite prejudice against the English. The writings by scholarly jurists, such as Joseph STORY's *Commentaries on the Constitution of the United States* (1833) and James KENT's *Commentaries on American Law* (1826–30) in the early 19th century, ensured the continuation of common law.

The United States Supreme Court. Before John MARSHALL's appointment as chief justice in 1801, the SUPREME COURT OF THE UNITED STATES was held in low esteem; it was disorganized and decided few cases. Marshall's concern was to establish a strong, independent judiciary. The decisions of his court did much to increase the power and prestige of the Court. In MARBURY V. MADISON (1803) the Supreme Court declared it had the power to determine the constitutionality of legislative acts.

In decisions such as McCULLOCH V. MARYLAND (1819) and GIBBONS V. OGDEN (1824) the Marshall court shaped the future of the law and the country. These decisions gave the consti-

tution the flexibility to meet the needs of a growing nation. As American society progressed, the functions of the Court expanded. An interesting and complicating feature of the U.S. legal system is the coexistence of two sets of law and jurisdictions—federal and state. The 14TH AMENDMENT (1868) had tremendous impact on the law and the future of the judicial system: it guaranteed EQUAL PROTECTION OF THE LAWS and DUE PROCESS of the law, allowing the federal courts to determine the constitutionality of state statutes that affect individual rights. Thus, the 14th Amendment increased the role and authority of the judiciary.

Civil Rights. The emphasis in U.S. law shifted from property rights in the late 19th and early 20th centuries to CIVIL RIGHTS and liberties in the middle and later part of the 20th century. The court outlawed segregation in public schools (BROWN V. BOARD OF EDUCATION OF TOPEKA, KANSAS, 1954); guaranteed the fundamental freedoms of religion, press, and speech (see FREEDOM OF THE PRESS; FREEDOM OF RELIGION; FREEDOM OF SPEECH); ensured the right to a trial by jury for criminal offenses; and added constitutional protections to those accused of crimes. The Court ruled that EVIDENCE obtained by illegal searches and seizures cannot be used in trials (*Weeks* v. *U.S.*, 1914, and MAPP V. OHIO, 1961), and it held that a criminal suspect must be informed of his or her right to remain silent (see SELF-INCRIMINATION) and to legal counsel (MIRANDA V. ARIZONA, 1966). The common law proved it could adapt to

During the 1950s the U.S. Supreme Court, under Chief Justice Earl Warren (1953–69), was composed of: (left to right, seated) William O. Douglas, Hugo L. Black, Earl Warren, Felix Frankfurter, Tom C. Clark; (standing) Charles E. Whittaker, John M. Harlan, William J. Brennan, Jr., and Potter Stewart. The liberal focus of the Warren Court resulted in landmark decisions in civil liberties and civil rights.

In September 1957, President Eisenhower ordered 1,000 federal troops to Little Rock, Ark., to effect the entrance of nine black students into the city's segregated Central High School. The unanimous 1954 decision of the U.S. Supreme Court (under Chief Justice Earl Warren) in Brown v. Board of Education, Topeka, Kansas ruled that racially segregated educational facilities were unconstitutional.

changing American society. An important function of the judiciary system has also been to protect the supremacy of law against abuses by the executive branch. In cases such as YOUNGSTOWN SHEET AND TUBE COMPANY V. SAWYER (1952) and UNITED STATES V. RICHARD M. NIXON (1974), the Supreme Court respectively upheld the primacy of statutory authority and overruled the assertion of executive privilege when it was faced with the fundamental requirements of due process of law.

Corporate Law. U.S. law is called upon to deal with increasingly complex issues, such as how to regulate the ubiquitous corporation. Formed to conduct business for profit, the corporation is a creation of the law. The ability of the U.S. legal system to adapt the common law to the requirements of a changing society is exemplified in BUSINESS LAW. Early Supreme Court decisions in DARTMOUTH COLLEGE V. WOODWARD (1819) and Bank of Augusta v. Earle (1839) provided impetus for corporate growth. As corporations grew in the late 19th and early 20th centuries, so did the demand for their control. Federal and state governments enacted legislation to regulate their development (see GOVERNMENT REGULATION). Corporate law involves the majority of businesses in American society from General Motors to the local grocery store and includes topics ranging from taxes to shareholder rights.

Administrative Law. Another recent and increasingly important addition to the U.S. legal system is ADMINISTRATIVE LAW, which governs the proliferating activities of governmental agencies and officials whose function is to execute legislative mandates. The first agency was the Interstate Commerce Commission formed in 1887. The many others that followed affect the gamut of American life from licensing of trades and professions to workers compensation to airline safety. Administrative law procedures differ substantially from traditional common law; but the fundamental principles of administrative law are at least in part derived from the U.S. Constitution.

American and other legal systems have been challenged by increasing demands. Aviation disasters can involve citizens and laws of many nations, and tremendous antitrust suits may involve multinational corporations. Larger law firms now have offices throughout the world to conduct INTERNATIONAL LAW. Both the importance and complexity of law has clearly increased since the era of Justinian.   STUART M. SPEISER

Bibliography: Carpenter, Williams S., Foundations of Modern Jurisprudence (1958); Dawson, John P., The Oracles of the Law (1968); Friedman, Lawrence M., A History of American Law (1973); Hart, Herbert L. A., The Concept of Law (1961); Holmes, Oliver Wendell, Jr., The Common Law (1881; repr. 1964); Jolowicz, H. F., Historical Introduction to the Study of Roman Law, 2d ed. (1952); Merryman, John, The Civil Law Tradition (1969); Pound, Roscoe, Interpretations of Legal History (1923); Schwartz, Bernard, The Law in America: A History (1974); Speiser, Stuart M., Recovery for Wrongful Death (1975); Wigmore, John H.,

Panorama of the World's Legal Systems (1928); Wormser, René A., The Story of the Law and the Men Who Made It, rev. ed. (1962); Zane, John M., The Story of Law (1927).

See also: CONTRACT; CRIMINAL LAW; LEGAL PROCEDURE; MARITIME LAW; MILITARY JUSTICE; PROPERTY; TORT.

Law, Andrew Bonar   [bah'-nur]

Andrew Bonar Law, b. Sept. 16, 1858, d. Oct. 30, 1923, led the British Conservative party for more than ten years and was briefly prime minister (1922–23). Born in Canada, he went to Scotland as a boy and made a substantial fortune in the iron trade of Glasgow. Elected to Parliament in 1900, he became leader of the Conservatives in 1911 on the resignation of Arthur BALFOUR. Law excelled in the delivery of vigorous debating speeches, replete with facts and statistics. The Liberal David LLOYD GEORGE remarked: "The fools have chosen their best man."

During World War I, Law proved himself an excellent administrator as colonial secretary (1915–16) in Herbert ASQUITH's coalition and as chancellor of the exchequer (1916–19) under Lloyd George. In 1922, Law opposed the continuation of the coalition government, and he succeeded to the post of prime minister in October. Mortal illness, however, forced him to resign after seven months, and he died soon after.   DAVID DILKS

Bibliography: Blake, Robert, The Unknown Prime Minister (1955).

Law, John

John Law, b. April 1671, d. Mar. 21, 1729, was a Scottish financier whose brilliant but overly speculative banking and stock market projects in France during LOUIS XV's minority created a spectacular but shortlived economic boom.

Law persuaded the near-bankrupt French government to test his theory that state credit schemes based on public confidence could greatly increase national wealth. In 1716 his government-chartered General Bank began to issue paper currency and provide low-interest loans to businesses. At the same time Law's Company of the West, organized in 1717, sold 100 million livres of stock based on the potential wealth of its monopoly over France's Louisiana Territory (see MISSISSIPPI SCHEME). In 1719 this company, renamed the Company of the Indies, absorbed all other French trading companies. By 1720, Law was controller general of finance. In that year he merged his bank and company into a vast financial organization that assumed control of state debts, coinage, and taxation. Panic public selling later that year destroyed the entire scheme. The idea of state banking was discredited for a century, and Law became a bankrupt exile.   A. LLOYD MOOTE

Bibliography: Hyde, H. M., John Law, rev. ed. (1969); Minton, Robert, John Law: The Father of Paper Money (1975).

law, physical

Physical laws give precise expression to observed regularities that occur in nature. They are necessary for describing, explaining, or predicting the development of natural phenomena. For example, KEPLER'S LAWS of planetary motion, established from observation, describe how the planets move in their orbits about the Sun. Newton's LAWS OF MOTION and his law of GRAVITATION explain mathematically the laws of planetary motion.

If the state of motion of a physical system is known at some initial time, then the laws of motion can, in principle, determine the system's state of motion at any later time. If, for example, the positions and velocities of all the bodies in the solar system were known at some instant, Newtonian mechanics could be used to calculate the positions and velocities of the bodies at any later time. An important property of most classical physical laws is that they do not contain statements about the initial state of a system; once the initial conditions have been specified, however, they describe subsequent physical behavior precisely.

The laws of electromagnetism are expressed by MAXWELL'S EQUATIONS, a set of partial differential equations for electric and magnetic fields. Here, the initial data are much more complex. The fields must be given at an initial instant at every point in space before Maxwell's equations can be used to predict the future condition of the electromagnetic field.

Einstein's special theory of RELATIVITY synthesized and unified mechanics and electromagnetic theory and led to a more general set of laws known as the classical laws of relativistic electrodynamics. Einstein also extended and generalized Newton's law of gravitation into a more accurate, far-reaching treatment known as the general theory of relativity.

Classical physical laws, however, lead to incorrect results when applied to atoms, nuclei, and elementary particles. Between 1900 and 1930 the laws of QUANTUM MECHANICS were discovered, developed, and successfully applied. Quantum laws can be written in the form of differential equations, which, as is true of the classical case, require that the initial data be specified. Heisenberg's UNCERTAINTY PRINCIPLE states that initial data cannot be specified with sufficient precision to apply classical laws; therefore, separate sets of laws apply to microscopic and macroscopic phenomena.

The basic physical laws share two surprising properties: they are all unproven and also unprovable. Developed from observation and experimentation, they are assumed valid as long as no natural violations of them can be found. It is presumed that natural physical laws exist and have always existed. It is the goal of scientists, mathematicians, and philosophers to discover and define those laws.

N. ASHBY AND W. E. BRITTIN

Bibliography: Duhem, Pierre, *The Aim and Structure of Physical Theory* (1906; trans. 1954); Hempel, C. G., *Philosophy of Natural Science* (1966); White, Harvey E., *Modern College Physics*, 6th ed. (1972).

See also: SCIENCE, PHILOSOPHY OF.

Law, William

William Law, b. 1686, d. Apr. 9, 1761, was an English theologian and mystic. Educated at Cambridge, Law was ordained a priest in the Church of England and remained as a fellow at Cambridge University. In 1714, however, he was dismissed because of his refusal to renounce his loyalty to the Stuart dynasty and swear allegiance to the Hanoverian George I. As a nonjuror he lost any possibility of advancing in the church. Law joined the household of the Gibbon estate in Putney (1727–37), where he tutored Edward Gibbon (father of the historian). Through the Gibbons he came to know the WESLEY family, who also sought his advice.

Influenced by Jakob BÖHME, Law became a mystic after 1734. In 1740 he retired to his birthplace at Kings Cliffe, Northamptonshire, accompanied by two disciples. Their aim was to cultivate a saintly existence of devotion, study, and service. A powerful foe of deism and mystical writer of note, Law is renowned for his devotional classic, *Serious Call to a*

Devout and Holy Life (1728). His works were collected in nine volumes after his death.

JAMES D. NELSON

Bibliography: Clarkson, George, *The Mysticism of William Law* (1978); Green, J. B., *John Wesley and William Law* (1945); Hobhouse, Steven, *William Law and Eighteenth Century Quakerism* (1927); Walker, A. K., *William Law: His Life and Thought* (1973).

Law of the Sea: see SEA, LAW OF THE.

Lawes, Henry   [lawz]

Henry Lawes, b. Jan. 5, 1596, d. Oct. 21, 1662, was an important developer of the British song tradition that ultimately led to Henry Purcell. A member of a musical family, he studied in London and was granted a series of royal appointments there. Lawes devoted great care to the text of his vocal music, granting each word its appropriate accent and duration. His works include several masques, among them a setting of Milton's *Comus* (1634), part songs, and anthems. His brother, William Lawes (1602–45), was an influential composer of instrumental ensemble music, as well as of anthems and masques.

KAREN MONSON

Bibliography: Evans, Willa M., *Henry Lawes, Musician and Friend of Poets* (1941).

Lawes, Sir John Bennett

English agriculturist John Bennett Lawes, b. Dec. 28, 1814, d. Aug. 31, 1900, founded the artificial fertilizer industry. In 1842 he patented a process for converting ground phosphate rock into SUPERPHOSPHATE by mixing it with sulfuric acid, and the next year he opened the first factory for mass-producing superphosphate. On his estate at Rothamsted, England, Lawes also built the world's first agricultural research station.

lawn bowls   [bohlz]

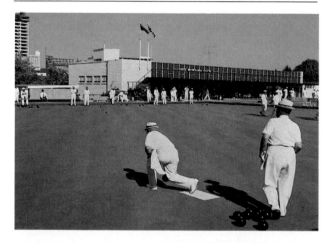

A player kneels to release a ball toward the jack, a smaller, white target ball, during a lawn bowling match in Sydney, Australia, the site of the first World Lawn Bowls Championship (1966). Play is governed according to the regulations of the International Bowling Board.

Lawn bowls, or simply bowls, involves rolling balls, the bowls, down finely manicured grass lanes so that they stop in close proximity to a smaller ball. Bowls is a game played either indoors or outdoors by both men and women in teams of 1 to 4 and is most popular in English-speaking countries.

Prehistoric in origin, it was played in various forms by the Egyptians, Greeks, and Romans, who brought their version, BOCCIE, to northern Europe. It was popular in England by the 12th century, and the Scots codified the rules in 1849.

The standard bowling green is 120 ft (36.58 m) by 120 ft and is divided into 6 parallel rinks or lanes. The first player rolls the jack, a white ball 2.5 in. (6.35 cm) in diameter and weighing 10 oz (283 g), along the rink. Then the players each roll their bowls, which are 4.75–5.13 in. (12.1–13 cm) in diameter and weigh between 3 lb 2 oz and 3 lb 8 oz (1.42 and 1.59 kg), with the teams alternating turns. At the completion of a round, or end, each bowl closer to the jack than an opponent's scores 1 point. The game is over either after a specified number of ends (usually 21 for 4-person teams) or at a specified game point (21 in singles). A common tactic is to use the curved-path rolls of the biased, or eccentrically balanced, bowls to knock opponents' bowls aside.

Bibliography: Maxwell, Harvey C., *Bowls: The American Lawn Bowler's Guide,* 4th ed. (1976).

lawnleaf

Lawnleaf, *Dichondra repens,* belongs to the morning glory family, Convolvulaceae. Native to the West Indies, it is a low-creeping perennial herb with mat-forming shoots, small, rounded or kidney-shaped leaves, and tiny greenish yellow flowers. Some authorities believe that the lawn-covering plant sold as *D. repens* is actually *D. micrantha*.

Lawrence

Lawrence (1980 pop., 63,175) is an industrial city in Essex County, northeastern Massachusetts, on the Merrimack River. First settled in 1655, it was chosen by Abbott Lawrence and other Boston entrepreneurs as the site of a planned industrial city, which was laid out in 1845. Lawrence soon became a major center for the manufacture of woolen textiles, its mills employing thousands of immigrant workers. In 1912 the Industrial Workers of the World led a famous strike of the Lawrence millworkers and won substantial concessions from the employers.

Bibliography: Cole, Donald B., *Immigrant City: Lawrence, Massachusetts, 1845–1921* (1963; repr. 1980).

Lawrence, Abbott

Abbott Lawrence, b. Groton, Mass., Dec. 16, 1792, d. Aug. 18, 1855, was a promoter of the New England textile industry. In 1814 he and his brother Amos established A. & A. Lawrence, which imported textiles and manufactured goods. By 1830 the firm was one of the most prominent companies in Boston. Lawrence was also a founder (1845) of the industrial town of Lawrence, Mass. He served in Congress (1835–37, 1839–40), was a member of the Northeast Boundary Commission (1842), and was U.S. minister to Great Britain (1849–52). Lawrence contributed money to Groton Academy, which became (1846) Lawrence Academy, and founded the Lawrence Scientific School at Harvard University.

Lawrence, D. H.

In the course of 20 years D. H. Lawrence published more than 40 volumes of narrative fiction, poetry, criticism, travel writing, and social commentary, probably doing more than any other writer of his time to alter the course of the novel in English. His importance, and his continuing notoriety, depend less on his technical accomplishments—which were considerable—than on his subject matter and intense personal convictions. Lawrence abandoned the traditional concerns of the English novel—worldly careers, courtship, and social manners—and regarded sexual relations as the decisive element in human behavior. For this reason two of his major novels—The RAINBOW (1915) and LADY CHATTERLEY'S LOVER (1928)—were banned, but Lawrence's forthright portrayal of sexuality was an integral part of his crusade against the constricting and sterile values of modern civilization. Although his language and subjects no longer offend, his fervent beliefs continue to demand response; reactions to his philosophy cannot be separated from valuations of his writing.

David Herbert Lawrence, the son of an illiterate coal miner and a schoolteacher, was born in the Nottinghamshire village of Eastwood on Sept. 11, 1885. He attended Nottingham University, qualified as a teacher in 1908, and worked in a London school until 1912. In the same year, Lawrence met Frieda

D. H. Lawrence, one of the outstanding British authors of the early 20th century, is best remembered for novels such as Women in Love *(1920) and* Lady Chatterley's Lover *(1928), which shocked some readers and critics because of their frankness in dealing with themes of love and sexual passion.*

Weekley (born von Richthofen), a married woman who left her husband and three children to live with him. For Lawrence their marriage (1914) exemplified many of the concerns of his fiction: the breaking down of social barriers, the flouting of moral conventions, and the conflict between the psychological and physical needs of men and women. The stresses of their relationship were portrayed in his volume of autobiographical verse *Look! We Have Come Through* (1917). Lawrence and his wife left England in 1919, returning only occasionally for brief visits. They traveled throughout Europe and also lived in Australia and New Mexico.

Lawrence's first novel, *The White Peacock* (1911), begun when he was 20 years of age, is closely modeled on his own boyhood and adolescence. Its style is romantic and owes something to Thomas Hardy and George Meredith, but the lyrical descriptions of rural England are all Lawrence's own and prefigure the spirituality of his later work. SONS AND LOVERS (1913) is generally acknowledged to be his first completely successful novel and is thought of by some critics as his finest. Certainly, Lawrence never excelled the realism of his psychological portrayal of a young man's struggle to cast off the imprisoning emotional ties of his own past and find physical and spiritual fulfillment. The quest is continued in *The Rainbow,* the beginning of an account of several generations of women that concludes with WOMEN IN LOVE (1920). In *The Rainbow* Lawrence began to experiment with technique. In this, and in many of his subsequent works, he deals with the irreconcilable polarity of sensual and spiritual values, portraying his characters' mental states through their relationship with nature. Both *The Rainbow* and *Women in Love* achieve unity of design and meaning through the use of symbolism—a device that Lawrence also exploited in his short stories. *Lady Chatterley's Lover,* Lawrence's last major novel, is an expression of Lawrence's belief in the possibility of personal fulfillment through sexual relations.

Lawrence's short stories, which some critics value above his novels, began to appear in 1909, and he continued to work in this form all his life. The sermonizing tone that often mars his lesser novels, such as *The Plumed Serpent* (1926), is absent from his stories and novellas, which include the masterpieces "Odour of Chrysanthemums" (1914), "The Fox" (1923), and "The Man Who Died" (1931). His poems, published in a collected edition in 1932, are variable in quality. Many are merely autobiographical effusions; others, such as "Piano," are extremely fine.

Lawrence's long exile produced several fine volumes of travel writing—which include *Mornings in Mexico* (1927) and *Etruscan Places* (1932)—and a vast correspondence that provides insight into his irascible but generous nature. He suffered greatly from the hostility of a prudish public, who thought of him as a pornographer, and did not live to enjoy the praise that his books began to receive in the 1950s. He died of tuberculosis in France on Mar. 2, 1930.

HOWARD BATCHELOR

Bibliography: Aldington, Richard, *D. H. L.: Portrait of a Genius, But. . .* (1950); Cavitch, David H., *D. H. Lawrence and the New World* (1969); Delaney, Paul, *D. H. Lawrence's Nightmare: The Writer and His Circle in the Years of the Great War* (1978); Draper, Ronald P., *D. H. Lawrence* (1964); Lawrence, D. H., *Collected Letters*, 2 vols., ed. by Harry T. Moore (1962), and *The Letters of D. H. Lawrence*, vol. 1 ed. by James T. Boulton (1979–   ); Leavis, F. R., *D. H. Lawrence, Novelist* (1955); Moore, Harry T., *The Priest of Love: A Life of D. H. Lawrence*, rev. ed. (1974); Nehls, Edward, *D. H. Lawrence: A Composite Biography*, 3 vols. (1957–59); Spender, Stephen, ed., *D. H. Lawrence: Novelist, Poet, Prophet* (1973); Spilka, Mark, ed., *D. H. Lawrence: A Collection of Critical Essays* (1963); Tedlock, E. W., *D. H. Lawrence: Artist and Rebel* (1963).

Lawrence, Ernest Orlando

The American physicist Ernest Orlando Lawrence, b. Canton, S.Dak., Aug. 8, 1901, d. Aug. 27, 1958, conceived (1929) and invented the CYCLOTRON, a high-energy particle ACCELERATOR, for which he was awarded the 1939 Nobel Prize for physics. After the construction of two small models by students, Lawrence built (1931) an 11-in.-diameter (28-cm) cyclotron that accelerated protons to an energy of 1,250,000 electron volts; this energy enabled him to disintegrate (1932) lithium, the first artificial disintegration of matter in the Western Hemisphere. Lawrence became associate professor (1928) and then full professor (1930) at the University of California, Berkeley. He was appointed (1936) director of Berkeley's Radiation Laboratory (since renamed the LAWRENCE BERKELEY LABORATORY), which was built to house the larger cyclotrons that he and his colleagues subsequently constructed. In the Manhattan Project, which produced the first atomic bomb, Lawrence was program chief in charge of developing an electromagnetic process for separating uranium 235.

CRAIG B. WAFF

Bibliography: Childs, Herbert, *An American Genius: The Life of Ernest Orlando Lawrence, Father of the Cyclotron* (1968); Davis, Nuel Pharr, *Lawrence and Oppenheimer* (1968).

Lawrence, Gertrude

One of the most popular and captivating stars of the British and American stages, Gertrude Lawrence, b. Gertrude Klasen, London, July 4, 1898, d. Sept. 6, 1952, began her acting and singing career as a child, making her American debut in *Charlot's Revue* in 1924. Her most memorable performances were in Noel Coward's *Private Lives* (1930), *Tonight at 8:30* (1935), *Lady in the Dark* (1941), and *Blithe Spirit* (1945), and as the English governess in the musical *The King and I* (1951). Her autobiography, *A Star Danced*, was published in 1945.

Bibliography: Aldrich, Richard Stoddard, *Gertrude Lawrence as Mrs. A.; An Intimate Biography of the Great Star* (1954).

Lawrence, Jacob

Jacob Lawrence, b. Atlantic City, N.J., Sept. 7, 1917, is a black American artist whose major works have chronicled the history and social progress of his race. Often using tempera, he favors a limited range of colors applied in flat areas; this technique, combined with a preference for angular, simplified forms, gives his paintings the look of posters. The social realism of his carefully researched works is well exemplified in his *Migration of the Negro* series (1940–41; Phillips Collection and the Museum of Modern Art, New York), whose 60 individual works focus on the tragic sufferings of blacks throughout modern history.

ABRAHAM A. DAVIDSON

Bibliography: Brown, Milton W., *Jacob Lawrence* (1974); Lawrence, Jacob, *Harriet and the Promised Land* (1968); Richardson, Ben, and Fahey, W. A., *Great Black Americans* (1976).

Lawrence, John Laird Mair Lawrence, 1st Baron

John Laird Mair Lawrence, b. Mar. 4, 1811, d. June 27, 1879, was viceroy of British India (1864–69). He arrived in Calcutta in 1830 as a magistrate and for 19 years served in various positions in northwestern India, mostly in and around Delhi, then the most turbulent part of the subcontinent. Determined to effect a land-tenure system that would create what he called a "fat, contented yeomanry," Lawrence restored order in the Punjab after the Sikh wars of the 1840s and welded the SIKHS into an army loyal and capable enough to stand behind the British during the INDIAN MUTINY of 1857. During the mutiny, John's older brother, Sir Henry Lawrence (1806–57), was killed in the siege of Lucknow. As governor-general, John Lawrence was responsible for expanding public works programs. He was made 1st Baron Lawrence in 1869.

MARCUS FRANDA AND VONETTA J. FRANDA

Bibliography: Edwardes, Michael, *The Necessary Hell: John and Henry Lawrence and the Indian Empire* (1958) and *British India, 1772-1947* (1968); Pal, Dharm, *Administration of Sir John Lawrence in India, 1864-69* (1952).

Lawrence, T. E.

T. E. Lawrence, a British soldier, scholar, and writer, both promoted and resisted his almost legendary identity as Lawrence of Arabia. An autobiographical account of his brilliant guerrilla exploits in the Arab Revolt during World War I was published privately in 1926 as Seven Pillars of Wisdom.

Colonel T. E. Lawrence, known as Lawrence of Arabia, was a guerrilla leader in the Arab Revolt of 1916–18, which expelled the Turks from western Arabia and Syria during WORLD WAR I. Lawrence was an aloof, complex, versatile, somewhat arrogant genius, and his exploits made him a popular, if enigmatic, hero in the Western world.

Thomas Edward Lawrence was born at Tremadoc, Wales, on Aug. 15, 1888. His father, Sir Thomas Robert Chapman, was an Anglo-Irish landholder who left his wife for his family's governess. Thomas was the second of five sons produced by this union. Adopting the name Lawrence, the family settled in Oxford, where Thomas eventually entered the university. Specializing in archaeology, architecture, and history, he began learning Arabic when he visited Syria and Palestine. After graduating in 1910, he worked as an archaeologist in the Middle East until early 1914.

After the outbreak of World War I, Lawrence returned to Egypt in December 1914 as an intelligence officer. In October 1916 he accompanied a British mission to aid HUSAYN IBN ALI of Mecca, who had launched the Arab Revolt against Ottoman Turkish rule. Shortly thereafter, he joined Husayn's son and army commander, Faisal (later King FAISAL I of Iraq), as an advisor. Together, Faisal and Lawrence proceeded to push back the Ottoman forces by raiding the Damascus-Medina railroad and overrunning Ottoman strongpoints. In October 1918 the Arabs took Damascus, and Lawrence returned to Britain.

As a member of the British delegation to the Paris Peace Conference (1919), Lawrence championed the cause of Arab independence, but without effect. Following a research fellowship at All Souls College, Oxford, he became a Middle Eastern advisor at the Colonial Office under Winston Churchill. Although he succeeded in having Faisal appointed king of Iraq, Lawrence had tired of fame and what he termed "the shallow grave of public duty." Resigning from his post in 1922, he completed his famous account of his Arabian experiences, the *Seven Pillars of Wisdom* (printed privately, 1926; published, 1935). Under the assumed names of Ross and, later, Shaw, he spent most of the remainder of his life as an enlisted man in the Royal Air Force and Tank Corps. He developed a passion for high-speed boats and motorcycles and died on May 19, 1935, after a motorcycle accident. Lawrence also wrote *The Mint* (1955), an account of his life in the air force.   ROBERT G. LANDEN

Bibliography: Aldington, Richard, *Lawrence of Arabia: A Biographical Enquiry* (1955; repr. 1976); Garnett, David, ed., *The Letters of T. E. Lawrence* (1938); Graves, Robert, *Lawrence and the Arabian Adventure* (1928); Knightley, Phillip, and Colin, Simpson, *The Secret Lives of Lawrence of Arabia* (1969); Lawrence, A. W., ed., *T. E. Lawrence by his Friends* (1937; repr. 1980); Liddell Hart, Basil, *Colonel Lawrence, The Man Behind the Legend*, rev. ed. (1964); Mack, John E., *A Prince of Our Disorder: The Life of T. E. Lawrence* (1975); Stewart, Desmond, *T. E. Lawrence* (1977); Tabachnick, S. E., *The T. E. Lawrence Puzzle* (1984).

Lawrence, Sir Thomas

This oil study, Charles William Lambton, typifies Sir Thomas Lawrence's darker and simpler late style. Lacking the high-keyed surface effects of his early portraits of aristocrats, such sober works disclose his debt to the old masters, although his paintings were occasionally marred by tinges of sentimentality. (1824–25; Collection Earl of Durham, London.)

The British artist Sir Thomas Lawrence, b. Apr. 13, 1769, d. Jan. 7, 1830, was the most successful portrait painter during the romantic period in England. Lawrence was a child prodigy, executing portrait drawings from the age of 10. He settled (1787) in London and attended the Royal Academy schools for a short period. Lawrence's success as a professional portrait painter was immediate. He was commissioned to paint Queen Charlotte in 1789 and in 1791 was made an associate of the Royal Academy. He became painter to the king on the death of Sir Joshua Reynolds in 1792 and was elected to the Royal Academy in 1794. His early portraits, such as the glittering *Eliza Farren* (1790; Metropolitan Museum of Art, New York City), are marked by a directness of vision and vivacity of handling that extended Reynolds's style and presaged the romantic era. In 1814 the prince regent (later George IV) selected him to paint what became a remarkable series of portraits of the leaders of the alliance against Napoleon, including the emperor of Russia, the king of Prussia, and Pope Pius VII. Lawrence was knighted in 1815 and succeeded (1820) Benjamin West as president of the Royal Academy, an office he held with distinction until his death; he was buried with great pomp in Saint Paul's Cathedral.   MALCOLM CORMACK

Bibliography: Armstrong, Walter, *Lawrence* (1913; repr. 1970); Garlick, Kenneth J., *Sir Thomas Lawrence* (1954); Goldring, Douglas, *Regency Portrait Painter* (1951).

Lawrence Berkeley and Lawrence Livermore laboratories   [burk'-lee]

The Lawrence Berkeley Laboratory is a multidisciplinary research center with activities in atomic and high-energy phys-

ics and in energy and environmental problems. It is the part of the center founded in 1931 as the Radiation Laboratory by Ernest LAWRENCE and is located in the Berkeley hills near San Francisco, Calif. The laboratory is operated by the University of California and funded by the U.S. Department of Energy. It was the location of the first CYCLOTRON accelerators and played a distinguished part in the early days of high-energy physics research with the 6 GeV proton synchrotron, called the Bevatron, now converted for heavy-ion acceleration.

The Lawrence Livermore Laboratory, formerly part of the Radiation Laboratory, became a separate institution in 1952. Located in Livermore, Calif., the laboratory's applied research deals with nuclear explosives (for both weaponry and peaceful purposes), fusion reactions, and health problems caused by artificial radiation. The laboratory conducts underground nuclear-explosion tests at a site in Nevada.

BRIAN SOUTHWORTH

lawrencium   [luh-rens'-ee-uhm]

Lawrencium is a synthetic radioactive metal, the last member of the ACTINIDE SERIES. Its symbol is Lr (originally Lw); its atomic number, 103; and its atomic weight, 260 (longest-lived isotope). Lawrencium does not occur naturally; it was first synthesized at the Radiation Laboratory in Berkeley, Calif., in 1961. By bombarding a mixture of californium isotopes with boron-II ions, Albert Ghiorso, T. Sikkeland, A. E. Larsh, and R. M. Latimer created ^{258}Lr, with a half-life of 4.2 seconds. The element was named for Ernest Lawrence, the inventor of the cyclotron. Other lawrencium isotopes have been created by bombarding other TRANSURANIUM ELEMENTS with heavy ions.

laws of motion

Newton's laws of motion are the three most fundamental natural laws of classical mechanics. Sir Isaac Newton stated them in his book *Principia Mathematica* (1686). Taken together, Newton's three laws of motion underly all interactions of force, matter, and motion except those involving relativistic and quantum effects.

Newton's first law of motion is also known as the law of inertia, which states that any object in a state of rest or of uniform linear motion tends to remain in such a state unless acted upon by an unbalanced external force. In effect, this is a definition of equilibrium; the branch of physics that treats equilibrium situations is STATICS. The tendency for matter to maintain its state of motion is known as inertia.

Newton's second law of motion, the most important and useful of the three, establishes a relationship between the unbalanced force applied to an object and the resultant acceleration of the object. This relationship states that an unbalanced force acting on an object produces an acceleration that is in the direction of the force, directly proportional to the force, and inversely proportional to the mass of the object. In other words, force equals mass times acceleration, or $F = ma$. Thus, a given force will accelerate an object of small mass more rapidly than it will a massive object. Similarly, doubling the applied force produces twice the acceleration of an object of arbitrary mass.

According to Newton's third law of motion, which is also known as the principle of action and reaction, every action (or force) gives rise to a reaction (or opposing force) of equal strength but opposite direction. In other words, every object that exerts a force on another object is always acted upon by a reaction force. The recoil of a gun, the thrust of a rocket, and the rebound of a hammer from a struck nail are examples of motion due to reaction forces.   GARY S. SETTLES

Bibliography: Cohen, I. B., *Introduction to Newton's Principia* (1971); Holton, Gerald, et al., eds., *Project Physics* (1975); McMullin, Ernan, *Newton on Matter and Activity* (1978).

Lawson, Henry

Henry Lawson, b. June 17, 1867, d. Sept. 2, 1922, was one of Australia's most accomplished short-story writers. Although he lacked much formal education and became totally deaf at age 14, his life in the Sydney slums and in the bush of Western Australia provided the realism, irony, and idiom of his fictional world. Among his works are *When the Billy Boils* (1896), *The Country I Come From* (1901), and *The Rising of the Court* (1910). Lawson also published poetry.

Lawton

Lawton (1980 pop., 80,054), a city in southwest Oklahoma, is the seat of Comanche County and a commercial center with diversified industries. The city is the site of Cameron University, and Fort Sill, the U.S. Army Field Artillery Center, is nearby. First inhabited by the Kiowa and Comanche, the area was opened to white settlement by lottery about 1901.

laxative: see CATHARTIC.

Laxness, Halldór Kiljan   [lahks'-nes]

Halldór Kiljan Laxness, b. Halldór Guðjonsson, in Reykjavik, Apr. 23, 1902, the most prominent figure in modern Icelandic literature, received the Nobel Prize for literature in 1955. His first successful novel, *Vefarinn mikli frá Kasmír* (The Great Weaver from Kashmir, 1927), reflects his discomfort with Roman Catholicism and his interest in expressionism and surrealism. In the 1930s, Laxness completed three sequences of novels: *Salka Valka* (1931–32; Eng. trans., 1936), a detailed account of a small fishing community at a time of social transition; *Independent People* (1934–35; Eng. trans., 1945), about a poor farmer's struggle against injustice; and *World Light* (1937–40; Eng. trans., 1969), about a poet living among people unable to comprehend his genius. During World War II, Laxness wrote his finest novel, *Íslandsklukkan* (Iceland's Bell, 1943–46), a trilogy set in the late 17th and early 18th centuries. In *The Atom Station* (1948; Eng. trans., 1961) he gives a satirical account of the decline in Icelandic culture that made possible the admission of U.S. military bases there. Laxness also wrote an autobiography entitled *Skáldatími* (A Writer's Schooling, 1963) and a documentary novel entitled *Innansveitarkronika* (A Parish Chronicle, 1970).   AAGE JØRGENSEN

Bibliography: Hallberg, P., *Halldór Laxness*, trans. by R. McTurk (1969).

Layamon   [lay'-uh-muhn]

The English poet Layamon, a Worcestershire priest who flourished in the early 13th century, is known only for his 16,000-line poem *The Brut* (c.1205), which includes the first account in English of King Arthur and his knights. Brut, a shortened name for Brutus, was the mythical founder of Britain. Layamon's poem is based on the *Roman de Brut* by Robert Wace of Jersey, which in turn is an adaptation of GEOFFREY OF MONMOUTH's *Historia Regum Britanniae*.   DAVID YERKES

Layard, Sir Austen   [lay'-urd]

Austen Henry Layard, b. Mar. 5, 1817, d. July 5, 1894, was a renowned English traveler, archaeologist, art collector, and politician. As a British government employee (1842–47), he traveled to Turkey and Persia, where he excavated at various ancient sites, including NIMRUD, which he then believed to be the ruins of NINEVEH. On a second expedition (1849–51), he confirmed the proper identity of Nineveh (at modern Kuyunjik) through his recovery of an extensive cuneiform library there. Returning (1851) to England, he became a member of Parliament (1852–57) and published the widely acclaimed *Discoveries in the Ruins of Nineveh and Babylon* (1853). He was reelected in 1860, serving as undersecretary for foreign affairs. He became minister to Spain in 1869. Layard retired from politics in 1880.   STEPHEN A. KOWALEWSKI

Bibliography: Brackman, Arnold C., *The Luck of Nineveh* (1978; repr. 1981); Waterfield, Gordon, *Layard of Nineveh* (1963; repr. 1968).

Laye, Camara   [lay, kam'-uh-ruh]

The Guinean author Camara Laye, b. Jan. 1, 1928, d. Feb. 4, 1980, was a leading French-language black African writer.

Educated in Islamic and French schools in Guinea, he lived for some years as an impoverished student in France. His first published work, *The African Child* (1953; Eng. trans., 1959), is a moving memoir of his village childhood. *The Radiance of the King* (1954; Eng. trans., 1956) renders in fictional terms Laye's belief that black and white cultures can achieve a positive synthesis. Many critics rank the work as the greatest African novel. Laye's last work, *The Guardian of the Word* (1978; Eng. trans., 1984), is a "translation" of an African legend told by a *griot,* keeper of tribal history. A critic of Guinea's leader Sékou Touré, Camara Laye died in exile in Senegal.

Bibliography: King, Adele, *The Writings of Camara Laye* (1981); Ogungbesan, K., *New West African Literature* (1980).

Lazarev, V. G.

The Soviet cosmonaut Vasily Grigoryevich Lazarev, b. Feb. 23, 1928, was the commander of the mission that suffered the first known failure to launch a manned spacecraft. A Soviet air force physician trained as a pilot, Lazarev and Oleg MAKAROV were launched into orbit on *Soyuz 12* on Sept. 27, 1973. Lazarev's second spaceflight was to have been a 2-month stay at the *Salyut 4* space station, but during the launch on Apr. 5, 1975, the booster rocket malfunctioned and crashed in the Altai Mountains of Siberia.   JAMES OBERG

Lazarus   [laz'-uh-ruhs]

In the New Testament, Lazarus was the brother of MARY AND MARTHA. After four days in the tomb, he was restored to life by Jesus (John 11–12). This was one of the most striking miracles of Jesus recorded in the Gospels.

Lazarus, Emma

The American poet and essayist Emma Lazarus, b. New York City, July 22, 1849, d. Nov. 19, 1887, is particularly remembered as the author of the inscription on the Statue of Liberty. The sonnet, "The New Colossus" (1883), is best known for the closing lines:
> Give me your tired, your poor,
> Your huddled masses yearning to breathe free,
> The wretched refuse of your teeming shore,
> Send these, the homeless, tempest-tost, to me,
> I lift my lamp beside the golden door!

Among her other works are *Songs of a Semite* (1882) and *The Dance of Death*, a historical drama about medieval Hebrew life. An ardent champion of the Jews victimized in the Russian pogroms of the 1880s, Lazarus also translated Spanish, Hebrew, and German poetry.

Bibliography: Vogel, Dan, *Emma Lazarus* (1980).

Lazio: see LATIUM.

lazurite: see LAPIS LAZULI.

Le Brun, Charles   [luh bruhn', sharl]

Charles Le Brun, b. Feb. 24, 1619, d. Feb. 2, 1690, a French painter, designer, politician, and courtier, held every important official post in the arts under Louis XIV. He was responsible for the creation of the characteristic Louis XIV style (see STYLES OF LOUIS XIII–XVI) and exercised far-reaching authority over the arts in France until the death (1683) of his protector, Jean Baptiste COLBERT. One of the founders of the French Royal Academy in 1648, Le Brun was given complete authority as chancellor in 1663; his reform of the Academy converted it into a fully equipped school for the training of young artists. In 1663, Le Brun was made the first director of the GOBELINS tapestry factory, for which he not only furnished cartoons for tapestry series, such as the *Story of Alexander* (1664), but also provided designs for and supervised the work of the goldsmiths, cabinetmakers, bronze workers, and other artisans employed there. Le Brun was responsible for the entire decorative program at the Palace of VERSAILLES (notably the Hall of Mirrors, 1678–84) including the sculptures in the park.

The "grand manner," with its technical discipline and esteem for history painting, predominated during the reign of Louis XIV. This decorative classicism is exemplified by The Chancellor Séguier in the Procession of Marie Thérèse's Entrance into Paris, 26 August 1660 *by Charles Le Brun. (Louvre, Paris.)*

Son of a master sculptor, Le Brun was an apprentice in Paris to the painters François Perrier (from 1632) and Simon Vouet (from 1634) and studied in Italy (1642–45) with Nicholas Poussin. From Poussin and Italian masters such as Pietro da Cortona he learned a sober, classicizing baroque idiom of careful groupings, powerfully conceived figures, and concentration of dramatic focus that was to define the French classical style of the later 17th century. Le Brun returned to Paris in 1646 and in 1658 was put in charge of all the artists at work on the decorations of Vaux-le-Vicomte, the chateau of Nicolas Fouquet, the king's ambitious minister of finance. In 1661, when Fouquet was disgraced, all the artists who had worked at Vaux were transferred to Versailles, and Le Brun, appointed principal painter to the king, was given his first royal commission—the decoration of the Apollo Gallery of the Louvre.

Bibliography: Razin, Germain, *Baroque and Rococo* (1964); Blunt, Anthony, *Art and Architecture in France, 1500–1700*, 2d ed. (1970); Hauser, Arnold, *The Social History of Art*, 4 vols., 2d ed. (1958).

Le Carré, John   [luh kah-ray']

John Le Carré is the pseudonym of David Cornwell, b. Oct. 19, 1931, an English writer who won international recognition in 1963 with the novel *The Spy Who Came in from the Cold* (film, 1966), a critically acclaimed look at modern espionage. Le Carré served (1961–64) in the British Foreign Service, and all of his work is derived from that experience. His heroes—chief among them George Smiley, a much abused master of British intelligence—are organization men who operate in a frigid world in moral limbo and who are likely to be in greater danger from their superiors than from their enemies. Le Carré's novels include *The Looking Glass War* (1965); the trilogy comprising *Tinker, Tailor, Soldier, Spy* (1974; television adaptation, 1980), *The Honourable Schoolboy (1977)*, and *Smiley's People* (1980; television adaptation, 1981); and *The Little Drummer Girl* (1983), in which he delves into the war between Israeli intelligence and Palestinian terrorists.

Bibliography: Bragg, Melvyn, "A Talk with John Le Carré," *New York Times Book Review*, Mar. 13, 1983; Le Carré, John, "In England Now," *New York Times Magazine*, Oct. 23, 1977.

Le Châtelier, Henri Louis   [luh shaht-ul-yay', ahn-ree' lwee]

The French chemist and metallurgist Henri Louis Le Châtelier, b. Oct. 8, 1850, d. Sept. 17, 1936, discovered (1884) the thermodynamic principle that every change in a system in stable chemical equilibrium results in a rearrangement of the system so that the original change is minimized. This phenomenon, known as Le Châtelier's principle, helps predict the outcome of a chemical reaction. Le Châtelier also made reliable high-temperature thermometers using a thermocouple consisting of platinum and a platinum-rhodium alloy.

JOHN T. BLACKMORE

Le Corbusier   [luh kor-boo-zyay']

Charles Édouard Jeanneret, known as Le Corbusier, b. La Chaux-de-fonds, Switzerland, Oct. 6, 1887, d. 1965, was a Swiss-French architect who played a decisive role in the development of MODERN ARCHITECTURE. He first studied (1908–10) in Paris with August Perret, and then worked (1910) for several months in the Berlin studio of industrial designer Peter Behrens, where he met the future BAUHAUS leaders Ludwig Mies van der Rohe and Walter Gropius. Shortly after World War I, Jeanneret turned to painting and founded, with Amédée Ozenfant, the purist offshoot of cubism. With the publication (1923) of his influential collection of polemical essays, *Vers une architecture* (*Towards a New Architecture*, Eng. repr. 1970), he adopted the name Le Corbusier and devoted his full energy and talent to creating a radically modern form of architectural expression.

In the 1920s and '30s, Le Corbusier's most significant work was in urban planning. In such published plans as *La Ville Contemporaine* (1922), the *Plan Voisin de Paris* (1925), and the several *Villes Radieuses* (1930–36), he advanced ideas dramatically different from the comfortable, low-rise communities proposed by earlier garden city planners. During this 20-year span he also built many villas and several small apartment complexes and office buildings. In these hard-edged, smooth-surfaced, geometric volumes, he created a language of what he called "pure prisms"—rectangular blocks of concrete, steel, and glass, usually raised above the ground on stilts, or *pilotis*, and often endowed with roof gardens in-

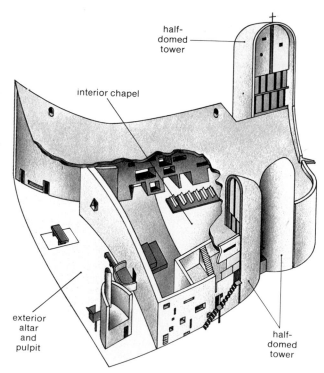

The organic forms of the chapel of Notre Dame du Haut (1950–54), Ronchamp, France, exemplify Le Corbusier's sculptural treatment of industrial materials and his post-World War II "anti-rational" architecture. The chapel, a pilgrimage site, is designed for interior and exterior use, featuring a pulpit both inside and out. Irregularly shaped and positioned windows provide illumination.

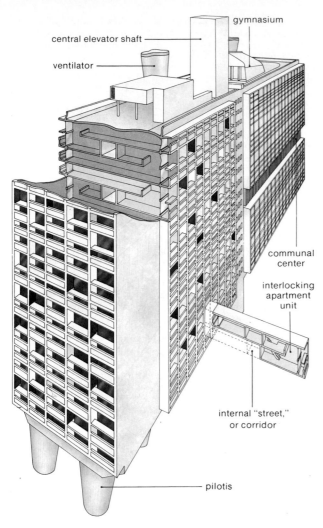

central elevator shaft

ventilator

gymnasium

communal center

interlocking apartment unit

internal "street," or corridor

pilotis

Le Corbusier's Unité d'Habitation (1946–52) in Marseilles, France, reflects his "modulor" concept of scaling architecture to human proportions. The honeycombed facade, devised by Le Corbusier in 1933, became a standard feature in later apartment designs.

tended to compensate for the loss of usable floor area at ground level.

After World War II, Le Corbusier moved away from purism and toward the so-called New Brutalism, which utilized rough-hewn forms of concrete, stone, stucco, and glass. Newly recognized in official art circles as an important 20th-century innovator, he represented (1946) France on the planning team for the United Nations Headquarters building in New York City—a particularly satisfying honor for an architect whose prize-winning design (1927) for the League of Nations headquarters had been rejected. Simultaneously, he was commissioned by the French government to plan and build his prototypical Vertical City in Marseilles. The result was the Unité d'Habitation (1946–52)—a huge block of 340 "superimposed villas" raised above the ground on massive pilotis, laced with two elevated thoroughfares of shops and other services and topped by a roof-garden community center that contained, among other things, a sculptured playground of concrete forms and a peripheral track for joggers.

His worldwide reputation led to a commission from the Indian government to plan the city of CHANDIGARH, the new capital of the Punjab, and to design and build the Government Center (1950–70) and several of the city's other structures. These poetic, handcrafted buildings represented a second, more humanistic phase in Le Corbusier's work that also was

reflected in his lyrical Pilgrim Church of Notre Dame du Haut at Ronchamp (1950–54) in the Vosges Mountains of France; in his rugged monastery of La Tourette, France (1954–59); and in the several structures he designed (from 1958) at Ahmedabad, in India. Le Corbusier drowned in a swimming accident off Cap Martin in the Mediterranean on Aug. 27, 1965, at the age of 77.   PETER BLAKE AND LELI SUDLER

Bibliography: Besset, Maurice, *Le Corbusier* (1976); Blake, Peter, *Le Corbusier: Architecture and Form* (1963) and *The Master Builders* (1976); Choay, Françoise, *Le Corbusier* (1960); Le Corbusier, *Oeuvre Complète*, ed. by Willy Boesiger, abr. ed. (1967); Serenyi, Peter, ed., *Le Corbusier in Perspective* (1975).

Le Guin, Ursula

Ursula Kroeber Le Guin, b. Berkeley, Calif., Oct. 21, 1929, is among the foremost writers of science fiction in the United States. Her most important work divides into two groups. The six novels of the "Hainish" cycle are concerned with earthly issues (for example, the distortions created by sexual role-playing, the ambiguities inherent in utopian idealism) as they might be played out on non-Earth worlds. Two of the novels, *The Left Hand of Darkness* (1969) and *The Dispossessed* (1974), won both the Hugo and the Nebula awards for best science fiction of their years. The Earthsea trilogy (*The Wizard of Earthsea,* 1969; *The Tombs of Atuan,* 1971; and *The Farthest Shore,* 1972) are fantasies written for older children. *Always Coming Home* (1985) describes a future utopia in stories, essays, poems, and—on an accompanying tape—music and song.

Le Havre   [luh ahv']

Le Havre, the second largest seaport of France, is located in northern France on the English Channel at the estuary of the Seine River. The city has a population of 198,700 (1982); that of the conurbation is 255,000. Le Havre is France's principal Atlantic port. Although passenger liner traffic has declined, the cross-channel trade in cargo has increased rapidly. Much cargo destined for Paris via the Seine River is transshipped here. Le Havre has a variety of industries, including petroleum refining, shipbuilding, food processing, chemicals, wood products, and nonferrous metals.

Once a small fishing village, Le Havre took on added significance in 1517 when Francis I began harbor improvements. The port was an important military base during both world wars. Le Havre was occupied by the Germans and suffered much damage from Allied bombing during World War II. Postwar Le Havre is virtually a new city. A new automated section (called Antifev) of the harbor was completed in 1976.
                                                    LAWRENCE M. SOMMERS

Le Mans   [luh mahn']

Le Mans is a city in the Loire Valley in northwestern France, at the confluence of the Sarthe and Huisne rivers, about 185 km (115 mi) southwest of Paris. An industrial and marketing center, it has a population of 145,976 (1982). Manufactures include railroad and automobile machinery, textiles, plastics, and tobacco products. The Le Mans 24-hour Grand Prix automobile race is held just south of the city.

Le Mans was settled as early as the 5th century BC. The old walled city, fortified by the Romans, is the site of the Saint-Julien Cathedral (11th–15th century), the church of Notre-Dame-de-la-Couture (10th–13th century), and the Church of Sainte-Jeanne d'Arc (begun 11th century). During the Hundred Year's War the city was besieged by the English five times, and the city was occupied by the Germans in 1871.

Le Nain brothers   [luh nan']

The three Le Nain brothers were French painters best known for their depictions of peasants and tradesmen in simple settings. All three brothers—Antoine, Louis, and Matthieu—were born in Laon, where they received their first training. From 1620 the brothers shared a studio in Paris. When they were received (March 1648) into the Royal Academy, Antoine and Louis were listed as *peintres de bambochades*, or painters of

The French painter Louis Le Nain's The Traveller's Rest marks a departure from previous portrayals of country people. In contrast to earlier painters, Le Nain rendered his peasants as dignified figures, and used a realistic rather than allegorical style. (Louvre, Paris.)

low-life—genre—scenes, and Matthieu was mentioned as portraitist. Early critics found the brothers' works so similar as to be virtually indistinguishable. Modern scholars, however, generally recognized three distinct groups within the Le Nain oeuvre, although the brothers' close association and their practice of signing works only with their surname make attribution difficult.

According to contemporary accounts, **Antoine Le Nain** (c.1588–1648) "excelled in miniatures and small portraits." Several of his small group portraits, such as the *Réunion de Famille* (1642; Louvre, Paris), show members of a bourgeois family placed before a neutral background. The diminutive, stiffly posed figures painted in strong, pure colors are naively arranged with little care for composition. Another of Antoine's characteristics, a love of children's amusements, can be seen in his *Village Pipe* (n.d.; Detroit Institute of Art).

Louis Le Nain (c.1593–1648) was by far the most talented of the three brothers. The impressive large-scale paintings associated with his name are carefully constructed and well-ordered compositions in which the colors tend toward a narrow range of cool grays, gray browns, and gray greens. Although early biographers refer to Louis as "Le Romain," there is no conclusive evidence that he ever visited Rome. Apparent in Louis's works, however, is the influence of the Dutch artist Pieter van Laer, called Il Bamboccio, who had worked in Rome and had specialized in genre painting. Louis, following van Laer, took as his subject lowly French peasants, whom he portrayed without grotesque or comic qualities. The family depicted in the *Peasants at Supper* (1645–48; Louvre, Paris) sits quietly in a simple interior, a dignified group posed with an ordered sensibility that gives the work a sense of calm and detachment.

Matthieu Le Nain (1607–77), in contrast, chose to portray the middle-class residents of Paris. He became (1633) master painter to the city of Paris and, later, a lieutenant in the city militia; many of his paintings reflect these responsibilities. His *Corps de Garde* (1643; private collection, Paris), for example, depicts a party of swaggering officers drinking in a candlelit interior.   J. PATRICK COONEY

Bibliography: Blunt, Anthony, *Art and Architecture in France: 1500–1700*, 2d ed. (1970); Thuillier, Jacques, and Châtelet, Albert, *French Painting from Le Nain to Fragonard* (1964).

Le Nôtre, André   [luh noht', ahn-dray']

The landscape architect André Le Nôtre, b. Mar. 12, 1613, d. Sept. 15, 1700, was the creator of the French formal garden.

His earliest royal post was first gardener to King Louis XIII at the TUILERIES in Paris, where he succeeded (1637) his father.

As buildings inspector for the royal works (from 1657), he was responsible for all the chief royal gardens, especially those at Saint Germain, FONTAINEBLEAU, and Clagny, and for the parks of the chief ministers of King Louis XIV.

Le Nôtre's best known work is the immense park of the Palace of VERSAILLES (1661–90), commissioned by Louis XIV and imitated throughout Europe. The principles of the *jardin français,* however, can be seen more clearly at the Château de VAUX-LE-VICOMTE, where Le Nôtre worked (1656–61) in collaboration with the architect Louis Le Vau and the designer Charles Le Brun. Whereas the design of the typical Renaissance garden consisted of individual geometric units laid side by side, with a strong sense of compartmentalization, the gardens designed by Le Nôtre were unified by a dominant central axis that firmly controlled the movement of the spectator through the various lawns, gardens, and pools. He also made use of the lay of the land for optical effects, closing the vista by funneling the lines of perspective. He also channeled water from terrace to terrace as it passed through the various cascades and fountains. His spacious, elegantly orchestrated works epitomized the opulent era of Louis XIV and played a key role in the development of LANDSCAPE ARCHITECTURE.
                                              ROBERT NEUMAN

Bibliography: Fox, Helen M., *André Le Nôtre: Garden Architect to Kings* (1962); Hazlehurst, F. Hamilton, *Gardens of Illusion: The Genius of André Le Nôtre* (1972); Tobey, G. B., *A History of Landscape Architecture* (1973).

Le Sueur, Eustache   [luh soo-ur', u-stahsh']

Eustache Le Sueur, b. Nov. 18, 1617, d. Apr. 30, 1655, was the most notable minor classical painter of his period in France. Together with Charles Le Brun and Pierre Mignard, he helped introduce the rich decorative style of Louis XIV. His teacher, Simon Vouet, was the major influence on Le Sueur's early work; later, the example of Nicolas Poussin became important. His first important commission, for the Hôtel Lambert, included *Venus Presenting Love to Jupiter* (1647; Louvre, Paris); his most important work was *The History of St. Bruno,* a series of 24 paintings for the Charterhouse of Paris (1645–48; Louvre, Paris).   SUZANNE WILSON

Bibliography: Blunt, Anthony, *Art and Architecture in France, 1500–1700*, 2d ed. (1970).

Le Vau, Louis   [luh voh', lwee]

Louis Le Vau, b. 1612, d. Oct. 11, 1670, was a leading French architect who, in collaboration with other artists, created architectural ensembles in which the arts were fused in a typically baroque manner. He was trained by his father, with whom he engaged in the speculative building of townhouses, termed *hôtels,* on the Île Saint Louis, Paris. His principal work from this period is the Hôtel Lambert (1634–44).

Commissioned by Louis XIV's finance minister, Nicolas Fouquet, to build the Château de VAUX-LE-VICOMTE, Le Vau created (1657–61) a building that greatly influenced the subsequent design of country houses, particularly through the innovative placement of an oval salon in the center of the garden facade. Despite a characteristic misunderstanding of the classical orders, Le Vau brilliantly realized in Vaux-le-Vicomte an overall effect of opulence and theatricality. Louis XIV was so impressed with the complex, which included a decor by Charles LE BRUN and gardens by André LE NÔTRE, that Le Vau soon was put to work on the enlargement of the Palace of VERSAILLES, where he designed (1669) a garden front that later was remodeled by Jules Hardouin Mansart.

Le Vau's chief projects in Paris were the Collège des Quatres Nations, commissioned (1661) by Cardinal Mazarin and modeled after Italian baroque ecclesiastical facades, and the completion of the LOUVRE Palace (1660s), for which Le Vau designed the colonnade of the east facade in collaboration with Le Brun and Claude PERRAULT.   ROBERT NEUMAN

Bibliography: Blunt, Anthony, *Art and Architecture in France: 1500–1700*, 2d ed. (1970); Norberg-Schulz, Christian, *Baroque Architecture* (1971).

Leach, Sir Edmund   [leech]

Sir Edmund Ronald Leach, b. Nov. 7, 1910, is an influential British social anthropologist. A faculty member of the London School of Economics (1947–53) and of Cambridge University (since 1953), he has done fieldwork in Southeast Asia. His early work emphasized cultural dynamics—the study of culture as "a process in time." Leach has worked to systematize the cross-cultural analysis of social structure, turning in recent years to the structuralist approach of Claude LÉVI-STRAUSS. Leach's writings include *Political Systems of Highland Burma* (1954), *Rethinking Anthropology* (1961), *Genesis as Myth* (1970), and *Lévi-Strauss* (1970).   STEPHEN A. KOWALEWSKI

Leacock, Stephen   [lee'-kahk]

Stephen Butler Leacock, b. Hampshire, England, Dec. 30, 1869, d. Mar. 28, 1944, became one of Canada's best-loved citizens. A professor at McGill University from 1903 to 1936, he wrote on economics, history, literature, and politics. He is chiefly remembered, however, as the author of many works of farcical humor, including *Literary Lapses* (1910) and *Sunshine Sketches of a Little Town* (1912).   MARY JANE EDWARDS

Bibliography: Curry, Ralph L., *Stephen Leacock, Humorist and Humanist* (1959); Davies, Robertson, *The Feast of Stephen* (1970); Legate, David, *Stephen Leacock* (1970).

lead

Lead is a lustrous, silvery metal that tarnishes in the presence of air and becomes a dull bluish gray. Soft and malleable, it has a low melting point (327° C). Its chemical symbol, Pb, is derived from *plumbum*, the Latin word for waterworks, because of lead's extensive use in ancient water pipes. Its atomic number is 82; its atomic weight is 207.19.

Occurrence. The Earth's crust is about 15 ppm lead. Four stable lead isotopes exist in nature; three of them—^{206}Pb, ^{207}Pb, and ^{208}Pb—are end products of the radioactive decay of uranium and thorium. It is assumed that all of the fourth isotope, ^{204}Pb, that exists in rocks has been there since the rocks were formed. The most valuable lead ore is galena (lead sulfide, PbS), which is almost always mixed with other valuable ores. The production of pure lead from ores involves several stages of purification. Much of the world production of bismuth, arsenic, antimony, and silver comes from the production of lead. Lead is also recycled from scrap metal.

Toxicity. Lead and lead compounds can be highly toxic when eaten or inhaled. Although lead is absorbed very slowly into the body, its rate of excretion is even slower. Thus, with constant exposure, lead accumulates gradually in the body. It is absorbed by the red blood cells and circulated through the body where it becomes concentrated in the soft tissues, especially the liver and kidneys. Lead can cause lesions in the central nervous system and apparently can damage the cells making up the blood-brain barrier that protects the brain from many harmful chemicals (see BRAIN). Symptoms of lead poisoning include appetite loss, weakness, anemia, vomiting, and convulsions, sometimes leading to permanent brain damage or death. Children who ingest chips of old, lead-containing paint may exhibit such symptoms. The newborn of mothers who had been exposed to lead levels even considered safe for children appear to show signs of slowed mental growth. Levels of environmental lead considered nontoxic may also be involved in increased hypertension in a significant number of persons, according to studies released in the mid-1980s. As a result, the U.S. Centers for Disease Control in recent years has been revising downward the levels of environmental lead that it would consider safe. At one time, lead poisoning was common among those who worked with lead, but such workplace hazards have been largely curtailed (see POLLUTANTS, CHEMICAL).

Uses. Lead has been used by humans since ancient times. It was used in ancient Egypt in coins, weights, ornaments, utensils, ceramic glazes, and solder. Lead is mentioned in the Old Testament. The Romans conveyed drinking water in lead pipes, some of which are still in operation. Roman slaves extracted and prepared the lead, and Pliny describes a disease among the slaves that was clearly lead poisoning. Because of their potential toxicity, lead water pipes are no longer being installed. The greatest single use of lead metal today is in the plates of storage batteries for automobiles.

The protective oxidation layer formed by lead in contact with such substances as air, sulfuric acid, and fluorine makes it highly resistant to corrosion, so lead has been used to make drainage pipes and lead chambers in sulfuric acid factories. It is also used as a roofing material. The softness and malleability of lead make it useful for sheathing telephone and television cables, and it is used in solder because of its low melting point. When combined with tin, lead forms solder alloys that are stronger than lead alone, with melting points lower than those of either original metal.

Lead has the highest density of all metals in common use, which, for example, makes it useful as a counterweight in the keels of ships. Because of their high density, lead bullets and shot encounter little air resistance and thus achieve excellent striking power. Shot is produced by allowing molten lead to drip down from heights up to 38.10 m (125 ft). The drops become spherical and are condensed by the cooling action of the air before being collected in a tank filled with water or oil. Lead's density and softness also make it highly suitable for damping sound and vibrations. To isolate them from vibration, heavy machinery and even whole buildings are placed on lead blocks. Because the effectiveness of shielding against gamma and X rays depends largely on the density of the shield, lead is used in the protective shielding of X-ray machines and nuclear reactors.

Lead can be alloyed with many metals. Lead alloys are important because they resist attack by sulfuric acid and are harder than pure lead.

Lead Compounds. Lead exists in the divalent or tetravalent oxidation state in compounds. A number of lead compounds are important in the paint industry. At one time, lead pigments were often used in ceramic glazes and interior paints; but because lead pigments are toxic, their use is now restricted. White lead, $Pb(OH)_2 \cdot 2PbCO_3$, is the most important lead pigment. Lead dioxide, PbO_2, is a vigorous oxidizing agent that is sometimes used in match heads.

Tetraethyl lead or tetramethyl lead has often been added to gasoline to improve engine efficiency and reduce gasoline consumption in automobiles. Because of the toxic effect of lead on the environment, however, plans call for phasing out this use (see GASOLINE). Lead azide, $Pb(N_3)_2$, is sensitive to striking and is highly explosive; it is frequently used as a detonator of explosives. Lead iodide, PbI_2, is a light yellow substance that is used as a dye in such processes as coloring bronze. It has light-sensitive properties comparable to those of silver salts.   STEPHEN FLEISHMAN

Bibliography: Chisholm, J. J., and O'Hara, D. M., *Lead Absorption in Children* (1982); Harrison, R. M., and Laxen, D. P., *Lead Pollution* (1981); Hehner, N. E., and Ritchie, E. J., *Lead Oxides* (1974); Nriagu, J. O., *Lead and Lead Poisoning in Antiquity* (1983); Rochow, E. G., and Abel, E. W., *The Chemistry of Germanium, Tin and Lead* (1975).

Leadbelly

The black singer and guitarist Leadbelly, b. Huddie Ledbetter in Mooringsport, La., Jan. 21, 1888, d. Dec. 6, 1949, spent most of his life as an itinerant laborer and street singer in the small towns of the deep South. Accompanying himself on his 12-string guitar, Leadbelly sang the work songs, blues, hollers, and dance tunes of the black country people of his time. The folk-song archivist John A. Lomax heard him in a Louisiana penitentiary, recorded his songs, and helped obtain his release. Leadbelly came to New York in 1934 and, from that year until his death, sang throughout the country and abroad, both in concert and on recordings. His posthumous influence on the folk music revival of the 1950s and '60s was enormous.

Bibliography: Asch, Moses, and Lomax, Alan, eds., *The Leadbelly Song Book* (1962); Lawless, Ray M., *Folksingers and Folksongs in America* (1960; repr. 1965); Lomax, John and Alan, *Negro Songs as Sung by Leadbelly* (1936); Palmer, Robert, *Deep Blues* (1981).

leadwort   [led'-wurt]

Cape leadwort, P. auriculata, or P. capensis, of South Africa, is an evergreen shrub. Its blue or white flowers open in late summer or early fall.

Leadwort is a genus, *Plumbago,* of mostly tropical perennial herbs, sometimes shrubby or climbing, in the plumbago family, Plumbaginaceae. They produce spikelike clusters of slender-tubed flowers that are blue, reddish, or white. The cape leadwort, *P. auriculata,* from South Africa, is a sparsely leaved evergreen shrub with short spikes of usually blue flowers. The Southeast Asian *P. indica* is a partially climbing evergreen shrub with branching stems and elongated clusters of red flowers.

leaf: see PLANT.

leaf beetle

Leaf beetles, family Chrysomelidae, order Coleoptera, are a group of about 25,000 species of leaf-feeding insects that occur throughout the world. They have brightly colored, oval bodies that are usually less than 13 mm (0.5 in) long, with short antennae about half their body length. Adult leaf beetles feed on the leaves and flowers of various plants, and larvae eat the leaves and roots. Many leaf beetles, such as the Colorado potato beetle, *Leptinotarsa decemlineata,* are important agricultural pests.

leafhopper

Leafhoppers are a very large group of insects constituting the family Cicadellidae in the order Homoptera. Most of the more than 2,000 species in North America are small, less than 10 mm (0.4 in) long. Leafhoppers are usually slender, often brightly colored, and have four wings and short hairlike antennae in front of and below the eyes. They have piercing, sucking mouthparts and feed on plant juices; some species are economically important plant pests. A clear, sugary liquid called honeydew, composed of unused sap and excretory products, is expelled from the anus of many leafhoppers and may attract other insects and cause plant surfaces to become sticky.   STEPHEN C. REINGOLD

League of Nations

The League of Nations was an organization established after World War I to promote international peace. Sixty-three nations were members, including all the major European powers at one time or another. The United States played an important role in setting it up but did not join. From its headquarters in Geneva, the league organized many social and economic welfare activities, although it concentrated on political matters. It was nominally responsible for the administration of many colonial territories under the mandate system.

An important instrument of diplomacy in the 1920s, the league was unable to fulfill its chief aims of disarmament and peace-keeping in the 1930s. It lost members and fell into disuse before World War II. Some of its technical services continued to function until the organization was formally termi-

nated on Apr. 18, 1946, when it was succeeded by the newly organized UNITED NATIONS.

Creation. The outbreak of World War I in 1914 led people in Britain, France, the United States, and several neutral countries to explore alternatives to traditional diplomatic methods for keeping the peace. As the war went on, various schemes for world organization were advanced and won popular support. Some government leaders, including U.S. President Woodrow WILSON, Jan SMUTS of South Africa, and Lord Robert Cecil, a member of the British cabinet, gave their support to the league ideal as a way to prevent future wars. This ideal was one of the FOURTEEN POINTS put forward by Wilson as the basis for a just peace, and by the time of the PARIS PEACE CONFERENCE it was a leading war aim of the victorious Allied powers. It brought to world politics the same liberal precepts that, in theory at least, guided the political experience of the Western democracies: a sense of moral purpose, a belief in parliamentary procedure, and a faith that differences could be resolved peacefully.

When the League of Nations was established on Jan. 10, 1920, it disappointed some of its early supporters. The Covenant, which was the basis for the league's operation, was included in the Treaty of Versailles imposed on defeated Germany. This made it appear that the league was a tool for the victors to use against their former enemies who were not members. The U.S. Senate refused to ratify the peace treaty and, in a blow to President Wilson, also kept the country out of the league. The USSR was also not a member at first, although like the United States it cooperated with the league disarmament conference and some other activities.

Organization. The purpose and rules for the organization were set forward in the League of Nations Covenant, which consisted of 26 short articles. In approach it was more legalistic than the United Nations Charter; it was assumed that member nations could work together without compromising their sovereignty. Outlined in the Covenant were three approaches to preventing war: arbitration in settling disputes, disarmament, and collective security.

Under the Covenant all member states were represented in an assembly, which held sessions at least once a year. Each nation had one vote, and unanimity was required for all decisions. The assembly regulated the budget and membership of the league and served as a sounding board for world public opinion. The main political work of the league and the settlement of international disputes were delegated to another, smaller body—the council. Permanent seats on the council were reserved for Britain, France, Japan, Italy, and, later, Germany and the USSR; other countries were elected to temporary representation on the council to make a total of 8, later raised to 10, and then 14 members. The third main organ of the league was the secretariat, which consisted of an international staff of several hundred officials who administered league activities. In addition, the league was linked to several other bodies, most notably the Permanent INTERNATIONAL COURT OF JUSTICE, or World Court, which met at The Hague, and the INTERNATIONAL LABOR ORGANIZATION.

Activities. In the early 1920s the league attempted to establish its position as a center of world affairs. The public enthusiasm that had helped launch it was hard to sustain in peacetime. It proved effective in finding peaceful solutions to several minor disputes, such as that between Sweden and Finland over the Åland Islands in 1920 and that between Greece and Bulgaria in 1925. Doubts remained about whether it could really stop aggression by a major power, however, and the position of Germany with regard to European security was still a major concern. Proposals to reinforce the Covenant and overcome these uncertainties did not win approval; the Geneva Protocol of 1924, which branded aggressive war as an international crime, failed because of British opposition. The collective security machinery of the league remained untested, and no international forces were assembled to secure it, although this was often proposed. Disarmament could not proceed while unease continued over security.

This situation did not change fundamentally in the late

1920s, but the league gained in prestige because the threat of war was remote. The LOCARNO PACT of 1925 reassured Germany's neighbors and paved the way for German admission to the league the following year. Foreign ministers and other government leaders attended sessions in Geneva, and the league's reputation was high. It gained support through its valuable nonpolitical work—combating the spread of opium and other illicit drugs, contributing to child welfare, improving health conditions around the world, and lowering the barriers against international trade.

The DEPRESSION OF THE 1930s and a series of international crises changed the political climate. The crisis ensuing from the Japanese invasion of MANCHURIA in September 1931 is often seen in retrospect as the first decisive challenge to the league system. At the time, however, the European statesmen on the league council did not so perceive it. In 1932 they sent a commission of inquiry to study the rights and wrongs of the war between China and Japan (see SINO-JAPANESE WARS). Japan soon left the league, but no effort was made to force it to give back the territory it had conquered.

Manchuria was far away, and many people hoped that the league would still be effective if aggression occurred closer to Europe. Nonetheless, this failure eroded confidence in collective security. Adolf HITLER's rise to power in Germany aggravated the crisis. In 1933 he pulled Germany out of the GENEVA CONFERENCE on disarmament and then out of the league itself. As Germany began to rearm and overturn the restrictions of the Treaty of Versailles, the league was slow to respond. Its supporters continued to press for disarmament when force was needed to deter Germany. They tried to win Hitler back to the organization rather than work to stop him.

Collective security was finally put to the test in 1935 when Italy attacked ETHIOPIA. After Ethiopia's emperor HAILE SELASSIE appealed for help, the league voted to impose economic sanctions against Italy until it stopped its aggression. Britain and France, whose cooperation was essential to this effort, acted timorously, as they did not want to antagonize the Italian dictator Benito MUSSOLINI. Hence they tried to work out various compromise solutions with him and did not attempt to cut off his vital oil supplies. Italy was able to overcome this half-hearted sanctions policy and complete its conquest of Ethiopia. Italy withdrew from the league in 1937 and went on to further foreign intervention, along with Germany and the USSR, in the SPANISH CIVIL WAR.

The league never recovered from this setback. It continued to meet in the late 1930s but could take no effective action. One reaction of its supporters was to try to use the league as the rallying point for an anti-fascist coalition built around Britain, France, and the USSR. Another conflicting tendency was to ask for revisions of the Covenant to prevent the league from imposing sanctions. This tactic was supposed to improve the league's position in nonpolitical humanitarian work such as assisting refugees. The league was all but ignored in the rush of events that led to the outbreak of World War II. It revived briefly in December 1939 to make the meaningless gesture of expelling the USSR for its attack on Finland.

Evaluation. Despite its eventual failure to halt the tide of war, the league was an important pioneering venture in international affairs. The recurrence of war only emphasized the world's need for an effective alternative to anarchy, and the United Nations followed the structure and methods of the league in its main outlines. The changes in emphasis in the new organization reflected some of the lessons of the league experience. The United Nations Charter is a more political and less legalistic document than the Covenant. It places more reliance on diplomacy and less on elaborate judicial procedures to prevent war. Moreover, the United Nations emphasizes nonpolitical work in economic development to a much greater degree than did the league. The United Nations is truly a worldwide group that tries to meet the needs of its members; the league was more limited in scope and membership.

DONALD S. BIRN

Bibliography: Baer, George W., *Test Case: Italy, Ethiopia and the League of Nations* (1977); Haigh, R. H., et al., *Soviet Foreign Policy, the League of Nations and Europe, 1917–1939* (1986); Kimmich, Christoph M., *Germany and the League of Nations* (1976); Northedge, F. S., *The League of Nations* (1986); Schiffer, Walter, *The Legal Community of Mankind* (1954; repr. 1972); United Nations Library (Geneva), *The League of Nations in Retrospect* (1983); Walters, F. P., *A History of the League of Nations* (1952; repr. 1986); Zimmern, Alfred, *The League of Nations and the Rule of Law, 1918–1935,* 2d ed. (1969).

League of Women Voters

Founded in Chicago in 1920, the League of Women Voters is an organization that attempts to further the development of political awareness through political participation. The league, an offshoot of the National American Woman Suffrage Association, was organized in 1920, the year of national enfranchisement of women, to educate the female electorate in the use of their right to vote. Though originally limited to women, the league voted in 1974 to extend membership to men; of the 1987 membership of 105,000, more than 4,000 were men. The league's activities are no longer limited to issues involving women's rights but center on any important national political or social concern.

The league consists of more than 1,200 state and local chapters. It conducts studies, distributes responsibly prepared information on candidates and issues, runs voter-registration drives, and takes stands on pending legislation. Biennial conventions are held to establish programs and policy decisions.

Leahy, William Daniel   [lay'-hee]

William Daniel Leahy, b. Hampton, Iowa, May 6, 1875, d. July 20, 1959, was an American admiral and diplomat. He graduated from Annapolis in 1897 and served in the Spanish-American War and World War I. In 1937, Leahy became chief of naval operations but retired two years later and became governor of Puerto Rico. In 1940, President Franklin D. Roosevelt named Leahy ambassador to Vichy France. Recalled to naval service in 1942, he was chief of staff to Roosevelt and to Harry S. Truman until 1949. In 1944, Leahy became the first fleet (five-star) admiral.

Bibliography: Leahy, William D., *I Was There* (1950).

Leakey   (family)   [leek'-ee]

The British anthropologists **Louis S. B. Leakey**, b. Aug. 7, 1903, d. Oct. 1, 1972, his wife **Mary**, b. Mary Nichol, Feb. 6, 1913, and their son **Richard**, b. Dec. 19, 1944, have made major contributions to the study of human evolution. Louis and Mary Leakey investigated early human campsites at OLDUVAI GORGE, Tanzania, and found important hominid fossils more than 1.75 million years old. Their son Richard has conducted research in the East TURKANA area of Kenya and has discovered even earlier hominid fossils dating from as much as 3 million years ago.

The son of a missionary in Kenya, Louis Seymour Bazett

The Leakey family of British archaeologists and anthropologists has made many important contributions to the study of human origins. Pictured here are Louis Leakey and his wife Mary. Together they conducted excavations at various fossil sites in East Africa.

Leakey studied archaeology at Cambridge University from 1922 to 1926. He then returned to Kenya, where he investigated Stone Age cultures in East Africa, then a pioneer field of research. From 1931 to 1959, Louis and his second wife, Mary, worked at Olduvai Gorge, reconstructing a long sequence of Stone Age cultures dating from approximately 2 million to 100,000 years ago. They documented the early history of stone technology from simple stone-chopping tools and flakes to relatively sophisticated, multipurpose hand axes. In 1959 the Leakeys discovered the skull of *Australopithecus boisei* (a species of the prehuman genus AUSTRALOPITHECUS). This skull was later dated at about 1.75 million years of age, using potassium-argon dating. The Leakeys also excavated another skull of a less robust individual in somewhat lower levels. Both new fossils were associated with stone choppingtools. Louis Leakey claimed that the less robust hominid, which the Leakeys called HOMO HABILIS, was the earliest toolmaker and a direct ancestor of modern humans. Many scientists disagreed, however, largely because the fossil fragments were so small. By 1965 the Leakeys had found several other fossils at Olduvai, including a HOMO ERECTUS cranium that is about 1 million years old.

Louis Leakey also experimented with techniques of making stone tools and attempted to understand how prehistoric hunter-gatherers obtained their food. In addition, he was a pioneer in primatological research, encouraging such well-known social scientists as Jane GOODALL and Dian Fossey to study chimpanzees and gorillas. Leakey believed that such studies would increase understanding of early humans.

After Leakey's death, Mary Leakey and their son Richard continued field research in East Africa. Mary Leakey did much of the fieldwork at Olduvai, and in recent years she has discovered *Homo* fossils more than 3.75 million years old at LAETOLIL, located 40 km (25 mi) south of Olduvai. Richard Leakey has worked in the OMO area of southern Ethiopia and has discovered more than 388 km² (150 mi²) of Lower Pleistocene deposits on the eastern shore of Lake Turkana (Rudolf) in northern Kenya. Here he found traces of australopithecines, as well as fragments of a more advanced hominid, perhaps an early *Homo*. This fossil, known as SKULL 1470, was dated by Leakey as 2.6 million years old. In 1984 he and his colleagues also found a nearly complete skeleton of a large *H. erectus*, dated as about 1.6 million years old.   BRIAN M. FAGAN

Bibliography: Cole, Sonia M., *Leakey's Luck: The Life of Louis Seymour Bazell Leakey, 1903–1972* (1975); Leakey, Mary, *Disclosing the Past* (1984); Leakey, Richard E., *One Life: An Autobiography* (1984).

Lean, David

David Lean, b. Mar. 25, 1908, is one of contemporary Britain's most prominent film directors. A noted film editor in the 1930s, Lean collaborated with Noel Coward during the war to codirect such Coward vehicles as *In Which We Serve* (1942) and *Brief Encounter* (1946). He consolidated his reputation with two Dickens films—*Great Expectations* (1946) and *Oliver Twist* (1948)—and *The Sound Barrier* (1952). Lean became an outstandingly successful international producer-director with *Bridge on the River Kwai* (1957), for which he won an Academy Award, *Lawrence of Arabia* (1962), which won another Oscar, *Dr. Zhivago* (1966), *Ryan's Daughter* (1970), and *A Passage to India* (1984). Polished craftsmanship and highly disciplined editing are Lean's hallmarks.   ROGER MANVELL

Bibliography: Anderegg, M. A., *David Lean* (1984).

leap year: see CALENDAR.

Lear, Edward

The writer and artist Edward Lear, b. London, May 12, 1812, d. Jan. 29, 1888, is known both for his many nonsense LIMERICKS and songs and for his drawings and paintings of landscapes and of birds. Having begun work as an artist before he was 16, he was commissioned to draw the menagerie of the earl of Derby. While working on the estate, he amused the earl's grandchildren with the limericks he later published as

A Book of Nonsense in 1846. By that time he had also become a landscape painter, and he gave a series of lessons to Queen Victoria. He published collections of sketches of scenes in southern Italy, Greece, Palestine, and Turkey. An enlarged edition (1861) of *A Book of Nonsense* became very popular and was followed by four other humorous books, containing such poems as "The Owl and the Pussy Cat" and "The Jumblies." Lear was a restless, lonely man; he traveled incessantly and settled down only toward the end of his life in San Remo on the Italian Riviera.   DONALD GRAY

Bibliography: Hofer, Philip, *Edward Lear as a Landscape Draughtsman* (1967); Lehmann, John, *Edward Lear and His World* (1977); Noakes, Vivien, *Edward Lear: The Life of a Wanderer* (1968).

Lear, Norman

Writer, producer, and director in television and films, Norman Milton Lear, b. New Haven, Conn., July 22, 1922, changed U.S. situation comedy with the debut (1971) of his most popular and important television series, "All in the Family." Mainly through its central character—Archie Bunker, a realistic blue-collar, likable bigot from Queens, N.Y.—Lear challenged his audience by presenting areas of controversy with unprecedentedly strong language.

Lear began writing television comedy in the 1950s and moved into movies in the 1960s (*Come Blow Your Horn*, 1963, and *The Night They Raided Minsky's*, 1968, for example). The "All in the Family" format spawned several other successful comedy series for Lear, among them "Maude" (debut, 1972), "Sanford and Son" (1972), "The Jeffersons" (1975), and "Mary Hartman, Mary Hartman" (1976).

learning disabilities

Learning disabilities is a category of handicapping conditions that may afflict children, youth, and adults. The most frequently used definition of the term is in the Education of All Handicapped Children Act of 1975: " 'Specific learning disabilities' means those children who have a disorder in one or more of the basic psychological processes involved in understanding or in using language, spoken or written, which disorder may manifest itself in imperfect ability to listen, think, speak, read, write, spell, or do mathematical calculations. Such disorders include such conditions as perceptual handicaps, brain injury, minimal brain dysfunction, dyslexia, and developmental aphasia. Such term does not include children who have learning problems which are primarily the result of visual, hearing, or motor handicaps, of mental retardation, of emotional disturbance, or environmental, cultural, or economic disadvantage."

Learning disabilities is the most recently defined handicap to be included in federal and state special education laws and to command the attention of legislators, parents, and professionals in many areas whose services are required by persons with specific learning disabilities. It is only within the past decade or so that the term has come into common usage. At least three areas have been defined: perceptual and perceptual-motor disorders; language and speech disorders; and reading disabilities, in both children and adults. These areas have determined the scope of training of specialists in learning disabilities and have defined the types of problems that have been thus diagnosed. An early emphasis on perceptual processes for their own sake has gradually given way to interest in perceptual processing as a prerequisite to academic achievement and language development and as an indicator of development among preschool children.

Research in the early 1960s indicated about 100 different kinds of learning disabilities, which were grouped into 15 categories, including perceptual-motor impairments, attentional deficits, hyperactivity, distractibility, and impulsivity. In regulations formulated by the U.S. Office of Education in 1977, learning disabilities in children were reduced to eight areas: oral expression, listening comprehension, written expression, basic reading skills, reading comprehension, mathematics calculation, mathematics reasoning, and spelling.

There appears to be little consensus on the precise characteristics of children with learning disabilities, although there is some agreement that these children are characterized by wide discrepancies in function, being able to do certain things at or above the normal level of achievement while being able to do other things only at a much lower level.

Estimates of children with learning disabilities in the school-aged population vary widely. Several studies have indicated that between 4 and 7 percent of the school-aged population need special education and related services because of learning disabilities. At present most states are serving significantly smaller percentages of the school-aged population as learning disabled, and some of these children might be better served in remedial programs.

The cause of learning disabilities is not known. Researchers have been attempting to determine the role played by central nervous system dysfunction as a result of prenatal, perinatal, or postnatal trauma, malnutrition, biochemical imbalance, infections and so forth. Genetic factors appear to play a part in some children whose learning disabilities may be characterized by specific symptoms such as reading disability or a less-specific developmental delay or maturational lag. Unless the cause involves a medically correctible condition, etiology is of little importance to the child's educational program. In general, a teacher needs to know the child's present level of performance in detail in order to set realistic goals and objectives in designing a program to remedy the deficits and improve the child's functioning in academic skills and adaptive behavior.

Methods of instruction for children with learning disabilities have varied widely, reflecting the needs of individual children, the philosophy of individual teachers, and prevailing trends. Three major remedial strategies have been defined: task training, in which the task to be learned is simplified or modified; ability or process training, in which efforts are directed toward remediation of the disability that seems to be interfering with normal learning; and the combination process-task (or ability-task) approach, which integrates remediation of the process dysfunction with a task analysis of the sequence of skills required and attempts to bring about a precise match between the demand of the task and the particular pattern of learning in the child.

In addition to these educational approaches, a variety of other procedures such as eye-training exercises, diet control, motor training, sensory training, and medication, including antihistamines, stimulants, and vitamins, have been advocated by some professionals in the field. Proponents of these approaches seem to be convinced of the value of their procedures; there are controlled studies being done with large groups of learning-disabled children to determine the effectiveness of such approaches. It is important to determine the characteristics of both the children who respond favorably to some of these less-traditional approaches and those who do not, and to tailor the approach to the particular needs of each child.

As school programs have developed in every state for learning-disabled children, the Association for Children with Learning Disabilities, founded in 1963 primarily for parents of such children, has grown into an influential national group, promoting the cause through state and local affiliates. The importance of learning in our society has apparently highlighted the difficulties in learning experienced by some of our children and has resulted in rapid growth in all aspects of the field of learning disabilities.   JEANNE M. McCARTHY

Bibliography: Adelman, Howard, and Taylor, Linda, *Learning Disabilities in Perspective* (1983); Kauffman, J. M., and Hallahan, D. P., eds., *Handbook of Special Education* (1981); Lerner, Janet, W., *Learning Disabilities*, 3d ed. (1981).

learning theory

Learning, in psychology, is a process by which relatively permanent changes in behavior occur as a result of practice or experience. Learning itself is not directly observable; it can only be inferred by observing changes in a person's or animal's behavior. Psychologists do not agree in their theories of learning. The various schools of thought differ in their methodology, their interpretation of what occurs in learning, and the extent to which they theorize about the process.

CLASSICAL CONDITIONING

A form of learning that has been studied intensively by Ivan P. PAVLOV and others is classical CONDITIONING, in which the mind learns to associate a response with a stimulus to which it was not originally related. Pavlov experimented with dogs, studying the flow of their saliva in response to the stimuli of food and a bell. When food was presented to a dog, the flow of saliva increased. Psychologists call this a natural or unconditioned stimulus-response sequence, food being the unconditioned stimulus (US) and salivation the unconditioned response (UR). Pavlov found that when another stimulus, such as the sound of a bell, was presented along with the food, the dog soon began to salivate when the second, or conditioned, stimulus (CS) was presented by itself. The latter response is called a conditioned response (CR).

Development of Conditioning. The CS-US time sequence is crucial. They must occur together or the CS must precede the US very briefly in order for conditioning to occur. If the CS precedes the US by more than five seconds, conditioning is weak, and if the US precedes the CS, conditioning does not occur. If the CS is repeatedly presented without the US, extinction occurs, consisting of a gradual reduction of the CR until it ceases. Pavlov also demonstrated two basic learning principles, those of generalization and discrimination. He found that his animals tended to give the same conditioned response to a number of different stimuli, such as bells of different pitch. They could be trained, however, to discriminate between bells of only slightly different pitch or other stimuli closely resembling each other. The training consisted of CS-US pairings concentrated on a single stimulus, interspersed with other stimuli without the US.

Experimental Neurosis. During his research on discrimination, Pavlov found that when the training had gone to the limits of the animals' ability to distinguish among different stimuli they became agitated, overreactive, and aggressive. They also developed a strongly generalized salivation to all stimuli, and salivated spontaneously so that they were no longer trainable using the salivation response. Some psychologists have contended that this provides the proper explanation of neurotic behavior in humans. Whereas Sigmund FREUD claimed that NEUROSES are the outcome of childhood and sexual traumas, John B. WATSON set out to show that they could be explained by classical conditioning (1920). Watson used a tame albino rat as the CS and an 11-month old infant named Albert as his subject. He conditioned a "phobia neurosis" to the rat in Albert. The phobia was generalized to things other than rats; Albert showed a fear of furry animals in general, and even of the color white, resembling the generalized fear often expressed by patients suffering from phobias.

OPERANT CONDITIONING

The methods of conditioning studied by B. F. SKINNER have produced the simplest, most powerful, and most accurate of learning methodologies. Operant conditioning, sometimes called instrumental conditioning, differs from classical conditioning because it is based on the reinforcement of a natural response (operating on the environment—thus the term "operant"). For example, a pigeon will naturally peck at objects placed before it. It can be trained to peck at a certain object, such as a disk, by giving it food whenever it does so. Operant conditioning can be measured with great accuracy. Continuous reinforcement quickly produces a high rate of response. The response can be made nearly permanent by reinforcing it at scheduled intervals.

A response can also be changed to a completely new response by shaping. Animals have been taught to perform complex tricks by carefully reinforcing certain responses and not reinforcing others. A pigeon can be trained to dance a circle by shaping the pecking response into a turning response and by selectively reinforcing its head thrusts in the desired direction.

Programmed Learning. Skinner developed TEACHING MACHINES using his discoveries in operant conditioning. Just as pigeons can be taught to dance in circles, people can be taught many things more quickly if the proper reinforcement and shaping procedures are followed. Such PROGRAMMED LEARNING involves gradually increasing the level of difficulty while continuously reinforcing correct responses and extinguishing incorrect responses. A teaching machine is a mechanical device for presenting the program in correct order and ensuring that the learner continues only if the correct response has been made. Programmed learning has demonstrated its effectiveness in education, although it has not lived up to its early promise.

Reinforcement. Many kinds of reinforcement have been studied. Reinforcement can be positive, as in giving a reward, or negative, as in terminating punishment when a proper response is given. Food or candy is a positive reinforcer; the stopping of an electric shock when a rat pushes the right lever is a negative reinforcer. A neutral reinforcer—one that is neither positive nor negative—can become a secondary reinforcer by virtue of being repeatedly associated with reinforcement. Thus money is a secondary reinforcer because it can be exchanged for positive reinforcers.

CONTROVERSIES AND EMPHASES IN LEARNING THEORY

Much of the recent research in learning has been conducted by behaviorists, who have regarded learning as overt, measurable behavior that can be studied simply by investigating the conditions that produce and control learning. The school of BEHAVIORISM is divided between those who, like Clark HULL, use theoretical constructs in explaining behavior, and a larger group who follow B. F. Skinner in rejecting theory altogether. Hull distinguished between permanent learning, or HABIT, and temporary performance that he analyzed as reflecting incentives and stimuli. Other approaches to psychology emphasize perceptual and cognitive processes and make extensive use of theory (see COGNITIVE PSYCHOLOGY; PERCEPTION).

S-R vs. S-S Theories. Behaviorists assert that all learning consists of responses to stimuli, or S-R connections. Other theorists have interpreted learning as an active organization of stimuli, or signs, in terms of their meanings (S-S connections). An illustration of the S-S approach can be found in the work of Wolfgang KÖHLER, who demonstrated (1917) that the great apes sometimes solve problems by a process of insight learning. Insight is the sudden occurrence of a new, correct, problem-solving response following a period of ineffective trial-and-error behavior. Insight gives the appearance of understanding and reorganization. For example, an ape can learn to reach a banana some distance away by putting together a distance-spanning combination of sticks. E. C. TOLMAN introduced the concept of place learning; he showed that rats in a maze are able to find an object by learning its location rather than through a response-chain of left or right turns.

Latent Learning. Investigators also disagree on the part played by reinforcement in learning. While behaviorists insist that all learning requires reinforcement, cognitive theorists assert that reinforcement does not actually produce learning but, rather, provides a signal about what to do or a reason for doing it. Tolman's discussion of latent learning is an example of this. He found that when rats obtained food after reaching a goal following a series of nonreinforced trials, an immediate increase in "learning" appeared. He concluded that the learning had already occurred, but that it had not found expression in performance until the reinforcement was given.

Two-Factor Theory. Some theorists believe that classical conditioning and operant conditioning represent two fundamentally different learning processes. One is trial-and-error learning, which requires reinforcement of right responses as in operant conditioning; it involves the central nervous system and the voluntary musculature. The other learning process is emotional learning, which occurs through the signal learning of classical conditioning; it involves the autonomic nervous system and the involuntary musculature. In some behaviors both trial-and-error learning and emotional learning may be involved.

FRED HEILIZER

Bibliography: Bolles, Robert C., *Learning Theory*, 2d ed. (1979); Estes, William K., et al., *Learning Theory and Mental Development* (1970); Hergenhahn, B. R., *An Introduction to Theories of Learning*, 2d ed. (1982); Hilgard, Ernest R., and Bower, Gordon H., *Theories of Learning*, 4th ed. (1975); Hill, Winfred F., *Learning: A Survey of Psychological Interpretations*, 3d ed. (1977); Kimble, Gregory, ed., *Foundations of Conditioning and Learning* (1967); Mowrer, Orval H., *The Psychology of Language and Learning* (1980); Schwartz, Barry, *Psychology of Learning and Behavior* (1978); Tighe, Thomas J., *Modern Learning Theory* (1982).

lease

A lease is a grant by one person (the lessor or landlord) to another (the lessee or tenant) of the right to possess and use property for a specific period of time. Leases can be either oral or written, although most states of the United States require leases for one year or more to be written. The two most common types of leases are residential and commercial. Residential leases concern the rental of houses and apartments, and commercial leases involve the rental of land, offices, and other property for commercial purposes. The laws governing these two types of leases are generally the same, but some states distinguish between the two in matters such as security deposits, evictions, and the landlord's duty to repair.

A valid lease must identify the parties by name and by status (such as landlord or tenant). It must describe the property with reasonable particularity. The commencement and duration of the leasehold must be specified, as must the amount of rent and when it is to be paid. A lease usually contains a series of covenants (promises) agreed upon by the parties concerned. In most jurisdictions these covenants are considered to be independent, that is, if one party does not perform his or her covenants, the other party is still liable to perform his or her own covenants. The only remedy for an aggrieved party is to sue the other party for breach of particular covenants. Express covenants are those written or orally agreed upon by the parties. Implied covenants are those covenants which the law treats as being usual and logical—for example, a tenant's duty to pay rent and a landlord's duty to provide quiet enjoyment of the property.

Residential leases tend to favor the landlord over the tenant. Although most reasonable lease provisions will be enforced by the courts, some states have enacted legislation protecting tenants against unreasonable lease clauses imposed upon them by landlords. In New Jersey, for example, the law provides that a security deposit may never exceed one and one half month's rent, and that interest on it must be paid to the tenant.

A security deposit is usually required in a lease. This is an amount deposited by the tenant with the landlord to cover any damages to the property other than reasonable wear and tear, and to insure against rent default by the tenant. Late payment of rent penalty provisions are often included. These are generally valid unless waived by the landlord's habitual acceptance of late rent without imposing the penalty. Many leases contain clauses prohibiting assigning or subletting without the landlord's consent. These clauses are usually upheld by courts. Usually the landlord will agree to repair residential premises. It is not uncommon, however, for a provision to be included whereby the tenant is required to make and pay for certain types of minor repairs. Other common provisions include the landlord's right to inspect and show the property to potential tenants or buyers at reasonable times, a provision determining who is responsible for paying the various utilities, and a provision stating that the premises are to be used only for specified purposes: a residential lease may state, for example, that commercial activities may not be conducted on the property.

Bibliography: Brue, Nordahl L., *Retailer's Guide to Understanding Leases* (1980); McMichael, Stanley L., and O'Keefe, P., *Leases: Percentage, Short and Long Term*, 6th ed. (1974).

Lease, Mary Elizabeth   [lees]

Mary Elizabeth Clyens Lease, b. Ridgway, Pa., Sept. 11, 1850, d. Oct. 29, 1933, was a populist who achieved fame by exhorting farmers to "raise less corn and more hell." The famous phrase, however, was probably not hers but that of a hostile reporter. A lawyer (by her own claim) in Kansas, Lease joined the Populist party and became a vigorous advocate of agrarian reform, woman suffrage, free silver, Prohibition, popular election of senators, government supervision of corporations, and nationalization of railroads. She was called Mary Yellin Lease by some opponents.

least-squares method

The least-squares method is a statistical procedure used to fit a set of measurements onto an approximate curve. It is a technique that allows researchers to identify trends based upon measurement values. Due to ERROR, measurement values generally deviate from their expected positions along a mathematical curve. Of the various curves based on correction formulas, the least-squares curve has the smallest sum of the squares of the individual measurement deviations.

German mathematician Carl Friedrich GAUSS developed the least-squares method in 1794. In 1801, Gauss successfully employed this method in an attempt to relocate the first known asteroid, Ceres, after it had been tracked for 41 days, then lost in the brightness of the Sun. Least-squares methods were used in reconstructing the trajectories of the Apollo spaceships as they hurtled toward the Moon. In that case statistical errors amounted to only about 19 cm (7.5 in) over a typical 100-km (62-mi) flight segment.   DONNA AND TOM LOGSDON

Bibliography: Draper, N. R., *Applied Regression Analysis,* 2d ed. (1981); Longley, James W., *Least Squares Computations* (1984); Mikhail, Edward M., *Observations and Least Squares* (1982).

leather and hides

Leather is the hide or skin of a mammal, reptile, bird, or fish that has been made pliable and resistant to decay through the chemical treatment called tanning. The surface area of hides and skins contains the hair and oil glands and is known as the grain side. The arrangement of hair pockets and the texture of the surface give each type of leather its distinguishing character, or grain. The flesh side of the hide or skin is much thicker and softer; in cattle hide it comprises about four-fifths of the total thickness.

One of the properties of animal hides and skins is their ability to absorb tannic acid, a plant extract, and other chemical substances that prevent them from decaying, make them resistant to wetting, and keep them supple and durable. In addition, the fibrous structure of hides and skins, which is retained in the leather, allows air and water vapor to pass through—thus, for example, perspiration will evaporate from leather shoes.

Properly treated leather is among the most long-lived of natural substances. Ancient pieces of leather clothing and utensils have been found throughout the world—sandals from Egyptian tombs, bits of leather garments brought up from Scottish bogs, and water and grain containers from Minoan Crete. About 500 years before the birth of Christ, the Athenian playwright Aristophanes referred to the tanner, who was already a well-established craftsman.

The Tanning Process. Before tanning, hides and skins must be cured to prevent putrefaction. Large hides are green salted: they are spread in layers for several days with salt between each layer. A faster process, used on smaller hides and skins, is brine-pickling—immersion in a salt-brine solution circulated by pumps or agitators.

At the tannery the hides and skins are trimmed, sorted into batches of the same size and thickness, and finally washed and soaked to remove excess salt and restore the fibers to a condition in which they can readily absorb tanning agents. Solutions of lime and enzyme materials are applied to loosen the hairs, and a dehairing machine leaves the surface smooth and the distinctive grain pattern visible. The hides and skins are then ready for one of several tanning processes.

Vegetable tanning with tannic acids is the oldest method. Used primarily for heavy cattle hides, the process may take a month or more. Tannin extracts come from the bark and wood of several trees: the South American quebracho, the Bornean mangrove, and the Indian and East Indian gambier,

as well as from the North American chestnut, oak, and hemlock. The hides are suspended in a vat containing a weak tanning solution; they are moved through a series of successively stronger solutions until the leather matures. The tanned leather is then bleached and impregnated with natural oils and greases. The final product of the vegetable tanning process is a firm, water-resistant leather used chiefly in shoe soles but also in upholstery, luggage, saddlery, and industrial belting.

Almost all leather made from lighter-weight cattle hides and from the skin of sheep, lambs, goats, and pigs is chrome-tanned, using a process developed in the latter half of the 19th century. Hides and skins are tumbled in huge drums partially filled with chrome-salt solutions that produce a light blue green leather, which is then cleaned, dried, and smoothed by machine. The natural oils and greases lost in tanning are restored by fat-liquoring: the application of emulsified oils, egg yolks, and clay. The chrome-tanning process is very quick—a matter of hours rather than the days required by vegetable tanning—and produces leathers for shoe uppers, garments, handbags, gloves, and other small leather goods.

Other tanning processes include tawing, or alum tanning, a mineral tanning technique that uses alum combined with salt; a recently developed fast process called Secotan, using dry-cleaning solvents as the tanning agents; and chamoising, in which sheepskin or calfskin is treated with oils and fats. Chamois leather is napped, or sueded, on both sides and is very absorbent.

Finishing. After the leather is tanned, machines split it into flesh and grain layers. The leather must now be dried. To prevent shrinkage it is often stretched on frames or smoothed flat on a glass or metal plate before being placed on a conveyor and passed through the drying cabinet. Dried leather is generally too stiff, and it may be conditioned by spraying with water until sufficient moisture has been absorbed to ensure flexibility.

Various types of finishes are then applied. Leathers are

LEATHER TYPES AND USES

Source	Market Name	Uses
Cattle	Cattle hide	Shoe uppers and soles, luggage, upholstery, belts, clothing
	Untanned rawhide	Machine belts, bindings, luggage
	Calf leather	Shoe uppers, handbags, belts
Goat and kid	Goatskin and kidskin	Shoe uppers, purses, apparel, gloves
Sheep and lamb	Sheepskin, lambskin	Shoe uppers and linings, gloves, apparel, bookbindings, chamois
	Shearling (wool is clipped and left on hide)	Coats, boots, slippers
Wild hog (peccary) and domestic hog	Pigskin	Shoes, gloves, wallets, luggage
Asian water buffalo		Shoes, luggage, handbags
Reptile	Snakeskin	Shoe uppers, handbags
Deer	Deerskin and buckskin (grain surface removed)	Apparel, gloves, shoes
Shark	Sharkskin	Shoe uppers, small leather goods
Horse	Horsehide and cordovan	Shoe uppers, apparel, baseball covers

buffed with fine abrasives to produce a suede finish; waxed, shellacked, or treated with pigments, dyes, and resins to achieve a smooth, polished surface and the desired color; or lacquered with urethane for a glossy patent leather. In boarding, the leather is folded and hand pressed with a board to produce tiny creases. In embossing, designs are pressed into the surface of cattle leather to give it the look of an exotic grain such as ostrich or reptile.

Sources of Leather. Cattle and calves are the largest single source of leather, and their hides and skins are used in almost every area where leather is needed—from machine beltings and furniture to shoes, gloves, and handbags. The United States, the USSR, Argentina, and Brazil are the largest cattle-hide producers.

Sheepskin is produced primarily in the USSR, Australia, and New Zealand; goatskin, in India and China. Leather is also obtained from the skins of wild and domestic hogs, Asian water buffalo, snakes (especially Indian cobra and South American python), alligators, deer, sharks, and horses.

The United States is the leading leather manufacturing country, followed by the USSR, India, Brazil, and Argentina.

Synthetic Substitutes for Leather. Since the 1950s, plastic materials have been developed that resemble leather in many respects, although they do not share leather's pliability and its ability to "breathe" and to retain its shape. Nevertheless, as natural products have become more costly, synthetic substitutes have been used to replace leather. Today they constitute a sizable share of the products sold under the term *leather goods,* and up to 80 percent of shoe soling. Because of their impermeability, however, synthetics have not found wide use in shoe uppers.   RITA V. COPELMAN

Bibliography: Gustavson, K. H., *The Chemistry of Tanning Processes* (1956); Leather Industries of America, *Leather in Our Lives,* rev. ed. (1975); O'Flaherty, Fred, and Roddy, William T., eds., *The Chemistry and Technology of Leather,* 4 vols. (1956-65; repr. 1978); Thorstensen, Thomas C., *Practical Leather Technology,* 2d rev. ed. (1969; repr. 1976); Waterer, John W., *Leather Craftmanship* (1968) and *Leather in Life, Art and Industry* (1946); Welsh, Peter C., *Tanning in the United States to 1850* (1964).

leatherback turtle

The leatherback turtle, *Dermochelys coriacea,* is the largest living species of turtle and the sole surviving member of the family Dermochelyidae. It reaches 1.8 m (6 ft) in shell length and up to 680 kg (1,500 lb) in weight. The shell is covered with smooth, leathery skin and has seven prominent lengthwise ridges on the top. This species lives in the open sea, apparently going ashore only to lay eggs. The leatherback, threatened because of overhunting (particularly of its eggs), is scarce but worldwide in distribution, occurring mostly in tropical waters.   JONATHAN CAMPBELL

Bibliography: Ernst, Carl H., and Barbour, Roger W., *Turtles of the United States* (1972).

Largest of all turtles, the leatherback turtle, D. coriacea, is usually found singly in warm oceans worldwide. Its shell consists of bony plates embedded in its dark brown or black leathery skin.

Leatherstocking Tales, The

The Leatherstocking Tales, a series of five popular novels by James Fenimore COOPER, constitute an epic of the American wilderness. Natty BUMPPO, the central character, embodies the spirit of the frontier in The DEERSLAYER (1841), where he is an idealized youth, and in *The Prairie* (1827), in which, as an old man, he is transfigured and dies. The other novels in the series are *The Last of the Mohicans* (1826), *The Pathfinder* (1840), and *The Pioneers* (1823).

leatherwood

Leatherwood is a deciduous, flowering shrub of North America in the family Thymelaeaceae. The species found in the northeastern United States, *Dirca palustris,* is also known as moosewood. It grows near wooded areas. The yellowish flowers occur in clusters and bloom in the spring. These yield a red or greenish berrylike fruit called a drupe, which ripens in May or June. The bark is toxic and can cause vomiting if eaten. Another species, *Dirca occidentalis,* is found in California.

Leaves of Grass

Leaves of Grass (1855), Walt WHITMAN's first published volume of poetry, consisted of 12 poems written without regular meter or rhyme. Until his death in 1892, Whitman revised and expanded his book until the ninth and final version contained hundreds of poems. Among the most famous are "Out of the Cradle Endlessly Rocking," "When Lilacs Last in the Dooryard Bloom'd," "O Captain! My Captain!" and "SONG OF MYSELF." The first edition contained a preface, later omitted, in which Whitman expounded a theory of the poet's vocation. The volume was not well received in the United States and found its first enthusiastic champions in England.

Bibliography: Cowley, Malcolm, ed., *Walt Whitman's "Leaves of Grass"* (1959); Marki, I., *The Trial of the Poet* (1976).

Leavis, F. R.   [lee'-vis]

Frank Raymond Leavis, b. July 14, 1895, d. Apr. 17, 1978, was an influential British literary critic whose teaching and writing profoundly affected the study of literature in British schools and universities. Unlike other major critics of his time, such as I. A. Richards, William Empson, or the American "New Critics" (see NEW CRITICISM), Leavis did not base his assessments of literature on close verbal analysis of the text. Although his arguments were based on concrete examples, he evaluated authors according to their capacity to experience life with maturity and sensitivity. His first book, *New Bearings in English Poetry* (1932), acknowledged a debt to the criticism of T. S. Eliot and praised the work of Eliot, Ezra Pound, and Gerard Manley Hopkins, but found that of W. H. Auden and W. B. Yeats adolescent and immature. His vehement judgments, which were often expressed with devastating scorn, found a wide audience through the journal *Scrutiny* (1932-53), which he edited with his wife, the scholar and critic Q. D. Leavis.

Revaluation (1936) examined the tradition of English poetry, and *The Great Tradition* (1948) deemed the novelists Jane Austen, George Eliot, Henry James, Joseph Conrad, and D. H. Lawrence "significant in terms of the human awareness they promote." Many readers regard *The Common Pursuit* (1952) his finest book. In the 1950s, Leavis became increasingly engaged in literary politics, and his later work, which includes *Dickens the Novelist* (1970), is marred by intemperate diatribes against contemporary British society.

HOWARD BATCHELOR

Bibliography: Hayman, Ronald, *Leavis* (1977).

Leavitt, Henrietta Swan   [lev'-it]

The American astronomer Henrietta Swan Leavitt, b. July 4, 1868, d. Dec. 12, 1921, established the PERIOD-LUMINOSITY RELA-

TION for CEPHEID variable stars. This led to the development of a new method for determining how far extremely distant stars and galaxies are from the Earth. She graduated from what is now Radcliffe College in 1892, and worked at Harvard College Observatory from 1902. There, her major task was conducting a program of photographic photometry initiated by Edward C. PICKERING, to determine the brightnesses of selected stars. Her study of VARIABLE STARS, of which she discovered 2,400, led to the discovery of the relationship between the period of variability and the luminosity of Cepheid variables. Harlow SHAPLEY later used this relationship to determine the distance of globular clusters.   STEVEN J. DICK

Bibliography: Hoffleit, Dorrit, *Notable American Women* (1971).

Lebanon   [leb'-uh-nuhn]

The Republic of Lebanon, a tiny country some 55 km (35 mi) wide and 215 km (135 mi) long, is located on the eastern shore of the Mediterranean Sea. It is bordered on the north and east by Syria and on the south by Israel. From earliest times (see PHOENICIA), Lebanon has been at the center of the tumultuous history of the Middle East. It was a French mandate from the end of World War I until 1943, when it gained full independence, and it gradually became the commercial and cultural hub of the Arab Middle East. Lebanon has long been known for its religious and cultural diversity. Its inhabitants generally coexisted peacefully until 1975, when rapid economic, social, and demographic changes, rising intersectarian rivalries, and regional and international tensions contributed to the outbreak of a devastating civil war. Since that time the country's very existence has been threatened by domestic conflict and external pressures.

LAND AND RESOURCES

Lebanon is made up of four contrasting physiographic regions running north to south parallel to the Mediterranean. The narrow, fertile coastal plain is dominated by the foothills and peaks of the rugged Lebanon Mountains, which rise to 3,088 m (10,131 ft) at Qurnat al-Sawda, the highest point in the country. Behind the Lebanon Mountains lie successively the narrow, fertile al-Biqa (Bekaa) Valley (the northern extension of the GREAT RIFT VALLEY, some 915 m/3,000 ft above sea level) and the Anti-Lebanon Range. The latter forms Lebanon's eastern frontier with Syria and is often considered to include Mount HERMON. Numerous swift small rivers flow down from the Lebanon Mountains to the sea. Lebanon's two major rivers, the Litani and the Orontes, rise in the al-Biqa Valley.

Climate. Lebanon's climate varies sharply from place to place. The narrow coastal plain receives an average of 900 mm (about 35 in) of rainfall annually. There, winters are mild and rainy, summers are warm, humid, and rainless. The foothills and mountains receive substantially more precipitation in the form of both rain and snow during the wet season (October to April). Drier weather prevails in the al-Biqa Valley, where annual rainfall and snow average about half that of the coastal plain.

Soils, Vegetation, and Animal Life. Geologically, Lebanon is formed of three successive layers: limestone at the surface, sandstone, then limestone. Because of the varied terrain and climate, a large number of crops are grown. Areas not cultivated—mostly above 1,200 m (4,000 ft)—are generally bare of vegetation due to overcutting and overgrazing by goats, and the great forests of cedar celebrated in the Bible have largely disappeared. The lower-lying hills, where not cultivated, are covered with thornbushes and seasonal wildflowers. Indiscriminate hunting has greatly reduced a once rich and varied bird and animal population, and pollution in the Mediterranean threatens coastal fishing.

Resources. In ancient times Lebanon was famous for its wood, iron, and copper. All of these resources are now essentially exhausted. Abundant limestone deposits are used by the construction industry and in making cement for export.

PEOPLE

Lebanon is an Arab country, and Arabic is the official language. French and English are widely spoken and taught in the schools, however. The people are ethnically diverse be-

cause of the area's long history of conquest and assimilation. Indeed, one of the fundamental principles of the social and political order is confessionalism—the proportionate sharing of power among the nation's various ethnic-religious communities. More than 15 such communities are officially recognized by law. Among them, the principal Christian sects (several of which are EASTERN RITE CHURCHES) are the Maronites, Greek Orthodox, Greek Catholics, Protestant Evangelicals, Roman Catholics, Armenian Orthodox, Armenian Catholics, and Armenian Protestants. SUNNITES, SHIITES, and DRUZES (an offshoot of Shiite Islam) comprise the principal Muslim communities. Jews, mainly oriental, numbered perhaps 5,000 before 1975. In many ways, Lebanon today is less a nation than a collection of feudallike baronies organized along religious lines, and more than a decade of civil strife has strengthened sectarian loyalties at the expense of national unity.

Demography. No official census has been taken since 1932, when Christians slightly outnumbered Muslims. That enumeration included emigrant Lebanese (primarily Christian). The two most populous and prosperous sects, the Maronites and the Sunnites, used the 1932 census as the basis for the formula allocating political power along religious lines at independence; this unwritten agreement guaranteed the Maronites control of Lebanon. Since that time the Muslims, particularly the poorer Shiites, have had a substantially higher birthrate than the Christians. Recent estimates indicate that Muslims may constitute as much as 60% of the population—25% Sunnite, 25% Shiite, and 10% Druze—whereas Maronites comprise only an estimated 30% of the current total. The arrival of as many as 400,000 predominantly Muslim Palestinian refugees after 1948 further threatened Lebanon's delicate balance. Since 1975, civil strife has also driven thousands of Lebanese from their homes. By the end of the 1980s, it was estimated that 35% of the population had become refugees. Also, many foreign investors and wealthy Lebanese left the country.

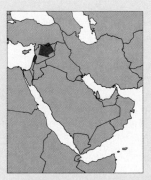

REPUBLIC OF LEBANON

LAND. Area: 10,452 km² (4,036 mi²). Capital and largest city: Beirut (1989 est. pop., 200,000).

PEOPLE. Population (1990 est.): 3,300,000; density: 315.7 persons per km² (817.6 per mi²). Distribution (1987): 80% urban, 20% rural. Annual growth (1989): 1.1%. Official language: Arabic. Major religions: Islam, Christianity, Druze.

EDUCATION AND HEALTH. Literacy (1985): 77% of adult population. Universities (1987): 5. Hospital beds (1982): 11,400. Physicians (1986): 3,509. Life expectancy (1989): women—70; men—65. Infant mortality (1989): 50 per 1,000 live births.

ECONOMY. GDP (1985): $1.8 billion; $690 per capita. Labor distribution (1986): agriculture—19%; manufacturing—18%; construction—6%; utilities, transportation, and communications—8%; finance—3%; trade—17%; public administration and services—29%. Foreign trade (1987): imports—$1.5 billion; exports—$1.0 billion; principal trade partners—Saudi Arabia, Italy, France, United States. Currency: 1 Lebanese pound = 100 piastres.

GOVERNMENT. Type: republic. Legislature: National Assembly. Political subdivisions: 5 governorates.

COMMUNICATIONS. Railroads (1988): 412 km (256 mi) total. Roads (1988): 7,100 km (4,412 mi) total. Major ports: 4. Major airfields: 1.

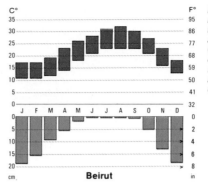

Bars indicate monthly ranges of temperatures (red) and precipitation (blue) of Beirut, the capital of Lebanon. Beirut has a Mediterranean climate.

LEBANON

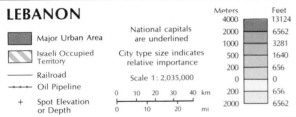

Major Urban Area	
Israeli Occupied Territory	
Railroad	
Oil Pipeline	
+ Spot Elevation or Depth	

National capitals are underlined

City type size indicates relative importance

Scale 1 : 2,035,000

Meters	Feet
4000	13124
2000	6562
1000	3281
500	1640
200	656
0	0
200	656
2000	6562

At least one-third of the population lives in the greater BEI-RUT area, and widespread urbanization has added to everyday tensions and increased demands for services that the weak and fragmented government is unable to provide.

Education and Health. Lebanon has long had one of the best systems of private education in the Middle East, with private elementary and secondary schools serving about half the student population. Public education, expanded during the 1960s, remains insufficient to meet demand or provide consistent quality. Lebanon has five institutions of higher education (see MIDDLE EASTERN UNIVERSITIES). The most notable is the

AMERICAN UNIVERSITY OF BEIRUT (1866), in which about half of the student body was once non-Lebanese. The Lebanese population's familiarity with foreign languages, high literacy rate, and relatively advanced educational level support a flourishing publishing industry and contribute to a still-vibrant cultural life. Before 1975, Lebanon's health-care system was one of the best in the region, although it concentrated services in urban areas, particularly Beirut. Since 1975 a growing refugee population has imposed great strains on community services.

ECONOMIC ACTIVITY

In modern times the Lebanese economy has been fundamentally transformed. Where once the majority of the population was engaged in agriculture, today a diversified economy is dominated by the service sector. The sharpest phase of economic transformation occurred after 1960 and benefited chiefly Christians and a few Sunni Muslims. By 1975 about 4% of the population controlled one-third of the wealth, a fact that contributed greatly to the current conflict.

Agriculture. As recently as 1960 nearly half the population was rural, although only one-quarter of the land was cultivated and agriculture generated less than one-fifth of the GNP. Most farmers in the mountains are small freeholders; those in the al-Biqa Valley, southern Lebanon, and the extreme north are mostly tenant farmers or sharecroppers for absentee landlords. The coastal areas yield citrus fruits, bananas, and olives, and the lower slopes of the Lebanon Mountains are terraced for the production of apples, grapes, pears, and peaches. These products were long valuable as exports to Arab countries, where demand for them was high. Grains, potatoes, melons, and vegetables flourish in the al-Biqa Valley.

Manufacturing and Services. Lebanon's manufacturing sector, though small, is nonetheless significant. By 1974 it employed some 120,000 workers and generated 16% of the GNP. The principal manufactures are textiles, cement, ironwork, wood products, plastics, ceramics, pharmaceuticals, and processed foods; refineries at TRIPOLI and near SIDON process oil piped from Iraq and Saudi Arabia to meet domestic require-

Beirut, located on the Mediterranean Sea, is the capital and largest city of Lebanon. The city has existed since biblical times. Since 1975 much of the city has been destroyed, and it has been divided by the so-called Green Line into predominantly Christian East Beirut and mostly Muslim West Beirut.

The cedars of Lebanon, famous since biblical times, became the symbol of the country and are shown on the national flag. Today they are found only in a few protected groves.

ments. Most industrial concerns are small-scale family firms. Manufacturing, concentrated in the Beirut area before the civil war, has since become decentralized; overall industrial exports have declined sharply since 1982.

Independent Lebanon prospered by attracting foreign investment. Its banking secrecy laws and uncontrolled foreign exchange market encouraged a strong banking sector. Some 80 major banks once served the Middle East from Beirut, which became the financial and commercial center of the region. Tourism, banking, finance, commerce, and other services accounted for nearly 70% of the GNP by 1973. The economy was shattered by the civil war and later events.

Power. In the early 1970s a long-standing power shortage was eliminated with the construction of more oil-fired generators and the completion of the Litani dam. Since 1975, however, Lebanon has been unable to meet its power needs.

Transportation. Lebanon's transportation system was one of its principal assets in regional and international trade. An important part of the port of Beirut, the country's leading port, is its "Free Zone" for transit trade. Tripoli and Sidon are also major ports. Since 1975 numerous illegal ports for smuggling weapons and contraband for the flourishing black market have emerged. More recently, entire sections of the country were cut off by occupying foreign armies. Civil air transportation is confined to Beirut International Airport. A government-owned railway connects Beirut with Tripoli and Damascus. A good road system is now much in need of repair. Trucks carry passengers and goods to and through Syria, which controls Lebanon's overland transportation links to other countries.

Trade. Lebanon's links to the outside world are critical to its economic viability. For decades Lebanon's trade deficit was offset by the reexport trade and by remittances from Lebanese working abroad. A sharp decline in these remittances since 1983—particularly after the 1990 Iraqi invasion of Kuwait—contributed to the virtual collapse of the Lebanese pound on foreign exchange markets.

GOVERNMENT

The Lebanese republic, independent since 1943, was established under French mandate by the Constitution of 1926 (since amended). The constitution provides for an executive branch (president, prime minister, and cabinet) balanced by an independent judiciary and a unicameral legislature elected to a four-year term by universal adult suffrage. (The current legislature, elected in 1972, has extended its life by special legislation.) Until 1990 an unwritten agreement known as the National Pact was as important as the constitution. It specified that the president be a Maronite Christian, the prime minister a Sunni Muslim, and the speaker of the legislature a Shiite Muslim. Legislative seats were apportioned among the various sects in accordance with a six-to-five ratio of Christians to Muslims, as were posts in the cabinet, bureaucracy, judiciary, and military. Under constitutional reforms set forth in a 1989 Arab-brokered peace accord and signed into law in September 1990, many of the powers of the Christian president were shifted to the half-Christian, half-Muslim cabinet, and the Muslim prime minister was to countersign presidential decrees. The legislature was to be evenly divided between Christians and Muslims.

HISTORY

Lebanon has been in the mainstream of history since recorded history began. Its strategic location has made it a transporter and transmitter of civilization, culture, and religion.

The earliest inhabitants were a Semitic people related to the Canaanites who came to coastal Lebanon from the Arabian Peninsula about 3500 BC. The Greeks named these seafaring people Phoenicians, and they established city-states (including BYBLOS, TYRE, Sidon, Beirut, and BAALBEK) and spread their 22-letter alphabet throughout the Mediterranean region. After being successively ruled by the Egyptians, Assyrians, Neo-Babylonians, Persians, and Greeks, Lebanon came under Roman rule in 64 BC. Christianity was firmly established there before AD 395. Lebanon later became part of the Eastern Roman (or Byzantine) Empire.

Particularly during the early Christian era, when theological controversies bred numerous sects, Lebanon became a refuge for persecuted minorities fleeing imperial authority. In the 660s one of these sects, which later became the Maronite church, settled in the Lebanon Mountains to avoid forcible conversion to Islam by the Arabs, who had completed their conquest of the region by 640. The attractiveness of Lebanon as a refuge persisted into Islamic times. Shiites found a haven there during the 9th century, Druzes in the 11th century.

The coastal plain and Lebanon Mountains fell temporarily to the Crusaders (see CRUSADES) early in the 12th century. Many Lebanese Christians fought alongside the Crusaders, and thousands of them were slaughtered by Muslims once the Crusaders had been driven out in the late 13th century by the MAMELUKS of Egypt. Generally, however, the mosaic of religions that Lebanon had become offered semiautonomy or independence for its various groups, each of which concentrated in specific areas until modern times. The Maronites lived in Mount Lebanon (the heart of present-day Lebanon, excluding the coastal cities), the Druzes in the mountains of southern Mount Lebanon, the Shiites to the south and east, and the Sunnites and various Christian minorities along the coast.

From 1516 to 1918, when Lebanon was formally part of the OTTOMAN EMPIRE, local leaders were granted relative autonomy as long as they paid taxes to their Ottoman rulers. One powerful Druze chieftain, Fakhr al-Din, gained control of Mount Lebanon and parts of Syria and Palestine. After his execution by the Turks in 1635, Druze power waned, paving the way for the rising influence of the Maronites, who established close ties with other Lebanese Christian sects. Under Ottoman rule, Lebanon developed commercial, educational, and religious ties with Europe. Open to the West, it became a center for political rivalries between various foreign powers, including France, England, and Russia. These powers assumed the protection of certain ethnic-religious groups, with France as the chief protector of the Maronites. Intermittent warfare between 1840 and 1860 cost both Maronite and Druze lives. A massacre of Maronites in 1860 prompted French and British inter-

Baalbek, an ancient Phoenician city, rose to prominence during the Roman occupation. Although the city was destroyed by earthquake in 1759, many fine examples of Roman architecture remain. Since 1975, Baalbek has been a headquarters for radical Shiites.

vention and the establishment (1864) by Turkey of a semiautonomous Christian-dominated province in Mount Lebanon.

After World War I, Lebanon became a French mandate, as promised by the secret Sykes-Picot Agreement of 1916. In 1920 the French created Lebanon's current boundaries by adding the al-Biqa Valley, the coastal cities, and areas to the north and south—with large Sunnite and Shiite populations—to predominantly Christian Mount Lebanon. The Republic of Lebanon, established by the Constitution of 1926, remained under French mandate until 1943, when it gained independence.

For a time, independent Lebanon was a model ecumenical society. Two grave weaknesses, however, eventually undid the Lebanese system. The first was the rigidity of the 1943 National Pact, which did not take into account changes in the demography and political consciousness of the various communities. The second was Lebanon's gradual involvement in the Arab-Israeli conflict. Lebanon did not participate militarily in the ARAB-ISRAELI WARS, but the influx of predominantly Muslim Palestinian refugees after the 1948 war helped to change the country's internal balance of power. In addition, Lebanese Muslims who identified with the Pan-Arab nationalism of Egyptian president Gamal Abdel NASSER were alienated when President Camille Chamoun was the only Arab head of state who refused to break diplomatic relations with France and Britain during the 1956 Suez Crisis. Civil war broke out in 1958, ending only when U.S. Marines landed in Beirut. Economic and social inequalities, Muslim demands for more political power, and the activities of PALESTINE LIBERATION ORGANIZATION (PLO) commandos (who operated virtually a state within a state and launched guerrilla raids against Israel from Lebanese soil) continued, laying the groundwork for the 1975–76 civil war.

The civil war pitted the Nationalist Movement (a mostly Muslim mixture of socialists, Communists, and Nasserite groups) against the Lebanese Front (a group dominated by the Maronite Phalange party but including right-wing Muslims). The PLO joined the fighting on the side of the Nationalist Movement. In June 1976, with the Nationalist Movement on the verge of victory, Syria (which at various times has supported different groups) intervened on behalf of the Lebanese Front. The Syrian military action was ratified in October by the Arab League, which helped to arrange a cease-fire.

Despite the Syrian presence, sporadic communal strife and the cycle of Israeli-Palestinian violence on Lebanese soil continued. Israeli forces briefly invaded southern Lebanon in 1978 but withdrew after a United Nations peacekeeping force (UNIFIL) was sent into the area. In 1982, Israeli forces again invaded, occupying Beirut and forcing the PLO to evacuate its headquarters there. Phalangist leader Amin GEMAYEL took office as president in September; at his request, a multinational peace force came in to try to restore order. In May 1983, Gemayel concluded a security agreement with Israel that provided for a continuing Israeli role in southern Lebanon. Syria, which had refused to withdraw its troops when its Arab League mandate expired, rejected the accord. Meanwhile, the Lebanese army was unable to halt fighting between Lebanon's numerous armed militias (including rival Palestinian groups), and terrorist bomb attacks on the multinational force, which was withdrawn in 1984. Gemayel then repudiated the unpopular Lebanese-Israeli security agreement and installed a new, pro-Syrian cabinet of national unity. The cabinet seldom met after Gemayel rejected a Syrian-brokered peace accord in January 1986, contributing to political and economic deterioration exacerbated by the activities of terrorist groups such as the Iranian-backed HEZBOLLAH and by the 1987 assassination of Prime Minister Rashid Karami. Most Israeli forces left Lebanon by June 1985, but conflicting Israeli and Syrian interests continued to compound Lebanon's formidable internal problems. In 1988 the legislature's inability to agree on a candidate to succeed Gemayel led to the formation of rival Christian and Muslim governments. In November 1989 the Lebanese parliament accepted an Arab-brokered peace accord and elected Maronite René Moawad president. Moawad was assassinated on November 22; his successor was Elias Hrawi. Christian prime minister Gen. Michel Aoun launched a "war of liberation" against the Syrian forces in Lebanon in March 1989. His surrender in October 1990, coupled with the 1990 constitutional revisions giving political parity to Muslims, raised hopes for peace.   KARL K. BARBIR AND LEILA S. AL-IMAD

Bibliography: Cobban, H., *The Making of Modern Lebanon* (1985); Fawaz, L., *Merchants and Migrants in 19th Century Beirut* (1983); Fisk, R., *Pity the Nation* (1990); Friedman, T. L., *From Beirut to Jerusalem* (1989); Gordon, D. C., *Lebanon* (1980) and *The Republic of Lebanon* (1983); Harik, I., *Politics and Change in a Traditional Society: Lebanon, 1711–1845* (1968); Hitti, P. K., *Lebanon in History*, 3d ed. (1967); Khaladi, W., *Conflict and Violence in Lebanon* (1979); Khalaf, S., *Persistence and Change in 19th Century Lebanon* (1979) and *Lebanon's Predicament* (1987); Khuri, F., *From Village to Suburb* (1975); Mackey, S., *Lebanon* (1989); Makdisi, J. S., *Beirut Fragments* (1990); Norton, A. R., *Amal and the Shia* (1987).

Lebedev, Valentin

The Soviet civilian cosmonaut Valentin Vitalyevich Lebedev, b. Apr. 14, 1942, was the flight engineer on *Soyuz 13*. Lebedev and commander Pyotr KLIMUK were launched into orbit on board *Soyuz 13* for an 8-day mission on Dec. 18, 1973. On May 13, 1982, Lebedev returned to space with Anatoly Berezovoy in *Soyuz T5*, remaining aboard *Salyut 7* for 211 days. Lebedev's account of this mission, *Diary of a Cosmonaut* (1983; Eng. trans., 1989), is a fascinating technical and psychological report on life in a space station.   JAMES E. OBERG

Lebesgue, Henri Léon   [luh-beg']

The French mathematician Henri Léon Lebesgue, b. June 28, 1875, d. July 26, 1941, revolutionized the field of integral calculus by his generalization of the Riemann integral. Up to the end of the 19th century, mathematical analysis was limited to continuous functions, based largely on the Riemann method of integration. Building on the work of others, Lebesgue developed (1901) his theory of measure. A year later he extended the usefulness of the definite integral by defining the Lebesgue integral, a method of extending the concept of area below a curve to include many discontinuous functions.
          HOWARD FRISINGER

lecithin   [les'-uh-thin]

Lecithin is a LIPID material that is found in all living cells, especially in nerve and brain tissue and in red blood cells. It is also a significant substance in egg yolk and in some vegetable oils and, for commercial use, is extracted from these substances and dried to form a waxy, colorless solid. Processed lecithin is used as an emulsifying agent in the manufacture of margarine, chocolate, and other foods where fats or oils must be mixed with water. Despite widespread popular claims, no clear evidence exists that lecithin protects against heart attacks or other diseases.

NINA L. MARABLE AND NOELLE KEHRBERG

Leclerc, Jacques Philippe

Jacques Philippe Leclerc, b. Nov. 22, 1902, d. Nov. 28, 1947, became famous as a commander of Free French forces in World War II. His real name was Philippe, vicomte de Hautecloque, but he adopted the alias Leclerc during the war. Trained at Saint Cyr Military Academy, he escaped from Vichy France in 1940 and took command of Free French forces in Africa. In December 1942–January 1943 he led troops overland from Lake Chad to Tripoli to take part in the Tunisian campaign. Leclerc commanded French troops in the 1944 Normandy Invasion and led the first division into Paris. Assigned to Indo-China in 1945, he soon resigned, frustrated by inadequate government support for his operations against the Viet Minh. On tour as inspector-general of the French armies in North Africa, Leclerc died in an air accident in Algeria.

DONALD J. HARVEY

Bibliography: Aron, Robert, *France Reborn: The History of the Liberation* (1964); Maule, Henry, *Out of the Sand* (1966).

Lecompton Constitution   [luh-kahmp'-tuhn]

Drafted in October–November 1857 at Lecompton, capital of the Kansas Territory, the Lecompton Constitution was designed to bring Kansas into the United States as a slave state. The passage of the KANSAS-NEBRASKA ACT (1854), which allowed settlers in those territories to decide whether they should have slavery or not, had polarized Kansan politics. The proslavery elements controlled the territorial legislature at Lecompton, while free-state forces set up an extralegal government at Topeka. Guerrilla warfare erupted between the two sides, turning the territory into "bleeding Kansas."

When the Lecompton Constitution was presented to the electorate in December 1857, the free-state forces boycotted the election. Nonetheless, President James Buchanan urged Congress to admit Kansas to statehood on the basis of the constitution, and the U.S. Senate complied. The House of Representatives, however, under the prodding of Stephen A. DOUGLAS, rejected the constitution, which was resubmitted to Kansan voters in August 1858. This time proslavery forces boycotted the election, and the Lecompton Constitution was defeated. Kansas was admitted to the Union as a free state in 1861.

Leconte de Lisle, Charles Marie   [luh-kohnt' duh leel']

Charles Marie René Leconte de Lisle, b. Oct. 22, 1818, d. July 17, 1894, was the leader and finest poet of the PARNASSIANS. His finest work—*Poèmes antiques* (Poems of Ancient Times, 1852), *Poèmes barbares* (Poems on the Barbarian Races, 1862), and *Poèmes tragiques* (Tragic Poems, 1884)—reveals his talent for depiction of savage nature and his profoundly pessimistic nihilism. He succeeded Victor Hugo in the Académie Française in 1886.

ALFRED ENGSTROM

Bibliography: Brown, Irving, *Leconte de Lisle* (1924); Denommé, Robert, *Leconte de Lisle* (1973); DiOrio, Dorothy, *Leconte de Lisle: A Hundred and Twenty Years of Criticism (1850-1970)* (1972); Putter, Irving, *Leconte de Lisle and His Contemporaries* (1951).

Leda   [lee'-duh]

In Greek mythology, Leda was the wife of Tyndareus, king of Sparta. ZEUS, who came to her as a swan, seduced her and was the father of one or more of her children. There are many variations of the legend. In one version Leda's daughter HELEN OF TROY was hatched from an egg. In another version

Leda bore two eggs, from which came Helen and CLYTEMNESTRA and CASTOR AND POLLUX. Helen and Pollux are commonly thought to have been the children of Zeus, whereas Clytemnestra and Castor were those of Tyndareus.

Ledbetter, Huddie: see LEADBELLY.

Lederberg, Joshua   [led'-ur-burg]

The geneticist Joshua Lederberg, b. May 23, 1925, Montclair, N.J., expanded research in genetics through his studies of heredity in bacteria. With Edward L. TATUM he discovered how bacterial genes are recombined, exchanged, and inherited. For this work both men shared the 1958 Nobel Prize for physiology or medicine with George BEADLE. Lederberg also showed how certain viruses could transfer genetic material from one bacterium to another, a process he called transduction.

Ledoux, Claude Nicolas   [luh-doo', klohd nee-koh-lah']

The French architect and theorist Claude Nicolas Ledoux, b. Mar. 21, 1736, d. Nov. 19, 1806, was one of the three major proponents of what is termed *revolutionary*, or VISIONARY, ARCHITECTURE, along with Étienne Louis BOULLÉE and Jean Jacques Lequeu. His prophetic concepts helped undermine architectural tradition and prepared the way for modern architecture. He was early influenced by Jacques François Blondel, with whom he studied (from 1748), and by the work of Andrea Palladio and Giovanni Battista Piranesi. His early works such as his Hôtel Hallwyl (1764-66; Paris) and Pavilion of Louveciennes (1770-71; Paris) were successful and popular designs in a traditional mode, although they contained the seeds of his more radical later works. A tendency toward austere and blocklike geometric forms in his late visionary work begins with his unexecuted plans for the utopian new town of Chaux, according to which all architectural forms were to imitate nature directly. Among Ledoux's designs that actually were erected, the Palladian saltworks at Arc-et-Senans (1775-79), the Theater of Besançon (1778-94; Paris, only exterior intact), and the Tollhouse of la Villette (1785-89; Paris) stand out. His extravagant and innovative projects and his tendency to monumentalize proved to be his undoing, however, and all but four of his 16 unpopular tollhouses were sacked and burned in 1789. After suffering imprisonment during the French Revolution, he died a ruined and disillusioned man, although not before publishing (1804) his prophetic and influential 2-volume treatise, *L'architecture considérée sous le rapport de l'art, des moeurs et de la législation* (The Relation of Architecture to Art, Custom, and Law).

SUZANNE WILSON

Bibliography: Kaufmann, Emil, *Three Revolutionary Architects: Boullée, Ledoux and Lequeu* (1952); Lemagny, J. C., *Visionary Architects: Boullée, Ledoux, Lequeu* (1968); Rosenau, Helen, *Boullée and Visionary Architecture* (1976) and *Ledoux and Utopian Architecture* (1977).

Lee   (family)

Richard Henry Lee, portrayed here by Charles Willson Peale, was an early American political leader. Both he and his brother, Francis Lightfoot Lee, signed the Declaration of Independence and served in the Continental Congress. As senator from Virginia, Richard Henry Lee pressed for adoption of the Bill of Rights. (National Historical Park Collection, Philadelphia.)

The Lees of Virginia were one of the most distinguished families of 18th- and 19th- century America. They traced their American roots to **Richard Lee,** d. 1664, who came to the colony about 1641, acquired land, and became a wealthy tobacco planter, shipowner, and merchant. In the tradition of the English gentry, he entered politics, holding both executive and legislative offices.

Richard Lee's great-grandsons were prominent in the next century. **Richard Henry Lee,** b. Jan. 20, 1732, d. June 19, 1794, and his brother **Francis Lightfoot Lee,** b. Oct. 14, 1734, d. Jan. 11, 1797, both served in the Continental Congress and signed the Declaration of Independence. As a U.S. senator from Virginia (1789-92), Richard Henry also played a major role in the adoption of the Bill of Rights. Two other brothers, **William Lee,** b. Aug. 31, 1739, d. June 27, 1795, and **Arthur Lee,** b. Dec. 21, 1740, d. Dec. 12, 1792, were diplomatic agents for the Continental Congress. The latter helped negotiate the 1778 pact with France, but he quarreled with his fellow diplomats, Benjamin Franklin and Silas Deane, and brought about Deane's disgrace.

Henry "Light Horse Harry" Lee, b. Jan. 29, 1756, d. Mar. 25, 1818, a cousin of the four brothers named above, was a distinguished cavalry commander in the American Revolution, a close friend of George Washington, a member of the Continental Congress (1785-88), governor of Virginia (1791-94), commander of the forces that suppressed the WHISKEY REBELLION (1794), and a member of the U.S. Congress (1799-1801). His brother **Charles Lee,** b. 1758, d. June 24, 1815, was U.S. attorney general (1795-1801).

The best-known member of the family was Light Horse Harry's son, Robert E. LEE. His sons, **George Washington Custis Lee,** b. Sept. 16, 1832, d. Feb. 18, 1913, and **William Henry Fitzhugh Lee,** b. May 31, 1837, d. Oct. 15, 1891, both served as Confederate generals in the Civil War. The former was later president of Washington and Lee University (1871-97), and the latter was a member of the U.S. Congress (1887-91). Their cousin **Fitzhugh Lee,** b. Nov. 19, 1835, d. Apr. 28, 1905, was a Confederate cavalry general, governor of Virginia (1886-89), U.S. consul general in Havana (1896-98), and a general in the Spanish-American War.   RICHARD M. MCMURRY

Bibliography: Hendrick, B. J., *The Lees of Virginia* (1935); Lee, Edmund Jennings, *Lees of Virginia, 1642-1892* (1895)

Lee, Ann

Ann Lee, b. Manchester, England, Feb. 29, 1736, d. Sept. 8, 1784, founded the SHAKERS in America. An illiterate cotton millworker and then a cook in Manchester, she married and had four children, all of whom died early. About 1758 she joined the Shakers, a faction of the Quakers. Personal experience and direct religious visions led her to embrace celibacy, which she believed could, in conjunction with attention to the spiritual promptings of God, bring those who accepted it to perfection. Her followers became convinced that the Second Coming was revealed in her.

Mother Lee and her small band of followers emigrated to America in 1774 and formed a community at Watervliet, N.Y., 2 years later. There she was heralded as both a prophetess and female messiah. The community that gathered around her welcomed everyone willing to share common property and seek release from bondage to the flesh. After Lee's death the movement based on her teachings and personality flourished for another century.   HENRY WARNER BOWDEN

Bibliography: Campion, Nardi R., *Ann the Word: The Life of Mother Ann Lee, Founder of the Shakers* (1976); Evans, Frank W., *Ann Lee* (1858).

Lee, Charles

Charles Lee, b. 1731, d. Oct. 2, 1782, was a controversial general during the American Revolution. Born in England, he served in the British army in America during the French and Indian Wars of 1754-63. Lee settled in Virginia in 1773, and when the Revolution began, Congress commissioned him a major general, second in rank only to George WASHINGTON.

Lee proved more a hindrance than a help to Washington. He was effective in 1776, planning New York City's defenses, and driving the British out of Charleston, S.C. Ambitious for supreme authority, he disregarded Washington's orders in December 1776 and was captured by the British in New Jersey. While a prisoner he prepared a plan for defeating the Americans, but it was ignored by the British commander William Howe. The Americans were unaware of it, and controversy over Lee's motives continues to this day.

He was exchanged in 1778, but his tactics at the Battle of Monmouth in June 1778 nearly caused an American defeat (see MONMOUTH, BATTLE OF). He was court-martialed and suspended for a year. Lee's criticism of Washington continued, and Congress dismissed him from the service in 1780.
GEORGE ATHAN BILLIAS

Bibliography: Alden, John R., *General Charles Lee, Traitor or Patriot?* (1951); Patterson, Samuel W., *Knight Errant of Liberty* (1958).

Lee, Jesse

The Methodist preacher Jesse Lee, b. Va. Mar. 12, 1758, d. Sept. 12, 1816, is considered one of the most influential figures in early American Methodism. He began preaching in the South and Middle Atlantic States, but from 1789 to 1798 he was a circuit rider in New England, pioneering Methodism in that predominantly Congregationalist area. He became Bishop Francis Asbury's assistant in 1797 and, in 1801, presiding elder of the South District of Virginia. He served as chaplain in both the House of Representatives and the Senate, and his *Short History of Methodism in America* (1810) is the first history of the Methodists in the United States.

Bibliography: Lee, Jesse, and Thrift, Minton, *Memoir of the Rev. Jesse Lee, with Extracts from His Journals* (1823; repr. 1969); Meredith, William, *Jesse Lee: A Methodist Apostle* (1909).

Lee, John Doyle

John Doyle Lee, b. Sept. 12, 1812, d. Mar. 23, 1877, was an American executed for participating in the MOUNTAIN MEADOWS MASSACRE of 1857. A native of Illinois, he was converted to Mormonism in 1838 and devoted his life thereafter to church and community service. In 1850, Brigham YOUNG sent Lee to establish Mormon settlements in southern Utah. Among other functions, he served as an Indian agent, and his work with the Indians led to his involvement with a band of Paiute in the 1857 massacre of California-bound immigrants in a wagon train at Mountain Meadows. Lee continued his colonization work until 1875, when he was tried for the crime. After two trials he was executed at the site of the massacre.   RONALD G. WATT

Bibliography: Brooks, Juanita, *John Doyle Lee, Zealot-Pioneer Builder-Scapegoat* (1962).

Lee, Robert E.

Robert E. Lee, the brilliant commander of Confederate forces during the U.S. CIVIL WAR, was one of the most famous and respected soldiers in American history. After the defeat of the South, he served as a symbol of courage in defeat, embodying the finest elements of the Southern heritage.

Early Life and Career. Robert Edward Lee was born on Jan. 19, 1807, at his family's home, "Stratford," in Westmoreland County, Va. His father, Henry "Light Horse Harry" Lee (see LEE family), had been a cavalry officer during the American Revolution and a close friend of George Washington. Henry Lee, a compulsive gambler, lost much of the family wealth in land speculation prior to his death in 1818. Robert grew up in genteel poverty in Alexandria, Va. Appointed to West Point in 1825, he graduated (1829) after compiling an enviable academic record. In 1831, Lee married Mary Ann Randolph Custis, great-granddaughter of Martha Washington by her first marriage. During the next 30 years he often lived at Arlington, the Custis mansion near Washington, D.C.

Commissioned in the Corps of Engineers in 1829, Lee held a variety of assignments, helping with construction work at several military posts and with river and harbor improvements

Robert E. Lee, outstanding Confederate general during the Civil War, refused an offer in 1861 to command Federal forces against his native South, becoming instead the commander of Confederate forces in Virginia and later of all Confederate forces. Called by Winston Churchill "one of the greatest captains known to the annals of war," Lee was renowned for his bold strategies and gracious character.

at St. Louis. Promotion was slow, however, and it was not until 1838 that he was made a captain. In the Mexican War, Lee was an engineering officer with Winfield SCOTT's force that fought its way to Mexico City. Lee's outstanding work won for him praise and a brilliant reputation. From 1852 to 1855 he was superintendent at West Point. In 1855 he was made lieutenant colonel of the Second Cavalry, and in 1859 he commanded the force that suppressed the John BROWN raid on Harpers Ferry.

Role in Civil War. A moderate, Lee was dismayed by the extremists on both sides of the North-South controversy in the 1850s. Nevertheless, believing that he owed his first loyalty to his own state, he declined an offer to command the Federal army, resigned his commission in the U.S. Army, and offered his services to Virginia when it seceded in April 1861. Confederate president Jefferson DAVIS appointed Lee a general in the Southern army. After an unsuccessful effort to repel an invasion of western Virginia, Lee was sent to prepare Atlantic coastal defenses. In March 1862 he returned to Virginia as an advisor to Davis. After Joseph E. JOHNSTON was wounded in May 1862 during the PENINSULAR CAMPAIGN, Lee became commander of the main Confederate army in Virginia—a force that he soon named the Army of Northern Virginia.

When Lee took command, the outlook appeared dim for the Confederacy. Federal troops were slowly gaining control of the Mississippi Valley, and a large enemy army was within sight of Richmond. In late June, Lee struck at the Unionists near Richmond and in the Seven Days' Battles drove them away from the capital. In August he defeated a Northern army in the second Battle of BULL RUN and chased it into the defenses of Washington, D.C. Lee followed up this victory by invading Maryland. During the Battle of ANTIETAM (Sept. 17, 1862) he fought a drawn battle with the Federals. Lee then withdrew to Virginia where he inflicted a costly defeat on his opponents at FREDERICKSBURG in December.

At CHANCELLORSVILLE (May 1863), Lee won his greatest victory and suffered his greatest loss. Boldly dividing his army into three parts, Lee assailed a larger Federal force. The Unionists were thoroughly befuddled and driven back with heavy casualties. Southern losses were also high, and among them was Lee's greatest general, Stonewall JACKSON, who died after the battle. Lee never again achieved the degree of success he had won with the cooperation of Jackson.

In the summer of 1863, Lee launched another invasion of the North. In early July he attacked a Federal army at Gettysburg, Pa., and was defeated in the greatest battle of the war (see GETTYSBURG, BATTLE OF). The Confederates fell back into

Virginia, and there, in 1864, Lee led them into a series of bloody battles against the Northern army, now commanded by Ulysses S. GRANT. Hampered by the loss of many good officers, such as James LONGSTREET (wounded May 6) and J.E.B. STUART (mortally wounded May 11), Lee maneuvered brilliantly against Grant and inflicted heavy losses on the Federals. Unable to seize the offensive, he was pushed back to Richmond and Petersburg and forced to defend those cities against a semisiege. Grant finally broke through the Southern lines in April 1865. Lee tried to escape with his army to join other Confederate forces in North Carolina, but Grant trapped him at APPOMATTOX COURT HOUSE and forced him to surrender on April 9. By then Lee had become the symbol of the Confederacy (and he had finally been appointed general in chief of all Confederate armies in February); when he surrendered, other Southern armies soon ceased fighting.

Postwar Life and Reputation. After the war, Lee became president of Washington College (now Washington and Lee University) in Lexington, Va. Accepting the results of the war, he devoted himself to education and to helping rebuild the South. Lee died on Oct. 12, 1870.

Lee had many weaknesses as a general. He was too considerate of others, and his politeness sometimes obscured the necessity for quick, total obedience to his orders. He entrusted too much discretion to subordinates who, except for Jackson, were not capable of handling it. He may not have paid sufficient attention to logistics, and he has been accused of devoting too much attention to Virginia to the neglect of other areas. Despite these weaknesses, many historians maintain that Lee was the most capable commander of the Civil War. Robert E. Lee was a fitting symbol of the South as well as an American hero.

RICHARD M. McMURRY

Bibliography: Anderson, N. and D., *The Generals: Ulysses S. Grant and Robert E. Lee* (1988); Connelly, Thomas L., *The Marble Man* (1977); Davis, Burke, *Gray Fox* (1956); Dowdey, Clifford, *Lee* (1965) and, as ed., *The Wartime Papers of R. E. Lee* (1961); Flood, C. B., *Lee: The Last Years* (1981); Freeman, Douglas S., *R. E. Lee: A Biography*, 4 vols. (1934–35), and *Lee's Lieutenants*, 3 vols. (1942–44); Fuller, J. F., *Grant and Lee* (1982); Miers, Earle S., *Robert E. Lee* (1956); Sanborn, Margaret, *Robert E. Lee*, 2 vols. (1966–67).

Lee, Tsung Dao

The Chinese-American theoretical physicist Tsung Dao Lee, b. Shanghai, Nov. 25, 1926, shared the 1957 Nobel Prize for physics with Chen Ning YANG for the postulation of the nonconservation of parity in weak interactions (see PARITY, physics). Lee went to the United States in 1946 and studied at the University of Chicago under Enrico Fermi and Edward Teller, earning his Ph.D. in 1950.

As a fellow at the Institute for Advanced Study at Princeton in 1951 he began his collaboration with Yang on the physics of the elementary particles known as K-mesons. This work led them to postulate that, in violation of parity, the same K-meson particle behaved in slightly different ways, depending on whether it was left-handed or right-handed. This conjecture was soon confirmed experimentally. In 1953, Lee joined the faculty at Columbia University.

JOHN GUINN MAY

Lee Kuan Yew

Lee Kuan Yew, b. Sept. 16, 1923, long-time prime minister of Singapore, was educated at Cambridge University, England. He helped found Singapore's People's Action party in 1954 and in 1955 was elected to the legislative council. He became prime minister in 1959, led (1963) Singapore into the Federation of Malaysia, and remained prime minister of independent Singapore after it seceded (1965) from the federation.

Lee, a staunch supporter of free-enterprise capitalism, is considered the architect of Singapore's remarkable postindependence economic growth. The rapid and orderly transformation of Singapore into a modern industrial state through detailed government social and economic engineering generated much popular support for Lee, particularly since prosperity was widely shared. His party's percentage of the popular vote in the 1985 and 1988 legislative elections declined, however, due to an economic slowdown and demands for political reform by an increasingly well-educated electorate. Lee retired as prime minister in November 1990 (replaced by Goh Chok Tong) but remained in the cabinet and still headed the party.

Bibliography: Minchin, J., *No Man Is an Island* (1987).

Lee Teng-hui

Lee Teng-hui, b. Jan. 15, 1923, the first native-born president of Taiwan, assumed his post after the death of President CHIANG CHING-KUO on Jan. 15, 1988. Lee was educated in Japan, Taiwan, and the United States, receiving a Ph.D. in agricultural economics from Cornell University in 1968. He entered government in 1972, serving as mayor of Taipei (1978–81), governor of Taiwan province (1981–84), and vice-president (1984–88) before succeeding to the balance of Chiang's term. Later named chairman of the ruling KUOMINTANG and elected president in his own right in March 1990, Lee continued the reforms begun with the lifting of martial law in 1987.

leech

This medicinal leech, Hirudo medicinalis, lives in ponds and swamps of Europe and Asia and grows to 10 cm (4 in) long.

Leech is the common name for more than 300 species of aquatic or terrestrial annelid worms, phylum Annelida, class Hirudinea, that prey on small invertebrates in fresh water or suck blood from vertebrate animals. Most leeches live in ponds and streams, where they feed upon worms, snails, and insect larvae or wait for the chance to attach themselves to a fish, turtle, or a wading bird or mammal to suck its blood. Some leeches are marine and get blood meals from fish or sea turtles. A few leeches inhabit tropical rain forests.

Leeches have flattened bodies and usually lack gills, breathing instead through their skin. They are generally black, brown, olive, or red in color and may be spotted or striped. Most leeches are from 2 to 5 cm (0.8 to 2 in) long, but they range from 1 cm (0.4 in) to 30 cm (12 in). Every leech has a muscular sucker at the rear end of the body; many have a second sucker around the mouth. These organs are used to hold the leech to a support or to a host while it is drawing blood.

Two types of feeding structures are found in leeches. Some leeches have an extendable, tubelike proboscis that is made rigid and forced into the tissues of the victim. Others lack the proboscis, having instead three knifelike jaws that slice through the host's skin. The wound area is anesthetized by an as yet unknown substance, so the victim feels no pain. Predatory worms feed rather frequently. Bloodsuckers feed only rarely but may consume many times their weight; water is removed from the ingested blood, and the remaining blood cells are digested slowly. The saliva of these leeches also contains an ANTICOAGULANT called hirudin, which prevents blood clots and can dissolve them as well. Members of the genus *Hirudo*, called medicinal leeches, were once widely used for bloodletting and the relief of blood congestion; they are still employed by surgeons to maintain circulation in small blood vessels during delicate operations. Researchers are investigating the usefulness of proteins in leech saliva in treating cardiovascular disease.   LORUS J. AND MARGERY MILNE

Bibliography: Mill, P. J., ed., *Physiology of Annelids* (1978); Sawyer, R. T., *Leech Biology and Behaviour*, 3 vols. (1986).

Leeds

Leeds is a city of north central England located in West Yorkshire (see YORKSHIRE). Situated on the navigable River Aire with a canal connecting it with Liverpool, Leeds is a major inland port. The population is 709,000 (1987 est.). One of Britain's leading garment manufacturing centers, Leeds also produces light machinery, electrical equipment, ceramics, leather, and paper. Kirkstall Abbey (1151) and Temple Newsam mansion (17th century) are landmarks. The city operates a museum, an art gallery, and a library and has varied sports facilities. It is the seat of the University of Leeds (1904).

The city was probably settled before Roman times, as the River Aire provides a strategic route through the Pennine mountain chain. It was a major woolen center from the 14th century until the Industrial Revolution. During the late 1700s it was renowned for pottery and linen manufacturing.

Leeds, Thomas Osborne, 1st Duke of: see

DANBY, THOMAS OSBORNE, 1ST EARL OF.

leek

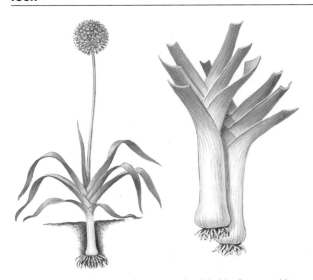

The leek, A. ampeloprasum, bears a single globelike flower and linear leaves. Its blanched leaf base (right) is eaten as a vegetable.

The vegetable leek, *Allium ampeloprasum*, family Amaryllidaceae, Porrum group, is a mild-flavored relative of the ONION. The plant produces a sheath of leaves about 4 cm (1.6 in) thick, but unlike the onion, it does not form a distinctive bulb. Plants are blanched by gradually building up the soil around their bases, a process that keeps the edible portion white and tender. The culture of leek is similar to that for onion. Leek seeds are sown directly in the soil, or seedlings may be transplanted. Plants are spaced about 5 cm (2 in) apart in the row and mature in about 150 days.   O. A. LORENZ

Leeuwenhoek, Antoni van   [lay'-vuhn-hook, ahn'-tohn-ee vahn]

Antoni van Leeuwenhoek, a self-taught Dutch scientist, built over 400 microscopes, whose focuses are amazingly accurate and clear. With them, he observed and carefully described diverse organic substances, including spermatozoa, blood, and bacteria.

Antoni van Leeuwenhoek, b. Oct. 24, 1632, d. Aug. 26, 1723, was a Dutch biologist and microscopist. He became interested in science when, as a Dutch businessman, he began grinding lenses and building simple microscopes as a hobby. Each microscope consisted of a flat brass or copper plate in which a small, single glass lens was mounted. The lens was held up to the eye, and the object to be studied was placed on the head of a movable pin just on the other side of the lens. Leeuwenhoek made over 400 microscopes, many of which still exist. The most powerful of these instruments can magnify objects about 275 times. Although future microscopes were to contain more than one lens (compound microscopes), Leeuwenhoek's single lens was ground to such perfection that he was able to make great advances and to draw attention to his field.

Leeuwenhoek was the first person to observe single-celled animals (protozoa) with a microscope. He described them in a letter to the Royal Society, which published his detailed pictures in 1683. Leeuwenhoek was also the first person, using a microscope, to observe clearly and to describe red blood cells in humans and other animals, as well as sperm cells. In addition, he studied the structure of plants, the compound eyes of insects, and the life cycles of fleas, aphids, and ants.

Reviewed by LOUIS LEVINE

Bibliography: De Kruif, Paul, *Microbe Hunters* (1926; repr. 1966); Dobell, Clifford, *Antony van Leeuwenhoek and His "Little Animals,"* 2d ed. (1958); Ford, B. J., *Single Lens* (1985); Schierbeek, A., *Measuring the Invisible World* (1959).

Leeward Islands   [lee'-wurd]

The Leeward Islands, extending from Puerto Rico to Guadeloupe, are the northern group of the Lesser Antilles (see ANTILLES, GREATER AND LESSER) in the Caribbean Sea. (The WINDWARD ISLANDS lie to the south.) From 1871 to 1956 the name Leeward Islands was used for the collectively administered British colonies in the area. The VIRGIN ISLANDS are sometimes included but sometimes not.

Lefebvre, Marcel   [luh-fev', mar-sel']

Marcel Lefebvre, b. Nov. 29, 1905, is a French churchman who heads a Roman Catholic traditionalist movement. He was excommunicated in 1988 and declared in schism for consecrating four bishops against the Vatican's wishes. Ordained a priest in 1929 and consecrated as a bishop in 1947, Lefebvre was archbishop of Dakar, Senegal, from 1955 to 1962 and then briefly bishop of Toul, France. He condemned the liberalizing changes introduced by the Second VATICAN COUNCIL (1962–65) and established (1965) his own seminary in Ecône, Switzerland. After Lefebvre ordained a number of traditionalist priests in 1976, Pope Paul VI suspended him from priestly duties. At the time of his excommunication Lefebvre had an estimated 100,000 followers.   J. DEAN O'DONNELL, JR.

Lefèvre d'Étaples, Jacques   [luh-fev' day-tahp'-luh, zhahk]

Jacques Lefèvre d'Étaples, c.1455–1536, was one of the most famous scholars and Christian humanists of the French Renaissance. After studying in Paris and entering the priesthood, he traveled in Italy, where he met many of the prominent Italian humanists. He returned to Paris, where, as librarian of the abbey of Saint-Germain-des-Prés, he taught and wrote philosophy and began editing classical texts and producing his own commentaries on the Bible. He also translated portions of the Bible into French.

In 1520, Lefèvre was named vicar-general of Meaux, where he gathered about him an impressive group of younger scholars who joined him in working for reform in response to church abuses. He served briefly as the royal librarian and tutor of King Francis I's children but spent his final years in the court of Margaret of Navarre in southern France. Like Erasmus, he refused to break openly with the Catholic church, but many of his followers became Protestants.   T. TACKETT

Bibliography: Hughes, P. E., *Lefevre* (1984); Steinmetz, David C., *Reformers in the Wings* (1971).

Lefschetz, Solomon   [lef'-shets, sahl'-uh-muhn]

Solomon Lefschetz, b. Moscow, Sept. 3, 1884, d. Oct. 5, 1972, was an American mathematician who was the main architect of the algebraic aspects of TOPOLOGY. He established certain fixed-point theorems, which deal with points that do not move under a given transformation (fixed points), and applied these theorems to developing important formulas for points that remain fixed when a manifold is subjected to a continuous mapping onto itself.   HOWARD FRISINGER

left-handedness: see HANDEDNESS.

legal aid

Legal aid (sometimes called legal services) is the mechanism for providing legal counsel for poor people. The lawyers may be paid by the government or by charitable organizations or they may be appointed to serve without compensation.

Legal aid may be available in either civil or criminal cases. From its start in 1876 until the mid-1960s, civil legal aid was financed almost exclusively by private donations to local legal-aid societies. These societies generally hired a few full-time or part-time lawyers to help as many poor people as they could with the societies' very limited resources.

Legal aid for criminal defendants has evolved along different lines, with government assuming more responsibility. Some states and localities employ public defenders for people who cannot afford legal fees. Other jurisdictions rely on an assigned counsel system under which the judge appoints private lawyers to represent poor persons. In 1963 the U.S. Supreme Court provided new impetus when it declared that every poor defendant charged with a felony is entitled to free counsel as a matter of constitutional right (see GIDEON V. WAINWRIGHT). This decision compelled every state and locality to make explicit provision for criminal legal aid. As a result, the number of public defenders multiplied several times as did government budgets for legal aid in criminal cases. In 1972 this right was extended to those charged with many kinds of misdemeanors (see ARGERSINGER V. HAMLIN).

Government neglect of civil representation ended in 1965 when the federal government started the Office of Economic Opportunity (OEO) Legal Services Program as part of the Johnson administration's "War on Poverty." During its first 18 months the OEO program increased eightfold the amount of civil legal aid available to poor people. In 1974, Congress created an independent public entity, the Legal Services Corporation, which assumed control of the OEO legal-aid program. Soon the corporation was financing several thousand full-time lawyers employed by locally controlled legal-services agencies. (In a few places, "judicare" clients are served by private lawyers who then bill the government.) Congress resisted President Reagan's call for its abolition to cut costs, but the corporation's budget diminished during his two terms.

Although no constitutionally protected right to free counsel for poor people in civil cases exists as yet, there appears to be a slight tendency in that direction. Some state supreme courts recently have found a constitutional right to counsel for certain kinds of civil cases, such as paternity issues and child-dependency hearings.

Three general types of legal aid in civil cases exist in other countries. In some countries, such as Britain and Germany, the government compensates, in varying degrees, private lawyers chosen by the court or defendant. In other countries—Italy, for example—courts appoint lawyers to serve without compensation. Still others—Sweden and Canada, for example—allow clients to choose between salaried lawyers or private attorneys.   EARL JOHNSON, JR.

Bibliography: Cappelletti, Mauro, et al., *Toward Equal Justice: A Comparative Study of Legal Aid in Modern Societies* (1975); Johnson, Earl, *Justice and Reform: The Formative Years of the American Legal Services Program*, rev. ed. (1978); Katz, Jack, *Poor People's Lawyers in Transition* (1984); Kessler, Mark, *Legal Services for the Poor* (1987).

legal procedure

Legal procedure consists of the methods used in enforcing legal rights and remedies. These include rules for initiating a lawsuit, conducting a trial, and appealing to a higher court and also the processes whereby one party secures redress or compensation from another.

American legal procedure is based on English COMMON LAW and equity (see EQUITY, law). All common-law countries, including the United States, Canada, and England, have modernized the traditional English procedure within the last century. In the United States, David Dudley FIELD's work (1848) on the New York code of civil procedure was influential in the development of modern U.S. legal procedure.

Preparation of a Legal Action. A lawsuit is initiated by the attorney for the plaintiff (the party bringing suit), who prepares a summons and a complaint. The summons is a notice to the defendant (the party against whom suit is brought) that he or she is being sued and specifies the time and place of the hearing and the nature of the demand being made. The complaint is a brief statement of the essentials of the plaintiff's case that is made under oath before an official who is empowered to charge people with offenses.

The summons and complaint are delivered to the defendant in person by a marshal or other qualified person. This action is called servicing a process, and from this point the court has authority, termed jurisdiction, over the defendant. If the defendant declines to appear in court for trial, a decision may nonetheless be entered against him or her. This procedure is termed a judgment by default.

Normally the defendant will forward the complaint to an attorney, and the attorney will prepare a document called the answer, which will contradict one or more assertions contained in the complaint. The answer will then be served on the plaintiff. If the defendant brings up some new matter in the answer, the plaintiff may respond with a reply. Various rules of pretrial discovery enable both plaintiffs and defendants to acquire more information about the case.

Exchange of the complaint, answer, and, if used, the reply constitute the pleading. The purposes of the pleading are to inform each party of the issues in the approaching trial and narrow the possible issues to those actually in contention.

The Trial. Following the pleading, the case will be tried. Either party may insist on a trial by JURY except for cases in equity, but often neither party desires a jury trial because trials in which the judge fills the role of the jury tend to proceed more quickly. If neither party insists on a jury trial, the case will be heard solely by the judge.

The trial begins with opening statements by the plaintiff's attorney and the defendant's attorney; they both present a broad outline of what they intend to prove. Opening statements may be and often are waived. Following the opening statements, the plaintiff's attorney presents EVIDENCE, generally elicited through direct examination or questioning of witnesses under oath. After a witness is examined, the defendant's attorney may cross-examine to test the witness's accuracy and veracity. After all the plaintiff's witnesses have been examined and cross-examined, the defendant is given an opportunity to present witnesses. Each witness also may be cross-examined by the plaintiff's attorney.

After the evidence has been presented, the attorneys make their closing arguments in which they present their clients' positions as best they can based on their view of the evidence. In a trial by jury, the judge then instructs the jury in the rules of law applicable to the case. The jury's task is to decide the facts, to apply the law as contained in the instructions to the facts, and to reach a verdict. In many states a jury must reach a unanimous verdict. The losing party may request a new trial. The judge may grant such a request if, for example, newly discovered evidence is presented.

Appeals. The usual basis for APPEAL is that an error of law was committed during the original trial. The facts as established by the jury may not be challenged unless the court of appeals determines that no reasonable jury could have decided as it did.

The party bringing an appeal is called the appellant, and the opposite party—the winner in the lower court—is the appellee or respondent. Appellate courts are presided over by a panel of judges, usually at least three and sometimes as many as nine, depending on the particular court . No jury sits in an appeal because the findings of fact were determined by the trial court.

Both parties to an appeal submit written briefs containing legal authorities and arguments. The actual hearing consists of an exchange of oral presentations by the two attorneys. After the court has reached a decision, one of the judges prepares an opinion that states the facts of the case, the legal issues, how the case was decided, and why.

Judgment and Execution. Most civil (in other words, noncriminal) cases are brought to secure money damages. If a jury awards damages to the plaintiff, the court enters a judgment entitling the plaintiff to collect a sum of money from the defendant. Judgments are not, however, self-enforcing. If the defendant refuses to pay, the plaintiff must locate money or property belonging to the defendant and submit certain papers to the sheriff, who can seize the money or property. This action is called an execution on the judgment. If property is seized, the sheriff can have it sold at auction to satisfy the plaintiff's judgment.   JON P. McCONNELL

Bibliography: Grilliot, H. G., *Introduction to Law and the Legal System,* 3d ed. (1983); Mayers, Lewis, *The Machinery of Justice* (1974); Mermin, Samuel, *Law and the Legal System,* 2d ed. (1982); Simon, P. N., *The Anatomy of a Lawsuit* (1984); Tullock, Gordon, *Trials on Trial: The Pure Theory of Legal Procedure* (1980).

See also: CRIMINAL JUSTICE.

legend

A legend originally was simply something to be read. The term may still be used in this restricted sense to refer to mottoes, titles, or inscriptions on coins and medals. The more general current meaning is illustrated by Washington Irving's title, ''The Legend of Sleepy Hollow'' (1820), in which the word denotes a tale of past exploits. Whether the legend is fact or fiction is unimportant, provided it is set in the past and centers on remarkable incidents.

Legendries, or lists of legends, however, were popularly accepted by their medieval readers as true histories. Many legendries were lists of the lives of saints that detailed the wonders and miracles associated with each saint. The best known is the *Legenda Aurea,* or *Golden Legend,* one of the medieval world's most loved books, written by Jacobus de Voragine, archbishop of Genoa, in the 13th century and translated into English by William Caxton in 1483. Although the central figures of legends are not necessarily saints, all share the ability to be single-minded, purposeful, and capable of extraordinary feats of valor or endurance. Geoffrey Chaucer's *Legend of Good Women* (1380–86), for instance, relates the stories of notable women of history whose lives or deaths witnessed to their passionate fidelity to love.

Many legendary figures are national heroes, usually historical figures like King Arthur or Charlemagne who attach to themselves cycles of legends, sometimes oral, sometimes written. These legends mix fact and fantasy and tell with relish not only the bare deeds of the heroes' lives but also the marvelous exploits credited to them, each bearing the hallmark of their dedication to a particular credo, or belief. Thus Arthur and the Knights of the Round Table are renowned for their legendary courtesy and valor, Robin Hood and his men for their loyalty and defense of the downtrodden. Similarly, the United States has its heroes and folk figures in Paul BUNYAN, Long Barney Beal, ''Oregon'' Smith, and Johnny Appleseed (see CHAPMAN, JOHN).   MARJORIE COLLINS

Bibliography: Cavendish, R., ed., *Legends of the World* (1982); Dorson, R. M., *America in Legend* (1974); Leach, M., and Fried, J., eds., *Funk & Wagnalls Standard Dictionary of Folklore, Mythology and Legends* (1984).

See also: ARTHUR AND ARTHURIAN LEGEND; CHANSON DE ROLAND; CHANSONS DE GESTE; FAUST; FLYING DUTCHMAN, THE; MYTHOLOGY; SAGA; WANDERING JEW.

Leger, Alexis Saint-Leger: see PERSE, SAINT-JOHN.

Léger, Fernand [lay-zhay', fer-nahn']

The Great Parade (1954) by the French cubist painter Fernand Léger marks an important change in his late work. In this painting Léger made line and color independent of one another, using color as a technique of composition. (Guggenheim Museum, New York City.)

The French painter Fernand Léger, b. Argentan, Feb. 4, 1881, d. Aug. 17, 1955, was a major figure in the development of CUBISM and a prime expositor of modern urban and technological culture. After moving (1900) to Paris he worked as an architectural draftsman and a photographic retoucher and also studied informally at the École des Beaux-Arts and the Académie Julien. By 1911, Léger had become a key member of the evolving cubist movement. His personal style of cubism is characterized by tubular, fractured forms and bright colors highlighted by juxtaposition with cool whites—a decorative scheme that conveys a sense of form in relief. Major works of this cubist period include La Noce (1911–12; Musée National d'Art Moderne, Paris), Woman in Blue (1912; Oeffentliche Kunstsammlung, Basel), and Contrasts of Forms (1913; Philadelphia Museum of Art).

Following World War I, Léger concentrated more and more on urban and machine imagery, which led logically to his association (1919–c.1925) with the purism of Le Corbusier and Amédée Ozenfant. In paintings such as The Mechanic (1920; National Gallery of Canada, Ottawa) and Three Women (1921; Museum of Modern Art, New York City), he favored sharply delineated, flat shapes, unmodeled color areas, and combinations of human and machine forms. After 1930, Léger's style favored precisely delineated and monumental forms modeled in planes and set in shallow space, and he concentrated on depicting scenes of proletarian life, such as his Great Parade (1954; Guggenheim Museum, New York City). MAGDALENA DABROWSKI

Bibliography: Buck, R. T., et al., Fernand Léger (1982); De Francia, Peter, Fernand Léger (1983); Green, Christopher, Léger and the Avant-Garde (1976); Rosenblum, Robert, Cubism and Twentieth Century Art, rev. ed. (1976).

Léger, Jules

Jules Léger, b. Saint-Anicet, Quebec, Apr. 4, 1913, d. Nov. 22, 1980, was governor-general of Canada from 1974 to 1979. After receiving his doctorate in literature from the University of Paris in 1938, Léger joined the Canadian foreign service in 1940. He served in a variety of posts abroad, including ambassador to Mexico, NATO, Italy, France, and Belgium.

Léger, Paul Émile

A Canadian cardinal and former archbishop of Montreal, Paul Émile Léger, b. Valleyfield, Quebec, Apr. 26, 1904, was educated for the priesthood in Montreal, where he was ordained a priest in 1929. He continued his studies in France, where he joined the Sulpicians. From 1933 to 1939 he headed a Sulpician seminary in Japan that he had founded. He returned to Canada in 1940 and served as vicar-general of the Valleyfield diocese until 1947, when he was called to Rome as rector of the Canadian Pontifical College. Léger became archbishop of Montreal in 1950 and was named a cardinal in 1953. In 1967 he resigned as archbishop in order to do missionary work among lepers in Africa. Upon his return to Canada he worked as a parish priest in Montreal (1974–75).

Bibliography: Bell, Ken, Man and His Mission: Cardinal Léger in Africa, trans. by Jane Springer (1977).

Leghorn: see LIVORNO.

legion, Roman

The legion was the basic combat unit of the ancient Roman army. Its early history is obscure, but by about 300 BC it had received its traditional form: a division of 3,000 to 6,000 men, consisting primarily of heavy infantry (hoplites), supported by light infantry (velites), and sometimes by cavalry. The hoplites were drawn up in three lines. The hastati (youngest men) were in the first, the principes (seasoned troops) in the second, and the triarii (oldest men) behind them, reinforced by velites. Each line was divided into ten maniples, consisting of two centuries (60 to 80 men per century) each. The cohort, which later superceded the maniple as the main tactical unit, was composed of one maniple from each line, plus the support forces. Under Julius Caesar, the commander of each legion was made directly responsible to the Senate. In 15 BC, 28 legions existed; under Septimius Severus, 200 years later, there were 33. Each carrying the standard of an eagle, the rigorously trained legions were the military key to the Roman conquest of the ancient world. The maniple formation (each was a tiny phalanx) gave them the tactical advantage of flexibility in fighting massed armies, such as those of the Greeks and Persians. They were vulnerable to more loosely organized opponents, however; in AD 9 the forces of the German chief ARMINIUS destroyed three legions in the Teutoburg Forest. From the 1st century AD on, the Romans relied increasingly on auxiliary forces of archers, light infantry, and cavalry (many of them recruited from the German tribes) to fend off the attacks of mounted barbarian armies.

Bibliography: Grant, Michael, The Army of the Caesars (1974); Webster, Graham, The Roman Imperial Army of the First and Second Centuries AD (1964).

Legion of Decency, National: see CENSORSHIP.

Legion of Honor: see MEDALS AND DECORATIONS.

Legionnaires' disease

Legionnaires' disease is a noninfectious respiratory illness that occurs as individual cases and sometimes in sporadic outbreaks. This disease, and a milder form known as Pontiac fever, are caused by several species of Legionella bacteria. The first recognized outbreak—caused by L. pneumophila—occurred at an American Legion convention in Philadelphia in 1976, during which 221 people became ill, of whom 34 died. The bacteria contaminate such damp areas as large air-conditioning towers and hot-water systems and are spread on water droplets. People inhale the bacteria, which infect the lungs and are parasitic to certain white blood cells called monocytes; pneumonia, mental confusion, and kidney and liver damage result, with about a 15 percent mortality rate. Pontiac fever is not fatal and does not result in pneumonia. Treatment for both diseases includes such antibiotics as erythromycin.

legislature

A legislature is a governmental decision-making body engaged in making law. Most legislators are popularly elected, although legislative bodies may contain some members who are appointed or who are entitled to membership because of their status in the society. Legislatures vary greatly in the extent of their impact upon law. Some, like the CONGRESS OF THE UNITED STATES, are full-fledged lawmaking bodies. Others, like the British House of Commons, largely follow the lead of the government of the day. Legislatures in authoritarian regimes have only the most formal and perfunctory role in lawmaking.

Representative assemblies like the senates of Greece and Rome have histories going back to ancient times, but the taproot of modern legislatures extends to the Middle Ages. The "mother of parliaments"—the British PARLIAMENT—began to take modern shape in the 13th century. Today, legislative bodies exist in some 140 countries, from the Albanian People's Assembly to the Parliament of Zimbabwe.

A notable structural feature of legislatures is the number of houses that compose them. Almost two-thirds of the world's national legislatures are unicameral—one house. (One U.S. state legislature has a single house, that of Nebraska.) Other national legislatures are bicameral, including the U.S. Congress (made up of the HOUSE OF REPRESENTATIVES and the SENATE). Bicameral legislatures tend to develop in federal systems, where one chamber represents the people directly and the other represents the states or provinces.

The constitutional role of the world's legislatures varies greatly. In congressional systems like that of the United States, where the doctrine of separation of powers means that members of Congress are elected separately from the chief executive, the legislature is quite independent. In parliamentary systems the political executive is a member of the legislature and the leader of the dominant party.

In general, legislators are elected in two types of election systems. The first, the single-member district, plurality vote system, is common to English-speaking countries and others following their example. In this system a country is divided into a number of constituencies equal to the number of representatives to be elected; in each district, the election is won by a plurality of the vote. The second type of system is PROPORTIONAL REPRESENTATION. Here, seats in the legislature are allocated to political parties in proportion to their shares of votes in the election. Some legislative bodies include appointed, rather than elected, members. For instance, Canadian senators are appointed by the governor general on the recommendation of the prime minister.

Legislatures perform three basic functions. First, legislatures endeavor to manage conflicts among diverse social, economic, or political groups. Often, managing conflict involves the passage of laws. Second, legislatures are involved in recruiting leaders. This function is limited in the United States, but the Senate does have the constitutional role of confirming presidential appointments. In parliamentary countries like Britain, the prime minister and cabinet members are responsible to the legislature and must maintain the support of a majority of its members to stay in power.

Third, legislatures provide important links between the government and the citizenry. Most countries are divided into districts from which legislators are elected. Once elected, these members serve as representatives from their geographical areas to the central government.   SAMUEL C. PATTERSON

Bibliography: Loewenberg, Gerhard, and Patterson, Samuel C., *Comparing Legislatures* (1979); Mezey, Michael L., *Comparative Legislatures* (1979); Wheare, K. C., *Legislatures* (1963).

See also: APPORTIONMENT; GOVERNMENT; REPRESENTATION.

legless lizard

Legless lizards are two species of snakelike lizards, *Anniella pulchra* and *A. geronimensis,* in the family Anniellidae, inhabiting sandy areas in western California and Baja California. They are burrowing, blunt-tailed lizards reaching about 25 cm (10 in) in length. They feed on insects and are ovoviviparous, bearing one to four living young. Legless lizards possess movable eyelids but lack external ear openings, characteristics that distinguish them from the limbless worm lizards (amphisbaenians), which lack movable eyelids, and the limbless glass snakes, *Ophisaurus,* and some European slowworms, *Anguis,* which have external ear openings.   JONATHAN CAMPBELL

Leguía y Salcedo, Augusto Bernardino   [lay-gee'-ah ee sahl-say'-doh, ow-goos'-toh bairn-ar-dee'-noh]

Augusto Bernardino Leguía y Salcedo, b. Feb. 19, 1863, d. Feb. 7, 1932, was twice president of Peru (1908–12, 1919–30). A prominent businessman, he served as minister of finance from 1903 to 1908. During his first term as president, Leguía broke diplomatic relations with Chile in the prolonged TACNA-ARICA DISPUTE. In 1919, after a period in England, he returned to Peru and overthrew President José Pardo. Leguía governed dictatorially, twice extending his term, but he also settled (1929) the Tacna-Arica Dispute, expanded Lima, developed the road and irrigation network, and enacted social and labor legislation. He was overthrown by a coup in 1930.

legume   [leg'-yoom]

Legumes comprise a large family, Leguminosae, of flowering plants, ranging from trees (acacia, carob, tamarind) to vegetables (beans, lentils, peas) and forage crops (clover, alfalfa). All legumes are distinguished by their fruit, which grows in the form of a pod that splits along its seams when mature and opens to reveal the seeds. Many legumes have nodule-bearing roots that contain nitrogen-fixing bacteria, which transform nitrogen in the air into a form that can be utilized by plants. Nitrogen-fixing fodder crops such as clover and alfalfa are additionally important in agriculture as green manures that are planted to enrich the soil.

Lehár, Franz   [leh'-har, frahnts]

The Hungarian-born composer Franz Lehár, b. Apr. 30, 1870, d. Oct. 24, 1948, achieved international fame with his operettas. He worked first as an orchestral violinist, and then, as his father had before him, he became a military bandmaster, working in Trieste (1896), Budapest (1898), and Vienna (1899–1902). During this time he made some attempts at writing opera, but then turned to operetta, where he found success particularly with *The Merry Widow* (1905), which established him among the foremost composers of the genre, the successor to von Suppé and Johann Strauss. The plot of *The Merry Widow* involves the successful intrigues of the ambassador from an imaginary Balkan country to bring about the marriage of a wealthy widow to one of his deputies in order to save the country from financial collapse. All this frivolity is accompanied by many waltzes and light songs. Among Lehár's other operettas are *The Count of Luxembourg* (1909), *Gypsy Love* (1910), *Paganini* (1925), and *The Land of Smiles* (1929).
    F. E. KIRBY

Bibliography: Grun, Bernard, *Gold and Silver: The Life and Times of Franz Lehár* (1970); MacQueen-Pope, W. L., and Murray, D. L., *Fortune's Favorite: The Life and Times of Franz Lehár* (1953).

Lehigh University   [lee'-hy]

Established in 1865, Lehigh University (enrollment: 6,000; library: 786,000 volumes) is a private coeducational institution in Bethlehem, Pa. It has colleges of arts and sciences, engineering, physical sciences, business, and economics, and awards bachelor's, master's, and doctorate degrees.

Lehman, Herbert H.   [lee'-muhn]

Herbert Henry Lehman, b. New York City, Mar. 28, 1878, d. Dec. 5, 1963, was an American banker and politician who became a leading spokesman for Democratic party liberals. In 1908 he joined the family investment firm Lehman Brothers. During World War I he held various posts, working for a time in the office of then Assistant Secretary of the Navy Franklin D. Roosevelt, with whom he was later closely associated. In 1928 he was elected lieutenant governor of New York, and in 1933 he succeeded Roosevelt as governor. In his 10 years in office, Lehman followed a liberal legislative program and attempted to clean up corruption in state politics. From 1943 to 1946, Lehman was director of the United Nations Relief and Rehabilitation Administration. He later served (1949–57) in the U.S. Senate, where he was one of the few to oppose Sen. Joseph R. McCarthy.

Bibliography: Ingalls, Robert P., *Herbert H. Lehman and New York's Little New Deal* (1975); Nevins, Allan, *Herbert H. Lehman and his Era* (1963).

Lehmann, Johann Gottlob [lay'-mahn, yoh'-hahn gawt'-lohp]

The German chemist and geologist Johann Gottlob Lehmann, b. Aug. 4, 1719, d. Jan. 22, 1767, was among the first to recognize that the history of the Earth might be deciphered in the vertical succession of layered rocks. After a brief career in medicine, Lehmann determined that mining and metallurgy interested him more. In 1756 he settled in Berlin, where he taught chemistry and geology at the Royal Prussian Academy of Sciences. He left Berlin in 1761 to teach chemistry at the University of Saint Petersburg in Russia.

The largest part of Lehmann's work was in chemistry, analyzing the chemical composition of rocks and ores. In the course of this work he discovered new metallic elements, including cobalt and tungsten. His most significant work, however, was in geology, where he described layers, or strata, of rock deposits and demonstrated the fact of their temporal succession. Georg Christian Füchsel, a contemporary of his, made similar observations. Lehmann also studied the origin of mountains and distinguished two classes. According to Lehmann, primitive mountains were older and formed of veined rock, whereas secondary mountains were younger and occurred in bedded deposits laid down by the action of water, such as the biblical flood.   ANNE MILLBROOKE

Bibliography: Adams, Frank Dawson, *The Birth and Development of the Geological Sciences* (1938).

See also: STRATIGRAPHY.

Lehmann, Lotte

One of the most acclaimed lyric-dramatic sopranos of her time, German-born Lotte Lehmann, b. July 2, 1885, d. Santa Barbara, Calif., Aug. 26, 1976, excelled in the operas of Richard Strauss, particularly in the role of the Marshallin in *Der Rosenkavalier*. She made her debut at the Hamburg Opera in 1909 and was a principal singer with the Vienna Opera from 1914 to 1938. There she created the roles of the composer in *Ariadne auf Naxos* and the dyer's wife in *Die Frau ohne Schatten,* both by Strauss. Lehmann sang at the Metropolitan Opera from 1934 to 1945, mostly in Wagnerian roles, and settled in California in 1938, following Hitler's annexation of Austria. She was an excellent pedagogue, and her masterclasses were attended by such singers as Marilyn Horne and Grace Bumbry. Lehmann's writings include the autobiographical volumes *Midway in My Song* (1938), *My Many Lives* (1948), and *Singing with Richard Strauss* (1964).

Discography: Schumann, Robert, *Dichterliebe;* Strauss, Richard, *Der Rosenkavalier* (excerpts); Wagner, Richard, *Tristan und Isolde* (excerpts) and *Die Walküre* (excerpts).

Lehmbruck, Wilhelm [laym'-bruk, vil'-helm]

Heinrich Wilhelm Lehmbruck, b. Duisburg, Germany, Jan. 4, 1881, d. Mar. 25, 1919, was a highly individualistic German sculptor and painter whose works addressed man's spiritual essence. While studying (1901–06) at the Düsseldorf Academy, Lehmbruck admired the works of Auguste Rodin and created conservative, classicized pieces. Upon settling (1910) in Paris, however, he discarded academicism. The *Kneeling Woman* (1911; Museum of Modern Art, New York City), his first mature work, shows the attenuated forms and the austere and melancholic aura that would remain hallmarks of his sculptural style.

With the outbreak of World War I, Lehmbruck fled first to Berlin (1914) and then to Zurich (1916). His subsequent themes, often violent and sexual in nature, are related indirectly to those of the German expressionist movement called *Die Brücke* and to those of the Norwegian expressionist painter Edvard Munch. The painting *Pietà I* (1916–17; Lehmbruck Museum. Duisburg) reveals his doleful state of mind during this period. Always a depressive personality, Lehmbruck was shattered by the tragic events of World War I and mortified by his failure to achieve an international style of art that would lead to a unified art epoch. In perhaps his most famous statue, *Seated Youth, or The Friend* (1918; Lehmbruck Museum, Duisburg), he created a poignant memorial to his dead compatriots and their foes. Burdened by despair for postwar Europe, he committed suicide after the end of the war at the age of 38.   HARRY RAND

Bibliography: Heller, Reinhold, *The Art of Wilhelm Lehmbruck* (1972); Hoff, August, *Wilhelm Lehmbruck: Life and Work* (1969).

Leibl, Wilhelm [ly'-bul, vil'-helm]

The German painter Wilhelm Leibl, b. Oct. 23, 1844, d. Dec. 4, 1900, was one of the most important advocates of realism in art in the 19th century. He studied painting in the late 1860s at the Munich Academy, where instruction emphasized the depiction of historical and allegorical subjects. Leibl rejected the academic tradition, however, preferring to paint portraits of his friends and scenes of real life among the Bavarian peasants. His work attracted the attention of the French realist Gustave Courbet, who invited him to Paris, where he spent several months (1869–70). Upon his return to Munich, Leibl became the leading member of a group of young painters who shared his interest in realism, the "Leibl Circle," which included Wilhelm TRÜBNER, Karl Schuch, and Fritz Schider. In 1873, Leibl left the city and went to live in Bavarian villages among the countryfolk, whom he depicted in such works as *Three Women in Church* (1878–82; Kunsthalle, Hamburg).   ELIZABETH PUTZ

Bibliography: Finke, Ulrich, *German Painting from Romanticism to Expressionism* (1974).

Leibniz, Gottfried Wilhelm von [lyb'-nitz]

Gottfried Leibniz was a pioneer in the advancement of intellectual and scientific thought that foreshadowed the German Enlightenment. Although his mathematical theories were respected by his contemporaries, it was not until the 19th and 20th centuries that the importance of his philosophical inquiries was acknowledged.

The German philosopher and mathematician Gottfried Wilhelm von Leibniz, b. July 1, 1646, d. Nov. 14, 1716, was a universal genius and a founder of modern science. He anticipated the development of symbolic LOGIC and, independently of Newton, invented the calculus with a superior notation, including the symbol $\int$ for integration and dx for differentiation. He expounded a theory of substance based on monads, which were metaphysical and animistically endowed points of force and perception. Leibniz also advocated Christian ecumenism in religion, codified Roman laws and introduced natural law in jurisprudence, propounded the metaphysical law of optimism (satirized by Voltaire in *Candide*) that our universe is the "best of all possible worlds," and transmitted Chinese thought to Europe. For his work, he is considered a progenitor of German idealism and a pioneer of the Enlightenment.

Leibniz was the son of a professor of moral philosophy at Leipzig. A precocious youth, Leibniz taught himself Latin and some Greek by age 12 so that he might read the books in his father's library. From 1661 to 1666 he majored in law at the University of Leipzig. When refused admission to its doctoral program in law in 1666, he went to the University of Altdorf, which awarded him the doctorate in jurisprudence in 1667.

In the tradition of Cicero and Francis Bacon, Leibniz chose to pursue the active life of a courtier. He thus declined a professorship at Altdorf because he had "very different things in view." After serving as secretary of the Rosicrucian Society in Nuremberg in 1667, he moved to Frankfurt to work on legal reform. From 1668 to 1673 he served the elector-archbishop of Mainz. He was sent to Paris in 1672 to try to dissuade Louis XIV from attacking German areas. Leibniz proposed a campaign against Egypt and the Levant as well as building a canal through the Isthmus of Suez. Although his proposals were unheeded, Leibniz remained until 1676 in Paris, where he practiced law, examined Cartesian thought with Nicolas de Malebranche and Antoine Arnauld, and studied mathematics and physics under Christiaan Huygens.

From 1676 until his death, Leibniz served the Brunswick family in Hanover as librarian, judge, and minister. After 1686 he served primarily as historian, preparing a genealogy of the Hanovers based on the critical examination of primary source materials. In search of sources, he traveled to Austria and Italy from 1687 to 1690. Because of his Lutheran background, he declined the position of custodian of the Vatican Library, which required his conversion to Catholicism.

In his later years, Leibniz attempted to build an institutional framework for the sciences in central Europe and Russia. At his urging, the Brandenburg Society (Berlin Academy of Science) was founded in 1700. He met several times with Peter the Great to recommend educational reforms in Russia and proposed what later became the Saint Petersburg Academy of Science.

Although shy and bookish, Leibniz knew no master in disputation. After 1700 he opposed John Locke's theory that the mind is a *tabula rasa* (blank tablet) at birth and that humans learn only through the senses. He strongly protested the Royal Society's charge (1712–13) of plagiarism against him regarding the invention of the calculus. In his final debate with Samuel Clarke, who defended Newtonian science, Leibniz argued that space, time, and motion are relative.

Leibniz's most important works are the *Essais de Théodicée* (1710; Eng. trans., 1951), in which much of his general philosophy is found, and the *Monadology* (1714; trans. as *The Monadology and Other Philosophical Writings*, 1898), in which he propounds his theory of monads. His work was systematized and modified in the 18th century by the German philosopher Christian WOLFF.   RONALD CALINGER

Bibliography: Broad, C. D., and Lewy, C., *Leibniz: An Introduction* (1975); Calinger, Ronald, *Gottfried Wilhelm Leibniz* (1976); Frankfurt, Harry G., ed., *Leibniz: A Collection of Critical Essays* (1976); Hostler, J. M., *Leibniz's Moral Philosophy* (1975); Ishiguro, Hide, *Leibniz's Philosophy of Logic and Language* (1972); Leclerc, Ivor, ed., *The Philosophy of Leibniz and the Modern World* (1973); Loemker, Leroy E., *Struggle for Synthesis* (1972); Parkinson, G. H., *Logic and Reality in Leibniz's Metaphysics* (1965); Rescher, Nicholas, *The Philosophy of Leibniz* (1967); Russell, Bertrand, *Critical Exposition of the Philosophy of Leibniz* (1900; 2d ed., 1961).

Leicester   [les'-tur]

Leicester, a city in central England on the River Soar, is the county town of Leicestershire. It lies about 160 km (100 mi) northwest of London and has a population of 280,324 (1981). Leicester produces footwear, knitted goods, office machines, plastics, and dyes. The center of the city has been rebuilt since World War II and includes a modern concert hall. Of historic interest are extensive Roman and Norman remains, several churches, the Guild Hall, and Trinity Hospital. In addition to the University of Leicester (1918), schools of art and technology are located in the city.

Leicester was founded, probably by the Romans, during the 1st century AD, at the site of a road crossing the Soar. The city's growth was slow until a railroad connected it to a nearby coal-mining region in the 19th century, after which it developed steadily as an industrial center.

Leicester, Robert Dudley, Earl of

Robert Dudley, b. June 24, 1532 or 1533, d. Sept. 4, 1588, was a favorite of Queen ELIZABETH I of England, who made him earl of Leicester in 1564. A son of John Dudley, duke of NORTHUMBERLAND, he was involved in his father's plan to secure the succession to the throne of Lady Jane GREY in 1553. When the scheme failed, he was condemned to death, but later pardoned.

Dudley's dashing personality and good looks made him Elizabeth's favorite courtier from the time of her accession in 1558. She considered marrying him and might have done so had not his first wife, Amy Robsart, died under unusual circumstances in 1560. Many suspected that Dudley had murdered her, but there is no evidence to implicate him, nor did he lose influence with the queen. He was given Kenilworth Castle, near Coventry, in 1563 and ennobled in 1564. In the latter year, Elizabeth also tried to marry him to MARY, QUEEN OF SCOTS, who rejected the proposal.

In 1578, Leicester did alienate Elizabeth by marrying the widow of the 1st earl of Essex. From 1585 to 1587 he commanded English forces participating in the DUTCH REVOLT and again angered the Queen by accepting the title of governor of the Low Countries. Leicester was also a notable patron of literature and drama.   STANFORD E. LEHMBERG

Bibliography: Jenkins, Elizabeth, *Elizabeth and Leicester* (1961).

Leicestershire   [les'-tur-shir]

Leicestershire is a county in the Midlands region of central England. A rich agricultural area covering 2,553 km^2 (986 mi^2), it has a population of 842,577 (1981). Leicester is the county town. Major rivers include the Avon, Soar, and Welland. The fertile western uplands produce wheat, barley, and vegetables, whereas sheep raising and dairying are important east of the Soar; some coal is mined in the west. Industries include footwear, textile (especially hosiery), and plastics manufacturing. Settled in Roman times, the county was invaded by the Angles and Danes; it became part of the Kingdom of Mercia in 653. Bosworth Field, the site of Richard III's defeat (1485) by the future Henry VII, is located there. The county was reorganized in 1974 to incorporate the former county of Rutland.

Leiden   [ly'-den]

Leiden (also Leyden) is a city in the South Holland province of the Netherlands, located close to the North Sea and about 15 km (10 mi) northeast of The Hague. Leiden's population is 103,457 (1982 est.). The well-known State University of Leiden (1575), the first institution of higher learning in Holland, makes Leiden a prominent intellectual center. The food-processing and printing industries are important, and the city has a large livestock market. The Netherlands' principal tulip fields are located in the sand dunes north of Leiden.

The city was founded near a 12th-century citadel at the confluence of the former Old and New branches of the Rhine River. A southward shift of the river's main channel curtailed shipping and stimulated creation of the canals for which Leiden is noted. The arrival of Flemish weavers brought prosperity from the 14th to the 16th century. The former cloth hall (1640) is now a museum. The city suffered during a siege by the Spanish (1574) during the Dutch Revolt. Leiden was the birthplace of the 17th-century painters Rembrandt and Jan Steen.   JONATHAN E. HELMREICH

Leif Eriksson   [leef air'-ik-suhn]

Leif Eriksson (or Ericsson), c.970–c.1020, was a Norse explorer who apparently reached North America c.1000. His exploits are known through the Icelandic SAGAS of the 13th century. Leif the Lucky was the son of ERIC THE RED, the colonizer of Greenland. He grew up in Greenland but c.999 visited Norway, where he was converted to Christianity. According to one saga, he was then commissioned by King Olaf I to convert the Greenlanders to Christianity, but he was blown off course, missed Greenland, and reached North America.

The other, more probable version describes Leif sailing on a planned voyage to lands to the west of Greenland that had been sighted 15 years earlier by Bjarne Herjulfsson. He landed at places called Helluland and Markland and wintered at Vinland. These may well have been Baffin Island, Labrador, and Newfoundland, respectively, but historians differ in their identifications of the sites. Leif went back to Greenland, but an expedition led by Thorfinn Karlsefni returned to settle Vinland. Leif may well have helped to Christianize Greenland.   Bruce B. Solnick

Bibliography: Jones, Gwyn, ed., *The Norse Atlantic Saga: Being the Norse Voyages of Discovery and Settlement to Iceland, Greenland, and America* (1964); Morison, Samuel Eliot, *The European Discovery of America: The Northern Voyages* (1971); Mowat, Farley, *Westviking: The Ancient Norse in Greenland and North America* (1965); Wahlgren, Erik, *The Vikings and America* (1986).

See also: L'Anse aux Meadow.

Leighton, Frederick, Baron Leighton of Stretton   [layt'-uhn, stret'-uhn]

The English painter Frederick Leighton, b. Dec. 3, 1830, d. Jan. 25, 1896, was trained in Germany under Edward von Steinle in the classically simple and precise style of the Nazarenes. After further study in Rome, Brussels, and Paris, Leighton settled in London in 1859. His extremely detailed paintings won him election to the Royal Academy in 1868. His dedication to that establishment brought him its presidency and a knighthood in 1878, followed by a peerage in 1896. During his academy career he painted popular, highly finished classical subjects, such as *Lachrymae* (c.1895; Metropolitan Museum, New York City).   Rowland Elzea

Bibliography: Gaunt, William, *Victorian Olympus*, rev. ed. (1975); Ormond, Leonee and Richard, *Lord Leighton* (1975).

Leinsdorf, Erich   [lynz'-dorf, ay'-rik]

The Austrian conductor Erich Leinsdorf, b. Feb. 4, 1912, is acclaimed for his versatility in the standard repertoire and as a champion of contemporary music. After an apprenticeship (1934) at the Salzburg Festival under Bruno Walter and Arturo Toscanini and subsequent appearances with European orchestras, he came to the United States and led (1938–43) the Metropolitan Opera, specializing in Wagner and the German repertoire. He went on to head the Cleveland Orchestra (1943) before serving in the U.S. Army, and afterward, the Rochester Philharmonic (1947–56) and the New York City Opera (1956–62). During his tenure (1962–69) as music director of the Boston Symphony, and as head of the Berkshire Music Festival, he brought some of the world's most promising young musicians to Tanglewood. Since 1969 he has toured the five continents as guest conductor of the leading European and American orchestras. During his career he has made a concerted effort to promote contemporary music and has given first performances of numerous operas and orchestral works by 20th-century composers. His writings include an autobiography, *Cadenza: A Musical Career* (1975), and *The Composer's Advocate* (1981), in which he gives his views on the art of conducting.   Ella A. Malin

Leinster   [len'-stur]

Leinster, a traditional province in southeastern Ireland, incorporates the areas of the ancient kingdoms of Leinster and Meath. It has an area of 19,632 km² (7,580 mi²) and a population of 1,790,521 (1981). Leinster contains the counties of Carlow, Dublin, Kildare, Kilkenny, Laoighis, Longford, Louth, Meath, Offaly, Westmeath, Wexford, and Wicklow; these are Ireland's most prosperous and populous counties. Dublin is the largest city. A dispute over the kingship of Leinster was the occasion for the first English invasion of Ireland in the 12th century, and in the later medieval period, Lein-

ster—especially the area around Dublin, known as the Pale—was the only part of the country effectively under English control.

Leipzig   [lipe'-tsik]

Leipzig, the second largest city of East Germany, lies at the confluence of three rivers in the Saxon lowlands. The city hosts the Leipzig Fair, which originated as a medieval trade fair and has developed into an annual commercial and industrial exposition.

Leipzig is the second largest city in East Germany and the capital of the Leipzig district (*Bezirk*), one of the 15 districts of East Germany. The city lies in the historic region of Saxony, in south central East Germany, where the foothills of the central German mountains give way to the fertile North German plains. Leipzig's area is 141 km² (54 mi²), and the population is 559,000 (1983 est.).

Leipzig's old town is located between the Parthe, Elster, and Pleisse rivers. In the center is the old market, the 16th-century town hall, the Church of Saint Nicholas (first mentioned 1017), and the 13th-century Church of Saint Thomas, where Johann Sebastian Bach served as cantor from 1723 to 1750. The walls encircling the old town were replaced in the 18th century by a ring of parks and promenades. Subsequently Leipzig expanded in all directions by gradually incorporating the suburbs that were growing up around it.

After East Berlin, Leipzig is the largest commercial and industrial center of East Germany and an important transportation hub. Its great trade fairs, which date back to the Middle Ages and attract business people from all over the world, have acquired world renown, as have Leipzig's book and fur trades (although the importance of furs has diminished since World War II). The city's suburbs now contain industrial parks whose factories produce iron and steel, heavy machinery, scientific instruments, chemicals and plastics, musical instruments, textiles, and toys.

Leipzig is the seat of the largest university in East Germany (Universitas Lipsiensis), which was founded in 1409; it was renamed Karl Marx University in 1952. The city also has a well-known conservatory of music, where both Bach and Felix Mendelssohn held positions.

Leipzig's name is derived from Lipsk, the original Slav settlement named for the lime tree (*lípa*). During the 10th century the German king Henry I destroyed the original settlement and erected a fort around which a new town began to grow. In 1174, Leipzig received its charter from the margrave of Meissen, and it soon became a flourishing trade center. In 1519, Martin Luther held his momentous disputation with Johann Eck in Leipzig's citadel. The city suffered heavily during the Thirty Years' War. In October 1813, Napoleon I's army was defeated near Leipzig in the famous Battle of Leipzig (sometimes referred to as the Battle of the Nations). During World War II the city was heavily damaged by Allied bombing.   Edward Taborsky

leishmaniasis   [leesh-muh-ny'-uh-sis]

Leishmaniasis is a group of three conditions, each caused by a different species of a protozoan parasite of the genus *Leishmania*. Leishmaniasis normally affects canines and rodents and is transmitted, by bites, to humans by sandflies of the genus *Phlebotomus* in regions where the disease is endemic. The parasites live and multiply inside certain tissue cells, called macrophages, in infected animals or humans. When multiplication causes these cells to burst, the released parasites invade fresh cells. Sandflies become infected when they feed on the blood of infected individuals.

Visceral leishmaniasis, or KALA-AZAR, is caused by *L. donovani* and affects inhabitants mainly in the Mediterranean area, equatorial Africa, Ethiopia, central Asia and China, and South America. This form of leishmaniasis most severely affects the spleen, liver, lymph nodes, intestines, bone marrow, and skin. The rate of fatality is nearly 90 percent in untreated cases, but under 10 percent when treated.

Cutaneous leishmaniasis, or Oriental sore, is caused by *L. tropica* and is found in the Mediterranean area, the Near East, China, and parts of India. The infection normally remains fairly localized in the region of the skin where the sandfly bite occurred—usually on the face, arms, and legs. Healing takes from 2 to 18 months, leaving depressed, often disfiguring, scars.

American leishmaniasis, or espundia, caused by *L. braziliensis*, occurs in southern Mexico and Central and South America but is most common in Brazil, Paraguay, and Peru. The disease is characterized by disfiguring skin lesions that spread into the oral and nasal cavities; it may persist for years, if untreated, resulting in death from secondary infection.

PETER L. PETRAKIS

Leisler, Jacob   [lyz'-lur]

Jacob Leisler, b. 1640, d. May 16, 1691, led a revolt against English authority in colonial New York in 1689–91. The German-born soldier arrived (1660) in the colony when it was still under Dutch rule. By the time the English took over in 1664, he had married a wealthy widow and become a prosperous merchant.

The Glorious Revolution, which drove the Roman Catholic James II from the English throne in 1688, sparked American rebellion against Sir Edmund ANDROS, governor of the Dominion of New England, which included New York. In New York, Leisler assisted in the seizure of Fort James in May 1689 and assumed command of the rebel army after Lt. Gov. Francis NICHOLSON fled in June. In December he proclaimed himself lieutenant governor. In March 1691 a new royal governor, Henry Sloughter, arrived in New York. When Leisler hesitated to relinquish power, he was arrested, convicted of murder and treason, and hanged. Parliament later reversed the conviction. Leisler generally represented Protestant, antiaristocratic interests in New York, and his popular, or anticourt, faction was a factor in the colony for another generation.

LARRY R. GERLACH

Bibliography: Lovejoy, David S., *The Glorious Revolution in America* (1972; repr. 1987); Reich, Jerome R., *Leisler's Rebellion* (1953).

Leisy v. Hardin

The U.S. Supreme Court case of *Leisy* v. *Hardin* (1890) dealt with the constitutional question of state control over articles shipped in interstate commerce. Leisy, a brewer in Peoria, Ill., had sent a quantity of beer in barrels and cases to Keokuk, Iowa. A local constable had seized the beer while in its original containers since it was against the law in Iowa to sell intoxicating liquors. Speaking for the Court, Chief Justice Fuller ruled that because the beer was a legitimate article of interstate commerce, the states could not interfere with it so long as it remained in its original package. Once the importer in Iowa had sold the beer and it had become mingled in the common mass of goods for sale in the state, the state's laws might take effect.

The Court was applying the "original package" doctrine (first enunciated in BROWN V. MARYLAND, 1827, by Chief Justice John Marshall), which holds that a state may not tax or seize or destroy an article of interstate commerce while it remains in its original package even though it has come to rest. Also applied in this case was the "Cooley Rule" (announced in COOLEY V. BOARD OF PORT WARDENS, 1851) that when a subject of commerce is national in character and requires a uniform rule, Congress alone can act upon it. As a practical matter the states could not make their prohibition laws against intoxicants effective until Congress passed the Webb Kenyon Act (1913), which permitted dry states to take immediate action against liquor in interstate commerce as soon as it entered the states.

ROBERT J. STEAMER

Leitrim   [lee'-trim]

Leitrim is a county in Connacht province in the north of the Republic of Ireland. With an area of 1,525 km² (589 mi²), it has a population of 27,609 (1981). The mountains in the north and wet lowlands in the south are divided by Lough Allen, a 36-km² (14-mi²) lake. The county town is Carrick-on-Shannon. Livestock raising is the mainstay of the economy, and potatoes are the main crop; coal is mined in the north. Leitrim was owned by the O'Rourke family from the 12th to the 16th century.

Leloir, Luis Frederico   [luh-loyr', loo-ees']

The Argentine biochemist Luis Frederico Leloir, b. Sept. 6, 1906, d. Dec. 4, 1987, was awarded the 1970 Nobel Prize for chemistry for his studies of the processes that break down body sugars into simpler molecules. Leloir has also studied the oxidation of fatty acids, the structure of lactose (milk sugar), and the synthesis of glycogen. He is director of the Instituto de Investigaciones Bioquimicas in Buenos Aires and also teaches at the University of Buenos Aires.

Lely, Sir Peter   [lee'-lee]

Sir Peter Lely, b. Pieter van der Faes, Sept. 14, 1618, d. Dec. 7, 1680, was the leading portrait painter at the court of Charles II, king of England. Of Dutch birth, Lely went to England in about 1641 and soon turned from figure and landscape compositions to portraiture. Through hard work and the influence of Sir Anthony Van Dyck, he became the most popular portrait painter of his time. He confidently expressed the luxurious character of the court; this was typified in his series of *Beauties* (Royal Collection, Hampton Court) and in *The Duchess of Portsmouth* (c.1679; J. Paul Getty Museum, Malibu, Calif.) in which the subjects display a languishing air and are in a state of undress. However, Lely also made striking portraits of men of action and affairs—for example, the *Admirals* at the National Maritime Museum, Greenwich, England. He had a large and active studio, lived luxuriously, and formed a notable art collection. His baroque style was to influence British portraiture for a century after his death.

MALCOLM CORMACK

Bibliography: Becket, R. B., *Lely* (1951); Millar, Sir Oliver, *Sir Peter Lely* (1978); Whinney, Margaret, and Millar, Sir Oliver, *English Art, 1625–1714* (1957).

LEM: see LUNAR EXCURSION MODULE.

Lem, Stanisław

Stanisław Lem, b. Sept. 12, 1921, is the most widely translated Polish writer since Henryk Sienkiewicz. In his fantasy-satires, philosophical essays, and science fiction, Lem probes moral questions involving modern science and technology. Perceiving human nature as flawed, because intelligence is inherently limited and chained to a biology that is the product of evolutionary accidents, Lem is pessimistic about the possibilities of future social improvement. The bitterness of his work, however, is often relieved by a highly idiosyncratic sense of fun and linguistic playfulness. Lem's fiction includes *Solaris* (1961; Eng. trans., 1970); *The Invincible* (1965; Eng. trans., 1973); *A Perfect Vacuum* (1971; Eng. trans., 1978–79), containing "perfect book reviews of nonexistent books" and first published in English in the *New Yorker*; *Memoirs Found in a Bathtub* (1971; Eng. trans., 1973); *The Chain of Chance* (1976; Eng. trans., 1978); *His Master's Voice* (1968; Eng. trans., 1983); and *Imaginary Magnitude* (1973; Eng. trans., 1984). He has also written such works of nonfiction as *Microworlds: Writings on Science Fiction and Fantasy* (1970; Eng. trans., 1986).

MICHAEL KANDEL

Bibliography: Ziegfeld, Richard E., *Stanisław Lem* (1986).

Lemaître, Georges Édouard   [luh-metr']

The Belgian priest and astronomer Georges Lemaître, b. July 17, 1894, d. June 20, 1966, is known for his research on the origin of the universe, especially for his proposal (1927) of an expanding model of the universe, which was explained in 1931 by the assumption that the universe originated in an enormous explosion—an early version of the now widely accepted BIG BANG THEORY.

Lemercier, Jacques   [luh-mair-syay', zhahk]

Jacques Lemercier, b. between 1580 and 1585, d. June 4, 1654, ranks with François MANSART as one of the great French classical architects of the 17th century. Lemercier studied (c.1607–14) in Rome under the architect Giacomo della Porta, and this Italian influence is fully evident in his early ecclesiastical designs in Paris: both the facade of the Church of the Sorbonne (begun 1635) and the portal of the Val-de-Grace—completed after Mansart's dismissal in 1646—are based on such Roman classical church facades as that of Il Gesù. Lemercier's major work for King Louis XIII was the enlargement of the LOUVRE Palace, to which he added the Pavillon de l'Horloge (1624).

After 1626 his chief patron was Cardinal Richelieu, from whom Lemercier received commissions for the Sorbonne (begun 1626), the château and church of Rueill (1630), the Palais Cardinal (1633; now the Palais Royal) in Paris, and the château, church, and town of Richelieu (from 1631).

Lemercier also contributed to the field of domestic architecture. In his remodeling of the Hôtel de Liancourt in Paris (1623), he cleverly exploited the traditional scheme of a town house set between court and garden to give the impression of a grand, symmetrical layout.

ROBERT NEUMAN

Bibliography: Blunt, Anthony, *Art and Architecture in France: 1500–1700* (1970).

lemming   [lem'-ing]

Lemmings, family Cricetidae, are rodents that are closely related to voles and meadow mice. The four genera are: *Lemmus,* true lemmings; *Synaptomus,* bog lemmings; *Dicrostonyx,* collared or Arctic lemmings; and *Myopus,* red-backed or wood lemmings. The animals live in open grasslands or tundras in north temperate or arctic regions. Lemmings are 8–13 cm (3–5 in) long and weigh only a small fraction of a kilogram. The fur is reddish or grayish brown above and lighter-colored below; the tail is stubby. Collared lemmings turn white in winter, an adaptation to their snowy environment. The animals burrow to make underground nests lined with

The Norway lemming, Lemmus lemmus, *of Scandinavia is best known for its mass migrational behavior.*

grass or moss. They eat grass, roots, sprouts, and other plant materials. The mating season lasts from spring to fall; the female bears up to 9 young after a 20-day gestation period.

The legend that lemmings deliberately join in a death march to the sea, where they drown, is untrue. Lemmings migrate periodically from their home area when their population begins to exceed the food supply. They swim across streams and rivers in order to find land with food. Sometimes, however, lemmings try to swim bodies of water that are too wide and may drown in great numbers.

EVERETT SENTMAN

lemon

The lemon, Citrus limon, *is a small tropical tree with fragrant white flowers. Its yellow, acidic fruit is an important source of Vitamin C.*

Lemons, *Citrus limon* of the Rutaceae family, are the most widely grown acid species belonging to the CITRUS group of fruits. They rank third among all citrus fruits in tonnage produced. The lemon is grown most successfully in mild, coastal climatic regions. The leading producing countries are the United States, Italy, Spain, India, Argentina, and Turkey. Over three-quarters of the lemons grown in the United States come from California. Most of the rest are from Arizona.

Lemon trees are similar in appearance and longevity to ORANGE trees but have a more upright growth habit. Propagation and cultivation are also roughly similar, although the lemon profits more from heavy pruning. Lemon fruits have an ellipsoid shape, often with a neck on the stem (peduncle) end and a nipple on the other (stylar) end. The rind is yellow when matured in a subtropical climate.

The fruit contains 30–45% juice depending on variety, climate, maturity, and storage. The acid in the juice is mostly citric. Much of the U.S. lemon crop is processed into frozen or concentrated juice and such by-products as citric peel oil, pectin, and cattle feed.

WALTER REUTHER

Bibliography: Sinclair, W. B., *The Biochemistry and Physiology of the Lemon and Other Citrus Fruits* (1983).

LeMond, Greg

Gregory James LeMond, b. Lakewood, Calif., June 26, 1961, is a leading cyclist in world competition. LeMond was the 1983 world champion, and in 1986 he became the first American to win the prestigious Tour de France. In 1987, LeMond was shot in the back in a near-fatal hunting accident, but he returned to form, winning the Tour de France in both 1989 and 1990 and another world championship (1989).

Lemoyne, Jean Baptiste   [luh-mwahn']

The sculptor Jean Baptiste Lemoyne the Younger, b. Feb. 19, 1704, d. May 25, 1778, represents the realist, nonclassical strain of French rococo art. Lemoyne studied with his father and with Robert Le Lorrain from 1723 to 1725 and won the Academy's first prize in the latter year. From 1731 to 1774 he was the official portraitist of Louis XV, for whom he also produced monuments and other works. Most of these were destroyed during the French Revolution. Lemoyne's sculptures have a pictorial quality and were frequently polychromed. The vitality of his work lies in his direct, honest, sometimes stark manner of representation. An example is the spontaneous and expressive *Portrait of Voltaire* (*c.*1748; Chateau de Challis, Oise, France). NANETTE SALOMON

Bibliography: Kalnein, Wend Graf, and Levey, Michael, *Art and Architecture of the Eighteenth Century in France* (1972).

lemur [lee'mur]

The ring-tailed lemur, L. catta, a highly social animal, is the most familiar of the lemurs because it can adapt well to life in zoos.

Lemurs are approximately 15 species of monkeylike primates, grouped into 6 genera, making up the family Lemuridae. They are found only on Madagascar and on the Comoro Islands, northwest of Madagascar, and are generally slender-bodied and long-limbed, with thick, woolly fur and long tails. Lemurs range in size from the mouse lemurs, genus *Microcebus* and *Phaner,* which at about 60 g (2 oz) are among the smallest primates, to the gentle lemurs, genus *Hapolemur,* which are about the size of a large cat. (Some zoologists group the mouse lemurs and dwarf lemurs, genus *Cheirogaleus,* in a separate family, Cheirogaleidae.) The golden bamboo lemur, *H. aureus,* was not discovered until 1987.

Some lemurs are nocturnal, others are active at dusk, and a few are diurnal. The dwarf and mouse lemurs may estivate during hot, dry periods. Lemurs are completely arboreal except for the ring-tailed lemur, *Lemur catta,* which spends about 15% of the daylight hours on the ground and enjoys sunning itself. Lemurs feed on leaves, flowers, fruits, or insects, and at least six species of nocturnal, flower-eating lemurs are significant pollinating agents for several Madagascar plants. Because of habitat loss, a number of lemur species are endangered. EDWIN E. ROSENBLUM

Bibliography: Else, J. G., and Lee, P. C., eds., *Primate Ecology and Conservation* (1986); Tattersall, I., *The Primates of Madagascar* (1982).

Lena River [lee'-nuh]

The Lena River rises in south central Siberia, USSR, west of Lake Baikal, and flows some 4,265 km (2,650 mi) north to the Laptev Sea, part of the Arctic Ocean. It is the third longest river in Asia and the seventh longest in the world. Over its early course it drops precipitously through a deep canyon. After it is joined by the Vitim River, the Lena becomes a deep, slow-moving river, 1.6 km (1 mi) wide and bordered by taiga vegetation. Its delta is over 160 km (100 mi) long and 400 km (250 mi) wide. Except for its first 804 km (500 mi) the Lena is navigable during the ice-free season. Summer commercial fishing is important. YAKUTSK, Osetrovo, and Peleduy are ports.

Lenard, Philipp Eduard Anton [lay'-nart]

The German physicist Philipp Eduard Anton Lenard, b. June 7, 1862, d. May 20, 1947, was prominent in early investigations

of the ELECTRON, for which he received the 1905 Nobel Prize for physics. Lenard confirmed (1892) that cathode rays consist of negatively charged particles, later termed electrons. His proposal that these particles are constituents of the atom was a step toward Ernest RUTHERFORD's nuclear atomic model. Lenard was the first to describe the characteristics of the photoelectric effect, which served as a basis for Einstein's photon theory of light. ROBERT SILLIMAN

Lenca [leng'-kuh]

The Lenca are a Chibcha-speaking Indian people living in an isolated part of Honduras and estimated to number several thousand. They grow maize, beans, squash, and chili peppers and keep dogs, chickens, ducks, and pigs. They also hunt game and gather wild plants. Lenca villages are laid out in the Spanish colonial fashion around a central plaza lined with municipal buildings, stores, a church, and the houses of notables. Houses are adobe brick with thatch or tile roofs. Villages are virtually independent; each is headed by a *cacique* (chief) and town council. A family head may have as many as three wives. Although nominally Catholic, the Lenca have preserved their traditional beliefs in sacred mountains and hills. They express adoration for the Sun and practice planting and harvest ceremonies. LOUIS FARON

Bibliography: Steward, Julian H., and Faron, Louis, *Native Peoples of South America* (1959).

Lend-Lease

The U.S. Congress passed the Lend-Lease Act, at President Franklin D. Roosevelt's request, in March 1941. Designed to allow Britain and China to draw on the industrial resources of the then nonbelligerent United States in World War II, the measure authorized the president to transfer, lease, or lend "any defense article" to "the government of any country whose defense the President deems vital to the defense of the United States." The bill was opposed by isolationists, such as Sen. Burton K. Wheeler of Montana, who termed it "the New Deal's triple A foreign policy; it will plow under every fourth American boy." Still, it passed the House by a vote of 260 to 5 and the Senate, by 60 to 31. By Aug. 21, 1945, when the program was terminated, almost $50 billion in Lend-Lease aid had been shipped to Britain, the USSR, China, and other Allied nations. From September 1942 the United States received "reverse lend-lease" from the British Commonwealth and the Free French in the form of $8 billion worth of goods and services provided to U.S. forces overseas. Financial settlements were made after the war, until 1972. RICHARD POLENBERG

Bibliography: Dobson, A. P., *U.S. Wartime Aid to Britain, 1940–1946* (1986); Kimball, Warren R., *The Most Unsordid Act* (1969).

Lendl, Ivan [len'-duhl, ee-vahn']

Ivan Lendl, b. Mar. 7, 1960, is a Czechoslovakian tennis player who, in the early 1980s, became one of the world's best. Lendl led his country to the Davis Cup title in 1980. In 1985–87 he was top ranked in the world. With his powerful serve and forehand, Lendl has risen to his ascendant position with 8 Grand Slam singles titles—the 1984 and 1986–87 French Opens, the 1985–87 U.S. Opens, and the 1989–90 Australian Opens.

L'Enfant, Pierre Charles [lahn-fahn', pyair sharl]

Pierre Charles L'Enfant, b. Aug. 2, 1754, d. June 14, 1852, was the French architect and engineer responsible for the design of Washington, D.C. The plan of the city is based on principles employed by André Le Nôtre in the palace and garden of Versailles, where L'Enfant's father had worked as a court painter, and on Domenico Fontana's scheme (1585) for the replanning of Rome under Pope Sixtus V. Through the use of long avenues joined at key points marked by important buildings or monuments, the city is a symbolic representation of power radiating from a central source.

On his arrival in America in 1777, L'Enfant joined the Revolutionary army and attained the rank (1783) of major of engineers. When Congress decided (1791) to build a capital city on the Potomac, George Washington asked L'Enfant to prepare a design but dismissed him in the following year because of his high-handed and discourteous behavior. L'Enfant also designed the old City Hall in New York (c.1787) and the town house of the financier Robert Morris in Philadelphia (begun 1793; demolished).   ROBERT NEUMAN

Bibliography: Caemmerer, Hans P., *The Life of Pierre Charles L'Enfant* (1950; repr. 1970).

Lenglen, Suzanne   [lahn-glen', soo-zahn']

French tennis star Suzanne Lenglen, b. May 24, 1899, d. July 4, 1938, completely dominated women's tennis from 1919 to 1926, losing only one match. At Wimbledon, Lenglen won 6 singles titles (1919–23, 1925) and 8 more in doubles. A brilliant strategist and groundstroker, she was nevertheless extremely cautious and rarely made an unforced error. Hampered by ill health and a moody temperament, Lenglen lost to champion Molla Mallory at the 1921 U.S. Championships and never played the tournament again.   STEVE FLINK

Lenin, Vladimir Ilich   [len'-in]

Vladimir Ilich Lenin, Russian revolutionary theorist and tactician, created the tightly organized Bolshevik party that won control of Russia in the October (November) Revolution of 1917. Lenin is regarded as the founder of Russian communism.

Vladimir Ilich Lenin, founder of the Russian Communist party, leader of the Bolshevik Revolution of 1917, and first head of state of the USSR, was also a masterful political thinker whose theories shaped Communist thought.

Early Life. V. I. Lenin was born Vladimir Ilich Ulyanov, Apr. 22 (N.S.; Apr. 10, O.S.), 1870, in the provincial city of Simbirsk (now Ulyanovsk, renamed in his honor) on the Volga River. By all accounts Lenin's middle-class family was warm and loving. Lenin's father was a secondary-school teacher who rose to become a provincial director of elementary education. His mother also taught. Both were deeply concerned with the popular welfare, and Lenin, along with his two brothers and two sisters, absorbed at an early age both a desire to learn and an intense commitment to improving the lives of ordinary Russians. In 1887, shortly after the death of his father, Lenin's older brother Aleksandr was arrested in Saint Petersburg (now Leningrad) for plotting against the tsar. He was convicted and hanged. The tragic event affected young Vladimir deeply, but there is no reason to believe that it caused him to embrace the revolutionary movement. Instead, he immersed himself in radical writings, particularly those of Karl MARX and Nikolai CHERNYSHEVSKY, and continued his education. Graduating from high school with a gold medal, he entered the University of Kazan but was expelled and exiled because of his developing radical views. In 1891, however, he passed the law examinations at the University of Saint Petersburg as an external student, scoring first in his

class. He practiced law briefly in Samara (now Kuibyshev) before devoting himself full time to revolutionary activities.

Communist Theoretician. Between 1893 and 1902, Lenin studied the problem of revolutionary change in Russia from a Marxist perspective and worked out the essential features of what has come to be called Leninism. Convinced with other Marxists that the development of industrial capitalism in Russia held the key to radical social change, Lenin remained troubled by the inability of Russian workers to develop spontaneously—as Marx had predicted—a radical consciousness capable of effective political action. In this the workers behaved like the peasants, whose failure to respond to radical appeals had frustrated populist revolutionaries for years. To solve the problem Lenin developed the notion that a radical consciousness had to be cultivated among workers through agitation by a well-organized revolutionary party.

It was during this period that he began using his pseudonym "Lenin" (sometimes "N. Lenin"). He also met and married Nadezhda Konstantinovna KRUPSKAYA. In 1895, Lenin was arrested, imprisoned, and sent in exile to Siberia with other members of the Marxist organization known as the Union of Struggle. Lenin went abroad in 1900 and with Georgy Valentinovich PLEKHANOV and others he organized the clandestine newspaper *Iskra* (The Spark), designed to "ignite" radical consciousness. In *Iskra*, Lenin vigorously rejected the notion of a political alliance with liberals or other elements of the bourgeoisie (he was convinced that they would only preserve a position of dominance over workers and peasants) and stressed the importance of social, rather than political, democracy, as the basis for individual freedom. This phase culminated with the publication of his pamphlet *What Is to be Done?* (1902) and the organization of the Bolshevik (see BOLSHEVIKS AND MENSHEVIKS) wing of the Russian Social Democratic Labor party in the summer of 1903. Lenin, like his populist predecessors in the Russian radical movement, stressed the need for a vanguard to lead the revolution.

Organizing for the Revolution. After 1903, Lenin struggled to develop this vanguard organization, a revolutionary leadership party that many historians regard as having mixed the concepts of populist Jacobinism with Marx's views of proletarian class revolution. Lenin became widely known in this period for his absolute dedication to revolution and his complete lack of personal vanity. On political issues he was merciless, lashing out ruthlessly at opponents and castigating adversaries with biting sarcasm and scorn. He also showed himself a masterful political tactician. Although he was in forced exile until 1917 (except for a brief period—1905–07—during and after the RUSSIAN REVOLUTION OF 1905) in London, Paris, Geneva, and other European cities, he maneuvered for control over party committees and publications. He condemned his Social Democratic opponents as Mensheviks (the Minority Group) despite being outnumbered by them.

Many of the Mensheviks were as radical as Lenin. They worried about the dictatorial propensities of his vanguard party concept, however, and urged instead the development of a mass popular base among the workers. But Lenin remained characteristically impatient and optimistic. He saw nothing to fear from a revolutionary elite dedicated to the welfare of workers and poor peasants; the danger lay instead with political liberals and a capitalist bourgeoisie, whose social system skimmed society's wealth from the people and whose imperialist wars led them to death and destruction.

Masterminding the Revolution. In 1917, Lenin published *Imperialism, The Highest Stage of Capitalism* (Eng. trans., 1933, 1939, 1947). In it he denounced World War I (in which Russia was engaged on the side of the Allies) as a fight among the imperialist powers for control of the markets, raw materials, and cheap labor of the underdeveloped world. Since neither the Allies nor the Central Powers offered any benefits to the working class, he urged all socialists to withhold their support from the war effort. Following his lead Russian Bolsheviks refused to support their government in its war efforts.

The German government, looking to disrupt the Russian war efforts further, allowed Lenin to return to his country from exile in Switzerland (traveling across Germany in a sealed train). He arrived at Petrograd (as the former Saint Petersburg was then called) on Apr. 16 (N.S.; Apr. 3, O.S.), 1917, and received a tumultuous welcome from his followers. In his "April Theses" (Eng. trans., 1951), published that year in *Pravda*, the Bolshevik newspaper, he denounced the liberal provisional government that had replaced the tsarist government, and he called for a socialist revolution. It was at this time that he gained the important support of Leon TROTSKY.

An abortive uprising against the government in July forced Lenin into exile once again (this time to Finland). It was a short-lived exile, however. In September, correctly perceiving the increasingly radical mood in Russia, he sent a famous letter to the party's central committee calling for armed insurrection. He slipped back into Russia and successfully brought the Bolsheviks to power through the "Military Revolutionary Committees"; and during the first week of November (N.S.; October by the old-style calendar—hence the name October Revolution) he succeeded in bringing down the government of Aleksandr KERENSKY. On November 7 (N.S.; Oct. 25, O.S.) the first Bolshevik government was formed; Lenin became its chairman. Thus he brilliantly engineered the final act of the revolution that had begun only months before (see RUSSIAN REVOLUTIONS OF 1917).

Head of Government. Lenin moved quickly to consolidate Bolshevik power. He reorganized the various party factions into the Russian Communist party, established a secret police (the Cheka), and totally reconstituted the desperate Russian economy along Marxist principles. In order to bring the country out of the war, he accepted a humiliating peace treaty with Germany in 1918 (see BREST-LITOVSK, TREATY OF). That same year civil war broke out, and he was forced to put a Red Army in the field against dissident forces. The dissidents, known as the Whites, were supported by the Allies and were not defeated until 1921.

By that time the Russian economy was in shambles, and discontent among peasants and workers was dangerously widespread. In the face of such problems Lenin was forced to back away from his pure Marxian policies, instituting the NEW ECONOMIC POLICY. He granted economic concessions to foreign capitalists in order to encourage trade; he placed some light industry and most retail operations back into private hands; and to appease the peasants he permitted them to sell their produce on the open market. Despite these minor concessions, Lenin continued to press forward toward his goal of a Marxist Russia—and eventually a Marxist world. He established the COMINTERN in 1919 to assure that the Russian Communist party would remain in control of the Marxist movement.

Although Lenin's power in the government was dictatorial and unquestioned, his control over party affairs was never absolute. The great rivalry between Trotsky and Joseph STALIN, which was to tear apart the Communist movement in later years, was already being formed at this period.

On May 25, 1922, Lenin suffered a stroke that left him partially paralyzed. A series of strokes followed, and he died on Jan. 21, 1924, at the age of 53, the most revered personage—apart from Marx himself—in the world of communism. The former capital city of Saint Petersburg (then Petrograd) was renamed Leningrad in his honor.

Lenin's mausoleum in Red Square, with his body embalmed and on display in a glass coffin, has become the greatest shrine in the Communist world. More important, Lenin's writings, along with those of Marx, form the basis for Communist theory; their legitimacy is accepted by all factions of the Marxist movement.   WILLIAM G. ROSENBERG

Bibliography: Deutscher, Isaac, *Lenin's Childhood* (1970); Fischer, Louis, *The Life of Lenin* (1964); Hill, Christopher, *Lenin and the Russian Revolution* (1978); Krupskaya, N. K., *Reminiscences of Lenin,* trans. by Bernard Isaacs, 2 vols. (1930–32; repr. 1970); Polan, A. J., *Lenin and the End of Politics* (1984); Trotsky, Leon, *Lenin: Notes for a Biographer,* trans. by Tamara Deutscher (1971); Ulam, Adam, *The Bolsheviks* (1965); Valentinov, Nikolai, *The Early Years of Lenin,* trans. by Rolf Theen (1969), and *Encounters with Lenin,* trans. by Paul Rosta and Brian Pearce (1968); Wolfe, Bertram D., *Three Who Made a Revolution* (1962).

Leningrad [len'-in-grad]

The Grand Cascade, a structure of gilt statues, fountains, and pools, descends from the northern facade of Peterhof, the summer residence built for Peter the Great outside modern Leningrad. Largely destroyed during World War II, the palace was rebuilt and is now a museum.

Leningrad, the capital of Leningrad oblast in the Russian republic of the USSR, is the country's second largest city. It is situated in the delta of the NEVA RIVER on the Gulf of Finland. The population of the city proper is 4,295,000; including suburbs under the city administration, it is 5,550,000 (1984 est.). These suburbs include the island naval base of Kronshtadt; the beach resort of Sestroretsk; the former tsarist palace towns of Pavlovsk, Petrodvorets (the former Peterhof), and PUSHKIN (formerly Tsarskoye Selo); and the industrial satellite town of Kolpino.

The city was founded in 1703 by PETER I (the Great) and was originally called Saint Petersburg. When World War I broke out in 1914, its Germanic name was Russified to Petrograd; and finally, on Lenin's death in 1924, the city was renamed Leningrad. One of the world's great cities, Leningrad flourished as the center of the Russian economy and culture while serving as the capital of the Russian Empire. Its role in science, education, and innovation was only slightly diminished after the nation's seat of government was moved back to Moscow in 1918.

Contemporary City. Leningrad has a distinctive layout. The historical center is situated on the left, or south, bank of the Neva River, and the city spreads out over large delta islands, including Vasilyevsky Ostrov (Vasily Island), to the right, or north, bank. Because of an abundance of river channels and canals, the city is sometimes referred to as the Venice of the North. Leningrad has been subjected to flooding when strong westerly winds drive Baltic Sea water through the funnel-shaped Gulf of Finland toward the city, raising the level of the Neva River. A protective dike across the gulf is being constructed to deal with this problem. The Neva freezes for a four-month period. Because of the city's northern location, the sun descends only briefly below the horizon in June and July, producing the so-called white nights of twilight.

Leningrad has five major railroad stations and is connected by rail with foreign cities as well as with all parts of the USSR. Local transportation is provided by a subway system and by bus and streetcar lines.

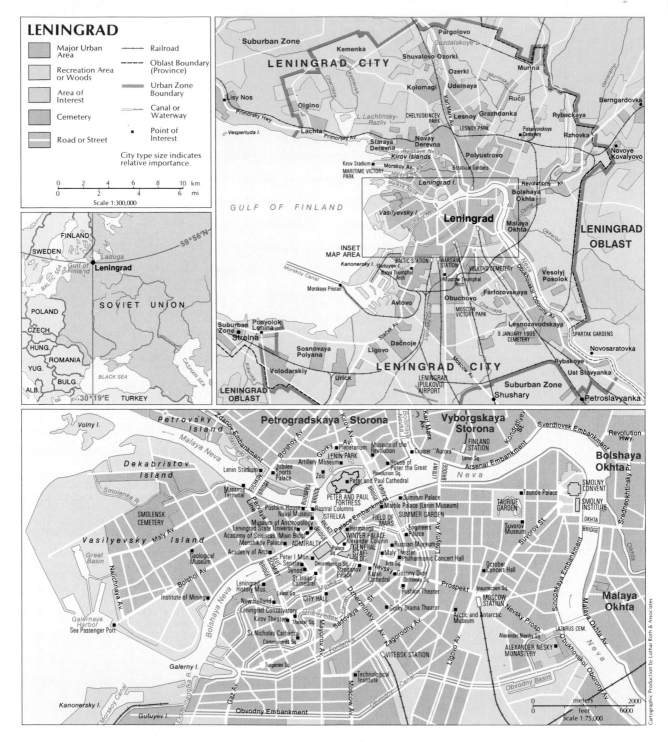

The city's population consists almost entirely of ethnic Russians; the largest minorities are Jews (4%) and Ukrainians (2.5%). Major commercial, cultural, and research institutions are concentrated in the city center on the left bank, where the city's main shopping street, the Nevsky Prospekt, is also located. Most industries have riverside locations along the Neva, upstream from the city center. As in most Soviet cities, residential high-rise developments are limited to the suburbs.

Leningrad, with its skilled labor force and old industrial traditions, is a highly diversified manufacturing center noted for the production of power-generating equipment and electrical goods, general industrial machinery, electronic components, chemicals and allied products, rubber goods, and plastics. The city is also a major shipbuilding center and seaport, handling a large portion of the USSR's exports and imports.

Often regarded as one of the world's most beautiful cities, Leningrad is distinguished by its sumptuous public buildings, designed for the tsars by Italian architects. Among the most prominent structures is the State HERMITAGE MUSEUM (founded 1754), one of the world's great art museums, which is housed in the tsar's former Winter Palace. Others include Saint Isaac's Cathedral (built 1818–1858), now a museum, and the Fortress

Leningrad, the second largest city of the USSR, lies along the Neva River's mouth on the Gulf of Finland. Originally named Saint Petersburg, the city was built as a fortress on land conquered from the Swedes by Tsar Peter the Great. It was the capital of Russia from 1712 to 1918.

of Saints Peter and Paul (built 1703–80), once a tsarist political prison. Leningrad State University, founded in 1819, ranks second in importance to Moscow State University.

HISTORY
Peter the Great chose the coastal site for his new capital to give the isolated, inward-looking Russian state a "window on Europe." Saint Petersburg soon replaced Arkhangelsk as Russia's foreign-trade port. Industrialization, begun in the second half of the 18th century and accelerated in the 19th, was based largely on raw materials imported from abroad. Unrest among the city's large industrial labor force was a factor in the overthrow of the tsar and the assumption of power by the Bolsheviks in 1917. Under Soviet rule, with national emphasis on economic self-sufficiency, Leningrad became more fully integrated with the economy. The city survived a 900-day siege (1941–44) by German forces in World War II.

THEODORE SHABAD

Bibliography: Gennady, Gubanov, *Leningrad* (1985); Miller, Wright W., *Leningrad* (1970); Salisbury, Harrison, *Nine Hundred Days: The Siege of Leningrad* (1969); Wechsberg, Joseph, *In Leningrad* (1977).

Leningrad State University

Founded in 1819 by Tsar Alexander I as the University of Saint Petersburg, A. A. Zhdanov Leningrad State University (enrollment: 20,000; library: 5,100,000 volumes) is a coeducational, free-tuition state institution in Leningrad, USSR. A full range of faculties in the humanities and the sciences offers programs leading to undergraduate and graduate diplomas and degrees. The university has research institutes, an astronomical observatory, and several museums.

Lenni-Lenape: see DELAWARE (Indian tribe).

lennoa [len'-oh-uh]

Lennoa are fleshy, brownish plants that live as parasites on the roots of desert shrubs and make up the family Lennoaceae of the order Polemoniales. They are found on beaches and other sandy areas of California and Mexico. Lennoa were once a source of food for desert-dwelling Indians.

Lennon, John: see BEATLES, THE.

Lenoir, Jean Joseph Étienne [luh-nwar' zhawn zhoh-zef' ay-tyen']

Jean Joseph Étienne Lenoir, b. Jan. 12, 1822, d. Aug. 4, 1900, is generally credited with designing the world's first INTERNAL-COMBUSTION ENGINE. Born in Belgium, he moved to Paris where his work with electroplating led him to other electrical inventions, among them a railway telegraph. Lenoir patented his first engine in 1860. Looking much like a double-acting STEAM ENGINE, it fired an uncompressed charge of air and illuminating gas with an ignition system of his own design. One of these engines powered a road vehicle in 1863; another ran a boat. Because of improved designs by Nikolaus OTTO and oth-

er inventors, the Lenoir engine became obsolete, and only about 500 Lenoir engines were built. DENNIS SIMANAITIS

Bibliography: Cummins, C. Lyle, *Internal Fire* (1976).

lens

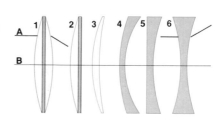

Converging lenses bend light (A) toward the axis (B); types include the double convex (1), plano-convex (2), and concavo-convex (3). Diverging lenses bend light outward; types include the convexo-concave (4), plano-concave (5), and double concave (6).

A lens, in OPTICS, is a piece of transparent material shaped to form an image by bending light rays (see REFRACTION). In ancient times lenses were called "burning glasses" because they could focus the Sun's rays to start fires. Their magnifying power has long been known (see EYEGLASSES; MICROSCOPE), but their use in TELESCOPES awaited the development of compound lenses. Other systems for focusing other kinds of beams are sometimes also called lenses (see ELECTRON MICROSCOPE). In astronomy, whole galaxies may function as lenses for more distant light (see GRAVITATIONAL LENS).

OPTICS OF LENSES
A simple lens has two opposing faces, at least one of which is curved. Most lenses have spherical surfaces, but other curvatures are used for special purposes.

Lens Shapes. A lens is called converging, or positive, if light rays passing through it are deflected inward. It is called diverging, or negative, if the rays spread out. Converging lenses are thicker at the middle, whereas diverging lenses are thicker toward the edges. A lens surface is concave (curved inward), plane, or convex (curved outward). A meniscus lens has one concave and one convex surface.

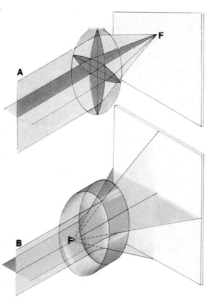

A simple lens consists of a piece of transparent material, such as glass, bounded by a curved surface—generally spherical—on one or both sides. Convex lenses (top) are positive lenses; light rays (A) entering parallel to the axis are converged at the focal point (F). Concave lenses (bottom) are negative lenses; light rays (B) entering parallel to the axis are spread out, appearing to originate from a negative focal point (F) called the virtual focus.

Image Formation. The focal length of a single lens is the distance from the lens to the point at which incoming parallel rays focus. Light converged in this manner can produce a real image, that is, an image that can actually be projected onto a screen. In a negative lens, rays do not actually come to a real focus, but appear to originate from a point called the virtual focus. The focal length of a diverging lens is considered to be negative.

When the diverging rays from a point source, which may be an actual source of light or a point on an extended object, are passed through a lens, the emerging rays produce an image that will be either real or virtual, depending on the type of lens and the location of the source.

A simple convex lens, or magnifying glass, will produce a virtual image if the object is either at the focal point or between the focal point and the lens. Light from the object passes through the lens, and the eye focuses it onto the retina. The object appears enlarged behind the lens. If the object is beyond the focal point of the same lens, a real image can be formed. A magnifying glass held in front of a light bulb will cause an image of the filament to be projected onto a screen or wall across the room.

The Lens Equation. Whether real or virtual images are formed, the image distance q can be calculated from the lens equation when the distance of the object to the lens, p, is known: $1/p + 1/q = 1/f$. Here f is the focal length of the lens, positive for a converging lens and negative for a diverging lens. The equation also shows whether the image is real or virtual; positive values of q indicate a real image and negative values correspond to a virtual image.

Image Defects. The ability of a simple lens to form a perfect optical image is limited by certain inherent defects called ABERRATIONS. Chromatic (color) aberration is a defect caused by different wavelengths of light refracted at slightly different angles, so that the focal length is slightly different for each color. This results in a colored fringe around an image. The defect can be corrected by a two-component design made with different kinds of glass. Color-corrected lenses are called achromatic lenses and are used in all fine optical instruments. Astigmatism, coma, and spherical aberration are defects that cause an image to be blurred.

The *f*-Number. The *f*-number of a lens is the ratio of the focal length to the lens diameter. Lenses of large diameter have small *f*-numbers and hence greater light-gathering power than lenses of small diameter or large *f*-number. Aberrations generally become more serious as the *f*-number decreases. This factor is particularly important in the design of camera lenses, the development of which dates from about 1840 with the introduction of the Petzval portrait lens, a combination of three components. Protar, Dagor, and Tessar camera lenses were developed during the latter part of the 19th century, and their basic designs are still used. Some modern camera lenses use 12 or more components. The advent of electronic computers has allowed rapid advances in their design.

Lens Materials. New kinds of optical glasses have been developed in recent years, such as rare-earth glass, having a relatively high INDEX OF REFRACTION. Techniques for making good-quality plastic lenses have been introduced in recent years. Such lenses have advantages in special applications, such as spectacle lenses.

Lenses for use in the ultraviolet and infrared regions of the spectrum must be made of special materials, because ordinary optical glass is opaque to these wavelengths. Quartz is the most common material for ultraviolet-transmitting lenses. Infrared lenses are made with calcium fluoride, sodium chloride (salt) or other alkali halides, or silicon.   GRANT R. FOWLES

LENSES OF OPTICAL INSTRUMENTS
The lens of a camera is a converging lens for forming a real image of the scene (object) that is to be recorded photographically. A simple convex lens theoretically focuses the incoming light beam, but in practice such a lens suffers from numerous types of defects, called aberrations, which cause blurring and distortion of the image.

A lens for an optical instrument such as a CAMERA, ENLARGER, or PROJECTOR generally consists of up to eight or more simple lenses, or lens elements. These elements may be used either separately or cemented together in a group called a lens component. Such arrangements are designed to reduce aberrations to a minimum. The degree of reduction or enlargement of an image with respect to the size of the object depends on the focal length of the lens used.

Aperture. The brightness of the image is determined by the relative aperture, or *f*-number (see APERTURE). In the same way that the amount of light falling on a wall opposite a circular window can be determined by calculating the ratio of the room length to the window diameter, the relative aperture is defined as the ratio of the focal length to the diameter of the effective aperture of the lens. This aperture can be varied by means of a diaphragm. For given lighting conditions, a lens of small aperture (large *f*-number) gives a dim image that requires a relatively long exposure. This shortcoming, however, is compensated by the decreased aberrations, and hence increased sharpness, of the image. On the other hand, wide-aperture (small *f*-number) lenses, which are required to give a bright and sharp image, need many lens elements to reduce aberrations and are therefore expensive and bulky.

Angle of View. The angle of view—the amount of the field that the lens will cover—depends on the lens's focal length. The field of a camera lens may be as small as about 15° or as large as about 140°. A standard lens may cover 60°; a wide-angle lens, 90°; and a telephoto lens, 30°.

A wide-angle lens forms an image of a wide field of view. The scene appears smaller and more distant than it actually is. Such a lens might be used, for example, to take a close-up shot of a tall building. Such lenses, however, may introduce considerable distortion, especially at the edges. A wide-angle portrait photograph may, for example, show hands that appear disproportionately large.

A telephoto lens is a lens combination that has a long focal length, without the bulk of a standard long-focus lens. It makes distant objects appear closer and larger but covers a narrower area than a standard lens.

A zoom lens is one with a focal length that may be varied; it is also called a variable-focus lens. The zoom lens consists of fixed and movable elements. The focal length is changed by moving one or more groups of variable elements mounted in a movable barrel along the axis. The variation is continuous, and in a reflex camera the effect may be followed on the ground-glass screen. In many situations it is more convenient to use a zoom lens than to interchange several lenses, especially in CINEMATOGRAPHY. Unfortunately, although zoom lenses continue to be improved, such lenses are expensive, and the definition of the image is somewhat inferior to that produced by lenses of fixed focal length.

LENS GRINDING
Lens grinding is the process by which optical lenses are manufactured from glass. (Transparent plastics, which are used to produce certain types of lenses, are molded rather than ground.) Fine lenses are made from specially prepared optical glass, which must be free of metallic impurities that might cause discoloration.

Optical glass is often cast in blocks, although it is also available in strips, panes, and rods, or it may be molded roughly into lens shape. A lens blank is cut off the glass block and then rough-ground, using a diamond abrasive on a grinding wheel, to a shape approximating its final dimensions. Fine grinding, or lapping, is accomplished by using carborundum or emery abrasives in a convex or concave lapping tool made of a rigid material: iron, for mass-produced lenses such as those made for eyeglasses; or glass, for high-precision optical lenses. A number of small lenses may be mounted together on a spherical block and lapped simultaneously.

For fine optical glass, the final polishing may take many hours, using a soft lapping tool that is shaped precisely to fit the lens. Harder polishing laps made of resin or plastic are used for lenses of lower accuracies. Both sides of the lens are usually polished, and the lens edge is ground so that its axis is centered and it has the correct diameter.

Bibliography: Freeman, Michael, ed., *Cameras and Lenses* (1988); Katz, Jerome, *How to Think Lenses and Focal Lengths* (1987); Miller, E. E., and Roesler, F. L., *Applied Optics* (1988); Twyman, Frank, *Prisms and Lens Making*, 2d ed. (1988); Welford, W. T., *Optics*, 2d ed. (1989).

Lent

For Christians, Lent is a 40-day penitential period of prayer and fasting that precedes EASTER. In the Western church, observance of Lent begins $6^{1}/_{2}$ weeks prior to Easter on ASH

WEDNESDAY; Sundays are excluded. In the Eastern church the period extends over 7 weeks because both Saturdays and Sundays are excluded. Formerly a severe fast was prescribed: only one full meal a day was allowed, and meat, fish, eggs, and milk products were forbidden. Today, however, prayer and works of charity are emphasized. Lent has been observed since the 4th century.

lentil   [len'-tul]

An annual plant, the lentil, *Lens culinaris*, of the LEGUME family, Leguminosae, is among the most ancient of cultivated vegetables. It is believed to be indigenous to southwestern Asia and was cultivated in Egypt and Greece long before the biblical era. In the Bible it is probably the pottage vegetable that Esau traded for his inheritance. Today the vegetable is widely grown in temperate and subtropical climates. About 2 million ha (5 million acres) of lentils are grown worldwide; India is by far the largest producer. In the United States lentils are raised mainly in Washington and Idaho.

Lentils are grown for their seeds, which are rich in protein, and for animal forage (see PULSE CROP). The round, flattened seeds are contained in pods and must be threshed during harvesting. They range in size from 3 to 9 mm (0.118 to 0.354 in) and in color from white to green, brown, orange, and violet blue. Like beans, lentils can be dried and stored. They are eaten whole in soups and stews and are also ground into a flour. Yields in the United States are about 1,200 kg per ha (more than 1,000 lb per acre); in India, the yield is about 470 kg per ha (about 450 lb per acre).   O. A. LORENZ

Bibliography: Duke, J. A., *Handbook of Legumes of World Economic Importance* (1981).

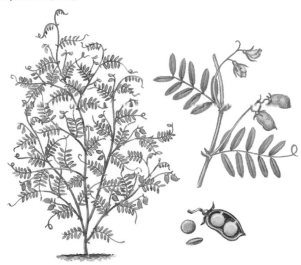

The lentil, L. culinaris, is a legume that is grown for its seeds, which are exceptionally rich in protein. Like beans, to which they are closely related, lentils vary widely in size and color.

Lenya, Lotte

The actress and singer Lotte Lenya, b. Karoline Blamauer in Vienna, Oct. 18, 1900, d. Nov. 27, 1981, popularized the songs of her husband, Kurt WEILL, especially those written in collaboration with playwright Bertolt Brecht. Lenya, a young dancer and actress in Germany, married Weill in 1926. She sang the lead in *The Little Mahagonny,* the first Weill-Brecht collaboration, in 1927, creating a sensation with her rendition of the "Alabama Song." She played her greatest role, that of the slavey Jenny in *The Threepenny Opera* (1928), and starred in the opera *The Rise and Fall of the City of Mahagonny* in 1930. In 1933, Lenya and Weill fled Germany for France and the United States. After Weill's death (1950), Lenya performed in

a long-running revival of *The Threepenny Opera* in New York City and established herself as an actress in Hollywood and on Broadway—notably, in the 1966 production *Cabaret.*

Lenz, Jakob

German poet and playwright Jakob Michael Reinhold Lenz, b. Jan. 12, 1751, d. May 24, 1792, is associated with the literary era of STURM UND DRANG. Lenz wrote plays that prefigured and influenced later naturalist and expressionist drama. In Strasbourg he became friendly with Johann Wolfgang von Goethe and invented his life's obsession, a passionate sense of rivalry with Goethe. Already showing signs of the mental derangement that was to blight his later years, Lenz nevertheless wrote his best work during the years in Strasbourg (1771–76)—his plays *The Tutor* (1774) and *The Soldiers* (1776), with their short swift scenes strung together in sometimes jolting juxtaposition, and his theoretical *Notes on the Theater* (1774).

Lenz's law   [lents'-iz]

Lenz's law is a basic law in electromagnetic theory for determining the direction of flow of induced currents (see ELECTROMAGNETIC INDUCTION). It was first stated by the Estonian physicist Heinrich Lenz (1804–65). According to the law, when a current is caused to flow in an electrical conductor by a change in the external magnetic field surrounding the conductor, the direction of flow of the current is such as to produce a magnetic field opposing the original change. This law is a particular case of the more general principle of Henri Louis LE CHÂTELIER, which states that changes in systems displaced from equilibrium react to restore that equilibrium.

Lenz's law explains the behavior of the inductance coil, or INDUCTOR. In this device, a changing current causes the inductor to develop its own electromotive force (emf) through self-inductance (see INDUCTANCE). If the current were decreasing, the induced emf would be in such a direction to sustain it. If the current were increasing, the emf would be in the reverse direction, opposing it. Thus an inductor tends to reduce or smooth out fluctuations in current. This is particularly the case with high-frequency components, which cause greater self-inductance than lower frequencies.

A. G. ENGELHARDT AND M. KRISTIANSEN

Leo

Leo (the Lion), the fifth constellation of the ZODIAC, is located between Cancer and Virgo and is best seen in the Northern Hemisphere in spring. The Sun passes southeastward through Leo from about August 23 to September 23, just prior to crossing the celestial equator at the autumnal equinox. Its brightest star is Regulus (Latin for "little king"), a blue-white star of magnitude 1.36 located 84 light-years from the Sun; Regulus has two dimmer companions, making it a triple star. Twice as close is the second brightest star, Denebola (Arabic for "tail of the lion"), which has a magnitude of 2.23. Leo is the apparent radiation point of the Leonid meteors, seen in November.

CRAIG B. WAFF

Leo III, Byzantine Emperor   (Leo the Isaurian)
[biz'-uhn-teen, ih-sor'-ee-uhn]

Leo III, b. *c.*685, d. June 18, 741, ruled (717–41) the BYZANTINE EMPIRE during a period of dire crisis. Of Isaurian, or Syrian, peasant stock, he rose through the imperial guard to military command and was brought to the throne by the army, displacing Theodosius III. A few months later, a large Muslim Arab army and fleet commenced a year-long siege of Constantinople (August 717–August 718). Only Leo's military ability, and timely Bulgarian help, saved the Byzantine capital. Thereafter, he strove successfully to repel the Arabs from Anatolia.

Internally, Leo reformed the legal code and extended the *theme* system (military administration of civilian provinces). In 726 he inaugurated a policy of ICONOCLASM, or opposition to image-worship, which marked the beginning of a long and bitter controversy in the empire. Leo himself did not push his campaign, especially after it caused revolts in Greece and the exarchate of Ravenna in Italy. The Byzantine hold on Italy was gravely weakened as a result. Leo was succeeded by his son, Constantine V.   C. M. BRAND

Leo VI, Byzantine Emperor   (Leo the Wise)

Leo VI, b. 866, d. May 12, 912, ruled the BYZANTINE EMPIRE from 886, in succession to his father, BASIL I. He completed his father's legal reforms by publishing the *Basilica* (Imperial Laws), the largest recodification since that of Justinian I. He also reorganized the imperial administration for greater efficiency. Leo's wars with the Bulgars and Arabs were unsuccessful: in 904 Arab corsairs sacked Thessalonika. His efforts to obtain an heir led him into a fourth marriage, which Byzantine churchmen vigorously opposed. His constructive reforms, however, survived these difficulties.   C. M. BRAND

Bibliography: Jenkins, Romilly, *Byzantium: The Imperial Centuries, A.D. 610–1071* (1966).

Leo I, Pope

Saint Leo I, called the Great, d. Nov. 10, 461, is acclaimed as one of the greatest popes in early Christian times. He assumed the pontificate in 440 and held it until his death. Leo had personal encounters with both ATTILA THE HUN (452) and GAISERIC, king of the Vandals (455), in which he persuaded the former not to attack Rome and the latter not to sack it.

The first pope to emphasize the divine origin of the power of the papacy, Leo was a strong-willed man of authority and government, as well as an extraordinary pastor, upholding discipline in faith. He defended the unity of the church against such heresies as MANICHAEISM, PELAGIANISM, and Priscillianism (see PRISCILLIAN) and defended Catholic teaching in the Nestorian-Monophysite Controversy. His *Letter (Tome) to Flavian* (449) provided the foundation for the Christological dogma of Chalcedon (see CHALCEDON, COUNCIL OF), defining the two natures and one person of Christ. Leo clearly and forcefully set forth the doctrines of the church on the incarnation, redemption, grace, and the sacraments. His teaching is contained in letters and sermons, which remain rich sources of inspiration and guidance for Christian spirituality. He is a Doctor of the Church. Feast day: Nov. 10 (formerly Apr. 11).   AGNES CUNNINGHAM

Bibliography: Jalland, Trevor G., *The Life and Times of Saint Leo the Great* (1941); Kelly, J. N., *Early Christian Doctrines,* 4th ed. (1968); Sellers, R. V., *The Council of Chalcedon* (1953).

Leo III, Pope

Saint Leo III was pope from 795 until his death in 816. He crowned the Frankish ruler CHARLEMAGNE emperor on Christmas Day, 800, an event of primary importance in Western history. The coronation had the dual effect of strengthening papal authority and creating in the West a ruler with status and prestige equal to that of the Byzantine emperor in the East. As pope, Leo first had to strengthen his position in Rome, which he did with Charlemagne's aid. The emperor also helped him defeat the Adoptionist heresy in Spain. In the controversy between the Eastern and Western churches over the doctrine of the procession of the Holy Spirit, Leo, while regarding the *Filioque* as dogmatically correct, refused Charlemagne's request to include it in the Nicene Creed (see CREED). During his pontificate Leo also renovated and beautified the churches in Rome. He was canonized in 1673. Feast day: June 12.

Leo IX, Pope

Leo IX, b. June 21, 1002, d. Apr. 19, 1054, was pope from 1048 to 1054. He was an Alsatian named Bruno of Egisheim. After he was elected pope, Leo insisted on confirmation of the election by the people and clergy of Rome. He sponsored an extensive reform program, in which he was assisted by Hildebrand (later GREGORY VII), the statesman and reformer Humbert of Silva Candida, and Saint PETER DAMIAN. During his pontificate, decrees were issued against simony, clerical marriage, and other abuses. In his campaign to enforce papal rights in southern Italy, however, Leo was defeated by the

Normans at Civitate in 1053 and was taken prisoner for nine months. In 1054, Humbert, whom Leo had sent as legate to Constantinople, precipitated the final schism between the Eastern and Western churches by excommunicating the Patriarch MICHAEL CERULARIUS. Feast day: Apr. 19.

Leo X, Pope

Pope Leo X, b. Dec. 11, 1475, d. Dec. 1, 1521, was pope from 1513 to 1521. The second son of Lorenzo de'Medici, he was called Giovanni and made a cardinal in his boyhood. He became head of his family before he was 30. Although he was a pious man, Leo's mild disposition and his concern for the advancement of the Medicis made him, in fact, an ineffectual pope. A patron of Raphael, he continued great artistic projects begun by his predecessor, JULIUS II, but initiated little new work. Leo presided at the Fifth Lateran Council (see LATERAN COUNCILS), but it failed in its efforts to reform the church. Perhaps Leo's most famous act was his excommunication of Martin LUTHER on Jan. 3, 1521.

JOHN W. O'MALLEY

Bibliography: Chamberlin, Eric R., *The Bad Popes* (1969); Gontard, Friedrich, *The Popes,* trans. by A. J. and E. P. Peeler (1964); Vaughan, Herbert M., *The Medici Popes* (1908; repr. 1971).

Leo XIII, Pope

Leo XIII, the former Cardinal Pecci, was elected to the papacy in 1878, succeeding Pius IX. Leo XIII is remembered for such diverse achievements as opening the Vatican archives to scholars, supporting social reform legislation in various nations, and encouraging the growth of the Catholic education system around the world.

Leo XIII, b. Mar. 2, 1810, d. July 20, 1903, was pope from 1878 to 1903. Born to a minor noble family at Carpineto, he was named Gioacchino Vincenzo Pecci. After his ordination in 1837, he entered the administrative service of the papacy and was appointed governor of Benevento (1838), governor of Perugia (1841), and nuncio to Brussels (1843). On diplomatic missions to other European cities, he gained a firsthand knowledge of modern social questions, an awareness that later characterized his pontificate. His years of diplomatic experience had given him a certain flexibility; he realized that the papacy would have to resolve its feud with Italy, which had seized Rome from PIUS IX in 1870. In February 1878 the cardinals elected as pope this frail, brilliant, hard worker to set a new policy for the church.

Leo XIII reversed much of the conservative political policy of Pius IX. He restored good relations with Germany by ending the KULTURKAMPF stalemate; improved relations with Great Britain, Russia, and Japan; and established (1892) an apostolic delegation in Washington, D.C. His policy failed, however, in Italy. Italy refused to restore papal sovereignty over Rome, and Leo maintained the increasingly useless posture of "prisoner of the Vatican." He also failed to persuade French Roman Catholic leaders to support the Third Republic; his last years saw increasingly anti-Catholic French legislation.

The pontificate of Leo XIII was especially important for the leadership he gave on social questions. His most famous encyclical was *Rerum Novarum* (May 15, 1891), on the condition of workers in the modern world. The document outlined the duties of both employers and workers, upholding the principles of collective bargaining, just wages, and private property. Leo also took an interest in education and opened the Vatican archives to all scholars. His pontificate was marked by an openness to scientific progress and concern for reconciling the church with the modern world.

J. DEAN O'DONNELL, JR.

Bibliography: Burton, Katherine, *Leo the Thirteenth, the First Modern Pope* (1962); Gargan, Edward T., ed., *Leo XIII and the Modern World* (1961); Jemolo, Arturo Carlo, *Church and State in Italy, 1850–1950,* trans. by David Moore (1960); Wallace, Lillian P., *Leo XIII and the Rise of Socialism* (1966).

León (Mexico) [lay-ohn']

León is the largest city in Guanajuato state in central Mexico. The city lies on the plain of the Gómez River about 50 km (30 mi) northwest of the city of Guanajuato, at an altitude of 1,884 m (6,182 ft). With 655,809 inhabitants (1980), it is the population center of the fertile Bajío region. León is primarily known for its shoe industry, as well as for leatherwork and silver-decorated saddles produced by local artisans.

León (Nicaragua)

León is the capital of León department in northwestern Nicaragua. The country's second largest city, with a population of 92,764 (1981 est.), it is an important commercial and agricultural center as well as the intellectual heart of Nicaragua, with a university (1812) and several museums and libraries. Rubén Darío, the famous poet, lived and studied in León and is buried in the city's cathedral. Until 1857, León served as the capital of Nicaragua.

León (Spanish city)

León is the capital of León province in northwestern Spain, at the confluence of the Bernesga and Torio rivers. The city's population is 131,134 (1981). Local industries include leather and brandy production, as well as lumbering, iron mining, and tourism. León is noted for its 13th-century Gothic cathedral with its 230 stained-glass windows, and the 11th-century Romanesque Church of San Isidoro.

León (Spanish region)

León, a region in northwestern Spain, comprises the provinces of León, Salamanca, and Zamora. The region covers 38,363 km² (14,812 mi²) and has a population of 1,110,397 (1981). The climate is dry, with hot summers and cold winters; much of the area consists of arid plateaus, but the periphery of the region has the well-watered Cantabrian Mountains. León's major rivers are the DOURO and Miño. Principal crops include cereals, flax, peas, and hops. Cattle and sheep (especially merino) are raised. Coal and iron mining and textile manufacturing complement the economy. The principal cities are León, SALAMANCA, Zamora, and Astorga.

In 217 BC, HANNIBAL captured the region for Carthage, and in the late 2d century BC most of the region was incorporated into the Roman province of LUSITANIA. In the early 8th century AD, León was conquered by the Moors. During the 9th century, Christians uniting to push the Moors out of Spain established their headquarters in León. Under King Ferdinand I of Castile, León and Castile were joined; this union lasted, with brief interruptions, from 1035 to 1157. During this period the powerful kingdom greatly expanded its holdings, and the Cortes, a parliament of local nobles, was established. In 1217, when FERDINAND III ascended to the throne, León was finally merged into Castile.

Leonard, Elmore

A writer of Westerns and thrillers, Elmore Leonard, b. New Orleans, La., Oct. 11, 1925, won literary fame in the 1980s, after three decades of modest commercial success with more than 20 novels and a substantial body of short stories and screenplays. His work is now compared to Hemingway's for the authenticity of its dialogue; his characters—usually, men living at the margins of society—have an uncanny authenticity of their own. *Hombre* (1961; film, 1967) is his most famous Western. His hard-boiled suspense thrillers include *Cat Chaser* (1982), *Stick* (1983), and *Glitz* (1985).

Leonardo da Vinci [lay-oh-nar'-doh dah vin'-chee]

The life and work of the great Italian Renaissance artist and scientist Leonardo da Vinci have proved endlessly fascinating for later generations. What most impresses people today, perhaps, is the immense scope of his achievement. In the past, however, he was admired chiefly for his art and art theory. Leonardo's equally impressive contribution to science is a modern rediscovery, having been preserved in a vast quantity of notes that became widely known only in the 20th century.

LIFE

Leonardo was born on Apr. 15, 1452, near the town of Vinci, not far from Florence. He was the illegitimate son of a Florentine notary, Piero da Vinci, and a young woman named Caterina. His artistic talent must have revealed itself early, for he was soon apprenticed (c.1469) to Andrea VERROCCHIO, a leading Renaissance master. In this versatile Florentine workshop, where he remained until at least 1476, Leonardo acquired a variety of skills. He entered the painters' guild in 1472, and his earliest extant works date from this time. In 1478 he was commissioned to paint an altarpiece for the Palazzo Vecchio in Florence. Three years later he undertook to paint the *Adoration of the Magi* for the monastery of San Donato a Scopeto. This project was interrupted when Leonardo left Florence for Milan about 1482. Leonardo worked for Duke Lodovico Sforza in Milan for nearly 18 years. Although active as court artist, painting portraits, designing festivals, and projecting a colossal equestrian monument in sculpture to the duke's father, Leonardo also became deeply interested in nonartistic matters during this period. He applied his growing knowledge of mechanics to his duties as a civil and military engineer; in addition, he took up scientific fields as diverse as anatomy, biology, mathematics, and physics. These activities, however, did not prevent him from completing his single most important painting, *The Last Supper.*

With the fall (1499) of his patron to the French, Leonardo left Milan to seek employment elsewhere: he went first to Mantua and Venice, but by April 1500 he was back in Florence. His stay there was interrupted by time spent working in central Italy as a mapmaker and military engineer for Cesare Borgia. Again in Florence in 1503, Leonardo undertook several highly significant artistic projects, including the *Battle of Anghiari* mural for the council chamber of the Town Hall, the portrait of Mona Lisa, and the lost *Leda and the Swan.* At the same time his scientific interests deepened: his concern with anatomy led him to perform dissections, and he undertook a systematic study of the flight of birds.

Leonardo returned to Milan in June 1506, called there to work for the new French government. Except for a brief stay in Florence (1507–08), he remained in Milan for 7 years. The artistic project on which he focused at this time was the equestrian monument to Gian Giacomo Trivulzio, which, like the Sforza monument earlier, was never completed. Meanwhile, Leonardo's scientific research began to dominate his other activities, so much so that his artistic gifts were directed toward scientific illustration; through drawing, he sought to convey his understanding of the structure of things. In 1513 he accompanied Pope Leo X's brother, Giuliano de'Medici, to Rome, where he stayed for 3 years, increasingly absorbed in theoretical research. In 1516–17, Leonardo left Italy forever to become architectural advisor to King Francis I of France, who greatly admired him. Leonardo died at the age of 67 on May 2, 1519, at Cloux, near Amboise, France.

ARTISTIC ACHIEVEMENTS

Early Work in Florence. The famous angel contributed by Leonardo to Verrocchio's *Baptism of Christ* (c.1475; Uffizi, Florence) was the young artist's first documented painting.

Other examples of Leonardo's activity in Verrocchio's workshop are the *Annunciation* (*c.*1473; Uffizi); the beautiful portrait *Ginevra Benci* (*c.*1474; National Gallery, Washington, D.C.); and the *Madonna with a Carnation* (*c.*1475; Alte Pinakothek, Munich). Although these paintings are rather traditional, they include details, such as the curling hair of Ginevra, that could have been conceived and painted only by Leonardo.

Other, slightly later works, such as the so-called *Benois Madonna* (*c.*1478–80; The Hermitage, Leningrad) and the unfinished *Saint Jerome* (*c.*1480; Vatican Gallery), already show two hallmarks of Leonardo's mature style: *contrapposto,* or twisting movement; and CHIAROSCURO, or emphatic modeling in light and shade. The unfinished *Adoration of the Magi* (1481–82; Uffizi) is the most important of all the early paintings. In it, Leonardo displays for the first time his method of organizing figures into a pyramid shape, so that interest is focused on the principal subject—in this case, the child held by his mother and adored by the three kings and their retinue.

Work in Milan. In 1483, soon after he arrived in Milan, Leonardo was asked to paint the *Madonna of the Rocks.* This altarpiece exists in two nearly identical versions, one (1483–85), entirely by Leonardo, in the Louvre, Paris, and the other (begun 1490s; finished 1506–08) in the National Gallery, London. Both versions depict a supposed meeting of the Christ Child and the infant Saint John. The figures, again grouped in a pyramid, are glimpsed in a dimly lit grotto setting of rocks and water that gives the work its name. Not long afterward, Leo-

(Above) *This drawing, a self-portrait of Leonardo as an elderly sage, was executed about 1512. The penetrating realism of the work testifies to the intensity of Leonardo's interest in the appearance and function of natural forms.* (Royal Library, Turin.)

(Left) Madonna of the Rocks *(begun 1490s; finished 1506–08) is a delicately sensuous, poetic vision of the infant John the Baptist adoring the infant Christ in the presence of the Virgin Mary and an angel. The work exemplifies Leonardo's technique of chiaroscuro, a method of painting in which three-dimensional modeling is achieved by means of light and shadow, creating a new unity between figures and their setting.* (National Gallery, London.)

nardo painted a portrait of Duke Lodovico's favorite, Cecilia Gallerani, probably the charming *Lady with the Ermine* (*c.*1485–90; Czartoryski Gallery, Krakow, Poland). Another portrait dating from this time is the unidentified *Musician* (*c.*1490; Pinacoteca Ambrosiana, Milan). In the great *The Last Supper* (42×910 cm/13 ft 10 in×29 ft 7½ in), completed in 1495–98 for the refectory of the ducal church of Santa Maria delle Grazie in Milan, Leonardo portrayed the apostles' reactions to Christ's startling announcement that one of them would betray him. Unfortunately, Leonardo experimented with a new fresco technique that was to show signs of decay as early as 1517. After repeated attempts at restoration, the mural survives only as an impressive ruin.

Late Work in Florence. When he returned to Florence in 1500, Leonardo took up the theme of the Madonna and Child with Saint Anne. He had already produced a splendid full-scale preparatory drawing (*c.*1498; National Gallery, London); he now treated the subject in a painting (begun *c.*1501; Louvre). We know from Leonardo's recently discovered Madrid notebooks that he began to execute the ferocious *Battle of Anghiari* for the Great Hall of the Palazzo Vecchio in Florence on June 6, 1505. As a result of faulty technique the mural deteriorated almost at once, and Leonardo abandoned it; knowledge of this work comes from Leonardo's preparatory sketches and from several copies. The mysterious, evocative portrait *Mona Lisa* (begun 1503; Louvre), probably the most famous painting in the world, dates from this period, as does *Saint John the Baptist* (begun *c.*1503–05; Louvre).

Leonardo da Vinci's La Gioconda (c.1503–05), or Mona Lisa, the name by which it is best known, is probably the most famous of all paintings. The mysterious smile of this fashionable Florentine lady has never failed to puzzle and fascinate. (Louvre, Paris.)

SCIENTIFIC INVESTIGATIONS

Written in a peculiar right-to-left script, Leonardo's manuscripts can be read with a mirror. The already vast corpus was significantly increased when two previously unknown notebooks were found in Madrid in 1965. From them we learn, among much else, how Leonardo planned to cast the Sforza monument.

The majority of Leonardo's technical notes and sketches make up the *Codex Atlanticus* in the Ambrosian Library in Milan. At an early date they were separated from the artistic drawings, some 600 of which belong to the British Royal Collection at Windsor Castle.

The manuscripts reveal that Leonardo explored virtually every field of science. They not only contain solutions to practical problems of the day—the grinding of lenses, for instance, and the construction of canals and fortifications—but they also envision such future possibilities as flying machines and automation.

Leonardo's observations and experiments into the workings of nature include the stratification of rocks, the flow of water, the growth of plants, and the action of light. The mechanical devices that he sketched and described were also concerned with the transmission of energy. Leonardo's solitary investigations took him from surface to structure, from catching the exact appearance of things in nature to visually analyzing how they function.

Leonardo's art and science are not separate, then, as was once believed, but belong to the same lifelong pursuit of knowledge. His paintings, drawings, and manuscripts show that he was the foremost creative mind of his time.

DAVID BROWN

Bibliography: Clark, Kenneth, *Leonardo da Vinci*, rev. ed. (1959); Cooper, Margaret, *The Inventions of Leonardo Da Vinci* (1968); Goldscheider, Ludwig, *Leonardo da Vinci* (1959); Gould, Cecil, *Leonardo: The Artist and the Non-Artist* (1975); Heydenreich, Ludwig H., *Leonardo da Vinci*, 2 vols. (1954), and *Leonardo: The Last Supper*, ed. by John Fleming and Hugh Honour (1974); Pater, Walter, *Leonardo Da Vinci* (1971); Payne, Robert, *Leonardo* (1978); Pedretti, Carlo, *Leonardo: A Study in Chronology and Style* (1973); Popham, A. E., *The Drawings of Leonardo da Vinci* (1945); Reti, Ladislao, ed., *The Unknown Leonardo*, trans. by Alan Morgan (1974); Richter, Jean P., *The Literary Works of Leonardo da Vinci*, 2 vols., 3d ed. (1970); Rosci, Marco, *The Hidden Leonardo* (1977); Wallace, Robert, *The World of Leonardo* (1966); Wasserman, Jack, *Leonardo da Vinci* (1975).

See also: ART; ITALIAN ART AND ARCHITECTURE; PAINTING; RENAISSANCE ART AND ARCHITECTURE.

Leonardo Pisano   [lay-oh-nar'-doh pee-zah'-noh]

Leonardo Pisano, b. *c.*1170, d. after 1240, also known as Leonardo of Pisa or Leonardo Fibonacci, was the first great mathematician of medieval Christian Europe. He played an important role in reviving ancient mathematics and made significant contributions of his own. *Liber abbaci* (Book of the Abacus, 1202), his treatise on arithmetic and elementary algebra, introduced the modern Hindu-Arabic system of numerals using ten symbols. His most important original work is in indeterminate analysis and number theory. The FIBONACCI SEQUENCE is named for him. *Mis practica geometriae* (Practice of Geometry, 1220) gave a compilation of the geometry of the time and also introduced some trigonometry.

JANICE A. HENDERSON

Bibliography: Gies, Joseph and Frances, *Leonardo of Pisa and the New Mathematics of the Middle Ages* (1969).

Leoncavallo, Ruggero   [lay-ohn-kah-vahl'-loh, rood-jay'-roh]

Ruggero Leoncavallo, b. Mar. 8, 1858, d. Aug. 9, 1919, is known today for a single work, *I Pagliacci*, one of the masterpieces of Italian VERISMO opera. After studying music and literature (preparing him to write both the music and librettos for his operas), he traveled for several years, earning his living as a café pianist, composer of light music, and music teacher. In an effort to adapt Wagner's epical German manner to Italian opera, he composed the trilogy *Crepusculum*, depicting major figures of the Italian Renaissance. Unable to obtain either publication or performance for this work, and noting the success of Mascagni's short *verismo* opera *Cavalleria Rusticana* (1890), Leoncavallo composed a comparable work, *I Pagliacci* (1892). This work achieved immediate and lasting success. Of his 18 other operas, *La Bohème* (1897) and *Zazà* (1900) were received favorably when first presented, but are no longer staged.

Leoni   (family)   [lay-ohn'-ee]

Leone Leoni and his son, Pompeo, were Italian Mannerist sculptors renowned for their work in bronze. **Leone Leoni,** b. 1509, d. July 22, 1590, a medalist and engraver, was principal engraver at the Papal mint in Rome (1538–40) and later became master of the imperial mint in Milan, a dependency of the Habsburg emperor Charles V. Leone visited the imperial courts in Brussels (1548–49, 1556) and Augsburg (1551), where he received commissions for portraits of members of the Habsburg family. He also executed (c.1579) 27 statues for the high altar of the Escorial Palace in Madrid. These statues were begun in Milan and completed in Madrid by his son, **Pompeo,** b. c.1583, d. Oct. 13, 1608, whose work also includes a marble statue of Isabella of Portugal (1572; Prado, Madrid) and monumental bronze groups of Charles V and Philip II with their families (in the Escorial Palace).   ROSA MARIA LETTS

Leonidas, King of Sparta   [lee-ahn'-ih-duhs]

Leonidas succeeded his half brother Cleomenes I as one of the two kings of Sparta about 488 BC. In 480, during the PERSIAN WARS, he led a small Greek army, including his royal guard of 300 Spartans, to hold the pass of THERMOPYLAE against the Persian army of XERXES I. All the Spartans, including Leonidas, were killed.

Leonids: SEE METEOR AND METEORITE.

Leonov, Aleksei   [lay-awn'-uhf, uhl-ek'-say]

The Soviet cosmonaut Aleksei Leonov, b. May 30, 1934, was the first man to walk in space. A jet pilot, he became a cosmonaut in 1960 and was the copilot of VOSKHOD 2, launched Mar. 18, 1965. During the flight he exited from the spacecraft and performed a space walk. Leonov was also commander of the Soviet part (July 15–21, 1975) of the APOLLO-SOYUZ TEST PROJECT, with flight engineer Valery Kubasov. Leonov has been called the "artist-cosmonaut" because of his paintings and caricatures.   JAMES OBERG

Leonov, Leonid Maksimovich   [lay-uhn-yeet' muhk-seem'-uh-vich]

Leonid Maksimovich Leonov, b. Moscow, 1899, is a leading Soviet novelist and playwright. He is among the few Soviet authors who favor the Dostoyevskian manner of writing—emphasis on psychological analysis, predilection for alienated protagonists, a flair for melodrama, and an atmosphere of mystery. These characteristics are particularly evident in Leonov's early works, such as *The Badgers* (1925; Eng. trans., 1947), in which the struggle between city and countryside is personified in two brothers, and *The Thief* (1927; Eng. trans., 1931), a story of a Communist officer turned criminal. *Invasion* (1942; Eng. trans., 1943), a play of World War II, features a social outcast whose patriotism outweighs his grievances against the Soviet regime. A similar theme may be found in *Evgenia Ivanovna* (1963), a novella.   MAURICE FRIEDBERG

Bibliography: Simmons, Ernest J., *Russian Fiction and Soviet Ideology* (1958); Struve, Gleb, *Soviet Russian Literature, 1917–1950* (1951).

Leontief, Wassily   [lee'-ahn-teef, vah-sil'-ee]

Wassily Leontief, b. Saint Petersburg (now Leningrad), Russia, Aug. 5 (N.S.), 1906, developed the INPUT-OUTPUT method of economic analysis. Used particularly in planned and develop-

Wassily Leontief, who is considered an American economist, emigrated in 1925 from the USSR at age 19. In 1973 he won a Nobel Prize for his influential work in economics. Today his "input-output" system of analysis, which explains how economic changes are dependent upon one another, is used in many countries for economic forecasting.

ing economies for determining the levels of resources necessary to produce according to a given plan, the theory won Leontief the 1973 Nobel Prize for economics.

A teacher of economics at Harvard University from 1931 to 1975, Leontief has been director of the Institute for Economic Analysis since 1978. His works include *Input-Output Economics* (1966) and the two-volume *Essays in Economics* (1976, 1978).

Bibliography: Silk, Leonard, *The Economists* (1976).

leopard   [lep'-urd]

The leopard, *Panthera pardus,* is one of the largest members of the cat family, Felidae. A large male may weigh more than 91 kg (200 lb), may stand 70 cm (28 in) high at the shoulders, and may be 1.5 m (nearly 5 ft) long, plus a 90-cm (35-in) tail. Leopards occupy a great diversity of habitats, including dry grasslands, scrubland, mountains, and jungles. They have the greatest geographic distribution of any wild cat, being found over most of Africa south of the Sahara and from the Middle East and India north into central Asia and south into the East Indies. The leopard's color varies from a pale yellowish gray to a yellowish red, with whitish underparts. Spots are present over the entire body, but on the back and sides they are formed into circles, or rosettes. Black leopards, or panthers, occur in the same litter with yellowish leopards.

Leopards are chiefly nocturnal and solitary, but a male and female commonly hunt as a pair during and for a time after the mating season. Usually two to four young are born after a gestation period of 90 to 105 days. Intensive hunting of leopards for their skins has eliminated or seriously reduced a number of subspecies or geographical races.

The snow leopard, or ounce, *Uncia uncia,* is similar in size and general appearance to the leopard. Its coat, however, has a dense woolly underfur and a long, thick outer coat. It is generally light yellowish gray to cream colored, with black to grayish rosettes on the upper parts of the body. Snow leopards are found in the highlands of central Asia from the Altai Mountains into the Himalayas. They inhabit rocky grasslands above the tree line. Breeding occurs in late winter, and usually two to four young are born after a gestation period of about 98 days. The snow leopard has become quite scarce mainly because of overhunting for its beautiful fur.

The clouded leopard, *Neofelis nebulosa,* weighs up to 23 kg (50 lb) and may be 80 cm (32 in) high at the shoulders and 1 m (40 in) long, plus a 90-cm (35-in) tail. It is grayish or yellowish to brownish yellow in color, with black spots and dashes on the head, legs, and tail and large black-bordered, "cloudlike" blotches on its sides. The blotches have pale centers and darker rear borders. Clouded leopards are forest inhabitants found from India to Taiwan south into Borneo. Gestation is about 90 days, with apparently two young to a litter.

The leopard, *P. pardus, is rarely seen, even by its prospective victims, because of its silent, wary habits. The black panther* (left) *is actually a leopard with black coat pigmentation.*

The clouded leopard, despite its rarity, is hunted for food, for its supposed medicinal properties (especially in China), and for its skin.   EDWIN E. ROSENBLUM

Bibliography: Edey, Maitland, ed., *Cats of Africa* (1968); Walker, Ernest, *Mammals of the World*, 2 vols., 4th ed. (1983).

leopard frog

The leopard frog, *R. pipiens, a North American frog, is distinguished by its light-bordered spots and pointed head.*

Leopard frogs, family Ranidae, are medium-sized frogs, 5 to 10 cm (2 to 4 in) in body length, with distinct spots on the back. Once thought to be a single species, *Rana pipiens*, the leopard-frog complex is now divided into at least six different but closely related species. As a group, leopard frogs are one of the most widely distributed amphibians in North America, ranging from Canada to Costa Rica. They are usually the frogs that are dissected in elementary biology courses. Leopard frogs were previously used in pregnancy tests; when the male is injected with urine from a pregnant woman, it causes the frog to extrude spermatozoa within about two hours.

JONATHAN CAMPBELL

Leopardi, Giacomo, Conte   [lay-oh-par'-dee, jah'-koh-moh, kohn'-tay]

Count Giacomo Leopardi, poet, philologist, and prose writer, b. Recanati, in the Marches, June 29, 1798, d. June 14, 1837, was 19th-century Italy's greatest lyric voice. Leopardi, when only 10, discovered his father's well-stocked library and set himself a regimen of voracious reading. By the age of 15, he had mastered ancient Greek, Latin, Hebrew, and several European languages. In 1816 he produced an amazingly scholarly history of astronomy. Although his intense work had caused

eye damage, he continued his literary studies and activities and in 1819 began writing the lyrics (*Canti*; Eng. trans., 1949) on which his reputation primarily rests. Love, sorrow, boredom, futility, patriotism, and the dire necessity for all men to be brothers, so as to survive the pain of living and the brutality of nature, are the major themes of his poetry.

At the age of 24 he left home and spent several months in Milan, Bologna, Rome, and (later on) Naples. Disappointed by what he saw, he returned to Recanati to write his poetry as well as his major prose work, the *Essays, Dialogues, and Thoughts* (1824–32; Eng. trans., 1905), a series of dialogues and narratives whose main characters are mythological and historical figures.   SERGIO PACIFICI

Bibliography: Caserta, Ernesto, *Giacomo Leopardi* (1976); Origo, Iris, *Leopardi: A Study in Solitude*, 2d rev. ed. (1953); Whitfield, J. H., *Giacomo Leopardi* (1954).

Leopold, Aldo   [lee'-uh-pohld, al'-doh]

Naturalist Aldo Leopold, b. Burlington, Iowa, Jan. 11, 1886, d. Apr. 21, 1948, aroused the first great public interest in wilderness conservation. He believed that undisturbed wilderness is a valuable asset and felt that people should enjoy wilderness areas but disturb them as little as possible. Although Leopold received worldwide acclaim as an authority on wilderness conservation, he was also an expert on wildlife management; his textbook *Game Management* (1933) has become a classic in the field. Leopold also wrote a number of essays on conservation, published in *A Sand County Almanac* (1949) and *Round River* (1953).

Bibliography: Flader, Susan L., *Thinking Like a Mountain: Aldo Leopold and the Evolution of an Ecological Attitude toward Deer, Wolves and Forests* (1969); Schoenfeld, C., "Aldo Leopold Remembered," *Audubon*, May 1978.

Leopold I, King of the Belgians

Leopold I, b. Dec. 16, 1790, d. Dec. 10, 1865, became the first king of the Belgians after Belgium had asserted its independence of the Netherlands in 1830. The youngest son of Duke Francis Frederick of Saxony-Coburg-Saalfeld, Leopold became a British subject when he married Charlotte (1796–1817), the only child of the future GEORGE IV of England. In 1830 he rejected election as king of Greece, but the following year he accepted the crown offered by the Belgian National Congress.

Leopold repelled the Dutch attempts to reconquer the country and finally secured Dutch recognition of Belgian independence in 1839. He loyally observed the constitution, which gave basic political power to the parliament, and he encouraged collaboration among the political parties. Although he

Leopold I, a German prince and uncle of Queen Victoria of England, was elected as the first king of the Belgians in 1831, shortly after Belgium had declared its independence from the Netherlands. Leopold organized resistance to Dutch efforts to recover control and maintained a policy of neutrality in disputes among the major powers of Europe.

Leopold III, king of the Belgians, was forced to abdicate because of the controversy concerning his conduct during World War II. When the Germans invaded Belgium in May 1940, Leopold declined to follow his government into exile and, as commander in chief, surrendered unconditionally to the Germans after 18 days.

After the Allied invasion in June 1944, Leopold was taken to Germany. He was liberated by American troops in Austria in May 1945. Much bitter opposition to his return existed in Belgium because of his wartime conduct. When finally the Catholic People's party obtained a majority in his favor in a referendum in 1950, he went home. He met such fierce hostility, however, manifested in strikes and other protests, that he abdicated on July 16, 1951, in favor of his son BAUDOUIN.

HERBERT H. ROWEN

Bibliography: Arango, Ergasto R., *Leopold III and the Belgian Royal Question* (1963); Page, James, *Leopold III: The Belgian Royal Question* (1961).

Leopold I, Holy Roman Emperor

Leopold I, b. June 9, 1640, d. May 5, 1705, was the second son of the Holy Roman Emperor FERDINAND III. Not until the sudden death of his older brother, Ferdinand, in 1654 did Leopold fall heir to the Austrian Habsburg titles and lands. He was elected king of Hungary (1655) and king of Bohemia (1656) and succeeded his father as emperor in 1658.

Leopold devoted his 47-year reign to consolidating his diverse family possessions in Austria, Hungary, and Bohemia. His persistent efforts to strengthen the centralized authority of the Vienna court and to extend Counter-Reformation Catholicism throughout his domains provoked vigorous opposition from his Hungarian subjects, who periodically rebelled.

Elsewhere in Europe the peace-loving Leopold confronted the expansionist policies of the French king LOUIS XIV and the revived power of the OTTOMAN EMPIRE in the Balkan peninsula. Following the unsuccessful Ottoman siege of Vienna in 1683, Leopold's generals won a series of victories over the Turks, culminating in EUGENE OF SAVOY's triumph at Zenta in 1697. By the Treaty of Karlowitz (1699) most of Hungary was recovered from the Turks. Leopold joined (1686) the defensive League of Augsburg (see AUGSBURG, LEAGUE OF) against France. Though preoccupied with the Turkish campaigns during the War of the GRAND ALLIANCE (1688–97), the imperial forces played a central role in the War of the SPANISH SUCCESSION (1701–13), which ensued from the conflicting Austrian Habsburg and French Bourbon claims to the Spanish throne. Leopold left to his son JOSEPH I not only this war but also an expanded Austrian monarchy.

JOHN A. MEARS

Bibliography: Kann, Robert A., *A History of the Habsburg Empire, 1526–1918* (1974); Spielman, John P., *Leopold I of Austria* (1977).

Leopold II, Holy Roman Emperor

Leopold II, Holy Roman emperor from 1790 to 1792, was a ruler of vision and political skill who saved the HABSBURG monarchy from revolution and initiated war with revolutionary France. The third son of Emperor FRANCIS I and MARIA THERESA, he was born on May 5, 1747, and brought up in Tuscany, succeeding his father as grand duke there in 1765. Influenced by the philosophical ENLIGHTENMENT, he reorganized Tuscan government, equalized taxes, abolished torture, and even drafted a constitution, based on American models, to encourage citizen participation. When opposition developed, however, he withdrew the plan.

married (1832) a daughter of Louis-Philippe of France, Leopold supported a policy of neutrality for Belgium. He was instrumental in arranging the marriage (1840) of his niece, Queen Victoria of England, to Albert of Saxe-Coburg-Gotha. His own daughter, Carlota, married (1857) Maximilian, the future emperor of Mexico.

HERBERT H. ROWEN

Bibliography: Richardson, Joanna, *My Dearest Uncle: A Life of Leopold I, King of the Belgians* (1961).

Leopold II, King of the Belgians

Leopold II, b. Apr. 9, 1835, d. Dec. 17, 1909, succeeded his father, Leopold I, to the Belgian throne in 1865. A constitutional, if strong-willed, monarch in Belgium, he ruled the Congo Free State (now ZAIRE) as a personal domain.

Interested in economic and colonial expansion from his youth, Leopold sponsored Sir Henry STANLEY's 1879–84 expedition to the Congo, and in 1885 he won recognition from the United States and the European powers as personal sovereign of the Congo Free State. Reports of outrageous exploitation and mistreatment of the native population, especially in the rubber industry, led to an international protest movement in the early 1900s. Finally, in 1908, the Belgian parliament compelled the king to cede the Congo Free State to Belgium. In domestic politics Leopold emphasized military defense as the basis of Belgian neutrality, but he was unable to obtain a universal conscription law until on his deathbed. He was succeeded by his nephew ALBERT I.

HERBERT H. ROWEN

Bibliography: Ascherson, Neal, *The King Incorporated: Leopold II in the Age of Trusts* (1964); Collins, Robert O., *King Leopold, England, and the Upper Nile, 1899–1909* (1968); Slade, Ruth, *King Leopold's Congo* (1962).

Leopold III, King of the Belgians

Leopold III, b. Nov. 3, 1901, d. Sept. 25, 1983, succeeded his father, ALBERT I, to the Belgian throne in 1934. A strong-willed monarch, he refused to go into exile after the German conquest of Belgium in 1940 and became the target of criticism so bitter that he abdicated in 1951.

An advocate of a more independent foreign policy for Belgium before World War II, Leopold twice urged mediation of the conflict between Nazi Germany and the Western Allies in the months immediately before and after the outbreak of war in 1939. After the German invasion in May 1940, he took command of the army and led its resistance for 2 weeks before surrendering. He rejected the government's appeal to join them in a government-in-exile and stayed in Belgium as a self-proclaimed prisoner of war in his castle at Laken.

Such flexibility was significant, for when he succeeded his brother JOSEPH II as emperor and ruler of the Habsburg lands in 1790, Leopold found the Austrian Netherlands and Hungary in rebellion, the imperial army tied down in a war with the Ottoman Turks, and the Prussians mobilized to exploit his troubles. Recognizing that Joseph's centralizing reforms had gone too far, the new emperor judiciously combined concession and force to restore order. In foreign affairs he thwarted Prussia by terminating (1791) the Turkish war and then enlisted Prussian aid in warning revolutionary France not to harm King Louis XVI and MARIE ANTOINETTE, Leopold's sister. The warning was embodied in the joint Declaration of Pillnitz (August 1791), which, though mild, was exploited in France to inflame relations. A month after Leopold's death, on Mar. 1, 1792, France declared war.   ENNO E. KRAEHE

Bibliography: Kann, Robert A., *A History of the Habsburg Empire, 1526–1918* (1974); Wangermann, Ernst, *From Joseph II to the Jacobin Trials* (1969).

Leopold II, Lake: see MAI-NDOMBE, LAKE.

Léopoldville: see KINSHASA.

Lepanto, Battle of   [lih-pant'-oh]

The naval Battle of Lepanto, fought off the coast of Greece on Oct. 7, 1571, was the first major defeat of the Ottoman Turks by the Christian states of western Europe. The allied fleet of Spain, Venice, and the papacy was commanded by Don JOHN OF AUSTRIA.

Bibliography: Beeching, Jack, *The Galleys at Lepanto* (1983).

lepidolite: see MICA.

Lepidoptera: see BUTTERFLIES AND MOTHS.

Lepidus, Marcus Aemilius   [lep'-ih-duhs]

Marcus Aemilius Lepidus was the name of several notable figures in Roman history. The first, d. 152 BC, who held the offices of consul (187, 175), triumvir (183), and censor (179), founded several cities and instituted a notable building program. His descendant Marcus Aemilius Lepidus, d. 77 BC, was consul in 78 but the following year led an army against Quintus Lutatius CATULUS, who, with Pompey's help, defeated him. His son, Marcus Aemilius Lepidus, d. 13 BC, was consul with Julius CAESAR in 46. He was a member of the Second TRIUMVIRATE with Mark ANTONY and Octavian (later AUGUSTUS) and, after the Battle of Philippi (42), governed Africa. In 36 BC he laid claim to Sicily, but Octavian forced him to retire.

leprechaun: see FAIRY.

leprosy   [lep'-ruh-see]

Leprosy, a chronic infectious disease known for many centuries, affects an estimated 12 to 20 million people worldwide. It occurs mainly in tropical, subtropical, and temperate regions of Southeast Asia, Africa, and South America; of the approximately 2,000 persons in the United States who have leprosy, most came from these regions. The only long-term treatment center for leprosy in the United States is the Public Health Service Hospital in Carville, La.

Cause. Once a disease so dreaded that its victims were isolated in so-called leper colonies, leprosy can now be controlled and its resulting disfigurements prevented. The infectious agent, *Mycobacterium leprae*, is a bacillus in the same family as the one that causes tuberculosis. (It was discovered in 1874 by a Norwegian physician, Gerhard Hansen, and leprosy is sometimes called Hansen's disease.) The agent is transmitted by skin-to-skin contact and nasal discharges. About 95 percent of the persons exposed to the bacterium are immune, however, so leprosy is not considered highly contagious. Because the bacterium is very slow growing, the incubation pe-

riod can range from 1 to 30 years, but the average is about 3 to 5 years. The organism invades the peripheral nerves, skin, and mucous membranes, damaging the nerves and causing anesthesia. The resulting insensitivity can lead to unnoticed and therefore neglected injuries; this accounts for many of the deformities—such as loss of fingers—that occur in leprosy. Paralysis may also result; in advanced cases, numbness of the eyes may lead to blindness through trauma or infection.

Forms of Leprosy. Two main forms of the disease are known: tuberculoid and lepromatous. The tuberculoid form mainly involves the skin and nerves. Plaques—such as a red, raised rim surrounding a pale, flat center—occur most often on the arms and legs. Nerves under the plaques are damaged, and the areas become numb; contraction and wasting of muscles often occur. The lepromatous form is a more generalized infection that involves skin, mouth, nasal passages, upper respiratory tract, eyes, nerves, adrenal glands, and testicles. Various skin eruptions may cover the entire body, but numbness is more patchy and less severe than in tuberculoid leprosy. In advanced stages, however, lepromatous leprosy can cause ulcers, eyebrow loss, collapse of the nose, enlarged earlobes and facial features, and blindness.

Treatment. The drugs now available for treating leprosy can prevent the disfigurement and disability once associated with the disease. The main drug used is dapsone, usually given with other bactericidal drugs because some patients become resistant to its effects. Clofazimine, approved for U.S. use in 1987 against lepromatous leprosy, is also usually given in combination with other drugs. By the mid-1980s, scientists had developed cloning techniques to produce in quantity some of the antigens to the disease, for the potential development of a leprosy vaccine. Another vaccine, produced by older means, was already undergoing clinical trials by that time.
WILLIAM A. CHECK

Bibliography: Hastings, R. C., ed., *Leprosy* (1986); Jopling, W. H., *Handbook of Leprosy*, 3d ed. (1984); Seghal, V. N., *Clinical Leprosy* (1980); Wulff, Robert, *Village of Outcasts* (1968).

Leptis Magna   [lep'-tis mag'-nuh]

The well-preserved remains of the ancient Roman port city of Leptis Magna are situated on the coast of Libya 120 km (75 mi) east of modern Tripoli. The site of a small natural harbor, it was first settled in the 6th century BC by Phoenician traders. The settlement grew rapidly after its absorption by the Roman province of Africa in 46 BC and, with the expansion of sea trade under the empire, gained regional importance.

During large-scale building projects in the 1st century AD at Leptis a series of street grids were organized around two avenues, and a forum, basilica, market building, amphitheater (the largest in Africa), and several triumphal arches were erected. Hadrian added huge public baths and Marcus Aurelius built a four-faced triumphal arch, but Septimius Severus (r. 193–211), a native of Leptis, was responsible for the city's major period of building. Among the public works he underwrote were cisterns, aqueducts, a new forum and basilica, a colonnaded street 366 m (1,200 ft) long, another four-sided arch, and a vast harbor complex protected by artificial breakwaters. Raids on Leptis by nomadic tribes from the interior and the gradual silting up of the harbor brought about its decline in the late 3d to 4th centuries.   JOHN P. OLESON

Bibliography: Bandinelli, B. R., et al., *The Buried City*, trans. by David Ridgeway (1966); Haynes, D. E. L., *An Archaeological and Historical Guide to the Pre-Islamic Antiquities of Tripolitania* (1956).

lepton   [lep'-tahn]

A lepton is a class of FUNDAMENTAL PARTICLES that includes electrons, neutrinos, muons, and their antiparticles. The name is derived from a Greek word meaning light weight, although leptons are best characterized by their atomic interactions. The behavior of leptons is governed by the so-called weak interaction, and they are not affected by the strong interaction (see FUNDAMENTAL INTERACTIONS).

Bibliography: Duff, B. G., *Fundamental Particles* (1986).

leptospirosis   [lep-tuh-spy-roh'-sis]

Leptospirosis, or Weil's disease, is an acute fever caused by a spiral bacteria, *Leptospira* (see SPIROCHETE), communicated from animals to humans, commonly through skin contact with rat-infested water or sewage. It often takes a fatal form characterized by jaundice and bleeding. *Leptospira* may also cause MENINGITIS. Treatment is with penicillin.

Lermontov, Mikhail   [lair'-muhn-tuf]

One of Russia's greatest poets, Mikhail Yurievich Lermontov, b. Moscow, Oct. 3 (O.S.), 1814, was killed in a duel on July 15 (O.S.), 1841, at the age of 26. In his short life, however, he established himself as the foremost Russian romantic poet, a pioneer in prose, and an uncompromising opponent of the reactionary policies that followed the unsuccessful Decembrist uprising of 1825.

Well tutored at home, Lermontov spent a short time at Moscow University and 2 years (1832–34) at the School of Cavalry Cadets in Saint Petersburg. He then received his commission in the Life Guard Hussars at Tsarskoye Selo. He first attracted attention with "Death of a Poet" (1837), inspired by the death in a duel of Aleksandr Pushkin; the poem was an indictment of the court society that Lermontov blamed for the tragedy. This led to his exile to a regiment in the Caucasus, but his grandmother's influence made possible his return in 1838. In 1840 he was again exiled to the Caucasus for dueling, but he returned to Saint Petersburg in 1841. Exiled yet once more, he went to Pyatigorsk, where he was killed.

Among the many influences on Lermontov, that of Byron was the strongest; he was preoccupied with the disillusioned Byronic hero. Inveighing against the injustices of God's world and against society's callous hypocrisy, he let his heroes take out their frustrations by wreaking sadistic vengeance on others. This applies to his best-known narrative poem, *The Demon* (1841; Eng. trans., 1930), as well as his novel, *A Hero of Our Time* (1840; Eng. trans., 1886). The hero of the former, an angel exiled from paradise, joylessly sows evil on earth; though moved to love by the beautiful Tamara, he ends up destroying her. The novel is a remarkable piece of psychological realism. Lermontov's antidote to *Weltschmerz* was a cynical, satirical humor, but a greater solace was provided by his profound love of nature. His mature work, notably the *Song of the Merchant Kalashnikov* (1837), reveals his interest in folk poetry.   WALTER N. VICKERY

Bibliography: Garrard, John, *Mikhail Lermontov* (1982); Kelly, Laurence, *Lermontov: Tragedy in the Caucasus* (1977); Lermontov, M. Y., *The Demon and Other Poems,* trans. by Eugene M. Kayden (1965), *A Hero of Our Time,* trans. by V. and D. Nabokov (1958), and *A Lermontov Reader,* trans. and ed. by Guy Daniels (1967); Lavrin, Janko, *Lermontov* (1959); Mersereau, John, *Mikhail Lermontov* (1962).

Lerner, Alan Jay, and Loewe, Frederick   [loh]

Alan Jay Lerner, lyricist, b. New York City, Aug. 31, 1918, d. June 14, 1986, and Frederick Loewe, composer, b. Vienna, June 10, 1901, d. Feb. 14, 1988, created scores for many of the classic American musicals. Their supreme achievement was *My Fair Lady* (1956), a production based on George Bernard Shaw's *Pygmalion.* This popular work had a record-breaking run on Broadway and the London stage and was produced in many other countries. The pair's other classics are *Brigadoon* (1947), *Paint Your Wagon* (1951), *Camelot* (1960), and the Oscar-winning film *Gigi* (1958).   DAVID EWEN

Bibliography: Ewen, David, *Composers for the American Musical Theatre* (1968) and *American Songwriters* (1987); Lerner, Alan J., *The Street Where I Live* (1978); Suskin, Steven, *Show Tunes, 1905–1985* (1986).

Les Combarelles   [lay kohm-bah-rel']

Les Combarelles, a prehistoric cave site discovered (1901) near Les Eyzies in Dordogne, France, contains important examples of Ice Age cave art (see PREHISTORIC ART). The main gallery, a narrow, winding tunnel, contains an outstanding collection of engravings and, near the entrance, a few worn paintings. The animal engravings include not only the commonly depicted mammoth, bison, reindeer, horses, and ibex, but also cave lions, cave bears, and wolves. Several anthropomorphic figures, as well as masklike images, are also depicted. The site has been dated to the Middle MAGDALENIAN phase of the Paleolithic (*c.*13,000–10,000 BC).   LYA DAMS

Lesage, Alain René   [luh-sahzh', ah-lan' ruh-nay']

Alain René Lesage (or Le Sage), b. May 8, 1668, d. Nov. 17, 1747, was a French novelist and playwright whose popularization of the picaresque novel influenced Henry Fielding and Tobias Smollett. A professional writer, he authored or coauthored approximately 100 farces or comedies of manners for the popular fairground theaters of Paris. Many of these were adaptations of Spanish originals, but his *Turcaret* (1709; Eng. trans., 1933) was a genuine creation on his part; it satirized the crooked practices of the period's financiers. Lesage's masterpiece, however, is the picaresque novel *The Adventures of Gil Blas Santillana* (Eng. trans., 1781), which he published in installments from 1715 to 1735. It is a lively panorama of contemporary life and manners, and its characters are drawn with vigorous, earthy strokes.

Bibliography: Crocker, Lester G., *An Age of Crisis: Man and World in Eighteenth Century French Thought* (1963); Green, Frederick C., *French Novelists, Manners and Ideas,* rev. ed. (1964); Mylne, Vivienne, *The Eighteenth-Century French Novel,* 2d ed. (1981).

lesbianism

Lesbianism is HOMOSEXUALITY in women. The name refers to the island of Lesbos, where the poet SAPPHO—whose love lyrics are often addressed to women—lived most of her life.

Lesbos   [lez'-bahs]

Lesbos, a Greek island in the Aegean Sea less than 25 km (15 mi) from the Turkish coast, covers 1,630 km² (630 mi²) and has a population of 104,620 (1981). Lesbos is an island with hilly terrain reaching 968 m (3,176 ft). Olives, vines, grains, and fruits are grown in the valleys. Olive exporting and sardine fishing are important. Mytilene (1971 pop., 23,426) is the largest city.

Lesbos was the site of Early Bronze Age settlements, and during the 2d millennium BC it was settled by the Aeolians. By the 7th century BC the island was a notable cultural center, home of the poets SAPPHO and ALCAEUS. Lesbos was captured by the Persians in 527 BC but joined the Delian League after the Persian defeat in 479. During the Peloponnesian War the island revolted (428–427) unsuccessfully against Athens and later fell (405) to Sparta. It was later held successively by the Macedonians, Romans, Byzantines, Seljuks, Genoese, and Ottoman Turks. It became part of modern Greece in 1913.

Lescot, Pierre   [les-koh', pyair]

One of the major French architects of the 16th century, Pierre Lescot, b. *c.*1500–15, d. Sept. 10, 1578, achieved this status by virtue of his excellent understanding of Italian Renaissance styles. This ability enabled him to expel from French architecture the lingering traces of the Gothic style. His major work involved the first phase of the rebuilding of the old medieval palace of the LOUVRE. In the Cour Carrée, Lescot combined a French system of pavilions with an Italianate elevation of superimposed orders (western wing, 1546–51). The facades were enriched with delicate low-relief sculpture designed by Jean GOUJON. The Fontaine des Innocents (*c.*1550) in Paris is another of his surviving major works.   ROBERT M. NEUMAN

Lesotho   [luh-soh'-toh]

Lesotho is a small, landlocked country in southern Africa that is entirely surrounded by the Republic of South Africa. Until 1966, it was the British colony of Basutoland. With limited mineral and agricultural resources, little industry, and insufficient development capital, Lesotho is heavily dependent upon South Africa for manufactured goods, transportation links, and employment.

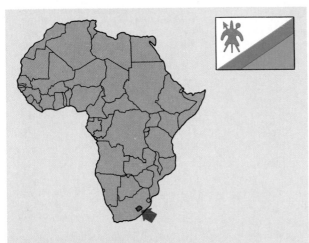

KINGDOM OF LESOTHO

LAND. Area: 30,355 km² (11,720 mi²). Capital and largest city: Maseru (1985 est. pop., 55,000).
PEOPLE. Population (1987 est.): 1,600,000; density (1987 est.): 52.7 persons per km² (136.5 per mi²). Distribution (1985): 6% urban, 94% rural. Annual growth (1986): 2.6%. Official languages: English, Sesotho. Major religions: Roman Catholicism, Protestantism, Anglicanism.
EDUCATION AND HEALTH. Literacy (1985): 60% of adult population. Universities (1986): 1. Hospital beds (1982): 2,300. Physicians (1982): 114. Life expectancy (1980–85): women—51.0; men—47.7. Infant mortality (1986): 106 per 1,000 live births.
ECONOMY. GNP (1985): $730 million; $470 per capita. Labor force (1984): subsistence agriculture—87%. Foreign trade (1983): imports—$450 million; exports—$30 million; principal trade partner—South Africa. Currency: 1 loti = 100 lisente.
GOVERNMENT. Type: limited monarchy. Legislature: National Assembly. Political subdivisions: 10 districts.
COMMUNICATIONS. Railroads (1986): 1.6 km (1 mi) total. Roads (1985): 4,221 km (2,623 mi) total. Major ports: none. Major airfields: 2.

A Basuto shepherd watches over his flock on the hilly terrain of Lesotho, a small African nation that is completely surrounded by South Africa. Because the nation has little industry and few natural resources, Lesotho's economy is heavily dependent upon livestock.

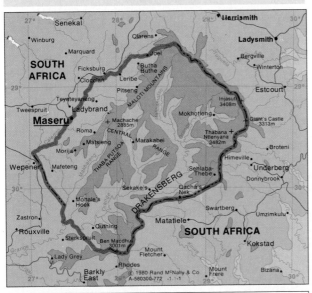

LESOTHO

——— Railroad

+ Spot Elevation

National capitals are underlined

City type size indicates relative importance

Scale 1:4,200,000

0 25 50 75 100 km

0   25   50   mi

Meters	Feet
4000	13124
2000	6562
1000	3281
500	1640

LAND AND PEOPLE

The eastern two-thirds of Lesotho are dominated by the rugged and sparsely populated DRAKENSBERG and Maloti ranges. They form a high plateau with an average elevation of almost 3,100 m (10,000 ft). The Orange (Senqu) and Tugela, two of southern Africa's most important rivers, rise near Thabana Ntlenyana (3,482 m/11,424 ft), Lesotho's highest mountain.

Western Lesotho is a narrow, lowland region at an average elevation of 1,700 m (5,500 ft). The area is densely populated, and most of the towns, including MASERU, the capital and largest town, are there. Temperatures throughout the country average 15° C (59° F) in January (the summer), and 3° C (37° F) in July (the winter). Average annual rainfall is 1,520 mm (60 in) in the east and 690 mm (27 in) in the west.

Lesotho is an ethnically homogeneous country. The Basuto tribal group constitutes more than 90% of the population. COLOUREDS, ZULUS, Tembus, and whites form small minorities. The white population consists primarily of missionaries, businessmen, and government advisors; they and other non-Basutos are prohibited from owning land. Both English and Sesotho are official languages. More than 70% of the people are Christian, mostly Roman Catholic and Lesotho Evangelist. The remainder of the population practices traditional animism.

All primary education in Lesotho is free, and about 67% of school-age children attend. Lesotho has one of the highest literacy rates in Africa. Very few students, however, advance beyond primary school. The National University of Lesotho is at Roma, near Maseru.

ECONOMIC ACTIVITY

Although only about 10% of Lesotho's land is suitable for agriculture, such activity provides about two-thirds of the domestic income, mostly in the form of subsistence farming. Maize (corn) is the leading crop, and wheat, sorghum, barley, and beans are important. Because agriculture suffers from severe soil erosion and poor farming practices, yields are low, and Lesotho must import food, primarily from South Africa. Cattle, ponies (used for transport), sheep, and goats are raised. Wool and mohair are the major agricultural exports.

The government is attempting to build up other sectors of the economy. The only major industries are light manufacturing (furniture, bricks, and cosmetics) and food processing (meat canning and beer brewing). Work on a giant water project began in 1988. Lesotho's beautiful, mountainous terrain has contributed to the growth of tourism. Because economic opportunities are scarce, about 140,000 Basutos, mostly men, leave Lesotho each year to work in South Africa.

HISTORY AND GOVERNMENT

Lesotho was sparsely populated by the SAN (Bushmen) until the late 16th century. During the 17th and 18th centuries refugees from tribal wars in the surrounding areas entered Lesotho. In the early 19th century, Paramount Chief MOSHESHWE, who ruled from about 1820 to 1870, welded the Basuto nation out of these diverse Bantu-speaking peoples. From 1858 to 1868 the Basuto were at war with the Boers. The latter won a large piece of Basuto land, and to prevent further loss, Mosheshwe requested British protection. Thus in 1868 the kingdom became a British protectorate. From 1884 to 1959 it was, like Botswana and Swaziland, a British High Commission territory. On Oct. 4, 1966, independence was granted.

Until 1970, Lesotho was a constitutional monarchy, with a hereditary king who appointed the prime minister and cabinet. That year, following a disputed election, prime minister Dr. J. Leabua Jonathan declared a state of emergency and took away all political authority from the king, Mosheshwe II. The state of emergency was lifted in 1983, but elections scheduled for 1985 were suspended. When Lesotho, long a haven for black South African refugees, refused to sign a nonaggression pact with South Africa, South Africa severely restricted the flow of imports. The resultant economic crisis and discontent with Jonathan's policies led to a military coup on Jan. 20, 1986. Gen. Justin Lekhanya, head of the ruling military council, was more conciliatory towards South Africa. In 1990 he stripped King Mosheshwe II of his powers, although the king remained titular head of state.   ALAN C. G. BEST

Bibliography: Bardill, J. E., and Cobbe, J. H., *Lesotho* (1985); Coates, A., *Basutoland* (1966); Machobane, L. B., *Government and Change in Lesotho, 1800–1966* (1990); Schwager, Coleen and Dirk, *Lesotho* (1975); Strom, G. W., *Development and Dependence in Lesotho* (1978).

lespedeza   [les-puh-dee'-zuh]

Lespedezas are several species of important crop plants, genus *Lespedeza*, widely grown for HAY and forage. Originally native to Asia, they are annual or perennial LEGUMES that generally stand about 30 cm (12 in) high, although some species are larger. The leaves consist of three leaflets marked by prominent veins or furrows. The inconspicuous flowers are usually bluish. Some species of lespedeza are also cultivated as ornamentals.

Lesseps, Ferdinand Marie, Vicomte de
[les-eps', fair-dee-nahn', vee-kohnt']

Ferdinand Marie de Lesseps, b. Nov. 19, 1805, d. Dec. 7, 1894, was responsible for building the SUEZ CANAL. Beginning in 1825 he served as a diplomat in the overseas service of the

The 19th-century French diplomat Ferdinand de Lesseps promoted and organized the construction of the Suez Canal, which connected the Red and Mediterranean seas.

French government in various cities, including Alexandria, Cairo, and Rome, but a diplomatic failure forced his retirement in 1849. In 1854 his friendship with Muhammad Said, made while in the diplomatic service, enabled him to secure an act of concession authorizing him to bridge the Isthmus of Suez with a canal from Port Said on the Mediterranean Sea to Suez on the Red Sea. The accession to the Egyptian throne of his friend Muhammad Said made it possible for him to bring forward the great scheme that he had long cherished. An international Suez Canal Company was incorporated in 1858 to carry out a scheme formulated by de Lesseps in conjunction with two prominent engineering surveyors. The French nation subscribed more than half the cost of construction, largely due to the enthusiasm and organizational ability of de Lesseps who was a superb administrator, politician, and public relations man. Construction of the canal began in 1859 and was completed in 1869; de Lesseps was acclaimed a national hero. For his role in the later transfer of the canal to British control, however, he suffered considerable temporary loss of popularity in France.

In 1879, de Lesseps, at age 74, began an attempt to carry out the construction of a canal across the Isthmus of Panama. A combination of his age and temperament and the extreme physical difficulties encountered led to the collapse of the undertaking and the liquidation of the company formed for the project. A political and financial scandal erupted, centering on de Lesseps and his son Charles.   W. A. McCUTCHEON

Bibliography: Beatty, C. R. L., *De Lesseps of Suez* (1956); Farnie, D. A., *East and West of Suez* (1969); Marlowe, John, *The Making of the Suez Canal* (1964); Pudney, John, *Suez, de Lesseps' Canal* (1968).

Lesser Antilles: see ANTILLES, GREATER AND LESSER.

Lessing, Doris

A major British novelist and short-story writer, Doris May Lessing, b. Oct. 22, 1919, has used her fiction to explore such important contemporary themes as political commitment, the male-female dynamic on its most fundamental level, women's search for identity, and the relationship between the artist and his or her work. She is probably best known for her long, experimental novel focusing on the lives of two talented professional women, *The Golden Notebook* (1962).

Although Lessing has lived in England since 1949, she was born in Persia and brought up in Rhodesia (Zimbabwe), the setting for her first novel, *The Grass Is Singing* (1950). Between 1952 and 1969 she published five novels centering on the character Martha Quest, collectively titled *The Children of Violence,* that traced Martha's search for an independent self against a background of impending global catastrophe. Later works such as *The Memoirs of a Survivor* (1974) continued the theme of apocalypse, whereas *Canopus in Argos* (1979) marked the start of a multivolume foray into science fiction. She returned to themes of contemporary society and the individual in *The Diaries of Jane Somers* (1984, originally published under the pseudonym Jane Somers), *The Good Terrorist* (1985), and *The Fifth Child* (1988).

Bibliography: Draine, Betsy, *Substance under Pressure* (1983); Knapp, Mona, *Doris Lessing* (1984); Sprague, Claire, and Tiger, Virginia, *Critical Essays on Doris Lessing* (1986); Sprague, C., *Rereading Doris Lessing* (1987); Whittaker, R., *Doris Lessing* (1988).

Lessing, Gotthold   [gawt'-hohlt]

The German dramatist and critic Gotthold Ephraim Lessing, b. Jan. 22, 1729, d. Feb. 15, 1781, was a vigorous and prolific writer on literary, philosophical, and theological subjects and the outstanding figure of the German Enlightenment. Lessing studied theology and medicine at the University of Leipzig and received a degree in medicine from the University of Wittenberg (1752). During his 30-year career as an author and journalist, he traveled throughout Germany, working in Berlin, Leipzig, Breslau, Hamburg, and Wolfenbüttel. His personal life was filled with disappointments. Unlucky in love during his youth, he finally married in 1776 but lost his wife in childbirth two years later. His hopes of becoming royal librarian in

Gotthold Ephraim Lessing, one of the most influential figures of the Enlightenment, is considered the creator of German literary criticism. In Laocoön, *which greatly influenced the young Goethe, Lessing countered the neoclassical view that art can represent only what is in the artist's mind by vividly describing his own thoughts while viewing a work of art.*

Berlin were disappointed, and he failed in an attempt to establish a national theater in Hamburg. He finally became a librarian in Wolfenbüttel (1770) and there had to suffer censorship on account of his controversial theological opinions.

His writing career began at Leipzig, where his first comedy, *The Young Scholar* (1748; Eng. trans., 1878), was performed. Two other comedies, *The Jews* (1749; Eng. trans., 1801) and *The Freethinker* (1749; Eng. trans., 1838), foreshadowed his later writings—the former a plea for racial and religious tolerance, the latter exposing a freethinker's intolerance. His finest comedy is *Minna von Barnhelm* (1767; Eng. trans., 1858).

In 1753, Lessing launched his *Briefe* (Critical Letters), containing a review of Samuel Gotthold Lange's translation of Horace. Lange's retort provoked Lessing to publish the annihilating tract *Ein Vademecum* (A Pocket Companion, 1754), which established him as a formidable controversialist. He continued to publish his critical writings in his periodical *Theatralische Bibliothek* (Theatrical Library, 1754–58). Here he made a break with the French style generally accepted in his time and adopted the English literary concepts exemplified by his own domestic tragedy, *Miss Sarah Sampson* (1755; Eng. trans., 1878). He returned to the denunciation of French dramatic style in his *Briefe die neueste Litteratur betreffend* (Letters on the Most Recent Literature, 1759–65) and provided a theoretical justification of middle-class tragedy in the *Hamburgische Dramaturgie* (Hamburg Dramaturgy, 1767–69). His own tragedy, *Emilia Galotti* (1772; Eng. trans., 1786), exerted a strong influence on the Sturm und Drang movement.

As an art critic Lessing made his mark with *Laocoön; or, The Limits of Poetry and Painting* (1766; Eng. trans., 1836). Here, taking issue with Johann Joachim WINCKELMANN, he defined coexisting objects as the field of painting and sculpture and consecutive events as that of poetry.

Lessing's last years were occupied by his polemics against the influential clergyman Johann Melchior Goeze. Silenced by a ban on further articles, Lessing again turned to drama to reassert his points, writing the parable of religious tolerance *Nathan the Wise* (1779; Eng. trans., 1781). His final work was *The Education of the Human Race* (1780; Eng. trans., 1938), in which he propounded a rational religion progressing through Christianity to humanitarianism.

HENRY B. GARLAND

Bibliography: Allison, Henry E., *Lessing and the Enlightenment* (1966); Garland, Henry B., *Lessing* (1937; repr. 1973); Lamport, F. J., *Lessing and the Drama* (1981); Michaelson, G. E., Jr., *Lessing's "Ugly Ditch"* (1985).

lethal injection

Lethal injection is a method of capital punishment by which a convicted criminal is injected with a deadly dose of barbiturates through an intravenous tube inserted into the arm. The procedure resembles the method used for a patient undergoing anesthesia before surgery. Although lethal injection has been adopted by several U.S. states since 1980, its first use (1982) stirred a debate over the ethics of using medical procedures and medical professionals to end a life.

Lethbridge [leth'-brij]

Lethbridge, located on the Oldman River in southern Alberta, Canada, is Alberta's third largest city, with a population of 58,841 (1986). Long an important coal town, Lethbridge also serves as the commercial and food-processing center for the surrounding farming district. It also has diversified manufacturing and is the seat of the University of Lethbridge (1967). The city was settled in about 1870 after extensive coal deposits were discovered in the area and originally called Coalbanks.

Lethe [lee'-thee]

In Greek mythology, Lethe was one of the five rivers in HADES. Souls drank from it to forget their earthly sorrows before passing into the ELYSIAN FIELDS.

Leto [lee'-toh]

In Greek mythology, Leto was the daughter of the Titans Coeus and Phoebe and the mother of ARTEMIS and APOLLO by Zeus. Leto wandered through many lands seeking a place to give birth to her children, because Hera, the wife of Zeus, had forbidden any place under the sun to receive her. In the most common version of the story, Leto gave birth while clinging to a palm tree on the island of Delos, which Poseidon had covered with waves to evade Hera's decree.

letter of credit

A letter of credit is a negotiable instrument issued by a bank, usually addressed to a correspondent bank, stating that it will accept drafts charged against it in the name of a person or company. Commercial letters of credit are often used by importers and exporters to finance the purchase of goods. A circular letter of credit is one not addressed to any particular bank. The TRAVELER'S CHECK is a form of letter of credit.

letterpress

Letterpress is the best known of the relief printing processes, in which the image is on a raised surface. It is the oldest printing process, with modern mechanical presses of this type going back to the presses of Johannes GUTENBERG (about 1450). In the letterpress process the image carriers can be cast-metal type, etched-metal plates, or photopolymer plates

In letterpress printing an inked image is transferred directly from a raised type surface to paper. Paper may be pressed against the inked image by a flat platen (A) or, in a flatbed press, by a cylinder (B). A rotary press (C) feeds paper between an impression cylinder and a plate cylinder. Metal type (D) consists of a face (1), shoulder (2), body (3), foot (4), and a nick (5) that aids typesetting. Newly cast zinc blocks (E) have metal trimmed (6) from around the design (7).

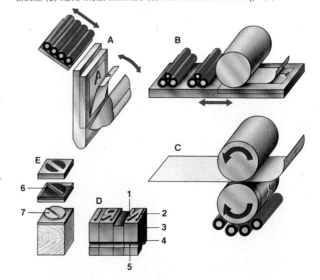

on which the image, or printing, areas are raised and the non-image areas are below the surface of the printing areas. Printing is done on a printing press, which provides means for inking the type or plates, transporting the substrate (usually paper), transferring the inked image directly to the substrate, and delivering the printed substrate as a sheet or folded signature. Presses suitable for letterpress printing include the Platen press, the FLATBED CYLINDER PRESS, and the ROTARY PRESS. On platen and flatbed cylinder presses the cast-metal type or plates are mounted on a flat surface that forms the printing bed of the press. Cast-metal type and flat metal plates cannot be used on rotary presses. The printing bed is a cylinder, so the image carriers must be curved. Printing can be done on sheets of paper using sheet-fed presses, or on rolls of paper using web-fed presses.

Sheet-fed letterpress on small platen and flatbed presses is used for short-run and medium-run job printing. Large sheet-fed letterpress is used for general commercial printing, books, catalogs, advertising, and packaging. Web letterpress is used for printing business forms, long-run magazines, and newspapers, especially the large metropolitan daily newspapers. Letterpress has the advantage that type can be either hand-set or machine-set (see TYPE AND TYPESETTING). It prints directly onto paper and is capable of long runs with reasonable consistency, high quality, and low paper waste. It has the disadvantage of high cost of photoengravings, time-consuming makeready (adjustments to compensate for high and low areas of type), and poor picture quality on rough papers such as newsprint. Because of these shortcomings and the advent of PHOTOTYPE-SETTING, letterpress is gradually being replaced by OFFSET LITHOGRAPHY for the short and medium runs and gravure, a form of INTAGLIO, for the long runs.   MICHAEL H. BRUNO

Bibliography: Adams, J. M., and Faux, D. D., *Printing Technology* (1987); Chappell, Warren, *A Short History of the Printed Word* (1980); Moran, James, *Printing Presses: History and Development from the 15th Century to Modern Times* (1973); Rothenstein, Michael, *Relief Printing* (1977); Simon, Herbert, *Introduction to Printing* (1980).

Lettish language: see BALTIC LANGUAGES.

Letts: see LATVIAN SOVIET SOCIALIST REPUBLIC.

lettuce   [let'-uhs]

Lettuce, *Lactuca sativa,* of the family Compositae, is the most popular of all salad crops. It is a cool-season vegetable, growing best at temperatures between 15 and 18° C (59 and 64° F). It will often bolt, or produce seed prematurely, if it is grown in midsummer heat. Of the four principal lettuce types, the most popular, the crisp-heading lettuces (iceberg is a well-known variety), have brittle, prominently veined leaves; butterhead types (Boston, for example) have softer leaves and a smooth texture; loose-leaf varieties, such as oak leaf, do not form heads but grow as clusters or bunches of leaves; and cos lettuce, or romaine, forms a long, loaf-shaped head. Cos is slower to bolt than other lettuces and is therefore useful as a warm-weather crop. No cultivated lettuce variety has been found growing in the wild, although there are many wild lettuces, and it is assumed that domesticated varieties may be cultivars of the weed *L. serriola* (prickly lettuce).

Lettuce is usually propagated by seeding directly in the soil, although head-lettuce types are sometimes transplanted. Leaf lettuce is harvested about 40 days after seeding, head lettuce from 70 to 90 days. Of the U.S. states, California is the major commercial lettuce producer, followed by Arizona and Florida. Lettuce shipped from these areas is often kept fresh by a process known as vacuum cooling, in which the tender leaves are cooled by rapid evaporation of water.   O. A. LORENZ

Leucippus   [loo-sip'-uhs]

Leucippus, fl. 5th century BC, was a Greek philosopher and the founder of ATOMISM. He maintained that atoms and empty space are the ultimate realities. Atoms are imperceptible, individual particles that differ only in shape and position. The intermingling of these particles in space gives rise to the world of experience. DEMOCRITUS developed and popularized the ideas of Leucippus.   ROBERT M. BAIRD

leucite: see FELDSPATHOID.

leucothoe: see FETTERBUSH.

leukemia   [loo-kee'-mee-uh]

Leukemia is a term given to a number of malignant, or cancerous, diseases of the BLOOD-forming organs. The acute and chronic leukemias, together with the other types of tumors of the blood, bone cells (myelomas), and lymph tissue (LYMPHOMAS), cause about 10% of all cancer deaths and about 50% of all cancer deaths in children and adults less than 30 years old.

Leukemias are characterized by the appearance of excessive amounts of white blood cells, with death resulting from the invasion of these cells into various tissues, particularly the bone marrow, spleen, and lymph nodes. Diagnoses of these diseases are generally made by two types of blood counts,

Of the many varieties of lettuce, L. sativa, *the most popular include* (left to right) *crisphead; oak leaf; butterhead; and cos, or romaine. Unlike the other types, the oak leaf is a loose-leaf variety and does not form a true head. Each lettuce is subtly differentiated in flavor and texture.*

"total" and "differential." The general diagnosis is invariably arrived at by noting a very large increase in the total number of white blood cells. A more specific diagnosis arises from comparing the relative numbers and types of white cells. Thus, the type of leukemia derives its name from the major cell type, for example, lymphoblastic and myeloblastic.

As with most human cancers, the exact cause of most leukemias has yet to be established. Some animal leukemias are induced by viruses, such as Rous chicken sarcoma, feline leukemia, and Rauscher mouse leukemia. More recently two RETRO-VIRUSES have been identified as causes of human T-cell leukemia. Certain chemicals, such as benzene, chloramphenicol, and procarbazine, as well as radiation, are also likely to be able to produce leukemia in humans. Genetic researchers, in addition, have been able to link certain chromosomal abnormalities with some forms of leukemia.

An individual with leukemia, more particularly the chronic rather than acute forms, may not be aware of it unless, for example, a blood count is done. As the condition progresses there may be weakness, fatigue, loss of appetite, weight loss, anemia, enlarged spleen, and bone pain. When untreated, acute leukemia is fatal in 1 to 2 years and often fatal within about 6 months of onset. Today's therapy produces 85 to 90% remissions for 3 or more years and apparent cure in 50% of the cases. Vigorous therapy is based on the premise that every leukemic cell must be destroyed.

In addition to radiation, the following drugs, usually in combinations with each other, are used to treat acute leukemias: vincristine, prednisone, methotrexate, mercaptopurine, cyclophosphamide, cytarabine, and teniposide. In chronic leukemia, busulfan, melphalan, and chlorambucil are used. These drugs tend to make patients quite ill. Patients are treated less vigorously while in remission and are able to lead relatively normal lives. A rare form of leukemia known as hairy-cell leukemia has been found to respond to some degree to INTERFERON treatment, and research is currently being devoted to the possibilities of treating myeloid leukemia with certain proteins that occur naturally in the body.

REGINALD L. REAGAN

Bibliography: Chanarin, Israel, et al., *Blood and Its Diseases*, 3d ed. (1984); Gale, R. P., ed., *Leukemia Therapy* (1986); Margolies, C. P., and McCredie, K. B., *Understanding Leukemia* (1983; repr. 1987); Pullman, M. E., et al., eds., *Retroviruses and Disease* (1989); Wiernik, P. H., *Leukemias and Lymphomas* (1985).

leukocyte: see BLOOD.

leukocytosis   [loo-kuh-sy-toh'-sis]

An abnormally high number of leukocytes, or white BLOOD cells, is known as leukocytosis. This normally occurs in pregnant women but otherwise indicates a pathological condition, usually a bacterial infection such as staphylococcus or streptococcus. It also often follows a large loss of blood. Leukocytosis may be local (an abscess) or systemic (pneumonia). LEUKEMIA results in leukocytosis in the form of overproduction of immature leukocytes.

leukoderma   [loo-kuh-dur'-muh]

Leukoderma, or vitiligo, is a disease of the skin of unknown origin. It causes white, often symmetric, patches primarily on the hands, face, neck, and upper torso. Hair in affected areas is also white. Patches start small and enlarge slowly. The pigment melanin, responsible for skin color, is either deficient, or there is an absence of melanocytes, which synthesize melanin, suggesting possible hereditary factors. Leukoderma affects 1 percent of the population but is only a cosmetic problem. Normal skin color rarely returns; there is no cure.

leukopenia   [loo-kuh-peen'-yuh]

Leukopenia is a deficiency of circulating white blood cells, or leukocytes. If the white-blood-cell count falls below 2,500 per cubic millimeter of blood, the body may become more susceptible to disease. Diseases and other conditions that de-

crease the production of white cells by the bone marrow can cause leukopenia. These include viral infections (such as infectious MONONUCLEOSIS), tuberculosis, connective tissue diseases, toxic reactions to certain drugs, and the presence of malignant cells in bone marrow. Leukopenia can also result from increased destruction of leukocytes by the spleen during the occurrence of such conditions as rheumatoid arthritis or cirrhosis of the liver.

DONALD L. RUCKNAGEL

leukorrhea   [loo-kuh-ree'-uh]

Leukorrhea, or vaginal discharge, is usually a symptom of infections of the vagina or cervix, or malignancies of the cervix, uterus, or vagina, or both. The major causes of vaginal infections are *Trichomonas vaginalis, Candida albicans,* and bacterial vaginitis. Trichomonads are protozoans commonly found in the urinary tract, and they do not cause infection unless they reach the vagina. There they can cause vaginitis with severe itching, ill smell, and painful urination. The vagina becomes engorged with excess blood, giving it a strawberrylike appearance (see TRICHOMONIASIS). *Candida albicans* is a fungus that causes CANDIDIASIS, the symptoms of which can include heavy leukorrhea and itching. Bacterial vaginitis is commonly caused by *Hemophilus vaginalis.*

Leukorrhea is a common symptom of genital cancers, second only to bleeding. Any vaginal discharge that persists or is resistant to treatment, or both, should be investigated to rule out any evidence of malignancy in the genital tract.

Bibliography: McPherson, Ann, *Women's Problems in General Practice,* 2d ed. (1988); Pauerstein, Carl, ed., *Gynecologic Disorders* (1981); Van Wertz, S. M., *Vaginitis* (1987).

Leutze, Emanuel   [loyt'-suh, ay-mahn'-oo-el]

The German-American artist Emanuel Leutze, b. May 24, 1816, d. July 18, 1868, is best known for his large painting *Washington Crossing the Delaware* (1851; Metropolitan Museum of Art, New York City), one of the most familiar works in American art. Leutze was born in Germany and immigrated to Philadelphia with his parents in 1825. After beginning his painting career, he returned to Germany to study at the Düsseldorf Akademie and spent much of the 1850s in that country. His last major work was the enormous mural *Westward the Course of Empire Takes Its Way* (1862) for the Capitol in Washington, D.C.

DAVID TATHAM

Bibliography: Groseclose, Barbara S., *Emanuel Leutze, 1816–1868: Freedom Is the Only King* (1975).

Levalloisian   [le-val-wah'-zee-uhn]

Levalloisian (or Levallois), in archaeology, is a technique of PALEOLITHIC tool manufacture in which flakes are struck off a previously prepared stone core. First discovered in the 19th century at the Parisian suburb of Le Vallois-Perret, it was originally conceived of as a distinct tool culture. The Levalloisian is now known to have occurred in many middle and late sites of the ACHEULEAN tradition and in several variations of the MOUSTERIAN in Africa, the Near East, and western Europe during the period from about 700,000 to 32,000 years ago.

The Levalloisian technique consists of the initial preparation of a core of flint by removing a series of peripheral flakes to form a ring of striking platforms. These platforms are used to remove a number of flat, converging flakes from the upper surface of the core, resulting in a residual core shaped somewhat like a tortoise back. Finally, a single, large flake is detached from the upper surface of the so-called tortoise core, thus yielding a preformed sharp-edged hand ax. Preformed triangular points are also produced by means of the Levalloisian technique. Acheulean or Mousterian tool assemblages having a large proportion of points and hand axes indicating Levalloisian technique are termed "Acheulean of Levallois tradition" or "Levallois-Mousterian."

DAVID S. BROSE AND ROY LARICK, JR.

Bibliography: Bordaz, Jacques, *Tools of the Old and New Stone Age* (1970); Gamble, C., *The Paleolithic Settlement of Europe* (1986); Wymer, J., *The Paleolithic Age* (1982).

Levant [luh-vant']

The Levant (from the Middle English *levaunt*, "east") is a name formerly applied to the areas along the eastern shore of the Mediterranean, including present-day Greece, Turkey, Syria, Lebanon, Israel, and Egypt; a more restricted definition includes only the non-European coastlands. The name is still sometimes used to refer to the former French mandates of Lebanon and Syria.

levee [lev'-ee]

A levee is an earthen embankment constructed along the side of a river or stream to prevent flooding of the adjoining land (see FLOODS AND FLOOD CONTROL). The world's largest system of levees, covering a total of 5,741 km (3,566 mi), is constructed along the Mississippi River and its tributaries. Other rivers with important levee systems include the Sacramento; the Yellow and Yangtze (China); the Rhône, Danube, and Rhine (Europe); and the Volga (USSR). DIKES in the Netherlands are essentially levees.

· A levee system is designed not only to prevent floodwaters from overrunning the land, but also, where possible, to slow the destructive velocity of a flood. For example, levees may be set back from riverbanks to create a broader flood channel. When the levee alignment has been determined, the area is cleared of trees and brush. A muck ditch or cutoff trench is dug on the levee's river side, down to the more impervious subsoil layers. It is refilled with the most impervious soil available, such as clay or clayey gravel, in order to prevent seepage of water along the base of the levee. The levee embankment is then constructed and its slopes planted with grass to protect it from erosion. Exceptionally vulnerable riverside sections may be paved with concrete.

The top of a levee is usually 1 to 1.5 m (3 to 5 ft) above the high-water mark and 1 to 3.5 m (3 to 12 ft) wide. The sides often have a slope of 1:2 or 1:3 on the land side and 1:3 or 1:4 on the river side; the lighter the construction material used, the flatter the slope. Many levees are provided with culverts or gate-controlled sluiceways to allow for natural drainage from behind the levee.   THOMAS CONCANNON

Levellers

The Levellers were members of an English radical political movement that came into being in 1646–47 at the end of the first ENGLISH CIVIL WAR. Its leaders were John Lilburne (c.1614–1657) and Sir John Wildman (c.1621–1693), both gentry involved in trade. Its appeal, however, was to the lower-middle classes, and it found support in the ranks of the army.

The Levellers advocated a wider parliamentary franchise, religious toleration, legal reform, and the abolition of tithes paid to the church, trading monopolies, and excise duties. They also called for parliaments to be held every 2 years, because all power was thought to lie with the people. This program was embodied in the Agreement of the People, a proposed constitution presented to the army's general council at the so-called Putney debates in October 1647. The army generals rejected the Agreement out of hand.

After the execution of King CHARLES I (1649), the Levellers opposed the new governing oligarchy headed by Oliver CROMWELL, and Lilburne published a pamphlet entitled *England's New Chains*. Several Leveller mutinies within the army were broken by Cromwell, and the movement petered out. The Levellers' aims are not easy to disentangle, but they were essentially individualistic—unlike the communistic Diggers, an even shorter-lived movement of the same period.

MAURICE ASHLEY

Bibliography: Morton, A. L., ed., *Freedom in Arms: A Selection of Leveller Writings* (1976); Shaw, Howard, *The Levellers* (1968).

lever [lev'-ur]

The lever is a SIMPLE MACHINE used, in its most basic form, for magnifying the force that can be exerted on an object. An early lever, known as the shadoof, was used in ancient Egypt. It

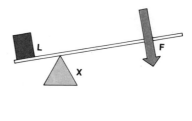

Three arrangements of levers are possible depending on where the force F is applied with respect to the fulcrum X, or point of support about which the lever turns, and the load L. In one case (top) the force and the load act on opposite sides of the fulcrum. In another case (center) the load lies between the fulcrum and the applied force. In a third arrangement (bottom) the force is applied between the load and the fulcrum. The amount of force required to move the load depends on the distance of each from the fulcrum.

consisted of a long bar pivoted near one end that enabled a person pulling down on the long arm to raise a bucket of water, many times his or her own weight, attached to the short arm.

Three possible arrangements and effects can be produced with a lever, all depending on the position of the pivot point, or fulcrum, relative to the points where the load and effort are applied. If the force exerted (F) and the load lifted (L) are just sufficient to keep the lever in balance, then the force-amplifying capacity, or mechanical advantage, of the lever is equal to the ratio of the load lifted to the force exerted. If a weight of exactly 45 kg (100 lb) could be raised by an effort of 9 kg (20 lb), the mechanical advantage would be 5. In this case the fulcrum is located at a point five times the distance from the force exerted as from the load lifted. In this form the lever principle is the reason for the gripping capacity of a pair of pliers and the load-lifting effectiveness of a pry bar.

If the fulcrum is shifted to the end of the bar the mechanical advantage is the ratio of the length of the bar to the distance from the load to the fulcrum. This form of the lever is found in a nutcracker and a wheelbarrow. In the latter the fulcrum is on the axis of the wheel, W is at the center of gravity of the load being lifted, and the effort is that exerted on the handles by the hands of the operator.

In the third form of the lever the mechanical advantage is less than 1, and the lever is not a force-multiplying device like the other two forms, but a motion-multiplying device. This form of the lever is found on foot-operated sewing machines, in which a relatively large force applied by the foot of the operator through a small distance on the treadle results in a lesser force moving the sewing machine wheel through a large angular distance. In all levers what is gained in motion is lost in force, so that the larger force always moves through the smaller distance.   ALEXANDER COWIE

Lever, William Hesketh, 1st Viscount Leverhulme [lee'-vur, hes'-keth, lee'-vur-hulm]

William Hesketh Lever, b. Sept. 19, 1851, d. May 7, 1925, turned a small soapworks in Warrington, England, into one of the most successful companies in Britain. The son of a grocer, Lever leased a soap factory in 1884 and with his brother built up the international firm Lever Brothers, which by 1925 had 250 associated firms. He created a model industrial village in Cheshire called Port Sunlight and embarked on a program of "prosperity-sharing" with his employees. Lever, who served in Parliament from 1906 to 1909, was made a baron in 1917 and a viscount in 1922.

Bibliography: Jolly, W. P., *Lord Leverhulme: A Biography* (1976).

Leverrier, Urbain Jean Joseph   [lu-vair-ee-ay']

The French astronomer Urbain Jean Joseph Leverrier, b. Mar. 11, 1811, d. Sept. 23, 1877, is best remembered for his work leading to the discovery of the planet NEPTUNE. His early work on an anomaly in the orbit of Mercury led him to propose the existence of a perturbing planet orbiting closer to the Sun than Mercury; the anomaly has since been accounted for by Albert Einstein's general theory of relativity. Leverrier's prediction of the position of an undiscovered planet (Neptune) that caused perturbations in the orbit of Uranus, although made some 9 months after a similar prediction by John Couch ADAMS, was the first to be observationally confirmed, by Johann Gottfried GALLE on Sept. 23, 1846.   STEVEN J. DICK

Levertov, Denise   [lev'-ur-tawf]

The American poet Denise Levertov, b. Ilford, England, Oct. 24, 1923, became closely associated with the BLACK MOUNTAIN SCHOOL OF POETRY after moving to the United States in 1948. Her early volumes, such as *The Jacob's Ladder* (1961), describe moments from everyday life in a simple, idiomatic style. In the 1960s her poetry dealt primarily with her antiwar convictions, but she returned to earlier modes in *Life in the Forest* (1978), *Candles in Babylon* (1982), and *Breathing the Water* (1987).

Bibliography: Marten, H., *Understanding Denise Levertov* (1988).

Lévesque, René   [lay-vek', ruh-nay']

The French-Canadian political leader René Lévesque, b. Aug. 24, 1922, d. Nov. 1, 1987, was elected premier of Quebec in November 1976. Formerly a broadcast journalist, he entered Quebec politics in 1960 as a member of the Liberal party. In 1967 he helped found the separatist Sovereignty Movement, which developed into the Parti Québécois in 1968. In May 1980, Quebec's voters rejected political sovereignty for the province, but Lévesque's party won again in general elections in April 1981. In June 1985, Lévesque resigned as party leader.

Levi, Primo   [lay'-vee]

The Italian writer Primo Levi, b. July 31, 1919, d. Apr. 13, 1987, is remembered chiefly for his three-volume autobiography, which combines reminiscence, philosophical writings, and accounts of his experiences as an inmate of Auschwitz, a Nazi concentration camp. Born into a middle-class Italian-Jewish family, Levi's life was relatively placid until the German occupation of Italy transformed him from chemist to partisan. Captured and sent to Auschwitz, Levi survived only because of his usefulness as a chemist. The autobiographical works are *Survival in Auschwitz* (1947; Eng. trans., 1959), *The Reawakening* (1958; Eng. trans., 1965), and *The Periodic Table* (1975; Eng. trans., 1984). Other works include the novels *The Monkey's Wrench* (1978; Eng. trans., 1986) and *If Not Now, When?* (1982; Eng. trans., 1985), several posthumous gatherings of essays and short stories, and his *Collected Poems* (1988).

Levi ben Gershon   [lee'-vy ben gur'-shuhn]

The Jewish astronomer, mathematician, and philosopher Levi ben Gershon (also called Gersonides and Ralbag), b. Bagnols, France, 1288, d. Apr. 20, 1344, was a controversial commentator on Aristotelian philosophy, the Bible, and parts of the Talmud. His most important mathematical work (1342) dealt with trigonometry. As an astronomer, he was an independent follower of the Ptolemaic tradition. Levi devised an instrument for measuring the angular separation between any two astronomical bodies, the JACOB'S STAFF, which was much used in navigation, especially in the 16th century.

Levi's major philosophical work, *Milhamot Adonai* (The Wars of the Lord, 1329), treats many of the critical philosophic problems of his time as an Averroist, that is, a follower of the Aristotelian commentator AVERROËS. Unlike Maimonides, who, when faced with an unresolvable contradiction between Aristotle and the Bible, accepted the biblical word as primary,

Levi tried to accommodate biblical ideas to those of Aristotle. Because of this he was suspected of heresy.   JOSEPH L. BLAU

Bibliography: Blumenthal, D. S., *Approaches to Judaism in Medieval Times* (1984); Sirat, Colette, *A History of Jewish Philosophy in the Middle Ages* (1985).

Levi-Montalcani, Rita   [lay'vee-mohn-tahl-cah'-nee]

Italian biochemist Rita Levi-Montalcani, b. Apr. 22, 1909, is noted for her research into the development of the nervous system. Obtaining a medical degree from the University of Turin in 1936, she pursued her studies of nerve cells thereafter. During the Nazi occupation of the country in 1943 and 1944, she used a laboratory she had set up in her own home. Following the occupation she served as a doctor among war refugees in Florence. She was invited in 1947 to join fellow investigators at Washington University in St. Louis, Mo., as they attempted to identify the protein called nerve growth factor. For her role in its successful isolation she shared the 1986 Nobel Prize for physiology or medicine with Stanley Cohen. From 1969 to 1978 she served as director of the Institute of Cell Biology in Rome. Her autobiography, *In Praise of Imperfection*, was published in English translation in 1988.

Lévi-Strauss, Claude   [lay-vee-strows', klohd]

The French anthropologist Claude Lévi-Strauss is one of the leading exponents of structuralism. Widely respected for intellectual achievement, he taught at the Collège de France from 1959 until his retirement in 1982. In 1973 he was elected to the Académie Française.

Claude Lévi-Strauss, b. Nov. 28, 1908, a leading French philosopher, social theorist, and anthropologist, is associated with the development of STRUCTURALISM as a method in both the social sciences and humanities. Aside from a period spent teaching in Brazil before World War II and a few years as an academic and diplomat in the United States during and after the war, Lévi-Strauss has lived and taught in France. His researches have focused on the massive amount of ethnological materials collected by field-workers worldwide. In the tradition of 19th- and early-20th-century French sociology (which included anthropology), pioneered by such figures as Émile DURKHEIM, Lévi-Strauss is a theorizer on a grand scale. By developing a sophisticated means of analyzing the cultural artifacts of preindustrial, nonliterate peoples, he has sought to discover underlying structures of thought that characterize not only so-called primitive societies—the anthropologist's specialty—but also the formal structures of human mentality generally.

Lévi-Strauss derived his structuralist method from structural linguistics (see APPLIED LINGUISTICS). Considering the perspective of structural linguistics appropriate for culture and thought, as well as for language, he attempted to demonstrate that the cultural features of tribal societies were assemblages of codes, in turn reflecting certain universal principles of human thought. Lévi-Strauss's first major work was *Elementary Structures of Kinship* (1949; Eng. trans., 1962), but his career project has been the structural study of mythology, realized in *Mythologiques* (4 vols., 1964–71; Eng. trans., 1970–81). Unlike previous analysts of myth, Lévi-Strauss holds that meaning does not reside in the intrinsic significance or symbolism of a particular element in a mythical story. Rather, a myth's meaning is hidden in the underlying relationships of all its elements, which can be discovered only through structuralist analysis.

As Lévi-Strauss's works became available in English in the 1960s, his structuralist method gained popularity in the United States in such fields as sociology, architecture, literature, and art, as well as anthropology. His writings include *Tristes Tropiques* (1955; Eng. trans., 1964), *Structural Anthropology* (1958; Eng. trans. in 2 vols., 1963 and 1976), and *The Savage Mind* (1962; Eng. trans., 1966). GEORGE E. MARCUS

Bibliography: Leach, Edmund, *Claude Lévi-Strauss,* rev. ed. (1974); Pace, David, *Claude Lévi-Strauss* (1983).

Leviathan   [luh-vy'-uh-thuhn]

In his political treatise *Leviathan* (1651), the English philosopher Thomas HOBBES compares the state, with its innumerable competing members, to the largest of natural organisms—the whale, or leviathan. By this analogy Hobbes argued that the state, like the whale, requires a single controlling intelligence to direct its motion.

In the state of nature, Hobbes observed, there is continual strife, and "the life of man is solitary, poor, nasty, brutish and short." Misery and anarchy, he proposed, can be avoided by a social contract between ruler and subjects. He justified the absolute power of his ideal monarch not by divine sanction, but on grounds of expediency; he antagonized contemporary opinion and allied himself with philosophers who are pessimistic concerning human nature.   JANE COLVILLE BETTS

Bibliography: Gauthier, David P., *The Logic of Leviathan* (1969); McNeilly, F. S., *The Anatomy of Leviathan* (1968).

Levine, Jack   [luh-veen']

The American painter Jack Levine, b. Boston, Jan. 3, 1915, approaches social themes with a satirical and often angry outlook on the excesses and corruption inherent in modern society. A poverty-stricken childhood and early training in the socially conscious Federal Arts Project of the Depression years helped mold Levine's artistic attitude, evident in *The Feast of Pure Reason* (1937; Museum of Modern Art, New York City), *Welcome Home* (1946; Brooklyn Museum, New York City) and *The Gangster's Funeral* (1953; Whitney Museum, New York City). Levine's paintings generally display rich, active surfaces combining both colored glazes and heavy impasto, the distorting effects of which he uses to great advantage in depicting his themes.

Bibliography: Getlein, Frank, *Jack Levine* (1966).

Levine, James   [luh-vyn']

The conductor and pianist James Levine, b. Cincinnati, Ohio, June 23, 1943, made his professional debut at the age of ten as piano soloist with the Cincinnati Symphony Orchestra. His piano teachers included Rosina Lhévinne at the Juilliard School and Aspen and Rudolf Serkin at Marlboro. Levine studied conducting with Jean Morel, Max Rudolf, Alfred Wallenstein, Fausto Cleva, and George Szell, who hired him as apprentice conductor (1964) of the Cleveland Orchestra. He soon became assistant conductor and appeared with the orchestra as piano soloist. His conducting debut (1971) at the Metropolitan Opera was followed within a year by his appointment as principal conductor (1973). He became musical director of the Metropolitan Opera in 1976, and in 1983 his appointment as its artistic director, effective in 1986, was announced. In addition to guest appearances with major orchestras throughout the United States and Europe, he was also appointed (1973) music director of the Ravinia festival, which includes a summer concert series by the Chicago Symphony Orchestra.   JEFFREY M. CORNELIUS

levirate: see MARRIAGE.

Levites   [lee'-vyts]

Members of the Israelite tribe of Levi, descended by tradition from the third son of JACOB, were called Levites. MOSES belonged to this tribe. They were a religious caste, some or all of whose members acted as priests for Israel. Lacking their own territory, they lived among the other tribes in special settlements called Levitical cities. In early Israel the priesthood had a predominantly teaching function, because the laity then were considered competent to sacrifice. Later, especially in postexilic times, the sacrificial duties of the priests at the Jerusalem Temple were increased. The biblical sources make it difficult to write a definitive history of the Israelite priesthood. Several priestly lines held the ascendancy in various times and places, for example, the house of Eli and the Zadokites. Eventually the high priest and priests competent to sacrifice were traced back to the house of AARON, while Levite became the term for lower-rank cultic attendants who maintained the temple, taught, and provided music for worship.   NORMAN K. GOTTWALD

Bibliography: Cody, Aelred, *A History of Priesthood* (1969).

Leviticus, Book of   [luh-vit'-ih-kuhs]

Leviticus is the third book of the Pentateuch, or TORAH, the first five books of the BIBLE, which are traditionally ascribed to MOSES. Its name is derived from the tribe Levi (the Levites), which had the responsibility for overseeing Israel's ritual worship. Leviticus consists primarily of laws regulating such activity, including sacrificial offerings, the installation of priests, cultic purity (which includes the dietary laws), and a more general legal collection known as the Holiness Code because of its emphasis on God's holiness. These major collections together with several shorter supplements are part of the P source, normally dated to *c.*450 BC. Thus, as a book, Leviticus is postexilic, but the individual laws and various collections within the book differ in age, and some are quite ancient.   J. J. M. ROBERTS

Bibliography: Levine, B. A., *In the Presence of the Lord* (1974); Milgrom, Jacob, *Cult and Conscience* (1976).

Levitt, William Jaird   [lev'-it]

William Jaird Levitt, b. Brooklyn, N.Y., Feb. 11, 1907, introduced mass-production methods into the building of low-cost HOUSING tracts. In 1947–51 his company turned 480 ha (1,200 acres) of Long Island potato fields 16 km (10 mi) from New York City into a residential community named Levittown, N.Y. He followed this project with another Levittown in Pennsylvania halfway between Philadelphia and Trenton, N.J., built in 1951–55. Both communities were preplanned, consisting of thousands of simple homes built on concrete slabs, together with schools, shopping centers, playgrounds, and community centers. Other Levittown-type communities later were built in New Jersey, Maryland, Florida, and elsewhere.

Bibliography: Gans, Herbert J., *The Levittowners: Ways of Life and Politics in a New Suburban Community* (1967).

Levittowns: see HOUSING.

Levnî, Ressam

Abdülcelil Chelebi of Edirne, d. 1732, widely known as Ressam Levnî, was the most celebrated Turkish miniaturist-painter of the 18th century. Although he was trained in the traditional Turkish style of strong and contrasting colors, he later excelled in the use of softer colors and subdued accents of goldleaf in his manuscript illuminations. The Ottoman sultans Mustafa II (r. 1695–1703) and Ahmed (Ahmet) III (r. 1703–30) gave him encouragement, and Levnî in turn immortalized them by preparing an album of 50 paintings that contained their portraits and those of their families and courts. Levnî's portraits of European gentlemen are marked by the influence of European rococo art, and his illustrations in the *Book of*

Festival of Ahmet III exhibit his great admiration for the activities of all classes of society, including the artisans who were his favorite subjects.   S. A. A. RIZVI

Bibliography: And, Metin, *Turkish Miniature Painting* (1974); Ettinghansen, Richard, *Turkish Miniatures from the Thirteenth to the Eighteenth Century* (1965).

levodopa   [leev'-uh-dohp-uh]

Levodopa, or L-dopa, is a drug used to treat PARKINSON'S DISEASE, which has been related to a depletion of the NEUROTRANSMITTER dopamine in the brain. The drug crosses the blood-brain barrier more easily than dopamine itself and is converted to dopamine in the brain's basal ganglia. L-dopa can have some serious side effects, however.

Lewes, George Henry   [loo'-is]

George Henry Lewes, b. Apr. 18, 1817, d. Nov. 30, 1878, was an English literary critic, journalist, and scientific writer best known for his liaison with novelist George ELIOT (Mary Anne Evans). Born to a London theatrical family, Lewes was for a time a medical student before becoming (1840) a free-lance journalist and critic. In that year he married and joined a communal marriage group in which he accepted his wife's affair with Thornton Hunt, son of poet Leigh Hunt. He left his wife, however, when he learned in 1850 that his youngest son was Hunt's. Lewes met Evans in 1851, and they lived together from 1854 until his death.

An early Darwinian, he studied physiological psychology and marine biology and wrote *Seaside Studies* (1858), *Physiology of Common Life* (1859–60), *Studies in Animal Life* (1862), and *The Problems of Life and Mind* (1874–79). He also wrote two novels and a number of philosophical and biographical works, most notably *The Life and Works of Goethe* (1855).

Bibliography: Hirshberg, Edgar W., *George Henry Lewes* (1970); Tjoa, Hock G., *George Henry Lewes: A Victorian Mind* (1977).

Lewin, Kurt   [le-veen']

The German-born American psychologist Kurt Lewin, b. Sept. 9, 1890, d. Feb. 12, 1947, developed field theory after doctoral studies in Gestalt psychology at the University of Berlin. His work subsequently influenced GROUP DYNAMICS and other areas of social psychology that study attitudes.

Lewin's field theory maintains that an individual's behavior is determined by his or her contemporary life space. What constitutes the individual's life space is not the objective environment in itself, but the way the individual perceives it. Lewin was one of the earliest psychologists to use mathematical models, presenting field theory in the language of topology and vector analysis.

Working in the United States from 1932 on, Lewin sought to combine theory and practical application. His aphorism, "There is nothing so practical as a good theory," is illustrated by the group dynamics work he was engaged in when he died. Out of this work developed the theoretically oriented group research of the Center for Group Dynamics (University of Michigan) and the applied group training procedures of the National Training Laboratories (Bethel, Maine).

                                    WILLIAM J. MCGUIRE

Bibliography: De Rivera, Joseph, *Field Theory as Human Science: Contributions of Lewin's Berlin Group* (1976); Lewin, Kurt, *Principles in Topological Psychology* (1936); Marrow, Alfred J., *The Practical Theorist: The Life and Work of Kurt Lewin* (1969; repr. 1977.)

Lewis, Sir Arthur

Sir William Arthur Lewis, b. Saint Lucia, West Indies, Jan. 23, 1915, is a Nobel prize–winning economist, so honored in 1979 for his studies of economic development and construction of theoretical models used to explain the problems of underdevelopment. Lewis, who was reared in London, was educated at St. Mary's College in St. Lucia (1924–29) and at the London School of Economics (Ph.D., 1940), where he was a lecturer (1938–47). He subsequently was associated with the Universi-

ty of Manchester (1948–58), the University of the West Indies (1959–63), and Princeton University (1963–83). In addition, he has been an economic advisor to many Third World governments. His most famous book is *The Theory of Economic Growth* (1955). He was knighted in 1963.

Lewis, C. Day: see DAY-LEWIS, CECIL.

Lewis, C. S.

C. S. Lewis wrote numerous works about Christianity and a series of fantasy novels, The Chronicles of Narnia. *A man of vivid imagination and precise logic, Lewis was also an acclaimed literary critic whose study of the conventions of allegory is considered a standard reference.*

The English scholar and writer Clive Staples Lewis, b. Nov. 29, 1898, d. Nov. 22, 1963, led two virtually distinct—and equally successful—careers as an author. *The Allegory of Love* (1936), written during his time as a fellow of Magdalen College, Oxford (1925–54), remains a standard work on medieval literature and the tradition of courtly love. It was followed by other important critical and scholarly works, which include *A Preface to Paradise Lost* (1942) and *English Literature in the 16th Century, Excluding Drama* (1954). In 1954 he was appointed professor of medieval and Renaissance literature at Cambridge University.

Lewis was known to a large public, however, as a persuasive and passionate advocate of conservative Christianity. In a science-fiction trilogy—*Out of the Silent Planet* (1938), *Perelandra* (1943), and *That Hideous Strength* (1945)—he placed the idea of Christian pilgrimage in a cosmic setting. His most brilliant work of Christian apologetics is perhaps *The Screwtape Letters* (1942; rev. ed., 1961), in which a seasoned old servant of the Devil instructs an apprentice in the art of capturing souls. Lewis also achieved success with *The Lion, the Witch, and the Wardrobe* (1950) and his other children's stories constituting *The Chronicles of Narnia*. He related his religious conversion in *Surprised by Joy* (1955).

Bibliography: Christopher, J. R., *C. S. Lewis* (1987); Glover, D. E., *C. S. Lewis: The Art of Enchantment* (1981); Griffin, W., *Clive Staples Lewis: A Dramatic Life* (1986); Hannay, M. P., *C. S. Lewis* (1981); Sayer, G., *Jack: C. S. Lewis and His Times* (1985).

Lewis, Carl

Hailed as the greatest track and field star since Jesse Owens, Frederick Carlton Lewis, b. Birmingham, Ala., July 1, 1961, at the 1984 Olympics in Los Angeles, won the same 4 gold medals as Owens did in 1936 (100 m, 200 m, long jump, 4 × 100-m relay). At the 1988 Olympics he repeated as gold medalist at 100 m and the long jump and earned a silver medal at 200 m. In 1981, Lewis received the Sullivan Award as the nation's finest amateur athlete.

by members who withdrew from the American Labor party, which itself had been founded in 1936 by a group of labor-union leaders and liberals. Those who withdrew included well-known New Deal liberals such as Adolf A. BERLE, Jr., David DUBINSKY, Reinhold NIEBUHR, and Alex Rose. They charged that the American Labor party contained a strong pro-Communist element. Since then the Liberal party has played an important balance-of-power role in New York politics, and through this a marginal role in national elections. It generally supports liberal Democrats.   JOHN H. FENTON

Bibliography: Bentley, Michael, *The Climax of Liberal Politics* (1987); Cook, Chris, *A Short History of the Liberal Party* (1976); Cyr, Arthur, *Liberal Politics in Britain*, rev. ed. (1988); Hamer, D. A., *Liberal Politics in the Age of Gladstone and Rosebery* (1972); Morgan, Kenneth, *The Age of Lloyd George*, 2d ed. (1978); Thorburn, Hugh, *Party Politics in Canada*, 5th ed. (1985).

Liberal Republican party

The Liberal Republican party was founded in the United States in 1872 by a group of moderate Republicans who were disillusioned both with the aura of political corruption surrounding Ulysses S. GRANT's administration and with the RECONSTRUCTION policy of the Radical Republicans. Besides advocating an end to Radical Reconstruction, the party platform called for civil service reform, local self-government, and the resumption of specie payment. Allied with the Democrats, the Liberal Republicans nominated Horace GREELEY for president and Benjamin Gratz Brown for vice-president in 1872, but Grant was reelected and the new party soon disbanded.

Bibliography: Ross, E. D., *The Liberal Republican Movement* (1919; repr. 1971).

liberalism

Liberalism, a political philosophy that emphasizes individual freedom, arose in Europe in the period between the Reformation and the French Revolution. During the 16th, 17th, and 18th centuries the medieval feudal order gradually gave way as Protestantism, the nation-state, commerce, science, cities, and a middle class of traders and industrialists developed. The new liberal order—drawing on Enlightenment thought—began to place human beings rather than God at the center of things. Humans, with their rational minds, could comprehend all things and could improve themselves and society through systematic and rational action.

Liberal thinking was hostile to the prerogatives of kings, aristocrats, and the church; it favored freedom—a natural right—from traditional restraints. These notions did much to precipitate the American and French revolutions and were important factors in various uprisings in the 19th century. Liberalism sought to expand civil liberties and to limit political authority in favor of constitutional representative government and promoted the rights to property and religious toleration. In the economic sphere, classical liberalism was opposed to direction by the state, arguing with Adam SMITH and David RICARDO that the forces of the marketplace were the best guide for the economy (see LAISSEZ-FAIRE).

One of the first thinkers to formulate a comprehensive liberal philosophy was the Englishman John LOCKE. As a political philosopher, Locke was widely influential. Thomas Jefferson drew upon his ideas in framing the Declaration of Independence, and the French Enlightenment philosophers VOLTAIRE and MONTESQUIEU were indebted to him. Leading liberal voices in the 19th century included Jeremy BENTHAM, John Stuart MILL, Alexis de TOCQUEVILLE, and Thomas Hill Green.

In its full flower in the 19th century, liberalism stood for limited government with a separation of powers among different branches such as the legislative, executive, and judicial and for free enterprise in the economy. Because of the reaction against the excesses of the French Revolution, however, liberalism shed some of its reliance on rationalism and began to base itself on utilitarianism. A link was thus forged between early revolutionary individualism and a new idealistic concern for the interests of society.

In England the Liberal party, which espoused liberal doctrines, came into being (1846) under the leadership of Lord John Russell (later Earl Russell) and William E. GLADSTONE. In France, liberalism developed in opposition to the policies of the restored Bourbon kings and became a major force in the Third Republic; leading French liberals were Léon GAMBETTA and Georges CLEMENCEAU. In the United States the most characteristic representative of liberalism was Woodrow WILSON.

By the 20th century, political and economic thinking among liberals had begun to shift in response to an expanding and complex economy. Liberals began to support the idea that the government can best promote individual dignity and freedom through intervention in the economy and by establishing a state concerned about the welfare of its people. With the rise of the WELFARE STATE, the new liberals also looked to government to correct some of the ills believed to be caused by unregulated capitalism. They favored TAXATION, MINIMUM WAGE legislation, SOCIAL SECURITY, ANTITRUST LAWS, public education, safety and health laws, and other measures to protect consumers and preserve the environment (see GOVERNMENT REGULATION). Some liberals became socialists, although opposing doctrinaire Marxism and communism. The more traditional liberals, who held to the ideas of Adam Smith and John Stuart Mill, found themselves classed as conservatives.

LENNART FRANTZELL

Bibliography: De Ruggiero, Guido, *The History of European Liberalism*, trans. by R. C. Collingwood (1927; repr. 1977); Eccleshall, Robert, *British Liberalism* (1986); Gerber, William, *American Liberalism*, rev. ed. (1987); Gray, John, *Liberalism* (1986); Hamby, Alonzo, *Liberalism and Its Challengers* (1985).

liberation theology

Liberation theology, a term first used in 1973 by Gustavo Gutiérrez, a Peruvian Roman Catholic priest, is a school of thought among Latin American Catholics according to which the Gospel of Christ demands that the church concentrate its efforts on liberating the people of the world from poverty and oppression. Many Protestant churchmen and church bodies have adopted similar positions.

The liberation-theology movement was partly inspired by the Second Vatican Council and the 1967 papal encyclical *Populorum progressio*. Its leading exponents include Gutiérrez, Leonardo Boff of Brazil, and Juan Luis Segundo of Uruguay. The liberationists have received encouragement from the Latin American bishops, especially in resolutions adopted at a 1968 conference in Medellín, Colombia; others in the Roman Catholic church have objected to their use of Marxist ideas, their support for revolutionary movements, and their criticisms of traditional church institutions. Vatican authorities censured Boff in 1985 but in a 1986 document supported a moderate form of liberation theology.

Bibliography: Berryman, Phillip, *Liberation Theology* (1987).

Liberia   [ly-bir'-ee-uh]

The Republic of Liberia is located on the Atlantic coast of West Africa and is bordered by Sierra Leone, Guinea, and Ivory Coast. An independent nation since 1847, Liberia is the only nation in black Africa never to have been under colonial rule. Partly settled by freed American slaves during the 19th century, Liberia has always maintained close ties with the United States. It is a developing nation, whose income is derived almost entirely from the export of raw materials.

LAND AND RESOURCES
Liberia's straight, sandy coast, 560 km (350 mi) long, is broken by lagoons and mangrove swamps and gives way to a low, rolling plain about 30 km (20 mi) wide. Further inland, foothills ranging in height from 200 to 300 m (600 to 1,000 ft) are found. They become mountains in the north and east whose ranges run southwest-northeast. High plateaus are interspersed between the ranges. In the north is Mount Wutuvi, the highest point in the country, which rises to 1,381 m (4,531 ft). Liberian rivers are short, flowing parallel to each other from the mountains to the ocean. The largest rivers are the Saint Paul, Saint John, and Cavalla.

Liberia's tropical climate is hot and humid. Average temperatures range from 17° C (63° F) to 31° C (87° F). Annual rainfall, as much as 4,500 mm (177 in) at the coast, gradually decreases inland to 1,750 mm (69 in). The monsoonal rainy season occurs between May and October. A dusty winter wind, the Harmattan, blows during December.

Liberia's vast timber resources include over 90 commercially exploitable species. Mineral resources include substantial deposits of iron ore, diamonds, and gold.

PEOPLE

The population consists of 16 indigenous ethnic groups, each with its own language, as well as the English-speaking Americo-Liberians. The largest groups are the Kpelle (19% of the population), the Bassa (14% of the population), and the Gio, Kru, Grebo, Mano, and Loma. The Americo-Liberians, who constitute only 5% of the population, are descendants of blacks who migrated to Liberia from the New World, mostly from the United States, between 1820 and 1865. The Americo-Liberians dominated Liberian society until the military coup of 1980. An earlier (1944) program of integration designed to reduce the imbalance had proved largely ineffective. After the coup, the government was dominated by the Krahn, allied with the Mandingo. After civil war began in late 1989, the army slaughtered many Gio and Mano, inflaming ethnic tensions. Liberia is officially Christian, but a majority practice traditional religions, and there is a Muslim minority.

Almost half of the urban population live in MONROVIA, the capital, which was badly damaged during the civil war. Earlier, Monrovia and the mining centers in the interior experienced rapid growth due to internal migration from rural areas.

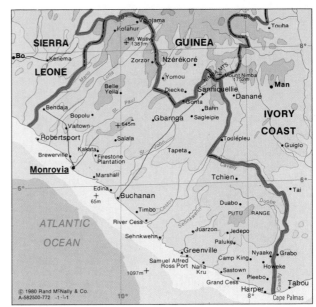

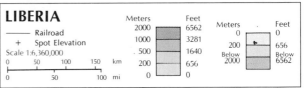

LIBERIA

	Meters	Feet	Meters	Feet
Railroad	2000	6562	0	0
+ Spot Elevation	1000	3281	200	656
Scale 1:6,360,000	500	1640	Below	Below
	200	656	2000	6562
	0	0		

Scale: 0 50 100 150 km / 0 50 100 mi

© 1980 Rand McNally & Co.
A-582500-772 -1-1-1

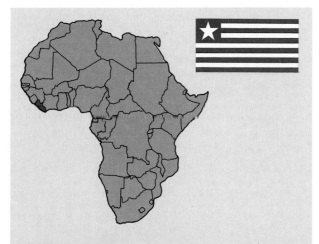

REPUBLIC OF LIBERIA

LAND. Area: 111,369 km² (43,000 mi²). Capital and largest city: Monrovia (1984 est. pop., 425,000).

PEOPLE. Population (1990 est.): 2,600,000; density: 23.3 persons per km² (60.5 per mi²). Distribution (1987): 42% urban, 58% rural. Annual growth (1985–90): 3.2%. Official language: English. Major religions: traditional religions, Christianity, Islam.

EDUCATION AND HEALTH. Literacy (1985): 35% of adult population. Universities (1990): 2. Hospital beds (1981): 3,000. Physicians (1983): 221. Life expectancy (1985–90): women—56; men—53. Infant mortality (1985–90): 87 per 1,000 live births.

ECONOMY. GNP (1987): $1.05 billion; $450 per capita. Labor distribution (1984): agriculture—72%; services—9%; trade—7%; mining—3%; transportation and communications—2%; manufacturing—2%. Foreign trade (1987): imports (1986)—$259 million; exports—$458 million; principal trade partners—United States, European Community. Currency: 1 Liberian dollar = 100 cents.

GOVERNMENT. Type: republic (rival governments proclaimed in 1990, none of which has effective control). Legislature: National Assembly (suspended). Political subdivisions: 13 counties.

COMMUNICATIONS. Railroads (1987): 490 km (304 mi) total. Roads (1987): 8,064 km (5,011 mi) total. Major ports: 4. Major airfields: 2.

Education was formerly provided by Christian missions, but most schools are now government operated. Although education is free and compulsory from ages 6 to 16, less than half of all school-age children attend, partly because of a teacher shortage. The University of Liberia (1862) is in Monrovia.

ECONOMIC ACTIVITY

Most of Liberia's workers are engaged in subsistence agriculture. Commercial crops (most notably rubber) are grown primarily on plantations, which employ about half the wage-earners. Fishing has always flourished along the coast, and mining and forestry are economically important. Iron ore replaced rubber as the leading export in 1961, and constituted about 57% of exports in 1987. Liberia also receives income from the registration of foreign ships, many of which fly the Liberian "flag of convenience" to avoid regulations and taxes. The industrial sector remains underdeveloped; machinery, transportation equipment, and food are imported.

Close economic relations are maintained with the United States. U.S. aid to Liberia totaled $500 million from 1980 to 1987—the largest amount per capita in sub-Saharan Africa—although economic mismanagement led to a subsequent reduction in assistance. Unable to pay its foreign debts for several years, Liberia was in a state of virtual economic collapse by 1990 due to the civil war. Homes and businesses were destroyed, the planting and harvesting of crops were disrupted, and famine threatened much of the population.

HISTORY AND GOVERNMENT

Liberia's tribal peoples migrated to the area between the 12th and 16th centuries. The Portuguese arrived in 1461 and began a trade in ivory and pepper, and later in slaves. In 1816 the AMERICAN COLONIZATION SOCIETY was founded in the United States to resettle former slaves in Africa. In 1820 the first colonists arrived, and their successful settlement was named Monrovia (for U.S. president James Monroe) in 1824. More colonists gradually arrived and established separate colonies. In 1847 the colonies amalgamated, and Liberia became the first independent republic in black Africa.

The new nation faced a variety of problems: resistance to the government by the indigenous tribes, decline in demand for Liberia's exports, and territorial encroachment by the

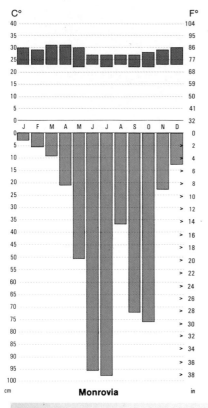

C° F°

Monrovia

cm in

(Left) *Bars indicate monthly ranges of temperature (red) and precipitation (blue) in Monrovia, the capital and largest city of Liberia. Monrovia, which is situated on the Atlantic coast, has a tropical wet climate.*

(Below) *A small clearing reveals workers' cottages on the 4,000-km² (1,500-mi²) Firestone Rubber plantation at Harbel, the world's largest. About 2% of the world's rubber is produced in Liberia, which is also one of the world's leading producers of iron ore. Falling prices for iron ore and rubber battered the economy in the 1980s. The situation worsened in 1990, when rebel forces occupied the Firestone Rubber plantation and halted production at the iron-ore mines in the Nimba Mountains, where the fighting began.*

British, French, and Germans. Liberia was able to maintain its independence only with U.S. support. In order to restore the languishing economy, a 99-year rubber-plantation concession was granted to the Firestone Company in 1926 in exchange for a large long-term loan from the U.S. government. After World War II, various development projects were constructed with U.S. financing. From 1878 to 1980, when the 1847 constitution was suspended after a military coup led by Sgt. Samuel K. DOE, politics were dominated by the Americo-Liberian True Whig party. William V. S. TUBMAN served as president from 1944 until his death in 1971. His successor, William R. TOLBERT, Jr., was killed in the 1980 coup. Liberian policies toward

the United States and foreign business remained unchanged after the 1980 coup. In 1984, voters approved a new U.S.-style constitution. Doe remained head of the civilian government installed following elections in 1985 from which the main opposition parties were barred.

In December 1989, as political repression increased and the economy neared collapse, rebels launched a war against the Doe regime. Backers of rebel leader Charles Taylor and one of his allies, Prince Johnson, later split into rival factions. Taylor gained control of most of the countryside, while Johnson battled Doe's armed guard in Monrovia. In August 1990 a multinational West African force entered Liberia to try to end the bloody three-way civil war, which had caused at least 5,000 deaths (mostly among civilians as a result of tribal rivalries exacerbated by the war) and forced another 400,000 Liberians to flee to neighboring countries. After Doe was killed by Johnson's forces on September 9, fighting between the multinational force and Taylor's rebels broke out. A late September cease-fire soon broke down, and prospects for a negotiated settlement remained dim.   RONALD D. GARST

Bibliography: Boley, G. E. S., *Liberia: The Rise and Fall of the First Republic* (1984); Dunn, D. E., and Tarr, S. B., *Liberia* (1988); Gershoni, Y., *Black Colonialism* (1985); Liebenow, J. G., *Liberia: The Evolution of Privilege* (1969) and *Liberia: The Quest for Democracy* (1987); Lowenkopf, M., *Politics in Liberia* (1976); Nelson, H. D., ed., *Liberia: A Country Study* (1985); Smith, J. W., *Sojourners in Search of Freedom: The Settlement of Liberia by Black Americans* (1987).

Liberty Bell

The Liberty Bell is a pre-Revolutionary War relic that was first hung in 1753 in the newly finished Pennsylvania State House, the building that would eventually become Independence Hall. Cast in a London foundry, the bell was inscribed with the words *Proclaim Liberty throughout all the Land . . .* (Lev. 25:10). It was rung on the adoption of the Declaration of Independence in July 1776, inaugurating an Independence Day tradition that was observed until 1846. That year a small crack enlarged to the point where the bell could no longer be sounded. Perhaps the most famous symbol of the colonial struggle for independence, it is now housed in Philadelphia's Liberty Bell pavilion.

Bibliography: Boland, C. M., *Ring in the Jubilee* (1973).

Liberty party

The first political party in U.S. history based exclusively on an antislavery platform, the Liberty party held its first convention in Albany, N.Y., on Apr. 1, 1840. It sought a middle path between such abolitionists as William Lloyd GARRISON, who refused to participate in the political process, and opponents of slavery who remained loyal to established parties.

James G. BIRNEY ran for the presidency on the Liberty party ticket in 1840 and 1844. The party was often strong enough in local elections to force major-party candidates to espouse abolitionism in order to win its backing. In 1848 it joined antislavery Whigs and Democrats in the new FREE SOIL PARTY.

libido   [li-bee'-doh]

In psychoanalysis, libido is the energy source used to satisfy sexual or general needs (Sigmund Freud), or psychic energy (Carl Jung). In general usage, libido means sexual drive.

Libra   [leeb'-ruh]

Libra (the Balance), the seventh constellation of the ZODIAC, is located between Virgo and Scorpius and is best seen in the Northern Hemisphere in spring. The Sun passes southeastward through Libra from about October 24 to November 22, during its sojourn south of the celestial equator. Among Libra's stars are three binaries: the two stars of Alpha Librae are just barely resolvable to the naked eye; Beta Librae, with the unusual color of green, is a spectroscopic binary; and Delta Librae is an eclipsing binary.

library

The library is a place where books, journals, microfilms, and audio and visual materials are kept and organized to support the cultural, informational, recreational, and educational needs of the general public or specific groups of users. Thus a public library houses materials of general interest and is open to everyone, whereas a corporate library limits its clientele and the scope of its holdings. Recent advances in computing and communication technologies have transformed the contemporary library: it is not only a repository, but now also an active member in a vast network of libraries and databanks through which users have access to a worldwide store of recorded knowledge.

The most common kinds of libraries are public libraries and those of schools, colleges and universities, and government. In addition, many specialized libraries serving industry, commerce, the media, and the professions have been established during the latter half of the 20th century. In the United States and Canada alone more than 135,000 libraries exist, ranging in size from the LIBRARY OF CONGRESS to the smallest elementary school facilities. Currently, American libraries are facing severe financial hardship caused by cutbacks in public funding and government support, escalating costs of materials and equipment, and a growing dependence upon initially costly communication and computing technologies.

Classification Systems and the Catalog. Library classification systems permit users to look for a particular book by title or author, or to discover what books on a particular subject are held by the library. Most libraries use one of three major classification systems: the Dewey Decimal System, invented by Melvil DEWEY; the Universal Decimal Classification, a European adaptation of Dewey; or a system developed by the Library of Congress.

The library's catalog not only lists the library's contents but also analyzes them, so that all works by an individual author, all works on a given subject, and all works in a specific category (dictionaries, sound recordings, or atlases, for example) can be easily located by readers. The modern catalog is a practical tool that is the result of the analysis of the subject, category, and contents of books, videocassettes, microfilms, compact discs, and a host of other informational vehicles.

The library's own card catalog is only one of the many forms in which catalog and bibliographic materials are available. Large libraries own the *National Union Catalog,* for example, a cumulative listing of the library resources of the Library of Congress and other major and specialized libraries in the United States and Canada. Specialized libraries may own or subscribe to such specialized catalogs as the *Eighteenth Century Short Title Catalog* (ESTC), a computerized database listing every publication—book, pamphlet, or single sheet—printed between 1701 and 1800 in English or, if in a foreign language, in English-speaking countries.

Cataloging and classifying are expensive processes. Many libraries economize by subscribing to a computerized bibliographic service. To locate materials that are not among its holdings, a library may query the Online Computer Library Center (OCLC) or the Research Libraries Information Network (RLIN), which are the two major national catalog networks. Through their computerized databases, these networks offer interlibrary loan services that can operate, if necessary, across the continent.

History. The earliest ancient libraries were clay-tablet repositories in ancient Mesopotamia. Ashurbanipal's library in Nine-

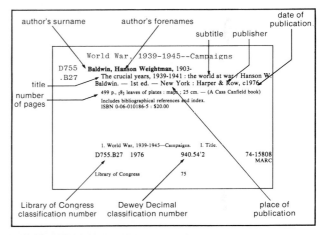

(Above) *A subject card from the card catalog details essential information about a book in the listed subject area and provides the classification code that locates it in the library's collection. An up-to-date catalog—now often in computerized form—is essential to efficient use of a library's resources.*

(Left) *The library of the University of Leiden, the Netherlands's oldest university, is portrayed in this Dutch engraving (1610). The political and religious upheavals of the Reformation led to the founding of many Protestant centers of learning, including both university and town libraries, to replace monastic centers of learning.*

(Left) *This cuneiform tablet (c.705 BC) was found at the palace of the Assyrian king Sargon II. Archives of Mesopotamian rulers were among the earliest libraries.* (Center) *This miniature of Saint Luke comes from the Ebbo Gospels (c.816–35), one of the many illuminated manuscripts now preserved in European libraries. (Municipal Library, Épernay, France.)* (Right) *Duke Humphrey's Library, founded by the duke of Gloucester in 1489, is part of Oxford University's Bodleian Library, a great repository of literary and historical manuscripts.*

veh (7th century BC) consisted of thousands of inscribed clay tablets recording laws, astronomical data, commercial transactions, narrative poems, and royal happenings. A 30,000-tablet library has been discovered at diggings in the ancient Sumerian city of Nippur, and other extensive libraries have been found throughout the Mesopotamian region.

The earliest large Greek library is attributed to Aristotle (4th century BC), but the greatest was established (3d century BC) by Ptolemy I in the museum at Alexandria, Egypt. Scholars there copied, revised, collated, and edited works of the classical Greek writers. Their copies of ancient works became the standard editions on which other ancient copyists and libraries depended and, ultimately, the basis of most of the manuscripts in European libraries. The library flourished for several centuries and held about 500,000 papyrus scrolls. Another great Hellenic library was at Pergamum, in what is now Turkey.

Libraries in the Middle Ages were established in monasteries throughout Europe, and in cathedrals that served as links between the monasteries and universities. Manuscripts were laboriously copied by hand on parchment pages that were assembled into wood-bound codices (see BOOK).

In the Muslim world, Damascus, Baghdad, and many other cities had libraries, but most were destroyed by the 13th century. In China the first libraries were established under the Ch'in dynasty (221–206 BC), when one copy of every book in the empire was placed in an imperial library and all other copies (with certain exceptions) were burned. In the 1st century AD the Han-dynasty Imperial Library owned 677 works, of which 47 survive. The Sui-dynasty library (7th century AD) had over 5,000 titles and divided its holdings into four categories: Confucian classics, philosophy, history, and belles lettres. This division was used until the 20th century.

In Europe the advent of printing in the 15th century brought down the cost of books by speeding up the process of copying. Private libraries became more common, and by the 17th century a few public libraries had come into being. Thereafter the number of libraries multiplied in both Europe and America. Users remained few in number, however, until literacy became more widespread during the 18th century.

In the 17th century, France's national library, the BIBLIO-THÈQUE NATIONALE, was founded in Paris. The BRITISH LIBRARY, originally a part of the British Museum, was set up during the 18th century. The first academic library in the United States was established by John Harvard at Harvard College in 1638. In 1731, Benjamin Franklin founded the Library Company of Philadelphia, the first subscription library in America. Dues paid by its members were used to buy books, which could then be borrowed, without charge, by the members. Franklin's library provided a pattern for the modern public library, a uniquely American institution where anyone may independently pursue self-education.

The first U.S. public library was opened in Salisbury, Conn., in 1803, the result of a gift of 150 books by a resident. New York State began to develop its free public libraries beginning in 1835, by legislating the establishment of tax-supported libraries in state school districts. Within states, library systems burgeoned under the administration of municipalities, counties, or regions. The U.S. federal government established national libraries of medicine and agriculture, as well as de-

This page from a 14th-century Bible Moralisée *exhibits the lavish illumination that had developed as an artistic mode in monastic libraries and scriptoria during the Middle Ages. Although the scarce, expensive manuscripts were generally confined to monastic and university libraries, extensive private book collections were formed during the late Middle Ages and early Renaissance. (Bodleian Library, Oxford.)*

(Above) *The reference desk of a public library provides professional assistance in locating information. Since the opening (1830s) of the first tax-supported libraries in the United States, public libraries have proliferated and steadily expanded their range of services.*

Rare-book collections are housed in such diverse settings as Yale University's strikingly modern Beinicke Library (above), designed (1963) by Gordon Bunshaft, and the luxurious East Room of the Pierpont Morgan Library (left), New York City. Vincent of Beauvais's Myrour of the Worlde (below left), printed by William Caxton in 1481, is one of many rare books in the Morgan's renowned medieval and Renaissance collections.

(Left) *Young children are encouraged to explore picture books and primers in a public library's juvenile department.*

(Below) *The John F. Kennedy Library in Dorchester, Mass., overlooking Boston Harbor, contains an extensive collection of tapes, documents, and studies concerning the late president's political career. This specialized library, designed by I. M. Pei, was dedicated in October 1979.*

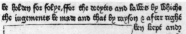

A librarian assists a researcher in the use of a microfilm reader. Such technological advances as microfilm, which contains data on film in miniature form, and computerized collections have greatly expanded the range of materials available to public libraries.

partmental and agency libraries; it supports the Library of Congress and provides some funding for the various public and institutional library systems in the country.

Most countries have now established their own national libraries, but their oldest university libraries often have richer collections of rare materials. Harvard and Yale in the United States and Oxford (the BODLEIAN LIBRARY) and Cambridge in England are famous for their bibliographical treasures. Government libraries for the most part date from the 19th and 20th centuries; the great public libraries—those of New York, Boston, Philadelphia, Chicago—though older, did not develop into anything even approaching their present size until late in the 19th century.

Both public and private libraries have benefited from the generosity of many benefactors. Andrew CARNEGIE helped establish over 2,000 public libraries. Notable private foundations in the United States include the MORGAN LIBRARY, the FOLGER SHAKESPEARE LIBRARY, the HUNTINGTON LIBRARY, and the NEWBERRY LIBRARY. In Europe, private collections such as the AMBROSIAN LIBRARY in Milan or the LAURENTIAN LIBRARY in Florence can trace their origins back to the Middle Ages or Renaissance times.

Two national libraries, one in Beijing (People's Republic of China) and the other in Taipei (Taiwan), opened their new buildings in 1987 and 1988, respectively. The Beijing library is among the largest in the world, with holdings of 14 million items. (The world's largest is the U.S. Library of Congress, with over 88 million items in 1988, including 14.5 million books and 36.5 million manuscripts.)

Library Trends. The trend of library policy is clearly toward the ideal of making all information available inexpensively and quickly to all people. Because of the information explosion and the issues raised by the control, manipulation, encryption, and preservation of knowledge, accomplishment of this goal is difficult. Retrenchment in public funding, the increase in paper-format (book) publishing, and rising costs of technology make it obligatory for conservationists, archivists, and librarians to cooperate in resolving their problems. For example, PAPER decay has plagued libraries for many years. Microfilm copying was adopted as a makeshift way of maintaining decipherability, but now, stress is being placed on conservation techniques to stem the decay of the volumes themselves. New standards for permanent paper are being proposed, as well as direct publication in nonprint media. Preservation, as the 21st century nears, extends beyond familiar maintenance and curatorial responsibilities. The problem of preserving not just the physical media (books, journals, and so on) but the transient information embodied in electronic

form must now be faced. Ambiguous public policy, costly technology, an adverse economy, and a growing shortage of qualified librarians are all conspiring to make the healthful survival of libraries one of the major issues of the 1990s.

ROBERT L. COLLISON
Reviewed by RICHARD S. HALSEY

Bibliography: *American Library Directory* (annual); *Bowker Annual of Library and Book Trade Information* (annual); Dekker, Marcel, *Encyclopedia of Library and Information Science*, vols. 1–43 (1968–88); Dickson, Paul, *The Library in America: A Celebration in Words and Pictures* (1986); Edelman, Hendrick, ed., *Libraries and Information Science in the Electronic Age* (1986); Jackson, Sidney L., *A Brief History of Libraries and Librarianship in the West* (1974); Thompson, James, *Ancient Libraries* (1940; repr. 1962) and *The Medieval Library* (1939; repr. 1967).

Library of Congress

The Library of Congress was created in 1800 to provide "such books as may be necessary for the use of Congress." Over the succeeding years, and supported largely by funds appropriated by Congress, it has grown to become the national library of the United States, serving all government branches and the public at large. Since the 1870s it has also administered the American copyright system. It publishes the *National Union Catalog*—a cumulative record of the books housed in 2,500 libraries in the United States and Canada—which serves as a basic bibliographic and catalog source (see LIBRARY); prints and distributes cataloging data for subscriber libraries; and has developed and popularized a numerical system of subject classification. The library's Congressional Research Service prepares reports on any topic at the request of congressmen.

The library's collections contain over 14 million books and 36 million manuscripts, including the personal papers of most U.S. presidents up to Calvin Coolidge. It also holds maps, music, art prints, photographs, motion pictures, videotapes, newspapers, pamphlets, recordings, and other materials—for a total of 88 million items. Because of its copyright function,

The reading room of the Library of Congress, the national library of the United States, contains the card catalog, information that is also available on computer. The library's vast collection includes all printed material subject to U.S. copyright laws.

it receives a copy of every book copyrighted in the United States. The American Folklife Center, administered by the library, collects and preserves American folklore; it supports research projects and presents performances and exhibitions of folk music, arts, and crafts.

The library was originally housed in the Capitol; most of its books were destroyed when the British shelled the building during the War of 1812. The major step in rebuilding the collection was taken in 1815, when Congress purchased the 6,000-volume personal library of Thomas Jefferson. With the purchase of the books of Dr. Otto H. F. Vollbehr in 1930, the library more than doubled the size of its collection of incunabula, which is now the largest in the Western Hemisphere. The main Library of Congress building was erected in 1897; the library also occupies the Thomas Jefferson building, formerly called the annex, and the new James Madison building.

The post of Librarian of Congress, appointed by the president with the advice and consent of the Senate, has often gone to eminent scholars and artists, as well as to professional librarians. Recent Librarians of Congress include Archibald MacLeish (1939–44), L. Quincy Mumford (1954–74), Daniel J. Boorstin (1974–87), and James H. Billington (1987–   ).

Bibliography: Goodrum, Charles A., *The Library of Congress* (1987) and *Treasures of the Library of Congress* (1980); Hilker, Helen-Anne, *Ten First Street, Southeast: Congress Builds a Library, 1886–1897* (1980); Rohrbach, P. T., *FIND: Automation at the Library of Congress* (1985); Schreyer, Alice D., *History of Books: A Guide to Selected Resources in the Library of Congress* (1987).

libration   [ly-bray'-shun]

A libration is a vibration around some equilibrium position (originally applied to a measuring balance). The word is often used in astronomy, as in the librations of the TROJAN asteroids around their triangular equilibrium positions in the Sun-Jupiter-asteroid system (see THREE-BODY PROBLEM).

The period of rotation of the Moon on its axis is equal to the period of its revolution around the Earth, so that, on the average, the Moon always has the same hemisphere turned toward the Earth. The librations of the Moon consist of four types of oscillations about this average situation. There are optical librations: in latitude, because the axis of rotation is not perpendicular to the plane of the orbit, and in longitude, because the line joining the Earth to the Moon does not revolve in space at a constant rate (because of the eccentricity of the Moon's orbit). Diurnal librations occur because the rotation of the Earth enables an observer to see the Moon from different directions. Physical librations are small oscillations caused by torques exerted gravitationally on the Moon, which is not quite spherical, by other bodies.   J. M. A. DANBY

libretto   [lib-ret'-oh]

A libretto (literally, "little book") is the text of an opera, operetta, oratorio, or—more recently—a musical comedy. The author of a libretto often works in conjunction with the composer, as in the famous collaborations of Mozart and Lorenzo DA PONTE, Verdi and Arrigo BOITO, Richard Strauss and Hugo von HOFMANNSTHAL, and GILBERT AND SULLIVAN. Many authors' works were set by more than one composer: librettos of Otavio Rinuccini were set by Cavalli and Monteverdi, those of Pietro METASTASIO by Alessandro Scarlatti, Handel, Mozart, and many others, and those of Eugène SCRIBE by Auber, Cilèa, Halevy, and Meyerbeer. In the 19th century Wagner wrote his own librettos to achieve a closer marriage of text and music.
                                                                    HOMER ULRICH

Bibliography: Groos, A., and Parker, R., eds., *Reading Opera* (1988); Smith, Patrick J., *The Tenth Muse* (1970; repr. 1975).

Libreville   [leeb-ruh-veel']

Libreville, the capital city of Gabon, lies on the Gabon Estuary, near the Gulf of Guinea. It has a population of 235,700 (1985 est.). The city is primarily an administrative center, but lumber, rubber, cacao, and palm products are shipped from its sheltered port, and an international airport is located 11 km

(7 mi) north. The National University of Gabon (1970) is there. Settled by the Pongoue people in the 16th century, Libreville was colonized by the French in 1849, who settled freed slaves there.

Librium   [lib'-ree-uhm]

Librium, the trade name for chlordiazepoxide hydrochloride, was the first of a class of drugs called benzodiazepines, which include VALIUM. Discovered in 1958, Librium rapidly became widely used as a TRANQUILIZER for patients suffering from anxiety and tension. Librium, which may be administered either by capsule or injection, is also indicated for use in treating the withdrawal symptoms of acute alcoholism. While excessively large doses can produce coma, fatalities from overdosage of Librium alone are very rare. Nevertheless, Librium and other minor tranquilizers can cause dependence and have come under strict control in the United States by the Food and Drug Administration (FDA).   RICHARD H. RUNSER

Libya   [lib'-yuh]

Libya, a petroleum-rich Arab nation located in North Africa, is Africa's fourth largest country. After centuries of rule by Ottoman Turks, three decades as an Italian colonial possession, and post–World War II combined British and French administration, Libya gained independence in 1951 as the United Kingdom of Libya. In 1969, Col. Muammar al-QADDAFI led a military coup that ended the monarchy and proclaimed the Libyan Arab Republic. In 1977 its name was changed to the Popular Socialist Libyan Arab Jamahiriya (the word *Jamahiriya* meaning "state of the masses"). The Mediterranean Sea

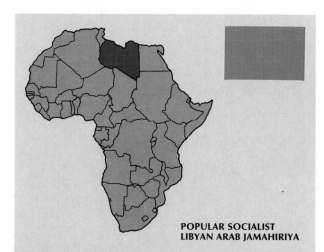

**POPULAR SOCIALIST
LIBYAN ARAB JAMAHIRIYA**

LAND. Area: 1,759,540 km² (679,362 mi²). Capital and largest city: Tripoli (1988 pop., 1,083,000).
PEOPLE. Population (1989 est.): 4,080,000; density: 2.3 persons per km² (6 per mi²). Distribution (1985): 65% urban, 35% rural. Annual growth (1985–90): 3.45%. Official language: Arabic. Major religion: Islam.
EDUCATION AND HEALTH. Literacy (1985): 74% of adult population. Universities (1990): 3. Hospital beds (1985): 20,000. Physicians (1985): 5,450. Life expectancy (1989): women—69; men—64. Infant mortality (1989): 70 per 1,000 live births.
ECONOMY. GNP (1988 est.): $20 billion; $5,410 per capita. Labor distribution (1985): construction—24%; services—17%; agriculture—17%; manufacturing—11%; transportation and communications—9%. Foreign trade (1988): imports—$5.0 billion; exports—$6.6 billion; principal trade partners—Italy, West Germany, United Kingdom, France. Currency: 1 Libyan dinar = 1,000 dirhans.
GOVERNMENT. Type: socialist state. Legislature: General People's Congress. Political subdivisions: 10 administrative provinces.
COMMUNICATIONS. Railroads (1990): none. Roads (1987): 19,300 km (12,000 mi) total. Major ports: 4. Major airfields: 2.

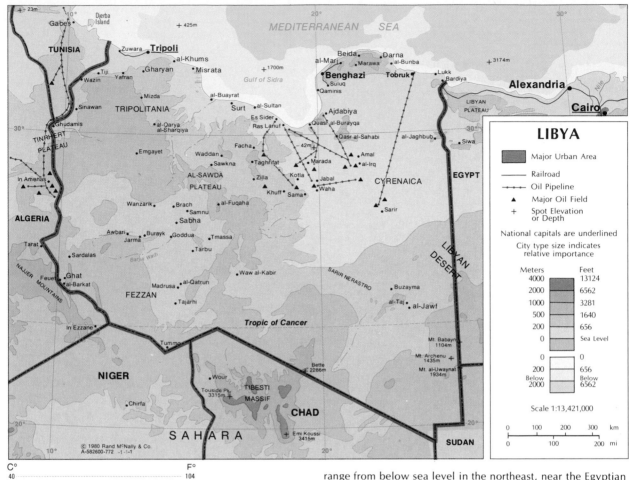

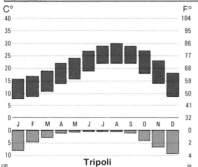

Bars on this annual climate chart indicate the monthly ranges of temperature (red) and precipitation (blue) in Tripoli, the capital and largest city of Libya. Tripoli, which has a Mediterranean climate, is cooler and wetter than most places in the country.

lies to the north, Egypt and Sudan to the east, Tunisia and Algeria to the west, and Chad and Niger to the south. Tripoli, on the Mediterranean coast, is the capital.

LAND AND RESOURCES

Libya consists of three distinct physical regions: the northwest coast, the northeast coast, and a vast desert region to the south that covers more than 90% of the nation. The northwest region, the historical province of Tripolitania, borders the Mediterranean Sea and rises southward in a series of steps from a narrow, often marshy, coastal plain to the 120-km-wide (75-mi) Jaffara Plain and the shrub-covered plateau of Jabal Nafusah, with elevations of about 600 to 900 m (2,000 to 3,000 ft). The northeastern region, which is the northern part of the historical province of CYRENAICA, lies east of the Gulf of Sidra on the Mediterranean. The land rises southward from the narrow al Marj plain near the sea to the tree-covered slopes of the Jabal al Akhdar, or Green Mountains, at elevations less than 915 m (3,000 ft). To the south stretch the semiarid and desert lands that are part of the SAHARA. Elevations

range from below sea level in the northeast, near the Egyptian border, to 2,286 m (7,500 ft) in Bette Peak, which is Libya's highest point and is located in the rugged Tibesti Massif near the border with Chad. Al-Kufrah, Ghat, and Ghudamis, three of the large oases, are located in depressions where groundwater reaches the surface or where the drilling of wells is feasible.

Climate. Some areas along the coast have a Mediterranean climate with moderate temperatures and enough rain during the winter months for grain farming. In Tripoli average temperatures are 30° C (86° F) in summer and 8° C (46° F) in winter; annual precipitation averages 380 mm (15 in) and falls mainly in winter. Semiarid conditions predominate in the al Marj and Jaffara plains, and in the southern deserts frequent periods of drought occur. A scorching wind called the *ghibli* occasionally blows into the usually humid coastal towns.

Resources. Libya has no perennial rivers and is drained by intermittent water courses (*wadis*) that flow only after heavy rains. Most water is obtained from shallow wells that tap vast underground artesian aquifers (water-bearing rock layers). Only the Jabal al Akhdar, covering about 1% of the country, is forested. Steppe vegetation, including esparto and other short grasses, is characteristic of northern semiarid areas, and xerophytic, or drought-resistant, vegetation predominates in desert areas. Petroleum and natural gas, first discovered in 1959 at Zaltan, are abundant and constitute the principal mineral resources; iron ore and potash deposits are also present.

PEOPLE

About 90% of Libya's population belong to the Arabic-speaking majority of mixed Arab-Berber ancestry. True BERBERS, who retain the Berber language and customs, are the largest non-Arab minority but form only 4% of the population; they are concentrated in small, isolated villages in the west. Other minorities are the Arabic-speaking Harratin, of Negroid and West African ancestry, who make up about 3% of the population and inhabit the southern oases; and the Berber-related TUAREG and Tebu in the south, who make up about 1% of the population. The official language is Arabic. The Sunni branch of Islam is the official religion and the nation's dominant political, cultural, and legal force.

The Mediterranean coastal areas, where 90% of the population live, are densely populated; other areas are only sparsely settled or uninhabited. TRIPOLI and BENGHAZI are the largest cities. About 20% of the population are nomadic, particularly in the east. Population growth is rapid, resulting from the disparity between a high birthrate and a low death rate. Nonetheless, Libya's development programs are hindered by a serious labor shortage; about 30% of the labor force is composed of foreigners. Primary education for children between the ages of 6 and 12 is now compulsory. Libya's petroleum revenues have been used in part to finance construction of schools, hospitals, and clinics. The University of Garyounis (1955) in Benghazi and Tripoli's Alfateh University (1973) are among the nation's higher-education institutes.

ECONOMIC ACTIVITY
Petroleum was discovered in 1959 and has since financed the transformation of Libya from a poor nation at the time of independence to a rich one that spends vast sums on social, agricultural, and military development. In 1987, Libya ranked 16th among world petroleum producers, with a governmentally regulated output of about 1.05 million barrels per day.

Manufacturing and other private-sector economic activities have been nationalized. The construction, food-processing, textile, petrochemical, and tanning industries, along with the production of traditional handicrafts, are the leading industrial activities. Land suitable for agriculture, located mainly in the coastal regions, constitutes less than 6% of the total area. Wheat, olives, and fruits and vegetables are the major crops. Livestock raising is the chief economic activity of the nomadic population. Investments in irrigation facilities, improved seed strains, and the reclamation of unstable dune areas have done little to reduce Libya's dependence on imported foods. Be-

High-grade Libyan petroleum extracted from well sites in the nation's interior is conveyed through pipelines to the Mediterranean coast for shipment to refineries in Western Europe and the United States. Libyan petroleum is particularly valued for its low sulfur content.

cause of the drop in world oil prices in the 1980s, Libya was forced to scale back many development plans. In 1984, however, Qaddafi inaugurated his most ambitious project—the construction of a great artificial river to transport water from aquifers beneath the Libyan Desert to coastal cities.

A modern highway network now connects the coastal towns with the desert oases and petroleum fields. Tripoli and Benghazi are the chief ports for cargo; Es Sidar, Ras Lanuf, and Marsa el Brega handle petroleum shipments. Petroleum accounts for more than 95% of all export income, although the petroleum industry employs less than 10% of the labor force. The value of petroleum exports far exceeds that of imports, dominated by machinery, foodstuffs, and armaments.

GOVERNMENT
Qaddafi has tried to transform Libya into an egalitarian, socialist state of the masses. In theory, there is no formal government. According to the 1977 constitution, the masses rule themselves through an interlocking network of people's committees that exercise control over virtually all governmental and nongovernmental activities. The highest of these bodies is the General People's Congress (GPC). Qaddafi, Libya's "Revolutionary Leader," has held no formal office since his resignation as secretary-general of the GPC in 1979.

HISTORY
Phoenicians, Greeks, and Romans all established colonies in the area of present-day Libya. Arab domination began in the 7th century. In 1510, Spain conquered Tripoli and ruled until 1551 when Turkish forces made Libya part of the OTTOMAN EMPIRE. In 1711 the area became virtually autonomous and enjoyed 125 years of prosperity based on piracy directed by the Karamanli family; Ottoman rule was reasserted in 1835, however. In 1911, Italy declared war on Turkey (see ITALO-TURKISH WAR) and annexed Libya, making it a colony in 1934.

Italian settlement was opposed by the nationalist Sanusi (conservative Sunni Muslims; see SANUSI, AL-), whose leaders returned from exile to fight alongside the Allies and drive Italian and German forces out of Libya during World War II. After the war, Libya was placed under British and French administration. Italy gave up attempts to regain control in 1947, and the United Nations granted Libya independence effective in 1951 as the United Kingdom of Libya; the Sanusi leader Muhammad Idris of Cyrenaica became King IDRIS I.

In 1969, Idris was deposed, and Qaddafi and the Revolutionary Command Council seized power. Qaddafi, known for his radical Arab nationalism, has been a persistent foe of Israel and has attempted unsuccessfully to merge Libya with Egypt, Syria, Sudan, Tunisia, Chad, Morocco, and Algeria. Qaddafi has been accused of interfering in the internal affairs of a number of African states; he sent troops to Uganda in 1979 in support of President Idi Amin and intervened militarily in a civil war in neighboring Chad in the 1980s. Qaddafi's activities also involved him in conflicts with the United States, France, and Great Britain in the 1980s. After the United States launched air attacks on Libyan targets in 1986 in retaliation for Qaddafi's support of international terrorism, government agencies were moved from Tripoli to remote villages. Qaddafi survived coup attempts in 1970, 1975, and 1984 and major military defeats in Chad in 1987. Faced with rising dissatisfaction at home, he released many political prisoners and moderated some of his radical economic policies in 1988. In 1989 he signed a peace treaty with Chad and celebrated the 20th anniversary of his rise to power.   GARY L. FOWLER

Bibliography: Anderson, L., *The State and Social Transformation in Tunisia and Libya* (1986); Cooley, J., *Libyan Sandstorm* (1982); Davis, J., *Libyan Politics* (1988); Deeb, M. J., *Libya's Foreign Policy in North Africa* (1988); Deeb, M. K. and M. J., *Libya since the Revolution* (1982); Harris, L. C., *Libya* (1986); Khader, B., and El-Wifati, B., eds., *The Economic Development of Libya* (1986); Waddams, F. C., *The Libyan Oil Industry* (1980); Wright, J. L., *Libya: A Modern History* (1982).

Libyan Desert

The Libyan Desert, the northeastern portion of the SAHARA, is located in northwestern Sudan, western Egypt, and eastern Libya. It covers about 1,950,000 km^2 (750,000 mi^2). Elevations vary from 133 m (436 ft) below sea level at the QATTARA DE-

PRESSION in northern Egypt, to 1,934 m (6,345 ft) at Jabal al-Uwaynat, where the three countries meet. The terrain is composed of sand-free, rocky plateaus and plains covered with sand dunes or gravel. The annual rainfall is less than 125 mm (5 in), and summer temperatures rise above 43° C (100° F). A few Berbers and Arabs live in the scattered oases, raising fruits and livestock. Potash, coal, salt, gypsum, and petroleum are extracted in the region. The Egyptian portion of the desert was the scene of important battles during World War II.

lice: see LOUSE.

lichen [ly'-kuhn]

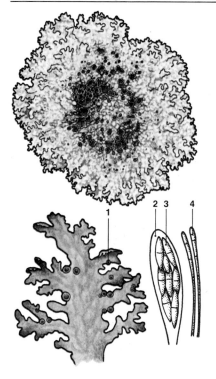

Parmelia (top) is a foliose, or leaflike, lichen found on deciduous trees in the southeastern United States. Lungwort, Lobaria pulmonaria (bottom), another common foliose lichen, reproduces sexually by means of apothecia (1), small, cup-shaped bodies borne on the surface of the lichen. The inner layer of the apothecia consists of sterile hairs, or paraphyses (2), and saclike asci (3), which contain ascospores (4). After the ascospores are dispersed, they germinate and reproduce the fungus, which must then combine with another alga to form a new lichen.

Lichens are dual organisms composed of an alga, called the phycobiont, and a fungus, called the mycobiont. The body, or thallus, of the lichen consists of algal cells mixed among the threadlike hyphae of the fungus; there are no true leaves, stems, or roots. The alga and the fungus live associated in a dependent symbiotic, or mutualistic, relationship; that is, they typically require each other to survive. Lichens are classified on the basis of the fungal component. The fungi are either Ascomycetes (sac fungi), Basidiomycetes (bracket fungi), or Deuteromycetes (fungi imperfecti). The algae are either green (Chlorophyta), blue-green (Cyanophyta), or yellow-green (Xanthophyta). Most lichens are composed of green algae and ascomycete fungi. In certain green algae lichens a secondary blue-green alga may also be present in restricted areas.

Lichens appear in a wide variety of habitats, including dry deserts, moist woods, mountaintops, under the soil, and in the ocean. They may be crustose (firmly attached to and encrusted on some surface); fruticose (projected out in upright, branched, or hanging stalks); or foliose (assume leaflike shapes). Lichens are slow-growing, some enlarging as little as 1 mm (0.04 in) per year, and are generally long-lived, with some Arctic lichens claimed to be 4,000 years old. Lichens play a role in the establishment of plant colonies on bare areas by accumulating soil debris beneath them and by limiting rock disintegration, which aid in soil formation.

The alga manufactures and provides itself and the fungus with a carbohydrate, either a simple sugar, such as glucose, or a sugar alcohol, such as sorbitol; the fungus converts it into a sugar alcohol, mannitol, which may serve as a storage food.

The alga also provides such vitamins as biotin and thiamine. Blue-green algae, in addition, are able to obtain, or fix, nitrogen from the air, which is also passed to the fungus. In turn, the fungus provides the alga with certain physical protection and obtains water vapor from the air, providing moisture for the alga. The water content of the lichen thallus is a critical factor in the rate of photosynthesis (sugar manufacture) and respiration. The fungus also manufactures various substances that often contain the pigment that gives the lichen its characteristic color, but whose function is not known. Few of the lichenized fungi or algae can survive alone, and the green alga Trebouxia, found in about half of all lichen species, has never been found in the free-living state.

Reproduction occurs in several ways. The alga or fungus may reproduce separately, in a manner identical to free-living forms. The alga commonly does this by reproducing asexually within the lichen thallus. The lichen as a whole may reproduce vegetatively by fragmentation or by various special algal-fungal combinations, such as soredia and isidia. A soredium is a package of one or more algal cells and some fungal hyphae, which are commonly released in great numbers through openings in the surface of the thallus. The isidium is a small projection from the surface of the thallus containing algal cells; it may break off and reproduce vegetatively. In some ascomycete lichens algal cells become associated and dispersed with the fungal spores.

Lichens of the genus Cladonia, known as reindeer moss, are a staple of caribou diet in North America. Old man's beard, Usnea, grows in long gray green streamers from branches in moist northern woods. Dyes and medicinal substances are extracted from lichens, but only the dye orchil, which is used as a food colorant and the source of litmus (a pH indicator), is commercially important.

EDWIN E. ROSENBLUM

Bibliography: Bland, John, Forests of Lilliput (1971); Hale, Mason E., The Biology of Lichens, 2d ed. (1974), and How to Know the Lichens (1969); Richardson, David, The Vanishing Lichens (1974).

Lichtenstein, Roy [lik'-ten-steen]

Roy Lichtenstein, b. New York City, Oct. 27, 1923, is a pop artist well known for his painted enlargements of banal comic strips (see POP ART). After studying and teaching at Ohio State University, Lichtenstein taught (1960–63) at Rutgers University and held his first one-man show in New York City in 1962. Comic-strip paintings such as Whaam (1963; Tate Gallery, London) humorously transpose the simplified violence and sentimentality of popular culture into huge, almost abstract, images. More recently, Lichtenstein has applied his distinctive style of dots and lines to adaptations of works by modern masters such as Pablo Picasso, and has produced sculptural parodies of the decorative styles of the 1920s and '30s.

Bibliography: Coplans, John, comp., Roy Lichtenstein (1972); Lichtenstein, Roy, Roy Lichtenstein: Drawings and Prints (1971).

In Okay, Hot-Shot (1963) and his other bold comic-strip "frames" from the 1960s, the American Pop painter Roy Lichtenstein conveys a double irony: slick, strong-colored images, very like the output of large commercial printing presses, are actually produced using intricate hand techniques; dialogue balloons contain terse, cryptic comments on popular culture. (Collection R. Morone, Turin.)

Licinius, Roman Emperor   [ly-sin'-ee-uhs]

Valerius Licinianus Licinius, AD c.250–325, was appointed emperor (augustus) in the West by GALERIUS in 308. Because this was a period of political confusion, with several rivals, including CONSTANTINE I, contending for the title of augustus, Licinius initially controlled only Illyria. After Galerius died in 311, however, he allied himself with Constantine and in 313 defeated another rival, Maximinus Daia, thus gaining control of the East. Beginning in 314, Licinius quarreled with Constantine, who made him give up all his European lands except Thrace. Subsequently, Licinius began persecuting the Christians. In 324 his forces were defeated by Constantine at Adrianople and at Chrysopolis, and Licinius was exiled. When he conspired to return to power he was executed.

Lick Observatory

Lick Observatory, constructed through a gift from James Lick and opened in 1888, is situated on the peak of Mount Hamilton (elevation: 1,283 m/4,200 ft), 65 km (40 mi) from Santa Cruz, Calif. The main building houses the 36-in (91-cm) and 12-in (30-cm) refractors. (The first, built by Alvin Clark and installed in 1888, is the second largest refractor in the world.) Separate domes house the 36-in (91-cm) Crossley reflector, the 22-in (56-cm) Tauchman reflector, the 20-in (51-cm) Carnegie double astrograph, the 24-in (61-cm) reflector, and the 120-in (305-cm) Shane reflector. The observatory headquarters is located at the University of California at Santa Cruz.

Bibliography: Donnelly, Marian, *A Short History of Observatories* (1973); Wright, Helen, *James Lick's Monument* (1987).

licorice   [lik'-uh-rish]

Licorice, Glycyrrhiza glabra, a Mediterranean herb, is related to the pea. Its root contains a substance that is 150 times sweeter than table sugar. Licorice-root extracts are used to flavor food, beverages, tobacco, and drugs such as cough syrup.

The word licorice refers both to the perennial herb *Glycyrrhiza glabra* of the legume family and to the flavoring produced from its roots. The plant grows to a height of about 1 m (3 ft) and has pealike blue flowers, flat pods, or legumes, and long, soft, flexible roots that are bright yellow inside. The roots are crushed, ground, and boiled to extract the juice, which is then thickened to produce hard black sticks of paste known as black sugar. The bittersweet flavoring is used in candy and tobacco, as a soothing ingredient in cough lozenges and syrups, as a laxative, and in the manufacture of shoe polish. Spain is the largest producer of licorice, but the plant is grown throughout the Mediterranean area, in parts of Asia, and in California and Louisiana. A wild species, *G. lepidota*, is native to North America.

Liddell Hart, Sir Basil   [lid'-ul hart, baz'-ul]

Sir Basil Henry Liddell Hart, b. Oct. 31, 1895, d. Jan. 29, 1970, was a British military historian and strategist. After serving in World War I, he retired from the British Army as a captain in 1927. As a newspaper correspondent and author of many books, Liddell Hart was an early advocate of tank warfare and air power. The Germans, however, made better use of his concept of the indirect approach than did the British War Office. His writings include *The Remaking of Modern Armies* (1927), *The Strategy of the Indirect Approach* (1929), *The Tanks* (1959), *Deterrent or Defence* (1960), and *A History of the Second World War* (1970).

Lidice   [lid'-yit-seh]

Lidice (est. pop., 500) is a coal-mining village in Bohemia, northwest Czechoslovakia. On June 10, 1942, German soldiers killed the adult male population, deported the women and children, and razed the village in retaliation for the assassination of Reinhard Heydrich, German administrator of Moravia and Bohemia. A new village was established in 1947 near the original site, which is now a national monument.

lidocaine   [lyd'-uh-kayn]

Lidocaine, also called xylocaine, is a widely used and highly effective local anesthetic. It is applied topically or by injection in general surgical or dental procedures. When administered with epinephrine, its duration of action is increased while toxicity is diminished. Especially important is lidocaine's antiarrhythmic activity on the heart—it decreases electrical excitability.   E. A. GREEN

Lie, Trygve Halvdan   [lee, troog'-veh hahlv'-dahn]

The Norwegian statesman Trygve Halvdan Lie, b. July 16, 1896, d. Dec. 30, 1968, became the first secretary-general of the United Nations. National secretary of the Norwegian Labor party from 1926 to 1946, he entered the cabinet as minister of justice in 1935. During World War II he served in London as foreign minister for the Norwegian government in exile.

Lie attended the San Francisco conference that drafted the UN charter in 1945. The following year he was elected secretary-general of the new organization. Lie disapproved of the cold war, which he thought Winston Churchill had helped to provoke. He believed that UN membership should be universal and urged in 1950 that Communist China be admitted. That same year he condemned North Korean aggression against South Korea, and the Security Council voted to intervene in the Korean War. The Soviet leadership never forgave Lie for his support of UN intervention in that war. In 1953, Dag HAMMARSKJÖLD was elected to succeed Lie in the United Nations. Lie remained active in Norwegian politics until his death.   J. R. CHRISTIANSON

Bibliography: Lie, Trygve, *In the Cause of Peace: Seven Years with the United Nations* (1954).

lie detector

Lie detector is the common name for the polygraph, an instrument used to record certain physiological changes that take place in response to questioning; these changes presumably indicate the truthfulness of the statements made by the person being questioned. The reliability of polygraphy depends heavily on the skill of the polygraph operator, who uses the instrument data as the basis for a judgment as to whether or not the test subject is telling the truth.

Attempts to correlate blood pressure and respiration rate with lying had been made since the late 19th century. The first practical polygraph was devised (1921) by John A. Larson, a medical student at the University of California. His instrument gave a continuous recording of blood pressure and respiration. Later, a technique was developed for measuring stress-induced variations in the electrical conductivity of the skin (galvanic skin reflex, or GSR); and a single three-channel instrument combining Larson's device with a GSR mechanism was marketed in the 1930s by Leonarde Keeler. Keeler's instrument quickly gained acceptance for use in criminal interrogation and for personnel selection and theft control in commercial institutions. In recent years the Psychological

Stress Analyzer—an instrument that measures stress-induced changes in the voice's tonal quality—is also widely used.

Polygraph use has given rise to important civil-liberties and legal questions—as well as the continuing question of reliability. In 1988, Congress prohibited private businesses from requiring workers and job applicants to take lie-detector tests, with some exceptions involving security services and employees suspected of financial crime. The law banning polygraphs does not apply to federal, state, or local governments. Courts of law generally deny the admissibility of polygraph evidence except when agreed to by both defense and prosecution with the judge's concurrence.　　　　　　　ROBERT F. BORKENSTEIN

Bibliography: Ferguson, R. J., et al., *Preemployment Polygraphy* (1984); Gale, Anthony, ed., *The Polygraph Test: Lies, Truth and Science* (1988).

Liebermann, Max　　[lee'-bur-mahn, mahks]

Considered the outstanding representative of German impressionist painting, Max Liebermann, b. July 20, 1847, d. Feb. 8, 1935, chose his subjects from the everyday world about him. He studied at the academies of Weimar and Düsseldorf and lived in Paris from 1873 until 1878, also visiting Holland in 1875 and many times thereafter. He seems to have been more influenced by Dutch genre painting and the Barbizon school than by the French impressionists. His work shows little of the French interest in light and atmosphere, being more concerned with the depiction of the lives of the humble. Liebermann lived in Munich (1878–84) and then settled in Berlin, where he taught at the Berlin Academy and later became its president. His basic antagonism to academic art, however, led him to serve as the first president (1898–1911) of the Berlin Secession, a group of progressive artists. After the Nazis rose to power, he was forbidden, as a Jewish artist, to paint or to exhibit.　　　　　　　ELIZABETH PUTZ

Bibliography: Haftmann, Werner, *German Art of the Twentieth Century* (1957; repr. 1972); Werner, A., "The Forgotten Art of Max Liebermann," *Art Journal* 23 (Spring 1964).

Liebig, Justus, Baron von　　[lee'-bik, yus'-tus]

Baron Justus von Liebig, a pioneer in the development of organic chemistry, became one of the most highly regarded chemists of his day through his systematic research, precise analytical techniques, and innovative methods of laboratory instruction. His Annals of Pharmacy, first published in 1832, remains a leading research journal.

Justus Liebig, b. May 12, 1803, d. Apr. 18, 1873, was a German chemist whose chief contributions were in the relatively new field of organic chemistry. They included the analysis and the establishment of the empirical formulas of many organic compounds, the discovery of new compounds, the theory of chemical RADICALS, the hydrogen theory of acids, and agricultural and physiological chemistry. Liebig became a full professor at the University of Giessen at the age of 23, and for the next 28 years the chemistry department there was famous throughout the world. Many of his students, such as August von HOFMANN, Friedrich KEKULÉ, and Charles Adolphe WURTZ, also became famous chemists.

Among Liebig's earliest research was the study of the compounds known as fulminates, which he showed to be isomers of cyanates. He and Friedrich WÖHLER collaborated on their famous paper (1832) on the benzoyl radical, the first to describe the persistence of a group of atoms in a series of reactions. They also worked on uric acid. Another of Liebig's earlier chemical investigations had to do with perfecting the methods of organic analysis. He devised a procedure of quantitative organic combustion that was used well into the 20th century. The soil fertility researches of Liebig and others created an interest in artificial mineral manures and led to the rise of the fertilizer industry, even though the fertilizer devised by Liebig was not successful because it was insufficiently soluble. The requirement of microorganisms for growth-accessory factors was postulated by Liebig in 1871.

Before Liebig began to publish his views on physiological chemistry, physiologists paid scant attention to the chemical aspects of their subject. His book *Animal Chemistry* (1842) drew attention to the need for research in this area even though it contained many erroneous ideas. The most important of Liebig's publications was *Annalen der Pharmacie* (Annals of Pharmacy), founded in 1832, which became the preeminent chemistry journal. It carried reports on current major developments, particularly those in organic chemistry. Wöhler became coeditor in 1840. In 1873, following Liebig's death, the name was changed to *Justus Liebig's Annalen der Chemie.*　　　　　　　VIRGINIA F. MCCONNELL

Bibliography: Farber, E., *Great Chemists* (1961); Fruton, Joseph S., *Molecules and Life* (1972); Moulton, F. R., ed., *Liebig and after Liebig* (1942); Partington, J. R., *A History of Chemistry*, vol. 4 (1964); Rossiter, Margaret, *The Emergence of Agricultural Science: Justus Liebig and the Americans, 1840–1880* (1975).

Liebknecht　　(family)　　[leeb'-knekt]

The Liebknecht family played a prominent role in the development of German socialism in the late 19th and early 20th centuries. **Wilhelm Liebknecht,** b. Mar. 29, 1826, d. Aug. 7, 1900, eschewed the previous family pursuits of theology and the civil service to take part in the Revolutions of 1848. He met Karl Marx while in exile in England (1850–62) and in 1869 formed a Marxian German socialist party with August BEBEL. This group subsequently merged (1875) with Ferdinand LASSALLE's party to form the Socialist Workers party. Elected to the Reichstag in 1874, Liebknecht was prominent in the Socialist INTERNATIONAL and edited the chief German Socialist newspaper, *Vorwärts,* from 1890 until his death.

Karl Liebknecht, b. Aug. 13, 1871, was Wilhelm's son. Elected to the Reichstag in 1912, he opposed German participation in World War I and founded (1916) the radical Spartacist League with Rosa LUXEMBURG. Imprisoned for revolutionary activity, he was released in 1918. In January 1919 the Spartacists—renamed the Communist party—attempted an uprising. Liebknecht and Luxemburg were arrested and murdered on Jan. 15, 1919.　　　　　FREDERIC B. M. HOLLYDAY

Bibliography: Meyer, Karl W., *Karl Liebknecht, Man without a Country* (1951); Trotnow, Helmut, *Karl Liebknecht* (1984); Walden, Eric, *The Spartacist Uprising of 1919* (1958).

Liebling, A. J.　　[leeb'-ling]

The American journalist Abbott Joseph Liebling, b. New York City, Oct. 18, 1904, d. Dec. 28, 1963, is remembered for his acerbic criticism of the press. His best criticism is collected in *The Wayward Pressman* (1947)—which also includes autobiographical accounts of his days as a newspaperman—and in *The Press* (1961). Both books contain many of his *New Yorker* articles. His other books include *The Earl of Louisiana* (1961), a portrait of Gov. Earl Long, and *The Most of A. J. Liebling* (1963).　　　　　　　ROBERT V. HUDSON

Bibliography: Midura, Edmund M., *A. J. Liebling: The Wayward Pressman as Critic* (1974).

Liechtenstein　　[lik'-ten-shtine]

The Principality of Liechtenstein is in western Europe, bordered on the south and west by Switzerland and on the east

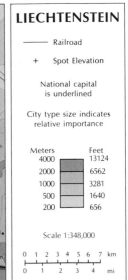

LIECHTENSTEIN

——— Railroad

+ Spot Elevation

National capital
is underlined

City type size indicates
relative importance

Meters	Feet
4000	13124
2000	6562
1000	3281
500	1640
200	656

Scale 1:348,000

0 1 2 3 4 5 6 7 km
0 1 2 3 4 mi

PRINCIPALITY OF LIECHTENSTEIN

LAND. Area: 157 km² (61 mi²). Capital and largest city: Vaduz (1985 est. pop., 4,872).

PEOPLE. Population (1986 est.): 28,000; density (1986 est.): 178 persons per km² (459 per mi²). Distribution (1984): 75% urban, 25% rural. Annual growth (1984): 0.9%. Official language: German. Major religions: Roman Catholicism, Protestantism.

EDUCATION AND HEALTH. Literacy (1986): 100% of adult population. Universities (1987): none. Hospital beds: not available. Physicians (1983): 20. Life expectancy (1980–84): women—77.8; men—71.1. Infant mortality (1985): 6.3 per 1,000 live births.

ECONOMY. GNP (1984 est.): $400 million; $15,000 per capita. Labor distribution (1985): industry, trade, and construction—54%; services—42%; agriculture and forestry—4%. Foreign trade (1984): imports $191 million (1983 est.); exports—$440 million; principal trade partners—European Community, Switzerland. Currency: 1 Swiss franc = 100 centimes.

GOVERNMENT. Type: constitutional monarchy. Legislature: Diet (Landstag). Political subdivisions: 11 communes.

COMMUNICATIONS. Railroads (1984): 18.5 km (11.5 mi) total. Roads (1985): 323 km (201 mi) total. Major ports: none. Major airfields: none.

breeding. Liechtenstein has a diversified industrial base, including the manufacture of machines and industrial equipment, precision instruments, dental supplies, textiles, ceramics, pharmaceuticals, and processed foods. More than 25,000 foreign businesses and banks have established nominal headquarters in Liechtenstein because of favorable tax policies. Tourism is important, especially during the winter skiing season. Liechtenstein's postage stamps, sold to collectors, are a lucrative source of income.

Vaduz, the capital of Liechtenstein, is situated on the Rhine River floodplain at the foot of the central Alps. The castle of Vaduz, which serves as residence of Liechtenstein's prince, overlooks the town that is home to approximately one-fifth of the nation's inhabitants.

by Austria. The country is approximately equal in size to Washington, D.C. The upper Rhine River flows along most of Liechtenstein's western border. The country maintains close relations with Switzerland, sharing customs, currency, and postal systems. This practice has enabled Liechtenstein to share in Switzerland's prosperity and, along with Liechtenstein's own industrial development, gives its citizens one of the world's highest per capita incomes.

LAND AND PEOPLE

Liechtenstein is divided into two traditional regions, the Upper and Lower Country. The western portion, the Lower Country, is the flat plain of the Rhine. Most of Liechtenstein, however, is the mountainous Upper Country, where the Alpine ranges run east-west. The highest point in the country is Vorder-Grauspitz (2,599 m/8,527 ft), in the south. Liechtenstein's 40 km² (16 mi²) of remaining forests are protected in preserves. Annual rainfall varies according to elevation, from an average of about 1,000 mm (40 in) in the lowlands to about 1,980 mm (78 in) in the mountains. Temperatures are mild—about −1° C (30° F) in January and 19° C (66° F) in July.

A homogeneous population, the residents speak Alemannish, a local dialect of German. The population is 90% Roman Catholic. Almost the entire population lives in the communities near the Rhine, with 20% of the total in Vaduz, the capital and largest city. Because of the employment opportunities in Liechtenstein, about one-third of the population is composed of resident foreigners. Liechtenstein's official literacy rate of 100% can be credited to its well-developed system of primary and secondary schools.

ECONOMIC ACTIVITY

Until the end of World War II, the economy of Liechtenstein was agricultural, but since 1945 an economic revolution has occurred. Today only a small percentage of the population are engaged in agriculture, specializing in dairying and stock-

HISTORY AND GOVERNMENT

Once part of the Roman province of Rhaetia, the area was occupied by the Alemanni tribe during the 6th century. After 1396, Liechtenstein was an autonomous fief of the Holy Roman Empire, and in 1719 the independent principality was established. Between 1815 and 1866 it was a member of the German Confederation. Liechtenstein maintained close ties with Austria-Hungary until 1918 and since then has developed close ties with Switzerland, with whom it formed an economically important customs union in 1923.

According to the 1921 constitution, Liechtenstein is a constitutional monarchy, hereditary in the male line. Prince Hans Adam succeeded to the throne in 1989 on the death of his father, Francis Joseph II. A 5-member government is appointed by the prince on the recommendation of the Landtag (parliament), whose 25 members are elected every 4 years by direct universal suffrage; women won the right to vote in 1984. Liechtenstein's foreign affairs are handled by Switzerland.

PAUL C. HELMREICH

Bibliography: Bently, James, *The House of Liechtenstein* (1988); Kranz, Walter, ed., *The Principality of Liechtenstein* (1973); Moore, Russell F., *The Principality of Liechtenstein: A Brief History* (1960); Raton, Pierre, *Liechtenstein* (1970).

Lieder: see SONG.

Liège [lee-ezh']

Liège (Flemish: Luik), the capital of Liège province in eastern Belgium, is about 100 km (60 mi) east of Brussels. The population is 200,312 (1988 est.). Situated at the confluence of the Meuse and Ourthe rivers, Liège has long been a transportation center and a city of cultural, military, and industrial importance. The city, home of the greatest concentration of French-speaking Belgians (Walloons), is the cultural center of the region and has produced movements in defense of Walloon rights.

Linked by the Albert Canal with Antwerp, Liège is the third largest river port in Europe. Located in the center of Belgium's coal-mining region, Liège also produces steel, transportation equipment, chemicals, rubber, textiles, and glass. An international fair of mining, metalworking, and machinery is held annually in Liège. The University of Liège (1817) is located in the city.

Liège was ruled by prince-bishops from the 7th century until 1792, when French Revolutionary forces took the city. Liège suffered severe damage during both world wars.

JONATHAN E. HELMREICH

lien [leen]

A lien is a claim on real or personal property used as security for a debt or other legal obligation. The possessor of a lien who properly records it in the appropriate public office is known as a secured creditor. Such a person has priority over general (or unsecured) creditors and is entitled to satisfy his or her claim regarding an unpaid debt from the sale of the secured property.

Liens are characterized as either general or particular. A general lien secures the creditor for all claims against the debtor. A specific lien secures a creditor only for claims arising from a particular transaction affecting a specific piece of property. Liens can be created by agreement, as with a MORTGAGE, or by operation of law. An example of the latter is the mechanic's lien, which gives a builder or contractor a claim on the property—both building and land—as security for payment for labor and materials. Other liens include the judgment lien (whereby a court can order a debtor to sell his or her property to pay the creditor) and the landlord's lien (whereby a landlord can secure payment of rent by a lien on a tenant's movable property).

Lifar, Serge [lee-fahr', sir-gay']

One of Serge DIAGHILEV's later discoveries, Serge Lifar, b. Kiev, Russia, Apr. 2 (N.S.), 1905, d. Dec. 15, 1986, went on from his days as a star of the BALLETS RUSSES DE SERGE DIAGHILEV to help revitalize French dance through his leadership at the Paris Opéra. Lifar was taken to Paris in 1923 by his teacher, Bronislava Nijinska. He became (1925) premier danseur of Diaghilev's company, creating the title roles in George Balanchine's *Apollon Musagète* (1928) and *Fils Prodigue* (*Prodigal Son*, 1929) and choreographing *Le Renard* (*The Fox*, 1929).

After Diaghilev's death, in 1929, Lifar became danseur étoile and maître de ballet at the Paris Opéra. He staged and danced in classics, such as *Giselle*, and choreographed and danced in original works, such as *Prométhée* (1929). From 1945 to 1947 he served as artistic director of the Nouveau Ballet de Monte Carlo. Lifar returned to the Paris Opéra in 1947, choreographing *Phèdre* (1950), *Blanche-Neige* (*Snow White*, 1951), and *Daphnis et Chloë* (1958), among many others, before he left the Opéra in 1958. The Institut Choréographique, since 1957 the Université de la Danse, was founded by Lifar in Paris in 1947. He wrote more than 25 books on various aspects of ballet and the dance world.

MICHAEL ROBERTSON

Bibliography: Lifar, Serge, *A History of Russian Ballet from Its Origins to the Present Day*, trans. by Arnold Haskell (1954), *Lifar on Classical Ballet*, trans. by D. M. Dinwiddie (1951), and *Ma Vie, from Kiev to Kiev: An Autobiography*, trans. by James Holman Mason (1970).

Life

A pioneer in American PHOTOJOURNALISM, *Life* magazine aimed, in the words of publisher Henry R. LUCE, "to see life; to see the world; to eyewitness great events." Originally published in 1883 as a magazine devoted to social satire, *Life* became a pictorial weekly when Luce purchased it in 1935. Its leading editor was Wilson Hicks, and its outstanding staff photographers included Margaret BOURKE-WHITE, Robert CAPA, Alfred EISENSTAEDT, and W. Eugene SMITH. The magazine broke circulation records in the 1960s, then declined, and was forced to stop publishing in 1972 when advertisers shifted to television. Success of occasional special issues led to *Life*'s rebirth as a monthly in 1978 under the direction of editor Hedley Donovan and photo editor John Loengard.

JAMES W. BROWN

Bibliography: Life Magazine Editors, *Life: The First Fifty Years* (1986).

life

The quality known as life is generally easy to recognize but has been difficult for biologists to define. Living forms—microbes, plants, and animals—have the properties of METABOLISM, GROWTH, and REPRODUCTION. Many also move and respond to external stimuli. Nonliving objects can have some of these properties, but by no means are they considered to be alive.

CHARACTERISTICS

Living material consists chiefly of the elements carbon, hydrogen, oxygen, and nitrogen. Metabolism is the ability of living forms to combine food and oxygen in order to obtain energy for their normal function. Plants, blue-green algae, and some bacteria produce oxygen by using light energy through PHOTOSYNTHESIS. Certain lower organisms known as ANAEROBES cannot use oxygen but instead depend on other chemical pathways to obtain energy.

AMINO ACIDS are the building blocks of proteins, and the NUCLEIC ACIDS DNA and RNA are the keys that link amino acids together to form proteins (see PROTEIN SYNTHESIS). Proteins, in turn, regulate the formation of CARBOHYDRATES and fats. Amino acids, nucleic acids, fats, proteins, and carbohydrates are found within the living CELL, a viscous sac of material encased in a membrane. The simplest living organisms are one-celled creatures and those having a chain of several cells. Cells of increasingly complex organisms are structured into tissues, organs, and organ systems.

In living forms, the genetic material DNA is copied, or reproduced, and passed on from parent to offspring (see GENETICS; HEREDITY). The offspring are never entirely identical to their parents because they acquire half the genes from each parent and also because of slight errors in passing on the par-

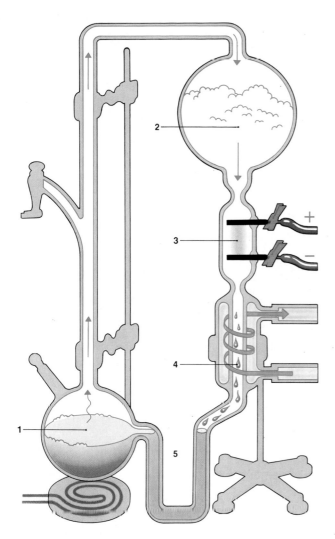

The creation of the conditions for life was demonstrated in 1953 by Stanley L. Miller, an American biochemist. He boiled a mixture of methane, ammonia, water, and hydrogen in a flask (1). These chemicals evaporated, and the vapors mixed in another flask (2). The vapors were subjected to electrical discharges (3) and were condensed (4). The vapors and products were returned to the boiling flask by way of a U-tube (5). After several days of recirculation and reaction, the mixture was tested for newly synthesized chemicals. Miller found that several chemicals necessary for life, such as simple amino acids, sugars, and urea, were present in the flask. He hypothesized that primitive life was formed in the oceans of the world by a similar process, in which the chemicals were evaporated by the Sun's heat, exposed to electrical storms, and condensed by cold air currents.

ents' hereditary information. As a result, some members of a species have a better chance of surviving changes in the environment than do others, an event known as adaptation. Genetic variation and adaptation are the bases of EVOLUTION from lower to higher forms of life. The offspring of many creatures begin life as fertilized eggs. In animals the offspring develop and grow to full size within a certain LIFE SPAN, whereas plants grow throughout their lives (see AGING; DEATH AND DYING). Many living creatures move freely about (see BIOLOGICAL LOCOMOTION). Many also have nervous or behavioral responses (see ANIMAL BEHAVIOR).

ORIGIN OF LIFE

The earliest forms of life known are bacterialike cells dating back to 3.5 billion years ago (see FOSSIL RECORD). How life was originally formed, however, is open to controversy. Various CREATION ACCOUNTS dating back thousands of years attempt to explain how life began. A version well known in the Western

world is the biblical account. Many people consider creationistic views to be correct and believe that life is so complex that it must have been formed by divine intent. Also, many believe that each form of life was created and did not evolve (see CREATIONISM). A more sophisticated outlook encompassing the findings of modern science is the so-called anthropic principle, which holds that the nature of the universe and the existence of life are causally related.

The Greek philosophers ANAXIMANDER and ARISTOTLE promoted the theory of SPONTANEOUS GENERATION—that life constantly arises from nonliving organic matter—for the origin of life. This theory was put in doubt by the work of the Italian physician Francesco Redi (1668) and the Italian scientist Lazzaro SPALLANZANI (1776), and discredited by the French chemist Louis PASTEUR (1861).

The British naturalist Charles DARWIN developed his theory of the evolution of species in the 19th century. The scientific community came to accept Darwin's theory, in modified form. Numerous scientists have since attempted to explain the initial development of life. In the 1920s the Russian biochemist Aleksandr Ivanovich OPARIN and the British geneticist J. B. S. HALDANE suggested that certain organic chemicals present in primitive oceans combined to form self-reproducing forms, reactions that were aided by electrical discharges and an atmosphere rich in hydrogen. This theory was tested in 1953 when the American chemists Stanley Lloyd MILLER and Harold C. UREY created a model of a primitive environment in the laboratory and produced amino acids and other organic compounds. Other scientists have argued, however, that the odds against life forming in the vast primitive oceans were prohibitively great, and that the environment of ancient sands and clays along the shores was more suitable.

In 1908, the Swedish chemist Svante August ARRHENIUS suggested in his Panspermia Theory that life reached Earth by means of spores from outer space, a notion also pursued by the British astronomer Fred HOYLE. Although the discovery of complex organic molecules in INTERSTELLAR MATTER might be taken to support the concept, it still does not explain how life began. One attempted explanation was the "life cloud" theory developed by a team of Canadian and British scientists in the 1970s, which proposes that the organic chemicals present in stellar dust clouds could react to form nucleic acids and proteins. These molecules could then settle on a planet to form living organisms. The space probes *Viking I* and *Viking 2* (both 1976) were equipped to test for life on Mars, thus far with no positive results. Astronomers are also using radiotelescopy to search for signs of life in the universe and, possibly, clues to the origin of life on Earth (see LIFE, EXTRATERRESTRIAL).

Reviewed by LOUIS LEVINE

Bibliography: Barrow, John, and Tipler, Frank, *The Anthropic Cosmological Principle* (1986); Cairn-Smith, A. G., *Seven Clues to the Origin of Life* (1985); Calvin, Melvin, *Chemical Evolution* (1969); Delbrück, Max, *Mind from Matter?* (1986); Fox, S. W., and Dose, Klaus, *Molecular Evolution and the Origins of Life*, 2d ed. (1977); Hoyle, Fred, and Wickramsinghe, N. C., *Lifecloud* (1979); Long, C. H., *The Myths of Creation* (1963); Polkinghorn, John, *One World* (1986).

life, extraterrestrial

The term *extraterrestrial life* encompasses all life, ranging from the lowest possible forms to those with suprahuman intelligences, that may exist beyond the Earth. In the most general sense such life may be based on principles far different from those which operate on Earth, thus extending the traditional definitions of life and providing insight into the nature of all living things. Although no compelling evidence has been presented to confirm the existence of extraterrestrial life, its possible occurrence has long been the subject of debate and continues to generate intense controversy.

HISTORY

The subject of life beyond the Earth was touched upon by the Pythagoreans in the 5th century BC and by the Greek atomists Democritus and Epicurus in the 4th century BC. Only in the 17th century, however, when the widespread acceptance of the heliocentric cosmology of Copernicus provided a framework in which the other planets could be viewed as similar to the Earth, did a serious debate arise about the possibility of planetary life. Johannes KEPLER, in the *Somnium* (*Dream,* 1634), and John WILKINS, in *The Discovery of a World in the Moone* (1638), defended the idea of life on the Moon. Later in the century, Bernard le Bovier de FONTENELLE, in his popular treatise *Entretiens sur la pluralité des mondes* (*Conversations on the Plurality of Worlds,* 1686), and Christiaan HUYGENS, in his *Cosmotheoros* (1698), postulated the existence of life on the planets revolving around the Sun and around other stars. Although many theological and philosophical objections remained, such 18th-century Newtonians as Immanuel KANT and Pierre Simon de LAPLACE placed the benefits of the belief to natural theology above all Scriptural objections. A strong measure of skepticism introduced by William Whewell's essay *Of the Plurality of Worlds* (1853) was countered by numerous writers, notably Sir David BREWSTER and Camille FLAMMARION and, above all, Percival LOWELL, with his claims of canals on MARS. When, in the 20th century, improved telescopes and spectroscopy provided strong evidence against the possibility of intelligent life in the solar system, attention increasingly turned to the possibility of planets outside the solar system.

CONDITIONS FOR LIFE

Three conditions are important when considering the possibility of life on other planets: temperature, the existence of water, and the existence of an atmosphere. Although these conditions need not be precisely the same as those on Earth for life to exist, certain tolerance limits for life as it is normally understood can be established. (Totally different life chemistries lie only in the realm of conjecture.) An ecosphere for any star is that small range of distances from the star within which temperatures are suitable for life, water may exist in liquid form, and an atmosphere may be retained without boiling off into space.

Within the Solar System. The ecosphere of the Sun includes the Moon and the planets Earth and Mars. The Moon and Mars present striking evidence that even within a star's ecosphere, planetary development may provide conditions inhospitable to life. The Moon lacks an atmosphere and water and is alternately scorched and frozen by temperatures ranging from 117° C (240° F) to −190° C (−310° F). Although small amounts of water may exist on Mars and temperatures at the equator may reach a comparatively mild 17° C (62° F), the average atmospheric pressure is only 6 millibars, compared to the standard atmospheric pressure of 1,013.25 millibars (about 14.7 psi) at mean sea level on the Earth, and the atmosphere is in the form of carbon dioxide.

Outside of the ecosphere of the Sun, Mercury and Venus, with temperatures of 430° C (800° F) and 485° C (900° F) respectively, are ruled out as abodes of life, as are the outer planets, where temperatures fall below −140° C (−220° F) even in the upper cloud layers of the closest gas giant, Jupiter. Although internal heat sources might generate milder temperatures in the lower cloud layers of Jupiter or on the surface of a volcanic satellite such as Io, that life could exist under these conditions is difficult to conceive.

Outside the Solar System. A large number of factors must be considered in attempting to estimate how many intelligent civilizations might have arisen throughout the Galaxy. One famous attempt at assessing these factors, originated by the radio astronomer Frank Drake, expresses the number of technical civilizations in the Milky Way Galaxy as $N = R \cdot f_p n_e f_l f_i f_c L$, where each of the letters on the right side of the equation represents a factor necessary to sustain intelligent life.

The first three factors may be characterized as physical and take into account the rate of star formation ($R \cdot$), the fraction of stars with planetary systems (f_p), and the number of planets in each system with conditions favorable to life (n_e). The next two factors are biological and estimate the fraction of those planets on which life develops (f_l) and the fraction with intelligent life (f_i). The last two factors incorporate societal evolution and represent the fraction of those planets with intelligent life that evolve technical civilizations capable of interstellar communication (f_c), and the lifetime of such a civilization (L).

Each of the factors in the Drake equation is extremely uncertain. Among the physical factors, for example, the most widely accepted theory of the origin of PLANETARY SYSTEMS asserts that planets condense out of a rotating nebula, of which the central star is itself the most prominent remnant, a circumstance that scientists have no reason to believe was unique to our solar system. This possibility is in contrast to an early rival theory, which held that our solar system was the chance result of the collision of another star with the Sun. Despite these theories, no other planets have ever been detected with certainty outside the solar system, in spite of claims made about perturbations of the motion of Barnard's star and others by possible planets. The cloud of material discovered around the star Vega in 1983, however, may indicate that a planetary system is forming there.

Theories of the origin of life are equally elusive. In 1953, Stanley MILLER demonstrated that if hydrogen, ammonia, methane, and water vapor were irradiated, organic molecules would be produced. Later experiments showed that components of DNA and RNA, the basis of life on Earth, could be produced in a similar manner. Some organic molecules have since been discovered floating in space (see ASTROCHEMISTRY). The limits of their formation and the subsequent evolution of life, however, are not well understood.

Even more conjectural is societal evolution. The only known example of a technical civilization capable of radio communication is our own; whether a scientist believes a civilization would take 50 years or millions of years to develop such a technology depends on the individual scientist's prejudices. As a result of such uncertainties, widely different numbers are used in the Drake equation, and scientists have estimated that as many as 10,000,000 technical civilizations exist in our galaxy or as few as 1, represented by the Earth.

SEARCH FOR LIFE

The search for life in our solar system reached its highest point to date with the successful landing (1976) of two VIKING spacecraft on Mars. Aboard were experiments designed to look for the biological processes of metabolism, photosynthesis, and respiration. In the metabolism, or labeled release, experiment, a Martian soil sample was covered with a nutrient containing radioactive carbon-14, on the assumption that any organisms in the soil would ingest the nutrient and give off carbon-14 gas. Astonishingly, large amounts of this gas were indeed detected. The other two experiments produced negative results, however, leading to speculation that a highly unusual chemical reaction, not necessarily biological, was taking place. Moreover, a gas chromatograph failed to detect the presence of organic molecules. The prevailing opinion is that Mars most likely does not support even low forms of life. The discovery in the late 1970s that lichens and other microorganisms can grow below the surface of porous rocks in the dry valleys of Antarctica and other desert regions, however, suggests to some scientists that the Martian subsurface might be a promising place to search.

Because manned interstellar travel is not now feasible and because no evidence has established beyond doubt that Earth has been visited by interstellar travelers (despite persistent reports of UNIDENTIFIED FLYING OBJECTS), the search for extraterrestrial intelligence (SETI) outside the solar system must at present be carried out with radio telescopes (see RADIO ASTRONOMY). Such telescopes could detect radio signals transmitted by intelligent beings on distant planets. The central problem with this approach is deciding which stars to listen to and at what frequencies. In a landmark paper (1959) in *Nature,* Philip Morrison and Giuseppe Cocconi suggested a frequency of 1,420 mHz, corresponding to a wavelength of 21 cm, as a universally recognizable communication channel, because that frequency is emitted when an electron reverses its spin in an atom of hydrogen, the most abundant element in the universe. The very abundance of hydrogen, however, may make this channel too noisy, and thus other, supposedly fundamental frequencies might be used. Once a frequency is decided on, nearby Sun-like stars would be logical early targets.

The first attempt at radio communication with extraterrestrial intelligence was made by Frank Drake in 1960 at the Na-

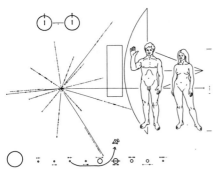

This drawing appeared on the plaques borne by the Pioneer 10 *and* 11 *space probes. The plaque, interpreted through a measurement (in binary code) derived from the hydrogen atoms represented at the top, indicates the Earth's position in relation to 14 pulsars* (left) *and within our solar system* (bottom).

tional Radio Astronomy Observatory in Green Bank, W.Va. This pioneering attempt, known as Project Ozma, focused on the stars Epsilon Eridani and Tau Ceti at a frequency of 1,420 mHz. Since 1960 about 45 searches for extraterrestrial intelligence were initiated around the world, all of limited duration and concentrating on a few Sun-like stars, usually at the 1,420-mHz frequency. One SETI program begun at Harvard University's Oak Ridge Observatory in 1983 uses a 25.6-m (84-ft) radio telescope to scan about 68 percent of the sky. Originally employing a multichannel spectrum analyzer that simultaneously scanned 131,072 channels (or frequency ranges), Oak Ridge's system was upgraded to 8.4 million channels in 1985. The National Aeronautics and Space Administration (NASA), in conjunction with Stanford University, is developing a 10–15 million-channel spectrum analyzer to be deployed by the early 1990s. NASA's effort will involve two approaches—a broad-band whole-sky survey that will utilize 3 existing 34-m (111.5 ft) antennas in Goldstone, Calif., Tidbinbilla, Australia, and Madrid; and a narrower-band "targeted search" of about 1,000 nearby stars that will use the same three antennas and several other antennas around the world.

SETI programs may be distinguished from communication with extraterrestrial intelligence (CETI), which implies actual two-way communication. The seriousness with which scientists take the possibility of life in the universe may be gathered from the appeal of Nobel Prize–winner Sir Martin Ryle that no signals be intentionally sent to other stars for fear of an invasion or a loss of human values if contact is made with a superior intelligence. For more than half a century, however, radio, television, and radar signals have been traveling away from the Earth at the speed of light, announcing our presence to the universe. Also, on the chance that another civilization might encounter them, the PIONEER 10 and 11 spacecraft each bears an engraved plaque with a message from Earth, and VOYAGERS 1 and 2 carry an elaborate recorded message of words and music. All four spacecraft are heading toward interstellar space.   STEVEN J. DICK

Bibliography: Billington, John, ed., *Life in the Universe* (1981); Christian, James L., ed., *Extraterrestrial Intelligence* (1976); Crowe, Michael, *The Extraterrestrial Life Debate, 1750–1900* (1985); Dick, Steven J., *Plurality of Worlds* (1982); Hart, Michael H., and Zuckerman, Ben, eds., *Extraterrestrials: Where Are They?* (1982); Papagiannis, Michael D., ed., *The Search for Extraterrestrial Life* (1986); Ponnamperuma, Cyril, and Cameron, A. G. W., *Interstellar Communication: Scientific Perspectives* (1974); Sagan, Carl, ed., *Communication with Extraterrestrial Intelligence (CETI)* (1973); Shklovskii, I. S., and Sagan, Carl, *Intelligent Life in the Universe* (1966).

life expectancy: see LIFE SPAN.

life insurance

Life insurance is a method by which numbers of individuals pool their funds so as to spread the risk of financial loss from death equally among them. Historically, the practice of life insurance dates back at least as far as the Romans whose burial clubs financed funeral expenses and made payments to families of the deceased. A primitive mortality table (calculations of risk of death for classes of people at certain ages) was

constructed as early as AD *c.*220, but it was only in 1693 that a true actuarial table was created by the astronomer Edmond Halley, more than a century after the first modern life insurance policy was issued (1583) in England. In the United States the first life insurance company was established (1759) by the Presbyterian Synod of Philadelphia for Presbyterian ministers, but life insurance did not become common until the middle of the 19th century. A century later life insurance had become a vast industry.

TYPES OF LIFE INSURANCE

The three basic types of life-insurance contracts are term, whole life, and endowment. A related type is the annuity.

Term Insurance. The simplest type of policy is term insurance, in which the policyholder buys protection only for the period of the contract, which may run from 1 to 20 years or more. Term insurance provides maximum protection for a minimum outlay at a given time. If the insured person dies within the period of the contract, the face value of the policy is paid to a beneficiary. The premium, or cost, of the term policy increases with the age of the insured.

Whole Life Insurance. A policy that is bought to cover the whole lifetime of the insured is called whole life, straight life, or ordinary life insurance. The younger the age when a person takes out a policy, the lower the rate of premium. This premium remains constant, since it is based on the expectation that the policy will be held for the person's lifetime. In early years the premium paid by the policyholder is more than the true cost of the insurance (the financial risk to the insurance company of a policyholder's death is more than covered by the premium rate), but in later years it is less. Thus in early years the policy builds up a cash value accruing from the difference between the premium paid in and the true cost of the insurance. The insured person can capture this cash value by borrowing on it or by discontinuing the policy and getting a refund. Since insurance companies invest the premiums paid in, they are required to guarantee the policyholder a certain rate of interest on the cash value; for this reason, whole life insurance requires lower cash outlay than other types of policies over a person's lifetime.

Variations on whole life insurance now include variable life schemes, where the policyholder has a choice of investment programs and cash value and death benefits (above a certain guaranteed minimum) change according to the performance of the program selected. The premium remains the same throughout. Universal life gives the policyholder the option of changing both premium and death benefit from time to time, adjusting them to his or her changing needs.

Endowment Insurance. An endowment policy is designed to accumulate savings over a period of years. Such a policy can be used to provide funds for a child's education or for retirement. However, it offers less protection in the event of early death than does a whole life policy. If the policyholder lives to a specific age he or she will be paid the face value of the policy, and if the policyholder dies within the period of the policy, the face value is also paid to a beneficiary.

Annuities. Closely related to life insurance is the ANNUITY. While life insurance may be said to protect against the risk of dying too young, an annuity protects against living too long. It assures that a person's accumulated funds will last for the remainder of his or her life. Thus a retired person with savings may decide to purchase an annuity that guarantees a specific income for as long as he or she lives. The price of the annuity is based on the average life expectancy for persons of a given age; those who die earlier than the average are, in effect, paying to support those who live longer.

Insurance Combinations. The three basic types of life insurance can be combined in various ways, with each other and with annuities, to fit many different requirements. Mortgage insurance, for example, is a term insurance policy that decreases in value as a mortgage is paid off, so that the policyholder's family will be able to continue payments should the policyholder die. It may be combined with another policy, such as whole life insurance, to provide additional income.

COSTS OF LIFE INSURANCE

The cost of a life insurance policy is affected by several factors: the amount and type of insurance being purchased, the age of the insured, the administrative and selling expenses of the insurance company, and the type of company from which it is purchased.

Whole life insurance requires the least cash outlay over a person's lifetime because part of its cost is paid from the interest on the accumulated value of the policy. Interest rates once were far lower than the rates obtainable from other forms of savings. Today, however, insurance companies compete with other financial organizations, and plans such as variable life offer the opportunity to invest in stock, bond, or money markets. Yields (minus fees) are therefore usually equivalent to those earned by direct investors. In addition, many policy holders appreciate the discipline of "forced" savings through regular premium payments.

Insurance companies vary in the amount of "loading"—the selling costs, administrative expenses, reserves, and profits that they add to the net insurance rate. For identical policies, the premiums of different companies may vary as much as 50 percent.

Group insurance is less expensive than an individual policy because the cost of selling and servicing a group policy is much less. Individual policies of comparable cost are available from savings banks in the states of Massachusetts, New York, and Connecticut, where savings banks are allowed to sell life insurance over the counter. They avoid much of the advertising and sales expense of private companies.

Mutual insurance companies, in which the insured becomes a stockholder in the company, pay dividends from time to time that reduce the amount of the premiums over a period of years. For this reason a policy whereby the insured participates in a mutual company's earnings is generally less expensive, in the long run, than the nonparticipating policy sold by other companies.   ROBERT S. CLINE

Bibliography: Consumer Reports Editors, *The Consumers Union Report on Life Insurance* (1981); Greene, Mark R., and Trieschman, James S., *Risk and Insurance* (1984); Huebner, Solomon S., and Black, Kenneth, Jr., *Life Insurance*, 10th ed. (1982); Institute of Life Insurance, *Life Insurance Fact Book* (annual); Mehr, Robert I., and Gustavson, Sandra G., *Life Insurance: Theory and Practice*, 3d ed. (1984).

Life of Samuel Johnson, The

James BOSWELL's *Life of Samuel Johnson LL.D.* is the most illustrious biography in English literature. Published in 1791, it describes the events of Dr. JOHNSON's life, especially his later years when Boswell knew him intimately, and records his conversations and witty remarks. Boswell dogged Johnson's footsteps, taking down verbatim what he said to others and querying Johnson about his opinions on all manner of subjects. The book creates a presence so magnificently that Johnson's fame perhaps derives more from this work than from his own writings. As Boswell boasted, Johnson is seen in his book "more completely than any man who has ever yet lived."

JANET M. TODD

Bibliography: Clifford, James L., ed., *Twentieth Century Interpretations of Boswell's Life of Johnson* (1970); Passler, David L., *Time, Form and Style in Boswell's Life of Johnson* (1971).

life span

Life span denotes the length of time intervening between conception and death, during which organisms undergo remarkable changes in structure and function. In the embryonic stage the fertilized egg progressively differentiates into a highly complex multicellular organism. After birth or hatching, the organisms enter the juvenile phase, which is characterized by growth in size until sexual maturation, when growth slows down and eventually ceases completely. After the peak of the reproductive period, physiological capacities of various organs begin an inexorable decline, with a consequent increase in the probability of death for an organism.

All organisms have a finite and species-characteristic life span that reflects the underlying rates of AGING. There is a tremendous variation in life span among different groups of or-

ganisms. Differences in the longevity of species, hybrids, mutants, sexes, and strains lend support to the view that life span is genetically determined. Accurate mortality records are available for only a small fraction of the known species.

Life span is measured either as the maximum age achieved by a member or as an average among the population. The former reveals the genetic potential, whereas the average life span reflects the hospitality of the environment and is a more meaningful measure. In general, organisms live longer in captivity than in the wild. Females usually live 10–15 percent longer than males. The maximum natural life spans of organisms range from about 8 days in some rotifers to over 150 years in tortoises and a few thousand years in some higher plants. Humans are the longest-living mammals and among the longest-living of all animals. As of 1985, the highest authenticated human age was 120 years.

PLANTS

Plants age as animals do, but defining age in plants is more difficult because of the structural differences. For example, a plant may germinate from a seed that had been lying dormant for thousands of years. Also, the embryonic tissue of plants contributes to growth and development for a much longer period of time than embryonic cells in animals, sometimes functioning for the life of the plant. Thus a tree may continually add new cells while some parts either die and slough off (bark and leaves) or die and remain part of the tree (wood of roots and trunk). A tree's age, however, may be at least roughly determined by counting its rings (new wood layers), which are added to the trunk with each growth period (see DENDROCHRONOLOGY). In addition, some plants propagate by developing offshoots that become genetically identical plants, or clones, whose ages, arguably, may be considered as extensions of the age of the original plant. On such terms, for example, a stand of CREOSOTE BUSH clones has been radiocarbon-dated as about 11,700 years old.

SINGLE CELLS

Bacteria and other unicellular organisms that reproduce asexually rather than sexually continue to divide indefinitely and thus cannot be said to age. Any bacterial cell divides to produce two young cells; thus, division for such organisms is a process of rejuvenation. By contrast, individual cells in multicellular organisms normally die as part of the developmental sequence. During the development of vertebrate limbs, for example, cell death and resorption shape the digits, thighs, and upper arm contours.

Recent experiments indicate that cells taken from animals and cultured in the laboratory also have a finite life span, and that death is an inherent property of cells themselves. Cul-

MAXIMUM LIFE SPAN FOR SOME ANIMALS AND PLANTS

Organism	Life Span (years)	Organism	Life Span (years)
Mammals		**Fish**	
Humans	120	Eel	55
Indian elephant	78	Sea horse	6
Dog	29		
Brown bear	22	**Invertebrates**	
Guinea pig	14	American lobster	50
White laboratory rat	5	Earthworm	10
		Ant	5
Birds		Housefly	0.2
Condor	72		
Bald eagle	44	**Conifers**	
Domestic pigeon	35	Bristlecone pine	4,900
American robin	12	Sierra redwood	750
		Swiss stonepine	544
Reptiles and Amphibians		Common juniper	417
Galápagos tortoise	152	European larch	2,300
Giant salamander	55		
Nile crocodile	40	**Flowering Plants**	
Bullfrog	16	English oak	1,500
		Linden	815
Fish		European beech	250
Sturgeon	82	Dwarf birch	80
Halibut	70		

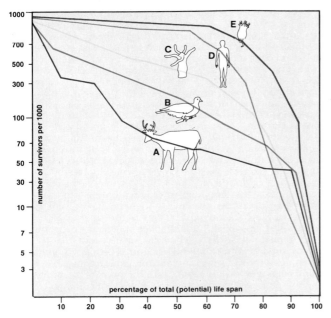

Graph shows survivorship curves of selected animal populations. White-tailed deer (A), display high mortality (low survival rate) in early years. The pigeon (B) and hydra (C) have a relatively constant death rate at different ages. Humans (D) and rotifers (E) have a very low mortality rate in early years.

tured normal embryonic cells undergo a finite number of population doublings by division and then die. Although the data are fragmentary, the doubling potential of normal embryonic cells of various animal species appears to be proportional to the average maximum life span for those species. If this relationship is eventually proven, it would then be possible to compute the life span for any animal species.

EVOLUTION AND LIFE SPAN

The limited life span of individuals appears to be necessary for ensuring the survival of the species during evolution. The alternative, immortality, has three main disadvantages as a survival strategy. First, it would be impossible for an immortal species to meet changes in the environment through trial changes in the organism. The necessary changes can arise only in organisms with new genetic combinations brought about by mutation and reproduction, so that the failures among the offspring die out, while those that succeed survive to reproduce the better-adapted genetic combinations.

Second, immortal parents would compete for food and mates with their offspring and thus threaten the survival of future generations. Third, the constant presence of radiation from space often results in damaged genes and defective offspring. The probability of birth defects increases with the age of the mother; a population of immortal parents would reproduce many children unable to survive.

LIMITING FACTORS

Senescence probably is due to an inability to fully restore damage inflicted at the molecular level. Whatever the nature of aging reactions may be, analysis of longevity in different mammals indicates a relationship between life span, brain weight, metabolic rate, and body weight. Animals with a higher brain-to-body weight ratio tend to have a longer life span. Metabolic rate is inversely proportional to life span. Smaller mammals have a more intense metabolic rate and a shorter life span than do larger ones. According to one concept, organisms have a fixed metabolic potential and the length of life is determined by the rate of depletion of this potential. In several species of domestic mammals, maximum energy consumed has been calculated to be about 200 kcal per gram of body weight during the life span. Those species with a higher metabolic rate achieve this limit earlier. The inverse relationship between life span and metabolic rate has

been most clearly established in cold-blooded animals, such as insects. They live much longer at lower temperatures than at higher temperatures. Elevation in temperature affects life span by increasing physical activity and metabolic rate. It does not, however, necessarily follow that physical activity in mammals shortens life span. On the contrary, it is essential for the maintenance of a healthy body.

Another factor that exerts a significant effect on both the average and the maximum life span is the restriction of caloric intake. The maximum longevity of rats on restricted food intake is about 5 years, as compared to about 3 years in rats fed freely. The reduced food intake tends to increase the life span by extending the phase of life prior to sexual maturity (juvenile phase). Food intake has a less-pronounced effect on the duration of the adult period. Several environmental factors also have an effect on average life expectancy. They include diet, humidity, temperature, population density, and so forth. In humans, moderate exercise, relaxed life-style, and balanced diet tend to prolong life, whereas smoking, excessive drinking, and mental stress shorten the life span. Dietary supplements such as vitamins or drugs have not as yet proven to have any significant beneficial effect on the rate of aging.

RAJINDER SINGH SOHAL

Bibliography: Andrew, Warren, *The Anatomy of Aging in Man and Animals* (1971); Bakerman, Seymour, ed., *Aging Life Processes* (1969); Brues, Austin M., and Sacher, G. A., ed., *Aging and Levels of Biological Organization* (1965); CIBA Foundation, *The Lifespan of Animals* (1959); Comfort, Alex, *The Biology of Senescence,* 3d ed. (1979); Emerson, Geraldine M., ed., *Aging* (1977); Finch, Caleb, and Hayflick, Leonard, eds., *Handbook of the Biology of Aging* (1977); Milne, Lorus and Margery, *The Ages of Life* (1968).

life-support systems

A life-support system is a system that provides, in surroundings hostile to life, a comfortable environment similar to that at the Earth's surface. Such systems range from the integrated group of subsystems characteristic of a spacecraft or an underwater vessel to individual devices such as scuba gear and the spacesuit. Multimanned life-support systems supply, at a minimum, air, water, food, and a controlled temperature and humidity. In addition, the system may collect, store, or dispose of bodily wastes and trash. In the future, particularly aboard very large multimanned space stations, the life-support system may also include a substitute for Earth's gravity. Underwater systems are discussed in articles on BATHYSCAPHE, SUBMARINE, OCEANOGRAPHY, and SCUBA; this article treats life-support systems in space.

SPACECRAFT LIFE-SUPPORT SYSTEMS

The three types of spacecraft life-support systems are open, semiclosed, and closed. The first type is now principally of historical interest, the second is used in all manned spacecraft, and the third is still a dream of the future.

Open Systems. The open system was used during the late 1940s and the 1950s when bacteria, insects, monkeys, and mice were sent in balloons, sounding rockets, and guided missiles to very high altitudes and into the lower fringes of space for relatively brief periods. They required little more than a supply of air. In a typical system supporting a monkey, temperature was controlled by means of metal foil and fiberglass materials. Oxygen was supplied from a compressed gas tank, and carbon dioxide was removed by baralyme, a chemical used for the same purpose on submarines. Because of the length of the mission, which was only a matter of minutes, neither food nor water was required. The waste-management subsystem was simply a diaper.

Semiclosed Systems. The semiclosed system evolved from the open system during the preparation to enter space. It was subsequently used in the manned space programs of both the United States and the USSR. Its first appearance, in 1961, was with the Soviet VOSTOK satellite. Essentially the same system was used in the American Mercury spacecraft launched in the same year (see MERCURY PROGRAM). With technological refinement over the intervening years it was employed in the GEMINI PROGRAM, APOLLO PROGRAM, SOYUZ, SKYLAB, SALYUT, and SPACE SHUTTLE.

The life-support system of the Skylab space station is a good example of a semiclosed type. It was composed of an environmental-control subsystem, food-and-water-management subsystem, and waste-management subsystem. In addition, it had provisions for sleeping, personal hygiene, emergency medical attention, and monitoring astronaut vital signs.

The environmental-control subsystem stored, distributed, purified, and conditioned Skylab's two-gas atmosphere. Unlike the Mercury, Gemini, and Apollo spacecraft, which used 100% oxygen, Skylab used a mixture of 72% oxygen and 28% nitrogen. The Soviet Soyuz and Salyut also use a mixture of the two gases, although the atmospheric pressure in Skylab was only 3.45 Newtons/cm² (5 lb/in²), compared to 10.13 Newtons/cm² (14.7 lb/in²s) in Soyuz and Salyut. The atmosphere was circulated by fans and ducts as in a home-heating and cooling system. Carbon dioxide, excess heat and water vapor, odors, and solid particles were removed from the air by two molecular sieve units containing mechanical filters, activated charcoal, and beds of zeolite (alumino silicates).

The food-and-water-management subsystem consisted of 950 kg (2,100 lb) of food and 2,720 kg (6,000 lb) of water. Four types of food were available: dehydrated, which could be made ready by adding water; intermediate moisture, precooked so that the moisture content was about 20% that of natural state; thermostabilized, precooked fresh food reduced to −23° C (−10° F) prior to launching; and frozen, precooked fresh food reduced to −23° C (−10° F) prior to launching; and frozen, precooked fresh food reduced to −40° C (−40° F) before launching. These were packaged in plastic envelopes or aluminum cans. The beverages were dehydrated powders made drinkable by the addition of hot or cold water to collapsible plastic bottles. Ten stainless-steel storage tanks each held 274 l (72 gal) of water, enough altogether for 140 days in space.

The waste-management system provided for the disposal of trash and bodily wastes. Garbage was dumped into the oxygen tank of the converted Saturn 5 third stage by means of a complicated airlock mechanism that required one astronaut to operate and another to read a checklist of nine steps printed on the inner lid. Bodily wastes from the crew were collected in a toilet, complete with handholds and a seatbelt, mounted on the wall instead of the floor. A stream of air was used to move solid and liquid wastes into plastic bags.

Closed Systems. In the closed life-support system of the future, every atom within the closed system is accounted for and recycled. Thus, garbage cannot be dumped, and new supplies of food, air, and water cannot be brought from Earth as occurs with the Soviet Salyut space station. All such life-supporting elements must be provided continuously by the system. The obvious model for a closed system is the ecology of Earth. Such a system is closed only with respect to matter, not energy; because of the laws of thermodynamics, energy cannot be drawn from an outside source. The Sun, which is the ultimate source of energy on Earth, provides this source within the solar system.

Most models for a closed life-support system envision one based upon the exchange of metabolic products between human beings and lower forms of life. The heart of a typical system is a photosynthetic exchanger, in which a colony of algae suspended in water and exposed to light produces oxygen and takes up carbon dioxide produced by the crew. Nutrients for the algal colony are also provided by the liquid and solid wastes of the crew. Food for the crew comes from dried algae, which consist of 40 to 60% protein, 10 to 20% fat, 20% carbohydrate, and vitamins and amino acids.

Some designers of closed systems suggest that they might include intermediate forms of life such as fish, eels, and water fleas that could live off the algae and in turn be eaten by hu-

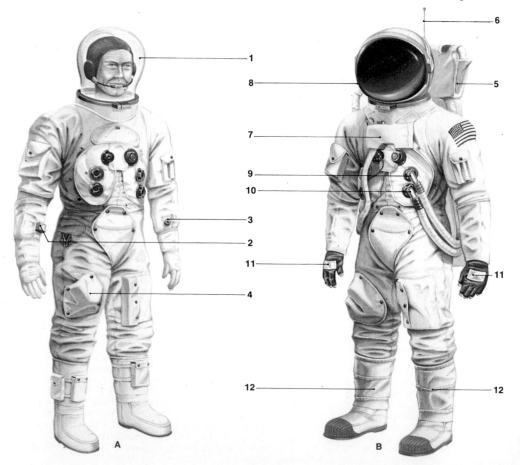

NASA developed two protective suits for astronauts on lunar missions. The space suit worn inside the vehicle (A) features an airtight helmet (1) to maintain neccessary pressurization, which is monitored on an external pressure gauge (2) and regulated by a relief valve (3). A flap (4) on the upper leg houses tubing used for the elimination of waste fluid and permits access to the thigh for injections. The suit worn on the lunar surface (B) has its own environmental unit. The Portable Life-Support System, or PLSS (5), contains a radio transmitter and aerial (6), oxygen, and an air-conditioning unit. Its control panel (7) is located on the upper chest. The helmet's visor (8) shields against solar radiation. The wearer is supplied with air through an inlet tube (9), and an outlet tube (10) draws off exhaled carbon dioxide. Gloves (11) and boots (12) are insulated to protect against heat and micrometeorites.

man beings. Soviet scientists for years have experimented with photosynthetic exchangers using plants such as sweet potatoes, lettuce, and cabbage grown in hydroponic beds.

SPACESUITS

The modern spacesuit permits an astronaut to leave the spacecraft and function outside it, either in open space or on the surface of extraterrestrial bodies. Thus it must be reasonably airtight, thermally insulated, contain its own air and water supply, provide protection against micrometeoroids, and be flexible enough to permit a wide range of movements.

The spacesuits developed for the early astronauts of Mercury, Gemini, Apollo, Skylab, Vostok, and Soyuz were tailor-made and very expensive. They were designed for use inside the spacecraft during potentially hazardous periods of a mission such as reentry into the atmosphere, or for the limited periods of time outside the spacecraft.

The Apollo A-7 spacesuit, also used in a modified form on Skylab, is typical of the modern suit. It consisted of an innermost layer of heat-resistant nylon, a neoprene-coated nylon bladder with a nylon restraint layer to contain the bladder. This pressure garment covered the entire body except the hands and head. The head was protected by a polycarbonate plastic helmet that permitted a full range of vision. The gloves were made of the same material as the pressure garment and attached to it by means of a clamp and bellows that permitted limited manual dexterity. When the suit was used outside the spacecraft or on the Moon, a special garment was worn over it. It was essentially an envelope made of fireproof fiberglass cloth within which was a set of alternating layers of aluminized plastic and fireproof marquisette cloth. These ensured thermal and micrometeoroid protection. Thermally insulated gloves and boots were also worn.

The A-7 suit was pressurized with oxygen to 2.6 newtons/cm² (3.7 lb/in²). In addition to providing the breathing gas for the astronaut, the oxygen also absorbed heat, water, vapor, and odors and transported them for removal. The oxygen entered the suit through a connector on the chest, flowed through ducts, and exited through another connector. The suit also had external connectors for a water-cooled undergarment used when the suit was worn outside the spacecraft. The garment was made of approximately 90 m (300 ft) of plastic tubing through which water circulated to remove heat generated by the body. External connectors on the suit also permitted cables from biosensors monitoring temperatures and heart rate of the astronaut to be attached.

A backpack containing sufficient water and oxygen for four hours made the suit independent of the spacecraft's life-support system. It was used for lunar-surface exploration and for retrieving film and experiments outside the Apollo command module on the return trip to Earth.

The United States and the USSR have also used a semirigid spacesuit in the Space Shuttle and the Salyut space station. It has a rigid plastic or metallic torso to which are attached fabric sleeves and legs similar to the Apollo suit. These spacesuits come in various sizes and use pure oxygen for breathing. Both suits have an integral backpack for life support outside the spacecraft and have provisions for radio communication built into the backpack. For untethered locomotion outside the Space Shuttle, the spacesuit can be attached, via the backpack, to a system called the manned maneuvering unit.

MITCHELL R. SHARPE

Bibliography: Gatland, Kenneth, *An Illustrated Encyclopedia of Space Technology* (1981); Holder, William G., and Siuru, W. D., *Skylab, Pioneer Space Station* (1974); Napolitano, L. G., ed., *Space: Mankind's Fourth Environment*, vol. 2 (1983); Von Braun, Wernher, et al., *Space Travel: A History*, rev. ed. (1985).

lifesaving and water safety

Lifesaving is the act of rescuing a person who is in danger of DROWNING and, if necessary, reviving the person by using artificial respiration (see CARDIOPULMONARY RESUSCITATION). Lifesaving is an aspect of water safety—specifically, how to deal with potential dangers in the water. The Red Cross offers instruction in water safety and lifesaving; it also certifies competence in these areas.

The history of formal lifesaving training follows that of swimming, which did not become a popular recreation until the 18th century. The first instructions in artificial respiration appeared in 1755 and the first description of lifesaving techniques in 1816. The Royal Life Saving Service began in England in 1891 and the United States Volunteer Life Saving Corps adopted similar methods early in the 20th century. The American Red Cross established a nationwide instructional program in 1914.

Three basic methods are commonly used to rescue a drowning person. The safest and easiest method is for the rescuer to remain on shore and throw a rope or float or to extend an object such as a pole or tree limb to the victim. The victim may also be approached in a boat. Only if these two methods cannot be used should the rescuer attempt the third and most risky method—that of swimming to and seizing the person in danger and dragging him or her to shore while swimming with a special sidestroke. The danger is that the drowning person may grab the rescuer and drag them both down.

Water safety involves common sense about an individual's swimming stamina and about the condition of the water. It also requires certain acquired skills such as knowing how to swim with clothes and shoes on, how to disrobe in the water, and how to survive in rough water.

Bibliography: American Medical Association, *The AMA Handbook of First Aid and Emergency Care* (1980); American National Red Cross, *Lifesaving, Rescue and Water Safety* (1974); Giambarba, Paul, *Surfmen and Lifesavers* (1985).

ligament   [lig'-uh-ment]

A ligament is a band of tough, flexible, dense, white, fibrous connective tissue that connects bones or cartilages, serving to support and strengthen joints. Ligaments are elastic only within narrow limits. One of the most important factors limiting joint movement is the tension of the ligaments, because they are designed to prevent excessive or abnormal joint movement. The majority of ligaments are within the joint capsule; a few accessory ligaments are extracapsular. Ligaments can also support organs. Certain folds of the peritoneum (the membrane lining of the abdominal cavity) are also called ligaments.

When ligaments are stretched beyond their elastic limits, mild strains (sprains) or more severe tears result. Treatment of extreme tears may involve the surgical grafting of TENDONS; in 1986 the Food and Drug Administration (FDA) approved the first synthetic ligament for the replacement of torn knee ligaments.

JANET VAUGHAN

ligand   [lig'-uhnd]

EDTA, a hexafunctional ligand

Ligands are ions or neutral molecules that are positioned geometrically around a central atom (usually a metal) to form a COORDINATION COMPOUND. A charged ligand may be a cation, such as a halogen, nitro group, cyanide group, hydroxyl group, or acetato group, or, more rarely, it may be an anion, such as a nitrosyl group. Examples of neutral ligands are ammonia, water, carbonyl, pyridine, and crown ethers—an entire family of organic molecules that can trap atoms within the center of a "crown" structure. In a coordination compound the central atom is usually a transition element, or ion, such as Cu^{2+} or Pt^{4+}. The overall charge of the complex is the sum of the charges of the central atom and the ligands. The number of attached ligands generally ranges from two to eight and is indirectly related to the valence of the central atom. The fixed geometric arrangement of ligands around the central atom may be linear, as in $Ag(NH_3)_2$, square planar, as in $Pt(NH_3)_2Cl_2$, octahedral, as in $Pt(Cl_6)^{2-}$, or any of a number of shapes determined by the nature and valence of the central atom. A single ligand, if large, may be capable of occupying more than one geometric site around the central atom. By bending, ligands such as ethylenediamine, $NH_2CH_2CH_2NH_2$, and ethylenedianinetetracetate (EDTA), $[(O_2CCH_2)_2NC_2H_4N(CH_2CO_2)_2]^{4-}$, can occupy multiple positions. The former is difunctional, whereas the latter is hexafunctional. A ligand that can wrap itself around a central atom in this manner is called a chelating agent. EDTA has such a strong attraction for metals that it can remove metals from enzymes, inhibiting their catalytic activity completely. Crown ethers are chelating agents used primarily as catalysts in organic reactions. In HEMOGLOBIN, an iron atom is at the center of a ring-shaped porphyrin structure (heme), and four of the iron's six valences are satisfied by linkages to the chelating ring.

Reviewed by JOHN TURKEVICH

Ligeti, György   [lee'-get-ee, dyurd]

The Hungarian composer György Ligeti, b. May 28, 1923, is a leader of the European musical avant-garde. Ligeti established his reputation with the orchestral *Atmosphères* (1961) in which he developed *Klangflächenkomposition,* music constructed with blocks of sound. In his mime-dramas *Aventures* (1962) and *Nouvelles Aventures* (1962–65) he used a meaningless language that resulted in a kind of musical theater of the absurd. An increasing interest in harmony can be discerned in the orchestral *Lontano* (1967), and beginning with his *Second String Quartet* (1968) he experimented with microtones. A subtle and complex polyphony characterizes most of Ligeti's music since the mid-1960s. His first opera, *The Grand Macabre,* was first performed in 1978. Music from his *Atmosphères* and *Requiem* (1963–65) was used in the film *2001: A Space Odyssey* (1968).

light

Light is ELECTROMAGNETIC RADIATION in the wavelength range extending from about 0.4 μ to about 0.7μ; or, perhaps more properly, the visual response to electromagnetic radiation in this range. By extension, the term is frequently applied to adjacent wavelength ranges that the eye cannot detect: ULTRAVIOLET LIGHT, infrared light (see INFRARED RADIATION), and black light. In addition to wavelength, FREQUENCY, in hertz, and wavenumber, in inverse units of length, are also used to specify and designate the character and quality of the radiation. Associated with wavelength or frequency is the visual response of COLOR. The term *monochromatic* is applied to the idealized situation in which the light in a beam is all of one wavelength.

CHARACTERIZATION OF LIGHT

Light is characterized not only by wavelength, essentially a temporal quality, but also by state and degree of polarization (see POLARIZED LIGHT), a geometric or directional quality, and by intensity, essentially a physical quality. The visual response to intensity is brightness. In the human visual system, at least, there is no counterpart response, to the state and degree of polarization, but ample evidence exists that certain arthropods—bees in particular—are sensitive to the state of polarization of sky light. There is some speculation that certain migrating birds may also respond to this quality of light.

Light is further characterized by its degree of coherence (see COHERENT LIGHT). Coherence, closely related to the degree of polarization and to the degree of monochromaticity, refers to the ability of a beam of light to interfere (see INTERFERENCE) with itself. Coherence is therefore an interferometric property of light. By the use of a Michelson INTERFEROMETER, most light sources can be made to produce interference fringes. These are clearest when the length of the two arms of the interfer-

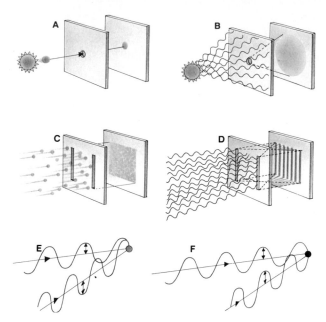

Both a particle and a wave theory of light explain reflection and refraction, but only the wave hypothesis can account for diffraction and interference effects. Particles of light (A) would pass straight through a pinhole and form a point image on a rear screen. Light waves (B), however, would diffract, or spread out, and form a large circular image. The passage of light particles (C) through two slits would form two bright lines. A series of light and dark bands (D) are seen, however, which can only be explained in terms of waves. Bright lines result when light waves (E) arrive at the screen in phase. Dark bands occur when waves (F) are out of phase.

ometer are equal. As one arm is lengthened, however, the contrast of the fringes is seen to decrease until they are no longer visible. Unfiltered light from an incandescent source will barely produce fringes under any circumstances. Light from a mercury arc lamp will produce fringes over a range of one or two centimeters. On the other hand, light from a continuous-wave gas laser has produced fringes at a distance of more than 100 meters.

Light is moving energy that travels at a speed of 300,000 km/sec (186,000 mi/sec). It can be regarded both as a particulate flow and as a wave phenomenon. These two apparently diametrically opposed views have been brought together in a theory that combines the best features of each. The particulate unit is the PHOTON, which has associated with it a central frequency or wavelength that determines (or is determined by) the amount of energy it contains. In a so-called monochromatic beam, the photons are all of the same energy and therefore have the same frequency. They can be made to interfere, which indicates a high degree of coherence as well as a more or less uniform state of polarization. If the distribution of the energy in the photons is more random, however, the beam will be less coherent and will have a lower degree of polarization.

It is also convenient to think of light as propagating as wavefronts (see HUYGENS'S PRINCIPLE). These waves, like the crest of an ocean wave, are surfaces on which the phase relationship is constant. Unlike an ocean wave, a wavefront or surface of constant phase is unobservable and undetectable. Light may be considered as energy being transported in a train of wavefronts. The direction of propagation (except for anisotropic media) is in a direction perpendicular to the wavefront. Rays can be conceived as trajectories of photons.

LIGHT PRODUCTION

Light, like any other electromagnetic radiation, results from either an accelerating electric charge or a nuclear fusion or fission reaction. In nuclear reactions, a photon is created in the same manner as other elemental partial products of the reaction. With the exception of sunlight and starlight, how-

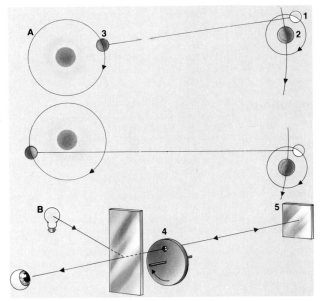

In 1675 a Danish astronomer, Olaus Roemer, was the first to find that light travels with a finite speed. The eclipse times (A) of Jupiter's moons (1) vary from the predicted times, depending on the distance between Jupiter (2) and Earth (3). Roemer calculated the velocity from the time difference and Earth's orbital diameter. In 1849 a French physicist, Armand Fizeau, determined the speed of light by sending a light beam (B) through a hole in a rotating disk (4) to a distant mirror (5). The disk's rotational speed was then adjusted until the reflected light could be seen through the hole. He calculated the speed of light from the disk's rotational speed and mirror distance.

ever, light usually is the result of changes in the electronic structure of atoms and molecules as they absorb and readmit energy.

The incandescent electric light has as its light source the heat that results from the ohmic resistance of the filament to the electric current. A red-hot poker absorbs heat directly from the fire resulting from the liberation of chemical energy. As the material in the filament or poker heats up, the atoms and molecules gain kinetic energy, which is realized by an increase in the number of collisions among the particles. Boiling off of some of the material is one mechanism that can be used to maintain an equilibrium temperature. Another mechanism is for the electrons associated with the various atoms in the metal to move to higher ENERGY LEVELS. When they drop back to lower energy levels they emit a photon, keeping the temperature of the material more or less constant despite the fact that energy is continually supplied. The excess energy is emitted as light.

Thermal production of light is essentially random and is idealized as BLACKBODY RADIATION. The light produced contains a mixture of wavelengths skewed around a central maximum λ_m, which is related to the temperature T of the material in degrees Kelvin. This relation, $\lambda_m T = $ constant, is known as the Wien displacement law. The spectrum produced by the light from such a source is continuous. Although there is a dominant wavelength, this light is not monochromatic. It is generally unpolarized and has a relatively short coherence length.

Another type of light source is energized plasma such as a flame or the gas in a discharge tube such as a neon bulb. Although light is produced by a mechanism similar to thermal emission, the atoms are in a gaseous phase and less random. The energy levels reached by the electrons depend more on the electronic structure of the atoms themselves, and therefore the photons emitted tend to be clustered around specific wavelengths. The spectrum produced by such a source is not at all continuous but consists of lines or bands that are characteristic of the atoms or molecules in the gas. Highly monochromatic light can be obtained from this type of source, par-

ticularly if the light is filtered. The light has a much longer coherence length but is generally unpolarized.

A third type of source is the LASER. Two principles are involved in laser operation. First, the lasing material is composed of atoms, or mixtures of atoms, that have a peculiar energy level structure. As they absorb energy, their electrons move up to higher energy levels, tending to accumulate at certain metastable levels. This is called population inversion. There they remain until stimulated by a photon of the proper frequency. Then the electrons drop to a lower energy level, emitting a photon of the same frequency and traveling in the same direction as the incident, stimulating photon. Because a single photon may stimulate the release of a large number of additional photons, the total number of photons is increased, thus increasing the intensity of the light within the medium. The process is referred to as gain.

The second principle is the geometry of the laser itself. The laser can be regarded as a hollow tube, much like an organ pipe, which is tuned to the wavelength of the emitted photons. The process can be visualized as a wavefront being reflected back and forth between the two ends of the laser, picking up more photons with each reflection. The portion of the light that is permitted to escape from the cavity is highly monochromatic, with a long coherence length. In some circumstances the laser output is highly polarized.

DUALISTIC NATURE OF LIGHT

The historical development of a theory of light, at least from the 17th century on, involved two apparently contradictory descriptions. One concept was the corpuscular theory, which envisioned light as a stream, or flow, of small particles. René DESCARTES modified this concept. He viewed light more as a pressure than as a flow—not as motion but as a tendency to motion. And since light was not motion it was not limited by a finite velocity. In other words, a beam of light required no time of transit. Pierre FERMAT held a different view. He believed not only that light propagated at a finite velocity, but also that its particles described trajectories or rays. Christiaan HUYGENS, on the other hand, was a believer that light was a wave phenomenon. Light propagated at a finite velocity in the form of a moving disturbance, just as a water wave moves as a ripple on a smooth pond.

As a ray of light passes across a surface from one medium to another (for example, from air to glass), its direction is changed—a phenomenon known as REFRACTION. The law of refraction, discovered first empirically by Willebrord SNELL, then subsequently derived formally by Descartes and Fermat, states that sin $r = K$ sin i, where i is called the angle of incidence, the angle between the incident ray and the normal (perpendicular) to the refracting surface. The angle of refraction, r, is the angle between the refracted ray and the surface normal.

Fermat and Descartes agreed on the form of the refraction law, but they disagreed violently on the meaning of the constant K. Fermat saw K as being proportional to the reciprocal of the velocity of propagation. Descartes, even though he believed that the velocity of propagation was infinite, concluded, on a different level of logic, that K was proportional to a velocity. The distinction is important because whether light speeds up or slows down as it passes into a denser medium determines the meaning of K.

Two opposing points of view evolved. Descartes and Fermat were both proponents of a corpuscular theory; Huygens believed in a wave theory. He also obtained a proof of the refraction law in terms of the existence of wavefronts, a construction now called Huygens's principle.

If light is a wave phenomenon, then a medium is required. Sound waves travel through the air but not through a vacuum; ripples require a watery medium. At first it was thought that air would be the medium that would support the propagation of light. The simple experiment of shining light through an evacuated jar, however, showed clearly that this theory was not correct. Theorists chose to hypothesize the existence of a medium called the ETHER.

Experimental evidence to support the wave theory of light was particularly strong. DIFFRACTION, the ability of light to bend around a sharp edge, certainly gave credence to the idea that light was a form of wave motion. Further support came with the discovery of polarization, which indicated that the undulations of a light wave were transverse to the direction of propagation and were not longitudinal, as were sound and water waves. Thus, if light was to be a wave phenomenon, the ether was required, and if so, then certain effects should be observed when a massive body passed through the ether. To detect such effects, telescope tubes were filled with water to determine the effect on starlight. No effect was observed. Experiments to detect an ether "drag" also failed.

On the other hand, James BRADLEY discovered stellar aberration in 1729 when he found that he had to aim his telescope a little in the direction of the Earth's motion ahead of the theoretical position of a star. This effect could be compared to a person in a rainstorm tilting his umbrella a little in front of him as he walks into the rain. Bradley's discovery supported a corpuscular theory, or at least it did not support the idea of an ether drag.

It was postulated, however, that if ether exists, then another observable phenomenon, ether "drift," must also exist. If both the Earth and light are moving through the ether, then the velocity of light observed on the Earth would depend on the direction of observation. The ether was regarded as stationary; the Earth and other planets, the Sun and the stars, and light moved through it. By measuring the apparent velocity of light in various directions, one could determine the absolute velocity and direction of motion of the Earth.

In the late 19th century A. A. MICHELSON and E. W. Morley (1838–1923) attempted to measure the absolute motion of the Earth through the ether (see MICHELSON-MORLEY EXPERIMENT). No ether drift was observed. The conclusion was the inconceivable notion that the velocity of light was constant and independent of the motion of the observer. This paradox led to Einstein's special theory of RELATIVITY, a cosmological theory of major significance.   O. N. STAVROUDIS

Bibliography: Basford, Leslie, and Pick, Joan, *The Rays of Light* (1966); Born, Max, and Wolf, Emil, *Principles of Optics*, 6th ed. (1980); Bragg, William, *The Universe of Light* (1959); Brown, Earle B., *Modern Optics* (1965; repr. 1974); Crawford, Frank S., *Waves*, vol. 3 (1965); Ditchburn, R. W., *Light*, 3 vols., 3d ed. (1977); Fowles, Grant R., *Introduction to Modern Optics* (1968); Heel, Abraham C. van, and Velzel, C. H., *What Is Light?*, trans. by J. L. Rosenfeld (1968); Jenkins, Francis A., *Fundamentals of Optics*, ed. by Robert A. Fry, 4th ed. (1975); Schawlow, Arthur L., *Lasers and Light: Readings from "Scientific American"* (1969).

light horses

Light horses, or light-horse breeds, are those intermediate in size between the heavy draft breeds and the small ponies. They range from 14-2 hands high (58 in/147 cm), the conventional upper size limit for ponies, to about 17-2 hands high (70 in/178 cm), which is taller than many of the heavy draft breeds; light horses weigh considerably less than the draft breeds, however, averaging about 545 kg (1,200 lb). Light horses are used for pleasure riding, racing and other sports, and light draft work. They are usually classified into warm-blooded and cold-blooded types, which refers to their ancestry and not to their blood temperature. Warm-blooded horses are those of Oriental ancestry, tracing their origins back to breeds from warm, dry, Asiatic regions. They can be characterized by a finer conformation, thinner skin, lighter coat, and spirited temperament. Cold-blooded horses trace their origins back to Europe and colder, damper climates. They have thick coats, a generally heavier build, and a more even temperament. Most light-horse breeds are of the warm-blooded type; among the cold-blooded breeds are the Finnish universal and the North Swedish trotter.   EDWIN E. ROSENBLUM

light meter: see ACTINOMETER.

light-year

A light-year is the distance light traverses in a vacuum in one year at the speed of 299,792 km/sec. With 31,557,600 seconds in a year, the light-year equals a distance of 9.46×10^{12} km

$(5.87 \times 10^{12}$ mi). One parsec, the distance at which the semimajor axis of the Earth's orbit (1 ASTRONOMICAL UNIT) subtends one arc second, is equal to 3.26 light-years. Astronomers commonly use the parsec and the light-year to measure astronomical distances. Alpha Centauri, the nearest star to the Sun, has a parallax of 0.76 arc second, equivalent to a distance of 1.3 parsecs, or 4.3 light-years.   K. AA. STRAND

lighthouse

A lighthouse is a structure designed to provide ships with a navigational point of reference by day and by night, and often to indicate dangerous rocks or shoals as well. Used since ancient times, lighthouses have evolved from beacon fires burning on hilltops to modern masonry or steel-frame towers that are capable of resisting the severest storms and are equipped with optical and sound signaling systems.

HISTORY

Although the Phoenicians and Egyptians are thought to have built lighthouses, there are no records of their accomplishments.

Construction. The first lighthouse for which a detailed account remains was the great Pharos of Alexandria, considered one of the SEVEN WONDERS OF THE WORLD. A stone structure about 107 m (350 ft) high with a wood fire at the top, the Pharos, built *c.*280 BC, took its name from the island on which it was built. After withstanding winds and waves for many centuries, it was toppled by an earthquake in the 14th century. The Romans built lighthouses along the European coastline, sometimes fortifying them for military use. Roman lighthouses still stand inside the walls of Dover Castle (England) and at Coruña, Spain.

Among noteworthy medieval lighthouses were two on the commercially important Tyrrhenian Sea, the famous Lanterna of Genoa (built *c.*1161) and the slightly later tower on the island of Meloria. Rebuilt in 1544, the Lanterna still stands today. An engineering feat of the late Middle Ages was the massive lighthouse built in 1584 by Louis de Foix on a half-submerged rock in the Gironde estuary, France. This was the first lighthouse ever built in the open sea.

In the 18th century rapid advances in equipment and construction occurred, and the first towers completely exposed to the sea were built. The Eddystone Light, off Plymouth, England, reflected in its successive forms increasingly scientific principles of design. The massive wooden tower built there in 1696–99 by Henry Winstanley stood 37 m (120 ft) high and had a solid base anchored to the rock by 12 iron stanchions. Destroyed by a storm in November 1703, it was rebuilt in 1708 by John Rudyerd, in the form of a slender and tapering wooden tower constructed around a central timber mast. When Rudyerd's tower burned in 1755, it was replaced by a masonry tower built by John SMEATON, who dovetailed the masonry blocks together and developed a curved, hyperbolic profile for wind and wave resistance that became standard for lighthouses. Smeaton's tower was in turn replaced in 1882 by one that still stands. This last structure is nearly twice as high as Smeaton's and rests on a solid masonry base, with the foundation stones dovetailed not only into each other but also into the reef. The Eddystone Light was the forerunner of many towers in similar isolated spots.

Illumination. Improvements over the old wood, coal, and oil illuminants were introduced at the end of the 18th century (see LIGHTING DEVICES). In 1782 the Swiss scientist Aimé Argand invented the Argand lamp—an oil lamp with a circular wick, protected by a glass chimney, and a central draft. The Argand lamp remained the principal lighthouse illuminant for over a century. The Welsbach gas-mantle lamp, which burned coal gas, was developed in the 1860s. Electric carbon-arc lamps were installed as early as 1858, in the South Forelands light on the English Channel. A new type of lantern invented by Arthur Kitson in 1901 vaporized kerosene under pressure, using the vapor to heat an incandescent mantle. Adapted by David Hood in 1921 to burn petroleum vapor, the vaporized-oil burner is used in lighthouses where electricity is unavailable.

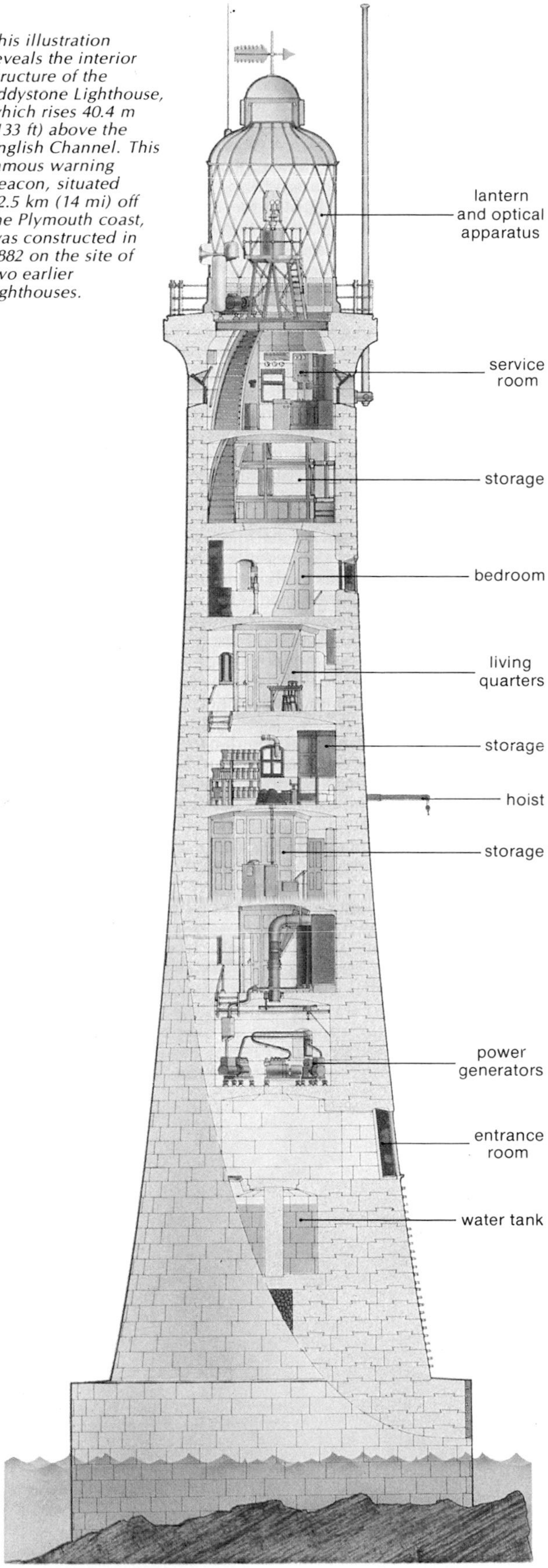

This illustration reveals the interior structure of the Eddystone Lighthouse, which rises 40.4 m (133 ft) above the English Channel. This famous warning beacon, situated 22.5 km (14 mi) off the Plymouth coast, was constructed in 1882 on the site of two earlier lighthouses.

lantern and optical apparatus

service room

storage

bedroom

living quarters

storage

hoist

storage

power generators

entrance room

water tank

The INCANDESCENT LAMP came into use in the 1920s and is standard lighthouse equipment today. An acetylene gas burner invented in 1906 by Nils Gustav Dalén of Sweden, and capable of automatic control, is still the normal illumination for unmanned lighthouses without electricity.

Optical Systems. At the same time, reflectors and refractors were developed to focus, or concentrate, the light into a single powerful beam. A catoptric reflector invented in 1777, which consisted of hundreds of mirror sections set in a plaster mold in the form of a parabolic curve, was later replaced by parabolic silvered copper reflectors. The resulting beam had to be rotated so that it would be visible from any direction. The first revolving light, operated by clockwork, was installed at Carlsten, Sweden, in 1781.

The dioptric system, an improvement on the catoptric reflector, was designed by the physicist Augustin Fresnel in the 1820s; it consisted of a curtain of prisms around a bull's-eye lens; this arrangement refracted the light into a narrow, horizontal beam. Later Fresnel added reflecting prisms above and below, producing the catadioptric system, the basis of all lighthouse optical systems in use today.

In 1890 a method was invented for rotating lights by floating the apparatus in a bath of mercury, almost eliminating friction and permitting revolutions as frequent as every 15 seconds. The technique led to a system of identifying lighthouses by the pattern of intervals of light and darkness. For identification in daylight, lighthouses are painted in distinctive patterns.

MODERN DEVELOPMENTS

Modern construction methods include the sinking of steel CAISSONS. This approach was first tried on the foundations of the Rothersand Shoal light in the Weser estuary in Germany in the 1880s. Prefabricated concrete construction was pioneered in Sweden in the 1930s, culminating in the telescopic method of lighthouse construction that emerged in the late 1950s. According to this method, two or more sections of closed-bottom caissons are constructed, one inside the other, and are floated to the site. The entire structure is first sunk. The outer section forms the foundation, and the inner telescopic sections are then raised by hydraulic jacks and locked into position to form the tower. In the 1960s the U.S. Coast Guard built a number of oil-rig–like towers of open steelwork. A tubular steel-braced framework was positioned on the seabed, piles were driven through the hollow legs to bedrock, and the space between the pile and tube in each leg was filled with concrete grout.

New illuminants include the xenon high-pressure arc lamp, which incorporates a powerful electric arc in a quartz bulb filled with the inert gas xenon (see ARC, ELECTRIC). Solar cells now provide some of the electricity needed to run a lighthouse. Lighthouse sound signals have increased in range—up to some 13 km (8 mi). At the same time, radio and radar beacons identify stations and give navigation bearings. BUOYS and lightships, used where stationary towers cannot be built, carry distinctive markings and, often, BEACONS.

Advances in the automation of electronic equipment have made it possible to maintain beacons from onshore. By the end of the 1980s, the last of the U.S. manned lighthouses—the Ambrose Beacon in New York City's harbor and several on the Maine coast—had been completely automated.

FRANCES GIES

Bibliography: Beaver, Patrick, *A History of Lighthouses* (1973); Engel, Norma, *Three Beams of Light: Chronicles of a Lighthouse Keeper's Family* (1986); Giambarba, Paul, *Lighthouses* (1985); Gibbs, James, *Lighthouses of the Pacific* (1986); Perry, Frank A., *The History of Pigeon Point Lighthouse* (1986); Snow, Edward, *Lighthouses of New England, 1716–1973* (1984); Woodman, Richard, and Smith, David, *View from the Sea* (1986).

lighting, stage: see STAGE LIGHTING.

lighting devices

Lighting, or artificial illumination, as opposed to the natural illumination of the Sun or Moon, was probably first furnished

Lindens, comprising about 30 species of deciduous trees of the northern temperate regions, belong to the genus *Tilia,* linden family, Tiliaceae. They are often called basswoods in North America. Lindens have sawtoothed, somewhat heart-shaped leaves and a tough, fibrous inner bark that has been used for cordage and mats. The small, fragrant yellow flowers of many species provide nectar for bees. The light, soft wood is used for containers, interior finish, and wood carving. *T. cordata,* the small-leaved European linden, is one of several European species planted as a shade tree in both Europe and North America.

Lindner, Richard   [lind'-nur]

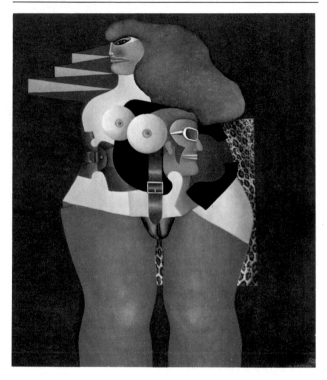

Richard Lindner's 1960s paintings, such as Leopard Lilly *(1966), have much in common with the Continental artistic milieu of the 1920s and early 1930s; metaphysical painting, analytic cubism, and expressionism influenced Lindner. (Museum Ludwig, Cologne.)*

The American painter and illustrator Richard Lindner, b. Hamburg, Germany, Nov. 11, 1901, d. Apr. 16, 1978, studied art in Nuremberg and Munich before emigrating first to France (1933) and then to the United States (1941). He worked as an illustrator for *Fortune, Harper's Bazaar,* and other leading periodicals, but in the 1950s he began to devote full time to painting the arresting, carefully shaded figures, usually of forceful women, that became his trademark—for example, *The Meeting* (1953; Museum of Modern Art, New York City). The solidity and vague sadism of these figures elicited comparisons with the art of the Weimar period in Germany, although analogies with POP ART have also been made.

PHIL PATTON

Bibliography: Ashton, Dore, *Richard Lindner* (1970); Kramer, Hilton, *Richard Lindner* (1975).

Lindow man

Lindow man was unearthed in 1984 in a peat bog near Manchester, England. The well-preserved corpse, approximately 2,200 years old, is remarkable because of the method of execution employed on him. Presumably a human sacrifice, he was first bludgeoned and garroted, then his throat was slit and he was dropped into a pool of water. The complexity of this ritual execution leads some archaeologists to believe that he was an important member of Celtic society, perhaps even a DRUID (see also CELTS).

In his stomach was found a piece of burnt bannock cake, a traditional last meal for Celtic sacrificial victims. Lack of bodily scars (other than those incurred during the sacrifice) tend to indicate he was from a noble, rather than a warrior, class. Lindow man's death is thought to resemble the deaths of TOLLAND MAN and other bodies found in Scandinavian peat bogs. If both Lindow man and the Scandinavian corpses are the remains of Druids, then the Druids' dominance of European culture may have extended geographically farther than previously believed.

Lindsay, Sir David   [lin'-zee]

Sir David Lindsay (or Lyndsay) of the Mount, b. *c.*1490, d. *c.*1555, was a pre-Reformation Scottish poet and dramatist. Active in court life, he was appointed guardian of the infant King James V in 1513 and became Lyon King of Arms, or chief herald, in 1531. Lindsay is best known for his morality play *The Satyre of the Thrie Estatis.* The play, which was first produced in 1540 and revised and expanded for a 1552 production, is the only Scottish drama of its kind that survives intact. It contains lively colloquial diction and comic character portrayal as well as moving and earnest satire of political and ecclesiastical corruption. Lindsay's support for his contemporary John Knox and his fervent belief in the need for just government and religious reform is also reflected in his allegorical poem *A Dialogue between Experience and a Courtier* (1553), which is in part an indictment of Roman Catholicism.

R. L. ABRAHAMSON

Bibliography: Lindsay, Sir David, *The Works of Sir David Lindsay of the Mount, 1490–1555,* ed. by Douglas Hamer, 4 vols. (1931–36; repr. 1972).

Lindsay, Howard, and Crouse, Russel

Howard Lindsay, b. Waterford, N.Y., Mar. 29, 1889, d. Feb. 11, 1968, and Russel Crouse, b. Findlay, Ohio, Feb. 20, 1893, d. Apr. 3, 1966, collaborated on a number of highly successful Broadway plays. *Life with Father* (1939), with 3,224 performances, had the longest run up to then in Broadway history, while another joint effort, *State of the Union* (1945), won the Pulitzer Prize in 1946. The team also prepared texts for such hit musicals as Rodgers and Hammerstein's *The Sound of Music* (1959) and Cole Porter's *Anything Goes* (1934).

Lindsay, John V.

John Vliet Lindsay, b. New York City, Nov. 4, 1921, was mayor of New York City from 1966 to 1973. A graduate of Yale Law School, he was elected (1958) to Congress where as a representative of Manhattan's "silk stocking" district he established a name as an independent liberal. In 1965, Lindsay was elected mayor of New York City on the Republican and Liberal tickets. His first administration was beset with strikes by municipal service unions, but was credited with keeping New York relatively peaceful when other large urban areas were being disrupted by race riots. Denied renomination in the 1969 Republican primary, Lindsay ran as the Liberal party nominee and won. In 1971, he switched to the Democratic party and in 1972 campaigned unsuccessfully to win nomination as the Democratic candidate.

Bibliography: Gottehrer, Barry, *The Mayor's Man* (1975).

Lindsay, Vachel   [vay'-chul]

Nicholas Vachel Lindsay, b. Springfield, Ill., Nov. 10, 1879, d. Dec. 5, 1931, was a poet who first received recognition for the celebrated "General William Booth Enters Into Heaven" (1913). Between 1906 and 1912, Lindsay toured the United States on foot, giving readings of his poetry in return for food and lodging. In his strongly rhythmical verse he sought to revive the art of oral poetry for a popular audience. His publications include *Rhymes To Be Traded for Bread* (1912), *Ad-*

ventures While Preaching the Gospel of Beauty (1914), and one of the earliest works of film criticism, *Art of the Moving Picture* (1915).

Bibliography: Camp, D., *Dictionary of Literary Biography* (1987); Flanagan, John T., *Profile of Vachel Lindsay* (1970); Massa, Ann, *Vachel Lindsay: Fieldworker for the American Dream* (1970); Masters, Edgar Lee, *Vachel Lindsay: A Poet in America* (1935; repr. 1969).

line

A line, or straight line, is one type of plane curve. In geometry, it is impossible to define all terms; some must be left undefined—for example, *set, point, line,* and *plane.* Although line is ordinarily not defined, it is possible to list some properties of a line. For example, a line is straight, has infinite length (hence, no endpoints), has neither width nor thickness, and is determined uniquely by any two of its points. Line segments, rays, and half-lines are subsets of lines.

Any point on a line separates the line into two half-lines. Any line in a plane separates the plane into two half-planes. The set of points between and including two fixed points *A* and *B* is called the line segment *AB.* A ray is the set of points on a line that lie on one side of a fixed point (called the origin of the ray).

In mathematics a line that has a COORDINATE SYSTEM marked off on it is called a number line. Two perpendicular number lines that intersect at the zero points on both form a rectangular coordinate system. An equation of the form $ax + by + c = 0$, with *a* and *b* not both zero, is called a LINEAR EQUATION (equation of a line). Equations of lines can be written in other forms, depending on the information given or desired. The study of sets of points in terms of the coordinates of the points is called ANALYTIC GEOMETRY. If (x_1, y_1) and (x_2, y_2) are the coordinates of two points *A* and *B,* then the line *AB* through them has equation

$$\frac{y - y_1}{x - x_1} = \frac{y_2 - y_1}{x_2 - x_1} \text{ where the expression } \frac{y_2 - y_1}{x_2 - x_1}$$

is called the slope of the line and is designated *m.* This is the two-point form of the equation of a line. The equation $y - y_1 = m(x - x_1)$ is called the point-slope form of the equation of the line through (x_1, y_1) having slope *m.* The equation $y = mx + b$ is the slope-intercept form of the line having slope *m* and *y*-intercept *b.* (The *y*-intercept is the value of *y* for $x = 0$.) If *a* and *b* are the *x*- and *y*-intercepts, respectively, then the equation can be written in the intercept form $(x/a) + (y/b) = 1$ for $a \neq 0$ and $b \neq 0$. A line in space has an equation of the form

$$\frac{(x - a)}{d} = \frac{(y - b)}{e} = \frac{(z - c)}{f}$$

where the numbers *d, e,* and *f* are called the direction numbers.   JOE K. SMITH

Bibliography: Leithold, Louis, *The Calculus with Analytic Geometry,* 5th ed. (1986); Meserve, Bruce E., and Sobel, Max A., *Introduction to Mathematics,* 5th ed. (1984).

lineage   [lin′-ee-uhj]

A lineage, in anthropology, is a group of persons who trace their descent unilineally, or through one parent, back to a known ancestor, either male or female. In a matrilineage, descent is determined according to the ancestry of the mother; in a patrilineage, according to that of the father.

Lineages are characteristic both of large-scale cultures such as that of traditional China and India and of small-scale tribal societies such as that of the Ashanti of Ghana. As a form of KINSHIP, lineages have greater depth than the EXTENDED FAMILY, consisting normally of at least four generations. They are considered permanent, outlasting their members, who ultimately become ancestors.

Lineage membership, because it is reckoned by unilineal descent, is unambiguous, and the lineage often acts as a unified body within a given society, assuming group functions. Lineages commonly serve as property-holding groups and as

legal groups, avenging wrongs or collecting and paying indemnities for wrongs committed. Often the lineage also has a political function; for example, chieftaincy or kingship often rests with a lineage. Political offices such as membership on a chief's council may also be vested in lineage.

JAMES LOWELL GIBBS, JR.

linear algebra

Linear algebra is the branch of mathematics that deals with vector spaces and linear functions that relate one vector space with another (see VECTOR ANALYSIS). MATRIX theory and the theory of LINEAR EQUATIONS are aspects of linear algebra. Since the early 1800s, linear algebra has played important roles in the development of algebra, calculus, and statistics, and in applications such as pure sciences and engineering.

The domain of linear algebra may be illustrated by considering vector spaces R_2 and R_3, consisting of vectors of two- and three-dimensional space, respectively. In R_2 addition of two vectors is defined by $(x,y) + (x′,y′) = (x+x′,y+y′)$, and multiplication of a vector by a scalar *a* is defined by $a \cdot (x,y) = (ax,ay)$. A function *T,* relating R_2 and R_3, is called a linear map if for any vectors $v = (x,y)$ and $v′ = (x′,y′)$, and any scalar *a,* $T(v+v′) = T(v)+T(v′)$ and $T(av) = aT(v)$.   J. L. BERGGREN

Bibliography: Barnett, Raymond A., and Ziegler, Michael R., *Linear Algebra* (1986).

Linear B

The syllabic script used from c.1500 to c.1400 BC for writing the Mycenaean Greek language is known as Linear B. Examples of Linear B script have been found on clay tablets at Knossos on Crete and at Mycenae and Pylos on the Greek mainland.

The Linear B script was first deciphered by a British architect, Michael G. F. VENTRIS, in 1952 and was shown to represent an archaic form of Greek about 500 years older than that used by Homer. Linear B was found initially at Knossos in central Crete, but later it also turned up at centers of Mycenaean civilization on the Greek mainland. Clay tablets were inscribed to form the archives of palaces at Pylos, Mycenae, and Tiryns in the Peloponnesus and at Thebes in Boeotia, as well as at Knossos. The Cretan tablets probably date from the early 14th century BC; those from the mainland, from the 13th. Some jars, probably Cretan, with short painted inscriptions, have also been found.

Linear B consists of about 90 signs, each representing a syllable, usually either a simple vowel or a consonant followed by a vowel. The interpretation is not straightforward, however, because the spelling gives only an outline of how the word was pronounced. *A-re-ka-sa-da-ra,* for example, is the woman's name Alexandra; *pa-ka-na* is *phasgana,* "swords," and *ko-wo* is *korwoi,* "boys." The language clearly shows characteristic Greek features, and some Semitic and other loanwords are already present. The numerals operate on the decimal system, though the weights and measures show traces of the Babylonian system of division into 60 parts.

At each site the tablets have been baked and hence preserved by the fire that destroyed the palace in which they were kept. The tablets yield inventories of personnel, livestock, agricultural produce, and manufactured goods such as textiles, storage vessels, furniture, weapons, and chariots. Of the more than 100 signs used as abbreviations for these commodities, many are simple pictures, though some have evolved into stylized patterns. Other tablets deal with land-holdings and religious offerings. Most of the classical Greek deities—Zeus, Hera, Poseidon, Athena, Hermes, and Dionysus—are mentioned, but unfamiliar names are also found.

Something of the Mycenaean social and administrative systems can likewise be deduced. The king was assisted by court officials and local governors. Artisans received payment in rations because no currency existed. A large force of working women (probably slaves) was maintained by the palace. The fact that some oxen at Knossos were recorded as having Greek names proves that, even on Crete, Greek was widely spoken and not merely the language of the overlords. There are no historical documents, but the Pylos tablets indicate that a sea raid was feared—perhaps from the people who shortly afterward destroyed the palace.

On Crete, Linear B superseded an earlier, Minoan script called Linear A, which had been in use since the 19th century BC. The identity of the language represented by Linear A remains an enigma. Although it has been assigned to either the Anatolian or Semitic group, convincing proof is lacking.

JOHN CHADWICK

Bibliography: Chadwick, John, *The Decipherment of Linear B,* 2d ed. (1967), and *The Mycenaean World* (1976); Palmer, Leonard R., *The Interpretation of Mycenaean Greek Texts* (1963); Pope, Maurice, *The Story of Decipherment* (1975); Ventris, Michael, and Chadwick, John, *Documents in Mycenaean Greek,* 2d ed. (1973).

See also: AEGEAN CIVILIZATION.

linear equation

A linear equation is an EQUATION whose variable or variables appear only to the first degree, or power; that is, no variable has an exponent greater than 1. A linear equation may contain any finite number of variables. For example, $2x = 7$, $3x - 2y = -5$, and $-4x + 6y - 8z = 10$ are linear equations containing, respectively, one, two, and three variables; the equation $2x^2 + 3x - 7 = 0$, however, is not linear but quadratic, since the variable x appears to the second degree. Another characteristic of a linear equation is the geometric property that its graph is always a straight LINE.

Many problems, both practical and theoretical, involve the solution of linear equations. An example is the following system of two linear equations in two unknowns (x and y):

$$2x + 5y = 11; \quad 4x - 7y = 5.$$

Such equations can be solved algebraically or graphically (see ALGEBRA). In the method of elimination, one of the unknowns is eliminated by suitable algebraic manipulation; a solution for the other unknown is then readily obtained; the solution of the above system is $x = 3$ and $y = 1$.

Bibliography: Hart, William L., and Waits, Bert, *College Algebra,* 6th ed. (1978); Lial, Margaret, and Miller, Charles, *Algebra and Trigonometry,* 3d ed. (1983).

linear programming: see OPERATIONS RESEARCH; PROGRAMMING, COMPUTER.

linear regression analysis: see CORRELATION AND REGRESSION.

linen

Linen is a yarn or a woven fabric made from the inner bark of the FLAX plant, *Linaceae usitatissimum.* Remnants of linen cloth that are many thousands of years old have been found. During the Middle Ages linen was the principal vegetable textile fiber, hence its name became the generic term for a large number of dress and household items—shirts, underwear, bedclothes, and tablecloths—that were then almost always made of linen.

Because linen fiber is relatively inelastic, attempts to mechanize the spinning and weaving of linen were unsuccessful until the early 19th century, and many of the technical innovations that were used to increase cotton production could not be applied to linen. In addition, once the cotton gin made possible the manufacture of a large volume of cotton fabrics, linen began to lose its importance. Its use today is relatively minor in clothing, although it is still important as an uphol-

stery and drapery fabric, and for fine handkerchiefs, tablecloths, and napkins.

Like cotton, linen consists principally of cellulose. It is resistant to sunlight and is stronger, cooler, absorbs moisture more readily, dries more quickly, has more luster, and soils less quickly than cotton. Aside from its cost—linen is still among the most expensive fibers because of the complexities of processing flax—a principal drawback in its use as a clothing fabric was its tendency to wrinkle. New finishing processes, however, have recently produced a wrinkle-resistant linen. The USSR is by far the largest flax-fiber and linen producer, although of relatively low quality. Belgium produces the best grades of flax. Great Britain, Ireland, and Belgium are the largest exporters of linen fabrics.   ISABEL B. WINGATE

Bibliography: American Fabrics Magazine, *Encyclopedia of Textiles,* 2d ed. (1972); Leggett, William F., *The Story of Linen* (1945); Potter, Maurice, *Textiles: Fiber to Fabric,* 5th ed. (1975).

lingua franca   [ling'-gwuh frang'-kuh]

A lingua franca is any auxiliary language, usually of a rudimentary kind, used as a medium of communication between people who speak different tongues. The term originally described a mixture of Italian and other languages (*lingua franca,* Frankish tongue) employed by traders in the Mediterranean during the Middle Ages. English, since it is spoken throughout the world, especially in its many PIDGIN forms, can be regarded as a lingua franca. In countries where many separate languages or dialects are spoken, one language may be chosen as the lingua franca of commerce and government. Examples include CREOLE, Mandarin Chinese, and SWAHILI, a Bantu language spoken throughout East Africa.

Bibliography: Hall, Robert A., *Pidgin and Creole Languages* (1966); Heine, Bernd, *Status and Use of African Lingua Francas* (1970).

linguistic geography: see GEOGRAPHICAL LINGUISTICS.

linguistics   [ling-gwis'-tiks]

Linguistics is the science of language; its subject is the pursuit of knowledge about the phenomenon of human language for its own sake. A common assumption is that linguists study only the histories and origins of languages. Even though these pursuits do constitute an important part of linguistics—the part called historical linguistics—they by no means exhaust the subject.

Most linguists also study foreign languages and frequently contribute to the development of materials and methods in language teaching. Neither of these activities, however, constitutes linguistics. The better understanding of foreign languages and the improved methods of teaching them come under the rubric of APPLIED LINGUISTICS and are by-products of linguistic analysis and research.

Implicit and Explicit Linguistic Knowledge. The acquisition of competence in foreign languages constitutes a tool of linguistics—an extremely useful and important tool, but only a tool, not the end or goal. The crucial distinction to be drawn is between implicit and explicit knowledge. A competent speaker of a language has implicit knowledge of that language; a linguist seeks to acquire explicit knowledge about it. Implicit knowledge of a language is reflected in speaking, understanding, reading, and writing—in short, in the ability to use the language, whether its properties are consciously understood or not. Explicit linguistic knowledge, on the other hand, has as its object the conscious understanding of a language's properties, whether or not the understanding is accompanied by the sort of unselfconscious utilitarian control over the language that is called implicit knowledge.

Traditional Grammar. In the West, speculation about language began with the Greeks. Although early philosophers such as PLATO went no further than to suggest hundreds of fanciful etymologies for Greek words, by the 1st century BC grammarians like DIONYSIUS THRAX had worked out an elaborate system—later called traditional grammar—that was by

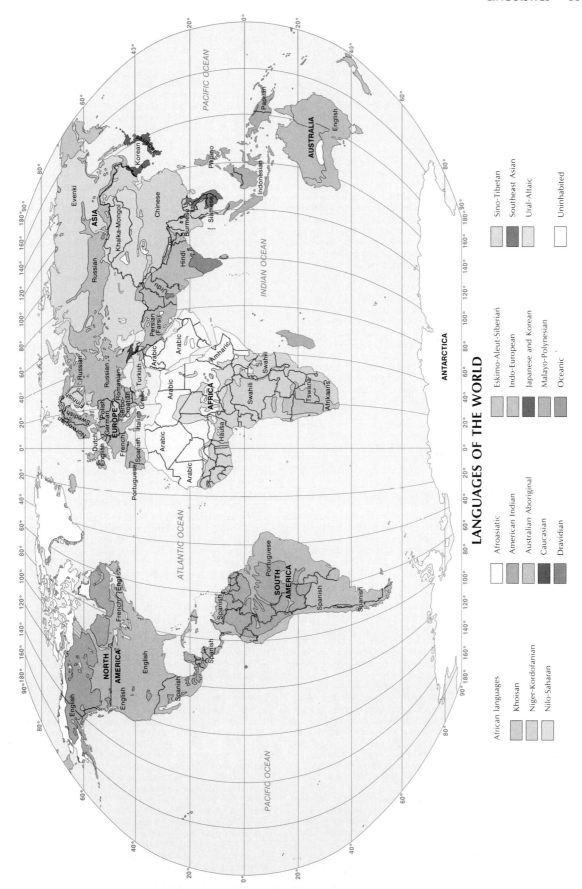

LANGUAGES OF THE WORLD

African languages
- Khoisan
- Niger-Kordofanian
- Nilo-Saharan

- Afroasiatic
- American Indian
- Australian Aboriginal
- Caucasian
- Dravidian

- Eskimo-Aleut-Siberian
- Indo-European
- Japanese and Korean
- Malayo-Polynesian
- Oceanic

- Sino-Tibetan
- Southeast Asian
- Ural-Altaic
- Uninhabited

and large faithful to the structure and properties of Greek. When the Roman grammarians Aelius DONATUS and Priscian (6th century AD) adopted this system for their own language, Latin, it worked well because Greek and Latin are both genetically related as INDO-EUROPEAN LANGUAGES and are structurally quite similar.

Difficulties with traditional grammar did not become evident until many centuries later when Latin had evolved into its descendant ROMANCE LANGUAGES such as Italian, French, and Spanish. The new languages were so different from Latin that the familiar analysis enshrined in the traditional grammars no longer had any contemporary relevance. Because of the high cultural esteem in which Latin was held, however, the false notion arose that the emerging Romance languages represented corrupt forms of classical Latin. Scholars urged that this presumed corruption should be countered by conscious adherence to the archaic language forms and patterns found in Latin, which were believed to be somehow better and purer. This fundamentally mistaken view—that language change is inherently pathological, and that hence a people's language should be kept immune from its normal course of development—is called linguistic prescriptivism.

With the Renaissance and the 15th-century boom in trade and exploration, information began to arrive in Europe about languages unrelated to and almost wholly different from Greek and Latin. Not surprisingly, traditional grammar was unsuited to cope with the new, exotic languages. One positive consequence of this confrontation of old norms and new languages was the development of philosophical interest in properties common to all languages, particularly with reference to canons of universal logic. This movement culminated in the so-called general grammars of the 17th century.

The Beginnings of Modern Linguistics. The English colonization of India during the 18th century uncovered the existence of Sanskrit, an ancient language of religion, philosophy, and literature (see INDO-IRANIAN LANGUAGES). Among the Hindus, Sanskrit occupied a place of importance and esteem analogous to that once held in Christian Europe by Latin.

Linguists noticed almost immediately that Sanskrit bore a remarkable resemblance to Greek and Latin, not only in the shapes of individual words—for example, *mātā,* "mother," and *asti,* "is," beside Greek *Mētēr* and *esti,* and Latin *mātēr* and *est*—but equally in the organization of morphology and syntax. Sanskrit had also been the object of native grammatical investigation dating back three millennia and preeminently represented by the work of PANINI. The Hindu approach in many respects surpassed the traditional grammar of the West for philosophic consistency and analytic thoroughness.

The soundness and rigor of Panini's Sanskrit grammar thereafter provided an intellectual model for European scholars, and Europeans sought an explanation of the unmistakable similarity of Sanskrit to Greek and Latin. In retrospect, modern linguists consider that the key insight is theorized by Sir William JONES, the first great European Sanskrit scholar, who in 1786 surmised that Sanskrit, Greek, and Latin may all "have sprung from some common source which, perhaps, no longer exists."

Jones's statement, made at the threshold of the 19th century, ignited the modern science of linguistics. For the next 100 years the interest of linguists was predominantly historical and comparative; they investigated the evolution and mutual relations of Sanskrit, Greek, and Latin, GERMANIC, CELTIC, and any additional Indo-European languages they could find. Other language families were also studied, most notably URAL-ALTAIC; but it was not until the 20th century that the pale of historical linguistics was extended significantly beyond Europe.

Synchronic Linguistics. During the last years of the 19th century linguists began turning their attention to nonhistorical aspects of language organization and function. They developed ways of studying a language independently of its own past history, as an object functioning at any given time or stage of its existence. An explicit and detailed exposition of the nonhistorical approach did not appear until the posthumous publication in 1916 of *Course in General Linguistics* by the Swiss linguist Ferdinand de SAUSSURE.. The new vantage on language came to be known as synchronic linguistics, in contradistinction to historical or diachronic linguistics. The recognition of these two analytic perspectives, which provide complementary rather than competing modes of linguistic investigation, has remained a cardinal feature of linguistics.

In the two decades after World War I, linguistic science showed rapid consolidation and development on both sides of the Atlantic; the science paid prime but not exclusive attention to synchronic linguistics. In Europe the Geneva school of linguists continued Saussure's pioneering work; significant brands of linguistics also developed in Denmark, under the direction of Otto JESPERSEN and Louis Hjelmslev, as well as in England in association with scholars like J. R. Firth. The most important European linguistic movement of the 1920s and '30s was Czechoslovakia's PRAGUE SCHOOL, led by Roman JAKOBSON, Nikolai Trubetzkoy, and others.

Behaviorism. During the 1920s synchronic linguistics underwent a profound development and wide expansion in the United States. American interest was fueled by the study and analysis of the rich variety of American INDIAN LANGUAGES. Particularly in its formative period, American linguistics developed in close association with SOCIAL ANTHROPOLOGY—Franz BOAS, Edward SAPIR, and Alfred L. KROEBER, for example, were all anthropologists as well as linguists. By the early 1930s, however, the descriptive work that had been dominating the field came more and more to be complemented by a search for theoretical foundations. Under the aegis of BEHAVIORISM, the sweeping, freshly formulated tenets of American linguistic thought were set down in 1933 by Leonard BLOOMFIELD in his book *Language.*

During World War II and in the decade that followed, linguistics continued to develop in the United States, aided and abetted by a variety of applied linguistic work, notably preparation of foreign language teaching materials begun in support of the war effort. European linguistics, on the other hand, was disrupted by the war, although it too began to pick up again in the 1950s with the work of such scholars as M. A. K. Halliday on systemic linguistics in England and André Martinet on functional linguistics in France. New or renewed progress also occurred after the war in Holland, Czechoslovakia, Poland, the USSR, and elsewhere.

The late 1940s and early 1950s saw much theoretical consolidation of American linguistics. The behavioristic program set forth by Bloomfield and others a generation earlier had been put to the empirical test of the world's languages, and the theoretical refinements of linguists like Bernard Bloch, Zellig Harris, Charles Hockett, Eugene Nida, and Kenneth Pike now converged on a coherent theory of language analysis known as neo-Bloomfieldian or structural linguistics—sometimes also called American structuralism to distinguish it from several coeval brands of linguistics that are also generally considered structural.

Because of its behaviorist foundations, American structuralism developed a variety of limitations to determine which linguistic phenomena might fall within the province of scientific inquiry. The specific limitations differed from time to time and from school to school, but they all reflected the structuralist tenet that scientific inquiry must be implemented by totally explicit and automatically replicable analytic methods—the so-called discovery procedures—and that the objects discovered or postulated by these methods must be physically defined. In the case of language, this procedure was tantamount to requiring that the defining properties of sentences, verbs, vowels, and so on be manifested behaviorally—that is, in the external behavior of speakers.

Transformational Grammar. Perhaps the single most serious limitation that the structuralists imposed on themselves was derived from their belief that meaning could not be scientifically studied because it showed insufficient physical manifestation to pass the rigorous behaviorist requirements. In the early 1950s, however, one of the most influential structuralists, Zellig Harris of the University of Pennsylvania, began an important series of investigations that ultimately led not only to the development of techniques for the scientific study of meaning, but also led to a revolution in linguistics. Harris explored the possibility of extending structuralist analysis beyond the limits of the sentence and developed formulas to capture systematic linguistic relations between sentences of different types—formulas that he called transformations. For example, a sentence in the active voice like *Harry drank the beer* was analyzed as being transformationally related to its passive-voice counterpart, *The beer was drunk by Harry.* To the extent that the transformation could be structurally stated, this theory was a breakthrough into a new realm, the linguistic study of meaning. What hitherto had been viewed purely as a relation of meaning—most structuralists had considered corresponding active and passive sentences equivalent in meaning but distinct in structure—could now be correlated with a structural relation as well, that of the transformation.

Though Harris continued developing his own brand of transformational linguistics, what is probably the most important single event in American linguistics since the appearance of Bloomfield's book in 1933 was the publication in 1957 of *Syntactic Structures* by Noam CHOMSKY of the Massachusetts Institute of Technology. A former student of Harris's, Chomsky took over the concept of transformation and incorporated it into a new linguistic theory now commonly known as transformational-generative, or simply generative, linguistics. The theory differs from structuralism in that it synthesizes theoretical and methodological elements from mathematics and the philosophy of language and abandons the structuralists' behaviorism for a philosophical position of neorationalism, which has roots going back to the 17-century concept of general grammar.

The descriptive-analytic power afforded by transformations, coupled with the much-widened analytic scope permitted by its nonbehaviorist philosophy, together account for the striking ascendancy of generative linguistics—and proportionate decline of structuralism—between 1960 and 1980. Although the battle between generativism and structuralism now appears to be waning, there are appearing brands of linguistics descended from generativism but no longer purely generative theoretically, such as relational theory. Currently linguistics is flourishing throughout the world, but theories are too much in flux to predict trends with any confidence.

THE MAJOR BRANCHES OF LINGUISTICS

Lay people commonly believe that a language operates through the element called words, which are strung together into sentences, which then are used to express thoughts. Although this view is an oversimplification and is frequently accompanied by distortions, it does reflect various fundamental truths about language.

According to the popular conception, words themselves have a dual role. First, they serve as building blocks for sentences; each individual word is viewed as having a meaning. Second, words have spellings, which are viewed as being more or less immutable and inviolable, but which in turn are coupled with pronunciations that are characterized by considerable instability and have a tendency to degenerate. The first of these views seems to be essentially correct, except that the popular conception of *meaning* is normally fuzzy and inaccurate in various ways. The second conception, however, is backwards, since both historically and functionally a word's pronunciation is primary, while its spelling not only is derivative but also is in fact dispensable. Even to this day many languages lack WRITING SYSTEMS; yet their words show no more variability or instability in pronunciation than do the words of English or any other language with an established orthography.

A word is an element coupling a meaning and a pronunciation, but comparisons between unrelated languages show the fundamental independence of meanings and pronunciations. For example, the English word *foot* may be compared with its nearest Hebrew equivalent, *regel*. The words differ in more than pronunciation; their meanings are not identical either. Both *regel* and *foot* designate the pedal extremity, but *regel* also designates the whole limb of which the pedal extremity is the end, a portion of the anatomy for which English uses the word *leg*.

Phonetics. PHONETICS is the branch of linguistics that studies the nature and mechanisms of human speech sounds independently of the meanings that those sounds are used to convey. The English word *mopper* ("one who mops"), for instance, is characterizable in terms of phonetics as beginning with and containing segments formed by certain significant lip movements (spelled *m* and *pp* in this case); as being pronounced more loudly on the first syllable (*mop*) than on the second (*per*); as differing only in the first segment from the word *hopper;* and so on.

Semantics. Semantics might be characterized as the branch of linguistics that studies the nature and organization of the meanings conveyed by human language independently of the speech sounds used to symbolize those meanings. Thus aspects of the word *mopper* of interest to semanticists include: delimitation of the real or imagined set of entities designable by the term *mopper;* the contribution of the constituents *mopp-* and *-er* to the word's overall meaning; the fact that *mopper*, "one who mops," bears a semantically relevant relation to *hopper* in the sense of "one who hops," but not also in the sense of "a container for transfering loose material"; the fact that a *mopper* is a kind of *cleaner* and that additional members of the same set include *sweeper* and *duster;* and so on.

Syntax. The relation between sentences and thoughts is not nearly so clear or foregone as was once assumed. The discipline of PSYCHOLINGUISTICS has shown that the term *thought* should be eschewed, where possible, in favor of more serviceable concepts. One such concept is *meaning:* human languages encode meanings into sounds through symbols called words, which enter into combinations called sentences.

The phonetic structure of a sentence is partially but not totally a sum of the phonetic structures of its component words. Likewise, the semantic structure of a sentence is partially but not completely determined by the meanings of its component words. If, however, the only organizational levels of language are the phonetic and the semantic, languages presumably can differ from one another solely in pronunciation or in meaning or in both simultaneously. For instance, English *foot* and German *Fuss* have the same meaning but differ in pronunciation, while English *foot* and Hebrew *regel* differ in both regards. A simple English sentence like *I don't know* may be considered. In its commonest sense it is a plea of ignorance with respect to some request for information. All languages have a sentence functionally equivalent to *I don't know,* and consequently all these sentences will be equivalent in meaning. If the only two levels of a language were the semantic and phonetic, then any two languages' versions of *I don't know* would differ only in pronunciation. This conclusion, however, is egregiously false, as a comparison of *I don't know* with, for example, the corresponding German version clearly shows. If German *Ich weiss nicht* differed only phonetically from the English version, then substituting English pronunciations for the German word by word—*I* for *Ich, know* for *weiss,* and *not* for *nicht*—should result in *I don't know.* It does not, of course, but rather results in *I know not,* which is not acceptable everyday English.

As a result, when the phonetic variances are abstracted out of the English and German sentences, an unaccounted-for residue of differences remains: elements present in one language but absent in the other (*do* appears only in the English version); elements receiving multiple representation (compare French *je ne sais pas,* literally translated as "I not know not"); and discrepancies in order of word placement (the negative precedes the verb in English, follows it in German, flanks it in French).

If these differences are neither phonetic nor semantic, what type of differences are they? Linguists tend to agree (although not unanimously) that the differences indicate the existence of a third level of language organization, the so-called syntactic level. Although the exact nature and properties of this level remain to be delimited, a largely uncontroversial sampling of syntactic facets of the word *mopper* would include: its derivational structure—that is, the PARTS OF SPEECH of both the word and its constituents, *mopp-* and *-er;* its inflectional structure—for example, the fact that a plural form, *moppers,* exists; and its possible syntactic functions—for example, that of subject in the sentence, "The mopper swabbed the deck."

Phonology. Evidence also exists for a fourth organizational level of language, phonology, which embraces aspects of both syntax and phonetics. Fundamentally, a language's phonological system specifies the deployment of its phonetic resources within the frames provided by the syntax. For example, the syntactic fact that the English nouns *mopper* and *mop* have plural forms *moppers* and *mops* is complemented by the phonetic fact that *-s* is pronounced differently in each instance—voiced (vibration of the vocal cords) in the case of *moppers,* but voiceless (vocal cords at rest) in the case of *mops.*

The phonological system provides the special relation between the voiced and voiceless sounds. This special relation is neither an exclusively phonetic fact—the final sounds of *moos* and *moose,* for instance, are phonetically identical with those of *moppers* and *mops,* yet lack the special relation found between the latter two sounds—nor an exclusively syntactic fact—the same special relation holds between the final sounds of the possessives *mopper's* and *mop's* and the verbs *slobbers* and *pops,* although these suffixes are quite distinct syntactically from the plural suffix.

Morphology and Lexicology. Most linguists recognize at least two additional organizational levels, morphology and lexicology (see LEXICOLOGY AND LEXICOGRAPHY). In traditional grammar, a language's morphology gives the patterns internal to a word; syntax examines the relations among words in a sentence. In what is perhaps the most prevalent contemporary usage, the functions of traditional morphology are distributed between syntax and phonology. Recently, however, some promising attempts have been made to grant morphology a more independent footing.

Lexicology is the branch of theoretical linguistics that corresponds to the applied science of lexicography and is thus concerned with the question of a language's repertory of words and other lexical items. In contemporary usage, a language's lexicological inventory, or lexicon, is viewed as either complementary or parallel to its semantics, syntax, morphology, and phonology.

LANGUAGE IN TIME AND SPACE

When a language is studied as an object of development and change through time, the study is called diachronic or historical linguistics. Alternatively, when a language is studied irrespective of its own past—as an object having specific properties at any given temporal point of its existence—the study belongs to the sphere of descriptive or synchronic linguistics.

Despite the importance of the distinction, these two modes of linguistic inquiry—the synchronic and the historical—were not kept sharply apart by linguists until the early part of the 20th century. An example of the difference between the synchronic and historical perspectives is provided by the English word *went.* Originally, *went* was the past tense of the verb *wend.* In time, however, it came to replace the original past tense (*yede,* from Old English *eode*) of the verb *go,* and the verb *wend* itself developed a new regular past tense form, *wended.* Because of this development, in modern English *went* is synchronically the past tense of *go,* but it is historically the past tense of *wend.* Both statements are equally true, but true from different vantages. To claim that *went* is the real past tense of *wend* would be clearly false, although statements of this type are frequently heard.

Just as language change through time constitutes the subject matter of historical linguistics, language variation in space provides the material for GEOGRAPHICAL LINGUISTICS, which includes both linguistic geography and dialectology. Linguistic geography studies differences of language usage in relation to differences of locality, with special attention to geographic and demographic conditions either favoring or hindering the diffusion of linguistic features. Dialectology is concerned with the development and mutual relations of regional and social varieties of a given language.

LANGUAGE, CULTURE, SOCIETY, AND THE INDIVIDUAL

Since language is an exclusive property of human beings, the object of the science of linguistics—unlike the object of sciences such as chemistry or biology—is exclusively human. This fact might be sufficient to put linguistics in a special relation to the other social sciences, except that language interpenetrates the various human faculties and institutions so thoroughly that specific branches of linguistics have had to be developed to study each aspect. ANTHROPOLOGICAL LINGUISTICS and ethnolinguistics are the studies of the relation of language to culture; SOCIOLINGUISTICS deals with its relation to society; and psycholinguistics examines the interaction between language and mind.

An especially close relation also obtains between language and literature and between language and philosophy; these include the well-established subdiscipline known as the philosophy of language. The study of writing cannot be separated from linguistics; various other disciplines study language as a special case of broader concerns. In semiotics, for example, language is a special but particularly important case of a symbolic system. COMMUNICATIONS includes such paralinguistic fields as ANIMAL COMMUNICATION, SIGN LANGUAGE, and gesturemics. Several branches of mathematics, notably LOGIC, CALCULUS, and automata theory (see AUTOMATA, THEORY OF), are also central to linguistics, as is CRYPTOLOGY, the analysis and decipherment of codes.

Applied linguistics is a term that includes a wide variety of practical uses of linguistic theory and methodology in fields as diverse as language teaching, speech therapy, and translating. Mathematical linguistics is dedicated to the study of the formal properties of language. Statistical linguistics refers to the application of probability theory to various analytical problems where quantitative significance must be reckoned with. Computational linguistics involves the computerization of linguistic data for practical or theoretical reasons. Neurolinguistics embraces the study of the anatomy and physiology of the brain as correlative to specific levels and patterns of language organization. Finally, onomastics is the linguistic study of names, particularly of persons and places.

JOSEPH L. MALONE

Bibliography: Bloomfield, Leonard, *Language,* rev. ed. (1951); Bolinger, Dwight, *Aspects of Language,* 2d ed. (1975); Chafe, Wallace L., *Meaning and the Structure of Language* (1970); Chomsky, Noam, *Language and Mind,* rev. ed. (1972), and *Syntactic Structures* (1957); Dineen, F. P., *An Introduction to General Linguistics* (1967); Greenberg, Joseph H., *Language, Culture, and Communication* (1971); Hayakawa, S. I., *Language in Thought and Action,* 3d ed. (1972); Hockett, Charles F., *Language in Culture and Society* (1964); Langacker, Ronald W., *Language and Its Structure,* 2d ed. (1973); Lyons, John, ed., *New Horizons in Linguistics* (1970); Pedersen, Holger, *Linguistic Science in the Nineteenth Century* (1931); Pei, Mario, *Invitation to Linguistics* (1965); Pike, Kenneth L., *Language in Relation to a Unified Theory of the Structure of Human Behavior* (1954); Quine, Willard V., *Word and Object* (1960).

linguistics, applied: see APPLIED LINGUISTICS.

linguistics, historical: see HISTORICAL LINGUISTICS.

Linked Ring Brotherhood

The Linked Ring Brotherhood was a London-based group of photographers devoted to the promotion of pictorial photography and the establishment of photography as a fine art. Founded in 1892 by Henry Peach Robinson, George Davison, and others, the group organized annual photographic salons to display the works of talented, innovative photographers. Membership included such important photographers as Alfred Stieglitz and Frederick H. Evans. The group was dissolved in 1910.

KEITH F. DAVIS

Bibliography: Gernsheim, Helmut, *The History of Photography* (1969).

Linlithgow, Victor Alexander John Hope, 2d Marquess of [lin-lith'-goh, mar'-kwes]

The 2d marquess of Linlithgow, b. Sept. 24, 1887, d. Jan. 5, 1952, was British viceroy of India from 1936 to 1943. Having served on commissions concerned with Indian affairs since 1926, he became viceroy shortly after passage of the Government of India Act (1935), which provided for provincial governments responsible to the Indian electorate. Linlithgow inaugurated the new system with skill. At the beginning of World War II (1939), however, he declared India a belligerent without consulting the Legislative Assembly. The offended Congress party leaders responded by resigning from the provincial ministries and later (1942) launching the "Quit India" movement. Linlithgow jailed the leaders of this civil disobedience campaign, including Mahatma GANDHI and Jawaharlal NEHRU. In 1943 he was replaced as viceroy by Lord WAVELL.

MARCUS FRANDA AND VONETTA J. FRANDA

Linnaeus, Carolus   [lin-ay'-uhs, kar-oh'-luhs]

Carolus Linnaeus, a Swedish botanist, developed the systematic use of two names for classifying plants, animals, and microorganisms. He coined the term Homo sapiens, *which means wise man, to classify humans. Linnaeus is portrayed in this 1739 oil painting by J. H. Scheffel.*

The Swedish biologist Carolus Linnaeus, b. May 23, 1707, d. Jan. 10, 1778, made two major contributions to the field of natural science: the classification of all known plants and animals, and a system of assigning a single scientific name to each plant and animal. This system, called binomial nomenclature, assigns a two-word Latin name to each organism. The first word is the genus to which the organism belongs; the second, often descriptive, is the species name. The house cat, for example, has the scientific name *Felis domesticus*. Its relative the lion is *Felis leo*.

Linnaeus became interested in classification while studying the stamens and pistils (male and female sex structures) of flowers. He then used the numbers of these structures to classify all known flowering plants. Although earlier publications existed, his classification of plants achieved its final form in his book *Systema Plantarum* (1753). The book *Systema Naturae* (1758) comprises the classification of more than 4,000 animals, even human beings. It was Linnaeus in this book who first gave humans the scientific name *Homo sapiens*. He was also the first to use the signs ♂ and ♀ for male and female.

In recognition of his work, Linnaeus was knighted by the Swedish government in 1761. Shortly afterward, he officially changed his name to Carl von Linné.

Reviewed by LOUIS LEVINE

Bibliography: Blunt, Wilfrid, *The Compleat Naturalist: A Life of Linnaeus,* with the assistance of William T. Stearn (1971); Fries, Theodore M., *Linnaeus (afterwards Carl von Linné); The Story of His Life* (1923); Goerke, Heinz, *Linnaeus,* trans. by Denver Lindley (1973); Gourlie, Norah, *The Prince of Botanists: Carl Linnaeus* (1953); Larson, James L., *Reason and Experience: The Representation of Natural Order in the Work of Carl von Linné* (1971).

Linotype   [line'-uh-tipe]

The Linotype is a mechanical type-composing machine that produces complete lines of type in solid metal (slugs). It was invented by Ottmar MERGENTHALER in the late 1880s and was

A linotype operator sets the type for a weekly newspaper in this 1949 photograph. Invented during the 1880s, the linotype was among the earliest and most widely used mechanical typesetting devices. It greatly decreased the cost and time requirements of typesetting.

the natural outcome of a demand for a quicker and cheaper method of composition than TYPESETTING by hand.

The machine consists of four main sections—keyboard, magazine, casting mechanism, and distribution mechanism. The keyboard resembles that of a TYPEWRITER. When the operator presses the appropriate button, a matrix is released from a channel in a storage magazine and transferred to an assembler box, gradually building up a line of matrices. A character stamped in a recess on one of the vertical edges of each matrix serves as a mold for casting. Before casting, wedge-shaped spacebands are inserted between words to justify the line, or make the line fill the measure. The line of matrices and spacebands is brought into contact with a mold; molten metal is then pumped into the mold to cast the entire line of type. (Hence, the machine was named the Linotype.) After casting, the line is automatically trimmed at the bottom and sides to the correct size and then ejected onto a galley with other lines already set.

As soon as the line is cast, the distribution mechanism comes into play. The spacebands are returned to their box and the matrices are transferred to a distributor bar suspended over the top of the magazine. The matrices move along this bar and drop into their correct channels according to combinations of teeth cut away on the matrices. The operation of the whole machine is entirely automatic; the operator can be tapping one line while another line is being cast and a third is being distributed. Slugs are more easily and speedily handled than individual letters, so Linotype saves a great deal of labor formerly spent in manually distributing type back into the type case. A disadvantage is the limited number of letters and symbols that can be set.

M. C. FAIRLEY

Bibliography: Hutchings, E. A., *A Survey of Printing Processes* (1970); Morton, Alan, *Mechanical Composition, Part 1: Line Composition* (1969).

linseed oil

Linseed oil, from the seeds of the FLAX plant, is used as a drying component in paints (see PAINT AND VARNISH) and as a binder in INKS. Flax produces the linen fiber, and linseed oil was originally a by-product of the linen industry; but in the United States the plant is now grown solely for its oil. The oil changes from a thin liquid to a tough, clear, water-resistant yet flexible film when exposed to oxygen. It responds to heating or liming to produce a heavier-bodied oil that has a high gloss and a faster dry and is more adaptable to paint and ink use. When chemically or physically combined with synthetic or natural resin, the blend produced is known as varnish.

JOHN J. OBERLE

lintel: see POST AND LINTEL.

Linz

Linz, the capital city of Upper Austria province, is in north central Austria on the Danube River, west of Vienna. Austria's third largest city, it has a population of 199,910 (1981). A busy river port and rail junction, Linz manufactures iron and steel as well as machinery and chemicals.

Originally the Roman fortress-settlement of Lentia (2d century AD), Linz became an important market town on the trade route from Italy to the Baltic during the Middle Ages. In the 15th century, during the residence of Holy Roman Emperor Frederick III, the city became a provincial capital. The Romanesque church of Saint Martin was begun in 799. The several notable baroque structures include the cathedral (17th century), where Anton Bruckner was an organist (1855–68).

lion

Lions, species *Panthera leo,* are among the great or roaring cats of the family Felidae. Though the male lion is called the king of beasts, it is the less heavy and majestic female lion that does most of the stalking and killing of prey and is the center of the lion pride (family). A male lion may be 1.8–2.4 m (6–8 ft) long, with the addition of a tufted tail of 58–89 cm (23–35 in), stand about 90 cm (3 ft) tall at the shoulder, and weigh 177–227 kg (390–500 lb). A lion's legs are short and massive, with large feet and heavy, sharp claws. In the male, the large head is usually framed with a ruff or mane. The coat is tawny yellow, with accents of black on the manes, ears, and tail tips of mature animals.

Within historic times the lion was common in many parts of Europe, Africa, and Asia. Today it is found only in protected

The lion, P. leo, *usually hunts in groups, one lion driving prey toward other lions lying in wait. The adult male* (right) *often takes no active role in the hunt but nevertheless will claim his portion of the kill. Lions live in groups called prides, each including several males, several females, and cubs. Common throughout central Africa, lions are in danger of extinction in India.*

areas south of the Sahara in Africa and in the Gir forest, a wildlife sanctuary in India. The Gir lions have some structural differences from the African lions. Lions favor open, grassy plains and thornbush country where water is available. They avoid dense forests. The prides are strongly territorial, defending against intrusion by other prides. Lions hunt at night and are a major factor in controlling the populations of grazing animals on the African savanna (see SAVANNA LIFE).

EVERETT SENTMAN

Bibliography: Adamson, Joy, *Born Free* (1960) and *Forever Free* (1963); Bertram, Brian, *A Pride of Lions* (1978); Chipperfield, Mary, *Lions,* ed. by Maurice Yonge (1977); Rudnai, Judith A., *The Social Life of the Lion* (1973); Schaller, George B., *The Serengeti Lion* (1972).

lionfish

Lionfish, or turkeyfish, is the common name for fishes of the genus *Pterois,* scorpionfish family, Scorpaenidae, inhabiting the coral reefs of the Indo-Pacific region. They are noted for the zebralike pattern of stripes that distinguish each species and for their venomous spines capable of inflicting painful, though rarely fatal, wounds. The species *P. volitans* has orange and white stripes, grows to about 30 cm (12 in) long, and is popular with aquarists. Lionfish bear their young alive.

A. R. EMERY

Lipchitz, Jacques   [leep-sheets', zhahk]

The French sculptor Chaim Jacob Lipchitz, known as Jacques Lipchitz, b. Lithuania, Aug. 22, 1891, d. May 26, 1973, was a vital figure in the development of modern sculpture. He achieved acclaim early in his long career for his cubist works, from which evolved the robust and solid forms characteristic of his mature style. Although Lipchitz's longevity as an artist allowed him to create a prolific and varied oeuvre, he always considered himself a cubist, and his work is unified by several recurrent themes, including musicians, maternities, portraits, and improvisations.

Arriving (1909) in Paris, Lipchitz enrolled in the École des Beaux-Arts and soon thereafter opened (1911) his own studio. During his early years in Paris, he befriended Juan Gris and

In the late 1920s and the 1930s, after a severely geometric cubist phase, the Lithuanian-American sculptor Jacques Lipchitz began creating more voluminous, undulating forms inspired by themes that had strong religious or mythic meaning for him, such as his joyous Song of the Vowels. (Kunsthaus, Zurich.)

Complex Lipids. Among the complex lipids, important structural types are phosphoglycerides, phosphosphingolipids, and glycolipids. The parent phosphoglyceride, phosphatidic acid (PA), is similar in structure to a triglyceride except that the 3-hydroxyl group of the glycerol moiety is esterified to phosphoric acid rather than to FA.

Further esterification of the phosphoric acid of PA with a variety of small, hydroxyl-containing molecules leads to a series of derived phosphoglycerides, including phosphatidyl choline (PC), commonly known as lecithin, and phosphatidyli ethanolamine (PE).

The phosphosphingolipids are derived from sphingosine. The formation of an amide with an FA at the 2-position yields ceramide. Esterification of the 1-hydroxyl of ceramide with phosphorylcholine gives sphingomyelin, the major phosphosphingolipid. If the 1-hydroxyl group of ceramide is linked instead to a simple sugar, a cerebroside glycolipid is formed. The further addition of several amino sugars yields more complex glycolipids, the gangliosides.

DISTRIBUTION AND FUNCTION
Lipids are found in all organisms as structural components of the cell membrane. In most animals the major membrane lipids are lecithin, phosphatidyl ethanolamine, and phosphatidyl serine and a sterol, cholesterol. Cell membranes of the central nervous system contain, in addition to the above, sphingo-

Pablo Picasso, two of the founders of CUBISM. Inspired by the cubist aesthetic, Lipchitz overcame his earlier restraint and executed such masterpieces as the pierced *Man with a Guitar* (1916; Museum of Modern Art, New York City). Although the flattened planes and angular masses remained prominent in his works of the 1920s and '30s, the *Bather* (1923–25; Marlborough Gallery, New York City) marked the end of his purely cubist phase and the beginning of his exploration of a sculpture of themes and ideas rather than of formal relationships.

In *Figure* (1926–30; Museum of Modern Art, New York City), Lipchitz synthesized his prior aesthetic examinations and made a decisive turn toward the monumentality expressed in his *Rape of Europa* (1941; Ingersoll Collection, Penllyn, Pa.), an allegorical comment on Hitler's conquest of Europe. After emigrating (1941) to the United States he developed a massive, vigorous style that culminated in his monument titled *Peace on Earth* (1967–69; Los Angeles Music Center).   HARRY RAND

Bibliography: Arnason, H. H., *Jacques Lipchitz: Sketches in Bronze* (1969); Hammacher, Abraham M., *Lipchitz*, trans. by James Brockway, rev. ed. (1975); Lipchitz, Jacques, and Arnason, H. H., *My Life in Sculpture* (1972); Van Born, Bert, *Jacques Lipchitz: The Artist at Work* (1966).

lipid   [lip'-id]

The term *lipid* describes a group of biological compounds that are insoluble in water but are relatively soluble in many organic solvents. Thus, unlike the other major groups of biological molecules—proteins, carbohydrates, and nucleic acids—lipids are categorized by a physical property rather than by structural features.

CLASSIFICATION
Lipids can be classified in three subgroups based on chemical composition: hydrocarbons, simple lipids, and complex lipids. Hydrocarbons contain carbon and hydrogen only. Simple lipids contain C, H, and O, and complex lipids contain one or more additional elements, such as phosphorus, nitrogen, or sulfur.

Simple Lipids. Simple lipids can be segregated into structural types, which are fatty acids (FA), waxes, triglycerides (TG), and sterols. A fatty acid is a long-chain monocarboxylic acid, and a wax is the ester of a long-chain alcohol and a fatty acid. A triglyceride is the ester of a glycerol that contains three FA molecules. Sterols are a special class of alcohols, containing a fused four-ring structure, or steroid nucleus. Sterols may combine with a fatty acid to form sterol esters.

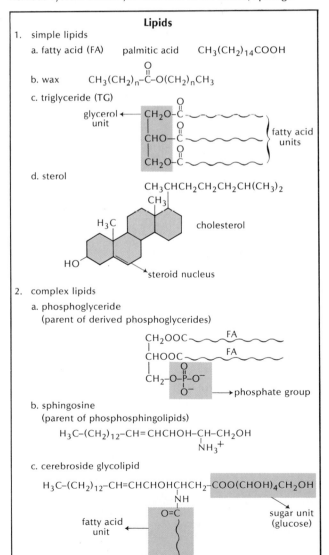

Lipids

1. simple lipids
   a. fatty acid (FA)   palmitic acid $CH_3(CH_2)_{14}COOH$
   b. wax $CH_3(CH_2)_n\!-\!\overset{\overset{O}{\|}}{C}\!-\!O(CH_2)_nCH_3$
   c. triglyceride (TG)

   glycerol unit / fatty acid units

   d. sterol

   $CH_3CHCH_2CH_2CH_2CH(CH_3)_2$

   cholesterol

   steroid nucleus

2. complex lipids
   a. phosphoglyceride
      (parent of derived phosphoglycerides)

   phosphate group

   b. sphingosine
      (parent of phosphosphingolipids)

   $H_3C\!-\!(CH_2)_{12}\!-\!CH\!=\!CHCHOH\!-\!CH\!-\!CH_2OH$
   $\overset{|}{NH_3^+}$

   c. cerebroside glycolipid

   $H_3C\!-\!(CH_2)_{12}\!-\!CH\!=\!CHCHOHCHCH_2\!-\!COO(CHOH)_4CH_2OH$

   fatty acid unit   sugar unit (glucose)

myelin, cerebrosides, and gangliosides. In higher plant membranes, lecithin and PE predominate, although phosphatidyl glycerol (PG) and phosphatidyl inositol (PI) are also present.

Cholesterol is absent, but other sterols, known as phytosterols, are commonly present. Bacterial membranes are unique in that lecithin is rarely present and sterols are completely absent; PE and PG are usually the major lipids.

Although triglycerides are not important membrane lipids, they are stored in most animals and plants as a metabolic energy reserve. In vertebrates, TG is located in adipose (fat) tissue, which is widely distributed in the body. In insects, TG is concentrated in a specific fat body that functions both as a depot and as a center for triglyceride metabolism. In higher plants, TG is found in the seeds of most plants and is the source of most vegetable oils. In a few plants, such as the avocado, the palm, and the olive, the fruit also contains large amounts of triglycerides.

Lipids have a number of specialized functions. In mammals living in cold climates, subcutaneous fat retards loss of body heat. Hydrocarbons and waxes on insect cuticle, as well as on plant leaves and fruit, aid in water retention. Certain cyclic FA, the prostaglandins, are involved in blood clotting and hormonal responses in mammals, and a variety of other FA derivatives serve as sex attractants and growth regulators in insects. Sex hormones and the adrenal corticoids of higher animals are lipids derived from cholesterol. Essential dietary lipids include certain polyunsaturated fatty acids as well as the vitamins A, D, E, and K.

METABOLISM

Triglycerides supply 30 to 50 percent of the calories of the average American diet. Ingested TG is hydrolyzed in the gut and absorbed as fatty acid and monoglyceride. Resynthesis of TG takes place within the intestinal cells and appears first in lymph and then in blood as the major component of chylomicrons, lipoproteins secreted by intestinal cells, which transport dietary lipid to adipose tissue and liver.

Lipid manufactured in the liver, chiefly from carbohydrates, is transported in the blood by three other lipoproteins that are named according to their behavior in an ultracentrifuge: extremely low-density lipoproteins (VLDL), involved in TG transport, low-density lipoproteins (LDL) for cholesterol transport, and high-density lipoproteins (HDL), the carriers of phosphoglycerides and cholesterol. In the capillaries of adipose tissue, the TG of chylomicrons and VLDL are hydrolyzed to glycerol and FA. The FA is taken up by adipose cells and again converted to TG for deposition. At the same time, TG within the cells is hydrolyzed and released into the blood as FA and transported to other tissues for oxidation. The heart, for example, normally obtains 70 percent of its metabolic energy by this process.

In order to produce energy, FA is first degraded into acetate units by a process known as β-oxidation, which is carried out in mitochondria. Acetate, in turn, is oxidized to carbon dioxide by means of enzymes of the citric acid cycle, also known as the KREBS CYCLE, resulting in the manufacture of the high-energy molecule adenosine triphosphate (ATP).

The basic building blocks for triglyceride synthesis, acetate and glycerol-3-phosphate (GP) can be derived from either carbohydrate or amino acid metabolism. Thus even in a fat-free diet, a caloric intake in excess of that needed for metabolic energy leads to a net increase of lipid in adipose tissue. In higher animals, the liver is the major site of fatty acid synthesis. FA, synthesized from acetate, combines with GP to yield phosphatidic acid. After enzymatic removal of the phosphate group of phosphatidic acid, the resulting diglyceride combines with another FA to yield triglycerides. The liver can then release these triglycerides into the blood as VLDL for transport to adipose tissue. Acetate is also the precursor for cholesterol synthesis, whereas phosphatidic acid is the direct precursor of the phosphoglycerides.   ARMAND J. FULCO

Bibliography: Brisson, G. J., *Lipids in Human Nutrition* (1981); Gurr, M. I., and James, A. T., *Lipid Biochemistry,* 3d ed. (1980); Simons, L. A., *Lipids* (1980); Smith, E. L., and Hill, R. L., *Principles of Biochemistry,* 7th ed. (1983); Wakil, Salih, *Lipid Metabolism* (1970).

See also: FATS AND OILS; LYMPHATIC SYSTEM.

Lipmann, Fritz Albert   [lip'-mahn, fritz ahl'-bairt]

Fritz Albert Lipmann, b. June 12, 1899, d. July 24, 1986, a German-American biochemist, discovered (1945) coenzyme A and its importance in metabolism and was awarded a share of the 1953 Nobel Prize for physiology or medicine for this work. Lipmann began studying the role of enzymes in metabolism in the 1930s. He later also studied the mechanisms involved in protein synthesis and eventually turned to the study of energy changes in living organisms.

Lippi, Filippino   [lip'-pee, fee-lip-pee'-noh]

Filippino Lippi, b. *c.*1457, d. Apr. 18, 1504, was a Florentine painter of the High Renaissance. A son and pupil of the painter Fra Filippo Lippi, he acquired his father's mastery of line and color. Later, working under Sandro Botticelli, he acquired his teacher's graceful expressiveness. In 1484, Lippi completed MASACCIO's frescoes in Florence's Brancacci Chapel, having modified his style to that of his predecessor. In the *Vision of Saint Bernard* (*c.*1486; Badia, Florence), Lippi demonstrated his ability to suggest nervous tension through the use of line—his most expressive device. After 1488 he painted many important frescoes in Rome (1489; Santa Maria sopra Minerva) as well as in Florence (1495–1502; Strozzi Chapel, Santa Maria Novella). The last of these—also the artist's last important works—project a sense of restless energy and drama that seems to foreshadow the Mannerism of a later period.

BARBARA CAVALIERE

Bibliography: Berenson, Bernard, *The Drawings of the Florentine Painters*, 3 vols. (1938; repr. 1969); Nielson, Katherine B., *Filippino Lippi* (1938; repr. 1972).

Lippi, Fra Filippo   [lip'-pee, frah fee-lip'-poh]

In Madonna and Child, *one of Filippo Lippi's soft-hued paintings from the 1440s, the solid and sober volumes of his earlier Masaccio-influenced sacred figures give way to a more colorful and decorative elaboration of line and form. (National Gallery of Art, Washington, D.C.)*

Fra Filippo Lippi, *c.*1406–1469, also called Lippo Lippi, was a leading painter of the Early Renaissance Florentine school. In his graceful portrayals of biblical personages and incidents he displayed the gifts of a superb draftsman and colorist as well as those of a natural storyteller.

Lippi, an orphan, was raised in a Carmelite monastery and became a monk at the age of 15. The religious life did not suit him, however, and he left the Carmelite order about 1431, later marrying Lucrezia Buti. Their son, Filippino Lippi, also became a prominent painter.

Lippi's earliest datable work is a *Madonna Enthroned* (1437; National Gallery, Rome), in which, like Masaccio (who may have been his teacher), he achieved a sense of grandeur by using monumental figures, heavy draperies, and lighting designed to heighten the sculptural effect. The detailed domestic scenery in the background suggests a link with the Flemish masters; he may also have drawn inspiration from the relief sculptures of Donatello and Lorenzo Ghiberti, then key figures in Florentine art. Lippi's synthesis of these influences enabled him to bring new ideas to painting and to advance the work of his pupils, for example, Sandro Botticelli and Il Pesellino.

Among Lippi's panel paintings is a *Coronation of the Virgin* (1441–47; Uffizi, Florence); here, the crowded yet controlled pictorial surface displays the painter's lyrical use of color. Lippi's frescoes in the Prato Cathedral (1452–65) show his mastery of the perspectival format, then relatively new. He painted (1466–69) a series of frescoes for the cathedral at Spoleto that portray a vision of Paradise. They were finished after his death by Fra Diamante.   BARBARA CAVALIERE

Bibliography: Berenson, Bernard, *Homeless Paintings of the Renaissance* (1970); Dewald, Ernest T., *Italian Painting: 1200–1600* (1961); Strutt, Edward C., *Fra Filippo Lippi* (1901; repr. 1971).

Lippizaner   [lip'-ih-zan-ur]

The Lippizaner's powerful haunches and strong back enable it to perform the intricate movements comprising the haute école airs for which it is so famous. Its graceful pirouettes, levades, and caprioles are executed in a crisp action possible only after years of training.

The Lippizaner is a breed of show horse bred and trained primarily at the Spanish Riding School in Vienna. The breed is noted for its strength, elegance, and ability to perform the intricate movements of haute école, a discipline of dressage now taught only at the Spanish Riding School. The breed was founded in 1580 at Lippiza, near Trieste, and its ancestors include the Arabian, the Italian, and the Kladruber of Bohemia. The Lippizaner is comparatively small and compact, with a long back, a short, thick neck, and powerful legs. Gray is the predominant color.   EVERETT SENTMAN

Bibliography: Reuter, Wolfgang, *The Lippizaners and the Spanish Riding School* (1969).

Lippmann, Gabriel   [leep-mahn' gahb-ryel']

Gabriel Lippmann, b. Aug. 16, 1845, d. July 13, 1921, was a French physicist who developed the first method for reproducing all colors in a single image on a plate slide. The Lippmann process involved the use of an emulsion film that, like an oil film on the surface of water, produced all colors of the spectrum by interference when light rays were passed

through it. He publicly explained the process in 1891 and was awarded the Nobel Prize for physics in 1908 for his discovery. The technique was slow and difficult to carry out and never became commercially practical. Lippmann worked at a number of scientific laboratories and invented several devices, including a capillary electrometer.

Bibliography: Newhall, Beaumond, *The History of Photography* (1964).

Lippmann, Walter   [lip'-mahn]

Walter Lippmann, a founder of the liberal weekly New Republic, *was one of the most influential political commentators of the 20th century. His Pulitzer Prize-winning syndicated column, "Today and Tomorrow," analyzed current social, political, and ethical issues for 36 years.*

The American journalist Walter Lippmann, b. New York City, Sept. 23, 1889, d. Dec. 14, 1974, was a major journalistic commentator of his time and has often been considered a renaissance man of the American press. He wrote brilliantly of politics, economics, and philosophy and was a syndicated columnist, a newspaper editor, and an author. He achieved such stature that many people reportedly awaited the newspapers bearing his column so that they would know "how to think" about the issues of the day.

Lippmann's education was broad. He was graduated from Harvard University in the famous class of 1909 and then worked as a graduate assistant to George Santayana. William James was one of his teachers; Lincoln Steffens became his mentor. With Herbert Croly he founded the *New Republic* in 1914, and after World War I he served as an aide to E. M. House preparing data for the Versailles peace conference. In 1921 he joined the *New York World,* and he was its editorial page editor from 1929 to 1931. He then became a special writer for the *New York Herald Tribune,* and his column was syndicated in several newspapers. His early books, such as *A Preface to Politics* (1913) and *Public Opinion* (1922), displayed an astute understanding of politics.

As a political commentator, Lippmann took stands varying from conservatism to liberalism. *The Public Philosophy* (1955) was almost a document of "the new conservatism." He was, however, a strong backer of President John F. Kennedy and, until he became disillusioned with the war in Vietnam, of President Lyndon B. Johnson. Lippmann wrote numerous books and in 1958 and 1962 won Pulitzer prizes in journalism.   CALDER M. PICKETT

Bibliography: Adams, Larry, *Walter Lippmann* (1977); Luskin, John, *Lippmann, Liberty and the Press* (1972); Schapsmeier, Edward and Frederick, *Walter Lippmann, Philosopher-Journalist* (1969); Wellborn, Charles, *Twentieth Century Pilgrimage: Walter Lippmann and the Public Philosophy* (1969).

Lippold, Richard   [lip'-ohld]

The American sculptor Richard Lippold, b. Milwaukee, Wis., May 3, 1915, is best known for his abstract wire pieces made in the tradition of Constructivism. His first small sculptures were made (1942) from available junk metal, but after he moved (1944) to New York City he concentrated on large, elegant, geometrically designed wire works that express a preoccupation with delineating space. *Variation No. 7: Full Moon* (1949–50; Museum of Modern Art, New York City), a major work of this period, was intentionally installed in semi-

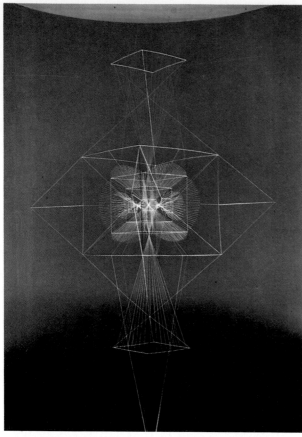

Richard Lippold's Variation No. 7: Full Moon *(1949–50) typifies his intricate constructions of wire and metal. Although possibly inspired by natural phenomena, these geometric suspensions fall within the constructivist heritage. (Museum of Modern Art, New York City.)*

darkness with spotlights on the wires so as to seem to float in space. Since the 1960s, and continuing into the 1980s, Lippold's work has increased to monumental size, and he has collaborated with several architects on designing wire pieces for public buildings.   LISA M. MESSINGER

Bibliography: Anderson, Wayne, *American Sculpture in Process: 1930/1970* (1975); Ashton, Dore, *Modern American Sculpture* (1968).

Lipscomb, William Nunn, Jr.   [lips'-kuhm]

The American chemist William Nunn Lipscomb, Jr., b. Cleveland, Ohio, Dec. 9, 1919, was awarded the 1976 Nobel Prize for chemistry for his studies of borines (boron-hydrogen compounds) and for contributing to the theory of molecular structure and bonding in electron-deficient compounds. Lipscomb received (1946) his Ph.D. degree in physical chemistry from the California Institute of Technology.

Lipset, Seymour Martin

The American sociologist and political theorist Seymour Martin Lipset, b. New York City, Mar. 18, 1922, is best known for his studies of democracy. He has taught at Columbia University (1950–56), the University of California at Berkeley (1948–50, 1956–66), and Stanford University (1975–   ). Maintaining that contemporary democracy though flawed "is the good society itself in operation," he welcomes a trend to supplant political ideology with sociological analysis. Among Lipset's many publications are *Political Man: The Social Bases of Politics* (1960; rev. ed. 1981); (as editor together with Reinhard Bendix) *Class, Status and Power in Comparative Perspective* (1966); *Revolution and Counterrevolution* (1968); (as editor)

Party Coalitions in the Nineteen Eighties (1981); and (with William Schneider) *The Confidence Gap* (1983).

lipstick: see COSMETICS.

Lipton, Sir Thomas

Sir Thomas Johnstone Lipton, b. Glasgow, Scotland, May 10, 1850, d. Oct. 2, 1931, was the founder of the tea and provision company, Lipton, Ltd. Lipton made his fortune primarily on cured meats, eggs, butter, and cheeses. His small store in Glasgow grew to include a chain of shops throughout the United Kingdom; he also owned foreign tea, coffee, cocoa, and rubber plantations; fruit orchards, bakeries, and jam factories in England; and a meat-packing house in Chicago. Lipton was knighted in 1898 and made a baronet in 1902. An ardent yachtsman, he tried unsuccessfully to win the America's Cup in the races of 1899, 1901, 1903, 1920, and 1930.

Bibliography: Lipton, Sir Thomas, *Leaves from the Lipton Logs* (1931); Smallwood, Robert Bartley, *Sir Thomas Lipton* (1953); Waugh, Alec, *The Lipton Story: A Centennial Biography* (1950).

liquefied natural gas: see PETROLEUM INDUSTRY.

liquefied petroleum gas   [lik'-wuh-fide puh-troh'-lee-uhm]

Liquefied petroleum gas (LPG) is a mixture of gases—primarily propane and butane—produced from natural gas, or through the fractionation of crude oil. Easily condensed to liquid form, LPG vaporizes easily and is similar to natural gas in combustion efficiency and controllability. It is transported in pressure tanks or pipelines as a liquid and is subsequently converted to a fuel gas by vaporization at lower pressures. LPG is used as a heating fuel, as a raw material in the chemical industries, and as an engine fuel.

liquid

Liquid is the state of matter in which molecules or atoms have sufficient KINETIC ENERGY to flow, but insufficient kinetic energy to rise out of a container. Like gases, liquids are fluids. Given enough energy, a solid substance will usually melt, becoming a liquid; also, a liquid, when given enough energy, will boil (or vaporize), becoming a gas.
General Properties. The properties of liquids are related to the properties they have in the gaseous or solid state. Thus a liquid, being in a condensed state, has a density near that of the solid; it is usually somewhat less dense, but in a few cases, such as the water-ice system, the liquid is more dense. Also, like solids, liquids are difficult to compress. A solid is incompressible because its molecules are oriented and are spaced at fixed intervals in geometric arrays. X-ray diffraction of liquids shows that although the molecules are mobile and randomly scattered, their mean separation is comparable to that in the solid. Because of their incompressibility and inability to support shear stress (sliding forces), liquids will transmit pressure in all directions (Pascal's law).
   Depending on their shape and the attractive forces present, the molecules of liquids are sometimes able to form loosely bound clusters. Long-chain molecules can form in parallel alignments. Organic molecules with hydroxyl or amino groups, such as DNA, are sometimes loosely joined by HYDROGEN BONDS, thereby creating a limited long-range order.
Surface Tension. The molecules in a liquid attract each other. A molecule in the interior is attracted equally in all directions, but a molecule at the surface is attracted only by other molecules beneath and beside it. This results in an unbalanced force at the surface called SURFACE TENSION. A combination of surface tension and adhesion (or nonadhesion) to the container causes the liquid surface to bend upward (or downward) at the edges, into a shape called a meniscus.
Electrical Conduction. Many liquids are conductors of electricity. Conduction can occur in various ways. If the liquid is

a molten metal, such as mercury at room temperature or any other metal at sufficiently high temperatures, conduction is by free electrons. Molten salts conduct current by the migration of the ions into which the salt has dissociated itself. A liquid that may be a poor conductor when pure can be a solvent of substances that readily yield ions to transport the electricity. Water, for example, is a surprisingly poor conductor when pure but is an excellent solvent for ion-producing substances that are good conductors.

Solutions. Without undergoing any chemical reaction, liquids can form solutions of solids, other liquids, and gases (see SOLUBILITY). Alcohol and water are miscible; in fact, they dissolve in each other so readily that the volume of their solution is less than the volume of the separate components. On the other hand, oil and water are immiscible. A carbonated beverage is an example of a solution of a gas in water.

A. F. SCHUCH AND E. R. GRILLY

Bibliography: Kohler, Friedrich, *The Liquid State* (1972); Metcalfe, H. Clark, et al., *Modern Chemistry* (1974); Murrell, J. N., and Boucher, E. A., *Properties of Liquids and Solutions* (1982).

See also: FLUID MECHANICS; KINETIC THEORY OF MATTER; PHASE EQUILIBRIUM; SUBLIMATION.

liquid crystal

Liquid crystals are substances that do not melt directly to the LIQUID phase but first pass through a paracrystalline stage in which the molecules are partially ordered. In this stage a liquid crystal is a cloudy or translucent fluid but has some of the optical properties of a solid CRYSTAL.

The three major types of liquid crystals—smectic, nematic, and cholesteric, or twisted nematic—are designated by the alignments of the rod-shaped molecules. Smectic liquid crystals have molecules parallel to one another, forming a layer, but within the layer no periodic pattern exists. Nematic types have the rodlike molecules oriented parallel to one another but have no layer structure. The cholesteric types have parallel molecules, and the layers are arranged in a helical, or spiral, fashion. The molecular structure can be altered easily by mechanical stress, electric and magnetic fields, pressure, and temperature. A liquid crystal also scatters light that shines on it, cholesteric types often in iridescent colors. Because of these properties, liquid crystals are often used to display letters and numbers on calculators and digital watches or to test for heat-sensitive areas on other materials.

A normally translucent liquid crystal can become turbulent in some regions when an electric field is applied to it. Light is scattered solely from the turbulent regions, and images are formed by controlling the size and shape of the turbulent areas. Flat, liquid-crystal television screens can replace bulky picture tubes but currently are confined to small applications (hand-held TVs) due to poor picture resolution.

Bibliography: Chandrasekhar, S., *Liquid Crystals,* rev. ed. (1980); De Gennes, P. G., *The Physics of Liquid Crystals* (1974).

liquor: see BRANDY; GIN; RUM; VODKA; WHISKEY

Lisboa, Antonio Francisco: see ALEIJADINHO.

Lisbon   [liz'-buhn]

Lisbon (Portuguese: Lisboa) is the capital, largest city, and chief port of Portugal. The population of the city is 812,385 (1981), and that of its metropolitan area is 2,061,600 (1981). More than 20% of Portugal's population live in Lisbon and its suburbs. The city lies on the northern shore of the Tagus River about 13 km (8 mi) from the Atlantic, on the westernmost piece of land in Europe. The estuary there is 3 km (2 mi) wide, but on the inland, or eastern, side of the city it expands into a large, shallow lagoon. Lisbon's harbor is one of the finest in southern Europe.

Contemporary City. The oldest part of Lisbon lies around a steep hill where the Castle of Saint George, built originally as a Moorish fortification, stands. This part of the city is characterized by steep, narrow, twisting streets. On the lower

Lisbon, the capital and largest city of Portugal, is situated along the Tagus River on the Atlantic Ocean. One of the world's great maritime cities, Lisbon was the center of the trading empire founded by Portuguese explorers during the 15th and 16th centuries.

ground to the west, the Baixa district was built after the earthquake of 1755, with straight, wide streets and spacious squares. Black Horse Square, planned as a formal entrance to the city from the harbor, is there. The docks stretch along the waterfront for 10 km (6 mi). Modern residential quarters have been built on the hills to the north and west. In 1966 a suspension bridge crossing the Tagus was completed.

Up to two-thirds of Portugal's seaborne trade passes through Lisbon, some of it in transit from Spain. The main imports are fuel and industrial raw materials. Exports include cork, timber, olive oil, and fish. The port is equipped to handle container ships and oil tankers. A manufacturing district has been developed to the south of the Tagus estuary, with petroleum refining, cement, steel, and consumer-goods industries (textiles, soap, foodstuffs).

Lisbon is the seat of the Portuguese government and is the country's chief cultural and educational center. The University of Lisbon (1290; reestablished 1911) is Portugal's largest university. The city also has numerous museums. Landmarks include the medieval cathedral; the Jerónimos Monastery, begun in 1502 to commemorate the opening of the sea route to India; and the nearby Tower of Belém, an elaborate Gothic building of the same era.

History. The origins of Lisbon are unknown, although it may have been founded (*c.*1200 BC) by the Phoenicians. Developed by the Romans during the 3d century BC as Felicitas Julia, it was captured by Germanic invaders in the 5th century AD. In the 8th century the city was taken by the Moors, who called it Lixbuna and held it until 1147, when it was taken by the Christian Portuguese coming from the north. In 1256 the seat of government was transferred there from Coimbra.

Lisbon began to grow significantly with the discovery of the sea route to India and the development of oceanic trade. It became one of Europe's leading cities and the chief port serving the vast Portuguese Empire. The city declined, however, during the period of Spanish rule (1580–1640) over Portugal. In 1755 much of Lisbon was destroyed in one of the most disastrous earthquakes known in Europe. It was rebuilt under the direction of the crown minister, the marquês de POMBAL. During the Napoleonic Wars, Lisbon was occupied by the French (1807–08) and then by the British (1808–1820).

NORMAN J. G. POUNDS

Bibliography: Wright, David, and Swift, Patrick, *Lisbon: A Portrait and a Guide* (1971).

Lismer, Arthur [lis'-mur]

The Canadian landscape painter Arthur Lismer, b. Sheffield, England, June 27, 1885, d. Mar. 23, 1969, was a member of the GROUP OF SEVEN. After emigrating from England in 1911, he worked for several years as a commercial artist. In 1913, Lismer made his first trip to the Georgian Bay region; this rugged scenery of northern Canada inspired much of his work throughout his career. During World War I, while in Halifax, Nova Scotia, he painted scenes of naval life in the busy harbor. Lismer returned frequently to the Maritime Provinces after 1930, particularly Cape Breton Island. During these years he gained a wide reputation as a progressive teacher in the field of children's art education.   DAVID WISTOW

Bibliography: Bridges, Marjorie, *A Border of Beauty: Arthur Lismer's Pen and Pencil* (1977); McLeish, John, *September Gale: A Study of Arthur Lismer of the Group of Seven* (1973); Mellen, Peter, *The Group of Seven* (1970); National Gallery of Canada, *The Group of Seven* (1970).

LISP

LISP, an acronym for List Processing Language, is a high-level COMPUTER LANGUAGE that is used widely in the study of ARTIFICIAL INTELLIGENCE (AI). Developed by John McCarthy in the late 1950s, LISP became popular with researchers at the Massachusetts Institute of Technology, who exploited its logical and economic structure in their studies of AI. LISP is an interactive language in which the user builds complex commands, or "lists," by putting together a series of related words, or "atoms," by means of expanding parentheses.

Liss, Johann: see LYS, JAN.

Lissajous figure [lee-suh-zhoo']

Lissajous figures are the interesting and often intricate patterns that are traced out when two mutually perpendicular periodic disturbances occur simultaneously. The resultant motion can be represented by a repetitive pattern on the plane containing the two perpendicular directions. The figures depend on the ratio of the frequencies of the disturbances and the phase difference between them. French physicist Jules A. Lissajous (1822–80) made an extensive study of these motions, and these figures are therefore named for him. Lissajous figures are conveniently displayed on an oscilloscope by applying periodic electrical signals across its vertical and horizontal inputs.   S. BHATTACHARYA

Lissitzky, El [lee-seet'-skee]

Eliezer Markovich Lissitzky, b. Nov. 10 (N.S.), 1890, d. Dec. 30, 1941, a Russian painter and designer, was one of the most enthusiastic advocates of ABSTRACT ART. It was largely through his efforts that suprematism and constructivism, both early forms of abstraction, were first understood in western Europe. He studied engineering in Germany and at the invitation of Marc Chagall returned to Russia in 1919 to teach at Vitebsk art school. About this time he began to paint what he called *Prouns*, geometrical abstractions influenced by the work of Kasimir MALEVICH, such as *Proun 2* (1920; Philadelphia Museum of Art). These convey an architectural feeling for clarity and order by the simple arrangement of lines, squares, and rectangles.

In 1922, as a result of the Bolshevik government's hostility to abstract art, Lissitzky returned to Germany where he contributed constructivist ideas to the Bauhaus and the Dada movement. He is also credited with the idea that modern abstract works should be viewed in a museum setting that is in accord with their style, an idea that he adopted for subsequent exhibitions. Lissitzky lived in Moscow from 1928, where he experimented with architectural and printing techniques.
                                        IRMA B. JAFFE

Bibliography: Lissitzky-Küppers, Sophie, *El Lissitzky: Life, Letters, Texts*, trans. by Helene Aldwinckle and Mary Whittall (1968).

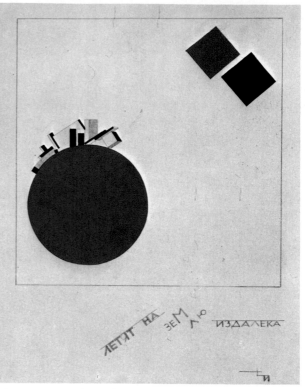

The Russian artist El Lissitzky's sketch (1920) for his Story of Two Squares *is one diagram from a lithographic series (published 1922) of geometrical abstractions. (Museum of Modern Art, New York City.)*

Lister, Joseph [lis'-tur]

The British surgeon Joseph Lister, b. Apr. 5, 1827, d. Feb. 10, 1912, was the first to use antiseptics to reduce infection after surgery (antisepsis). In 1865, Lister began dipping bandages and ligatures into carbolic acid and pouring the acid into wounds to sterilize them, greatly decreasing the rate of death from gangrene. His article "On the Antiseptic Principle in the Practice of Surgery" (1867), however, was not initially accepted in England or the United States. In 1897, Lister was made a baron by Queen Victoria, on whom he had once operated. Among his other contributions was the method of draining abscesses using a rubber tube.

Bibliography: Cameron, H. C., *Joseph Lister, the Friend of Man* (1948); Fisher, Richard B., *Joseph Lister* (1977); Truax, Rhoda, *Joseph Lister, Father of Modern Surgery* (1944).

Joseph Lister revolutionized surgery with his antiseptic practices. By applying Pasteur's germ theory, he concluded that microorganisms caused infection of wounds, and began using carbolic acid to destroy the germs. Lister later introduced gauze dressings and sterile catgut ligatures.

Liszt, Franz   [list, frahnts]

Liszt, a 19th-century Hungarian composer, gave his first piano concert at the age of nine and eventually became the acknowledged master pianist of his day. A prolific composer, he produced more than 700 works, including the Faust Symphony (1854–57) and his 20 Hungarian Rhapsodies. The inventor of the symphonic poem, he also anticipated 20th-century harmonic methods.

Franz (Ferencz) Liszt, b. Raiding, Hungary, Oct. 22, 1811, d. July 31, 1886, was the most celebrated pianist of the 19th century and one of its most innovative composers. As a small child he showed immense musical gifts. When he was 10, he and his family moved to Vienna, where he studied with Carl Czerny and Antonio Salieri and played for Beethoven. In 1823 his family moved to Paris, but Liszt was denied admission to the conservatory because of his youth and foreign origin. He had no further formal piano instruction, even though he studied composition with both Ferdinando Paër and Anton Reicha.

Liszt toured for several years as a recitalist before he settled (1834) in Geneva, Switzerland, with the Countess Marie d'Agoult. One of their three children, Cosima, married the conductor Hans von Bülow and then the composer Richard Wagner; another, Blandine, married Emile Ollivier, premier of France at the outbreak of the Franco-Prussian War of 1870–71. In 1839, Liszt embarked on a series of concert tours throughout Europe.

In 1844, Liszt was appointed musical director in Weimar; he settled there in 1848 and abandoned concertizing to devote himself to conducting and composition. From these Weimar years come his best-known large compositions: the two piano concertos, the *Totentanz* (Dance of Death) for piano and orchestra, the *Dante Symphony* (1856), and the monumental *Faust Symphony* (1854–57). Liszt also invented a new form, the SYMPHONIC POEM, an orchestral composition that follows a literary or other program; it consists of a single movement, generally organized either as a loose sonata form, as in *Tasso*, or as a one-movement symphony, as in *Les Preludes* (see PROGRAM MUSIC). Eleven of his twelve symphonic poems date from his first Weimar period. Liszt unified his larger works by deriving their thematic materials from one or more short motifs. The *Hungarian Rhapsodies* are solo piano works that are based on Hungarian urban popular music rather than on folk music.

Liszt left Weimar for Rome in 1859 with the Princess Carolyne von Sayn-Wittgenstein, whom he met on a concert tour in Russia in 1847 and with whom he lived until 1863. After they separated, Liszt turned to writing religious music, including two masses, the *Legends* for piano, and the oratorio *Christus* (1863). In 1865 he received minor orders and was made an abbé by Pope Pius IX. Liszt returned to Weimar in 1869, but after his appointment as president of the New Hungarian Academy of Music in Budapest in 1875 he divided his time between Budapest, Weimar, and Rome.

The works of Liszt's late years, misunderstood by his contemporaries, are surprisingly modern in concept and anticipate many of the devices of Claude Debussy, Maurice Ravel, Béla Bartók, and the Austrian expressionists. He died while attending the Wagner festival in Bayreuth, Germany.

Liszt was one of the great altruists in the history of music: he performed the large piano works of Robert Schumann and Frédéric Chopin when they were physically unable to do so; he provided opportunities for Hector Berlioz, Wagner, and Camille Saint-Saëns to have their music performed; and he also arranged for piano much music in other media—from Bach's organ works to Wagner's operas. His piano writing incorporates both the orchestral style of Beethoven and the delicate pianistic effects of Chopin. He was also a distinguished piano teacher. Though many of Liszt's works contain passages of bombast or sentimentality, his innovations in harmony, musical form, and writing for the piano make him one of the most important and influential composers of the 19th century.

R. M. LONGYEAR

Bibliography: Fay, Amy, *Music Study in Germany* (1880; repr. 1965); Liszt, Franz, *Letters of Franz Liszt*, 2 vols. (1980); Longyear, R. M., *19th Century Romanticism in Music*, 2d ed. (1973); Newman, Ernest, *The Man Liszt* (1934; repr. 1970); Perenyi, Eleanor, *Liszt: The Artist as Romantic Hero* (1974); Searle, Humphrey, *The Music of Liszt*, 2d ed. (1966); Sitwell, Sacheverell, *Liszt*, rev. ed. (1967); Walker, Alan, *Franz Liszt: The Virtuoso Years, 1811–1847* (1983) and, as ed., *Franz Liszt: The Man and His Music* (1970).

litany   [lit'-uh-nee]

The litany is a Christian prayer form consisting of a series of petitions sung or said by a deacon, priest, or cantor, to which the congregation repeats a fixed response. The form originated at Antioch in the 4th century and spread from there throughout the Eastern churches and then to the West. It has remained more important in the East, where litanies led by a deacon are the major form of participation by the congregation in the LITURGY. In the West, the Litany of the Saints is the only liturgical litany for Roman Catholics; the Book of Common Prayer contains a litany for Anglican churches. Nonliturgical litanies include the Litany of Loretto (or of the Blessed Virgin Mary).

litchi   [lee'-chee]

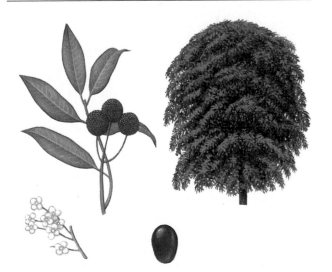

The tropical litchi fruit, L. chinensis, is usually eaten fresh or canned and is a common dessert in oriental restaurants in the West.

The litchi or lychee (*Litchi chinensis*) is a southeast Asian fruit tree of the Sapindaceae family, which includes the SOAPBERRY tree native to tropical America, the Akee tree, and the subtropical LONGAN.

The plum-sized litchi fruit has a thin, tough, bright red peel and juicy, sweet-to-tart white flesh surrounding a single large, smooth seed. Although the seed is inedible, the dried fruit is often called a litchi nut.

The tree was introduced to India over 200 years ago and more recently to South Africa, Florida, and other subtropical regions. It fruits regularly under subtropical conditions that include annual chilling (but not freezing) and also under tropical conditions at moderately high altitudes. Near sea level in the tropics, litchis fruit poorly.   R. J. KNIGHT, JR.

literacy and illiteracy

Literacy is an ability to read and write. The level of ability has been defined in many ways. In the late 19th century, the U.S. government considered literacy to be the ability to read and write one's name. Today, UNESCO classifies it as understanding and producing a simple statement on everyday life. Other proposed definitions involve even more complex skills. Whatever the definition, the extent of literacy and illiteracy reflects social, economic, and educational conditions.

Literacy first arose in the ancient Near East. About 3100 BC, the Sumerians developed, or perhaps borrowed, a system for representing speech—not ideas, as in earlier systems—by means of a set of standardized visual symbols. The introduction of this script seems to have been in response to (and later helped promote) an increasingly complex commercial and administrative structure. Over the next 2,000 years similar requirements led to the introduction of writing systems in other countries, particularly Egypt and China.

Although early scripts were a more precise way to record and preserve information than were prelinguistic systems, they were cumbersome (having hundreds of symbols), ambiguous (not representing all speech sounds), or both. These shortcomings, along with other factors, usually economic, sharply limited the number of people who became literate. (See WRITING SYSTEMS, EVOLUTION OF.)

The development of the Greek alphabet during the 9th and 8th centuries BC dramatically increased the potentials of literacy. This alphabet consisted of a small, easily mastered set of symbols for representing accurately all the sounds of the Greek language. In conjunction with the development of a democratic form of government and a growing appreciation of education, the alphabet spread throughout Greece, which became the world's first truly literate society.

Although debate continues about the extent of literacy in ancient Greece, a more germane debate has arisen over what constituted this literacy. Greek literacy may not have required significantly more critical ability on the part of most people than had been required in earlier societies. Little was available to be read, thus few opportunities to improve reading skills existed. Much of what was written down was direct transcription or reworking of well-known stories. Most people learned what had been written down by hearing it read aloud.

On the other hand, it was during this period that novel, nonpoetic, critical thoughts were first written down. The composition and understanding of such works would seem to require careful, analytical skills on the part of writers and readers. In fact, Plato, who criticized some uses of writing, believed that by carefully rendering and scrutinizing prose statements, people could learn to examine and evaluate objectively both the world and themselves.

Ancient Rome adopted the Greek's appreciation and promotion of literacy. The Germans who conquered Rome during the 5th century AD, however, were illiterate and attached little value to literacy. Literacy was eradicated to such an extent that by the year 1000, probably only 1 or 2 percent of Europe's population was literate.

Outside Europe, the degree of literacy was somewhat greater. Islam had, from its beginning in the 7th century, a strong "tradition of the book." As Islam spread through Asia, North Africa, and southern Europe, this tradition was carried with it. Throughout the period of Europe's Dark Ages, literacy continued to be esteemed in China and India.

The sole protector and nurturer of literacy in medieval Europe was the Roman Catholic church. In abbeys and monasteries over the continent, clerics carefully copied and studied religious texts. Again, however, as was true of pre-Greek times, little of what was written or read was original. Creativity found expression in the development of competing, ornamental styles of writing the alphabet, which, ironically, resulted in the production of texts that were difficult to decipher, if not unintelligible altogether. In addition, literacy was preserved in Latin and not in the vernacular languages of the masses.

After 1000, literacy slowly began to reemerge and spread through Europe. After the Reformation, Protestant countries encouraged people to read the Bible. By 1700, Europe's literacy rate ranged from 30 to 40 percent; by 1850, 50 to 55 percent; and by 1930, 90 percent.

Until at least the time of the Renaissance, literacy served mnemonic purposes; reading was a laborious process of identifying words. Before long, however, this situation changed. The use of writing to convey, and sometimes refine, the succession of revolutionary ideas that were molding the Western world, the establishment of universities, and the invention of the printing press combined, resulting in the development of creative, analytical, and inferential literacy skills that could be used to understand and assess new ideas and put them into practice. At first, however, only elite groups gained such skills. Out of a fear of the impact literacy might have, or as a result of underestimating people's ability to learn, literacy instruction for the lower classes stressed rote learning, not analysis or evaluation. The industrialization of the 19th century made it necessary to teach more people to read and write, although until the 20th century, most were taught only to comprehend, recall, and respect standard political or religious materials.

The 20th century has been marked by a number of significant developments. Building on the gains made during the 19th century, the developed world has virtually eliminated illiteracy. Moreover, in many of the developed countries, efforts have long been under way to ensure that all people can do more than merely recite and minimally understand what they read. Several nations—including the USSR, Cuba, Mexico, China, and Argentina—which at the beginning of the 20th century had illiteracy rates of 70 percent or higher, have especially since 1945 greatly reduced or nearly eliminated illiteracy. In addition, governments and international agencies have been seeking ways to combat illiteracy.

Most modern literacy programs in both developed and developing countries aim to make people functionally literate. This concept originated during World War I, when the United States Army found that, although many recruits and draftees could read and write, they could not do so at a level that would make them effective soldiers. Programs were quickly begun to raise the literacy level of these men. Since that time, functional literacy has been variously defined.

One approach equates functional literacy with a level of reading achievement, which, as defined by the U.S. Bureau of the Census, is a sixth-grade reading level. Another defines functional literacy in terms of some external goal, such as improvement in the economic spheres of life, that literacy can facilitate. The most common definition equates functional literacy with the skills needed to perform everyday reading, writing, and arithmetic tasks. Several assessments conducted from this perspective have identified from 13 to more than 50 percent of American adults, especially those who are poor, undereducated, or members of minority groups, as being functionally illiterate. Although these results are the subject of much concern, they are also controversial. Skeptics question whether the methods used to assess illiteracy are based on empirical examination of the literacy tasks that people confront in their daily lives. Nonetheless, it has been established that millions of Americans read too poorly to function successfully in the everyday world.

The spread of literacy and the achievement of high levels of literacy have been slow but, generally steady. It is uncertain whether the development and spread of electronic and computer technology will increase the spread of literacy or diminish the need for it and result in an oral culture overwhelming the present written one.   EUGENE RADWIN

Bibliography: Bhola, H. S., *Campaigning for Literacy* (1985); Carroll, J. B., and Chall, Jeanne, eds., *Toward a Literate Society* (1975); Cressy, David, *Literacy and the Social Order* (1980); Goelman, Hillel, et al., eds., *Awakening to Literacy* (1984); Goody, Jack, ed., *The Domestica-*

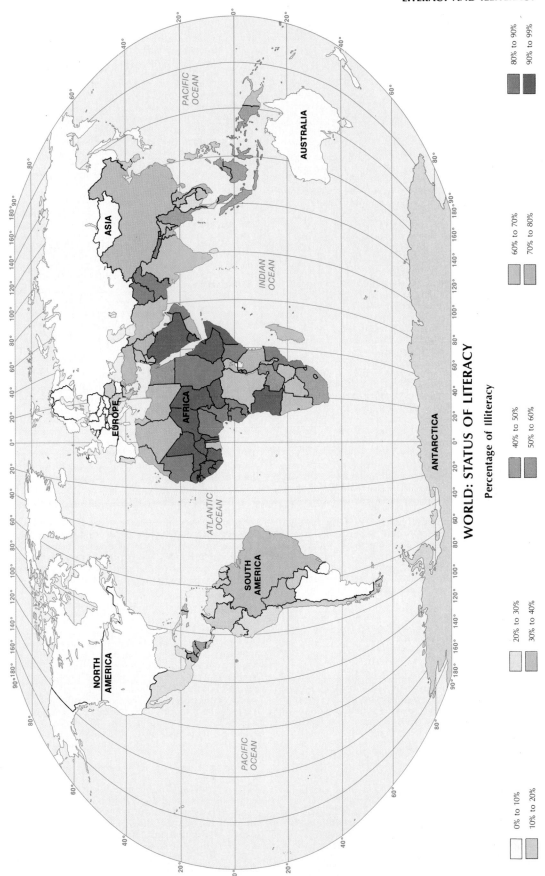

WORLD: STATUS OF LITERACY

Percentage of Illiteracy

0% to 10%
10% to 20%

20% to 30%
30% to 40%

40% to 50%
50% to 60%

60% to 70%
70% to 80%

80% to 90%
90% to 99%

tion of the Savage Mind (1977); Judy, S. N., *The ABC's of Literacy* (1980); Kozol, Jonathan, *Illiterate America* (1985); Olson, D. R., and Torrance, Nancy, eds., *Literacy, Language and Learning* (1984).

literary criticism: see CRITICISM, LITERARY.

literary fraud

Literary fraud is the counterfeiting and disseminating of spurious manuscripts, printed works, or memorabilia. Documents have been forged for political or other purposes from early times; such fabulous works as the famous *Travels of Sir John Mandeville,* composed in the mid-14th century—most probably by a French physician—were translated into many languages, and their incredible tales accepted as true narrations. Not until the 18th century, however, were there enough antiquarians and connoisseurs to make the forging of literary works a profitable enterprise. The *Poems of Ossian* (1762), which its author, James MACPHERSON, claimed comprised an epic translated from 3d-century Gaelic sources, was widely accepted as genuine. Only gradually, in the face of Macpherson's refusal to exhibit his "originals," were the poems recognized as a fabrication.

Shakespeare has been a particularly fruitful subject for literary fraud. William H. V. Ireland (1777–1835) forged several Shakespearian manuscripts, including a complete play that was produced at Drury Lane. Ireland later published a confession, demonstrating how he had contrived the inks, seals, and signatures used in his bogus work. A more dangerous forger was the respected scholar John Payne Collier (1789–1883), whose fraudulent manuscript corrections and altered dates created a host of problems for later researchers. Another specialist in fraud was Thomas James Wise (1859–1937), who printed spurious first editions of major Victorian writers, and used his own authority to certify and sell them.

Modern laboratory analysis and a more stringent scholarship have almost put an end to the common literary forgery, although faked letters of Byron, Poe, and others still confront autograph dealers. Forgeries of material relating to Adolf Hitler have become common. A spectacular contemporary hoax was the near acceptance by scholars and publishers of 60 handwritten volumes that surfaced in 1983, represented as Hitler's diaries, but actually the work of a German dealer in Nazi memorabilia. Even more remarkable was the work of American Mark W. Hofmann, a scholar whose forgeries of Mormon documents fooled every expert for years. Hofmann also sold papers he claimed were written by such authors as Dickens and Twain, and would have sold a "rare" 17th-century document to the Library of Congress—except that his price was too high. Hofmann was jailed in 1987 for the murder of two accomplices who had threatened to reveal his forgeries.   LAWRENCE SENELIK

Bibliography: Barker, N., and Collins, J., *A Sequel to an Enquiry: The Forgeries of Forman and Wise Reexamined* (1984); Farrer, J. A., *Literary Forgeries* (1907; repr. 1969); Trevor-Roper, H. R., *The Hermit of Peking: A Hidden Life of Sir Edward Backhouse* (1976).

literary modernism

A general term describing an innovative style of 20th-century literature in its first few decades, modernism meant, first of all, a rejection of the traditional literary forms and values of 19th-century literature. In many ways the modernist tendency in literature paralleled the various antitraditionalist movements in "modern" art, beginning with the CUBISM and ABSTRACT ART of the early 1900s. Both literary and artistic movements were profoundly influenced by the new psychologies of Freud and Jung, and by anthropologist Sir James Frazer's *The Golden Bough* (1890). Both art and literature emphasized the central role of the unconscious mind, the importance of the irrational, the intuitive, and the primitive, and the use of myth. Many of the variant modernist movements were both literary and artistic: DADA, FUTURISM, SURREALISM, VORTICISM.

In rejecting traditional exposition, literary modernists often replaced it with STREAM OF CONSCIOUSNESS as a narrative mode. Internal experience was emphasized over outward "reality,"

and conventional chronology and causality frequently yielded to a more subjective order.

The 1920s were modernism's golden age, a decade that saw the publication of its principal icons: PIRANDELLO's *Six Characters in Search of an Author* (1921), T. S. ELIOT's *The Waste Land* and James JOYCE's *Ulysses* (both 1922), Ezra POUND's *A Draft of XVI Cantos* (1925), Franz KAFKA's *The Trial* (1925) and *The Castle* (1926), Thomas MANN's *The Magic Mountain* (1925), and William FAULKNER's *The Sound and the Fury* (1929).

Although other major writers of the time, and of the decades to follow, may have been less obviously "modernist," all were, in a literal sense, children of the movement. It is impossible to conceive, for instance, of the works of such writers as Günter Grass, Thomas Pynchon, or Jorge Luis Borges within a context that does not include many of the ideas and techniques of literary modernism.

Reviewed by LILIAN R. FURST

Bibliography: Ellmann, R., and Feidelson, C., Jr., eds., *The Modern Tradition* (1965); Ortega y Gasset, J., *The Dehumanization of Art* (1925); Howe, I., ed., *Literary Modernism* (1967); Rosenberg, H., *The Tradition of the Avant-Garde* (1962); Schwartz, S., *The Matrix of Modernism* (1985).

literature

The term *literature*, which originally designated all written language, is now restricted to examples of literary GENRES such as DRAMA, EPIC, LYRIC, NOVEL, and POETRY. For the literature of particular cultures and countries, see ARABIC LITERATURE; ENGLISH LITERATURE, and so forth. For literary theories and techniques, see CRITICISM, LITERARY; NARRATIVE AND DRAMATIC DEVICES; and VERSIFICATION.

literature for children: see CHILDREN'S LITERATURE.

lithium   (drug)   [lith'-ee-uhm]

The term lithium, in medicine, refers to the salts of the metal lithium that are used in preventing recurrent attacks of MANIC-DEPRESSIVE PSYCHOSIS and in correcting sleep disorders in manic patients. In the United States the salt approved for psychiatric use is lithium carbonate.

Therapeutic dosages of lithium do not affect normal individuals, and their mode of action in manic patients is not yet understood. The salts are taken orally; careful control of dosage is necessary, because toxic levels can occur near the therapeutic levels. Early signs of lithium intoxication include diarrhea, lack of coordination, and vertigo; acute intoxication can lead to seizures and death. Lithium therapy has shown mixed results in other disorders and is best used with patients who have otherwise normal heart and kidney functions.

Bibliography: Johnson, F. N., *Handbook of Lithium Therapy* (1980) and *The History of Lithium Therapy* (1984).

lithium   (element)

Lithium is a chemical element of the ALKALI METALS, group IA in the periodic table; the chemical symbol is Li. Its atomic number is 3 and atomic weight is 6.941, the lowest weight of all metals. Soft and silvery-white, lithium quickly becomes covered with a gray oxidation layer when exposed to air. In nature, lithium is always found in bonded form. Lithium is found in the minerals spodumene, $LiAlS_2O_6$; petalite, $LiAlSi_4O_{10}$; and eucryptite, $LiAlSiO_4$. Lithium metal is prepared by electrolysis of molten lithium chloride, $LiCl$. In 1978 the world resources of lithium were estimated at more than 10 million metric tons.

Although a highly reactive element, lithium is less active than the other alkali metals. Like the others, it easily yields an electron, forming monovalent positive ions. Lithium reacts with water to form lithium hydroxide, $LiOH$, which is used as a carbon dioxide bonding agent in the ventilating systems of submarines and spaceships. Other important lithium compounds are lithium carbonate, Li_2CO_3, and lithium borate, $Li_2B_4O_7$, which are used in the ceramic industry as glaze constituents, and lithium perchlorate, $LiClO_4$, which like all perchlorates is a very powerful oxidizing agent. It has been suggested for use in solid fuels for rockets. Lithium salts are used as antidepressant drugs (see MANIC-DEPRESSIVE PSYCHOSIS).

Lithium hydride, LiH, is used to inflate lifeboats and balloons. It is also a powerful reducing agent. Lithium hydride, composed of the lithium-6 isotope and deuterium, is called lithium deuteride, LiD. LiD can be converted into helium in a nuclear fusion reaction. Lithium deuteride is the explosive material of the hydrogen bomb and may eventually be the fuel of controlled fusion reactors.

Bibliography: Johnson, F. N., *The History of Lithium Therapy* (1984); Zimmerman, Roy, *Adverse Effects of Lithium* (1987).

lithograph   [lith'-oh-graf]

The French artist Henri de Toulouse-Lautrec helped raise lithography from a commercial process to an art with bold, vivid posters such as La Goulue at the Moulin Rouge *(1891).* The clearly defined contours and flat planes characteristic of Toulouse-Lautrec's work derived in part from the nature of the lithographic process. *(Musée Toulouse-Lautrec, Albi, France.)*

A lithograph is a print made with a planographic (flat surface) process discovered in the 1790s by the German playwright Aloys SENEFELDER. To make a lithograph print in the original manner the artist uses a greasy crayon or an oily wash to draw on the surface of a limestone slab. After the stone is treated with an acid solution the areas touched by crayon or wash will reject water rubbed on the stone but retain ink. When the stone is placed on a press the inked design on its surface will print on a sheet of paper. By 1834 specially treated zinc plates began to replace the heavy stones in making lithographs, but limestone from Bavaria long remained the favored material.

Soon after its invention lithography came to be valued as an artistic medium as well as a convenient reproductive technique. Benjamin WEST made the first lithographs attributed to a well-known artist (a series titled *Specimens of Polyautography,* 1801–07). In the period 1815–30 romantic painters such as Francisco de GOYA and Eugène DELACROIX exploited lithography's advantages as a medium that preserved the liveliness of drawing without demanding the complicated preparation and slower execution of etching. Because they were cheap to produce and an excellent vehicle for lively characterization, they also gained widespread favor among mid-19th-century newspaper and magazine illustrators. The French painter and illustrator Honoré DAUMIER was one of the first artists to reach a mass audience with his satiric lithographs.

The development of color lithography was perfected by Paul GAVARNI in his 12 color lithographs *Physiognomies of the Population of Paris* (1831). Although Édouard MANET and Edgar DEGAS, along with others in the impressionist movement, executed original and important lithographs, the dazzling, colorful posters of Henri de TOULOUSE-LAUTREC played the most

prominent role in gaining lithography an esteemed position among the art processes used in the late 19th century. Toulouse-Lautrec's daring use of color lithography was widely emulated by European artists of the 1890s and 1900s—especially Édouard VUILLARD and Pierre BONNARD—and by American lithographers such as Edward Penfield and William Bradley. Not all lithographic artists preferred to work in color, however. Monochrome lithography was popular with many German artists, including Ernst BARLACH and Käthe KOLLWITZ, and the Norwegian expressionist Edvard MUNCH worked with great originality in both color and black-and-white.

Chromolithography, a technique for printing color pictures using a separate plate for each color, produced an inexpensive and popular form of art from the mid-1700s. "Chromos," or oleographs, reproduced, sometimes garishly, many of the famous pictures of the time. CURRIER AND IVES prints were all oleographs, many printed with great skill.

In the 20th century, the development of photolithography and the use of lithography in combination with other graphic techniques have vastly increased the artistic range of the lithograph. Yet for contemporary artists, as much as for Delacroix and Toulouse-Lautrec, the attractiveness of lithography remains its flexibility and liveliness.   BARBARA CAVALIERE

Bibliography: Adams, Clinton, *American Lithographers, 1900–60* (1983; repr. 1987); Gilmour, Pat, *Lasting Impressions* (1988); Man, F. H., *Artists' Lithographs: A World History* (1970); Porzio, Domenico, ed., *Lithography: 200 Years of Art, History, and Techniques* (1983); Saltman, David, and Forsythe, Nina, *Lithography Primer* (1986); Senefelder, Alois, *A Complete Course of Lithography* (1819; repr. 1977).

See also: GRAPHIC ARTS.

lithography, offset: see OFFSET LITHOGRAPHY.

lithosphere   [lith'-uhs-feer]

The lithosphere (from the Greek word *lithos,* "stone") is the solid portion of the Earth, as contrasted to the ATMOSPHERE and the HYDROSPHERE. In a more restricted sense, it is the crust, or outer, rigid shell, of the Earth, as opposed to the mantle and core, which together comprise the barysphere, or centrosphere (see EARTH, STRUCTURE AND COMPOSITION OF).

lithothamnion   [lith-oh-tham'-nee-uhn]

Plants belonging to the genus *Lithothamnion* form a heavily calcified external cover or crust (often pink) on rocks and corals. These red, calcareous algae, which belong to the family Corallinaceae of the division Rhodophycophyta, are found throughout most of the world's oceans. They are notably abundant, however, on the outer edge of CORAL REEFS, where, together with other species (particularly those of the genus *Porolithon*), they form a lithothamnion ridge, which rises about 1 m (3 ft) above the reef and extends 6 to 7 m (20 to 23 ft) below sea level.   TIMOTHY R. PARSONS

lithotripsy   [lith'-uh-trip-see]

Lithotripsy is a widely used, noninvasive medical technique for crushing small KIDNEY STONES. Its full name is extracorporeal shockwave lithotripsy, or ESWL (see ULTRASONICS). ESWL is an alternative to surgery that eliminates the pain and risk associated with surgical incisions. The device used, called a lithotripter, was developed and first tested in West Germany in 1980. Clinical trials are also being conducted of ESWL use for gallstone crushing.

The anesthetized patient is placed in a water bath. The bath contains a small electrode that generates brief but numerous and noisy shock waves, typically over a one-hour period. The patient is positioned so that the waves focus on the kidney stone and cause it to fragment. The fragments are later passed naturally in the urine, and the patient usually returns to normal activity in a few days. Some physicians express concern, however, that ESWL has the potential of causing kidney damage in some patients, which in turn can lead to hypertension problems.   SUSAN D. ROGERS

Lithuania   [lith-oo-ayn'-ee-uh]

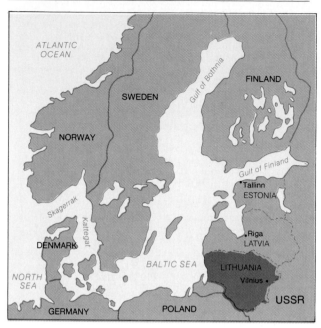

Located on the eastern shore of the Baltic Sea, Lithuania is bounded on the north by Latvia, on the east by Belorussia, and on the southwest by Poland and the Kalingrad oblast of the Russian republic. Its area is about 65,200 km² (25,174 mi²), and its population is 3,690,000 (1989). The capital city is VILNIUS, with a population of 582,000 (1989). From 1940 to 1990, Lithuania was a soviet socialist republic, one of the 15 constituent republics of the USSR. Its current political status is ambiguous and transitional. On Mar. 11, 1990, it declared its independence and changed its name to the Republic of Lithuania, but the USSR did not recognize its independence.

Land and People. Lithuania's topography is of glacial origin, forming an extension of the East European plain. It is dotted with lakes and rivers. The highest elevation is about 300 m (960 ft). Most of the Baltic shoreline is separated from the open sea by a long narrow strip of sand dunes called the Courland Spit; the body of water behind the spit is the Courland Lagoon. Klaipeda, Lithuania's only commercial port, is situated where the lagoon meets the open sea. Lithuania has a moderate climate, with cool summers and mild winters. Precipitation ranges from 559 to 864 mm (22–34 in). The principal river is the NEMAN (Nemunas).

Ethnic Lithuanians constitute 79.6% of the population; 9.3% are Russians, and 7% are Poles (1989); most of the remainder are Belorussians, Ukrainians, and Jews. Lithuanians speak a Baltic language related to Latvian. Roman Catholicism is the predominant religion, but Protestant and Orthodox minorities also exist. Sixty-eight percent of the population is urban (1989). The principal cities, in addition to Vilnius and Klaipeda, are KAUNAS (an industrial center and the country's former capital), Siauliai, Panevezys, and Alytus.

Economy. Lithuania's natural resources include clays and sands that are used to make cement, glass, and ceramics. It also has modest deposits of oil and natural gas, but for most of its energy needs it is dependent on oil and natural-gas imports and on its giant nuclear power station near Ignalina. About 60% of Lithuania's gross national product is industrial, and about 25% agricultural. Industries include metalworking, oil refining, ship building, machine construction, paper, chemical products, construction materials, and furniture. Light industry concentrates on textiles and food processing. Lithuania has a large oceangoing fishing fleet. Its agriculture specializes in meat and dairy production; fodder crops, cereal grains, sugar beets, potatoes, vegetables, and flax are grown.

History. The Lithuanians, with the Latvians, are survivors of the Baltic family of peoples who lived in the region in ancient times and traded with the Romans, primarily in amber. Lithuania emerged as a united nation under Grand Duke Mindaugas in the 13th century. Mindaugas's successors founded an empire extending as far south as the Black Sea. In 1386, Grand Duke JAGELLO (Jogaila) accepted the Polish crown, introduced Christianity, and established a personal union between Poland and Lithuania. In 1569 the two states were merged into a commonwealth, and Lithuania gradually was submerged into Poland as a province.

When Poland was partitioned in 1795, Lithuania was annexed by Russia. A Lithuanian nationalist movement developed during the 19th century, and after the collapse (1917) of the Russian Empire, Lithuania regained its independence (Feb. 18, 1918). It began its life as a democracy, but after a coup d'etat in December 1926, authoritarian rule was set up under Antanas Smetona, who remained president until Lithuania was forcibly annexed by the USSR in 1940.

Except for the German occupation of 1941–44, the country remained under Soviet rule for the next half century. The Soviet regime was resisted by a partisan war (1944–52) that caused an estimated 40,000–60,000 casualties. More than 350,000 were deported or perished in Soviet labor camps. In the decades that followed the economy was industrialized, and an attempt was made to Russify the population.

In the late 1980s the advent of Mikhail Gorbachev's PERESTROIKA reform campaign brought an opportunity for change. In 1988 the non-Communist Sajudis (Lithuanian Reform) movement conducted a successful campaign to restore Lithuanian as the official language and to legalize the old national symbols. In December 1989 the Lithuanian Communist party separated itself from the Soviet Communist party, and Lithuania became the first Soviet republic to permit a multiparty system. In February 1990, Sajudis won an overwhelming majority in free parliamentary elections, and in March independence was proclaimed. Moscow responded with an economic blockade that brought Lithuanian industry and transportation to a standstill. The republic's premier, Kazimiera Prunskiene, visited Western capitals in an attempt to attract international support. Foreign leaders declined to intervene, but urged both sides to show moderation. In June the Lithuanians agreed to suspend their independence declaration while negotiations were held to reach a solution.   V. STANLEY VARDYS

Bibliography: Misiunas, Romuald, and Taagepera, Rein, *The Baltic States: Years of Dependence, 1940–1980* (1983); Vardys, V. Stanley, ed., *Lithuania under the Soviets* (1965).

See also: BALTIC STATES.

Lithuanian language: see BALTIC LANGUAGES.

litotes: see FIGURES OF SPEECH.

Little Bighorn, Battle of the

The Battle of the Little Big Horn (June 25, 1876), also called "Custer's Last Stand," was the last major Indian victory in the INDIAN WARS of the American West. The Sioux and Cheyenne peoples resisted incursions of whites prospecting for gold on Indian land in the Black Hills of Dakota beginning in 1874. In 1876 the U.S. Army sent an expedition to subdue the Sioux leaders, SITTING BULL and CRAZY HORSE. On June 24, Col. George Armstrong CUSTER, commanding the 7th Cavalry, located their camp on the Little Big Horn River in Montana. Underestimating his opponents' strength, he attacked them with a small force of about 225 men the following day. In the ensuing battle, Custer and all of his men were killed. Despite their victory, most of the Sioux had been expelled from the Black Hills by the end of 1876. The site of the battle is now a national monument.

Bibliography: Graham, W. A., *The Story of the Little Bighorn*, 2d ed. (1959; repr. 1988); Miller, David, *Custer's Fall: The Indian Side of the Story* (1985); Sandoz, Mari, *Battle of the Little Big Horn* (1966).

Little Dipper

A group of seven faint stars, the Little Dipper is part of a larger group, the constellation Ursa Minor, the Little Bear. The group contains POLARIS, the North Star, which lies very close to the celestial north pole at the end of the dipper's handle. The second brightest star in the group, Kochab, was closer to the pole about 2,000 years ago; hence its name is derived from the Arabic word meaning polestar.

Little Entente   [ahn-tahnt']

In 1920–21, Czechoslovakia, Romania, and Yugoslavia entered into a defensive alliance known as the Little Entente. These countries had emerged wholly or in part from the dismemberment of the Austrian Empire, which had occurred at the end of World War I. They joined together to preserve the postwar territorial settlement. Their alliance was mainly at Hungary, but also at Germany and Italy. France, the major power most sympathetic to the Little Entente, bolstered it with an alliance with Czechoslovakia (1924) and treaties of friendship with Romania (1926) and Yugoslavia (1927).

The Little Entente was effective until the mid-1930s; in 1933 its members concluded a new treaty setting up a permanent alliance organization. The resurgence of German power under the Nazis, however, forced the smaller states of Eastern Europe to modify their policies, and the Little Entente was weakened. It finally collapsed after France and Britain agreed to the dismemberment of Czechoslovakia at the MUNICH CONFERENCE (1938).   DONALD S. BIRN

Bibliography: Machray, R., *The Struggle for the Danube and the Little Entente, 1929–1938* (1938) and *The Little Entente* (1929; repr. 1970).

little grass frog

The little grass frog, *Limnaoedus ocularis*, in the tree frog family, Hylidae, is the tiniest North American frog, usually not exceeding 16 mm (5/8 in). Its color is variable, ranging from tan to red, but a distinctive dark line, passing through the eye onto the sides of the body, is almost always present. Little grass frogs prefer the grassy edges of ponds and rarely climb, but sometimes are found on low vegetation. They are distributed from southeast Virginia to the southern tip of Florida. Their shrill, chirping call is higher pitched than the hearing range of many people.   JONATHAN CAMPBELL

Little League baseball

Little League baseball is an international program consisting of teams in leagues for children from ages 8 to 12. This network of approximately 7,000 leagues is managed by Little League Baseball, Inc., with operations in more than 30 countries.

The first Little League was started by Carl E. Stotz in 1939, when 3 teams were established in Williamsport, Pa. The concept spread quickly in the United States, and by the 1950s teams were organized in other countries. Local leagues have 4 to 10 teams with 12 to 15 players each. In 1947 a Little League World Series was held at Williamsport. Since then the champions from 4 geographic regions in the United States have met annually to compete in playoffs, with the two finalists meeting in the Series. The World Series became international in 1969, was confined to North American teams for the 1975 season, and then was returned to international status in 1976. Since 1969, Taiwan has dominated.

Little League games are played on smaller-than-regulation-size fields, with bases 60 ft (18.3 m) apart and the pitcher's mound 44 ft (13.4 m) from home plate. In 1974 girls started playing on Little League teams.

Little Rock

Little Rock, a city in central Arkansas, is the capital and largest city of the state and the seat of Pulaski County. A port on the Arkansas River, it is the state's cultural, administrative, and economic center. Its population is 158,461 (1980). Little Rock is surrounded by farmland, and poultry, cattle, and a variety of agricultural products are processed in the city. Manufactures include lumber, concrete products, paper, clothes, and metal products. Bauxite and other minerals are mined nearby. The city is the site of the University of Arkansas at Little Rock (1927), Philander Smith College (1868), and Arkansas Baptist College (1884). Among Little Rock's landmarks are three capitol buildings: the restored territorial capitol, the Old State House, and the present capitol (completed 1916).

A French trader, Bernard de la Harpe, established a trading post on the site in 1722. Little Rock became the territorial capital in 1821 and the state capital in 1836. During the Civil War, the Battle of Little Rock was fought in 1863. The city drew wide attention in 1957 when federal troops enforced a Supreme Court ruling against segregation in public schools.

Little Turtle

Little Turtle, 1751?–1812, the great MIAMI Indian chief, led the Indians to victory over Gen. Josiah Harmar (1790) and Gen. Arthur St. Clair (1791), blocking American expansion into the Lake Michigan region. He later led his people against Gen. Anthony Wayne at the Battle of Fallen Timbers (1794) but was defeated by the Americans and deserted by his British allies. Thereafter he counseled peace and accommodation. While signing the Treaty of Greenville in August 1795, he proclaimed, "I am the last to sign it, and I will be the last to break it," and, true to his word, he refused to aid the Shawnee chief TECUMSEH in later years.   JAMES A. CLIFTON

Bibliography: Dockstader, F., *Great North American Indians* (1977).

littoral zone   [lit'-uh-ruhl]

The littoral zone, the bottom environment on the perimeter of the ocean, extends from high water on the shoreline seaward to a depth of about 200 m (660 ft) at the continental shelf break. It covers about 8 percent of the world's oceans and is subdivided into the eulittoral (nearshore) zone and sublittoral (shelf) zone. The eulittoral zone, usually considered to extend up to a depth of 50 m (165 ft), is the area most affected by waves, tides, and current action. Some scientists restrict the eulittoral to the zone between high- and low-tide levels. In areas of tectonic uplift, volcanism, or glacial scouring, the littoral substrate may be rocky and gravelly. Sand and gravel bottoms characterize the littoral zone along stable coastal plains.   HAROLD R. WANLESS

See also: BEACH AND COAST; BENTHONIC ZONE.

liturgy   [lit'-ur-jee]

Liturgy, from two Greek words meaning "people" and "work," refers to the formal public rituals of religious worship. In the Christian tradition, it is used as a specific title for the EUCHARIST and in general designates all formal services, including the DIVINE OFFICE. Both the written texts of the rites and their celebration constitute liturgy. Among Protestants, the term describes a fixed rather than free form of worship. Outside the Christian church, liturgy is also used to designate the form of prayer recited in Jewish synagogues.

The historic Christian liturgies are divided into two principal families: Eastern and Western. The Eastern liturgies include the Alexandrian (attributed to Saint Mark), the Antiochene (Saint James, Saint Basil, Saint John Chrysostom), and the East Syrian (Assyrian) or Chaldean (Addai and Mari), as well as the Armenian and Maronite rites. The Byzantine liturgies (those attributed to Saint John Chrysostom and Saint Basil) are used today by all Orthodox Christians in communion with Constantinople. The Western liturgies are the Roman and the Gallican. The only Gallican liturgy still in use is the Ambrosian Rite of Milan, although the Mozarabic (Spanish), the Celtic, and the Franco-German Gallican were widely used until the 8th century.

Traditional Anglican and Lutheran liturgies have been based on the local uses of the Roman rite revised according to 16th-century Reformation principles. Reformed (Calvinist) churches attempted to replace historic liturgies with the forms of worship of the early Christian communities.

In the 20th century a movement has arisen among the Roman Catholic and Protestant churches to revise the liturgies to make them more contemporary and relevant while retaining the basic beliefs of the church. In the Roman Catholic church, the Constitution on the Sacred Liturgy of the Second VATICAN COUNCIL substituted the use of vernacular languages for Latin in the Mass and allowed the participation of the laity in public worship. The Anglican (Episcopalian) church has revised the Book of Common Prayer, and the Lutheran churches have issued a new Lutheran Book of Worship. Revised liturgies also are contained in Methodist, Congregationalist, and Presbyterian church hymnals.

L. L. MITCHELL

Bibliography: Dalmais, L. H., *Eastern Liturgies*, trans. by Donald Attwater (1960); Dix, Gregory, *The Shape of the Liturgy*, 2d ed. (1945); Klauser, Theodor, *A Short History of the Western Liturgy*, trans. by John Halliburton, rev. ed. (1979); McManus, William D., *Sacramental Liturgy* (1967); Sheppard, L. C., ed., *The New Liturgy* (1970); Van Allmen, J. J., *Worship: Its Theology and Practice* (1965).

Litvinov, Maksim Maksimovich   [leet-vee'-nuhf]

Maksim Litvinov, b. July 17 (N.S.), 1876, d. Dec. 31, 1951, was the Soviet commissar for foreign affairs from 1930 to 1939. A Jew from Russian Poland, originally named Meir Walach, he joined the Russian Social Democratic Workers' party in 1898 and was associated with the Bolsheviks from 1903. In exile in London at the time of the Russian Revolutions of 1917, he was arrested (1918) and was later exchanged for Bruce Lockhart, formerly the British consul general, who had been arrested in Moscow. In the 1920s Litvinov was deputy to Foreign Affairs Commissar Georgy Vasilyevich Chicherin. Succeeding to Chicherin's office, he served as chief Soviet delegate at the Geneva conference on disarmament (1932) and conducted negotiations that led to the establishment of diplomatic relations with the United States (1933) and Soviet entry into the League of Nations (1934). Replaced by Vyacheslav Mikhailovich Molotov in 1939, Litvinov was later (1941–43) Soviet ambassador to the United States.

Bibliography: Craig, Gordon A., and Gilbert, Felix, eds., *The Diplomats, 1919–1939* (1963); Mastny, V., "Cassandra in the Foreign Commissariat: Maxim Litvinov and the Cold War," *Foreign Affairs*, January 1976; Pope, Arthur E., *Maxim Litvinoff* (1943).

Liu Shao-ch'i   (Liu Shaoqi)   [lyoo show-chee]

The Chinese Communist Liu Shao-ch'i, 1898–1969, served (1959–68) as head of state of the People's Republic. A stalwart of the Chinese Communist party from its founding in 1921, he became the party theoretician, second only to MAO TSE-TUNG in political authority. His manual *How to Be a Good Communist* (1939) was the orthodox text for the indoctrination of cadres. Liu, who had studied in Moscow and served as chief labor agitator for the party, succeeded Mao as head of state in 1959. Bitterly attacked during the CULTURAL REVOLUTION, he was purged from office in 1968 and imprisoned until his death. In 1980 he was posthumously rehabilitated.

Bibliography: Li, T'ien-min, *Liu Shao-ch'i* (1971); Liu Shao-ch'i, *Quotations from President Liu Shao Ch'i*, intro. by C. P. Fitzgerald (1968).

liver

The liver, an organ found in all vertebrates, is the largest organ in the human body. It is a spongy, reddish brown gland that lies just below the diaphragm in the abdominal cavity. It serves to metabolize CARBOHYDRATES and store them as glycogen; metabolize LIPIDS (fats, including cholesterol and certain vitamins) and PROTEINS; manufacture a digestive fluid, bile; filter impurities and toxic material from the blood; produce blood-clotting factors; and destroy old, worn-out red blood cells (see CIRCULATORY SYSTEM).

Two large lobes, the right and the left, make up most of the liver; attached to the right lobe are the smaller quadrate and caudate lobes. The lobes are made up of lobules—six-sided cells arranged in sheets one cell thick—that are closely arranged around blood vessels, bile ducts, lymph vessels, and nerves. Certain reticuloendothelial cells (Kupffer cells) line these lobules and play a role in immunity.

Approximately three sides of each cell are in contact with a blood vessel, and three are adjacent to a bile duct. The lobules are grouped in clusters so that the bile manufactured by each lobule passes down a common duct, which connects to larger ducts that lead to the common hepatic duct. This duct joins with the cystic duct of the GALLBLADDER and enters the duodenum along with the pancreatic duct of Wirsung. Once in the intestines, bile salts aid in emulsifying fats and enhancing the METABOLISM of fats and proteins by enzymes.

The liver is a highly vascular tissue. It receives 25% of its blood from a hepatic artery. The other 75% of the liver's blood supply comes from the portal vein, which transports digested nutrients and hormones from the intestines, hormones from the pancreas, and old red blood cells and bilirubin—a component of bile—from the spleen. Blood leaves the liver by the inferior vena cava, which goes to the heart.

The liver is able to regenerate itself after being injured or diseased; if, however, a disease progresses beyond the tissue's capacity to regenerate new cells, the body's entire metabolism is severely affected. Two common liver diseases are HEPATITIS (inflammation of the lobules) and CIRRHOSIS, or a scarring of the lobules. Many disorders can affect the liver and interfere with the blood supply, the hepatic and Kupffer cells, and the bile ducts. Bile consists of such substances as lecithin, bile salts, and cholesterol, the last two of which can form GALLSTONES under certain conditions and result in obstruction of bile ducts. JAUNDICE, yellow skin discoloration, is a symptom of a variety of liver disorders. Liver cancer is fairly rare but generally incurable. Severely impaired livers are sometimes replaced, and in the early 1980s the one-year survival rate for such operations was 70 percent. In 1984 the U.S. Department of Health and Human Services shifted liver transplantation in children to a nonexperimental basis (see TRANSPLANTATION, ORGAN).

Bibliography: Chen, T. S. and P. S., *Essential Hepatology* (1977); Johnson, L. R., *Gastrointestinal Physiology*, 2d ed. (1981); Sherlock, S. V., *The Human Liver* (1978).

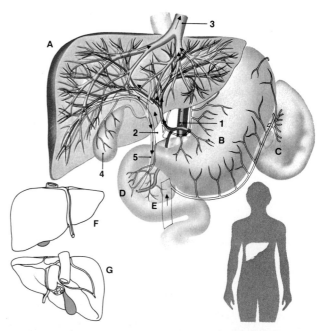

The liver (A) is situated in the upper abdomen below the diaphragm on the right side of the body. A part of the digestive system, it lies next to the stomach (B) and spleen (C) and above the duodenum (D) and pancreas (E). The liver performs at least 500 functions, more than any other organ. Oxygenated blood enters through the hepatic artery (1), and blood containing nutrients enters through the portal vein (2). After being processed by the liver, the blood exits through the hepatic vein (3). Bile is stored in the gallbladder (4) and is released into the duodenum through the bile duct (5). The relative positions of the liver and gallbladder are shown in front (F) and rear (G) views.

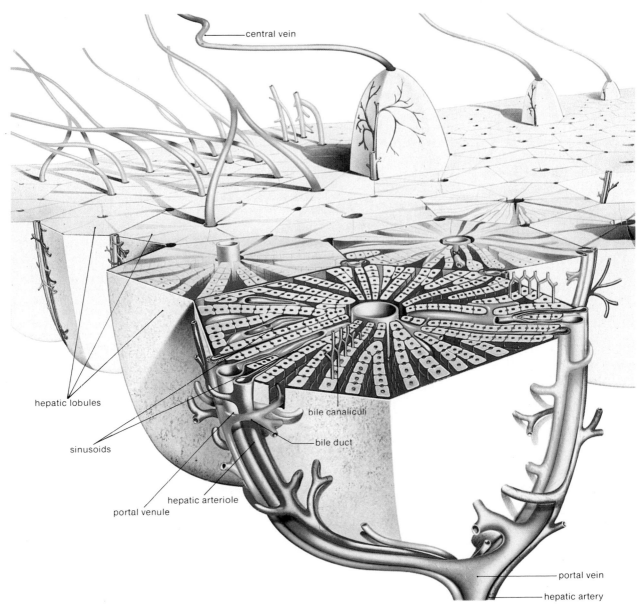

central vein

hepatic lobules

sinusoids

bile canaliculi

bile duct

hepatic arteriole

portal venule

portal vein

hepatic artery

The liver is the largest single organ in the body, weighing about 1.5 kg (3 lb). As shown in this cross-sectional representation, it is composed of many six-sided units called hepatic lobules, each of which consists of a central vein surrounded by liver cells arranged in sheets. Oxygenated blood from the heart arrives via the hepatic artery and reaches the liver cells through the arterioles. Blood from the intestines, which contains digested nutrients, enters through the portal vein and passes through the venules to the cells. There an exchange of materials occurs; nutrients and toxic wastes are removed from the blood, while glucose, proteins, and vitamins are added. The blood then flows through the sinusoids to the central veins, into the hepatic veins, and thence into the inferior vena cava and the heart. Bile, which is important in the digestion of fats, is also produced by hepatic cells. It passes through the bile canaliculi into a branch of the bile duct and then into the gallbladder.

Liverpool

Liverpool is an industrial city and major port in northwestern England on the northeastern shore of the Mersey Estuary. The population of the city is 509,981 (1981); that of the metropolitan county of Merseyside is 1,513,070 (1981). The city center is 5 km (3 mi) from the sea, but docks extend for 8 km (5 mi) northward along this flat coast. The Mersey Estuary is linked by ship canal with Manchester and other industrial cities in the hinterland. The Queensway Tunnel under the Mersey links Liverpool with the industrial city of Birkenhead to the south.

As a port Liverpool is second only to London in national importance, and it is the main port for the highly industrialized north of England. Traditionally, it handles most of

Britain's imported raw cotton and wool, but it also imports sugar, grain, oilseeds, minerals, and crude petroleum and exports manufactured goods of all kinds. It is developing as a container port. Liverpool's manufacturing industries were at first those associated with its foreign commerce, such as grain milling and soap making, but automobile and electrical engineering, chemicals, and petroleum refining have been added and are now more important.

Liverpool is a cultural and educational center. The University of Liverpool was chartered in 1881, and the city's museums and galleries contain some of the finest collections in Great Britain. There is also a well-known orchestra. Liverpool is the seat of an Anglican bishopric and a Roman Catholic bishopric. The Roman Catholic cathedral was begun in 1933 according to a design by Sir Edwin LUTYENS. Only part of it was completed by his death (1944), however, and the main circular, centralized structure was designed by Frederick Gibberd and completed in 1967. The Anglican cathedral (1904–79), a vast Gothic Revival building, was designed by Sir Giles Gilbert Scott.

Liverpool was settled in 1207, after King John granted a charter for a new, planned town. It developed during the mid-17th century as the main port linking England with Ireland. In the 17th and 18th centuries it developed an important colonial trade and became the center of the slave trade with Africa and North America. With the Industrial Revolution Liverpool became the port for the manufacturing region of Lancashire and West Yorkshire.

Liverpool, Robert Banks Jenkinson, 2d Earl of

The 2d earl of Liverpool, b. June 7, 1770, d. Dec. 4, 1828, served as prime minister of Great Britain from 1812 to 1827, years in which the British were victorious in the Napoleonic Wars and experienced an aftermath of social and economic unrest. Entering the House of Commons as a Tory in 1790 and moving to the House of Lords in 1808, he was foreign secretary (1801–04), home secretary (1804–06, 1807–09), and secretary of war (1809–12) before succeeding the assassinated Spencer Perceval as prime minister.

Liverpool's long tenure as prime minister—unprecedented for a member of the House of Lords and one who was, by the standards of the day, incorrupt—makes Benjamin Disraeli's description of him as the "Arch-Mediocrity" untenable. Liverpool's talent lay in diplomatic handling of his cabinet colleagues and of the prince regent, who eventually became George IV, and in his acute sense of the changing political temper of the nation. During the difficult war and postwar years, he sensed Britain's conservative mood, but in the 1820s he was quick to perceive the growing liberal sentiment that accompanied the rise of the middle classes. Liverpool was thus able to work with both Lord Castlereagh and the latter's enemy George Canning, and in 1822 he replaced his reactionary home secretary Lord Sidmouth with the reformer Robert Peel. The collapse of existing political alignments when a paralytic stroke forced his retirement in 1827 testifies to Liverpool's skills.

DONALD SOUTHGATE

Bibliography: Brock, William R., *Lord Liverpool and Liberal Toryism,* 2d ed. (1967); Cookson, J. E., *Lord Liverpool's Administration* (1975); Petrie, Charles, *Lord Liverpool and His Times* (1954).

liverwort

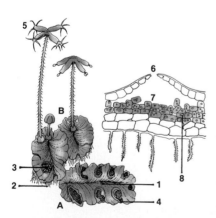

A liverwort commonly found on damp brickwork, L. cruciata, *comprises a thallus, or flat plant body* (1), *held to the ground by rhizoids, or rootlets* (2). *Male* (A) *and female plants* (B) *have lens-shaped structures* (3) *for asexual reproduction, as well as male* (4) *and female* (5) *sex organs. Air pores in the thallus* (6) *lead to an air chamber* (7) *above cells containing chlorophyll* (8).

Three hundred genera of green, terrestrial plants are known as liverworts; they comprise 10,000 species and belong to the class *Hepaticae* in the division Bryophyta. They play a definite role in stabilizing bare soils; they also promote soil formation from rock surfaces and downed logs by retaining water and breaking down minerals. Liverworts derive their name from a supposed resemblance of some species to lobes of the liver.

Liverworts are small plants, ranging in size from nearly mi-

croscopic, such as *Cephaloziella,* to more than 20 cm (8 in) in length, such as *Dumortiera* and *Monoclea.* Most abundant in the cool mountain forests of the tropics, liverworts inhabit all of the continents, including Antarctica. Along with mosses and lichens, they form the dominant surface vegetation in many parts of the tundra. Some liverworts are entirely aquatic, such as *Riella* and *Ricciocarpus;* most are restricted to regions of abundant moisture. They frequently are found growing along shady stream banks, over rocks, and on trunks of trees. A few, however, such as *Riccia,* have adapted to drier habitats.

The plant body of a liverwort is relatively simple. Although certain species have distinguishable internal tissues, such complex tissues as xylem and phloem are absent. Two basic body types exist, one that is characteristic of leafy liverworts and the other of thallose liverworts. Leafy liverworts are elongated and flattened and have two or three rows of leaves. They have structures that resemble stems (caulidia) and leaves (phyllidia). Thallose liverworts may grow in circular rosettes, such as *Riccia* and *Sphaerocarpo,* or, more typically, as elongated, lobed blades. They appear as straps or ribbons and are anchored to their substrate by one-celled rhizoids. They may or may not have a conspicuous midrib.

In reproduction the plant body often fragments, and leaves and stems regenerate. In addition, many species produce special cells (gemmae), found on leaves, on stems, or in cuplike structures, that propagate asexually. The sexual life cycle of liverworts is similar to that of mosses except for certain morphological details. The dominant phase, the gametophyte, is photosynthetic and alternates with the sporophyte, which is entirely dependent upon the gametophyte for nutrition. As with mosses, sperms of liverworts are flagellated; hence, fertilization of eggs can take place only when water is present. The spore-producing capsules lack both a peristome and a central column of sterile tissue (columella), features that are typical of moss capsules. The capsule normally opens by splitting from the top downward along four lines. The spore mass contains sterile cells known as elaters, which twist and jerk with changes in humidity, aiding in spore dispersal.

DANA GRIFFIN

Bibliography: Bold, Harold, *Morphology of Plants,* 3d ed. (1973); Conard, H. S., *How to Know the Mosses and Liverworts,* rev. ed. (1956); Grout, A. J., *Moss Flora of North America,* 3 vols. (1928–40); Watson, E. V., *The Structure and Life of Bryophytes,* 3d ed. (1971).

livestock: see ANIMAL HUSBANDRY.

Livia Drusilla   [liv'-ee-uh droo-sil'-uh]

Livia Drusilla, b. Jan. 30, 58 BC, d. AD 29, was the second wife of the Roman emperor Augustus and the mother of his successor, Tiberius. The daughter of an adopted member of the Drusus family, she first married (43 or 42) Tiberius Claudius Nero, by whom she had two sons: Tiberius and Nero Claudius Drusus. In 39, however, she divorced Nero to marry Octavian (later Augustus). Livia became Augustus's esteemed counselor and ran his domestic life with integrity and grace. She used her influence to ensure the succession of Tiberius in AD 14, but he thwarted her attempt to gain greater personal power during his reign.

Living Theatre

The Living Theatre is an American theater collective formed in 1947 by actors Judith Malina (b. 1926) and her husband Julian Beck (1925–85). At first dedicated to the text-oriented dramas of Brecht, García Lorca, Gertrude Stein, and Paul Goodman, the Living Theatre eventually evolved a performance style based on the nonverbal acting techniques of Antonin Artaud. Pioneers in the off-Broadway movement, the Living Theatre performed poetic dramas until 1956. In 1959 they presented Jack Gelber's play about drug addiction, *The Connection.* Ever since, their work has been largely dedicated to social and political issues reflecting their pacifist and anarchist beliefs. In 1963 the group produced Kenneth Brown's *The*

This scene is from Seven Meditations, *a 1976 performance by the Living Theatre, an innovative American Off-Broadway theater collective begun in 1946. The group stresses physicality and ritualistic improvisation and incorporates audience participation.*

Brig, which was set in a military prison. That same year the building in which the Living Theatre performed was closed for tax delinquency and the group went into exile. From 1964 to 1969 it performed throughout Europe, where it developed its most important pieces—*Antigone,* based on Sophocles and Brecht, *Frankenstein, Mysteries and Smaller Pieces,* and the revolutionary *Paradise Now.* In Brazil in 1970 the group began developing its epic work, *The Legacy of Cain.* Beck and Molina returned to New York in 1979. Their innovative performance techniques, mostly in the service of political and sexual ideologies, made them the most influential of the experimental groups of the 1960s and '70s.   BONNIE MARRANCA

Bibliography: Biner, Pierre, *Living Theatre* (1972).

Livingston   (family)

The Livingston family was a dominant social and political force in 18th-century New York. The founder of the clan, **Robert Livingston**, 1654–1728, was born in Scotland and raised in the Netherlands. He arrived in New York in 1674 and soon married (1679) Alida Schuyler Van Rensselaer, thus merging the Livingstons with the prominent Schuyler and Van Rensselaer families. In 1686 he obtained the second largest manor in the colony, a 65,000-ha (160,000-acre) estate below Albany east of the Hudson River. Livingston Manor eventually passed to his son Philip; his son Robert received Clermont, 5,250 ha (13,000 acres) around the manor house.

Three of Philip's sons achieved distinction. **Robert** became third lord of the manor. **Philip**, b. Jan. 15, 1716, d. June 12, 1778, a politician and merchant, signed the Declaration of Independence. **William**, b. Nov. 30, 1723, d. July 25, 1790, lawyer and member of the Federal Convention of 1787, was the first governor of the state of New Jersey (1776–90). William's son, **Henry Brockholst Livingston**, b. Nov. 25, 1757, d. Mar. 18, 1823, was a Continental army officer, associate justice of the U.S. Supreme Court (1806–23), and founder (1805) of the New-York Historical Society.

The Clermont branch of the family also had its noteworthy members. **Robert R. Livingston**, b. Nov. 27, 1746, d. Feb. 26, 1813, a statesman and diplomat, served as chancellor of New York (1777–1801) and negotiated the LOUISIANA PURCHASE (1803). **Henry Beekman Livingston** (1750–1831) was a Revolutionary War officer. **Edward Livingston**, b. May 28, 1764, d. May 23, 1836, was a lawyer, congressman (1795–1801), and mayor of New York City (1801–03); after moving to New Orleans in 1803 he compiled the first law code in the United

States (1821) and served as state legislator (1820–23), congressman (1823–29), senator (1829–31), Andrew Jackson's secretary of state (1831–33), and minister to France (1833–35).
          LARRY R. GERLACH

Bibliography: Brandt, Clare, *American Aristocracy: The Livingstons* (1986); Dangerfield, George, *Chancellor Robert R. Livingston of New York, 1746–1813* (1960); Leder, Lawrence H., *Robert Livingston, 1654–1728, and the Politics of Colonial New York* (1961); Livingston, Edwin B., *The Livingstons of Livingston Manor* (1910).

Livingstone, David

By a series of journeys in the mid-19th century, David Livingstone contributed more than any other single person to the opening of Africa to the West.

Born in Blantyre, Scotland, on Mar. 19, 1813, Livingstone went to work in a cotton mill at the age of ten. Later he resumed his education, becoming a doctor of medicine in 1838 and an ordained minister in 1840. After being rejected for missionary work in China, he was sent by the London Missionary Society to Kuruman (part of the modern Cape Province, South Africa), arriving in 1841. Never satisfied with the routine of missionary life, Livingstone began his dramatic explorations in 1849, when he guided the first successful European crossing of the Kalahari Desert to Lake Ngami. There he learned of a great river to the north and peoples who had not been reached by missionaries.

Obsessed with a desire to open up inner Africa to new forms of commerce and religion in order to end the slave trade and advance civilization as he understood it, Livingstone investigated central Africa between 1853 and 1856. From the Chobe River (in modern Botswana) he traveled up the Zambezi River with a small group of Africans. Passing through Barotseland (modern Zambia), he followed African trade paths across the Cuango River into Portuguese Angola. He arrived at Luanda on the Atlantic coast in 1854. Livingstone then plunged back into the African interior. Following the Zambezi River downstream from the point of his earlier departure, he discovered (1855) and named the Victoria Falls. He continued east across what is now Zambia and Mozambique until he emerged at Quelimane on the Indian Ocean in 1856, becoming the first non-African to cross the continent from west to east.

Livingstone's return to London shortly thereafter set in motion efforts to introduce commercial and missionary enterprise into much of east and central Africa. The accounts of his experiences also stimulated the exploring endeavors of others such as Sir Richard BURTON and Henry Morton STANLEY. Livingstone himself made another expedition in 1858–63, when he became the first Briton to describe Lake Nyasa and the Shire Highlands of what is now Malawi. From 1866 to 1873 he sought the source of the Nile and Congo rivers and

The Scottish missionary David Livingstone explored Africa's interior in an attempt to introduce Christianity and eliminate slavery by developing channels of commerce. His explorations furnished Great Britain with claims to parts of Africa. He was the first European to sight the Zambezi River (1851) and Victoria Falls (1855), which he named.

investigated how the great African lakes related to each other and to the great rivers. In the process he discovered lakes Mweru and Bangweulu (in modern Zambia) and reached the Lualaba tributary of the Congo River. In 1871, Stanley found the sick Livingstone at Ujiji on Lake Tanganyika. Livingstone insisted on continuing his explorations, however, and, malarious and emaciated, he died on May 1, 1873, near Bangweulu.

Livingstone's accounts of his travels in Africa—*Missionary Travels* (1857) and *The Zambezi and Its Tributaries* (1865)—were bestsellers, and he achieved widespread fame.

ROBERT I. ROTBERG

Bibliography: Helly, Dorothy, *Livingstone's Legacy* (1986); Jeal, Tim, *Livingstone* (1973); Martelli, George, *Livingstone's River: A History of the Zambezi Expedition, 1858–1864* (1970); Seaver, George, *David Livingstone: His Life and Letters* (1957).

Livius Andronicus   [liv'-ee-uhs an-druh-ny'-kuhs]

Lucius Livius Andronicus, b. *c.*284 BC, d. *c.*204 BC, though non-Roman by birth and brought to Rome as a war captive from southern Italy, earned glory as the "father of Roman literature." Combining a mastery of earlier Greek poetry with a command of the Latin language, he produced (240 BC) the first Latin comedy and the first Latin tragedy. The development inaugurated the dynamic flourishing of Roman drama over the next century. His translation of Homer's *Odyssey* in Saturnian meter also influenced subsequent Roman epic poetry.

WILLIAM S. ANDERSON

Livonia   [liv-oh'-nee-uh]

Livonia is a historical region in the USSR, comprising the present-day areas of northern Latvia and southern Estonia. Its original inhabitants were the Livs, a Finnic people who arrived between the 5th and 7th centuries seeking better fishing grounds. They settled in the area of the Dvina and Gauja rivers, adjacent to the shores of the Gulf of Riga.

At the beginning of the 13th century the German Order of the Brothers of the Sword (known as the Livonian Knights after they merged with the TEUTONIC KNIGHTS in 1237) conquered and Christianized the Livs, whose land they called Livonia. In 1207 the bishopric of Livonia became a principality of the Holy Roman Empire with the bishop as its prince. Between 1558 and 1583, Russia fought a series of wars against the knights—the so-called Livonian Wars. Unable to defend themselves, the knights disbanded in 1561 and dismembered Livonia. Poland gained control of the area in 1569 but ceded most of it to Sweden in 1660. During the Great NORTHERN WAR, Russia conquered Livonia, retaining it at the Peace of Nystad (1721). Russia received Polish Livonia in 1772 as part of the first Partition of Poland, and in 1783, Livonia became a province of the Russian Empire. At the end of World War I, historic Livonia was divided between the two new Baltic republics of Estonia and Latvia. This division remained when the two countries were absorbed into the USSR in 1940.

DONALD L. LAYTON

Bibliography: Kirchner, W., *The Rise of the Baltic Question* (1954).

Livorno   [lee-vor'-noh]

Livorno (English: Leghorn) is the capital of Livorno province in the central Italian region of Tuscany. Situated on the Ligurian Sea and on the ancient Roman Aurelian Way, it is a thriving commercial, industrial, and tourist center and one of Italy's main ports. The city has a population of 176,298 (1983 est.). A canal completed in 1938 connects Livorno with Pisa. Livorno's imports include coal, cereals, fertilizers, and minerals, and the main exports are marble, plate glass, wine, olive oil, and copper. The city's plants produce chemicals, refined petroleum, and metals. Livorno is the seat of the prestigious Italian Naval Academy. The 16th-century cathedral (restored in 1954–59) and part of the 17th-century city walls are notable historic landmarks.

In the 16th century the original fishing village developed into a busy trading town when Cosimo I de'Medici began the construction of the Porto Mediceo (Medici Harbor) in 1571.

Ferdinand I de'Medici, grand duke of Tuscany, made Livorno a free port in 1590 and opened the city to political and religious refugees. In 1860, Livorno became part of united Italy.

DANIEL R. LESNICK

Livy   [liv'-ee]

The ancient Roman historian Livy (Titus Livius), b. 64 or 59 BC, d. AD 17, wrote a history of Rome that was recognized as a classic during his lifetime. He was born in Patavium (Padua) but spent most of his life in Rome, where he witnessed civil wars, the fall of the republic, and the establishment of the principate by Augustus. Little else is known of his life. From his writings, it is evident that he read extensively in Greek and Latin literature and was influenced by Cicero.

Livy immersed himself in the past. His *History of Rome* covers the period from the arrival of Aeneas in Italy and the "foundation" of the city of Rome to 9 BC. Of the original 142 books, only 35 are extant—Books 1–10 and 21–45, dealing with the years 753–293 BC and 218–167 BC. Some fragments of other books remain, however, and summaries exist of all but one. Livy was not a critical historian; he perpetuated many inaccuracies of earlier writers. He demonstrated little knowledge of military matters. His genius lay in his vivid style and gift for dramatic composition. Livy followed an annalistic arrangement of events but focused on the characters of the leading figures in the episodes. He viewed history through representative individuals and extolled the old Roman virtues of discipline, piety, and patriotism. Despite its republican sentiments, his history gained the favor of Augustus.

J. LINDERSKI

Bibliography: Luce, T. J., *Livy: The Composition of His History* (1977); Walsh, Patrick G., *Livy: His Historical Aims and Methods* (1961).

lizard   [liz'-urd]

Lizards are reptiles that are closely related to snakes. Well-adapted to life on land, lizards possess a dry, scaly body covering; limbs suited for rapid locomotion; internal fertilization; and hard-shelled eggs for the protection of the embryo. Lizards feed mostly on insects, although a certain number of them eat plants. Only two species are venomous, the Gila monster (*Heloderma suspectum*) and the Mexican beaded lizard (*H. horridum*).

LIZARDS AND SNAKES

Both snakes and lizards are classified in the same order, Squamata, but lizards are separated into their own suborder, Sauria. Lizards generally can be distinguished from snakes by the presence of two pairs of legs, external ear openings, and movable eyelids, but these convenient external diagnostic features, while absent in snakes, are also absent in some lizards. Lizards can be precisely separated from snakes, however, on the basis of certain internal characteristics. All lizards have at least a vestige of a pectoral girdle (skeletal supports for the front limbs) and sternum (breastbone). The lizard's brain is not totally enclosed in a bony case but has a small region at the front covered only by a membranous septum. The lizard's kidneys are positioned symmetrically and to the rear; in snakes the kidneys are far forward, with the right kidney placed farther front than the left. The lizard's ribs are never forked, as are one or two pairs in the snake.

DISTRIBUTION AND HABITAT

There are over 3,000 known species of lizards, making them one of the largest and most successful groups of reptiles. They are found on all the continents except Antarctica. The greatest diversity of species occurs in the tropics, but lizards range as far north as the Arctic Circle in Eurasia (*Lacerta vivipara*) and as far south as southern Chile in South America (*Liolaemus, Diplolaemus*). In North America lizards barely range into southern Canada. Lizards live at elevations exceeding 4,500 m (15,000 ft) in the Himalayas, in the Andes, and among the volcanoes of Mexico.

Although no living species of lizard can truly fly through the air, as did some reptiles of the past, lizards occupy practically every other habitat. Some lizards live in areas of rain

When threatened by an enemy, the Australian frilled lizard, C. kingii, rears on its hindlegs, whips its tail threateningly, opens its mouth and hisses, and unfolds its enormous neck frill—giving the impression of a fierce adversary several times larger than its original size.

Horned lizards, Phrynosoma, will sometimes squirt blood from their eyes as a defense. The blood is released from an inner eyelid in a fine stream that may spurt up to 1 m (3 ft) and break into droplets.

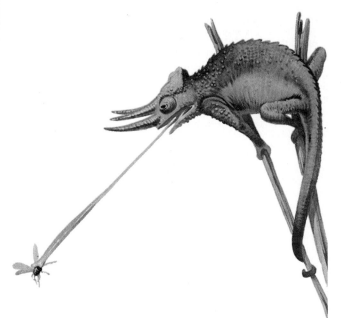

Like all chameleons, Jackson's chameleon, C. jacksonii, catches prey by shooting out its tongue—longer than its body—trapping the prey on the tongue's sticky tip, and then quickly pulling in its catch.

The Turkish gecko, H. turcicus, like many lizards, can break off its tail to escape from a predator—the violently thrashing tail distracts the enemy while the lizard escapes. The tail, which is severed by muscular contraction, will later regenerate.

and cloud forests soaked by daily rains. Others—such as the crocodile lizard, Shinisaurus, of China, which feeds on fish and tadpoles, the snail-eating caiman lizard, Dracaena, of tidal marshlands in South America, and the brown water lizard, Neusticurus, of South America—have become semiaquatic. Conversely, some lizards have adapted to deserts that receive only 200 mm (about 8 in) or less of rainfall annually. The gecko, Palmatogecko rangei, has extensive webbing on its feet for walking over fine sand. Arboreal forms may exhibit various adaptations, including climbing pads, zygodactylous feet (having the toes arranged into two opposing groups), prehensile tails, and strongly recurved claws. The flying dragons, Draco, of Southeastern Asia have sheets of skin attached to their elongated ribs and are capable of gliding. Burrowing lizards often have reduced eyes and limbs, reduced head plates, smooth scales, and conical heads with rigid skulls to make for easier burrowing. The marine iguana, Amblyrhynchus cristatus, of the Galapagos Islands freely enters the ocean to feed on algae (seaweed) and may forage 15 to 20 m (50 to 65 ft) underwater. This species has salt-secreting glands in the head.

GENERAL FEATURES

Lizards range in size from 20 to 75 mm (0.75 to 3 in) in exceptionally small forms (Brookesia, Sphaerodactylus) to over 3 m (10 ft) in the Komodo dragon (Varanus komodoensis), but most are closer to 400 mm (16 in) in length.

Limbs. Limbs are generally well developed, and some species demonstrate bipedalism, standing up and running on their hind legs (Basiliscus, Chlamydosaurus). The racerunners, Cnemidophorus, are particularly quick and have been clocked at almost 30 km/h (19 mph). Burrowing forms often have degenerate limbs, and legless lizards move in the same manner as snakes. In some species in the genus, such as the marine iguana, Amblyrhynchus, the tail is vertically flattened, from side to side, an adaptation to swimming.

Skin and Teeth. The lizard's skin is dry and scaly. The scales are derived from the epidermis and hence are not identical to fish scales, which are derived from another part of the skin, the dermis. Scales may vary from small granules, as in the gecko, to those bearing prominent spines, as in the horned lizard. Many lizards have osteoderms beneath the epidermal skin. These bony nodules are often in a one-to-one ratio with the epidermal scales, providing them with internal support. The lizard's skin is shed periodically, but, unlike that of most snakes, it is shed in patches. A few species in the family Aguinidae shed their skin in its entirety.

Skin glands are not numerous in lizards. Most lizards have scent glands at the base of the tail, and males often have glands in front of the anus (preanal) or on the thigh (femoral) that become filled with a hard, waxy, yellow substance. This material may extend from the glands in hairlike columns that rub off on rocks and other surfaces. The significance of these glands is not precisely known, but because they are larger in males, whereas some females lack them completely, and are active during the breeding season, they appear to play a role in courtship.

Metachrosis, or the ability to change color under the influence of external stimuli, is a common characteristic of lizards. Many species can darken or lighten their color in response to light, temperature, or emotional state, and a few (chameleons) have developed the ability to alter their color to a remarkable degree. The green anole, *Anolis carolinensis,* called the American chameleon and found in the southeastern United States, can change from a bright green to brown. A cave lizard, *Proctoporus,* of Trinidad, is reported to be luminous. Four types of pigment-bearing cells (chromatophores) have been identified in lizards: melanophores, with black or brown pigment; guanophores (leucophores), with whitish pigment; lipophores (xanthophores), with yellow to orange red pigment; and allophores, with red pigment. Lizard coloration may be structural as well as pigmental. Structural colors result from the presence of tiny particles, such as purine crystals, which themselves may be colorless but which selectively reflect the shorter, or bluer, wavelengths of light, making the object appear blue. A combination of structural blue and pigmental yellow can produce green.

Lizards bear teeth on the palatines and pterygoids—which are two sets of paired bones in the roof of the mouth—and on the dentaries, or lower jaw. A uniform shape for all the teeth is most common, but in certain species in the families Agamidae and Teiidae the teeth are more or less differentiated into conical and molar types (heterodonty). Lizards' teeth are not set in separate sockets but are fused either to the upper surface of the jaws (acrodont) or to the inside edges (pleurodont). The teeth are generally sharp and conical but may be extremely elongated in some predatory species or serrated or blunt in the larger herbivorous forms or among species with certain feeding specializations. In general, there is little chewing of food among lizards. Many lizards simply seize their prey, bite it and move it about the mouth, and then swallow it.

Senses. Lizards recognize prey either by visual clues or by chemoreception (scent and taste). The lizard's eye is different from that of a snake in that focusing is accomplished by the contraction of the ciliary muscle of the eye directly squeezing the lens and causing it to change shape. In snakes, focusing is generally accomplished by muscular deformation of the eyeball, which increases its internal pressure and forces the lens forward. Nocturnal lizards usually have a vertical pupil, lack a fovea, and have numerous retinal rods (highly sensitive sensory cells) that distinguish different light intensities. Diurnal species generally have rounded pupils, a fovea, and retinal cones instead of rods; cones distinguish wavelengths of light (color) and hence provide more-detailed daytime vision. Many diurnal lizards have yellow oil in their retinal cones that acts to filter out the shorter wavelengths of light, thereby reducing the amount of unequal refraction (chromatic aberration) characteristic of these wavelengths. In addition to the pair of eyes possessed by most vertebrates, many lizards have a third, or parietal, eye located on the upper rear surface of the head.

In some North American species in the family Iguanidae the parietal eye is well developed, having a cornea, a lens, and a retina with sensory elements. The parietal eye has been shown to act as a sort of light meter that helps to regulate the amount of time a lizard exposes itself to the sun.

The majority of lizards have eardrums (tympanic membranes), usually located nearly flush with the surface of the skin or just below it. Behind the eardrum is the middle ear cavity, which leads to the middle ear. The ear provides a sense of balance as well as hearing. Some species, such as *Holbrookia,* appear to lack ears because the ear opening is covered by scaly skin. In burrowing species the external ear opening is small or absent and the middle ear degenerated.

The Jacobson's organs are important to the lizard's sense of smell. These organs are paired chambers in the front area of the roof of the mouth that have a connection to the olfactory (scent) lobes of the brain. These chambers detect not only particles present in the mouth cavity but also particles brought to them by the lizard's tongue. By protruding its tongue, a lizard is able to pick up airborne particles, which dissolve in the fluid on the tongue; these particles are then transferred by the tongue to the Jacobson's organs. This process is most efficient in lizards with deeply forked tongues, the tips of which are placed against or thrust into the chambers. In such lizards the sense of smell is relatively keen. The lizard's tongue is not ordinarily used directly in feeding, as an amphibian's is; in chameleons, however, the tongue is long and unforked (and the Jacobson's organs are rudimentary) and is used to catch prey.

Internal Features. Lizards depend almost entirely on paired lungs to aerate the blood. The heart is three-chambered: the right atrium, which receives deoxygenated blood from the body, is separate from the left atrium, which receives oxygenated blood from the lungs; but the ventricle, which pumps blood to both the body and the lungs, is single. There is, however, an incomplete septum, or wall, across part of the ventricle that essentially separates the two bloodstreams.

Female lizards, like other reptiles but in contrast to mammals, have saclike (saccular) ovaries rather than solid ones, and their eggs are polylecithal (large-yolked). Males have two copulatory organs called hemipenes, one on each side of the base of the tail. These are generally short and broad, with pleats or folds, but may also be forked. Either one of the two hemipenes may be used in mating. The majority of lizards lay eggs, but at least half of the lizard families have species that bear live young, with varying degrees of placental formation (mother-embryo connection).

BEHAVIOR

Parental care is unknown in lizards, but in some forms the female broods, or cares for, the eggs. Growth rates vary greatly, and sexual maturity may be reached in the first breeding season after birth in small species, or not for several years in larger species. Lifespans are poorly documented, but generally the small forms live short lives of 1 to 5 years, whereas larger forms may live for 10 to 20 years or even longer. A notable exception is the small European slow worm, *Anguis fragilis,* a captive specimen of which reportedly reached 54 years of age.

Temperature is one of the most important environmental factors influencing lizard behavior; it directly determines a lizard's metabolic rate. Lizards are ectothermic (cold-blooded) and thus depend primarily on an external heat source to regulate their body temperature. This does not mean, however, that a lizard's body temperature will be the same as that of its immediate environment. Lizards can control their temperature by various behaviors, such as by basking directly in the sun (heliothermy), by positioning themselves (such as under a sunlit rock) in such a way as to gain heat through conduction (thigmothermy), or by seeking shade. A lizard's temperature may be 20 to 30 C degrees (35 to 55 F degrees) higher than the ambient (surrounding) temperature.

Most lizards exhibit marked seasonal changes in activity. In order to avoid harsh weather conditions, lizards hibernate in temperate regions during the winter, generally seeking refuge beneath the frost line, or they may estivate during hot, dry climatic conditions, often in deep crevices or fissures in the ground, where they can best retain body moisture.

Many lizards are cryptically colored and thereby avoid detection. When disturbed, however, lizards have a variety of defensive actions that include threatening with an open mouth, hissing, inflating the body, positioning the body in such a fashion as to appear as large as possible, biting and scratching, and lashing with the tail. With very few exceptions, only the geckos have a voice and can produce threat calls. Many species are equipped with spinelike scales that make it difficult for a predator to swallow them. Some forms expose brightly colored surfaces in an attempt to frighten enemies. Horned lizards, *Phrynosoma,* may eject blood from their eyes. Many lizards break their tails (autotomy) when they are confronted by an enemy or roughly handled. This break does not occur between the vertebrae (tail bones) but rather in a zone of weakness in a vertebra itself. These specialized vertebrae can be voluntarily split by muscular con-

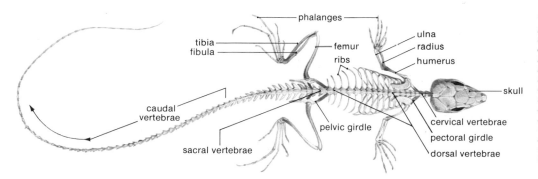

phalanges

tibia
fibula

femur

ribs

ulna
radius

humerus

skull

caudal
vertebrae

cervical vertebrae

pelvic girdle

pectoral girdle

sacral vertebrae

dorsal vertebrae

The lizard's skeleton includes a skull with two temporal openings separated by no more than one bony arch, and the brain is not completely enclosed by bone. The sternum and pectoral girdle are present in all lizards; many species also have special break points in the tail vertebrae.

With more than 3,000 known species, lizards are one of the largest and most diverse groups of modern reptiles, ranging in size from 2-cm (0.75-in) geckos to Komodo dragons of more than 3 m (10 ft). Body form varies greatly. For example, marine iguanas have broad, flat tails for swimming; glass snakes are burrowing lizards with no legs; flying dragons use winglike flaps of skin to glide from tree to tree.

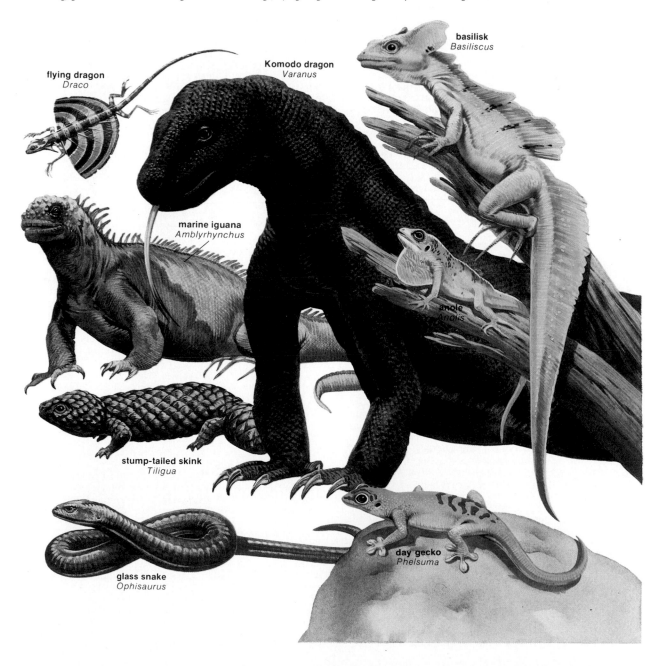

basilisk
Basiliscus

flying dragon
Draco

Komodo dragon
Varanus

marine iguana
Amblyrhynchus

anole
Anolis

stump-tailed skink
Tiligua

glass snake
Ophisaurus

day gecko
Phelsuma

traction; sphincter muscles in the tail stump close off the caudal artery to prevent excessive bleeding. Predators are often attracted to the thrashing, dismembered tail, which allows the lizard to escape. Although tail autotomy may seem like a drastic measure, in actuality it does the lizard little harm, for a new tail is soon regenerated. The new tail, however, is not identical to the original. Its skeletal support consists of a fibrocartilaginous rod instead of vertebrae; its musculature is nonsegmental; its scales are different in size and form; and its color is usually subdued or otherwise altered.

EVOLUTION

Lizards probably arose from early eosuchian reptiles, particularly such genera as *Prolacerta,* which lived during the Lower Triassic Period, about 220 million years ago. Fossils of lizards have been discovered in Europe in deposits of Triassic age. Several extinct forms (*Kuehneosaurus, Icarosaurus*) resembled the flying dragon, *Draco,* which is still found in southeastern Asia. During the Cretaceous Period, about 100 million years ago, certain lizards took to the sea and evolved into the giant MOSASAURS, some species reaching 9 m (30 ft) in length. Marine reptiles such as ichthyosaurs and plesiosaurs may also have evolved from ancestral lizard forms, but this is not certain.

CLASSIFICATION

The lizards are classified in the order Squamata, suborder Sauria (or Lacertilia). Although authorities may differ on various groupings, the suborder is usually divided into four infraorders. The infraorder Gekkota contains three families: Gekkonidae, Pygopididae, and Xantusiidae (some authorities consider them a single family, Gekkonidae, with four subfamilies). The infraorder Iguania also contains three families: Iguanidae, Agamidae, and Chamaeleonidae. The Anguinomorpha comprises five families: Anguinidae, Xenosauridae, Helodermatidae, Lanthonotidae, and Varanidae. The Scrincomorpha is composed of four families: Cordylidae, Lacertidae, Scrincidae, and Teiidae.   JONATHAN CAMPBELL

Bibliography: Fitch, H. S., *The Reproductive Cycles of Lizards and Snakes* (1970); Goin, C. J., et al., *Introduction to Herpetology,* 3d ed. (1978); Grzimek, Bernhard, ed., *Grzimek's Animal Life Encyclopedia,* vol. 6 (1975); Hartman, J. E., *Looking at Lizards* (1978); Huey, R. B., et al., eds., *Lizard Ecology* (1983); Mattison, Christopher, *Lizards of the World* (1989); Smith, H. M., *Handbook of Lizards* (1946).

lizardfish   [liz'-urd]

Lizardfishes are marine fishes with cigar-shaped bodies, large mouths, and long, sharp teeth. Most are less than 30 cm (12 in) long. They commonly sit on the sea bottom, propped up in front by the two pectoral fins. Lizardfishes, classified in the family Synodontidae, order Myctophiformes, are distributed worldwide, mostly in inshore tropical waters.

                                        ALFRED PERLMUTTER

lizard's tail

Lizard's tail, *Saururus cernuus,* is a perennial succulent herb of the family Saururaceae, native to bogs and swamps of eastern North America. Known also as water dragon or swamp lily, the plant bears soft, white flowers densely packed into a long, slender, partly drooping spike said to resemble a lizard's tail. It grows to 1.5 m (5 ft) high. The only other species in the genus is a smaller Chinese lizard's tail, *S. loureiri.*

Ljubljana   [lee-oo-blee-ahn'-uh]

Ljubljana, the capital of the republic of Slovenia in northwest Yugoslavia, is situated on the Ljubljanica River near its junction with the Sava, about 50 km (30 mi) south of the Austrian border. The city of Ljubljana's population is 253,061 (1981). Manufactures include hydroelectric equipment, textiles, paper, footwear, drugs, and glass. The city is also a rail and road hub. Notable landmarks are a medieval fort and the Renaissance cathedral of Saint Nicholas. A university, founded in 1595, and the Slovene Academy of Sciences and Arts are located there.

In 34 BC the Romans founded a city called Emona on the site. It was destroyed by the Huns in 451, but the Slavs later built a new community, which was named Ljubljana in the 12th century. From 1277 until the creation of Yugoslavia in 1918 the city belonged to the Habsburg empire.

llama   [lah'-muh]

The llama, L. peruana, *a relative of the camel, can carry loads of 45 kg (100 lb) for 16–32 km (10–20 mi) a day over rugged slopes at high altitudes. Besides being a means of transportation in parts of South America, the llama also furnishes wool used for clothing and blankets.*

The llama, *Lama peruana,* is a South American member of the CAMEL family, Camelidae. It stands 1.2 m (4 ft) high at the shoulders and may be more than 1.2 m (4 ft) long (plus a short tail) and 140 kg (300 lb) in weight. Its body is covered with a fine, fairly long wool. The llama was domesticated as a wool and pack animal as long as 4,000 years ago by the Indians of Peru from either a now-extinct wild llama or from the guanaco, *L. guanacoe.*

Llanos   [yah'-nohs]

The Llanos are wide, mostly treeless, grassland plains of northern South America, surrounded by the Andes mountains to the north and west, the Guaviare River and Amazon rain forest to the south, and the lower ORINOCO RIVER and Guiana Highlands to the east. Drained by the Orinoco and its western tributaries, the sparsely populated Llanos cover about 582,747 km² (225,000 mi²), divided between Venezuela (about 56%) and Colombia. The economic mainstay of the region is cattle raising; oil fields in part of the Venezuelan Llanos are also of economic importance.

Llewellyn, Richard

Richard Dafydd Vivian Llewellyn Lloyd, b. Dec. 8, 1906, d. Nov. 30, 1983, was a Welsh writer most famous for his widely acclaimed first novel, *How Green Was My Valley* (1939; National Book Award, 1940; film, 1941), a warm, captivating story of the hard lives of Welsh coal miners and their families. Though Llewellyn never matched the success of that novel, he went on to write about 20 others, including *None but the Lonely Heart* (1943; film, 1944). He was also a playwright (*Poison Pen,* 1938), journalist, and scriptwriter.

Lloyd, Harold   [loyd]

Harold Lloyd, b. Burchard, Nebr., Apr. 20, 1893, d. Mar. 8, 1971, was one of the most popular screen comedians of the 1920s, a living symbol of the shy but optimistic all-American

In this scene from Safety Last *(1923), Harold Lloyd finds himself in typically precarious, zany circumstances. In his heyday in the 1920s, Lloyd, who never used a double, was Hollywood's highest paid actor.*

boy. This ingratiating character started evolving in 1910–20 but crystallized only after he became a major star in such 1920s silent films as *Grandma's Boy* (1922) and *The Freshman* (1925). Lloyd's trademarks were a straw hat and horn-rimmed glasses, but he is perhaps best remembered for the "thrill comedy" of films like *Safety Last* (1923). Snippets from his many early films appeared in two 1963 screen compilations: *Harold Lloyd's World of Comedy* and *Harold Lloyd's Funny Side of Life.* His unpretentious approach to comedy received wider attention after his "rediscovery" in the 1970s.

LEONARD MALTIN

Bibliography: Lloyd, Harold, *An American Comedy* (1928; repr. 1971); Maltin, Leonard, *The Great Movie Comedians* (1978); Reilly, Adam, *Harold Lloyd: The King of Daredevil Comedy* (1977); Schickel, Richard, *Harold Lloyd: The Shape of Laughter* (1974).

Lloyd, Henry Demarest

A leading opponent of business monopolies, Henry Demarest Lloyd, b. New York City, May 1, 1847, d. Sept. 28, 1903, was one of the pioneer MUCKRAKERS of the late 19th century. He developed his antimonopoly theme as financial writer and editor (1872–85) at the *Chicago Tribune,* and in books. His *Wealth against Commonwealth* (1894) was a major denunciation of big business; later works included the three reform tracts *Labour Copartnership* (1898), *A Country without Strikes* (1900), and *Newest England* (1900).   ERNEST C. HYNDS

Bibliography: Destler, Chester, *Henry Demarest Lloyd and the Empire of Reform* (1963); Jernigan, E. Jay, *Henry Demarest Lloyd* (1976).

Lloyd George, David, 1st Earl Lloyd-George of Dwyfor   [doo-ee'-vor]

David Lloyd George, a British statesman and prime minister (1916–22), led social reform efforts of the Liberal party before his controversial rise to the premiership. A forceful leader during World War I, he proved a significant moderating voice at the Versailles peace negotiations. The varied achievements of his parliamentary career did much to shape the modern British state.

David Lloyd George was one of the commanding figures in 20th-century British politics and the only person of Welsh extraction to become prime minister. Born in Manchester, England, on Jan. 17, 1863, he was raised by his uncle, a village shoemaker and sectarian lay preacher in North Wales. In 1878 he was apprenticed to a solicitor (nontrial lawyer), and he opened his own law practice in 1884. As "the poachers' lawyer," willing to defend clients accused of breaking the harsh game laws, Lloyd George acquired a loyal following among North Wales tenant farmers and quarrymen. In 1890 he was elected to Parliament as a Liberal, beginning a 55-year career at Westminster.

Lloyd George acquired recognition speaking for the interests of Welsh nonconformists—including temperance, disestablishment of the Anglican church in Wales, nondenominational education, and local autonomy. He was viewed as an unorthodox, independent Liberal, a reputation enhanced by his uncompromising opposition to the South African War (1899–1902). Later he won national prominence as leader of the nonconformist opposition to the Conservative government's Education Act of 1902. When Sir Henry CAMPBELL-BANNERMAN formed his Liberal cabinet in 1905, he included Lloyd George as a representative of nonconformist interests. In the post of president of the Board of Trade, Lloyd George was highly successful as a champion of business and labor negotiator. Prime Minister Herbert ASQUITH promoted him to chancellor of the exchequer in 1908.

Lloyd George became an active social reformer, horrifying traditionalists by using the annual government budget to construct policy as well as to raise money. His "people's budget" of 1909, with its land taxes, provoked a clash with the Conservative-dominated House of Lords, ending in curtailment (1911) of the House of Lords' power to veto legislation. In 1911, Lloyd George guided through Parliament his pioneering National Health Insurance Act. This act, in conjunction with his Old Age Pensions Act (1908), is often identified as the foundation of the British welfare state.

At first reluctant to approve Great Britain's entry (August 1914) into WORLD WAR I, Lloyd George soon advocated a knockout blow against Germany, demanding greater vigor and efficiency from the government. As munitions minister in 1915–16, he ensured that a steady supply of guns and shells reached the western front, becoming a hero of the press but making many political enemies. He became minister of war shortly before he joined with the Conservative leaders to maneuver Asquith out of office in December 1916. Lloyd George then became prime minister and the dominant figure in the new 5-member coalition war cabinet.

Lloyd George imposed an effective regime of "war socialism" upon the British people, but he quarreled with his generals, particularly Douglas HAIG, and was unable to cut the heavy casualties on the western front. Nevertheless, he was popularly regarded as the man who won the war, and he exploited this reputation to win a huge election victory for his coalition following the 1918 armistice.

The last 4 years of Lloyd George's premiership (1918–22) were anticlimactic. He was the principal British negotiator at the PARIS PEACE CONFERENCE and five subsequent international parleys, but his "conference diplomacy" failed to mitigate postwar tensions. His government's housing program ("homes for heroes") was a disaster; there was mounting unemployment and labor unrest; and a major recession began in 1921. In Ireland he initially adopted a policy of harsh repression against the nationalist rebels, but he finally negotiated the treaty (1921) that established the Irish Free State. This settlement was his one major postwar success, but it damaged his relations with the Conservatives, on whom his government depended. The Conservatives finally withdrew their support after the CHANAK CRISIS (1922) in which Lloyd George brought Britain to the brink of war with Turkey.

After the coalition fell in October 1922, Lloyd George was reunited with the Asquithian Liberals. He later split with Asquith again, but he succeeded him as Liberal party leader (1926–31). With the decline of Liberalism, Lloyd George's fortunes waned. He never again held office, although he was a leading parliamentary critic of Labour and, more so, Conservative foreign and domestic policies. He was awarded an earldom shortly before his death on Mar. 26, 1945.

DON M. CREGIER

Bibliography: Cregier, Don M., *Bounder from Wales* (1976); Fry, Michael, *Lloyd George and Foreign Policy*, vol. 1 (1977); Grigg, John, *Lloyd George,* 2 vols. (1979, 1985), and *The Young Lloyd George* (1973); Morgan, Kenneth, *Consensus and Disunity* (1979); Woodward, David, *Lloyd George and the Generals* (1983).

Lloyd's of London   [loydz]

Lloyd's of London is an association of insurance underwriters who provide all types of insurance coverage throughout the world. Lloyd's is actually a market in which members (26,000 in 1985) form several hundred syndicates specializing in such categories as marine, motor, and aviation insurance. A person wishing to insure with Lloyd's approaches a Lloyd's broker, who in turn approaches one or more syndicates. Observers have often said that anything that cannot be insured at Lloyd's cannot be insured at all. Lloyd's takes its name from the late-17th-century London coffee house of Edward Lloyd, where marine insurers met to do business. Lloyd's began to handle nonmarine insurance in the late 1880s. Hanging in Lloyd's headquarters is the Lutine bell, which was salvaged (1857) from a shipwreck; it tolls once for good news and twice for bad news. In 1986, Lloyd's moved into new "high-tech" headquarters, designed by Richard Rogers.

Bibliography: Hodgson, Godfrey, *Lloyd's of London* (1984).

LNG: see NATURAL GAS.

loach   [lohch]

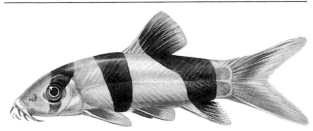

The clown loach, Botia macracanthus, *is a hardy freshwater fish of Borneo and Sumatra. Some have lived as long as 25 years in tanks.*

Loaches are small, often slim, elongated fishes making up the family Cobitidae in the minnow order Cypriniformes. They have tiny scales, 6 to 12 barbels around the mouth, soft-rayed fins, and usually teeth in the pharynx (throat) but never on the jaws. In some species there is a movable spine located either below or in front of each eye. Many loaches are about 10 cm (4 in) in length. Some species have an unusual accessory breathing adaptation: they gulp and swallow air, and the intestinal walls absorb oxygen; carbon dioxide and unused gases are then expelled through the anus. One species, *Misgurnus fossilis,* appears to be so sensitive to weather that its increased activity is said to indicate a change in the weather, hence the name weatherfish. Loaches are common throughout Europe and Asia and locally in Morocco and Ethiopia. The greatest number of species occurs in Southeast Asia. Many are spectacularly colored and are popular aquarium fishes.

A. R. EMERY

loam: see SOIL.

Lobachevsky, Nikolai Ivanovich   [luh-buh-chef'-skee]

Nikolai Ivanovich Lobachevsky, b. Dec. 1 (N.S.), 1792, d. Feb. 24 (N.S.), 1856, was a Russian mathematician who is best noted for his work in the field of NON-EUCLIDEAN GEOMETRY,

sometimes called Lobachevskian geometry. His major work, "Geometriya," completed in 1823, was not published in its original form until 1909. Since the time of Euclid mathematicians had been trying to prove Euclid's fifth postulate as a theorem, either by assuming implicitly an equivalent statement or by directly substituting another postulate for the statement that, given a line and point not on it, *only one* coplanar line may be drawn through the point not intersecting the given line. Lobachevsky's geometry derives from the concept that a geometry in which all of Euclid's axioms except the fifth postulate are demonstrably true is not in itself contradictory. Lobachevsky categorized EUCLIDEAN GEOMETRY as a special case of a more general system.

THEODORE ALLEGRI

Bibliography: Bell, Eric T., *Men of Mathematics* (1937); Bonola, Roberto, *Non-Euclidean Geometry: A Critical and Historical Study of Its Developments,* trans. by H. S. Carslaw (1912; repr. 1955); Kagan, Veniafin F., *N. Lobachevsky and His Contributions to Science* (1957).

lobbyist

A lobbyist is a person who attempts to influence legislators in favor of SPECIAL-INTEREST GROUPS. The word was originally used in the 1830s to describe those who frequented the lobbies of U.S. public buildings, particularly those of federal and state governments, and talked with legislators. Organizations that maintain lobbyists in Washington, D.C., and state capitals range from large business corporations to citizens' groups such as the AMERICAN CIVIL LIBERTIES UNION, COMMON CAUSE, and the NATIONAL RIFLE ASSOCIATION OF AMERICA. They may be concerned with a specific law or amendment or with an array of laws and regulations.

Lobbyists attempt to influence decision makers by direct contact, by affecting public opinion through the use of the media, and by mailing campaigns. Although its reputation has been frequently marred by such practices as bribery—the Korean lobby scandal of the late 1970s, for example—lobbying has become a familiar and accepted political activity. It is regarded by many as essential to the modern, complex process of government. Lobbyists, for instance, provide the busy legislator with practical information that helps in the drafting of technical legislation, and they work with administrative agencies to obtain clarifications and rulings on regulations.

Lobbying is protected by the U.S. Constitution, especially by the 1st Amendment's guarantees against interference with freedom of speech and the right to petition. Under the Federal Regulation of Lobbying Act (1946), persons who receive remuneration for such activities, as their principal purpose, must register with the secretary of the Senate and the clerk of the House of Representatives and file quarterly reports, which are then printed in the *Congressional Record.* These reports disclose on whose behalf lobbyists are acting, their objectives, and the amounts they receive and spend. In 1981, 5,662 lobbyists registered under this law; the number of registered lobbyists had grown to 20,400 in 1986. Many successful lobbyists are former legislators or government officials who are familiar with government procedures and who have wide contacts in Washington. Congress in 1986 began considering new rules to limit lobbyists' activities, prompted by news accounts of former (but quite recently departed) officials, including White House aides, whose lobbying clients included foreign governments.

MARTIN TORODASH

Bibliography: DeKieffer, Donald, *How to Lobby Congress* (1982); Hayes, M. J., *Lobbyists and Legislators* (1981; repr. 1984); Howe, Russell, and Trott, Sarah, *The Power Peddlers* (1977); Hrehenar, R. J., and Scott, R. K., *Interest Group Politics in America* (1982); Levitan, Sar A., and Cooper, Martha, *Business Lobbies* (1983); Wootton, Graham, *Interest Groups* (1971).

lobelia   [loh-beel'-yuh]

Lobelia is a genus of about 375 species of herbs, shrubs, and some trees in the lobelia family, Lobeliaceae. In many classifications it is placed in the bellflower family, Campanulaceae. More than 250 varieties of annuals and perennials are grown as ornamentals. Lobelia flowers are blue, violet, red, yellow, or white in color and commonly have petals formed into two projecting lips. The flowers are borne mostly in elongated spires (racemes).

The cardinal flower, *L. cardinalis*, is a perennial found in moist meadows and along streams throughout the eastern half of Canada and the United States. It produces short offshoots at its base and, from July to September, bears terminal spikes of cardinal-red flowers. The giant lobelia, *L. gibberoa*, native to Central and East Africa, is a treelike form reaching 9 m (30 ft) in height. It sends up solitary, hollow stalks bearing 60-cm (2-ft) leaves and long, spikelike clusters of tiny greenish white flowers.

Lobengula, King of the Ndebele   [loh-beng-goo'-luh]

Lobengula, b. *c.*1836, d. January 1894, was the second and last king of the NDEBELE, or Matabele, an African people who inhabited Matabeleland, now part of Zimbabwe. After the death (1868) of his father, Mzilikazi, the founder of the Ndebele kingdom, Lobengula's claim to the throne was challenged by a half-brother, Nkulumane, who attracted both dissident Ndebele and European allies. Lobengula, who succeeded to the throne in 1870, also sought European allies. In 1888 he granted rights to the minerals of his kingdom to agents of Cecil RHODES, who soon received a royal charter creating the British South Africa Company. Rhodes interpreted the concession as granting his company territorial rights over all Ndebele lands. Many conflicts then followed; they included disputes between Lobengula and dissidents within his kingdom and disputes between the king and representatives of the British. By the early 1890s, however, Lobengula's army—formerly much feared—had grown weak and dispirited. He died of smallpox while fleeing the advancing British forces.

ROBERT R. GRIFFETH

Bibliography: Bhebe, A. H., *Lobengula of Zimbabwe* (1977).

lobster

The Norway lobster, N. norvegicus, a small species of lobster with slender pincers, is found along the northeastern Atlantic coast.

Lobsters are large marine crustaceans in the order Decapoda; they are closely related to crayfish and shrimp. The tasty white meat of the lobster is widely prized as a delicacy. In some areas, lobster fishing is an important industry.

The lobster's body is made up of two main parts: the front section (cephalothorax) and the tail (abdomen). Several pairs of appendages perform a variety of functions. Two pairs are antennae, or feelers, and five pairs are legs. In most lobsters, one pair forms two large and differently shaped claws. One claw, the narrower one, is called the cutter because it is used to slice dead fish, one of the lobster's favorite foods. The heavier claw, called the crusher, has toothlike bumps used for crushing clam shells and other hard objects. The only lobsters without these large claws are the spiny lobsters, which have sharp body spines instead.

Perhaps the largest lobster is the American lobster, *Homarus americanus*, which lives along the Atlantic coast from Labrador to Virginia. It has been known to reach a length of 90 cm (3 ft) and a weight of 20 kg (44 lb). A popular European lobster is the Norway lobster, *Nephrops norvegicus*. Spiny lobsters in the family Palinuridae are caught off the coasts of California, Florida, Australia, New Zealand, and South Africa.

Bibliography: Bliss, Dorothy, *Shrimps, Lobsters, and Crabs: Their Fascinating Life Story* (1982); Prudden, T. M., *About Lobsters* (1962); Taylor, Herb, *The Lobster: Its Life Cycle* (1975).

Local Group of galaxies

The Local Group of galaxies is the small cluster of galaxies that surrounds our galaxy to distances within about one million parsecs (3,260,000 light-years). At least 28 members of the group are known. The exact number is unknown because of difficulties in identifying dim galaxies, especially dwarf galaxies, that are close to the galactic plane with its heavy interstellar absorption. Even some of the accepted members in the Local Group have still not been adequately studied.

The two giant members of the Local Group are our Milky Way Galaxy and the ANDROMEDA GALAXY (M 31). There is a subclustering about these two giants: 13 galaxies in the Milky Way group and 9 galaxies in the M 31 group, with 5 galaxies outside both groups. Aside from the two giant galaxies, the Local Group also includes an average spiral (M 33); the Large MAGELLANIC CLOUD; more than a half dozen dwarf Magellanic irregular galaxies, including the Small Magellanic Cloud and its recently determined offshoot, the Mini Magellanie Cloud; and perhaps a dozen dwarf ellipticals. The range in absolute magnitude is about 12 (from −9 to −21), corresponding to a range in absolute luminosity of 63,000. Most of the luminosity and mass of the Local Group are in M 31 and the Milky Way. The total mass of the Local Group is about 700 billion solar masses. One of the lowest luminosity systems is Leo II, an extreme dwarf elliptical system with a mass of only a million solar masses, comparable in size to globular clusters. Even more extreme dwarf systems down to star-cluster size probably exist but so far have not been observed.

The Local Group is important because individual stars can be studied in detail within each member and because the most common type of galaxy, the dwarf elliptical, is best observed there.

JOHN B. IRWIN

Bibliography: Abel, George O., *Drama of the Universe* (1978); Berman, Louis, and Evans, J. C., *Exploring the Cosmos*, 2d ed. (1977); Hartmann, William K., *Astronomy* (1978); Jastrow, Robert, and Thompson, Malcolm H., *Astronomy*, 3d ed. (1977); Mitton, Simon, *Exploring the Galaxies* (1976); Motz, Lloyd, and Duveen, Anneta, *Essentials of Astronomy*, 2d ed. (1977); Pasachoff, Jay M., *Astronomy Now* (1978); "The Three Magellanic Clouds," *Sky & Telescope*, April 1984.

See also: EXTRAGALACTIC SYSTEMS.

Locarno   [loh-kar'-noh]

Locarno is a town in the Italian-speaking canton of Ticino in southern Switzerland. It has a population of 14,103 (1980). Located on the northern shore of Lake MAGGIORE, it is a popular holiday and health resort. Industries include machinery and electrochemicals. Notable among the historic buildings are the Church of Madonna del Sasso (1480) and the castle of the dukes of Milan (14th century). Settled in prehistoric times, Locarno was under Milanese rule from 1342 to 1512, when it was taken over by the Swiss.

Locarno Pact

The Locarno Pact was a group of treaties signed in 1925 at Locarno, Switzerland, by representatives of Belgium, Britain,

Czechoslovakia, France, Germany, Italy, and Poland. These agreements were an attempt to settle security problems left unresolved at the end of World War I. The main treaty, which confirmed Germany's western borders with France and Belgium, was signed by the powers directly concerned and guaranteed by Britain and Italy. Germany signed treaties with its eastern neighbors, Poland and Czechoslovakia, but they were not given the same protection. France, however, concluded an agreement with the latter countries promising to help them if Germany broke its commitment to settle any future disputes with them peacefully. The Locarno Pact made Germany's entry into the LEAGUE OF NATIONS possible and was followed by a short era of international harmony.

DONALD S. BIRN

Bibliography: Jacobson, Jon, *Locarno Diplomacy* (1972).

Loch Ness: see NESS, LOCH.

Loch Ness monster   [lahk nes]

The Loch Ness monster is a legendary animal said to live in the depths of Loch Ness in northern Scotland. Belief that a mysterious creature lives in the lake goes back to the Middle Ages and the legend of the water horse, or kelpie, which lured travelers to their deaths. The first recorded sighting dates back to AD 565, when Saint COLUMBA came upon the burial of a man said to have been bitten to death by a monster while he was swimming in Loch Ness. According to one writer, Saint Columba himself later saw the monster.

Although many sightings have been reported in the subsequent centuries, not until 1933 did the Loch Ness monster become a subject of worldwide fascination. In that year a man and woman driving along a road at the side of the lake noticed a great surging of water in the middle, and for several minutes they watched "an enormous animal rolling and plunging." The incident was widely reported by the press.

Since then many investigators have attempted to get evidence of the creature's existence, using equipment ranging from telescopes and cameras to sonar and even a submarine. Many purported photographs of the monster have turned out to be inconclusive or outright hoaxes. Speculation as to what type of mysterious animal might inhabit the loch is endless.

In 1972 and 1975 an American expedition sponsored by the Academy of Applied Science used sophisticated scientific equipment to obtain some startling underwater time-lapse pictures that some researchers believe show a large animal swimming submerged in Loch Ness. Using sonar equipment, a British expedition failed to detect the presence of such a creature in 1987. Most scientists remain skeptical of the existence of the "monster."

PETER L. PETRAKIS

Bibliography: Bauer, Henry H., *The Enigma of Loch Ness* (1986); Campbell, Steuart, *The Loch Ness Monster: The Evidence* (1986); Dinsdale, Tim, *The Loch Ness Monster*, 4th ed. (1982).

Lochner v. New York   [lahk'-nur]

In the case of *Lochner* v. *New York* (1905) the Supreme Court invalidated a maximum-hour labor law enacted by the state of New York. Joseph Lochner had been found guilty of violating an 1897 law that prohibited employers from allowing employees to work more than 60 hours per week or 10 hours per day in bakeries. The purpose of the law was to protect the health of bakers who worked long hours in the heat generated by the ovens. The Court, through Justice Rufus W. Peckham, declared the law unconstitutional on the grounds that it violated "freedom of contract" implicitly guaranteed by the due process clause of the 14th Amendment. The statute, said Peckham, interfered with the right of employees and employers to make a contract of labor.

The idea that due process constituted a substantive as well as procedural limitation on government was not new. In DRED SCOTT V. SANDFORD (1857), Chief Justice Taney argued that the Missouri Compromise was void because it violated the due process clause of the 5th Amendment. In *Lochner* the Court's

majority used due process to prevent government regulation of economic matters. Most of the justices believed strongly in laissez-faire economics and Social Darwinism. Justice Holmes wrote an often-quoted dissent, in which he chastised the majority for deciding the case on "an economic theory which a large part of the country does not entertain." Accusing them of distorting the Constitution, he declared that "the Fourteenth Amendment does not enact Mr. Herbert Spencer's social statics." Liberty of contract lost most of its vitality when *Lochner* was implicitly overruled in the case of *West Coast Hotel* v. *Parrish* (1937).

ROBERT J. STEAMER

lock, canal: see CANAL.

lock and key

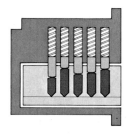

The cutaway diagram illustrates the process by which a key opens its corresponding lock. When the key is inserted until it meets the shear point (A), spring-loaded drivers (B) force the pins (C) to align with the grooves along the key. This permits the key to turn, opening the lock.

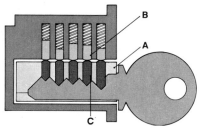

A lock is a fastening contrivance consisting of a bolt and the mechanisms for propelling it. Locks are opened by keys designed to fit and move the bolt mechanism.

Early Development. The oldest known lock, found in the ruins of the Near-Eastern palace of Khorsabad near ancient Ninevah, dates from about 2000 BC. A forerunner of the modern pin-tumbler lock, this so-called Egyptian lock consists of a large wooden bolt pierced with holes; pins from the lock housing drop through the holes to secure the bolt. The key, a long wooden bar fitted on one end with a pattern of pegs corresponding to the pins in the bolt, lifts the pins and permits the bolt to slide.

Other ancient Mediterranean cultures produced their own versions of locking devices. The early Greeks are credited with first employing keyholes. Roman contributions include the first metal locks, the earliest padlocks, the introduction of small keys, and the development of warded locks. The warded lock employs projections (wards) inside the lock casing that obstruct any key except one cut with notches that correspond to the projecting ward.

Warded construction, although fairly easy to open with a picklock, continued as the standard lock design until the late 1700s. In medieval and Renaissance Europe skilled locksmiths devised ingenious variations and adorned them with elaborate decorations. The principle of the combination lock probably originated in China; it appeared in southern Germany in the 16th century and resurfaced in England in the following century. This keyless device depends on the correct alignment of numbers or letters on a dial to actuate the unlocking mechanism.

Modern History. In 1778, Robert Barron, an Englishman, patented his double-acting, lever-tumbler lock. His invention had two tumbler plates, which in the locked position fitted into slots in the bolt and required a key to raise each tumbler to a specific height. Barron's design is the basis for the lever-tumbler locks in use today, primarily on safe-deposit boxes.

In 1784, Joseph BRAMAH received a British patent for a lock that required a cylindrical key to push down and turn aside an arrangement of thin metal slides set in a barrel-shaped plug holding the bolt in place. Bramah and his assistant Henry MAUDSLAY are credited with successfully introducing mass-production techniques to 18th-century industry.

The modern pin-tumbler lock was invented by Linus Yale and Linus YALE, Jr. Inspired by the ancient Egyptian pin lock, the senior Yale patented (1851) a lock with radial pin tumblers; his son patented improvements and began the manufacture of what proved to be the prototype of the modern cylinder lock. Housed in a cylindrical plug, the pin tumblers stood in a row along the cylinder's turning axis. Use of the correct flat, serrated key lifted all the pins to the proper height, permitting the key to turn the bolt mechanism. The Yale design's improved security, small size, and adaptability to mass production account for its widespread use.

Today, new security technologies threaten the dominance of the metal lock and key. The keycard, developed in the early 1980s for use in hotels, has a magnetically imprinted code allowing its holder to enter the room he or she has rented. The code is changed when the person checks out. Newer technologies depend on the identification of person rather than card. Sophisticated sensor-computer systems can scan and identify the unique patterns of blood cells inside a person's eye; recognize fingerprints or the distinctive profile of a hand; or respond to a voice whose digitized sound was previously stored in the system.   CARLENE STEPHENS

Bibliography: Allen, Sam, *Locks and Alarms* (1984); Rogers, S. L., *The Personal Identification of Living Individuals* (1986); Roper, C. A., *The Complete Book of Locks and Locksmithing* (1983); Spilker, B., *Keys and Locks in the Collection of the Cooper-Hewitt Museum* (1987).

Locke, Alain

An American educator, critic, and anthologist, Alain LeRoy Locke, b. Philadelphia, Sept. 13, 1886, d. June 9, 1954, gained immediate recognition as an authority on the cultural achievements of American blacks with his anthology *The New Negro* (1925; repr. 1968). Locke was active in the HARLEM RENAISSANCE movement, which he helped broaden to encompass artists and musicians as well as writers, and to include persons outside of New York City. The first black American Rhodes Scholar, Locke completed (1918) his Ph.D. at Harvard and taught philosophy at Howard University for 36 years. His later anthologies were *The Negro and His Music* (1936; repr. 1968), *Negro Art—Past and Present* (1936; repr. 1969), and *The Negro in Art* (1940; repr. 1971).

Bibliography: Harris, T., ed., *Afro-American Writers before the Harlem Renaissance* (1986) and *Afro-American Writers from the Harlem Renaissance to 1940* (1986).

Locke, David Ross: see NASBY, PETROLEUM V.

Locke, John

John Locke, b. Aug. 29, 1632, d. Oct. 28, 1704, was an English philosopher and political theorist, the founder of British EMPIRICISM. He undertook his university studies at Christ Church, Oxford. At first, he followed the traditional classical curriculum but then turned to the study of medicine and science. Although Locke did not actually earn a medical degree, he obtained a medical license. He joined the household of Anthony Ashley Cooper, later 1st earl of SHAFTESBURY, as a personal physician. He became Shaftesbury's advisor and friend. Through him, Locke held minor government posts and became involved in the turbulent politics of the period.

In 1675, Locke left England to live in France, where he became familiar with the doctrines of René Descartes and his critics. He returned to England in 1679 while Shaftesbury was in power and pressing to secure the exclusion of James, duke of York (the future King JAMES II) from the succession to the throne. Shaftesbury was later tried for treason, and although

John Locke, an English philosopher of the 17th century, is best known as an advocate of civil and religious liberties. He denied the divine right of kings, arguing that government is based on the consent of the people. He also developed a theory of understanding in which he asserted that knowledge of the outside world is limited by the extent of ideas, or experience, gained through the five senses.

he was acquitted, he fled to Holland. Because he was closely allied with Shaftesbury, Locke also fled to Holland in 1683; he lived there until the overthrow (1688) of James II. In 1689, Locke returned to England in the party escorting the princess of Orange, who was to be crowned Queen MARY II of England. In 1691, Locke retired to Oates in Essex, the household of Sir Francis and Lady Masham. During his years at Oates, Locke wrote and edited, and received many influential visitors, including Sir Isaac Newton. He continued to exercise political influence. His friendships with prominent government officers and scholars made him one of the most influential men of the 17th century.

Locke's *Essay Concerning Human Understanding* (1690) is one of the classical documents of British empirical philosophy. The essay had its origin in a series of discussions with friends that led Locke to the conclusion that the principal subject of philosophy had to be the extent of the mind's ability to know (see EPISTEMOLOGY). He set out "to examine our abilities and to see what objects our understandings were or were not fitted to deal with." The *Essay* is a principal statement of empiricism and, broadly speaking, was an effort to formulate a view of knowledge consistent with the findings of Newtonian science.

Locke began the *Essay* with a critique of the rationalistic idea that the mind is equipped with INNATE IDEAS, ideas that do not arise from experience. He then turned to the elaboration of his own empiricism: "Let us suppose the mind to be, as we say, white paper, void of all characters, without any ideas; how comes this to be furnished? . . . whence has it all the materials of reason and knowledge? To this I answer, in a word, from experience." What experience provides is ideas, which Locke defined as "the object of the understanding when a man thinks." He held that ideas come from two sources: sensation, which provides ideas about the external world, and reflection, or introspection, which provides the ideas of the internal workings of the mind.

Locke's view that experience produces ideas, which are the immediate objects of thought, led him to adopt a causal or representative view of human knowledge. In perception, according to this view, people are not directly aware of physical objects. Rather, they are directly aware of the ideas that objects "cause" in them and that "represent" the objects in their consciousness. A similar view of perception was presented by earlier thinkers such as Galileo and Descartes.

Locke's view raised the question of the extent to which ideas are like the objects that cause them. His answer was that only some qualities of objects are like ideas. He held that primary qualities of objects, or the mathematically determinable qualities of an object, such as shape, motion, weight, and number, exist in the world, and that ideas copy them. Secondary qualities, those which arise from the senses, do not exist in objects as they exist in ideas. According to Locke, secondary qualities, such as taste, "are nothing in the objects themselves but powers to produce ideas in use by their primary qualities." Thus, when an object is perceived, a person's ideas of its shape and weight represent qualities to be found in the object itself. Color and taste, however, are not copies of anything in the object.

One conclusion of Locke's theory is that genuine knowledge cannot be found in natural science, because the real essences of physical objects that science studies cannot be known. It would appear that genuine certainty can be achieved only through mathematics. Locke's view of knowledge anticipated developments by later philosophers and exercised an important influence on the subsequent course of philosophical thought.

Locke's considerable importance in political thought is better known. As the first systematic theorist of the philosophy of LIBERALISM, Locke exercised enormous influence in both England and America. In his *Two Treatises of Government* (1690), Locke set forth the view that the state exists to preserve the natural rights of its citizens. When governments fail in that task, citizens have the right—and sometimes the duty—to withdraw their support and even to rebel. Locke opposed Thomas HOBBES's view that the original state of nature was "nasty, brutish, and short," and that individuals through a SOCIAL CONTRACT surrendered—for the sake of self-preservation—their rights to a supreme sovereign who was the source of all morality and law. Locke maintained that the state of nature was a happy and tolerant one, that the social contract preserved the preexistent natural rights of the individual to life, liberty, and property, and that the enjoyment of private rights—the pursuit of happiness—led, in civil society, to the common good. Locke's notion of government was a limited one: the checks and balances among branches of government (later reflected in the U.S. Constitution) and true representation in the legislature would maintain limited government and individual liberties.

A Letter Concerning Toleration (1689) expressed Locke's view that, within certain limits, no one should dictate the form of another's religion. Other important works include *The Reasonableness of Christianity* (1695), in which Locke expressed his ideas on religion, and *Some Thoughts Concerning Education* (1693).   THOMAS K. HEARN, JR.

Bibliography: Aaron, Richard I., *John Locke*, 3d ed. (1971); Collins, James D., *The British Empiricists: Locke, Berkeley, Hume* (1967); Cranston, Maurice, *John Locke: A Biography* (1957); Dunn, John, *Political Thought of John Locke* (1969); Gough, J. W., *John Locke's Political Philosophy: Eight Studies*, 2d ed. (1973); Mabbott, J. D., *John Locke* (1973); Sahakian, Mabel L. and William S., *John Locke* (1975); Yolton, John W., *John Locke and the Way of Ideas* (1956) and, as ed., *John Locke: Problems and Perspectives* (1969).

lockjaw: see TETANUS.

lockout

A lockout is the closing of a place of business by management in order to prevent employees from working and thus to pressure a labor union into settling a dispute in management's favor. The lockout is analogous to the STRIKE; it is a last resort. In U.S. labor history, lockouts were sometimes used to frustrate union organizers. This use of a lockout was outlawed by the National Labor Relations Act of 1935, which requires employers to bargain "in good faith" with representatives of their employees. An employer is not required under the law to agree to demands made by a union and may decide to endure a strike until the union comes to terms. For this reason a strike is sometimes called a lockout by workers involved in a dispute. During a lockout, an employer may continue to do business by hiring temporary replacements.

Lockwood, Belva Ann Bennett

Belva Lockwood, b. Royalton, N.Y., Oct. 24, 1830, d. May 19, 1917, was the first woman lawyer admitted to practice before the U.S. Supreme Court and the first woman candidate for the U.S. presidency. Rejected by many law schools on the ground that she was a woman, she finally entered the National University Law School and was admitted to the District of Columbia bar in 1873. She won the right to present cases before the Supreme Court in 1879. Lockwood was a leading litigator and lobbyist on behalf of women's rights. In 1884 and 1888 she was nominated as the presidential candidate of the National Equal Rights party.

Bibliography: Stern, Madeleine, *We the Women*, rev. ed. (1975).

Lockyer, Sir Joseph Norman

The English astronomer Sir Joseph Norman Lockyer, b. May 17, 1836, d. Aug. 16, 1920, was an early researcher in the field of astrophysics. With the crude spectroscope of the 1860s Lockyer studied the spectra of sunspots and prominences. Together with Edward Frankland, Lockyer found evidence in the Sun for a new element that he named helium—a discovery for which he was knighted in 1897. Lockyer also discovered and named the Sun's chromosphere, proposed that atoms might be broken down into simpler constituents, and developed a "meteoritic hypothesis" of the evolution of the universe. He founded the journal *Nature* in 1869 and was its editor for a half century.   STEVEN J. DICK

Bibliography: Meadows, A. J., *Science and Controversy: A Biography of Sir Norman Lockyer* (1972).

locomotion, biological: see BIOLOGICAL LOCOMOTION.

locomotive

A locomotive is a vehicle that runs on rails and is self-propelled by any of several forms of energy for the purpose of moving railroad cars. In the 19th century the railroad, along with the steam locomotive, was considered by many persons to be the true symbol of the new industrial age. During its long history the railroad locomotive has experienced a complex technical development moving in turn from steam to electric and finally to diesel power.

HISTORY

Some of the first RAILROADS (called railways in Britain) used horses for motive power, but the development and acceptance of the steam locomotive was needed to make railroads a practical mode of transportation.

Steam Locomotive. England was the birthplace of the steam locomotive, which is essentially a STEAM ENGINE mounted on and used to propel a wheeled vehicle on rails. The first steam locomotive was built in 1804 by Richard TREVITHICK for the Penydarren Iron Works in Wales. It was able to haul a sizable load (25 tons) but was too heavy for the track and was converted to a stationary steam engine; it did, however, encourage others to build steam locomotives. George STEPHENSON built the engine *Locomotion* for the Stockton and Darlington Railway, which was opened in 1825. This engine, with a single flue and outside coupling rods, had a boiler capacity more suited for freight than passenger service. Far more powerful was the ROCKET, an engine designed primarily by George Stephenson's son Robert. The *Rocket* was the winning entry in the 1829 Rainhill Trials, a locomotive competition organized by the Liverpool and Manchester Railway; the *Rocket*'s performance convinced the railway directors of the practicability of steam motive power. The *Rocket*, which had a multitube boiler and an efficient method of exhausting the steam and creating a draft in the firebox, generated a boiler pressure

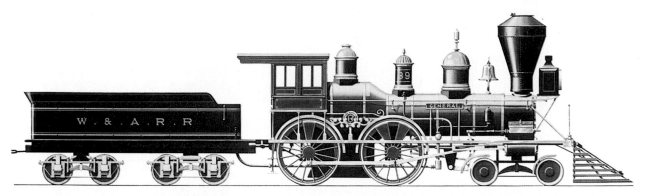

Western & Atlanta's "General," built in 1855, typifies American locomotives of that vintage. It had 4 leading wheels, 4 drivers, and no trailing wheels; hence it was designated 4-4-0. The General was built by Thomas Rogers, a carpenter turned locomotive builder, who was the first to use a steam whistle in an American engine. Rogers was largely responsible for making Paterson, N.J., known as "The City of Iron Horses."

Robert Stephenson's "Rocket" was the first steam engine to use the multitube boiler. This, along with other improvements, allowed the locomotive to reach the unprecedented speed of 46 km/h (29 mph) with a full load. The Rocket won the Rainhill competition in England in 1829.

of 3.4 atm (50 psi), sufficient to complete the trials at an average speed of 24 km/h (15 mph) with a top speed of 46 km/h (29 mph).

English locomotives also played a role in early American railroad history. Because the United States then had such a limited manufacturing capacity, U.S. railways imported more than 100 English locomotives between 1829 and 1841. One of the first was the STOURBRIDGE LION, imported in 1829 by the Delaware & Hudson Railroad. One of the company's engineers, Horatio Allen, decided that the English engine was too heavy and rigid for American track. More successful was the JOHN BULL, which the Camden & Amboy Railroad imported in 1831. Before long, this locomotive was furnishing passenger service across New Jersey in 7 hours.

The Americans soon began building their own locomotives. In 1830, Peter Cooper's tiny (1.43 hp) TOM THUMB lost its famous race against a horse-drawn coach but still convinced officials of the Baltimore & Ohio Railroad that they should use steam power rather than horses. On Christmas Day, 1830,

in South Carolina, the BEST FRIEND OF CHARLESTON—the first locomotive built for sale in the United States—carried 141 passengers on the first scheduled steam railroad train in America. Unlike the *Rocket*, which had a single pair of drivers, the *Stourbridge Lion*, the *John Bull*, and the *Best Friend of Charleston* all had four drivers, a connected pair on each side. John B. Jervis, a civil engineer who worked for the Mohawk & Hudson Railroad, was not happy with the rigid front axle and poor turning characteristics of such engines. In 1832 he built the *Experiment*, an engine with a single pair of drivers and a four-wheeled bogie (a swivel truck under the front of the locomotive). The new engine negotiated most curves with ease and later proved capable of much higher speeds.

Other American innovations quickly followed. In 1836, Henry Campbell of Philadelphia designed an eight-wheeled engine (bogie truck plus four drivers); it was known as the American-type locomotive, and this type was to dominate U.S. locomotive design for half a century. Joseph Harrison, also of Philadelphia, in 1839 invented the equalizing beam, which permitted equal pressure by each driver, even on rough track. Earlier in the decade, Isaac Dripps, of the Camden & Amboy, invented the pilot, or "cowcatcher," and placed the first one on the *John Bull*. Such additional equipment was necessary in America, where few tracks were protected by fencing. Night rail travel was fairly common within 12 years, and by the 1840s the conventional large headlight, burning kerosene in front of tin reflectors, was quite common. The sandbox (to provide better driver traction) was first used in Pennsylvania in 1836 when a plague of grasshoppers threatened to stop all train movements in the state. Canvas, and later wooden, cabs were often added to the engines in northern states for protection against freezing winter weather. Both locomotive bells and whistles were soon found on most engines as a warning signal at railroad crossings; the whistle was later also used for signaling the train crew.

By the 1850s, British and American locomotives tended to differ considerably. British engines were shorter, with generally smaller tenders and cabs. They rarely used the bogie or pony swivel truck in front, and the American-type pilot was never seen on English engines. Naturally in each country the engine builders built to meet the differing needs and requirements of their own railroads. Both countries exported many locomotives to developing nations during the 19th century.

The Union Pacific "Big Boy," built by the American Locomotive Company during World War II, was one of 25 locomotives designed to haul freight from Omaha, Neb., to Cheyenne, Wyo., negotiating the Wasatch Mountains. Powerful enough to handle extreme tonnages at high speeds, the Big Boy weighed nearly 100 tons and could reach 128 km/h (80 mph).

Great Northern Railway's single-driver locomotive, designed by Patrick Stirling, operated on Great Britain's east-coast line between King's Cross and York. These famous engines pulled London-Southend expresses in the 1890s.

The London and North Eastern Railway's Pacific "Mallard," designed by Sir Nigel Gresley, broke the world speed record for a steam locomotive in 1938 by reaching a speed of 202 km/h (126 mph).

The Santa Fé Class 2900 is a good example of a large American fast freight locomotive. A 4-8-4 (four wheels in front, eight drivers, four wheels under the cab), it was built in 1943.

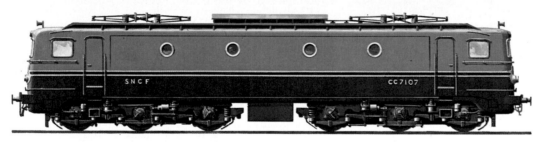

The French National Railway's Class CC 7100 electric locomotive broke the world rail speed record in March 1955 by reaching 331 km/h (205 mph).

Great Northern's diesel engine, built by General Motors, is a typical large American general-purpose diesel locomotive. Diesel power began to replace steam power in the 1950s, and soon most major rail lines owned no steam engines at all.

The New Tokaido Line, a high-speed electric line, runs between Tokyo and Osaka, Japan. It completes the 512-km (320-mi) journey in about three hours.

By the eve of the Civil War, the favorite locomotive design in America was the eight-wheel American type. This was known as a 4-4-0 (four wheels in front, four drivers, no wheels under the cab), according to the Frederic M. Whyte system of engine classification. In 1860 the average American-type locomotive had a functional cowcatcher, large headlight, balloon smokestack, and a name rather than a number; cost $8,000 to $10,000 to build; and used wood, or possibly coal, for fuel. Between 1850 and 1860 the average weight of the 4-4-0 increased from 15 to 25 tons. By 1870 most of them were heavier, more powerful, and coal-burning, and they were providing about 85% of the motive power in the United States.

In the half century between the Civil War and World War I, a new emphasis was placed on strength, bulk, and power in the manufacture of American locomotives. One change was the increase in the number of drivers. The Baltimore & Ohio increasingly turned to Ten-Wheelers (4-6-0, according to the Whyte classification), and still more tractive power was possible when the Lehigh Valley introduced the Consolidation type (2-8-0). The need for a larger firebox was met by moving the firebox from between the rear pair of drivers, making it broader, and placing it over a trailing truck of smaller wheels. This resulted in the Atlantic type (4-4-2) in 1895. A few years later the Missouri Pacific achieved still greater power with its Pacific locomotive (4-6-2). The increase in power and wheel complexity is shown in the accompanying table.

WHYTE CLASSIFICATION OF LOCOMOTIVES BY WHEEL ARRANGEMENT

Symbol	Wheel Arrangement (front to back)	Type Name
0-6-0	OOO	Six-wheel switcher
0-8-0	OOOO	Eight-wheel switcher
2-6-0	oOOO	Mogul
2-6-2	oOOOo	Prairie
2-8-0	oOOOO	Consolidation
2-8-2	oOOOOo	Mikado
2-8-4	oOOOOoo	Berkshire
2-10-0	oOOOOO	Decapod
2-10-2	oOOOOOo	Santa Fé
2-10-4	oOOOOOoo	Texas
4-4-0	ooOO	American
4-4-2	ooOOo	Atlantic
4-6-0	ooOOO	Ten-Wheeler
4-6-2	ooOOOo	Pacific
4-6-4	ooOOOoo	Hudson (Baltic)
4-8-2	ooOOOOo	Mountain
4-8-4	ooOOOOoo	Northern
4-8-8-4	ooOOOO OOOoo	"Big Boy"

Improvements in U.S. steam locomotives continued during the first half of the 20th century. During World War I, the U.S. Railroad Administration purchased 1,930 locomotives, all built to standard specifications, with about half of the engines being Mikado (2-8-2) freight locomotives. During the prosperous 1920s, 15,000 new locomotives were purchased by American railroads, some of the largest being the huge mallet or articulated models, steam engines with two sets of drivers powered by a single firebox and boiler. During World War II, the Union Pacific commissioned 25 giant "Big Boys," huge articulated engines 35.1 m (117 ft) in length, with 170-cm (68-in) drivers, and capable of producing 7,000 hp. By 1950 the most powerful steam engines had roughly three times the tractive effort of those 50 years earlier.

Electric Locomotive. Late in the 19th century, steam motive power was challenged by the electric locomotives, both in Europe and in America. By the turn of the century the Baltimore & Ohio and the New York, New Haven & Hartford lines had successfully installed short electrified routes. Later the Milwaukee electrified much of its mountain line as it built west to the Pacific. In the 1920s and '30s the Pennsylvania did the same for its lines from New York City to Harrisburg, Pa., and to Washington, D.C. By the mid-1950s, U.S. railroads were operating a total of 3,900 km (2,400 mi) of electrified route. The increasing popularity of the diesel locomotive, however, has led to a reduction in electrified sections of railroads. Between 1955 and 1976, the electrified mileage was reduced by half.

Diesel Locomotive. The invention of the diesel locomotive made possible great increases in operating efficiency. The DIESEL ENGINE was invented in the 1890s by Rudolf DIESEL, a French-born German mechanical engineer. The first diesel-electric locomotive was used by the Central Railroad of New Jersey for switching operations in New York City in the mid-1920s. In the mid-1930s the Burlington and the Union Pacific both used diesel power for their new streamliner passenger trains, and in 1941 the Santa Fé successfully used diesel power for freight service. During and after World War II, the conversion to diesel power was rapid. By 1945, diesel power was performing 7% of the freight, 10% of the passenger, and 25% of the yard switching service; by 1952, for the first time, diesel units exceeded steam locomotives; and by 1957 the new form of motive power performed 92% of the freight, 93% of the passenger, and 96% of the switching service in the United States. A similar trend was occurring worldwide.

COMPARISON OF OPERATION OF LOCOMOTIVE TYPES

The long century and a quarter history of the steam locomotive accompanied the birth and growth of a viable rail industry that tended to peak in many industrial nations in the second quarter of the 20th century. In contrast, the appearance of both electric and diesel power came at a time when the railroad industry was near, or even past, its peak in mileage and economic importance. Without doubt the greater efficiency of the diesels eased the financial strain that accompanied the decline of the industry. Today most railroads in industrial nations use either electric or diesel locomotives. Steam is still quite extensively used, however, in many underdeveloped countries in Africa, Asia, and South America.

In the diesel locomotive an oil-burning diesel engine supplies the power. It is possible to transmit this power to the driving wheels by using a mechanical or hydraulic transmission, but the indirect, flexible electric transmission is more commonly used, and such a locomotive is called a diesel-electric. In this type, the diesel engine turns electric GENERATORS; these, in turn, power several electric MOTORS, normally one for each axle. This form of power offers several advantages over the steam locomotive. Although diesels are expensive (costing probably double the price of steam engines of comparable horsepower) the higher initial costs are offset by the economic advantages of high fuel efficiency, low maintenance costs, and a high degree of availability of the diesel. While the average steamer requires extensive daily attention to its firebox and boiler, the diesel can run thousands of miles with only incidental maintenance. The diesel-electric transmits power to the wheels smoothly, without the reciprocating motion of the steam-engine drivers that subjects the track to heavy pounding. Like electric locomotives, the diesel can also reverse its motors to act as brakes on downgrades. Diesels are more flexible in usage, in that extra units can be added to the lead diesel unit, all the units being controlled by a single engine crew.

Many of the advantages of the diesel are also found in the electric locomotive. In addition, electric units are cleaner, because electric motors do not pollute the environment, and power is supplied from a large generating plant, which produces its power more efficiently and cleanly than individual diesel locomotives do. Electric locomotives are relatively simple in construction, have a low maintenance cost, and may have a longer economic life than diesel units. The major disadvantage of electrified service is the high original capital cost of the fixed plant of overhead wire, power substations, and other necessary equipment. Further, electric locomotives lack the flexibility of diesel power, because they can operate only where trolley wires are in place. Electric operation is generally economically profitable only in areas of large population or dense traffic. Such conditions prevail in several countries in Europe as well as in Japan.   JOHN F. STOVER

Bibliography: Alexander, Edwin P., *Iron Horse: American Locomotives, 1829–1900* (1941); Bruce, Alfred W., *The Steam Locomotive in America*

(1952); *Encyclopedia of Railroads* (1977); Morgan, Bryan, ed., *The Great Trains* (1973); Roberts, Arthur J., *The American Diesel Locomotive* (1976); Stover, John F., *The Life and Decline of the American Railroad* (1970); Tuplin, William A., *The Steam Locomotive* (1980); Weissenborn, Gustavus, *American Locomotive Engineering Illustrated* (1967); White, John H., Jr., *A History of the American Locomotive: Its Development, 1830–1880* (1980).

locoweed

Locoweed is the name given to a number of poisonous plants causing erratic behavior and sometimes death when eaten by livestock. Horses are the most susceptible. Commonly the name locoweed is applied to species of *Astragalus* in the pea family, Leguminosae; among the more toxic are the purple loco, *A. mollissimus*, and the western loco, *A. wootonii*. Another locoweed, *Oxytropis lambertii*, of the same family, is similar and is sometimes classified in *Astragalus*. The poison larkspur, *Delphinium glaucum*, and closely related species have a similar effect and are sometimes called locoweeds.

locust   (insect)

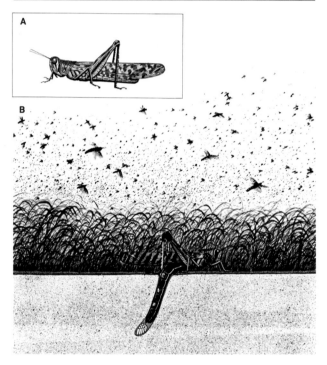

Locusts, superfamily Acridoidea, is the name given to a few species of grasshopper that migrate in huge swarms, ruining vegetation in the course of their flight. In its solitary phase (A), a locust is light colored and behaves like any other grasshopper. When an area is overpopulated with locusts or food is scarce, solitary locusts undergo a gregarious change (B); their skin turns dark and they swarm. A female is shown laying her eggs underground (bottom).

Locust is the common name for about nine GRASSHOPPER species in the short-horned grasshopper superfamily, Acridoidea. These species are distinguished from other grasshoppers by sometimes swarming and taking part in mass migrations, during which periods they change their habits and appearance. Because the swarms are difficult to control and can have a devastating effect on crops and vegetation, they are greatly feared. The species mentioned in the Old Testament is the desert locust, *Schistocerca gregaria,* family Catantopidae, which roams over central and north Africa, the Middle East, and India. Other *Schistocerca* species also swarm in these regions and in South America, while in North America the best-known swarming locust is *Melanoplus sanguinipes.* Swarms of *Locusta* and *Locustana* species, family Acrididae, occur from Europe through Africa and Asia and in New Zealand.

When populations of locusts are sparse in a region, the individuals live separate lives and migrate singly at night, like other grasshoppers. As their numbers increase, however, they respond to more frequent encounters with each other by becoming more and more gregarious, active, and conspicuous. They form mobs of "hoppers" (nymphs) and adults, which migrate by day in a uniquely itinerant mode of life, mating and reproducing as they travel. The swarming and nonswarming forms are known, respectively, as the gregarious and solitary phases. The solitary phase is always present, whereas the gregarious phase appears only sporadically and only in areas where food supplies and other factors vary markedly. Under sufficiently crowded conditions, a solitary hopper will mature into a gregarious adult, with longer wings, shorter legs, and other identifiable characteristics. As more and more of the gregarious types appear, characterized by their restless movement, migratory swarms build up. Once started, a locust plague may last for several years while generations of the swarms overrun regions in which the solitary phase cannot maintain itself. The swarms eventually die out and scatter, leaving only the solitary phase.

Other grasshoppers and the periodic CICADA are also sometimes referred to as locusts.   J. S. KENNEDY

Bibliography: Barrass, Robert, *The Locust* (1975); Brown, V. K., *Grasshoppers* (1983).

locust   (plant)

The various trees and shrubs of the genus *Robinia*, pea family, Leguminosae, are known as locusts. Native to North America, they bear pinnately compound leaves, fragrant flowers in drooping clusters, and small, flat seed pods. The most important tree species is the black locust, *R. pseudoacacia*, or false acacia, which is native to the eastern and central United States but has been naturalized in Europe and Asia. Its heavy and durable lumber is valued for fence posts, insulator pins, and railroad ties. Other species include the clammy locust, *R. viscosa*, and the New Mexican locust, *R. neomexicana*.

lodestone: see MAGNETITE.

Lodge   (family)

Several members of the Lodge family of New England have held prominent public office as Republicans and have played leading roles in American foreign affairs. **Henry Cabot Lodge**, b. Boston, May 12, 1850, d. Nov. 9, 1924, wrote several historical biographies before becoming a Republican representative from Massachusetts (1887–93). He championed civil service reform and helped write the SHERMAN ANTI-TRUST ACT (1890). Lodge subsequently served in the U.S. Senate (1893–1924), where he favored a strong navy and endorsed President Theodore Roosevelt's aggressive nationalism. As Senate majority leader (1918–24) and chairman of the Foreign Relations Committee (1918–24), he led the successful opposition to U.S. membership in the League of Nations in 1919. His grandson, **Henry Cabot Lodge, Jr.**, b. Nahant, Mass., July 5, 1902, d. Feb. 27, 1985, was also a Republican senator from Massachusetts (1937–44, 1947–53). He served as U.S. ambassador to the United Nations (1953–60) and was the unsuccessful Republican vice–presidential nominee in 1960. He was ambassador to South Vietnam (1963–64, 1965–67), ambassador-at-large (1967–68), and ambassador to West Germany (1968–69). He also led (1969) the American delegation to the Vietnam peace talks in Paris. His brother, **John Davis Lodge**, b. Washington, D.C., Oct. 20, 1903, d. Oct. 29, 1985, was a Republican representative from Connecticut (1947–51), governor of Connecticut (1951–55), and U.S. ambassador to Spain (1955–61), Argentina (1969–74), and Switzerland (1983–85).

Bibliography: Garraty, John A., *Henry Cabot Lodge* (1953); Hatch, Alden, *The Lodges of Massachusetts* (1973).

Lodge, Thomas

Thomas Lodge, b. *c.*1557, d. 1625, was an English poet, dramatist, and writer of prose romances. He received a degree from the University of Oxford in 1578 and went on to study law but abandoned it for a literary career. Sometime between 1584 and 1589, Lodge joined an expedition to the Canaries and the Azores. On the voyage he completed *Rosalynde*, a pastoral romance modeled on the style of his contemporary John Lyly; the work was later used by William Shakespeare as the main source of his play *As You Like It*. Lodge later studied medicine and became an eminent physician.

Bibliography: Rae, Wesley D., *Thomas Lodge* (1967).

Łódź   [looj]

Łódź, the capital of Łódź province and the second largest city in Poland, lies about 120 km (75 mi) southwest of Warsaw. The population is 848,500 (1983 est.). An important transportation and industrial center, Łódź is primarily known for its textiles. The city has several colleges and technical schools. Dating from the 14th century, Łódź was a small village until the 19th century, when it developed into an industrial city.

loess   [loh'-es]

Loess cliffs along the Yukon River in Canada are thick, unstratified deposits of yellow brown and uniformly fine-grained silt, sand, and clay. The sediments are believed to have been formed by windblown dust from dried-up beds of ice-age lakes and streams.

Loess (German for "loose") is a loose surface sediment commonly thought to have been formed by WIND ACTION during the ICE AGES of the PLEISTOCENE EPOCH; its origin, however, is still debated. Widespread deposits of loess 10 to 15 m (33 to 49 ft) thick are not uncommon; on the Loess Plateau of China, deposits 180 m (about 590 ft) thick have been reported. Loess usually lacks internal layering, but some deposits display multiple strata, perhaps indicating episodic emplacement. Its gray or yellowish color is caused by iron-oxide minerals. Loess contains silt-size grains (0.01–0.05 mm/0.004–0.0020 in), mostly of quartz but also smaller amounts of clay minerals, feldspar, mica, hornblende, and pyroxene. Carbonate minerals may amount to 40 percent but are not universally regarded as essential constituents. The silt in the deposits may have come from broad areas of barren till (see TILL AND TILLITE) and glacial outwash before they were stabilized by vegetation. Often highly porous, loess is always stable, holding near vertical walls in which birds of certain species dig their nests and some Chinese dig cave houses.

Major deposits of loess are found in North America, Eurasia, and Argentina. In North America, loess occurs in an area extending east from the Rocky Mountains to Pennsylva-

nia and south to the Mississippi Delta. In Europe, it occurs from the Atlantic coast to the Ural Mountains but most extensively in Eastern Europe. In Asia, loess covers large areas of northern China.

Loess deposits may indicate formerly dry, continental climates having moderate to strong prevailing winds; otherwise, they have no consistent paleoclimatic significance.

PAUL A. KAY

Bibliography: Smalley, I. J., ed., *Loess: Lithology and Genesis* (1975).

Loewe, Frederick: see LERNER, ALAN JAY, AND LOEWE, FREDERICK.

Loewy, Raymond   [loh'-ee]

Raymond Loewy, b. Nov. 5, 1893, d. July 14, 1986, was an engineer and industrial designer known for his promotion of the "streamlined look." Born in France, he emigrated to the United States after World War I and founded his own design firm in 1927. Loewy's first major success was the award-winning Coldspot refrigerator, commissioned by Sears Roebuck in 1935. He subsequently designed everything from automobiles, ocean liners, and locomotives to furniture, toothbrushes, and electric shavers, dramatically changing the appearance of the industrial products used by the American consumer.

Logan, James

James Logan, b. Oct. 20, 1674, d. Oct. 31, 1751, was an associate of William Penn, the founder of Pennsylvania, who brought him to America in 1699. He held a number of government posts in colonial Pennsylvania, including provincial secretary (1701–17), councilor (1702–47), mayor of Philadelphia (1722), and chief justice of the Pennsylvania Supreme Court (1731–39). A scholar and a bibliophile, Logan wrote extensively—especially on botany and mathematics; on his death, his 3,000-volume library greatly augmented the collections of the Library Company of Philadelphia, a subscription library that became an important cultural institution in that city.

LARRY R. GERLACH

Bibliography: Armistead, Wilson, ed., *The Memoirs of James Logan* (1851; repr. 1976); Tolles, Frederick B., *James Logan and the Culture of Provincial America* (1957; repr. 1978).

Logan, John

Captain John Logan, *c.*1725–80, also known as James Logan or as Tahgahjute, was a leader of the Mingo, bands of Iroquois-speaking Indians who lived near the headwaters of the Ohio River in western Pennsylvania. Born a CAYUGA on the Susquehanna River, Logan became a vigorous defender of whites after moving to the Ohio region. Embittered when his kin were slaughtered by colonists during the Yellow Creek Massacre of 1774, Logan, with the blessings of the British, made numerous retaliatory raids against American settlers. After his defeat (1774) at the Battle of Point Pleasant, Pa., he delivered an eloquent speech that was much admired at the time and later cited by Thomas Jefferson.

WILLIAM HERRICK

Logan, John Alexander

John Alexander Logan, b. Murphysboro, Ill., Feb. 9, 1826, d. Dec. 26, 1886, was an American politician and Union general in the Civil War. After studying law, he served in the Illinois legislature and in 1858 and 1860 was elected Democratic congressman from Illinois. In 1861 he resigned his House seat and entered the Union army as colonel of the 31st Illinois Infantry, which he organized. A good combat leader, Logan served at Fort Donelson (1862) and in the Vicksburg campaign (1862–63). By 1862 he was a general, and in 1864 he briefly commanded the Army of the Tennessee.

After the war, Logan returned to Illinois and reentered politics. He was elected to the U.S. Congress as a Republican, serving in the House (1867–71) and Senate (1871–77 and 1879–86). In 1884 he was the Republican candidate for vice-president. Logan was active in many veterans' groups; in 1868 he inaugurated the observance of Memorial Day to commemorate the Civil War dead. RICHARD M. MCMURRY

Bibliography: Jones, James P., *Black Jack: John A. Logan and Southern Illinois in the Civil War Era* (1967).

Logan, Mount

Mount Logan, the highest mountain in Canada and the second highest in North America (after Mount McKinley), is situated in the southwestern Yukon in the St. Elias Mountains. The tallest of its several peaks reaches an altitude of 6,050 m (19,850 ft). Mount Logan is difficult to climb because of glaciers; the central peak was first ascended in 1925 by A. H. MacCarthy and his Canadian-American team.

loganberry: see BLACKBERRY.

logarithm   [lawg'-uh-rithm]

A logarithm is an exponent. The exponential equation $y = b^x$ can be equivalently expressed by the logarithmic equation $\log_b y = x$, which can be read, "the logarithm to the base b of y is x." Because logarithms are exponents, logarithms satisfy the same properties as exponents:

1. $\log_b (xy) = \log_b x + \log_b y$
2. $\log_b (x/y) = \log_b x - \log_b y$
3. $\log_b x^y = y \log_b x$
4. $\log_b \sqrt[y]{x} = (1/y) \log_b x$

These properties of logarithms can be used to simplify computations that might otherwise be very long and cumbersome. They are particularly useful when carrying out computations involving very large or very small numbers.

Any positive number other than 1 can be used as a base for a logarithm. The bases used most often are base 10 (which is particularly useful in computing because the ordinary number system uses base 10) and base e ($e = 2.7182818284590 . . .$), which is often used in science and technology because it simplifies many calculations (see separate article on e). Logarithms to base 10 are called common logarithms, and logarithms to base e are called natural logarithms. When common logarithms are used, it is customary to dispense with any mention of the base. For example, log 100 = 2 means that the logarithm to the base 10, or common logarithm, of 100 is 2. In other words, $10^2 = 100$.

Each common logarithm has two parts, a characteristic and a mantissa. The characteristic is the number to the left of the decimal point in the logarithm and represents the greatest power of 10 that is less than the number whose logarithm is being found. For example, to find the common logarithm of 526 one must determine the highest power of 10 that is still less than 526. Because $10^2 = 100$ and $10^3 = 1,000$, and 526 is between 100 and 1,000, the logarithm of 526 must be between 2 and 3. Thus the characteristic of log 526 is 2. The characteristic of the common logarithm of a number can also be determined by counting the number of digits to the left of the first whole unit in that number. The mantissa of a logarithm is the part that follows (is to the right of) the decimal point. It is normally determined by referring to a MATHEMATICAL TABLE of logarithms.

The discovery of logarithms (c.1614) is attributed to John NAPIER of Scotland and Jobst Biirgi of Switzerland. Logarithmic tables were developed in the early 1600s by Henry BRIGGS of England and Adriaen Ulacq of the Netherlands and remained in use into the 20th century. Until recently, before the advent of electronic calculators, logarithms provided one of the few practical means of simplifying difficult numerical calculations. The use of logarithms reduces the calculations of 2.67^{10}, for example, from 10 steps to just 3 basic steps:

$$y = 2.67^{10}$$
$$\log y = \log 2.67^{10} = 10 \log 2.67 = 10 \times 0.42651 = 4.26510$$
$$y = 18,370$$

JOHN M. PETERSON

Bibliography: Swokowski, Earl, *Fundamentals of Algebra and Trigonometry*, 4th ed. (1978).

loggerhead turtle

The loggerhead turtle, C. caretta, *like other sea turtles, has large, oarlike flippers as forelimbs. It is primarily aquatic.*

The loggerhead turtle, *Caretta caretta,* in the family Cheloniidae, is the most common sea turtle in North American waters and appears to be less tropical than others in its family. Characteristically, it has a large head and a reddish brown upper shell, which has five or more large scales, or laminae, on each side of the midline. Two subspecies are recognized: the Atlantic loggerhead, *C. c. caretta,* found in the Atlantic Ocean from Nova Scotia and Scotland to Argentina and South Africa and in the Mediterranean Sea; and the Pacific loggerhead, *C. c. gigas,* found in the Pacific and Indian oceans from Japan and southern California to South Africa, Australia, and Chile. Loggerheads feed on marine organisms such as mollusks and crustaceans and also eat seaweed. They are the largest hard-shelled turtles and are second in size only to the leatherback. Records of specimens reaching 2.1 m (7 ft) long and 450 kg (1,000 lb) exist, but individuals of 140 kg (300 lb) are considered large. JONATHAN CAMPBELL

logging

Logging is the practice of harvesting trees and transporting logs from forest lands to wood-manufacturing facilities. Logs used for LUMBER are at least 20 cm (8 in) thick and 2.4 m (8 ft) long. Logs used to make veneers, called veneer bolts, must have fewer knots and other defects than lumber logs. Poles for use in power or telephone lines are typically longer and thinner than saw logs and veneer bolts. Pulpwood, timber logged for the manufacture of paper products, may be as small as 10 cm (4 in) in diameter.

Cutting is usually done with hand-held, power-driven chain saws. For timber less than 61 cm (24 in) in diameter at ground level, tree-felling machines with hydraulic shears instead of saws are often used. The branches of felled trees are trimmed off, and the logs may be cut into shorter lengths.

After the timber is felled and trimmed, large tractors move the logs to a loading area, in a process known as skidding. When the ground is impassable for tractors, large suspended metal cables may be used to drag or lift logs to the loading deck. Where soil and site disturbance must be minimized, balloons or helicopters have been used for skidding.

Although water transportation was once the principal means of moving harvested logs to a sawmill or factory, the method was slow and massive log jams often clogged waterways and damaged riverbanks. Today, U.S. trucks and railroads carry much of the log harvest. In the South, barge transport is sometimes used for pulpwood. ROBERT S. MANTHY

Bibliography: Conway, Steve, *Logging Practices,* rev. ed. (1982); Lucia, Ellis, *The Big Woods and Lumbering* (1979); MacKay, Donald, *The Lumberjacks* (1978); Wackerman, Albert E., et al., *Harvesting Timber Crops,* 2d ed. (1966); Williams, Richard L., *The Loggers* (1976).

See also: FORESTRY.

(Left) *A logger trims limbs from a felled tree using a motor-driven chain saw. Before lumber can be transported, limbs are removed and the trunk is cut into logs of a manageable size in a process known as bucking. Although it has traditionally been a manual operation, machines have recently been developed to fell the trees and then buck the logs.*

Hundreds of logs are stored in a holding pond prior to being drawn into the mill along conveyor belts. In addition to making the heavy logs easier to handle, the water prevents them from drying and splitting and protects against damage from insects, fungi, or fire.

logic

Logic is the systematic study of reasoning that provides standards by which valid reasoning can be recognized. It clarifies the reasoning process and provides a means for analyzing the consistency of basic concepts. Logic has played an important role in the history of PHILOSOPHY.

TRADITIONAL LOGIC

The history of Western logic can be traced to ancient Greece. Logic had developed independently in China and India but apparently had little influence in the West. ARISTOTLE is usually considered the first major Western logician, although earlier contributions to logic were made by PLATO, SOCRATES, ZENO OF ELEA, and others. Aristotle's logical system treated the categorical SYLLOGISM and the laws of logic. His many books on logic became the basis for its study up to the 19th century. The next school of logicians, the Megarians, flourished in the 4th century BC. Rather than study categorical inferences, they sought to define the conditions under which a conditional, "if A, then B," is true. The Stoics, especially one of their leaders, Chrysippus, took over and developed the logical ideas of the Megarians (see STOICISM). Aristotle had set forth a logic of terms; Chrysippus worked out a logic of propositions. Stoic thinkers after Chrysippus apparently did not contribute further to the development of logic. Other late Greek and Roman logicians mainly codified the work of their predecessors, although Galen (AD 129–199) added some theories about special kinds of syllogisms.

The logic of the Greeks endured in the Middle East after the fall of Rome and the conquest of western Europe by the barbarian tribes. In the Middle Ages logic was again brought to the attention of the Western world by logicians of the Islamic empire, mainly those working in Baghdad and southern Spain. Many of Aristotle's writings as well as commentaries preserved by heretical Christian sects were available to these logicians. Al-Farabi (870–950), one of the greatest Muslim logicians, wrote commentaries on most of Aristotle's logical works. Other logicians translated other Greek works on logic into Arabic. (From Arabic they were usually translated by Jewish scholars into Hebrew, and then from Hebrew into Latin; in this way these texts became available to scholars in Christian Europe.) The great Muslim philosopher AVICENNA made logic independent of the teachings of Aristotle and the Stoics. By the 14th century, intellectuals were reading handbooks on logic by various Muslim scholars, instead of the classics.

Meanwhile, the logical materials that were being studied in the Islamic empire became known in Christian Europe. The Christians had previously had only a few of Aristotle's works and a few commentaries. The first significant logician of the Christian Middle Ages, Peter ABELARD, wrote before most of the Aristotelian materials became available but developed detailed and critical evaluations of the material that had been preserved in the West. The rest of Aristotle's logical writings became available by about 1200, resulting in the emergence of the *logica moderna,* a "new logic" taught mainly in the arts faculties of the universities rather than in the theological schools. Perhaps the greatest of the modern logicians was WILLIAM OF OCCAM, who wrote the *Summa Logicae* (1326?). Other logicians restructured the domain of logic so that the Aristotelian heritage was incorporated into a broader logic.

As the renaissance began, so did an attack on medieval (Scholastic) thought and on the Aristotelian theories that provided its basis. The major Renaissance opponent of Aristotelian logic was the 16th-century French Protestant thinker Petrus RAMUS, who is supposed to have debated "that every proposition in Aristotle is false." Ramus attacked nearly all of Aristotle's logical doctrines and proposed instead that there be a logic of invention or discovery and a logic of judgment.

With the rejection of Aristotle's metaphysics by the great 17th-century thinkers Francis Bacon, René Descartes, Baruch Spinoza, and John Locke, a search began for a new logic that would fit with a new picture of reality. Gottfried Wilhelm von Leibniz made major contributions to this new logic, although most of his logical work did not become generally available until the end of the 19th century. Leibniz tried to work out a universal logical language, and he also developed a logical calculus. He was apparently not ready to reject Aristotelian logic, but his examinations of other possibilities when discovered at the end of the 19th century nevertheless aided in the development of modern logic.

RICHARD H. POPKIN

MATHEMATICAL LOGIC

Logic is the theory of argument and reasoning. Mathematical logic is that branch of logic which uses exacting formal methods to achieve precision and objectivity in explaining what it is to be logical in argument and reasoning. It concentrates on the explanation and development of proof and on the nature of formal systems used in constructing proofs. Although its greatest successes have been in application to mathematics and computers, its generality makes it potentially applicable to virtually any field. Different branches of mathematical logic treat different types of questions. Alethic modal logics have been applied to such diverse questions as the nature of God and the structure of scientific laws; deontic logics, to normative systems of legal and moral behavior.

Mathematical logic developed from the desire to provide systematic foundations for the practice of mathematics, explaining the nature of numbers and the laws of arithmetic and replacing intuition with rigorous proof. Noteworthy among its founders is the Italian mathematician Giuseppe Peano (1858–1932), but the German mathematical philosopher Gottlob Frege (1848–1925) is considered the father of mathematical logic. Their early work was advanced by Bertrand Russell and Alfred North Whitehead in *Principia Mathematica* (3 vols., 1910–13), and by many others, including Alonzo Church, Kurt Gödel, David Hilbert, Emil Post, and Alfred Tarski. Among important precursors of modern logic were Aristotle, George Boole, Augustus De Morgan, Gottfried Wilhelm von Leibniz, Charles Sanders Peirce, and Ernst Schröder.

Valid argument is basic to mathematical logic. An argument is composed of a *conclusion*, which is argued for, and *premises*, which are the reasons for the conclusion. In a valid argument the conclusion follows from the premises: the argument is of such a form that no argument having that form can have true premises and a false conclusion. Thus, the following argument is valid, and its corresponding form exemplifies a logical way of thinking.

Argument I	Form I
No one putting profits first is putting human rights first	No *F* is *G*
This person is putting profits first	This *H* is *F*
Therefore:	Therefore:
This person is not putting human rights first	This *H* is not *G*

In contrast, the following argument and corresponding form are invalid, as is shown by the counterexample.

Argument II	Form II	Counter-example II
All communists are dissenters	All *F* are *G*	All tigers are cats
All communists are subversives	All *F* are *H*	All tigers are striped
Therefore:	Therefore:	Therefore:
All dissenters are subversive	All *G* are *H*	All cats are striped

Counterexample II shows Form II to constitute an illogical way of thinking, in which truth can lead to falsehood. Arguments I and II are deductive: certainty of the premises would be intended to make the conclusion certain (see DEDUCTION). In contrast, inductive arguments seek probability rather than certainty (see INDUCTION). Some theorists posit other kinds of arguments: Peirce, the abductive; Aristotle, the practical. The nature and significance of nondeductive arguments remains to be fully investigated.

Alternative deductive logics are produced by changes in the conception of validity. The best-known such school is intuitionist logic, founded by the Dutch mathematician L. E. J. Brouwer (1881). Many-valued logics, which reject the assumption, questioned since the time of Aristotle, that there are only two values—truth and falsehood—have been rigorously developed, beginning with the work of the Polish logician Jan Łukasiewicz in the 1920s.

Mathematical logic achieves precision, clarity, and manipulability through the use of artificial languages (see LANGUAGES, ARTIFICIAL), symbol systems deliberately constructed for use in logic. Sentences of such a system may represent sentences of natural languages like English, directly representing logical words such as *no* or *all* and suppressing structures considered irrelevant. To represent "All communists are dissenters," one abbreviates to "All *C* are *D*," which corresponds to its representation "*(x) (Cx ⊃ Dx)*" via the paraphrase "For any one whatsoever, if that one is *C*, then that one is *D*." The universal quantifier "*(x)*" corresponds to "for any one whatsoever," the conditional "(. . . ⊃ . . .)" to "if . . ., then . . .," and the variable *x* to "that one" having "for any one whatsoever" as

grammatical antecedent. With *m* and *n* for names like *Carter* or *Brezhnev*, instances of the universally quantified sentence are "*(Cm ⊃ Dm)*" and "*(Cn ⊃ Dn)*." Negatives, as in "*n* is not *C*," may be represented as "*~Cn*." Formation rules, analogous to grammatical rules in natural languages, explain the forms of the sentences. Transformation rules (or rules of proof or of inference) state which forms may be validly concluded from others. Universal instantiation (UI) allows an instance of a universally quantified sentence to be concluded from the sentence. Modus ponens (MP), with "*A*" and "*B*" standing for full sentences, allows "*B*" to be concluded from premises "*A*" and "*(A⊃B)*." Proofs string together valid arguments in accordance with such formal rules. Thus "*Dn*" may be proved from "*Cn*" and "*(x) (Cx ⊃ Dx)*" by applying UI to the second to obtain "*(Cn⊃Dn)*," and then applying MP to that and "*Cn*" to obtain "*Dn*." In this way, formal methods free proofs of appeals to intuition and make assumptions explicit and open to debate.

Formation and transformation rules deal only with form and so are purely syntactic. SEMANTICS relates forms to the world via rules of valuation, which determine how logical operators like quantifiers and conditionals affect truth and falsehood and thus how form affects content. A rule of valuation states that the truth value of an atomic sentence like "*Dn*" is determined by whether the predicate "*D*" truly applies to the thing referred to by the name *n*; the sentence is true if the predicate applies, and otherwise false. Another rule for conditionals states that a conditional is false in case its left constituent (such as "*Cn*") is true and its right constituent (such as "*Dn*") is false; in any other case the conditional is true. Another rule handles the universal quantifier, and so on. These rules explain how complex sentences may be understood on the basis of simpler ones and bring out the conditions required for the proper application of the formal system to a given subject matter. They also make it possible to study the logical properties of the system.

Because validity is the formal impossibility of true premises and false conclusion, the semantics yields an explanation of validity independent of the transformation rules. The consistency (validity of the rules) and completeness (capacity to prove all valid arguments that are expressible) may thus be studied in a metalogic (logical theory of a logical system). These and other systemic properties have been brilliantly as well as successfully investigated by Hilbert, Post, Tarski, Church, Gödel, Leopold Löwenheim, Thoraf Skolem, and other philosophers.

Relational logic treats many-place predicates, which have more than one place for a name or variable, unlike "*C*" and "*D*" above. Examples are "*x* is between *y* and *z*," "*x* has a greater volume than *y*," and "*x* spoke to *y*." The inclusion of relational predicates greatly increases the scope of the system, far surpassing the traditional syllogism of Aristotle. A special relation is identity, expressing the idea that something is one and the same thing as something. This concept is essential to expressing the concept of another—one thing different from the first—and is thus essential to counting.

SET THEORY, or the theory of classes, is often considered a step beyond elementary logic. It adds a relation of class membership to the basis already described. "*m* ε the class of presidents" would say that Carter is a member of the class of presidents. Such a class is an abstract grouping independent of physical proximity. With the relation of class membership and systemic expressions for referring to classes, all the basic concepts of arithmetic have been explained, including the kinds of numbers and arithmetic operations in general, without appeal to any undefined arithmetic concept. Such an explanation was what Russell and Whitehead first accomplished, based on Frege's work.

Modal logics deal with necessity and possibility, or "must" and "can." They have recently been given a rigorous semantics that has stimulated discussion of their application to such concepts as essential natures (METAPHYSICS); laws of nature (philosophy of science; see SCIENCE, PHILOSOPHY OF); what *would* be true if something that is not true *were* to be true (subjunctive conditionals); what ought to be done (ETHICS);

what was or will be true (time and tense); and what is known (EPISTEMOLOGY). The assumptions involved in such application are, however, deeply controversial.

Pragmatics goes beyond syntax and semantics in relating the interpreted forms to the language users in contexts of use. Such rules would specify the conditions of appropriate use and are especially important in regard to the theory of natural languages in the field of linguistics. This kind of investigation is still in its infancy.   JACK CUMBEE

Bibliography: Bochenski, Innocenty, *A History of Formal Logic,* 2d ed. (1970); Copi, Irving M., *Symbolic Logic,* 5th ed. (1979); Lemmon, Edward J., *Beginning Logic,* rev. ed. (1978); Prior, Arthur N., *Formal Logic* (1962); Stolyar, A. A., *Introduction to Elementary Mathematical Logic* (1983).

logical positivism

Logical positivism is a 20th-century philosophical movement in the tradition of ANALYTIC AND LINGUISTIC PHILOSOPHY. Like earlier forms of POSITIVISM, it had close ties to British EMPIRICISM and was marked by respect for natural science and hostility to metaphysical speculation.

The movement originated with a group of German and Austrian philosophers known as the Vienna Circle. At first just a discussion group, the Vienna Circle later became a more formal organization, publishing its own philosophical journal. Organized by Moritz Schlick (1882–1936), who came to the University of Vienna as professor of philosophy in 1922, it also included Herbert Feigl, Kurt GÖDEL, Hans Hahn, Friedrich Waismann, and, after 1926, Rudolf CARNAP.

The Circle was decisively influenced by Ludwig WITTGENSTEIN, though he was never really a member of it. In his *Tractatus Logico-Philosophicus* (1921), Wittgenstein put forward a general theory of linguistic representation, according to which propositions are "logical pictures" of possible facts. This implied that a proposition is not meaningful unless it determines a precise range of circumstances in which it is true. A partial exception was made for tautologies (such as "Either it is raining or it is not raining") and contradictions (such as "It is raining and it is not raining"). Such propositions say nothing, since they are, respectively, true or false no matter what; they show, however, the workings of the "logical constants," "not," "or," "and," and so forth. In metaphysics, however, philosophers have often tried to say something about reality as a whole, making claims supposedly so general and fundamental as to be indifferent to the particular facts of the world. On Wittgenstein's theory of language, such claims are literally nonsensical, words without meaning.

The logical positivists used this argument for the meaninglessness of metaphysical propositions but interpreted it in a way that Wittgenstein almost certainly did not intend. Wittgenstein had distinguished in an abstract way between elementary and complex propositions. The positivists took his elementary propositions to be reports of observations. This was the origin of their central idea, the verification principle, which said that any meaningful proposition, other than the tautological or, as they came to be called, "analytic" propositions of logic and pure mathematics, had to be verifiable by means of observation. Propositions belonging to traditional metaphysics—such as those about the existence of God, for example—were deemed not to meet this condition and were declared meaningless. Metaphysical statements were not the only ones to fail the test. Ordinary moral judgments seemed to fail it too. One way this was dealt with was by saying that such judgments were expressions of emotion, rather than genuine propositions.

With the elimination of metaphysics, the business of philosophy was seen as the logical clarification of scientific statements and theories: for example, putting informally stated theories in strict axiomatic form, so as to distinguish clearly their analytic from their empirical elements.

Nevertheless, a good deal of controversy centered on the interpretation of the principles of logical positivism itself. One problem concerned observation statements: were they about an individual's private perceptual experiences, as Schlick thought, or publicly accessible events? Another concerned the verification of scientific laws that, because they apply to a potentially infinite number of instances, cannot be verified with absolute conclusiveness. Eventually, the original strong notion of verification gave way to a weaker notion of confirmation. Attempts to make this notion precise by constructing a formal inductive logic met with only limited success, however. In general, the more the verification principle was qualified, the harder it became to distinguish logical positivism from other forms of logical empiricism.

With the advent of nazism, most members of the Vienna Circle chose exile, many settling in the United States. This marked the end of logical positivism as an organized movement. In England it had found an able spokesman in the young Alfred Jules Ayer, whose *Language, Truth and Logic* (1936) is a classic statement of the positivist outlook. Logical positivism's subsequent influence, however, was stronger in the United States. In contemporary philosophy, especially in the United States, the spirit of logical positivism can be seen in the respect for science, distrust of highflown jargon (or what is thought to be such), and insistence on clarity and rigorous argument. Its specific theoretical ideas are no longer accepted in their original form.   MICHAEL WILLIAMS

Bibliography: Ayer, A. J., *Language, Truth and Logic,* 2d ed. (1946; repr. 1966), and, as ed., *Logical Positivism* (1959; repr. 1978); Schilpp, Paul A., ed., *The Philosophy of Rudolf Carnap* (1963).

LOGO

LOGO is an instructional COMPUTER LANGUAGE developed in the 1970s by Seymour Papert of the Massachusetts Institute of Technology. Aimed at young learners, LOGO involves the recognition and uses of colors, shapes, directions, letters, words, and sounds. LOGO teaches concepts such as planning, problem solving, and experimentation, and it introduces children to computer use. In practice, LOGO involves the manipulation of "sprites" and "turtles," forms that can be moved around the computer screen to draw or erase lines.

logos

The word *logos* (from the root of the Greek verb *lego,* "to say") figures prominently in a number of Greek and Christian philosophical doctrines. Although the word's earliest meaning probably was "connected discourse," by the classical period it already had a wide variety of other meanings: "argument," "rational principle," "reason," "proportion," "measure," and others. For this reason, it is difficult to interpret the logos doctrines of philosophers and dangerous to assume a single history for these doctrines.

HERACLITUS was the earliest Greek thinker to make logos a central concept. He urges that attention be paid to the logos, which "governs all things" and yet is also something people "encounter every day." One should probably emphasize the linguistic connections of logos when interpreting Heraclitus' thought. In efforts to understand the world, one should look to language and the order embodied in it, rather than to scientific or religious views that neglect this.

In the 3d century BC the proponents of STOICISM borrowed the idea of logos from Heraclitus (neither Plato nor Aristotle had given the term prominence) and used it for the immanent ordering principle of the universe—represented, at the level of language, by humankind's ordered discourse. Nature and logos are often treated as one and the same, but logos is nature's overall rational structure, and not all natural creatures have logos, or reason, within them. Humans are urged to "live consistently with logos."

In the New Testament, the Gospel According to Saint JOHN gives a central place to logos; the biblical author describes the Logos as God, the Creative Word, who took on flesh in the man Jesus Christ. Many have traced John's conception to Greek origins—perhaps through the intermediacy of eclectic texts like the writings of PHILO OF ALEXANDRIA. More recently, however, scholars have emphasized that the Old Testament contains a doctrine of the Word of God, and in Aramaic paraphrases the "Word of God" takes on some of the functions of God. Later Christian thinkers clearly did incorporate the Stoic logos doctrine; logos was associated particularly with Christ and later, in ARIANISM, no longer identified with God.

MARTHA C. NUSSBAUM

Bibliography: Ong, W. J., *Presence of the Word* (1967).

logwood

Logwood is a DYE extracted from the heavy red heartwood of the logwood tree (*Haematoxylum campechianum*), which is native to Mexico and Central America and is cultivated in the West Indies. The dye, which is extracted by boiling logwood chips in water, produces colors ranging from dark purple and black to blues and violets, on wool, cotton, and silk fabrics.

Loire River   [lwar]

The Loire River, with a total length of 1,006 km (625 mi), making it the longest river in France, rises on Mont Gerbier de Jonc in the MASSIF CENTRAL. Initially, it flows north toward the Paris Basin, but at ORLÉANS it arcs toward the west, passing Blois, TOURS, and NANTES before flowing through a 56-km (35-mi) estuary to the Atlantic Ocean at Saint Nazaire on the Bay of BISCAY. Its tributaries include the Maine, Vienne, Cher, Allier, and Indre rivers, and its drainage area is 116,550 km^2 (45,000 mi^2), more than a fifth of France.

The Loire has an irregular flow and is subject to sudden floods. Much of the river is lined by levees. Formerly, commercial navigation along the Loire and the canals that connect it with the Rhône and Seine river systems was very important. Today, however, the valley of the Loire is famous for its chateaus, especially those of CHAMBORD, CHENONCEAUX, Amboise, Azay-le-Rideau, and Chinon.

Bibliography: Dunlop, Ian, *Chateaux of the Loire* (1969).

Loisy, Alfred Firmin   [lwah-zee']

Alfred Firmin Loisy, b. Feb. 28, 1857, d. June 1, 1940, was a French Roman Catholic modernist theologian and a biblical scholar. In 1881 he became professor of Hebrew at the Institute Catholique. Dismissed 12 years later and accused of heresy during a controversy over the inerrancy of the Bible, he began a long struggle with the church. Loisy became a leader of the MODERNISM movement, which applied the tools of scientific and historical criticism to the Bible. In 1903 five of his books were placed on the Index of Forbidden Books; later the body of his work was condemned by the Holy See. In 1908 he was excommunicated. Having given up the Christian faith, Loisy taught the history of religions at the Collège de France (1909–27) and wrote extensively on the problems of religion in general.

JOHN BOOTY

Bibliography: Ratté, John, *Three Modernists: Alfred Loisy, George Tyrrell and William L. Sullivan* (1968); Vidler, Alec, *A Variety of Catholic Modernists* (1970).

Loki   [loh'-kee]

In Norse mythology Loki was the spirit of fire, strife, and envy. The son of a giant, he lived among the gods at ASGARD, where he continually caused them trouble but aided them with his cunning. After he contrived the death of BALDER, however, the gods chained him to a rock below a serpent whose mouth dripped venom. Loki was to remain bound until the final battle of RAGNAROK, in which he would lead the forces of evil against the gods.

Lollards   [lahl-urdz]

The Lollards, followers of the English religious reformer John WYCLIFFE, were members of a widespread Christian movement of the late 14th and early 15th centuries that was highly critical of the power and wealth of the church. The Lollards were led by Wycliffe's "poor priests," who used an English translation of the Bible and preached a nonsacramental Christianity that minimized clerical authority and emphasized poverty, ethical purity, and devotional intensity. The movement spread rapidly during the decade following Wycliffe's death (1384), enjoying the support of Oxford scholars, powerful nobles and country gentlemen, wealthy merchants, and masses of common people. Its preachers based their teachings on personal faith, divine election, and on the Bible. They taught that the commonly held doctrines of transubstantiation (see EUCHARIST), INDULGENCES, and hierarchical church organization were unscriptural.

After the usurpation of the English throne by HENRY IV in 1399, the Lollards were subject to increasing persecution. Despite strong Lollard resistance in the House of Commons, the statute *De haeretico comburendo* (On the Burning of the Heretic) was passed by Parliament in 1401. Martyrdoms followed as more organized repression developed. HENRY V, determined to break the support of Lollardism by rural aristocrats, brought his friend, the popular Sir John Oldcastle (*c.*1378–1417), to trial and, finally, to the stake. Meanwhile, the Council of Constance (1414–18; see CONSTANCE, COUNCIL OF) officially condemned Wycliffe, and the Lollards were driven underground, where they survived to make a formative impact on the English REFORMATION. The PIERS PLOWMAN poems classically represent the Lollard spirit.

JAMES D. NELSON

Bibliography: Carrick, John Charles, *Wycliffe and the Lollards* (1908); McFarlane, K. B., *John Wycliffe and the Beginning of English Nonconformity* (1952) and *Lancastrian Kings and Lollard Knights* (1972); Thomson, J. A. F., *The Later Lollards,* (1965).

Lomax   (family)   [loh'-maks]

The field of American folk-song study is founded in the work of **John Avery Lomax**, b. Goodman, Miss., Sept. 23, 1875, d. Jan. 26, 1948, and his son, **Alan Lomax**, b. Austin, Tex., Jan. 31, 1915. John was an English professor and banker who studied folklore as an avocation. In the early 1900s, equipped with an Ediphone cylinder recording machine, he traveled the backroads of the Southwest, collecting songs that had never appeared in print before the publication of his book, *Cowboy Songs and Other Frontier Ballads* (1910). In 1933, with his son, Alan, and with a recorder built into the back of his car, Lomax traveled the South and West again. The results were published as *American Ballads and Folk Songs* (1934). The materials were given to the newly formed Archive of American Folksong of the Library of Congress, and Lomax was made honorary curator—a post later filled by Alan, who continues to collect and record both in America and in Europe.

Bibliography: Lomax, John, *Adventures of a Ballad Hunter* (1947; repr. 1971); Lomax, John and Alan, *Folk Song U.S.A.* (1947) and *Our Singing Country* (1939).

Lombardi, Vince   [lahm-bard'-ee, vins]

Vincent Thomas Lombardi, b. Brooklyn, N.Y., June 11, 1913, d. Sept. 3, 1970, was an American football coach who, as head coach of the Green Bay Packers of the National Football League (NFL) from 1959 to 1967, won 89 games, lost 29, and tied 4. His success paralleled the growth of professional football in the United States, and his disciplined approach to

Vince Lombardi, himself an outstanding football player at Fordham University, compiled an enviable record of success as a coach of high school, collegiate, and professional football teams. During a nine-year span, Lombardi guided the Green Bay Packers to five NFL championships through his authoritarian coaching methods, developed to motivate athletes to perform to the height of their abilities.

football fundamentals became the standard training method used by contemporary coaches. The Packers, while coached by Lombardi, won five National Football League titles (1961, 1962, 1965–67) and the first two Super Bowls (1967, 1968). Lombardi got his football start at St. Francis Prep School and then played as a lineman on Fordham University's famed "Seven Blocks of Granite" team in the mid-1930s. He coached high school football in New Jersey until he was 35 years old, then served as an assistant coach at Fordham University and the United States Military Academy and as offensive coach for the professional New York Giants before joining the Packers in 1959. In 1968 he resigned as coach of the Packers but remained for another year as general manager. He also coached (1969) the Washington Redskins to their first winning season in 14 years as the team posted a 7–5–2 record during the fall before he died. In 1971, Lombardi was inducted into the Pro Football Hall of Fame.   JIM BENAGH

Bibliography: Dowling, Tom, *Coach: A Season with Lombardi* (1970); Flynn, George L., ed., *Vince Lombardi on Football* (1981); Lombardi, Vince, and Heinz, W. C., *Run To Daylight* (1967).

Lombardo   (family)   [lohm-bar'-doh]

The name Lombardo was given to a family of sculptors and architects from Lombardy, Northern Italy, who worked in Venice during the 15th and 16th centuries. Their proper surname may have been Solari. **Martino,** an architect, was the first of the family to settle in Venice, and his son, **Pietro** (*c*.1435–1515), was one of the most important sculptors working in Venice in the 15th century. His sculpture was based on antique models and was quite conservative, as was much Venetian art at that time, but he prepared the way for the Venetian Renaissance sculpture of the 16th century. As an architect, he supervised work on the Doge's Palace after 1498 and is also thought to have designed the Vendramin Palace on the Grand Canal (*c*.1500–*c*.1509). Pietro's sons **Tullio** (*c*.1460–1532) and **Antonio** (*c*.1458–*c*.1516) worked with him and dominated the family sculpture workshop after 1500. Tullio's head of a warrior from the Vendramin monument (1492–95; Santi Giovanni e Paolo) clearly shows his adherence to the realistic sculpture style of ancient Rome. Three of Antonio's sons, **Aurelio** (1501–63), **Girolamo** (*c*.1504–*c*.1590), and **Lodovico** (*c*.1507–1575), were also sculptors.   ROWLAND ELZEA

Bibliography: Seymour, Charles, *Sculpture in Italy, 1400–1500* (1966).

Lombards   [lahm'-bardz]

The Lombards, a Germanic people, were first mentioned by classical writers in the 1st century AD. They are thought to have fought against the Romans as early as AD 6. In the 4th century they moved southeastward from their home on the lower Elbe River. By the 6th century the Lombards had converted to Arian Christianity (see ARIANISM), and about 547 the emperor JUSTINIAN I gave them land in Pannonia and Noricum (modern Hungary and eastern Austria) for attacking the Gepids, another Germanic tribe that was destroyed in 567.

In 568 the Lombards, under King Alboin, invaded Italy, and by 572 they held the north as well as Spoleto and Benevento to the south. Shortly after this conquest the Lombard monarchy ceased to exist (574), and the Lombard territories were divided among various dukes, who ruled until 584, when the monarchy was restored under King Authari. During the 7th and much of the 8th century the Lombards strengthened their hold on Italy and fought off the Franks, the Byzantines, and several coalitions raised against them by the popes. The kingdom reached its zenith under Liutprand (r. 712–44), who accepted Roman Christianity and made notable changes in the law and administration to consolidate his rule.

In 754–56, Pope Stephen II allied with the Frankish king PEPIN THE SHORT, who forced the Lombards to return a considerable amount of territory—the so-called Donation of Pepin—to the papacy. In 773–74 the Lombard king Desiderius (r. 756–74) was defeated by CHARLEMAGNE, and the kingship passed to the Frankish monarch.   BERNARD S. BACHRACH

Bibliography: Hallenbeck, J. T., *Pavia and Rome* (1982); Hodgkin, Thomas, *Italy and Her Invaders*, vols. 5, 6 (1885; repr. 1967).

Lombardy   [lahm'-bar-dee]

Lombardy (Italian: Lombardia), an Italian region that borders on Switzerland in the north, is the country's chief commercial and industrial region. With an area of 23,834 km² (9,202 mi²) and 8,891,318 inhabitants (1984 est.), it is Italy's most populous region—16% of the total Italian population live in Lombardy, although it comprises only about 8% of the land area. The capital is MILAN, and other major cities and provincial capitals are BERGAMO, BRESCIA, COMO, CREMONA, PAVIA, Mantua, Sondrio, and Varese. Lombardy's manufactures include iron and steel, automobiles, machinery, textiles, and furniture. Grain is an important product in the southern agricultural region. The Alpine lakes COMO, GARDA, and MAGGIORE are well-known tourist attractions.

After the 3d century BC, Lombardy formed part of the Roman Empire. From 568 to 774 it was the center of the kingdom of the Lombards, a Germanic people, and in the 8th century it was conquered by the Franks. Free city-states, first established in the 11th century, formed the Lombard League in 1167 and subsequently defeated Holy Roman Emperor FREDERICK I. Lombardy was ruled by Spain (1535–1700), Austria (1714–97), France (1797–1814), and again by Austria (1814–59).   DANIEL R. LESNICK

Lombroso, Cesare   [lohm-broh'-soh, chay'-say-ray]

An Italian professor of psychiatry and anthropology, Cesare Lombroso, b. Nov. 6, 1835, d. Oct. 9, 1909, started the scientific discipline of criminology (see CRIME). Lombroso believed in an inherited disposition to criminal behavior, evidenced in recognizable physical characteristics. Such ideas have since been rejected.

Bibliography: Mannheim, Hermann, ed., *Pioneers in Criminology*, 2d ed. (1972).

Lomé   [loh-may']

Lomé is the capital and primary city of Togo. Located on the Gulf of Guinea in western Africa, Lomé has a population of 366,476 (1983 est.). The city's excellent deep-water harbor is used for the export of raw cotton, cocoa, coffee, copra, palm nuts, and phosphates. The University of Benin (1965) is located there. As the capital of German Togoland (1897–1914), Lomé quickly became a prosperous colonial capital with an elaborate rail and road system. Lomé remained the capital while under Anglo-French rule (1914–22) and French rule (1922–60) and after Togo achieved independence in 1960.

Loménie de Brienne, Étienne Charles de
[loh-may-nee' duh bree-en', ay-tyen' sharl]

In the months immediately preceding the French Revolution the government of Louis XVI was headed by the French churchman Étienne Charles de Loménie de Brienne, b. Oct. 9, 1727, d. Feb. 19, 1794. As archbishop of Toulouse (1763–88), Loménie de Brienne gained a reputation as an aristocratic, freethinking supporter of Enlightenment ideas. In 1787 he was named to the Assembly of Notables, a body summoned by the king at the urging of finance minister Charles Alexandre de CALONNE for the purpose of reforming France's tax policy—a reform that meant in effect taxing the nobility and clergy. Loménie de Brienne led the opposition to Calonne's reforms, forcing him out of office. Louis XVI then appointed Loménie de Brienne as "principal minister" to replace Calonne. Loménie de Brienne's efforts at fiscal reform caused such an uproar in the Paris PARLEMENT that the king was forced to convoke the STATES-GENERAL. That body quickly became radicalized, and its actions led to revolution. Loménie de Brienne was dismissed from office in 1788. The same year he was created a cardinal, but he was later deprived of that office after taking an oath to the 1790 Civil Constitution of the Clergy. He died in prison.   A. LLOYD MOOTE

Bibliography: Egret, Jean, *The French Prerevolution, 1787–88*, trans. by Wesley D. Camp (1977).

Lomonosov, Mikhail Vasilevich [luh-muh-naw'-suhf]

The Russian scientist and man of letters Mikhail Vasilevich Lomonosov, b. Nov. 19 (N.S.), 1711, d. Apr. 15 (N.S.), 1765, was the son of a prosperous fisherman. His outstanding abilities won him a scholarship to study (1736–41) at the German university of Marburg, where he began to write lyric poetry. After his return to Saint Petersburg Lomonosov was appointed (1745) professor of chemistry at the university and in 1757 he became a councillor of Moscow University, which he had helped to found. Lomonosov made numerous discoveries in chemistry and physics and is equally well known for studies of Russian grammar that simplified the language of his time into a suitable vehicle for literary expression.

Lomonosov Ridge

Lomonosov Ridge is the major topographic feature of the Arctic Ocean basin. Extending for 1,800 km (1,100 mi) between the New Siberian Islands and Ellesmere Island, Canada, it separates the Arctic Ocean floor into the Canadian and the Eurasian basins. The ridge is about 3 km (2 mi) high. Its rather flat summit, lying at water depths of between 1,000 and 1,600 m (3,300 and 5,300 ft), appears to have been planed off by wave erosion during a period when sea level was much lower. The ridge displays neither seismic activity nor unusual magnetic anomalies, so it is not a mid-oceanic ridge. It appears instead to be a fragment that was formerly part of the Siberian continental shelf. The Lomonosov Ridge was discovered by Soviet scientists, who set up stations on drifting ice islands in the 1950s. ROBERT S. DIETZ

Lon Nol [lahn nohl]

The Cambodian military and political leader Lon Nol, b. Nov. 13, 1913, d. Nov. 17, 1985, was ousted as president of the Khmer Republic (now Kampuchea) by Communist forces in 1975. He served as a provincial governor and army district commander before becoming chief of general staff and minister of national defense, posts he held from 1955 to 1966. He became commander in chief (1960), deputy prime minister (1963), and then prime minister (1966–67, 1969–72). In 1970 pro-Western Cambodian officers led by Lon Nol overthrew Prince NORODOM SIHANOUK and proclaimed the Khmer Republic. In 1972, Lon Nol became president of the Khmer Republic and suspended the constitution. His attempts to eliminate Communist influence in Cambodia with the aid of the United States led to civil war. In May 1975 the Communist KHMER ROUGE defeated Lon Nol's forces and captured the capital city of Phnom Penh. Lon Nol went into exile in Hawaii.

London (England)

London is the capital and largest city of the United Kingdom. The city (coterminous with the county of Greater London) covers 1,580 km² (610 mi²) and has a population of 6,756,000 (1984 est.). The first settlement, the Roman Londinium, was founded in AD 43 on a terrace near the north bank of the River Thames, 64 km (40 mi) from its estuary on the North Sea. The river is tidal, and London has been a port for seagoing vessels since the Roman period. London's size and population mirror the city's economic importance; it is one of the world's leading financial and insurance centers, as well as an important industrial city.

London's climate is one of mild winters, with an average temperature of 6° C (43° F) in January; summers are cool, with a July average temperature of 18° C (64° C). The average rainfall is 585 mm (24 in) and is heaviest in the months of October and November. The city has a reputation for severe fog as a result of the damp air combined with atmospheric pollution. The pollution, however, has been much reduced in recent years.

THE CONTEMPORARY CITY

London is a multiracial city, with a large immigrant population from Britain's former colonies, especially from South Asia and the West Indies. Some quarters of the city are dominated

A famous London landmark is the clock tower of the Houses of Parliament, containing the bell known as Big Ben. This complex of buildings, properly known as Westminster Palace, stands on the bank of the River Thames; it dates from the mid-1800s.

by specific ethnic groups, for example, Paddington, Notting Hill, and Brixton.

Economy and Transportation. London is Great Britain's foremost manufacturing center, with light and consumer-goods industries predominating. Food processing is important, as are electronics, light metals, pharmaceuticals, and printing. Most branches of heavy industry are located to the east, near the docks, and include petroleum refining and metalworking. London is also the country's main banking and financial center and contains the chief commodity markets. London is one of the largest ports in the United Kingdom. The docks formerly were located near London Bridge in the city center. In recent years these inner docks have been replaced by larger and more modern facilities to the east. The important Tilbury docks are located more than 10 km (6 mi) outside the city limits. London attracts millions of visitors each year, and tourism, especially in the summer, is a major industry and contributor to the economy.

London is linked with all parts of the country by roads and railroads that radiate from the city. Transportation within the city is by means of a complex but efficient system of subways—the Underground—and by an even more complex system of surface transportation by bus. The principal airport is at Heathrow, 26 km (16 mi) to the west of the city center, although it is supplemented by Gatwick to the south and Stansted to the north.

Government. Since 1965 the city of London has been coterminous with the county of Greater London. Thus the city is composed of the Corporation of the City of London (the historic core of the city covering only 2.6 km²/1 mi²); the 12 inner boroughs surrounding the City; and the 20 outer boroughs. Each borough elects its own government council, and, until March 1986, the elected Greater London Council (GLC) coordinated regional planning and services. With the abolition of the GLC, most of its functions went to centrally appointed boards, although some devolved to the borough councils.

Education and Culture. Because of London's long history as Britain's leading city, it abounds with major educational and

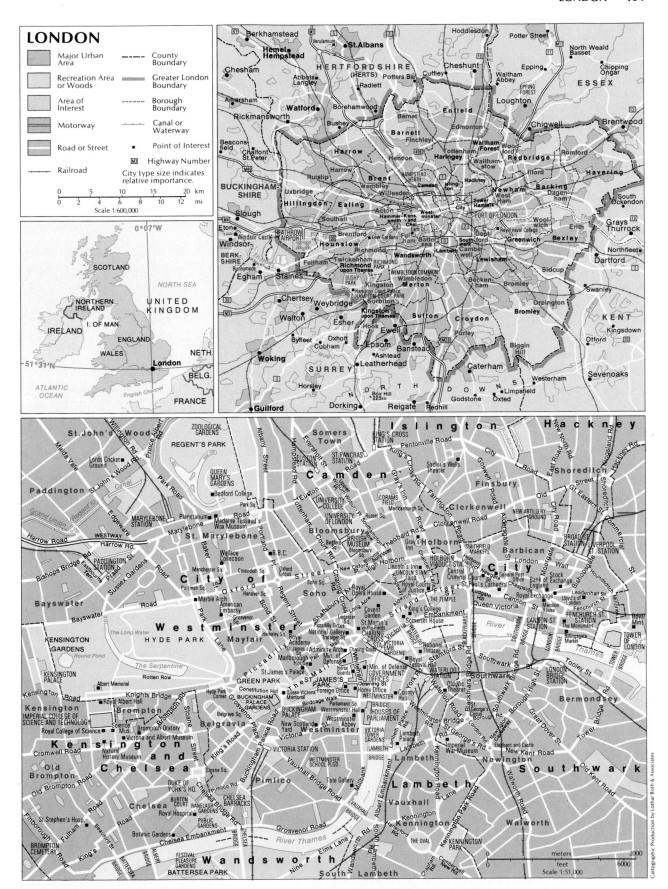

cultural institutions. The University of London (see LONDON, UNIVERSITY OF) is the largest institution of higher education in the United Kingdom. Its 14 colleges, scattered throughout the city, enroll 76,100 students (1979–80). The BRITISH LIBRARY houses one of the finest general collections in the world, and many specialized libraries contain significant collections. Museums and galleries are of exceptional importance, notably the BRITISH MUSEUM, the NATIONAL GALLERY, the TATE GALLERY, and the VICTORIA AND ALBERT MUSEUM. London also contains the headquarters of most of the United Kingdom's learned and cultural societies. Several orchestras and other musical groups as well as ballet, opera, and theater companies perform in the city's many halls, including COVENT GARDEN and the modern Royal Festival Hall (built 1951). London is no less a center of sports, especially tennis (the famed Wimbledon championships are played in the city), soccer, and cricket.

Historic Sites. One of London's oldest landmarks is the TOWER OF LONDON. The former royal residence located along the Thames was begun by William I (the Conquerer) about 1079 and later served as a prison. Tower Bridge, a distinctive Victorian structure, crosses the Thames beside the Tower. To the west lies the City, the heart of London and its financial district. The 17th-century SAINT PAUL'S CATHEDRAL is located there, as are the Bank of England, Mansion House (residence of the lord mayor), and many other landmarks. One of the bridges flanking the City is LONDON BRIDGE; the original wooden bridge (built 963–75) has been replaced many times, and it is now a six-lane concrete structure. West of the City, the Thames bends about 90° to the south, where the borough of Westminster is located on the west bank. The Houses of Parliament (see WESTMINSTER PALACE) are topped by the famous clock tower, Big Ben. WESTMINSTER ABBEY stands beside them. Many government buildings, including 10 Downing Street, the residence of the British prime minister, are nearby. Trafalgar Square contains the famous statue of Lord Nelson, commemorating his victory at the Battle of Trafalgar. The Mall, a long road cutting through Saint James's Park, ends at BUCKINGHAM PALACE, the residence of the royal family. SOHO, where many of London's restaurants and nightclubs are located, is near the main shopping district of Regent and Oxford streets and Piccadilly. North and east of Piccadilly Circus lies the theater district. Regent's Park (the site of London Zoo) is located to the north of this general area, and to the west is Hyde Park where the Marble Arch and Speaker's Corner are found; Kensington Gardens adjoins Hyde Park on the west. To the south lie Belgravia, Knightsbridge, Kensington, and Chelsea, all fashionable residential areas. The last also became famous in the 1960s as a center of bohemian life.

HISTORY

London was founded as the Roman town of Londinium in AD 43, and the Roman wall, patched and repaired, continued to protect the medieval city. The importance of London declined following the 5th century, during the period of Anglo-Saxon and Scandinavian invasions. Gradually, however, the importance of the city's site along the Thames reasserted itself, and it became a prosperous trade center. In the early 11th century London became the seat of government of the last Anglo-Saxon kings, and in 1066, when the Normans invaded Britain, William the Conqueror granted London its charter and made the city his capital.

Throughout the Middle Ages London was the political center, largest city, and chief port of England. New palaces replaced the Tower as the royal residence—notably Westminster, WHITEHALL, and SAINT JAMES'S. The royal court was located in London much of the time, and the city became a great cultural center. London reached a new level of preeminence during the reign (1558–1603) of Queen ELIZABETH I. William Shakespeare's plays were first performed in the GLOBE THEATRE, book publishing began, and London became the center of England's newly emerging foreign trade.

By the 17th century London was a crowded city of narrow and twisting streets. Outbreaks of the plague between 1625 and 1665 claimed more than 75,000 lives. Buildings were largely of wood, and a disastrous fire in 1666 consumed much of the city. The rebuilding of the city was distinguished by the work of the architect Sir Christopher WREN. He rebuilt Saint Paul's Cathedral and more than 50 city churches in his own classical style.

In the 18th century the city again began to grow. Elegant housing was built to the west and northwest of the old city, and London became the focus not only of politics but also of literary and artistic society.

During the 19th century building activity continued, especially in the inner boroughs, with industrial suburbs spreading to the northeast and east of the city and the docks and dock-related industries spreading downriver. At the same time, straight, elegant streets were constructed through the congested inner city and open spaces such as Trafalgar Square were created. The 19th century was also a period of reform and establishment of municipal services: in 1829, Sir Robert PEEL established the Metropolitan Police Force, whose "bobbies" were named after him; in 1890 the world's first electric underground railroad was built.

During the 20th century the suburbs continued to grow until 1935, when a Green Belt law was instituted to control further growth beyond a ring of parks. During World War II, London suffered heavy bombing, resulting in about 30,000 casualties and destroying entire sections of the city. The greatest change of recent years has come from the subsequent rebuilding; the London skyline is today one of tower blocks rather than of spires and church towers. In 1963 the Greater London Council was established, with governmental jurisdiction over Greater Metropolitan London, newly created from the former London and Middlesex counties. This elected unit was abolished in 1986.

NORMAN J. G. POUNDS

Bibliography: Borer, Mary C., *The City of London: A History* (1978); Marsden, P., *Roman London* (1981); Pritchett, V. S., *London Perceived* (1962); Trease, Geoffrey, *A Concise History of London* (1975).

London (Ontario)

London, a Canadian city with a population of 269,140 (1986), is located in southeastern Ontario about 250 km (105 mi) southwest of Toronto. London is a rail and highway junction and an important distribution center for the surrounding agricultural valley. Its manufactures include beer and wine, flour, breakfast cereals, textiles, furniture, machinery, and transportation equipment. The University of Western Ontario (1878) is located there. The site was chosen in 1792 as the planned capital of Upper Canada, but it was not settled until 1826. Subsequently it served as a British military post.

London, Jack

John Griffith London, b. San Francisco, Jan. 12, 1876, d. Nov. 22, 1916, was easily the most successful and best-known writer in America in the first decade of the 20th century. His vigorous tales of men and animals at odds with each other and with their environment—in Alaska, the South Seas, and elsewhere—made him an earlier Hemingway, a writer whose adventurous personal life seemed as exciting as his books.

An illegitimate child who later adopted his stepfather's name, London grew up in poverty and deprivation in the

Jack London, one of the most widely read American authors of the early 20th century, is best known for moving novels of conflict and adventure, such as The Call of the Wild (1903) and The Sea-Wolf (1904). London's fiction and political works express a strong commitment to his philosophic amalgam of socialism and individualism.

Oakland slums and poor farms nearby. While still in his teens he became an oyster pirate and gang leader in the Oakland docks, experiences that later formed the basis for such boys' adventure stories as *The Cruise of the Dazzler* (1902) and *Tales of the Fish Patrol* (1905). At 17 he ran away to sea on a sealing ship bound for the North Pacific; his brutal experiences on this voyage were the material for his best novel, *The Sea-Wolf* (1904), which is about a "superman" captain. Afterward he became a hobo and spent 30 days in jail, an experience he found so degrading that he resolved to educate himself for a better life. His passionate concern for the outcasts of society later found expression in *The People of the Abyss* (1903), which pictured London slum life, and *The Road* (1907), the first of the vagrant novels in a tradition subsequently taken up by John Steinbeck and Jack Kerouac.

London worked his way through high school and the Oakland public library, taking jobs in canneries and laundries to support himself. His overwork to become a self-taught writer is recorded in his autobiographical novel, *Martin Eden* (1909); his hatred of the exploitation of factory labor, in his short story "The Apostate" (1906).

London's year in the Klondike, where he participated in the Gold Rush of 1897–98, yielded no gold but did give him the raw material for his best short stories. These strong, bold tales of the struggle for survival in the Far North were influenced by Herbert Spencer's sociology, Darwin's evolutionary theories, and Kipling's style, and they made London's reputation. Many were collected in *The Son of the Wolf* (1900), *The God of His Fathers* (1901), *Children of the Frost* (1902), *Love of Life* (1907), and *Smoke Bellew* (1912). His two short novels of dogs and wolves in the northland, *The Call of the Wild* (1903) and *White Fang* (1906), are regarded as classics because of their allegory of the struggle in man and beast between savagery and civilization.

London had two daughters by his first wife, then, following his divorce, married his "mate" Charmian Kittredge. On Apr. 23, 1907, they embarked on a not-to-be-completed cruise around the world in his ketch the *Snark*; after his return to California (1909), he retreated to his ranch near Sonoma, where he slowly began to die from a variety of diseases, physical ailments, and drug treatments. London later tempered his Marxism with an inconsistent addiction to racism, nationalism, and, above all, untrammeled individualism. The prescience of his apocalyptic novel about 20th-century industrial society, *The Iron Heel* (1908), together with his socialist tendencies, nevertheless makes him one of the most popular American writers in the Soviet Union today. The author of 50 books in 20 years, London lived the proverbial nine lives before dying at the age of 40, already a legend for his strength of will.   ANDREW SINCLAIR

Bibliography: Barltrop, Robert, *Jack London* (1976); Foner, Philip S., *Jack London, American Rebel*, rev. ed. (1969); Labor, Earle, *Jack London* (1974); London, Joan, *Jack London and His Times* (1939; repr. 1968); O'Connor, Richard, *Jack London* (1964); Sinclair, Andrew, *Jack* (1977); Stone, Irving, *Jack London: A Sailor on Horseback* (1938).

London, treaties and conferences of

London, the capital of Great Britain, has been the site of many international conferences and treaty negotiations.

At the London Conference of 1827–32 the major European powers determined the status and boundaries of the newly independent Greece. When the Belgians rebelled against Dutch rule in 1830, the conference also recognized Belgian independence. By the Treaty of London of 1839, the Netherlands confirmed that independence and the European powers guaranteed Belgian neutrality. The Germans, however, derided this treaty as a "scrap of paper" when they violated (1914) Belgian neutrality at the beginning of World War I.

The Treaty of London of 1852 recognized the disputed region of SCHLESWIG-HOLSTEIN as an autonomous province under the Danish crown although this settlement proved short-lived. Another Treaty of London (1867) guaranteed the independence and neutrality of the Grand Duchy of Luxembourg.

During the BALKAN WARS delegates of the major powers met in London and produced (May 30, 1913) a preliminary peace treaty, under which Turkey agreed to surrender its Balkan territories and a state of Albania was to be created. This peace lasted less than a month, however. In World War I the Entente powers concluded (Apr. 26, 1915) the secret Treaty of London with Italy, which pledged to enter the war in exchange for territorial concessions. Although Italy fulfilled its obligation, it received only part of the territories promised when peace was concluded (1918–19).

Subsequent conferences held in London include the 1930 Naval Conference, at which Britain, France, Italy, Japan, and the United States agreed to regulate submarine warfare and to limit ship construction until 1936. Britain, Japan, and the United States also accepted a treaty limiting the size of battleships. In 1933 a World Monetary and Economic Conference met in London but failed to reach agreement on methods needed to halt the worldwide depression.

London, University of

Established by royal charter in 1836, the University of London in London, England, is a federation of educational institutions. The first colleges, University (1826) and King's (1829), were established independently. The university originally offered no instruction but granted degrees by examination to students of approved British universities. In 1868 it became the first university in the United Kingdom to admit women to its degree program. After 1900 the university was reorganized to accept as constituent schools private university-level colleges in London, and thereafter it became a teaching as well as an examining body. Before 1949 all universities and colleges in England and Wales were part of the university's external degree system. As a result, their curricula strongly resembled London's. The university became the model for many Commonwealth universities.

Each of the university's constituent institutions, all but three of which are in London, has its own residence hall and library. The Centre of International and Area Studies, a marine biological station in Scotland, and a reactor center in Berkshire are units of the university, as is the Athlone Press (1949). The central library contains one million volumes.

Two types of students receive degrees from the university. The internal student, registered at one of the constituent colleges, receives university instruction. The external student takes courses on a part-time basis or at a private institution in the United Kingdom but is examined by the university in London or at centers elsewhere.

The University of London's executive and governing body in all academic affairs is the senate, consisting of the chancellor, vice-chancellor, chairman of convocation, principal, and representatives of faculties and heads of some schools. The senate appoints professors and readers. To ensure future financial resources and to maintain the quality of its academic programs, the university initiated a major reorganization in 1983.

EDUCATIONAL INSTITUTIONS OF UNIVERSITY OF LONDON

Institution	Date Founded*	Enrollment	Volumes in Library
Nonmedical Colleges			
Bedford	1849 (1909)	1,650	200,000
Birkbeck	1823 (1926)	2,365	160,000
Chelsea	1891 (1972)	2,395	106,000
Imperial College of Science and Technology	1907 (1907)	4,570	289,000
King's	1829 (1829)	3,140	380,000
London School of Economics and Political Science	1895	3,650	685,000
Queen Elizabeth	1908 (1953)	1,020	40,000
Queen Mary	1887 (1934)	3,100	210,000
Royal Holloway, Egham, Surrey	1883	1,485	145,000
Royal Veterinary	1791 (1875, 1956)	397	26,000

Institution	Date Founded*	Enrollment	Volumes in Library	Institution	Date Founded*	Enrollment	Volumes in Library
School of Oriental and African Studies	1916 (1916)	978	510,000	Guy's Hospital Medical School	1769 (1948)	850	35,000
School of Pharmacy	1842 (1952)	365	11,000	Guy's Hospital Dental School	1888 (1948)	435	35,000
University	1826 (1907)	6,000	840,000	King's College Hospital	1831	640	21,000
Westfield	1882 (1933)	1,085	125,000	London Hospital	1785 (1900)	910	27,000
Wye, Ashford, Kent	1447 (1948)	485	30,000	Middlesex Hospital	1835	645	13,500
Institutes				Royal Dental Hospital of London	1858 (1948)	260	5,500
Courtauld Institute of Art	1932	265	41,000	Royal Free Hospital	1874 (1938)	555	25,000
Institute of Advanced Legal Studies	1947	495	130,000	St. Bartholomew's Hospital	1662 (1921)	1,000	30,000
Institute of Archaeology	1936	215	16,000	St. George's Hospital	1734	290	20,000
Institute of Classical Studies	1953	145	50,000	St. Mary's Hospital	1854 (1948)	550	24,000
Institute of Commonwealth Studies	1949	530	75,000	St. Thomas's Hospital	13th century	570	34,000
Institute of Education	1902	2,365	180,000	University College Hospital	1828 (1907)	480	30,000
Institute of Germanic Studies	1950	No registered students	45,000	Westminster	1834	275	10,000
Institute of Historical Research	1921	2,090	119,000	**Theological Schools**			
Institute of Latin American Studies	1965	520	2,000	Heythrop College (Roman Catholic)	1926	160	150,000
School of Slavonic and East European Studies	1915	250	190,000	King's College, Theological Department (Anglican)	1846	180	60,000
Institute of United States Studies	1965	No registered students	1,000	**Postgraduate Medical Schools**			
Warburg Institute	1944	46	200,000	British Postgraduate Medical Federation	1945 (1947)	6,890	
British Institute in Paris	1894	6,025	60,000	London School of Hygiene and Tropical Medicine	1924 (1924)	270	70,000
Undergraduate Medical and Dental Schools				Royal Postgraduate Medical School	1931 (1931)	1,650	24,000
Charing Cross Hospital	1818 (1883)	600	30,000				

Institutions with Recognized Teachers Goldsmiths' College (1,200), Jews' College (20), London Graduate School of Business Studies (220), Royal Academy of Music (20), Royal College of Music (30), Trinity College of Music (1).

* Date of university charter appears in parentheses.

London Bridge

Old London Bridge was not just a means of crossing the Thames; for centuries it was a thriving business and residential area as well. Constructed on broad piers, the bridge so constricted the river's flow that at high tide the water rushed through with a loud noise.

At least three permanent structures known as London Bridge have spanned the Thames River. Old London Bridge (begun 1176) was designed by Peter of Colechurch, who had been in charge of the last of the timber bridges built (1163) over the Thames. Consisting of 19 pointed masonry arches varying in span from 4.6 to 10.4 m (15 to 34 ft) and founded on wide, protected piers, Old London Bridge was the first of its kind to be built over a swiftly flowing river with such a large tidal range (5 m/16 ft).

Although its wooden shops and houses were damaged by fire many times and were finally removed in 1763, Old London Bridge survived until 1831, when it was replaced by a five-arched, masonry structure designed by John RENNIE. Upon being dismantled in 1967, the masonry facade of Rennie's bridge was sold to a private developer and reerected at Lake Havasu City, Ariz. The present London Bridge (completed 1972) is a six-lane, prestressed concrete structure.

SIR HUBERT SHIRLEY-SMITH

London Company

The London Company, properly called the Virginia Company of London, was chartered by King James I of England in 1606 for the purpose of establishing a colony in North America between 34° and 41° north latitudes. At the same time the Virginia Company of Plymouth was granted the right of settlement between 38° and 45° north latitudes. The Plymouth Company soon lapsed into inactivity, but the London Company founded JAMESTOWN in Virginia in 1607.

The London Company was a joint-stock trading company, and its principal objective was to turn a profit for its investors. Some investors probably expected their profits to be earned through peaceful trade with the Indians of Virginia; others hoped to find gold and silver and to meet with military success against the Spanish and Indians. The company attempted initially to pursue a peaceful policy, but the Virginia settlers soon provoked the Indians, who struck back.

Plagued with difficulties, the company underwent a series of reorganizations. In 1609 the bounds of its jurisdiction were redefined, the company and its council were given authority to appoint a governor, and the colonists were offered stock in the company. The colony of Jamestown still did not prosper, however, and a new charter—designed to attract new settlers and fresh capital—was issued in 1612. The company's governance of the colony was altered in 1619, when a "grand charter of liberty," creating an elected assembly, was issued. Factional quarrels among the leaders of the company, continued conflict with the Indians in Virginia, and the uncertain progress of Virginia's tobacco economy all worked to undermine the authority of the company. A commission of inquiry finally ruled that the management of both the company and the colony had been mishandled, and in 1624 the charter of the London Company was recalled. Virginia then became a royal colony.

The PILGRIMS received their original settlement authorization from the London Company. They landed (1620) to the north of its jurisdiction, however, and their PLYMOUTH COLONY was repatented by the Council of New England, successor to the Plymouth Company.   RICHARD R. BEEMAN

Bibliography: Craven, Wesley F., *The Dissolution of the Virginia Company* (1932; repr. 1964).

Londonderry   (city)

Londonderry, seat of the former County Londonderry in northwestern Northern Ireland, lies at the head of Lough Foyle on the Foyle River, about 150 km (95 mi) northwest of Belfast. It has a population of 95,100 (1982 est.). A shipbuilding and textile-manufacturing city, Londonderry also serves as the commercial center for local agricultural products. Magee University College (1865) is located there.

The town grew around a monastery founded by Saint Columba in 546. Following an unsuccessful Irish revolt against the English in the early 17th century, James I gave (1613) the town as a land grant to the City of London; the original name,

Derry (from the Gaelic *doire*, "oakwood"), then became Londonderry. In 1689 the city withstood a 105-day siege by the army of JAMES II; the event is commemorated every year. Londonderry was a center of violence in the religious and political strife that plagued Northern Ireland from the late 1960s into the 1980s. The "Derry Massacre" occurred on Jan. 30, 1972; during a Roman Catholic protest march in the city, British paratroopers fired into the crowd, killing 13 people.

Londonderry   (county)

Londonderry is a former county in northwestern Northern Ireland on the Atlantic Ocean. Londonderry is the chief town; other important towns include Coleraine and Portstewart. With an area of 2,082 km² (804 mi²), the region has a hilly surface with elevations of more than 670 m (2,200 ft) in the Sperrin Mountains. Stock raising, the cultivation of oats and potatoes, and salmon fishing are important. Industry—including brewing, the manufacture of textiles and fertilizers, and shipbuilding—is limited mainly to Londonderry and Coleraine. Remains of prehistoric settlements dating from at least 2000 BC are scattered over much of the area. Part of the ancient kingdom of ULSTER, Londonderry was long under the influence of the O'Neill family. It came under English control in 1609 and was a county from 1613 until the local government reorganization of 1974.

Lonely Crowd, The

The Lonely Crowd: A Study of the Changing American Character (1950) is a famous presentation, written by David RIESMAN (with Nathan GLAZER and Reuel Denney), of social patterns in middle-class America at the middle of the 20th century. The authors discuss character types that have declined or developed as a result of major population shifts and technological developments and try to probe the effects of these changes on the urban American middle class. Although the book was based on a Yale research program (poll data, interviews, and observations), some critics say it was a simplification of a complicated process. A sequel, *Faces in the Crowd*, by Riesman and Glazer, was published in 1952.

Long   (family)

Huey Long, governor of Louisiana (1928–32) and a U.S. senator (1932–35), rose to prominence as a spokesman for the poor and established dictatorial control over the state of Louisiana. Despite his methods his policies, including a plan for a redistribution of the nation's wealth that would make "every man a king," elicited enthusiasm. Long had begun to campaign for the presidency when he was assassinated in 1935.

The Long family of Louisiana has dominated the political life of that state for more than 50 years. The founder of the political dynasty was **Huey Pierce Long, Jr.**, b. Winnfield, La., Aug. 30, 1893, d. Sept. 10, 1935. After studying law at Tulane University and gaining admission to the bar (1915), Long served on the state's public service commission, making a reputation as a foe of corporate interests. A Democrat, he served as governor from 1928 to 1932. Long sponsored reforms that endeared him to the rural poor. He provided free textbooks for schoolchildren, built roads and bridges, and repealed the poll tax. Ruthless, cynical, and ambitious, Long ruled Louisiana in a dictatorial fashion and created a powerful political machine. In 1932 he left the governorship to serve in the U.S. Senate, where he gained a large following outside Louisiana by his advocacy of the "share-our-wealth" plan. By imposing high taxes on the rich, he promised to provide every family with a $5,000 homestead allowance and a guaranteed annual income of at least $2,000. By 1935 the Kingfish, as he was called, was a vitriolic critic of the New Deal, and he was considered a possible third-party candidate for the 1936 presidential election. On Sept. 8, 1935, however, he was shot by an assassin; he died two days later.

Earl Kemp Long, b. Winnfield, La., Aug. 26, 1895, d. Sept. 5, 1960, inherited his brother Huey's mantle. Elected lieutenant governor in 1936, Earl Long served briefly as governor in 1939–40 and was elected to 4-year terms in 1948 and 1956. Although he padded the state payroll with political cronies, he also delivered free lunches to schoolchildren, provided pensions for the elderly, and equalized the pay of white and black schoolteachers.

Huey's son, **Russell B. Long**, b. Shreveport, La., Nov. 3, 1918, was educated at Louisiana State University, receiving a law degree in 1942, and served in World War II. In 1948 he was elected as a Democrat to fill a 2-year vacancy in the U.S. Senate. Reelected six times, he served until 1987. Russell Long was chairman of the Senate Finance Committee from 1966 to 1980. He was thus an influential figure in all legislation pertaining to taxation.   RICHARD POLENBERG

Bibliography: Liebling, A. J., *The Earl of Louisiana* (1961; repr. 1970); Martin, Thomas, *Dynasty* (1960); Williams, T. Harry, *Huey Long* (1969; repr. 1981).

Long, Huey: see LONG   (family).

Long, Stephen H.

Longs Peak, in northern Colorado, one of the tallest of the Rocky Mountains, was first sighted (1820) and named by the American explorer Stephen Harriman Long, b. Hopkinton, N.H., Dec. 30, 1784, d. Sept. 4, 1864. Long became a U.S. Army engineer in 1814 and 3 years later was sent to explore the upper Mississippi and the portage of the Fox and Wisconsin rivers. In 1820 he headed a Rocky Mountains expedition and, like Zebulon Montgomery Pike before him, reported that the area that is now Colorado was uninhabitable. This view influenced U.S. expansion for almost 4 decades. Long examined the sources of the Minnesota River and the adjacent northern boundary of the United States in 1823. He subsequently was an advisor to various railroad companies.

Bibliography: Wood, Richard G., *Stephen H. Long, 1784–1864* (1966).

Long Beach

Long Beach, a suburban port city located in southern California, is situated on San Pedro Bay about 30 km (19 mi) south of Los Angeles. The city has a population of 361,334 (1980). Long Beach is an oil production center; the oil, discovered in 1921, is pumped from both land-based and offshore wells. Other industries include the manufacture of aircraft, electronic equipment, missiles, automobile parts, chemicals, and canning. Tourism and conventions are also important. Connected to Los Angeles harbor by a channel, Long Beach is the site of a large naval station, a shipyard, and a drydock. Points of interest include 14 km (9 mi) of beaches; the Long Beach Museum of Art; La Casa de Rancho Los Cerritos (1834), a preserved adobe ranch house; and the ocean liner *Queen Mary,* bought by the city in 1967 and docked there.

The site of Long Beach was originally an Indian trading camp and in 1784 became part of Rancho Nieto. The city was first called Willmore City for W. E. Willmore, who laid it out in 1881 and promoted it as a seaside resort. The name was changed to Long Beach in 1888.

Long Day's Journey into Night

The four-act drama *Long Day's Journey into Night* was written by American playwright Eugene O'NEILL in 1941 but was first produced in 1956 (film, 1962), three years after his death. It is regarded by many critics as his greatest work. O'Neill had originally requested that no performance be given of this autobiographical work until 25 years after he died. It follows the course of 18 tortured hours in the life of Edmund Tyrone (O'Neill) as he and his family—a miserly actor father, a delicate mother who has returned to drug addiction, an alcoholic elder brother—vent their guilts and frustrations upon one another.

Long Island

Long Island (1980 pop., 6,728,074), in southeastern New York, extends about 190 km (120 mi) east from the mouth of the Hudson River into the Atlantic Ocean; it is separated from the New York and Connecticut shores by Long Island Sound. The island's 3,615-km² (1,396-mi²) area is divided into four counties: Kings (Brooklyn) and Queens (both boroughs of New York City), Nassau, and Suffolk. Of glacial origin, Long Island is dominated by two east-west ridges. At the eastern end these form two narrow peninsulas—Orient Point and Montauk Point—divided by Peconic Bay.

Long Island has experienced enormous urban and suburban growth since World War II. Agriculture (truck farming, potato growing, and duck raising) and fishing are still important in the east, and many tourists are attracted by its beaches.

Delaware Indians inhabited the island when the Dutch arrived in the 1630s. English settlement followed soon after, and the English took control in 1664. The 1776 Battle of Long Island took place in Brooklyn.

Long Island, Battle of

The Battle of Long Island, fought between the forces of George WASHINGTON and William Howe on Aug. 27, 1776, opened the British campaign to seize New York City during the American Revolution. It was the first large-scale battle of the war. From American headquarters on Manhattan Island, Washington had sent about a third of his troops across the East River to Brooklyn Heights, where they constructed strong entrenchments. He erred, however, by sending forward 4,000 men to occupy the Heights of Guana and then failing to protect this left flank adequately. On August 22, Howe arrived from Staten Island with 20,000 men, whom he landed at Gravesend Bay, an inlet of lower New York Bay. In the early morning of August 27, Howe made a thrust against the American right. Simultaneously, he dispatched a column that passed undetected around the American left flank under Israel PUTNAM and attacked the Americans' rear position. The Americans lost more than 1,000 men; Howe lost 400. The American troops retreated to their Brooklyn entrenchments, and during the night of August 29–30, Washington ferried his demoralized army back to Manhattan.   DON HIGGINBOTHAM

Long Island Sound

Long Island Sound, a part of the Atlantic INTRACOASTAL WATERWAY, is a partially enclosed inlet of the Atlantic Ocean that separates Long Island, N.Y., from the Connecticut shore. The sound is 145 km (90 mi) long and 32 km (20 mi) across at its widest point. In the west it narrows to a tidal strait, the East River, which runs into the Upper New York Bay along the eastern side of Manhattan Island. BRIDGEPORT, NEW HAVEN, and NEW LONDON, located on the Connecticut shore, are Long Island Sound's main ports.

long jump: see TRACK AND FIELD.

Long March

Sometimes called the most extraordinary march in human history, the Long March was the 10,000-km (6,000-mi) epic journey across China undertaken by the Chinese Communists in 1934–35. In October 1934 about 85,000 troops and another 15,000 auxiliary personnel of the Red Army escaped from a Nationalist cordon in Kiangsi province, in southeastern China. Beginning in January, the army, led by MAO TSE-TUNG, marched across mountains and rivers in a circuitous westerly route through the wilderness of southwest China, arriving in a remote area of Shensi province in October 1935. Thousands perished, but the Long March inspired many Chinese to join the Communist party, which established its headquarters in Yen-an, Shensi province, in December 1936. From the survivors came the Chinese Communist leadership group—CHOU EN-LAI, CHU TEH, LIN PIAO, and P'eng Teh huai—who, with Mao, shaped the first quarter century of the People's Republic of China.

Bibliography: Salisbury, Harrison, *The Long March* (1985); Wilson, Dick, *The Long March, 1935* (1971).

Long Parliament

In November 1640, King CHARLES I of England summoned a Parliament that retained legal identity for an unprecedented 20 years; it is called the Long Parliament. The Parliament immediately quarreled with the king and substantially reduced his powers. Royalist and parliamentary forces eventually fought the ENGLISH CIVIL WAR (1642–48), from which Parliament emerged victorious. The parliamentary army under Oliver CROMWELL then took control of the country and expelled (December 1648) hostile members of Parliament in what became known as Pride's Purge. The remainder, known as the Rump Parliament, then voted for Charles's execution. Cromwell later dissolved (1653) the Rump Parliament; he appointed a quasi legislature known as Barebone's Parliament but actually ruled without a Parliament. After Cromwell's death in 1658 the Rump Parliament was reconvened. On Mar. 26, 1660, after readmitting those members expelled in Pride's Purge, the Long Parliament dissolved itself. A newly elected Parliament arranged the RESTORATION of King Charles II.

Bibliography: Hill, Christopher, *The Century of Revolution, 1603–1714,* 2d ed. (1982).

longan [lahng'-guhn]

The longan (*Euphoria longan,* family Sapindaceae) is a Southeast Asian fruit tree related to LITCHI and other SOAPBERRY relatives. The tree grows to 15 m (50 ft) or more and casts a dense shade. The yellowish brown, smoothly pebbled fruits, borne in clusters of 25 to 150 or more, are the size of a small plum. The crisp, juicy flesh is mild and sweet and surrounds one dark-brown, smooth, inedible seed. The fruit is consumed fresh, canned, or frozen. Dried, it has been important in commerce for centuries. The longan is grown today in Florida and Hawaii as well as in Asia.   R. J. KNIGHT, JR.

longevity: see LIFE SPAN.

Longfellow, Henry Wadsworth

Henry Wadsworth Longfellow was one of the most widely read poets of the 19th century, although today his work is considered sentimental. Longfellow's scholarly translations of European literature, such as Dante's Divine Comedy, acquainted him with a variety of styles; his incorporation of these styles into his own work helped familiarize the American public with foreign verse forms.

Henry Wadsworth Longfellow, b. Portland, Maine, Feb. 27, 1807, d. Mar. 24, 1882, was the most popular and influential American poet of the 19th century and had the widest range and greatest technical skill of all the poets of "the flowering of New England." He exercised a profound influence upon the poetic taste of generations of readers throughout the English-speaking world. Combining gentility with the common touch, he was equally successful in lyric and narrative poetry and during his later years became a master of the sonnet. Ballads like "The Wreck of the Hesperus" and "Paul Revere's Ride" were familiar to every schoolchild, and *Evangeline* (1847) became the first enduringly successful long poem written in the United States. His exploration of Indian lore in *The Song of Hiawatha* (1855) showed his skill in the use of American subject matter, and as a pioneer in the teaching of modern languages, he helped introduce Americans to the literature of Europe.

Longfellow was educated at Bowdoin College, from which he graduated in 1825. He then pursued further studies in Europe and in 1829 became a professor at Bowdoin. From 1835 to 1854 he was Smith Professor of Modern Languages at Harvard. He was twice married, first to Mary Storer Potter in 1831 (she died in 1835) and then, in 1843, to Fanny Appleton, who became the mother of his six children; their extremely happy married life ended tragically in 1861 when she was burned to death. Longfellow's last visit to Europe (1868–69) was a triumphal tour during which he received honorary degrees from both Oxford and Cambridge. In 1884, 2 years after his death, he became the first American to be honored with a bust in the Poets' Corner of Westminster Abbey, London.

Changing tastes in poetry have undermined Longfellow's reputation during modern times, and anthologists who have persisted in reprinting such poor poems as "A Psalm of Life," which was much admired in its time, have done him no good. For his contemporaries, he was a "new poet" who was sometimes reproached for lacking the didacticism that modern readers now complain of in his work. A learned man, he valued spontaneity and simplicity and believed that the purpose of the imagination was not "to devise what has no existence, but rather to perceive what really exists, not creation but insight." A Christian humanist, he generally avoided the sentimental nature pantheism popular in his time, and his essay "The Defence of Poetry," published in the *North American Review* (1832), anticipated much of what Ralph Waldo EMERSON would say, 5 years later, in his address "The American Scholar" to the Harvard Phi Beta Kappa Society.

EDWARD WAGENKNECHT

Bibliography: Arvin, Newton, *Longfellow, His Life and Work* (1963; repr. 1977); Hilen, Andrew, ed., *The Letters of Henry Wadsworth Longfellow,* 4 vols. (1966–72); Longfellow, Samuel, *The Life of Henry Wadsworth Longfellow,* 3 vols. (1891; repr. 1985); Thompson, Lawrance, *Young Longfellow* (1938; repr. 1969); Wagenknecht, Edward, *Longfellow: A Full-Length Portrait* (1955) and *Henry Wadsworth Longfellow: His Poetry and Prose* (1986); Williams, Cecil B., *Henry Wadsworth Longfellow* (1964).

Longford

Longford is a county in Leinster province in east central Ireland. The area is 1,044 km^2 (403 mi^2), and the population is 31,140 (1981). Longford is the county town. Part of the Irish central plain, Longford consists mainly of low, fertile valleys dotted with marshes and small lakes. The chief river is the SHANNON. The area is well suited for cattle raising, which is the economic mainstay. The major farm crops are potatoes and oats. It was known as Annaly when owned by the O'Farrell family prior to the 12th century. Longford was established as a shire in 1569.

longhaired cats

All longhaired cats are frequently, but incorrectly, called Persian or Angora cats because two of the oldest and best-known types are known by those names. The Persian-type longhair is believed to have originated in Persia (Iran), but the evidence is inconclusive. A Persian-type longhair has a short, compact body, a short tail, and a large, rounded head

The most popular of the longhaired breeds, the Persian cat has a massive head with large, widely spaced eyes. The Persian requires regular grooming to maintain its long, fine-textured coat.

with a short nose and small ears. Its coat tends to stand away from its body. Persian cats, officially called longhairs in Britain, are bred in a wide variety of coat colors and patterns; there is even a shorter-nosed variety called the peke-face. The Angora-type longhair is believed to have originated in Turkey or possibly Armenia and is presumably named for the superficial resemblance of its coat to that of the Angora goat. The Angora is finer-boned and longer-bodied than the Persian, with longer legs and a longer tail. Its head is relatively smaller and more tapered, and it has larger ears. Its coat is not quite as long or as dense as that of the Persian, and it tends to lie closer to the body.

Persian and Angora types were interbred for many years around the turn of the century in Britain and the United States, and the Angora characteristics disappeared in favor of the more numerous and popular Persian types. Recent efforts, using white cats imported from Turkey, have reestablished the Angora breed. White is presently the only accepted color for Angora cats in America.

Another longhaired breed from Turkey is the Van cat or Turkish cat. Its coat lacks an underfur and is not as dense as that of the Persian. Its head is wedge-shaped, with large ears and a medium-length nose. It is white in color, with reddish markings on the top of the head and light and dark reddish markings on the tail. A fourth Asiatic breed is the Birman cat of Burma. It is somewhat heavy-bodied like the Persian but has a longer head and tail. Its coloring is unique. Like the Siamese, it has dark points—face, ears, legs, and tail—but its body is cream colored and its paws white. The Birman should not be confused with another cat from Burma, the short-haired Burmese.

A relatively old longhaired breed is the Maine coon cat of the United States, which is believed derived from random breedings of Angora-type cats in the late 1800s in the New England states, particularly Maine. It is a large cat with Angora-like body structure and a variety of coat patterns. A new breed of longhaired cat is the Balinese, which is essentially a longhaired Siamese cat, having the same body structure, coloring, and personality but long hair. It is different from the Himalayan, which is a Persian-type cat with Siamese-like markings.

Bibliography: Fireman, Judy, ed., *The Cat Catalog* (1976); Pond, Grace, ed., *The Complete Cat Encyclopedia* (1972).

Longhena, Baldassarre   [lohng-gay'-nah]

The Italian architect Baldassarre Longhena, b. 1598, d. Feb. 18, 1682, created a Venetian version of Roman baroque architecture in his major work, the Church of Santa Maria della Salute in Venice. Longhena began his career as a pupil of Vincenzo Scamozzi, and his early work in Venice, such as the Palazzo Giustinian-Lolin (c.1623), reveals his debt to his predecessors Andrea Palladio, Michele Sanmicheli, and Jacopo Sansovino. In 1630 the city of Venice, which had been ravaged by

plague, chose to build a church dedicated to the Virgin to be called Santa Maria della Salute (Mary of Health). Longhena won the competition for its design, and construction began in 1631. Consisting of an octagon surrounded by an ambulatory, the church is the first of its kind in the post-Renaissance period. Its plan was probably derived from the Byzantine Church of San Vitale in nearby Ravenna. In addition, Longhena designed the Palazzo Rezzonico (begun 1667) in Venice and the cathedral at Chioggia (1624–47).

NICHOLAS ADAMS

Bibliography: Wittkower, Rudolf, *Art and Architecture in Italy: 1600-1750* (1958).

Longhi, Pietro   [lohng'-gee, pee-ay'-troh]

Pietro Longhi, b. 1702, d. May 8, 1785, was the primary artistic chronicler of the bourgeois character of 18th-century Venetian society through the genre known as the conversation piece. He studied with Antonio Balestra in Venice, and his early works were influenced by his study in Bologna with Giuseppe Maria Crespi. Although he began his career as a painter in the grand manner, Longhi did not devote himself to large-scale works; he chose the small cabinet format for his pleasant if somewhat bland depictions of polite society. *The Concert* (1741; Accademia, Venice), his first Venetian genre scene, displays the poetic intimacy he achieved through a combination of frankness and sympathy toward his subject. During the 1740s he executed a religious series, *The Seven Sacraments* (Pinacoteca Quirini Stampalia, Venice). After 1760 he depicted brothels, gambling houses, and other diversions. Some critics have suggested that Longhi, in his anecdotal treatment of these subjects, drew on the tradition of Dutch genre painting. Longhi was one of the first members of the Venetian Academy and the father of the portraitist Alessandro Longhi (1733–1813).

THOMAS SOKOLOWSKI

Bibliography: Maxon, John, and Rinshel, Joseph, eds., *Painting in Italy in the Eighteenth Century* (1970); Pignatti, Terisio, *Pietro Longhi*, trans. by Pamela Waley (1969).

The 18th-century Venetian painter Pietro Longhi was a keen observer of his social milieu. His genre scenes, such as Viewing the Rhinoceros, *depicted cosy boudoir and salon activities as well as worldly diversions. (Palazzo Ca' Rezzonico, Venice.)*

longhorn cattle: see CATTLE AND CATTLE RAISING.

Longinus   [lahn-jy'-nuhs]

Cassius Longinus, AD c.213–273, was a Greek Neoplatonist philosopher, a teacher of rhetoric in Athens, and a counselor to Zenobia, Queen of Palmyra. When his policies failed, Zenobia delivered him to the Romans, who executed him as a traitor. A work of literary criticism entitled *On the Sublime*, long attributed to Longinus, had actually been written by an unknown writer 2 centuries earlier. It became popular in Europe in the French translation by Nicolas Boileau-Despreux (1674) and during the 18th century helped to inspire the romantic movement in poetry and painting.

GEORGE KENNEDY

Bibliography: Grube, G. M., *The Greek and Roman Critics* (1965); Monk, Samuel H., *The Sublime: A Study of Critical Theories in XVIII-Century England* (1960).

longitude   [lawn'-jih-tood]

Longitude is a position on the Earth's surface indicating the distance east or west of Greenwich, England, the PRIME MERIDIAN. The distance—expressed in degrees, minutes, and seconds—is measured along a LATITUDE line. The imaginary half-circles connecting the points of the same longitude, from the North Pole to the South Pole, are called MERIDIANS. On the opposite side of the globe from Greenwich is the international date line, 180° West or East. At the equator, one degree of longitude equals 111.32 km (69.17 mi)—at the poles, it is zero.

ROBERT S. WEINER

longitudinal waves: see WAVES AND WAVE MOTION.

longshore drift

When waves propagate into shallow water toward a beach, the net transport of water in the direction of propagation increases substantially, an excess that must eventually escape. A longshore current flowing parallel to the beach usually develops inside the breaker zone; it is directed away from the oncoming waves if they approach the shore at an angle. The longshore currents, most well developed along long, straight coasts, often feed rip currents, which flow offshore through the surf zone at discrete places.

These currents are extremely important to the longshore drift, or transport, of sand and sediment suspended by wave action in the surf zone or introduced by streams and rivers. The currents tend to deposit this material when they are slowed at places of increased depth, such as at the end of a sandspit or at the mouth of a harbor. Longshore drift is of great importance to beach development and to the maintenance of a supply of sand to beaches (see BEACH AND COAST). Jetties that interrupt the longshore drift can have significant effects on the beach downstream of the structure (see COASTAL PROTECTION).

ROBERT E. WILSON

Bibliography: Shepard, Francis P., *Submarine Geology*, 3d. ed. (1973).

Longshoremen's Union: see INTERNATIONAL LONGSHOREMEN'S UNION.

longspur

Longspurs are any of four species of small, seed-eating birds of the genus *Calcarius*, in the finch family, Fringillidae, named for their unusually long hind claw. Longspurs are migratory, ground-nesting birds, about 15 cm (6 in) long, inhabiting open country in North America. One species, the Lapland longspur, *C. lapponicus*, also occurs in Eurasia; it may be the most abundant nesting bird on the Arctic tundra. The longspur's upper body plumage is streaked in dead-grass colors, and, in breeding season, the males develop bold markings around the head. Females lay 3 to 6 eggs, which they incubate for 10 to 13 days. Both parents feed insects to the young.

The Lapland longspur, Calcarius lapponicus, is a songbird native to both North America and Eurasia. The male (top) *has a black crown, face, and breast in summer; both sexes have white-edged black tails.*

Longstreet, James

After the American Civil War, James Longstreet, b. Edgefield District, S.C., Jan. 8, 1821, d. Jan. 2, 1904, became embroiled in a long controversy about his conduct as a Confederate general during the war. After graduating from West Point in 1842, Longstreet served in the U.S. Army until 1861, when he joined the Confederate Army. Commissioned a general, he led troops in most of the major battles in the Virginia theater—including the two battles of BULL RUN and the Battle of FREDERICKSBURG—and at CHICKAMAUGA in Georgia before he was wounded (1864) in the WILDERNESS CAMPAIGN. When he recovered, Longstreet returned to duty and fought until the war ended in 1865. He was a solid, usually dependable subordinate, although he preferred to fight on the defensive rather than to attack. He performed poorly in independent command in Virginia and Tennessee in 1863.

After the war, Longstreet became a Republican and was appointed to several federal posts by his friend President Ulysses S. Grant and by later Republican presidents. This political connection hurt him in the eyes of ex-Confederates as did his criticism of Robert E. Lee, who had become a symbol of heroism to the South. Longstreet was blamed (unjustly it now seems) by Gen. Jubal A. Early and others for the Southern defeat at the Battle of GETTYSBURG.

RICHARD M. MCMURRY

Bibliography: Sanger, Donald, and Hay, Thomas, *James Longstreet* (1952); Tucker, Glenn, *Lee and Longstreet at Gettysburg* (1968).

James Longstreet, like many West Point graduates, elected to serve the Confederacy at the outbreak of the Civil War and became one of Robert E. Lee's most able subordinate generals despite his reputation as an overly cautious tactician. Following the war, Longstreet alienated his former comrades-in-arms by joining the Republican party and accepting a federal post as U.S. minister to Turkey.

Longueuil, Charles Le Moyne, Sieur de
[lohn-gur'-yuh, sharl luh mwahn, sur duh]

Charles Le Moyne, b. Aug. 2, 1626, d. February 1685, was a leading French colonist in Canada. Arriving in Canada in 1641, he worked with the Jesuits among the Huron Indians and became expert in Indian languages. He settled (1646) at Montreal, where he served both as an interpreter and as a soldier against the Iroquois Indians. As a reward he was made seigneur of Longueuil and of Châteauguay. Several of his children became famous, notably Sieur d'IBERVILLE, founder of Louisiana, and Sieur de BIENVILLE, founder of New Orleans.

Longus   [lawng'-guhs]

Longus, a Greek who is thought to have lived in Lesbos in the 3d century AD, was the author of the first pastoral romance (see PASTORAL LITERATURE), *Daphnis and Chloe*. The story concerns a shepherd boy and girl who gradually discover their love for each other.   GEORGE KENNEDY

Bibliography: McCulloh, William E., *Longus* (1970).

loom

A loom is a device for WEAVING, the interlacing of threads or yarns to form a fabric. The earliest looms were probably simple stick frames on which was wound a series of parallel lengthwise threads, the warp. The weaver used fingers or a needle to lace the filling threads, called the weft, over and under alternate warps. (Children's hand looms are still worked in this fashion.) Only when a means was found to lift alternate warp threads mechanically did looms become capable of weaving significant quantities of cloth. A simple loom, such as the one illustrated here, has several such devices, called heddles—wooden slats with holes through which alternate warp threads are strung. When a heddle is lifted, its load of warp threads is lifted at the same time, and an open area, the shed, is created, through which the weft thread is passed. It is pressed tight, or beaten in, against the previous rows of weft by a batten, or reed, a fine comb originally made of reed and now usually made of wire. By using a number of heddles, the order of lifted warp threads can be varied, and different patterns created.

Early Looms. The earliest loom of which we have any histori-

A craftsman demonstrates a treadle loom patterned after those used in early American household industry. The simple treadle loom may have been introduced into Europe as early as the 13th century and was widely used until the invention of automated looms during the 1800's.

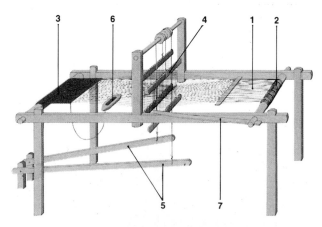

Although the loom originated thousands of years ago, the basic method of interlacing warp and weft remains the same. Parallel threads, known collectively as the warp (1), are strung tautly between two rollers, originating with the warp beam (2) and terminating with the breast beam (3). As the warp traverses the loom it passes through the two or more frames known as heddles (4), which are activated by treadles (5) causing the warp to move alternately up and down. The shuttle (6), carrying the cross thread (weft), passes through the "shed," the open space between the warps. The newly laid weft is compressed against the previously laid weft with a toothed comb, called a reed or beater. When the lever (7) is depressed, more warp is fed out from the warp beam as fabric accumulates on the breast beam.

cal knowledge was that used by the ancient Egyptians. It was a horizontal loom consisting of two beams (the warp, or back beam, and the breast, or front beam, of a modern hand loom) mounted on four posts that lifted the beams off ground level. Weaving took place at the breast beam. As the cloth was woven, it was wound around the breast beam, while additional warp threads were wound off the back beam. The weft thread was at first wound around a stick; later, a spool of weft, or bobbin, was inserted into the shuttle, a slim, hollow container that could be passed quickly through the shed, the weft thread pulling out through a hole in the side of the shuttle.

Early looms were often vertical. The warp hung down from an upper beam suspended from rope. When lengths of cloth were to be made longer than the length of the loom, the additional warp lengths were wound around a bottom beam, to be unwound as weaving progressed. Some vertical looms had no bottom beam; instead, groups of warp threads were tied onto stone weights. The vertical loom continued in use in Europe until late medieval times and is still used by carpet weavers in the Middle and Far East.

The Draw Loom. By the 1500s in Europe the heddle and shed operation was controlled by treadles, and intricate patterns could be produced by working several heddles in varied order or by operating two or more in unison. With the development of the draw loom, silk weaving, perfected long before in China, became a Western art as well. In the draw loom, certain warp threads in each heddle group were tied to overhead slip cords. Operated by a drawboy, who sat on top of the loom, the cords with their attached warp threads could be drawn up whenever the complexities of the pattern required it. The first automated loom, the Jacquard loom (1805; see JACQUARD, JOSEPH MARIE), used hooks instead of slip cords. The hooks were activated at each weft insertion by being pressed against a revolving chain of punched cards. Jacquard cards adapted for power looms are in use today.

The Flying Shuttle. In 1733, John KAY, an English broadcloth weaver, invented the flying shuttle. Broadcloth—so called because it was woven on a wide loom—required two weavers to operate the shuttle. Kay designed a driver mechanism that allowed the weaver, by pulling a cord, to send the shuttle mechanically across the width of the loom. Kay's son, Robert, later invented the drop box, in which several shuttles, each with a different weft, could be stored and retrieved automatically.

Power Looms. Mechanical devices to operate the heddles, the beating in, and the movement of the shuttle were invented in large numbers, and by the 19th century many of the looms that incorporated these devices were being powered by steam. Modern powered looms, although far more complex than even the late-19th-century versions, still carry out the same basic operations. The most significant advances have been (1) a device that senses when the weft on a bobbin is about to run out and replaces it with a full bobbin; and (2) the use of shuttleless looms, which carry the weft thread at enormous speed, either via a small steel projectile (a dummy shuttle), or via a flexible steel tape that reels out and in, or on a jet of air or water.   RICHARD HILLS

Bibliography: Blum, Herman, *The Loom Has a Brain,* rev. ed. (1966); Duxbury, V., and Wray, G. R., eds., *Modern Developments in Weaving Machinery* (1962); Hooper, Luther, *Hand Loom Weaving* (1979); Reed, Jim, *The Loom Book* (1973); Robinson, Harriet H., *Loom and Spindle* (1976); Roth, Henry, *Studies in Primitive Looms* (1918; repr. 1973); Singer, Charles, et al., *History of Technology,* 7 vols. (1954); Vincent, J. J., *Shuttleless Looms* (1979); Weibel, Adele C., *Two Thousand Years of Textiles* (1952).

See also: INDUSTRIAL REVOLUTION; TEXTILE INDUSTRY.

loon

The common loon, G. immer, *shown in summer* (foreground) *and winter* (background) *plumage, is found in North America and Iceland.*

Loons, also known as divers, belong to a single genus, *Gavia,* of the bird family Gaviidae, order Gaviiformes. All four species are found in northern areas of the Northern Hemisphere and are migratory. Loons measure 61–102 cm (24–40 in) in length and have an elongated body and sharp, pointed bill. They are strong swimmers and propel themselves when diving by using their webbed feet. The legs are attached far back on the body, a characteristic that permits ease of movement when swimming but causes great difficulty when the loon walks on land. Loons are unique among living birds because their legs are encased within the body all the way to the ankle. They are good fliers but become airborne only after an extensive run along the top of the water. Nests are placed on land near the water's edge, often on small islands. Usually two eggs are laid, and both sexes, which are similar in color, incubate the eggs and care for the young.

The common loon, *Gavia immer,* inhabits northern lakes of the New World and rivers throughout the world. It has a call that sounds like yodeling. The three other species are the yellow-billed loon, *G. adamsii;* the red-throated loon, *G. stellata;* and the arctic loon, *G. arctica.*   GARY D. SCHNELL

Bibliography: Bent, Arthur C., *Life Histories of North American Diving Birds* (1919); Lehtonen, Leo, "Loons," in *Grzimek's Animal Life Encyclopedia,* ed. by Bernhard Grzimek, vol. 7 (1975).

Loos, Adolf   [lohs, ah'-dawlf]

The Austrian architect Adolf Loos, b. Dec. 10, 1870, d. Aug. 23, 1933, played a seminal role in the development of modern European architecture. Trained as an architect in Dresden, Loos spent several years in the United States, where he was impressed by the functional design of American industrial buildings. He returned to Vienna in 1896. The buildings he subsequently designed were primarily residences. They echoed in form the principles he outlined in his widely-read essay "Ornament and Crime" (1908). Reacting against the excessive use of ART NOUVEAU and other ornamental styles, Loos condemned the use of ornament insofar as it had no useful purpose and was not an organic outgrowth of contemporary culture. The exteriors of his buildings, which were often built of the new, reinforced concrete, were spare and unadorned, but his interiors were sumptuous and visually delightful. Le Corbusier was among the prominent architects whose work was influenced by Loos.

Bibliography: Benedetto, G., *Adolf Loos: Theory and Works* (1982).

Loos, Anita   [loos]

Actress, screenwriter, and playwright Anita Loos, b. Mt. Shasta, Calif., Apr. 26, 1893, d. Aug. 18, 1981, won instant fame with her novel *Gentlemen Prefer Blondes* (1926). Its heroine, flapper Lorelei Lee, is remembered for her fractured grammar and her hard-nosed romanticism: "Kissing your hand can make a girl feel good, but a diamond bracelet lasts forever." A play, two musicals, and two movies are based on the book. Loos' screenwriting career spanned the film industry's history from the earliest silents to sound hits of the 1930s and '40s. She wrote several successful plays, notably *Happy Birthday* (1946), three volumes of autobiography, and many humorous books, including the posthumous collection *Fate Keeps On Happening* (1984).

loosestrife

Loosestrifes are typically moisture-loving, sometimes slender plants of several different genera. They include 165 or more species classified in the genus *Lysimachia,* in the primrose family, Primulaceae. These are mostly leafy-stemmed perennial herbs of wide distribution in temperate regions. *L. vulgaris,* the common or garden loosestrife, is native to Eurasia but now grows wild in North America. It is a coarse, bushy plant, growing to 1 m (3 ft) or more in height, and bears leafy clusters of dark-margined yellow flowers.

The name loosestrife is also applied to several species of plants in the genus *Lythrum* and to its family, Lythraceae. The purple loosestrife, *Lythrum salicaria,* which exhibits a superficial resemblance to several species of *Lysimachia,* is

Purple loosestrife, Lythrum salicaria, *a perennial that grows best in damp soil, bears long, spikelike flower clusters. The name loosestrife is sometimes confined to plants of the genus* Lysimachia, *of which it is an approximate English translation (*lysis, *loosening;* mache, *strife). According to tradition, the Macedonian king* Lysimachus *once stopped a maddened bull by waving one of these plants in its face.*

native to Eurasia but has become naturalized in North America. It is an erect, somewhat downy perennial, growing to 1.8 m (6 ft) in height, with stalkless, narrow leaves and long spikes of red purple flowers. The water willow, *Decodon verticillatus*, of the same family, is sometimes called the swamp loosestrife. The 75 species of aquatic or marsh plants of the genus *Ludwigia*, in the evening primrose family, Onagraceae, are collectively called false loosestrifes.

Lop Nor   [lahp nohr]

Lop Nor, an area of salt marshes and occasional lakes, is the lowest spot (elevation, 760 m/2,493 ft) in the Tarim Basin of southern Sinkiang Uighur Autonomous Region, China. It is surrounded by sparsely populated semidesert. The People's Republic of China tests its nuclear weapons at Lop Nor. The first Chinese-made atom bomb (a fission device) was tested there on Oct. 16, 1964; the first guided missile on Oct. 27, 1966; and the first thermonuclear (fusion) device on Dec. 28, 1966. In the early 20th century the area was visited by the explorers Sir Aurel Stein and Sven Hedin.

Bibliography: Hedin, Sven, *The Wandering Lake* (1946).

Lopburi   [luhp-bur-ee']

Lopburi, the capital of Lopburi province in south central Thailand, was an ancient city of the Buddhist MON people from the 7th to the 10th century AD. Few remains survive of the splendid art of this period, except for some brick shrine-towers and fragments of Buddha icons. From the early 11th to the early 13th century, Lopburi became a provincial center of the KHMER EMPIRE. Of the substantial remains of Khmer-influenced art styles, the late-12th-century P'ra Prang Sam Yot is the best surviving example of local work in brick and stucco imitating ANGKOR Wat. In the early 14th century Lopburi lost much of its importance to Ayutthia.   PHILIP RAWSON

Lope de Rueda: see RUEDA, LOPE DE.

Lope de Vega: see VEGA, LOPE DE.

López, Francisco Solano   [loh'-pays, frahn-sees'-koh soh-lah'-noh]

Francisco Solano López, b. July 24, 1827, d. Mar. 1, 1870, the president of Paraguay from 1862 to 1870, pursued a disastrous course of military adventurism that sank his country into a state from which it needed two generations to recover. He is, nevertheless, considered a national hero in Paraguay.

The son of President Carlos António López, Francisco López became a brigadier general at the age of 19, then a special envoy to Europe empowered to conclude commercial treaties (1853–54), minister of war (1855), and vice-president. In Europe he nurtured a Napoleonic image of himself, and after succeeding (1862) his father in office, he forged a despotism that enabled him to pursue his whims without opposition. His pet project was his army, which he built into one of the largest in the Southern Hemisphere, and he used it to play the role of power broker in the Río de la Plata area. After Brazil sent (1864) its troops into Uruguay, López issued Brazil an ultimatum to desist. When it was ignored, he invaded southwestern Brazil. During the invasion Paraguay violated Argentina's border and was soon embroiled in war with that country as well as Brazil and Uruguay. This War of the TRIPLE ALLIANCE (1864–70) proved disastrous for Paraguay. Much of the country's male population was killed or died of disease, and its economy was ruined. López himself fell in battle.

Bibliography: Brodsky, Alyn, *Madame Lynch and Friend* (1975); Cunninghame Graham, R. B., *Portrait of a Dictator: Francisco Solano López* (1933).

Lopez, Nancy

Hall of Fame member Nancy Lopez, b. Torrance, Calif., Jan. 6, 1957, emerged in the late 1970s as the fastest rising woman professional golfer in history. After an outstanding collegiate

and amateur record, Lopez joined the Ladies' Professional Golf Association (LPGA) tour in mid-1977. In 1978 she won 9 tournaments, including a record 5 straight and the LPGA championship tournament, and her earnings totaled $189,814, then an LPGA record. In 1979 she won 8 tournaments and $197,489. In 1978, 1979, and 1985, Lopez was named Player of the Year, in addition to winning the Vare Trophy, awarded annually to the player with the best average score per round. In 1985 and 1989 she won LPGA championships again, and in 1988, another Player of the Year award. By the late 1980s, Lopez had won over $2.7 million and over 40 tournaments.

López Portillo y Pacheco, José   [loh'-pays por-teel'-yoh ee pah-chay'-koh, hoh-say']

Under President José López Portillo, Mexico gained new prestige as a leading petroleum producer. His moderately conservative policies appealed to both business interests and opposition parties. Formerly a law professor, López Portillo has written books of law, political science, and fiction.

José López Portillo y Pacheco, b. June 16, 1920, was president of Mexico from 1976 to 1982. López Portillo was a professor of political science at the University of Mexico before entering government service in 1959. He served in a number of government posts, distinguishing himself especially as secretary of finances and public credit (1973–75) under President Luis Echeverría Alvarez. In July 1976 he was elected to the presidency as the candidate of Mexico's dominant Institutional Revolutionary party (PRI).

As president, López Portillo attempted to steer a middle course, moving away from the leftist policies of his predecessor. In foreign affairs he became one of the leading spokesmen of the Third World countries and was critical of U.S. policies. In the early years of his administration the Mexican economy benefited from the exploitation of the country's vast petroleum resources. When oil prices fell in the early 1980s, however, the boom ended, and the government was faced with a serious financial crisis. During his last year in office, López Portillo was forced to devalue the peso and nationalize Mexico's banks. He was succeeded in the presidency by Miguel de la Madrid Hurtado.

López Portillo has written books on economics and political science, as well as a volume of literary criticism and two novels, *Don Q* (1969; Eng. trans., 1976) and *Quétzalcóatl* (1965; Eng. trans., 1976).

López Velarde, Ramón   [loh'-pays vay-lahr'-day, rah-mohn']

Ramón López Velarde, b. June 15, 1888, d. June 19, 1921, was a Mexican lyric poet and an important contributor to the postmodern period in Mexican literature. Although he earned a degree in law in 1911 and served briefly as a judge, he dedicated himself to writing. He was widely recognized after the publication of his first book of poems, *La Sangre devota* (Devout Blood, 1916). This was followed by *Zozobra* (Anguish, 1919), a powerfully imaginative re-creation of the writer's recollections of Mexican regional life. Feelings of personal anguish and religious doubt and the deeply felt torment of erotic yearnings and the desire for spiritual peace permeate his work. *El son del corazón* (The Sound of the Heart), posthumously published in 1932, contains some uncollected pieces including the poem "La Suave Patria" (Sweet Fatherland), which was written as a tribute to his native Mexico.

lophophorate   [lahf-uh-for'-ayt]

Three related phyla of water-dwelling invertebrates—the BRACHIOPODS, BRYOZOANS, and PHORONIDS—are termed lophophorates because they all possess the distinctive feeding organ called a lophophore. Surrounding their mouths they have a crown of tentacles covered with vibratile cilia (tiny, vibrating hairlike structures) with which they entrap food. They also share some other features characteristic of a sessile existence, that is, permanently attached to a surface.

loquat

The loquat, *Eriobotrya japonica*, is a small evergreen tree of the rose family, Rosaceae, native to warm and temperate parts of China and Japan. It grows to 9 m (30 ft) tall and bears large, coarsely toothed, glossy green leaves with rusty, woolly undersides. The fragrant white flowers mature into clusters of yellow or orange pearlike fruits with a pleasant, slightly tart taste. Loquat fruits are juicy, with white or orange flesh surrounding smooth, brown seeds. The tree has been introduced to many parts of the tropics and warm-temperate areas.

The fruit of the loquat tree, E. japonica, *is eaten throughout Asia. The plum-shaped yellow-to-orange fruit has a slightly tart taste and is often jellied or preserved in syrup. Warm temperatures are required to mature the fruit.*

LORAN: see NAVIGATION.

Lorca, Federico García: see GARCÍA LORCA, FEDERICO.

Lord of the Flies

In *Lord of the Flies* (1954), the first novel of British writer William GOLDING, the author contends that civilization is merely a thin veneer covering humanity's savage instincts. A group of British schoolboys are stranded on an uninhabited island. Initially, they struggle to reproduce British society but soon revert to a barbarism replete with bloody rituals and taboos. The novel is seen as a powerful work, although some critics doubt its premise.   CHARLOTTE D. SOLOMON

Bibliography: Baker, J. R., ed., *Critical Essays on William Golding* (1988); Whitely, J. S., *Golding: Lord of the Flies* (1970).

Lord Haw-Haw

During World War II, William Joyce (nicknamed Lord Haw-Haw), b. Brooklyn, N.Y., Apr. 24, 1906, broadcast Nazi propaganda in English over German radio. At the war's end, he was captured in Germany by the British, who claimed jurisdiction, despite his U.S. birth, because Joyce held a British passport. He was convicted of treason and hanged on Jan. 3, 1946.

Lords, House of: see PARLIAMENT.

Lord's Prayer

The Lord's Prayer, or Our Father, is the only formula of PRAYER attributed to JESUS CHRIST. It appears twice in the New Testament: in Matt. 6:9–13 and in a shorter version in Luke 11:2–4. In Matthew the prayer is composed of an invocation and seven petitions, the first three asking for God's glorification, the last four requesting divine help and guidance. A final doxology, "For thine is the kingdom . . .," is found in some ancient manuscripts. Protestants customarily include the doxology in their recitation of the prayer; Roman Catholics do not, although it is added in the new order of Mass. The prayer, known in Latin as the Pater Noster, is the principal prayer and a unifying bond of Christians.   L. L. MITCHELL

Bibliography: Boff, L., *The Lord's Prayer* (1983).

Lord's Supper: see EUCHARIST.

Loren, Sophia   [luh-ren', suh-fee'-uh]

The Italian film actress Sophia Loren appears here in a scene from Two Women *(1961), a film for which she received an Academy Award. Although her early films exploited her reputation as one of the world's most beautiful women, Sophia Loren is recognized as a talented performer and has excelled in both dramatic and comedic roles.*

Beautiful, sensuous, and stately, the Italian film star Sophia Loren, b. Sophia Scicolone, Sept. 20, 1934, first came to international attention in *Woman of the River* (1955). Quickly adopted by Hollywood for such films as *The Pride and the Passion* (1957), *Desire Under the Elms* (1958), and *El Cid* (1961), Loren enjoyed greater critical success in the Italian comedies *Yesterday, Today and Tomorrow* (1963) and *Marriage Italian Style* (1964) and in the dramatic roles afforded by *The Key* (1958), *Two Women* (1961), for which she won an Academy Award, and *A Special Day* (1977). Since 1957 she has been married to producer Carlo Ponti.   LESLIE HALLIWELL

Bibliography: Hotchner, A. E., *Sophia, Living and Loving* (1979).

Lorentz, Hendrik Antoon   [lohr'-ents, hen'-drik ahn'-tohn]

The Dutch theoretical physicist Hendrik Antoon Lorentz, b. July 18, 1853, d. Feb. 4, 1928, made significant contributions to the theory of electromagnetic radiation, for which he received the 1902 Nobel Prize for physics jointly with Pieter ZEEMAN. His postulation that there are contractions in the lengths of objects at relativistic speeds is now known as the FITZGERALD-LORENTZ CONTRACTION.

Lorentz received his doctorate from the University of Leiden in 1875 and in 1877 accepted the newly created chair in theoretical physics at Leiden. Even before Joseph J. THOMSON proved the existence of electrons, Lorentz proposed that light waves were due to oscillations of an electric charge in the atom. From 1892 to 1904, Lorentz developed his electron theory, which mathematically distinguished the electromagnetic fields from matter. He attracted large numbers of physicists to Leiden with his Monday lectures on current problems in phys-

In his doctoral dissertation submitted when he was 21 years old, Hendrik Antoon Lorentz, a 19th-century Dutch physicist, stated his electron theory of matter, a milestone in theoretical physics. Lorentz, who spent most of his life in isolated study, achieved international recognition in physics.

ics, and he served as president of the Solvay Congresses—a series of international science conferences sponsored by the Belgian industrial chemist Ernest Solvay—from the first in 1911 until 1927.   J. Z. FULLMER

Bibliography: De Haas-Lorentz, G. L., ed., *H. A. Lorentz: Impressions of His Life and Work* (1957).

Lorenz, Konrad   [lohr'-ents, kohn'-raht]

Konrad Lorenz, a founder of modern ethology, described imprinting in geese during the 1930s. He is known for comparative studies of behavior—especially instinct—in birds, fish, and other animals. Lorenz's later ideas on human aggression, however, have been controversial.

Austrian ethologist Konrad Zacharias Lorenz, b. Nov. 7, 1903, d. Feb. 27, 1989, is often called the founder of ETHOLOGY, the comparative study of behavior in human beings and other ani-

mals. It was for his pioneering work in this field that Lorenz shared the 1973 Nobel Prize for physiology or medicine with animal behaviorists Karl von Frisch and Nikolaas Tinbergen.

Lorenz received his medical degree (1928) and his Ph.D. in zoology (1933) at the University of Vienna. In the early 1930s he and his colleague Oskar Heinroth studied and described the process of IMPRINTING that occurs at a very early age in some animals. He found, for example, that when goslings hatched in his presence and their mother's absence, they learned to follow him about and came to identify him as their mother in that way, even when they later saw their real mother. Lorenz found that some instinctive behavior patterns of this sort occur throughout all members of a species (see INSTINCT), and he reclassified certain species based on similarities and differences in such patterns.

Lorenz later turned his attention to human behavior, particularly aggression. Although he found aggressive behavior patterns instinctive to some degree, he maintained that they were no longer necessary for survival and could be altered to become socially useful behavior. His views, presented in *On Aggression* (1963; Eng. trans., 1966), aroused controversy but received wide attention. Lorenz also wrote *King Solomon's Ring* (1949; Eng. trans., 1952), *Man Meets Dog* (1950; Eng. trans., 1954), *Studies in Animal and Human Behavior* (1965; Eng. trans., 1970–71), and *The Waning of Humaneness* (1981; Eng. trans., 1987).   Reviewed by LOUIS LEVINE

Bibliography: Evans, Richard I., *Konrad Lorenz: The Man and His Ideas* (1975); Montagu, Ashley, ed., *Man and Aggression*, 2d ed. (1973); Nisbett, Alec, *Konrad Lorenz: A Bibliography* (1977).

Lorenzetti brothers   [lor-aynt-set'-ee]

The brothers Ambrogio and Pietro Lorenzetti, fl. first half of the 14th century, were among the most innovative Sienese painters of their time. They sometimes collaborated but usually worked independently, and each made distinctive contributions to the development of Italian painting.

Pietro Lorenzetti, on the basis of contemporaneous documents, seems to have been the elder. His earliest works recall the tenderness and the sinuous linearity of Duccio di Buoninsegna's paintings, but these qualities soon yield to a dramatic intensity and to a preference for broader forms that reflect a knowledge of the work of the great Florentine Giotto di Bondone. Pietro's new fervor is conveyed eloquently in the frescoes (date uncertain) of Christ's Passion in the Lower Church of San Francesco at Assisi. In the *Descent from the Cross,* for example, the harsh, angled contours of Christ's gaunt body and the stark anguish expressed by Mary and the other

The 14th-century Italian painter Ambrogio Lorenzetti's frescoes for the Palazzo Pubblico in Siena, Allegories of Good and Bad Government *(c.1338), are striking in their handling of perspective and a convincingly natural depiction of medieval urban life, going well beyond the decorative Sienese tradition of Duccio and Martini.*

mourners prefigure the poignancy of the altarpieces painted in the following century by the Netherlandish master Rogier van der Weyden. Even more notable is Pietro's rendering of deep and naturalistic space in his altarpiece *Birth of the Virgin* (1342; Museo dell'Opera del Duomo, Siena).

Ambrogio Lorenzetti's *Purification of the Virgin* (Uffizi, Florence), like his brother's *Birth of the Virgin*, was painted in 1342 for the Cathedral of Siena, and it anticipates even more closely the vanishing-point perspective developed in 15th-century Florence. Other representations of the Virgin by Ambrogio embody the homely, down-to-earth approach to Christian mysteries characteristic of his time. Ambrogio's most unprecedented work, however, is an enormous panoramic fresco known as *Good Government* (1337–39; more than 12 m/40 ft wide), in the Palazzo Pubblico of his town, portraying in vivid detail secular life in city and country under the beneficent government of Siena.   EDITH W. KIRSCH

Bibliography: Borsook, Eve, *The Mural Painters of Tuscany from Cimabue to Andrea del Sarto* (1960); Dewald, Ernest T., *Pietro Lorenzetti* (1930); Meiss, Millard, *The Great Age of Fresco* (1970); Rowley, George, *Ambrogio Lorenzetti*, 2 vols. (1958); White, John, *Art and Architecture in Italy: 1250 to 1400* (1966).

Lorenzo di Credi   [loh-rent'-soh dee kray'-dee]

The Florentine painter, sculptor, and goldsmith Lorenzo di Credi, b. Lorenzo d'Andrea d'Oerigo, c.1456–60, d. Jan. 12, 1537, developed a meticulous technique under the tutelage of the painter and sculptor Andrea del Verrocchio. Unlike his contemporaries in Verrocchio's studio, Leonardo da Vinci and Perugino, Credi was resistant to the stylistic innovations of the High Renaissance. His numerous images of seated madonnas with attendant angels reveal an artistic personality of scant imagination and often monotonous repetitiveness. Credi's consistently fine draftsmanship, however, is evident in his *Self-Portrait* (c.1490; National Gallery of Art, Washington, D.C.). Handpicked as his teacher's successor, Credi became the director of the most flourishing artistic workshop in Florence.   THOMAS W. SOKOLOWSKI

Bibliography: Freedberg, Sidney, *Painting in Italy 1500–1600* (1970); Seymour, Charles, *The Sculpture of Verrocchio* (1971).

Lorenzo Monaco   [moh'-nah-koh]

Lorenzo Monaco, b. Piero di Giovanni, c.1370–1425, was an early-Renaissance painter and miniaturist of the Florentine school who acquired the name Lorenzo the Monk on entering a monastery in Florence in 1391. Lorenzo was born in Siena and his earliest works reveal the influence of the Sienese school. His later paintings, however, are in the international Gothic style exemplified by his *Christ as Man of Sorrows* (1404; Accademia, Florence). In the *Monte Oliveto Altarpiece* (1410; Uffizi, Florence) and the *Coronation of the Virgin* (1414; Uffizi) Lorenzo used delicately patterned forms that are both decorative and naturalistic. His principal late works are the monumental frescoes of the *Life of the Virgin* (1420–22; Bartolini Chapel, Santa Trinità, Florence) and the *Adoration of the Magi* (1422; Uffizi).

Bibliography: Fremantle, Richard, *Florentine Gothic Painters* (1975); Hartt, Frederick, *History of Italian Renaissance Art* (1969).

Loricifera

Loriciferans, microscopic invertebrate animals that live in marine sands and gravels, were first observed in 1974 but not established as a separate phylum, Loricifera, until 1983. They share some features with bottom-dwelling invertebrates of similar size, but other features are sufficiently unique to justify their separate classification. Both larval and adult loriciferans have a flexible mouth cone, surrounded by a mass of spines, that can be withdrawn into the body along with the head. The larvae also have swimming appendages, but the adults are apparently sedentary and may live as ectoparasites. The name Loricifera, which means ''girdle wearer,'' refers to the series of cuticle platelets surrounding the midsections of the animals.

loris   [lor'-is]

The slow loris, N. coucang, is a primitive primate native to the jungles of Southeast Asia. It tightly grips tree branches as it slowly moves in search of food at night.

A loris is one of three species of small, nocturnal, tree-dwelling primates of Southern Asia characterized by extremely slow movements. The slender loris, *Loris tardigradus*, grows to about 26 cm (10 in) in length and weighs about 350 g (12 oz). The slow loris, *Nycticebus coucang*, grows to 38 cm (15 in) in length and weighs about 1.5 kg (3.5 lb). The lesser slow loris, *N. pygmaeus*, reaches only 20 cm (8 in) in length. Lorises feed on insects, lizards, birds and bird eggs, and fruit.

Lorrain, Claude   [loh-ren', klohd]

The French landscape painter Claude Gelée, b. Chamagne, Lorraine, 1600, d. Rome, 1682, is also known as Claude Lorrain, or simply as Claude. He moved to Rome as an adolescent and, but for a brief spell in Nancy, northeast France (1625–26), remained in Italy for the rest of his life. Not surprisingly, his work is more Italian than French in style.

Claude began his career as a fresco painter in Rome and Naples, but by the mid-1630s was producing small, finely detailed landscapes such as *View of Rome with the Trinità dei Monti* (1632; National Gallery, London). By the late 1630s he was the most celebrated landscape painter in Italy and about that time began compiling a record of his work in order to distinguish it from imitations and forgeries. The *Liber Veritatis*, a group of 195 carefully drawn copies of his paintings that is now in the British Museum, London, is an invaluable record of Claude's stylistic development. When reproduced in engravings at a later date, these drawings exercised a profound influence on landscape painters of the 19th century such as J. M. W. Turner and the French impressionists.

Claude may be said to have established the European tradition of LANDSCAPE PAINTING, but the true subject of his art was

Claude Lorrain's Odysseus Restoring Chryseis to Her Father *(1647) exemplifies the luminous lighting and evocative atmosphere characteristic of his work. Lorrain is considered one of the greatest exponents of 17th-century landscape painting. (Louvre, Paris.)*

the beauty and variety of natural light. His intense interest in light led, in many of his early paintings, to the relegation of human figures and physical objects such as trees and classical ruins to a position of secondary importance. Typically, the light in his earlier work emanates from a point low in the sky, flooding through the composition and suffusing it with a radiant glow. In later classical and biblical landscapes, such as *The Marriage of Isaac and Rebekah* (1648; National Gallery, London) and the *Embarkation of Saint Ursula* (1644; National Gallery), light is more diffused and imparts an idyllic atmosphere to the pastoral scene. Human figures are rarely the focus of interest in Claude's landscapes, but *The Sermon on the Mount* (1656; Frick Collection, New York City) is an exception. Although Claude's works were executed in the studio, their details were based on the numerous sketches that he made in the countryside near Rome. Nearly 1,000 of these are preserved in collections—notably that of the British Museum.

ROWLAND ELZEA

Bibliography: Cotté, Sabine, *Claude Lorrain* (1970); Kitson, Michael, *Claude Lorrain: Liber Veritatis* (1978); Mannocci, Lino, *The Etchings of Claude Lorrain* (1988); Röthlisberger, Marcel, *The Claude Lorrain Album* (1971).

Lorraine: see ALSACE-LORRAINE.

Los Alamos National Scientific Laboratory

Los Alamos National Scientific Laboratory, a research center devoted to the applications of nuclear energy and to national defense, occupies a 199-km² (77-mi²) site in the Jemez Mountains in north central New Mexico. The laboratory, founded in 1943 as the Atomic Research Laboratory, is operated by the University of California and funded by the U.S. Department of Energy. Scientists at Los Alamos developed the first ATOMIC BOMB (see also MANHATTAN PROJECT) and the first U.S. hydrogen bomb. The laboratory program has now extended to the peaceful uses of atomic energy and basic research in such fields as physics, biology, chemistry, geothermal energy, medicine, and metallurgy. Major facilities include magnetic-fusion-energy devices, tandem Van de Graaff generators, and an 800-MeV proton linear accelerator (see ACCELERATOR, PARTICLE) called LAMPF (Los Alamos Meson Physics Facility).

BRIAN SOUTHWORTH

Bibliography: Badash, Lawrence, et al., eds., *Reminiscences of Los Alamos, 1943–1945* (1980); Kunetka, James, *City of Fire: Los Alamos and the Birth of the Atomic Age 1943–1945* (1978); Lyon, Fern, and Evans, Jacob, *Los Alamos: The First Forty Years* (1984).

Los Angeles [laws an'-juh-les]

Los Angeles, located on the Pacific coast of southern California, is the seat of Los Angeles County. With 3,420,000 (1990 prelim.) inhabitants, Los Angeles is the second most populous city in the United States, having overtaken Chicago for that position during the decade of the 1980s with a growth rate of 15.3%. Metropolitan Los Angeles County, with a population of 8,700,000 (1990 prelim.), stretches eastward for about 160 km (100 mi) to the San Gabriel Mountains and includes LONG BEACH, PASADENA, SANTA MONICA, Beverly Hills, and about 100 other independent cities.

Numerous geologic faults cause periodic tremors, and the strong, dry Santa Ana winds pose the threat of fires spreading into the brush-covered hills around the city. The climate of Los Angeles is Mediterranean, with long, dry summers and rain from occasional winter storms. Annual precipitation averages 305 mm (12 in). Temperatures vary greatly between the milder coastal areas and the interior. In summer, cool sea air drawn in under hotter air creates a temperature inversion, trapping air pollutants from industry and the huge number of automobiles, and causing smog.

About 25% of the city's water needs are supplied from local wells; the remainder is piped in through aqueducts from the Owens River and the Sierra Nevada, from the Colorado River across the desert from the east, and from the Feather River in northern California.

Contemporary City. The city's layout today is marked by shopping centers and industrial parks scattered among tract housing, with the whole tied together by freeways. Public transportation is poorly developed; the private automobile is almost the sole means of mobility. The original Los Angeles, "Downtown L.A.," is only one of many commercial centers.

The population is composed of many minorities set in a basic matrix of Anglo-Americans, many of whom are retired people from other parts of the United States. Blacks—who totaled 505,208 persons in 1980—are the primary occupants of the area from Watts and Huntington Park to Culver City. Inmigration is strong, chiefly from rural areas of the South, and the black population is increasing rapidly. The Chicano group is growing more rapidly as a result of heavy emigration from Mexico. The Japanese-Americans have been integrated into the Anglo-American society and economy. Other groups include Koreans, Filipinos, Cubans, Chinese, and Vietnamese.

The economy of Los Angeles was once dependent on agriculture, but industry is much more important today. Modern Los Angeles industry falls largely into two groups: motion picture-recording-advertising and aerospace-electronics-engi-

Part of the vast urban agglomeration of Los Angeles is surveyed in an aerial photograph. "Downtown L.A." (center) is the site of major banks, hotels, and high-rise office and shopping complexes, but the area is only one of several major commercial centers. To the north, the Santa Monica Hills and San Gabriel Mountains (background) extend in an east-west direction above the Los Angeles basin. A national forest and wilderness preservation areas protect the San Gabriels from urban development.

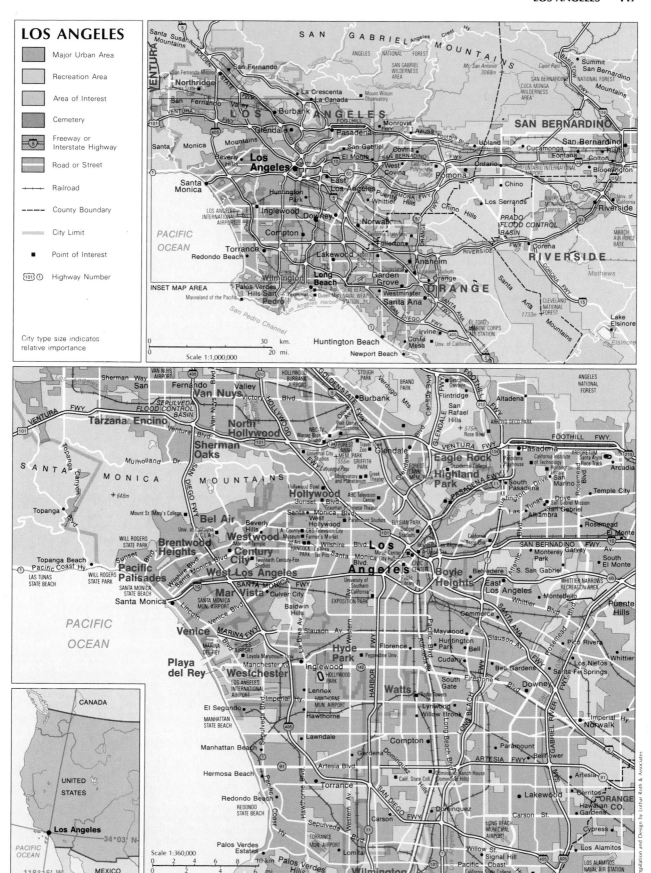

LOS ANGELES

▨	Major Urban Area
▨	Recreation Area
▨	Area of Interest
▨	Cemetery
5	Freeway or Interstate Highway
	Road or Street
+—+	Railroad
- - -	County Boundary
	City Limit
▪	Point of Interest
101 ①	Highway Number

City type size indicates relative importance

INSET MAP AREA

0   30 km.
0   20 mi.
Scale 1:1,000,000

PACIFIC OCEAN

San Gabriel Mountains, **San Bernardino**, **Riverside**, **Orange**, **Los Angeles**, **Long Beach**

Scale 1:360,000

0 2 4 6 8 10 km.
0   2 4 6 mi.

PACIFIC OCEAN

CANADA
UNITED STATES
Los Angeles — 34°03′ N
PACIFIC OCEAN
MEXICO
118°15′ W

Compilation and Design by Lothar Roth & Associates

neering-research. Manufactures include automobiles, farm machinery, chemicals, and textiles. Food processing, printing, and furniture making are also important. Petroleum, first discovered in 1892, is produced from several fields, some of which are highly productive, and the city has networks of buried pipelines supplying large refineries and storage "tank farms." The need for shipping petroleum spurred construction of the port of Los Angeles; the harbor, begun in 1899, is now one of the world's largest artificial harbors.

Included among the many institutions of higher education in the area are the CALIFORNIA INSTITUTE OF TECHNOLOGY (1891), the University of Southern California (1880), Occidental College (1887), and the University of California at Los Angeles (1919; see CALIFORNIA, STATE UNIVERSITIES AND COLLEGES OF). Among the numerous public parks are DISNEYLAND, Griffith Park, and Magic Mountain. The missions of San Gabriel (1771) and San Fernando (1797), El Pueblo de Los Angeles Historical Monument, and the WATTS TOWERS are notable landmarks. The GETTY MUSEUM, the Los Angeles County Museum of Art, the Museum of Contemporary Art, the George C. Page La Brea Discoveries Museum, and the Norton Simon Museum attract many visitors, as do the Hollywood Bowl and the Music Center for the Performing Arts. Government consists of an elected mayor and 15 elected council members.

History. The Spaniard Gaspar de PORTOLÁ camped near the site of Los Angeles in 1769. The settlement itself was founded in 1781 by Felipe de Neve, who named it El Pueblo de Nuestra Señora la Reina de los Angeles de Porciúncula (The Town of Our Lady, the Queen of the Angels of Porciúncula). U.S. forces won the city in 1847 during the Mexican War and gained all of California in the same year.

The arrival of two railroads—the Southern Pacific in 1876 and the Santa Fe in 1885—encouraged immigration. Los Angeles's rapid growth continued into the 20th century, and the city's population tripled between 1900 and 1910. During World War II defense industries underwent great expansion. The postwar years have brought Los Angeles face to face with the problems of older cities, but the area continues to attract many new residents. Among more recent highlights were the election in 1973 (and subsequent reelections) of Tom BRADLEY as the first black mayor of Los Angeles and the city's successful hosting of the 1984 Summer Olympics (it had also been the site of the 1932 Olympics).   RICHARD F. LOGAN

Bibliography: Lawson, G., *Los Angeles* (1984); Moore, C., et al., *The City Observed: Los Angeles* (1984); Parker, R. M., *L.A.* (1984).

Los Angeles County Museum of Art

Founded in 1910, the Los Angeles County Museum of Art has notable collections in a number of fields, including Egyptian, classical, Oriental, European, and American art. The Gothic period is particularly well represented by prime examples of stained glass and tapestries, and the museum has significant holdings dating from the Renaissance to the present.

One of the few major art museums in Southern California, it was made the beneficiary of the de Sylva bequest, a large collection of abstract paintings by such contemporary artists as Jackson Pollock, Mark Rothko, and Robert Motherwell. A spacious new complex of buildings was opened in 1966, designed by the controversial architect William L. Pereira. Additional new galleries were inaugurated in 1983.   CARTER RATCLIFF

Los Millares   [lohs meel-yar'-ays]

Situated on a promontory above the Andarax River in southeast Spain, Los Millares has been prominent in discussions of western Mediterranean prehistory since its partial excavation around 1900. The site consists of circular and rectangular huts inside an enclosure wall, four stone-built circular forts situated nearby, and a cemetery of about 80 burials of passage-grave type (see MEGALITH), some set within beehive-shaped stone structures called *tholos* tombs. Rich in copper tools and painted pottery, Los Millares is regarded as the type site for the Chalcolithic (Copper Age) Millaran culture. Radiocarbon dating has proved Los Millares to have been built before 3000 BC.   LLOYD R. LAING

Losey, Joseph   [loh'-zee]

The American-born film director Joseph Losey, who went to England during the McCarthy era of the 1950s, became one of Britain's foremost directors. This scene is from The Servant (1963), which brought Losey international recognition. Dirk Bogarde plays the title role in this film scripted by Harold Pinter, who collaborated with Losey on several films.

Although forced to abandon his career in the United States when blacklisted in the 1950s, Joseph Losey, b. La Crosse, Wis., Jan. 14, 1909, d. June 22, 1984, went on to become an important director in the British film industry. After extensive stage experience, Losey made his first feature film, *The Boy with Green Hair*, in 1948. This was followed by several taut melodramas—*The Lawless* (1950), *The Prowler* (1951), *M* (1951; a remake of Fritz Lang's classic), and *The Big Night* (1951)—that some still consider his best work. In 1952, during a period in which he was forced to work pseudonymously, he moved to London. There Losey gained international recognition with *The Servant* (1963), a film that marked the beginning of a fruitful collaboration with playwright Harold PINTER, later resumed in *Accident* (1967) and *The Go-Between* (1971). The charged atmospherics of these films also characterized such later Losey efforts without Pinter as *The Romantic Englishwoman* (1975) and *Mr. Klein* (1977).   WILLIAM S. PECHTER

Bibliography: Hirsch, Joseph, *Joseph Losey* (1980); Leahy, James, *The Cinema of Joseph Losey* (1967).

Lost Generation

"You are all a lost generation," Gertrude Stein said to Ernest Hemingway. The epithet refers to a group of American writers who came of age during World War I, and has been taken to mean that these authors were alienated both from traditional prewar values and from their roots in the United States: many of them (John Dos Passos, Hart Crane, F. Scott Fitzgerald) lived and worked in Europe. Hemingway used the phrase as the epigraph of his novel *The Sun Also Rises* (1926), whose characters do indeed seem to have lost their moral bearings. Yet the words mean little when applied to the work of the postwar literary generation, which produced a body of writing of extraordinary originality and vitality.

lost-wax process

The lost-wax process, also known as the investment casting process and by its French name *cire perdue*, is a precision casting method in which a pattern of wax or some other expendable material is used. The pattern is surrounded by a refractory slurry, commonly plaster; after the slurry mold has set, the wax is melted or vaporized out of the mold cavity. The metal is then poured into the space where the wax had been, and when the metal has cooled the slurry mold is removed. The method is a very old one and has been used for many years in casting bronze dental inlays, dentures, and jewelry. New techniques and materials have been devised to adapt the process to the casting of high-melting-point alloys such as those used in superchargers and gas turbines.

Patterns for the lost-wax process, formed in metal dies, must be made of materials, such as waxes or plastics, that will melt, vaporize, or burn completely and leave no residue. In order to produce the fine surface finish desired on precision castings, the patterns may be dipped in, or sprayed with, a

In industrial usage, the lost wax process is called investment casting and is used to make intricate precision parts by means of an expendable mold. In casting a turbine blade, the two halves of a steel mold are machined to the desired blade shape (A). The mold halves are then clamped together and wax is poured into the mold opening (B). After solidifying, the wax pattern is removed from the mold (C) and attached along with many other patterns to a common runner known as a tree (D). The tree assembly is dipped into a refractory slurry (E) to build up a coating that is dried and then sintered by heating. The wax melts and runs out (F), leaving a hollow ceramic mold into which molten metal is poured (G). The ceramic coating is chipped away and the solidified metal blade is removed from the tree (H) and machine finished (I).

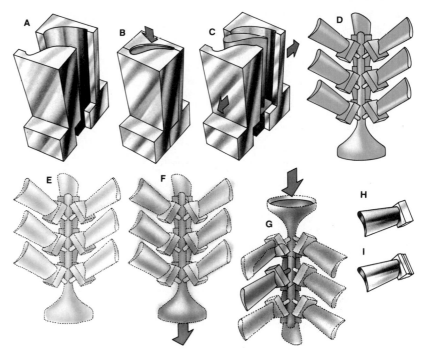

slurry of fine refractory powder before being surrounded by the plaster slurry. Complete setup and curing time for the mold may vary from half an hour to 24 hours, depending on the type of slurry used.

The most important use of the lost-wax process is in the casting of alloys and shapes that are difficult or impossible to manufacture by forging or machining procedures. However, the smoothness and dimensional accuracy that may be obtained by the process decreases as the castings get larger. In addition, the cost of the process is high because of the many steps involved, and it cannot compete with the screw-machining process where large production volumes are required.

MERLE C. NUTT

Bibliography: American Society for Metals, *Forging and Casting* (1970); Flinn, Richard A., *Fundamentals of Metal Casting* (1963); Kowal, Dennis, and Meilach, Dona, *Sculpture Casting* (1972).

Lot [laht]

In the Bible, Lot was the son of Abraham's brother Haran and lived in Sodom until it was destroyed by God (Genesis 19). He and his family escaped, but his wife turned into a pillar of salt when she looked back at the burning city. Through incestuous relations with his daughters, Lot was an ancestor of the Moabites and Ammonites.

Lothair, King of Lotharingia [loh-thair', lahth-uh-rin'-juh]

Lothair, b. *c*.835, d. Aug. 8, 869, was the second son of Frankish Emperor Lothair I. When the latter abdicated in 855 he left his namesake the northern part of the Frankish Middle Kingdom, which came to be called LOTHARINGIA. Most of Lothair's energy seems to have been spent in the effort to divorce his childless wife, Teutberga, and marry his mistress, Waldrada, so that his son by the latter would be recognized as his heir. This ploy failed because of the opposition of Pope NICHOLAS I. In 863, Lothair inherited the kingdom of Provence from his brother Charles. After Lothair's death, his kingdom was divided between his uncles LOUIS THE GERMAN and the future Emperor CHARLES II by the Treaty of Mersen (870).

BERNARD S. BACHRACH

Lothair I, Frankish Emperor

Lothair, b. 775, d. Sept. 29, 855, the eldest son of Emperor LOUIS I, came to rule the Middle Frankish Kingdom, which in-

cluded most of what is now the Low Countries, Alsace-Lorraine, Switzerland, and northern Italy. Lothair was designated to succeed his father as emperor in 817. In 822 he became king of Italy, and the next year he was crowned coemperor by the pope. Friction with Louis over the future of Lothair's half brother Charles (later Emperor CHARLES II) led to open conflict in 830 and again in 834 between the emperor and his coemperor.

When Louis I died in 840, civil war erupted between Lothair, his brother LOUIS THE GERMAN, and Charles. Lothair was defeated by his brothers at the Battle of Fontenoy (841), and in 843 he concluded the Treaty of Verdun (see VERDUN, TREATY OF), by which the Frankish empire was divided into three parts. Lothair received the Middle Kingdom as well as the imperial title. After dividing his kingdom among his three sons, Lothair entered the monastery of Prüm in 855.

BERNARD S. BACHRACH

Lothair II, King of Germany and Holy Roman Emperor

Lothair II (sometimes called Lothair III), b. 1075, d. Dec. 4, 1137, was German king (1125–37) and Holy Roman emperor (1133–37). The son of Gebhard, count of Supplinburg, Lothair was made duke of Saxony by Holy Roman Emperor HENRY V in 1106. When Henry died in 1125, the electors chose Lothair as his successor rather than Henry's nephew. Lothair had led the opposition against Henry, and his election thus represented a victory of princely independence over heredity. He encouraged the eastward expansion of Germany (see DRANG NACH OSTEN) and the spread of Christianity. Compliant toward the church and his advisor BERNARD OF CLAIRVAUX, Lothair supported Innocent II after the disputed papal election of 1130. Until 1135 he battled the HOHENSTAUFENS and strengthened his son-in-law, Henry the Proud of Bavaria, by grants of Italian and Saxon lands. On his deathbed, Lothair designated Henry as his successor, but the princes chose instead his former rival CONRAD III of Hohenstaufen.

RAYMOND H. SCHMANDT

Lotharingia [lahth-uh-rin'-juh]

Lotharingia was a region in early medieval Europe that comprised much of the present-day Low Countries and ALSACE-LORRAINE. When the Frankish empire was divided by the Treaty of Verdun in 843, Emperor LOTHAIR I received the portion called the Middle Kingdom. Shortly before his death in

855, however, he divided his kingdom; the northern segment was given to his son Lothair (see LOTHAIR, KING OF LOTHARINGIA) and came to be known as Lotharingia, or Lothair's kingdom.

After the younger Lothair's death (869) without an heir, his uncles the future Emperor CHARLES II and LOUIS THE GERMAN divided Lotharingia between them by the Treaty of Mersen (870). The western parts in general went to Charles and the West Frankish Kingdom, and the more easterly areas were taken by Louis and his East Frankish Kingdom. The East Frankish king Louis the Younger won control of all Lotharingia in 879–80, but during the next half-century Lotharingia passed from East Frankish domination to West Frankish domination and then back to the East in 925. Finally, Archbishop Bruno of Cologne, brother of Holy Roman Emperor Otto I, divided (959) Lotharingia into two duchies: Upper and Lower Lorraine. The latter soon broke up, but Upper Lorraine, soon known simply as Lorraine, continued as a duchy until 1766. The area was contested between France and Germany into the 20th century.   BERNARD S. BACHRACH

Bibliography: McKitterick, Rosamund, *The Frankish Kingdoms under the Carolingians* (1983).

Lothian   [loh'-thee-un]

Lothian is an administrative region in southern Scotland. Bordered by the rivers Tweed and Forth, the region has an area of 1,753 km² (677 mi²) and a population of 745,229 (1985 est.). A highly developed region, Lothian is a major agricultural and industrial center. The chief crops are wheat, barley, and vegetables, and manufactures include paper and engineering products, textiles, and heavy metals. Some coal mining and fishing also take place. The principal cities are EDINBURGH, Haddington, and Linlithgow.

Lothian was a part of the English shire of Northumberland before coming under the influence of the Scots in the 11th century. In 1333 the region was taken by Edward III of England, but it was eventually returned to the Scots. In 1975, during the reorganization of local government in Scotland, Lothian was created from parts of the former counties of East and West Lothian and Midlothian.

lottery

A lottery is a popular form of GAMBLING in which the players pay to participate, and the winners are determined by chance. (It is also a method of selection, as in a lottery to choose which groups of men will be conscripted into the army.) In most lotteries, players buy numbered tickets at fixed prices. At a subsequent drawing, the winning numbers are picked at random (by lot) or are selected on some other unpredictable basis—such as the results of a horse race.

Over the centuries, lotteries of various types have been organized for a variety of purposes and have realized huge sums for their promoters. Governments have frequently used lotteries as a source of revenue or as a supplement to, or substitute for, taxation. The earliest state lotteries were organized in France in 1520. In 1680, England held a historic lottery to raise funds for improving London's water supply equipment. Spain developed the *gordo*, and Ireland, the sweepstakes. Lotteries were popular in the United States, although dishonest practices in both private and public lotteries eventually forced the federal government to prohibit (1890) the transportation of lottery tickets by mail or in interstate commerce. The states also took prohibitive action, and between the 1890s and 1963, no government-sponsored lotteries were held in the United States.

In 1963, however, New Hampshire authorized a sweepstakes lottery and designated a proportion of the moneys made to be spent on its education system. The lottery proved so profitable that, by the end of the 1980s, more than half of the states (and the District of Columbia) had approved lotteries—among them, California, Massachusetts, New Jersey, New York, and Pennsylvania. The practice of the states is to reserve a certain percentage of the lottery take for expenses, a large percentage for the state itself, and a lesser percentage

for prizes. Resisting the growing popularity of state lotteries, North Dakota voters rejected one in 1988.

Lotteries have remained an important feature of life in other countries as well. In 1976, Canada sponsored a lottery to help pay for the Olympic Games in Montreal; by the time the games started the lottery had netted an unexpected $200 million. Today that country has a number of provincial and national lotteries. The Soviet Union introduced several national lotteries to help develop Soviet sports and to finance construction of facilities for the 1980 Olympic Games.

Bibliography: Adler, Bill, *The Lottery Book* (1986); Lang, John T., *Digest of State Lotteries* (1983); Wagman, Robert, *Instant Millionaires: Cashing in on America's Lotteries* (1986).

Lotto, Lorenzo   [loht'-toh, loh-rent'-soh]

Lorenzo Lotto, b. c.1480, d. 1556, was one of the first great Venetian artists of the High Renaissance to see the art of central Italy and Rome. From 1509 to 1511 he worked with a number of artists in the Vatican Stanze—the apartments of Pope Julius II—which were later to be completed by Raphael (see VATICAN PALACE). Lotto's introverted and peripatetic nature led him to work in the provincial towns of northern Italy, especially in those of the provinces called the Marches, rather than in the large artistic centers. His austere and elegant religious pictures, such as the *Madonna and Child with Saints* (c.1520s; Kunsthistorisches Museum, Vienna), are founded on a strong base of 15th-century religiosity that recalls northern European types, especially those of Albrecht Dürer. His use of strong, clear lighting is patterned after that in Giovanni Bellini's work, and he always used a perspectival grid overlaid with ornamental detail.

After short stays in Florence and Bergamo, Lotto returned to Venice about 1526, where he produced such highly original works as his *Portrait of Andrea Odoni* (1527; Royal Collections, Hampton Court Palace), which could be mistaken for a much later Mannerist painting. In 1552, Lotto ceased his wanderings and sought refuge at the Sanctuary of the Holy House in Loreto; two years later he became an oblate (lay member). To this period belongs his last masterpiece, *The Presentation of Christ in the Temple* (after 1552; Palazzo Apostolico, Loreto). Lotto's long sequence of portraits have become his most admired works; his paintings done in the ¾-length Venetian portrait mode are among the most riveting images of the 16th century.

Bibliography: Berenson, Bernard, *Lorenzo Lotto* (1895; repr. 1956).

lotus   [loh'-tuhs]

Lotuses are five species of water lilies, three in the genus *Nymphaea* and two in *Nelumbo*; both genera are members of the water-lily family, Nymphaeaceae. Lotus is also the name of a genus in the pea family, Leguminosae, which contains such plants as the bird's-foot trefoil, *Lotus corniculatus*.

Nymphaea lotus, the Egyptian white lotus, is believed to be

The lotus Nymphaea lotus *bears many-seeded, berrylike fruit and leathery, floating leaves that may reach 50 cm (20 in) across. The cup-shaped flowers of the lotus were often represented in ancient Egyptian art and architecture.*

the original sacred lotus of ancient Egypt. It and the Egyptian blue lotus, *N. caerulea*, were often pictured in ancient Egyptian art. The white lotus is a shallow-water, night-blooming plant with a creeping rootstock (rhizome) that sends up long-stalked, nearly circular, dark green leathery leaves, which float on the surface. The flowers, up to 25 cm (10 in) across, remain open until midday. The blue lotus is a smaller, less showy day-blooming plant. The Indian blue lotus, *N. stellata*, differs from the blue Egyptian species largely in its leaves.

Nelumbo contains but two species. The American lotus, *N. lutea*, is found in the eastern half of the United States into southern Canada. It has thick, spreading rootstock and large bluish green circular leaves that are usually raised above the surface of the water. The pale-yellow flowers usually open on three successive days. Both the seeds and the rootstock (rhizomes) were eaten by the Indians. The East Indian lotus, *N. nucifera*, found in southern Asia, was introduced into Egypt about 2,500 years ago but is no longer found there. The lotus has been a sacred symbol in many cultures and is particularly prominent in Buddhism.　　　　　EDWIN E. ROSENBLUM

Lotus-Eaters

In Greek mythology, the Lotus-Eaters (or Lotophagi) were a North African people who subsisted on the fruit of the lotus tree, which made them forget the past and live in blissful indolence. In the *Odyssey*, some of ODYSSEUS's crew tasted the lotus fruit, forgot their homes and families, and had to be forcibly carried back to the ships by their companions.

Lotze, Rudolf Hermann　　[loht'-seh]

Rudolf Hermann Lotze, b. May 21, 1817, d. July 1, 1881, was a German philosopher who attempted to reconcile the concepts of mechanistic science with the principles of romantic idealism. A student of both medicine and philosophy at Leipzig, he later lectured there in both fields, becoming a professor in 1842. In 1844 he succeeded J. F. Herbart as professor at Göttingen, and in 1881 he joined the faculty at Berlin.

Lotze combined a firm belief in the universality of scientific law with a conviction of the need for metaphysics. He insisted that philosophy is rooted in the natural sciences, because human beings are subject to the same natural laws as inanimate objects. He protested against attempts to deduce reality from mere principles; knowledge, he held, is the result of observation and experimentation, not of logical dialectic. The task of metaphysics is therefore to analyze and systematize concepts that the sciences produce.

According to Lotze, nature is governed by mechanical law, but the system of nature is a set of means to a divinely appointed end. He considered all things as immanent in God (see IMMANENCE, DIVINE); what the scientist sees as mechanical causality is simply the expression of the divine activity. So-called laws are the divine action itself, the mode of God's operation. Lotze's principal work was *Mikrokosmos* (1856–64; Eng. trans., 1899).　　　　　PETE A. Y. GUNTER

Bibliography: Santayana, George, *Lotze's System of Philosophy*, rev. ed. (1971); Thomas, E. E., *Lotze's Theory of Reality* (1921).

loudspeaker

A loudspeaker, or speaker, is one of several devices that convert electrical energy into mechanical energy. Such devices are called electromechanical TRANSDUCERS. In a loudspeaker the mechanical energy is in the form of vibrations that are transmitted to the surrounding air, producing sound (see SOUND AND ACOUSTICS).

Types of Speakers. Theoretically, a number of operating principles can be used for a loudspeaker. In practice, however, one particular type is most popular because of its efficiency and wide-range response; it is known as an electrodynamic, dynamic, magnetic, or magnetodynamic loudspeaker. Less popular, but also in use, is the electrostatic loudspeaker.

Operation. In the electrodynamic loudspeaker an electromagnet or permanent magnet produces a magnetic field. A voice coil situated within or surrounding the magnetic field is

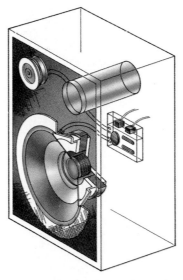

A bass reflex speaker, with its large woofer and small tweeter, also contains a port, or vent—the cylinder directly above the woofer—which enhances bass tones. The box on the cabinet's rear contains terminals for the wires connecting speaker and amplifier and the electronics for the crossover network.

energized by the electrical signal. Hence a variable magnetic field is generated in the coil, and the coil is alternately attracted to and repelled from the magnet. The coil is linked to a diaphragm, which vibrates and causes the surrounding air to vibrate, re-creating the original sound. In the electrostatic loudspeaker the diaphragm is a conducting plate. Surrounding it are two fixed grids. When the signal voltage is applied to the grids, the electrostatic force produced causes the diaphragm to vibrate.

Most speaker transducers, known as drivers, require a surrounding structure called an enclosure to efficiently transfer sound energy to the surrounding air. A large driver, or woofer, with a diaphragm up to 76 cm (30 in) in diameter, and large enclosure are required for efficient low-frequency reproduction; at high frequencies a small driver, the tweeter (as small as 2.5 cm/1 in) is more efficient. Many speaker systems also have a midrange speaker, intermediate in size, that operates most efficiently at the middle frequencies. An electrical network called a crossover divides the audio spectrum into frequency bands suitable for each driver, which is then driven in the appropriate frequency band.

Types of Speaker Systems. In theaters, stadiums, and similar locations, driver/radiator combinations are often large, freestanding components. In high-fidelity systems for the home, however, all elements of the speaker system are usually contained in one multipurpose radiator called an enclosure.

Narrow-band speakers have been developed specifically to reproduce the narrow frequency band of speech; such speakers are used in public-address systems. The other extreme is the single speaker designed to cover the widest possible frequency band, as in small radios, televisions, and headphones.

Two sound channels are used to create STEREOPHONIC SOUND, a technique where sound is recorded simultaneously on right and left bands to fabricate the illusion of hearing the sounds live. To reproduce stereo sound, two speakers are needed.　　　　　KENNETH C. ROBERTSON

Bibliography: Colloms, M., *High Performance Loudspeakers*, 3d ed. (1985); Dearborn, L., and Dasheff, B., *Good Sound* (1987); Fantel, H., and Berger, I., *New Sounds of Stereo* (1986).

Louganis, Greg

Diver Gregory Louganis, b. San Diego, Calif., Jan. 29, 1960, was only 16 when he won a silver medal in the platform dive at the 1976 Olympics. Since then his accomplishments in both platform and springboard competition are unapproached: 4 of 4 Olympic gold medals (1984, 1988), 6 of 6 Pan American Games gold medals (1979, 1983, 1987), 5 of 6 world championships (1978, 1982, 1986), and 47 U.S. titles. Louganis was awarded the 1984 Sullivan Award as the finest U.S. amateur athlete.

Louis, Joe

Joe Louis Barrow, b. Lafayette, Ala., May 13, 1914, d. Apr. 12, 1981, who fought as Joe Louis—nicknamed "the Brown Bomber"—was the longest-reigning world heavyweight boxing champion in history. Louis fought his first amateur bout in 1932, and 2 years later he won the Amateur Athletic Union (AAU) light-heavyweight title. He turned professional in 1934 and won the heavyweight title on June 22, 1937, by knocking out James J. Braddock in 8 rounds. On Mar. 1, 1949, he retired as champion after holding the title 11 years 8 months and defending it 25 times, a record for any division. He returned to the ring in financial straits in 1950 and lost a 15-round decision to Ezzard Charles in another title bout. After being knocked out in the 8th round the following year by Rocky Marciano, Louis retired permanently. He was a dexterous two-fisted fighter and is regarded by some as the greatest heavyweight ever. His only loss prior to his first retirement was in 1936 to Max Schmeling of Germany in a nontitle fight. In 1938, after he had become champion, Louis avenged the loss and knocked out Schmeling in the first round in one of the most famous fights in history; many sport fans saw the fight as a symbolic showdown between American democracy and German dictatorship. He defeated such fighters as Primo Carnera, Billy Conn, Lou Nova, Jack Sharkey, and Jersey Joe Walcott. During his professional career Louis recorded 68 victories (54 by knockout) and lost only 3 fights.

Bibliography: Astor, Gerald, . . .And a Credit to His Race: The Hard Life and Times of Joseph Louis Barrow, a.k.a. Joe Louis (1974); Louis, Joe, et al., Joe Louis: My Life (1978); Young, Andrew S., Negro Firsts in Sports (1963).

Joe Louis, a former national amateur champion, won the world heavyweight boxing championship in 1937 and defended his title 25 times before retiring in 1949. Among his most dramatic bouts was his first-round knockout of Max Schmeling in 1938, avenging a previous loss to Schmeling that Adolf Hitler had claimed as evidence of Aryan racial supremacy.

Louis, Morris

Morris Louis, originally named Morris Bernstein, b. Baltimore, Md., Nov. 28, 1912, d. Sept. 7, 1962, was an abstract color-field painter and one of the leading members of the Washington Color School. He was awarded a scholarship to the Maryland Institute in 1929 and during the late 1930s worked in New York for the Works Progress Administration's Federal Arts Project. After moving to Washington, D.C., in 1952, Louis taught painting at the Washington Workshop Center for the Arts and at the Corcoran School of Art until his death.

The trademark of Louis's mature color-field style was his technique of pouring thinned, acrylic paint onto unprimed canvas to create soft, glowing effects, an idea inspired in 1953 by Helen FRANKENTHALER's work. His 1954 paintings, called "veils," consisted of layers of transparent paint. These were followed by "florals," composed of bursts of color that radiate from the center of the painting. His later, "unfurled," works exhibit large central areas of raw canvas, with stripes of color flowing diagonally across the lower corners. Louis's last paintings, called "stripes," were more formal, exhibiting only parallel lines of bright color.   HARRY RAND

Bibliography: Fried, Michael, Morris Louis (1970); Hunter, Sam, American Art of the 20th Century (1972).

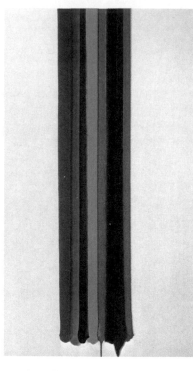

The American artist Morris Louis's Pillars of Dawn (1961), part of a series of paintings composed of stripes of color, exemplifies his technique of applying veils of transparent color to absorbent canvas. (Wallraf-Richartz Museum, Cologne.)

Louis, Victor

Victor Louis, b. May 10, 1731, d. July 3, 1800, was a leading architect during the reigns of Louis XV and Louis XVI and a major exponent of the neoclassical style in France. He worked primarily in the realm of public architecture: the theater in Bordeaux (1772–88), with its grandiose succession of stair and auditorium spaces, became an important model for later theater building; the novel use of cast iron in the Comédie Française (1787–90), Paris, was equally innovative. His favorite motif was the continuous row of giant columns or pilasters, as seen in his best-known work, the wings enclosing the garden of the Palais Royal (1781–84), Paris.   ROBERT NEUMAN

Louis decorative styles: see STYLES OF LOUIS XIII–XVI.

Louis the German, East Frankish King

During the reign of the Carolingian king Louis the German, b. c.804, d. Aug. 28, 876, the separation of Germany from the Frankish state began. One of the sons of Frankish Emperor LOUIS I, Louis the German was involved in the civil wars of his father's reign, which culminated in the Treaty of Verdun (843; see VERDUN, TREATY OF). This agreement divided the Carolingian state into three parts: Louis received the lands of the German-speaking peoples; his half brother, Charles the Bald (later Frankish Emperor CHARLES II), the French-speaking areas; and his brother Emperor LOTHAIR I, a middle kingdom comprising Italy and the area later called LOTHARINGIA.

Much of Louis's reign was devoted to gaining control of the lands assigned to his brothers. In 860 he was promised Alsace, and in 870 he and Charles partitioned the remainder of Lotharingia by the Treaty of Mersen. Louis exercised some limited authority over the Slav tribes east of the Elbe River and protected Bishop Ansgar of Hamburg-Bremen's mission to convert Sweden. In his last years Louis worked in vain to acquire the imperial crown and Italy for his son Carloman.   RAYMOND H. SCHMANDT

Louis Napoléon: see NAPOLEON III, EMPEROR OF THE FRENCH.

Louis Philippe, King of France

The reign of Louis Philippe, the "citizen king" of France, marked the triumph of the wealthy bourgeoisie over the aristocracy. Assuming power after the July Revolution (1830), Louis sought friendship with Britain and supported colonial expansion; France conquered Algeria during his reign. Resisting political reform, Louis Philippe antagonized the lower middle and working classes and was forced to abdicate in the Revolution of February 1848. (Portrait by F. X. Winterhalter, Versailles.)

Louis Philippe, b. Oct. 6, 1773, d. Aug. 26, 1850, was the last king of France. A member of the ORLÉANS family, the younger branch of the ruling Bourbon house, he was the son of Philippe Égalité. He served as an officer in the royal army and fought in the republican army in early battles of the French Revolutionary Wars. In 1793, suspected of involvement in a conspiracy to restore the monarchy, he fled the country. For the remaining years of the Revolutionary and Napoleonic period, Louis Philippe lived in exile. While in Sicily for a time, he married (1809) Marie Amélie, daughter of Ferdinand IV of Naples and a descendant of LOUIS XIV of France.

In 1814, Louis Philippe returned to France and with his large family took up residence in Paris. His political sympathies were with the liberal opposition to the restored Bourbon regime, but there is no firm evidence that he was significantly involved in politics. In 1830, however, when the JULY REVOLUTION drove CHARLES X from Paris and forced his abdication, Orléanist supporters won over both deputies and streetfighters to accepting Louis Philippe as king of the French.

As king, Louis Philippe observed the forms of parliamentary government, but by selection of amenable first ministers, manipulation of elections, parliamentary intrigue, and judicious granting of favors he achieved a high degree of personal rule. He resisted all attempts to make the government more representative and responsive, and his rule became increasingly ill-adapted to the needs and expectations of a country entering a period of revolutionary economic and social change. On Feb. 23, 1848, a minor demonstration turned into insurrection, and Louis Philippe found himself without effective support, either political or military. He abdicated on February 24, and the Orléanist monarchy ended on that day with the proclamation of the Second Republic. Louis Philippe fled to England, where he died.   DAVID H. PINKNEY

Bibliography: Howarth, T. E. B., *Citizen King* (1961); Pinkney, David H., *The French Revolution of 1830* (1972).

Louis I, King of Bavaria

Louis, or Ludwig, I, b. Aug. 25, 1786, d. Feb. 29, 1868, ruled Bavaria from 1825 until 1848, when he was forced to abdicate. A patron of the arts, he made Munich, his capital, one of the world's major art centers. Succeeding his father, MAXIMILIAN I, Louis initially pursued moderate, liberal policies. He aided the Greek revolt against the Ottoman Empire; his second son became king of Greece as OTTO I in 1832. Louis rapidly turned reactionary, however, and his unpopularity was increased by his affair with Lola MONTEZ. The REVOLUTIONS OF 1848 displaced him in favor of his son Maximilian II.

ROBIN BUSS

Louis II, King of Bavaria

Louis, or Ludwig, II of Bavaria, b. Aug. 25, 1845, d. June 13, 1886, is remembered for his patronage of the composer Richard WAGNER, for his lavish buildings, and for his eccentricities.

Succeeding his father, Maximilian II, as king in 1864, Louis supported Austria in the SEVEN WEEKS' WAR (1866) but allied with Prussia in the FRANCO-PRUSSIAN WAR (1870–71) and joined the new German Empire in 1871. Soon disillusioned with the Prussian-dominated empire, he abandoned politics and involved himself totally in his cultural pursuits and his homosexual love life.

In 1864, Louis had invited Wagner to Munich, giving him a pension to complete his opera-cycle *The Ring of the Nibelungs*. Although public hostility soon forced Louis to renounce his friendship with the composer, he continued his financial support of Wagner. Increasingly cut off from reality, the king developed a mania for building elaborate castles and palaces, where he created a fantasy world. Pronounced insane in 1886, he drowned himself a few days later.

Bibliography: Blunt, Wilfrid, *The Dream King: Ludwig II of Bavaria* (1970); Chapman-Huston, Desmond, *Bavarian Fantasy* (1956).

Louis II's Bavarian palaces

The three country palaces of Louis II, king of Bavaria (r. 1864–86), also called "Mad Ludwig," are among Bavaria's most popular and profitable tourist attractions.

Schloss Neuschwanstein (begun 1869), a many-turreted mock castle perched on a crag near Füssen in the Bavarian Alps, was built as a shrine to three of Richard WAGNER's operas: *Lohengrin*, *Parsifal*, and *Tannhäuser*. Although some of the interiors remain unfinished, the king's suite was completed. The large neo-Romanesque minstrel's hall recalls the setting for act 2 of *Tannhäuser*—the Hall of Song in the Wartburg. The 2-story throne room, with its resplendent gold and polychrome mosaics, galleried arcades, and central dome, closely resembles a Byzantine church.

Schloss Linderhof (1870–79), his only completed project, was the king's favorite residence. The diminutive palace, a white rococo confection set in a rugged alpine valley near Neuschwanstein, was intended to memorialize the Bourbon King Louis XIV. The charming result is an amalgam of French, Franconian, and Bavarian rococo, particularly evident in the lush fittings, furniture, tapestries, and crystal chandeliers. The four principal chambers form a cross, with a stair hall at its center to the ground floor. Four salons in the corners connect the rooms to form a rectangular suite. In the extensive surrounding park is a huge underground re-creation of the Venusberg Grotto, the setting for the opening scene of *Tannhäuser*, complete with waterfall, lake, and colored lights.

Schloss Herrenchiemsee (begun 1878), on an island in the Chiemsee, was designed to glorify the principle of absolute monarchy. Louis intended a full-scale facsimile of Versailles (see VERSAILLES, PALACE OF), but only the great central block was completed before his death in 1886. The splendid staircase is a meticulous replica of the *Escalier des Ambassadeurs* (destroyed in 1752) at Versailles, and the magnificent Hall of Mirrors outdoes the *Galerie des Glaces* in opulence. The sumptuously embellished state apartments were not intended for occupancy; a separate suite was created for the king's use. In the vast gardens many features, such as the Grand Canal and the Apollo and Latona fountains, recall their counterparts at Versailles.   EDWARD T. MCCLELLAN

Louis I, King of France: see LOUIS I, FRANKISH EMPEROR   (Louis the Pious).

Louis IV, King of France   (Louis d'Outremer)
[doo-truh-mair']

Louis d'Outremer ("from overseas"), b. 921, d. Sept. 10, 954, was king of France from 936. Son of King CHARLES III (Charles the Simple), he was taken to England as a child by his mother Eadgifu, daughter of the Anglo-Saxon king Edward the Elder. Recalled to France to succeed King Raoul (r. 923–36), Louis struggled against Hugh the Great, count of Paris, through most of his reign. While attempting to conquer Normandy, he was captured in 945 and became Hugh's prisoner until 946. With the aid of the German king OTTO I, he eventually defeated Hugh, who made peace in 950.

Louis VI, King of France   (Louis the Fat)

Louis VI, b. 1081, d. Aug. 1, 1137, succeeded his father, PHILIP I, as king of France in 1108. As early as 1100, however, he had begun to take over the military leadership of the monarchy from his aging and lethargic father. During this period the French princes were virtually independent, and the king had effective power only in the royal domain consisting essentially of the Île-de-France. Even this region was infested with unruly barons who used their castles as bases from which to terrorize the countryside, plunder churches, and disrupt transportation. In 30 years of almost constant fighting, Louis VI, with strong support from the clergy, forced these barons to accept his discipline, won the respect of the princes, and laid the foundations for the future growth in monarchical power. Although not an eager supporter of church reform, Louis had good relations with the popes, one of whom was his wife's uncle. He held his own against such dangerous and powerful neighbors as the duke of Normandy, who was HENRY I of England, and the count of Blois. He also led an army that repelled a German invasion in 1124, although he was less successful when he tried to intervene in Flanders in 1127. In the latter year he reduced the power of the Garlande family, which had sought to dominate the royal administration, and thereafter his main advisors were Raoul, count of Vermandois, and SUGER, abbot of Saint-Denis, who became his biographer. Shortly before Louis's death in 1137, ELEANOR OF AQUITAINE became his ward and married his son and successor, Louis VII.   JOHN B. HENNEMAN

Bibliography: Fawtier, Robert, *The Capetian Kings of France*, trans. by Lionel Butler and R. J. Adam (1960); Petit-Dutaillis, Charles E., *The Feudal Monarchy in France and England from the Tenth to the Thirteenth Century*, trans. by E. D. Hunt (1936).

Louis VII, King of France   (Louis the Young)

Louis VII, b. 1121, d. Sept. 18, 1180, the second son of Louis VI of France, became heir to the throne on the death (1131) of his elder brother. He succeeded his father in 1137, a few days after marrying ELEANOR OF AQUITAINE. Louis inherited not only a prosperous, well-pacified royal domain, but also two experienced counselors, Raoul of Vermandois and SUGER. His youth and inexperience led Louis into over-ambitious projects during the first 15 years of his reign. One of these was the Second CRUSADE (1147–49), which was a military disaster, although it enhanced the visibility, and hence the prestige, of the French crown. In 1152, Louis had his marriage to Eleanor annulled, and she promptly married Henry, count of Anjou and duke of Normandy, who became HENRY II of England in 1154. The addition of Aquitaine to Henry's other possessions made him much more powerful than Louis, and he was a frequently hostile neighbor. With Suger and Raoul both dead by the end of 1152, Louis had to reconstruct his government around new advisors. He established close ties with the counts of Flanders and Champagne, collaborated with the church, encouraged the growing towns, and carefully managed the resources of the royal domain. Between Henry II and the Holy Roman emperor FREDERICK I, he reestablished strong royal influence in Burgundy and Languedoc. He also supported the intrigues of Henry's rebellious sons. In 1165, Louis's third wife, Adèle of Champagne, gave birth to a long-desired male heir, who was to succeed to the throne as PHILIP II. Louis barely managed to hold his own against his rival, Henry II, with his vast holdings. He left to his son, Philip, however, a stronger and better-respected French monarchy than he had inherited.   JOHN B. HENNEMAN

Bibliography: Fawtier, Robert, *The Capetian Kings of France*, trans. by Lionel Butler and R. J. Adam (1960); Petit-Dutaillis, Charles E., *The Feudal Monarchy in France and England from the Tenth to the Thirteenth Century*, trans. by E. D. Hunt (1936).

Louis VIII, King of France

Louis VIII, b. Sept. 5, 1187, d. Nov. 8, 1226, was the son of PHILIP II of France and Isabella of Hainaut. He married (1200) BLANCHE OF CASTILE, niece of King JOHN of England. In 1214, Louis blocked John's Poitou campaign, and in 1216 he invaded England, supporting the rebellious barons and laying claim to the throne. After a defeat at Lincoln he was persuaded to leave in 1217. Louis succeeded to the French throne in 1223 and conquered Poitou from the English in 1224. Throughout his career he was also heavily involved in the crusade against the ALBIGENSES. He made expeditions to southern France in 1215 and 1219 and returned as king in 1226 to pacify the region.   JOHN B. HENNEMAN

Louis IX, King of France   (Saint Louis)

Louis IX (Saint Louis), a Capetian king of France, appears at prayer in this medieval miniature. He led the Seventh Crusade to the Holy Land in 1248 and died during a later crusade. Louis, who came to be regarded as the model Christian king, was canonized in 1297 by Pope Boniface VIII. (Bibliothèque Nationale, Paris.)

Louis IX of France, later known as Saint Louis, most closely approached the medieval ideal of chivalric kingship. Born on Apr. 25, 1214, he was the oldest son of the future king LOUIS VIII and BLANCHE OF CASTILE. He came to the throne as a child in 1226, and the early years of his reign were marked by princely uprisings. The queen mother, Blanche, successfully overcame this opposition and in 1229 concluded a treaty with the count of Toulouse that gave the crown a foothold on the Mediterranean and terminated the crusade against the ALBIGENSES. Louis himself removed the last threat to royal authority in Poitou by defeating the English at Taillebourg in 1242. He had attained his majority in 1234, although Blanche was to remain influential until her death (1252).

A man of great piety and a strong pacifist in dealing with fellow Christians, Louis was bitterly intolerant of heretics and non-Christians. In 1245, while recovering from a serious illness, he resolved to lead a CRUSADE to the Middle East. Before he left, he dispatched commissioners called *enquêteurs* to discover and correct governmental abuses in France. He then departed for the Levant in 1248, leaving Blanche as regent.

Louis was accompanied on the crusade by Jean, sire de JOINVILLE, whose biography of Louis remains an important historical source. The Crusaders captured the Egyptian port of Damietta, but afterward Louis was defeated and taken prisoner at Mansura in 1250. After his release he remained in the Middle East for several years before returning to France in 1254.

In his later years, Louis promoted internal reforms and made treaties with Aragon (1258) and England (1259) that were intended to establish permanently peaceful relations. Before the end of the century, however, France fought wars with both these countries, and Louis was subsequently criticized for being too conciliatory. In 1270 he undertook another crusade, this time against Tunis; he became ill and died near Tunis on Aug. 25, 1270. Admired for his prowess, his piety, and his strong sense of justice, Louis was revered as a saint well before his canonization by the church in 1297. Feast day: Aug. 25.   JOHN B. HENNEMAN

Bibliography: Joinville, Jean de, *The Life of Saint Louis*, ed. by Natalis de Wailly, trans. by René Hague (1955); Labarge, Margaret W., *Saint Louis: Louis IX, Most Christian King* (1968).

Louis XI, King of France

Louis XI, called by his enemies "the universal spider," was an able but unpopular ruler. Seeking to centralize power in the crown, Louis enlisted the support of bourgeois officials, successfully curbed the power of the great nobles, and encouraged the growth of industry and professional guilds. Fearing assassination, he spent his final years in seclusion near Tours. (Brooklyn Museum.)

Louis XI was a highly successful French monarch whose enemies dubbed him the Spider. He was born on July 3, 1423, when his father, CHARLES VII, was at the nadir of his political fortunes. Louis did not get along with his father, and at the age of 17 he joined an unsuccessful princely revolt called the Praguerie. In the 1440s he held a number of important commands, but in 1447 he retired to the Dauphiné, the province that he held as heir to the throne (see DAUPHIN). He ruled efficiently there until Charles seized the land in 1456 and drove him into exile at the Burgundian court. Louis's continuing feud with his father was partly the product of misunderstandings purposely encouraged by their respective advisors.

Louis returned from exile in 1461 to succeed Charles as king. Reversing many of his father's policies, he soon antagonized a large part of the kingdom. A princely coalition called the League of the Public Weal rebelled in 1465, and Louis had to make significant concessions to dissolve this group. He then realized that an effective monarchy required the weakening of the princes and that this goal could be achieved more easily by capitalizing on their mutual jealousies than by resorting to force. In general he endeavored to cooperate with the families of Bourbon and Anjou, to isolate Brittany, to crush the dissident Gascon lords, and to break the power of the duke of Burgundy by subsidizing the latter's other enemies, notably the Swiss. Louis's greatest successes derived from the death of CHARLES THE BOLD, duke of Burgundy, in 1477 and the extinction of the princely house of Anjou in 1481, both of which brought the crown substantial territory and eliminated dangerous rivals.

These successes were largely a matter of luck, a fact that makes assessing the importance of Louis XI difficult. His reign is rich in narrative sources—mainly chronicles, memoirs, and the reports of Italian ambassadors. These writings portray a king with many bizarre characteristics who enhanced the greatness of his realm through guile and cunning; he appears as an inveterate schemer who earned the hatred of his subjects by tripling taxes but who was able to liquidate serious threats to the monarchy without recourse to costly wars. Yet the vast administrative documents of Louis's reign have not been carefully studied, and the memoirs of Philippe de Com-

mynes, long the most respected narrative source, has been discredited by recent scholarship. Louis, who died on Aug. 30, 1483, remains an enigma.   JOHN B. HENNEMAN

Bibliography: Cleugh, James, *Chant Royal* (1970); Comines, Philippe de, *Memoirs: The Reign of Louis XI*, trans. and intro. by Michael Jones (1972); Kendall, P. M., *Louis XI, The Universal Spider* (1971).

Louis XII, King of France

Throughout his reign, Louis XII, who ruled France from 1498 to 1515, was involved in foreign wars, most notably the ITALIAN WARS. Louis was born on June 27, 1462, the son of Charles, duc d'ORLÉANS and thus the great-grandson of king Charles V. Forced to marry (1476) the deformed daughter of Louis XI, Louis was still childless when he succeeded his cousin CHARLES VIII as king in 1498. He had his first marriage annulled in order to marry (1499) Charles's widow, ANNE OF BRITTANY, by whom he had two daughters. Brittany, however, was not incorporated into the royal domain until the reign of FRANCIS I, Louis's cousin and successor, who married Louis and Anne's older daughter, Claude, in 1514.

Charles VIII had invaded Italy (1494) in pursuit of a rather remote claim to the throne of Naples. Louis XII inherited this claim and had a much stronger claim of his own to Milan, derived from his grandmother Valentina Visconti, whose family had ruled Milan until 1447. These French claims in Italy had already alarmed FERDINAND II of Aragon, inducing that Spanish monarch to conclude marriage alliances with the Austrian Habsburg dynasty, which had recently secured the Burgundian inheritance in the Low Countries. The wars of Louis's reign were waged against this backdrop of complex dynastic politics and territorial claims.

First invading Italy in 1499, Louis was generally successful in the north, holding Milan from 1500 to 1512. He and Ferdinand agreed in 1500 to divide the kingdom of Naples, but as they carried out the division, they quarreled. Defeats by Spanish forces at Cerignola and Garigliano in 1503 forced France to abandon Naples. In 1508, Louis joined the League of Cambrai against Venice and defeated the latter at Agnadello (1509). Once again his allies turned against him after securing their shares of the spoils. Pope JULIUS II organized (1511) a Holy League against France comprising the papacy, Aragon, Venice, the Swiss Confederation, England, and the Holy Roman Empire. Defeated at Novara and Guinegate in 1513, Louis lost all his Italian conquests. Although duped and defeated abroad, Louis was a popular king because he did not demand excessive taxes and provided the nobles with military employment and opportunities for glory. He died on Jan. 1, 1515.
JOHN B. HENNEMAN

Bibliography: Bowen, Marjorie, *Sundry Great Gentlemen* (1928; repr. 1968); Law, Joy, *Fleur de Lys: The Kings and Queens of France* (1976).

Louis XIII, King of France

Louis XIII, b. Sept. 27, 1601, d. May 14, 1643, allowed his minister Cardinal RICHELIEU to rule France for most of his reign. The son of HENRY IV and MARIE DE MÉDICIS, he succeeded to the throne in 1610 at the age of eight. Louis was stubborn and sickly as a boy and grew up to be proud, secretive, and devout. However, he was determined to be just and showed genuine concern for his subjects. In 1615, while still under his mother's regency, the young king married ANNE OF AUSTRIA, daughter of Philip III of Spain. Two years later he ended the regency, exiling his mother to Blois and suppressing the two subsequent attempts she made to recover her authority. In 1620, Louis annexed the formerly autonomous and largely Protestant province of Béarn, and he commanded his troops in several campaigns to reimpose Catholicism there and in French Navarre. His chief advisor in this period was his falconer, Charles d'Albert, duc de Luynes, who died in 1621.

In 1624, Louis entrusted Richelieu with total authority. While the cardinal crushed the French Protestants (HUGUENOTS), he allied France with the Protestant powers against Spain during the THIRTY YEARS' WAR. Richelieu made himself so indispensable that he survived the many plots to undermine his influence with the king.

Louis largely ignored his wife, who for a time dallied with the English duke of BUCKINGHAM—the incident fictionalized in Alexandre Dumas Père's *The Three Musketeers*. The king formed close friendships with several other women and, from 1639, with the young marquis de Cinq-Mars. In 1642, however, he sanctioned the latter's execution when Richelieu proved that Cinq-Mars was plotting with Spain. The cardinal died in December 1642, and Louis survived him by only six months. He was succeeded by his young son, Louis XIV.

J. H. M. SALMON

Bibliography: Chapman, Hester, *Privileged Persons* (1966); Tapié, Victor L., *France in the Age of Louis XIII and Richelieu*, ed. and trans. by D. McN. Lockie (1975).

Louis XIV, King of France

Louis XIV, the French "Sun King," epitomized absolutism in his long (1643-1715) reign. Louis's strong personal rule brought the extension of France's boundaries, the decline of the power of the nobility, and the promotion of industry and art. He appears here in a painting by Hyacinthe Rigaud. (Louvre, Paris.)

Louis XIV, France's Sun King, had the longest reign in European history (1643-1715). During this time he brought absolute monarchy to its height, established a glittering court at VERSAILLES, and fought most of the other European countries in four wars. The early part of his reign (1643-61), while Louis was still young, was dominated by the chief minister Cardinal MAZARIN. In the middle period (1661-85) Louis reigned personally and innovatively, but the last years of his personal rule (1685-1715) were beset by problems.

Minority. Born on Sept. 5, 1638, Louis was the first, regarded as "god-given," child of the long-married Louis XIII and his Habsburg wife, ANNE OF AUSTRIA. He succeeded his father on the throne at the age of four. While his mother was regent the great nobles and the judges of the PARLEMENT of Paris launched a major but uncoordinated revolt (the FRONDE of 1648-53) in reaction to the centralizing policies of Louis XIII's minister Cardinal RICHELIEU and his successor, Mazarin. The royal family was twice driven out of Paris, and at one point Louis XIV and Anne were held under virtual arrest in the royal palace in Paris.

Mazarin finally suppressed the Fronde and restored internal order. The Peace of Westphalia (1648; see WESTPHALIA, PEACE OF) which ended the Thirty Years' War, together with the Peace of the Pyrenees (1659), which concluded prolonged warfare with Spain, made France the leading European power. The latter treaty was sealed by Louis XIV's marriage (1660) to Marie Thérèse (1638-83), the daughter of PHILIP IV of Spain.

Personal Administration. On Mazarin's death in 1661, Louis astounded his court by becoming his own chief minister, thereby ending the long "reign of the cardinal-ministers." A sensational 3-year trial (1661-64) of the powerful and corrupt finance minister Nicolas FOUQUET sent the would-be chief minister to prison for life. The king thereafter controlled his own government until his death, acting through his high state council (*conseil d'en haut*) and a few select ministers, whom he called or dismissed at will. The most famous and powerful of the ministers were Jean Baptiste COLBERT in internal affairs and the marquis de LOUVOIS in military matters.

Breaking with tradition, Louis excluded from his council members of his immediate family, great princes, and others of the old military nobility (*noblesse d'épee*); his reliance on the newer judicial nobility (*noblesse de robe*) led the duc de SAINT-SIMON to call this, mistakenly, "the reign of the lowborn bourgeoisie." Local government was increasingly placed under removable INTENDANTS.

Period of Glory. The early personal reign of Louis was highly successful in both internal and foreign affairs. At home the parlements lost their traditional power to obstruct legislation; the judicial structure was reformed by the codes of civil procedure (1667) and criminal procedure (1669), although the overlapping and confusing laws were left untouched. Urban law enforcement was improved by creation (1667) of the office of lieutenant general of police for Paris, later imitated in other towns. Under Colbert commerce, industry, and overseas colonies were developed by state subsidies, tight control over standards of quality, and high protective tariffs. As controller general of finances, Colbert sharply reduced the annual treasury deficit by economies and more equitable, efficient taxation, although tax exemptions for the nobility, clergy, and some members of the bourgeoisie continued.

Colbert and the king shared the idea of glorifying the monarch and monarchy through the arts. Louis was a discriminating patron of the great literary and artistic figures of France's classical age, including Jean Baptiste MOLIÈRE, Charles LEBRUN, Louis LE VAU, Jules MANSART, and Jean Baptiste LULLY. His state established or developed in rapid succession academies for painting and sculpture (1663), inscriptions (1663), French artists at Rome (1666), and science (1666), followed by the Paris Observatory (1667) and the academies of architecture (1671) and music (1672). The literary Académie Française also came under formal royal control in 1671.

Money was lavished on buildings. In Paris the LOUVRE was essentially completed with the classical colonnade by Claude PERRAULT. At Versailles, Louis XIII's hunting lodge was transformed into a remarkable palace and park, which were copied by Louis's fellow monarchs across Europe. When the king moved permanently to Versailles in 1682, an elaborate court etiquette was established that had the aristocracy, including former rebel princes, vying to participate in Louis's rising (*levé*) and retiring (*couché*) These ceremonies led to the saying that, at a distance, one could tell what was happening at the palace merely by glancing at an almanac and a watch.

In foreign affairs, the young Louis XIV launched the War of DEVOLUTION (1667-68) against the Spanish Netherlands, claiming that those provinces had "devolved" by succession to his Spanish wife rather than to her half brother CHARLES II, who had inherited the Spanish crown. The war brought him some valuable frontier towns in Flanders. Louis turned next against the United Provinces of the Netherlands in the third ANGLO-DUTCH WAR (1672-78). The intent this time was to revenge against Dutch intervention in the previous war and to break Dutch trade. By the Peace of Nijmegen (1678-79) he gained more territory in Flanders, and the formerly Spanish FRANCHE COMTÉ was added to France's eastern frontier, now fortified by the great siege expert, Sébastien Le Prestre de

VAUBAN. Now at the height of his power, the king set up "courts of reunion" to provide legal pretexts for the annexation of a series of towns along the Franco-German border. More blatantly, he seized both the Alsatian city of Strasbourg and Casale, in northern Italy, in 1681.

Period of Decline. The turning point in Louis's reign between the earlier grandeur and the later disasters came after Colbert's death (1683). In 1685 the king took the disastrous step of revoking the Protestant (HUGUENOT) minority's right to worship by his Edict of Fontainebleau, often called the revocation of the Edict of Nantes (see NANTES, EDICT OF). Many Huguenots—who constituted an industrious segment of French society—left the country, taking with them considerable capital as well as skills. In addition Louis's display of religious intolerance helped unite the Protestant powers of Europe against the Sun King.

In September 1688, Louis sent French troops into the Palatinate, hoping to disrupt his enemies who had formed the League of Augsburg (see AUGSBURG, LEAGUE OF) against him. The 9-year war of the GRAND ALLIANCE ensued. France barely held its own against the United Provinces and England, both under WILLIAM III, as well as Austria, Spain, and minor powers; but the Treaty of Rijswijk (1697) preserved Strasbourg and Louis's "reunion" acquisitions along the Franco-German border.

The aging ruler was almost immediately drawn into the disastrous War of the SPANISH SUCCESSION (1701–14), in which he defended his grandson PHILIP V's inheritance of Spain and its empire on the death of Charles II. The genius of the English general the duke of MARLBOROUGH and his Austrian counterpart, EUGENE OF SAVOY, was almost too much for the ducs de VILLARS, BERWICK, and VENDÔME, who were Louis's principal generals. The terrible French winter of 1709 and near fiscal collapse also took their toll. Nonetheless, France rallied. By the Peace of Utrecht (see UTRECHT, PEACE OF) France retained most of its earlier conquests, and the Spanish empire was divided between Philip V, who received Spain and its overseas colonies, and Holy Roman Emperor CHARLES VI, who acquired the Spanish Netherlands and Spain's Italian possessions. Louis was forced to agree that the crowns of France and Spain would remain separate despite the Bourbon dynastic connection.

During the post-1685 period the once personal monarchy became increasingly bureaucratized. A long and bitter quarrel (1673–93) with the pope was concluded when the king withdrew the French clergy's Four Gallican Articles of 1682, in which they had claimed quasi-independence from the papacy for the French church (see GALLICANISM). Reconciliation with the papacy aided Louis's attempt to suppress JANSENISM. The Jansenist convents of Port-Royal were closed (1709–10), and in 1713 the pope issued, at Louis's request, the anti-Jansenist bull *Unigenitus.*

After a series of celebrated liaisons with mistresses, notably Louise de la Vallière and Madame de MONTESPAN, Louis settled down to a more sedate life with Madame de MAINTENON, whom he secretly married about 1683. She shared with Louis the grief of lost battles and the successive deaths of all but two of his direct descendants. The two who survived him were his grandson Philip V of Spain and a great-grandson who became Louis XV when the Sun King died on Sept. 1, 1715.   A. LLOYD MOOTE

Bibliography: Gaxotte, Pierre, *The Age of Louis Fourteenth,* trans. by Michael Shaw (1958; repr. 1970); Goubert, Pierre, *Louis XIV and Twenty Million Frenchmen,* trans. by Anne Carter (1970); Hatton, Ragnhild, *Louis XIV and His World* (1972); Lewis, W. H., *The Splendid Century* (1954); Ogg, David, *Louis Fourteenth,* 2d ed. (1967); Rule, John, ed., *Louis XIV and the Craft of Kingship* (1969); Wolf, John B., *Louis XIV* (1968).

Louis XV, King of France

Louis XV, who succeeded his great-grandfather Louis XIV as king of France in 1715, was dominated by court factions, his own sensual pleasures, and his mistresses, notably the marquise de POMPADOUR and the comtesse DU BARRY. His reign's disastrous wars, mounting fiscal crisis, and conflicts with JAN-

SENISM and the PARLEMENTS, which repeatedly vetoed tax reforms, prepared the way for the French Revolution of 1789.

Born on Feb. 15, 1710, to the duc de Bourgogne (Burgundy) and Marie Adélaide of Savoy, Louis was a minor under the regency of the duc d'Orléans (see ORLÉANS, PHILIPPE, DUC D') from 1715 to 1723. Orléans reversed Louis XIV's policy of governing without the parlements and nobility and backed financier John LAW's ill-fated MISSISSIPPI SCHEME. From 1726 to 1743 the young king was guided by his former tutor, André Hercule de FLEURY, who governed cautiously and economically. In the War of the POLISH SUCCESSION (1733–38), France backed the former Polish king STANISŁAW I, who was the father of Louis's wife Maria Leszczyńska. After the war Stanisław acquired Lorraine, which passed to France in 1766.

On Fleury's death (1743) Louis tried to be his own chief minister, but his ineffectualness increased court divisions. French participation in the War of the AUSTRIAN SUCCESSION (1740–48) proved costly and territorially unrewarding, and the king failed to back Controller-General Jean Baptiste de Machault's attempt to raise government funds by including the clergy, nobles, and parlementary judges in a new universal tax (the *vingtième,* 1749). In the SEVEN YEARS' WAR (1756–63) France was not only committed to another bout of costly continental fighting but also lost most of its overseas empire (including its North American colonies; see FRENCH AND INDIAN WARS) to Britain.

The naval and army reforms of the duc de CHOISEUL and the acquisition (1768) of Corsica were not enough to restore the king's plummeting popularity. Although he had been called the well-beloved after a near fatal illness in 1744, he narrowly escaped assassination in 1757. Belatedly, Louis moved to support the reform efforts of his chancellor, René de Maupeou, who secured abolition of the parlements' tax-vetoing power in 1771. The reform was promptly overturned when the king died on May 10, 1774, and was succeeded by his grandson, Louis XVI.   A. LLOYD MOOTE

Bibliography: Behrens, C. B. A., *The Ancien Régime* (1967); Gooch, G. P., *Louis XV: The Monarchy in Decline* (1956; repr. 1976); Gramont, Sanche de, *Epitaph for Kings* (1967); Lough, John, *Introduction to Eighteenth-Century France* (1961).

Louis XVI, King of France

Louis XVI, grandson and successor of Louis XV as king of France, was neither interested in politics nor capable of dealing with the FRENCH REVOLUTION, which engulfed his reign. Absorbed in family life, eating, hunting, and mechanical arts (he was a skilled locksmith), he allowed a mounting financial crisis to culminate in the destruction of the once powerful absolute monarchy and French aristocratic society, and he lost his own life to the revolution.

Born on Aug. 23, 1754, to the Dauphin Louis and Maria Josepha of Saxony, Louis became heir to the French throne on his father's death in 1765. In 1770 he married the Austrian

Louis XVI, the last Bourbon monarch of France with absolute powers, was a well-intentioned but weak-willed and indecisive ruler. Engulfed by the French Revolution (1789), Louis outwardly accepted the establishment of a constitutional monarchy but secretly attempted to sabotage the efforts of the new regime. He was convicted of treason and on Jan. 21, 1793, was guillotined in the Place de la Révolution in Paris. (Portrait by J. S. Duplessis, Versailles.)

archduchess MARIE ANTOINETTE, and in 1774 he succeeded his grandfather to the throne.

Louis's first fateful act as king was to restore the political power of the reactionary PARLEMENTS, which Louis XV had virtually abolished in 1771. The new king appointed (1774) the fiscal reformer Baron TURGOT as controller-general of finance but dismissed (1776) him in the face of parlementary opposition. Jacques NECKER, the next director of finances, floated huge loans, but he too was dismissed (1781) when his reform efforts incurred the courtiers' hostility. French participation (1778–83) on the rebel side in the American Revolution increased the government's debts and fueled demands for liberty at home.

After the failure of Charles CALONNE, controller-general from 1783 to 1787, to steer tax reform past a royally appointed Assembly of Notables, Louis gave in to the popular demand for an elected STATES-GENERAL to discuss the financial crisis. When it met in 1789 the king's indecisiveness over voting procedure and lack of a royal reform program allowed revolutionary middle-class delegates to dominate events and declare themselves a National Assembly. When Louis halfheartedly summoned troops against the assembly, a Parisian mob stormed the BASTILLE (July 14), signaling the beginning of violent revolution.

In October 1789 a mob forced the royal family to leave Versailles for Paris, where they were housed in the Tuileries palace. Although Louis had publicly accepted the revolutionary changes, he remained under suspicion because of footdragging on revolutionary legislation. An abortive attempt to flee France (the so-called Flight to Varennes, June 1791) and popular fear of Louis's collusion with the Austrians and Prussians, who invaded France in 1792, led to a mob uprising against the monarchy in August 1792. A republic was declared on September 21. Evidence that Louis had intrigued with the Austrians was used in his trial for treason in December. He was condemned by a complicated, close multiple vote in the republic's Convention and executed by guillotine on Jan. 21, 1793.   A. LLOYD MOOTE

Bibliography: Cobban, Alfred, *A History of Modern France*, vol. 1, rev. ed. (1963); Cronin, Vincent, *Louis and Marie Antoinette* (1975); Faÿ, Bernard, *Louis XVI; Or the End of a World*, trans. by Patrick O'Brian (1968); Furneaux, Rupert, *The Last Days of Marie Antoinette and Louis XVI* (1971); Padover, Saul K., *The Life and Death of Louis XVI*, rev. ed. (1963).

Louis XVII, King of France

Although Louis XVII, b. Mar. 27, 1785, was proclaimed king of France by royalist exiles after the execution (January 1793) of his father, Louis XVI, he remained a prisoner until his death. The second son of Louis and MARIE ANTOINETTE, he became heir to the throne on the death (1789) of his elder brother. After the overthrow of the monarchy in 1792, he was first imprisoned with his family. In July 1793 he was removed from his mother and placed for a time in the care of a shoemaker, Antoine Simon. Neglected, he became ill and almost certainly died on June 8, 1795. Rumors that he had escaped enabled a number of people to claim later that they were Louis XVII.

Bibliography: Francq, H. C., *Louis Seventeenth* (1970).

Louis XVIII, King of France

Louis XVIII, b. Nov. 17, 1755, d. Sept. 16, 1824, became king of France in 1814, when the Bourbon monarchy was restored following the Revolutionary and Napoleonic period. A younger brother of Louis XVI, he fled France early in the French Revolution and in 1795, on the death of his nephew, Louis XVII, he proclaimed himself king of France. He did not recover the throne, however, until after the abdication of NAPOLEON I in 1814, and he was forced into exile again during Napoleon's brief return to power (1814–15).

When he came back to France in 1814, Louis understood that the revolution and Napoleon had fundamentally changed the country and that there could be no turning back. He granted (June 4, 1814) a constitution that guaranteed parliamentary government, a free press, and essential legal and so-cial reforms, and he exercised a wisely restraining influence on the reactionary Ultraroyalists. In the 1820s, however, he yielded increasingly to pressures from the Ultras and sanctioned policies favoring the nobility and the clergy. He was succeeded by his younger brother, CHARLES X.

DAVID H. PINKNEY

Bibliography: Bertier de Sauvigny, Guillaume de, *The Bourbon Restoration* (1966); Stewart, John H., *The Restoration Era in France, 1814–1830* (1968).

Louis IV, King of Germany and Holy Roman Emperor   (Louis the Bavarian)

Louis, or Ludwig, IV, b. Apr. 1, 1282, d. Oct. 11, 1347, overcame a disputed election to the German kingship and intense papal opposition in the last major medieval church-state conflict. When Emperor HENRY VII of the house of Luxemburg died, the German electors sought a king from another dynasty. They divided, however, between Louis, who was duke of Bavaria and a member of the WITTELSBACH family, and the HABSBURG Frederick the Fair of Austria. Both were elected king in 1314, and a long war ensued. Louis finally won with a decisive victory in the Battle of Mühldorf in 1322.

At this point Pope JOHN XXII, living in Avignon, intervened, claiming the right to veto Louis's election. When Louis denied this right, John excommunicated him. Supported by philosophers MARSILIUS OF PADUA and John of Jandun, as well as by some disaffected Franciscan friars, Louis entered Italy in 1327. He had himself crowned emperor by lay officials in Rome in 1328 and set up an antipope, Nicholas V. Most of the German princes came to back Louis against increasingly fierce papal denunciations, and in 1338, by the Declaration of Rense, the electors asserted that they alone had the power to elect the German kings, who automatically became emperors-elect. Louis's decree *Licet juris* enacted that statement as law.

Louis continued to negotiate, to no avail, with John's successors, Benedict XII and CLEMENT VI. In the meantime he alienated his German supporters by his expansion of his family's domains. To acquire the Tyrol he annulled (1341) the marriage of its heiress, Margaret Maultasch, by royal decree and induced her to marry his own son, thus contravening canon law. In 1346 the electors finally accepted the papal deposition of Louis and elected CHARLES IV of the house of Luxemburg as king. Louis was preparing to fight when he died while hunting.   RAYMOND H. SCHMANDT

Louis I, King of Hungary   (Louis the Great)

Louis the Great, b. Mar. 5, 1326, d. Sept. 10, 1382, was king of Hungary (1342–82) and of Poland (1370–82). One of the greatest and most beloved rulers of Hungary, he made that country into a significant power in Central and Eastern Europe. The son and successor of CHARLES I (Charles Robert), Louis was the second ANGEVIN king of Hungary. He typified the so-called knightly ruler; under his rule Hungary experienced a cult of knightly virtues. Louis's expansive foreign policy brought him considerable success in the Balkans (Dalmatia, Serbia, Bulgaria, Walachia). But because of papal opposition, his efforts to gain control over the Kingdom of Naples, where his family had come from, were doomed to failure. After the death of his maternal uncle CASIMIR III of Poland (1370), Louis also gained the Polish throne. But being an absentee king, he was less than successful as ruler of Poland. Of his two surviving daughters, Maria inherited Hungary and JADWIGA ascended to the Polish throne.   S. B. VARDY

Bibliography: Kosary, D. G., and Vardy, S. B., *History of the Hungarian Nation* (1969); Lukinich, Imre, *A History of Hungary in Biographical Sketches* (1937; repr. 1968).

Louis II, King of Hungary

Louis, or Lajos, II, b. July 1, 1506, d. Aug. 29, 1526, was the last king of the JAGELLO dynasty to rule Hungary and Bohemia. The son of Ulászló II, he succeeded to the throne as a minor in 1516. Sickly and frivolous, he remained under control of the Hungarian magnates after he was declared of age in 1521.

In 1522 he married the Habsburg Maria of Austria. When the Ottoman Turks invaded Hungary, Louis led a force of 20,000 against them in 1526. His army was crushed in the Battle of MOHÁCS, and Louis himself drowned during the retreat. His crowns then passed to his wife's brother Archduke Ferdinand (later Holy Roman Emperor FERDINAND I).

Louis I, Frankish Emperor (Louis the Pious)

Although Louis I, b. 778, d. June 20, 840, was an able ruler and energetic military commander, his reputation has suffered because he was not as successful as his father, CHARLEMAGNE. Louis was crowned king of Aquitaine at the age of three and after reaching his majority, he established a vigorous Carolingian presence in Spain. His brothers having died, he was crowned coemperor in 813, and in 814 he succeeded Charlemagne as sole ruler of the Frankish empire.

Louis sought to develop the imperial ideal, working closely with the church. However, squabbles among his sons for greater shares in what was to be their inheritance led to civil war. In 817, Louis made his eldest son, LOTHAIR I, coemperor and allocated parts of the empire to his other sons, LOUIS THE GERMAN and Pepin. The birth of another son, the future Emperor CHARLES II, to Louis's second wife, Judith of Bavaria, started the trouble. Louis's attempts to provide for Charles precipitated a series of revolts by the older sons. The invasions of Vikings and Muslims further weakened Carolingian power. By the time of Louis's death the empire was in serious decline.   BERNARD S. BACHRACH

Bibliography: Cabaniss, Allen, *Son of Charlemagne* (1961); Duckett, Eleanor, *Carolingian Portraits* (1962; repr. 1988).

Louis II, Frankish Emperor

Louis II, b. *c.*822, d. Aug. 12, 875, was the eldest son of the emperor LOTHAIR I. Designated to rule Italy in 839, Louis was crowned king by the pope in 844, and in 850 he was made coemperor with his father. He became sole emperor in 855 after his father's abdication, although his rule was confined to Italy. Louis spent most of his career trying to expel the Saracens (Arabs) from southern Italy, an endeavor in which he was hindered by the Lombard princes. Despite victories over the Arabs at Bari (871) and Capua (872), he failed to win control of the south. On the death (863) of his brother Charles, Louis gained much of the Provence. When his other brother, LOTHAIR II, died in 869, however, Louis received no part of the kingdom of Lotharingia, which was partitioned by his uncles LOUIS THE GERMAN and Charles the Bald (later Emperor CHARLES II).   BERNARD S. BACHRACH

Louisbourg   [loo'-is-burg]

Louisbourg (1986 pop., 1,355) is a town on Cape Breton Island, northeastern Nova Scotia. Fish processing and packing is the economic mainstay. Louisbourg was settled in 1713 by the French, who constructed (1720–40) there a great fortress designed by Sébastien le Prestre de VAUBAN. The town was taken by the British in 1745 during King George's War (see FRENCH AND INDIAN WARS) but was restored to France by the Treaty of Aix-La-Chapelle in 1748. During the final French and Indian War the British again captured (1758) the fortress; they evacuated the French and used Louisbourg as a base for capturing much of Canada. The old fortress has been extensively restored and is now a national historic park.

Louise, Lake

Lake Louise is a picturesque lake in the Canadian Rockies in southwest Alberta. Within Banff National Park, the small (2.4-km-long/1.5-mi) lake lies at an altitude of 1,728 m (5,670 ft) and is framed by tall, glacier-topped peaks. It drains eastward to the Bow River. Discovered in 1882, Lake Louise is a popular year-round resort.

Louisiana

Located in the southeastern United States, Louisiana lies entirely within the Gulf Coastal Plain. It is shaped like a capital

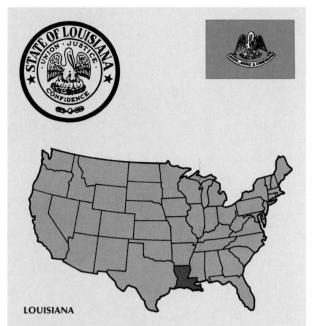

LOUISIANA

LAND. Area: 123,677 km² (47,752 mi²); rank: 31st. Capital: Baton Rouge (1988 est. pop., 235,000). Largest city: New Orleans (1988 est. pop., 532,000). County equivalents (parishes): 64. Elevations: highest—163 m (535 ft), at Driskill Mountain; lowest— −2.4 m (−8 ft), at New Orleans.

PEOPLE. Population (1990 prelim.): 4,180,831; rank: 21st; density: 36.3 persons per km² (93.9 per mi²). Distribution (1988 est.): 69.2% metropolitan, 30.8% nonmetropolitan. Average annual change (1980–90): −0.06%.

EDUCATION. Public enrollment (1988): elementary—581,095; secondary—205,588; higher—149,349. Nonpublic enrollment (1980): elementary—88,500; secondary—28,400; combined— 40,100; higher (1988)—26,682. Institutions of higher education (1987): 34.

ECONOMY. State personal income (1988): $54.2 billion; rank: 23d. Median family income (1979): $18,088; rank: 33d. Nonagricultural labor distribution (1988): manufacturing—170,000 persons; wholesale and retail trade—360,000; government— 314,000; services—327,000; transportation and public utilities— 107,000; finance, insurance, and real estate—83,000; construction—84,000. Agriculture: income (1988)—$1.9 billion. Fishing: value (1988)—$317 million. Forestry: sawtimber volume (1987)—70.7 billion board feet. Mining: value, nonfuels only (1987)—$424 million. Manufacturing: value added (1987)— $16.5 billion. Services: value (1987)—$13.6 billion.

GOVERNMENT (1991). Governor: Charles E. (Buddy) Roemer, Democrat. U.S. Congress: Senate—2 Democrats; House—4 Democrats, 4 Republicans. Electoral college votes: 10. State legislature: 39 senators, 105 representatives.

STATE SYMBOLS. Statehood: Apr. 30, 1812; the 18th state. Nickname: Pelican State; bird: Eastern brown pelican; flower: magnolia; tree: bald cypress; motto: Union, Justice, Confidence; songs: "Give Me Louisiana" and "You Are My Sunshine."

L, approximately 530 km (330 mi) at its widest, and about 450 km (280 mi) from north to south. Louisiana is bordered by Mississippi on the east, the Gulf of Mexico on the south, Texas on the west, and Arkansas on the north. Sighted by the Spanish in 1519, Louisiana was first explored by Pánfilo de NARVÁEZ of Spain, who navigated its coast in 1528. Later, Robert Cavelier, sieur de LA SALLE, named the region Louisiane in honor of the French king Louis XIV, claiming it for France in 1682. The state's long and varied history, diverse population, abundant energy resources, and strategic location at the mouth of the Mississippi River are valued attributes. The problems that exist in Louisiana stem from its prolonged recovery after the Civil War, its relatively slow industrial growth, and its heavy dependence on extractive industries.

LAND

Louisiana is part of a sedimentary plain that slopes gently

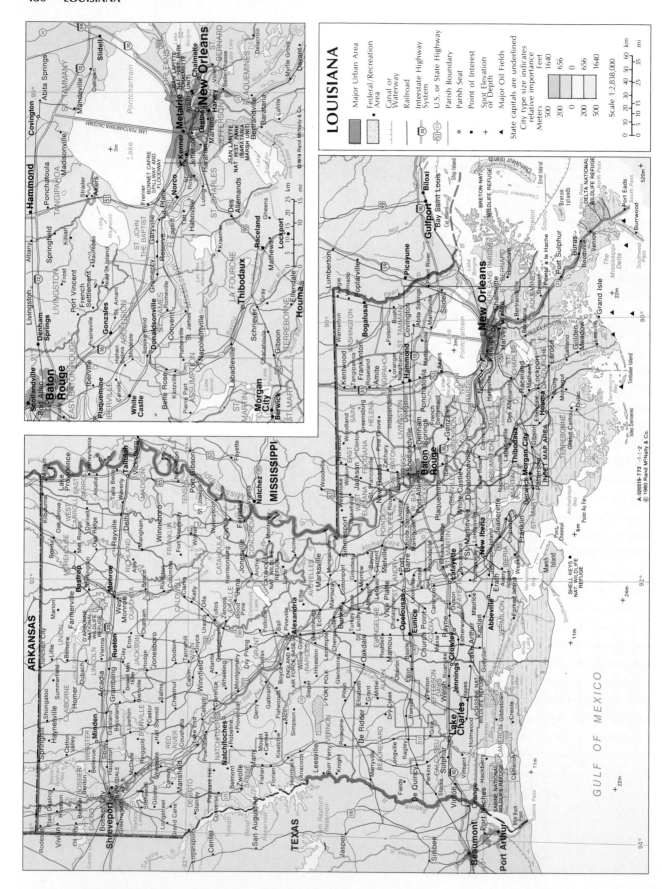

LOUISIANA

Major Urban Area

Federal/Recreation Area

Canal or Waterway

Railroad

Interstate Highway System

U.S. or State Highway

Parish Boundary

Parish Seat

Point of Interest

Spot Elevation or Depth

Major Oil Fields

State capitals are underlined

City type size indicates relative importance

Meters	Feet
500	1640
200	656
0	0
200	656
500	1640

Scale 1:2,838,000

© 1979 Rand McNally & Co.

A-500519-772 -1.1 -2
© 1980 Rand McNally & Co.

The Mississippi River branches out into channels in the Delta region of Louisiana before ending its winding, 10-state journey at the Gulf of Mexico. The wooded swampland and salt marshes of the Delta are rich in shrimp, oil, oysters, and waterfowl.

These trawlers are a small segment of the fleet of Louisiana shrimping boats that fish the Gulf coastal waters. Louisiana's fishing industry is among the most productive in the United States, ranking (1976) first in the quantity of fish caught and third in the value of its catch.

toward the Gulf of Mexico. The tilted strata that constitute this plain are pierced in the northwest and coastal area by enormous plugs of salt called salt domes. The most pronounced relief in the land surface is found in the northern hills and the area north of Lake Pontchartrain. The flattest terrain is on the coastal marshes. The dominant physical feature of the state is the Mississippi River.

Five natural regions are recognizable. The coastal marshes have either a firm surface or are soft, depending on the salt content. The gently sloping alluvial valley of the Mississippi lies toward the east, with its channels forming a bird-foot-shaped delta. The Red River valley, running northwest to southeast, follows the Mississippi's pattern on a much smaller scale. The terraces comprise the prairies in the southwest and the flatwoods to their north. The loessial bluffs flanking the Mississippi and containing moderate relief are also part of the terraces. The hill region, found in the northwest, is the oldest and highest part of the state.

Drainage. The most important rivers in Louisiana are the MISSISSIPPI, RED, Atchafalaya, and Ouachita. Stream patterns are usually dendritic, resembling the branches of a tree. The Mississippi flood plain, however, is lower than the natural levees along the main watercourse, and water therefore drains away from the river. As a result, tributaries of the Mississippi in the state are insignificant. Much of Louisiana's terrain is related to the Mississippi.

Lakes, including an increasing number of artificial reservoirs such as Toledo Bend, are found throughout the state. Along the Mississippi and Red are a number of bayous or oxbows, formed as the rivers cut across their own meanders or when channels were cut off for flood control. False River and Raccourci Old River on the Mississippi are examples. Some larger lakes such as PONTCHARTRAIN and Maurepas are the result of subsurface faulting. In the west, shallow lagoons that formed behind beach ridges eventually created Sabine and Calcasieu lakes. To the east, subsidence of deltaic sediments formed round lakes. At the time of Spanish exploration, logjams had dammed the Red River and its tributaries, forming temporary raft lakes.

Soils. Louisiana's immature transported, or alluvial, soils comprise the most fertile land. They are associated with the Mississippi and Red River flood plains. The organic marsh soils are high in natural fertility but poorly drained and subject to flooding.

Residual soils of the uplands are derived from older sediments and are sandy and infertile. They are used primarily for grazing and forestland. The finely grained terrace soils of the prairies are older alluvial soils underlain by a claypan layer. This stratum of clay, coupled with low relief, causes slow drainage. Flatwoods soils are older and of low fertility.

Climate. Louisiana's humid subtropical climate is relatively uniform throughout the state. The chief factors influencing climate are the subtropical latitude, location along the Gulf of Mexico, the continental landmass to the north, and the prevailing southerly winds. Annual average precipitation ranges from 1,175 mm (46 in) in the northwest to more than 1,625 mm (64 in) in the southeast. Although precipitation is for the most part evenly distributed throughout the year, February and March tend to be slightly wetter. Diurnal summer temperatures range from 29° to 35° C (84° to 95° F) in the afternoons to 16° to 24° C (61° to 75° F) in the early morning. Temperatures of at least 38° C (100° F) occur in almost all years. Louisiana is subject to tropical storms in summer and hurricanes in summer and fall, often accompanied by tornadoes. The cooler seasons are more variable, influenced by both cold polar air and warm tropical air. Winter temperatures drop as low as 5° C (41° F).

Vegetation and Animal Life. The number of plant species in the state is estimated at 4,500. Present vegetation regions differ greatly from what would be the natural vegetation as a result of human habitation. Treeless plains fringe the Gulf of Mexico, while freshwater marshes support floating plants. At slightly higher elevations stands of moss-festooned live oaks characterize the landscape. The prairie grasses in the southwest, inland from the marsh, are divided by gallery forests

New Orleans is the second largest port in the United States and an important shipbuilding center. Wharves line the Mississippi River as it loops around the city. The Algiers district (foreground) was once a depot for the slave trade. In the distance is Lake Pontchartrain.

growing along streams. Longleaf pines grow north of the prairies in the west and north of Lake Pontchartrain in the east. The northwestern corner of the state supports drought-resistant loblolly pine, oak, and hickory. Along smaller streams dogwood, redbud, and hackberry can be found. The floodplains of the major rivers have hardwoods on the well-drained soils and cypress in the swamps. In the lower swamps, blackgum, red maple, and palmetto grow with the cypress. Bluff land hardwoods include oak, maple, dogwood, tulip, and hickory.

Louisiana has always had abundant animal life. Squirrels, turkeys, beavers, muskrat, mink, raccoon, opossums, and alligators are common today. Nutrias have increased following their introduction in the 1930s, and large numbers of armadillos have migrated from the Southwest. A variety of fish is found inland and in the adjacent Gulf waters.

Resources. Louisiana's mineral resources are few in number but are economically important. Deposits of petroleum are found in the Mississippi delta area. To the west, increasing amounts of natural gas occur with petroleum. Large quantities of these minerals have also been extracted to the north, but since the 1940s drilling has moved offshore, with some rigs operating more than 95 km (60 mi) from the coast. Much of Louisiana's petroleum is associated with coastal salt domes. Extraction of salt is now mostly from the domes in the southern part of the state, particularly from the Five Islands—Avery, Belle Isle, Côte Blanche, Jefferson, and Weeks. Sulfur, sand, gravel, clays, lime, shell, and gypsum are also extracted. Lignite occurs in the northwest.

Because of concern for the preservation of the natural environment, a number of state environmental protection agencies have been formed. Louisiana also operates commissions

The French Quarter of New Orleans is distinguished by its narrow streets and balconies with ornamental grillwork. Also known as the Vieux Carré, or Old Square, it was the original settlement at New Orleans and is now noted for jazz, nightlife, and restaurants.

for the protection of wildlife and participates in the research work of the Gulf States Marine Fisheries Commission.

PEOPLE

Louisiana's population increased 15.4% from 1970 to 1980; from 1980 to 1985 it increased 6.5%. The state has become increasingly urban, with ten cities with populations of more than 50,000. The largest are NEW ORLEANS, BATON ROUGE, SHREVEPORT, and Metairie. During the period 1970–85, Louisiana experienced a net total in-migration of 129,000. A relatively small number of persons are foreign-born; most of these live in New Orleans.

Culturally, Louisiana is one of the most diverse states, having grown from settlement by French, Spanish, English, and American populations. Early French traits have been retained by CREOLES and CAJUNS in southern Louisiana. A Spanish influence was added to this culture in the southern and western portions of the state. People of Anglo-Saxon descent migrated to eastern and northern Louisiana, and blacks were brought into the plantation areas. Although French is no longer widely spoken as a first language, the French Roman Catholic core of southern Louisiana may still be distinguished from the English-speaking Protestant majority of northern Louisiana and the east. Baptists form the largest Protestant denomination.

Education and Health. The first school in the state is believed to have been the Ursuline Convent for girls in New Orleans, dating from 1728. Public schools developed slowly until 1841, when New Orleans established free public schools supported by poll and property taxes. There are over 30 public and private institutions of higher education operating in Louisiana (see LOUISIANA, STATE UNIVERSITIES OF). The state's per capita expenditures on public education perpetually lag behind the national annual average. Possibly reflecting this fact, Louisiana's literacy rate ranks among the lowest of all the states.

Health facilities in rural areas suffer from a lack of readily available medical services. The number of active physicians per 100,000 people is below the national average; the birthrate and infant mortality rate are above average. During the 1980s the death rate, formerly relatively high, declined. Carville, in southeast Louisiana, is the site of the only leprosarium in the continental United States.

Culture. Louisiana maintains a number of cultural institutions—primarily in New Orleans, Baton Rouge, and Shreveport—which include art galleries, historical museums, planetariums, and historical sites. The Louisiana State Museum, housed in the Cabildo in New Orleans, is probably the most famous. Other museums include the Louisiana State Exhibit Building and R. W. Norton Art Gallery in Shreveport, and the art gallery of the Louisiana Art Commission in Baton Rouge. Orchestras of note include the New Orleans Philharmonic, the Baton Rouge Civic Symphony, and the Shreveport Symphony. New Orleans and Shreveport have opera associations.

Several historic sites have been designated, including the prehistoric Indian areas of Poverty Point, northeast of Monroe, and Marksville, southeast of ALEXANDRIA; the Mansfield Battle Park and Museum; and the Acadian House and Museum at Longfellow-Evangeline State Park in Saint Martinville near New Iberia. Chalmette National Historical Park is at the site of the Battle of New Orleans (1815). The state has recreational facilities consisting of numerous parks. A health resort is located at Hot Wells, near Alexandria, and many antebellum plantations are open to the public. The most notable arena for sports is the Superdome in New Orleans; when completed (1975), it was the largest U.S. structure of its kind.

The most famous of Louisiana's daily newspapers is the *New Orleans Times-Picayune*; it is also the paper with the widest circulation. The state has ample numbers of television as well as AM and FM radio stations.

ECONOMIC ACTIVITIES

Manufacturing. The leading industries in value added by manufacture are chemicals and allied products, petroleum products, and food and food products. The worldwide oil glut of the mid-1980s was very damaging to Louisiana's economy, causing not only high unemployment in the petroleum industry but also markedly reduced state revenues from petroleum

(Left) *Oak Alley Plantation at Vacheries, La., was so named because of the navelike alley of oaks leading to the mansion. The architecture reflects Greek Revival influences adapted to the American South.*

(Below) *The Texaco plant at Baton Rouge is part of Louisiana's vast petrochemical industry. Petroleum products are a mainstay of the state's economy. With reserves throughout the state and its offshore waters, Louisiana is one of the largest producers of oil in the United States.*

taxes. The leading centers for manufacturing in Louisiana are the largest urban hubs, particularly New Orleans, Baton Rouge, and Shreveport. The state's leading manufactured or processed products, in addition to those based on petroleum, coal, and natural gas, include salt, drugs, fertilizers, processed rice, and sugar.

Energy. Louisiana generates almost all its power from hydrocarbons (petroleum and natural gas) extracted from within the state. There is a small nuclear-power capacity. In 1985, Louisiana's electric utilities produced approximately 44.3 billion kW h.

Agriculture, Forestry, and Fishing. Until World War II, Louisiana was basically an agricultural state. Since then, although agriculture remains a significant factor in the economy, the number of farms in operation has greatly decreased. The number of large farms increased markedly, however, whereas small farms nearly vanished. Major agricultural commodities include soybeans, sugar and sugarcane, rice, and cotton, along with dairy products, cattle, and calves. Specialty crops include hot peppers grown on Avery Island, which are made into Tabasco sauce, and the world's supply of pungent perique tobacco. By the 1930s the virgin forests had been depleted and the landscape scarred. Although the huge cypress and hardwood stands of the past are gone, Louisiana's climate has allowed the reforestation of rapid-growing pines to take place.

Louisiana leads all other states in volume of fish caught. Menhaden is most important, and buffalo, catfish, flounder, and spotted sea trout are commercially significant. Crabs, crayfish, oysters, and shrimp are important in both volume and value. Louisiana's fur industry has grown in recent years with the development of a stable market for nutria (an aquatic rodent that resembles a miniature beaver).

Tourism. Tourist traffic to Louisiana is served by a number of airlines, four interstate highways, and state and federal roadways. Tourism is generally focused on the metropolitan centers, with New Orleans most important. The city attracts large numbers of Mardi Gras visitors. Some 7.3 million people visited the New Orleans World's Fair between May and November 1984. The Acadian, or Cajun, country of the southwest is also a popular tourist area.

Transportation and Trade. Several thousand miles of railway track cross the state, serving primarily to move freight. Approximately 300 airports serve Louisianans. The highway and road network is extensive.

Foreign trade is important to Louisiana's economy; New Orleans handles the bulk of the state's overseas trade. Louisiana is a principal U.S. exporter of chemicals, petroleum, primary metals, rice, cotton, and fish products. Imports include animal, fish, and vegetable oils and fats, foodstuffs, and crude rubber.

GOVERNMENT AND POLITICS

Since 1812, Louisiana has operated under 11 constitutions, the most recent dating from 1974. The Louisiana legislature is composed of two houses—a 39-member senate and a 105-member house of representatives. Legislative sessions are annual. Legislators are elected for concurrent terms of 4 years. Judicial power is vested in the supreme court, the courts of appeals, and the district courts. The executive branch is headed by a governor elected to a 4-year term. Other major elected state officials include the lieutenant governor, secretary of state, attorney general, and treasurer.

The state is divided into 64 parishes. The original territory was divided into 12 somewhat indefinitely bounded counties, coinciding with parish boundaries established by the Roman Catholic church during colonial times. Since 1845 the term "parish" has been used for these political subdivisions. The eight parishes north of Lake Pontchartrain and east of the Mississippi, known as the Florida Parishes, were once a part of Spanish Florida. Parishes, with a few exceptions, are governed by elected bodies called police juries.

From 1877 until after World War II, Louisiana was controlled by Democrats. Since the 1950s, however, Republican U.S. presidential candidates have frequently won the state's electoral votes. In 1964, for the first time in this century, two Republicans were elected to the state legislature (others followed). In 1979 a Republican, David C. Treen, was elected governor.

HISTORY

The earliest known Indian occupancy dates to perhaps 10,000 years ago. These people, probably big-game hunters, left little evidence of their habitation. A hunting and gathering economy is thought to have continued until about 2,000 years ago,

Louisiana's many swamp areas, such as this swamp near the Pearl River on the Mississippi border, are excellent hunting and fishing grounds. Water oaks, cypresses, tupelo gum, wild turkeys, deer, frogs, and various species of fish are found in these regions.

when farming began. The fertile flood plains were gardened, producing squash, sunflowers, beans, and maize. The Poverty Point excavation, nearly 1.6 km (1 mi) across, has revealed a highly organized society dating from about 700 BC.

Written accounts after the arrival of Europeans document the decline and disappearance of many Indian groups. A reasonable estimate of the Indian population in AD 1700 would be 15,000, formed of six linguistic groups: CADDO in the northwest, NATCHEZ near the middle Mississippi, Atakapa on the prairies of the southwest, Chitimachan in the Atchafalaya Basin, Muskogean east of the Mississippi, and Tunican in the northeast. Most were sedentary village farmers who also hunted and fished.

Permanent European settlement was begun by France almost 200 years after the Spanish had entered the area. Robert Cavelier, Sieur de La Salle, explored the Mississippi downstream to its mouth, and he claimed the entire drainage basin for France in 1682. La Salle's efforts at colonization failed, but the French continued in their attempt to establish a permanent settlement. Eventually, the colony, which had also failed at BILOXI, moved upstream on the Mississippi to the foot of the Great Raft on the Red River, establishing the first permanent settlement in the Louisiana Territory at Natchitoches in 1714. Colonization proceeded under the direction of Pierre Le Moyne, Sieur d' IBERVILLE and his brother, Jean Baptiste Le Moyne, Sieur de BIENVILLE.

The early history of the colony is a tragic one, as the first settlers were ill-suited to the rigors of frontier life. In 1717, France granted a monopoly on commerce to John LAW in order to promote development of the territory. His MISSISSIPPI SCHEME was designed to entice investment in what he claimed was a land of fabulous mineral wealth. The scheme fell apart in 1720, with no financial rewards to the investors, but the territory gained population as a result of Law's promotion.

German peasants from the Upper Rhine area contributed to the betterment of the region when they began to settle land upstream from New Orleans in the 1720s. Louisiana became a French crown colony in 1731. Crops, grown on plantations, included indigo, rice, and tobacco; trade was primarily by water, and the few roads ran along the levees. To this day, the arpent system, based on an old French unit of measure approximating 0.35 ha (0.85 acres), is evident in the property lines running back from the streams.

In 1762, Louisiana was ceded to Spain as a result of the French and Indian War, and Great Britain gained control of Florida, which extended to the east bank of the Mississippi.

At the same time, Acadians, driven from Nova Scotia by the British, began migrating to Louisiana. The Acadians settled in the eastern prairies around the present site of Saint Martinville and later along the Lower Mississippi and Bayou Lafourche.

The Spanish made feeble attempts to offset the growing French population, but were eventually absorbed themselves. In 1800 they returned Louisiana to France by the Treaty of San Ildefonso. Although Napoleon I originally intended to establish a new empire in America, he sold Louisiana to the United States in 1803. The $15-million LOUISIANA PURCHASE represented about 4 cents an acre. Louisiana became the 18th state on Apr. 12, 1812, comprising the territory south of 33° North latitude, which had been the Territory of Orleans. The rest became the Missouri Territory. Not until 1819, however, were the Florida Parishes and the lands west of the Red River added to form the present state boundaries.

During the WAR OF 1812, British ships moved up the Mississippi River to New Orleans. On Jan. 8, 1815, Gen. Andrew Jackson's troops defeated the British at New Orleans. The battle ended 15 days after the Treaty of Ghent was signed, ending the war. Jean LAFITTE aided the American cause.

By 1860 the population exceeded 700,000, and a class system based on plantations with slave labor had developed. At the same time, yeoman farmers were practicing subsistence farming—Anglo-Saxons in the hills and Acadians to the south. During the Civil War, the importance of the port of New Orleans and Louisiana's strategic position on the Mississippi made it an early Union target; the state's economy was devastated.

Streams had been the major routes since the beginning of settlement. By the 1860 peak of steamboat travel, nearly all of the state could be reached by these craft. As railroads improved, steamboat traffic declined. Rail travel grew in the early 20th century. Much of the modern settlement of the prairies is attributable to the access rail travel gave the area. Highway development began after the 1920s. The prairies began to change from the arpent-strip farms of the Acadians (or Cajuns, as they came to be known) and the rectangular Spanish *sitio* grants for ranching, to vast rice fields farmed by migrants from the Middle West who arrived at the beginning of the 20th century.

Louisiana had come a long way from the earliest Spanish explorers and French settlers, through the Civil War and Reconstruction. In 1928 a Winnfield lawyer, Huey Pierce Long, Jr. (see LONG family), had obtained the governorship, and from 1930 to 1935 he served as a U.S. senator. His program of road building and free schoolbooks, based on tax revenue from petroleum, appealed to the grass roots population, but his methods became increasingly suspect. Scandals, which had begun by the mid-1930s, accelerated after Long was assassinated in 1935, but his career marked a turning point in Louisiana history. For much of the period since World War II the petroleum industry sparked the economic development of the state (with the notable exception of the oil slump that took place during the mid-1980s). By the 1960s Louisiana had become a major space-age industrial center; as industry grew, the state became urbanized. Urgent environmental problems of the 1980s included industrial pollution, disposal of toxic waste, and erosion of the coastline.   JOHN W. HALL

Bibliography:

GENERAL: Core, Lucy, and Calhoun, David, eds., *The Louisiana Almanac 1984–85* (1984).

DESCRIPTION AND GEOGRAPHY: Davis, Edwin A., and Suarez, Raleigh A., *Louisiana: The Pelican State,* 5th ed. (1985); Federal Writers' Project, *Louisiana: A Guide to the State,* rev. ed. (1971); Lockwood, C. C., *Discovering Louisiana* (1986); Newton, Milton B., *Atlas of Louisiana* (1972).

LAND AND PEOPLE: Kniffen, Fred B., and Hilliard, Sam B., *Louisiana: Its Land and People,* rev. ed. (1987); Read, William A., *Louisiana French,* rev. ed. (1963).

HISTORY: Davis, Edwin A., ed., *Louisiana: A Narrative History,* 3d ed. (1971), and *The Rivers and Bayous of Louisiana* (1968); Neuman, Robert W., *An Introduction to Louisiana Archaeology* (1984); Newton, Lewis W., *The Americanization of French Louisiana* (1981); O'Neill, Charles Edwards, et al., *Louisiana: A History,* ed. by Bennett H. Wall (1984); Rushton, William F., *The Cajuns: From Acadia to Louisiana* (1979); Taylor, Joe G., *Louisiana: A Bicentennial History* (1976; repr. 1984); Tunnell, Ted, *Crucible of Reconstruction: War, Radicalism, and Race in Louisiana, 1862–1877* (1984).

ECONOMICS, POLITICS, AND GOVERNMENT: Bolner, James, ed., *Louisiana Politics: Festival in a Labyrinth* (1982); Cook, Bernard A., and Watson, James R., *Louisiana Labor: From Slavery to "Right-to-Work"* (1985); Michels, Greg, ed., *Governments of Louisiana, 1986* (1985); Reeves, Miriam G., *Governors of Louisiana,* 3d ed. (1980); Sindler, Allan P., *Huey Long's Louisiana: State Politics, 1920–1952* (1956; repr. 1980); Taylor, Joe G., *Louisiana Reconstructed, 1863–1877* (1975).

Louisiana, state universities of

There are two coeducational multicampus universities in Louisiana. All of their constituent schools are coeducational, and all grant both undergraduate and graduate degrees. The Louisiana State University system consists of **Louisiana State University and Agricultural and Mechanical College** (1855; enrollment: 29,500; library: 2,000,000 volumes), a land-grant institution at Baton Rouge that has colleges of liberal arts and sciences and schools of law, veterinary medicine, music, and library science, and branches, having programs in liberal arts and education, in New Orleans (1931), where the medical center, with schools of dentistry, nursing, and medicine, is located, and in Shreveport (1964; enrollment: 4,600; library: 168,300 volumes), which also has a medical school (1965). The university has a number of agricultural research stations throughout the state, where work is done on sugar, rice, and sweet potatoes. The **University of New Orleans** (1956; enrollment: 16,700; library: 578,000 volumes) is also part of the university system.

The Southern University system consists of **Southern University and Agricultural and Mechnical College** (1880; enrollment: 13,200; library: 326,000 volumes) at Baton Rouge, a land-grant school with undergraduate and graduate programs in liberal arts, education, and technical training, and a law school, and its New Orleans campus (1959; enrollment: 3,200; library: 128,000 volumes), which offers an undergraduate program for commuters.

Other state universities offering liberal arts and education curricula are **Grambling State** (1901; enrollment: 4,800; library: 178,000 volumes) at Grambling, founded as a liberal arts and teacher education college for blacks; **McNeese State** (1939; enrollment: 8,000; library: 203,000 volumes) at Lake Charles; **Northeast Louisiana** (1936; enrollment: 11,600; library: 439,000 volumes) at Monroe; and **Northwestern State**

University of Louisiana (1884; enrollment: 6,200; library: 265,000 volumes) at Natchitoches.

Additional universities are **Louisiana Tech** (1894; enrollment: 10,900; library: 290,000 volumes) at Ruston; **Nicholls State** (1948; enrollment: 7,400; library: 229,000 volumes) at Thibodaux; **Southeastern Louisiana** (1925; enrollment: 9,000; library: 250,000 volumes) at Hammond; and the **University of Southwestern Louisiana** (1898; enrollment: 16,350; library: 545,200 volumes) at Lafayette.

Louisiana Purchase

By a treaty signed on Apr. 30, 1803, the United States purchased from France the Louisiana Territory, more than 2 million km² (800,000 mi²) of land extending from the Mississippi River to the Rocky Mountains. The price was 60 million francs, about $15 million; $11,250,000 was to be paid directly, with the balance to be covered by the assumption by the United States of French debts to American citizens.

In 1762, France had ceded Louisiana to Spain, but by the secret Treaty of San Ildefonso (1800) the French had regained the area. Napoléon Bonaparte (the future Emperor Napoleon I) envisioned a great French empire in the New World, and he hoped to use the Mississippi Valley as a food and trade center to supply the island of Hispaniola, which was to be the heart of this empire. First, however, he had to restore French control of Hispaniola, where Haitian slaves under TOUSSAINT L'OUVERTURE had seized power (1801; see HAITI). In 1802 a large army sent by Napoleon under his brother-in-law, Charles Leclerc, arrived on the island to suppress the Haitian rebellion. Despite some military success, the French lost thousands of soldiers, mainly to yellow fever, and Napoleon soon realized that Hispaniola must be abandoned. Without that island he had little use for Louisiana. Facing renewed war with Great Britain, he could not spare troops to defend the territory; he needed funds, moreover, to support his military ventures in Europe. Accordingly, in April 1803 he offered to sell Louisiana to the United States.

Concerned about French intentions, President Thomas Jefferson had already sent James Monroe and Robert R. Livingston to Paris to negotiate the purchase of a tract of land on the lower Mississippi or, at least, a guarantee of free navigation on the river. Surprised and delighted by the French offer of the whole territory, they immediately negotiated the treaty.

Jefferson was jubilant. At one stroke the United States

Troops fire a salute as the American flag is raised, replacing the tricolor of Napoleonic France, during the ceremonies on Dec. 20, 1803, marking the transfer of the vast Louisiana Territory from France to the United States.

LOUISIANA PURCHASE

would double its size, an enormous tract of land would be open to settlement, and the free navigation of the Mississippi would be assured. Although the Constitution did not specifically empower the federal government to acquire new territory by treaty, Jefferson concluded that the practical benefits to the nation far outweighed the possible violation of the Constitution. The Senate concurred with this decision and voted ratification on Oct. 20, 1803. The Spanish, who had never given up physical possession of Louisiana to the French, did so at New Orleans on Nov. 30, 1803. In a second ceremony, on Dec. 20, 1803, the French turned Louisiana over to the United States. Disputes with Britain and Spain over the boundaries of the purchase took years to resolve.   MORTON BORDEN

Bibliography: Barry, James P., *The Louisiana Purchase, April 1803* (1973); Chidsey, Donald B., *The Louisiana Purchase* (1972); DeConde, Alexander, *This Affair of Louisiana* (1976); Lyon, Elijah Wilson, *Louisiana in French Diplomacy* (1974); Sprague, Marshall, *So Vast So Beautiful a Land: Louisiana and the Purchase* (1974).

Louisville   [loo′-ee-vil]

Louisville, the largest city in Kentucky, is located in the north central part of the state at the falls of the Ohio River. It is the seat of Jefferson County and has a population of 298,451 (1980). The city is a major river port and one of the South's leading industrial, commercial, and shipping centers. Whiskey, tobacco products, and appliances are among its chief manufactures. Louisville has also become a cultural center; its orchestra and theater group have won national acclaim for commissioning and performing new works. The homes of George Rogers Clark and President Zachary Taylor are of historic interest. The University of Louisville (1798) is the oldest municipal university in the nation. The KENTUCKY DERBY, held annually at Churchill Downs since 1875, draws an international crowd of racing fans.

Louisville's site was surveyed in 1773 but was not settled until 1778, when George Rogers CLARK built a fort as a base of operations against the British and Indians. After a canal bypassing the falls was built (1830) and the Louisville and Nashville Railroad was extended (1880s) to Florida, Louisville developed as a major transportation center. During the Civil War it was a military and supply depot for Union forces. The city was torn by racial rioting in 1968 and again in 1975 by antibusing disturbances. FORT KNOX, the national gold depository, is nearby.

Lourdes   [loord]

Lourdes is a town in southwestern France in the foothills of the Pyrenees on the Gave du Pau (river). It has a population of 17,425 (1982). The town has been a pilgrimage center known for its miraculous cures since 1858 when 14-year-old Bernadette Soubirous (see BERNADETTE, SAINT) had numerous religious visions in a nearby grotto. A basilica was built on the site in 1876, and nearly 3 million tourists visit the shrine annually. An underground church was completed in 1958. The fortified town was a medieval stronghold.

Lourenço Marques: see MAPUTO.

louse   [lows]

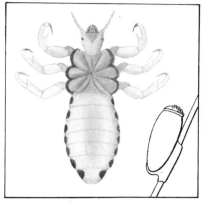

A body louse, Pediculus humanus, *is a small, wingless insect that lives on humans, sucking its host's blood. A louse egg, or nit (lower right), is shown attached to hair.*

Louse (pl. lice) is a name applied to several different invertebrates that are either external parasites (harmful to the host) or commensals (not harmful). Included are certain crustaceans, such as the parasitic fish louse, *Argulus*. Most commonly, however, the name refers to two groups of flattened, wingless insects living on warm-blooded animals. They are usually regarded as separate orders: Mallophaga, or chewing lice, and Anoplura, sucking lice. Chewing lice are found on mammals, but mostly inhabit birds. They chew feathers, hair, and skin and sometimes draw blood. Most species of chewing lice are limited to a single host species. Sucking lice feed only on the blood of mammals, most commonly rodents but others too. The crab louse and the head and body louse are sucking lice and the only lice that parasitize humans, the crab louse occurring chiefly in the pubic region. Both lice glue their eggs, or nits, to hair, but the body louse may also fasten its eggs to clothing. The immature lice look like tiny adults.

In addition to the uncomfortable itching caused by its bites, the body louse may transmit the pathogens that cause typhus, relapsing fever, or trench fever. The spread of these diseases, and of lice themselves, is closely associated with crowded, unsanitary conditions. The first widespread use of DDT was to control lice and prevent an epidemic of typhus in Naples during World War II.   DAVID J. HORN

Bibliography: Snow, Keith R., *Insects and Disease* (1974).

Lousma, Jack   [lows′-mah]

The American astronaut Jack Robert Lousma, b. Grand Rapids, Mich., Feb. 29, 1936, a Marine jet pilot when selected as an astronaut in 1966, spent 59 days in space as a pilot of the *Skylab 3* (see SKYLAB) mission (July 28–Sept. 25, 1973). With fellow crewmen Alan Bean and Owen Garriott, Lousma helped deploy a sunshade to protect Skylab. He logged more than 11 hours outside Skylab on two spacewalks. In 1982 he served as commander of the third flight (Mar. 22–30) of the SPACE SHUTTLE *Columbia*.   DAVID DOOLING

Louth   [lowth]

Louth is a county in Leinster province in northeastern Ireland, on the Irish Sea. The smallest of the Irish counties, it has an area of 821 km² (317 mi²). The county's population is 91,698 (1986). Dundalk is the county town. Louth is situated on an extensive plain. The land is mainly used for cattle and sheep raising, but there is some cultivation of vegetables and oats. Industry is limited to the towns and includes the manufacture of textiles, beer, and food products. Tourism is also important.

Loutherbourg, Philippe Jacques de   [loo-tair-boor′, fee-leep′ zhahk duh]

Philippe Jacques de Loutherbourg, a painter and theatrical designer of Alsatian origin, b. Oct. 31, 1740, d. Mar. 11, 1812,

The glass pyramid in the central courtyard of the Louvre was opened in March 1989; it contrasts dramatically with the adjacent 19th-century portions of the museum complex. The pyramid, designed by the U.S. architect I. M. Pei, serves as the main public entrance to the Louvre. Also, it is a skylight for the main hall of the vast new underground Louvre. This subterranean addition contains cafeterias, an auditorium, and information and education facilities for visitors, as well as storage and work areas.

won his reputation as a painter of romantic landscapes and battle scenes. He was chiefly influential, however, for the innovative atmospheric sets and romantic scenic designs he introduced (1773–1785) at London's Drury Lane Theatre.

Louvain   [loo-van']

Louvain (Flemish: Leuven) is a university town in Brabant province, Belgium, about 24 km (15 mi) east of Brussels. Its population is 84,583 (1987 est.). In medieval times Louvain was a textile center and capital of the duchy of Brabant. Today its main industry is brewing. The Catholic University of Louvain, originally founded in 1425, was closed during the French Revolution and reestablished in 1834. Beginning in the late 19th century it was a leading center in the revival of SCHOLASTICISM. In 1970 it was divided into two universities, one for Flemish-speaking and one for French-speaking students.

Louvois, François Michel Le Tellier, Marquis de   [loo-vwah', frahn-swah' mee-shel luh tel-yay']

The marquis de Louvois, the second of three members of the Le Tellier family to serve as French war minister under LOUIS XIV, was the dominant figure in the royal council from 1683 to 1691. Born c.1639, François Michel Le Tellier was groomed for the war ministry by his father, Michel Le Tellier (1603–85), who held that office from 1643. He assisted his father officially after 1662, in effect shared the office from 1666, and formally succeeded to the post when his father became chancellor in 1677. He also gained the postal superintendency (1668) and ministerial entry to the king's inner council (1672). In 1683, with the death of his rival Jean Baptiste COLBERT, he became superintendent of buildings, arts, and manufactures.

Although the governmental roles of the Le Tellier father and son and the monarch are difficult to separate, Louvois was a harsh disciplinarian who controlled the army created by his father, established unprecedented civilian dominance over noble officers, and ensured adequate army supplies. He apparently set military objectives and even influenced the foreign policy of the Sun King. Louvois's name is associated with implacable persecution of French HUGUENOTS and the brutal French devastation (1688) of the Palatinate, which triggered the War of the GRAND ALLIANCE. Military defeats after 1689 diminished royal favor, but Louvois's secretarial post passed to his son, the marquis de Barbézieux, after his sudden death on July 16, 1691.   A. LLOYD MOOTE

Bibliography: Treasure, G. R., *Seventeenth Century France* (1966).

Louvre   [loovr]

The Louvre, one the world's great art museums, houses many works of fundamental importance in Western cultures, including the Victory of Samothrace and Leonardo da Vinci's Mona Lisa. Originally a royal fortress and palace built (12th century) for Philip II, the Louvre is an immense complex of buildings erected in Paris over a span of four centuries. Most of the structures that constitute the museum follow the French Renaissance style of the architect Pierre LESCOT, who in 1546 was commissioned by King Francis I to erect what is now the west wing of the complex. In founding the Louvre's collection, Francis I was guided by the Italian artists Andrea del Sarto and Francesco Primaticcio, whose works, along with those of their fellow expatriate Leonardo da Vinci, formed the nucleus of the museum's original holdings. The Louvre complex grew as the royal collections expanded. The Grande Galerie was completed under Henry IV (r. 1589–1610), and Jacques LEMERCIER was commissioned (1624) by Louis XIII to plan extensions to the Louvre, of which the Pavillon de l'Horloge is the most notable. The impressive east façade (begun 1667) was designed primarily by Claude PERRAULT, with Jean Baptiste Colbert, the royal minister, overseeing the construction.

Throughout the 17th century, as France assumed a dominant role in Europe, the Louvre's holdings increased dramatically. Particularly important acquisitions during this period were major works by the great Dutch and Flemish masters. In the 18th century the annual SALON exhibitions were established. The first state museum was opened in the Louvre in 1793. The central position held by the Louvre in artistic life was magnified by Napoleon I, who began its Egyptian collection. The overall museum complex was completed under Napoleon III (r. 1852–70).

Subsequently, the Louvre expanded its collections greatly through gifts and bequests. Its departments include Oriental (ancient Mesopotamian) antiquities, Greek and Roman antiquities, and Egyptian antiquities; sculpture from the Middle Ages to modern times; furniture and objets d'art; and European paintings and drawings.

In 1984 the French government launched a decade-long expansion and modernization program for the Louvre, under the direction of the U.S. architect I. M. PEI, involving a large underground addition.   CARTER RATCLIFF

Bibliography: Bazin, Germain, *The Louvre*, trans. by M. I. Martin, rev. ed. (1971); Gauthier, Maximillien, *The Louvre: Sculpture, Ceramics and Objets d'Art* (1962); Gowring, Lawrence, *Paintings in the Louvre* (1987); Laclotte, M., and Cuzin, J. P., *The Louvre* (1983); Schneider, P., *Louvre Dialogues*, trans. by P. Southgate (1971).

lovage   [luhv'-ij]

Lovage, *Levisticum officinale*, is a branching perennial herb growing to 1.8 m (6 ft) in height native to the mountains of southern Europe but now found wild across the United States from New Jersey to New Mexico. A member of the parsley family, Umbelliferae, lovage is cultivated as an ornamental and for its celery-flavored leaves; for its aromatic fruits, which are used as a flavoring; and for its oil, which is used in perfumes, liqueurs, and tobacco blends.

Love Canal: see POLLUTANTS, CHEMICAL.

Lovecraft, H. P.

The writer Howard Phillips Lovecraft, b. Providence, R.I., Aug. 20, 1890, d. Mar. 13, 1937, was remarkable for the macabre imagination he displayed in his fantasy and horror tales. A precocious child and reclusive man, Lovecraft wrote of dislocations in the web of time and space that exposed unspeakable monsters. He created the Cthulhu mythos to support his vision of the horrible origins of the world. Some of his best writing is found in *The Dunwich Horror and Other Weird Tales* (1939; repr. as *The Dunwich Horror*, 1945) and *Best Supernatural Stories of H. P. Lovecraft* (1945). Five volumes of his *Selected Letters* (1965–76) have appeared.

Bibliography: De Camp, L. Sprague, *Lovecraft: A Biography* (1975); Shreffler, Philip A., *The H. P. Lovecraft Companion* (1977).

Lovelace, Richard   [luhv'-luhs]

Richard Lovelace, 1618–58, an English CAVALIER POET, is remembered for two exquisite love lyrics: "To Lucasta, Going to the Wars" and "To Althea, from Prison." Lovelace, who remained loyal to the deposed King Charles I, was twice imprisoned for his royalist beliefs and died in poverty, having spent his fortune in the king's cause.

Lovelace published *Lucasta* (1649), the only volume of his poems to appear during his life, while in prison. A second volume bearing the same title was published by his brother in the year following his death.

Lovell, Sir Bernard   [luhv'-ul]

The English astronomer Sir Alfred Charles Bernard Lovell, b. Aug. 31, 1913, is known for his work leading to the construction of the 76-m (250-ft) radio telescope at the Jodrell Bank Experimental Station (now called the NUFFIELD RADIO ASTRONOMY LABORATORIES), which he founded in Cheshire, 32 km (20 mi) south of Manchester.

After graduation from the University of Bristol, Lovell joined the staff of Manchester University and was appointed (1951) professor of radio astronomy and director of Jodrell Bank. There he began work on the 250-ft (76-m) radio telescope, at the time the world's largest fully steerable dish. In *The Story of Jodrell Bank* (1968) and *Out of the Zenith* (1973), Lovell describes the construction and use of the telescope.

STEVEN J. DICK

Lovell, James

The American astronaut James Arthur Lovell, Jr., b. Cleveland, Ohio, Mar. 25, 1928, was command module pilot of Apollo 8, the first manned mission to orbit the moon (Dec. 21–27, 1968; see APOLLO PROGRAM). Lovell served as a U.S. Navy test pilot and was selected as an astronaut in 1962. On Gemini 7 (Dec. 4–18, 1965; see GEMINI PROGRAM), he and commander Frank Borman spent 14 days in space, a record at that time. On Gemini 12 (Nov. 11–15, 1966), commander Lovell and pilot Edwin E. Aldrin conducted rendezvous tests. Lovell was commander of Apollo 13 (April 11–17, 1970), intended as the third manned lunar landing but aborted because of an explosion. After serving as Deputy Director of Science and Applications at the Johnson Space Center, Lovell resigned from the navy and NASA in 1973 to become senior executive vice-president of Bay-Houston Towing Company. He is now president of Fisk Telephone Systems, Inc., also in Houston.

DAVID DOOLING

Bibliography: Cooper, Henry S. F., Jr., *Thirteen: The Flight That Failed* (1973).

Low, Seth

Seth Low, b. Brooklyn, N.Y., Jan. 18, 1850, d. Sept. 17, 1916, was an American political reformer and educator. A well-to-do merchant, Low became interested in municipal reform; he was elected mayor of Brooklyn in 1881 and served until 1885. He became president of Columbia University in 1890 and greatly expanded the university and effected its move to its present site on Morningside Heights. In 1901 he was elected mayor of New York City, which by then included Brooklyn, as a fusion, anti-Tammany candidate. As mayor, Low instituted numerous reforms but was defeated for reelection in 1903.

Bibliography: Kurland, Gerald, *Seth Low: The Patrician as Social Reformer* (1971); Low, Benjamin R., *Seth Low* (1925; repr. 1971).

Low Countries, history of the

The Low Countries are the region in northwest Europe lying on the coast of the North Sea between France and Germany. They now comprise the three countries of BELGIUM, the NETHERLANDS, and LUXEMBOURG. The name *Netherlands*, which is adapted from the Dutch form of *Low Countries*, was originally applied to the whole area, but in the last two centuries it has been restricted to the Kingdom of the Netherlands. Belgium takes its name from the ancient Gallic tribe of the Belgae, who were conquered by the Romans; Renaissance humanists revived the name for the whole of the Low Countries, and it was adopted by the southern Netherlands when they declared their independence from Austria in 1789. The Low Countries were also often called Flanders, after the province of that name, until the 17th century.

The Low Countries did not become a distinct political entity until late in the Middle Ages. The region was recognized as a geographical unit, often called Frisia (or Friesland), in the early Middle Ages, although it was always divided in its language and culture. North of a line stretching roughly west to east across modern Belgium, the people have spoken a Germanic language for more than 1,000 years. It was called Netherlandish (*Nederlands*), Hollandish (*Hollands*), or Flemish (*Vlaams*) by those who spoke it; but in England it was called Dutch (from *Deutsch*, meaning *German*), and this is still the English name. South of the line, the people spoke a French dialect called Walloon. The formation of the modern nations of the Netherlands and Belgium was not based on the separation of Dutch and Walloon, and there has been a sharp conflict between Dutch- and French-speakers in Belgium for more than a hundred years.

EARLY HISTORY

The once-fashionable theory that the distinction between the Dutch and the Belgians was a fundamental one, extending back to the beginning of the Middle Ages, has now been abandoned. The Romans, whose conquest of the area began with a victory by Julius CAESAR over the Belgae in 57 BC, established their military and political frontier along the line of the Rhine River. However, they made allies of the Germanic peoples—the Batavi and other tribes—who had recently settled to the north of the river. The principal Roman route to

In 1547, Holy Roman Emperor Charles V declared the 17 provinces of the Netherlands hereditary Habsburg possessions. The Leo Belgicus, *an imaginative representation of the area, suggests the power perceived in the thriving Low Countries by a 16th-century mapmaker.*

Britain, across the North Sea, passed through this region.

When Roman power began to recede in the 3d and 4th centuries AD, another Germanic people, the FRANKS, moved into the Low Countries, settling south of the Rhine and to the south of the present language boundary. They began to penetrate into GAUL early in the 5th century and under CLOVIS (r. 481–511) established their rule over all of Gaul; the latter became known as *Frank-land*, from which comes the name of France. As part of the Frankish kingdom, the Low Countries were converted to Christianity in the 6th century. When the grandsons of the Frankish emperor CHARLEMAGNE divided his realm in 843, the Low Countries became part of the middle kingdom called LOTHARINGIA. However, that kingdom was soon partitioned into the East Frankish (German) and West Frankish (French) kingdoms. Thus, by the 10th century, the more northerly and easterly part of the Low Countries was incorporated into the HOLY ROMAN EMPIRE, while the westerly and southerly part came under French rule.

The Low Countries were far from the centers of power in both Germany and France, and the local potentates who arose were almost independent of their overlords. The development of wool manufacture made FLANDERS and BRABANT the most important industrial districts in northern Europe, while HOLLAND, which then included Zeeland, developed large fishing and shipping industries. These provinces became densely populated, and numerous cities arose. The wealth created by industry and trade provided the base for the growth of political institutions within the provinces, sometimes in alliance with local rulers (as in Brabant) and sometimes in rebellion against them (as in Flanders).

Most of the inland provinces remained primarily agricultural. Those in the southeast (Hainaut, Artois) saw the full development of feudalism and manorialism, but the peasantry in the far north (Friesland) remained free. Although marriage alliances occurred frequently among the ruling families, no general political unity developed in the region. It was deeply involved in the HUNDRED YEARS' WAR (1337–1453) between France and England, but different provinces were often on opposite sides.

BURGUNDIAN AND HABSBURG RULE

Political unification and centralization of the Low Countries began when PHILIP THE BOLD, duke of Burgundy, who had married the heiress of Flanders, acquired Artois and became count of Flanders in 1384. Over the next century and a half the dukes of Burgundy acquired possession of all the northeastern lands of the Low Countries, some by dynastic marriage and some by military conquest. During the 15th century the key provinces were already in their hands, and they not only followed the same policies in all of them but also began to form common political institutions over them, notably the STATES-GENERAL. Resistance to loss of local autonomy was strong, however, and rebellions recurred, especially in the Flemish city of GHENT. Nonetheless the immense economic resources of the Low Countries enabled them to play a major independent role in European affairs. Since the dukes of Burgundy were also leading political figures in France, the Low Countries were involved in French civil wars as well as in the second phase (1415–53) of the Hundred Years' War.

Duke CHARLES THE BOLD attempted to create a new independent middle kingdom between France and Germany, but he was killed in battle with the Swiss in 1477. His heiress, MARY OF BURGUNDY, married (1477) the future Holy Roman emperor MAXIMILIAN I, thereby combining the Burgundian inheritance with that of the Austrian HABSBURGS. Their son, Philip the Handsome (see PHILIP I of Castile), married the Spanish princess JOAN THE MAD, and the eldest son of this marriage became both king of Spain (1516) and Holy Roman emperor (1519) as CHARLES V. The Low Countries were thus incorporated again in an immense empire.

Although Charles was born in Flanders, he subordinated the interests of the Low Countries to the general interests of his dynasty and especially to the political needs of Spain. This policy was continued by his son, PHILIP II, who received the Low Countries along with Spain on his father's abdication in 1555–56. Philip's effort to govern the Low Countries from

Dutch noblemen, threatened by Philip II's efforts to enforce antiheretical edicts and to limit local political power, inaugurated the Dutch Revolt when they journeyed to Brussels in April 1566 to petition the regent Margaret of Parma. Philip's delayed response to the petitioners sparked violent anti-Catholic riots.

Spain, to intensify centralization of power, and to persecute the Protestants led to the DUTCH REVOLT.

The insurrection began in 1566 in the southern provinces, Flanders in particular, and spread throughout the north only after the rebels' capture of Brielle (Brill) in 1572. Efforts at suppression by the Spanish armies had only limited success until the Calvinists became the driving force of the rebellion and began to alienate the Walloon provinces. WILLIAM I, prince of Orange (William the Silent), was the leader of the rebels, and he sought to maintain the unity of the Low Countries against Spanish domination. He failed because of religious differences between the Calvinist north and the Roman Catholic south.

The rebellion began to turn into a Dutch war of indepen-

The Council of Troubles, dubbed the Council of Blood for its unscrupulous methods and ruthless convictions, was convened in 1567 by the duque de Alba to try Protestants and opponents of Spanish rule. Two of the purported 18,000 victims are pictured (inset).

LOW COUNTRIES, 1609-48

Territories gained by
United Provinces, 1609-48

United Provinces, 1648

Spanish Netherlands, 1648

Boundary of the
Holy Roman Empire, 1648

o   Sieges

| 0 | km | 150 |
| 0 | mi | 100 |

Cartographic Production by Lothar Roth & Associates

lic, which renounced allegiance to Philip II in 1581. The surrender of ANTWERP to Spanish besiegers under Parma in 1585 marked the end of effective resistance to Spain in the south. In the north, however, the rebellion continued under the leadership of MAURICE OF NASSAU, son of the assassinated William the Silent, and Johan van OLDENBARNEVELT. Spain gave temporary recognition to Dutch independence during the Twelve Years' Truce (1609–21) and then final recognition in the Peace of Westphalia (1648).

THE UNITED PROVINCES

The Dutch Republic, known formally as the United Provinces of the Netherlands, took shape as a federal state of seven provinces—Friesland, Gelderland, Groningen, Holland, Overijssel, Utrecht, and Zeeland—but it was dominated by the merchants of Holland. It was able to continue the fight against Spain both because of its highly defensible position behind the mouths of the Rhine, Scheldt, and Maas and because of the immense wealth provided by the commerce and industry that continued in Holland in the midst of war.

The 17th century became the Golden Age of the Dutch. The Dutch EAST INDIA COMPANY, founded in 1602, and the DUTCH WEST INDIA COMPANY, founded in 1621, established colonies and trading posts in Asia, Africa, and America, and Dutch shipping carried a major portion of the world's trade. AMSTERDAM became the financial center of Europe and the United Provinces one of the great European powers. All this was accompanied by a remarkable cultural flowering. Earlier, Flanders had been preeminent in the arts of the Low Countries; now the northern provinces, with political independence, developed their own distinctive Dutch styles (see DUTCH ART AND ARCHITECTURE; FLEMISH ART AND ARCHITECTURE). From the mid-17th into the 18th century Dutch politics

dence, directed against both Spain and the southern provinces of the Netherlands, with the arrival of a new Spanish commander, Alessandro FARNESE, duke of Parma, in 1578. A gifted military and political leader, he turned the situation to Spain's favor for a decade. In 1579 two unions, or leagues, of provinces were established that laid the basis for the separate political development of north and south. The first, the Union of Arras, brought about the reconciliation of the southern provinces with Spain, while the second, the Union of Utrecht, became the basis for an independent Dutch Repub-

(Above) *The assassination (1584) of William the Silent deprived the Dutch Revolt of its most influential leader. The prince's death, however, did not end the war, and the independence of the seven northern provinces—the United Provinces—was finally secured in 1648.*

(Left) *Patriot militiamen flee Utrecht in September 1787 as Prussian forces invade the city. The Patriots, a popular party supporting democratic and Enlightenment ideals, seized power from stadholder William V in 1785 when disillusionment with his rule became widespread. The Prussian restoration of William V in 1787 led to repression of the Patriots, with many fleeing to Belgium and France. When French revolutionary armies invaded the Netherlands in 1794–95, the Patriots again seized power and established the Batavian Republic, a French protectorate.*

were dominated by a struggle for power between the merchant patricians of Holland and the princely house of ORANGE, which provided the elected stadholders (provincial governors). When WILLIAM II, prince of Orange, died in 1650, leadership passed to the merchants in the province of Holland, who gave (1653) effective control to Johan de WITT. Under de Witt, commercial rivalry led to two naval wars with England (1652–54, 1665–67; see ANGLO-DUTCH WARS). In a third war, beginning in 1672, LOUIS XIV of France allied with the English and overran much of the United Provinces. This debacle led to the murder (1672) of de Witt and the restoration of the stadholdership to the house of Orange. The new stadholder was William III, who in 1688–89 became King WILLIAM III of England and who was a major force in the European opposition to Louis XIV's expansionism (see AUGSBURG, LEAGUE OF; GRAND ALLIANCE, WAR OF THE; and SPANISH SUCCESSION, WAR OF THE).

When William died (1702) the stadholdership was again left vacant until 1747, when William IV of Orange-Nassau was recognized as stadholder by hereditary right. The republic was now in a period of decline, having lost commercial preeminence to England and France. Beginning about 1780, a new party called the Patriots arose; it combined traditional republicanism with the new ideas of the ENLIGHTENMENT. It sought to displace both the patricians and the Orangists in favor of a wider democracy, and this action brought about a reconciliation of the former foes, especially after the Patriots seized power in 1785. The Patriots were turned out by a Prussian army of intervention 2 years later, but they returned to power in 1795 when a French revolutionary army invaded the country and the Republic of the United Provinces was replaced by the French-sponsored Batavian Republic (see FRENCH REVOLUTIONARY WARS).

THE SPANISH AND AUSTRIAN NETHERLANDS

The southern Low Countries spent the two centuries after the Union of Arras under Habsburg rule, first of the Spanish and then of the Austrian branch. The Spanish kings accepted the basic compromise worked out in 1579 by the duke of Parma: Spanish sovereignty maintained in collaboration with the native nobility and the urban patricians and the religious monopoly of Catholicism without the rigors of the Inquisition. Any possibility of an attempt to seek reunification of the Low Countries by alliance with the Dutch against Spain was generally removed by the intolerance of the Dutch Calvinists. Economic prosperity returned to the rich southern provinces, although the base shifted from trade and industry to agriculture and the area was a major battleground in Louis XIV's wars.

The southern Netherlands passed from Spanish to Austrian hands by the Peace of Utrecht (1713–14), which concluded the War of the Spanish Succession. However, the basic policy of collaboration between the foreign sovereign and the local nobility, who maintained their internal domination, remained unchanged until the reign (1765–90) of Holy Roman Emperor JOSEPH II. For his Low Countries territories, Joseph's enlightened despotism meant establishing effective control from Vienna, weakening the position of the Catholic church, and eliminating the dominance of the nobility. A rebellion—the so-called Brabant Revolution—against his authority broke out in 1789, when the States-General proclaimed a republic of the United States of Belgium. Emperor LEOPOLD II reimposed Habsburg authority in 1790, but the country was annexed by revolutionary France in 1795.

FRENCH DOMINATION AND LIBERATION

French occupation brought profound changes in both parts of the Low Countries. The Batavian Republic, established in the north in 1795, replaced the antiquated Dutch political institutions with a unitary state. In 1806, Emperor NAPOLEON I placed his brother Louis Bonaparte (see BONAPARTE family) over the Dutch as king of Holland. When Louis proved too sympathetic with his subjects, Napoleon incorporated the country into the French Empire in 1810. Throughout this period Dutch economic activity declined disastrously. Not only did the French drain off resources through requisitions, but the Dutch lost most of their overseas trade as a result of the

British blockade in retaliation against Napoleon's CONTINENTAL SYSTEM.

The situation was different in Belgium, as the country was called after the Brabant Revolution, where incorporation into the French state brought a rapid rise of industry in the Walloon, or French-speaking provinces. Despite popular resistance, the middle classes gladly accepted French rule, and the French language became the language of the educated classes in Flanders, no less than in the Walloon provinces.

The removal of French control brought a temporary political unification of the Low Countries. Dutch patriots seized power in the north in 1813 and brought the son of the last stadholder back as sovereign prince. In 1815, the Congress of Vienna (see VIENNA, CONGRESS OF) made him king, as WILLIAM I, of the United Netherlands, in which the Belgian provinces were joined with the Dutch. He also became grand duke of Luxembourg, which was a member of the German Confederation.

William ruled as a constitutional monarch although the parliament's role was limited to lawmaking and some budgetary control. His efforts to unify the two regions did not win adequate support in the south, however, and the Belgian Revolution of 1830 broke the kingdom in two. The Belgians invited a German prince, Leopold of Saxe-Coburg, to become their king (as LEOPOLD I) in a constitutional and parliamentary monarchy. William finally recognized the independence of Belgium in 1839, and he abdicated the following year. His successor, WILLIAM II, accepted constitutional reforms that made the Netherlands a parliamentary monarchy in 1848.

Luxembourg also received a new constitution in 1848. After the collapse of the German Confederation in 1866, WILLIAM III of the Netherlands created a crisis (1867) by agreeing to sell Luxembourg to France. The Prussians, who garrisoned the

A contemporary caricature of the intransigent Dutch king William I depicts the monarch as a fortified Edam cheese, an ethnic slur mocking his florid defensive might and stolid immovability. William's autocratic methods and his flagrant disregard of the distinct cultural, religious, and economic interests of the southern (Belgian) provinces, which were united with the north as the kingdom of the Netherlands in 1815, provoked the Belgian revolution of August 1830. Although French intervention late the following year put an end to the king's efforts to reconquer Belgium, William refused to recognize the new state for another seven years. Faced with unrest at home over his dictatorial rule, he abdicated in 1840.

(Left) *Constantin Meunier's painting of the battle for Brussels of September 1830, the first major engagement of the Belgian revolution, conveys the severity of the 3-day clash. This Dutch invasion united Belgian groups behind the revolutionary movement and prompted their declaration of independence on October 4, 1830. (Musées Royaux des Beaux-Arts, Brussels.)*

(Below) *Demonstrations against the return of Belgian King Leopold III, who was exiled in 1945 for alleged cooperation with the Nazi regime, erupted on July 9, 1950. Continued unrest forced the monarch's abdication the following year.*

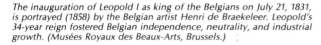

The inauguration of Leopold I as king of the Belgians on July 21, 1831, is portrayed (1858) by the Belgian artist Henri de Braekeleer. Leopold's 34-year reign fostered Belgian independence, neutrality, and industrial growth. (Musées Royaux des Beaux-Arts, Brussels.)

duchy, threatened war, and a conference of the European powers made the grand duchy a neutral territory. The house of Orange continued to rule there until the accession (1890) in the Netherlands of Queen WILHELMINA. Salic law prevented her from inheriting Luxembourg, which passed to a collateral line of the family.

MODERN NATIONS

Belgium and the Netherlands followed similar paths of development in the 19th and 20th centuries. Belgium became heavily industrialized, first in the Walloon provinces and later, after World War II, in Flanders. The Netherlands continued to concentrate on commerce and agriculture well into the 20th century, but then developed a large-scale industrial base, notably in electronics. Parliamentary authority was supreme in both countries, and the electorate was expanded by the introduction of universal manhood suffrage (Belgium, 1893; the Netherlands, 1917) and women's suffrage (after World War II). The Netherlands inherited colonies (in South America and the East Indies) from the republican period, while Belgium took over the Congo (now ZAIRE) from the personal rule of King LEOPOLD II in 1908.

Belgium had been declared neutral by the European powers at its founding, but its neutrality was violated by Germany in 1914. Unable to halt the German advance, despite heroic resistance, the country was occupied throughout World War I. The Netherlands remained neutral during World War I. In World War II both countries were occupied by the Germans from 1940 until 1944–45. Governments-in-exile were established in London; the Dutch one was under Queen Wilhelmina, but the Belgians formed theirs without LEOPOLD III, who chose to remain in his occupied country.

After the war, both countries became firm members of

NATO. As early as 1944, Belgium and the Netherlands joined with Luxembourg in forming a customs union called Benelux. Subsequently, all three became (1957) founding members of the EUROPEAN ECONOMIC COMMUNITY (or Common Market).

The postwar period also brought colonial divestment. After a bitter conflict the Dutch granted independence to Indonesia in 1949, and in 1963 the former Dutch New Guinea (now Irian Jaya) was joined to Indonesia. In the Western Hemisphere the Netherlands Antilles and Suriname became autonomous units of the Dutch state in 1954, and Suriname became independent in 1975. The Belgians relinquished their one colony, the Congo (now Zaire), suddenly in 1960, and chaos ensued (see CONGO CRISIS).

Queen Wilhelmina, ruler of the Netherlands for half a century (1890-1948), symbolized resistance to the Germans during World War II as she encouraged the nation by radio from her London exile. Her popular reign saw the expansion of the electorate and the maintenance of political stability.

Internal conflicts between the monarch and parts of the population occurred in both countries. The Dutch royal family, headed from 1948 by Queen JULIANA, came under attack because of the unpopular marriages of several princesses. Nonetheless, the eldest, BEATRICE, succeeded to the throne without incident on the abdication of her mother in 1980. In Belgium, Leopold III's wartime role had caused controversy, and he was forced to abdicate in favor of his son, BAUDOUIN I, in 1951. Belgium was also torn by conflict between its Dutch- and French-speakers. In 1980 the Belgian parliament voted to federalize the government, creating regional assemblies for the Dutch-speaking north and the French-speaking south.   HERBERT H. ROWEN

Bibliography: Huggett, F. E., *Modern Belgium* (1969); Lijphart, Arend, *The Politics of Accommodation: Pluralism and Democracy in the Netherlands*, new ed. (1976); Parker, Geoffrey, *The Dutch Revolt* (1977); Schöffer, Ivo, *A Short History of the Netherlands*, 2d ed. (1973).

low-pressure region

A portion of the ATMOSPHERE with fewer molecules than adjacent portions is called a low-pressure region, area, or cell, or simply a low. In such a region a column of air exerts less pressure on the Earth's surface than do nearby columns. Because air is generally rising in such systems, they are cloudy, usually rainy, and often stormy. Low-pressure cells may be less than 1 km (0.6 mi) across in a TORNADO, about 100 km (60 mi) across in a hurricane (see HURRICANE AND TYPHOON), or more than 1,000 km (600 mi) across in a mature midlatitude CYCLONE. The largest are the semipermanent lows around Iceland and the Aleutian Islands, the low-pressure belt encircling Antarctica, and the region (variously called the DOLDRUMS, the tropical rainy belt, or the intertropical convergence zone) where the trade winds end in a region of warm, rising air near the equator.   ARNOLD COURT

Lowell   [loh'-ul]

Lowell, a city in northwestern Massachusetts, is located about 48 km (30 mi) northwest of Boston, at the confluence of the Merrimack and Concord rivers. One of two county seats of Middlesex County (the other is Cambridge), Lowell has a population of 92,418 (1980). The city has electronics, chemical, and plastics industries. The birthplace of the painter James McNeill Whistler, Lowell is also the seat of the University of Lowell—established by the 1975 merger of Lowell State College (1894) and Lowell Technological Institute (1895). First settled in 1653, Lowell became an important textile center in the 19th century when the waters of the Merrimack were harnessed to provide power for the mills and the Middlesex Canal system was completed.

Lowell, Abbott Lawrence

Abbott Lawrence Lowell, b. Boston, Dec. 13, 1856, d. Jan. 6, 1943, was an influential president (1909–33) of Harvard University. He was the brother of the astronomer Percival Lowell and of the poet Amy Lowell. A graduate of Harvard (1877) and its law school (1880), he practiced law before returning to Harvard in 1897 as a professor of the science of government. He was appointed president in 1909, succeeding Charles William Eliot, who had replaced a required curriculum with a system of free electives. Lowell partially returned to a structured curriculum by having students concentrate on a major subject. He introduced a general examination and a system of tutorials. He also created the Harvard system of residential "houses." The enrollment doubled, endowment increased dramatically, and several professional schools were added during Lowell's tenure. Lowell is also known as a defender of academic freedom.

Bibliography: Bragdon, Henry W., *Woodrow Wilson and Lawrence Lowell, an Original Study of Two Very Different Men* (1943); Yeomans, Henry A., *Abbott Lawrence Lowell, 1856–1943* (1948; repr. 1977).

Lowell, Amy

Amy Lawrence Lowell, b. Brookline, Mass., Feb. 9, 1874, d. May 12, 1925, a descendant of a wealthy and distinguished New England family, is best known as the leading American advocate of IMAGISM in poetry. With untiring energy and shrewdness she created a reputation as a discerning critic of modern poetry, as a literary biographer—her massive study, *John Keats,* was published in 1925—and as a poet. Lowell wrote her first poems, published in *A Dome of Many-Coloured Glass* (1912), in the tradition of English romanticism. Her acquaintance with the experimental verse of Ezra Pound and F. S. Flint is reflected in the free-verse sections of *Sword Blades and Poppy Seed* (1914). She also experimented with polyphonic prose, an unsatisfactory union of prose and traditional poetry. In subsequent volumes there appeared the popular "Patterns," "Lilacs," and other poems that seem imagistic in their concreteness, particularity, and absence of direct message. In *Fir Flower Tablets* (1921; publ. 1946) Lowell tried to outdo Pound by translating some ancient Chinese poems. Among her critical works are *Six French Poets* (1915), *Tendencies in Modern American Poetry* (1917), and *A Criti-*

Amy Lowell, an American poet of the early 20th century, became a leading advocate of imagism through her collections of poetry, lectures, and literary criticism. Lowell was posthumously awarded a Pulitzer Prize for her volume of verse What's O'Clock *(1925).*

cal Fable (1922), in which her highly eccentric personality comes to life. *The Complete Poetical Works* of Amy Lowell, edited by Louis Untermeyer, appeared in 1955.

JAMES A. HART

Bibliography: Damon, S. Foster, *Amy Lowell: A Chronicle* (1935; repr. 1966); Gould, Jean, *Amy: The World of Amy Lowell and the Imagist Movement* (1975); Gregory, Horace, *Amy Lowell* (1958); Wood, Clement, *Amy Lowell: A Critical Study* (1926).

Lowell, Francis Cabot

Francis Cabot Lowell, b. Newburyport, Mass., Apr. 7, 1775, d. Aug. 10, 1817, was a Boston merchant who helped launch the U.S. textile industry. In 1810-12 he visited England, where he observed the workings of the Lancashire cotton mills; on returning home he began building a cotton mill in Waltham, Mass. Lowell worked with designer Paul Moody to construct the first American power loom and other equipment required to turn raw cotton into cloth. After his death, his brother-in-law, Patrick T. Jackson, carrying out Lowell's dreams of a textile city, built mills on land which in 1826 became Lowell, Mass.

Lowell, James Russell

James Russell Lowell, b. Feb. 22, 1819, Cambridge, Mass., d. Aug. 12, 1891, was one of the finest New England poets of the 19th century and a distinguished literary critic. His humorous poetry, such as *The Biglow Papers* (1848), is highly valued by modern readers, but he also dealt with lyrical themes and public affairs and wrote charmingly of the New England countryside. *The Vision of Sir Launfal* (1848) combines medievalism with modern social consciousness; *A Fable for Critics* (1848) tempers criticism with humor. The first series of *The Biglow Papers* was propaganda against the Mexican War and war itself, and *The Cathedral* (1870) is one of the important religious poems of the century, in some ways anticipating Henry Adams's *Mont-Saint-Michel and Chartres* (1913). Among the finest of his critical essays—historical, aesthetic, and didactic in method and more concerned with the appreciation of individual writers than general critical principles—are the studies of Chaucer, Dante, Shakespeare, and Spenser.

Lowell graduated from Harvard Law School in 1840 but disliked the law and gave it up in 1843. The following year he married Maria White, a poet, abolitionist, and devotee of social causes; during their marriage he wrote much on abolition. Maria died in 1853, and in 1857 he married Frances Dunlap. From 1855 to 1875, Lowell held the Smith Professorship at Harvard, succeeding Henry Wadsworth Longfellow. He was the first editor (1857-61) of *The Atlantic Monthly* and coedited (1863-72) *The North American Review* with Charles Eliot Norton. He served as minister to Spain (1877-80) and to England (1880-85). At the time of his death, Lowell was generally regarded as the most distinguished man of letters in America.

EDWARD WAGENKNECHT

Bibliography: Duberman, Martin, *James Russell Lowell* (1966); Greenslet, Ferris, *James Russell Lowell, His Life and Work* (1905; repr. 1973); Howard, Leon, *Victorian Knight-Errant: A Study of the Literary Career of James Russell Lowell* (1952; repr. 1971); Scudder, Horace E., *James Russell Lowell, A Biography*, 2 vols. (1901; repr. 1973); Wagenknecht, Edward, *James Russell Lowell, Portrait of a Many-Sided Man* (1971).

Lowell, Percival

The American astronomer Percival Lowell, b. Boston, Mar. 13, 1855, d. Nov. 12, 1916, is best known for his belief in the existence of artificial canals on MARS. Lowell was a businessman and traveler in the Far East before becoming obsessed with Giovanni SCHIAPARELLI's report (1877) of *canali* ("channels") on Mars. He founded (1894) the Lowell Observatory near Flagstaff, Ariz., especially for studying the Martian surface, and for more than a decade he charted the apparently crisscross markings of Mars. Although other astronomers vehemently denied the existence of canals on Mars, Lowell maintained that not only did they exist, they had also been built by intelligent beings. Not until the Mars probes of the 1960s were Lowell's claims conclusively disproved.

Despite the controversy over the Martian canals, Lowell Observatory has contributed substantially to studies of the planets and the stars. Lowell himself predicted the position of a perturbing planet beyond Neptune, later discovered by Clyde TOMBAUGH and named Pluto.

STEVEN J. DICK

Bibliography: Hoyt, William Graves, *Lowell and Mars* (1977); Lowell, Abbott L., *Biography of Percival Lowell* (1935).

Lowell, Robert, Jr.

Robert Lowell, a leading poet of post–World War II America, voiced his dismay at the spiritual impotence of individuals and society in such poems as "For the Union Dead" (1948) and "Skunk Hour" (1958). The winner of two Pulitzer prizes and a National Book Award, he has been greatly praised for his tightly constructed verse and his arresting honesty.

Photo Jill Krementz © 1975

Robert Traill Spence Lowell, Jr., b. Boston, Mar. 1, 1917, was the spokesman for a generation of American poets who came to prominence during World War II. Lowell felt that individuals must not become depersonalized by war and by the constant pressure of violence in society. A number of his finest poems—"The Quaker Graveyard at Nantucket" (1946), "Mother Marie Therese" (1948), "Skunk Hour" (1958), and "For the Union Dead" (1960)—both dramatized this issue and found broad moral significance in the tension between his obligation to American social and religious traditions and his own private interests.

Lowell was descended from several old and prominent American families. While a student at preparatory school he came under the influence of Elizabeth Drew's *Discovering Poetry* (1933). An interest in Roman Catholicism dominates his earlier volumes *Land of Unlikeness* (1944), *Lord Weary's Castle* (1946), and *The Mills of the Kavanaughs* (1951). Lowell attended (1935-37) Harvard University before transferring to Kenyon College to complete an undergraduate degree in classics. His teachers at Kenyon included the distinguished poet John Crowe Ransom. In 1940, the year of his graduation, he married the fiction-writer Jean Stafford and was converted to Catholicism. They were divorced in 1948, and Lowell married another prominent writer, Elizabeth Hardwick. After college Lowell worked as an editor and teacher. During World War II he refused to enter military service and was imprisoned for five months. *Land of Unlikeness* (1944), which appeared shortly after his imprisonment, was greeted by mixed reviews. With *Lord Weary's Castle* (1946), for which he won a Pulitzer Prize, Lowell was acknowledged as America's foremost young poet. His next important work, *Life Studies* (1959), broke with traditional poetic form and diction and introduced a personal, less declaratory tone to his work.

During the 1960s, Lowell remained preoccupied with political and social issues. In 1965 he refused to attend a White House Arts Festival because of American policies abroad, and in 1970, by way of protest, he left the United States and took up residence in England. His output during these years was prolific: two books of translations; *The Old Glory* (1965), a trilogy of plays; and such verse works as *For the Union Dead* (1964), *Near the Ocean* (1967), and *Notebook* (1969). *The Dolphin* (1973) won him a second Pulitzer Prize. His final work, *Day by Day* (1977), published shortly before a fatal heart attack on Sept. 12, 1977, cut short his brilliant career.

JEROME MAZZARO

Bibliography: Axelrod, Steven G., *Robert Lowell: Life and Art* (1978); Fein, Richard J., *Robert Lowell* (1970); Mazzaro, Jerome, *The Poetic Themes of Robert Lowell* (1965); Meiners, Roger, *Everything to Be Endured: An Essay on Robert Lowell and Modern Poetry* (1970); Parkinson, Thomas, ed., *Lowell: A Collection of Critical Essays* (1968).

lower class: see CLASS, SOCIAL.

Lowry, Malcolm   [low'-ree]

Malcolm Lowry, b. July 28, 1909, d. June 27, 1957, was a British novelist whose major work, *Under the Volcano* (1947), expresses many of the problems of his own life, generation, and educated class. A victim of chronic alcoholism, several mental breakdowns, and alienation from his country and family, Lowry had a grand scheme for a trilogy of novels on hell, purgatory, and heaven. *Volcano*, which Lowry called "a drunken Divine Comedy," is his inferno, the story of an ex-consul to Mexico named Geoffrey Firmin. Lowry's other writings, edited posthumously by his second wife, Marjorie Bonner, include the novel *Lunar Caustic* (1968) and the short stories in *Hear Us O Lord From Heaven Thy Dwelling Place* (1961) and *Dark As The Grave Wherein My Friend Is Laid* (1968).

JANE COLVILLE BETTS

Bibliography: Bradbrook, Muriel C., *Malcolm Lowry: His Art and Early Life* (1975); Costa, Richard H., *Malcolm Lowry* (1975); Day, Douglas, *Malcolm Lowry: A Biography* (1973).

Loyalists

In American history, the Loyalists, or Tories, were the men and women who refused to renounce allegiance to the British crown after July 1776; they demonstrated that the AMERICAN REVOLUTION was a civil war as well as a quest for independence. Approximately 500,000 persons, 20 percent of the white population, actively opposed independence; probably a like number were passive Loyalists. There were Loyalists in every colony, but they were most numerous in the Mid-Atlantic states and in the South.

Although the incidence of loyalism was greatest among crown officials, Anglican clergy, social and economic elites, and cultural minorities, the king's friends came from all racial, religious, ethnic, economic, class, and occupational groups. Some, like Joseph GALLOWAY of Pennsylvania, were Whig-Loyalists who opposed British policies but also rejected secession from the empire. Sometimes families were divided; Benjamin Franklin's son William was a Loyalist. Vested interest, temperament, or political philosophy could separate Patriot from Loyalist.

As much as the Patriots did, the Loyalists put their lives, fortunes, and honor on the line during the Revolution. Be-

This cartoon, printed in London in 1774, depicts a Loyalist in the American colonies being tarred and feathered by Patriots. Crown supporters, about one-fifth of the white population, suffered physical violence and loss of property throughout the Revolutionary War period.

sides those who served in the regular British Army, some 19,000 men fought in over 40 Loyalist units, the largest of which was Cortlandt Skinner's New Jersey Volunteers. Refugees gathered in British-occupied New York City, where the Board of Associated Loyalists, headed by William Franklin, helped direct military activities. During the war crown supporters suffered physical abuse, ostracism, disenfranchisement, confiscation of property, imprisonment, banishment, even death. However, only 4,118 Loyalists requested compensation from Britain's Royal Claims Commission after the war, receiving a total of about £3,000,000.

The Revolution forced approximately 100,000 persons, 2.4 percent of the population (compared with 0.5 percent in the French Revolution), into exile. Some refugees went to England, others to Florida or the Caribbean; at least half went to Canada, where the new colony of NEW BRUNSWICK was created (1784) to meet their demands for lands and recognition. The United Empire Loyalists, a hereditary organization created by the Canadian government in 1789 to honor those who rallied to the crown before the peace of 1783, remains today the Loyalist counterpart to the Sons and Daughters of the American Revolution.

LARRY R. GERLACH

Bibliography: Brown, Wallace, *The Good Americans* (1969); Calhoon, Robert M., *The Loyalists in Revolutionary America* (1973).

Loyola University   [loy-oh'-luh]

Established in 1870 (enrollment: 15,200; library: 1,200,000 volumes), Loyola is a coeducational university conducted by the Jesuits in Chicago. It has graduate schools of law, medicine, and dentistry.

LPG: see LIQUEFIED PETROLEUM GAS.

LSD

LSD, or D-lysergic acid diethylamide, also known as LSD-25 and "acid," is a prototype of the hallucinogenic drug class. The mental effects of LSD were discovered in 1943 when a small amount was accidentally ingested by the Swiss chemist Albert Hofmann. The first to synthesize the drug, Hofmann did so while studying derivatives of alkaloids from the ERGOT fungus, a parasitic fungus of rye and wheat. LSD may stimulate the sympathetic nervous system, but its action is complex and as yet not fully known. It produces dilation of the pupils and increases in pulse rate, blood pressure, and temperature. Acting on the brain, LSD can cause sensory distortions, with vivid visual and sometimes auditory hallucinations. Emotional and subjective responses vary widely and may include difficulty in concentration, loss of identity, feelings of unreality, seemingly magical insights, depression, anxiety, and sometimes panic and terror. LSD does not produce physical dependence, but psychological dependence and tolerance can develop. LSD is potent in very small doses; as little as 35μ can produce measurable effects. It has been used experimentally in the study of mental illness and has also been used to treat various psychiatric conditions and alcoholism. At present, however, LSD has no proven and accepted medical use and its general use, manufacture, and sale is illegal in the United States. In the late 1950s and early '60s, LSD was a popular drug of abuse, frequently used socially on college campuses (see DRUG ABUSE).

CHARLES W. GORODETZKY

Bibliography: Barron, Frank, *LSD, Man and Society*, ed. by Richard DeBold and Russell Leaf (1967; repr. 1975); Blum, Richard H., et al., *The Utopiates* (1964); Cohen, Sidney, *Beyond Within: The LSD Story*, rev. ed. (1967); Ray, Oakley S., *Drugs, Society and Human Behavior*, 2d ed. (1974); Ungerleider, J. Thomas, ed., *The Problems and Prospects of LSD* (1972).

Lu Hsün   (Lu Xun)   [loo sheun]

Chinese writer Lu Hsün (pseudonym of Chou Shu-Jen), 1881–1936, is known for stories and essays that humorously censure social and moral values. While studying medicine in Japan with his brother, the essayist Chou Tso-Jen, he read Western and Russian literature and philosophy and abandoned his studies to become a writer. During the literary revolution launched by Hu Shih in 1917, Lu Hsün won acclaim for short stories set in his native Chekiang province and written in colloquial language. These include *Huang-jen Jih-chi* (Diary of a Madman, 1918), based on a work of the same title by Gogol in which a lunatic suspects that he alone is sane, and Lu Hsün's most famous work, *A Q Cheng-chuan* (1921; trans. as *The True Story of Ah Q*, 1956), in which the hero, a village boor who is able to face reality only through self-deception, symbolizes reactionary forces in Chinese society. His later stories, collected in *Ku-shih Hsin-pien* (Old Tales Retold, 1935), are more ideological than his earlier work. He also wrote poems and many widely read newspaper articles.

Bibliography: Huang Sung-k'ang, *Lu Hsün and the New Culture Movement of Modern China* (1957); Lee, L. O., ed., *Lu Xun and His Legacy* (1985); Tsi-an Hsia, *The Gate of Darkness: Studies on the Leftist Literary Movement in China* (1968).

Lü-shun   (Lüshun)   [lue shoon]

Lü-shun, formerly Port Arthur, is an important port and naval base in China's northeast (formerly called Manchuria). Located at the southern tip of the Liaotung Peninsula, Lü-shun guards the entrance to the Pohai (Gulf of Chihli). Lü-shun and Ta-lien (Da-lian), which lies 32 km (20 mi) to the northeast, form one urban center called Lü-ta (Lüda). The twin cities are connected by rail and a highway. Because of warm offshore currents, the natural harbor of Lü-shun stays ice free all year.

Although the site was used as a Chinese military post from the 2d century BC, modern Lü-shun dates from the mid-19th century. The British occupied the area in the 1850s, and the Russians developed the settlement into a seaport in the late 19th century. The Russians obtained a lease on the port in 1898, but after their defeat in the Russo-Japanese War (1904–05) they were forced to cede it to Japan, which held it until 1945.   JAMES CHAN

Lü-ta   (Lüda)   [lue-dah]

Lü-ta (1985 est. pop., 1,630,000), an autonomous subprovincial municipality, occupies the tip of the Liaotung Peninsula in Liaoning province, China. The component cities of Lü-ta are Lü-shun and Ta-lien, once known as Port Arthur and Dairen, respectively. Lü-ta serves as an ice-free port for southern Manchuria and is a leading industrial center.

Luanda   [loo-ahn'-duh]

Luanda, the capital of Angola and of Luanda district, is a port located on the Atlantic Ocean. Connected by rail to Quela, Luanda exports cotton, coffee, sugar, diamonds, and manganese ore. The city has a population of 1,134,000 (1988 est.). Industries include an oil refinery, fisheries, and factories that manufacture foodstuffs, beverages, textiles, motor vehicles, and construction materials. Luanda has an international airport, and it is the seat of an archdiocese and of the University of Angola (1963). Founded by the Portuguese in 1576, Luanda was the site of a large slave market from the mid-16th to the mid-19th century.

Luang Prabang   [lwahng pruh-bahng']

Luang Prabang (Louangphrabang), a city in Laos, is the religious center of the country and the former royal capital. It lies on the Mekong River, about 200 km (125 mi) northwest of Vientiane. The population is 46,000 (1975 est.). The city is an important river port and a market town for fish, agricultural and forest produce, and some handicrafts. The Gold Buddha (Prabang), a sacred Sinhalese carving, was probably brought to the city in 1356.

Established as the capital of Laos by King Ngoun in 1353, the city was originally named Moung Swa. Its present name dates from 1563. It continued to serve as the royal residence until 1975, when the People's Democratic Republic of Laos was established.   ASHOK K. DUTT

Luba   [loo'-buh]

The Luba, a Bantu-speaking people in Zaire related to the Lunda and Bemba peoples, have for many centuries been at the forefront of ethnic politics in the region. Their home area in the province of Shaba (formerly Katanga) may have been one of the central areas from which Bantu-speakers spread across Africa. By the 9th century AD the Luba were prominent in long-distance trade and had attained considerable technical skill and elegance in making pottery and in working copper, ivory, and iron. The forms of political organization that they developed by the 16th century were widely imitated by their neighbors, many of whom now claim Luba origins. Their empire was extensive before the onset of European colonial rule in the 19th century, and it was governed through subordinate rulers under a powerful king who succeeded through the mother's line. Among the earliest labor migrants to Upper Katanga, the Luba were also among the first to form voluntary ethnic associations. A Luba state led by Albert Kalonji existed briefly in Zaire's Kasai region in 1960–61. The Luba numbered more than 5 million in the 1980s.   RICHARD WERBNER

Bibliography: Bustin, Edouard, *Lunda under Belgian Rule: The Politics of Ethnicity* (1975); Reefe, T., *The Rainbow and the Kings* (1981).

Lubbers, Ruud

Rudolph Frans Marie Lubbers, b. May 7, 1939, is prime minister of the Netherlands. A wealthy industrialist, Lubbers entered parliament as a member of the Catholic People's party in 1972 and served as economics minister in the government of Johannes den Uyl from 1973 to 1977. A Christian Democrat after 1980, he became prime minister as head of a center-right coalition in 1982, winning endorsements from the voters in 1986 and 1989.

Lubbock   [luhb'-uhk]

Lubbock, a city in northwest Texas, is the seat of Lubbock County. The trade center for the cotton- and grain-producing South Plains region, it has a population of 173,979 (1980). Manufactures include cottonseed oil, heavy agricultural and petroleum equipment, irrigation pipe and pumps, mobile homes, and electronic components. Texas Tech University is located in the city, and Reese Air Force Base is nearby. Quakers settled in the area in the 1870s. Present-day Lubbock was formed from the merger of Old Lubbock and Monterey in 1890.

Lubbock, John, 1st Baron Avebury   [ayv'-bur-ee]

Sir John Lubbock, 1st Baron Avebury, b. Apr. 30, 1834, d. May 28, 1913, English prehistorian, naturalist, banker, and politician, produced influential early writings on archaeology and entomology. In his book *Pre-Historic Times* (1865) Lubbock coined the terms *paleolithic* and *neolithic,* and in *The Origin of Civilization and the Primitive Condition of Man* (1870) he treated prehistoric cultures as part of human evolutionary development. As a naturalist, he wrote *On the Senses, Instincts, and Intelligence of Animals* (1888).

Bibliography: Grant Duff, U., ed., *The Life-work of Lord Avebury* (1924).

Lübeck   [lue'-bek]

Lübeck is a city in the West German state of Schleswig-Holstein, on the Trave River near the Baltic Sea. The most important Baltic seaport of the country, it has a population of 209,159 (1987 est.). The city's economy is heavily concentrated on port activities. Manufactures include ships, iron and steel, cement, machinery, furniture, rugs, and food products. Among the city's landmarks are the Romanesque cathedral (begun 1173) and the 13th-century Rathaus (city hall).

Founded on the site of a ruined Slavic settlement, Lübeck was destroyed by fire in 1157. The present city dates from 1159, when it was rebuilt. It developed as an important economic and cultural center for the entire Baltic area; in 1358 it was chosen as the administrative headquarters for the HANSE-ATIC LEAGUE. Its importance lasted until the 15th century, when the league began to crumble. Napoleon I made it part of his empire in 1806, and after 1815 it was part of the German Confederation. Lübeck later became part of the North German Confederation and, in 1871, part of the German Empire. The Elbe-Lübeck Canal, opened in 1900, brought new prosperity. In 1937 Lübeck was attached to Schleswig-Holstein. During World War II the city was heavily bombed, but much of the devastated area has been rebuilt.

Lubitsch, Ernst   [loo'-bich, airnst]

Ernst Lubitsch, b. Berlin, Jan. 28, 1892, d. Nov. 30, 1947, was a German-American film director known for his sophisticated comedies of manners. He had already achieved success as an actor and director in Europe when Mary Pickford brought him to Hollywood to direct her in *Rosita* (1923); Lubitsch's subsequent silent films—*The Marriage Circle* (1924), *Forbidden Paradise* (1924), *Lady Windermere's Fan* (1925), and *So This Is Paris* (1926)—established his reputation as a master of urbane, sardonic humor.

The "Lubitsch touch" survived the transition to sound. In the 1930s, beginning with *The Love Parade* (1930), he directed musicals, often using the team of Maurice Chevalier and Jeanette MacDonald. The cynical wit that was his trademark was especially evident in *Trouble in Paradise* (1932); *Ninotchka* (1939), starring Greta Garbo; and *To Be Or Not To Be* (1942), which satirized nazism. He departed from his usual brand of humor in *The Shop around the Corner* (1940), another comedy directed at the Nazi threat.

Bibliography: Paul, William, *Ernst Lubitsch's American Comedy* (1983); Poague, Leland A., *The Cinema of Ernst Lubitsch* (1978).

Lublin   [loo'-blin]

Lublin, an industrial and commercial city in southeastern Poland, lies about 160 km (100 mi) southeast of Warsaw. The population is 324,100 (1984 est.). Manufactures include motor vehicles, farming equipment, and food products. Lublin has several colleges, a Roman Catholic university, and many museums.

Founded in the late 9th century, the city grew around a 12th-century castle and was chartered in 1317. It was already a prosperous commercial center in 1569, when the Union of Lublin (between the Kingdom of Poland and the Grand Duchy of Lithuania) was signed there. Under Austrian rule from 1795, Lublin passed to Russian Poland in 1815 and to the Polish republic in 1918. In 1941 the Germans established the Majdanek concentration camp on the outskirts of the city; the camp is now a museum.

Lubovitch, Lar   [loo'-buh-vich]

One of the new generation of choreographic synthesizers, Lar Lubovitch, b. Chicago, Apr. 9, 1945, strives to combine ballet and modern dance in his lyrical choreography. His dance studies and performing included work in the José Limón and Martha Graham techniques as well as in classical ballet at the Juilliard School. Lubovitch has choreographed for the American Ballet Theatre, Pennsylvania Ballet, and Ballet Rambert, among others. He founded his own company in 1968 to produce works in his innovative style, including *Scriabin Dances* (1977), *Marimba* (1977), *Up Jump* (1979), *Big Shoulders* (1983), and *A Brahms Symphony* (1985).

MICHAEL ROBERTSON

Bibliography: Gruen, John, *The Private World of Ballet* (1975).

lubrication

Lubrication is the introduction of a substance, called a lubricant, between two moving surfaces in contact in order to reduce FRICTION. This reduction of friction greatly reduces the wear of the surfaces and thus lengthens their service life. It also reduces the energy required for the motion.

TYPES OF LUBRICATION

Friction occurs whenever one surface slides over another. To overcome this friction, a force greater than the frictional resistance must be applied. The force required depends on the roughness of the surfaces and on the load—the force with which the two surfaces are pressed together. Dry, or unlubricated, sliding takes place when no lubricant is used. If a film of lubricant is used but is so thin that some contact still occurs between the surfaces, the process is called boundary, or thin-film, lubrication; the resistance is still considerable. Boundary lubrication commonly occurs when the load is heavy and during starting and stopping of machinery. In fluid-film lubrication, a lubricant film that is thick enough to completely separate the surfaces is introduced between the moving surfaces. The lubricant must be under pressure in order to keep the surfaces separated. In hydrostatic lubrication, the pressure in the lubricant film is generated by an external source, such as a pump.

Pressure can also be generated as a result of the shape and motion of the surfaces (hydrodynamic lubrication); for example, a rotating shaft in a BEARING forces lubricant into the wedge-shaped space between the shaft and the bearing, generating a pressure whose magnitude depends on the clearance between the bearing and the shaft, the load on the shaft, the speed of rotation, and the viscosity of the lubricant. Solid lubricants, which are discussed below, can also be used. Solid lubrication is often used under extreme conditions of load and temperature, under which normal lubricants break down and lose their effectiveness.

FUNCTIONS OF A LUBRICANT

Although the basic function of a lubricant is to reduce friction and wear, a lubricant may also perform a number of other functions. It may carry off heat that is generated, thus functioning as a coolant. This function is its primary purpose in some machine-tool operations, especially in grinding. It may help to control corrosion by coating parts with a protective film; this protection can be enhanced by adding a corrosion inhibitor to the lubricant. It may also help remove contaminants. In metalworking this flushing action is used to remove chips of metal. In automobile engines a detergent additive removes sludge deposits from inside the engine (see INTERNAL COMBUSTION ENGINE).

TYPES OF LUBRICANTS

Lubricants may be made from animal products, such as sperm oil, lard oil, and goose grease; vegetable products, such as soybean, cottonseed, and linseed oil; and mineral products, including petroleum lubricants and various inorganic solid lubricants. Animal and vegetable products have been used since ancient times, but they have rapidly been superseded by the more effective and stable mineral products. Petroleum lubricants are predominantly hydrocarbons that are refined from crude petroleum by various methods, including a distillation. Solid lubricants include inorganic compounds such as graphite, molybdenum disulfide, and talc; and organic compounds such as metallic soaps and animal waxes. Synthetic lubricants have been developed to meet the more demanding requirements of modern machinery. Examples are polymer films and silicones. A lubricating grease consists of a liquid lubricant with a thickening agent added to it. A grease is sometimes preferable to an oil, because grease acts as a seal to keep the lubricant in and contaminants out, and it requires less frequent applications.

SYSTEMS FOR APPLYING LUBRICANTS

Modern machinery requires not only a proper lubricant but also an effective system for applying it. At first, lubricants were applied by hand or by the use of an oil can. (Oil is simply a lubricant that is a liquid.) Although simple, this method was not precise. Mechanical devices called lubricators were developed to apply the lubricant. A simple type is a small container with a hole or valve placed over the part to be lubricated. This arrangement is called drop-feed lubrication. In wick-feed lubrication a wick immersed in an oil reservoir is pressed against the moving part; the wick supplies the oil by capillary action.

Bath lubrication or splash lubrication may be used for

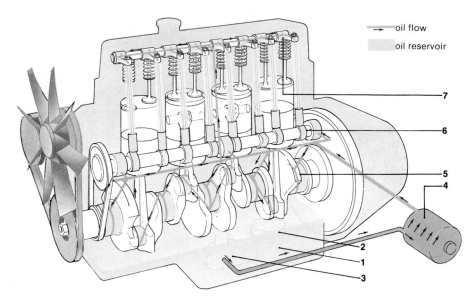

The lubrication system of an automobile engine furnishes clean, cool oil to moving parts to reduce friction and wear and to help remove heat. The oil in a sump (1) is sucked through a screened oil intake (2) into an oil pump (3). The pump forces the oil through a filter (4) to a main gallery line from which branch passages conduct it to moving parts, such as main crankshaft (5) and camshaft (6) bearings, valve rockers (7), and connecting rod bearings. Cylinder walls are sprayed with oil from rotating parts. The oil returns by gravity to the sump.

oil flow
oil reservoir

gears, chains, bearings, and other moving parts that can be partly submerged in an oil reservoir. In the bath system the part simply picks up oil as it dips into the reservoir and carries it to other parts along its path. The splash system increases the efficiency by attaching a special splash ring to a moving part so that the oil is splashed against other parts that need to be lubricated. This is similar to oil-mist lubrication, in which the oil is atomized in a stream of air. Force-feed lubrication uses an oil pump to force the oil under pressure to the parts to be lubricated. Some parts are self-lubricating and require no external lubrication; the lubricant may be sealed in against loss as in sealed ball bearings, or a porous material such as porous bronze can be used so that oil impregnated in the material can penetrate to the point of contact of the moving parts through pores in the material. In small two-stroke gasoline engines the oil is mixed in with the fuel to bring it to the moving parts inside the engine.

Although lubricating oil is used elsewhere in a car, the lubrication of the engine is of greatest importance because it reduces the friction and wear between moving metal parts and also removes heat from the engine. A supply of oil is kept in the engine crankcase. An oil pump, which is powered by the engine, forces oil from the crankcase under pressure to the cylinder block. Passages in the engine channel the oil to various moving parts, and the oil eventually drains back down in the crankcase. An oil filter is inserted in the oil circuit to filter out metal shavings, carbon deposits, and dirt. Because the filter is not completely effective, the oil eventually becomes contaminated, breaks down (decomposes), and loses its effectiveness. That is why routine auto maintenance calls for changing the oil and the oil filter periodically.

ARTHUR BIDERMAN

Bibliography: Bowden, Frank Philip, and Tabor, David, *Friction* (1973); Cameron, Alastair, *Basic Lubrication Theory*, 3d ed. (1982).

Lubumbashi   [loo-boom-bah'-shee]

Lubumbashi (until 1966, Elisabethville) is the third largest city in Zaire, with a population of 543,268 (1984 est.), and the capital of Shaba (formerly Katanga) province. It lies in the southern part of the country, near the border with Zambia, in the heart of a rich copper-mining region. The region also contains cobalt, zinc, and cadmium deposits. Lubumbashi is the administrative seat of the state-owned mining concern. A railway links it with Angola and with South Africa through Zimbabwe (Rhodesia). A branch of the National University of Zaire is located there.

Founded in 1910, Lubumbashi became the administrative capital of the Katanga region. In 1960–63 the city was the capital of the secessionist state of Katanga.

EDOUARD BUSTIN

Lucan   [loo'-kuhn]

Marcus Annaeus Lucanus, or Lucan, nephew of the philosopher Seneca, was a Latin epic poet, b. Spain, Nov. 3, AD 39, who committed suicide at the age of 26, Apr. 30, 65, when detected in a conspiracy against the emperor Nero. His only surviving work, the *Bellum Civile,* sometimes called the *Pharsalia,* is an account of the Roman civil wars that pitted Julius Caesar against the senatorial class.   STEELE COMMAGER

Bibliography: Ahl, Frederick W., *Lucan: An Introduction* (1976); Morford, M. P. O., *The Poet Lucan: Studies in Rhetorical Epic* (1967).

Lucas, George

The American film director, screenwriter, and producer George Lucas, b. Modesto, Calif., May 14, 1944, is best known for his fantastically popular trilogy of space fantasy movies—*Star Wars* (1977), *The Empire Strikes Back* (1980), and *Return of the Jedi* (1983). After his first feature, *THX-1138* (1971), Lucas made *American Graffiti* (1973), a nostalgic look at adolescence in 1962. He collaborated with filmmaker Steven Spielberg on *Raiders of the Lost Ark* (1981) and *Indiana Jones and the Temple of Doom* (1984), then coproduced *Mishima* (1985), a film about the famous Japanese writer.

Lucas van Leyden   [loo'-kahs vahn ly'-duhn]

Lucas van Leyden, also known as Lucas Hugensz, 1494–1533, was one of the greatest engravers of the Netherlandish Renaissance. Although he began his career as a painter, studying with his father Hugh Hugensz and later with Cornelis Engelbrechtsz, Lucas's work in this medium is completely overshadowed by his proficiency in ENGRAVING. His earliest-known engraving, *Mohammed and the Monk Sergius* (1508), displays a precocious mastery of technique and expertise in the handling of detail and pictorial space. In the so-called Circular Passion series (1510), he adopted a tondo, or round, format to depict scenes from the life of Christ in landscape settings.

The major influence on his style was Albrecht Dürer, whose work inspired Lucas's two most celebrated engravings, *The Milkmaid* and *Ecce Homo* (both 1510). Lucas is thought to have learned the technique of etching from Dürer, whom he met in Antwerp in 1521, and it is certain that Lucas, after this meeting, began to engrave on copper, rather than on steel plates—a technique that allowed him to achieve the effects of engraving and etching in the same work. Lucas's later prints, such as *Venus and Mars* (1530), were executed in a rather mannered style and lack the force of his earlier work. Among Lucas's finest paintings are *The Last Judgment* (1526; Stedelijk Museum, Leiden) and *Moses Striking the Rock* (1527; Museum of Fine Arts, Boston).

In his painting Lot and His Daughters *(c.1509), the Netherlandish Renaissance artist Lucas van Leyden uses the sinuous line of his engraving to create a bold, dramatic composition to the night scene. Flashes of light lend spectral effects. (Louvre, Paris.)*

Bibliography: Jacobowitz, Ellen, and Stepanek, S. L., *Prints of Lucas van Leyden and His Contemporaries* (1983); Lavalleye, Jacques, comp., *Pieter Bruegel the Elder and Lucas van Leyden (1967)*.

Lucca [luc'-cah]

Lucca (1981 pop., 91,097), the capital of Lucca province in the region of Tuscany, Italy, lies about 16 km (10 mi) northeast of Pisa. A market center for the surrounding farming region, Lucca produces flour, olive oil, tobacco products, and wine. Silk fabric has been a major export since the 1300s. Lucca is rich in historic architecture. Its Cathedral of San Martino, consecrated in 1070, contains a famous crucifix. Other major structures include the churches of San Frediano (6th century) and San Michele (12th century).

Of Ligurian origin, Lucca became a Roman Latin colony in 180 BC and the seat of a Lombard duchy in the 6th century. A commune from the 12th century, it was a prosperous commercial and artistic center. From 1322 to 1328 the city was ruled by the mercenary Castruccio Castracani. A period of rule by Florence and Pisa ended in 1369, when Lucca bought its independence. It remained an independent republic until taken by the French in 1799. Lucca became a principality under Napoleon's sister Élisa in 1805, an independent duchy under the Spanish infanta María Luisa in 1815, and a part of Tuscany in 1847. It was annexed to the Kingdom of Italy in 1860.

Luce, Clare Boothe [loos]

The playwright, journalist, and politician Clare Boothe Luce, b. New York City, Apr. 10, 1903, d. Oct. 9, 1987, started her career in publishing in 1930, working first on *Vogue* and then as a top editor (1931–34) of *Vanity Fair*; her sketches for the

Clare Boothe Luce, an American writer and public official, became the first American woman to hold a major diplomatic post with her appointment (1953) as ambassador to Italy. Luce, also a successful playwright and journalist, served two terms (1943–47) as a congresswoman from Connecticut.

latter magazine appeared in *Stuffed Shirts* (1933). Following her marriage in 1935 to publishing magnate Henry R. Luce, she wrote three successful Broadway plays: *The Women* (1936; film, 1939), a satire; *Kiss the Boys Goodbye* (1938; film, 1941), a comedy; and *Margin for Error* (1940; film, 1943), an anti-Fascist melodrama. A tour of Western Europe in 1940 led to a perceptive study, *Europe in the Spring* (1940), and other wartime journalistic assignments (1940–42) for *Life*. Entering politics as a critic of the Roosevelt administration, Luce served two terms (1943–47) as Republican congresswoman from Connecticut. Her appointment by President Eisenhower as U.S. ambassador to Italy (1953–57) made her the first American woman ever to hold a major diplomatic post. With the one-act play *Slam the Door Softly* (1970), Luce returned to her earlier interest in feminism. ELEANOR M. GATES

Bibliography: Shadegg, Stephen C., *Clare Boothe Luce: A Biography* (1970); Sheed, Wilfred, *Clare Boothe Luce* (1984).

Luce, Henry Robinson

Henry Robinson Luce, b. Apr. 3, 1898, to missionaries in Tengchow (now P'eng-lai), China, d. Feb. 28, 1967, was the leading innovator and publisher of magazine journalism in this century. With fellow Yale graduate Briton Hadden (1898–1929), Luce founded TIME (1923) as a weekly news summary. Despite the Depression, a second magazine, *Fortune* (1930), soon became profitable. LIFE, which Luce began in 1936, grew into the most popular weekly picture magazine and was revived as a monthly in 1978 after a 6-year absence. *Sports Illustrated* (1954) likewise became the foremost periodical of its type. Luce purchased *Architectural Forum* in 1932, and although it

Henry Luce, an American editor and publishing magnate, founded a financial empire based on successful magazines he had established, including Time *(1923),* Fortune *(1930),* Life *(1936), and* Sports Illustrated *(1954). The editorial stance of Luce's publications often reflected his staunch conservatism, and he became highly influential in American politics before retiring as editor in chief of* Time, Inc., *in 1964.*

was unprofitable, he published it for more than three decades. He retired as editor in chief of the magazines in 1964.

After graduating from Yale, Luce and Hadden raised money from friends to pursue their idea of a newsweekly. When the *Literary Digest* folded in 1938, *Time* became the leader in circulation in its field—a position it has never relinquished. The magazine's news summary approach was adapted to radio and film under the *March of Time* title. A fervent anti-Communist, Luce used his publications and prestige to influence U.S. policy favorably toward Chiang Kai-shek on the mainland of China and later on Taiwan. Luce was influential in Republican party policy and in drafting Eisenhower as a presidential candidate. Luce's journalism often was criticized for its bias, but public acceptance of his magazines was consistently high.   SAM KUCZUN

Bibliography: Elson, Robert T., *Time Inc.: The Intimate History of a Publishing Empire* (1968) and *The World of Time Inc.*, 2 vols. (1973); Swanberg, W. A., *Luce and His Empire* (1972).

Luce, Stephen B.

Stephen Bleecker Luce, b. Albany, N.Y., Mar. 25, 1827, d. July 28, 1917, an American naval officer, inspired the establishment of the Naval War College at Newport, R.I. While teaching at the Naval Academy at Newport during the Civil War he wrote *Seamanship* (1863), which became a standard text. After the war Luce lobbied for improved training of enlisted men, higher standards for the merchant marine, and a postgraduate college for naval officers. On Oct. 6, 1884, the secretary of the navy created the Naval War College and appointed Luce its first president. Luce persuaded Alfred Thayer MAHAN to join the faculty. Mahan's lectures were published in 1890 as *The Influence of Sea Power upon History, 1660–1783*. Luce retired as a rear-admiral in 1889.   KENNETH J. HAGAN

Lucerne   [loo-surn']

Lucerne (German: Luzern), the capital of the Swiss canton of Lucerne, lies about 40 km (25 mi) southwest of Zurich on the Reuss River at Lake Lucerne. The city is an important tourist resort and textile center. The population is 61,041 (1985 est.). Two of the seven bridges crossing the Reuss date from the 13th and 14th centuries. Other notable structures include the Hofkirche (cathedral; 8th century), the town hall (built 1601–06), Am Rhyn House (1617), and the Mariahilf Church (1676–81). An international music festival is an annual summer event. Technical and vocational schools are in the city.

Lucerne was settled around the monastery of Saint Leodegar in the 8th century. It flourished as a trade center under Habsburg rule (1291–1332) and then joined the Swiss Confederation. It led the Catholic cantons of Switzerland in the civil wars of the Reformation (1529–31) and the *Sonderbund* (1847) and served (1798–1803) as the capital of the Helvetic Republic.

Lucerne, Lake

Lake Lucerne (German: Vierwaldstätter See) is a picturesque, mountain-ringed lake in central Switzerland. At an altitude of 434 m (1,424 ft), the lake is 39 km (24 mi) long and 3 km (2 mi) wide. Its outlet and principal tributary is the Reuss River. The lake is one of Switzerland's most popular resort areas.

Luchow: see HOFEI.

Lucia di Lammermoor

The novels of Sir Walter Scott left their mark on composers of opera in the early-to-mid 1800s, among them, Gaetano Donizetti. His most renowned score, based on Scott's *The Bride of Lammermoor*, is *Lucia di Lammermoor* (libretto by Salvatore Cammarano), first heard at the Teatro San Carlo, Naples, on Sept. 26, 1835. Two eminent singers of the day, Fanny Persiani and Gilbert-Louis Duprez, starred in the premiere.

In the opera, hostility has long existed between two noble Scottish families: the Ashtons—headed by Enrico—and the house of Ravenswood—of which Edgardo is master. Despite this bitter feud Edgardo is in love with Lucia Ashton, whom he meets secretly in the park of her family's castle, Lammermoor. Her brother, Enrico, sees political advantage in a marriage between Lucia and Lord Arturo Bucklaw. Enrico is enraged to hear of the romance between his sister and Edgardo. Enrico convinces Lucia by means of a forged letter that Edgardo, in traveling to France, has abandoned her. Chagrined, she agrees to wed Arturo. Just as she has signed the marriage document Edgardo returns unexpectedly and denounces her. The girl's morale is shattered, her mind unhinged. In a fit of insanity she murders her husband and, in one of the most famous of mad scenes, imagines she is being wed to Edgardo. Meanwhile the hero, fancying that Lucia and Arturo are celebrating their wedding night, broods among the tombs of his ancestors. On hearing the funeral knell and learning of Lucia's death, he stabs himself.   ROBERT LAWRENCE

Bibliography: Ashbrook, William, *Donizetti* (1965).

Lucian   [loo'-shuhn]

Lucian, c.120–c.180, was a Greek satirist of the Roman period who worked in a variety of genres. Born in Samosata in Syria, he studied rhetoric, traveled widely, and later served the Roman Empire as an official in Egypt. Eighty-two writings are attributed to Lucian; most of these are short dialogues showing the influence of Plato, although some take the form of letters; by contrast, his fantasy, *The True History,* is an amusing novellike narrative of a journey to the Moon. Typical of Lucian's innovative satirical works are the *Dialogues of the Gods* and *Dialogues of the Dead,* in which he ridicules Greek philosophy, religion, and mythology and pictures humankind as hypocritical and foolish. In the dialogue *Timon* the characters include an Athenian misanthrope, Zeus, Wealth, and Poverty. It is not clear that Lucian's satire, bitter as it is, reflects a deepseated skepticism on his part; his objective may have been literary: to attract and startle his readers. In any case, he is often considered the forerunner of such biting, latter-day satirists as Swift and Voltaire.   GEORGE KENNEDY

Bibliography: Allinson, F. G., *Lucian, Satirist and Artist* (1930; repr. 1950); Robinson, C., *Lucian and His Influence in Europe* (1979).

Lucifer: see SATAN.

Lucilius   [loo-sil'-ee-uhs]

Gaius Lucilius, c.180–103 BC, is known as the inventor of Roman SATIRE. Although his family was distinguished, he rejected politics and business, preferring the life of poet and sardonic commentator. His 30 books of *Satires,* widely admired, began the tradition that later inspired Horace, Persius, and Juvenal.
                                            WILLIAM S. ANDERSON

lucite: see PLASTICS.

Luckman, Sid

Hall of Fame football player Sidney Luckman, b. Brooklyn, N.Y., Nov. 21, 1916, played quarterback when he starred both in college (Columbia, 1935–39) and as a professional in the National Football League (Chicago Bears, 1939–50). Considered one of the NFL's greatest passers, Luckman completed 904 of 1,744 passes for 14,683 yd and 139 touchdowns while leading the Bears to 4 NFL titles. He was the NFL's MVP in 1943, first-team All-League 5 times, and the leader in average gain per pass attempt 7 times (unapproached). Luckman still shares the NFL record of 7 touchdown passes thrown in a single game.

Lucknow   [luhk'-now]

Lucknow is the capital of Uttar Pradesh state, northern India. Situated on the Upper Ganges Plain, it is about 420 km (260 mi) southeast of New Delhi. The population of 895,721 (1981) is mostly Hindu but includes a large Muslim minority.

Industries include food processing, sugar refining, distilling, and cotton weaving, as well as handicrafts. A paper mill is also located in the city. An administrative and cultural center, Lucknow is the site of Lucknow University, founded in 1921. Chawk, the thriving business center of the city since the 18th century, is noted for gold, silver, and other retail shops. Points of interest include the Great Imambara, a courthouse (1784); the Husainabad Imambara (1837), which contains several tombs and a mosque; and the State Museum (1863).

The legendary founder of Lucknow was Lakshman, famous from the RAMAYANA epic. In the 13th century the sheikhs of Bijnor built a fortress on the site. Modern Lucknow, however, is largely the creation of the nawabs of Oudh, who ruled from 1724 to 1856. During the Indian Mutiny, Lucknow was besieged for 12 weeks (June–November 1857) by Indian rebels. By the time it was relieved about 500 British, including Sir Henry Lawrence, had been killed.   ASHOK K. DUTT

Lucretia   [loo-kree'-shuh]

In Roman legend, Lucretia was a virtuous and beautiful Roman matron, whose rape by Sextus, son of TARQUINIUS SUPERBUS, led to the overthrow of the Tarquin dynasty in Rome and the establishment of a republic (traditionally 509 BC). Lucretia made her husband and father vow to avenge her dishonor before she committed suicide. The story is the subject of William Shakespeare's *Rape of Lucrece.*

Lucretius   [loo-kree'-shuhs]

Titus Lucretius Carus, c.95–55 BC, Rome's most distinguished philosopher-poet, achieved his place in Latin literature on the basis of one work, *De Rerum Natura (On the Nature of Things),* a didactic poem, in dactylic hexameter, comprising six books. This made available to a Latin audience the ideas of the Greek philosopher Epicurus.

The object of Epicureanism was pleasure, but pleasure of an austere kind involving primarily freedom from fear of the gods and of an afterlife. According to Epicurus, although the gods did exist, they had no concern for humans, either to punish or to reward them. Furthermore, because the soul was mortal, dying with the body, to fear the torments of an afterlife was quite unnecessary.

A good part of *De Rerum Natura* deals with the physical nature of the universe, which Lucretius explains in terms that approximate modern atomic theory and that were based on the theories of DEMOCRITUS. But the purpose of his physical arguments is ethical: to present a universe explicable in scientific terms, and so banish fear of the unknown and free people's minds from superstition.   STEELE COMMAGER

Bibliography: Hadzsits, George D., *Lucretius and His Influence* (1930; repr. 1963); Santayana, George, *Three Philosophical Poets* (1910; repr. 1971); Sikes, Edward E., *Lucretius, Poet and Philosopher* (1936; repr. 1971); West, David, *The Imagery and Poetry of Lucretius* (1969).

Lucullus, Lucius Licinius   [loo-kuhl'-uhs, loo'-shuhs ly-sin'-ee-uhs]

A leading Roman noble, Lucius Licinius Lucullus, c.117–56 BC, began his political career as quaestor under Lucius Cornelius SULLA in 88 or 87 BC. He continued to serve Sulla in the eastern war against MITHRADATES VI of Pontus. After serving as aedile (79) and praetor (78), he governed the province of Africa and was elected consul for 74.

In that year Lucullus obtained command in the renewed war against Mithradates. Although he occupied much of Pontus and invaded Armenia, taking its capital in 69, a series of mutinies among his troops weakened his political position. He also came under attack from powerful interests in Rome whose hopes of profit from the Asian conquests had been frustrated by Lucullus's judicious handling of financial matters. POMPEY THE GREAT began to intrigue for the Asian command, with some help from Lucullus's brother-in-law, Publius CLODIUS, and in 66 he finally received it. With CATO THE YOUNGER, and for a while with Marcus CRASSUS, Lucullus led the opposition to Pompey until the latter proved too power-

ful. After 59 BC he retired to a life of self-indulgent luxury before being overtaken by insanity and death.
                ALLEN M. WARD

Bibliography: Ward, A. M., *Marcus Crassus and the Late Roman Republic* (1977).

Lucy, Saint

Saint Lucy, d. c.304, was a Christian martyr executed in Sicily during the persecution of Diocletian. Her name, suggestive of light in Latin, was probably the reason that she was popularly invoked against eye diseases. In art she is frequently depicted holding her own eyes, plucked out in her martyrdom, on a dish. Feast day: Dec. 13.

Luddites   [luhd'-yts]

To protest unemployment caused by the Industrial Revolution in the early 19th century, English workers known as Luddites resorted to a campaign of breaking machinery, especially knitting machines. Their name may come from a legendary boy named Ludlam, who, to spite his father, broke a knitting frame. The Luddites revived the name by signing their proclamations "General Ludd," "King Ludd," or "Ned Ludd." The movement began in the hosiery and lace industries around Nottingham in 1811 and spread to the wool and cotton mills of Yorkshire and Lancashire. The government dealt harshly with the Luddites—14 were hanged in January 1813 in York. Although sporadic outbreaks of violence continued until 1816, the movement soon died out.

Bibliography: Liversidge, Douglas, *The Luddites: Machine-Breakers of the Early Nineteenth Century* (1972); Thomis, Malcolm I., *The Luddites: Machine-Breaking in Regency England* (1970).

Ludendorff, Erich   [loo-den-dorf, ay'-rik]

Erich Friedrich Wilhelm Ludendorff, b. Apr. 9, 1865, d. Dec. 20, 1937, was a German general in WORLD WAR I. A career officer, he entered the elite Prussian general staff before World War I and distinguished himself in the opening days of the war by capturing the Belgian fortress-city of Liège. He was thereupon made chief of staff to Gen. Paul von HINDENBURG, who had just been called from retirement to come to the rescue of East Prussia, which the Russians were overrunning. Stunning victories at TANNENBERG and the Masurian Lakes in the late summer of 1914 saved the eastern front and made the two generals national heroes.

In 1916, Emperor William II gave Hindenburg and Ludendorff, with joint operational responsibility, virtually dictatorial control of the German supreme command. They consolidated the German lines on the stalemated western front and in 1917 commenced unrestricted submarine warfare, which resulted in the entry of the United States into the war against Germany. When their last great offensive failed in 1918, Hindenburg and Ludendorff insisted on an armistice. It was finally granted on Nov. 11, 1918, but on terms that caused Ludendorff to resign in protest.

In 1923, Ludendorff participated in Adolf HITLER's abortive MUNICH PUTSCH. He was a National Socialist member of the Reichstag from 1924 to 1928 but played no part in the Third Reich.   DONALD S. DETWILER

Bibliography: Goodspeed, D. J., *Ludendorff: Genius of World War I* (1966); Ludendorff, Erich, *My War Memories, 1914–18*, trans. anon., 2 vols. (1919).

Ludlow, Roger

Roger Ludlow, b. 1590, d. after 1664, was one of the founders of colonial Connecticut. A director of the Massachusetts Bay Company, he left England for Massachusetts in 1630. He served (1634) briefly as deputy governor there, and in 1635 he joined in the organization of a new colony on the Connecticut River. In 1636, Ludlow presided over Connecticut's first court (held at Windsor), and in 1639 he founded the town of Fairfield, on Long Island Sound. He is credited with drafting the Fundamental Orders, a constitution adopted in January 1638 or '39, that remained the basis of Connecticut's government until 1818, and Ludlow's Code, or the Code of 1650, a compilation of the colony's laws. In 1654, Ludlow went to Ireland in the service of the Cromwellian government and remained there, probably until his death.

Ludovice, João Pedro Frederico   [loo-doh'-vee-chay]

João Pedro Frederico Ludovice, b. Johann Peter Friedrich Ludwig in Swabia, 1670, d. 1752, became known for his architectural designs in Portugal. Before arriving in Lisbon in 1701, he worked as a goldsmith in Germany. Ludovice was commissioned (c.1711) as the architect of what later became the great palace-monastery complex of Mafra, completed (1770) after his death. Based on Italian Renaissance and Central European baroque models, Mafra became Portugal's principal rococo-style architectural masterpiece. Ludovice also designed the apse of the Évora Cathedral (dedicated 1746) and the library of the University of Coimbra (1717–23).

EDWARD J. SULLIVAN

Bibliography: Kubler, George, and Soria, Martin, *Art and Architecture in Spain and Portugal and Their American Dominions, 1500 to 1800* (1959).

Ludwig, Christa

Christa Ludwig, a mezzo-soprano, b. Berlin, Mar. 16, 1928, grew up backstage in opera houses where her parents were singing. She has been a star of the Vienna Opera since 1955 and of the Metropolitan Opera since 1959. Her wide vocal range, from contralto to dramatic soprano, encompasses a varied repertoire, from soubrette (a light, comic role) to Wagnerian music drama. Among her roles are Kundry in *Parsifal*, Octavian in *Der Rosenkavalier*, and Cherubino in *The Marriage of Figaro*.

Bibliography: Ewen, David, ed., *Musicians since 1900* (1978).

Ludwig, Emil

Emil Ludwig, b. Jan. 25, 1881, d. Sept. 17, 1948, German historian, journalist, and essayist, is best known for his highly original biographies. Ludwig focused on the personalities of his subjects rather than on their deeds. He used actual and invented dialogue in his works, occasionally sacrificing accuracy for the sake of drama. His fascinating psychological studies include *Goethe* (1920; Eng. trans., 1928), *Napoleon* (1925; Eng. trans., 1926), *Bismarck* (1926; Eng. trans., 1927), and a controversial profile of Christ, *The Son of Man* (1928; Eng. trans., 1928). Ludwig became a Swiss citizen in 1932 and in later years was a frequent visitor to the United States.

JOSEPH A. REITER

Ludwig: for German kings of this name, see LOUIS.

Ludwig, Jack

Jack Barry Ludwig, b. Winnipeg, Manitoba, Aug. 30, 1922, is a writer, editor, and critic whose short stories have won him two O. Henry Awards (1961, 1965) and an Atlantic First Award (1960). Some of his stories are collected in *Confusions* (1963). Ludwig has written a semiautobiographical novel, *Above Ground* (1974), and he frequently writes about sports, as in *Five Ring Circus: The Montreal Olympics* (1976). He has taught college and lived in the United States since 1949.

Ludwig, Otto

The German novelist, playwright, and critic Otto Ludwig, b. Feb. 12, 1813, d. Feb. 25, 1865, began his career studying music with Felix Mendelssohn. Ludwig turned to literature in 1840, his most important work being *Shakespeare-Studien* (Shakespearean Studies, 1871), a collection of short essays on the history and theory of drama.

Ludwig favored realism in literature and drama, as in his play *The Forest Warden* (1850; Eng. trans., 1912), a convincing look at a portion of the middle class in Thüringen. He consid-

ered the idealism of Schiller escapist. By no means a crude naturalist, however, Ludwig believed strongly in poetic realism, as exemplified in *Between Heaven and Earth* (1856; Eng. trans., 1911).

CARL R. MUELLER

Bibliography: McClain, W. H., *Between Real and Ideal* (1963; repr. 1973); Turner, David, *Roles and Relationships in Otto Ludwig's Narrative Fiction* (1975).

Lug

In ancient Celtic mythology Lug was a major divinity, often identified with the Roman god MERCURY. According to Irish legend, he was a member of the Tuatha Dé Danann (people of the Goddess Danann), a divine race from which the Irish people are descended. He ensured the triumph of the Tuatha over their rivals, the Fomoire, by slaying Balor, the Fomoire chief, who was his own grandfather. Known for his versatility, Lug was a skilled warrior, harpist, poet, sorcerer, and carpenter. Lugdunum, the name of several towns in ancient Gaul, including what are now the French cities of Lyon and Laon, probably means ''hill (or fort) of Lug.''

Lugano, Lake   [loo-gah'-noh]

Lake Lugano lies astride the border of Ticino canton, Switzerland, and the Lombardy region of Italy. Located in the Alps at an altitude of 271 m (889 ft), it is 35 km (22 mi) long, approximately 3 km (2 mi) wide, and reaches a maximum depth of 288 m (945 ft). Fed by mountain streams, it is drained by the Tresa River into Lake MAGGIORE.

Lugard, Frederick John Dealtry Lugard, 1st Baron   [lou-gard']

The British colonial administrator Frederick Lugard, b. Jan. 22, 1858, d. Apr. 11, 1945, played an important role in opening Africa to European influence. After a brief period of attendance at the Royal Military College, Sandhurst, he served as an army officer in India, Afghanistan, the Sudan, Burma, and Nyasaland (now Malawi). In 1889 he entered the service of the Imperial British East Africa Company. He not only secured British supremacy in Uganda but was also instrumental in persuading the British government to declare Uganda a protectorate in 1894.

In 1900, Lugard was appointed high commissioner of Northern Nigeria, where he introduced a system of indirect rule through traditional tribal rulers. Between 1907 and 1912 he served as governor of Hong Kong, but in 1912 he returned to Nigeria, where he combined Northern and Southern Nigeria into a single country (1914), staying as governor-general until 1919. He was made Baron Lugard of Abinger in 1928. Lugard published *The Rise of Our East African Empire* (1893) and *The Dual Mandate in British Tropical Africa* (1922), the classic defense of British colonialism.

L. H. GANN

Bibliography: Kirk-Greene, A. H., ed., *Lugard and the Amalgamation of Nigeria* (1968); Perham, Margery F., *Lugard: The Years of Adventure, 1858–1898* (1956) and *Lugard: The Years of Authority, 1898–1945* (1960).

luge

A luge is a small sled for one or two riders used for a type of TOBOGGANING in recreational and competitive settings. Its main portion, or shell, is made of fiberglass and wood; the two runners are made of fiberglass, wood, plastic, and steel. Riders are usually prone, on their backs, feet first. Steering is accomplished with subtle movements of the body and feet. In competition, luge speeds can exceed 97 km/h (60 mph). The first European lugeing championship was held in 1914. A Winter Olympics sport since 1964 (one- and two-man and one-woman), luge is governed worldwide by the Fédération Internationale de Luge de Course (founded 1957).

Lugeon, Maurice   [loo-zhohn', mor-ees']

The work on Alpine tectonics of the Swiss geologist Maurice Lugeon, b. July 10, 1870, d. Oct. 23, 1953, was a brilliant synthesis of the geologic surveying done in the 19th century. In a pioneering paper (1901) that explained the overall structure of the Alps and the interrelationships of Alpine features, Lugeon established the basic terminology and concepts of modern tectonics (the study of the large features of the Earth's upper crust), as well as new comprehensive theories.

Lugones, Leopoldo   [loo-goh'-nays, lay-uh-pohl'-doh]

The Argentine poet, storyteller, essayist, and historian Leopoldo Lugones, b. June 13, 1874, d. Feb. 19, 1938, was the dominant figure in the poetry of his country during the first three decades of the 20th century and a major force in Spanish-American modernism. The poems in his first important collection, *Las montañas del oro* (Mountains of Gold, 1899), were ultramodern, full of deliberately shocking imagery. In his next collection, *Los crepúsculos del jardín* (Twilights of the Garden, 1905), he softened the tone of his poetry, emphasizing form rather than content in the style of the French Parnassians. He collected his stories of the fantastic in *Las fuerzas extrañas* (Strange Forces, 1906) and *Cuentos fatales* (Fatal Tales, 1924). Lugones committed suicide in 1938.

JAIME ALAZRALCI

Lugosi, Bela   [luh-gohs'-see, bel'-uh]

Bela Lugosi stares malevolently while abducting the heroine in the classic horror film Dracula *(1931)*. Because of his vivid performance, the Hungarian-born actor was typecast in a series of horror films, mostly of mediocre quality. At his death in 1956, a consequence of his drug addiction, Lugosi was buried in the flowing black cloak he had made famous in his role as Count Dracula.

A respected Hungarian stage actor who made a hit in Hollywood as the Transylvanian vampire Count Dracula in the film *Dracula* (1931) after creating the role on Broadway (1927), Bela Lugosi, b. Béla Blaskó, Oct. 20, 1882, d. Aug. 16, 1956, failed through his imperfect command of English to utilize his full range and became typecast in cheap horror films. He was at his best in *White Zombie* (1932), *The Black Cat* (1934), *Son of Frankenstein* (1939), and *Abbott and Costello Meet Frankenstein* (1948).

LESLIE HALLIWELL

Bibliography: Lennig, Arthur, *The Count: The Life and Films of Bela "Dracula" Lugosi* (1974).

lugworm

Lugworms are annelid (segmented) marine worms of the genus *Arenicola* in the class Polychaeta. These worms, which may reach lengths of more than 30 cm (12 in), live in U-shaped, tubular burrows up to 60 cm (2 ft) deep in the bottoms of shallow marine waters. The light-colored body in-

creases in diameter as it nears the small head, which is often dark red. The lugworm can evert, or extend, its pharynx into a proboscis, which is used both for burrowing and for ingesting food particles.

STEPHEN C. REINGOLD

Bibliography: Russell-Hunter, W. D., *A Biology of Lower Invertebrates* (1968).

Luisetti, Hank

Angelo "Hank" Luisetti, b. San Francisco, Calif., June 16, 1916, changed the character of basketball in the 1930s when he popularized the one-handed jump-shot, which is now standard. As a player at Stanford University, Luisetti was such a scoring threat that his teammates often carried the offense when he was double-teamed. Stanford became a powerhouse and broke with the old style of setting up players for two-handed shots, a time-consuming procedure. Luisetti, who was 1 m 90.5 cm (6 ft 3 in) tall, led Stanford to a stunning upset of Long Island University in December 1936, stopping LIU's 43-game winning streak. In 1938 he scored a record 50 points in a game against Duquesne University. Luisetti was elected to the Naismith Memorial Basketball Hall of Fame in 1959.

Lukács, György   [loo'-kahch]

György Lukács, b. Apr. 13, 1885, d. June 4, 1971, was a Hungarian Marxist philosopher, literary critic, and writer. One of the foremost Marxist theoreticians during the first half of the 20th century, Lukács developed a Marxist aesthetic drawing a link between art and social struggle. His earliest works—such as *The Soul and the Forms* (1910; Eng. trans., 1978) and *The Theory of the Novel* (1920; Eng. trans., 1971)—were heavily influenced by the thoughts of Max Weber as well as Karl Marx.

After moving to Vienna, Lukács wrote his major reevaluation of Marxism, *History of Class Consciousness* (1923; Eng trans., 1971). He was, however, promptly labeled a revisionist because he departed from standard Marxist-Leninist orthodoxy. After Hitler's rise to power in 1933, he lived in Moscow where he worked at the Marx-Engels Institute and at the In-

György Lukács, a Hungarian philosopher and critic, sought to define a humanistic Marxist aesthetic in his essays and critical studies. His works, including History of Class Consciousness *(1923), were viewed with suspicion by some doctrinaire Marxists, but they sparked much important discussion.*

stitute of Philosophy of the Soviet Academy of Sciences.

Following World War II, Lukács returned to Hungary to become a professor of philosophy and aesthetics in Budapest. Because of his idealist interpretation of Marxism, however, he often became the center of ideological controversy. His involvement in the revolution of 1956 pushed him into the background, but in 1965 he was rehabilitated.

AGNES HUSZAR VARDY

Bibliography: Bahr, Ehrhard, and Kunzer, Ruth G., *Georg Lukács* (1972); Lichtheim, George, *Georg Lukács*, ed. by Frank Kermode (1970); Parkinson, George H., *Georg Lukács* (1970).

Luke, Gospel According to

The Gospel According to Luke is the third book of the New Testament of the BIBLE. Because of its similarities to the Gospels According to Mark and Matthew, it is classified with them as the synoptic Gospels. Although the Gospel was traditionally ascribed to Luke, a companion of Paul (Philem. 24; 2 Tim. 4:11), most modern scholars think that it was written between AD 80 and 90 by a Gentile Christian who wrote the ACTS OF THE APOSTLES as a sequel. The Gospel characteristically teaches a message of universal salvation addressed to all people, not only to the Jews.

Luke's Gospel can be divided into five major sections: a prologue (1:1–4); infancy narrative (1:5–2:52); ministry in Galilee (3:1–9:50); journey to Jerusalem (9:51–21:38); and the passion and resurrection (22:1–24:53). The conclusion sets the scene for the spread of the Christian word, as recounted in the Acts.

In common with the other Gospels, Luke relates the principal events of Christ's public life. Passages peculiar to Luke include the parable of the good Samaritan (10:25–37), the prodigal son (15:11–32), and Christ's words to the women of Jerusalem and to the good thief (23:27–31, 43). Commentators point out the prominence given to women. Examples include the story of Elizabeth (1:5–66), Mary's part in the infancy narrative (1:5–2:52), and the widow of Naim (7:11–17). Luke also contains three hymns that have become an important part of liturgy: the Magnificat (1:46–55), the Benedictus (1:68–79), and the Nunc Dimittis (2:29–32).   ANTHONY J. SALDARINI

Bibliography: Caird, G. B., *The Gospel of St. Luke* (1963); Danker, Frederick, *Jesus and the New Age According to St. Luke* (1972).

Luke, Saint

Saint Luke, traditionally considered to be the author of the third Gospel and the Acts of the Apostles, was a companion and fellow worker of Saint PAUL. According to Colossians 4:11–14, he was a Gentile and a physician. Later legend made him an artist, and during the Middle Ages the picture of the Virgin Mary in Santa Maria Maggiore, Rome, was ascribed to him. He is the patron saint of physicians and artists. Feast day: Oct. 18.

Bibliography: Jervell, Jacob, *Luke and The People of God: A New Look at Luke–Acts* (1972); Marshall, I. Howard, *Luke: Historian and Theologian* (1971).

Luks, George   [looks]

A member of the Ashcan school, George Luks, b. Williamsport, Pa., Aug. 13, 1867, d. Oct. 29, 1933, was an American painter and graphic artist noted for his vigorous studies of New York City life.

Luks studied at the Pennsylvania Academy of the Fine Arts in Philadelphia and in Europe. Returning to the United States in 1894, he began working as a newspaper illustrator, first for the Philadelphia *Press* and in 1896 as a cartoonist for the New York *World*.

Luks began painting scenes of urban life, specializing in lively figure and character studies in a vigorous style inspired partly by the work of Frans Hals, for example, *The Spielers* (1905; Addison Gallery of American Art, Phillips Academy, Andover, Mass.). He also produced a number of fine portraits, including *Otis Skinner as Col. Bridau in "The Honor of the Family"* (1919; The Phillips Collection, Washington, D.C.).

Bibliography: Young, Manhonri, *American Realists* (1977) and *The Eight: The Realist Revolt in American Painting* (1973).

Lull, Raymond

Raymond Lull (also Llull and Lully), c.1235–1316, was a Catalan poet, philosopher, and Christian mystic. The son of wealthy parents, he was reared at the royal court of Majorca. At the age of 30, he claimed to have a vision of Christ crucified. He abandoned his life at the court and dedicated himself to the conversion of Muslims in North Africa after studying Arabic, oriental mysticism, theology, and philosophy.

The author of almost 300 works, Lull was important in the development of the Catalan language. His interest in finding a common ground between Christianity, Islam, and Judaism made him one of the earliest ecumenists.

Lull's principal work, *Ars magna* (The Great Art), was a philosophic defense of Christianity against the teachings of AVERROËS. The 21-volume critical edition of his writings in Catalan, published between 1905 and 1952, enjoys wide popularity.   THOMAS E. MORRISSEY

Bibliography: Hillgarth, J. N., *Ramon Lull and Lullism in Fourteenth Century France* (1971); Peers, Edgar, *Ramon Lull: A Biography* (1929; repr. 1969).

Lully, Jean Baptiste   [lue-lee']

Jean Baptiste Lully was one of the most influential figures in the development of opera in France. Lully, who controlled French operatic production during the latter half of the 17th century, introduced the "French overture," influenced the form of French recitative, and, collaborating with Molière and Quinault, produced a brilliant body of compositions for opera and ballet.

Although Italian by birth, Jean Baptiste Lully, b. Nov. 28, 1632, d. Mar. 22, 1687, became one of the most significant French composers in history. Taken to France in 1646, Lully was employed by a cousin to the king of France, who recognized his musical ability. In 1652 he entered the service of the 14-year-old Louis XIV to play the violin and later to compose court ballets and dance in them, sometimes with the king himself participating. He also organized *Les Petits-Violons du Roi*, which became the king's personal orchestra. Through musical and managerial talent, enormous ambition, and shrewdness, Lully rose quickly in position and authority, and in 1662 he was appointed music master to the royal family. Between 1663 and 1671 he collaborated with Molière and produced comic masterpieces such as *Le Bourgeois Gentilhomme*. In 1672, having been given almost sole authority to develop French opera, he turned from ballet to the *tragédie-lyrique*, a term Lully applied to all his operas. He produced, in collaboration with his librettist Quinault, 20 operas in 14 years. Lully developed unprecedented standards of performance that became a model for all of Europe. He also raised the quality of declaiming French to music, and he reshaped traditional dry recitative to an orchestrally accompanied style. Lully's death came at the peak of his career. While conducting a concert and beating time with a heavy baton, he accidentally struck his foot; the resulting gangrene caused his death.
          JEFFREY M. CORNELIUS

Bibliography: Scott, Ralph Henry Forster, *Jean-Baptiste Lully* (1973).

lumbago   [luhm-bay'-goh]

Lumbago is a general term for low backache characterized by pain and tenderness originating in the fibromuscular tissue. The pain may be due to local inflammations in the spine, its ligaments, or its muscles, or it may be reflected to the back in disorders of the pelvic or abdominal organs. One common cause of lumbago is having legs of unequal length; even the smallest discrepancy in length causes the back muscles to work harder. If such a person is employed in an occupation that requires long periods of standing, the back muscles may become excessively strained and go into a painful spastic condition. Lumbago is common in women and is usually due to gynecologic causes. Osteoporosis, a degeneration of bone that can involve the spine, can also be a cause of lumbago in postmenopausal women and in very old people of either sex.

PETER L. PETRAKIS

lumber

Lumber is timber that is cut from forests and prepared for use in the construction of buildings, floors, woodwork, furniture, and a wide variety of other products. More than 30 percent of the world's commercial timberland is in the USSR, and about 18 percent is in North America. Both regions predominate in softwoods, those relatively nonporous woods that are derived from conifers, or cone-bearing TREES. Some countries, such as Japan, support a lumber industry largely dependent on softwoods imported from the United States, Canada, and the USSR. Others, such as India, export valuable hardwoods, those usually derived from deciduous trees that lose their leaves in autumn. These include rosewood, mahogany, sandalwood, ebony, and teak. Softwood lumber, which constitutes 80 percent of U.S. production, is used mostly for building houses; hardwood lumber is used primarily for furniture and floors (see also WOOD).

(Above) Logs are mechanically loaded onto a heavy truck. Although logs are still floated downriver in some areas, trucks and railroads are today the most common means of transportation to the mill.

(Right) As logs are drawn along a conveyor, they pass through a debarking machine before reaching the first saws. The machine removes bark with scraping blades or with jets of high-pressure water.

The wooden frame of this house under construction indicates one of the important uses of lumber. More than half of all timber harvested in the United States is used to produce lumber for the construction industry. The remainder is processed into plywood, pulp for paper, and chemical by-products such as cellophane and artificial fibers.

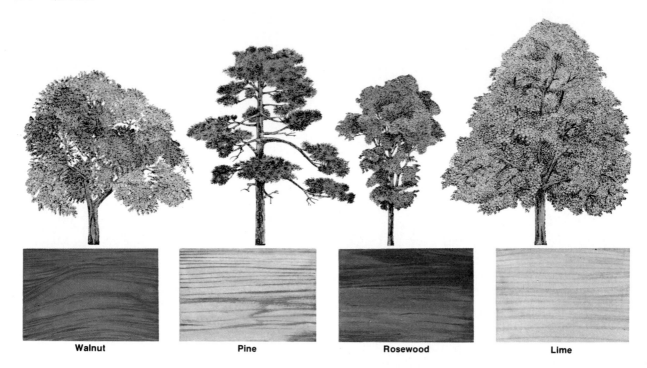

Walnut   **Pine**   **Rosewood**   **Lime**

(Above) *Walnut, a native American and European hardwood timber, is highly valued for its hardness, strength, elasticity, and velvety surface. It is used in making furniture, cabinets, and gun stocks. Pine is a widely distributed softwood timber. Although low in strength and elasticity, its availability, smooth surface, and ability to take paints and varnishes well have led to its extensive use in paneling, cabinetmaking, and construction. Rosewood is an important hardwood timber from tropical countries. It has an attractive combination of hardness, elasticity, strength, and extremely high resistance to decay. Uses include the manufacture of fine furniture, ships, and handles for tools. Lime, a smooth, soft, and lightweight hardwood timber, is found in Europe and America; it is of little commercial value.*

(Below) *Beech is a hardwood timber from northern temperate regions. The wood, which is of even texture, dense, strong, and hard, is used in the manufacture of underwater piles, chairs, and furniture. Teak is a hardwood timber from Burma and neighboring countries. Noted for its hardness, dimensional stability, strength, resistance to decay, and pleasing appearance, it is used in making fine furniture, cabinets, and interior trim. Oak is among the world's most important timbers. A widespread hardwood that is tough, elastic, and decay resistant, it is widely used for shipbuilding, flooring, interior woodwork, and furniture. Spruce, a major softwood timber of Europe and North America, is used mainly as a source of pulpwood in the manufacture of paper. Small amounts are used for construction joists and boxes.*

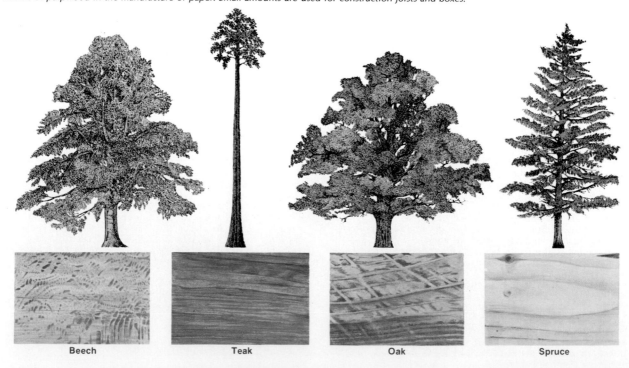

Beech   **Teak**   **Oak**   **Spruce**

Cedar | Mahogany | Fir | Ash

Cedar, a widely used softwood, is grown in Europe and the Americas. Although low in strength and elasticity, it is prized for its high resistance to insects and decay and is used in making posts, lawn furniture, shingles, and storage chests. Mahogany, a hardwood timber from tropical America, is one of the most valuable of woods. An excellent combination of strength, toughness, durability, and luster make it an ideal lumber for use in high-quality cabinets, furniture, and ships. Fir is one of the most valuable softwood timbers in the Americas. Hard, strong, and available in long lengths, it is used for heavy structures, poles, fences, and plywood. Ash is a hardwood native to North America and Europe. Outstanding in strength, toughness, and elasticity, it is used mainly for sports equipment and tool handles.

DEVELOPMENT OF THE LUMBER INDUSTRY

The logging of forests for timber and the sawing of logs into lumber have been major human activities since ancient times. It was necessary, however, to invent (c.1500 BC) the frame saw—a straight saw held in the center of a long wooden frame—before the cutting of wood planks out of logs could be accomplished with any efficiency. The first mechanized saws were powered adaptations of the frame saw. The most successful was the 17th-century Dutch Paltrok mill, a wind-driven sawmill with several saw blades mounted vertically on a movable wood frame. Two or three boards could be sawed simultaneously. The Paltrok was a forerunner of the gang saw, which—powered first by water, later by steam, and finally by an engine—is still used today.

The first steam-powered sawmill, built in 1663 in London, caused riots among sawyers who feared that such a machine would deprive them of jobs. Steam-powered sawmills did not come into general use until the early 1800s. Most early saw-mills were water powered and situated on rivers and streams where logs could easily be floated or rafted.

The U.S. lumber industry began in New England, and by 1675 there were over 50 water-powered sawmills—called "gang mills" after the gang saws they used—in northern Massachusetts, New Hampshire, and Maine, producing barrel staves and board lumber. The best Northeastern white pines were not sawed but were marked by the British as property of the king and were used for ships' masts.

Timbering in the South began later, and after independence the U.S. Navy reserved much of the southern forest lands for ship lumber.

After the Civil War, the lumber industry shifted to the lake states of Michigan, Wisconsin, and Minnesota. From 1870 to 1900 these states led the nation in lumber production. The huge tracts of white pine found in the lake states, however, were eventually logged over and converted to farmland. In addition, despite the considerable forests that remained unlogged, the lake states could be logged only on a seasonal basis, with cutting done in the fall and early winter, hauling during the winter, and transportation to mills in the spring when the rivers were at their fullest.

In the South forests could be harvested and logs moved to mills almost year-round, and huge, fast-growing stands of timber were available for conversion to lumber. By 1930, however, the best timber had been cut, and the lumber industry shifted to the West. Today the major lumber-producing states are Oregon, California, Washington, and Idaho. Forests in and west of the Rocky Mountains supply almost half the nation's lumber.

The development of the lumber industry in Canada closely parallels that of the United States. The first Canadian lumber was exported to France in 1653 in the form of timbers up to 9 m (30 ft) long, hand hewed and squared with a broadax. Since 1917, British Columbia has led all Canadian provinces in lumber production.

IMPORTANT U.S. TIMBER SPECIES

The major U.S. timber species now used for lumber are Douglas fir, loblolly and other southern pines, ponderosa pine, fir, hemlock, and spruce. These and other softwoods account for nearly two-thirds of the lumber produced in the United States.

In the West, Douglas fir, ponderosa pine, sugar pine, red-wood, fir, cedar, hemlock, and spruce are the primary timber species supplied to sawmills. In the South loblolly pine, long-leaf pine, shortleaf pine, and slash pine are used extensively for lumber. Southern hardwoods, such as the sweet gum, tupelo, and bald cypress, are also important lumber species. In the lake states, maple, beech, birch, elm, ash, cottonwood, and aspen are the dominant lumber species. Many of the more valuable hardwoods, such as cherry, yellow poplar, hickory, and walnut (used mostly for veneer for furniture and paneling), are in relatively short supply.

THE LUMBER-MAKING PROCESS

In the forest trees are cut with large power saws, loaded onto trucks, and transported to sawmills. The old method of floating logs to the mill is now impractical for the most part and has been replaced by truck and rail transportation. Many of the old logging rivers have been dammed to produce hydroelectric power. In addition many of the forests near watercourses were logged first, forcing modern loggers to shift to forests that are not near navigable rivers and streams.

Environmental concerns about pollution and about rivers becoming clogged with debris have also been instrumental in ending water transportation of logs (see LOGGING).

Because rafting is no longer used, most of today's lumber mills do not have millponds for log storage. Instead, logs delivered by truck and rail are stacked in yards, or decks, outside the mill, where they are usually sprayed with water to prevent insect damage. Once inside the sawmill, logs are processed into board.

A machine first strips the bark from the wood either by grinding or by high-pressure water jets. Stripped logs go to a headsaw where they are squared. Whenever possible, the slabs removed in this process are trimmed and sawed into boards. The squared log, called a cant, is then sent through a series of saws to be cut into boards of desired thickness. These boards are trimmed to desired length and width and placed on a moving belt, called a green chain, to be sorted for later drying.

Boards are dried either in open-air sheds or in large ovens called KILNS. The rough surfaces are smoothed by planing or sanding, and smoothed boards are then ready to be transported to markets. Sawmills also produce waste products in the form of sawdust, trimmings, and slabs. These manufacturing residues are reused to make PAPER, particle board, hardboard, and chipboard. These last three products are sheets of wood chips or particles of varying sizes that are bonded together by glue or resins and molded into large sheets.

Most of the dimension lumber, common lumber, flooring, studs, and beams produced in U.S. sawmills are used in the construction of homes, apartments, and other buildings. Some lumber products are treated with chemicals to resist decay, insects, or fire. CREOSOTE and pentachlorophenol (PCP) are two of the more common chemicals used. Wood treated with these chemicals will last longer when exposed to wind, insects, weather, and water.

Market needs determine the lumber products a sawmill will produce. During the construction of the transcontinental railroad many sawmills made only railroad ties. Later, many of these mills diversified to produce lumber and other wood products needed to serve the towns that grew up near the mills and the railroad tracks.   ROBERT S. MANTHY

Bibliography: Brown, N. C., *Lumber*, 2d ed. (1958); Carroll, Charles F., *The Timber Economy of Puritan New England* (1973); Larson, Agnes M., *History of the White Pine Industry* (1949; repr. 1972); Pike, Robert E., *Tall Trees, Tough Men* (1967; repr. 1984); Shepherd, Jack, *The Forest Killers* (1975); Smith, David C., *A History of Lumbering in Maine, 1861–1960* (1972); Stenzel, George, et al., *Logging and Pulpwood Production* (1984); Wells, Robert W., *Daylight in the Swamp* (1978); Williston, M., ed., *Lumber Manufacture* (1976); Wood, Nancy, *Clearcut: The Deforestation of America* (1971).

See also: FORESTS AND FORESTRY; PLYWOOD.

lumen   [loo'-men]

In photometry, the lumen is the SI unit of luminous flux, the rate at which radiant energy reaches a surface. It is defined as the flux emitted by a uniform point source of one CANDELA intensity in a cone having a solid angle of one steradian.

Lumet, Sidney

Sidney Lumet, b. Philadelphia, June 25, 1924, is one of several prominent television directors who made the transition to films in the 1950s. Lumet's first film, *Twelve Angry Men* (1957), was a successful version of a play he had directed for television, and his subsequent films included *A View from the Bridge* (1961), *Long Day's Journey into Night* (1962), *Fail Safe* (1964), and *The Pawnbroker* (1965).

Later, Lumet departed from the rough look and small-scale concentration of such work for the greater polish and bigger budgets of The *Anderson Tapes* (1971), *Serpico* (1974), *Murder on the Orient Express* (1974), and, with livelier results, *Dog Day Afternoon* (1975) and *Network* (1976). Lumet has comfortably worked in several different genres, directing slick entertainment vehicles such as *The Wiz* (1978), *Deathtrap* (1981), and *The Morning After* (1986), while also exploring social issues in such films as *Prince of the City* (1981), *The Verdict* (1982), and *Running on Empty* (1988).

WILLIAM S. PECHTER

Lumière, Louis and Auguste   [loo-mee-air']

Louis Jean Lumière, b. Oct. 5, 1864, d. June 6, 1948, and Auguste Marie Lumière, b. Oct. 19, 1862, d. Apr. 10, 1954, were French inventors of an early motion-picture projector and pioneer filmmakers. The two brothers took over management of their father's photographic supply factory in Lyons in 1893. There Louis developed (1895) the Cinématographe, a single machine that functioned both as camera and projector. Its unique feature was a system of claws that moved the film mechanically but held each frame long enough for viewers to perceive the image.

The Cinématographe was first demonstrated before a paying audience in Paris on Dec. 28, 1895, with the showing of 10 of the brothers' films, including *Workers Leaving a Factory* and a comic sequence, *The Sprinkler Sprinkled*. The public exhibition marked the beginning of cinema history. In the next few years the Lumières continued to produce short, 2-minute films that were records of everyday life; they also made documentaries, newsreels, and a historical film, *The Life and Passion of Jesus Christ* (1897).

Bibliography: Quigley, Martin, Jr., *Magic Shadows: The Story of the Origin of Motion Pictures* (1969).

luminescence

Luminescence is the emission of light by relatively cold materials. It is distinct from incandescence, in which materials emit light as a result of their high temperatures. Luminescence includes the phenomena of FLUORESCENCE (prompt radiation-stimulated emission of light) and PHOSPHORESCENCE (radiation-stimulated emission of light that continues to occur for prolonged periods after the stimulation is removed).

Luminescent emission arises from atoms and molecules that have been energized in some manner without appreciably heating the bulk material, and that release the excess energy in the form of light. Excitation can be caused by absorption of visible light, ultraviolet radiation, X rays, and gamma rays, by collision with charged particles; by chemical reactions, and by other means.

The earliest observed forms of luminescence were the natural phenomena of ELECTROLUMINESCENCE, such as the AURORAS, and BIOLUMINESCENCE, the light produced by fireflies, glowworms, and many varieties of marine life. Bioluminescence is a form of chemiluminescence, which is the emission of light as a result of a chemical reaction.

Many elements, chemical compounds, and minerals can demonstrate fluorescence (see FLUORESCENCE, MINERAL). NEON and other gases will fluoresce when a beam of electrons is passed through them. Solid material that will fluoresce—such as the coatings of fluorescent light tubes and television picture tubes—are known as PHOSPHORS. Certain minerals fluoresce in vivid colors when irradiated.

Triboluminescence is luminescence caused by friction; some minerals, such as corundum (aluminum oxide), give off light flashes when scraped by metal. Thermoluminescence occurs in minerals such as barite (barium sulfate) that will glow after being heated to a temperature below that of red heat. Sonoluminescence, a relatively recently observed phenomenon, is luminescence that occurs in some liquid hydrocarbons when they are irradiated with high-frequency sound waves.

Bibliography: Deluca, M., and McElroy, W., eds., *Bioluminescence and Chemiluminescence* (1981); Leverenz, H. W., *Introduction to Luminescence of Solids* (1969); Pankove, J. I., ed., *Electroluminescence* (1977).

Luminism

A recent term of art historians, coined by John I. H. Baur in 1954, *Luminism* describes the work of a group of American landscape painters active between 1848 and 1876. Their spacious compositions, most of which emphasize the horizontal and infinite aspects of nature, usually portray the coastal wetlands and rocky shorelines of New England and the frontier wilderness of North, and later of South, America. A suffused, incandescent light floods their vistas, which symbolize a reasoned awareness of, and faith in, the physical grandeur and moral potential of the American continent. In exploring the effects of light, the Luminists made full use of new, intense cadmium pigments.

As much concerned with "a meteorology of feeling as of weather," the Luminists include Fitz Hugh LANE (their first representative), Martin Johnson HEADE, Frederick Edwin CHURCH, John Frederick KENSETT, and Sanford Gifford (1823–80). Some of these painters, such as Church and Kensett, are also included in the HUDSON RIVER SCHOOL, the culmination of which is now seen to be Luminism. During the 1860s the Luminists became more painterly and poetic. A subtle, brooding interplay of atmospheres can be seen in works such as Heade's *Storm Over Narragansett Bay* (1868; collection of Ernest Rosenfeld, New York City) and Gifford's *Twilight on Hunter Mountain* (1866; Vose Galleries of Boston); more exotic locales are exemplified in such works as Church's *Aurora Borealis* (1865; National Collection of Fine Arts, Washington, D.C.) and *Morning in the Tropics* (1877; National Gallery of Art, Washington, D.C.).   BARBARA CAVALIERE

Bibliography: *Luminist Landscapes: The American Study of Light, 1860–75* (1966); Hills, Patricia, *The American Frontier: Images and Myths* (1973); Novak, Barbara, *American Painting of the Nineteenth Century* (1974); Wilmerding, John, *American Light* (1980) and *American Art* (1976).

Lumley, Henry de

Henry de Lumley, b. Aug. 14, 1936, a French archaeologist at the Université de Provence, Marseille, is noted for his excavation of early human habitation sites in Europe. Working (1966) at the 400,000-year-old site of TERRA AMATA, near Nice, he found extensive cultural remains of HOMO ERECTUS, the immediate ancestor of the modern human species. In 1968 he and his wife excavated a cave near Lazaret, in the French Pyrenees, and found tentlike shelters used by the NEANDERTHALERS. In 1971, at Arago, also in the French Pyrenees, the de Lumleys found a skull considered intermediary between *Homo erectus* and the more evolved Neanderthal hominid species.

Lummer, Otto

The German physicist Otto Richard Lummer, b. July 17, 1860, d. July 5, 1925, developed with Eugen Brodhun the Lummer-Brodhun photometer (1889) and with Ernst Gehrcke the Lummer-Gehrcke interference spectroscope (1901–02), which had greater resolving power than the classical Fabry-Perot instrument (1897).

In 1900, with Ernst Pringsheim, Lummer performed experiments of blackbody radiation that led Max Planck to his formulation of the quantum theory. After working (1887-1901) at the Physikaloisch-Technische Reichsanstalt in Berlin, Lummer taught at the University of Berlin (1901–04) and the University of Breslau (1904–25).   CARL A. ZAPFFE

lumpfish

Lumpfish is the common name for various fishes belonging to the family Cyclopteridae and characterized by a rounded, flabby body and a broad suction disc on the chest, formed from modified pelvic fins. The suction disc serves to attach the fish to rocky inshore areas.

lumpy jaw: see FUNGUS DISEASES.

Lumumba, Patrice   [loo-moom'-bah]

Although his tenure as the first prime minister of the independent Republic of the Congo was brief (June–September 1960), Patrice Lumumba achieved enduring fame from his defiance of Western interests in seeking armed suppression of the secession of Katanga. Dismissed from office, he was subsequently murdered in Katanga, becoming a martyr to the cause of African nationalism.

Patrice Emergy Lumumba, b. July 2, 1925, the first prime minister of the independent Democratic Republic of the Congo (now Zaire), was killed early in 1961 during the CONGO CRISIS. A member of the Batetela people, he was born in Kasai province in what was then the Belgian Congo.

Originally pro-Belgian in politics, Lumumba became an increasingly militant nationalist and an admirer of Kwame Nkrumah. In 1958 he helped to form the Congolese National Movement, aiming at an independent and unitary Congolese state. Lumumba participated in the 1960 Belgo-Congolese conference at Brussels that led to independence, and in June 1960 he was appointed prime minister by President Joseph KASAVUBU.

The Congo was immediately engulfed in crisis when Moise Kapenda TSHOMBE launched a Belgian-backed separatist movement in Katanga province (now Shaba). Lumumba was determined to crush the secession, appealing first to the United Nations and then to the USSR for aid. On Sept. 5, 1960, however, he was dismissed from office by Kasavubu, and within days the army leader Col. Joseph Mobutu (later MOBUTU SESE SEKO) seized power.

Still claiming to head the government, Lumumba was captured by Kasavubu's troops on December 2. He was turned over to the Katanga regime, which announced on Feb. 13, 1961, that he had been killed by villagers. Lumumba's supporters, however, believed that the Congolese government was responsible for his murder. Lumumba's views were published in English in *Congo: My Country* (1962) and *Lumumba Speaks: The Speeches and Writings of Lumumba, 1958–1961* (1972).   L. H. GANN

Bibliography: Kanza, Thomas R., *Conflict in the Congo: The Rise and Fall of Lumumba* (1972); McKown, Robin, *Lumumba: A Biography* (1969).

Luna   (mythology)

In Roman mythology, Luna was the moon goddess. Her Greek counterpart was SELENE. In art she is often represented driving a chariot with two white horses over the clouds.

Luna   (spacecraft)

Luna, a series of Soviet space probes (see SPACE EXPLORATION) developed for the exploration of the Moon, produced the first probes to pass near, to impact, and to photograph the Earth's only natural satellite, and the first spacecraft to land on, to orbit around, and to automatically return samples from this celestial object. The first three achievements were accomplished in 1959 by *Lunas 1, 2,* and *3.* Each of these spacecraft weighed about 275 kg (600 lb).

A series of heavier Luna probes, each weighing about 900 kg (2,000 lb), began in 1963 with the goal of a hard but

LUNA FLIGHTS

No.	Launch Date	Results
1	Jan. 2, 1959	Passed within 5,965 km (3,728 mi) of the Moon.
2	Sept. 12, 1959	Impacted on the Moon.
3	Oct. 4, 1959	Circumnavigated the Moon; photographed the back side.
4	Apr. 2, 1963	Missed the Moon by 8,451 km (5,282 mi).
5	May 9, 1965	Impacted on the Moon; soft landing failed.
6	June 8, 1965	Missed the Moon by 160,000 km (100,000 mi).
7	Oct. 4, 1965	Impacted on the Moon; soft landing failed.
8	Dec. 3, 1965	Impacted on the Moon; soft landing failed.
9	Jan. 31, 1966	Soft landed in western Oceanus Procellarum (Ocean of Storms); photographed lunar surface.
10	Mar. 31, 1966	Orbited the Moon; sent scientific data.
11	Aug. 24, 1966	Orbited the Moon; sent scientific data.
12	Oct. 22, 1966	Orbited and photographed the Moon; sent scientific data.
13	Dec. 21, 1966	Soft landed in Oceanus Procellarum (Ocean of Storms); sent soil-density data and photographed lunar surface.
14	Apr. 7, 1968	Orbited the Moon; studied the Moon's gravitational field and the Earth-Moon mass relationship.
15	July 13, 1969	Impacted on lunar surface after 52 orbits of the Moon.
16	Sept. 12, 1970	Soft landed in Mare Fecunditatis (Sea of Fertility) on September 20; soil-sample payload launched September 21 and successfully recovered on the Earth.
17	Nov. 10, 1970	Soft landed in Mare Imbrium (Sea of Rains) on November 17; Lunokhod 1, an automated roving vehicle, ranged several miles on lunar surface.
18	Sept. 2, 1971	Impacted on lunar surface (September 11) after 54 orbits of the Moon.
19	Sept. 28, 1971	Orbited the Moon and conducted photographic survey.
20	Feb. 14, 1972	Soft landed in highlands northeast of Mare Fecunditatis (Sea of Fertility) on February 21; soil-sample payload launched (February 22) and successfully recovered (February 25) on the Earth.
21	Jan. 8, 1973	Soft landed at the eastern edge of Mare Serenitatis (Sea of Serenity) on January 16; Lunokhod 2 explored neighboring area.
22	May 29, 1974	Orbited the Moon and conducted photographic survey.
23	Oct. 28, 1974	.Lunar-surface landing (November 16) damaged drill, preventing soil-sample return.
24	Aug. 9, 1976	Soft landed in southeastern part of Mare Crisium (Sea of Crises); soil-sample payload launched (August 19) and successfully recovered on the Earth (August 22).

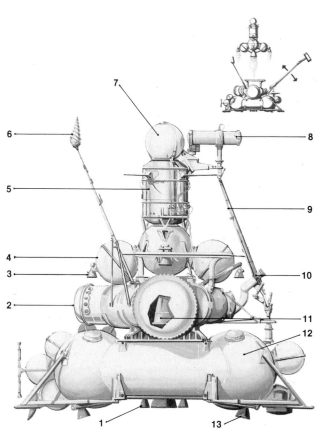

The Soviet Luna 16, 20, and 24 missions successfully returned lunar soil samples to Earth. The Luna comprised a descent vehicle for landing on the Moon, an ascent stage for lift-off, and a small reentry capsule for returning the lunar soil samples to Earth. Numbers indicate: rocket engines (1) of the descent stage; instrument compartment (2) of the descent stage; small motors (3), for in-flight control of the ascent stage; one of three ascent stage propellant tanks (4); instrument compartment of the ascent stage (5); antenna (6); reentry capsule (7), 50 cm (20 in) in diameter, which carried 10 g (0.22 lb) of soil sample during the Luna 16 mission; housing (8) for a 35-cm (14-in) sample drill, and shaft (9) of drill, both of which are lowered to lunar surface; photometer (10); rocket engine (11) of ascent stage; one of four descent stage propellant tanks (12); one of four vernier thrusters (13), for stabilization of descent stage. The detail (upper right) shows lift-off from the Moon's surface.

survivable landing on the Moon. After an agonizing series of failures and near misses, Luna 9 made a landing on Feb. 3, 1966, and several television images of the surface were sent back to the Earth. Luna 10 was placed into orbit around the Moon in 1966, becoming the first artificial lunar satellite. The newest and heaviest versions of Luna, each weighing about 4,500 kg (10,000 lb), began flight-testing in 1969, but a long series of booster and spacecraft failures plagued this program. The heavy spacecraft were designed for particular tasks: Lunas 16, 20, and 24 picked up samples of lunar soil and returned them to the Earth; Lunas 17 and 21 carried LUNOKHOD "moon jeeps" that traversed the Moon's surface under remote control; and Lunas 19 and 22 carried out extended lunar orbital surveys.

JAMES OBERG

Bibliography: Smolders, Peter L., *Soviets in Space* (1971; trans. by Marian Powell, 1974); Woods, D. R., "A Review of the Soviet Lunar Exploration Programme," *Spaceflight*, July–August 1976.

See also: SPACE EXPLORATION.

Lunar Excursion Module

The Lunar Excursion Module (LEM), better known as the Lunar Module (LM), was the transport vehicle used in the APOLLO PROGRAM to ferry two astronauts between the command module in lunar orbit and the surface of the Moon. The lunar-orbit rendezvous eliminated the need to land the entire Apollo spacecraft on the Moon on a direct ascent flight path from Earth orbit, and thus made possible a lighter load of fuel. Nine LMs were flown during the Apollo program, and six landed on the Moon.

The two-stage LM was designed and built by the Grumman Aircraft Engineering Corporation under a $1.6-billion contract with the National Aeronautics and Space Administration. Because little was known about the lunar surface when construction began in 1962, engineers designed the cantilever landing gear—consisting of four sets of legs, each ending in a dish-shaped pod—so that the vehicle could land safely and remain upright on a variety of surfaces. With its legs extended, the LM was 7 m (23 ft) high and 4.3 m (14 ft) across. The descent stage, which stood slightly more than 3 m (10 ft) high, had an engine whose thrust could be controlled within a range of 44,500 to 4,600 newtons (4,530 to 475 kg, or 10,000 to 1,050 lb). To ensure a soft landing, the engine was fired

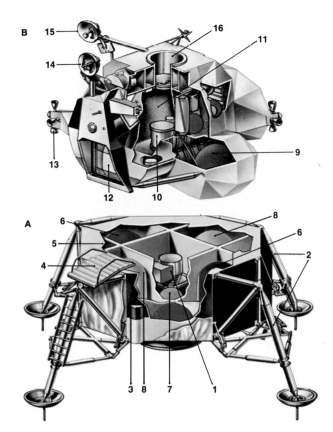

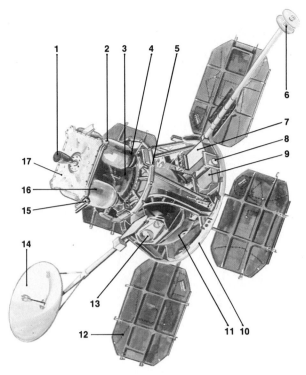

The Apollo lunar excursion module comprised two sections. The descent stage (A) contained the main engine (1), landing gear (2), scientific equipment bay (3), egress platform (4), and water (5), fuel (6), oxygen (7), and oxidizer (8) tanks. The ascent stage (B) contained a pressurized two-man cabin (11), ascent engine (10), fuel tank (9), forward hatch (12) for lunar egress and ingress, thruster assembly (13), rendezvous radar antenna (14), steerable radio antenna (15), and overhead hatch and tunnel (16) to the command module.

The Lunar Orbiter, 1.7 m (5.5 ft) tall, carried a 69-kg (152-lb) photographic laboratory to assist in the selection of landing sites for the United States Apollo Program. Orbiter's major structures were: 454-kg (1,000-lb) thrust velocity control engine (1); attitude control thrusters (2); upper structural module weighing 321 kg (708 lb) (3); oxidant tank (4); micrometeoroid detectors (5); omnidirectional, low-gain antenna (6); flight programmer (7); Canopus star tracker (8), for orientation; inertial reference unit (9); Sun sensor (10), beneath instrument deck; lower structural module, photographic laboratory (11); solar panel (12); telephoto and wide-angle cameras (13), each with film for 212 exposures; high-gain dish antenna (14); attitude control thrusters (15); fuel tank (16); and heat shield (17).

continuously during descent from lunar orbit. The crew rode in the ascent stage, which was equipped with an engine of 15,550 newtons (1,600 kg, or 3,500 lb) thrust. Both descent and ascent were made with the aid of a sophisticated guidance and navigation system that included a radar altimeter.

At launch, the LM was carried atop the third stage of a Saturn 5 rocket. As the vehicle system left Earth orbit on a translunar trajectory, the pilot of the Apollo Command and Service Module turned the spacecraft around and docked it nose to nose with the LM. In lunar orbit, two crew members transferred from the Apollo Command Module to the LM ascent stage through a docking tunnel, undocked the LM, and landed on the Moon. To leave the Moon, the crew fired the ascent-stage engine (using the descent stage as a launch platform), ascended to lunar orbit, and docked with the Apollo spacecraft. The descent stage was left on the Moon and the ascent stage was jettisoned in lunar orbit.   RICHARD LEWIS

Bibliography: Lewis, Richard, *Appointment on the Moon* (1969).

Lunar Orbiter

The Lunar Orbiter program was a series of five U.S. spacecraft used for a broad-scale lunar mapping effort, in contrast to the preceding RANGER spacecraft, which zeroed in on specific targets on their way to crash landings. The five Orbiter missions, all of them successful, were launched at approximately three-month intervals from Aug. 10, 1966, through Aug. 1, 1967.

The general area of interest for Apollo (see APOLLO PROGRAM) landing sites was a rectangle extending 5° north and south of the lunar equator and 45° east and west of the lunar

prime (essentially earth-centered) meridian. Lunar Orbiter 1 was launched to photograph the southern part of the rectangle, while Lunar Orbiter 2 was concerned with the northern half. A dozen promising Apollo landing sites were selected from these batches of images, and the third probe in the series was used for additional photos of the chosen sites. Lunar Orbiter 4 was placed in a higher-altitude orbit around the Moon, giving wider coverage while still showing the surface from a near-vertical aspect that cannot be seen from Earth except near the center of the lunar disk. Lunar Orbiter 5 was also used to complete Apollo site studies, but the success of the four previous Lunar Orbiters enabled much of the photography of the fifth mission to be devoted to targets of primarily scientific interest. Altogether, 95 percent of the Moon's surface was photographed by the Lunar Orbiters.

Some of the photos were also used to help pinpoint the locations of some of the unmanned SURVEYOR landing craft, and Lunar Orbiters 1 and 5 took pictures of the Earth. The Orbiters also discovered MASCONS (mass concentrations) on the Moon.   JONATHAN EBERHART

Bibliography: Lewis, Richard, *Appointment on the Moon* (1968).

Lunar Rover

The Lunar Rover, or Lunar Roving Vehicle, was a wire-wheeled, battery-powered vehicle used by the *Apollo 15, 16,* and *17* astronauts to explore the Moon's surface at greater distances than previously possible from the landing sites (see APOLLO PROGRAM). Built by the Boeing Company, the 310-cm-long (122-in), 114-cm-high (45-in), 218-kg (480-lb) vehicle was

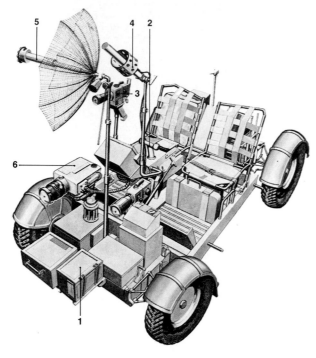

Lunar roving vehicles were used by the Apollo 15, 16, and 17 astronauts to carry scientific equipment, tools, and lunar rocks across the Moon's surface. Each rover was powered by two 36-volt batteries (1) and equipped with a hand controller (2) for steering and braking, a 16-mm camera (3), a low-gain antenna (4), a high-gain antenna (5) for direct transmission to Earth, and a color television camera (6).

stored folded in the Lunar Module's descent stage. Capable of supporting twice its own weight, the Lunar Rover could move at a speed of 13 km/h (8 mph), ascend slopes of up to 20°, and pass over 0.3-m-high (1-ft) obstacles and 0.6-m (2-ft) crevices.

Lunda   [loon'-duh]

The Lunda are an ethnic group of Central Africa. They live in Angola, Zambia, and Zaire and numbered over 1.5 million in the late 1980s. The Lunda take pride in a single, ancient, and glorious origin, a legendary Congolese empire ruled by the Mwata Yamvo. Some say that their name is derived from a word for friendship, the amity that once held between many small groups, each under its own chief, within a loose federation prior to the empire. Today, however, the Lunda are culturally and socially diverse and politically disunited. The diversity is so great that, although Northern and Southern Lunda are both West Central Bantu languages, they are not mutually intelligible.

The northerners, living in the original territory of the Lunda, are patrilineal; the southerners and the easterners, including the Ndembu and the peoples of the Luapula valley, are matrilineal, although the Kazembe, Luapula's paramount chief, claims to be of the same patrilineal dynasty as the founders of the legendary Lunda empire. Luapula society is stratified and hierarchically organized, but the Ndembu are egalitarian in social organization. The notion of Lundahood may be something of a fiction, but it is a fiction that, since the 1950s, has taken on political significance. Leaders, such as the late Moise-Kapenda TSHOMBE, who led the secession attempt (1960–63) by Zaire's Shaba (former Katanga) province, have gained Lunda support by capitalizing on the mystique of a restored Lunda empire.   RICHARD WERBNER

Bibliography: Bustin, Edouard, *Lunda under Belgian Rule: The Politics of Ethnicity* (1975); Turner, Edith, *The Spirit and the Drum* (1987); Turner, V. W., *Schism and Continuity in an African Society: A Study of Ndembu Village Life* (1954).

Lundmark, Knut   [lund'-mark, kuh-noot']

The Swedish astronomer Knut Emil Lundmark, b. June 14, 1889, d. Apr. 23, 1958, is known for his determinations of absolute stellar magnitudes and his early belief, shared by Heber D. CURTIS, in the now-established island universe theory. This theory, that certain nebulae are located outside of our galaxy and themselves represent other galaxies, was based on his measurements of the extremely small PROPER MOTIONS of the spiral nebulae and was strenuously opposed by Adriaan van Maanen.   STEVEN J. DICK

Lundy, Benjamin   [luhn'-dee]

Benjamin Lundy, b. Sussex County, N.J., Jan. 4, 1789, d. Aug. 22, 1839, was an American Quaker abolitionist during the early years of the republic. A saddlemaker who settled in Ohio in 1815, he founded (1821) *The Genius of Universal Emancipation,* an abolitionist journal that circulated principally among Scotch-Irish, Moravian, and Quaker freeholders in the upper South. In 1828 he persuaded William Lloyd GARRISON to become a coeditor of the *Genius* and thus helped to launch the career of that leading abolitionist. Lundy spent his last years in fruitless negotiations with the Mexican government, hoping to open areas of Texas for settlement by emancipated slaves.   JAMES BREWER STEWART

Bibliography: Dillon, Merton L., *Benjamin Lundy and the Struggle for Negro Freedom* (1966); Earle, Thomas, ed., *The Life, Travels and Opinions of Benjamin Lundy* (1847; repr. 1971).

lung, artificial: see HEART-LUNG MACHINE; IRON LUNG.

Lung-men   (Longmen)

At Lung-men, 16 km (10 mi) south of Lo-yang, in Honan province, China, is a complex of Buddhist cave temples decorated with stone sculptures ranging in date from AD 494 to the mid-8th century. Sculptures in the Pin-yang cave (completed 523), which contains the finest examples dating from the Northern Wei period (386–535), are characterized by highly spiritualized, ethereal-looking figures robed in elegant cascading drapery.

A colossal group measuring more than 15 m (50 ft) high and located in the Fêng-hsien temple (built 672–75), is the most significant sculptural group of the 7th century. These figures, modeled in the sensuous forms and clinging draperies typical of the T'ang period (618–907), reveal affinities with the Gupta style of India.

Bibliography: Sickman, Laurence, and Soper, Alexander, *The Art and Architecture of China,* rev. ed. (1956); Sirén, Osvald, *Chinese Sculpture from the Fifth to the Fourteenth Century,* 2 vols. (1925; repr. 1970).

Lung-shan: see CHINESE ARCHAEOLOGY.

lungfish

Lungfishes are members of an ancient group of fishes and are characterized by functional lungs, a direct circulatory connection from the lung to the heart (as in mammals), a partial division of the atrium and ventricle of the heart into double chambers, and nostrils opening into the mouth cavity. Lungfishes were often formerly classified with the lobe-fin fishes (Crossopterygii) in a single subclass, Sarcopterygii, of the modern bony fishes (class Osteichthyes), but they are now generally placed in a separate subclass of their own, Dipnoi.

The African lungfish Protopterus (shown) may be descended from the extinct lungfish Dipterus, which lived about 275 million years ago.

The most primitive lungfish is the Australian lungfish, *Neoceratodus forsteri.* It grows to 1.8 m (6 ft) long and 45 kg (100 lb) in weight. It has a compressed body, flipperlike paired fins, large scales, four pairs of holobranchs (complete gills), and a single lung. It is not dependent upon its lung for survival, nor does it estivate, or become dormant, during the dry season. The South American lungfish, *Lepidosiren paradoxa,* grows to about 1.2 m (4 ft) long. It has threadlike pectoral fins, somewhat featherlike pelvic fins, and three pairs of holobranchs. The African lungfishes, *Protopterus,* consist of four species, which may reach 2.1 m (7 ft) in length. They have two pairs of holobranchs, and both the pectoral and pelvic fins are threadlike.

Both the South American and African lungfishes have cylindrical bodies, small scales, and paired lungs. They obtain more than 95% of their oxygen supply from their lungs and will drown if denied access to air. Both the South American and African lungfishes build breeding nests by burrowing into the mud, and both estivate at the bottom of a mud burrow during the dry season. The African lungfishes form a mucus-lined mud cocoon that dries and hardens around them. They have been kept alive out of water in these cocoons for four years. The lungfish absorbs muscle tissue for energy when it estivates, and stores urea in its body tissues and eliminates it only after estivation.

Lungfishes first appeared in the middle of the Devonian Period, about 370 million years ago. They are important in biogeography. Their present distribution in Australia, Africa, and South America are thought to represent the scattered remnants of a once-continuous lungfish distribution on the ancient land mass Gondwanaland.   EDWIN E. ROSENBLUM

lungs

The lung is an organ of the RESPIRATORY SYSTEM of air-breathing vertebrates and some fishes and amphibians that takes in atmospheric oxygen, needed for energy production, and at the same time expires carbon dioxide, a waste product of this

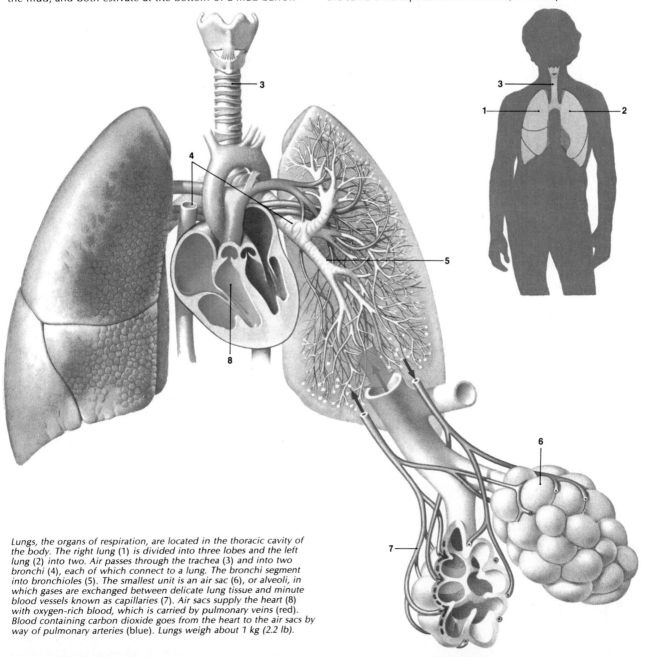

Lungs, the organs of respiration, are located in the thoracic cavity of the body. The right lung (1) is divided into three lobes and the left lung (2) into two. Air passes through the trachea (3) and into two bronchi (4), each of which connect to a lung. The bronchi segment into bronchioles (5). The smallest unit is an air sac (6), or alveoli, in which gases are exchanged between delicate lung tissue and minute blood vessels known as capillaries (7). Air sacs supply the heart (8) with oxygen-rich blood, which is carried by pulmonary veins (red). Blood containing carbon dioxide goes from the heart to the air sacs by way of pulmonary arteries (blue). Lungs weigh about 1 kg (2.2 lb).

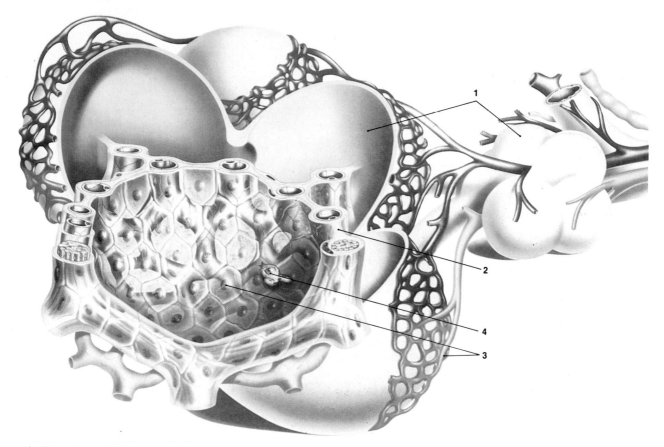

Alveoli, or air sacs, of the lung are the basic units of respiration. Each lung contains about 300 million alveoli, which are arranged in clusters (1). Each air sac has a wall of elastic and collagenous connective tissue (2) that is no more than 0.7 microns thick. The wall lines a network of capillaries (3) that surround each air sac. The walls of the capillaries and the air sacs are thin enough that oxygen and carbon dioxide exchange can occur by means of diffusion, or passive transfer. A phagocyte (4) moves around inside an air sac, engulfing debris that had been breathed in.

metabolism. The lungs of most animals consist of two elastic chambers, usually located in the thorax, with thin linings across which gaseous oxygen and carbon dioxide are exchanged between blood capillaries and the air within the chamber.

In evolutionary terms, lungs are the counterparts of the gills of fish and crustaceans, which are adapted for extracting oxygen from water, and the tracheae of insects, which pipe oxygen directly to the tissues. The development of the lung during evolution permitted the eventual evolution of air-breathing mammals, which need large amounts of oxygen, which can be extracted more quickly from air than from water.

The greatly increased surface area of the lung in higher vertebrates results from a subdivision of the inner surface into pockets, or folds. The mammalian lung is honeycombed with almost a half billion tiny sacs, called alveoli, each of which is less than 1 mm (.04 in) in diameter. Gas exchange takes place in the alveoli. The total exchange surface area in humans is about 70 m². thus ensuring great efficiency.

In humans, air first passes into the nose or mouth, through the pharynx (throat) and the larynx (voice box) and then into the trachea (windpipe). The generous blood supply of the nose, mouth, and pharynx brings incoming air to body temperature and humidity. The trachea splits to form two main stem bronchi, which in turn split to supply each of the five lobes that comprise the lung.

Each bronchus divides into 10 bronchopulmonary segments, or branches. Within each lobe the branches divide,

giving rise to even finer branches. The smallest branches are called bronchioles. If greater than 1 mm in diameter, they have walls made of smooth muscle that expands or contracts in response to the nervous system and are supported by discontinuous rings of CARTILAGE. Both the muscle and cartilage are incorporated into a framework of connective tissue. Their inner surfaces are covered by ciliated epithelium interspersed with mucus-secreting goblet cells. The mucus acts as an escalator, on which particles that have passed into the bronchial tree are carried upward by the beating of the cilia and toward the throat, where they are cleared. Foreign bodies that do reach the alveoli are engulfed and disposed of by ameboid cells, the alveolar macrophages. In bronchioles smaller than 1 mm in diameter, cartilage, ciliated cells, and goblet cells gradually disappear. The walls of the smallest airways and the entrance to the alveoli receive their support from an external network of connective tissue, the interalveolar septum. The bronchioles eventually terminate in pouches of air sacs, each sac comprising a cluster of alveoli.

The capillaries permeating the walls of the alveoli arise from the multiple branching of the pulmonary artery, which carries mixed venous blood from the heart. As the capillaries leave the lung they rejoin to form the superior and inferior pulmonary veins, which return oxygenated blood to the heart. The vessels of the pulmonary circulation are accompanied by lymph vessels, which serve to return plasma water lost through the capillaries to the circulation.

The lobes of the lung are contained within the chest cavity and are separated from each other and the chest wall by a double membrane called the pleura. The pleura reduces friction between the adjoining structures.

Bibliography: Coles, E. J., *Lung Function*, 3d ed. (1975); Levitzky, M. G., *Pulmonary Physiology*, 2d ed. (1986); Randall, D. J., et al., *The Evolution of Air Breathing in Vertebrates* (1981).

See also: RESPIRATORY SYSTEM DISORDERS.

lungwort

Lungwort is the common name for herbaceous plants of the genus *Pulmonaria,* family Boraginaceae, and a LICHEN (tree lungwort, *Lobaria pulmonaria*) that were formerly used in treating lung diseases. *Pulmonaria* species are garden flowers common in Europe; their drooping pink flowers turn blue, and their leaves are covered with stiff hairs.

Lunokhod   [loo-noh-koht']

The Lunokhods were remote-controlled moon rovers that the Soviet LUNA spacecraft successfully carried to the Moon's surface in 1970 and again in 1973. The purpose of the vehicles was to roll across the Moon's surface, sending back panoramic stereoscopic television images and making soil measurements. In shape and size the Lunokhods resembled bathtubs with four wheels on each long side. Total weight was about 900 kg (2,000 lb). A lid over the roof was raised in the daytime to expose solar power cells. A small radioisotope unit was used to maintain a survivable temperature.

The first successful Lunokhod (carried by *Luna 17*) landed

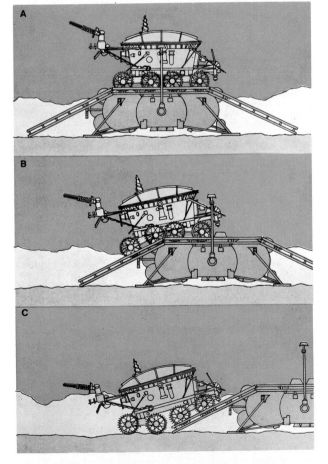

The Soviet Lunokhod 1 *was a remote-controlled, self-propelled vehicle that landed on the Moon on Nov. 17, 1970, as part of the unmanned* Luna 17 *spacecraft. On radio command from Earth, a ramp (A) was lowered from the descent stage, and Lunokhod was driven down (B) from its support platform onto the ground (C). Analyses of the lunar soil's properties at various points were telemetered to Earth.*

in the Mare Imbrium on Nov. 17, 1970. It operated for 11 months under the control of a 5-man team at a communications center near Moscow and covered a total of 10 km (6 mi) while crisscrossing the landing site. The second Lunokhod (carried by *Luna 21*) landed on the Moon on Jan. 16, 1973, inside the crater Le Monnier in the Mare Serenitatis. It covered 35 km (22 mi) in 5 months before apparently becoming stuck while exploring a deep ravine.   JAMES OBERG

Bibliography: Johnson, Nicholas L., *Handbook of Soviet Lunar and Planetary Exploration* (1979).

Lunt, Alfred, and Fontanne, Lynn   [luhnt, fahn-tan']

Alfred Lunt and Lynn Fontanne, a celebrated team in the American theater, entertained audiences for more than 40 years with their sophisticated light comedies. When Lunt died in 1977 the lights of Broadway's marquees were dimmed for one minute as a final tribute.

The actors Alfred Lunt, b. Milwaukee, Wis., Aug. 19, 1892, d. Aug. 3, 1977, and Lynn Fontanne, b. Woodford, England, Dec. 6, 1887, d. July 30, 1983, married in 1922 and during their 40-year professional career together gained the reputation of being the best acting couple on the American stage. They joined the Theatre Guild in 1924 and became famous for their wit and sophistication in such comedies as Molnár's *The Guardsman* (1924), Shaw's *Pygmalion* (1926), Noel Coward's *Design for Living* (1933) and *Quadrille* (1952), Shakespeare's *Taming of the Shrew* (1935), and Robert Sherwood's *Idiot's Delight* (1936). Their final stage appearance was in 1958–60, in Friedrich Dürrenmatt's chilling drama *The Visit.*
                                            ANDREW J. KELLY

Bibliography: Freedly, George, *The Lunts* (1958); Zolotow, Maurice, *Stagestruck: The Romance of Alfred Lunt and Lynn Fontanne* (1965).

Luo   [luh-woh']

The Luo (also called Kavirondo) people inhabit parts of northern and southeastern Uganda and western Kenya. Speakers of an Eastern Sudanic language, they are the southernmost of the Nilotic tribes (see NILOTES); they numbered about 3 million in the 1980s.

Once nomadic, the Luo are now a sedentary people living in clusters of politically autonomous villages. They cultivate sorghum, millet, and cotton, which is grown as a cash crop. Both fishing and cattle contribute to their economy.

Dominant patrilineal clans provide leadership in local communities. Traditionally, each tribe (a clan-family) was a self-contained, landholding, political and ritual unit. Today the small, extended, polygynous family is the primary element of social organization. The payment of bride-price in the form of cattle and separate mother-child households (*ot*) for plural wives are common. Their traditional religious beliefs centered on worship of a supreme deity and ancestors. Today most Luo adhere to Roman Catholicism.   JAMES W. HERRICK

Bibliography: Ogot, Bethwell, *A History of the Southern Luo* (1967); Wilson, Gordon, *Luo Customary Law and Marriage Customs* (1961).

Lupercalia   [loo-pur-kay'-lee-uh]

The Lupercalia was a Roman festival believed to have been in honor of FAUNUS, the god of flocks and fertility. Celebrated on February 15, it was intended to ensure the fertility of people, fields, and flocks for the new year. After sacrificing goats and a dog on the Palatine Hill, young men called Luperci raced around the borders of the hill striking those they met with whips made of the goatskins. Women who were struck were ensured of fertility and of easy delivery of children. The festival survived until the 5th century AD.

lupine   [loo'-pin]

The annual lupine, L. hirsutus, *is an ornamental herb native to the northwest United States. Its flowers grow in tall, colorful spires.*

Lupine is the common name for about 200 species of annual and perennial flowering herbs, members of the genus *Lupinus* of the PEA family, Leguminoseae. They are characterized by deeply cut leaves with lancelike leaflets radiating from the tip of the leaf stalk. The flowers are predominantly blue, yellow, white or rose in color and are borne on long-stemmed spikes in May and June.

Mostly native to the United States, lupines are cultivated chiefly as ornamentals in gardens; some, however, are grown as cover and forage crops.

lupus erythematosus   [loo'-puhs air-uh-theem-uh-toh'-suhs]

Lupus erythematosus is a disease of the connective tissue, as is arthritis. Abundant evidence indicates it is an autoimmune disorder. The immune system appears to react to the body's own tissues as if they were harmful invaders. Discoid lupus erythematosus (DLE) is one form of the disease; it is a skin disorder, forming red lesions usually on the face and scalp. In systemic lupus erythematosus (SLE), the other form of the disorder, the abnormal immune reaction can cause damage to the kidneys, heart, lungs, liver, nervous system, joints, and skin. In almost half of all cases of both DLE and SLE the patient has a characteristic facial rash shaped like a butterfly. The symptoms of SLE include arthralgias (pain in the joints), arthritis (tenderness and warmth in the joints), nephritis (inflammation of the kidney), and fever. Lupus erythematosus cells, white blood cells that destroy other white cells, appear in the majority of cases (50 to 90 percent), and their appearance is a diagnostic aid.

Lupus erythematosus occurs five to ten times more frequently in females than males, predominantly in the 15-to-55-year age group. According to recent estimates, 75 percent of all patients with the disease survive an average of 5 to 10 years. The most frequent cause of death is uremia (buildup of toxic wastes in the body due to kidney failure, followed by bacterial infection, heart failure, and hemorrhage.

Some patients have spontaneous remissions, whereas others respond favorably to treatment with corticosteroids or agents that inhibit the body's immune reactions. Antiinflammatory drugs and analgesics are also prescribed.

PETER L. PETRAKIS

Bibliography: Blau, Sheldon, *Lupus: The Body Against Itself* (1977); Dubois, Edmund, *Lupus Erythematosus*, 2d ed. (1974).

Luray Caverns   [lur-ay']

The Luray Caverns cover 26 ha (64 acres) near the town of Luray in the Shenandoah Valley of northern Virginia. Many of the limestone chambers in the caverns surpass heights of 43 m (140 ft), and most are studded with colorful stalagmites, stalactites and columns formed by underground rivers and dripping water.

The caverns were discovered by two brothers, William and Andrew Campbell, in 1878. The Caverns, indirectly lighted and connected by passages, bridges, and stairs, are a major tourist attraction.

Lurçat, Jean   [loor-sah', zhawn]

The French painter and designer Jean Lurçat, b. July 1, 1892, d. Jan. 6, 1966, is best known for reviving tapestry as a 20th-century art form. Lurçat was trained as a painter; initially, he pursued the ideas developed by Paul Cézanne and, later, those of the cubists. He began (1933) producing designs for the Aubusson workshop in France, the major tapestry-production center, but after 1936 devoted himself to the design and weaving of his decorative, colorful tapestries in a distinctive modern manner.

In 1939, in conjunction with the weaver François Tabard, Lurçat was instrumental in establishing a center for the making of modern tapestries at Aubusson, and he took part in the 1946 Paris exhibition that drew attention to the revival of tapestry as an architectural decoration. Lurçat described his art in his book *Designing Tapestry* (1950). He also designed for the theater and worked in ceramics, book illustration, and lithography.

Luria, Aleksandr Romanovich   [lur'-ee-uh]

A. R. Luria, b. July 16, 1902, d. Aug. 14, 1977, was a noted Soviet psychologist and a founder of neuropsychology. Luria graduated from Kazan University in 1921 and from the First Moscow Medical Institute in 1937. In 1945 he became a professor at Moscow State University. Among other honors, he received the Order of Lenin, the Order of the Badge of Honor, and the Lomonosov Prize.

Luria's psychological studies of the 1920s and '30s centered on the function of speech. He was especially concerned with the role of language in controlling the affective processes, and with the relationship between speech and the mental development of children. According to Luria, the development of speech is inextricably linked to a child's intellectual development.

While studying the relationship between language and thought, Luria became interested in types of speech pathology, including aphasia. His work on aphasia led Luria to investigate brain correlates of aphasia and then to study the brain in general. During World War II, Luria made important advances in the rehabilitation of brain-injured casualties, using, among other methods, the study of handwriting to determine the location of brain damage.

As in the work of most Soviet psychologists, Luria's studies show a bias toward materialist and behaviorist explanations. For example, his explanation of mental retardation stresses damage to the central nervous system and rejects genetic and cultural causes. Luria's more than 200 scientific works include *The Nature of Human Conflicts* (1932), *The Restoration of Brain Functions After War* (1963; Eng. trans., 1966), and *The Human Brain and Psychological Processes* (1963; Eng. trans., 1966).

Bibliography: Cole, M., "Alexander Romanovich Luria: 1902–1977," *American Journal of Psychology*, June 1978; Lindzey, Gardner, *A History of Psychology in Autobiography* (1974); Simon, J., "Scientist and Educationist: A. R. Luria," *Forum*, Summer 1978.

Luria, Isaac ben Solomon

Isaac ben Solomon Luria, b. 1534, d. Aug. 5, 1572, a Jewish mystic, led the development of later KABBALAH, a school of Jewish mysticism. He was born in Jerusalem, the son of immigrant German parents. After studying the Talmud and the *Zohar*, the basic work of Kabbalah, he settled (*c.*1570) in Safed, Palestine, where he developed a circle of disciples.

Luria's thought was a combination of kabbalistic mysticism and messianism. He held a form of emanationism, teaching that, by voluntary self-contraction (*tsimtsum*), God made room for creation, which took the form of an emanation, or "overflowing," of the divine light. When the divine light was enclosed in finite "vessels" (*kelim*), they shattered (*shevirat ha-kelim*), and darkness (evil) came into creation and mingled with the light. Before the Messiah comes, humankind must release the divine sparks from this mixture so there may be a restoration (*tikkun*) of the pure light of God. This can be achieved by practicing saintliness and asceticism. Luria's influence was far-reaching and is especially evident in HASIDISM. His school of mysticism is referred to as Lurianic Kabbalah. Although Luria wrote little, his ideas have been recorded in the many works of his disciple Hayyim Vital.

JOSEPH L. BLAU

Bibliography: Ashlag, Yehudah, *The Kabbalah: A Study of the Ten Luminous Emanations from Rabbi Isaac Luria* (1969); Scholem, Gershom, *Major Trends in Jewish Mysticism*, 3d rev. ed. (1954; repr. 1967).

Luria, Salvador   [loo'-ryah]

Salvador Edward Luria, b. Aug. 13, 1912, an Italian-American biochemist, shared the 1969 Nobel Prize for physiology or medicine with Alfred Day HERSHEY and Max DELBRÜCK for his discoveries concerning the replication mechanism and genetic structure of viruses. Working with Delbrück in 1943, he showed that genetic mutations can occur in bacteriophages, viruses that infect bacteria.

Lurie, Alison   [lur'-ee]

An American novelist and university professor, Alison Lurie, b. Chicago, Sept. 3, 1926, writes ironic fiction generally focused on the beleaguered, out-of-step relations between the sexes. Lurie's works zero in on contemporary events and fads. They include *The Nowhere City* (1965), *Imaginary Friends* (1967), *Real People* (1969), the highly successful *The War Between the Tates* (1974), *Only Children* (1979), and *Foreign Affairs* (1984), which won the 1985 Pulitzer Prize for fiction. Lurie also writes about children's literature.

Luristan

The western Iranian province of Luristan (1984 est. pop., 1,306,000) is the site of numerous unearthed ornamental bronze objects dating from the 9th to the 6th century BC; two earlier groups of bronzes have also been discovered dating from the late 3d millennium and the 14th–12th centuries BC.

Excavations in the Zagros Mountains since the late 1920s have revealed hundreds of burials containing horse and chariot fittings, jewelry, weapons, and other implements. The objects display abstract motifs and highly stylized animal and human forms, some of which also appear in early Iranian art. The Luristan bronzes, dating from the 1st millennium BC, were probably produced for Cimmerian, Median, or other nomadic warriors, although scholars are still uncertain about their stylistic origins.

Bibliography: Porada, Edith, *The Art of Ancient Iran* (1965).

Lusaka   [loo-sah'-kah]

Lusaka is the capital and largest city of Zambia, with a population of 535,830 (1980 est.). It is in the south central part of the country, about 95 km (60 mi) from the border with Zimbabwe. An important rail junction, it is a trading center for corn, wheat, tobacco, potatoes, and dairy cattle and produces building materials, tobacco products, foodstuffs, footwear, and textiles. The University of Zambia (1965) is there. Lusaka was founded by Europeans in 1905 as a railroad depot and named for the leader of a nearby African village. It replaced Livingstone as the capital of Northern Rhodesia (now Zambia) in 1935 because of its pleasant climate.

Lushai   [loo'-shy]

The Lushai people, speakers of a Tibeto-Burman language, inhabit the Mizo hills on the borders of India and Burma. They are estimated to number about 500,000. Traditionally, the Lushai practiced slash-and-burn agriculture, frequently moving their hilltop villages to new cultivable areas. Their stratified society included chiefs, commoners, serfs, and slaves. Traditional Lushai religion centered on ancestor cults and the propitiation of numerous gods through sacrificial offerings, especially of buffaloes. The status of male leaders depended in large part on the size and the frequency of their sacrifices. Until the late 19th century, when the British took control over this area, feuding and head-hunting among various groups were common, and Lushai villages were heavily fortified. Today their traditional culture has been drastically altered, and most Lushai have become Christians.

HILARY STANDING AND R. L. STIRRAT

Lusitania   (Roman province)   [loo-sih-tayn'-ee-uh]

Lusitania was an ancient Roman province in the Iberian Peninsula. By the reign (17 BC–AD 14) of Augustus it included western Spain and all of central Portugal. Its fierce inhabitants, the Lusitani, stood successfully independent of Roman rule until 139 BC, when they were defeated. During the 1st century BC the Roman general Quintus Sertorius led them in a rebellion against Roman rule, but they were conquered by POMPEY THE GREAT in 73 BC. Under the empire, the region prospered; its economy was enriched by trade in domestic animals, metal, and wood.

Lusitania   (ship)

The *Lusitania* was a British passenger ship that was sunk by a German submarine in the Atlantic on May 7, 1915. About 1,200 people were drowned, including 128 Americans. The sinking provoked a massive outcry in the United States, and President Woodrow Wilson protested strongly to Germany, demanding reparations and the cessation of unrestricted submarine warfare. The German government justified the action on the grounds that the *Lusitania* carried munitions, but it privately ordered German submarines not to sink passenger ships without warning. The incident contributed to the deterioration in U.S.-German relations that eventually led the United States to enter World War I.

Bibliography: Bailey, Thomas A., and Ryan, Paul B., *The Lusitania Disaster* (1975); Simpson, Colin, *Lusitania* (1972; repr. 1983).

On May 7, 1915, the Lusitania, a British passenger ship, was torpedoed by a German submarine off the Irish coast. Of the more than 1,900 people aboard, 1,198 drowned. The incident contributed to the rising sentiment in favor of U.S. entry into World War I.

theses directly criticized papal policies, they were put forward as tentative objections for discussion.

Copies of the 95 theses were quickly spread throughout Europe and unleashed a storm of controversy. During 1518 and 1519, Luther defended his theology before his fellow Augustinians and publicly debated in Leipzig with the theologian Johann Eck, who had condemned the ideas of Luther. Meanwhile, church officials acted against him. The Saxon Dominican provincial charged him with heresy, and he was summoned to appear in Augsburg before the papal legate, Cardinal Cajetan. Refusing to recant, he fled to Wittenberg, seeking the protection of the elector Frederick III of Saxony. When the Wittenberg faculty sent a letter to Frederick declaring its solidarity with Luther, the elector refused to send Luther to Rome, where he would certainly meet imprisonment or death.

Reforms. In 1520, Luther completed three celebrated works in which he stated his views. In his *Address to the Christian Nobility of the German Nation,* he invited the German princes to take the reform of the church into their own hands; in *A Prelude Concerning the Babylonian Captivity of the Church,* he attacked the papacy and the current theology of sacraments; and in *On the Freedom of a Christian Man,* he stated his position on justification and good works. The bull of Pope Leo X *Exsurge Domine,* issued on June 15 that same year, gave Luther 60 days to recant, and *Decet Romanum Pontificem* of Jan. 3, 1521, excommunicated him.

Summoned before Holy Roman Emperor Charles V at the Diet of Worms in April 1521, Luther again refused to recant and was put under the ban of the empire. He took refuge in the Wartburg castle, where he lived in seclusion for eight months. During that time he translated the New Testament into German and wrote a number of pamphlets. In March 1522 he returned to Wittenberg to restore order against enthusiastic iconoclasts who were destroying altars, images, and crucifixes. His reforming work during subsequent years included the writing of the Small and Large Catechisms, sermon books, more than a dozen hymns, over 100 volumes of tracts, treatises, biblical commentaries, thousands of letters, and the translation of the whole Bible into German.

With Philipp Melanchthon and others, Luther organized the Evangelical churches in the German territories whose princes supported him. He abolished many traditional practices, including confession and private mass. Priests married; convents and monasteries were abandoned. These were difficult times. Luther lost some popular support when he urged suppression of the Knights' Revolt (1522) and the Peasants' War (1524–26); his failure to reach doctrinal accord with Ulrich Zwingli on the nature of the Eucharist (1529) split the Reform movement. Nonetheless, Luther found personal solace in his marriage (1525) to a former Cistercian nun, Katherina von Bora; they raised six children.

At Worms, Luther had stood alone. When the Evangelicals presented the Augsburg Confession to Charles V and the Diet of Augsburg in 1530, many theologians, princes, and city councils subscribed to that classic Protestant statement of faith. By the time of Luther's death, a large part of northern Europe had left the Roman Catholic church for new Evangelical communities. Late in 1545, Luther was asked to arbitrate a dispute in Eisleben; despite the icy winter weather, he traveled there. The quarrel was settled on Feb. 17, 1546, but the strain had been very great and Luther died the next day.

Luther left behind a movement that quickly spread throughout the Western world. His doctrines, especially justification by faith and the final authority of the Bible, were adopted by other reformers and are shared by many Protestant denominations today. As the founder of the 16th-century Reformation, he is one of the major figures of Christianity and of Western civilization.   Lewis W. Spitz

Bibliography: Althaus, Paul, *The Theology of Martin Luther* (1966); Atkinson, James, *Martin Luther and the Birth of Protestantism* (1968) and *The Trial of Luther* (1971); Bainton, Roland, *Here I Stand: A Life of Martin Luther* (1951); Boehmer, Heinrich, *Road to Reformation* (1946; repr. 1978); Edwards, Mark, *Martin Luther and the False Brethren* (1975); Erikson, Erik H., *Young Man Luther* (1958); Fife, Robert H., *The Revolt of Martin Luther* (1957); Green, V. H. H., *Luther and the Reformation* (1964); Luther, Martin, *Luther's Works,* 56 vols., trans. and ed. by Jaroslav Pelikan and H. T. Lehmann (1955–   ), Pelikan, Jaroslav, ed., *Interpreters of Luther* (1968); Ritter, Gerhard, *Luther: His Life and Work,* trans. by John Riches (1964); Rupp, Gordon, *Luther's Progress to the Diet of Worms* (1964); Schwiebert, Ernest G., *Luther and His Times* (1950); Tierney, Brian, et al., eds., *Martin Luther, Reformer or Revolutionary?* 3d ed. (1977).

Luther v. Borden

The case of *Luther* v. *Borden* (1849) grew out of a dispute between two rival governments in the state of Rhode Island. Instead of drafting an entirely new constitution after the American Revolution, Rhode Island's constitution was—except for a few minor changes—essentially the colonial charter of 1663. Dissatisfied with this constitution's provision for limited suffrage, a group of citizens wrote a new constitution and elected a new governor, Thomas Dorr, in 1842 (see Dorr's Rebellion). When Dorr attempted to assert the authority of the new government, the charter government declared martial law and eventually succeeded in dispersing the rival group. Under the martial law declaration, Borden, a state militiaman, broke into the house of Luther, a Dorr supporter, in an attempt to arrest him. Luther sued for trespass, claiming that martial law had been declared by an illegitimate government. The important issue before the Supreme Court was whether the judiciary had the authority to determine which was the lawful government of the state.

The opinion by Chief Justice Roger B. Taney held that Congress, in the event of a dispute, should decide "what government is the established one in a state." The crucial point of the opinion was Taney's contention that questions of state sovereignty are "political questions" to be answered by Congress and the president, the final determination to be binding on the courts. To this day the doctrine remains as an important restraint on judicial authority.   Robert J. Steamer

Lutheranism

Lutheranism is the branch of Protestantism that generally follows the teachings of the 16th-century reformer Martin Luther. The Lutheran movement diffused after 1517 from Saxony through many other German territories into Scandinavia. In the 18th century it spread to America and, thereafter, into many nations of the world, and it has come to number more than 70 million adherents. As such, it lays claim to being the largest non-Roman Catholic body in the Western Christian church.

Lutheranism appeared in Europe after a century of reformist stirrings in Italy under Girolamo Savonarola, in Bohemia under John Huss, and in England under the Lollards. The personal experience of the troubled monk Luther gave shape to many of the original impulses of the Protestant Reformation and colors Lutheranism to the present. Like many people of conscience in his day, Luther was disturbed by immorality and corruption in the Roman Catholic church, but he concentrated more on reform of what he thought was corrupt teaching. After he experienced what he believed to be the stirrings of Grace, he proclaimed a message of divine promise and denounced the human merits through which, he feared, most Catholics thought they were earning the favor of God.

Lutheranism soon became more than the experience of Luther, but it never deviated from his theme that people are made right with God *sola gratia* and *sola fide*—that is, only by the divine initiative of grace as received through God's gift of faith. Because Luther came across his discoveries by reading the Bible, he also liked to add to his motto the exhortation *sola scriptura,* which means that Lutherans are to use the Bible alone as the source and norm for their teachings.

The Lutheran movement gained popularity quickly in Germany at a time of rising nationalism among people who resented sending their wealth to Rome. The early Lutherans were strongly based in the universities and used their learning to spread the faith among an international community of scholars. By 1530 they were formulating their own confes-

SIONS OF FAITH and proceeding independently amid the non-Lutheran reform parties that proliferated across most of northern Europe. By 1580 and through the next century, these confessions became increasingly rigid scholastic expressions, designed to define the church in formal terms. Ever since, Lutheranism has been known as a doctrinal and even dogmatic church.

Lutheranism did not and could not live only by the teaching of its professors. In the late 17th century its more gentle side, which grew out of the piety of Luther, appeared in the form of a movement called PIETISM. Nominally orthodox in belief and practice, the Pietists stressed Bible reading, circles of prayer and devotion, and the works of love. This pietism was somewhat unstable; in its downgrading of doctrine it helped prepare Lutherans for the age of Enlightenment, when many leaders and some of the faithful turned to rationalism. Subsequently, theology under Lutheran influence has often taken on a radical character, especially in Germany. As a result, there is often a considerable gap between intellectual expressions of Lutheranism and the liturgy and preaching of its congregations.

From the beginning, Lutheranism had to wrestle with the problem of its relation to civil authorities. Although Luther was a rebel against papal teaching, he was docile about reforming the civil order and rejected radical revolts by the peasants (see PEASANTS' WAR). Fearing anarchy more than authoritarianism, the Lutherans gravitated to biblical teachings that stressed the authority of the state more than the civil freedom of its citizens. Most of them were content not to separate church and state, and in the Peace of Augsburg (1555; see AUGSBURG, PEACE OF) approved the principle that the ruler determined the faith of the ruled. Later Lutherans have enthusiastically embraced republican and democratic government as applications of the principle that God is active in different ways through the two realms of civil and churchly authority. Many German Lutherans were silent or cooperative, however, when the Nazi regime took over the church; only the Confessing Church, led by Martin NIEMÖLLER, opposed the regime outright.

Lutherans have been more ready than many other Christians to see the permanence of evil in the powers of the created and fallen world, that is, the world under the influence of sin. Consequently, they have put more of their energies into works of welfare and charity—into orphanages, hospitals, and deaconesses' movements—than into social schemes to transform the world.

In Europe most Lutheran churches are episcopal, that is, ruled by bishops, and the churches of Denmark, Finland, Iceland, Norway, and Sweden are established (see CHURCH AND STATE). In North America and elsewhere Lutherans prefer congregational and synodical forms of government, in which local churches link together for common purposes. In the United States, Lutherans have united in three main bodies: the Lutheran Church in America (membership, 2.9 million), the Lutheran Church–Missouri Synod (2.6 million), and the American Lutheran Church (2.3 million). The American Lutheran Church, the Lutheran Church in America, and a third group, the Association of Evangelical Lutheran Churches, united in 1987 to form the Evangelical Lutheran Church in America.

Lutheranism is generally friendly to the ecumenical movement, and with some exceptions, Lutheran churches have participated in worldwide gatherings of Christians across confessional and denominational boundaries. Lutherans consider themselves to be both evangelical and catholic because they have points in common with the other Protestant churches on the one hand, and with Orthodox, Roman Catholic, and Anglican Christians on the other. In the ecumenical age, however, they have kept a very distinct identity through their general loyalty to the teachings of 16th-century Lutheranism.

MARTIN E. MARTY

Bibliography: Bergendoff, C., *The Church of the Lutheran Reformation* (1967); Bodensieck, J., ed., *Encyclopedia of the Lutheran Church*, 3 vols. (1965); Braaten, Carl, ed., *The New Church Debate: Issues Facing American Lutheranism* (1984); Swihart, A. K., *Luther and the Lutheran Church* (1960).

Luthuli, Albert John   [luh-thoo'-lee]

The South African religious and political leader Albert Luthuli is shown here at a 1966 meeting with Robert F. Kennedy. Luthuli gained worldwide recognition and a Nobel Peace Prize for his work in seeking a nonviolent path to end racial discrimination and apartheid laws.

The South African civil rights leader Albert Luthuli (or Lutuli), b. 1898, d. July 21, 1967, was the first African to receive the Nobel Peace Prize (1960). After attending Adams College, an American Board of Missions teacher-training institution, he taught there for 15 years. In 1936, Luthuli was elected chief of a Zulu community in Natal province. He joined the African National Congress in 1945, advocating full citizenship for all South Africans; in 1951 he became president of the Natal branch of the Congress and in 1952 its president-general.

Luthuli was strongly influenced by his religious convictions and also by the American civil rights struggle. His views were summed up in a message issued to white voters in 1958: "We shall never rest content until the democratic principle which is conceded for Europeans is extended to include the entire population. . . . Our aim is neither white supremacy nor black supremacy, but a common South African multiracial society." Luthuli opposed armed insurrection, putting his trust in passive resistance.

Repeatedly arrested and finally confined (1959) by the government to his own rural neighborhood for promoting "hostilities," he was allowed to leave the country for a short period to receive the Nobel Prize, awarded to him for his peaceful struggle against racial discrimination. When he returned to South Africa he faced even stricter limitations on his freedom. In 1960 the African National Congress was outlawed and forced to operate underground or in exile. In 1962 the government banned publication of Luthuli's statements.

Luthuli died when he was struck by a train at Stranger, South Africa. His autobiography, *Let My People Go,* was published in 1962.   L. H. GANN

Bibliography: Benson, Mary, *Chief Luthuli of South Africa* (1963); Callan, Edward, *Albert John Luthuli and the South African Race Conflict*, rev. ed. (1965); Walshe, Peter, *The Rise of African Nationalism in South Africa: The African National Congress, 1912–1952* (1971).

Lutosławski, Witold   [loo-toh-swav'-skee]

One of Poland's most celebrated composers, Witold Lutosławski, b. Jan. 25, 1913, has acquired renown and respect in the West. After World War II, in which he was a German prisoner of war, he devoted himself to composition and teaching. As his works became known, he was invited to give seminars in Western Europe and in the United States. His music through the 1950s—such as his Concerto for Orchestra (1954) and *Musique funèbre* (1958)—expresses his nationalism, merging Polish folk elements with techniques introduced by Béla Bartók. As he became more familiar with Western European styles, he experimented with the twelve-tone system and with aleatory music, of which *Jeux vénitiens* (Venetian Games, 1961) is an outstanding example. Such later works as the Second Symphony (1967) are rich in orchestral scoring. The Double Concerto for Oboe, Harp, and Chamber Orchestra (1980) draws upon his entire orchestral idiom of the preceding three decades.

Lutyens, Sir Edwin Landseer   [luh'-chuhanz]

The British architect Sir Edwin Landseer Lutyens, b. Mar. 29, 1869, d. Jan. 1, 1944, is considered the last major architect to create significant works using traditional styles. Self-taught in architecture, Lutyens began his career by designing several distinguished country homes, such as the Deanery Garden, Sonning, Berkshire (1900–01), that reflect the influence of Philip Webb (1831–1915) and the Arts and Crafts movement. As a result of this influence, Lutyens's designs demanded a high level of craftsmanship, for which his domestic architecture is noted.

As he moved from domestic to public architecture, Lutyens developed a style that was classical in outline and inspiration yet stamped with his own personality. His largest public project was the planning (1912–14) of NEW DELHI, India, which came to include one of his most notable designs, the Viceroy's House (1920–31). In great demand following the New Delhi project, Lutyens designed several war memorials noted for their classical simplicity, such as the Cenotaph in London (1920) and the Thiepval Memorial Arch in France (1924), where he developed the idea of the three-dimensional triumphal arch.   VALENTIN TATRANSKY

Bibliography: Brown, Jane, *Gardens of a Golden Afternoon* (1982); Butler, A. S. G., *The Architecture of Sir Edwin Lutyens*, 3 vols. (1950); Hussey, Christopher, *The Life of Sir Edwin Lutyens* (1950); Irving, Robert, *Indian Summer—Lutyens, Baker, and Imperial Delhi* (1981).

Lutyens, Elisabeth

Elisabeth Lutyens, b. London, July 9, 1906, d. Apr. 14, 1983, was one of the few women of her generation to establish an international reputation as a composer. She studied at the Royal College of Music in London and at the École normale in Paris. Her compositional style progressed from romanticism to expressionism, in which she cultivated the twelve-tone technique; with this change she discarded everything she wrote before 1935. Her works include operas, chamber concertos, string quartets, choral and piano music, a dramatic scene, *The Pit* (1949), and the choral work *Essence of Our Happiness* (1970). She also composed for films and radio.

KAREN MONSON

Luxembourg   (city)

Luxembourg (1981 est. pop., 78,900) is the capital city of the Grand Duchy of Luxembourg. The city is a transportation, financial, and banking center, and its industries manufacture clothing, electrical machinery, chemicals, and processed foods. The Romans built a fort on the site, because of its strategic location overlooking the Alzette River; by the 10th century Luxembourg was one of Europe's strongest walled towns. The fortress was razed according to the terms of the Treaty of London (1867). During both world wars the city was occupied by Germany.

Luxembourg   (country)

The Grand Duchy of Luxembourg is an independent European country. It is bordered on the north and west by Belgium, on the east by West Germany, and on the south by France. Because of its central location, Luxembourg has been subject to foreign invasions and domination for much of its history. During the 20th century Luxembourg has been one of the strongest supporters of economic and political cooperation with other Western European countries. At the same time the people maintain a strong national identity.

LAND AND PEOPLE
The northern third of Luxembourg, called Oesling, is an extension of the forested, gently rolling Belgian ARDENNES. At the northern tip is the Burgplatz, at 559 m (1,835 ft) the country's highest elevation. The southern portion, called Gutland or Bon Pays ("good earth" in German and French, respectively), is an extension of the French Lorraine Plateau. Luxembourg is laced with rivers and streams; most drain eastward into the two major rivers, the MOSELLE and the Sûre (German: Sauer).

The climate is cool, with mean temperatures of about 1° C (30° F) in January and 17° C (62° F) in July. Average annual rainfall varies by region from 1,015 mm (40 in) to 685 mm (27 in).

Luxembourg's native population is primarily of French and German descent. Approximately one-quarter of the population is composed of foreign workers, who come to the country because of employment opportunities there. The predominant spoken language is Letzeburgesch, of German origin, but French and German are the two official languages. About 97% of the population is Roman Catholic. Education is free and compulsory from the ages of 6 to 15.

ECONOMIC ACTIVITY
A heavily industrialized economy gives Luxembourg one of the highest standards of living in Europe. Industry is concentrated in the southern portion of the country, where extensive iron deposits are mined. The iron and steel industry, the economic heart of Luxembourg, accounts for almost half of the industrial production. In recent years industry has become more diversified, and today chemicals, plastics, rubber, and synthetic fibers are produced.

Agriculture, which employs only a tiny fraction of the labor force, is concentrated in central Luxembourg.

Tourism, also important to the economy, is centered in the north, because of the scenic landscape and castle ruins.

In 1948, Luxembourg joined the Benelux customs union, and in 1958, the EUROPEAN ECONOMIC COMMUNITY.

HISTORY AND GOVERNMENT
Luxembourg (or Luxemburg) emerged as a separate political entity in the Middle Ages, when it was a powerful fief of the Holy Roman Empire. In 1308 its ruling count was elected German king (later Holy Roman emperor) as HENRY VII. His son, John of Luxembourg (1296–1346), became king of Bohemia in 1310; although blind, he died fighting on the French side in the Battle of Crécy. John's grandson, Holy Roman Emperor

GRAND DUCHY OF LUXEMBOURG

LAND. Area: 2,586 km² (998 mi²). Capital and largest city: Luxembourg (1981 est. pop., 78,900).
PEOPLE. Population (1985 est.): 400,000. Density: 155 persons per km² (400 per mi²). Distribution: 78% urban, 22% rural. Annual growth (1985–90): −1.5%. Official languages: French, German, Letzeburgesch. Major religion: Roman Catholicism.
EDUCATION AND HEALTH. Literacy (1984): 99% of adult population. Universities (1984): 1. Hospital beds (1982): 4,816. Physicians: 580. Life expectancy (1985): 72. Infant mortality: 11.2 per 1,000 live births.
ECONOMY. GNP (1982): $3.4 billion; $9,289 per capita. Labor distribution (1981): agriculture—0.5%; industry and commerce—42%; services—45%; government—12%; unemployed—1%. Foreign trade (1982): imports—$1.9 billion; exports—$1.6 billion; principal trade partners—Belgium, West Germany, France, Netherlands. Currency: 1 franc=100 centimes.
GOVERNMENT. Type: constitutional monarchy. Legislature: Chamber of Deputies. Political subdivisions: 3 districts.
COMMUNICATIONS. Railroads (1981): 270 km (168 mi) total. Roads (1982): 5,108 km (3,174 mi) paved. Airfields (international, 1984): 1.

LUXEMBOURG

——— Railroad

+ Spot Elevation

Scale 1:1,087,000

0   5   10   15   20   25 km

0   5   10   15 mi.

City type size indicates relative importance

National capitals are underlined

	Meters	Feet
	1000	3281
	500	1640
	200	656
	0	0

When Belgium gained its independence from the Netherlands it received (1839) a portion of the grand duchy (now the Belgian province of Luxembourg). Finally, the London Conference of 1867 recognized the independence and neutrality of the grand duchy.

When Queen WILHELMINA succeeded to the Dutch throne in 1890, Luxembourg passed to a collateral branch of the house of Nassau. Germany violated the neutrality of Luxembourg and occupied the duchy in both world wars. The present grand duke is Jean, who succeeded on the abdication of his mother, Charlotte (r. 1919–64).

Luxembourg is a constitutional monarchy headed by the grand duke. He appoints the 7-member council of ministers. The council, however, is responsible to the 59-member chamber of deputies, elected by universal suffrage. A 21-member advisory council of state, whose members are appointed by the grand duke and serve for life, is required to review and advise on all legislation before it comes before the chamber of deputies.

PAUL C. HELMREICH

Bibliography: Gunther, F. G., *The Benelux Countries* (1959; repr. 1972); Herchen, Arthur, *History of the Grand Duchy of Luxembourg,* trans. by A. H. Cooper-Prichard (1950); Nelson, Nina, *Belgium and Luxembourg* (1975); Riley, R. C., and Ashworth, Gregory, *Benelux: An Economic Geography of Belgium, the Netherlands and Luxembourg* (1975); Taylor-Whitehead, W. J., *Luxembourg: Land of Legends* (1976).

See also: LOW COUNTRIES, HISTORY OF THE.

Luxembourg Palace

The Luxembourg Palace in Paris, the first great example of French classical architecture during the 17th century, was the culmination of the long tradition of the CHÂTEAU as a building type. It was commissioned in 1615 by Marie de Médicis, regent of France, for a site on the Left Bank then occupied by the Hôtel du Luxembourg, from which the name was derived. The regent favored an Italianate structure, but the architect Salomon de BROSSE followed a typically French layout of wings surrounding a court, with the chief living quarters and chapel facing the garden. The west wing was the original site of the paintings (1622–25; Louvre, Paris) by Peter Paul RUBENS depicting the regent's life.

During the 19th century the palace was extensively remodeled: the garden facade was added (1836–41) by Alphonse de Gisors, and a cycle of paintings (1845–47) by Eugène Delacroix was added to the library. The building now houses the French Senate.

ROBERT NEUMAN

Bibliography: Coope, Rosalys, *Salomon de Brosse* (1972).

CHARLES IV made (1354) Luxembourg a duchy under his brother Wencelas. (Bohemia and the imperial crown passed to Charles's sons, first Wencelas and later Sigismund.)

In 1443, Luxembourg was seized by Philip the Good of Burgundy. It subsequently passed (1477) to the Habsburg dynasty and was under Spanish and (after 1714) Austrian rule. It was twice (1684–97 and 1795–1814) annexed by France. The Congress of Vienna (1814–15) made Luxembourg a grand duchy but bestowed the ruling title on WILLIAM I, king of the Netherlands, and provided for a Prussian garrison in the city of Luxembourg.

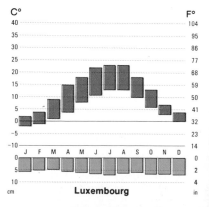

(Above) *Bars indicate monthly ranges of temperature (red) and precipitation (blue) of the city of Luxembourg which has a marine climate.*

(Right) *The historic city of Luxembourg is a center of trade, industry, and transportation.*

Luxemburg, Rosa

Rosa Luxemburg, b. Mar. 5, 1871, d. Jan. 15, 1919, was a leading socialist theorist and founder of the German Communist party. Born into a prosperous Jewish business family in Russian Poland, she engaged in revolutionary activity from 1887. In 1889 she was forced into exile in Switzerland, where she helped found (1893) the antinationalist Polish Socialist party.

Acquiring German citizenship by marriage, Luxemburg became a leader of the extreme left wing of the German Social Democratic party. She was active in the Second INTERNATIONAL, fighting the trend toward nationalism within the socialist movement.

While in prison (1916–18) for revolutionary activity during World War I, Luxemburg wrote the so-called Spartacus Letters. With Karl Liebknecht (see LIEBKNECHT family) she founded (1916) the radical Spartacus League, which, on Dec. 30, 1918, became the German Communist party. Both Liebknecht and Luxemburg were murdered by German troops after the abortive Spartacist uprising of January 1919. Luxemburg's chief work, presenting her theory of imperialism, was *Accumulation of Capital* (1913; Eng. trans., 1951).

FREDERIC B. M. HOLLYDAY

Bibliography: Bronner, S. E., *A Revolutionary for Our Times* (1981; repr. 1987); Bruno, Stephen, ed., *The Letters of Rosa Luxemburg* (1979); Ettinger, Elzbieta, *Rosa Luxemburg: A Life* (1986); Frölich, Paul, *Rosa Luxemburg: Her Life and Work,* trans. by Johanna Hoornweg (1972); Geras, Norman, *The Legacy of Rosa Luxemburg* (1976; repr. 1984); Nettl, J. P., *Rosa Luxemburg,* 2 vols. (1966).

Luxor [luhk'-sohr]

Luxor (1983 est. pop., 113,400), a city in upper Egypt, is located at the site of ancient THEBES. Located 740 km (460 mi) south of Cairo on the Nile River, it was the capital of ancient Egypt during the 11th dynasty (c.2130–1990 BC) but particularly in the New Kingdom (c.1570–1085 BC). In ancient times Luxor was called Waset, or No, meaning "the city" (Ezek. 30:14 and Nah. 3:8). Nothing can be seen of the ancient city except two of Egypt's finest pharaonic temples, those of Luxor and KARNAK, which stand on the east side of the river. On the west are the famous colossi of Amenhotep III (c.1417–1379 BC), the VALLEY OF THE KINGS and Valley of the Queens, the Ramesseum and other royal mortuary temples, and the finely decorated tombs of high officials. I. E. S. EDWARDS

Bibliography: Cury, Alexander R., *Luxor: How to See It* (1965); Kamil, Jill, *Luxor: A Guide to Ancient Thebes,* 2d ed. (1976); Nims, Charles F., *Thebes of the Pharaohs* (1965).

Luzon [loo-sohn']

Luzon is the northernmost and largest (104,688 km^2/40,420 mi^2) of the Philippine Islands. With 22,598,000 inhabitants (1980), Luzon is also the most populous island of the nation. MANILA, the largest city, capital, and chief port of the Philippines, is located on Luzon. The fertile central plain north of Manila is the largest tract of arable land in the archipelago. The southernmost part of Luzon consists of a series of elongated peninsulas, whereas the mountainous north has a more even coastline. The mean annual temperature is 27° C (80° F), and precipitation averages 2,030 mm (80 in) with the heaviest concentration occurring during the typhoon season (June–September).

Most of the inhabitants of Luzon are ethnic Filipinos, although remote parts of the island are occupied by small tribal groups (IGOROT and NEGRITO). Aside from manufacturing centered in Manila, Luzon is largely agricultural. Leading crops include rice (almost half the nation's rice harvest comes from Luzon), corn, coconuts, sugar, tobacco, and abaca. Tropical hardwoods, iron, gold, manganese, copper, and chrome are exported.

Ferdinand Magellan was the first European to discover the archipelago, in 1521. The Spaniards established Manila in 1570. During World War II the battles of Bataan and Corregidor took place on Luzon. MICHAEL McINTYRE

Luzzatto, Moses Hayyim [lut-saht'-toh]

Moses Hayyim Luzzatto, b. Padua, Italy, 1707, d. 1746, was a Jewish writer who ranks as one of the founders of modern Hebrew literature. His writings—chiefly, his ethical treatise *Mesillat Yesharim* (1740; *The Path of the Upright,* 1936)—were notable for the clarity of their language, a departure from the complex style of contemporary literary Hebrew. During his lifetime, however, Luzzatto was known principally as a charismatic mystic and interpreter of the KABBALAH. Alarmed by his messianic pronouncements, and fearing a repetition of the furor caused by the false Messiah SABBATAI ZEVI, the Italian rabbinate expelled Luzzatto, who died in Palestine.

Bibliography: Ginzburg, Simon, *The Life and Works of M. H. Luzzatto* (1931).

Lvov [lyuh-vawf']

Lvov is the capital of Lvov oblast in the western Ukrainian Soviet Socialist Republic of the USSR. The city has a population of 767,000 (1987 est.). Lvov is a transportation center, at the junction of railroads and highways, as well as an important manufacturing city. Lvov's industries, based primarily on its skilled labor force, produce motor vehicles such as buses and forklift trucks, light bulbs, television sets, and gas ranges. A petroleum refinery processes crude petroleum from the nearby Carpathian petroleum fields. The Lvov Ivan Franko State University, one of the oldest in the USSR, dates from 1661.

The history of Lvov is complex. Founded about 1256, it was named for Lev, a ruler of the early Russian principality of Galich. Together with the rest of the surrounding region of GALICIA, the city was transferred in the 14th century to Poland and was called Lwów. In 1772 it became part of Austria and was renamed Lemberg.

Much of Lvov's modern development dates from the Austrian period. The city reverted to Poland in the period 1918–39, between the two world wars, and, with the rest of the western Ukraine, was then absorbed by the USSR.

THEODORE SHABAD

Lwoff, André [luh-wawf', ahn-dray']

The French microbiologist André Lwoff, b. May 8, 1902, discovered that the genetic material (DNA) of a bacteriophage becomes incorporated into the genetic material of the bacterium that the virus infects—a process termed lysogeny. Earlier Lwoff found, when studying protozoa, that genetic material could exist outside the cell's nucleus. He shared the 1965 Nobel Prize for physiology or medicine with Jacques MONOD and François JACOB for his discoveries concerning the regulatory function of some genes.

Lyakhov, Vladimir [lee-ah'-kof]

Soviet cosmonaut Vladimir Lyakhov, b. July 20, 1941, and crewmember Valery Ryumin spent 175 days in space in 1979, a record at the time. Launched on February 25 aboard SOYUZ *32,* they docked with the SALYUT *6* space station and returned to Earth on August 19 aboard *Soyuz 34,* an originally pilotless craft that had docked with *Salyut 6* on June 8. On June 27, 1983, Lyakhov and cosmonaut Aleksandr Aleksandrov orbited in *Soyuz T-9,* docking a day later with *Salyut 7* and a linked, unmanned supply spacecraft called *Cosmos 1443.* They returned to Earth on Nov. 23, 1983. CRAIG B. WAFF

Lyallpur [ly'-ul-pur]

Lyallpur, renamed Faisalabad in 1979, is a city in Punjab province in northeastern Pakistan. It has a population of 1,092,000 (1981). It is the site of many experimental farms. Its economy is based on the production of textiles, fertilizers, vegetable oils, grains, and wheat flour. Pakistan Agricultural University (1961) and several colleges affiliated with the University of Punjab are located there. The city was founded by the British in 1892.

Lyautey, Louis Hubert   [lee-oh-tay', lwee ue-bair']

The French statesman and soldier Louis Hubert Gonzalve Lyautey, b. Nov. 17, 1854, d. July 21, 1934, administered French Morocco as its first resident general. Lyautey served in Algeria, Indochina, Madagascar, and France before 1904, when he was sent back to French Algeria—soon after France and Spain had secretly agreed to partition neighboring Morocco. As commandant at Aïn Sefra and later at Oran, Lyautey extended Algeria's territory by pushing the frontier westward into Morocco—especially after the Algeciras Conference of 1906, which allowed France to patrol the border. He returned to France in 1910 but in 1912 was appointed resident general of the new French protectorate of Morocco.

Except for 1916–17, when he served as French war minister, Lyautey administered the protectorate until 1925. He supported traditional Arab institutions while developing the Moroccan economy, promoting the port of Casablanca, and extending the protectorate's borders. He was successful in pacifying native Moroccan resistance movements, but he resigned his post in 1925 as the campaign against Berber tribes led by ABD EL-KRIM was nearing its conclusion.

Bibliography: Maurois, André, *Lyautey*, trans. by Hamish Miles (1931); Scham, Alan, *Lyautey in Morocco* (1970).

lycée   [lee-say']

In France the lycée is a state secondary school for students from the age of 11 to 18 or 19. First established in 1802 and reformed in 1959 to be more democratic and comprehensive, lycées, which can be for boys or for girls, prepare students for the *Baccalauréat,* the degree required for university admission. Classical, modern, and technical studies aim at developing the students' critical thinking.

lyceum

Lyceum was a 19th-century movement organized in the United States to provide town and village audiences with literary and scientific knowledge. Founded at Millbury, Mass., in 1826 by Josiah Holbrook, the movement sponsored lectures, debates, concerts, and publications. Local community leaders as well as such luminaries as Ralph Waldo Emerson, Henry David Thoreau, and Daniel Webster were among the participants. A forerunner of the CHAUTAUQUA and other adult education programs, the lyceum was named for the ancient Athenian gymnasium where Aristotle taught.

Lycia   [lish'-uh]

Lycia, an ancient country of southwestern Anatolia, occupied a mountainous promontory on the Mediterranean coast. The Lycian chieftains Sarpedon and Glaucus figure in Homer's *Iliad* as allies of Troy in the Trojan War. Conquered by the Persians in 546 BC, Lycia was subsequently dominated by Alexander the Great, the Ptolemies, the Seleucids, and finally the Romans. In AD 43 it was incorporated into the Roman province of Lycia-Pamphylia.

Lycurgus   [ly-kur'-guhs]

According to tradition, Lycurgus was the founder of the constitution of SPARTA and the lawgiver who designed that ancient Greek city-state's unique social and military structure. Herodotus mentions him as living about 900 BC, but later writers dated him to the early 8th century BC.

The limited and conflicting information about Lycurgus and the probability that the Spartan social system evolved gradually have led modern scholars to doubt his existence. If he was a real person, he was probably associated with the governmental and social reforms that followed the revolt of the enslaved population of Messenia in the mid–7th century BC.

Another Lycurgus, c.390–c.324 BC, was an Athenian orator and statesman in the period following Athens's defeat by Mac-edonia in the Battle of Chaeronea (338). He administered the state finances and an extensive building program.

Lydgate, John   [lid'-gayt]

John Lydgate, c.1370–c.1450, a monk of Bury Saint Edmunds, was the most prolific Middle English poet. Two of his best early works, *A Complaint of a Lover's Life* (c.1400) and *The Temple of Glass* (c.1403), closely imitate poems by Geoffrey Chaucer. Lydgate's later works include the encyclopedic *Troy Book* (1412–20) and *Fall of Princes* (c.1431–39).

DAVID YERKES

Bibliography: Ebin, Lois A., *John Lydgate* (1985); Pearsall, Derek, *John Lydgate* (1970).

Lydia   [lid'-ee-uh]

In ancient times Lydia was the name of a fertile and geologically wealthy region of western Anatolia. It extended from Caria on the south to Mysia on the north and was bounded by Phrygia on the east and by the Aegean on the west. Lydia first achieved prominence under the rule of the Mermnadae in the early 7th century BC. It is best known as the first ancient state to use coinage. In 547 BC, CROESUS, the powerful king of Lydia, was defeated by CYRUS THE GREAT of Persia; the Lydian capital SARDIS then became the seat of a Persian satrap (governor). Lydia absorbed and reflected both Oriental and Greek culture and interacted politically with Greek cities throughout the Persian period. The country passed to the Romans in 133 BC.

LOUIS L. ORLIN

lye: see CAUSTIC CHEMICALS.

Lyell, Sir Charles   [ly'-ul]

The British geologist Sir Charles Lyell, b. Nov. 14, 1797, d. Feb. 22, 1875, was the author of texts that were required reading in geology throughout the 19th century. The first volume (1830) of his *Principles of Geology* contained a vigorous indictment of catastrophism, the then-popular view that most of the Earth's history could be relegated to a short period of violent upheaval and flooding. Lyell argued instead that geological phenomena could be explained in terms of currently observed natural processes operating gradually over long periods of time, a concept termed UNIFORMITARIANISM. The second volume (1832) dealt with physical processes and introduced a number of new terms, including *metamorphic* to describe sedimentary rocks changed by high temperatures adjacent to igneous rocks. By the time the third volume—emphasizing stratigraphy and paleontology—appeared in 1833, second editions of the first two volumes had already been published. Lyell prepared many additional editions, the twelfth and last appearing in 1875.

Because of his success as an author, Lyell is sometimes classified as one who simply was facile in synthesizing the work of others. The criticism is without substance. The son of well-to-do Scottish parents, Lyell studied law at Oxford. His interest in geology was kindled by the lectures (1817) of William Buckland, one of the leading geologists of his day. Following his studies at Oxford his parents sent him on a tour of the continent. This journey was the first of several trips throughout Europe, occasions when he made many geologic observations. Later in his career he made several trips to the United States, again to observe geologic formations. These opportunities—especially at a time when the rocks in many parts of the world were first being described and classified—placed Lyell in a uniquely favorable position to assemble a unified view of Earth history.

Lyell was also a skilled zoologist. He drew on both geology and zoology in classifying the Tertiary rocks of northern Italy. Instead of relying on differences in rock types, as did most of his colleagues, he emphasized faunal distinctions. He sought to define "different tertiary formations in chronological order, by reference to the comparative proportion of living species of shells found fossil in each." The approach was unusually successful. He defined, from youngest to oldest, four periods,

Sir Charles Lyell, a British geologist, challenged the theory of catastrophism—the prevailing belief that geological conditions are largely shaped through sudden violent upheavals of the Earth. In his influential three-volume work, The Principles of Geology *(1830–33), Lyell argued that geological conditions are brought about gradually through ongoing processes, such as erosion and volcanism.*

now known as epochs: Newer Pliocene (subsequently renamed by him Pleistocene), Older Pliocene, Miocene, and Eocene. His nomenclature, with some modifications, is still used today.

Lyell's *Principles* was avidly read by Charles Darwin prior to the latter's voyage (1831–36) on the *Beagle.* Lyell's depiction of the vastness of geologic time undoubtedly established a frame of mind that prepared the way for Darwin's development of the theory of evolution. After Darwin's return he and Lyell became friends and were active correspondents. Lyell was instrumental in getting the ideas of Darwin and Alfred Russel Wallace published simultaneously. Ironically, Lyell himself was a late (although enthusiastic) convert to Darwin's ideas, primarily because he was troubled by Darwin's inability to describe the mechanism whereby progressive biologic change was accomplished.   THOMAS A. MUTCH

Bibliography: Bailey, Edward B., *Charles Lyell* (1962); Chorley, Richard J., et al., *The History of the Study of Landforms* (1964); Eiseley, Loren C., *Darwin's Century: Evolution and the Men Who Discovered It* (1958); Gillespie, Charles, *Genesis and Geology* (1951; repr. 1970); Lyell, Charles, *Life, Letters, and Journals of Sir Charles Lyell,* 2 vols., ed. by Katherine M. Lyell (1881; repr. 1983); North, F. J., *Charles Lyell* (1965); Wilson, Leonard G., *Charles Lyell: The Years to 1841* (1972) and, as ed., *Sir Charles Lyell's Scientific Journals on the Species Question* (1972).

Lyly, John   [lil'-ee]

John Lyly, c.1554–1606, was an English dramatist and the author of *Euphues, the Anatomy of Wit* (1578) and *Euphues and his England* (1580). These popular and influential romances created a fashion for elaborate, polished rhetoric (euphuism) and brought a new elegance to Elizabethan prose.

Lyly's comedies, like his prose works, are in the tradition of courtly, refined wit and based on classical mythology and legend. Shakespeare caricatured Lyly's artificial style in his early comedy *Love's Labour's Lost.*   ROBIN BUSS

Bibliography: Houppert, Joseph W., *John Lyly* (1975); Saccio, Peter, *The Court Comedies of John Lyly* (1969); Wilson, John Dover, *John Lyly* (1905; repr. 1969).

See also: ELIZABETHAN AGE.

Lyman, Theodore   [ly'-muhn]

The American experimental physicist Theodore Lyman, b. Brookline, Mass., Nov. 23, 1874, d. Oct. 11, 1954, investigated the far ultraviolet region of the electromagnetic spectrum. Lyman spent 6 years constructing a vacuum spectrometer for this work. In 1906 he obtained accurate measurements of lines below 2,000 angstroms (Å) and in 1917 he extended his ultraviolet research to 500 Å. He discovered (1914) a fundamental series of ultraviolet hydrogen lines, which were named in his honor. The discovery played a major role in supporting Niels Bohr's quantum theory of the atom.   RICHARD HIRSH

lyme disease

Lyme disease is a mild to serious bacterial disease that is transmitted by ticks. Since its first recognition in the northeastern United States (it is named for Lyme, Conn.), the disease is now known to occur in midwestern and western states as well as in many other countries. The tiny ticks, of genus *Ixodes,* infest animals such as white-footed mice and white-tailed deer. When a human is bitten by a tick, the minute spirochete *Borrelia burgdorferi* enters the bloodstream. Within a month a painless rash may appear, often accompanied by severe headaches, fatigue, chills, and fever. Severe inflammation of the heart muscle or nervous system may follow in the next few months, causing heart problems, meningitis, and severe migratory pains. In some cases, neither of these stages is observed. Within two years, however, arthritic attacks may develop that can become chronic if untreated. Scientists have recently found that humans may have a genetic predisposition that increases their susceptibility to chronic arthritis. Antibiotics used in the early stages of the disease are effective treatments.

Bibliography: Steere, Allen C., "Lyme Disease," *New England Journal of Medicine* 321, no. 9 (1989).

lymphatic system   [lim-fat'-ik]

The lymphatic system, composed of widely spread and structurally distinct tissues, provides vertebrates, including humans, with immune defenses, filters foreign substances and cell debris from blood and destroys them, and produces lymphocytes, which circulate in blood and lymph vessels.

The lymph vessels comprise a network of capillaries, which filter blood impurities; they contain a clear, colorless fluid (lymph). Lymph passes from capillaries to lymph vessels and flows through lymph nodes that are located along the course of these vessels. Cells of the lymph nodes phagocytize, or ingest, such impurities as bacteria, old red blood cells, and toxic and cellular waste. Finally, lymph flows into the thoracic duct, a large vessel that runs parallel to the spinal column, or into the right lymphatic duct, both of which transport the lymph back into veins of the shoulder areas.

Tissues of the lymphatic system include the spleen, thymus, bone marrow, and aggregates of lymphatic tissue located in the intestines, tonsils, and adenoids. The spleen, thymus, and bone marrow manufacture lymphocytes, which are the major cell type of the system. The spleen also is involved with destruction of old cells and other substances by phagocytosis, and plays a role in immune responses. The thymus, in humans, is considered the central organ that controls lymphocyte production and antibody formation. Lymphatic tissues of the intestines are known as lacteals—they absorb digested fat (lipids), which eventually are transported in the form of chyle to blood and finally to the liver. Lymph fluid from lacteals is milky white because of the fat globules that are present.

Lymph nodes are round and encapsulated, comprising an outer cortex and inner medulla. The cortex contains a dense mass of lymphocytes, and the medulla has lymphocytes and plasma cells that are arranged in cordlike structures. Lymph vessels that bring fluid into the node are called afferent vessels; efferent vessels drain the node. Nonencapsulated tissues, known as nodules, are located in the upper respiratory tract, intestines, urinary tract, and bone marrow.

The most common cell of the system is the lymphocyte. The majority of lymphocytes are small, mononuclear white cells. Lymphocytes can be classified as T cells (thymus-derived) or B cells (bone-marrow-derived). T cells are active in cell-mediated immunity and are responsible for delayed hypersensitivity reactions, rejection of tissue grafts, and rejection of antigenically altered tissue within the organism itself. B lymphocytes in humans are responsible for immunoglobulin secretion. Other cells include histiocytes, which are responsible for structural support of lymph tissue and for phagocytosis; monocytes, which are white blood cells that also function to ingest foreign substances; and plasma cells, which synthesize and release immunoglobulins.

Lymph, or lymphatic fluid, which transports nutrients to tissues and collects tissue wastes, is carried by the lymphatic system, a network of interconnecting vessels (1). The pressure of blood circulating through the capillaries (2) forces lymph out into tissue spaces (3). This fluid is collected by the lymphatic vessels and eventually returned to the bloodstream through ducts that empty into large veins near the collarbones (4). Lymph is moved by contractions of body muscles and of the vessels themselves, which have valves (5) to prevent backflow. Lymph nodes (6), which are distributed throughout the system, remove wastes and other particles and contain large concentrations of white blood cells, which attack invaders such as bacteria and viruses. The spleen (7), thymus (8), tonsils (9), and adenoids (10), all composed of lymphoid tissue, are also part of the immune system.

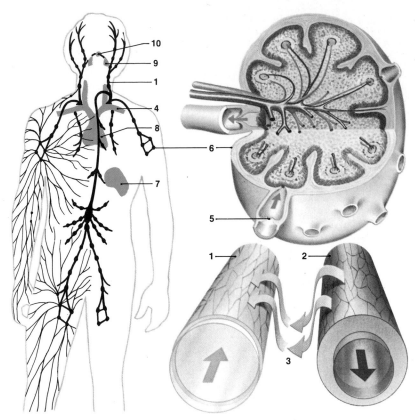

The lymphatic system can be affected by several disorders. Low white blood cell levels (LEUKOPENIA) and high white blood cell levels (LEUKEMIA) sometimes are disorders related to abnormal production of lymphocytes. Lymphedema, or obstruction of lymph circulation, can result from the presence of a tumor or an infection such as FILARIASIS. Degeneration of the lymph nodes, spleen, thymus, intestinal tissue, tonsils, and adenoids will impair the function of the lymphatic system and weaken the body's immune responses to infection. LYMPHOMAS, or cancers of the lymphatic system, include such disorders as HODGKIN'S DISEASE.

Bibliography: Battezati, Mario, *The Lymphatic System,* trans. by Vilfrido Cameron-Curry (1972); Foldi, Michael, *Diseases of Lymphatics and Lymph Circulation* (1969); Marchalonis, John J., ed., *The Lymphocyte: Structure and Function* (1977).

See also: BLOOD; CIRCULATORY SYSTEM; IMMUNITY (biology).

lymphocyte: see BLOOD; LYMPHATIC SYSTEM.

lymphoma   [lim-foh'-muh]

A lymphoma is a tumor of lymphatic tissue, which is the principal tissue in the lymph nodes, spleen, tonsils, and thymus gland. The benign or malignant tumor may involve any one of the various kinds of specialized cells of lymphatic tissue. The major sign of lymphoma is a painless enlargement of one or more lymph nodes. Patients may also experience fever, weight loss, nighttime sweating, liver and spleen enlargement, and gastrointestinal and kidney disturbances. One major type of lymphoma is HODGKIN'S DISEASE.

PETER L. PETRAKIS

Lynch, Benito

The Argentine writer Benito Lynch, b. 1885, d. Dec. 25, 1951, exalted rural life in his novels and short stories, contrasting it with life in the city. Two of his best novels are *Los caranchos de la Florida* (The Vultures of Florida Ranch, 1916) and *El inglés de les güesos* (The Englishman of the Bones, 1924).

JAIME ALAZRAKI

Lynch, Charles

Charles Lynch, b. 1736, d. Oct. 29, 1796, a patriot leader in Bedford County, Va., during the American Revolution, supposedly gave his name to the practice of LYNCHING. A colonel in the militia, he set up his own court to try and sentence Loyalists accused of aiding the British. Lynch did not execute people; his usual sentence was flogging.

Lynch, John

The Irish political leader John Mary "Jack" Lynch, b. Blackpool, Aug. 15, 1917, was prime minister of the Republic of Ireland from 1966 to 1973 and again from 1977 to 1979. Before entering the field of law in 1945, Lynch had been a famous hurling athlete. He was elected (1948) to the Dail (parliament) as a Fianna Fáil party member, became (1957) a minister for education in Eamon de Valera's cabinet, and later became (1959) minister for industry and commerce. Made minister of finance in 1965, he succeeded Sean Lemass as prime minister of Ireland in November 1966. Lynch led Ireland into the Common Market in 1973 and sought, without success, to play a peacemaking role in the sectarian conflict in Northern Ireland.

Lynchburg

Lynchburg (1980 pop., 65,743) is a city on the James River in the foothills of the Blue Ridge Mountains in central Virginia. Its economy is balanced between manufacturing (shoes, textiles, paper, and metal products) and agriculture (tobacco and grains). Several colleges are located in the city. Founded by Quakers in 1757, Lynchburg flourished economically after the completion of the Kanawha Canal (1840) and the arrival of the railroad (1850).

lynching

Lynching is the unlawful killing of a person by a mob, usually by hanging. The term is thought to have been derived from the activities of Charles LYNCH, a Virginia patriot in the American Revolution who tried and punished suspected Loyalists in his own court. Although forms of summary, extralegal justice have existed at some time in every country where conditions were unsettled and official justice distant or nonexistent, the practice of lynching in relatively recent times is most closely associated with the Southern United States, both before the Civil War, when abolitionists and others aiding escaped slaves were the most common victims, and beginning again during Reconstruction (1865–77), when the Ku Klux Klan and other white supremacist groups attempted to disenfranchise blacks through intimidation and violence. Victims were usually blacks accused of murdering or raping whites. Lynching was also a common form of frontier justice in the American West of the 19th century.

Lynching reached its peak in the South in the late 19th century and declined sharply after 1935. Increased news coverage and public awareness of lynching incidents, combined with progress in civil rights, may have ended the practice: there has been no reported case since the early 1960s.

Bibliography: Chadbourn, James H., *Lynching and the Law* (1933; repr. 1970); Grant, Donald L., *The Anti-Lynching Movement, 1883–1932* (1975); Hofstadter, Richard, and Wallace, Michael, eds., *American Violence: A Documentary History* (1971); Randel, William, *Ku Klux Klan* (1965); Raper, Arthur F., *The Tragedy of Lynching* (1933; repr. 1969).

Lynd, Robert S.

Robert Staughton Lynd, b. New Albany, Ind., Sept. 26, 1892, d. Nov. 1, 1970, was a sociologist who studied complex social organizations. He is best known for his careful analysis of daily life in middle America. Together with his wife, Helen Merrell Lynd, b. Mar. 17, 1894, d. June 30, 1982, he wrote *Middletown: A Study in Contemporary American Culture* (1929) and *Middletown in Transition: A Study in Cultural Conflicts* (1937). These classic works analyze how social change occurs in advanced industrialized society and provide a model of why modernization takes place. The Lynds' approach was the pragmatic application of traditional sociology to the problems of society, specifically, to a study of Muncie, Ind. ("Middletown"). Lynd was a professor of sociology at Columbia University from 1931 to 1960.

Lynen, Feodor   [lee'-nuhn, fay-oh'-dor]

The German biochemist Feodor Lynen, b. Apr. 6, 1911, d. Aug. 8, 1979, shared the 1964 Nobel Prize for physiology or medicine with Konrad Bloch for his research on the metabolic processes involved in the breakdown and synthesis of fatty acids and cholesterol. Lynen also helped discover the role of the vitamin biotin in lipid metabolism.

Lynn

Lynn is a city in northeastern Massachusetts, on Massachusetts Bay, about 18 km (11 mi) northeast of Boston. Its population is 78,471 (1980). Once an important shoe manufacturing center and site of the country's first ironworks (1643), it now supports a wide range of industries, producing electrical equipment, jet engines, and machinery. Lynn has more than 5 km (3 mi) of beaches and a 809-ha (2,000-acre) park, Lynn Woods. The town was the home of Mary Baker Eddy, founder of Christian Science.

Settled in 1629 as Saugus, it was laid out in 1631 and named for King's Lynn, England, in 1637. Shoemaking developed from 1635 as a cottage industry. In 1848 the first shoe-sewing machine was introduced, and the factory system of production began.

lynx   [links]

The lynx, *Felis lynx,* is a small member of the cat family, Felidae. It weighs up to 18 kg (40 lb), measures 1.1 m (3.5 ft) in length, and stands about 61 cm (24 in) high at the shoulder. It

The Spanish lynx, L. lynx pardina, a subspecies of the European lynx, is distinguished by its prominent spots. The lynx's large, padded paws and long legs enable it to move easily in snow and ice.

has black ear tufts and a stumpy tail. The lynx has a tawny or grayish brown coat with darker spots and stripes. Its winter coat, much prized by furriers, is dense, silky, and long. The lynx lives in forested areas of Europe, Asia, and northern North America. It usually hunts at night, killing foxes, rabbits, rodents, deer, and some domestic animals. It is a good climber and swimmer.   EVERETT SENTMAN

Lyon   [lee-ohn']

Located at the confluence of the Rhône and Saône rivers, about 274 km (170 mi) north of Marseille, Lyon (or Lyons) is the third largest city in France. The city has a population of 413,095; the population of the metropolitan area is 1,173,000 (1982).

Lyon is a significant inland port connected with Marseille by both canal and river. The city has long been famous as a silk manufacturing center, but today the textile industry consists mostly of spinning, weaving, and dyeing of artificial fibers. Chemical and charcoal manufacturing, food processing, and metallurgy are also leading industries. Warehouses and shipping facilities are located along the riverfront.

The University of Lyon (1896) and several museums and theaters are located in the city. Lyon is noted for its fine cuisine as well as for the locally produced Beaujolais and Mâconnais wines.

To the west, the city is dominated by the Fourvière Ridge, on which Notre Dame Basilica (built 1871–94) is located. Nearby are the Roman odeon and theater. The central business district is located on the peninsula formed by the juncture of the two rivers. The city is compartmentalized by its hills and the rivers, and auto traffic is disrupted by these features and by Lyon's many bridges.

Lyon originated as a fishing village during the Roman period and, as Lugdunum, became the capital of Gaul. After the introduction of Christianity into Gaul, Lyon became a major ecclesiastical center. The powerful archbishop of Lyon controlled the city until 1307; two important ecumenical councils were held in Lyon, in 1245 and 1274. Lyon was annexed to the French crown in 1312 and quickly began to prosper as a cultural and commercial center. By the 16th century it was an important silk manufacturing center. It suffered economically during the French Revolution and did not emerge as a prominent city again until the early 20th century. During World War II, Lyon was an anti-German resistance center and conse-

The oldest section of Lyon, a city in east central France, includes the medieval Cathedral of Saint Jean (foreground) and the Place Bellecour, between the Rhône and Saône rivers. Founded (43 BC) as a Roman colony, Lyon is a major French commercial center.

quently suffered much damage. It was freed from German control by the joint efforts of the resistance leaders and the French and U.S. armies in 1944.   LAWRENCE M. SOMMERS

Lyon, councils of

The councils of Lyon were two ecumenical councils (see COUNCIL, ECUMENICAL) of the Roman Catholic church. The First Council of Lyon (1245) was convened by Pope INNOCENT IV in the midst of his struggle with Holy Roman Emperor FREDERICK II over the control of Italy. Frederick was formally excommunicated and deposed. The council also attempted to assist the Christian forces fighting in the Holy Land and to organize a defense against the Mongol invasion of Europe.

The Second Council of Lyon (1274) was convoked by Pope Gregory X to bring about church reform, the launching of a new Crusade to the Holy Land, and union between the Eastern and Western churches. A tenuous reunion of the two churches was worked out with the Byzantine emperor Michael VIII, but it was never actually accepted by the Eastern clergy. Among the better-known participants in the council were ALBERTUS MAGNUS and Saint BONAVENTURE. Saint Thomas AQUINAS died on his way to the council.   T. TACKETT

Lyon, Mary   [ly'-uhn]

Mary Lyon, b. Feb. 28, 1797, d. Mar. 5, 1849, was an American educator and the founder (1836) of Mount Holyoke College, one of the first colleges for women. She served as president for nearly 12 years, guiding the institution to stability and prominence.

Bibliography: Gilchrist, Beth B., *The Life of Mary Lyon* (1910); Goodsell, Willystine, *Pioneers of Women's Education in the United States* (1931; repr. 1970); Lyon, Mary, *Mount Holyoke Female Seminary* (1903).

Lyon, Matthew

The Irish immigrant Matthew Lyon, b. July 14, 1750, d. Aug. 1, 1822, became prominent in Vermont and, later, Kentucky politics. After settling in Vermont he married (1771) Ethan Allen's niece and served with Allen during the American Revolution.

As a U.S. representative from Vermont (1797–1801), Lyon strongly opposed the policies of the Federalist party. In 1798 he was fined and sentenced to a 4-month prison term under the Sedition Act for criticizing President John Adams. Lyon later moved to Kentucky and represented that state in Congress (1803–11). In 1820 he went to Arkansas as U.S. agent to the Cherokee Indians.

Lyon, Nathaniel

Nathaniel Lyon, b. Ashford, Conn., July 14, 1818, d. Aug. 10, 1861, was a Union general in the U.S. Civil War. Assigned (March 1861) command of the Saint Louis arsenal, he successfully attacked Camp Jackson, where Missouri's secessionist governor, Claiborne F. Jackson, had garrisoned the state militia. In June 1861 the pro-Southern militia under Sterling PRICE was reinforced by Confederate troops from Arkansas. Lyon attacked them at Wilson's Creek on August 10 but was killed in the battle.

Bibliography: Adamson, Hans C., *Rebellion in Missouri* (1961).

Lyonnais   [lyoh-nay']

Lyonnais is a historic province in east central France, comprising the area of the modern departments of Rhône and Loire. Its chief cities are LYON, SAINT-ÉTIENNE, and Roanne. The land is used for grazing, and industries include the manufacture of textiles, perfume, chemicals, and steel.

Part of the Holy Roman Empire from 1032, it passed to France in 1307 and was enlarged in 1531 with the addition of Beaujolais and Forez. It became the department of Rhône-et-Loire in 1790 and was divided into two departments in 1793.

Lyons, Joseph Aloysius   [ly'-uhnz, al-oh-wish'-uhs]

Joseph Aloysius Lyons, b. Sept. 15, 1879, d. Apr. 7, 1939, was prime minister of Australia from 1931 to 1939. A school teacher, he entered the Tasmanian legislature in 1909, served as Tasmania's first Labor premier (1923–28), and was elected to the federal Parliament in 1929.

Lyons held office in the Labor government until 1931, when he broke away to form the more conservative United Australia party in coalition with former Nationalists. As prime minister he was able to restore some economic stability as the Depression of the 1930s began to wane. He also expanded Australia's forces in response to the threat of Japanese aggression. He died in office.

Lyons, Leonard

The American columnist Leonard Lyons, originally Leonard Sucher, b. New York City, Sept. 10, 1906, d. Oct. 7, 1976, wrote a popular Broadway column, the "Lyon's Den," for the *New York Post*. While in law school he began sending articles to columnist Walter Winchell, and in 1934 he was chosen over 500 other candidates to write for the *Post*. His lighthearted column retained its popularity throughout Lyons's career and was syndicated to newspapers with a total circulation of 15 million.   RICHARD HIXSON

Lyot, Bernard Ferdinand   [lyoh]

The French astronomer Bernard Lyot, b. Feb. 27, 1897, d. Apr. 2, 1952, was the inventor of the CORONAGRAPH (1930), which allows observations of the Sun's corona by producing an artificial solar eclipse. A graduate of the University of Paris, Lyot improved techniques for astronomical photography and for the detection of polarized light. The Lyot filter, which filters out all but the single wavelength of light to be studied, is named for him.   STEVEN J. DICK

Lyra   [ly'-ruh]

Lyra (the Harp) is a small but important northern constellation located between Hercules and Cygnus. Its brightest star, Vega (magnitude 0.04), is the fifth brightest in the heavens. Located 26 light-years from the Sun, Vega will be the pole star in about 12,000 years because of the precession of the Earth's axis. The second-brightest star, Sheliak (from the Arabic al-shalyaq, meaning "harp"), is an eclipsing binary. Another object in the constellation, Epsilon Lyrae, is resolvable, with keen eyesight or binoculars, into two stars; a telescope reveals that each of them in turn is double. Other important objects include the Ring Nebula in Lyra (M 57, or NGC 6720)—a planetary nebula shaped like an elliptical smoke ring—and the prototype RR LYRAE variable star.
CRAIG B. WAFF

lyre   [lire]

The Greek lyra, one of the two types of lyre played in ancient Greece, was an instrument of the amateur musician. Lighter than the kithara, it had a bowl-shaped resonator and seven strings and was generally used to accompany vocal music. Popular in the ancient Middle East and medieval Europe, the lyre is known' today in parts of East Africa and Siberia.

The lyre is a stringed instrument consisting of a resonance box or bowl with strings suspended from the base to a crossbar supported by two arms parallel to its surface. The earliest-known instruments were box lyres about three-and-a-half feet in length found in Sumerian civilization about 3000 BC. The instrument passed from that region in smaller forms to Israel within the second millennium BC, to Egypt in the New Kingdom (c.1500 BC), and to Greece, where Homer and other bards used it to accompany their epic poems.

The research of the musicologist Curt Sachs reveals a basic pentatonic (5-tone) tuning even when the number of strings had reached 11, as in the Greek kithara of the 5th century BC. A basic playing technique involved plucking the strings with a large plectrum while the fingers of the left hand damped unwanted strings. Another and more elaborate method involved the use of both plectrum and bare fingers. The lyre spread southward to Ethiopia and the headwaters of the Nile and Congo, where it is still played. It spread from Greece across Europe, changing construction in medieval times. A bowed instrument after 1000 BC, the lyre was ubiquitous during the Middle Ages and survived until recently in Wales, Estonia, and Finland.   ROBERT A. WARNER

Bibliography: Baines, Anthony, "Ancient and Folk Background," in Musical Instruments Through the Ages, ed. by Anthony Baines (1961); Marcuse, Sybil, Survey of Musical Instruments (1975); Sachs, Curt, History of Musical Instruments (1940).

lyrebird

Chickenlike birds of the forests of eastern Australia, lyrebirds constitute two species of large perching birds in the family Menuridae, order Passeriformes. Lyrebirds are splendid vocalists and mimics. Best known is the superb lyrebird, Menura superba, once hunted nearly to extinction.

The male possesses an ornate tail up to 60 cm (2 ft) long. There are 16 tail feathers: the 2 outer feathers form the shape of a Greek lyre when spread, whereas the 12 inner feathers are filamentous and the 2 innermost feathers wirelike. Males are polygamous and display from a small mound in a clearing, spreading the magnificent tail over the entire back and head as a lacy cloak. Females build the bulky nest and care for the single chick.   JOSEPH R. JEHL

lyric

A lyric (from the Greek lyrikos) was originally a song written for musical accompaniment by a lyre. The term now refers to poems that, although not necessarily intended to be sung, are melodious in meter and rhythm.

Lyrics tend to be subjective and emotional rather than intellectually complex and are generally written in the first person. The genres of elegy and ode are both lyrical in expression. The lyric is often distinguished from two other broad categories of poetry—the narrative and the dramatic—but both long narrative poems and verse plays frequently resort to the devices of lyricism.

Bibliography: Grierson, Herbert J. C., Lyrical Poetry of the Nineteenth Century (1929); Kinneavy, J. L., A Study of Three Contemporary Theories of Lyric Poetry (1957); Murray, Gilbert, The Classical Tradition in Poetry (1930).

Lyrical Ballads

The Lyrical Ballads (1798) is a volume of poetry by Samuel Taylor COLERIDGE and William WORDSWORTH. The contents include Wordsworth's LINES COMPOSED A FEW MILES ABOVE TINTERN ABBEY and Coleridge's RIME OF THE ANCIENT MARINER. The preface, which Wordsworth added to a second edition (1800), is regarded as the earliest and most important theoretical statement of the principles of the English romantic movement. In the preface Wordsworth rejected the artificial, consciously poetic diction of his predecessors and proposed to write in the "language really used by men," to illustrate "the primary laws of our nature" in the lives of humble, rustic people. His celebrated definition of poetry as "the spontaneous overflow of powerful feelings" is too personal to be inclusive, but it aptly describes the movingly introspective "Tintern Abbey."

Bibliography: Brett, R. L., and Jones, A. R., eds., Lyrical Ballads (1965); Owen, W. J. B., Wordsworth as Critic (1971).

Lys, Jan   [lees]

Jan Lys, or Johann Liss, b. c.1597, was a German baroque artist who infused new life into Venetian painting, then in decline. Living in Venice by 1621, he combined the exuberant, robust subjects of his Dutch teachers with the spirited brushwork and translucent color characteristic of Venetian artists, as in The Toilette of Venus (n.d.; private collection, Pommersfelden, West Germany). Eschewing the standard practice of drawing from antique statuary, Lys instead studied the 16th-century Venetian masters. He died of the plague in 1629 or 1630.   THOMAS W. SOKOLOWSKI

Bibliography: Cleveland Museum of Art catalog, Johann Liss (1975); Hempel, Eberhard, Baroque Art and Architecture in Central Europe (1965).

Lysander   [ly-san'-dur]

The Spartan general Lysander, d. 395 BC, was largely responsible for the ultimate Spartan victory in the PELOPONNESIAN

WAR. As admiral of the Peloponnesian fleet in 408–407 BC he improved its condition with the assistance of CYRUS THE YOUNGER, the Persian viceroy, who was placed in charge of Anatolia by his father, Darius II. Lysander won the important Battle of Notium (406), causing ALCIBIADES to leave Athenian service. In 405, Lysander crushed the Athenian fleet at Aegospotami (in the Hellespont). By blockading Athens he helped to establish the rule of the Thirty Tyrants after Athens capitulated.

Regarded at first as the savior of the Greeks, Lysander won their enmity and that of the Spartan authorities by arbitrarily arranging the governments of the cities that he had liberated from Athens.

After failing to make the Spartan kingship an elective monarchy Lysander made a bid for power by supporting (399) the succession of AGESILAUS II to a disputed kingship. Once he was in power, however, Agesilaus ignored Lysander. Lysander died in the Corinthian War.   CHARLES W. FORNARA

Bibliography: Ferguson, W. S., and Cary, M., *The Cambridge Ancient History,* vol. 5 (1953); Hammond, Nicholas G., *The History of Greece to 322 B.C.,* 2d ed. (1967); Plutarch, *Plutarch's Lives,* ed. and trans. by Bernadotte Perrin, 11 vols. (1914–26).

Lysenko, Trofim Denisovich   [lih-seng'-koh, truh-feem' duh-nees'-uh-vich]

Soviet agronomist Trofim Denisovich Lysenko, b. Sept. 29, 1898, d. Nov. 20, 1976, is best remembered not for any important scientific contributions but for his adverse influence over Soviet biological and agricultural research.

As a plant breeder, Lysenko believed that he could improve the spring wheat crop by vernalization—keeping the seeds cool and moist before sowing them. He came to support the Lamarckian theory that acquired characteristics can be inherited, and he rejected the widely accepted Mendelian theory of heredity.

Although Lysenko was opposed by many Soviet scientists, he was noticed and supported by Joseph Stalin. In 1940 he became director of the Institute of Genetics of the Soviet Academy of Sciences. Politically ambitious, he then banished many scientists and insisted that only his views be taught in the schools.

After Stalin's death, in 1953, Lysenko's career began to wane. In 1965, after the retirement of Nikita Khrushchev, Stalin's successor, Lysenko lost favor completely.

Bibliography: Huxley, Julian, *Soviet Genetics and World Science: Lysenko and the Meaning of Heredity* (1949); Joravsky, David, *The Lysenko Affair* (1970); Medvedev, Zhores A., *The Rise and Fall of T. D. Lysenko,* trans. by I. M. Lerner (1969).

Lysias   [lis'-ee-uhs]

Lysias, *c.*445–*c.*380 BC, was an ancient Greek orator, 34 of whose speeches survive. The most important is *Against Eratosthenes* (403 BC), written in prosecution of the man who had caused the execution of his brother; his most successful speeches, however, were those he wrote for clients to deliver in the Athenian law courts.

Lysias was especially successful at character portrayal and became the model of the "plain style" in the eyes of later students of rhetoric.   GEORGE KENNEDY

Bibliography: Dover, Kenneth J., *Lysias and the Corpus Lysiacum* (1968); Jebb, R. C., *The Attic Orators,* 2d ed. (1893); Kennedy, George, *The Art of Persuasion in Greece* (1963); Lysias, *Lysias,* trans. by W. R. Lamb (1943; repr. 1977).

Lysimachus, Macedonian King   [ly-sim'-uh-kuhs]

Lysimachus, *c.*360–281 BC, a senior Macedonian officer under ALEXANDER THE GREAT, was assigned rule over Thrace after Alexander's death in 323. He pacified the natives, then joined the alliance against ANTIGONUS I, and in 306–305 assumed the royal title.

After expanding his power to the north, Lysimachus took part in the final victory (301) over Antigonus and gained most

of Anatolia. In alliance with PYRRHUS of Epirus, he drove DEMETRIUS I POLIORCETES from Macedonia, then expelled Pyrrhus and won sole control of Macedonia and northern Greece. Lysimachus was weakened by court intrigues; he was attacked by SELEUCUS I NICATOR and died in battle.

E. BADIAN

Lysippus   [ly-sip'-uhs]

The career of the Greek sculptor Lysippus, who helped pave the way from pure classical to Hellenistic sculpture, spanned the latter half of the 4th century BC.

Lysippus was born in Sicyon, a city with a tradition of both painting and sculpture. He is said to have lived to an old age and to have made about 1,500 bronze statues of athletes, divinities, and notable personages, including Alexander the Great, who reportedly preferred him to all other sculptors. Of his works not a single known original remains, although some of Lysippus's athletes may be preserved in Roman marble copies. One such work in the Vatican museums is probably the *Apoxyomenos,* or *The Scraper,* a statue beloved by the emperor Tiberius. Another, the *Agias* in the Museum of Delphi, may be a contemporary replica. These statues, together with some comments by the Roman writer Pliny the Elder, suggest something of Lysippus's style, which introduced naturalism to the sculpture of his time.

Lysippus changed the system of proportions, elongating the body and reducing the size of the head to one-eighth the total height of the figure. More important, he departed from the principle of a uniform frontal plane for statuary, letting the limbs of his statues project in various directions, thus giving depth and a feeling of motion to his figures.

ANASTASIA DINSMOOR

Bibliography: Bieber, Margarette, *The Sculpture of the Hellenistic Age,* rev. ed. (1961); Johnson, F. P., *Lysippos* (1927; repr. 1968); Richter, G. M. A., *The Sculpture and Sculptors of the Greeks,* 4th ed. (1970); Robertson, C. M., *A History of Greek Art,* 2 vols. (1975).

See also: FARNESE HERACLES; GREEK ART.

Lysistrata   [lis-is-trah'-tuh]

Lysistrata, an antiwar play by the Greek comic dramatist ARISTOPHANES, is built around the idea that the women of Greece can put an end to the Peloponnesian War if they but deny the men fighting it their sexual favors. In the play, first performed in 411 BC, when Greece was torn by civil war, the women, led by the proud Lysistrata, unite in chastity against their husbands and lovers until the love-starved men succumb and peace is restored.

The plot of *Lysistrata* is simple, the language ribald, and the situations often hilarious, yet it has remained a powerful statement against war through the ages. In modern times it is an often-revived favorite with antiwar and feminist groups.

JAMES J. WILHELM

Bibliography: Lord, Louis E., *Aristophanes: His Plays and His Influence* (1930); Murray, Gilbert, *Aristophanes: A Study* (1933; repr. 1964).

lysosome   [lis'-uh-sohm]

The lysosome is an intracellular organelle consisting of a membrane-enclosed sac containing ENZYMES, such as lysozymes, that catalyze the digestion of most substances in living cells, including proteins, nucleic acids, some carbohydrates, and possibly fats. Disruption of the lysosomal membrane and release of the enzymes results in rapid digestion and dissolution of the cell. Lysosomes normally digest food stored in the cell or break down foreign particles engulfed by white blood cells (phagocytes). They also destroy aged cells and dissolve the structures surrounding the egg cell during the act of fertilization by sperm.

Lytton, Edward Robert Bulwer-Lytton, 1st Earl of: see BULWER-LYTTON, EDWARD ROBERT, 1ST EARL OF LYTTON.

"K,L"

INDEX

Key to Index Use

K

Finland 8:98
Ural-Altaic languages 19:475
KAREN (people) 12:27
KARĘN LANGUAGES
Sino-Tibetan languages 17:324
Southeast Asian languages 18:110–
111
KARENGA, M. RON
Kwanzaa 12:142
KARHULA (Finland)
map (60° 31′N 26° 57′E) 8:95
KARIBA (Zimbabwe)
map (16° 30′S 28° 45′E) 20:365
KARIBA, LAKE
map (17° 0′S 28° 0′E) 20:365
KARIBA DAM 1:143 illus.; 20:354
illus.
KARIMATA STRAIT
map (2° 5′S 108° 40′E) 11:147
KARIMGANJ (Bangladesh)
map (24° 52′N 92° 22′E) 3:64
KARINSKA, BARBARA 12:27 bibliog.
KARINTHY, FRIGYES
Hungarian literature 10:306
KARISIMBI, MOUNT
map (1° 30′S 29° 27′E) 16:378
KARL-MARX-STADT (East Germany)
12:27
cities
Zwickau 20:384
map (50° 50′N 12° 55′E) 9:140
KARLFELDT, ERIK AXEL 12:27
KARLOFF, BORIS 12:28 bibliog.
KARLOVAC (Yugoslavia)
map (45° 29′N 15° 34′E) 20:340
KARLOVY VARY (Czechoslovakia)
12:28
Carlsbad Decrees 4:152
map (50° 11′N 12° 52′E) 5:414
KARLOWITZ, TREATY OF
Köprülü (family) 12:110
Russo-Turkish Wars 16:374
KARLSEFNI, THORFINN see
THORFINN KARLSEFNI
KARLSKIRCHE
Fischer von Erlach, Johann Bernhard
8:111
KARLSKOGA (Sweden)
map (59° 20′N 14° 31′E) 18:382
KARLSKRONA (Sweden)
map (56° 10′N 15° 35′E) 18:382
KARLSRUHE (West Germany) 12:28
map (49° 3′N 8° 24′E) 9:140
KARLSTAD (Minnesota)
map (48° 35′N 96° 31′W) 13:453
KARLSTAD (Sweden)
map (59° 22′N 13° 30′E) 18:382
KARLSTADT 12:28 bibliog.
KARLUK
Turks 19:347
KARMA 12:28
Buddhism 3:539
Hinduism 10:170
sin 17:317
transmigration of souls 19:274
KARMAL, BABRAK 12:28
Afghanistan 1:135
KÁRMÁN, THEODORE VON 12:28
bibliog.
KARMEL, MOUNT
map (32° 44′N 35° 2′E) 11:302
KARNAK (Egypt) 12:28 bibliog.
Khons, Temple of 2:130 illus.;
19:95 illus.
Luxor 12:473
temple 19:94–95
Thebes 19:155
KARNAK (Illinois)
map (37° 18′N 88° 58′W) 11:42
KARNAPHULI RESERVOIR
map (22° 42′N 92° 12′E) 3:64
KARNATAKA (India) 12:28–29 bibliog.
cities
Bangalore 3:63
Mysore 13:692
map (14° 0′N 76° 0′E) 11:80
Tippu Sultan, Sultan of Mysore
19:207
KARNES (county in Texas)
map (28° 52′N 97° 53′W) 19:129
KARNES CITY (Texas)
map (28° 53′N 97° 54′W) 19:129
KAROK (American Indians)
Yurok 20:347
KARPATHOS (Greece)
Dodecanese 6:212
map (35° 40′N 27° 10′E) 9:325
KÁRPATHOS STRAIT
map (35° 50′N 27° 30′E) 9:325
KARPOV, ANATOLY 12:29 bibliog.
KARRE MOUNTAINS
map (6° 33′N 15° 40′E) 4:251
KARRER, PAUL 12:29
KARS (Turkey)
map (40° 36′N 43° 5′E) 19:343

KARSAVINA, TAMARA PLATONOVNA
12:29 bibliog.
Ballets Russes de Serge Diaghilev
3:48
KARSH, YOUSEF 12:29 illus.
Sir Winston Churchill 4:426 illus.
KARST TOPOGRAPHY
cave 4:222
China 4:361 illus.
KARTALA MOUNTAIN
map (11° 45′S 43° 22′E) 5:153
KARTHAUS (Pennsylvania)
map (41° 7′N 78° 7′W) 15:147
KASAAN (Alaska)
map (55° 32′N 132° 24′W) 1:242
KASAI RIVER
map (3° 6′S 16° 57′E) 20:350
KASAR AL KABIR (Morocco)
map (35° 1′N 5° 54′W) 13:585
KASAVUBU, JOSEPH 12:29 bibliog.
Africa, history of 1:160
Mobutu Sese Seko 13:488
KASDAN, LAWRENCE 8:89 illus.
KÄSEBIER, GERTRUDE 12:29 bibliog.
KASHAN (Iran)
map (33° 59′N 51° 29′E) 11:250
KASHEGELOK (Alaska)
map (60° 50′N 157° 50′W) 1:242
KASHGAR (China) 12:29
climate 4:364 table
map (39° 29′N 75° 59′E) 4:362
KASHI (China) see KASHGAR (China)
KASHMIR (India) 12:29–30 map
cities
Srinagar 18:207
India-Pakistan Wars 11:93
Indo-Iranian languages 11:145
map (34° 0′N 76° 0′E) 11:80
KASHUBIAN LANGUAGE 17:357
KASILOF (Alaska)
map (60° 23′N 151° 18′W) 1:242
KASKASKIA
Illinois (American Indians) 11:45
KASKASKIA RIVER
map (37° 59′N 89° 56′W) 11:42
KASOS STRAIT
map (35° 30′N 26° 30′E) 9:325
KASPAROV, GARY 12:30
KASPROWICZ, JAN
Polish literature 15:398
KASSALA (Sudan)
map (15° 28′N 36° 24′E) 18:320
KASSEBAUM, NANCY LANDON
12:184
KASSEL (Germany) 12:30
map (51° 19′N 9° 29′E) 9:140
KASSFM, ABDUL KARIM
Iraq 11:256
KASSITES 12:30 bibliog.
Mesopotamia 13:318
KASTLER, ALFRED 12:30
KASTRIOTI, GEORGE see
SKANDERBEG
KATA
martial arts 13:177–178
KATABATIC WIND see MOUNTAIN
AND VALLEY WINDS
KATAHDIN, MOUNT
map (45° 55′N 68° 55′W) 13:70
KATANGA (Belgian Congo) see SHABA
(Zaire)
KATANGA PLATEAU
map (10° 0′S 26° 0′W) 20:350
KATAYEV, VALENTIN PETROVICH
12:30
KATERINA, MOUNT
map (28° 31′N 33° 57′E) 7:76
KATERÍNI (Greece)
map (40° 16′N 22° 30′E) 9:325
KATHMANDU (Nepal) see KATMANDU
(Nepal)
KATIOLA (Ivory Coast)
map (8° 8′N 5° 6′W) 11:335
KATMAI, MOUNT 12:30
map (58° 17′N 154° 56′W) 1:242
national parks 14:38–39 map, table
Valley of Ten Thousand Smokes
19:508
KATMANDU (Nepal) 12:30–31
climate 14:87 table
map (27° 43′N 85° 19′E) 14:86
KATO KOMEI see KATO TAKAAKI
KATO TAKAAKI 12:31
KATOWICE (Poland) 12:31
map (50° 16′N 19° 0′E) 15:388
KATRINEHOLM (Sweden)
map (59° 0′N 16° 12′E) 18:382
KATSINA ALA RIVER
map (7° 48′N 8° 52′E) 14:190
KATSOYANNIS, MICHAEL
insulin 11:198
KATSUKAWA SHUNRO see HOKUSAI
KATSURA TARO 12:31
KATSUSHIKA HOKUSAI see HOKUSAI

KATTEGAT 12:31
map (57° 0′N 11° 0′E) 6:109
KATTWINKEL, WILHELM
Olduvai Gorge 14:376
KATWIJK AAN ZEE (Netherlands)
map (52° 13′N 4° 24′E) 14:99
KATYDID 11:192 illus.; 12:31 illus.
grasshopper 9:298–299
KATZ, SIR BERNARD 12:31
KATZ v. UNITED STATES
privacy, invasion of 15:556
wiretapping 20:183
KATZENJAMMER KIDS, THE 5:135 illus.
Dirks, Rudolph 6:188
KAU DESERT
map (19° 21′N 155° 19′W) 10:72
KAUAI (Hawaii)
Hawaii (state) 10:73; 10:75 illus.
map (22° 0′N 159° 30′W) 10:72
KAUAI CHANNEL
map (21° 45′N 158° 50′W) 10:72
KAUFBEUREN (Germany, East and
West)
map (47° 53′N 10° 37′E) 9:140
KAUFFMANN, ANGELICA 12:31
bibliog.
KAUFMAN (Texas)
map (32° 35′N 96° 19′W) 19:129
KAUFMAN (county in Texas)
map (32° 38′N 96° 18′W) 19:129
KAUFMAN, DENIS see VERTOV,
DZIGA
KAUFMAN, GEORGE S. 12:31–32
bibliog.; illus.
Connelly, Marc 5:197
Ferber, Edna 8:52
KAUIKEOULI see KAMEHAMEHA
(dynasty)
KAUKAUNA (Wisconsin)
map (44° 17′N 88° 17′W) 20:185
KAUKAUVELD (plateau)
map (20° 0′S 20° 30′E) 14:11
KAUMAKANI (Hawaii)
map (21° 6′N 157° 2′W) 10:72
KAUMALAPAU (Hawaii)
map (20° 47′N 156° 59′W) 10:72
KAUNAKAKAI (Hawaii)
map (21° 6′N 157° 1′W) 10:72
KAUNAS (USSR) 12:32
KAUNDA, KENNETH D. 12:32 bibliog.
KAURA NAMODA (Nigeria)
map (12° 35′N 6° 35′E) 14:190
KAURI PINE 12:32
Lacandón 12:158
KAUTSKY, KARL JOHANN 12:32
bibliog.
socialism 18:21
KAVAD, KING OF PERSIA 15:183
KAVAJË (Albania)
map (41° 11′N 19° 33′E) 1:250
KAVALA (Greece)
map (40° 56′N 24° 25′E) 9:325
KAVARRATI
Laccadive Islands (India) 12:158
KAVIENG (Papua New Guinea)
map (2° 35′S 150° 50′E) 15:72
KAVIR DESERT
map (34° 40′N 54° 30′E) 11:250
KAVIRONDO see LUO
KAW (American Indians) see KANSA
(American Indians)
KAW (French Guiana)
map (4° 29′N 52° 2′W) 8:311
KAW (Oklahoma)
map (36° 46′N 96° 50′W) 14:368
KAWABATA YASUNARI 12:32 bibliog.
KAWAIKINI (peak)
map (22° 5′N 159° 29′W) 10:72
KAWASAKI (Japan) 12:32
map (35° 32′N 139° 43′E) 11:361
KAWASAKI DISEASE 12:32
KAWATAKE MOKUAMI
Kabuki 12:4
KAWM UMBU (Egypt) see OMBOS
KAY (county in Oklahoma)
map (36° 50′N 97° 10′W) 14:368
KAY, CONNIE
Modern Jazz Quartet 13:498
KAY, JOHN 12:32–33
flying shuttle 20:84 illus.
KAY, MARSHALL
paleogeography 15:36
KAYAK 4:113 illus.
Eskimo 7:240
KAYAKING see CANOEING AND
KAYAKING
KAYE, DANNY 12:33 bibliog.
KAYE, NORA
American Ballet Theatre 1:337
KAYENTA (Arizona)
map (36° 42′N 110° 16′W) 2:160
KAYES (Mali)
map (14° 27′N 11° 26′W) 13:89
KAYSERI (Turkey)
map (38° 43′N 35° 30′E) 19:343

KAZAKH 12:33 bibliog.
KAZAKH SOVIET SOCIALIST REPUBLIC
(USSR) 12:33 bibliog.
cities
Alma-Ata 1:305
Kara Kum 12:26
people
Kazakh 12:33
KAZAKH STEPPE
map (49° 0′N 72° 0′E) 19:388
KAZAKHSTAN see KAZAKH SOVIET
SOCIALIST REPUBLIC (USSR)
KAZAKHSTANIA (ancient landmass)
plate tectonics 15:354 map
KAZAKOV, MATVEI
Russian art and architecture 16:362
KAZAN (USSR) 12:33
map (55° 49′N 49° 8′E) 19:388
KAZAN, ELIA 12:33–34 bibliog.
Actors Studio 1:90
KAZANLUK (Bulgaria)
map (42° 37′N 25° 24′E) 3:555
KAZANTZAKIS, NIKOS 12:34 bibliog.,
illus.
KAZBEK, MOUNT
map (42° 42′N 44° 31′E) 4:218
KAZERUN (Iran)
map (29° 37′N 51° 38′E) 11:250
KAZIN, ALFRED 11:34
KDKA (radio station) 16:54
KEA 12:34
KEAAU (Hawaii)
map (19° 37′N 155° 2′W) 10:72
KEAHOLE POINT
map (19° 44′N 156° 3′W) 10:72
KEAMS CANYON (Arizona)
map (35° 49′N 110° 12′W) 2:160
KEAN (family) 12:34–35 bibliog., illus.
KEAN, CHARLES
Kean (family) 12:34–35
theater, history of the 19:149
KEAN, EDMUND
Kean (family) 12:34 illus.
KEANSBURG (New Jersey)
map (40° 27′N 74° 8′W) 14:129
KEARNEY (Missouri)
map (39° 22′N 94° 22′W) 13:476
KEARNEY (Nebraska)
map (40° 42′N 99° 5′W) 14:70
KEARNEY (county in Nebraska)
map (40° 30′N 98° 50′W) 14:70
KEARNS (Utah)
map (40° 39′N 111° 59′W) 19:492
KEARNY (Arizona)
map (33° 3′N 110° 55′W) 2:160
KEARNY (county in Kansas)
map (38° 0′N 101° 20′W) 12:18
KEARNY (New Jersey)
map (40° 46′N 74° 9′W) 14:129
KEARNY, PHILIP 12:35 bibliog.
KEARNY, STEPHEN WATTS 12:35
bibliog.
Mexican War 13:352 map; 13:354–
355
Santa Fe (New Mexico) 17:68
KEARSARGE (ship) 5:32 illus.
Winslow, John Ancrum 20:180
KEATING, GEOFFREY
Irish literature 11:268
KEATON, BUSTER 12:35 bibliog., illus.
film, history of 8:82–83
KEATON, DIANE 12:35
KEATS, JOHN 7:198 illus.; 12:35–36
bibliog., illus.
Adonais 1:107
Endymion 7:171
Hunt, Holman 10:311
KEBAN, LAKE
map (38° 50′N 39° 15′E) 19:343
KEBLE, JOHN 12:36 bibliog.
Oxford movement 14:475
KEBLE COLLEGE (Oxford University)
14:474
Butterfield, William 3:593
KEBNE, MOUNT
map (67° 53′N 18° 33′E) 18:382
KECHI (Kansas)
map (37° 48′N 97° 17′W) 12:18
KECK TELESCOPE 19:84 illus.
KECSKEMÉT (Hungary)
map (46° 54′N 19° 42′E) 10:307
KEDAH, TELL EL- see HAZOR (Israel)
KEDGWICK (New Brunswick)
map (47° 39′N 67° 21′W) 14:117
KEDIRI (Indonesia)
map (7° 49′S 112° 1′E) 11:147
KEELE PEAK
map (63° 26′N 130° 19′W) 20:345
KEELER, CHRISTINE
Profumo scandal 15:562
KEELER, JAMES E.
extragalactic systems 7:343
KEELER, LEONARDE
lie detector 12:323

luster

Luster is the appearance of a mineral's surface in reflected light. Minerals such as pyrite and galena have a metallic luster; such minerals are frequently dark and opaque, even on thin edges. Light-colored minerals have various nonmetallic lusters: adamantine or brilliant (diamond), greasy (nepheline), resinous (sphalerite), silky (asbestos minerals), pearly (the micas), and vitreous, or glassy (quartz).

lusterware: see POTTERY AND PORCELAIN.

lute

A small, 16th-century lute with 12 strings has intricate inlay work on its back. Lutes were popular instruments in Renaissance Europe.

Lute, a generic name for stringed instruments composed of a body and of a neck that serves as a handle and holds strings stretched across the instrument, is also the specific name of the European short-necked instrument of the Renaissance, for which a vast and significant musical literature was composed in the 16th and 17th centuries. Appearing early in antiquity, the lute had little impact on Europe until the late Middle Ages. By 1500 the classic lute was formed with six courses of strings stretching over a fretted fingerboard from the holder glued to the belly of its light, pear-shaped, paneled body, across the beautifully carved rose and the broad neck to a pegbox tilted back at a sharp angle. About 1600, in order to adapt to new musical styles, an enlarged compass was obtained by additional low strings, usually unstopped and suspended from a separate and higher pegbox (*theorbo* and *chittarone*), and tunings were often altered. By the end of the baroque period (about 1750), the lute was largely abandoned.

The sheer loveliness of the instrument's appearance inspired the finest art of builders, performer-composers, and painters. Few unaltered instruments remain, but many printed volumes of lute TABLATURE testify to the lute's popularity and the high level of skill demanded of its performers. The recent revival of old music has produced many fine modern makers and players. The delicacy and finely shaded tone of the lute make it essentially an instrument for intimate performance.

ROBERT A. WARNER

Bibliography: Birch, Albert, "The Lute," in *Musical Instruments Through the Ages,* ed. by Anthony Baines (1961); *The Lute Society Journal* (1959–); Panum, Hortense, *The Stringed Instruments of the Middle Ages,* rev. and ed. by Jeffrey Pulver (1939; repr. 1970); Marcuse, Sybil, *Survey of Musical Instruments* (1975); Sachs, Curt, *History of Musical Instruments* (1940).

luteinizing hormone: see GONADOTROPHIN; HORMONES; PITUITARY GLAND.

lutetium   [loo-tee'-shee-uhm]

Lutetium is a chemical element, a silvery white metal of the LANTHANIDE SERIES. Its symbol is Lu, its atomic number 71, and its atomic weight 174.97 (the average weight of the two natu-ral isotopes, ^{175}Lu and ^{176}Lu. ^{176}Lu is radioactive, with a half-life of 2.2×10^{10} years. Lutetium was discovered in 1907 by Georges Urbain, who called it Lutetia after the ancient Roman name for Paris.

Luther, Martin

Martin Luther was a German theologian and a major leader of the Protestant REFORMATION. He is sometimes called the father of Protestantism, and one of the major branches of Protestantism—Lutheranism—is named after him.

Early Life. Luther, the son of a Saxon miner, was born at Eisleben on Nov. 10, 1483. He entered the University of Erfurt when he was 18 years old. After graduation he began to study law in 1505. In July of that year, however, he narrowly escaped death in a thunderstorm and vowed to become a monk. He entered the monastery of the Augustinian Hermits at Erfurt, where he was ordained in 1507. The following year he was sent to Wittenberg, where he continued his studies and lectured in moral philosophy. In 1511 he received his doctorate in theology and an appointment as professor of Scripture, which he held for the rest of his life. Luther visited Rome in 1510 on business for his order and was shocked to find corruption in high ecclesiastical places.

He was well acquainted with the scholastic theology of his day, but he made the study of the Bible, especially the epistles of Saint Paul, the center of his work. Luther found that his teachings diverged increasingly from the traditional beliefs of the Roman church. His studies had led him to the conclusion that Christ was the sole mediator between God and man and that forgiveness of sin and salvation are effected by God's GRACE alone and are received by faith alone on the part of man. This point of view turned him against scholastic theology, which had emphasized man's role in his own salvation, and against many church practices that emphasized justification by good works. His approach to theology soon led to a clash between Luther and church officials, precipitating the dramatic events of the Reformation.

Dispute over Indulgences. The doctrine of INDULGENCES, with its mechanical view of sin and repentance, aroused Luther's indignation. The sale by the church of indulgences—the remission of temporal punishments for sins committed and confessed to a priest—brought in much revenue. The archbishop of Mainz, Albert of Brandenburg, sponsored such a sale in 1517 to pay the pope for his appointment to Mainz and for the construction of Saint Peter's in Rome. He selected Johann TETZEL, a Dominican friar, to preach the indulgences and collect the revenues. When Tetzel arrived in Saxony, Luther posted his famous 95 theses on the door of the castle church at Wittenberg on Oct. 31, 1517. Although some of the

Martin Luther, whose 95 theses of 1517 catalyzed the events of the Protestant Reformation, intended to provoke reform within the Catholic church when he nailed his assertions to the Wittenberg church door. Driven by a restless mind and conscience, Luther engaged in an intense internal struggle before making salvation by faith alone the central tenet of his doctrine.

candlepower 4:107
measurement 13:255
Purkinje, Jan Evangelista 15:630
interference (physics) 11:207–209
lens 12:285–286
lumen 12:458
luminescence 12:458
measurement 13:255
angstrom 2:7
diffraction grating 6:169–170
Fitzgerald-Lorentz contraction 8:131
fluorometer 8:188
footcandle 12:339
photometer 15:273–274
Newton, Sir Isaac 14:173–174
optical computing 5:160g
optics 14:409–413 illus.
phosphor 15:256
phosphorescence 15:256
photochemistry 15:257–259
photoelectric cell 15:259–260
photoelectric effect 15:260
photography 15:261–265
photometry, astronomical 15:274
photon 15:274
phototaxis
taxis 19:48
physics, history of 15:284–285
polarized light 15:394–395
optical mineralogy 14:409 illus.
prism (physics) 15:553–554 illus.
production 12:334–335
incandescent lamp 11:73
quantum mechanics 16:9–11 illus.
reduction
extinction 7:340
reflection 16:119
luster, mineral 12:468
parabola 15:74
refraction 16:123–124
atmospheric refraction 2:304
rainbow 16:77 illus.
Rømer, Ole 16:304–305
scattering
liquid crystal 12:365
Tyndall, John 19:363
semaphore 17:194–195
sky 17:346
sources 12:334–335
magnesium 13:54
tritium 19:303
spectroscope 18:169 illus.
spectrum 18:172–173 illus.
speed 12:335 illus.
Einstein, Albert 7:93
Michelson, Albert Abraham 13:375–376
stroboscope 18:301
transformation
absorption, light 1:63
trapping
photosynthesis 15:276–277
tropism 19:309–310 illus.
twilight 19:360
ultraviolet light 19:379
velocity
atomic constants 2:311 table
wave theory 12:334 illus.
Arago, François 2:107
Euler, Leonhard 7:264–265
Huygens, Christiaan 10:325
Huygens's principle 10:325–326
X rays 20:309–311
zodiacal light 20:371
LIGHT AMPLIFICATION BY STIMULATED EMISSION OF RADIATION see LASER
LIGHT-EMITTING DIODE (LED)
diode 6:183
rectifier 16:183
semiconductor 17:197
LIGHT IN AUGUST (book)
Faulkner, William 8:36
LIGHT HORSE HARRY see LEE, HENRY "LIGHT HORSE HARRY"
LIGHT HORSES 10:243 illus.; 12:336
horse 10:244
LIGHT METER see ACTINOMETER
LIGHT PEN (computer term) 5:160h
LIGHT RAPID TRANSIT see STREETCAR
LIGHT-WATER REACTOR 14:281; 14:284
LIGHT-YEAR 12:336
LIGHTFOOT, JOSEPH BARBER
prehistory 15:517
LIGHTHOUSE 12:336–337 bibliog., illus.
Barnegat Lighthouse 14:128 illus.
Cape Hatteras 14:245 illus.
Eddystone Lighthouse
Smeaton, John 17:365
illumination
Fresnel, Augustin Jean 8:328

Montauk Point (New York) 14:152 illus.
Nubble Lighthouse (Maine) 19:417 illus.
Pharos of Alexandria 17:218 illus.
LIGHTING, CINEMATOGRAPHIC 4:433
LIGHTING, PHOTOGRAPHIC 15:262–264 illus.
LIGHTING, STAGE see STAGE LIGHTING
LIGHTING DEVICES 12:337–339 bibliog., illus.
black light, scheelite 17:118
candle 4:107
chandelier 4:279
coal gas
Murdock, William 13:648
Farmer, Moses 8:24
fluorescent light 8:186–187
houseplants 10:276
incandescent lamp 11:73
krypton 12:133
lamp 12:175–176
lighthouse 12:336–337
limelight
Drummond, Thomas 6:282
neon 14:85
searchlight 17:175
stage lighting 18:210
stroboscope 18:301
technology, history of 19:67 illus.
Tiffany lamp 2:211 illus.; 9:204 illus.; 19:196 illus.
Welsbach, Carl Auer, Baron von 20:101
LIGHTNING 12:339–340 bibliog., illus.
ball lightning 12:340
cause 12:339
death and injury, U.S. 12:339
discharge, electrical 6:189
electricity 7:107–109 illus.
forest fires 12:340
formation 12:339–340
Franklin, Benjamin 8:283
lightning rods 12:340
shock wave 17:279
static electricity 18:234
thunderstorms 12:339
weather modification 20:80
whistler 20:134
LIGHTNING BUG see FIREFLY
LIGHTNING ROD
Franklin, Benjamin 8:283
lightning 12:340
LIGHTSHIP see LIGHTHOUSE
LIGNIN 12:340 bibliog.
white rot fungus 20:138
LIGNITE 12:340
coal and coal mining 5:76; 5:77 map
sedimentary rock 17:185
LIGNITE (North Dakota)
map (48° 53′N 102° 34′W) 14:248
LIGONIER (Indiana)
map (41° 28′N 85° 35′W) 11:111
LIGONIER (Pennsylvania)
map (40° 15′N 79° 14′W) 15:147
LIGURIA (Italy) 12:340
cities
Genoa 9:96a illus.
La Spezia 12:149–150
LIGURIAN SEA
map (43° 30′N 9° 0′E) 11:321
LIHOLINO, ALEXANDER see KAMEHAMEHA (dynasty)
LIHUE (Hawaii)
map (21° 59′N 159° 22′W) 10:72
LIJ YASU
Haile Selassie, Emperor 10:13
LIK RIVER
map (18° 31′N 102° 31′E) 12:203
LIKASI (Zaire)
map (10° 59′S 26° 44′E) 20:350
LIKOUALA RIVER
map (1° 13′S 16° 48′E) 5:182
LIKUD (political party)
Begin, Menachem 3:168
Israel 11:306
LI'L ABNER (comic strip)
Capp, Al 4:127
LILAC 8:170 illus.; 12:340 illus.
LILBOURN (Missouri)
map (36° 35′N 89° 37′W) 13:476
LILBURNE, JOHN
Levellers 12:302
LILIENTHAL, DAVID 12:340–341 bibliog.
LILIENTHAL, OTTO 1:211 illus.; 12:341 bibliog.
glider 9:208
LILIOM (play)
Molnár, Ferenc 13:512
LILITH 12:341

LILIUOKALANI, QUEEN OF HAWAII 12:341 bibliog.
LILLE (France) 12:341
map (50° 38′N 3° 4′E) 8:260
LILLINGTON (North Carolina)
map (35° 24′N 78° 49′W) 14:242
LILLO, GEORGE 12:341
LILLOOET (British Columbia)
map (50° 42′N 121° 56′W) 3:491
LILLOOET RIVER
map (49° 45′N 122° 8′W) 3:491
LILONGWE (Malawi) 12:341
map (13° 59′S 33° 44′E) 13:81
LILY (botany) 8:170 illus.; 12:341–342 bibliog., illus.
adder's-tongue 1:99
aloe 1:307
Amaryllis 1:322
asparagus fern 2:261–262
aspidistra 2:262
bear grass 3:141–142
carrion flower 4:168
fritillary 8:335
grape hyacinth 9:290
grass tree 9:298
greenbrier 9:350
lily of the valley 12:342
meadow saffron 13:252
sarsaparilla 17:79
sego lily 17:188
Solomon's seal 18:57
spikenard 18:183
squill 18:204
star-of-Bethlehem 18:226
Sternbergia 18:261
tulip 19:330
water lily 20:49
LILY (periodical)
Bloomer, Amelia Jenks 3:340
LILY-OF-THE-FIELD see STERNBERGIA
LILY PAD see WATER LILY
LILY OF THE VALLEY 12:342 illus.
LIM BAY CHANNEL
map (56° 55′N 9° 10′E) 6:109
LIMA (Montana)
map (44° 38′N 112° 36′W) 13:547
LIMA (Ohio)
map (40° 46′N 84° 6′W) 14:357
LIMA (Peru) 12:342 illus.; 15:192 illus.
climate 15:193 table
Latin American art and architecture 12:224 illus.
map (12° 3′S 77° 3′W) 15:193
Pizarro, Francisco 15:324
LIMA, ALMEIDA
schizophrenia 17:124
LIMA BEAN 12:342–343 illus.
LIMA NUEVA (Honduras)
map (15° 23′N 87° 56′W) 10:218
LIMANN, HILLA
Ghana 9:166
LIMASSOL (Cyprus)
map (34° 40′N 33° 2′E) 5:409
LIMBE (Malawi)
Blantyre 3:328
LIMBIC SYSTEM 10:296i illus.
brain 3:446; 3:447
drug 6:276 illus.
LIMBOURG, POL 12:343
LIMBOURG BROTHERS 12:343 bibliog., illus.
Flemish art and architecture 8:160
International Style (Gothic art) 11:223
medieval feast 5:238 illus.
Très Riches Heures du Duc de Berry (book) 3:384 illus.; 7:284 illus.; 11:48 illus.; 12:343 illus.; 13:394 illus.
LIME (chemical compound) 12:343
calcium 4:23
compost 5:158
LIME (fruit) 12:343–344 illus.
citrus fruits 4:447
lumber 12:456 illus.
LIME VILLAGE (Alaska)
map (61° 21′N 155° 28′W) 1:242
LIMELIGHT
Drummond, Thomas 6:282
stage lighting 18:210
LIMERICK (city in Ireland) 12:344
map (52° 40′N 8° 38′W) 11:258
LIMERICK (comic verse) 12:344
Lear, Edward 12:259
LIMERICK (county in Ireland) 12:344
cities
Limerick 12:344
LIMESTONE 12:344–345 bibliog., illus.
calcite 4:22
calcium 4:22–23
calcium carbonate 4:23
chalk 4:271
coquina 5:257
Devonian Period 6:145
Earth, geological history of 7:12

emery 7:155
evaporite 7:314
formations
cave 4:222
coral reef 5:258
karst landscape 4:361 illus.
stalactite and stalagmite 18:213
geochemistry 9:96e
geode 9:96f
Grand Canyon 12:344 illus.
Greek architecture 9:336
idocrase 11:31
Illinois 11:44 illus.
Indiana 11:113 illus.
lapis lazuli 12:205
lithograph 12:371
marble 13:144
mining and quarrying 13:449
oolite 14:396
petroleum 15:208
sedimentary rock 17:184–185 illus.
siderite 17:294
smithsonite 17:372
speleology 18:177
sphalerite 18:180
stonewort 18:284
stratigraphy 18:292 illus.
stromatolite 18:302
willemite 20:154
LIMESTONE (county in Alabama)
map (34° 50′N 87° 0′W) 1:234
LIMESTONE (Maine)
map (46° 55′N 67° 50′W) 13:70
LIMESTONE (county in Texas)
map (31° 35′N 96° 35′W) 19:129
LIMIT (mathematics) 12:345 bibliog.
convergence 5:233
differential calculus 6:167–168
infinity 11:168–169
integral calculus 11:200–201
mathematics 13:222
sequence 17:207
LIMITATIONS, STATUTE OF see STATUTE OF LIMITATIONS
LIMITED TEST BAN TREATY (1963)
arms control 2:170
LIMNERS 12:345 bibliog.
folk art 8:197–198 illus.
Freake limner 8:289
Oliver, Isaac 14:379
portraiture 15:446
LIMNOLOGY 12:345
ecology 7:42–46
Hutchinson, George Evelyn 10:322–323
hydrologic sciences 10:342
lake (body of water) 12:167–169
LIMOGES (France) 12:345–346
Hundred Years' War 10:305 illus.
Limoges ware 12:346
map (45° 50′N 1° 16′E) 8:260
LIMOGES WARE 12:346 bibliog.
LIMON (Colorado)
map (39° 16′N 103° 41′W) 5:116
LIMÓN (Costa Rica)
map (10° 0′N 83° 2′W) 5:291
LIMÓN, JOSÉ 12:346 bibliog.
LIMONITE 12:346 illus.
LIMOSIN, LÉONARD 12:346 bibliog.
LIMOUSIN (France) 12:346–347 map
LIMPET 12:347; 13:510 illus.
Atlantic plate limpet 11:229 illus.
gastropod 9:57–58 illus.
intertidal life 11:230
Lister's keyhole limpet 11:229 illus.
rough limpet 11:229 illus.
LIMPKIN 12:347
LIMPOPO RIVER 12:347
map (25° 15′S 33° 30′E) 18:78
LIN BIAO see LIN PAIO (Lin Biao)
LIN PAIO (Lin Biao) 12:347 bibliog.
Mao Tse-tung (Mao Zedong) 13:135
LINACRE COLLEGE (Oxford University) 14:474
LINARES (Chile)
map (35° 51′S 71° 36′W) 4:355
LINARES (Mexico)
map (24° 52′N 99° 34′W) 13:357
LINARES (Spain)
map (38° 5′N 3° 38′W) 18:140
LINCH (Wyoming)
map (43° 37′N 106° 12′W) 20:301
LINCOLN (Argentina)
map (34° 52′S 61° 32′W) 2:149
LINCOLN (Arkansas)
map (35° 57′N 94° 25′W) 2:166
LINCOLN (county in Arkansas)
map (33° 57′N 91° 47′W) 2:166
LINCOLN (California)
map (38° 54′N 121° 17′W) 4:31
LINCOLN (county in Colorado)
map (39° 0′N 103° 30′W) 5:116
LINCOLN (England) 12:347
map (53° 14′N 0° 33′W) 19:403